University of Kentucky Book Award

Presented to :

Mohammad Abou
EL EZZ

Date:

May 2, 2017

Congratulations on your outstanding
achievements and best wishes for
continued academic success!

UNIVERSITY OF
KENTUCKY®
Alumni Association

Special thanks to
The *University Press of Kentucky.*

The Kentucky
African American
Encyclopedia

The Kentucky African American Encyclopedia

Edited by
Gerald L. Smith, Karen Cotton McDaniel,
and John A. Hardin

Copyright © 2015 by The University Press of Kentucky

Scholarly publisher for the Commonwealth,
serving Bellarmine University, Berea College, Centre
College of Kentucky, Eastern Kentucky University,
The Filson Historical Society, Georgetown College,
Kentucky Historical Society, Kentucky State University,
Morehead State University, Murray State University,
Northern Kentucky University, Transylvania University,
University of Kentucky, University of Louisville,
and Western Kentucky University.
All rights reserved.

Editorial and Sales Offices: The University Press of Kentucky
663 South Limestone Street, Lexington, Kentucky 40508-4008
www.kentuckypress.com

Library of Congress Cataloging-in-Publication Data

The Kentucky African American encyclopedia / edited by
Gerald L. Smith, Karen Cotton McDaniel, and John A. Hardin.
pages cm
Includes bibliographical references and index.
ISBN 978-0-8131-6065-8 (hardcover : alk. paper)—
ISBN 978-0-8131-6066-5 (pdf)—ISBN 978-0-8131-6067-2 (epub)
1. African Americans—Kentucky—Encyclopedias.   I. Smith, Gerald L., 1959– editor.
II. McDaniel, Karen Cotton, 1950– editor.   III. Hardin, John A., 1948–, editor.
E185.93.K3K46 2015
920.0092960769—dc23
2015014610

This book is printed on acid-free paper meeting
the requirements of the American National Standard
for Permanence in Paper for Printed Library Materials.

Manufactured in the United States of America.

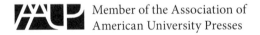 Member of the Association of
American University Presses

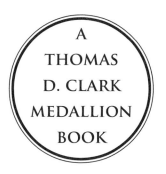

A
THOMAS
D. CLARK
MEDALLION
BOOK

Editorial Staff

Sallie L. Powell, Associate Editor

Aimee Briley

Dana Caldemeyer

Chris Chance

Kelcey Eldridge

Joshua D. Farrington

Erin Wiggins Gilliam

Shannon Guerrant

Elizabeth Hagee

Anthony Hartsfield Jr.

Evangeline Johnson

David Lai

Stephen Pickering

Jeremy Ridgeway

Elizabeth Schaller

Theda Wigglesworth

Sponsors

University of Kentucky, Office of the President, Lee Todd

University of Kentucky, Office of the Provost, Kumble R. Subbaswamy

University of Kentucky Graduate School, Jeannine Blackwell

University of Kentucky, College of Arts and Sciences, Mark Kornbluh

University of Kentucky Libraries, Carol Pitts Diedrichs and Terry Birdwhistell

University of Louisville, College of Arts and Sciences, J. Blaine Hudson

Helen Howard Hughes

Thomas Brumley

Don and Mira Ball Charitable Fund

Tubby Smith Foundation

Western Kentucky University

Eastern Kentucky University

Berea College

Centre College

Northern Kentucky University

Morehead State University

Transylvania University

Mark Neikirk

Connie Goodman

John and Lee Carroll

Nana Lampton

Orme Wilson

Sherry Jelsma

Melanie Kilpatrick

Bill Giles

Martha Johnson

Mike and Kit Hammons

Stan MacDonald

Virginia Fox

Bennie Ivory

Alice Stevens Sparks

Myra Leigh Tobin

Jane Beshear

Mark Davis

Aloma Dew

Warren Rosenthal

First Baptist Church, Lancaster

Kentucky American Water

Kevin and Jaquata Sykes

Richard and Oloroma Fowler

Viola Gross

Alpha Beta Lambda Chapter Education Foundation

Audrey Rooney

R. P. Formisano

Robert and Sandra Ireland

Sue Speed

James and Freda Klotter

Lexington Herald-Leader

Greensburg Green County Civic Club

James Host

John Kleber

John Merchant

Kenneth Roberts

Lila Rankin

Mary Hughes

Richard Weigel

Senator Georgia Powers

William and Deatra Newell

William and Janet Marshall

Francie Chassen-Lopez

Allan Rhodes Sr.

Beaumont Middle School

Betty Gabehart

Country Clubbers

Cynthia Lyons

Jackson and Carol Bennett

Jimmy and Lois Tevis

Juanita Laurie

Kentucky Historical Society Foundation

Lee Worful

Morning Star Baptist Church

Ellen Furlough

Taylor Chapel AME Church

Gary W. and Wanda P. Brown

Mollie M. Bradley

Susan L. F. Isaacs

Paul L. Whalen

Mark Russell

Antioch Missionary Baptist Church

Carol Crowe-Carraco

Vicky Miller

Ruby Wilkins Doyle

Benjamin Luntz

Eric James

Anne S. Butler

UK Office of Undergraduate Research, Bessie Guerrant

GOLD Community Fund

Authors

Adams, Luther
Amadife, Nkechi
Anders, Tisa M.
Anyanwu, Ogechi
Bartlett, Jennifer
Bash, Lee
Baskin, Andrew
Belue, Ted Franklin
Bogert, Brenda K.
Bogert, Cornelius
Bogert, Pen
Boyd, Douglas A.
Bradshaw, Dan
Brock, Peggy M.
Bryant, Jessica
Bulluck, Debra
Burch, John R., Jr.
Burnside, Jackie
Butler, Anne S.
Caldemeyer, Dana
Carraco, Carol Crowe
Christianson, Eric Howard
Claiborne, Karen
Clark, Aaron
Clark, Holly Jones
Clark, Kris
Coon, Diane Perrine
Craig, Berry
Crawford, Byron
Crews, Steve
Dallas, Fenobia I.
Dennis, Kenneth
Dew, Lee A.
Drane, Shannon M.
Dunston-Coleman, Aingred G.
Ellison, William L., Jr.
Embry, Jim
Faber, Charles F.
Farrington, Joshua D.
Fenton, Michele

Fitzpatrick, Benjamin
French, Robert Bruce
Garbett, Jannes W.
Gershtenson, Joseph
Gilbert, Karen L.
Gilliam, Erin Wiggins
Gonzalez, Vincent
Greene, Jojuana Leavell
Grimes, LeDatta
Hampton, Dantrea
Hardaway, Roger D.
Hardin, John A.
Harris, Theodore H. H.
Harrison, Benjamin T.
Henson, Gail
Hogg, Kevin
Hollenbeck, Hope L.
Hollingsworth, Randolph
Hoover, Amanda
Howell, Kristy
Hudson, J. Blaine
Hutchins, Walter W.
Jackson, David H., Jr.
Jackson, Eric R.
Johnson, Larry L.
Johnson, Wardell
Johnston, Joellen Tyler
Jones, Rev. LaMont, Jr.
Kennedy, Rick
Kindler, Christine
Klee, John
K'Meyer, Tracy E.
Knox-Perkins, Jessica
Kreinbrink, Jeannine
Lai, David
Lang, Stephanie M.
Lile, Joanna
Little, Harold T., Jr.
Lucas, Marion B.
Lucas, Mary Ellen

Marshall, Nancy Richey
Martin, John Franklin
Marty, Debian
McClintock, Jonathan
McDaniel, Karen Cotton
McDaniel, Kimberly Renee
McGee, Sharon R.
Merrill, Boynton, Jr.
Miller, Caroline R.
Minter, Patricia Hagler
Montell, William Lynwood
Muhammad, Lawrence
Mullins, Lashé D.
Neary, Donna M.
Nelson, Paul David
Newberry, Anthony
Nguyen, Kim
Nudd, Myrte
Oliver, Nettie
Onkst, Wayne
Parke, Julia C.
Partee, Angela
Patterson, Susan
Perrin, Anne Gray
Pickering, Stephen
Powell, Sallie L.
Pressley, Sheila
Rawlins, Benjamin
Ray, Maxine
Reliford, Hannah
Renau, Lynn S.
Richardson, Michael A.
Richey, Nancy
Robertson, John E. L.
Sanderfer, Selena
Savage, Steven P.
Schaller, Elizabeth
Schlipp, John
Sears, Richard D.
Simpson, Kareem A.

Smith, Gerald L.
Sorrell, Ashley
Spearing, Deborah
Stroup, Daniel G.
Sweeney, Michael R.
Thomas, Toni
Thompson, Charles
Threadgill-Goldson, Norma E.
Turley, Alicestyne
Turner, William H.
Tyler, Bruce M.

Vaughn, George
Waldrop, Evelyn L.
Wallen, Paul
Wasielewski, Alice
Watkins, Andrea S.
Wax, Darold D.
Wedekind, Carl
Weeter, Joanne
Weigel, Richard
Wessling, Jack
White, Juanita

Wilkinson, Doris
Williams, Rebecca J.
Williams, Shannen Dee
Willigen, John van
Wise, Stephen V.
Wood, Timothy
Yater, George H.
Yohe, Kristine
Young-Brown, Fiona

Contents

Acknowledgments

From the beginning, there has been an enormous outpouring of verbal support for this project. Everyone we met believed in the importance of this work and the contributions it would make to expanding interest in and knowledge of Kentucky history for years to come. Some persons, however, demonstrated unwavering faith in and support of this encyclopedia that exceeded words of encouragement. Among those individuals is Dr. Lee T. Todd, a past president of the University of Kentucky. President Todd provided major funding for this project. Had it not been for Dr. Todd, it would not have been possible to establish the infrastructure needed to complete a project of this magnitude. The website, office supplies, equipment, furniture, and hiring of students were all made possible because of his support. The former dean of the W. T. Young Library, Carol Pitts Diedrichs, welcomed the project into prime space in the library. This space provided access to library resources and gave the project the campus visibility it needed. Her successor, Dean Terry Birdwhistell, continued offering this kind of support, including updating the editors' computing system.

The late Dean J. Blaine Hudson of the University of Louisville's College of Arts and Sciences, a distinguished teacher and scholar of African, African American, and Kentucky history, was a true friend of this work. While serving in his position, he made sure that the project received needed funds to hire graduate students. His knowledge, wisdom, and friendship are truly missed. Dean Mark Kornbluh of the University of Kentucky's College of Arts and Sciences also encouraged our research and writing with funding on behalf of the college. Berea College and Eastern Kentucky University provided in-kind support in order for Karen Cotton McDaniel to work on the encyclopedia for uninterrupted periods of time. Western Kentucky University graciously provided similar assistance and support for John Hardin. Eastern Kentucky University also hosted an on-campus event to promote the significance of the encyclopedia. Berea College, Centre College, Morehead State University, Northern Kentucky University, and Transylvania University each made meaningful donations that helped to cover general expenses. Contributions of Thomas Brumley and his wife, Helen Howard Hughes, came at critical times during the preparation of the encyclopedia. We will never forget their generosity. The Don and Mira Ball Charitable Fund and the Tubby Smith Foundation were among the early supporters. Their generous support sustained the work during difficult periods of fund-raising. We are also very appreciative of the gifts of Warren Rosenthal and John and Lee Carroll, who saw the value of this volume in its early stages.

We also appreciate donations we received from Alpha Beta Lambda Chapter Education Foundation, Beaumont Middle School, Jackson and Carol Bennett, Mollie Bradley, Jerry Bransford, Gary and Wanda Brown, Lisa Brown, Vickie Carson, Francie Chassen-Lopez, First Baptist Church of Lancaster, Theresa Fitzgerald, Judy Fleming, R. P. Formisano, Richard and Loroma Fowler, Ellen Furlough, Betty Gabehart, Greensburg/Green County Civic Club, Michael Hammons, the Thomas D. Clark Foundation, James and Patricia Host, Mary Hughes, Robert and Sandra Ireland, Susan L. F. Isaacs, Kentucky American Water, Kentucky Historical Society Foundation, Melanie Kilpatrick, John Kleber, Dr. James and Freda Klotter, Juanita Lauarie, Cynthia Lyons, Joy Lyons, Mammoth Cave National Park, William and Janet Marshall, John C. Merchant, Morning Star Baptist Church, William and Deatra Newell, Georgia Powers, Lila Rankin, Allan Rhodes Sr., Kenneth Roberts, Audrey Rooney, Mark Russell, Sammons Estate, Sue Speed, Kevin and Jaquata Sykes, Taylor Chapel African Methodist Episcopal Church, Jimmy and Lois Tevis, Richard Weigel, and Paul L. Whalen.

The encyclopedia received early endorsements from: President Gary Ransdell (Western Kentucky University), Wayne D. Andrews (Morehead State University), James Ramsey (University of Louisville), Larry Shinn (Berea College), James C. Vortruba (Northern Kentucky University), John Roush and Richard Trollinger (Centre College), Charles Shearer (Transylvania University), Mary Evans Sias (Kentucky State University), Doug Whitlock

(Eastern Kentucky University), and John Chowning (Campbellsville University).

As the general coeditors traveled the state to give presentations about this project and raise funds, we met some wonderfully kind county librarians, local historians, city officials, and friends of this work. Among the places and people who opened their doors to us were Kim Bland (Hardin County Public Library); Carol Elliott (Nelson County Public Library); Amanda Clark and Judy Fleming (Boyd County Public Library); Brenda Vance (Bath County Public Library); Suzanne Kaufman (Anderson County Public Library); John Murskin (Clark County Public Library); Dianne Dehoney (Paul Sawyier Library), Frankfort; Wayne Riley (Laurel County African American Heritage Center, Incorporated); Joan Tussey (Garrard County Public Library); Patty Burnside and Melissa Gibson (Scott County Public Library); Kathy Crouch and Abigail Harris (Madison County Public Library); Lori Acton and Meghann Holmes (Laurel County Public Library); Kay Peppard (Lincoln County Public Library); John Maruskin and Julie Maruskin (Clark County Public Library); the Cynthiana–Harrison County Public Library; Irma Johnson, Hettie Oldham, and Vickie Miller (Paul G. Blazer Library, Kentucky State University); the Helen Williams Rowan County Public Library; the Scott County Public Library; James Chesney, Mount Moriah Baptist Church, Middlesboro, Kentucky; Ronnie Hampton, Greater Mount Sinai Baptist Church, Lynch, Kentucky; Hazard Community Technical College; Gary Pilkington and Dave Schroeder (Kenton County Public Library System); Mark Adler (Paris–Bourbon County Public Library); Charlotte Keeney (Pulaski County Public Library); Lana Hale (Knox County Public Library); Martha Nell Thomas (Mary Wood Weldon Memorial Public Library); Greater Campbellsville United; Mayor Brenda Allen; Judge Eddie Rogers, Campbellsville; Mayor George Cheatham II, Jerry Cowherd, James Washington, and Wanda Washington, Greensburg; Cumberland College; Mary Beth Garriott and Stan Campbell (Centre College, Grace Doherty Library); Danna Estridge (Woodford County Historical Society); Linda Kompanik (Logan County Public Library); Michael Morrow; Pam Yeager and Marcy Rae Werner, Archives and Special Collections, University of Louisville; and Carol Yates-Bennett. The University of Kentucky supported this project in numerous ways. Dean of the Graduate School, Jeannine Blackwell, provided support to hire graduate student research assistants. Bessie Guerrant and the office of Undergraduate Research at the University of Kentucky and former UK provost Kumble R. Subbaswamy provided financial support. Karen Petrone, chair of the UK History Department, allocated monies to help with the hiring of a postdoctoral fellow. The encyclopedia also received assistance from Jackie Burnside, Joan Shropshire, John Sterling, Mark Denommone, John Soward, Jr., Esther Edwards, Jason Flaherty, Louise Jones, Kent Whitworth, Darrell Meadows, Jennifer Duplaga, James C. Klotter, John Kleber, Dierdre Skaggs, Matthew Harris, Sarah Dorpinghaus, Gordon Hogg, Jeanette Dean, William "Bill" Turner, Calvert McCann, Vickie Miller, Doug Boyd, J. H. Atkins, Carolyn Sunday, Sam Coleman, Michael Douglass Lowery, Craig Wilkie, David Cobb, Allison Webster, Melissa Barlow, Sharon McGee, Tina Hagee, Charles Reed Mitchell, Hugo Freund, Mary Quinn Ramer, Kurt Holman, Jerry Bransford, Joy Medley Lyons, Susan Isaacs, Charles Mills, George C. Wright, Michael T. Hughes, Winston Mitchill, Nick Rowe, Laura Sutton, Ruby Wilkins Doyle, Connie Mitchell, Ron Garrison and the *Lexington Herald-Leader*, and the University of Kentucky Public Relations and Marketing Department.

It was a pleasure working with several undergraduate students who enthusiastically accepted varied assignments, from organizing and photocopying materials and researching newspapers, books, and articles to typing and mailing correspondence. Special thanks are extended to Elizabeth Hagee, Anthony Hartsfield Jr., Jeremy Ridgeway, Chris Chance, Christian Kindler, Lametta Johnson, Evangeline Johnson, Grant T. Mills, Sarah Smith, and Theda Wigglesworth. Elizabeth Schaller did a fine job writing some of the entries for the volume. Elizabeth and Kelcey Eldridge were especially helpful with the organization of the project. Kelcey did an amazing job of helping get the manuscript prepared to send to the Press. Her typing skills, efficiency, and impressive organizing methods were a wonderful contribution to the overall project.

As for graduate students, we benefited from the work of Western Kentucky University graduate student Aimee Briley, who assisted with identifying entries to be considered for inclusion in the encyclopedia during the early stages of our work. The contributions of University of Kentucky graduate students cannot be overemphasized. Shannon Guerrant researched entries, organized documents, and facilitated the planning of public presentations around the state. Erin Wiggins Gilliam and Evangeline Johnson helped identify and research entries and offered general office support. A core group of graduate students wrote a number of entries. Dana Caldemeyer, Joshua Farrington, Stephen Pickering, Sallie L. Powell, and David Lai brought a solid level of research and writing skills to the project that allowed for the completion of numerous entries. Sallie, Joshua, and Stephen became the core in-house writers of entries and deserve much credit for their writing. Sallie and Joshua eventually completed their doctorates. Joshua accepted a teaching position, and Sallie became an associate editor of the encyclopedia and was hired as a postdoc for a year and a half. She has served multiple roles with the encyclopedia. She provided office support, trained undergraduate students, wrote more entries than any other contributor, and served as a diligent researcher, editor, and passionate supporter of the volume. We are truly indebted to her for the enormous contributions she made to this work.

None of what we have done would have taken place had it not been for the vision and encouragement we received from Steve Wrinn, director of the University Press of Kentucky. He has championed this work in every phase. His wise counsel has kept the project on course and given us the confidence that we could get the book done. More than anything else, he has been our friend.

Gerald L. Smith wishes to extend special thanks to his wife, Teresa, his daughters, Elizabeth and Sarah, and his mother and mother-in-law, Mary Crawford and Octavene Turner, and the Pilgrim Baptist Church members. Special thanks to Sarah for accompanying him on research trips around the state, taking notes, and helping set up the presentations. John A. Hardin expresses his thanks to his understanding wife, Maxine Randle Hardin, for the countless times the project took him away. Karen Cotton McDaniel wishes to express her gratitude to her husband, Rodney, for his encouragement and support. She also thanks her daughter, Kimberly, for writing several entries and proofing others. Sallie L. Powell offers her sincere appreciation to the coeditors for their individual contributions to this gallant undertaking. Special credit goes to Gerald L. Smith who struggled to locate funding for not only myself, but also the many student workers. My gratitude also goes to my parents, Gene and Marie Powell, and my brothers, Mahlon, Mason, and Ben, who frequently listened patiently to my enthusiastic comments about this project.

The editors recognize that we may have omitted names of persons who gave us a name, event, or location of a part of Kentucky African American history and culture. These omissions are not intentional; every contribution helped us move forward to understand the cultural and historical complexity of the Bluegrass State. As Kentucky African American poet Frank Walker wrote, "Some of the bluegrass is black." We hope that this finished project makes this clear to all.

Introduction

In many ways, this encyclopedia is an extension of the early research and writings of an African American schoolteacher in Logan County, Kentucky, named Alice Dunnigan. In the 1930s, Dunnigan was teaching a course on Kentucky history and discovered that none of the textbooks referenced the contributions African Americans had made to the state's history and culture. She began preparing a "daily 'fact sheet'" on the role African Americans had played in the history of Kentucky. This information was later published in the *Louisville Defender* in a weekly column titled "The Achievements of the Kentucky Negro." The column generated a great deal of interest in local communities and even attracted national attention.[1]

William Ferris in a 1939 essay published in the *National Review* was optimistic that Dunnigan could publish a book on the subject. "It will render a two-fold service," he penned. "It will inform the Negro that handicapped as he has been since his emancipation from bondage, he has done something else besides sing and dance, fight, shoot craps and drink whiskey. It will show that he has not only made cultural advances, but has also built up a few business enterprises, which have been able to withstand the shock of the depression. It will give the Negro child information which will inspire him. In other words, it will banish the inferiority complex which is a weight around the black man's neck, dragging him down and back."[2]

In 1942, Dunnigan moved to Washington, DC, and became a highly respected journalist. Six years later, she became the first African American to hold the title of White House correspondent. Two generations of African American children would be born before her book, *The Fascinating Story of Black Kentuckians: Their Heritage and Traditions,* was finally published in 1982. The work provided numerous pen portraits of African American men and women with Kentucky roots and connections who lived before and after the Civil War. It included passages of information on African American newspapers and institutions of higher learning, as well as a number of photographs of African Americans. Dunnigan's volume provides an impressive and useful list of names and interesting historical anecdotes.

Her work argued that Kentucky African Americans have been part of the Commonwealth of Kentucky from its inception. They were an integral part of pioneer history as explorers and settlers who first witnessed the rich soil, vast forests, and varied wildlife the land offered. They worked alongside whites in opening the land for transportation, development, and agriculture. However, these black settlers did not migrate to Kentucky by choice. They came as slaves with no rights and no promises of a bright future. In the 1790s, Daniel Drake, from his settlement in Maysville, recalled seeing "caravans of travelers, mounted on horseback, and the gangs of negroes on foot."[3] Some slaves arrived from Virginia without their masters, who chose to stay behind until their property was ready to be occupied. Future U.S. attorney general John Breckinridge sent his overseer, John Thompson, ahead with a group of slaves to prepare their land. It was an arduous journey. Thompson informed his boss, "Our Negroes [were] Every day out of heart & sick." He added: "When the Negroes were wet & almost ready to give out, then I came forward with my good friend whiskey & Once every hour unless they were Sleep I was Oblige[d] to give them whiskey."[4]

Slavery grew rapidly in Kentucky. In 1790, there were 11,830 slaves in the state. This number had increased to 165,231 by 1839 and to over 200,000 by the end of the Civil War. J. Blaine Hudson writes that "enslaved African Americans were the farm machines and the household appliances of this era, which whites believed necessary both for their comfort and for the productivity of their lands and other enterprises."[5] Kentucky slaves labored in tobacco and hemp fields, salt pits, iron furnaces, rope factories, and river docks. They worked in all aspects of farm and domestic labor and in many public venues in the state. Central Kentucky had the highest percentage of slaves, followed by the western part of the state. Although slavery did exist in eastern Kentucky and the Jackson Purchase region of the state, it did not evolve to the extent it did in the other areas of the state, given the proximity of these areas to rivers as gateways of escape.

To be sure, slaves resisted their condition in many ways. Some escaped to the North, while others protested in performing their work assignments by destroying tools, working slowly, or pretending that they were physically unable to do the job because of illness. Not all blacks in the state were slaves. There were 114 free blacks counted in the state as of 1790, and the number gradually increased over the years. Members of this group of blacks were either born free, were emancipated by their owners through a will, or were granted their freedom because of some special service they rendered to whites. There were also slaves who were able to purchase their freedom from owners who had allowed them to earn and keep money from working for other white employers.

Despite these singular instances of nominal emancipation, slavery created an ongoing, relentless, and oppressive environment for Kentucky African Americans. Still, there were Kentuckians of African descent who overcame the circumstances of this era to leave their mark both in and beyond Kentucky. **Molly Logan** was a pioneer slave woman near present-day Stanford. Molly along with her white mistresses fought against and survived a hostile Indian attack when they were outside milking cows. "Captain" **Jack Hart** was a slave and frontiersman who contributed to and witnessed early phases of Kentucky's history. In 1846, the Kentucky General Assembly honored Hart with a declaration because he "endured the perils, privations and hardships incident to the pioneers." **Stephen Bishop,** while still a slave, explored historic passages in Mammoth Cave. **John Ballard** was born in Kentucky and became an early pioneer in Los Angeles. **George French Ecton** of Winchester was a runaway slave who, after leaving Kentucky, became the first African American to serve in the Illinois General Assembly during the 1880s. **Josiah Henson** was a slave in Daviess County who helped inspire Harriet Beecher Stowe to publish her classic novel *Uncle Tom's Cabin.* **John Milton Clarke** of Madison County became a distinguished abolitionist in the North. In 1870, he became the first African American elected to a public office in the city of Cambridge, Massachusetts. Some black achievements have been preserved, but the bravery, sacrifices, creativity, and contributions of many other African Americans who lived during this period may never be known.

With the end of statutory slavery in 1865, African Americans anticipated great opportunities. Instead, they encountered racial violence and segregation by custom and state laws. Lynchings, "legal lynchings," and mob rule limited political and economic opportunities and therefore dictated where blacks could live and work.[6] **Jim Crow** or racial segregation laws kept the races apart in transportation, recreation, and public accommodations. African Americans were forced to live in inferior neighborhoods, attend segregated schools with secondhand books and supplies in overcrowded buildings, and work in low-paying unskilled jobs. They were shuttled into black communities such as Pinnacle in Anderson County, Cole Ridge in Cumberland, Kentucky, and Chicken Bristle and Booneyville in Lincoln County. In 1904, Carl Day, a white representative from Breathitt County, successfully led the passage of a historic law in the Kentucky General Assembly that officially segregated public and private learning institutions. The **Day Law** assured that the races would not share the same learning environment for the next 50 years. Meanwhile, whites exploited racial stereotypes that depicted African Americans as inferior. African American women were deemed ugly, and black men were characterized as brutes. From eastern Kentucky's coal fields, northern Kentucky's "Gateway to the South," and the environs of the Jackson Purchase to the heart of the Bluegrass State, African American accomplishments were overlooked and dismissed. It was against this backdrop that African American parents, educators, and religious leaders pressed onward to overcome racial barriers and highlight black achievements.

Individual names, places, and institutions central to the African American experience stood a better chance of being preserved because of the efforts of generations of blacks born free and prepared to leave written or oral testimony relating to African American history. As the individual entries in this volume reveal, Kentucky African Americans have played significant roles as activists, athletes, builders, coal miners, doctors, educators, entrepreneurs, lawyers, nurses, organizers, and religious leaders. African American churches of all denominations have been pivotal institutions in making these achievements possible. Black churches housed schools, raised funds, trained leaders, and accommodated statewide and local meetings. African American pastors and preachers have served as educators, politicians, and civil rights leaders as they sought to establish and support black schools. A number of African American churches were erected during slavery. They include **Burks Chapel A.M.E. Church** in Paducah, **St. Paul A.M.E. Church** in Lexington, **Church of Our Merciful Savior,** an Episcopal Church in Louisville, and the **First African** and **Historic Pleasant Green**

Missionary Baptist Churches in Lexington. In 1824, the Roman Catholic **Sisters of Loretto** accepted the first African American women into their sisterhood. Historically, Baptist churches have been among the oldest and largest churches in Kentucky. Several of these churches are located in Louisville, the largest city in the state and the one with the highest concentration of African Americans. At present, Louisville's St. Stephen Baptist Church, with campuses in Kentucky and Indiana, has over 10,000 members.

With historical ties to the church, African American women have been instrumental in building, organizing, and promoting religious, cultural, educational, and social programs and activities. They have addressed health care and political issues, as well as recreational needs in the black community. Kentucky black women were affiliated with the National Association of Colored Women, which was founded in Washington, DC, in 1896. In 1903, the **Kentucky Association of Colored Women's Clubs** was formed. Operating under the motto "Looking upward not downward, outward not inward, forward not backward," local clubs were organized around the state. More than 200 of these clubs have been established since the founding of the association.

Bessie Lucas Allen was an early advocate of child welfare in Louisville. A staunch believer in the moral development of children, Allen established the newsboys' Sunday School, which met in the city's Odd Fellows Building. She later opened the Booker T. Washington Community Center, which offered vocational training to boys and girls. **Anna Simms Banks** helped organize a hospital movement in Winchester. In 1920, she became the first African American woman elected to serve as a delegate to a political convention in Kentucky. **Osceola Aleese Dawson** was the secretary of the **National Association for the Advancement of Colored People** in Paducah and the entire state during the 1950s. As a civil rights activist, she was known as "a symbol of hope." The contributions of these women and many others remain a testament to the relentless spirit of blacks in the Bluegrass State. Together with black men, they were determined to create a vibrant statewide community that met their social, political, and economic needs.

Under the state's segregation laws, blacks built thriving business districts in cities and towns, established hospitals for the ill, supported public schools and teachers' colleges, and established cemeteries to bury their loved ones. They worked long, hard hours in the hemp and tobacco fields of the state. African American women labored as **domestic workers** in the homes of wealthy whites. In eastern Kentucky, black men provided for their families by working in the most physically challenging jobs in the coal mines of Harlan County. Middle-class African Americans operated thriving businesses in Kentucky and other states. During the 1920s, the **African American Businessmen's Association of Covington** was organized. Real estate agents and the owner of a restaurant and bar were among its members. "Old **Walnut Street**" in Louisville and **Deweese Street** in Lexington were two prominent black business districts in the state, but other cities in the state had streets lined with African American businesses. The **First Standard Bank,** which opened in Louisville in 1921, was the first black bank in the state. The **American Mutual Savings Bank** welcomed customers the following year. African American businesses such as **Mammoth Life and Accident Insurance Company** and **Domestic Life and Accident Insurance Company** not only offered attractive employment opportunities but also gave African Americans the chance to plan for the future.

On the local level, African Americans also owned and operated barbershops, beauty shops, funeral homes, restaurants, bars, tailoring and dry cleaning shops, and grocery stores, among other establishments. **Aaron Hall Cabell** owned a successful grocery store in Henderson, Kentucky. In 1904, he became the first African American in the state to own a park after he purchased a park in the city and renamed it Cabell Park. African Americans also owned and operated newspapers in Bowling Green, Danville, Elizabethtown, Frankfort, Hopkinsville, Lexington, Louisville, Mt. Sterling, Owensboro, and Paducah. The National Colored Press Association was formed in Louisville in 1880. Some African Americans launched lucrative businesses outside the state. **Junius George Groves** from Green County became a wealthy landowner and entrepreneur in Kansas. Known as the Potato King, Groves amassed 500 acres and shipped produce around the country. He also operated a merchandise store and owned stock in mining and banking ventures.

African American businesses contributed to the growth of black culture in the state. African Americans created their own cultural and recreational opportunities. **African American theaters** offering music, motion pictures, and vaudeville acts entertained patrons in Kentucky cities during the first decade of the twentieth century. In 1908, **Caroline B. Bourgard** founded the Louisville Music Teacher's Association. She was a cofounder of the first art college for blacks in the city less than 20 years later. Kentucky African Americans have made broad contributions to the American music scene. Bowling Green native

Ernest Hogan (born **Reuben Crowdus**) was credited for his influence on the creation of **ragtime** music. **Sarah Martin** and **Sylvester Weaver** were appreciated for their talents in recording **blues** music. Vibraphonist **Lionel Hampton**, vocalist and dancer **John "Bubbles" Sublett**, and vocalist **Helen Humes** were among the **jazz** performers with national reputations. Lexington-born brothers Jason and Clay Coffey, known as **Black Coffey,** and **Midnight Star,** a band established in the 1970s by students at **Kentucky State University,** contributed to the twentieth-century rhythm and blues musical genre.

Blacks experienced individual success on racetracks as jockeys, in the boxing ring as fighters, in high school and college athletics as football and basketball players, and on baseball fields by operating their own teams. The Owingsville Giants, the **Lexington Hustlers,** the Winchester Hustlers, the Versailles Bearcats, and the Nicholasville Nicks were among the black baseball teams that played between 1930 and 1960. The story of African American sports in the state is a rich history that, like so much of the black experience, is waiting to be told.

In 1971, the Kentucky Commission on Human Rights published *Kentucky's Black Heritage,* a 161-page supplement to Kentucky history textbooks. This paperback study gave students and the general public the first overview of Kentucky African American history. Since then, doctoral dissertations, master's theses, and articles in scholarly journals have treated a number of topics and themes central to Kentucky African American history. In 1992, the Kentucky Historical Society published the two-volume *History of Blacks in Kentucky.* This impressive publication, authored by Marion Lucas and George Wright, chronicled the state's black past in a way in which it never had been before. Lucas examined the period from the frontier to 1891. His narrative provided a solid treatment of slavery and the post–Civil War years in the state. He contributed to the African American perspective on slave labor, living conditions, the lives of free blacks, and the conditions of the slave trade in the state. African American education, religion, recreation, and work were the primary topics he explored after emancipation. Wright wrote the second volume, which centered on race relations, education, and the civil rights struggle. Their work provided an engaging and solidly documented account of the state's black past.

Lucas and Wright's work has since been complemented by biographies and memoirs of famous black Kentuckians, including **Muhammad Ali, Whitney Young Jr., Lyman T. Johnson, Mae Street Kidd, Rufus Atwood, Isaac Murphy,** and **Ted Poston.** These works, as well as monographs on various special topics in Kentucky life, have created a growing interest in Kentucky African American history. *The Kentucky Encyclopedia* (1992), *The Encyclopedia of Louisville* (2001), and *The Encyclopedia of Northern Kentucky* (2009) each included entries on African Americans. These contributions have been a tremendous help in assembling *The Kentucky African American Encyclopedia.* More than 200 of the entries published in these three volumes were selected for reprint in this encyclopedia. However, some of the entries were revised to conform to the presentation of this encyclopedia and to make updates to the original entry.

The Kentucky African American Encyclopedia provides a comprehensive survey of research on the black experience in the commonwealth. From the frontier years to the present, it includes individuals, events, places, organizations, movements, and institutions that have shaped the state's history. Included are Kentucky African Americans who have been identified as having played significant roles in Kentucky life. Some of the entries are on Kentucky-born African Americans who later assumed important national roles, while others became Kentuckians by identification and migration.

The first of its kind, this volume was challenging to assemble. A number of important questions had to be considered as we prepared this encyclopedia. Who and what would merit inclusion in the book? Would the volume seek out all the African American "firsts" in the state? Should the work include white Kentuckians who influenced the shaping of the black experience? What topics should be represented in the book? What sources needed to be consulted in the selection of entries and the verification of historical facts?

The editors determined that we wanted to include as many counties as possible in this publication and as many little-known facts as possible about African Americans in the state. Although many of the entries have connections to Lexington and Louisville, we have made every effort to reach beyond these two cities to capture stories throughout Kentucky and even outside it. To do so, the editors traveled around the state in 2006 and 2007 to make public presentations at community organizations and county libraries, visit African American heritage museums, and experience driving tours in communities with an organized African American heritage.

It was clear from visiting various counties and what we read or heard that there is a strong interest in preserving local African American history. Lexington, London,

Louisville, and Franklin, Kentucky, have museums or heritage centers devoted to African Americans. Maysville has turned the Bierbower House into the **National Underground Railroad Museum,** and the Warren Thomas Museum houses black history in Hickman, Kentucky. Lexington has opened the **Isaac Scott Hathaway** Museum. Plans are also in the works to open an African American museum in Bowling Green. Although historic Kentucky sites such as the **Farmington** Plantation in Louisville and **Camp Nelson** Heritage Park in Jessamine County include references to the black experience, we learned that local communities are actively working to preserve their black history as well. Green and Taylor Counties and the city of Berea have compiled an information and tour brochure that showcases historic sites significant to black history in those areas. Paducah, Kentucky, has a heritage tour that includes the **Washington Street Missionary Baptist Church,** the Hotel Metropolitan, and Hamock Funeral Home, where **Charles "Speedy" Atkins** was embalmed in 1928, preserved, and displayed in public before he was finally buried almost 70 years later.

The more we observed and learned about Kentucky African American history, the more difficult making decisions on what to include became. African Americans were breaking racial barriers on the local, state, and national levels in all aspects of life. Given the broad and genuine interest in the African American experience across the state, we encouraged local historians, graduate students, teachers, university professors, and others to submit the names of possible entries and to serve as contributors. Gathering suggestions was not a challenge, but our effort to recruit authors was not as successful as we had hoped. Fewer than 150 writers contributed essays. To include only African American firsts would dismiss other meaningful black contributions. Although the decisions we made were difficult, we were careful and thoughtful in choosing the African American firsts represented in the book. In the end, we narrowed our choice of entries on the basis of two criteria: available writers and reliable sources. To maintain historical accuracy and provide as much rich information as possible, this volume contains over 1,000 entries.

We recognize that a number of white Kentuckians have played a critical and historic role in the construction of the black experience. U.S. senator Henry Clay favored the colonization of slaves and was president of the American Colonization Society; Robert Wickliffe was one of the largest slaveholders in the state; and Carl Day sponsored the **Day Law.** There were also white Kentuck-

ians who risked their lives, sacrificed opportunities, provided funding, and extended political, legal, and moral support to advance freedom and equality for African Americans. Their place in history is not intended to be minimized.

No one rises higher in shaping the discourse of African American history than Abraham Lincoln, the nation's 16th president. He was at the center of the slavery issue years before the Civil War began. During the Lincoln-Douglas debates of 1858, he was not "in favor of making voters or jurors of negroes, nor qualifying them to hold office, nor to intermarry with white people." In the sixth debate, he acknowledged that there was "no reason in the world why the negro is not entitled to all the rights enumerated in the Declaration of Independence—the right of life, liberty, and the pursuit of happiness."[7] Once in office, Lincoln signed the **Emancipation Proclamation,** which freed slaves in states of rebellion as of January 1, 1863. Although the act did not directly free Kentucky slaves, it clearly affected the final outcome of slavery; moreover, African Americans subsequently held annual **Emancipation Day** celebrations in various parts of the state.

White Kentuckians such as James G. Birney, John G. Fee, and Calvin Fairbank were among those who went to extraordinary lengths during slavery to free blacks from bondage. Cassius Marcellus Clay and Robert Jefferson Breckinridge, while more conservative in their antislavery beliefs, affected black history as well. Fee, on the other hand, was even more instrumental after slavery by promoting integrated education and an interracial community in Berea.

In 1896, U.S. Supreme Court justice and Kentucky native **John Marshall Harlan** was the only justice to offer a dissenting opinion in the landmark ruling on the case ***Plessy v. Ferguson,*** which set in place a constitutional protection for segregation. In the twentieth century, white Kentucky civil rights activists Anne and Carl Braden and Governors Edward Breathitt and Bert Combs, among many others, played significant roles in the struggle for civil rights. The lives and contributions of these individuals have been covered in other works, and rightly so. Their places are well rooted in the narrative of Kentucky history.

Aside from Harlan, the prominent names listed above were not included in this volume. Yet we do present entries on whites such as William Shreve Bailey, Isham and Lilburne Lewis, Delia Webster, and Joe Elsby Martin, among a few others. We believe this sampling will offer readers an interesting perspective on black life in the state. We also believe entries on historic places in the state, not owned by African Americans, will allow for a more diverse range of historical context and understanding.

While a few white subjects are included in the encyclopedia, this volume seeks to intentionally highlight African American agency with an emphasis on black life and culture. It sheds light on what African Americans did for themselves in their respective worlds. It reaches outside and beyond the traditional narrative of Kentucky history to capture hidden and forgotten stories that deserve inclusion in the making of Kentucky and American history. To accomplish this objective, numerous books, newspapers, magazines, journal articles, and websites were consulted in selecting and writing entries. The *Louisville Courier-Journal,* the *Lexington Herald,* the *Lexington Leader,* the *American Baptist,* the *New York Times,* the **Louisville Defender,** and the **Louisville Leader,** along with many other local newspapers, offered previously untapped information. Major databases such as Ancestry.com, the African American Biographical Database, Google News, Newsbank, the **Notable Kentucky African Americans Database,** and the Kentucky Digital Library provided access to a wealth of resource material. Once entries were selected, hard-copy data folders on each entry were created to save and document the research completed on the subject.

From an array of sources, it became distinctly clear that Kentucky African Americans have blazed trails both inside and outside the state since the frontier years. We have sought to preserve as much of this history as possible by identifying fifteen different topics: arts and culture, business, cemeteries, civil rights, communities, eastern Kentucky coal fields, education, law and politics, medicine, military, organizations, religion, slavery, sports, and women. Every effort has been made to ensure geographic diversity. More than 85 of the state's 120 counties are referenced in this work.

The vast majority of the entries in this book are on individuals. In most cases, there is a snapshot of the person's family history, followed by her or his significant contributions to Kentucky or the United States. The writings on organizations and institutions document their origins and attempt to present their status at the time of publication. We hope that the information shared on Kentucky African Americans will generate new research, new questions, and new debates on black life in a border state. We believe that it will complement the list of names, places, institutions, and organizations referenced in the amazing Notable Kentucky African Americans Database located at the University of Kentucky. In the end, we have tried in earnest to present a volume that will have lasting intellectual integrity and inspire future historians and community leaders to look even more closely with the intention of preserving Kentucky's rich black heritage.

In the words of the noted historian John Hope Franklin, "Every generation has the opportunity to write its own history, and indeed it is obliged to do so. Only in that way can it provide its contemporaries with the materials vital to understanding the present and to planning strategies for coping with the future. Only in that way can it fulfill its obligation to pass on to posterity the accumulated knowledge and wisdom of the past, which, after all, give substance and direction for the continuity of civilization."[8] We hope this volume contributes to fulfilling that obligation.

NOTES

1. Alice Allison Dunnigan, comp. and ed., *The Fascinating Story of Black Kentuckians: Their Heritage and Traditions* (Washington, DC: Associated Publishers, 1982), xvii.
2. William Ferris is quoted in Dunnigan's book. Ibid., xviii.
3. Gerald L. Smith, "Slavery and Abolition in Kentucky: 'Patter-Rollers' Were Everywhere," in *Bluegrass Renaissance: The History and Culture of Central Kentucky, 1792–1852,* ed. James C. Klotter and Daniel Rowland (Lexington: Univ. Press of Kentucky, 2012), 77.
4. Ibid.
5. Ibid., 78.
6. For more on racial violence in Kentucky after the Civil War, see George C. Wright, *Racial Violence in Kentucky, 1865–1940: Lynchings, Mob Rule, and "Legal Lynchings"* (Baton Rouge: Lousiana State Univ. Press, 1990).
7. Quoted in J. Blaine Hudson, "Abraham Lincoln: An African American Perspective," *RKHS* (Summer/Autumn 2008): 516–17.
8. John Hope Franklin, "On the Evolution of Scholarship in Afro-American History," in *The Harvard Guide to African-American History,* ed. Evelyn Brooks Higginbotham (Cambridge, MA: Harvard Univ. Press, 2001), xxiii.

Guide for Readers

The encyclopedia entries were written by an array of contributors between 2009 and 2013. These writers included longtime educators, university professors, and graduate and undergraduate students. The vast majority of the entries were written by a *Kentucky African American Encyclopedia* staff of University of Kentucky graduate students who worked diligently on the project year-round. Their dedicated research led to the uncovering of obscure facts in newspapers and magazines that had never been mined for information before.

The general coeditors and associate coeditor also served as authors and then screened all entries carefully and objectively, making sure the final work represented the academic integrity it richly deserves. We are now pleased to present these subjects, both old and new, in a historical context that highlights and captures the essence of the black experience in the form of a tightly organized volume.

The following entries are presented in a slightly different form from those in *The Kentucky Encyclopedia, The Louisville Encyclopedia,* and *The Northern Kentucky Encyclopedia.* The title of each entry is followed by a written snapshot of the entry's significance. Individual persons' birth and death dates and the place in which they occurred are in parentheses. Uncertain exact dates appear with "ca." No dates appear in the heading when the information was not found or could not be confirmed.

The encyclopedia draws information from a number of online newspaper databases. These sources were useful as primary sources and offered important details that otherwise might have been overlooked. Staff writers of the encyclopedia, in particular, have worked extensively with Ancestry.com and other sources to clarify and confirm contradictory information found in other sources on the entries included in the encyclopedia.

Selection of Entries

In preparing the encyclopedia, an entry selection criterion was established similar to that created for the other encyclopedias published by the University Press of Kentucky. Individuals must have been born in the state or have lived the formative years of their lives in Kentucky and must have made significant contributions to the state, the nation, or the world. Individuals could also have been born elsewhere, moved to Kentucky, and achieved success in the state or migrated to Kentucky, established a career, and then moved out of the state and gained a notable reputation. This volume is not limited to deceased persons. Living individuals noted for being barrier breakers and achieving state, national, or international recognition are also represented. And, a few non-African American individuals and places were included for contextual reasons.

Places and historic events were selected based on their significance in shaping regional history. African American institutions and publications have been included on the basis of their pioneering contributions, historic reputations, national affiliations, and long-standing commitments to service in the black community. Although there are numerous churches, schools, and social organizations that are qualified to fit any of these categories, the entries included in the encyclopedia seek to reflect the state's geographic diversity. We have included a few cemeteries, parks, and communities to further reveal the depth of segregation in Kentucky. Court cases and civil rights acts have been included to document the changes in American legal history that affected the status of race in Kentucky. There are a few topical essays in the encyclopedia. Essays on business, the civil rights movement, eastern Kentucky coalfields, education, and women provide a deeper and broader exploration of the Kentucky African American past. These topics are placed in the context of Kentucky history and may include names and places that are not among the published entries.

Cross-Referencing and Index

All names, places, events, organizations, and institutions that appear in the encyclopedia are printed in boldface type in order to distinguish their appearance as both an entry and a connecting reference to other entries. A few of these boldfaced entries appear in the Introduction and are intended to assist readers in grouping them under different topics. Specific entry names appear in the index, but readers will also be able to locate entries under a specific topic. For example, under "African American organizations," readers can find the Kentucky Negro Educational Association or Kentucky Negro Education Association.

Citations and Bibliography

The encyclopedia provides a limited number of source materials at the end of most entries. Many of the entries were based on newspaper sources. Unless otherwise noted, birth, death, marriage, Social Security Index, U.S. Federal Census, World War I and II Enlistment Records among other similar documentations are drawn from the Kentucky Section or another section of the website AncestryLibrary.com. Some authors and newspapers included titles for the articles and the paper's page number, but some did not, according to the information that was available. The following abbreviations of frequently cited newspapers and periodicals have been used:

AB	*American Baptist*
BAA	*Baltimore Afro-American*
BGDN	*Bowling Green Daily News*
CE	*Cincinnati Enquirer*
CJ	*Covington Journal*
CP	*Cincinnati Post*
DRF	*Daily Racing Form* (Chicago)
FCHQ	*Filson Club History Quarterly*
HK	*Hopkinsville Kentuckian*
IF	*Indianapolis Freeman*

JNH	*Journal of Negro History*
KE	*Kentucky Enquirer*
KNE	*Kentucky New Era*
KNEAJ	*Kentucky Negro Educational Association Journal*
KP	*Kentucky Post*
KTS	*Kentucky Times-Star*
LCJ	*Louisville Courier-Journal*
LD	*Louisville Defender*
LH	*Lexington Herald*
LHL	*Lexington Herald-Leader*
LL	*Lexington Leader*
NYT	*New York Times*
OMI	*Owensboro Messenger-Inquirer*
PD	*Plaindealer* (Kansas)
PES	*Paducah Evening Sun*
PS	*Paducah Sun*
RKHS	*Register of the Kentucky Historical Society*
WN	*Winchester News*
WP	*Washington Post*

Internet websites are also cited. These types of sources usually list the author's name, title of the article, website address, and date the site was consulted by the writer. Last, readers will find that some very useful source information was drawn from census records published over different decades. This source citation will appear as "U.S. Federal Census" followed by the year or years in parentheses.

In order to organize many of the sources cited in this publication into one section, a selected bibliography is provided. This bibliography consists of books, newspapers, journal and magazine articles, and Internet sites. This list will give readers an exhaustive source of references on many subjects pertinent to the African American experience in Kentucky.

The Kentucky
African American
Encyclopedia

A

ABBINGTON, VALLATEEN VIRGINIA DUDLEY (b. 1907?, IN; d. 2003, Los Angeles, CA), teacher, social worker, and civic leader who filed a lawsuit to equalize teacher salaries in Louisville. Born in rural Indiana to a family of eight children, Valla Dudley Abbington sold newspapers as a teenager. After the death of her parents, she worked her way through Michigan State Normal College and pledged **Alpha Kappa Alpha Sorority.** In 1938, she married Jesse Matthew Abbington.

Abbington began her 18-year teaching career in North Carolina before moving to Kentucky to teach at Louisville's Jackson Junior High School. The Louisville Board of Education paid African American teachers nearly $300 less than white teachers. In 1940, she became the plaintiff in a lawsuit brought by the Louisville NAACP to equalize teacher salaries. Thurgood Marshall, representing the national NAACP legal committee along with Charles H. Houston and Prentice Thomas, served as the local NAACP counsel in the case, *Valla Dudley Abbington v. Louisville Board of Education.* With support from the *Louisville Courier-Journal,* the school board equalized pay for African American teachers in Louisville in 1941.

Abbington later moved to St. Louis, MO, and earned a master's degree in social work. While living there, she sought to desegregate low-income public housing and promoted the integration of her local church, Trinity Episcopal. Widowed since 1962 and childless, Abbington died on October 13, 2003, in Los Angeles, CA. She is buried at Jefferson Barracks National Cemetery, St. Louis, MO.

"Alumna, 96, Remembered as Strong-Willed Activist." *Exemplar: Eastern Michigan University,* Winter 2004, 5. http://igre.emich.edu /news/exemplar.pdf (accessed September 29, 2008).
Hardin, John A. *Fifty Years of Segregation: Black Higher Education in Kentucky, 1904–1954.* Lexington: Univ. Press of Kentucky, 1997.
"Vallateen Virginia Dudley Abbington." East St. Louis Action Research Project, Univ. of Illinois at Urbana-Champaign. http://riverweb .cet.uiuc.edu/IBEX/clayton/women/a-b/abbington_valla.htm (accessed September 29, 2008).

—*Sallie L. Powell*

ADAMS, FLORENCE "FRANKIE" VICTORIA (b. 1902, Danville, KY; d. 1979, Atlanta, GA), social worker, educator, author, and community activist. Florence "Frankie" Victoria Adams was a native of Danville, KY. Her father, James T. Adams, was a farmer. Frankie graduated from Knoxville College in 1925. Two years later, she earned her diploma from the New York School of Social Work. By 1930, she had returned to Danville and worked in social services at the YMCA while living with her parents. Her father died the next year, and she began her tenure at the Atlanta School of Social Work (later known as the Atlanta University School of Social Work). She helped develop the social work curriculum and influenced the profession on the national level.

According to the 1940 U.S. federal census, Adams lived in Danville with her 75-year-old mother, Minnie Adams, and earned $900 a year while she was employed by the college in social work. Four years later, she authored *Soulcraft: Sketches on Negro-White Relations Designed to Encourage Friendship.* In the late 1950s and into the 1960s, she wrote journal reviews and articles, including "Cruelty to Children in England," "The Community-wide Stake of Citizens in Urban Renewal," and "Juvenile Delinquency—Its Causes and Cures." After 33 years at the Atlanta University School of Social Work, Adams retired as associate dean but continued working with neighborhood service centers.

After her death on August 29, 1979, Adams was buried at Hilldale Cemetery in Danville, KY, near her parents. Her book, *The Reflections of Florence Victoria Adams,* was published posthumously in 1981.

Fleming, G. James, and Christian E. Burckel, eds. *Who's Who in Colored America.* 7th ed. *Supplement.* Yonkers-on-Hudson, NY: Christian E. Burckel & Associates, 1950.
"Frankie V. Adams Collection." Atlanta Univ. Center, Robert W. Woodruff Library, Archives and Special Collections. http://www.auctr.edu /rwwl/FindingAids%5Cfvadams.pdf (accessed November 14, 2012).
Georgia Deaths, 1919–1998.
U.S. Federal Census (1910, 1920, 1930, 1940).

—*Sallie L. Powell*

ADAMS, HENRY (b. 1803, Franklin Co., GA; d. 1872, Louisville, KY), Baptist minister. In 1839, Henry Adams came to Louisville to become pastor of a small black Baptist congregation that worshipped in a house on Market St. between Seventh and Eighth Sts. He established a school in the church, and the congregation grew dramatically under his leadership. In April 1842, Adams led the congregation out of the white First Baptist Church and organized the First Colored Baptist Church of Louisville. Under Adams's vigorous leadership,

Rev. Henry Adams.

the church established itself by 1848 on Fifth St. south of Walnut. Ten years later the original structure was replaced by a handsome building designed by famed Louisville architect Gideon Shryock. It later became known as the **Fifth Street Baptist Church.** Adams remained as pastor of the church until his death on November 3, 1872.

Lucas, Marion B. *A History of Blacks in Kentucky.* Vol. 1, *From Slavery to Segregation, 1760–1891.* Frankfort: The Kentucky Historical Society, 1992.
Weeden, H. C. *Weeden's History of the Colored People of Louisville.* Louisville, KY: H. C. Weeden, 1897.

—*Cornelius Bogert*

ADAMS, JOHN QUINCY "J. Q." (b. 1848, Louisville, KY; d. 1922, St. Paul, MN), **first president of the Colored Press Association of the United States.** The son of Rev. Henry Adams, renowned pastor of the **Fifth Street Baptist Church** in Louisville, KY, John Quincy Adams had careers in education and politics before he became a journalist. Born on May 4, 1848, Adams attended private schools in Fond du Lac, WI, and Yellow Springs, OH. After graduating from Ohio's Oberlin College, he began a teaching career before he was elected as an engrossing clerk for the Arkansas Senate in 1873. He later held the positions in Arkansas of assistant superintendent of public instruction and deputy commissioner of public works.

After returning to Kentucky, he served on the Republican Party's State and City Executive Committees and as a delegate to the Republican National Convention of 1880. Afterward, he was appointed as granger and storekeeper in the U.S. Revenue Service for Kentucky's Fifth District. In 1879, he and his younger brother, Cyrus Field Adams, created the *Bulletin,* a weekly newspaper in Louisville. In 1885, he and his brother sold the *Bulletin* to the **American Baptist.** In 1880, J. Q. Adams persuaded the first Colored Press Association of the United States to meet in Louisville. He was elected the organization's first president.

In 1886, Adams left for St. Paul, MN, where he soon became the editor of the *Western Appeal,* later known as the *Appeal.* In 1888, he moved the newspaper's headquarters to Chicago. It was published there, as well as in St. Paul and Louisville. Adams used his journalistic skills to challenge white newspapers, which presented African Americans as criminals. He cautioned that white people read only of the "offcasts and outcasts" instead of "the thousands of benevolent and Christian enterprises" that dominated African American lives. He warned that this type of journalism was "a misfortune to both races."

On May 4, 1892, Adams married Ella Bell Smith of St. Paul, and they had four children, Adina, Margaret, Edythella, and John Jr. They lived at 527 St. Anthony Ave. in St. Paul. As he was returning from a gospel meeting, Adams, while boarding a streetcar, was struck by a car. He died the following day, September 4, 1922, and his beloved newspaper quickly went out of circulation.

Northrop, Henry Davenport, Joseph R. Gay, and I. Garland Penn. *The College of Life or Practical Self-Educator.* Chicago: Chicago Publication and Lithograph, 1895.

Penn, I. Garland. *The Afro-American Press, and Its Editors.* Springfield, MA: Willey and Co., 1891.

Taylor, David V. "John Quincy Adams: St. Paul Editor and Black Leader." *Minnesota History* 43, no. 8 (1973): 282–96.
—*Sallie L. Powell*

AFRICAN AMERICAN BALL (Lexington), a celebration of African American community and culture. On September 21, 1993, leaders in Lexington's black community founded the African American Forum to "address the Lexington-Bluegrass Region's limited arts and cultural offerings that reflected the African American experience." As part of wide-ranging efforts by the group to promote the arts in the region, John E. Cole III, Debbie Elery, and Shirley Hayden-Whitley organized a gathering designed to "showcase excellence in art, culture, and entertainment by African-Americans in the Lexington area." On January 22, 1994, the African American Forum held the first African American Ball in the ballroom of the Continental Inn, with proceeds benefiting arts programs in local schools.

Established as an annual event to be held each January, the African American Ball featured a cross section of African American arts and entertainment. One consistent element of each ball was the performance of music, primarily by local artists and deejays. Each gathering also included a display of artwork, with an emphasis on some of the state's finest black artists. Perhaps the most popular feature has been a fashion show in which models showcase clothes influenced by traditional African styles. Additions to later balls have included poetry readings, performances of plays, and a silent auction.

Originally a relatively small affair, with 300 attendees at the first gathering, the African American Ball became one of the most popular social events for Lexington's black community. In 1997, the ball turned its first profit, and organizers created the African American Forum Fund of the Blue Grass Community Foundation to better direct proceeds from the event into its supported charities two years later. In 2004, the African American Ball changed its location to the Lexington Center's Bluegrass Grand Ballroom, where organizers hoped to attract a more diverse crowd and pull from Louisville and northern Kentucky.

Since its foundation in 1994, the African American Ball has served as a significant showcase of the state's African American art and culture, with notable guests including poet **Frank X Walker** and sculptor **Edward Hamilton Jr.** It has also performed an important role in promoting a diverse array of charitable endeavors, supplementing its initial focus on the arts in elementary schools with efforts in later years to fight cervical cancer in the black community.

African American Forum, Inc. "Message from Our Founders." http://www.aafinc.com/message_from_founders.htm (accessed on January 23, 2012).

Newspapers: "African American Ball, Jan. 21," *LHL,* January 4, 1995, 7; "Ball to Showcase Black Culture," *LHL,* January 12, 1997, J1; "Ball Keeps Growing, Getting Better," *LHL,* January 16, 1998, 9; "A Good Time and More," *LHL,* January 18, 2002, 8; "African-American Ball Invites All," *LHL,* October 12, 2003, F1; "Reveling in the Revelry, All for Good Causes," *LHL,* January 25, 2009, E10.
—*Stephen Pickering*

AFRICAN AMERICAN BASEBALL, a popular pastime for blacks during the period of segregation. Although Jackie Robinson is famously known for integrating baseball in the modern era, his predecessor, Moses Fleetwood Walker, played for Ohio integrated teams in the late 1880s. On August 23, 1881, the *Louisville Commercial* claimed that "the quadroon Walker . . . was not allowed to play" in Louisville because some players of the Louisville Eclipse, a white team, refused to play Walker and his team, the White Sewing Machine Company team from Cleveland. However, in May 1884, Walker, considered by many the first African American major leaguer, returned to Louisville, playing catcher for the Toledo Blue Stockings in what some scholars claimed to be the first integrated major-league baseball game. The *Louisville Courier-Journal* said of Walker that "the colored catcher, who has been spoken of as something of a wonder, appeared to be badly rattled, and managed to make all the errors himself." The newspaper defensively claimed that the Louisville fans were "very orderly." The *Louisville Commercial* maintained in stereotypical form of the era that Toledo's loss was "all on account of a coon."

Before Walker's Kentucky debut, Louisville African Americans had formed a team named the Fall City in 1883. Four years later, it joined the newly formed League of Colored Base Ball Players, also known as the League of Colored Base Ball Clubs. This first African American baseball league, which included seven other teams from various states, lasted only a week or two weeks, depending on the source. Years later the *Paducah Sun* announced on June 11, 1904, that a "Colored League Is Being Formed, . . . the First in the South."

Throughout the early part of the twentieth century, various Louisville teams, such as the White Sox, the Black Caps, and the Black Colonels, competed. However, Louisville was not the only Kentucky community with African American baseball. Teams sprouted all over the state. In 1899, the *Lexington Leader* noted a push for an African American baseball league in the Bluegrass region. Early 1900s teams in the surrounding area included the Danville Corn Crackers, the Covington Stars, the Frankfort Royal Giants, the Paris Quicksteps, the Lancaster All-Stars, the Midway Giants, and the Mt. Sterling Halls. Lexington produced two teams, the Gem Theaters and the Heavy Hitters, the latter captained by Charles C. Beauchamp. There were also African American community teams, such as the Smithtown Reds and the Brucetown Heavy Hitters. The **Lexington Hustlers** began around 1904, and the team name continued as squad variations dominated the community's baseball scene through the early 1950s. The Lexington Hustlers played against and defeated white teams. During the era Jackie Robinson was integrating the white major leagues, the Lexington Hustlers, under the leadership of **John William "Scoop" Brown,** was becoming "the first integrated baseball team in the South," with an invitation to white player Bobby Flynn to join the team. Even the famous Leroy "Satchel" Paige pitched for the Lexington Hustlers in July 1950.

Meanwhile, Kentucky's smaller communities continued to form teams and travel out of state to play ball games. In 1900, a Hickman team journeyed to Columbus, OH, to compete. A year later, a Paducah team traveled across the Ohio River to play in Cairo, IL, against a team from Charleston, MO. This team, later named the Paducah Nationals, under the leadership of **Ben Boyd,** competed and usually won against teams in Memphis, New Orleans, Chicago, Little Rock, Atlanta, St. Louis, and Keokuk, IA. Boyd arranged for reserved seating for white baseball fans at Paducah's Eureka Park. In April 1905, the Nationals lost to a white team in Quincy, IL, considered "one of the strongest white independent teams in the middle states."

Males were not the only baseball players in Kentucky. On December 26, 1908, the *Indianapolis Freeman* reported plans for the organization of women's baseball teams in Springfield, OH, and Louisville, KY. Because Louisville had "the best woman baseball expert in the country," Mrs. Henry Newboy, the city would within months have a women's team. Mr. and Mrs. Newboy had been training a women's baseball team for the upcoming season.

Jules Tygiel, in *Baseball's Great Experiment: Jackie Robinson and His Legacy,* described Louisville's "hybrid form" of **Jim Crow** in the 1940s as one in which segregation existed, but not in every public arena. There was great concern how Louisville would respond to playing against Jackie Robinson and the Montreal Royals, the leading Dodger farm club. Even though Parkway Field was segregated and allowed only 466 African Americans in the Jim Crow section, people found ingenious ways to see Jackie Robinson play his first professional playoff game. Some of those methods included purchasing tickets from whites and watching the game from vantage points outside the ball park. Nonetheless, the majority white crowd hurled racist insults at Robinson, but editorial letters in the *Louisville Courier-Journal* reprimanded the fans for their demonstrations of prejudice.

Between the 1930s and the 1960s, several African American teams entertained baseball fans in Kentucky, including the Winchester Hustlers, the Georgetown Athletics, the Versailles Bearcats, the Nicholasville Nicks, the Covington Tigers, Seagram's Seven Crowns, the Owingsville Giants, the Aetna Hawks, and the Lexington Hard Hitters, organized by Robert Hayes and managed by Arthur Higgins. Many teams offered not only serious baseball playing but also entertainment through stunts and comedy. The Louisville Black Zulus, also known as the Zulu Cannibals, dressed in grass skirts and face paint to play against the House of David, whose players wore long beards as orthodox rabbis.

Baseball was a relaxing and enjoyable form of entertainment for African Americans despite the existence of segregation. African American athletes brought a creative style of play and energy to this pastime that served to revolutionize the game.

Newspapers: "Base Ball," *LC,* August 23, 1881, 4; "A Brilliant Opening," *LCJ,* May 2, 1884, 8; "A Fine Home Victory," *LC,* May 2, 1884, 2; "Colored League Is Being Formed," *PS,* June 11, 1904, 1; "To Play with Chicago," *PS,* October 30, 1905, 2; "Documentary Shows How Hustlers Became Legends," *LHL,* February 14, 2003, 11.

Peterson, Robert. *Only the Ball Was White: A History of Legendary Black Players and All-Black Professional Teams.* New York: Oxford Univ. Press, 1970.

Tygiel, Jules. *Baseball's Great Experiment: Jackie Robinson and His Legacy.* New York: Vintage Books, 1984.

Zang, David W. *Fleet Walker's Divided Heart: The Life of Baseball's First Black Major Leaguer.* Lincoln: Univ. of Nebraska Press, 1995.

—*Sallie L. Powell*

AFRICAN AMERICAN BOY SCOUTS, organization that played an important role in the development of many young African American boys. The first African American Boy Scout troop to be officially recognized and promoted by the Boy Scout Council was Negro Troop 75 in Louisville, KY, which the **Church of Our Merciful Savior,** an African American Episcopal church, sponsored beginning in 1916. Soon after, Louisville quickly became a city with one of the largest African American Boy Scout memberships in the nation, having more than 500 black scouts by the late 1920s. Separate from the main office, the Colored Division of Scouting in Louisville was housed by the Pythian Temple on Chestnut St. (today the building is the **Chestnut Street YMCA**). Numerous African American churches throughout the city sponsored troops, including the **Grace Hope Presbyterian** mission on Hancock Street, R. E. Jones Methodist Temple, First Virginia Avenue Baptist Church, **Plymouth Congregational Church, Quinn Chapel,** and Emmanuel Baptist Church.

Throughout much of the 1920s and early 1930s, the Colored Division in Louisville was chaired by black educator and businessman William Baxter Matthews. During the late 1930s, the National Council gave three African American men professional full-time positions in Nashville, Cincinnati, and Louisville. Louisville's appointee was Steward Pickett, an original member of Troop 75, who remained an influential community and scout leader in the city in future decades. During the 1937 flood in Louisville, for example, Pickett and his older Boy Scout members helped evacuate the sick and elderly from the West End, volunteered at "Tent City," and set up a 24-hour food stop at Troop 44's building on W. Madison St.

African American Boy Scout troops flourished throughout the state as well. There were active troops in Paducah and Mays Lick. Central Kentucky was a major center of African American scouting in Kentucky. Rev. **Horace H. Greene,** who led a troop at Gunn Tabernacle Church in Lexington, noted that scouting among black boys was at its height in the 1940s and early 1950s in the region. As chairman of the Negro Division of the Bluegrass Area Council of Scouts, Greene recalled that during this period, "every church that could afford it" had its own troop. The Negro Division was made up of about 30 troops in the Bluegrass region, which included Georgetown, Cynthiana, Lancaster, and Danville. Every year, hundreds of African American scouts from across the Bluegrass region would meet and have a dinner.

African American Boy Scout troops were also closely tied to the **Kentucky Negro Education Association** (KNEA). In 1933, **Atwood Wilson,** secretary-treasurer of the KNEA and editor of its journal, was awarded the Silver Beaver for 15 years of scouting leadership. He was only the third African American to receive the national honor. Boy Scouts also volunteered and participated in the KNEA's annual meetings.

"Boy Scouts of Kentuckiana." In *The Encyclopedia of Louisville,* edited by John Kleber, 110–11. Lexington: Univ. Press of Kentucky, 2001.
Greene, Horace H. Interview by Edward Owens, August 2, 1978. Lexington, Univ. of Kentucky, Louie B. Nunn Center for Oral History, Blacks in Lexington Project, 78OH121 KH81.
Kentucky Negro Educational Association Journal 1, no. 1 (October 1930); and 3, no. 2 (January–February 1933).
Pickett, Steward. Interviews by Mary Bobo, May 23 and June 4 and 25, 1979. Univ. of Louisville Archives, tapes 764, 765, 766.

—*Joshua D. Farrington*

AFRICAN AMERICAN BUSINESSMEN'S ASSOCIATION OF COVINGTON, organization of Covington businessmen. The African American Businessmen's Association of Covington was begun in Covington during the late 1920s. Its first members included real estate agents, a funeral director, a grocer, an operator of a dry cleaning and tailor shop, and the owner of a restaurant and bar. Their businesses were located primarily on the east side of Covington, although they served the entire African American community. Each businessman was a member or leader of various other civic, patriotic, and fraternal organizations. For the

youth of the community, they sponsored an annual picnic at the Shinkle Farm in Crestview Hills. The model for this association was the National Negro Business League, developed by Booker T. Washington. The charter members of the local organization included Charles L. Deal, Clarence Frateman, Wallace Grubbs, Richard "Uncle Dick" Johnson, **Charles E. Jones,** Gene Lacey, **William H. Martin,** and **Horace S. Sudduth.** Their unofficial meeting place was the C. E. Jones Funeral Home at 635 Scott St.

Charles L. Deal was an agent for the Mutual Fire Insurance Company and also sold real estate. He was born in October 1877. His early years were spent in Latonia, along Winston Ave. and Main St., while he was working for the railroad. In 1928, he opened a real estate business at 1109 Russell St. in Covington. A few years later, he moved the business to his residence at 1421 Russell St. In the late 1930s, he established his office at 804 Greenup St., where it remained until the mid-1950s. After integration opened up the real estate market in Cincinnati, he moved to the Avondale neighborhood of that city and continued to work in real estate until his retirement in the 1960s. Deal died on March 10, 1969.

Clarence Frateman was the nephew of Richard Johnson. No information is available about the type of business he operated in Covington.

Wallace Grubbs was a businessman who for a long time owned a restaurant and bar at 301 E. 11th St. in Covington. Grubbs was born on February 2, 1894. He was a veteran of World War I, having served in the U.S. Army, Company A, 308th Labor Battalion, Quartermaster Corps, and was a member of Charles L. Henderson American Legion Post No. 166. Grubbs died on May 8, 1964.

Richard "Uncle Dick" Johnson was the consigliere of the association. For years, he owned property at 317 Scott St. Johnson was a grandfather of John "Jack" Price, whose other grandfather was **Jacob Price.** Johnson was also the uncle of fellow association member Clarence Frateman. Uncle Dick Johnson died on October 9, 1957.

Charles E. Jones in 1913 purchased the funeral home owned by **Wallace A. Gaines** at 633–635 Scott St. Jones expanded the business and changed its name to C. E. Jones Funeral Home. It continued in business until 1972. Jones married Anna Watkins, daughter of Covington's first African American physician, **Dr. Simon J. Watkins.**

Eugene F. Lacey opened his first grocery store in Covington in 1918, at 508 Scott St., while residing at 839 Craig St. He opened his second Covington store at 205 E. Robbins St.; this one was called the Gene and Bess Store. He and his wife Bessie formed two companies, the Lacey Sausage Company and the Lacey Paper Company. In 1926, Lacey closed his store at 508 Scott St. He was a grade school classmate of Horace Sudduth.

William H. Martin's dry cleaning and tailor business was first located at Athey Ave. and Craig St. in Cincinnati. He was a U.S. Army veteran of World War I and a member of Charles L. Henderson American Legion Post No. 166. In 1928, Martin moved his business to 508 Scott St., Covington, the site formerly occupied by Eugene Lacey's grocery. In 1932, Martin opened a second dry cleaning business at 1015 Greenup St., near the corner of Clinton and Scott Sts. In the late 1930s, Martin closed the Greenup St. location to concentrate on his Scott St. business. In 1948, Martin moved from 508 Scott St. to 522 Scott St.

The leader and organizer of the group was Horace S. Sudduth, a native Covingtonian who was astute in the development of modern business practices. Sudduth founded the Horace Sudduth and Associates Real Estate Agency and owned the Manse Hotel in Cincinnati, where influential African American visitors stayed. He served as president of two national organizations, the National Negro Business League and the Industrial Federal Savings and Loan Association. Sudduth was married to Melvina Jones, the sister of Charles E. Jones, the funeral director.

These businessmen and the businesses they operated faced and overcame constant challenges, such as the Great Depression and competition from emerging corporate business chains. The community activities they sponsored indicated their love of their community and benefited the people who participated. In 1941, at the beginning of World War II, a number of these activities, along with the African American Businessmen's Association itself, ceased and were never reinstituted. Most of the African American businesses struggled on until they disappeared in the 1950s because of changing demographics in the community.

Newspapers: "Police Raids Bring 17 into Covington Court," *KP*, March 15, 1930, 1; "Johnson, Richard," *Kentucky Times-Star,* October 12, 1957, 4A; "Grubbs, Wallace," *KP*, May 9, 1964, 5K; "Reader Recollection," *KP*, March 2, 1992, 4K.

—*Theodore H. H. Harris*

AFRICAN AMERICAN CATHOLIC MINISTRIES, ministry in the Archdiocese of Louisville. The office of African American Catholic Ministries (OAACM) was established on August 1, 1988. Archbishop Thomas C. Kelly acted on the advice of the African American Catholic community and the committee for African American Catholic planning. With the establishment of the office of multicultural ministry in 1997, the OAACM was referred to as African American Ministries (AAM). The AAM works in collaboration with all offices and agencies in implementing the archdiocesan strategic plan and the national black Catholic pastoral plan through the following activities:

Serving as a vehicle to provide spiritual, cultural, educational, and social nourishment for African American Catholics
Providing a voice and representation at the decision-making level within the archdiocesan structure
Assisting archdiocesan agencies in the development, coordination, and implementation of programs and activities that involve the African American community
Identifying African American leadership within the Archdiocese of Louisville
Encouraging archdiocesan participation in African American organizations
Providing opportunities, through programs, to address racism
Representing the Archdiocese of Louisville at state and national African American Catholic conferences and other functions

—*Angela Partee*

AFRICAN AMERICAN GIRL SCOUTS (1940 to mid-1950s), organization for girls. Kentucky's first African American Girl Scout troop was officially formed in Louisville during the Girl Scouts' annual luncheon at the Pendennis Club in 1940. The or-

ganization quickly spread to other cities, such as Bowling Green, Lexington, and Paducah. By April 1942, Kentucky had roughly 150 African American Girl Scouts who sold over 4,000 dozen cookies in the year's campaign.

Despite this achievement, most African Americans within the Girl Scout organization were painfully aware of the racism within it. **Murray B. Atkins Walls,** Girl Scout leader and member of the organization's interracial committee, recalled that although the white and black Girl Scouts worked side by side, they were still divided by race. "They had their own cookie money. We had our own cookie money," she claimed. Even their camp sites were separated, so that the African American Scouts were prohibited from attending the white girls' camp. In response to this, Walls helped secure and organize a camp for the girls at Camp Dan Beard, named for a white Boy Scout leader, in Jefferson Co. in 1943 and 1944.

Roughly 100 girls attended the camps in the first year, and attendance gradually increased. By 1945, the African American Girl Scouts were able to establish a permanent campsite at Camp Lincoln Ridge at the **Lincoln Institute.** Former Scout Bettye Foster Baker recalled that in the early years the girls slept in tents raised on planks and dined in a large tent with a ditch dug around it to prevent flooding. In 1949, the camp built its first permanent building, which held a dining room, kitchen, and recreation hall and cost $6,000 to construct.

By the 1950s, Murray Atkins Walls had become the first African American woman to serve on the Girl Scouts' Board of Directors and actively pushed for integration within the organization. Walls's efforts paid off in the mid-1950s when the Girl Scouts decided to lead by example and desegregated their troops before Kentucky desegregated its public schools. "We just had the feeling that our girls needed to know each other," Walls recalled, "and if they did, it would help them in their school situation when they came together."

Baker, Bettye Foster. E-mail message to *Encyclopedia* staff, June 30, 2009.
Newspapers: "Negro Girl Scouts Organized," *LCJ*, February 21, 1940, sec. 2, p. 3; "Negro Girl Declared Scout Cookie Champion," *LCJ*, April 22, 1942, sec. 2, p. 3; "Negro Girl Scouts Encamp Today Near Middletown," *LCJ*, July 7, 1943, p. 3; "Girl Scouts to Dedicate Camp," *LCJ*, June 26, 1949, p. 15.
Walls, John, and Murray A. Walls. Interview by Dwayne Cox, July 27, 1977. Univ. of Louisville Archives, tapes 398 and 399.

—*Dana Caldemeyer*

AFRICAN AMERICAN HAMLETS, small rural communities established by white and black landowners. In the immediate years after the abolition of slavery, a myriad of rural segregated African American communities evolved throughout Kentucky. Many of these communities were near urban centers such as Lexington or Louisville. Residents worked on farms or as domestics in these cities and others throughout the state. These hamlets existed on the outskirts of downtown cities or in pockets of a city. Schools, churches, and grocery stores were typically the cornerstones of these residential areas. Surrounding Lexington, African American hamlets included **Bracktown, Brucetown, Cadentown,** Centerville, **Coletown, Fort Spring,** Goodlowtown,

Jimtown, Jonestown, Keene, Kinkeadtown, **Maddoxtown,** Nihizertown, Pricetown, Smithtown, Taylortown, and **Uttingertown.** In Louisville, **Berrytown, Brownstown, Griffytown, Harrods Creek,** Jeffersontown, Newburg, Prospect, and **Smoketown** provided community for African Americans.

Some counties proudly announced the existence of these segregated hamlets. For instance, in 1903, the *Paducah Sun* announced that Muhlenberg Co. "boasted having the only exclusively Negro town in Kentucky." Clarksville, three miles south of Central City on the Owensboro and Nashville railroad line in Muhlenberg Co., flourished with 150 citizens and black officials, but it was not the only African American community in Kentucky or even in Muhlenberg Co. Three miles southeast of Greenville in Muhlenberg Co., Salsberry Free Negro Settlement was created in 1860 after the death of slaveholder Mrs. Thomas Salberry.

African American hamlets were vulnerable to attacks by whites who resisted their independence. In February 1908, night riders posted notices warning African Americans in Birmingham (Marshall Co.) to leave. When they refused to abandon their rich farmland, the night riders resorted to murder. Law enforcement neglected protection for black citizens, thus forcing them to hastily desert their homes.

Former slaves Ezekiel and Patsy Ann Coe purchased land on a desolate, nearly inaccessible ridge in Cumberland Co. in 1866. For almost a century, **Coe Ridge** (also called Coetown and Zeketown) citizens endured assaults from whites who tried to remove them. The inaccessible geographic landscape protected Coe Ridge, but in the 1930s, improved transportation opened the hamlet to the white world, and the community ceased to exist within twenty years.

The Bluegrass region contained a diverse group of African American hamlets. **Claysville** and Ruckerville subsisted near Paris in Bourbon Co. Former slaves created the communities of Boneyville, Chicken Bristle, and Logantown in Lincoln Co. Other settlements included Anderson Co.'s Peanickle and Meaux Settlement, **Sleettown** near Perryville, **Bobtown** (also known as Joe Lick) and **Farristown** in Madison Co., Nicholas Co.'s Henryville, Mountain Island in Owen Co., and **Firmantown** (also called Fermantown) in Woodford Co. In Scott Co., the all-black community of **New Zion** was the home of five buffalo soldiers, and three of them are buried there.

Not all African American hamlets were established immediately after the Civil War. In the 1920s, Sanctified Hill in Harlan Co. was named for a preacher known for his "sanctifying sermons." Twenty homes formed the community. In 1973, a landslide forced the evacuation of the residents. When the federal government condemned the area, homeowners moved to another hillside known as Pride Terrace.

Residents of these communities remain proud of their historical roots and identity.

Lucas, Marion B. *A History of Blacks in Kentucky.* Vol. 1, *From Slavery to Segregation, 1760–1891.* Frankfort: Kentucky Historical Society, 1992.
Montell, William Lynwood. *The Saga of Coe Ridge: A Study in Oral History.* Knoxville: Univ. of Tennessee Press, 1970.
Newspapers: "Strictly Colored Town," *PS,* June 9, 1903, 1; untitled article, *HK,* March 24, 1908, 4; "A Four of Fayette County's Black Communities," *LHL,* May 20, 2001, H-2; "Mayor Hopes Dump Can Be Transformed," *HDE,* October 6, 2005.
Smith, Peter C., and Karl B. Raitz. "Negro Hamlets and Agricultural Estates in Kentucky's Inner Bluegrass." *Geographical Review* 64, no. 2 (April 1974): 217–34.
Wright, George C. *Racial Violence in Kentucky, 1865–1940: Lynchings, Mob Rule, and "Legal Lynchings."* Baton Rouge: Louisiana State Univ. Press, 1990.

—*Sallie L. Powell*

AFRICAN AMERICAN JOCKEYS, highly skilled athletes during slavery and throughout the late nineteenth and early twentieth centuries. For more than 100 years, African Americans dominated the Kentucky horse industry as owners, trainers, grooms, stable workers, and jockeys. African American jockeys "competed alongside whites in America's first national pastime." In the inaugural Kentucky Derby in 1875, 13 of the 15 riders were African American. A crowd of 10,000 witnessed **Oliver Lewis** ride Aristides to victory that historic day. Two years later, **William "Billy" Walker,** born in Woodford Co., KY, rode the winning horse in the Kentucky Derby. Other Kentucky Derby winners included **George Garrett Lewis** (1880), **"Babe" Hurd** (1882), **Erskine "Babe" Henderson** (1885), **Isaac Lewis** (1887), **Alonzo "Lonnie" Clayton** (1892), and **James "Soup" Perkins** (1895). **William "Willie" Simms** (1896 and 1898) and **Jimmy "Wink" Winkfield** (1901 and 1902) won the Kentucky Derby twice. The most famous jockey, **Isaac Murphy,** won the Kentucky Derby three times (1884, 1890, and 1891). Seven of these Kentucky Derby winners were from Lexington, KY.

Most jockeys were not as fortunate as these Kentucky Derby winners. Dale Austin, **Shelby "Pike" Barnes, Thomas "Tommy" Britton, James "Jimmy" Lee,** and **Alfred "Monk" Overton** had outstanding racing careers but never won the derby. Overton competed in the Run for the Roses eight times.

Horse racing was an extremely dangerous sport. Shortly after his 1880 Kentucky Derby victory, George Garrett Lewis died at age 17 in a race accident in Missouri. Cash Tankersley died from a fall at Latonia race track in 1886. In 1909, Leslie "Snowball" Day barely survived when he was dragged 75 feet after he caught his foot in one of the stirrups.

Many jockeys, such as "Goldie," John Clay, and June Doty Perkins, suffered serious injuries when a horse threw them. What happened to "Goldie" after the fall is unknown. Clay's plunge ended his jockey career. He became a trainer and a wealthy real estate mogul in Lexington, KY. Although many thought that Perkins's injuries would cause his death, he continued to race for at least 10 years after the accident.

Like John Clay, "Babe" Hurd, Albert "Monk" Overton, William "Willie" Simms, and James "Soup" Perkins, **Edward Dudley "Brown Dick" Brown** began his career in the horse industry as a jockey before becoming a trainer. Born a slave in Fayette Co. in 1850, Brown Dick exemplified the possibility of "riding from slavery to freedom." Brown became one of the most successful and richest independent horse trainers in the country. Like trainers Eli Jordon, Abe Perry, Bryan McClelland, and Dudley Allen, Brown trained the horse ridden by an African American Kentucky Derby–winning jockey. William "Billy" Walker, the 1877

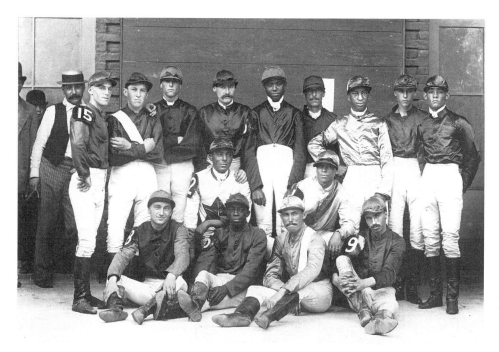

Jockeys photographed at Morris Park in New York in 1891. Anthony Hamilton is in the front row. Isaac Murphy is in the middle row seated behind Hamilton and to the left of Willie Simms.

Kentucky Derby winner, after his jockey career became not only a trainer but also later a turf correspondent.

In 1902, Fayette Co.'s **Jimmy "Wink" Winkfield** became the last African American jockey to win the Kentucky Derby. Like **Anthony "Tony" Hamilton,** William "Willie" Simms, and Andress Thomas, he left the country to continue his jockey career abroad. In 1908, James "Jimmy" Lee was the last African American to win a major stakes race. Horse racing offered African American men economic and athletic opportunities in the 1880s to the early 1900s. Tom Blevins, Jim Brooks, James Crutcher, Clarence "Pick" Dishman, Green Dunham, **John Hathaway,** Albert Isom, Bob Isom, Jim Juison, James "Sunny Jim" Lock, Alfred Neil, James Pearsall, Chippie Ray, William Scott, John Stoval, John Todd, William Tyler, and William "Tiny" Williams were among the many well-known black jockeys from Kentucky. During the twentieth century, the presence of African Americans on the track significantly declined. In 1902, the *Lexington Leader* reported that the demise of African American jockeys resulted from the established horse business resembling a family unit where the races did not mix. Roscoe Goose, a white jockey who won the 1913 Kentucky Derby, maintained that "violence in the saddle drove black jockeys away." In 1921, Henry King rode Planet in the Kentucky Derby. It would be decades before another African American jockey would ride in the Kentucky Derby.

The early African American horsemen paved the way for the entry of Cheryl White, the first African American female jockey, in 1971. White's father, Raymond, an eminent horse owner and trainer at Ohio and Kentucky tracks, had a horse in the 1932 and 1944 Kentucky Derbys. In 2000, **Marlon St. Julien** became the first African American jockey in the Kentucky Derby in seventy-nine years. Over a decade later, on May 4, 2013, Kevin Krigger rode Goldencents in the Kentucky Derby.

Hotaling, Edward. *The Great Black Jockeys: The Lives and Times of the Men Who Dominated America's First National Sport.* Rocklin, CA: Forum, 1999.

———. *Wink: The Incredible Life and Epic Journey of Jimmy Winkfield.* New York: McGraw-Hill, 2005.

Leach, George B. *The Kentucky Derby Diamond Jubilee.* Louisville, KY: Gibbs-Inman Co., 1949.

Newspapers: "The Commonwealth," *HC,* June 4, 1886, 1; "Horse World," *LL,* January 14, 1902, 7; "Jockey Is Hurt," *PES,* March 31, 1909, 1; "Ranks of Negro Jockeys Thinned by Grim Reaper," *Pittsburgh Press,* October 16, 1911, 15; "Passing of Negro Rider," *Daily Racing Form* (Chicago), April 8, 1923, 1–2.

Renau, Lynn S. *Racing around Kentucky.* Louisville, KY: L. S. Renau, 1995.

Saunders, James Robert, and Monica Renae. *Black Winning Jockeys in the Kentucky Derby.* Jefferson, NC: McFarland, 2003.

—*Sallie L. Powell*

AFRICAN AMERICAN MIGRATION, movements in which a large number of blacks chose to leave the South and moved to the West or to the North for social, political, and economic reasons. As slaves, African Americans were among the first migrants to the Commonwealth of Kentucky. In 1790, slaves constituted 16 percent of the total population. By 1860, the number of blacks in the state had grown exponentially, and there were approximately 250,000 slaves and 10,684 freed blacks living in the state.

In 1822, the American Colonization Society and the **Kentucky Colonization Society (KCS)** began sponsoring the migration of free blacks to Liberia. The KCS continued to fund the exodus of former slaves from Kentucky to Liberia as late as 1856. Private efforts also assisted in the migration of former slaves to Africa. In 1833, a Kentucky slave owner freed 32 of his slaves and funded their trip to Liberia. Henry Clay, one of the state's most preeminent politicians, was a major supporter of the American Colonization Society. A group of former slaves from Kentucky settled in a Liberian town and named it Clay Ashland in his honor.

After emancipation and the Civil War, many newly freed slaves migrated to states outside Kentucky. Between 1860 and

1870, almost 14,000 blacks left the state for the North, and between 1850 and 1880, the African American population of the state dropped from 21 percent of the total population to 16.5 percent.

Kansas proved to be a particularly attractive destination for African Americans. During the 1870s, almost 10,000 blacks from Tennessee and Kentucky participated in the exodus to Kansas. One of the most famous of all black settlements is **Nicodemus, KS,** formed by a group of African Americans from Lexington in 1877. W. J. Niles, a black businessman, and W. R. Hill, a white minister who had speculation interests in Kansas, actively recruited African Americans in Fayette and Scott Counties and later became prominent leaders of the settlement. Nicodemus inspired further migration of Kentuckians and the creation of other black settlements. For example, the settlers of Kinsley, KS, formed in 1878, modeled themselves on Nicodemus and were primarily emigrants from Harrodsburg and Lexington. **Junius Groves,** well known as the Potato King of the World, whose farm at one time produced more potatoes than any other, was among the thousands of black Kentuckians to migrate to Kansas.

In-state migration to urban areas also flourished after Reconstruction as African Americans became more concentrated in the state's cities. By 1890, over a third of the state's blacks lived in urban settings, and African Americans made up large percentages of residents in Louisville, Lexington, Winchester, Frankfort, and Hopkinsville. In 1910, African Americans made up approximately 20 percent of all people living in the state's cities. This figure jumped to 55 percent by 1940.

Reasons for migration varied on an individual basis, but almost all sought to avoid racism or to acquire better educational and economic opportunities. Many African Americans migrated north and west seeking better, industrial jobs, expanded educational options, and escape from the racial violence and segregation that plagued Kentucky. Similarly, many migrated to Louisville and other urban centers because of poor pay and exploitation as tenant farmers and sharecroppers in rural areas. Cities also provided some of the only public education open to African Americans in the state.

African Americans continued to migrate out of state during the Great Migration of the World War I years and the second Great Migration of the 1930s and 1940s. In 1860, more than 20 percent of Kentucky's population was African American, but the percentage had dropped to under 7 percent a hundred years later. Louisville's African American population increased in the twentieth century as more than 17,000 black migrants moved to the city between 1930 and 1970.

The staggering migration numbers in Kentucky illustrate the racial challenges of living in rural Kentucky, but also the determination of African Americans to seek better economic and educational opportunities for their families. For many years, African Americans "voted with their feet" against racial violence, labor exploitation, and the lack of educational opportunities for their children.

Adams, Luther. "'Way Up North in Louisville': African-American Migration in Louisville, Kentucky, 1930–1970." PhD diss., Univ. of Pennsylvania, 2002.

Hogan, Roseann Reinemuth. *Kentucky Ancestry: A Guide to Genealogical and Historical Research.* Salt Lake City, UT: Ancestry Inc., 1992.

Painter, Nell Irvin. *Exodusters: Black Migration to Kansas after Reconstruction.* New York: W. W. Norton, 1992.

Wright, George C. *A History of Blacks in Kentucky.* Vol. 2, *In Pursuit of Equality, 1890–1980.* Frankfort, KY: Kentucky Historical Society, 1992.

—*Joshua D. Farrington*

AFRICAN AMERICAN NEWSPAPERS, publications that have served as vital means of communication since the nineteenth century. From the mid-nineteenth century onward, African American men and women voiced their thoughts and concerns about their communities in newspapers printed by and for African Americans. In March 1867, Philip H. Murry, from Reading, PA, and John Patterson "J. P." Sampson, from Wilmington, NC, published the *Colored Kentuckian* in Louisville. Most of the earliest known newspapers began printing in the 1870s and covered a wide range of issues. In 1872, the *Louisville Weekly Planet* (1872–1875) began publication under the direction of lawyers T. F. Cassels and **Nathaniel R. Harper.** The paper was a nonpolitical organ dedicated to "the Intellectual and Moral interests of the colored people." Reverend **George W. Dupee** edited Paducah's *Baptist Herald* (1873–1879), which functioned as the respected voice of the **General Association of Baptists in Kentucky.** During its publication, the *Herald* printed sermons and materials for Kentucky ministers and Sunday school teachers throughout the state. Lexington's **Henry Scroggins** and a handful of faculty members of **Berea College** printed the *American Citizen* (1874–unknown), focusing on the challenges to black education.

Although many of these newspapers during this period did not remain in print for more than a few years after their first issue, the number of Kentucky's African American newspapers continued to grow, and they connected with other newspapers throughout the nation. In 1880, editors of the nation's African American newspapers convened in Louisville to form the Colored Press Association of the United States. During the convention, *Louisville Bulletin* editor **John Quincy Adams** was elected president of the new association.

Many leaders in this early period contributed to and edited multiple newspapers. After founding and editing an Indiana paper, Rev. **Eugene Evans** moved to Kentucky, where he published Elizabethtown's *Christian Pilot* and Lexington's *Fair Play* before editing Bowling Green's *Watchman* (1888–1892). One of the *Watchman*'s founders, Reverend **Chasteen C. Stumm,** and his wife also contributed to newspapers like the *Standard*, Paducah's *Baptist Herald,* the *Pilot* of Nashville, TN, and Danville's *Tribune* (1878–1892).

Kentucky had at least 13 African American newspapers by 1890; by 1905, the number had increased to 24. Two of the most prominent newspapers during this period were the *American Baptist* (1879–present), a religious newspaper edited by **William Henry Steward** and **William J. Simmons,** and the *Lexington Standard* (1892–1912), established by **William Decker Johnson** and later purchased by **Robert Charles O'Hara Benjamin,** who published it until his death in 1900. The *Lexington Standard,* at different times, operated as a Republican and then a Democratic newspaper before it became the *Lexington Weekly News* under **Edward D. Willis** in 1912.

The turn of the century also produced a host of smaller local newspapers throughout the state. Robert T. and George W. Berry established Owensboro's *Kentucky Reporter* while maintaining their tailor shop. A few years later, J. Edmund Wood began editing Danville's *Torch Light* (1902–1932). Although few articles from either of these papers remain, both papers tended to be Republican leaning and moved to Louisville and Lexington, respectively, between 1910 and 1912. According to the *Freeman,* before the *Torch Light*'s relocation, its subscribers could pay for their newspaper with eggs, meat, and other items.

The relocations of the *Reporter* and the *Torch Light* reflected a pattern many local newspapers followed in the second decade of the twentieth century. During this period, many small newspapers consolidated with larger papers or shut down operations entirely. Indeed, 14 out of Kentucky's 30 known African American newspapers terminated publication in this decade alone. In 1912, Lebanon's *Freeman,* **Dr. John A. Gwynn**'s *Richmond Sentinel,* and Bowling Green's *Liberty* all ceased publication. Despite surviving a fire in 1910, Mt. Sterling's *Reporter* closed its doors in 1915. After nearly two decades of publishing, Dr. **Edward E. Underwood**'s *Blue Grass Bugle* in Frankfort printed its last issue that same year.

But even as these newspapers faded, those that remained gradually grew more stable, and new publications emerged. T. A. Lawrence's *Paducah Light House,* which began in 1908, remained in print until 1937. In 1912, **William Warley** launched the *Louisville News* to speak against racism and segregation. Although the *News* never enjoyed a broad readership, it was nonetheless one of the foremost black newspapers of the period until it closed during World War II.

In 1933, a new Louisville newspaper emerged that challenged the hold of the *News* on the city. The *Louisville Defender* (1933–present), under **Frank L. Stanley Sr.**'s editorship, quickly became the most recognized African American newspaper in the commonwealth, reaching an estimated 17,000 readers by 1948. It distinguished itself as an advocate for integration in Louisville and greater Kentucky in the 1950s and 1960s.

Additionally in Louisville, three female journalists, Lucille E. St. Clair, **Alice A. Dunnigan,** and Mrs. M. S. Kimbley, edited and published the short-lived *Tri-Weekly Informer* in 1939. Dunnigan had also worked with Douglas Dawson on the *Hopkinsville Globe.* As white newspapers began printing stories of interest to African American communities and hired black reporters, the number of African American newspapers decreased, leaving only a select few in print in the twenty-first century, including the *American Baptist* and the *Defender.* In 1987, Donald Cordray founded, published, and edited the *Community Voice Newsjournal,* which halted production in 2001. Detroit native Patrice Muhammad and her husband, LaMaughn, printed the first edition of their newspaper, the *Key Newsjournal,* in January 2004.

Dunnigan, Alice Allison, comp. and ed. *The Fascinating Story of Black Kentuckians: Their Heritage and Traditions.* Washington, DC: Associated Publishers, 1982.
Henritze, Barbara K. *Bibliographic Checklist of African American Newspapers.* Baltimore: Genealogical Print Company, 1995.
Newspapers: "News Brevities," *Detroit Free Press,* March 27, 1867, 2; "The Planet," *Elevator,* February 22, 1873, 3; "The Colored Editors," *LCJ,* August 26, 1880, 4; "Meeting of Colored Editors." *NYT,* August 26, 1880; "Bridgeport," *FR,* September 30, 1882; "The Week in Society," *Washington Bee,* May 18, 1903, 5; "The Torchlight," *LL,* January 12, 1910; "The Reporter," *HGH,* February 3, 1910, 3; "Short Flights," *Freeman,* May 13, 1911, 2; "Black Voice to Fall Silent for a While," *LHL,* February 20, 2001, A-1; "Paper to Feature Black News," *LHL,* January 15, 2004, C1; "Frank Stanley, Jr., Champion of Civil Rights in Louisville, Dies at Age 70," *LCJ,* March 2, 2007, B4.
Pegues, A. W. *Our Baptist Ministers and Schools.* Springfield, MA: Willey and Co., 1892.

—*Dana Caldemeyer*

AFRICAN AMERICAN THEATERS, major business enterprises that provided entertainment opportunities. Although African Americans were either denied entry or segregated in the balcony in white theaters, some communities supported black-owned theaters that offered live entertainment and first-run films. In May 1910, the *Paducah Evening Sun* newspaper promoted the Lyceum Theater, "the new colored theater," by announcing, "Don't miss the show."

Larger communities like Lexington and Louisville sustained a multitude of theaters. Lexington's Frolic Theater, identified as "the only exclusive Colored theater in the south," opened on September 28, 1907, on Water St. near Mill St. Managers Webster Thompson, a paperhanger, and Peter Walker, from Louisville, offered free shows to entice business there in October. A November local newspaper ad encouraged African Americans to come where they were welcomed. Thompson and Walker portrayed the Frolic as a friendly, genteel meeting place. Robert Geary, a machinist, and C. B. Combs, a laborer, launched the Pekin Theater at 415 W. Main St. in September 1909. Charles J. Parker managed the 250-seat theater, which closed in November 1910.

More successful than the Frolic or the Pekin, the Gem Theater, under owners John Clark and Chester Brady, Cincinnati businessmen, opened in November 1910 with motion pictures, vaudeville performances, and local musical entertainers. The Gem Theater's competition, the Lincoln Theater, originated across the street at 415 W. Main St., which had been the previous home of the Pekin Theater. In May 1911, the Collins brothers of Piqua, OH, acquired the Lincoln Theater. After it closed in December 1911, "Senator" R. F. Bell, then the proprietor of the Gem Theater, purchased the Lincoln and controlled the Lexington African American theater market. Bell, an entrepreneur and realtor, expanded the Gem Theater Company into nearby Winchester in May 1912 and also sponsored a Lexington baseball team, the Gem Theaters. Willis E. Burden acquired the Gem Theater in April 1914. He stopped employing vaudeville acts and local entertainers and only showed movies. The Gem Theater no longer existed by 1918.

Proclaimed as the "nation's finest colored theater" in 1948, Lexington's **Lyric Theatre** hosted first-run movies and live entertainment such as Duke Ellington and Ella Fitzgerald. In April 1950, Marva Louis, the former wife of heavyweight boxing champion Joe Louis, modeled her own clothes in a fashion show held at the Lyric. The Art Deco–style building attracted people from across the state and became the city's leading cultural center for the African American community. Integration of white theaters precipitated the Lyric's closing in 1963.

Louisville's African Americans could spend a day in various theaters in the early 1900s. In August 1908, Edward D. Lee opened the first African American–owned moving picture theater in Louisville, located at Thirteenth and Walnut Sts. In October of that year, Lee established another 600-seat theater, the New Odd Fellows Theatre. By 1910, Luther Edwards founded the Taft Theatre on Cedar St., and the New Tick Houston Theatre opened on Walnut St., between Ninth and Tenth Sts. In the late 1920s, Ralph N. Dunn, secretary of the Colored Men's Branch of the YMCA, managed the Palace Theater. R. L. Ranshaw managed the prominent Lyric and Grand Theaters.

African Americans experienced segregated balcony seating in those Kentucky white theaters that allowed them entrance. The movie theaters were desegregated as a result of the civil rights movement. Lexington's Lyric Theatre, operational from 1948 to 1963, reopened its doors as a cultural arts center in 2010.

Dunnigan, Alice Allison, comp. and ed. *The Fascinating Story of Black Kentuckians: Their Heritage and Traditions.* Washington, DC: Associated Publishers, 1982.

Newspapers: "The Local News," *PES*, May 4, 1910, 5; "Colored Notes," *LL*, January 4, 1912, 11; "Short-Lived Lyric Left Lasting Memories," *LHL*, February 20, 2002, 14; "A Look Inside Lyric—Some Get First Peek, Others Reminisce," *LHL*, February 27, 2006, B1.

Sampson, Henry T. *The Ghost Walks: A Chronological History of Blacks in Show Business, 1865–1910.* Metuchen, NJ: Scarecrow Press, 1988.

Waller, Gregory A. *Main Street Amusements: Movies and Commercial Entertainment in a Southern City, 1896–1930.* Washington, DC: Smithsonian Institution, 1995.

—*Sallie L. Powell*

AFRICAN AMERICAN UNDERTAKERS, funeral directors and morticians responsible for burying the dead. African American undertakers, like ministers and educators, were leaders in Kentucky's African American communities. Many of them owned other businesses and actively participated in politics and civic work. Their funeral businesses frequently included members of their families. Segregation through **Jim Crow** laws presented possibilities and limitations in the early years for Kentucky's African American funeral commerce.

In 1867, Virginia native **J. H. Taylor** became the first African American mortician in Louisville when he joined Yarmouth Carr to establish an undertaking establishment. Shortly after his death, his wife, Mary H. Taylor, managed the business. Born in slavery, **Jordan Carlisle (J. C.) Jackson Jr.** exemplified the industrious undertaker. As a prosperous businessman and attorney, he served twice as a delegate to the Republican National Convention. He joined William M. Porter and formed the first African American funeral business in Lexington in 1892. In the same year, Louisville's Minnie Watson graduated at the top of her class at Clarke School for Embalming (later known as Cincinnati College of Mortuary Science) and then joined her husband, William, in the funeral profession.

Brothers **Aaron** and **George Cabell,** grocers, were involved in Henderson's Cemetery and Burial Company. Aaron's unsuccessful 1881 bid for a Henderson City Council seat made him the first African American to run for public office in the town. Hopkinsville's two undertakers, **James L. Allensworth Sr.** and **Edward W. Glass,** were most likely the first African American elected officials in Kentucky. Allensworth, a Baptist preacher, defeated a white physician to become coroner in 1894. In 1896, Glass won a city council seat. Both men worked on local newspapers. **Henry Botts** created the first African American funeral home in Montgomery Co. In 1901, he and James E. Bean were elected to Mt. Sterling's city council, becoming that community's first elected African American officials. That same year, the Falls City Undertaking and Embalming Company in Louisville was founded and later managed by Mt. Sterling native **James Harris Hathaway.** After his death, his daughter, Columbia, along with her husband, assumed ownership and made Hathaway and Clark the oldest African American–owned and operated funeral home in Louisville.

Besides caring for those who had died of natural causes, African American undertakers were frequently responsible for the bodies of persons who had been lynched. In 1901, a body was delivered to James H. Corbin, the Paris undertaker. In 1906, after one body hung for 44 hours near Hopkinsville, James L. Allensworth Sr. was officially notified. He buried the corpse about 50 yards from where the man had been hanged. Ten years later, an unnamed Paducah black undertaker handled the remains of two lynching victims that had been completely destroyed by fire.

In August 1904, Hopkinsville's Edward W. Glass, John Chafin, and other Kentucky African American undertakers applied for membership in the white Funeral Directors Association of Kentucky. Their denied membership resulted in the formation of the Colored Funeral Directors Association of Kentucky, and Glass was selected as its president. Other future officers would include Lexington's Jordan C. Jackson, Louisville's James H. Hathaway, **Lucas B. Willis, Alonzo B. McAfee,** Covington's W. A. Gaines, Frankfort's **Thomas K.** and **Jackson K. Robb,** and Mt. Sterling's Henry Botts. No other state African American funeral directors' association existed at this time, but along with educating its members in the latest scientific embalming techniques, the organization's objective was to grow into a national organization, which occurred 20 years later.

In the 1800s, undertakers were not required to secure a license to open a funeral business. By the early 1900s, that was changing, and African American undertakers earned their embalming license. Paducah's Andy Watkins obtained his license in 1904. Several years later, Walter Thomas was the first African American from Maysville to acquire his license. By 1910, **Daisy Morgan Saffell,** a teacher, had become an undertaker in Shelbyville, while her husband, **George William Saffell,** remained a high school principal. Daisy later served as an officer in the Colored Funeral Directors Association of Kentucky and the National Association of Colored Funeral Directors. Her husband managed the funeral home after her death and became the first president of the newly formed Independent National Funeral Directors Association in 1924. According to the *Louisville Courier-Journal,* **Georgia Cleopatra Williams** was the "first Negro woman embalmer" in Kentucky when she was in her early 20s and operated G. C. Williams Funeral Home in Louisville, beginning in 1929. In 1961, Calvin R. Winstead purchased the business.

Louisville's W. T. Shumake and Daughters Funeral Home, the only "and daughters" funeral home in Kentucky, opened its doors in 1981. The next year, 22-year-old Dwight Hughes continued a family legacy when he became the licensed funeral director of Hawkins Funeral Home in Lexington. His great-grandfather, John Hawkins, had founded the establishment in 1927. Although their numbers are diminished, Kentucky's African American undertakers have continued to serve various Kentucky communities.

Majors, Monroe A. *Noted Negro Women: Their Triumphs and Activities.* Jackson, TN: M. V. Lynk Publishing House, 1893.

Newspapers: "Judge Lynch," *BN,* February 12, 1901, 3; "Negroes Excluded," *HK,* August 12, 1904, 8; "First Negro Woman Embalmer in State Dies," *LCJ,* September 26, 1945, sec. 2, p. 9; "Mortician Carrying On a Family Tradition," *LL,* February 16, 1982, C2.

Parrish, C. H. *Golden Jubilee of the General Association of Colored Baptists in Kentucky: From 1865–1915.* Louisville, KY: Mayes Printing Co., 1915.

Smith, Suzanne E. *To Serve the Living: Funeral Directors and the African American Way of Death.* Cambridge, MA: Belknap Press of Harvard Univ. Press, 2010.

W. T. Shumake and Daughters Funeral Home. http://www.shumake anddaughters.com/about.html (accessed September 20, 2012).

—*Sallie L. Powell*

AFRICAN CEMETERY NO. 2, Lexington's oldest known cemetery established by African Americans in Kentucky. In the 1850s, former slaves organized the Benevolent Society "to take care of the sick, bury the dead and perform other deeds of charity." The **Union Benevolent Society** of Lexington, KY, established the African Cemetery No. 2 in 1870. The eight-acre cemetery, located at 419 E. Seventh St. in Lexington, contains over 5,000 graves and approximately 1,200 markers. Over 100 of the bodies have been identified as Civil War veterans. The cemetery was also the burial site of the famed jockey **Isaac Murphy** after his death in 1896. In 1967, his remains were relocated to the Kentucky Horse Park.

In 1979 and 1980, the African American community of Lexington rallied behind a restoration effort to improve and maintain the cemetery. According to the *Lexington Herald-Leader* in 1980, the cemetery "has been in a state of neglect and disrepair" since the 1940s, and dozens of tombstones had been damaged by vandals. Contributions from private individuals, local businesses, and the Urban Co. government paid for the restoration, which cost an estimated $150,000.

In 2003, a historical marker was dedicated in the cemetery, commemorating its historical roots and the African American community leaders buried there. The cemetery is under the direction of a nonprofit board, African Cemetery No. 2, Inc., and is the site of Veterans Day memorials and Juneteenth celebrations.

Newspapers: *Kentucky Leader,* February 3, 1892; "Black Community Rallies to Restore Historic Cemetery," *LHL,* March 25, 1979, A1; "Fresh Start," *LHL,* June 3, 1980, A3; "Volunteers Are Needed for Cemetery Cleanup," *LHL,* November 4, 1998, 4; "Rediscovering Juneteenth," *LHL,* June 16, 2002, B1.

—*Joshua D. Farrington*

ALEXANDER, SHAUN EDWARD (b. 1977, Florence, KY), football player. The son of Curtis and Carol Alexander, Shaun Edward Alexander was raised in Florence, KY. His football stardom began at Boone County High School when as a junior tailback he rushed for 2,401 yards and scored 42 touchdowns (setting a national record) to lead the Rebels to the Class AAAA state semifinals in 1993. He was voted Offensive Player of the Year. In high school, he primarily played offense but also occasionally played defense. In 1994, he was awarded Kentucky's Mr. Football honor.

Recruited by numerous colleges, Alexander chose the University of Alabama. In one game, he set a school record by carrying the ball for 291 yards. He was a leading Heisman Trophy candidate in 1999. He became Alabama's all-time leading rusher with 3,465 yards in four seasons. In 2000, the Seattle Seahawks signed the 5-feet-11, 220-pound running back to a $6.5-million, five-year contract in the first round of the draft. He made three trips to the Pro Bowl (2003, 2004, and 2005). His best playing year of professional football was 2005, when he rushed for 1,880 yards and was awarded Most Valuable Player, and the Seahawks went to the Super Bowl. The Seahawks released him after seven years. He went to the Washington Redskins and then retired in 2008.

Alexander has formed the Shaun Alexander Foundation and has written two books that relate his football experiences and his Christian faith. His hometown of Florence honored him by naming a street on the Boone County High School campus Shaun Alexander Way.

Alexander, Shaun. *The Walk: Clear Direction and Spiritual Power for Your Life.* Colorado Springs, CO: WaterBrook Press, 2010.

Alexander, Shaun, with Cecil Murphey. *Touchdown Alexander: My Story of Faith, Football, and Pursuing the Dream.* Eugene, OR: Harvest House Publishers, 2007.

"Florence People: Shaun Alexander." Florence Kentucky Online. http://www.florencekyonline.com/sports/ (accessed August 1, 2013).

Newspapers: "Football All-Stars—Alexander Earns Offensive Honor," *KP,* December 18, 1993, 14K; "Alexander the Great," *Mobile Register,* November 10, 1996, C1; "Alexander Falls Hard from MVP," *LHL,* October 29, 2008, C1.

—*Wardell Johnson*

ALGEE, JOHN ALFORD (b. 1931, Hickman, KY; d. 1998, Tulsa, OK), medical doctor. Born in Hickman, KY, John Alford Algee moved to Oklahoma at a young age. He shined shoes to pay for his education. He graduated from Langston University in Langston, OK, and earned his master's degree in physiology from the University of Illinois. He taught biology and physiology at Savannah State University before earning his medical degree from Howard University. He served his internship at Howard University Hospital and his residencies at Duke University Medical Center and D.C. General Hospital.

Algee's prime medical interests included gerontology. He served as a consultant for numerous organizations, including the National Council on Black Aging and the Departments of the Army, the Navy, Labor, Justice, and Health, Education, and Welfare. He also chaired the Advisory Health Committee on Aging for the Black Caucus Brain Trust. In 1966, he was recognized for his work on aging by the Office of Economic Opportunity.

Algee spent the majority of his career in Washington, D.C., where he served on the staffs of D.C. General and Howard

University Hospitals. As section chief of the D.C. Health Department's Neighborhood Health Centers, he organized the Union Medical Center, a private health care center. He also worked as the medical director of J. B. Johnson Nursing Home in Washington. He was chief of geriatrics of the D.C. Health Department when he retired. In two of his articles in the *Journal of the National Medical Association,* Algee argued for the importance of caring for the aged. In March 1990, as a doctor at the Benning Heights Neighborhood Health Center in northeast Washington, Algee maintained his support for troubled Washington mayor Marion Barry, "We've got a medical problem and we're making it a criminal justice problem. We're going to put him [Mayor Barry] in jail for being sick. It just doesn't seem right. What is the crime?"

Algee was divorced from Maebelle Algee and the father of one daughter, Teal Algee, when he died at age 66 of renal failure in Tulsa, OK, on February 15, 1998.

Dunnigan, Alice Allison, comp. and ed. *The Fascinating Story of Black Kentuckians: Their Heritage and Traditions.* Washington, DC: Associated Publishers, 1982.
Kentucky Birth Index, 1911–1999.
Newspapers: "Core Group of True Believers Standing by Mayor Barry," *Washington Post,* March 12, 1990, B1; "Obituaries," *Washington Post,* February 23, 1998, D6.
Social Security Death Index.

—*Sallie L. Powell*

ALI, MUHAMMAD (b. 1942, Louisville, KY), boxer. Kentucky Athlete of the Century and arguably the most recognized person in the contemporary world, Ali was born Cassius Marcellus Clay Jr. to Cassius Marcellus Clay Sr. and Odessa (Grady) Clay of Louisville. The Clay family lived at 3302 Grand Ave. in what was then the African American section of the **Parkland** neighborhood.

Louisville during and immediately after World War II, when Ali came of age, was a rigidly segregated city in which African Americans were concentrated in a few neighborhoods in its western and eastern sections. The African American community had a long history, dating to the 1820s, and a long record of moderate but effective political activism. However, limited gains in education and politics over time had neither blurred the local color line nor translated into significant economic opportunities; most black adults worked as industrial, service, or domestic laborers, with a small contingent of professionals and small-business owners. Although Louisville African Americans were spared the blatantly overt racism and endemic racial violence that typified social dynamics in the Deep South, they were nonetheless expected to keep to their separate and unequal place. As a nuclear, working-class family, Ali, his brother Rudolph (now Rahaman Ali), and their parents were perhaps far more representative of African Americans in Louisville than were the better-known black leaders of the period.

Muhammad Ali's boxing career began inauspiciously in October 1954 when the theft of his bicycle prompted him to seek boxing instruction from **Joe Martin,** an Irish American Louisville policeman. Ali trained at Columbia Gym, developed under Martin's tutelage, and soon began appearing on *Tomorrow's Champions,* a local television program featuring amateur boxing. His extraordinary talent became increasingly apparent, and by 1960 Ali had fought in 167 bouts, winning 161, including 6 Kentucky and 2 National Golden Glove tournaments and 2 national Amateur Athletic Union titles.

In 1960, Ali graduated from Louisville Central High School and, later that summer, defeated Zbiegniew Pietrzykowski to win the Olympic gold medal as a light heavyweight. By the time he turned professional, Ali had become well known as a brash, cocky, and extremely vocal fighter. No other African American athlete since the legendary Jack Johnson had been so outspoken, and, against the backdrop of the civil rights era, the impact of Ali's words, actions, and choices extended far beyond the bounds of his profession. Although race relations in the United States were changing, Ali discovered that his achievements and celebrity did not insulate him from discrimination. In his own memorable account, he threw his Olympic gold medal into the Ohio River after receiving such treatment following his return to Louisville. Still, race was not always a barrier—or not always the same barrier in all situations. Thus, as controversial as the Louisville Lip was becoming, black attorney **Alberta Jones** arranged for a group of prominent white Louisville businessmen to form a syndicate to promote Ali's professional career in return for 50 percent of his earnings. The Sponsoring Group included Archibald M. Foster, Patrick Calhoun Jr., Gordon Davidson, William S. Cutchins, J. D. Stetson Coleman, William Faversham Jr., James R. Todd, Vertner D. Smith Sr., George W. Norton IV, William Lee Lyons Brown, E. Gary Sutcliffe, and Robert Worth Bingham III. Ali's relationship with this group lasted until 1966.

Ali won his first professional fight on October 29, 1960, defeating Tunney Hunsaker in a six-round decision. After hiring Angelo Dundee as his trainer, Ali began predicting the round in which he would knock out his opponents. Although his cocky flamboyance infuriated many, Ali's flair for self-promotion was exceeded only by his talent. His knockout predictions were correct in 13 of 17 fights, and his drawing power grew as increasing numbers of boxing fans were willing to pay in hopes of witnessing his defeat. Victory followed victory as Ali moved ever higher in the rankings. Although Ali was not a power puncher in the mold of Joe Louis, his unique combination of heavyweight size and middleweight speed and the cumulative effect of his lethal left jab and flurries of combinations took a heavy toll on fighters who underestimated him. This unusual ability to "float like a butterfly, sting like a bee" stunned the nation when, on February 25, 1964, Ali won the heavyweight championship by defeating the heavily favored Charles "Sonny" Liston in Miami, FL.

In a press conference the next morning, Ali announced that he was a member of the Nation of Islam, commonly known as the Black Muslims. On March 6, 1964, he changed his name officially from Cassius Clay to Muhammad Ali, as decreed by Elijah Muhammad, then the leader of the Nation. Although the announcement of Ali's conversion surprised many, his actual association with the Nation dated to 1961, and, through relationships with Muslim ministers such as Jeremiah Shabbazz and Malcolm X, his actual conversion had occurred in 1962. Ali's relationship with Malcolm X has been the subject of considerable speculation and analysis, but Elijah Muhammad himself was the strongest influence on Ali at this time, and Ali remained loyal to Elijah Muhammad after Malcolm X left the Nation in 1964. Perhaps more than anything, the Nation offered a strong and spiritual basis for racial and gender identity that was profoundly appealing to many young African Americans, including Muhammad Ali. After the death of Elijah Muhammad in 1975, his son, Wallace, directed the Nation and Ali away from its image as an antiwhite sect and along the path of Islamic orthodoxy, with its emphasis on universal justice and peace.

Had Ali declared himself a Muslim before 1964, he might never have been permitted to contend for the heavyweight championship. Once he became champion, the racial and religious controversy surrounding his public declaration could not derail his career, particularly because so many boxing fans were still willing to pay in hopes of seeing him lose. Denying them their wish, Ali defeated Liston again on May 25, 1965, and easily bested his other challengers. However, although he could not be defeated in the ring, he could be driven from it, and his next and perhaps his most difficult challenge was unrelated to boxing. After his requests for a military draft deferment and exemption from service as a conscientious objector were denied in 1966, Ali refused to take one step forward at the Houston induction center on April 28, 1967. This stand was entirely consistent with the Muslim emphasis on uprightness, spirituality, and strong black manhood. It was complemented by a commitment to pacifism, as exemplified by Elijah Muhammad's imprisonment for being a conscientious objector during World War II. The New York Athletic Committee promptly suspended his boxing license, stripped him of his title, and awarded it to Joe Frazier. The following week, a federal grand jury in Houston indicted him for resisting the draft. Ali was sentenced to five years in prison and a $10,000 fine. Ali posted bail and subsequently appealed.

Ali's principled opposition to war at a time when U.S. involvement in Vietnam was deepening daily aroused both hatred and admiration, but he rose in stature as a man as he drifted into limbo as an athlete. Many prominent African American athletes rallied to his defense, including Lew Alcindor (soon to become Kareem Abdul-Jabbar) of UCLA, Bill Russell of the Boston Celtics, and Gale Sayers of the Chicago Bears. Furthermore, although he was barred from boxing, antiwar groups across the nation clamored for Ali's services as a speaker. His college lectures and his brief movie and theatrical career—Ali even starred in a Broadway musical, *Big Time Buck White*—provided a livelihood during his 29-month exile from the ring. Finally, on June 28, 1970, the U.S. Supreme Court reversed Ali's conviction after learning that the FBI had tapped Ali's telephone illegally. Ali regained his boxing license and on October 26, 1970, defeated Jerry Quarry in his first return bout. On March 8, 1971, he fought to regain his title from "Smokin'" Joe Frazier in the first of their three titanic battles but lost a 15-round decision for his first defeat as a professional. Ali suffered his second defeat and a broken jaw on March 31, 1973, in a bout with Ken Norton. As a 32-year-old fighter, Ali could easily have retired, but he persevered and scored two of his most memorable victories late in his career.

By 1974, George Foreman was world champion, and after Ali defeated Joe Frazier on January 28, 1974, rising fight promoter Don King arranged for Ali to fight Foreman for a purse of $5 mil-

lion for each boxer. On October 30, 1974, in Kinshasa, Zaire, in the "Rumble in the Jungle," Ali abandoned his customary dancing style and allowed the heavily favored Foreman to punch himself out in the early rounds. Ali knocked out the weary and confused Foreman in the eighth round and reclaimed his championship after nearly eight years. Joe Frazier challenged Ali one last time in what many boxing aficionados consider to be the greatest heavyweight fight in history, the "Thrilla in Manila" on September 30, 1975. Ali won again and defended his title until he lost to Leon Spinks on February 15, 1978. Then, at age 36, Ali became world champion for the third time by defeating Spinks on September 15, 1978. He lost his championship to Larry Holmes, a former sparring partner, on October 2, 1980, and retired in 1981 with a 56–5 record and 37 knockouts.

The last great challenge of Muhammad Ali's life followed his boxing career. Ali developed Parkinson's syndrome, a condition that left his mental faculties intact but slurred his speech and slowed his movements. As a Muslim committed to peace and harmony and as perhaps the best-known person in the world, Ali overcame his physical limitations and became a global ambassador in the 1980s. His international stature was never more obvious than when he lit the flame for the 1996 Summer Olympic Games and was greeted with a thunderous and sustained ovation.

An assessment of the life of any living person, particularly someone as vital and engaged in life as Muhammad Ali, is impossible because so many important chapters in his personal history may remain unwritten. Still, much can be said about the meaning and impact of his life in the last half of the twentieth century. In this context, Muhammad Ali rose to prominence as a boxer during an era that witnessed the transformation of the sport. The Olympic Games in 1952, 1956, and 1960 became an international arena in which many athletes achieved celebrity through the new medium of television and through which many lucrative professional careers were launched. Congressional probes into the involvement of organized crime and, as colonialism ended, the emergence of numerous boxers of color in Third World nations forced far-reaching changes both in how the sport was governed and in its racial demography. The World Boxing Association and the World Boxing Council, both formed in the early 1960s, were far more representative internationally, and African American fighters became major figures in the heavier weight classes regulated by each organization.

Transcending his celebrity as a boxer, Muhammad Ali achieved international recognition as a symbol of black masculinity, pride, and racial consciousness against the backdrop of social revolution in the 1960s and the beginnings of the decolonization of Africa and other regions of the non-European world. Beyond the practiced theatrics of his youth, the mature Ali forced the boxing establishment and the American and global public to respect him on his own terms. In so doing, he not only insisted on and preserved his own dignity but also epitomized the courage to stand on a principle and defy injustice. Ali became a hero to millions throughout the world. As Arthur Ashe concluded, "In retrospect, one must agree with Ali's self-assessment: He was 'The Greatest.'"

Ali was married four times, first to model Sonji Roi in 1964. After his divorce from Roi in 1966, he married Kalilah Tolona (formerly Belinda Boyd) in April 1967, with whom he had three daughters and a son. In June 1977, Ali married Veronica Porshe, and, in November 1986, he married Yolanda "Lonnie" Williams of Louisville. Fittingly, on September 13, 1999, the Kentucky Athletic Hall of Fame recognized Ali as Kentucky Athlete of the Century. On October 7, 1998, Ali and his wife announced plans to build the Muhammad Ali Center near the downtown Louisville waterfront. The seventy-five-million-dollar center opened to the public on November 21, 2005. Educational programs, an interactive museum, and special events highlight the center's activities.

Ali, Muhammad, with Richard Durham. *The Greatest: My Own Story.* New York: Random House, 1975.

Ashe, Arthur R., Jr. *A Hard Road to Glory: A History of the African-American Athlete since 1946.* New York: Warner Books, 1988.

Frazier, E. Franklin. *Negro Youth at the Crossways: Their Personality Development in the Middle States.* Washington, DC: American Council on Education, 1940.

Gorn, Elliot J., ed. *Muhammad Ali: The People's Champ.* Urbana: Univ. of Illinois Press, 1995.

Hauser, Thomas. *Muhammad Ali: His Life and Times.* New York: Simon & Schuster, 1991.

Reemtsma, Jan Philipp. *More Than a Champion: The Style of Muhammad Ali.* New York: A. A. Knopf, 1998.

Wright, George C. *Life Behind a Veil: Blacks in Louisville, Kentucky, 1865–1930.* Baton Rouge: Louisiana State Univ. Press, 1985.

—*J. Blaine Hudson*

ALLEN, BESSIE LUCAS (b. 1887, Louisville, KY; d. 1944, Louisville, KY), social worker. By the time of her death, Bessie Allen was one of the most active social workers in Louisville. After graduating from State University (later known as **Simmons College of Kentucky**), Allen served as the head of the city's newly formed Colored Division of Probation Work. She worked directly with many young delinquents and understood the importance of promoting child welfare, vocational training, and religion.

As part of her emphasis on the moral development of children, she founded the newsboys' Sunday School, which met every Sunday afternoon in the Odd Fellows Building and gathered children from several blocks. After running the nonsectarian Sunday school program successfully for several years, she received financial assistance from local white philanthropists and opened the Booker T. Washington Community Center, located at Ninth and Magazine Sts. The center offered vocational training, like woodwork and shoe repair, to boys and home economics classes for girls. During the summer months, she also started the Daily Vacation School to keep children off the streets and teach them similar skills.

Allen organized a marching band of students who regularly attended the Sunday school. The band became a badge of honor to many of the young children in the neighborhood. Each member of the marching band was given a uniform and a musical instrument. The band performed in various local parades. Notable African American musicians, such as Johan Jones, **Helen Humes, Dicky Wells, Bill Beason,** and Russell Bowles, received their early musical training in "Mrs. Allen's Marching Band."

During the second decade of the twentieth century, Bessie Allen also founded the Kentucky Home Society for Colored

Children, an orphanage, in Louisville. Many of these young persons participated in activities at the Booker T. Washington Center and joined the marching band. Besides her contributions to education, Allen served as the only African American on Louisville's Tenement House Commission. She organized the Newsboys Improvement Club, which met weekly to discuss community development and address local problems. Bessie Allen died in 1944 and was survived by her daughter, famed novelist and nonfiction writer **Ann Allen Shockley.**

Pike, Bill. "African-American Orphanages Fought to Care for Children." *LCJ,* February 19, 2003, 1N.

Powell, Jacob W. *Bird's Eye View of the General Conference of the African Methodist Episcopal Zion Church with Observations on the Progress of the Colored People of Lousiville and a History of the Movement Looking toward the Elevation of Rev. Benjamin W. Swain, D.D. to the Bishopric, 1920.* Boston: Lavalle Press, 1918.

Wright, George C. *Life Behind a Veil: Blacks in Louisville, Kentucky, 1865–1930.* Baton Rouge: Louisiana State Univ. Press, 1985.

—*Joshua D. Farrington*

ALLEN, ELMER LUCILLE HAMMONDS (b. 1931, Louisville, KY), one of the first black female chemists, founder of the Afro-American Coalition for Artists, and ceramic and fabric artist. On August 23, 1931, Elmer Lucille Hammonds became the firstborn child of Elmer and Ophelia Guinn Hammonds and was named for her father. Her father was a Pullman porter and her mother was a **domestic worker.** When her parents had a son a year later, he, too, was named Elmer, so the family called her by both names, Elmer Lucille. She later married Ray Allen.

In 1953, Elmer Lucille graduated from Spalding University (formerly Nazareth College) with a degree in chemistry, making her one of the first African American female chemists in the country. However, she could not find a job as a chemist in Kentucky. Instead, she accepted a position as a clerk/typist at Fort Benjamin Harrison in Indiana. Afterward, she worked as a research chemist at the University of Louisville's School of Medicine. In 1966, she became the first African American chemist at the Brown-Forman Company in Louisville. She began as a junior chemist and retired 31 years later as senior analytical chemist in 1997.

In 2002, at the age of 71, Allen earned a master of arts degree in creative arts with a major in ceramics from the University of Louisville. She worked in dual media of textiles and ceramics in shades of blue and black. In creating her textiles, she used the Japanese technique of shibori, which involves folding, crumpling, and binding cloth before dyeing it. As a charter member of the Arts Council of Louisville, she became the curator of the Wayside Expressions Gallery and founded the short-lived Afro-American Coalition for Artists.

Allen developed Kentucky's first African American Arts Directory and belonged to the **Alpha Kappa Alpha Sorority.** Her life served as the subject of the 2003 play *She Moves Like the Wind* by Nancy Gall-Clayton. She was the first recipient of the Community Arts Lifetime Local Achievement Award in 2004 and was honored by the Center for Women and Families as a Woman of Distinction that same year. In 2007, she was one of the Women of Spunk honorees and was recognized in Portraits of Grace, a portrait collection of feminist women in their 80s whose lives have made a positive impact on Louisville.

Allen's work has been exhibited widely; venues include the Kentucky Artisan Center in Berea, KY, the Kentucky Museum of Art and Craft in Louisville, **Kentucky State University**, the Kentucky Capitol, the Actors Theatre of Louisville, the Owensboro Museum of Fine Art, and the Bernheim Arboretum and Research Forest. Her art can be found in private collections, as well as the collections of Spalding University, the Brown-Forman Corporate Collection, and the Office of Multi-cultural Affairs at Purdue University.

Davis, Karen R. "Elmer Lucille Allen, Artist Interview." *Seamless Skin blog.* http://karoda.typepad.com/seamless_skin/2010/11/elmer-lucille-allen-artist-interview.html (accessed September 3, 2013).

"The First Time: Elmer Lucille Allen, Working in Shibori." http://www.courier-journal.com/article/20101107/SCENE05/311070013/The-First-Time-Elmer-Lucille-Allen-working-shibori (accessed September 3, 2013).

Kentucky Artisan Center. kyartisancenter.ky.gov/gs_artisans476.aspx (accessed September 2, 2013).

Kentucky Department for Libraries and Archives. *Kentucky Birth, Marriage, and Death Databases: Births, 1911–1999.* Frankfort: Kentucky Department for Libraries and Archives.

Newspapers: "Actors Theatre Will Honor Women of Spunk," *LCJ*, December 2, 2007, I1–I2; "Life Lessons: Elmer Lucille Allen, Artist, Scientist," *LCJ*, April 21, 2011, E3.

Potter, Eugenia K., ed. *Kentucky Women: Two Centuries of Indomitable Spirit and Vision.* Louisville, KY: Big Tree Press, 1997.

U.S. Federal Census (1940) and *U.S. School Yearbooks.*

—*Karen Cotton McDaniel*

ALLENSWORTH, ALLEN (b. 1843, Louisville, KY; d. 1914, Monrovia, CA), cofounder of Allensworth, CA. Allen Allensworth was born of slave parents, Levi and Phyllis, in Louisville, KY. Sold as a child, he lived with different masters in Henderson Co., KY, and New Orleans, LA. He returned to Louisville as a slave in 1861, but the following year he left the city with soldiers and obtained his freedom by joining the U.S. Navy.

After his tenure in the navy, he attended Ely School and the Nashville Institute. After a brief stint as a teacher in Georgetown, KY, Allensworth served as the pastor of churches in Louisville, Bowling Green, and Cincinnati. In 1880 and 1884, he became the first black delegate from Kentucky to attend the Republican National Convention. Later, while pastoring Union Baptist Church in Cincinnati, he was appointed by President Grover Cleveland as chaplain of the army's 24th Infantry and was promoted to lieutenant colonel, the first African American to receive that rank, in 1906.

After his service in the Spanish-American War, Allensworth retired and moved to Los Angeles, where he became the president and cofounder of the California Colony and Home Promoting Association in 1908. The organization sought to establish an all-black community in the state and encouraged African American migration from across the country. By 1914, the community was officially named Allensworth, with an all-black local government, and became the first African American school district in California.

Beasley, Delilah. *The Negro Trailblazers of California.* New York: Negro Universities Press, 1969.

Oder, Barron Krieg. "Education, 'Race-Adjustment,' and the Military: The Life and Work of Chaplain Allen Allensworth, 24th Infantry, U.S. Army." PhD diss., Univ. of New Mexico, 1994.

Simmons, William. *Men of Mark: Eminent, Progressive and Rising.* Cleveland: George M. Rewell, 1887.

—*Joshua D. Farrington*

ALLENSWORTH, JAMES L., SR. (b. 1845, Hopkinsville, KY; d. 1922, Hopkinsville, KY), Christian Co.'s first African American coroner. Probably born in slavery in Christian Co., KY, James L. Allensworth Sr. enlisted at age 19 in the 13th U.S. Colored Heavy Artillery on September 24, 1864. By 1870, he and his first wife lived in Hopkinsville, KY, where he worked as a painter. Ten years later, he was also a Baptist minister and editor of the *Baptist Monitor*. By 1892, Allensworth served as the state grand chief and Kentucky delegate for the National Grand Council of the Independent Order of Good Samaritans and Daughters of Samaria of North America.

On November 9, 1894, the *Hopkinsville Kentuckian* reported that Rev. Allensworth had won the election for coroner against Dr. Jacob M. Dennis, white, by 41 votes, making him among the first African Americans elected to a local office in Kentucky. The next year, he was elected chaplain of the Kentucky Department of the **Grand Army of the Republic.** He married his second wife, Gracie, in 1899. In 1902, while serving as a peace officer at the lodge of the Order of Good Samaritans, Allensworth suffered a flesh wound as he attempted to grab the pistol of an assailant. That same year, he was the chairman of the board of education at **Hopkinsville Male and Female College.** In September 1905, he served as the **Emancipation Day** marshal.

As coroner, Allensworth dealt with the mundane and the macabre. His inquests included infanticides, suicides, murders, and train deaths of African Americans and whites. In some cases, he was left to bury the body. In April 1909, the *Hopkinsville Kentuckian* provided a detailed account of the lynching of Ben "Booker" Brame, whose body hung from a dogwood tree for nearly two days. Allensworth cut down the body, held an inquest, supplied the coffin, and buried Brame near the location of his death.

About a week later, Allensworth easily won his fourth consecutive term as coroner. After eight months, he resigned. He addressed the public through a column in the local newspaper itemizing 10 of his 15 years as coroner. He had investigated 30 train deaths, 69 murders, 15 manslaughter crimes, and 125 sudden deaths. Although his name was mentioned again in 1911 for city council, Allensworth never held another public office but continued his work as a painter and Baptist minister. He died of pneumonia on December 18, 1922, and was buried in Cave Springs Cemetery.

Glazier, Jack. *Been Coming through Some Hard Times: Race, History, and Memory in Western Kentucky.* Knoxville: Univ. of Tennessee Press, 2012, 143–44.

Kentucky Death Records, 1852–1953.

Newspapers: "Here and There," *HK*, September 16, 1892, 3; "A Clean Sweep," *HK*, November 9, 1894, 2; "Good Samaritans," *HK*, September 26, 1902, 1; "Celebrated Emancipation," *HK*, September 23,

1905, 2; "Coroner's Work for Ten Years," *HK,* January 1, 1910, 8; "No Nomination," *HK,* October 3, 1911, 6.

U.S. Colored Troops Military Service Records, 1861–1865; U.S. Federal Census (1870, 1910, 1920).

—*Sallie L. Powell*

ALLIED ORGANIZATIONS FOR CIVIL RIGHTS, organization formed in 1964 to pressure the General Assembly into passing a public accommodations law. In 1963, the **Kentucky Commission on Human Rights** drafted a proposed public accommodations bill to be presented to the General Assembly. In January 1964, legislators **Arthur Lloyd "A. L." Johnson Jr., James "J. E." Smith,** and Norbert Blume officially introduced the bill. Soon after, Governor Edward T. Breathitt met with an interracial group of civil rights leaders from Louisville led by **Frank L. Stanley Jr.** Although Breathitt supported the bill, Stanley and others believed that he was dragging his feet on the issue, and they immediately organized the Allied Organizations for Civil Rights (AOCR).

The AOCR was an interracial coalition of over 100 organizations across the state whose sole purpose was to pass the law banning discrimination in public accommodations and enact a fair-employment law. Frank Stanley Jr. and Olof Anderson, the white pastor of Central Presbyterian Church, cochaired the organization. Eric Tachau, a white businessman, served as treasurer, and John Loftus, dean of Bellarmine College, was secretary. Although the public face of the organization was all men, women served critical roles behind the scenes. **Georgia Powers** and Lukey Ward did critical but often unacknowledged work managing the office and organizing AOCR activities.

Operating out of the Eli H. Brown building in downtown Louisville, at the corner of Third and Main, the AOCR was initially funded by the national office of the **National Association for the Advancement of Colored People.** In addition to private donations, it also raised money by forming its own "stock market," which sold one-dollar shares in "the Interest of Human Dignity." The shares quickly became prized possessions in black households in the city.

The group was also met with opposition. Congressman M. Gene Snyder often criticized the organization in his public remarks and labeled NAACP leader Roy Wilkins an "outside agitator" after he spoke at an AOCR rally. Louisville's **Congress of Racial Equality** leader, Bishop **Charles Eubank Tucker,** embittered that he was not included in the organization's leadership, was also a vocal critic.

The major event sponsored by the AOCR was the **March on Frankfort** on March 5, 1964, which included over 10,000 participants. Frank Stanley Jr., Martin Luther King Jr., Jackie Robinson, and others led the march and demonstrated for the passage of a state public accommodations bill. After the General Assembly continued to delay passage of the bill, the AOCR organized a fast and sit-in in Kentucky's House of Representatives. The General Assembly failed to pass a bill in 1964, and the AOCR office was closed.

Herbers, John. "Gov. Breathitt Losing Support of Rights Advocates in Kentucky." *NYT,* February 23, 1964, 21.

———. "Kentucky Capitol Ignoring Fasters." *NYT,* March 18, 1964.

K'Meyer, Tracy E. *Civil Rights in the Gateway to the South: Louisville, Kentucky, 1945–1980.* Lexington: Univ. Press of Kentucky, 2009.

Powers, Georgia Davis. *I Shared the Dream: The Pride, Passion, and Politics of the First Black Woman Senator from Kentucky.* Far Hills, NJ: New Horizon Press, 1995.

—*Joshua D. Farrington*

ALPHA KAPPA ALPHA SORORITY, INCORPORATED (1908–present), first women's black Greek-letter organization. On January 15, 1908, Ethel Hedgeman Lyle and eight other women founded the Alpha Kappa Alpha (AKA) Sorority at Howard University. With the motto "By culture and by merit" and colors salmon pink and apple green, the sorority was the first African American Greek-letter sorority in the nation. It was one of the original organizations incorporated into the National Pan-Hellenic Council when it formed in May 1930.

Although AKA members pushed for education and uplift from the outset and the organization had expanded into several states, in 1922 Eta Omega Alumnae Chapter of Louisville became the first AKA chapter chartered in Kentucky, while the state's first undergraduate AKA chapter, Beta Zeta, was chartered on the **Kentucky State University** campus on February 25, 1933. Around the state, the AKAs initially did not generate much attention. From the mid-1930s on, however, AKA chapters throughout the nation became more active, holding public conferences to discuss issues pertinent to education, crime, housing, health, financial credit systems, and African American uplift.

Alpha Kappa Alpha Sorority members at the old Holiday Inn in Frankfort, KY, for a Founder's Day celebration, ca. 1983.

When the AKAs held their 19th Boule (the sorority's governing convention) in 1937 in Louisville, the region's leading African Americans congregated at the **Quinn Chapel Church** for a tea at which the keynote speaker, Hazel Mountain Walker, addressed the theme Race Building and emphasized "the economic cultural and political advancement of the race." During the event, attendees such as **Rufus E. Clement** of the **Louisville Municipal College,** Dr. **Pruitt Owsley Sweeney,** and other prominent citizens delivered speeches praising the sorority's achievements. The event ended with an elegant banquet and dance held at the Allen Hotel. Such soirees were common among AKA chapters, which strove to showcase the sophistication and class of the African American intelligentsia, in stark contrast to the stereotypes of the day.

The AKAs received more attention in the late 1940s and early 1950s when they hosted Fashionetta events as fund-raisers in which sorority sisters modeled the latest fashions. During Lexington's third annual Fashionetta at the **Lyric Theatre** in 1950, Marva Louis, the former wife of heavyweight boxing champion Joe Louis, and six local sorority members modeled clothes for the event, which funded educational scholarships. The fund-raisers were a success and soon became a staple tradition; Lexington's 2011 Fashionetta cotillion awarded over $26,000 in scholarships.

In 1936, the AKAs formed the National Non-partisan Council on Public Affairs to push for civil rights and inform the public about issues pertinent to the African American community. By 1948, other Greek-letter organizations had joined the effort, forming the American Council on Human Rights (ACHR). The council devoted its attention to segregation and other inequality issues, particularly surrounding education and living standards. In some states, sororities in the ACHR launched boycotts against stores that discriminated against black patrons, while other chapters worked to assist students arrested for nonviolent demonstrations. By 1960, all chapters associated with the ACHR were instructed to cancel their normal and free events to hold fund-raisers to support the ACHR Emergency Fund.

Because of the AKAs' reputation for helping local communities and their commitment to education, many of Kentucky's prominent women were members of the organization. Writer **Margaret Buckner Young** was a member of the sorority, and teacher **Marie "Maude" Brown** served as the organization's supreme basileus.

Alpha Kappa Alpha Sorority, Incorporated. http://www.aka1908.com (accessed June 6, 2013).

Brown, Tamara L., Gregory S. Parks, and Clarenda M. Phillips, eds. *African American Fraternities and Sororities: The Legacy and the Vision.* Lexington: Univ. Press of Kentucky, 2005.

Dickerson, Dennis C. *Militant Mediator: Whitney M. Young Jr.* Lexington: Univ. Press of Kentucky, 2004, 29.

"K.N.E.A. Kullings." *Kentucky Negro Educational Association Journal* 3, no. 1 (October–November 1932): 29.

Newspapers: "Brilliant Address and Splendid Music Mark of Alpha Kappa Alpha Boule in Louisville," *Negro Star,* January 8, 1937, 3; "World's Flashlight," *Negro Star,* May 13, 1938, 4; "Former Wife of Heavyweight Champ Models Here," *LL,* April 16, 1950, 19; " 'We'll Wear Rags' to Fight for Freedom, Sorority Women Vow," *Tri-State Defender,* April 9, 1960, 3; "Alpha Kappa Alpha Sorority Presents Cotillion," *LHL,* December 28, 2011.

—*Dana Caldemeyer*

ALPHA PHI ALPHA FRATERNITY, INCORPORATED, first African American Greek-letter fraternity. Faced with racial prejudice both socially and educationally, several African American students at Cornell University in Ithaca, NY, wanted to create a venue for closer contact with one another outside the classroom. Because they attended a predominantly white institution at the turn of the twentieth century, many black students found themselves scattered throughout different departments at the university and excluded from many of the opportunities for mutual help that were available to white students. On December 4, 1906, seven of these students founded Alpha Phi Alpha Fraternity, Incorporated, "the first national inter-collegiate Greek letter fraternity established for black college men." The founders, called "Jewels" by members, were Henry Arthur Callis, Charles Henry Chapman, **Eugene Kinckle Jones,** George Biddle Kelley, Nathaniel Allison Murray, Robert Harold Ogle, and Vertner Woodson Tandy.

Alpha Phi Alpha expanded with the establishment of its second chapter at Howard University in Washington, DC, in December 1907. Howard is a historically black institution and became a center for the founding of other African American Greek organizations. Five black Greek-letter organizations that began in the first two decades of the 1900s were founded at Howard University: Omega Psi Phi, **Phi Beta Sigma, Alpha Kappa Alpha, Delta Sigma Theta,** and **Zeta Phi Beta. Kappa Alpha Psi Fraternity** was founded at Indiana University, and **Sigma Gamma Rho** Sorority was organized at Butler University in Indiana. Although Kappa Alpha Psi was formed in Indiana, two of its founders had transferred from Howard University and were likely influenced by the black Greek-letter opportunities that had evolved there.

African American fraternities and sororities spread quickly throughout the country, becoming a mainstay especially at many historically black colleges and universities. On January 13, 1911, Alpha Lambda, a graduate chapter of Alpha Phi Alpha, was established in Louisville, KY. Founder **Eugene Kinckle Jones,** an employee at Louisville High School at the time, was instrumental in establishing this chapter.

On April 28, 1933, the first undergraduate chapter of Alpha Phi Alpha in Kentucky was founded at Kentucky State College (later known as **Kentucky State University**). It had 15 charter members and was under the leadership of H. A. Merchant and **Frank Stanley Sr**. Members **Rufus B. Atwood,** the president of the college, and William W. Warren, head of the Science Department, were instrumental in the establishment of the fraternity's chapter at the school.

A little over a year later, on May 7, 1934, another Alpha Phi Alpha chapter was organized at **Louisville Municipal College** in Louisville, KY. Other undergraduate chapters in the state were founded after the desegregation of white higher learning institutions. The fraternity continues to uphold its principles of scholarship, good character, fellowship, and the bettering of humanity. Nationally known members include Martin Luther King Jr., John Hope Franklin, Thurgood Marshall, W. E. B. DuBois, Edward Brooke, Paul Robeson, and Adam Clayton Powell Jr.

Mason, Herman, Jr. *The Talented Tenth: The Founders and Presidents of Alpha.* Winter Park, FL: Four-G Publishers, 1999.

Ross, Lawrence C. *The Divine Nine: The History of African American Fraternities and Sororities*. New York: Kensington Publishing Corp., 2000.

Wesley, Charles H. *The History of Alpha Phi Alpha: A Development in College Life*. Chicago: Foundation Publishers, 1981.

—*David H. Jackson Jr.*

AMERICAN BAPTIST (1879–present), longest-running African American newspaper in Kentucky. In 1869, Kentucky's African American Baptists formed the **General Association of Baptists in Kentucky.** In less than a year, the association launched the *Baptist Herald* under Reverend **George W. Dupee**'s editorship. Although it was designed to "enable our ministers and Sunday School teachers to preach and teach the word of God intelligently," the Paducah-based newspaper also included non-Baptist columns that pertained to Kentucky's African American community, particularly on racial issues.

In 1879, constituents changed the paper's name to the *American Baptist* and moved its publication office to Louisville. **William Henry Steward,** a freedman and secretary of the General Association, assumed editorship of the paper and eventually purchased it from the General Association when it faced financial difficulties. With the help of his daughter, Carolyn Steward Blanton, and **William J. Simmons**, president of Simmons University, Steward ran the paper for 56 years until his death in January 1935.

In its early years in Louisville, the *American Baptist* was printed at the *Courier-Journal*'s presses, but under Steward's direction, the newspaper gradually grew to support itself. According to the newspaper's historians, in a time when other black newspapers started and faded quickly, Steward not only maintained the newspaper but increased its scope to include an independent press that printed announcements, pamphlets, and private materials for the community in addition to the paper. In particular, Steward used it to generate awareness about **State Colored Baptist University** (later known as **Simmons College of Kentucky**) activities and to raise funds for the school. Because of Steward's efforts, the paper was so widely read and respected that it became the largest African American Baptist paper and served as the National Baptist Convention's official organ.

When Steward's health failed, he appointed and trained Dr. W. H. Ballew to take his place and transferred ownership of the newspaper to the General Association. When Steward died, Ballew briefly acted as editor, but unable to balance pastoring one of Louisville's largest churches with overseeing the paper, he passed his editing duties to Henrietta Butler while still acting as the paper's manager.

Despite financial hardship during the Great Depression, the paper continued in print thanks to *Louisville Leader* founder and editor I. Willis Cole. Cole allowed the paper to be printed at the I. Willis Cole printing plant until the paper could purchase a new building at 1715 W. Chestnut St. in 1943. When Ballew died in 1959, Butler assumed the paper's managerial duties, serving for over 40 years. After Butler's retirement, the *American Baptist* expanded to include a publishing board and had a number of managers and editors, including Rev. Victor McKinney Jr., Rev. Thurmond Coleman, and Rev. Bernard Crayton.

Litwack, Leon, and August Meier. *Black Leaders of the Nineteenth Century*. Urbana: Univ. of Illinois Press, 1988, 280–81.

McKinney, Victor, Jr. and H. W. Jones Jr. "A Short History of the *American Baptist.*" In *The American Baptist Newspaper Centennial Volume*, 2–7. Louisville, KY: American Baptist Newspaper, 1978.

Simmons, William. *Men of Mark: Eminent, Progressive and Rising*. Cleveland: George M. Rewell, 1887, 46.

—*Dana Caldemeyer*

AMERICAN CIVIL LIBERTIES UNION OF KENTUCKY, affiliate of the national American Civil Liberties Union. The American Civil Liberties Union of Kentucky was founded in 1955 as an affiliate of the national American Civil Liberties Union (ACLU) and was at first called the Kentucky Civil Liberties Union. The mission of the ACLU of Kentucky is specifically to protect and defend the Bill of Rights of the U.S. Constitution. The principal organizers were Patrick Kirwan, Arthur Kling, and Louis Kesselman. They and a few others were responding to a move by the commonwealth's attorney's office in Louisville against feared Communist influence, and specifically the criminal trial of Carl Braden, charged with sedition against the Commonwealth of Kentucky.

The Braden case raised basic issues of freedom of speech and assembly, freedom of the press, and freedom from unreasonable search and seizure, all freedoms guaranteed by the Bill of Rights. Since its founding, the ACLU of Kentucky has played a role in practically every major civil rights issue arising in Kentucky. Some of the principal volunteer attorneys have been Grover Sales, Louis Lusky, Bob Sedler, Thomas Hogan, Robert Delahanty, Edward Post, William Stone, Joseph Freeland, and David Friedman. They and many others have participated in numerous lawsuits defending individual rights. Most of the ACLU court cases have gone to the Kentucky Supreme Court, and five have gone to the U.S. Supreme Court, where four were won.

The ACLU of Kentucky is frequently involved in controversy because of its willingness to defend those individuals most likely to be involved in unpopular causes. It believes that every defendant, no matter the charge, must receive due process, adequate counsel, and a jury of his or her peers. The ACLU of Kentucky holds that the lessening of a fundamental right for any individual is the lessening of freedom for all.

For these reasons, the ACLU of Kentucky led the struggle for the integration of Kentucky public schools, was the major defender of objectors to the war in Vietnam, is a leading advocate of reproductive freedom and gay and lesbian rights, and is involved on almost a continuous basis in issues regarding separation of church and state. It objects to government-sponsored prayer in public schools and to government-sponsored religious displays and ceremonies. Issues of equal protection of the law, due process, police brutality, prison conditions, and capital punishment are major concerns of the ACLU of Kentucky, both in the courts and in the state legislature.

In 1992, Everett Hoffman, an attorney, was appointed executive director of the ACLU of Kentucky. Jeffrey E. Vessels, an Owensboro native with a background in social work, was hired in April 1999 to replace Hoffman, who returned to the private practice of law.

ACLU of Kentucky. *A Celebration, 1955 to 1995.* Madison, WI, 1995.

Braden, Anne. *The Wall Between.* New York: Monthly Review Press, 1958.

Davis, Jeffery. "A Kentucky Response: The Founding of the Kentucky Civil Liberties Union, 1955–1960." MA thesis, Univ. of Washington, 1981.

Newspapers: *LCJ,* April 14, 1999.

—*Carl Wedekind*

AMERICAN MISSIONARY ASSOCIATION, religious antislavery organization. The American Missionary Association (AMA) was founded in 1846 in Albany, NY, with the express purpose of developing Christian missions to nonwhite people and promoting antislavery. The association became the primary sponsor of the growth of evangelical abolitionism in Kentucky and the strongest antislavery organization working in the state. Before the Civil War, Rev. John G. Fee spearheaded AMA missionary efforts in Kentucky from Berea, KY. Under the auspices of the AMA, Fee and his fellow missionaries established many free churches in which doctrines of evangelical abolitionism were regularly preached, as well as sponsoring schools where antislavery views were promoted and integration was considered possible, even in a time and a place where such a policy seemed unfeasible. Before slavery ended in Kentucky, the AMA had integrated grade schools in Rockcastle Co. and Jackson Co. **Berea College** supported the AMA by funding teachers and staff. **Gabriel Burdett** was one of the African American missionaries. The AMA also contributed to all-black institutions, such as **Ariel Academy** at **Camp Nelson** and **Ely Normal School** in Louisville.

After the abolition of slavery, the AMA promoted social equality among the races; the organization's position on this burning issue in Kentucky was clarified at **Camp Nelson** when Fee hired a young woman of African descent, E. Belle Mitchell (later known as **E. Belle Mitchell Jackson**), to teach in the school there. Many of the AMA-salaried teachers on the staff refused to eat in the same dining room with a person of color; when Fee—conducting a deliberate test case of attitudes toward race—and Mitchell sat down in the hall, the other teachers walked out in protest. The AMA, in disciplining its workers, established social equality as a standard for their behavior. Throughout the nineteenth century, the *American Missionary* magazine published articles about Kentucky that were written by Fee. These essays emphasized the conditions and needs of black people in the state and included reports on missions, educational goals, and the advancement of social equality.

Sears, Richard D. *The Day of Small Things: Abolitionism in the Midst of Slavery; Berea, Kentucky, 1854–1864.* Lanham, MD: Univ. Press of America, 1986.

———. *A Utopian Experiment in Kentucky: Integration and Social Equality at Berea, 1866–1904.* Westport, CT: Greenwood Press, 1996.

AMERICAN MUTUAL SAVINGS BANK (1922–1933), African American–owned bank in Louisville, KY. The economic successes in the 1910s reached into Louisville, KY, where aspiring African American businessmen hoped to increase and safeguard their gains. **William H. Wright,** community leader and founder of the **Mammoth Life and Accident Insurance Company,** founded the American Mutual Savings Bank to further encourage economic development within Louisville's African American community. It opened on February 18, 1922, with Wright as president and **Henry E. Hall** as secretary. Architect **Samuel Plato** designed its new building, located on 608 W. Walnut St., which the *Louisville Leader* claimed was one of the most modern banks in the nation, "equipped with the highest class office and banking fixtures and furnishings."

With the motto "The bank of personal service," the American Mutual Savings Bank fostered a vibrant African American business culture in Louisville and actively gave back to the community. It offered accounting services for small businessmen, assisted local churches, and taught patrons the value of thrift. By May 1922, the bank launched a new home-building program that built new homes, designed by Samuel Plato, available on an easy payment plan.

Such efforts made the American Mutual Savings Bank an instant success. Upon conducting a surprise inspection in September 1922, state bank examiners gave the bank a rating of "excellent" that further legitimized the institution in the minds of many residents. One newspaper observed, "Such ratings as this go a long way toward dispelling doubt in the minds of Colored people as to the ability of members of their race to conduct financial institutions." Just six months later, the bank boasted of having over 5,000 depositors and more than $300,000 in resources. By May 1924, its resources had increased to over half a million dollars.

Despite its prestige among Louisville's African American business community, the American Mutual Savings Bank was not strong enough to withstand the Great Depression. In 1930, the white-owned National Bank of Kentucky, the depository for American Mutual, collapsed. In an effort to survive, American Mutual and the **First Standard Bank,** another African American institution, merged to form the Mutual Standard Bank in January 1931. However, the economic tumult ultimately shook clientele faith in the security of the institution. As patrons closed their accounts, Mutual Standard launched a series of public campaigns to educate the public on the bank's soundness but ultimately had little choice but to close its doors permanently in May 1931.

Newspapers: "American Mutual Bank Open to Public," *LL,* February 25, 1922, 1; "The American Mutual Savings Bank in Thrift Campaign," *LL,* May 13, 1922, 1, 8; "Negro Bank Receives Excellent Rating," *Plaindealer,* September 22, 1922; "American Mutual Savings Bank a $300,000 Mark," *LL,* March 24, 1923, 1; "Mutual Bank on Top," *LL,* May 3, 1924, 1; "Mutual Standard Bank Announces Program; National President Writes," *LL,* February 28, 1931, 1, 8; "Officers and Directors Close the Mutual Standard Bank," *LL,* May 9, 1931, 1.

—*Dana Caldemeyer*

ANDERSON, CHARLES W., JR. (b. 1907, Louisville, KY; d. 1960, Louisville, KY), attorney, legislator, United Nations delegate. Charles W. Anderson Jr. was born on May 26, 1907, the son of Dr. Charles W. and Tabatha Murphy Anderson. He attended Kentucky State College (later known as **Kentucky State University**) (1925) and received a bachelor's degree from

Wilberforce University (1927) and an LLB from Howard University (1930). He was also awarded an honorary LLD from Wilberforce (1936). Anderson was admitted to the Kentucky bar in 1933 and began practicing law with Willie C. Fleming, Harry S. McAlpin, O. B. Hinnant, and J. Earl Dearing in Louisville. Anderson was an excellent trial attorney and served as a mentor and trainer of new attorneys in the firm.

In November 1935, Anderson became the first African American to be elected to the Kentucky House of Representatives and the first African American legislator in the South since Reconstruction. A Republican, he was reelected and served from 1936 to 1946. During his legislative career, Anderson was instrumental in seeing that issues relative to African Americans remained before the Kentucky legislature. As a representative, he successfully helped defeat the Senate's resolution that opposed a federal antilynching law (1938) and also succeeded in making electrocution mandatory in all Kentucky death cases. The **Anderson-Mayer State Aid Act** provided funds for African Americans to attend graduate school outside Kentucky and included a provision that allowed married women to teach, thereby providing extra income for many families. The legislation also provided for minimum wages and improved working conditions for **domestic workers** in the state.

Anderson was a strong advocate for education and supported better educational opportunities for all Kentuckians. He enhanced rural high school educational facilities for all students through his legislative action, led the fight for the integration of the state universities in Kentucky, and introduced legislation to integrate the nursing schools and postgraduate hospital training and residency programs in the state. These pieces of legislation improved the economic and educational conditions of poor whites as well as blacks. He also fought and defeated a bill to segregate people by race on Kentucky buses and trains and in schools, libraries, and other public places.

Anderson resigned from the General Assembly to become assistant commonwealth's attorney for Jefferson Co. in May 1946. This was another first for Kentucky and for the South. He served in this capacity until 1952. Anderson received the GOP nomination for judge in the Louisville Third District municipal court in 1949 but was defeated in the election.

President Dwight D. Eisenhower appointed Anderson as an alternate U.S. delegate to the United Nations' 14th General Assembly in 1959. As a member, he helped draft documents that protected the rights of children against abuse, exploitation, and neglect. Other documents prohibited any practices that allowed discrimination based on race, religion, or other criteria.

Anderson married Victoria McCall of Detroit on November 30, 1948. They had two children, Charles III and Victoria. He was killed on June 14, 1960, when his car was struck by an Ashland-bound Chesapeake and Ohio passenger train. He is buried in Louisville's Eastern Cemetery.

Anderson was the recipient of numerous awards and honors for his achievements in government and public service. In 1940, he received the Lincoln Institute Award for outstanding service to blacks. In 1945, he was awarded the Howard University Alumni Award for distinction in law and government. He was the first black to receive a Kentucky colonel's commission. In 1971, the

Kentucky Human Rights Commission honored Anderson in its poster series of Kentucky's Outstanding African Americans. On June 14, 1997, the 37th anniversary of his death, a historical marker honoring Anderson's distinguished career was unveiled in Louisville in front of the Jefferson County Hall of Justice. Another lasting tribute to Anderson is the Anderson Medal, which Governor Wallace Wilkinson's Equal Employment Opportunity Conference and the Department of Personnel created in 1989 as a perpetual memorial prize to be given to a Kentuckian who has "enhanced the opportunity for equality" in the workplace, classroom, or marketplace. The medal is given to individuals only.

Smith, Jessie C., ed. *Notable Black American Men.* Detroit: Gale Research, 1998.

—*Karen Cotton McDaniel*

ANDERSON, DENNIS HENRY (b. 1866, Claybrook, TN; d. 1952, Paducah, KY), educator, founder, and president of West Kentucky Industrial College. D. H. Anderson was born on a farm in Claybrook, TN, to William and Lucinda Anderson. After his graduation from Lane College in Jackson, TN, Anderson moved to western Kentucky, organized a black education league, and built three new schoolhouses in Fulton and Mayfield. In 1909, seeing firsthand the need for qualified teachers in his new schools; Anderson founded the West Kentucky Industrial College for Colored Persons (later known as **West Kentucky Community and Technical College**) in Paducah. Classes in education, agriculture, and various vocational skills were initially taught from a single wood-frame building that Anderson himself helped build. While serving as president of the college, Anderson received doctor of divinity and master of science degrees from Princeton Normal and Industrial University, Indiana, in 1914.

Initially surviving off money from Anderson's own pocket and private donations, WKIC struggled financially. In 1912 and 1918, Anderson launched a series of unsuccessful lobbying efforts at local state representatives to procure state funds. In 1914 and 1916, the Kentucky Senate passed a bill to provide public funding for West Kentucky Industrial, but the House refused to support it. In 1918, the legislature did pass an appropriations bill that paid for the salary of Anderson, his wife, Artelia, and three additional teachers.

Anderson's career was marred, however, by several indiscretions. During a personal feud with J. H. Alston, the principal of Paducah's black Lincoln High School, Anderson encouraged a young female to make false accusations of a lewd relationship with Alston. Throughout the 1920s and early 1930s, numerous reports and remarks by school administrators alleged poor bookkeeping and mismanagement of funds. Anderson received further criticism from the college's trustees for his insistence that the school emphasize vocational training over liberal arts education. In 1935, he was stripped of most of his responsibilities and power and was left only the title of president, and in 1937, he was replaced completely by **Harvey Clarence Russell Sr.**

Despite his mixed legacy, D. H. Anderson helped fill an educational void in western Kentucky for young African Americans with his construction of elementary schoolhouses and the establishment of West Kentucky Industrial College. Anderson died in 1952.

Hardin, John A. *Fifty Years of Segregation: Black Higher Education in Kentucky, 1904–1954.* Lexington: Univ. Press of Kentucky, 1997.

Mather, Frank Lincoln, ed. *Who's Who of the Colored Race: A General Biographical Dictionary of Men and Women of African Descent.* Vol. 1. Chicago: Momento Edition, 1915.

Wright, George C. *A History of Blacks in Kentucky.* Vol. 2, *In Pursuit of Equality, 1890–1980.* Frankfort: Kentucky Historical Society, 1992.

—*Joshua D. Farrington*

ANDERSON, ELIJAH (b. 1808, Fluvana Co., VA; d. 1861, Frankfort, KY), conductor in the Underground Railroad. Dubbed the "General Superintendent" of the **Underground Railroad** (UGRR) by Rush R. Sloane, an abolitionist in northwestern Ohio, Elijah Anderson became a major conductor, bringing hundreds of runaway slaves to freedom from northern Kentucky counties.

Born a free person of color in Virginia, Anderson was forced from his native state by restrictive black laws passed after the 1831 Nat Turner Rebellion. Sometime before 1835, he relocated to Cincinnati. Because he was trained as a blacksmith and skilled in making wrought-iron undercarriages and decorative fences, he found ready employment as a laborer fixing metal and steam fittings on Ohio River steamboats. He developed strong friendships with other free blacks: George De Baptiste, Chapman Harris, John Lott, and John Carter, a Lexington native who had settled in Cincinnati among the large free black community. Carter fled to Canada during the 1830 riots and then returned when things calmed down.

Both De Baptiste, a barber, and Carter, a grocer, worked as stewards, a high-ranking position for free blacks. According to Lott, these men were introduced to the Ohio Underground Railroad leaders through Rev. Henry Ward Beecher, who, during the 1830s, was at Cincinnati's Lane Seminary and also was serving in his first pastorate, at the Lawrenceburg (IN) Presbyterian Church. Between December 1837 and early 1840, all five of these free blacks relocated to Madison, IN, and soon provided energy and impetus to the UGRR's operations there. Anderson met and married May J., a native of Ohio 10 years his junior. Their only child, Martha, was born in 1840 in Madison. Elijah Anderson established his blacksmith shop on the southeast corner of Third and Walnut Sts. He prospered and before early 1842 had purchased a brick town home valued at $800 and taxed at $3.00 in the Georgetown section of Madison on Walnut St. near Fifth St. He was listed as the owner and taxpayer on that property through 1847.

Anderson soon attained leadership in the Madison UGRR. He excelled at opening and developing secure routes. Often he went over into Kentucky, particularly along the Kentucky River artery, contacting free blacks and slaves on plantations. He developed a solid relationship with free blacks in Carrollton and Frankfort, KY, and Lawrenceburg, IN, and also worked well with white abolitionists. By 1845, the black conductors in Madison managed most of the Ohio River crossing points. These free blacks shifted Madison's UGRR operations from a passive to an active state. De Baptiste claimed to have aided 108 runaways before 1846; Anderson said that he brought 200 through before 1850.

In 1845, two top agents of the American Anti-Slavery League, William Phelps and George Whitfield, who were originally from Wheeling, VA (West Virginia today), but had most recently worked out of Cincinnati, came to Madison and over the next three years developed routes on Kentucky soil, giving recruited plantation slaves information on safe routes and pickup times and places. Later that year, a wealthy black abolitionist, John Simmons, was welcomed to Madison. Shortly thereafter, major routes were compromised and near captures occurred. Anderson, Harris, Lott, and a number of other activists believed that Simmons had betrayed their cause for monetary reward; they beat Simmons severely and threatened him with death. Simmons sued in Indiana's Jefferson Co. court, and the legal fees over six years caused Anderson to lose his property in Madison.

A 100-man posse of Kentuckians and local sympathizers marauded through Madison targeting the UGRR leadership. Free black activists, charged with inciting a riot, were fined sums of $50 and $25. De Baptiste fled to Detroit, MI, and became active there. Lott headed for Canada. Harris hunkered down in Eagle Hollow, IN, three miles east of Madison, and became a major leader during the 1850s. Griffin Booth, known for assisting runaway slaves, was nearly drowned in the Ohio River by a mob. Amos Phillips was shot several times; he recuperated in Lancaster, IN, and then moved to the Little Africa settlement south of Vernon, IN. It took Harris and Carter three to five years to rebuild the UGRR base back to its original capabilities.

As a result of increased danger, the fines levied against him, and the Madison riots, Anderson moved his base of operations to Lawrenceburg, IN. Both Elijah and his wife were fair skinned, and in the 1850 Dearborn Co., IN, census, they both apparently passed as white. Since he spent months on the road away from his blacksmith business, it seems quite likely that at this time Anderson became an agent of the American Anti-Slavery League or was funded in part by Detroit's African American leadership. His Madison experience was helpful because Lawrenceburg, IN, was hostile to free blacks and by 1861 was trying to evict them from the city. During the early 1850s, Anderson was frequently linked to Cincinnati and to routes to Cleveland and Sandusky, OH.

As an experienced conductor, Anderson realized that bringing fugitives across by ones and twos was inefficient and likely to run afoul of the runaway-slave patrollers. Working with William Wyman, station master in Aurora, IN, with American Anti-Slavery League peddlers and ferrymen agents, and with his own local free black recruits, Anderson soon was able to bring large groups of fugitives out through Boone Co., KY. Results showed almost immediately. In 1847, the David Powell family of 6 vanished from the John Norris plantation between the Lawrenceburg and Aurora, IN, ferry landings. In May 1848, 8 slaves owned by Benjamin Stevens opposite Rising Sun, IN, made their escape. Gabriel Smith, an aged free black from Brookville, IN, participated in helping Anderson bring 50 slaves north to Sandusky, OH. Boone Co. slave owners reported that 29 slaves had escaped between September 1 and November 17, 1852; in April 1853, they lost another 40 slaves.

During the summer of 1856, after Anderson took a group of fugitives to Cleveland via the railroad's network, he sought work to earn money before returning to Lawrenceburg. An abolitionist gave him the name of a person in Detroit, and Anderson worked in Detroit through the fall of 1856 and then returned through Cincinnati and boarded a steamboat there. In a case of mistaken identity, a Madison UGRR activist, William J. Anderson, was arrested in Carrollton, KY, and accused of pirating hundreds of runaway slaves and carrying incendiary abolitionist materials into Kentucky. William J. Anderson, who claimed in his defensive autobiography that he had never worked south of the Ohio River and only had loaned his carriage to the UGRR, was defended by antislavery lawyers from Madison and released. Within a day or so, Elijah Anderson was recognized in Cincinnati or turned in, and Delos Blythe of the Alan Pinkerton Detective Agency in Louisville came up to arrest him once the steamboat that he was on had set off. The free black community in Madison was certain that William J. Anderson had bought his way out of jail by turning in Elijah Anderson, and Elijah was forced to flee to safer ground in Indianapolis.

At Carrollton, KY, Elijah Anderson was accused of enticing a slave owned by Gen. William O. Butler. The charge was peculiar because Butler had emancipated some of his slaves when he returned from the Mexican War in the late 1840s. It was among Butler's freed slaves living near the mouth of the Kentucky River that Elijah Anderson likely had established a solid base for UGRR routes from the Bluegrass State. One of those freed slaves, Sandy Duncan, moved to Madison. James T. Allison, an antislavery attorney from Madison, represented Anderson in Carrollton and won acquittal. But on the steps of the courthouse in Bedford, KY, the Trimble Co. sheriff arrested Anderson and incarcerated him. In Bedford, Anderson was accused of assisting and abetting a Negro boy named George in running away from his master, who lived in Henry Co., KY. Anderson claimed to have gone north for work. Found on his person was a chatty letter he had written but not mailed to his wife, Mary J., that gave the names of several abolitionist friends in Cleveland and Detroit. Sensational newspaper accounts in Louisville claimed that finding the letter broke the back of a ring of abolitionists that had been stealing slaves in Kentucky. Depositions from G. W. Burrows of Cleveland stated that Elijah Anderson was in Cleveland on September 1, 1856, and had sought employment from him, and that he had referred Anderson to a friend in Watertown, WI. A second disposition from John P. Clark stated that he had hired Anderson from November 1 to December 13, 1856, at his blacksmith shop at a Springwell, MI, dry dock.

But it was the eyewitness testimony of Wright Ray, who headed a ring of slave-catchers operating in southeastern Indiana, that led to Elijah Anderson's 10-year sentence in the Kentucky State Penitentiary in Frankfort. Ray testified that he had seen Anderson in Madison on May 11, 1856, ascending the Texas deck of a mail boat headed to Cincinnati. Anderson had a carpetbag and was in the company of a boy answering the description of George, a runaway slave owned by John Scott of Henry Co. The boy had escaped on May 8, and Scott had come to seek the services of Ray at Madison on May 12, 1856.

During the next few months, Chapman Harris, then a leader of the free blacks and slaves active in the Madison UGRR, attempted twice to mount a posse to free Anderson from the penitentiary. Meanwhile, the antislavery attorneys at Madison tried to negotiate an interstate gubernatorial pardon. When Anderson's daughter, Martha, came to Frankfort to pick him up in April 1861, he was found dead in his cell of unexplained causes. The body was released to his family for burial. According to Wilbur Siebert and the *Firelands Pioneer*, Elijah Anderson claimed to have brought out more than 1,000 runaway slaves, 800 of them after passage of the 1850 Fugitive Slave Act.

Annotated plat C., 1848–1850, Madison, IN.

Bordewich, Fergus M. *Bound for Canaan: The Underground Railroad and the War for the Soul of America.* New York: Amistad, 2005.

Commonwealth of Kentucky v. Elijah Anderson. Trimble Co. Circuit Court, Governors Papers, Kentucky Libraries and Archives, Frankfort.

Deed Book 6: 320, Jefferson Co., Madison, IN.

Griffler, Keith P. *Front Line of Freedom: African Americans and the Forging of the Underground Railroad in the Ohio Valley.* Lexington: Univ. Press of Kentucky, 2004.

Hudson, J. Blaine. *Fugitive Slaves and the Underground Railroad in the Kentucky Borderland.* Jefferson, NC: McFarland, 2002.

Israel Moody v. Trustees of the African Methodist Episcopal Church (January 1, 1853). Dearborn Co. Civil Cases, Lawrenceburg, IN.

Lawrenceburg Register, May 11, 1848; November 17, 1852; November 14, 1853.

Siebert, Wilbur. *The Underground Railroad from Slavery to Freedom.* New York: Macmillan, 1898.

Tax Assessment Book 2: 1838–1847, Madison, IN.

—*Diane Perrine Coon*

ANDERSON, EZZRETT "SUGARFOOT" (b. 1920, Arkansas), professional football player.

Ezzrett "Sugarfoot" Anderson was born and raised in Arkansas and attended Kentucky State College (later known as **Kentucky State University**). In 1946, the National Football League officially admitted black players. The following year, Anderson was signed by the Los Angeles Dons and became one of the first players from a predominantly African American school to play professional football. He lived in Los Angeles for two years and had minor roles in several films, including *The Story of Seabiscuit* and *Samson and Delilah*.

In 1949, Anderson was recruited by Coach Les Lear of the Calgary Stampeders to help revive the troubled Canadian Football League. Although his wife, Virnetta, was reluctant to move to the remote Canadian city, Anderson was ready to leave the racially charged environment of the National Football League. He played out the last nine years of his career as a tight end for Calgary, which became his home. The Stampeders inducted him into its Wall of Fame in 1990, and the Canadian Sports Wall of Fame inducted him in 1974.

Heritage Community Foundation and Black Pioneer Descendant's Society, Alberta's Black Pioneer Heritage. "Virnetta and 'Sugarfoot' Anderson." Alberta, Canada, 2007. http://blackpioneers.albertasource.ca/people/anderson.html (accessed January 26, 2009).

Platt, Michael. "As Barack Obama Becomes the First Black U.S. President, Another Recalls the Breaking of Alberta's Political Color Barrier." *Calgary Sun,* January 20, 2009.

Ross, Charles. *Outside the Lines: African Americans and the Integration of the National Football League.* New York: New York Univ. Press, 2001.

—*Joshua D. Farrington*

ANDERSON, FELIX SYLVESTER (b. 1893, Wilmington, NC; d. 1983, Louisville, KY), minister and politician. Felix Sylvester Anderson was born in Wilmington, NC, on October 3, 1893, but spent his formative years as a child in Boston, MA. As a teenager, he returned to North Carolina to attend high school and college at Livingstone College, completing his studies in 1920. He then attended Hood Theological Seminary, also in North Carolina, and Western Theological Seminary in Michigan, where he received his doctor of divinity degree. During the late 1920s and 1930s, Anderson preached in Elizabeth City and Edenton, NC, and Tuscaloosa and Mobile, AL. He served as president of the Mobile Civic Organization from 1942 to 1948.

In 1948, Anderson moved to Louisville and served as pastor at Broadway Temple American Methodist Episcopal (A.M.E.) Zion Church, located at the corner of Thirteenth St. and W. Broadway. He became involved in city politics and was elected as a representative from Jefferson Co.'s 42nd Congressional District in 1954. He was the first African American Democrat elected to the General Assembly and the fourth to serve in the state legislature. He was reelected in 1956 and 1958. During his last term in the legislature, he chaired the Committee of Suffrage, Elections, and Constitutional Amendments, the first African American to chair a standing committee in the Kentucky House of Representatives. In this capacity, he expressed regret by presenting a gift to Iris King, the mayor of Kingston, Jamaica, when she had been refused service at a Louisville store in November 1958.

In 1960, the General Conference of the African Methodist Episcopal Zion Church elected Anderson bishop. In 1967, he became ill and retired from public service and his church. He lived the remainder of his life in Louisville until his death in 1983. He was interred at Cave Hill Cemetery in Louisville.

Anderson, Felix. Interview by Kenneth Chumbley, October 19, 1978. Louisville, KY, Univ. of Louisville.

Newspapers: "Negro Heads Kentucky Panel," *NYT,* January 18, 1958, 9; "Store Bars Negro Mayor," *Pittsburgh Post-Gazette,* November 29, 1958, 16; "Two Bishops Are Elected," *NYT,* May 15, 1960, 79; "Black History Month," *LCJ,* February 4, 2008, 1B.

—*Joshua D. Farrington*

ANDERSON, NANCY "OLD BOSS" (b. ca. 1812, Jessamine Co., KY; d. 1888, Lexington, KY), orator and entrepreneur. Nancy Anderson was born a slave in Jessamine Co. and made her way to Lexington, KY, in 1835, where she worked as a ragpicker. Known by most residents as "Old Boss," Anderson was a stocky woman with a booming voice and distinct laugh that could be heard a block away. Although she was impoverished and easily dismissed in Lexington society, Anderson achieved notoriety through her entertaining speeches that she delivered on Lexington's city streets. Despite her illiteracy, Anderson's orations caught the attention of locals who enjoyed her off-the-cuff language that praised local whites.

By the mid-1870s, Anderson was a local celebrity whom Lexington visitors frequently asked to see. Druggists Sarah A. and Joseph G. Smith named a popular cigar "Old Boss" in her honor and placed her photo on the box. The events on July 5, 1880, however, were likely the most memorable of Anderson's life. On that

Nancy Anderson.

day, she was featured in Lexington's Rag Tag parade, riding in a horse-drawn carriage with a gingham dress, fancy hat, and new shoes. At the request of the crowd, Anderson delivered a speech praising Lexington's kindness while circulating a box for donations. Unfortunately, excitement turned to tragedy when the evening's celebratory bonfires destroyed Anderson's papers and rags. The *Daily Press* observed that "all the tears and entreaties of the heroine of the day could not avail to the protection of her property at night."

Anderson's experience in 1880 was just one example of her hard life. Despite having her photo included with other distinguished Lexington residents in the Fayette County Courthouse's cornerstone in 1883, Anderson's fame never brought her fortune. Just five years after her photo was placed in the cornerstone, Anderson crawled under a freight train to collect a few scraps of paper on the track. As she did so, a switch engine crushed her legs just above her ankles. Although she was taken to the hospital and her legs were amputated, Anderson died a week later, on March 8, 1888. Despite her celebrity and a front-page obituary praising her life, Anderson was buried in one of Lexington's colored cemeteries in a pauper's grave.

Anderson's persona persisted in Lexington lore. In 1938, newspaper writer John Skain included her biography in a *Lexington Leader* article heralding Lexington's notable "Characters of the 1880s." In it, Skain described her as a lively "character" and a "remarkable" woman.

Newspapers: "The National Holiday," *Lexington Daily Press,* July 6, 1880, 1; "Old Boss," *Lexington Morning Transcript,* March 9, 1888, 1; "John Skain Writes about Many of the Outstanding People of the City," *LL,* June 30, 1938, 11; "Ragpicker Was Local Celebrity," *LHL,* February 25, 2007, A1.

U.S. Federal Census (1870).

—*Dana Caldemeyer*

ANDERSON, ROBERT BALL (b. 1843, Greensburg, KY; d. 1931, Lincoln, NE), former slave and largest African American landowner in Nebraska. Robert Ball Anderson, farmer and Civil War volunteer, was born a slave on March 1, 1843, in Greensburg, KY. He was a field hand on the property of Robert Ball when the Civil War began. In 1864, Anderson fled behind Union lines and enlisted in the U.S. Army. His unit, the 125th Colored Infantry, was training for combat when the war ended; he spent the remainder of his three-year enlistment at military posts in the Southwest.

After his discharge at Louisville, he went west and eventually acquired an 80-acre farm in Butler Co. in eastern Nebraska. Poor economic conditions caused Anderson to move on to the panhandle of western Nebraska, where he obtained a quarter section of land under the provisions of the 1873 Timber Culture Act. In 1922, at the age of 79, he married 21-year-old Daisy Graham. She encouraged him to write his memoirs, which were published in 1927. Anderson died in an automobile accident near Lincoln, NE, on December 3, 1931. At the time of his death, his 2,080 acres made him the largest landowner among blacks in the state. He was buried at Hemingford, NE.

Anderson, Robert. *From Slavery to Affluence: Memoirs of Robert Anderson, Ex-Slave.* Steamboat Springs, CO: Steamboat Pilot, 1967.
Wax, Darold D. "Robert Ball Anderson, a Kentucky Slave, 1843–1864." *Register of the Kentucky Historical Society* 81 (Summer 1983): 255–73.

—*Darold D. Wax*

ANDERSON, WILLIAM H. (b. 1843, Vigo Co., IN; d. 1919, Evansville, IN), challenged segregated seating on railroad cars in Kentucky. William H. Anderson was born in Vigo Co., IN. In 1864, he enlisted in the army and served in the 13th U.S. Colored Infantry Regiment until the end of the Civil War. Self-educated, he became the pastor at Lost Creek Baptist Church in Rockville, IN, in 1871. Two years later, he took charge of the Third Baptist Church of Terre Haute, IN. He spent most of his pastoral career at McFarland Chapel, Evansville, IN, where he was the editor of the Indiana Baptist *Watch-Tower* and one of the most active supporters of the National Baptist Convention.

On October 30, 1893, Rev. W. H. Anderson and his wife, Sarah, challenged the 1892 **Separate Coach Law** when they refused to transfer from the train's white section to the colored car once they crossed over the Ohio River from Indiana en route to Madisonville, KY. They were put off the train by the Louisville and Nashville Railroad Company, a Kentucky corporation, in Henderson. They immediately purchased two first-class tickets on the next train to Madisonville. During this second challenge, they refused to move to the compartment for blacks and were removed from the train at Robard's Station, 30 miles north of Madisonville in Henderson Co. They filed a lawsuit against the Louisville and Nashville Railroad in the U.S. district court in Owensboro, and on June 4, 1894, Judge John W. Barr announced that Kentucky's statute was unconstitutional because it attempted to regulate interstate commerce. Two years later, in a separate case, the U.S. Supreme Court ruled that "separate but equal" railroad coaches were constitutional in ***Plessy v. Ferguson.***

Anderson v. Louisville & N.R. Co., 62 F. (C.C.D. Ky. 1894).
Pegues, A. W. *Our Baptist Ministers and Schools.* Springfield, MA: Willey and Co., 1892.
Penn, I. Garland. *The Afro-American Press, and Its Editors.* Springfield, MA: Willey and Co., 1891.
Wright, George C. *A History of Blacks in Kentucky.* Vol. 2, *In Pursuit of Equality, 1890–1980.* Frankfort: Kentucky Historical Society, 1992.

—*Joshua D. Farrington*

ANDERSON-MAYER STATE AID ACT, law that provided funding for African Americans to attend graduate school out of state. In 1936, **Charles W. Anderson Jr.,** the first African American member of the Kentucky legislature, along with a fellow politician from Louisville, Senator Stanley Mayer, cosponsored a bill requiring the state of Kentucky to appropriate funds to assist African American students to attend graduate school outside the state. Anderson wrote the bill in response to the **Day Law** of 1904, which forbade African Americans and whites to attend the same college or university. The act was intended to assist students who wished to pursue majors not offered at the state's black colleges.

The Anderson-Mayer Act initially required the legislature to appropriate a total of $5,000 a year and a maximum of $175 per student. In order to qualify, African American students had to qualify for matriculation at the University of Kentucky and major in programs not offered at **Kentucky State College,** West Kentucky Industrial College, or **Louisville Municipal College.** The act also contained a provision that allowed married women (white or black) to teach, which provided needed extra income for many families. It also provided for minimum wages and improved working conditions for **domestic workers** in the state.

During the 1936–1937 school year, 52 students received financial support from the act. First-year beneficiaries of the grants included Caroline E. Johnson, who received $95.50 to attend Columbia University Library School, and Bessie T. Russell, who received $62 to attend the Hampton Institute.

Although the Anderson-Mayer Act certainly provided needed financial assistance to many black students, it was not a solution to segregated education in higher education. It reaffirmed the Day Law by taking college integration off the legislature's agenda, and the initial appropriation of $5,000 was not enough to meet the needs of qualified applicants. Between 1936 and 1938, the state spent over $2,000 of emergency fund money to support the tuition payment plan. Also in 1938, the law was amended to allow counties with small black populations to pay tuition fees and provide transportation to nearby school districts. This allowed many counties to avoid having to establish high schools for their black residents.

In 1942, under increased pressure from African Americans to integrate Kentucky's colleges, the legislature raised the appropriations of the program to over $17,000. That same year the Department of Education gave Rufus Atwood of Kentucky State College authorization to administer the out-of-state funds. Many black leaders saw this as a way to avoid the more pressing issue of the integration of higher education. In 1948, the *Kentucky Negro*

Educational Association Journal wrote that African Americans supported the initial bill only "as a temporary device" to be used while they continued to press for the integration of the state's colleges. The Anderson-Mayer Act was officially repealed in 1966.

"The Anderson-Mayer Law," *The Kentucky Negro Educational Journal* (November–December 1948): 11.

Geiger, Roger. *History of Higher Education Annual.* Vol. 17, *1997.* Piscataway, NJ: Transaction Publishers, 1997.

Jones, Reinette. *Library Service to African Americans in Kentucky, from the Reconstruction Era to the 1960s.* Jefferson, NC: McFarland, 2001.

"Report of the Legislative Committee," *Kentucky Negro Education Association Journal* (October–November 1937): 31.

Smith, Gerald L. *A Black Educator in the Segregated South: Kentucky's Rufus B. Atwood.* Lexington: Univ. Press of Kentucky, 1994.

Wright, George C. *A History of Blacks in Kentucky.* Vol. 2, *In Pursuit of Equality, 1890–1980.* Frankfort: Kentucky Historical Society, 1992.

—*Joshua D. Farrington*

ANDERSON SLAVE PEN, prison structure for slaves in Mason Co., KY.

The Anderson Slave Pen is a two-story structure built of hewn logs that has one large, rectangular room on each floor and a 10-foot-wide chimney. Now located at the National Underground Freedom Museum in Cincinnati, it was first constructed and used in Mason Co. Its history began when Moses Frazee bought 100 acres of land from Lewis Craig in 1804. Frazee may have built the log building, or he may have taken over an existing log building on the 100-acre tract. At this time, the slave pen contained a 10-foot-wide chimney with a cooking fireplace at the north end of the building. On the east side, off-center, the structure had a single doorway with a rectangular transom over the door, and the door had a small brass doorknob, probably mounted with a surface lock to facilitate access. The doorway may have been constructed to reflect the Federal stylistic conventions that were popular at the time. The original building had at least one window with glass panes. Internally, the building exhibits evidence of shelves and divisions of the second floor.

Frazee sold the 100 acres to John W. Anderson in 1825, and Anderson bought additional land over the next nine years that totaled more than 900 acres. He apparently built himself a house, referred to as a mansion, in the adjacent field sometime between 1825 and 1834. He was certainly living there by the time of his death in 1834, because his widow, Susan S. Anderson, claimed the 100 acres as her "home farm" when she filed her claim for dower rights in early 1835. After Anderson constructed his mansion, the slave-pen building would not have been needed as a residence for his family. When he ceased using the slave-pen building as a house, he converted it to a very different purpose. The addition of iron rings, chains, and barred windows altered the building and its history forever. Its original purpose was obscured. It became a prison for the slaves he bought from friends and neighbors. He had made it into a commercial building, a nonpersonal structure that became a hidden part of the local landscape.

Anderson built up his slave-export business during the late 1820s and early 1830s. He became a major local dealer and exporter of humans from Kentucky to the Deep South, making

yearly trips to either Natchez, MS, or New Orleans between 1830 and 1833. Enslaved persons, horses, and produce such as wheat were the products he transported. In three sales between November 1832 and May 1833, Anderson sold more than $38,000 worth of persons (at least $800,000 in 2005 dollars). Major Lexington slave dealers of the same period claimed sales only in the $5,000 to $8,000 range. Anderson was a major player in the Kentucky-to-Natchez slave trade during his lifetime.

After Anderson died suddenly in July 1834, his widow, Susan Anderson, claimed dower rights over the 100 acres on which the slave pen was situated. She apparently lived there until her death in 1851 and was buried in the adjacent cemetery next to John W. Anderson and several of their daughters.

Newspapers: "Slave Pen Battles Continue," *KP,* January 17, 2000, 2K; "Log 'Slave Pen' Won't Let Us Forget," *Cincinnati Enquirer,* February 8, 2004, A1.

—*Jeannine Kreinbrink*

ANTI–SEPARATE COACH MOVEMENT, coordinated attempt led by African Americans to defeat Kentucky's law to separate the races on railroad cars.

The Anti–Separate Coach Movement was formed in December 1891, in Frankfort, KY, one month before the introduction of the railroad segregation bill in Kentucky's General Assembly. It coordinated black political activism across the state, including local grassroots activities against railroads, lawsuits alleging unfair treatment, and statewide lobbying efforts against the bill. These civil rights activities reflected an early paramount organizing effort by African Americans to fight the legal and political culture of white supremacy.

Upon learning of the Kentucky Railroad Commission's recommendation that lawmakers consider a law modeled on Tennessee's 1891 separate coach law, black leaders in Frankfort organized swiftly statewide, realizing that separate would not be equal. Professor **C. C. Monroe** of the State Normal School (later known as **Kentucky State University**) was elected chair, and the Reverend **S. E. Smith** became the movement's main chronicler. The organization consisted mainly of black ministers and teachers but also included lawyers, doctors, and merchants. Many teachers were women who testified about the horrors of traveling alone in **Jim Crow** cars. They believed that they could stop **Jim Crow** by demonstrating racial uplift to their white counterparts and described the bill as "the worst species of class legislation," which "the better class of white people would [never] sanction." They gained sufficient prominence that the *Louisville Courier-Journal* covered their activities.

Testifying on January 29, 1892, before the Joint Railroad Committee, members of the organization came "200 strong, representing 80 counties in the State and 300,000 Negroes," armed with petitions and letters against the proposed bill. Seven black men spoke, arguing that their class, not their race, should determine their status. Black women testified, emphasizing female frailty, vulnerability, and domesticity; Lexington teacher **Mary E. Britton,** who later became a medical doctor, gave an impassioned speech, immortalized in an 1893 poem by Paul Laurence Dunbar. Speakers addressed rights and citizenship. Taking a conservative approach, they realized that fear of equality, both social and political, motivated many white segregationists. One speaker assured lawmakers that they were not "seeking social rights, but civil rights," to avoid exclusion from first-class facilities. The *Courier-Journal* speculated that their eloquence would sway white lawmakers against the legislation. Kentucky's debate was the region's longest discussion of the separate coach issue, and the vote was relatively close. Despite their efforts, however, the bill passed in the House 59 to 25, and by 18 to 10 in the Senate. Governor John Y. Brown signed Jim Crow transit into law on May 31, 1892.

This was not the movement's final act, however. After passage, members of the movement urged black Kentuckians to "vindicate our race pride with our pocketbooks" and therefore financed the test case *Anderson v. Louisville and Nashville Railroad.* On October 30, 1893, Reverend **William H. Anderson** and his wife boarded a first-class ladies' coach from Evansville, IN, to Madisonville, KY. In Henderson, the conductor asked them to move to the second-class smoking car; when they refused, the conductor ejected them from the train. Staging a second test, the Andersons boarded a ladies' car from Henderson to Madisonville, en route to Nashville, TN; when they refused to leave, the conductor ejected them. Three days later, the Andersons sued in federal court. In 1894, Sixth Circuit judge John W. Barr of Owensboro not only found in their favor but also struck down Kentucky's 1892 Jim Crow law on grounds that its comprehensive language embraced all passengers and therefore unconstitutionally restrained interstate commerce. This nullified the Kentucky statute until the U.S. Supreme Court's decision two years later in ***Plessy v. Ferguson.***

Marshall, Anne E. "A Crisis in Our Lives: African-American Protest and the Kentucky Separate Coach Law, 1892–1900." *Register of the Kentucky Historical Society,* no. 3 (Summer 2000): 241–60.

Minter, Patricia Hagler. "The Codification of Jim Crow: The Origins of Segregated Railroad Transit in the South, 1865–1910." PhD diss., Univ. of Virginia, 1994.

Smith, S. E. *History of the Anti–Separate Coach Movement in Kentucky.* Evansville, IN: National Afro-American Press, 1895.

Wright, George C., *Life Behind a Veil: Blacks in Louisville, Kentucky, 1865–1930.* Baton Rouge: Louisiana State Univ. Press, 1985.

—*Patricia Hagler Minter*

ANTISLAVERY, a reform movement in the nineteenth-century United States. Although Kentucky was committed to slavery, the state also contained an active antislavery movement. From 1792 to 1799, the early antislavery movement in Kentucky was led by white clergy who attempted to secure a constitutional means to end slavery. In 1792, Presbyterian minister David Rice laid the intellectual groundwork for Kentucky's antislavery movement in his pamphlet "Slavery Inconsistent with Justice and Good Policy," in which he attacked the institution on moral and humanitarian grounds while advocating the gradual emancipation of slaves. That same year, proslavery forces at the state constitutional convention succeeded in including Article IX, which prohibited the legislature from passing emancipation laws, in the constitution despite the efforts of David Rice and other emancipationists. By 1799, another constitutional convention had been called, and

once again, the proslavery forces soundly defeated the antislavery delegates and adopted Article IX verbatim into the new state constitution.

After this defeat, clergymen created their own antislavery churches and organizations. In 1807, Baptist ministers David Barrow and Carter Tarrant met in Mason Co. and organized the largest antislavery association in the state, the Baptized Licking-Locust Association, Friends of Humanity. The association was composed of nearly a dozen congregations and established strict slaveholding rules. In 1808, Barrow and Tarrant created the **Kentucky Abolition Society (KAS).** By the late 1820s, the state had eight such societies with roughly 200 members. The KAS called for gradual emancipation with compensation to masters, prohibition of the slave trade, and education for freed blacks. In 1822, the society began publishing the *Abolition Intelligencer and Missionary Magazine,* edited by Rev. John Finley Crowe. Although the publication was short lived, it effectively disseminated the influential ideas of Barrow among other society members and was one of only two antislavery papers published in the country during this period.

Even though they espoused gradual emancipation, these antislavery churches and societies had little success because most whites were apprehensive about increasing the free black population. By the 1820s, the colonization movement began gaining support in Kentucky among churches. Colonization appealed to Kentuckians because it promoted repatriating freed blacks to Africa, which was not as extreme as abolitionism. In 1829, the **Kentucky Colonization Society** was founded, and by 1832, there were 31 such societies throughout the state. Despite these efforts, the promoters of colonization failed to achieve meaningful success. Between 1829 and 1859, the state society sent only 658 blacks to Liberia, an inconsequential number compared with the state's growing slave population during this period.

By the 1840s and 1850s, Kentucky did not contain one united antislavery movement but a hodgepodge of antislavery ideologies. It was during this period that two of the most outspoken antislavery supporters, Cassius M. Clay and John G. Fee, rose to prominence. Clay was an emancipationist who had started forming his antislavery views while attending Yale. By the 1840s, Clay had established his antislavery credentials by publicly supporting the Slave Non-importation Act of 1833 and by basing his opposition to slavery on what he believed was the economic degradation caused by the institution. By the early 1850s, Clay formed a tenuous partnership with abolitionist minister John G. Fee. In 1853, Fee and some followers founded the antislavery community of Berea, and in 1855, the Bereans constructed a one-room schoolhouse that would later become **Berea College.** The school was tasked with the mission of educating both blacks and whites. In 1859, because of the sectional tensions exacerbated by John Brown's raid on Harper's Ferry, proslavery men from Madison Co. forced the Bereans to leave the state within 10 days.

In the end, antislavery advocates were unsuccessful in their attempts to end slavery in Kentucky. The Civil War ultimately led to the end of human bondage in the Bluegrass State. Antislavery groups in Kentucky were a reflection of the diverse viewpoints of people in the state on this controversial subject.

Allen, Jeffrey Brooke. "The Debate over Slavery and Race in Ante-bellum Kentucky: 1792–1850." PhD diss., Northwestern Univ., 1973.

Harrison, Lowell H. *The Antislavery Movement in Kentucky.* Lexington: Univ. Press of Kentucky, 1978.

Howard, Victor B. *The Evangelical War Against Slavery and Caste: The Life and Times of John G. Fee.* London: Associated Univ. Press, 1996.

Peck, John M. "Brief View of the Baptist Interest in Each of the United States." *American Quarterly Register* 14, no. 1 (August 1841): 50.

—*Benjamin Fitzpatrick*

ARIEL ACADEMY, school for African Americans staffed by the American Missionary Association. Established in 1868 at **Camp Nelson,** KY, Ariel Academy was an extension of the schools founded there by Rev. John G. Fee during the Civil War. The village near the school was sometimes known as Ariel (a symbolic name for a freed slave, as in Shakespeare's *Tempest*), but it was also called Hall; eventually, both names disappeared, and the region became known again simply as Camp Nelson, with Ariel renamed Camp Nelson Academy. At first, the school was partially sponsored by the **Freedmen's Bureau.** In the spring of 1868, the bureau purchased the buildings that had been part of the school complex built for refugees while Camp Nelson continued to function as a Union Army installation. The bureau's purchase, for $1,520, included a large boardinghouse, with wings suitable for a schoolhouse and a chapel. Ariel Academy opened its doors to students only after the population of African Americans living at Camp Nelson had been drastically reduced by the operations of the Freedmen's Bureau. In 1871, the school had 100 students. As a normal school, Ariel Academy trained many black students to become teachers, but the number of pupils was never as large after the war as it had been while Camp Nelson was an active military camp, supply depot, and refugee center.

The school was never actually integrated, although it had been designed to be, since its constitution was modeled verbatim on that of Berea College. The white students who attended Ariel were typically children of teachers and staff. For many years, the **American Missionary Association** (AMA) supplied teachers for Ariel. During the academy's most prosperous period, Howard S. Fee, Fee's second son, was superintendent. Fee, who had been the prime mover in the school's establishment, was a trustee, as was his friend Rev. **Gabriel Burdett,** a black minister whom Fee had met and befriended at Camp Nelson. Burdett, certainly Ariel Academy's chief worker, spent almost a decade teaching and supervising there. After he left Kentucky, the school became increasingly less viable, even though AMA teachers continued the work. Although he moved to Berea permanently, John G. Fee continued to support the educational enterprise at Camp Nelson until he died in 1901; in his will he left bequests to Ariel Academy, but the school was already very near failure. In 1902, the trustees of the school at Camp Nelson appealed to Berea College, asking to become a part of that institution, but the request was denied. In 1904, the last of the school's property was sold to the Board of Missions for Freedmen of the Presbyterian Church in the United States of America.

Sears, Richard D. *Camp Nelson, Kentucky: A Civil War History.* Lexington: Univ. Press of Kentucky, 2002.

———. *A Utopian Experiment in Kentucky: Integration and Social Equality at Berea, 1866–1904.* Westport, CT: Greenwood Press, 1996.

—*Richard D. Sears*

ARNOLD, ADAM SHIRLEY, JR. (b. 1922, Lexington, KY), educator. After serving in the U.S. Army during World War II, Lexington native Adam Shirley Arnold Jr. earned his BA from West Virginia State College in 1947. He continued his education at the University of Wisconsin, where he earned both an MBA and a PhD in finance. While Arnold was a professor at Prairie View A&M College in Texas, an abstract of his 1951 dissertation, "The Investments of Seven Negro Life Insurance Companies," was published in the *Journal of Finance* in 1954. He also participated in the organization of the 1955 convention of the National Negro Business League. In 1957, upon his hiring by Father Ted Hesburgh in the Finance Department, Arnold became the first African American faculty member at the University of Notre Dame. After receiving tenure in 1961, Arnold, the first African American to earn tenure at Notre Dame, continued his work as professor of finance there for nearly 30 more years. Throughout those years, he was a mentor of African American students across the campus.

After retirement, Arnold and his wife, Helen, resided in Hampton, VA. In 2002, he received Notre Dame's prestigious William P. Sexton Award, an annual award for a nonalumnus "who has performed outstanding service to the University and whose life exemplifies the spirit of Notre Dame."

Arnold, Adam Shirley, Jr. "The Investments of Seven Negro Life Insurance Companies." *Journal of Finance* 9, no. 1 (March 1954): 55–57.

"Arnold Honored with Sexton Award," *Notre Dame Business Magazine Online,* issue 11, 2004. http://www.nd.edu/~ndbizmag/issue11/news7.shtml (accessed May 11, 2009).

"Notre Dame Alumni Briefs," *Notre Dame Magazine,* 2002–2003. http://magazine.nd.edu/news/14759-notre-dame-alumni-briefs-3 (accessed May 25, 2010).

"Planning for Business League Session," *Arkansas State Press* (Little Rock), September 9, 1955, 1.

—*Joshua D. Farrington*

ATKINS, CHARLES HENRY "SPEEDY" (b. 1875?, TN; d. 1928, Paducah, KY), mummified through an experimental embalming method and then placed on display. The pauper Charles Henry "Speedy" Atkins became famous in death. In life, he earned his nickname through his swiftness as a tobacco worker for the Dixon Tobacco Company. In 1928, he drowned in the Ohio River while fishing and drinking home-brewed liquor. W. P. Howe found Atkins's body and had it sent to A. Z. Hamock, an African American funeral home director in Paducah. Atkins had no known survivors and was embalmed by Hamock with a secret embalming fluid that remains a mystery today. Speedy's well-preserved body was placed on display for tourists. It was washed away in the 1937 Paducah flood but was later found and returned. Speedy's corpse became a celebrity, appearing on national television three times. In August 1994, Hamock's widow, Velma, recognized the 100th anniversary of the founding of Hamock's Funeral Home as the oldest continuously operating black-owned business in Paducah. To mark the occasion, Speedy's body was finally buried in Paducah's Maplelawn Cemetery. His grave marker reads: "Lived 53 years as a pauper embalmed by A. Z. Hamock Buried 66 Years Later August 5, 1994 As A Celebrity."

"Black Man Who Died 66 Years Ago Is Finally Buried," *Jet* 86, no. 17 (August 29, 1994): 56–59.

Holland, Jeffrey Scott. *Weird Kentucky: Your Travel Guide to Kentucky's Local Legends and Best Kept Secrets.* New York: Sterling Publishing Co., 2008.

McQueen, Keven. *Offbeat Kentuckians.* Kuttawa, KY: McClanahan Publishing House, 2001.

—*Sallie L. Powell*

ATWOOD, RUFUS BALLARD (b. 1897, Hickman, KY; d. 1983, Frankfort, KY), sixth president of Kentucky State College (later known as Kentucky State University). Rufus Ballard Atwood, educator and civic leader, was born on March 15, 1897, in Hickman, KY, the youngest child of Pomp and Annie (Parker) Atwood. Raised in a family that emphasized the importance of education, Atwood graduated from Fisk Academy in Nashville in 1915 and then enrolled at Fisk University there. He left Fisk in 1918 to volunteer for service in the army. As a member of the Negro Signal Corps, he received a Bronze Star for gallantry in action. Atwood held bachelor's degrees from both Fisk and Iowa State University, as well as a master's degree in administration from the University of Chicago.

Atwood served as dean of agriculture at Prairie View State College in Texas from 1923 to 1929. In 1929, he became the sixth president of **Kentucky State University** in Frankfort, serving until 1962. During his presidency, Kentucky State was accredited as a four-year college, and educational and administrative programs were revised and expanded. His work to improve black education statewide and nationwide and his contributions to numerous civic organizations brought Atwood numerous awards. The University of Kentucky honored him with the Algernon Sydney Sullivan Citizen Medallion at its commencement ceremonies in 1962. Atwood was the first black to receive the award, established in 1925 and conferred by 25 colleges and universities in the South.

Atwood married Mabel Campbell on June 28, 1921. Atwood died on March 18, 1983, and was buried in the Frankfort Cemetery.

Smith, Gerald L. "Mr. Kentucky State: A Biography of Rufus Ballard Atwood." PhD. diss, Univ. of Kentucky, 1988.

—*Gerald L. Smith*

Rufus Atwood (left) and Lyman T. Johnson. Johnson filed a lawsuit that ultimately led to the desegregation of the University of Kentucky graduate school in 1949.

AUBESPIN, MERVIN R. (b. 1937, Opelousas, LA), artist, reporter, associate editor, and former president of the National Association of Black Journalists. Louisiana native Mervin R. Aubespin joined the *Louisville Courier-Journal* in the mid-1960s as the newspaper's first black graphic artist. In the summer of 1968, he hastily made the transition from artist to reporter when he and a white reporter traveled to western Louisville to cover racial turbulence over the arrest of a black businessman. The white reporter fearfully deserted the area, and Aubespin spent 48 hours calling his reports into the *Courier-Journal*'s office via a pay phone. When a police officer jabbed a shotgun into his chest, Aubespin told him that he was a reporter for the *Courier-Journal*. The officer retorted, "There aren't any nigger reporters at the *Courier*."

Aubespin graduated from Tuskegee University in 1958. He soon moved to Louisville to teach junior high school industrial arts. After covering the civil rights movement for the *Courier-Journal*, he attended Columbia University in 1971 to improve his reporting and writing skills. The following year, he became a staff writer for the *Courier-Journal* and later the founder of the National Association of Black Journalists' first affiliate, the Louisville Association of Black Communicators. He received the Ida B. Wells Award for recruiting other African American journalists when he was associate editor beginning in the mid-1980s. In 1991, the Association of Schools of Journalism and Mass Communications awarded him the Distinguished Service to Journalism Award.

In 2002, artist and African art collector Aubespin retired and became a consultant for the *Courier-Journal*. He was inducted into the National Association of Black Journalists' Hall of Fame in 2007. Three years later, he won Louisville's Dr. Martin Luther King Jr. Freedom Award. Known as "Uncle Merv" by the thousands of young journalists whom he had influenced, Aubespin had followed in the journalist footsteps of **Robert T. Berry,** who was an African American investigative reporter for the *Courier-Journal* in 1913.

Marriott, Michel. "Merv Aubespin." National Association of Black Journalists. http://www.nabj.org/newsroom/publications/committed/story/418p-587c.php (accessed February 19, 2009).

Newspapers: "U.S. Editors Described as Remiss on Reporting the Plight of Blacks," *NYT,* April 12, 1985, A15; "Retired C-J Editor Enters Hall of Fame," *LCJ,* August 18, 2007, 4B; "They Were First," *LCJ,* January 18, 2009, 1A; "Former C-J Editor Wins MLK Freedom Award," *LCJ,* January 8, 2010, B3.

—*Sallie L. Powell*

AUGUST 8TH EMANCIPATION CELEBRATION, celebration of emancipation from slavery historically observed by western Kentucky communities on this date. August 8th Emancipation Celebrations have multiple origins. One source suggests that they recognized the abolition of slavery in the British West Indies in 1834. Another version follows the news that Tennessee's military governor, Andrew Johnson, had freed the slaves in his jurisdiction on August 8, 1864. Given these circumstances, western Kentucky communities have used this date to celebrate with picnics, musical concerts, dances, ball games, family reunions, beauty pageants, and church services. A small group of former slaves originated the celebration in the 1890s in a field at Rum Springs about a mile from Allensville in Todd Co., KY. This first celebration was held at Jim Phillips's barn, where people expressed gratitude to God for their freedom with songs and prayers. The event grew in popularity, and African Americans from all over the country came to Allensville for what became known as Annual Homecoming Day for Black People. The celebration generally lasted a week and ended with a picnic on August 8th.

In the early 1900s, Paducah was the site of the largest August 8th Emancipation Celebration. Thousands traveled to the city on the Illinois Central Railroad, which ran special trains from Hopkinsville and Louisville to Paducah at the round-trip rate of $1.25. A special train from Beaver Dam to Paducah cost $1.75 round-trip. In 1906, the Hopkinsville newspaper warned its readers to stay away from the Paducah celebrations because of "the feeling against negroes in the First district, growing out of the Mayfield and Hickman affairs." The paper never precisely identified the problem, but on the same day, the Paducah newspaper noted a request from "the Committee on Invitation" to disregard the deceptive advice. It was not able to name the culprit but claimed that a warning had reached Memphis and that a letter to the mayor of Owensboro cautioned that a race war might occur on August 8th. In 1907, a Hopkinsville railroad agent sold 650 tickets on 13 train cars for the August 8th trip. A newspaper writer maintained that it was mostly young people who took the trip because "the older ones, those who were really emancipated, preferred to stay at home and save their money."

In August 1908, African American celebrators encountered night riders who fired into their coaches. No one was injured. Five days later, the Hopkinsville newspaper alleged that Paducah African Americans had requested that their mayor stop the August 8th Emancipation Celebration. The ostensible reason for this ap-

peal was that the event brought "many dissolute negroes, with whom the local colored folk do not care to associate and whose presence is a menace to the peace of the community." However, possibly the fear of more attacks from night riders influenced this request. The following year, 1909, even though the crowd was a little smaller, thousands still attended the celebration in Paducah; consequently, the Hopkinsville newspaper's claim of the demise of Paducah's August 8th celebration was inaccurate. People arrived not only from Kentucky but also from Illinois, and the largest crowd came from Tennessee. Even though the crowds were peaceful, the local constable, in an intimidating act, "cleaned out his gatling [*sic*] gun" in what he claimed was preparation for any potential trouble. For the next few years, police expected the worst, but no major problems occurred.

"The 8th of August" Emancipation Celebration has continued into the twenty-first century. In Paducah, the Robert Coleman Park and the W. C. Young Community Center have hosted activities. The celebration has included music, a parade, a breakfast, a memorial service, a picnic, a golf tournament, vendors, and other activities that last over several days. In 2013, Russellville held its 27th annual Emancipation Celebration.

Bigham, Darrel E. *On Jordan's Banks: Emancipation and Its Aftermath in the Ohio River Valley.* Lexington: Univ. Press of Kentucky, 2005.

Glazier, Jack. *Been Coming through Some Hard Times: Race, History, and Memory in Western Kentucky.* Knoxville: Univ. of Tennessee Press, 2012.

Newspapers: "Emancipation Celebration," *HK,* July 24, 1900, 5; *HK,* August 4, 1906, 2; "Negroes Warned to Stay Away from Paducah Because of Bitter Feeling," *PES,* August 4, 1906, 1; "Negroes Flocked to Paducah Thursday to Celebrate," *HK,* August 10, 1907, 5; "Night Riders," *HK,* August 15, 1908, 7; "Cut Out Big Day," *HK,* August 20, 1908, 4; "Emancipation Day Quietly Celebrated," *PES,* August 10, 1909, 1; "Emancipation Celebration Highlights Weekend," *News-Democrat and Leader* (Russellville), August 2, 2013, A1.

"Paducah Kentucky Distinctively Creative." http://www.paducah.travel/includes/events/?action=displayDetail&eventId=15689 (accessed August 15, 2013).

Todd County Historical Society. *Todd County, Kentucky, Family History.* Todd Co., KY: Turner Publishing Company, 1995.

Wiggins, William H., Jr. *O Freedom! Afro-American Emancipation Celebrations.* Knoxville: Univ. of Tennessee Press, 1987.

—*Sallie L. Powell*

AUNT CHARLOTTE (unknown), freed slave and businesswoman. Several accounts of Aunt Charlotte's early life, although unsubstantiated by historical records, indicate that she was born and raised in slavery in Virginia before moving with her owner to Lexington, KY. Upon her owner's death, she received her freedom and perhaps some property as well. She proceeded to earn her living as a baker and street vendor in Lexington. It was in this manner that she earned enough money to purchase William "King" Solomon when he was auctioned off as an indentured servant in 1833.

According to the narrative first published by James Lane Allen in 1891, Solomon was a poor, white miscreant whose unruly behavior led the sheriff of Lexington to hire him out to the highest bidder. A hemp factory owner started the bid with $1. A medical student, who had joked that he would dissect Solomon after his death, offered an additional 50 cents. The price had increased to $10 when Charlotte entered the bidding. She purchased Solomon for $13 and freed him, and the two remained friends. He has been remembered for burying the bodies of those who succumbed to the outbreak of cholera in Lexington in 1833.

Records do not indicate whether Aunt Charlotte survived the cholera epidemic, and nothing has been uncovered about her life after the purchase of Solomon. In 1939, despite objections from the Negro Civic League of Lexington regarding her relative obscurity, the Charlotte Court public housing complex for African Americans in Lexington was named after Aunt Charlotte.

Allen, James Lane. *Flute and Violin and Other Kentucky Tales and Romances.* New York: Harper and Brothers, 1891.
Hollingsworth, Randolph. "Mrs. Boone, I Presume?" In *Bluegrass Renaissance: The History and Culture of Central Kentucky, 1792–1852,* edited by James Klotter and Dan Rowland, 93–130. Lexington: Univ. Press of Kentucky, 2012.
Milward, Burton. *William "King" Solomon, 1775–1854.* Lexington, KY: Larkspur Press, 1990.

—*Elizabeth Schaller*

AUSTIN, HELEN CLOUD (b. 1925, Harlan, KY), second African American student to attend the University of Louisville's Raymond A. Kent School of Social Work and first African American chief of social services at San Antonio State Hospital. Helen Cloud, the daughter of Tip and Ellen Cloud, was born in Harlan, KY. After earning her master of science degree at the University of Louisville in 1953, she worked as a social worker at Chicago's Cook County Hospital. In 1957, she moved to Cincinnati, OH, and became chief of the Outpatient Department at Longview State Hospital. She and her husband, George J. Austin, a civil service worker, moved to San Antonio, TX, when he was transferred to Kelly Air Force Base in 1962. Austin attempted to get a social worker position at San Antonio State Hospital but was denied employment because of the "no blacks hired as professional" policy. She had learned as a University of Louisville student about the nonviolent philosophy of Martin Luther King Jr. and had adopted it for herself. With Congressman Henry B. Gonzalez's assistance, the prejudicial policy was changed, and Austin became the first African American professional hired at the hospital in 1965. Years later, she claimed that she was hired because she and Gonzalez had "stayed in the background."

Austin not only aided patients with bus rides and excursions for their family and friends but also coordinated efforts to encourage short-term patients to register and vote in political elections in 1980. In the early 1980s, her social work was recognized when she became San Antonio Social Worker of the Year, Texas State Social Worker of the Year, and the nation's Social Worker of the Year. In 1985, she was inducted into the San Antonio Women's Hall of Fame, and four years later, she was included in the National Council of Negro Women's *Salute to Black Women Who Make Things Happen.*

In 1987, Austin retired from San Antonio State Hospital. She lost part of her left leg to diabetes. After 43 years of marriage, her husband, George, died in 2002. Because he had prepared their meals during the course of their marriage, she decided to move to an assisted-living facility in San Antonio. Austin gave her papers to the University of Texas because, as she stated, "Throughout your career, if you don't document it, then it didn't happen."

Newspapers: "Honors in Abundance: Woman Who Broke through Color Barrier Continues Her Legacy," *San Antonio Express-News,* February 25, 2003, 8B; "Know Warning Signs of Poor Diet," *San Antonio Express-News,* October 20, 2003, 1D; "Retired Social Worker Recalls King's Teachings," *San Antonio Express-News,* February 9, 2010, 11A.
University of Texas at San Antonio. "Helen Cloud Austin Papers, 1944–2008." http://www.lib.utexas.edu/taro/utsa/00049/utsa-00049.html (accessed February 20, 2009).
University of Texas at San Antonio, Oral History Collection. "Interview with Helen Cloud Austin, May 27, 1997." http://digital.utsa.edu/cdm/ref/collection/p15125coll4/id/2069 (accessed May 17, 2013).

—*Sallie L. Powell*

AYERS, RHODA MAE (b. 1931, Rock Island, IL; d. 1984, Fort Thomas, KY), first African American elected to political office in Newport, KY. Rhoda Mae Ayers, the first African American to be elected to political office in Newport and in Campbell Co., was born on July 26, 1931, the daughter of George and Lauretta Reynolds. Ayers moved to Newport, KY, from Rock Island, IL, in 1972, after the death of her husband, to live with her mother. Upon arriving in Newport, Ayers got involved in youth and other community activities; her service in those areas gave her the name recognition necessary for her first attempt at election to the Newport Board of Education. In the 1976 election, she ran on a "poor people's" platform. She won the election, placing third among the candidates, and served for four years on the board. During her tenure on the Board of Education, she strove to ensure fairness for students and teachers alike. When she ran for reelection in 1980, the Newport Teachers Association endorsed her, but despite that support, Ayers lost. Afterward, she was appointed to the Newport Recreation Commission and served as a member of the Community Action Commission advisory board. Ayers was also a board member of the Brighton Center. Employed at the U.S. Postal Service Annex in Cincinnati, she became the Postal Union's recording secretary. Ayers died on February 21, 1984, at St. Luke Hospital in Fort Thomas and is buried in the New St. Joseph Cemetery, Cincinnati.

Newspapers: "Tax Stands Help Elect Newport 4," *KP,* November 3, 1976, 4; "Election Brings No Surprises, No Mixup," *Kentucky Enquirer,* November 4, 1976, C1; "School Board Reactions Run Hot in Ludlow; Others Cool," *KP,* November 5, 1980, 3K; "Rhoda Ayers, Active in Community," *KP,* February 24, 1984, 12A.

—*Theodore H. H. Harris*

B

BACCHUS, PERCIVAL L. (b. 1902, Virgin Islands, West Indies; d. 1962, Cincinnati, OH), doctor whose medical license was revoked after he was accused of performing an illegal abortion. Percival L. Bacchus was an African American medical doctor who practiced in Newport for more than three decades. He was born in the Virgin Islands on May 2, 1902, but when he was young, his family moved to New Jersey. Bacchus attended Meharry Medical College in Nashville, TN, and graduated in the late 1920s. He practiced for a short time in Nashville before coming to Kentucky, where he passed the Kentucky State Medical Examination and, on August 10, 1931, was licensed to practice.

Bacchus was instrumental in revitalizing the long-dormant Newport Masonic Lodge PHA No. 120 and served as master of the lodge for many years. Meetings were held in the basement of his office at 341 Central Ave. The practice of medicine and the Masonic lodge were the two greatest passions of his life.

In December 1955, Bacchus was tried in Campbell Co. Circuit Court on a charge of performing an illegal abortion. The jury failed to reach a verdict, and a second trial took place in April 1956. The second jury also failed to return a decision. In August 1956, the State Board of Health revoked Bacchus's medical license on the grounds that he had "committed an unlawful abortion."

Bacchus was a 33rd-degree Mason, a Shriner, and the illustrious potentate of Aleikum Temple No. 96 in Covington. He died at General Hospital in Cincinnati on June 3, 1962, and was buried in Mary E. Smith Cemetery in **Elsmere.**

Kentucky Board of Medical License Records, Louisville, KY.
Newspapers: "Bacchus, Dr. Percival L.," *Cincinnati Times Star,* June 6, 1962, 40; "Journey's End, Bacchus, Dr. Percival L.," *CE,* June 6, 1962, 24.

—*Theodore H. H. Harris*

BACON, MAMIE B. (b. ca. 1873, Shelbyville, KY; d. unknown), organizer. While living in Ohio, Mamie B. Bacon actively participated in a myriad of social and fraternal organizations, including membership in the Household of Ruth, which was the women's auxiliary of the Grand United Order of Odd Fellows (GUOOF); the Good Samaritans; and the Daughters of Samaria. She held various positions in numerous organizations, like past grand master Council GUOOF, past grand worthy inspectrix, grand worthy lecturer of the Ohio Grand Court of Calanthe, and supreme representative to the biennial session of the Supreme Court of Calanthe, Louisville, KY, August 16–22, 1925. She founded and organized the Independent Sons and Daughters of America. She was also energetically involved in her church, Park Street Methodist Episcopal, and for 18 years was the secretary of its Official Board. She also served on the Executive Committee of Five in the reception of St. Paul (later Calvary) Methodist Episcopal Church and functioned as a charitable worker of the Woman's Home Missionary Society of the Methodist Episcopal Church.

The only daughter of John and Belle Howard, Bacon was educated in Kentucky and Indiana. She completed a business course at Benton College in 1898. She was married to H. Leonard Bacon and had two daughters, Leota K. Dixon and Carrie B. King, from a previous marriage.

Dabney, Wendell P. *Cincinnati's Colored Citizens: Historical, Sociological and Biographical.* Cincinnati: Dabney, 1926.
Yenser, Thomas, ed. *Who's Who in Colored America, 1941–1944.* 6th ed. Brooklyn, NY: Thomas Yenser, 1942.

—*Sallie L. Powell*

BAILEY, WILLIAM SHREVE (b. 1806, Centerville, OH; d. 1886, Nashville, TN), abolitionist and newspaper editor. William Shreve Bailey, an abolitionist, editor, and proprietor of several **antislavery** newspapers, was born on February 10, 1806, the son of John and Rebekah Shreve Bailey. He married Caroline A. Withnall in Wheeling, VA (now West Virginia), on December 13, 1827. Bailey was trained as a mechanic; in 1839, he moved his family to Newport, where he opened a machine shop. He wrote numerous articles in the *Newport News* that advocated abolition, thereby causing difficulties for the newspaper's owner, a man named Ryan. Bailey was encouraged to purchase the newspaper and its press.

Besides the *Newport News,* Bailey published several other newspapers dedicated to antislavery, such as the *Kentucky Weekly News,* the *Newport and Covington Daily News,* and the *Free South.* Bailey's sentiments gained the attention of other abolitionists, but in contrast to most of them, who were concerned about religious and moral issues, Bailey's opposition to slavery was based on economic principles. He believed that all workers should be paid for their efforts. Prominent abolitionist John G. Fee thought that Bailey lacked the intelligence and correct principles for abolition work, and he communicated his opinion to the **American Missionary Association.** Fee even refused to associate with Bailey.

Bailey's newspapers were constantly in need of financial help. In 1851, his office and presses were destroyed by fire. Proslavery Kentuckians also were pressuring his supporters in Cincinnati. Although Fee did not agree with Bailey's efforts, he believed that the newspaper would be a useful tool in the antislavery efforts in Kentucky. In a rare instance of communication with Bailey, Fee recommended William Goodell, a northern antislavery minister and writer, as a possible editor.

In 1858, Bailey requested and received financial help for his *Free South.* In 1859, a few days after John Brown's raid at Harper's Ferry, VA, a mob entered Bailey's office and destroyed his presses and type. Bailey had the advantage of being in Newport, just across the Ohio River from Cincinnati, so in 1860 he brought suit in a Cincinnati court against some Campbell Co. residents for the destruction of his printing office. He was then warned to leave the state, but he ignored the warnings and continued to publish his paper. Bailey was arrested after the reappearance of the *Free South,* charged with incendiarism, and jailed. He was granted bail and departed for England. He later returned to Kentucky, but his trial never took place because the Civil War had begun.

During the war, Bailey continued publishing the *Free South,* reporting on the activities of the Lincoln administration and pertinent antislavery actions. In 1867, he was arrested and sued for libel in Campbell Co. Circuit Court by J. R. Hallam. Bailey agreed to print a retraction and to pay Hallam's attorney fees. He moved to Nashville, where he died on February 20, 1886. He was buried in Nashville.

Allen, L. P. *The Genealogy and History of the Shreve Family from 1641.* Greenfield, IL: Privately printed, 1901.

Aptheker, Herbert. *Anti-racism in U.S. History.* New York: Greenwood Press, 1992.

Newspapers: "Fire in Newport," *CJ,* October 11, 1851, 2; "Aid for 'The Free South,'" *Free South,* September 3, 1858, 2; "The Title of Our Paper," *Free South,* September 3, 1858, 2; "Married," *Free South,* January 7, 1859, 3; "William S. Bailey," *CJ,* February 4, 1860, 2; "Newport," *Cincinnati Daily Enquirer,* April 1, 1867, 1.

Steely, Will Frank. "William Shreve Bailey: Kentucky Abolitionist," *FCHQ* 31 (1957): 274–81.

—*Theodore H. H. Harris*

BAKER, DAVID (b. 1881, Louisville, KY; d. unknown), inventor. David Baker was born in Louisville, KY. He was educated in New Orleans, LA, and married Celena Le'Cleac on April 18, 1903. They had one child, Hilda Katherine.

Baker lived in Los Angeles, CA, and held patents on the following inventions: a railway-signal apparatus, a signal device for indicating high water for bridges, and interliners to prevent tire punctures. His railway-signal apparatus, patent 1,054,267, patented on February 24, 1913, was designed for the twofold purpose of indicating the conditions of a stream and also of the switch end of a siding track. Baker believed that his device was "simple in construction, economical to install and maintain, and effective in use."

On September 21, 1915, Baker's signal apparatus for high water, patent 1,154,162, was patented. The invention's purposes were to indicate various water levels on bridges and the probable effect on bridge safety. The invention included a warning signal connected to an auxiliary battery, which would operate when other signals failed and have the float automatically in the raised position holding a contact arm that indicated when the bridge was unsafe. Baker's additional goals were that the apparatus be simple, economical, and effective.

Patent 1,620,054 for Baker's last patented creation, the interliner, was granted on December 10, 1924. The interliner provided resilient tread armor to protect the outer periphery of a tire tube from radial puncture. Baker believed that his conception was not only simple to construct and install but also neat and durable. He also invented scales for use in elevators to prevent overloading and a streetcar transom opener.

Mather, Frank Lincoln, ed. *Who's Who of the Colored Race: A General Biographical Dictionary of Men and Women of African Descent.* Vol. 1. Chicago: Memento Edition, 1915.

U.S. Patent and Trademark Office. http://www.uspto.gov/ (accessed June 30, 2009).

—*Sallie L. Powell*

BALLARD, JOHN (b. 1829, Kentucky; d. 1905, Los Angeles, CA), early settler in Los Angeles, CA. In the late 1850s, John Ballard left a life of slavery in Kentucky to move west with his wife, Amanda. He settled in Los Angeles, CA, where he worked as a teamster and accumulated enough wealth to establish himself in the frontier city. In 1869, he helped found the First African Methodist Episcopal Church, but a population boom and increased segregation forced him to move to the Santa Monica Mountains to work on 320 acres he and his daughter claimed through the Homestead Act.

Although Ballard had some wealth in the form of property in the city, he lived in simplicity in a rundown shack. As the first African American settler in the region, he was the object of both curiosity and some scorn, and local whites attempted to intimidate him into leaving the area by burning his home. He persevered, however, and remained on the land until shortly before his death in a county hospital in 1905.

The mountain on which he lived was named derogatively in acknowledgment of his presence, and until the first decade of the twenty-first century it was still officially known as Negrohead Mountain. On February 24, 2009, the Los Angeles County Board of Supervisors approved a plan to rename it Ballard Mountain in honor of one of the city's first black pioneers.

Newspapers: "Life of Early Black Settler Studied," *Ventura County Star,* February 16, 2006, Local; "LA County Urges Name-Change for Negrohead Mountain," Associated Press, February 25, 2009; "Mountain of Respect Called Overdue," *Los Angeles Daily News,* February 25, 2009, A4.

Russell, J. H. *Heads and Tails . . . and Odds and Ends.* Los Angeles: Thomas Litho and Printing Co., 1963.

—*Stephen Pickering*

BALLARD, WILLIAM HENRY, SR. (b. 1862, Franklin Co., KY; d. 1954, Lexington, KY), proprietor of the first African American–owned drugstore in the state. Born on Halloween to Dowan and Matilda (Bartlett) Ballard, William Henry Ballard Sr. studied with a private tutor until the establishment of a Kentucky public school system for blacks in 1874. He graduated from Louisville High School in 1880 and then attended Roger Williams University in Nashville, TN, from 1879 to 1882. He taught at several Tennessee and Kentucky schools. In 1892, he graduated with a degree in pharmacy from Northwestern University in Evanston, IL. He promptly married Bessie Brady from Nashville, TN.

On March 1, 1893, Dr. Ballard, along with James E. Nelson, opened the first African American–owned and operated pharmacy in Kentucky. Nelson remained with Ballard and Nelson Pharmacy for only two years, but the firm, Ballard Pharmacy, continued. At the time, Ballard was the only Kentucky African American member of the Drug Association. He actively participated in various civic and fraternal organizations, including the new Negro Business League of Lexington and Fayette County, the Greenwood Cemetery and Realty Company, the Masons, and the Kentucky State Blue Grass Medical Society. He served as one of the directors of Lexington's first African American YMCA, an officer of the True Sisters of Israel, a delegate to the 1898 Republican National Convention, deputy state grand chancellor of the Knights of Pythias, a representative to the 1908 annual national meeting of the Negro Business League in Baltimore, MD, president of the Emancipation and Civic League, a trustee at **St. Paul**

African Methodist Episcopal Church, and grand master of the **United Brothers of Friendship** of the State of Kentucky.

A Lexington newspaper indicated Dr. Ballard's popularity in the community when it announced a surprise 44th birthday party given by friends. Ballard gave back to the public in 1912 by helping **Lexington's Colored Orphan Industrial Home** hold a successful fund-raiser with the Tuskegee Band concert. In 1913, he joined other community leaders chosen "to speak for race" and confer with city and county officials periodically regarding pertinent issues, especially the issue of proposed parks for African Americans. His pharmaceutical influence resulted in four Kentucky drugstores managed by former Ballard Pharmacy clerks.

Ballard and his wife had six children; four survived to adulthood. Sons William Henry Jr., Orville Lee, and Edward Hunter entered the medical profession. A Howard University graduate, Orville Lee worked as a resident physician at Waverly Hills Sanatorium, Louisville. Dr. William Henry Ballard Sr. died on May 28, 1954, in Lexington.

Hamilton, G. P. *Biographical Sketches of Prominent Negro Men and Women of Kentucky.* Memphis: E. H. Clarke & Brother, 1911.
Mather, Frank Lincoln, ed. *Who's Who of the Colored Race: A General Biographical Dictionary of Men and Women of African Descent.* Vol. 1. Chicago: Memento Edition, 1915.
Newspapers: "Colored Doctors Meet," *LL,* May 12, 1901, 6; "Colored Notes," *LL,* November 2, 1906, 2; "Negroes Selected to Speak on Race," *LL,* January 10, 1913, 1; "Colored Notes," *LL,* June 23, 1914, 12.
Richardson, Clement. *The National Cyclopedia of the Colored Race.* Montgomery, AL: National Publishing Company, 1919.
Wright, Richard Robert, Jr. *Encyclopaedia of the African Methodist Episcopal Church.* 2nd ed. Philadelphia: Book Concern of the A.M.E. Church, 1947.

—*Sallie L. Powell*

BANKS, ANNA SIMMS (b. ca. 1862, Brandenburg, KY; d. 1923, Winchester, KY), Republican convention delegate and civic activist. According to Kentucky's Death Records, Anna (a.k.a. Annie) was born in Brandenburg, Meade Co., KY. Her mother's name was Isabelle (or Isabella). The 1870 U.S. federal census recorded Anna Corby living in Louisville, KY, with her mother, Isabella, a domestic servant, Marquis (or Marcus) Simms, a barber, and Edward and Gerrard Corby. The 1880 census listed Annie Simms as the daughter of Marcus Simms. By 1890, Annie was a schoolteacher living with Marcus on East Jacob Ave. She continued in the teaching profession until she married **William Webb Banks** (a.k.a. Webb or W. W.), a Winchester, KY, journalist, on July 10, 1906.

Annie Simms Banks joined her husband in his active involvement in civic activity, religious work, and politics. In 1908, she contributed to the **Berea College** Industrial School fund. She accompanied her husband to New York City and Washington, DC, when he was Kentucky's commissioner to the Emancipation Exposition in 1913. She was one of the organizers of a hospital movement for African Americans in Winchester. Her husband had served as Clark Co.'s delegate to the Republican State Convention in the late 1880s, and Annie found her own political niche.

On March 3, 1920, the Republicans of the Seventh Congressional District, the district formerly represented in Congress by Henry Clay, met in La Grange, Oldham Co., KY. A group of African American women attended the convention. Annie Simms Banks, "the lady from Clark," became "the first negro woman delegate ever elected to a political convention in Kentucky" at a time when Kentucky women could vote in the presidential election but still did not have full suffrage. Appointed to the Rules Committee, she helped prepare reports. She announced to the audience, "We are just beginning to open our eyes in politics, but before long we are going to make ourselves felt, and you can depend on Annie Simms Banks, of Winchester, to do her part for the grand old party."

Three years later, Annie Simms Banks died of pneumonia. Her obituary, most likely written by her husband, proclaimed her a "prominent race leader." She was buried in the Winchester Cemetery. Two years later, her husband was buried beside her.

Kentucky Death Records, 1852–1953.
Mather, Frank Lincoln, ed. *Who's Who of the Colored Race: A General Biographical Dictionary of Men and Women of African Descent.* Vol. 1. Chicago: Memento Edition, 1915.
Newspapers: "Hon. W. W. Banks," *IF,* November 14, 1891, 4; "Contributions for the Colored School," *WN,* December 18, 1908, 3; "Colored Column," *WN,* March 4, 1920, 6; "Negro Woman Sits as Delegate in Ky. Republican Convention," *New York Tribune,* March 4, 1920, 3; "Kentucky Women in Political Arena," *Cleveland Advocate,* March 20, 1920, 1; "Prominent Race Leader Dies," *Winchester Sun,* February 2, 1923, 6.
U.S. Federal Census (1870, 1880, 1900, 1910, 1920).

—*Sallie L. Powell*

BANKS, WILLIAM WEBB (b. 1862, Winchester, KY; d. 1928, Winchester, KY), newspaper correspondent. William Webb Banks was born to Patrick and Catherine Banks in Winchester, KY, on July 4, 1862. After graduating from State Colored Baptist University (later known as **Simmons College of Kentucky**) in Louisville in 1886, he returned to Winchester, where, over the course of the following 20 years, he taught school, worked as a custodian, and dabbled in real estate. His most prominent part-time labor during this time was as a correspondent with various black and white newspapers in Winchester, including the *Winchester Chronicle* and the *Winchester News.* During the early 1900s, he served as editor of the "Colored Column" for the *Winchester News,* a position from which he could write favorable columns regarding the city's black community.

Married to **Annie Simms Banks,** he was also active in the city's community life, including serving as steward of the local Elks Club. In the 1890s, he was part of the **Anti–Separate Coach Movement,** joining protestors before the General Assembly in Frankfort. He served as a local representative to the important Emancipation Exposition of 1913 in New York. He was also active in Winchester's religious life, serving as president of the Baptist Sunday School Convention, recording secretary of the Consolidated Baptist Association, and a messenger to the General Association of Kentucky Baptists.

"Colored Column," *WN,* January 2, 1909, 4.
Mather, Frank Lincoln, ed. *Who's Who of the Colored Race: A General Biographical Dictionary of Men and Women of African Descent.* Vol. 1. Chicago: Memento Edition, 1915.

—*Joshua D. Farrington*

BAPTIST WOMEN'S EDUCATIONAL CONVENTION OF KENTUCKY, organization of Baptist women. Baptist Women's Educational Convention of Kentucky held its first session on Tuesday, September 19, 1883, at the **Fifth Street Baptist Church** in Louisville, KY. Its initial purpose was to establish a committee within the network of Kentucky African American Baptist churches to raise funds for State University in Louisville, KY. The university was later renamed Simmons College due to its success under the guidance of its second president and the architect of the Baptist Women's Educational Convention, Reverend **William J. Simmons.**

At the first meeting called to order by Rev. Simmons, Amanda V. Nelson of Lexington was elected president and Amanda Redd of Georgetown was elected first vice president. Laura Scudder of Richmond was elected second vice president and Mrs. M. B. Wallace of Georgetown was elected secretary. Mrs. C. V. Paris of Lexington was elected assistant secretary and Mrs. Bell Smoot of Paris was elected treasurer.

This convention was the first statewide organization of African American Baptist women in the United States and was the leading example for other women's religious organizations across the nation. Between 1883 and 1900, the women's convention contributed over $12,000 to the school. Because of the Baptist Women's Educational Convention of Kentucky, State Colored Baptist University (later known as **Simmons College of Kentucky**) was able to build a women's dormitory and help retire the school's accumulated debt. Members within the organization worked hard for the convention and their own churches to make education a priority in the African American community and church.

The Baptist Women's Educational Convention of Kentucky remains active as an auxiliary of the General Association of Baptists in Kentucky. The Convention at-large formally meets annually, but remains quite active in the African American Baptist Church across the state and in the realm of education.

Higginbotham, Evelyn Brooks. *Righteous Discontent: The Women's Movement in the Black Baptist Church, 1880–1920.* Cambridge, MA: Harvard Univ. Press, 1994.
Minutes of the Baptist Women's Educational Convention of Kentucky, 1883–1885. American Baptist Historical Society. Atlanta, GA.
—*Erin Wiggins Gilliam*

BARBOUR, J. BERNI (b. 1881, Danville, KY; d. unknown), composer and entertainer. On April 22, 1881, J. Berni Barbour was born in Danville, KY, to Morris and Nicey Barbour. After he graduated from State Colored Baptist University (later known as **Simmons College of Kentucky**) in 1896, he moved to Chicago to attend the Schmoll School of Music, where he studied under Theodore Thomas and other musical luminaries. After his graduation in 1899, he traveled throughout the country as the director of various small musical groups.

In 1903, Barbour joined with N. Clark Smith to form a music-publishing company in Chicago. According to the *Indianapolis Freeman,* it was the first black-owned African American music-publishing house, and its first publication was "Baby, I'm Learning to Love You." By 1909, he had a studio in Seattle, WA. Renowned white composer Henry Hadley, the first conductor of the San Francisco Symphony, was so impressed with Barbour's interpretations of Beethoven, Chopin, and others that he named him "the Black Gabrilovich" after famed Russian composer Ossip Gabrilovich. Pleased with the nom de plume, Barbour used it in a self-promotion article in one newspaper.

In 1919, Barbour became manager of W. C. Handy's Memphis Blues Orchestra and worked as a writer for the Pace and Handy Music Company. Throughout the 1920s, he composed numerous original operas, including *Arrival of the Negro, Redemption,* and

Board of Baptist Women's Educational Convention of Kentucky.

Ethiopia, that were staged in New York City. He also had numerous collaborations with Billy King and Joseph Burroughs, many of which were performed on Broadway, including *Cabarabian Knights Revue* and *Over the Top.* In 1927, he became a writer for Edward B. Marks Music Company and oversaw the creation of an all-black-cast version of *Showboat* that was performed on Broadway.

Barbour continued to be in demand in the early 1930s. Over 150 people were in the chorus and cast of his production of *Arrival of the Negro* in Nashville, TN. The cast consisted of drama students from Pearl High School. At this time, research has yet to uncover where and when Barbour died.

Boris, Joseph J., ed. *Who's Who in Colored America, 1928–1929.* New York: Who's Who in Colored America Corp., 1929.
Newspapers: "Barbour and Smith, Music Publishers," *IF,* January 2, 1904, 6; "Brief Sketch of a Noted Pianist," *IF,* December 20, 1913, 5; "Hits and Bits," *Chicago Defender,* May 9, 1931, 5; "J. Berni Barbour," *Chicago Defender,* May 30, 1931, 5.
Southern, Eileen. *Biographical Dictionary of Afro-American and African Musicians.* Westport, CT: Greenwood Press, 1982.
—*Joshua D. Farrington*

BARFIELD, RUFUS LENRO (b. 1929, Hickman, KY), educator and college president. Rufus Lenro Barfield was born in Hickman, KY, to Carlos and Kattie Barfield in 1929. He was named after Hickman native **Rufus B. Atwood,** who had just been named president of Kentucky State Industrial College for Colored Persons (later known as **Kentucky State University**) earlier in 1929.

Barfield patterned much of his life after Atwood's. In 1952, he graduated from Kentucky State with a degree in education and sociology. Four years later, he completed his MA in education at the University of Kentucky. Over the course of the next 20 years, he did postgraduate work at the University of Cincinnati, Ohio State University, the University of Wisconsin at Madison, and Harvard University and received his PhD in educational administration from Miami University in Oxford, OH, in 1972.

In 1969, he became principal of the Columbian School of Cincinnati while working on his doctorate degree. After completing his education, he served as administrative assistant to the president and then as professor of education and dean of academic services at Kentucky State University. In 1975, he was appointed by Governor Julian Carroll to serve on the Commission of Higher Education. In 1978, he was named president of Bowie State College (now Bowie State University) in Maryland and served in that position until his resignation in 1983. He resided in Prince George's County's Enterprise Estates neighborhood.

"Bowie State President, Rufus Barfield, Resigns." *Jet,* February 14, 1983, 24.
Dunnigan, Alice Allison, comp. and ed. *The Fascinating Story of Black Kentuckians: Their Heritage and Traditions.* Washington, DC: Associated Publishers, 1982.
"Great Society Programs and How They Helped Shape Prince George's County," http://www.gettyimages.com/detail/news-photo/dr-rufus-l-barfield-a-former-president-of-bowie-state-news-photo/492188483 (accessed July 23, 2014).
—*Joshua D. Farrington*

BARNES, MARGARET ELIZABETH SALLEE (b. 1879, Monticello, KY; d. 1947, Oberlin, OH), editor, clubwoman, and civic activist. The daughter of former slaves James and Rebecca Sallee, Margaret Elisabeth Sallee graduated in 1900 from Kentucky State Normal School for Colored Persons (later known as **Kentucky State University**) in Frankfort and then taught in Kentucky for eight years. On August 24, 1904, she married James D. Barnes. They moved to Oberlin, OH, and had five children, including **Margaret Ellen Barnes Jones,** who later served with the only African American military women's unit sent overseas during World War II.

Active in community and civil rights organizations, Barnes, as a laundry operator, developed the Ohio Federation of Colored Women's Clubs in the early 1930s. The Margaret Barnes Welfare Club, the oldest African American women's club in Elyria, was named in her honor. This club worked to provide college scholarships for outstanding Elyria High School African American graduates. Beginning in 1933, Barnes served as president of the Federation of Colored Women, Ohio State, and edited the *Girl's Guide,* plus the *Queen's Gardens,* the official publication of the Ohio Federation of Colored Women's Clubs. She was a member of the Eastern Star and the Women's Christian Temperance Union. She also worked as a field representative of the Administrative Committee of the National Association of Colored Women. In 1939, Ohio governor John Bricker appointed her a trustee at Wilberforce University, where she led a million-dollar fund drive. A campus building was named in her honor, and the school awarded her an honorary doctor of humanities degree. In 1940, she served as a delegate-at-large to the Republican State Convention. She died seven years later.

Newspapers: "Club Head," *PD,* April 30, 1937, 4; "Re-instate Four Dismissed Teachers at Wilberforce," *PD,* September 29, 1939, 1; "Politics Said to Be Cause of Trouble at Wilberforce," *PD,* June 7, 1940, 2.
U.S. Federal Census (1900, 1920, 1930).
Yenser, Thomas, ed. *Who's Who in Colored America, 1938–1940.* Brooklyn, NY: Thomas Yenser, 1940.
—*Sallie L. Powell*

BARNES, SHELBY "PIKE" (b. 1871, Beaver Dam, KY; d. 1908, Columbus, OH), jockey. One of the winningest jockeys who never won the **Kentucky Derby,** Shelby "Pike" Barnes began his racing career at age 14 working with Robert Tucker. Another writer credited African American trainer Eli Jordon with molding Barnes, along with jockeys **Thomas Britton** and **Isaac Murphy** of Lexington, KY. In 1887, Barnes won six races in Lexington. He was named national champion jockey for two consecutive years because he had 367 victories, the most wins of any jockey. In 1888, he was the first jockey to win over 200 races a year. In his prime, it was said that Barnes rode the "choicest mounts."

Barnes was described as looking like an eight-year-old, and his size may have cost him a Kentucky Derby victory in 1889, when he was unable to control his horse, Proctor Knott, in the home stretch. He finished in second place, but ahead of famed jockey Isaac Murphy. Even though the horse had almost thrown Barnes twice before the race began, had made several false starts, and had supposedly been frightened by a spectator who caused it to bolt, Barnes praised the horse as the greatest horse he had ever ridden and took the blame for the loss by maintaining that he "was too light to hold him."

Some said that Barnes "lost his nerve" after his horse in a Chicago race ran over a fallen jockey and killed the young rider. Even though Barnes competed in more races and won the Brooklyn Handicap, he retired in 1891 and joined another jockey, "Tiny" Williams, in purchasing a saloon in Chicago.

Known as second only to the famed Isaac Murphy and the "king bee of jockeys," Barnes died of pneumonia at age 37 in Columbus, OH, on January 8, 1908. He was survived by his wife, Mary, and his brother, Frank, living in Columbus, and a sister, Josephine Barnes, of Beaver Dam, KY.

Hotaling, Edward. *The Great Black Jockeys: The Lives and Times of the Men Who Dominated America's First National Sport.* Rocklin, CA: Forum, 1999.
———. *Wink: The Incredible Life and Epic Journey of Jimmy Winkfield.* New York: McGraw-Hill, 2005.
Newspapers: "Racing News and Notions," *NYT,* November 9, 1891, 2; "In the World of Sports," *IF,* November 11, 1905, 6; "Noted Jockey Dead," *IF,* February 1, 1908, 6; "Ranks of Negro Jockeys Thinned by Grim Reaper," *Pittsburgh Press,* October 16, 1911, 15.
Wills, Ridley, II. *The History of Belle Meade: Mansion, Plantation, and Stud.* Nashville: Vanderbilt Univ. Press, 1991.

—*Sallie L. Powell*

BARNES TEMPLE A.M.E. CHURCH, African Methodist Episcopal church in Elsmere, KY. The Barnes Temple African Methodist Episcopal (A.M.E.) Church of Elsmere was established in the late nineteenth century by Rev. Daniel W. Ellison, an evangelical minister who had stopped in nearby Florence to deliver one of many sermons in the area. During his visit, Ellison envisioned the establishment of a small Methodist church. As a result, during the Christmas holiday season of 1896, he and several followers, while traveling house to house sponsoring prayer meetings, decided to hold services regularly at the local railroad station depot on Woodside Ave. Because the city of **Elsmere** was incorporated that same year, the new church became the African Methodist Episcopal (A.M.E.) Church of Elsmere.

Ellison served as pastor for only two years, until 1898; however, even though it had no permanent spiritual leader for several years, the church continued to grow and prosper. During this period, the church moved to a building in Elsmere on Spring St. and later to a facility in town along Shaw St. From there, the church was relocated to the Brittle House on Fox St. and then to a small building at the end of Palace Ave. While the congregation met at this location, it made plans to construct a permanent building along Fox St. on land donated by members of the Carneal family, who were well known throughout the community.

Over the next half century, several worship facilities were built at the Fox St. site. In 1905 or 1906, under the leadership of Rev. C. E. Carson, a small wood-frame building was constructed; in 1934, a "suspicious" fire destroyed it. The next year, under the direction of Rev. H. L. Barnes, a stone church building was begun. One year later, the cornerstone of the facility was laid, and the church was renamed the Barnes Temple African Methodist Episcopal (A.M.E.) Church of Elsmere. From 1940 to 1948, the Barnes Temple A.M.E. allowed the Erlanger-Elsmere Board of Educa-

tion to use part of the building to educate first- through third-grade African American students from the local community.

After several years, some church leaders decided that a new facility was needed. During the 1950s and 1960s, under the pastorates of Rev. Robert E. Mitchell and Rev. **Edgar L. Mack,** another church building was constructed at the Fox St. location. Modifications and additions to this facility, such as a remodeled sanctuary and a larger parking lot, were built during the late 1990s and the early years of the twenty-first century. The Barnes Temple A.M.E. Church continues to serve the citizens of Elsmere, both black and white, with a strong emphasis on spirituality, inclusiveness, and social justice.

Barnes Temple African Methodist Episcopal Church. http://www.barnestemple.com/ (accessed November 26, 2007).
"Barnes Temple A.M.E. Church Pamphlet." Northern Kentucky African American Heritage Task Force Collection, W. Frank Steely Library, Northern Kentucky Univ.
Bradford, Bill "Billy," mayor. Interview by Eric R. Jackson, Elsmere, KY, June 15, 2006.
Elsmere Centennial Committee. *City of Elsmere—Centennial Celebration Booklet, 1896–1996.* Elsmere, KY: City of Elsmere, 1996.
Newspapers: "Black Churches Offered Stability in Troubled Times," *KP,* January 20, 1997, 4K; "Park to Be Rededicated," *KP,* July 23, 2002, 2K; "Barnes Temple A.M.E.," *KP,* August 19, 2004, 4K.

—*Eric R. Jackson*

BARROWS CEMETERY, Lincoln Co. cemetery containing the remains of Civil War African American veterans. Barrows Cemetery was established in 1893. It is located on Ridgeway Drive, Old Highway 27, Stanford, KY. Six Civil War African American soldiers are buried in the cemetery: 1st Sergeant Richard Faulkner and Private Allen Smith, both of Company K, 12th Colored Heavy Artillery; Private Isaac Hayes, Company D, 114th Colored Infantry; Corporal Spencer Higgins, Company B, 5th Colored Cavalry; and Privates Rhodes Lackey and Waller Lackey, both of Company C, 6th Colored Cavalry.

Restoration of the cemetery began in 2000. In 2006, Barrows Cemetery received a grant of almost $2,000 from Kentucky's Cemetery Preservation Fund. The money was used for landscaping and fencing. Thirty-five loads of dirt had to be hauled into the cemetery to fill holes because headstones had sunk into the ground. A brick fence was erected, and new headstones were placed on the Civil War veterans' graves.

Edwards, Brenda S. "Ceremonies Honor Black Soldiers for Their Role in Civil War." *Danville Advocate Messenger,* October 9, 2006.
Kentucky Kin Folk. "Barrows Cemetery, Lincoln County." http://kykinfolk.com/lincoln/cemeteries/barrows.htm (accessed March 12, 2009).

—*Sallie L. Powell*

BATE, JOHN W. (b. 1854; d. 1945, Danville, KY), principal often referred to as "Kentucky's Booker T. Washington." John William Bate, distinguished Kentucky educator, was born a slave at Woodside, a plantation a few miles from Louisville. Bate was the son of his owner, John Throckmorton Bate, and a slave woman named Nancy Dickerson. Through his father, Bate was directly descended from many of the most distinguished families of colo-

John W. Bate.

nial Virginia. Five Bate families, all quite wealthy, owning nearly 100 slaves, lived next to one another on the River Road in Jefferson Co. in 1860. John William Bate was born into this enclave of relatives, both white and African American. His father freed his mother and her four children in 1863. The family moved to Louisville, where Nancy became ill, leaving the children, especially John, the eldest, to fend for themselves in an unwelcoming city.

In later years, Bate remembered being an unwashed child scrounging for garbage in back alleys; all his siblings died, and he faced direst poverty in this period of his life. He was befriended by an **American Missionary Association** teacher named Kate Gilbert, whom he admired so much that he followed her to **Berea College** when that institution hired her. At Berea he received a BA in 1881 and an MA in 1891. In 1882, he began his teaching career in the one-room dilapidated school that had been built for black students by the **Freedmen's Bureau** in Danville, KY. Bate was the sole instructor of only six pupils. As principal and teacher at the school for 59 years, Bate transformed it into an accredited high school emphasizing industrial and domestic sciences, with 15 teachers, 600 students, 20 rooms, and an auditorium seating 700 people. The building was eventually renamed in his honor and became Bate Middle School after the integration of schools.

Bate died in his home in Danville on September 13, 1945, aged 91. His funeral service was held in Bate Auditorium, and he was buried in Greenwood Cemetery (now Cove Haven) in Lexington. Frequently described as Kentucky's Booker T. Washington, Bate was very highly esteemed by the citizens of Danville and was honored by his alma mater, Berea College, as its oldest graduate and as a sterling representative of Berea's principles. He was twice married: his first wife, the mother of all his children, was Ida White, whom he married in Danville on October 24, 1885. They had three sons, Clarence, John W. Jr., and **Langston Fairchild Bate,** and two daughters, Helen and Vivian. He was survived by his second wife, Letty Rome.

John William Bate File, Berea College Archives.
Sears, Richard D. *A Utopian Experiment in Kentucky: Integration and Social Equality at Berea, 1866–1904.* Westport, CT: Greenwood Press, 1996.

—*Richard D. Sears*

BATE, LANGSTON FAIRCHILD (b. 1899, Danville, KY; d. 1977, Austin, TX), educator and chemist. Langston Fairchild Bate was born to Ida W. and **John W. Bate** in Danville, KY, in 1899. After his early education where his father served as principal, Langston Bate graduated from Kentucky Normal and Industrial Institute for Colored Persons (later known as **Kentucky State University**) in Frankfort in 1917. After receiving a second undergraduate degree from Illinois Normal College (now Illinois State University), he enrolled in graduate school at the University of Chicago, where he received an MA and a PhD in organic chemistry at the age of 26.

Bate taught at Kentucky Normal for two years before being appointed chair of the chemistry department at Lincoln University in Missouri. He was the first black PhD to teach at the college. Three years later, Bate was named chairman of the chemistry department at Virginia State College. In 1935, he joined the chemistry faculty of Miner Teachers College in Washington, DC (later named the University of the District of Columbia). After nine years, he was appointed chair of the department and served in that position from 1944 to 1954. Bate authored numerous articles published in the *Journal of the American Chemical Society* and *Science Education.* After his retirement, Bate and his wife Violet moved to Texas, where he died of a heart attack in 1977.

Dunnigan, Alice Allison, comp. and ed. *The Fascinating Story of Black Kentuckians: Their Heritage and Traditions.* Washington, DC: Associated Publishers, 1982.
Holland, Antonio Frederick. *Nathan B. Young and the Struggle over Black Higher Education.* Columbia: Univ. of Missouri Press, 2006.
"Langston Bate, Division Head at Miners College." *WP,* July 17, 1977, Obituaries, 49.

—*Joshua D. Farrington*

BATHER, PAUL C. (b. 1947, New York, NY; d. 2009, Houston, TX), community activist and politician. Paul C. Bather graduated from Fairfield University in Connecticut with a liberal arts degree in 1968, earned a master's degree in social work in 1970 from the City University of New York, and obtained his MBA from the University of Louisville in 1980. He began his community activism in the early 1970s as the director of the New York Manhasset–Great Neck Economic Opportunity Council, which served low-income black and Hispanic communities. Unlike former administrators, he viewed the council's obligation as assisting the poor in helping themselves, and his methods for accomplishing that goal included assisting African American groups with organizational skills, working with the Head Start program, and establishing "black capitalism" through economic development programs.

Bather's managerial skills led him into politics. He served for five years as the treasurer of Jefferson Co., KY. Through his policies, the county earned over $10 million in investment income. In 1986, the American Center for International Leadership acknowledged him as the National Alumnus of the Year. He was also a U.S. representative in an American-Soviet leadership exchange program. From 1986 to 2000, as a Democrat, Bather served as a member of the Louisville, KY, Board of Aldermen. In 2000, he was elected to the 43rd District seat of the Kentucky House of Representatives. He was reelected in 2002; he retired after two terms in office.

Bather was married to Coretta Waddell, a cousin of **Muhammad Ali,** and was the father of twin sons, Omar and Amir. On February 10, 2009, Bather died in Houston, TX, after a battle with pancreatic cancer.

Hawkins, Walter L. *African American Biographies: Profiles of 558 Current Men and Women.* Jefferson, NC: McFarland, 1994.

Newspapers: "An Operation Bootstrap Seeks to Aid the Frightened L.I. Poor," *NYT,* November 14, 1971, A8; "Rich and Poor Join to Help Each Other," *NYT,* May 25, 1975, 93; "Bather Won't Seek Reelection," *LCJ,* August 28, 2003, 1A; "Paul Bather Dies in Houston," *LCJ,* February 12, 2009, 1B.

—*Sallie L. Powell*

BEARD, ALFRED "BUTCH," JR. (b. 1947, Hardinsburg, KY), basketball player for the University of Louisville. Alfred "Butch" Beard Jr., basketball player and coach, son of Alfred and Mable (Moorman) Beard, was born on May 4, 1947, in Hardinsburg, KY. He played basketball at Breckinridge County High School and entered the University of Louisville in 1966. Joining the varsity team in 1967, Beard, along with **Wes Unseld,** led the team in several outstanding seasons, including two National Collegiate Athletic Association tournament appearances. In 1969, Beard was named an All-American. During his playing years at Louisville (1967–1969), the high-scoring guard netted 1,580 points, which in 1990 placed him 10th on the university's career scoring list. His average of 19 points per game was the second best in Louisville basketball history. He was selected by the American Basketball Association (ABA) Dallas Chaparrals in 1969 and in the first round of the 1969 National Basketball Association (NBA) draft by the Atlanta Hawks. Beard played for five NBA teams—the Hawks (1969–70), the Cleveland Cavaliers (1971–1972 and 1975–1976), the Seattle SuperSonics (1972–1973), the Golden State Warriors (1973–1974), and the New York Knicks (1975–1979)—and was an NBA All-Star in 1972. After his playing career, Beard became an assistant coach with the Knicks from 1979 to 1982 and then moved into the broadcast booth, serving as a commentator for both the Knicks and the Hawks. In 1988, he returned to coaching as an assistant with the New Jersey Nets. He was head basketball coach at Howard University in Washington, DC, from 1990 to 1994 and an assistant coach with the Washing-

ton Wizards from 1999 to 2000. In 2001 he was named head coach at Morgan State University and held this positon until 2006. In 2013 Beard was inducted into the Kentucky High School Basketball Hall of Fame.

"Basketball: Coach Don Morris Recalls Butch Beard's Talents." http://www.thenewsenterprise.com/content/basketball-coach-don-morris-recalls-butch-beard%E2%80%99s-talents (accessed July 24, 2014).

"Butch Beard." http://www.spiffbox.com/S/com.spiff.member.S_M_View?id=29264 (accessed July 24, 2014).

"Morgan State Names Butch Beard as Men's Basketball Coach." http://onnidan.com/2000-01/news/june/msu0612.htm (accessed July 24, 2014).

BEASON, WILLIAM "BILL" (b. 1908, Louisville, KY; d. 1988, New York, NY), jazz musician. William "Bill" Beason was born in Louisville, KY, and first played drums in **Bessie Allen**'s local Booker T. Washington Center marching band. At the age of 16, he attended Wilberforce University in Ohio and was the drummer for Horace Henderson's Collegians from 1924 to 1928. Over the course of the next 10 years, Beason recorded with Ferdinand Joseph LaMothe (Jelly Roll Morton), Teddy Hill, John Birks "Dizzy" Gillespie, and Don Redman. In 1937, he toured Europe and recorded with **William "Dicky" Wells,** who was born in Centerville, TN, and played in Bessie Allen's band. From 1939 to 1941, Beason replaced the terminally ill William Henry "Chick" Webb and played drums alongside Ella Fitzgerald in Chick Webb's Orchestra.

During the 1940s, Beason recorded with John Kirby and reunited with Horace Henderson, but by the early 1950s, he lost interest in his music career and settled in the Bronx, NY. In his musical career of the 1930s and 1940s, Beason recorded over 60 different songs. Some of his most popular and influential pieces include "Lady Be Good / Dicky Wells Blues" (1937) with Dicky Wells and "King Porter Stomp" (1937) with Teddy Hill.

Kernfeld, Barry, ed. *The New Grove Dictionary of Jazz.* 2nd ed. New York: Grove's Dictionaries, 2002.

Larkin, Colin, ed. *The Encyclopedia of Popular Music.* 3rd ed. New York: Muze, 1998.

Nicholson, Stuart. *Ella Fitzgerald: A Biography.* New York: Da Capo Press, 1995.

—*Joshua D. Farrington*

BEATTY, ANTHANY (b. 1951, Lexington, KY), first African American police chief in Lexington. Anthany Beatty grew up in public housing at Lexington's Bluegrass-Aspendale complex and graduated from Henry Clay High School in 1969. In 1973, he joined the city's police department and became the public face of the department by 1978. Working with the Community Services Bureau for over a dozen years, Beatty participated in a cable television program called *Lexington Crime Check,* in addition to meeting frequently with students, senior citizens, and neighborhood groups.

While working in the police force and raising a family of two boys with his wife, Eunice, Beatty furthered his education, earning a BA in police administration from Eastern Kentucky University in 1978 and an MA in public administration from

Kentucky State University in 1980. Over the course of the next 20 years, Beatty advanced through the ranks of Lexington's police department, being promoted to sergeant, lieutenant, captain, major, and assistant chief of patrol. In August 2001, Beatty became the first African American police chief in Lexington.

As chief of police, Beatty oversaw a policy banning racial profiling and upgraded the force's equipment. The *Lexington Herald-Leader* credited him with bringing more professionalism to the force and improving relations between the community and law enforcement. His experience with the Community Services Bureau was particularly helpful in his efforts to improve community relations. In 2001, for example, he personally met with community leaders in the Dunbar neighborhood, who had concerns about the prevalence of drugs and violent assaults. By 2005, in large part because of Beatty's efforts as police chief, the neighborhood's crime rate had fallen considerably.

In 2007, after 34 years of law-enforcement service in Lexington, Beatty retired and was appointed assistant vice president for public safety at the University of Kentucky, bringing much-needed diversity to the university's upper-level administration. Beatty oversaw the school's Police Department and the Departments of Parking and Transportation, Environmental Health, and Safety and Emergency Management. He has served as a deacon and treasurer at New Vine Baptist Church, a member of the YMCA Board of Directors, and a member of the Executive Board of the Boy Scouts of America Bluegrass Council.

Newspapers: "The Chief—Lexington's New Top Police Officer Knows the Power of Public Perception and the Value of a First Impression," *LHL,* August 19, 2001, A1; "Beatty Says Profiling Banned," *LHL,* February 2, 2002, B3; "Farewell to the Chief—Beatty a Good Addition to UK Administration," *LHL,* August 14, 2007, A8.

—*Joshua D. Farrington*

BECKETT, WILLIAM (b. 1910, Baltimore, MD; d. 1963, Louisville, KY), Louisville alderman, civil rights advocate, and businessman. William W. Beckett was born in Baltimore, MD, and grew up in St. Louis, MO. He returned to Baltimore to receive his BS degree from Morgan State College and studied embalming in Washington, DC, and St. Louis. After his education, he became the owner of Ridley Funeral Home in Louisville, KY, which he later renamed W. W. Beckett Funeral Home.

In 1951, Beckett was elected a Democratic alderman in Louisville. During his 10-year service in that position, Beckett played a key role in prompting Mayor Andrew Broaddus's integration reforms. These included the integration of the fire and police departments, golf courses, swimming pools, and public parks. In his most important act as alderman, Beckett helped launch the public-accommodations protests of 1960 and 1961 in Louisville by submitting a public-accommodations ordinance to the Board of Aldermen on February 10, 1960. As the only African American on the board, Beckett was the only vote for the bill. He reintroduced the bill in March with the backing of Attorney General John Breckinridge, but it was defeated once again. The defeat of Beckett's ordinance was instrumental in launching the sit-ins, stand-ins, and pickets of segregated restaurants, theaters, and hotels that filled the city in 1960 and 1961.

Despite his influential role in presenting the public-accommodations ordinance, Beckett was criticized by many African Americans for his continued support of Louisville's Democratic establishment and was defeated by a black Republican, Russell Lee, in the 1961 municipal Republican landslide. Beckett died two years later at the age of 53. In 2003, he was honored alongside six other Louisville civil rights leaders with a street sign bearing his name in the city's **Park DuValle** neighborhood.

Dunnigan, Alice Allison, comp. and ed. *The Fascinating Story of Black Kentuckians: Their Heritage and Traditions.* Washington, DC: Associated Publishers, 1982.
Farrington, Joshua. "Standing in the Wings: Black Voters in Louisville, Kentucky, and the Elections of 1960 and 1961." MA thesis, Univ. of Kentucky, 2008.
Newspapers: "Beckett Introduces 'Accommodations' Law," *LD,* February 11, 1960, 1; "Aldermen Turn Down Demands for Accommodations Ordinance: Milburn Says Beckett Proposed Bill Political," *LD,* June 15, 1961, 1; "Park DuValle's Street Names Honor Seven 'Vibrant' Black Leaders," *LCJ,* May 14, 2003, 1N.

—*Joshua D. Farrington*

BELL, J. W. (b. unknown; d. unknown), minister, book agent, and editor. Rev. J. W. Bell pastored the Center Street Colored Methodist Episcopal (C.M.E.) Church in Louisville, KY, in the early 1870s. On March 19, 1873, Bell was elected secretary at the second General Conference of the C.M.E. Church held in Trinity Church in Augusta, GA. Bishop **William Henry Miles,** "the only bishop of the Church" and from Winchester, KY, conducted the services. He also appointed Bell as an agent along with Alexander Austin from Winchester and W. P. Churchill and R. E. Marshall from Hopkinsville to raise funds for establishing a school in Louisville for men to be educated in the ministry. Miles praised Bell and the other pastors in a letter to southern African Americans and whites as trustworthy and stated that all could be assured that the money collected would "be most faithfully applied to this great charity."

Bishop Miles was also the chairman of the Book Committee, which was responsible for the offices of book agent and editor of the *Christian Index,* the C.M.E.'s monthly news publication. In March 1873, E. B. Martin was elected to the position of book agent and editor but resigned in September, claiming that the work was overwhelming. Bishop Miles, along with two other bishops, selected J. W. Bell in November to replace Martin. At that time, it was decided that the paper and the publishing house, called the Book Concern, would be moved to Louisville. Bell declared the following month that the obligations "were too onerous" and insisted that the business manager and the Publishing Committee separate the Book Concern from the editorship. W. P. Churchill was immediately appointed book agent. Subsequently, discord occurred between Bishop Miles and Bell that resulted in Bell's dismissal not only from his editorship but also from his pastorate at Center Street Church by January 1874.

On January 26, 1900, the *Hopkinsville Kentuckian* reported that Rev. J. W. Bell, the pastor of the local Colored Methodist church, had held a revival for three weeks, with one more week before it would end. There had been 35 conversions during the revival.

"Bell, J. W." Notable Kentucky African Americans Database, Univ. of Kentucky. http://nkaa.uky.edu/all.php?sort_by= (accessed July 24, 2014).
"Big Revival." *HK,* January 26, 1900, 4.
Phillips, C. H. *The History of the Colored Methodist Episcopal Church in America.* Jackson, TN: Publishing House C.M.E. Church, 1925.
—*Sallie L. Powell*

BELL, JAMES WILLIAM (PROF.) (b. ca. 1874, Tennessee; d. 1937, Memphis, TN), educator. In December 1903, Hopkinsville superintendent / principal James William "J. W." Bell joined eight other men, including **Edward W. Glass,** in petitioning Christian Co. Circuit Court judge Thomas P. Cook to adjudicate "a fair and speedy trial" for some African American men accused of murdering a white man near Pembroke, KY. Along with community activism, Bell was an ardent educator. In 1905, he presented an address to the eighth annual session of the Second Congressional District Association of Negro Teachers at the First Baptist Church in Henderson, KY. The following year he gave a lecture, "Preparation and Service," to the Colored Teachers' Institute.

After 10 years of teaching experience, Bell, a graduate of Roger Williams University, arrived in Hopkinsville after his marriage to Annie in 1902. He was surprised to learn of his dismissal from the Hopkinsville school system in 1907. Bell was responsible for 57 graduates in five years; all his predecessors had graduated only 14. Even though he had received assurance that he would be reelected to the $75-a-month principal's job, the trustees of the Hopkinsville colored schools assigned the position to the board chairman's wife. Bell complained "bitterly" about his perceived mistreatment by the trustees and asserted that he was "severely handicapped" by the late notice of his dismissal. He applied to the Evansville, IN, schools.

In 1910, Earlington, about 25 miles north of Hopkinsville, hired Bell to head its schools. The local newspaper praised Bell as "one of the best colored educators in the South." This appointment allowed Bell the opportunity to travel across the state, and he became known as a great orator. In June 1911, he lectured at **Eckstein Norton Institute** in Cane Springs, KY, and a month later in Owensboro for the Baptist Women's Missionary Convention. The next year, he attended the **General Association of Kentucky Baptists** in Frankfort.

In 1915, Bell, as a member of the **Kentucky Negro Educational Association** (KNEA), pushed for the preparation of African American youths for higher education. He maintained that a broad liberal arts education would be of greater value to African Americans than a rigidly defined vocational education; otherwise, blacks would be able to work only as manual laborers and semiskilled craftsmen. Bell, the chairman of the KNEA's Committee on Legislation in 1916, wrote in the organization's resolutions, "Any kind of education that is good for the white man is good for the Negro." In 1925, Bell represented Louisville at the KNEA and joined others, including James Bond, in fighting not only for education for African Americans but also for justice and better health conditions.

By 1935, Bell had returned to his native state and was teaching in Memphis, TN. He died of pneumonia on September 25, 1937, and was buried in Mount Carmel Cemetery in Memphis.

Hardin, John A. *Fifty Years of Segregation: Black Higher Education in Kentucky, 1904–1954.* Lexington: Univ. Press of Kentucky, 1997.
Newspapers: "Colored Citizens Act," *HK,* December 15, 1903, 5; "Handed a Lemon," *HK,* July 23, 1907, 3; "Prof. Bell Is Engaged," *Earlington (KY) Bee,* May 5, 1910, 1; "Memphis, Tenn.," *PD,* December 15, 1933, 3.
Proceedings of the Kentucky Negro Educational Association, April 25–28, 1916, and April 22–25, 1925.
Tennessee Death Records, 1908–1958.
U.S. Federal Census (1910, 1920).
—*Sallie L. Powell*

BELL, JESSE BURNETT (b. 1904, Tallulah, LA; d. 1998, Louisville, KY), physician. Jesse Burnett Bell was born on April 20, 1904, and graduated from Morehouse College in Atlanta and then from Meharry Medical College in Nashville in 1931. The following year, he moved to Frankfort, KY, and began practicing medicine.

In 1935, Bell moved to Louisville and worked at the Waverly Hills Sanatorium and then the city's health department. In 1946, he began his own practice. He became a member of the Mount Lebanon Baptist Church, where he eventually served on the board of trustees. He also served as vice chairman of the **Louisville Urban League** and was a member of the Jefferson County Medical Society, the Falls City Medical Association, the American Heart Association, the Bureau of Health Services for Kentucky, and the Kentucky Commission on Higher Education. In October 1965, Bell became the first African American to serve on the University of Louisville Board of Overseers, a board of 51 voting members elected by the board of trustees to advise the university's president.

Bell died in Louisville on November 27, 1998, and is buried in Cave Hill Cemetery.

LCJ, November 29, 1998.

BENJAMIN, ROBERT CHARLES O'HARA (b. 1855, St. Kitts, Caribbean Sea; d. 1900, Lexington, KY), newspaper editor, lawyer, and activist. Known throughout his illustrious career as R. C. O. Benjamin, Robert Charles O'Hara Benjamin was born on the island of St. Kitts in the Caribbean in 1855. As a boy, he served on numerous trade ships that traveled across the world. Although he never graduated, as a young teenager, Benjamin attended Trinity College at Oxford University. In 1869, at the age of 14, he settled in New York City and befriended former abolitionist Henry Highland Garnet, who many believe helped Benjamin receive his first job as a sales representative for the *New York Star.* Within less than a decade, Benjamin had become a reporter and editor for the New York–based magazine *Progressive American.*

In 1876, Benjamin became active in politics and worked for the presidential campaign of Rutherford B. Hayes. After the Republican candidate won the election, Benjamin was rewarded with a post in the New York City postal service; however, he quickly became bored with the work and decided to travel throughout the South. His first stop was in Kentucky, where he taught at a school in Hodgenville. He also began reading law books and befriended a white Larue Co. attorney, Dave Smith, who assisted him with his studies. Although he never attended law school, Benjamin eventually was admitted to the bar of an estimated 12 states throughout his legal career. During the rest of the 1870s and the early 1880s, Benjamin taught, practiced law, and contributed to black newspapers in Alabama, Arkansas, and Virginia. In 1884, he received notoriety in Richmond, VA, after his black client was acquitted of murder.

In the mid-1880s, Benjamin served briefly as a writer and editor of the *Chronicle* in Evanston, IN, and the *Colored Citizen* of Pittsburgh. In 1888, he moved to California, where he became the first African American to be admitted to the state's bar. He also worked as an editor for the *Los Angeles Observer* and the *San Francisco Sentinel* and frequently contributed columns denouncing violence against African Americans in the South. He became the first black man in California to edit a white newspaper when he was named a local editor for the *Los Angeles Daily Sun.* Throughout the 1880s and the early 1890s, Benjamin also became a prolific writer, publishing a biography of Toussaint L'Ouverture and numerous books that exposed and condemned the southern practice of lynching. These included *A Statistical Record of Lawless Doings, Southern Outrages,* and *The Negro Problem and Its Solution.*

In 1897, Benjamin, his wife, Lula, and their two children moved to Lexington, KY, where he was named the editor of the *Lexington Standard.* As editor, he became a vocal critic of local politicians and voter intimidation of blacks. On October 2, 1900, Benjamin chastised a white man, Michael Moynahan, who was harassing a group of black men who sought to register to vote. Moynahan responded by beating Benjamin with a revolver. Although he was arrested for assault, Moynahan was released from jail that evening and waited outside Benjamin's house. When Benjamin returned home, he saw Moynahan, turned to run, and was shot in the back six times. At the trial, Moynahan pleaded not guilty and argued that he acted in self-defense. After just two hours from the beginning of the trial, the judge sympathized with Moynahan's defense and dismissed the case.

R. C. O. Benjamin was buried in Lexington's **African Cemetery No. 2.** The local branch of the Knights of Pythias, which Benjamin served as vice chancellor, later erected a monument in his honor that stands alongside his grave.

Penn, I. Garland. *The Afro-American Press, and Its Editors.* Springfield, MA: Willey & Co., 1891.

Simmons, William. *Men of Mark: Eminent, Progressive and Rising.* Cleveland: George M. Rewell, 1887.

Smith, J. Clay, Jr. *Emancipation: The Making of the Black Lawyer, 1844–1944.* Philadelphia: Univ. of Pennsylvania Press, 1993.

Wright, George C. *Racial Violence in Kentucky, 1865–1940: Lynchings, Mob Rule, and "Legal Lynchings."* Baton Rouge: Louisiana State Univ. Press, 1990.

—*Joshua D. Farrington*

BENTLEY, DANIEL S. (b. 1850, Madison Co., KY; d. 1916, McKeesport, PA), minister and writer. Daniel Bentley was born in Madison Co., KY. As a teenager, he attended **Berea College,** where he converted to Christianity and was baptized by the school's founder, Rev. John G. Fee. In 1869, he began preaching in Danville, KY, and furthered his ministerial training at Danville's Presbyterian Theological Seminary. After leading various churches in Louisville and Frankfort for 14 years, Bentley was transferred to Indiana in 1884. Three years later, he moved to Pittsburgh, PA, to lead Wylie Avenue A.M.E. Church.

In Pittsburgh, Bentley founded the *Afro-American Spokesman* newspaper, which was owned by Spokesman Stock Company, of which Bentley was also president. In addition to his writing for the *Spokesman,* many of Bentley's publications can be found in the *Christian Recorder,* the oldest existing black periodical in America. He served as vice president at the Parliament of Religions in Chicago in 1893.

Bentley received a doctor of divinity degree from Livingstone College in North Carolina. In 1900, he wrote a small book titled *Brief Religious Reflections* and served as an alternate delegate to the meeting of the Ecumenical Council in London. In 1916, while standing in the pulpit of his pastorate, St. Paul A.M.E. Church in McKeesport, PA, Bentley suddenly died.

"Dr. Bentley Dead." *Cleveland Gazette,* December 9, 1916, 2.

Penn, I. Garland. *The Afro-American Press, and Its Editors.* Springfield, MA: Willey & Co., 1891.

Talbert, Horace. *The Sons of Allen: Together with a Sketch of the Rise and Progress of Wilberforce University, Wilberforce, Ohio.* Xenia, OH: Aldine Press, 1906.

Wright, Richard R. *The Centennial Encyclopedia of the African Methodist Episcopal Church.* Philadelphia: n.p., 1916.

—*Joshua D. Farrington*

BEREA COLLEGE, integrated, coed educational institution. In 1855, John G. Fee, a radical evangelical abolitionist minister from Bracken Co., KY, founded Berea College in Berea, KY. Gathering together a group of like-minded men and women in southern Madison Co., in a slaveholding state, Fee organized a church and school and preached "a *gospel* of impartial love." Repeatedly harassed and threatened by mobs, he and his followers persevered. In July 1859, they drafted a charter for Berea College, but in December they were driven from the state by a proslavery *posse comitatus* from Richmond, the county seat. They returned after the Civil War and opened a new integrated school for black and white students in 1866. That year, 187 students attended: 96 black, 91 white. By 1870, more than 40 black families had settled in the integrated village of Berea to take advantage of the school.

In 1869, E. Henry Fairchild became the first president of Berea College, and the first college class was enrolled. Throughout the next two decades, Fairchild, with Fee's support, maintained a student body that was around 300, deliberately apportioned at about half black, half white. The college was also coeducational by design. Although sometimes terrorized by hostile segregationist neighbors, Fairchild and his little community adhered to these principles until Fairchild's resignation in 1889.

With the appointment of William Goodell Frost as president in 1892, Berea College dramatically altered its mission. Frost, who had "discovered" Appalachia, transformed the school into an institution that primarily served the southern mountain region. Within a decade, white Appalachian enrollments were increased ninefold, while black enrollments remained steady. Moreover, Frost segregated the campus, reducing contacts between the races at Berea. Fee, as well as black Bereans such as **James S. Hathaway,** vociferously opposed these measures, but Frost was unmoved. In 1904, the Kentucky legislature enacted the **Day Law,** aimed directly at Berea College, which made it illegal for any school in Kentucky to be "integrated" or to establish an integrated branch within 25 miles of the parent institution. Berea fought the law in the courts, but in 1908, the Supreme Court of the United States ruled against the college in the historic case *Berea College v. Kentucky.* In 1912, Berea founded **Lincoln Institute** for black students in Shelby Co., while retaining the main campus for white students.

In 1950, when the **Day Law** was amended to allow white colleges and universities to integrate, Berea immediately admitted 3 black students into a student body of 1,400. Since then, the college has gradually reasserted the importance of its interracial commitment, incorporating required black studies courses into its general education curriculum and increasing the size of the black student enrollment. The college has actively striven to maintain black student enrollments at 20 percent and seeks to hire black instructors and staff.

Nelson, Paul David. "Experiment in Interracial Education at Berea College, 1858–1906." *JNH* 59 (1974): 13–27.

Sears, Richard D. *A Utopian Experiment in Kentucky: Integration and Social Equality at Berea, 1866–1904.* Westport, CT: Greenwood Press, 1996.

Wilson, Shannon H. *Berea College: An Illustrated History.* Lexington: Univ. Press of Kentucky, 2006.

—*Paul David Nelson*

BERRY, JULIUS S. (b. 1939, Lexington, KY; d. 2001, Lexington, KY), high school basketball all-star and civil rights activist. Julius Berry was born in Lexington to Rev. and Mrs. E. S. Berry. As a six-feet-five basketball player for **Dunbar High School** in the 1950s, he scored over 3,000 points and was selected as an all-state player for two consecutive years. In 1959, he was selected as the "star of stars" in the Kentucky-Indiana All-Star Game. Berry received scholarships to play college ball at the University of Dayton and at Kentucky State College (later known as **Kentucky State University**) and subsequently earned a master's degree in management and labor relations from Rutgers University in New Jersey.

Upon his return to Lexington, Berry worked with the **Congress of Racial Equality** and focused on school integration issues and the lack of employment opportunities for African Americans in the city. One summer, Berry single-handedly shut down a liquor store near Douglass Park through months of picketing it by himself. During the early 1970s, he worked for the A. Philip Randolph Education Fund, where he helped minorities obtain apprenticeships in the construction business. In 1975, Berry was appointed to the position of citizens' advocate for the Lexington–Fayette Urban County Government, where he was responsible for overseeing complaints against the city government.

During the early 1980s, Berry worked in the private sector as a public-relations representative for Ashland Oil Company and was self-employed in the horse industry as a breeder, seller, and Thoroughbred bloodstock agent. Berry also served as the president of the Bluegrass Black Business Association, an organization that encouraged black entrepreneurship and represented over 200 African American businesses and professional practices, during

the late 1980s. In 1984, Lexington mayor Scotty Baesler appointed Berry to the post of affirmative-action officer, where he managed the city's affirmative-action plan and investigated discrimination complaints. He was also responsible for helping minority and women contractors assemble competitive-bidding packages for city government jobs and helped them obtain bid and performance bonds. Berry was inducted into the Kentucky High School Hall of Fame in 1996. He died five years later in Lexington of cardiac arrest.

Berry, Julius. Interview by Edward Owens, Lexington, KY, July 20, 1978. Blacks in Lexington Project, Louie B. Nunn Center for Oral History, Univ. of Kentucky, 78OH111 KH73.

Newspapers: "Julius Berry Returns to Government," *LHL,* June 1, 1984, B1; "Black-Owned Firms Prosper," *LHL,* November 27, 1989, D1; "Aide to Lexington Mayor Dies—Dunbar Basketball Star during 1950s," *LHL,* December 3, 2001, B1.

—*Joshua D. Farrington*

BERRY, ROBERT T. (b. 1874, Kentucky; d. 1967, Louisville, KY), editor, political activist, and publisher. Robert T. Berry's World War I draft registration card in September 1918 documented his birth date as June 7, 1874, and his nearest relative as his mother, Mollie, of Glasgow, KY. It recorded his address as 445 Seventh St. in Louisville. In 1900, Berry and his older brother, George W., were tailors in Owensboro, KY, who also ventured into the newspaper business. A 1902 Owensboro *Kentucky Reporter* masthead listed R. T. as the editor and G. W. as the manager, but the men were still in the tailoring business since their newspaper included an advertisement for Berry Brothers Tailoring on W. Main St. The newspaper provided citizens with not only the international and national news but also the state and local news. The Berrys claimed to be "devoted to the Political, Religious, Educational and Industrial interest of the Negro." Although they published notices of births, marriages, deaths, and community events, they also challenged the status quo of the segregated society.

In early 1904, R. T. Berry announced in his newspaper his candidacy for delegate-at-large to the Chicago Republican National Convention. He proclaimed that the Republican Party and President Theodore Roosevelt held the people's interest better than any other party. Identified as "the most forceful Negro politicians [*sic*] of the State, an able writer and a fluent speaker," Berry expressed the desire to be "a member of the 'Big Four' in the Republican National Convention" in the March 17, 1908, edition of the *Lexington Leader.* The newspaper predicted Berry's success because of the high esteem in which he was held by Kentucky's black citizens and "quite a number of the white politicians." The journalist praised Berry's political insight. His *Kentucky Reporter* was "the first Negro paper to declare for Vice President Fairbanks for President" on July 12, 1907. Charles Warren Fairbanks was the 26th vice president of the United States under President Theodore Roosevelt, 1905–1909.

In 1910, the Berry brothers' parents, George W. and Mollie, lived with their adult daughters in Glasgow, KY. The brothers moved to Louisville in 1912. George worked as a U.S. storekeeper and gauger. Robert restarted the publication of the *Kentucky Reporter* at his print shop on Seventh St. He also worked as a city sanitary inspector and a *Courier-Journal* investigative reporter. In October 1913, Berry reported in the newspaper his research on an overpopulated black neighborhood in Louisville's Clay St. area. He provided a detailed account of the horrid conditions of people sleeping on floors, 15 inhabitants in a single room, rank odors, and disease-ravaged individuals.

In 1921, Berry moved his *Kentucky Reporter* office into the same building with other African American newspapers in Louisville's African American business district. That same year, in a September issue of the **Louisville Leader,** Rev. Noah W. Williams discussed the issue of political parties paying newspapers to advocate for them. Williams maintained, "Everybody knows that every newspaper in the city, white and colored, are paid for the use of them during every political campaign." He provided Robert T. Berry as one of many examples, reporting that Berry had given away 10,000 copies of his paper supporting the Republican Party. Williams argued that he did not do it for free, indicating that the politicians had paid for the distribution.

When Berry died on July 28, 1967, the *Louisville Courier-Journal* simply noted that he had been "the editor of a small Negro-community newspaper."

Kentucky Death Index, 1911–2000.
Kentucky Virtual Digital Library-Historic Kentucky Newspapers-Description of the *Kentucky Reporter* (Owensboro), http://kdl.kyvl.org/catalog/xt7gb56d3c6t_1.
Newspapers: *Kentucky Reporter* (Owensboro), March 22, 1902, 2; "Editor Berry a Candidate," *LL,* February 7, 1904, 3; "R. T. Berry," *LL,* March 17, 1908, 7; "R. T. Berry," *Barbourville Mountain Advocate,* March 27, 1908, 4; "Rev. Williams the News, Leader and 'Reporter,'" *Louisville Leader,* September 17, 1921, 1.
U.S. Federal Census (1900, 1910, 1930).
World War I Draft Registration Cards, 1917–1918.
Wright, George C. *Life Behind a Veil: Blacks in Louisville, Kentucky, 1865–1930.* Baton Rouge: Louisiana State Univ. Press, 1985.

—*Sallie L. Powell*

BERRY, THACKERY LOUIS (b. 1892, Hopkinsville, KY; d. 1944, Franklin, KY), medical doctor and surgeon. Thackery Louis Berry was born to Louis and Josephine Berry in Hopkinsville, KY, on October 17, 1892. He received an AM degree at the age of 18 from **Hopkinsville Male and Female College** and earned MD and PhD degrees from Meharry Medical College in Nashville, TN, in 1915. Immediately after graduating, he was named surgeon in chief at the newly opened **Winnie A. Scott Memorial Hospital** in Frankfort. He became one of the best-known surgeons in Kentucky. The segregated hospital served African Americans in Frankfort from 1915 until desegregation in 1959. At one time, Berry worked alongside two other prominent Kentucky medical doctors, Charles W. Anderson and **E. E. Underwood,** at the hospital.

In 1924, Berry moved to Cincinnati and took a position at Mercy Hospital. During his medical career, he was a member of the National Medical Association, the Cincinnati Medical Association, and the Kentucky State Medical, Dental, and Pharmacy Association. By 1940, Berry and his wife, Lelia Pearl, had returned to Frankfort, where he established a private practice. According to his death certificate, Berry died from pistol shots to his chest in 1944. No other sources have been located to clarify who murdered him. Frankfort's **Thomas K. Robb** Funeral Home handled the burial arrangements in Cave Spring Cemetery, Hopkinsville, KY.

Boris, Joseph J., ed. *Who's Who in Colored America, 1927.* New York: Who's Who in Colored America Corp., 1927.
Dabney, Wendell P. *Cincinnati's Colored Citizens: Historical, Sociological and Biographical.* Cincinnati: Dabney, 1926.
Dunnigan, Alice Allison, comp. and ed. *The Fascinating Story of Black Kentuckians: Their Heritage and Traditions.* Washington, DC: Associated Publishers, 1982.
Kentucky Death Records, 1852–1953.

—*Joshua D. Farrington*

BERRY, THEODORE MOODY (b. 1905, Maysville, KY; d. 2000, Cincinnati, OH), lawyer, politician, and first African American mayor in Ohio. Theodore Berry was born in Maysville, KY, in 1905. He met his white father, Daniel Berry, only once and was raised by his deaf mother, Cora Parks, with whom he communicated by using sign language. After moving to Cincinnati's West End, he won a local high school essay contest under the pseudonym Thomas Playfair after having been initially rejected when using his own surname by an all-white panel. In 1924, he became Cincinnati's first African American to serve as class valedictorian when he graduated from Woodward High School.

Ted, as he was known to his family and friends, attended the University of Cincinnati for both his undergraduate and law degrees. He worked at steel mills in Newport, KY, to pay his tuition. From 1932 to 1936 and again from 1943 to 1946, he served as president of the Cincinnati branch of the **National Association for the Advancement of Colored People.** In 1938, he was appointed the first black assistant prosecuting attorney in Cincinnati.

During World War II, Berry moved to Washington, DC, and served as a morale officer for the Office of War Information. After returning to Cincinnati, he was elected to the city council in 1950 and became vice mayor in 1955. In 1965, he was appointed by President Lyndon Johnson to head the newly created Community Action Programs division of the Office of Economic Opportunity. In that position, Berry oversaw Head Start, the Job Corps, and Legal Services. After the Johnson presidency, he returned to Cincinnati and became the city's first African American mayor in 1972. A street and a park in Cincinnati were named in his honor.

Fleming, G. James, and Christian E. Burckel, eds. *Who's Who in Colored America.* 7th ed. *Supplement.* Yonkers-on-Hudson, NY: Christian E. Burckel & Associates, 1950.
"Milestones," *The New Crisis,* November–December, 2000, 8.

—*Joshua D. Farrington*

BERRYTOWN, African American community in Anchorage, KY. The predominantly African American community known as Berrytown is located on the eastern boundary of the city of Anchorage. The community had its origins in the post–Civil War Reconstruction era, when many new patterns of rural settlement developed in Jefferson Co.

Several African Americans purchased land adjoining the Louisville, Cincinnati, and Lexington Railroad at the Forest Station in the 1870s. This group began the subdivision of land that is the core of Berrytown, along the road running between LaGrange Rd. and English Station Rd. The trustees of the First Colored Baptist Church of Anchorage, also known as the Little Flock Church, also purchased land. These initial purchases created the nucleus for the community.

Berrytown was named for Alfred Berry, one of several African Americans who bought 10-acre parcels in 1874. Other original landowners were Kidd Williams, William Butler, and Sallie Carter. The land was purchased from Samuel L. and Mary E. Nock, who had acquired the land from the estate of John B. Heafer in 1868. Nock sold additional parcels throughout the 1890s.

The introduction of the interurban railroad at the turn of the century facilitated travel to Louisville and La Grange. The neighborhood was enlarged in 1901 when the tract of land on the north side of Berrytown Rd. became the Marr and Gaddie's Subdivision.

The community of Berrytown was expanded to the south as part of an urban-renewal project in the 1960s. The plan, which called for the entire redevelopment of Berrytown, was resisted by residents. As a result, most of the original pattern of streets was preserved. In the late twentieth century, new construction altered the rural village profile of the community to one more resembling the surrounding suburban development.

Louisville and Jefferson County Planning Commission. *Berrytown Redevelopment Plan.* Louisville, KY: The Commission, 1976.

—*Donna M. Neary*

BETHEA, RAINEY (b. ca. 1910; d. 1936), the last person publicly executed by state sanction in the United States in 1936. In 1910, the Kentucky General Assembly determined that the Kentucky State Penitentiary in Eddyville would implement death sentences by electrocution. After the execution of accused rapist and murderer **Will Lockett** in Lexington, KY, the General Assembly amended the death penalty for rape to be execution by hanging in the county of the offense. Kentucky's death-sentence numbers gradually increased between 1910 and 1928.

Research has yet to locate much information on Rainey Bethea's life before his arrival in Kentucky. Most sources claim that he was born to Rainey and Ella Bethea in Roanoke, VA, sometime between 1909 and 1913. However, the 1910 U.S. federal census listed a 5-year-old Rainey Bethea as the stepson of Strans and Beulah Bethea in Bethea, SC. Ten years later, the 1920 census recorded 11-year-old Rainey Bethea living with his father, Rainey Bethea, and his younger brother, Bennie Bethea, in Mullins, SC. By the early 1930s, Bethea intermittently performed manual labor at various Owensboro homes. He also had several encounters with the law. On June 1, 1935, Bethea was sent to Eddyville's State Penitentiary for a one-year prison term for grand larceny. He was paroled on December 1, 1935, and returned to Owensboro.

On Sunday, June 7, 1936, 70-year-old Lishia Edwards, a widow and mother of Dr. Philip Rarick Edwards, a University of Kentucky professor and bacteriologist, was found dead in her upstairs apartment in Owensboro, KY. Edwards had been brutally raped and strangled. Some of her jewelry and personal items were missing. The killer had left behind his muddy footprints, fingerprints, and an Eddyville prison ring with the initial "R."

Bethea, who had worked for Edwards, was quickly arrested and, after a "speedy" trial of four and a half minutes, was found guilty of criminal assault and murder. He provided several confessions, one of which included the location of Edwards's personal items. Louisville African American attorneys **Charles Ewbank Tucker,** Stephen A. Burnley, **Charles W. Anderson Jr.,** Harry E. Bonaparte, and R. Everett Ray worked on his appeal. Governor Albert B. "Happy" Chandler scheduled Bethea to hang on August 14, 1936.

The state of Kentucky had previously publicly executed several convicted rapists, but this time, the county sheriff responsible for the execution was a woman. Florence Katherine Shoemaker Thompson, age 43 and the mother of four children, took the job after the death of her husband, Sheriff Joseph Everett Thompson. Her deputies handled the majority of the arrests, and she mainly performed administrative duties. She struggled with her role as executioner. Depression-era media latched onto the concept of a white female law-enforcement officer hanging an accused African American male criminal, portraying her as "the hangman in skirts." The *New York Daily News* flew reporters to Owensboro, and the *Chicago Times* equipped a truck with a photographic developing room. When a former Louisville policeman, Arthur Hash, voluntarily took the executioner job, the media turned their attention from Thompson to the crowd. Anywhere from 10,000 to 20,000 spectators, including children, attended the "carnival of sadism." Accounts surfaced of vendors selling popcorn, ice cream, and other food items. Sources maintained that many Owensboroans held "hanging parties" the evening before the execution, while others engaged in "necktie breakfasts" the morning of the hanging. Reports claimed that viewers were "jeering savagely," but eyewitnesses maintained that "a hush fell over the crowd" when Bethea was escorted to the gallows.

Shortly after 5:30 a.m., Bethea, standing about 5-feet-5 and weighing barely 128 pounds, dropped through the trap door. He was pronounced dead about 14 minutes later. Sheriff Thompson observed everything from a car. The hearse struggled through the crowd to get to Bethea's body. He was buried in Rosehill Elmwood Cemetery.

Many people responded with outrage. One editorial argued that "legalized murder" had become "a commercial racket." Criticism included the question of the humanity of American civilization. On March 12, 1938, the Kentucky General Assembly passed a law that all executions would be performed in private and by electrocution within the walls of the Kentucky State Penitentiary in Eddyville.

Dew, Lee A. "The Hanging of Rainey Bethea." *Daviess County Historical Quarterly* 2 (July 1984): 51–59.
Newspapers: "Crowd Rushes Gallows while Negro Hangs," *Reading (PA) Eagle,* August 14, 1936, 1, 18; "Voice of the People," *Indianapolis Recorder,* August 29, 1936, 10; "Protests Get 2D KY. Hanging Postponement," *Indianapolis Recorder,* September 5, 1936, 2; "There Was a Reason They Outlawed Public Executions," *NYT,* May 6, 2001, WK5.
Ryan, Perry T. *The Last Public Execution in America.* KY: P. T. Ryan, 1992.

—*Sallie L. Powell*

BIBB, CHARLES LEON (b. 1922, Louisville, KY), folksinger and actor. Leon Bibb was born in Louisville, KY, on February 7, 1922. He was trained in classical baritone singing in New York City and initially earned his fame on Broadway. He performed in the play *The Cat* and the musical *Annie Get Your Gun,* with Ethel Merman. During this time, he also performed as a folksinger in Greenwich Village.

Following the example of his idol, Paul Robeson, Bibb performed in Russia in 1964. Despite being blacklisted from many venues during the rest of the 1960s, Bibb continued to rise in fame. During the decade, he was an opening act for Bill Cosby and acted in numerous films alongside actors Sidney Poitier and Henry Fonda. In 1967, he was nominated for a Tony Award for Best Supporting Actor (Musical) for his performance in *A Hand Is on the Gate.*

In 1969, Bibb moved to Vancouver, Canada, and, while occasionally performing in musicals, has focused primarily on his folk music career. He has recorded over a dozen albums, including *This Is Leon Bibb* (1970), *Shenandoah* (1997), and *Lift Every Voice and Sing* (2003). As a folksinger, he has recorded and sung live with Arlo Guthrie, Pete Seeger, and Peter, Paul, and Mary. His son, Eric Bibb, also entered the music business as a **blues** singer and songwriter.

Dykk, Lloyd. "The Leon King." *Vancouver Georgia Straight,* November 1989, 10–17.
Newspapers: "Music in 'Annie Get Your Gun,'" *NYT,* December 15, 1946, X3; "Reaching into the Soul," *WP,* October 26, 1969, 167; "Leon Bibb Sings with Ailey Dancers in McKayle Work," *NYT,* May 15, 1973, 29.

—*Joshua D. Farrington*

BIBB, HENRY WALTON (b. 1815, Shelby Co., KY; d. 1854, Windsor, Ontario, Canada), author, abolitionist, editor, political activist, and fugitive slave. Henry Bibb was born in Shelby Co., KY, the oldest son of seven children born to Mildred Jackson, who was herself a former slave. Like many enslaved persons of color, young Bibb never knew his father, but one rumor alleged that he was the son of James Bibb, a Kentucky state senator. However, years later this account was proved incorrect.

Known as Walton by his owner, David White, at an early age young Bibb was hired out regularly to work on several nearby plantations, where he routinely received harsh treatment. Bibb recalled years later, "I was taken away from my mother, and hired out to labor for various persons, eight or ten years in succession. . . . It was then I first commenced seeing and feeling that I was a wretched slave." During these years, young Bibb also witnessed the destruction of his family when his sisters and brothers were sold away, one by one, to the highest bidder.

In 1833, Bibb married a biracial enslaved African American woman named Malinda, the daughter of a free black American who lived in nearby Trimble Co., KY, with whom he had one daughter, Mary Francis. Fatherhood, however, reignited Bibb's desire for freedom. Thus, in 1837, after promising his family that he would return for them, Bibb successfully escaped from bondage and traveled to Cincinnati, OH. From there, with the help of some local African Americans and a group of abolitionists, Bibb moved

to Perrysburgh, OH. Settling in Perrysburgh, he returned to Kentucky in 1839 to rescue his wife and daughter, but the entire family quickly was caught and imprisoned in a Louisville, KY, jail.

Eventually the Bibb family was placed on a steamboat bound first for Vicksburg, MS, and later New Orleans, LA. During the next few years, Bibb continuously tried to escape. However, these efforts proved unsuccessful until 1841, when Malinda and his daughter were sold to a gambler and Bibb himself became the property of a local Native American tribe. After months of searching, with no hope of recovering his family, Bibb turned his attention to securing his own freedom and becoming very active in the abolition movement.

In 1848, Bibb remarried. He soon became a prominent abolitionist and orator, published his autobiography, *Narrative of the Life and Adventures of Henry Bibb, an American Slave* (1849), and eventually moved to Windsor, Ontario, Canada. On January 1, 1851, with the help of his second wife, Mary, Bibb published the first successful Canadian abolitionist newspaper, *Voice of the Fugitive.* In addition, Bibb assisted in the construction of a local Methodist church, helped start an all-black school, and became a staunch activist for his fellow fugitives and free black Americans who had reached Canada. Unfortunately, on August 1, 1854, at the young age of 39, Bibb suddenly died of unknown causes. However, his legacy continued for decades.

Bibb, Henry. *Narrative of the Life and Adventures of Henry Bibb, an American Slave.* New York: privately printed, 1849.
Cooper, Afua. "The Fluid Frontier: Blacks and the Detroit River Region, a Focus on Henry Bibb." *Canadian Review of American Studies* 30 (2000): 129–49.
Heglar, Charles J. *Rethinking the Slave Narrative.* Westport, CT: Greenwood Press, 2001.
"Henry Bibb Is Dead," *Frederick Douglass' Paper* (Rochester, NY), August 11, 1854, 2.
Hudson, J. Blaine. *Encyclopedia of the Underground Railroad.* Jefferson, NC: McFarland, 2006.

—*Eric R. Jackson*

BICKERSTAFF, BERNARD TYRONE "BERNIE," SR. (b. 1943, Benham, KY), first African American from Kentucky to be named a head coach in the National Basketball Association. After graduating from high school in Benham, KY, Bernard Tyrone Bickerstaff attended Kentucky Wesleyan College but left because of racial tensions. He then worked in the coal mines until he enrolled in the University of San Diego, California, where he played basketball and later worked as an assistant coach (1967–1970). At age 25, he became the head coach (1970–1973) at the University of San Diego, the youngest college coach at the time.

Bickerstaff had never played or coached above the Division II college level, but in 1973, the new head coach of the Washington (DC) Bullets, K. C. Jones, picked Bickerstaff as his assistant coach (1973–1985), the youngest assistant coach in the National Basketball Association (NBA). In 1985, Bickerstaff was named head coach of the Seattle Supersonics. In 1987, he was named NBA Coach of the Year after guiding the Supersonics to the Western Conference finals. In 1990, he became general manger and vice president of basketball operations for the Denver Nuggets and worked in various capacities for the organization until 1997. He coached the Washington Bullets/Wizards (1997–1999), was basketball director and coach of the Harlem Globetrotters, and served as the general manager of the Charlotte Sting (WNBA) (2003) and the head coach of the Charlotte Bobcats (2004–2008). He then coached the Chicago Bulls (2008–2010) and the Portland Trail Blazers (2010–2012). In 2012, the Los Angeles Lakers hired him as a coaching consultant, and he was quickly promoted to interim head coach. The following year, the Cleveland Cavaliers hired him as assistant coach, giving him 40 years in the NBA organization.

Bickerstaff's hometown of Benham celebrated his achievements with Bernard Bickerstaff Day in 1991. A parade was organized in his honor; Governor Wallace Wilkinson named him a Kentucky Colonel; and the street of his childhood home was renamed Bernard Bickerstaff Blvd. In July 2014, Bickerstaff received the Chuck Daly Lifetime Achievement Award from the National Basketball Coaches Association.

"Bernie Bickerstaff." http://www.nba.com/coachfile/bernie_bicker staff/ (accessed November 13, 2013).

"Denver Nuggets' G. M. Bernie Bickerstaff Honored in Kentucky Hometown," *Jet,* October 28, 1991, 52.

Dunnigan, Alice Allison, comp. and ed. *The Fascinating Story of Black Kentuckians: Their Heritage and Traditions.* Washington, DC: Associated Publishers, 1982.

Escamilla, Brian. "Bernie Bickerstaff." In *Contemporary Black Biography: Profiles from the International Black Community,* vol. 21, edited by Shirelle Phelps, 18–21. Farmington Hills, MI: Gale Group, 1999.

Kentucky Birth Index, 1911–1999. (While other sources give February 11, 1944, as his birth date, this source claims that his birth date is November 2, 1943.)

National Basketball Association, "Basketball Operations, Bernie Bickerstaff" (NBA). http://www.nba.com/media/bobcats/Pg27-36_basket ballops.pdf (accessed July 20, 2009).

Newspapers: "Black Coaches in N.B.A. Have Shorter Tenures," *NYT,* March 22, 2005, A1; "Harlan Boasts Globetrotters Connections," *LCJ,* May 8, 2005, 1B; "Black Pioneers Paved Way for Today's NBA," *New Pittsburgh Courier,* February 21, 2007, C6.

"Trail Blazers Assistant Coach Bernie Bickerstaff Wins NBA's Chuck Daly Award." http://www.oregonlive.com/blazers/index.ssf/2014/06/former_trail_blazers_assistant_coach_bernie_bicker.html (accessed July 24, 2004).

—*Sallie L. Powell*

BIGGERSTAFF, THOMPSON BURNAM (b. 1902, Richmond, KY; d. 1969, Lexington, KY), dentist. Born on August 26, 1902, to James W. and Ellen (Noland) Biggerstaff, Thompson Burnam Biggerstaff had to grow up quickly. His father, a hotel waiter, died of influenza when Thompson was 16. His mother raised him and his older sister, Lucille, on a laundress's wages. He graduated from Richmond High School in 1919, Knoxville College in 1921, and dental school at Meharry Medical College in Nashville, TN, in 1925. His first wife, Mattie Huggins, from Nashville, died the year before he graduated from dental school. He married his second wife, Mattie C. Carnes, in 1936. He had four children.

Biggerstaff practiced dentistry in Pikeville, Richmond, Frankfort, Danville, and Lexington. He served as the vice president of the Blue Grass Medical Society, state secretary of the Elks, a member of the Blue Grass Athletic Club Board of Directors, president of the Young Men's Club, and a member of the National Dental Association, the J. A. Andrews Clinical Society, the Chicago Dental Society, the **National Association for the Advancement of Colored People,** the YMCA, and **Kappa Alpha Psi Fraternity.** In 1945, he served as a part-time dentist at Kentucky State College (later **Kentucky State University**). He served as chairman of the Lexington Negro Division of the Boy Scouts of America in 1950.

"Colored Notes," *LL,* June 26, 1950, 14.

Fleming, G. James, and Christian E. Burckel, eds. *Who's Who in Colored America.* 7th ed. *Supplement.* Yonkers-on-Hudson, NY: Christian E. Burckel & Associates, 1950.

Kentucky Death Records, 1852–1953.

"Kentucky State College Notes," *KNEAJ* 17, no. 1 (October–November 1945): 13.

Social Security Death Index.

U.S. Federal Census (1910, 1920, 1930).

—*Sallie L. Powell*

BIGGERSTAFF, WILLIAM (b. 1854, Lexington, KY; d. 1896, Helena, MT), condemned criminal who allowed his image to be photographed before his execution. On April 6, 1896, William Biggerstaff, a former slave from Lexington, KY, was hanged in Helena, MT. He had been charged and convicted of murdering "Dick" Johnson, an African American, in June 1895. Biggerstaff pleaded self-defense.

African American daguerrean James Presley "J. P." Ball photographed a series of picture cards of William Biggerstaff in 1896 that provided a framed narrative of the end of his life. The first image of Biggerstaff was a typical studio portrait with the subject exhibiting the signs of middle-class respectability in a three-piece suit, wearing a handkerchief in his coat pocket and a boutonnière in his lapel, and sitting in a chair, with his chin resting on his right hand as his elbow was positioned on the chair's arm. The backdrop presented a soft-focused angelic cherub leaning over Biggerstaff's head. Whether Biggerstaff hired Ball or someone else paid for the photo, the reason for this studio photograph is unknown.

Ball's next two images of Biggerstaff were taken after the hanging with white officials standing next to the hooded, dead body and the noose still around the neck. The final picture revealed Biggerstaff's body in a coffin. He apparently was wearing the same jacket he had worn in the studio photograph but was dressed in a different vest. Unlike the posed photo when he was alive, Biggerstaff's left hand displayed a wedding band. It is unknown when or whom he married.

Ball had led Biggerstaff's clemency committee and may have photographed his death to "memorialize" Biggerstaff's life.

American Studies at the University of Virginia. "Representing Death," http://xroads.virginia.edu/~MA02/amacker/photo/death.html (accessed April 3, 2009).

California Supreme Court and other states. *State v. Biggerstaff,* 43 P. 709 (January 30–March 26, 1896).

Goldsby, Jacqueline. *A Spectacular Secret: Lynching in American Life and Literature.* Chicago: Univ. of Chicago Press, 2006.

Willis, Deborah, ed. *J. P. Ball: Daguerrean and Studio Photographer.* New York: Garland, 1993.

—Sallie L. Powell

BINGHAM, REBECCA TAYLOR (b. 1928, Indianapolis, IN), librarian. Growing up in what she recalled as "a bookish household" in Wanamaker, IN, Rebecca Taylor Bingham was instilled with a love of books from the beginning of her life. She followed this love and received a bachelor's degree from Indiana University in 1950, an MA degree from the University of Tulsa in 1961, and an MLS degree from Indiana University in 1969. In 1971, Bingham became the first black president of the Kentucky Library Association and also served as the director of library media services for the Jefferson Co. public schools beginning in 1975.

According to the *Louisville Courier-Journal,* Bingham's "most significant contribution" was organizing the first national conference of the American Association of School Librarians in 1979. She arranged for the conference to be held in Louisville, and over 1,000 librarians from across the country attended. That same year, she was nominated to serve on the White House Conference on Library and Information Services. In 1998, President Bill Clinton named her to the National Commission on Libraries and Information Science. In 2005, Bingham's contributions were recognized by the American Association of School Librarians, which awarded her the Distinguished Service Award. That same day, Louisville mayor Jerry Abramson proclaimed June 27 Rebecca Bingham Day.

"President Clinton Names Rebecca T. Bingham and Martha B. Gould as Members of the National Commission on Libraries and Information Science." *American Library Association Washington Office Newsline* 7, no. 13 (February 4, 1998).
Williams, Keith. "Neighborhood Newsmaker: Rebecca T. Bingham," *LCJ,* July 27, 2005, B3.

—Joshua D. Farrington

BISHOP, STEPHEN (b. 1817, Glasgow, KY; d. 1857, Edmonson Co., KY), cave guide and explorer. Stephen Bishop won lasting fame as one of the earliest and most widely known Mammoth Cave guides. Bishop was born enslaved. His owner, Frank Gorin, a Glasgow attorney, purchased Mammoth Cave in 1838 and moved Bishop there to work as a guide. Gorin, however, lacked sufficient capital to develop the cave as a profitable tourist attraction, and, in 1839, Dr. John Croghan of Locust Grove in Jefferson Co. bought the property and Bishop for $10,000. Croghan added tours, expanded the inn, and had roads built.

Only 20 miles of the cave had been explored when Bishop arrived. In 1838, he was the first person to cross the Bottomless Pit. He later discovered Mammoth Dome, the River Styx, Dismal Hollow, Bandits' Hall, the sightless creatures of the cave depths, and other famous and previously unknown sections of the cave. Bishop is still credited with exploring more of Mammoth Cave than any other individual. In 1842, while visiting Locust Grove, he drew from memory a remarkably accurate map of Mammoth Cave.

Along with being a first-rate and daring explorer, Bishop was an even more remarkable guide. Described as a short, wiry, "charismatic," and "incredibly handsome" mulatto, he led tours by

Stephen Bishop.

lantern light and educated himself by watching, listening to, and discreetly questioning the many learned visitors who followed him into the subterranean darkness. In time he learned to speak some Latin and Greek and amazed visitors with his knowledge of history and geology. Although other black guides, such as brothers Masterson and Nicholas Bransford, were hired to assist him, Bishop himself became almost as great an attraction as Mammoth Cave itself by the mid-1840s. His fame was even more extraordinary given that his role as guide placed him in authority over whites, authority that could be exercised safely only with a mixture of deference and affability.

On his 1842 trip to Locust Grove, Bishop "married" Charlotte, another slave of John Croghan (under the Kentucky Constitution, slave marriage was not recognized by law). Charlotte returned with him to Mammoth Cave and worked as a maid at the nearby inn. When Croghan died in 1849, his will stipulated that Bishop and his family, including his son, Thomas, born in 1843, be emancipated in 1856 and assisted in emigrating to the West African nation of Liberia, which had been established in the early 1820s as an African site to which free blacks could be "returned." Instead, Bishop, who was officially emancipated in February 1856, saved his money and bought property near Mammoth Cave. Unfortunately, he was unable to enjoy his new freedom and died suddenly and mysteriously in the summer of 1857. Bishop is buried in the "Old Guide's Cemetery" near the Mammoth Cave entrance.

Finch, Marianne. *An Englishwoman's Experience in America.* London: Richard Bentley, 1853.
Jefferson Co. Will Book 4, 121.
LCJ, February 22, 1996.

Lucas, Marion B. *A History of Blacks in Kentucky.* Vol. 1, *From Slavery to Segregation, 1760–1891.* Frankfort: Kentucky Historical Society, 1992.

Schmitzer, Jeanne C. "The Sable Guides of Mammoth Cave." *FCHQ* 67 (April 1993): 240–58.

Thomas, Samuel W., Eugene H. Connor, and Harold Meloy. "A History of Mammoth Cave, Emphasizing Tourist Development and Medical Experimentation under Dr. John Croghan." *RKHS* 68, no. 4 (October 1970): 319–41.

—*J. Blaine Hudson*

BLACK, ISAAC E. (b. 1848, Kentucky; d. 1914, Louisville, KY), political leader in Covington, KY. African American lawyer Isaac Black was born in Kentucky in June 1848 and lived his early years in Covington. In 1869, he resided at the Old Hotel Building across from the Kenton County Courthouse in Covington, where he served as janitor and law librarian. One day in the early 1870s, while Black was working at the law library, John G. Carlisle, an eminent attorney and politician, sparked in him an interest in legal matters. Carlisle noticed the young man reading paperback novels and suggested that he instead devote his time to reading law. According to Robert S. Tate's biographical sketch of Carlisle, Black engaged in some law study under Carlisle's direction and, furthermore, was the only African American who had that privilege.

Black's community activism embraced many areas, from education and voter rights to civil rights and politics. These challenges in Covington, an arena of conflict between the heavily Democratic majority and an influential Republican minority, demanded much of him, but he rose above the circumstances. As long as he remained in northern Kentucky, even during the segregation of the Reconstruction era, the former slave was able to develop both personal and professional relationships with Kentuckians of both races.

In 1869, Black, **Jacob Price,** and **William Blackburn** were members of a delegation representing Covington at the **Freedmen's Bureau** for Education convention in Louisville. After the convention, Black and the other Covington delegates took the initiative and began to organize a board of trustees for the city's proposed black schools.

On February 25, 1870, a statewide African American political convention was scheduled for Frankfort. Some of the newly enfranchised African Americans wanted to vote the straight Republican ticket. However, Black, Price, and Blackburn favored voting for anyone who supported policies that were in the best interest of Covington's African American community. This political position later benefited the community by giving it a voice with politicians from both major parties. For example, William Grant, an influential businessman and a Covington City Council member, asked Black and other African American community leaders for their support. He said that if the African American voters supported him in his attempt to gain the Democratic nomination for the Kenton Co. district's seat in the Kentucky General Assembly, he would have the city charter of Covington amended to provide for an African American public school. Grant won the election, and as he had promised, the new Covington city charter soon provided for an African American school. Black's political wisdom had been demonstrated.

In August 1870, Black took a break from the rigors of politics and education to become president of the Starlight baseball club. The club remained organized for only a short period and was the last organized African American amateur baseball club formed in Covington until the turn of the century.

In early 1875, during the Easter holidays, an incident occurred when Black tried to attend Covington's Trinity Episcopal Church. He was denied a seat downstairs among the "quality" people. Black walked out of the church in disgust, but although the church had anticipated a lawsuit because of the incident, no suit was filed. Black moved to Atlanta, GA, where he studied theology. Thereafter, he established a law practice in Louisville and returned to Covington only for short visits. On April 18, 1914, Black died at age 66 in Louisville and was buried in the Louisville Cemetery.

Harris, Theodore H. "Creating Windows of Opportunity: Isaac E. Black and the African American Experience in Kentucky, 1848–1914." *RKHS* 98, no. 2 (Spring 2000): 155–77.

Tate, Robert S. "John G. Carlisle—Truly a Mental Giant." *Papers of the Christopher Gist Historical Society* 2 (1950–1951): 147–67.

Tenkotte, Paul A. "Rival Cities to Suburbs: Covington and Newport, Kentucky, 1790–1890." PhD diss., Univ. of Cincinnati, 1989.

—*Theodore H. H. Harris*

BLACKBURN, CHARLES HENRY "JACK" (b. 1883, Versailles, KY; d. 1942, Chicago, IL), boxer and trainer of Joe Louis. As a teenager in Versailles, KY, Charles Henry "Jack" Blackburn, son of a preacher, delivered newspapers and read headline stories about famous pugilists John L. Sullivan and "Gentleman Jim" Corbett. These stories influenced his dream to enter the sport of boxing. He left Kentucky for Indiana when he was 16 years old. He later sparred with future world heavyweight boxing champion Jack Johnson and gave him a bloody nose.

After a move to Baltimore, Blackburn suffered what he claimed to be his only loss as a lightweight prize fighter from 1902 to 1923 when Joe Gans won a 15-round bout by decision on points on March 25, 1904. Gans outweighed the 135-pound Blackburn by 15 pounds. Most of Blackburn's opponents outweighed him. He was known for his swift legs, fast hands, cunning, and knockout blows. Some believed that he was the lightweight version of Jack Johnson.

In January 1909, Blackburn's life took a detour when he was charged with murder and imprisoned for defending his white common-law wife, Maud Pillian. In 1916, he returned to the boxing world when he fought in the Harlem Sporting Club. In 1923, he retired as a fighter. Afterward, he became a trainer for Joe Louis, who nicknamed him Chappie. Blackburn taught Louis not only the finer points of boxing techniques but also the psychological aspects. He trained Louis to use a foot-shuffling method to maintain his balance when delivering a punch, which led to a popular dance, the Joe Louis shuffle.

Blackburn was a trainer, a surrogate father, and best friend to Joe Louis. When Blackburn died in Chicago on April 24, 1942, Louis mourned his loss. He and his wife named their first child, Jacqueline, after Blackburn.

Dunnigan, Alice Allison, comp. and ed. *The Fascinating Story of Black Kentuckians: Their Heritage and Traditions.* Washington, DC: Associated Publishers, 1982.

Erenberg, Lewis A. *The Greatest Fight of Our Generation.* New York: Oxford Univ. Press, 2006.

Miller, Patrick B., and David Kenneth Wiggins, eds. *Sport and the Color Line: Black Athletes and Race Relations in Twentieth-Century America.* New York: Routledge, 2004.

Newspapers: "'Joe' Gans Won from Blackburn," *NYT,* March 26, 1904, 13; "Jack Blackburn Shoots Two," *IF,* January 23, 1909, 7; "Boxer, Veteran of 150 Battles, Admits His Career Is Ended," *NYT,* March 11, 1923, S4; "Sports of the Times," *NYT,* June 20, 1935, 26; "Wants to Attend Services," *NYT,* April 25, 1942, 18.

"People and Events: Jack 'Chappie' Blackburn (1883–1942)." Public Broadcasting Service American Experience. http://www.pbs.org/wgbh/amex/fight/peopleevents/p_blackburn.html (accessed July 22, 2009).

—*Sallie L. Powell*

BLACKBURN, THORNTON (b. ca. 1814, Maysville, KY; d. 1890, York, Ontario, Canada), and BLACKBURN, LUCIE (RUTH) (b. ca. 1805, unknown; d. 1895, York, Ontario, Canada), escaped Kentucky slaves. On Independence Day, 1831, Thornton Blackburn and his bride Ruth (Rutha or Ruthie) Blackburn arrived free in Cincinnati after fleeing slavery in Louisville, KY. They traveled farther north on the **Underground Railroad** to Detroit, where they lived for two years before a white Kentuckian recognized Thornton and reported him as an escaped slave. Under the Fugitive Slave Law of 1793 and the Northwest Ordinance of 1787, Michigan was required to return the runaway slaves to Kentucky. African American Detroit citizens were incensed at this prospect. One couple, under the premise of consoling and praying with Ruth in her prison cell, managed to help her escape by trading places with her.

Ruth escaped to Ontario, Canada, and changed her name to Lucie (Lucy), but her husband, Thornton, remained in jail. On the same day on which Ruth was discovered missing from her cell, Monday, June 17, 1833, the sheriff and jailer led Thornton out of the jail, where a crowd of about 200 armed and angry African American women and men confronted them. In the ruckus later known as the Blackburn Riots of 1833, the first racial riots in Detroit, Thornton escaped to Canada.

In Canada, the Blackburns were arrested, and Michigan moved to extradite them, which precipitated the first serious legal dispute between Canada and the United States over the issue of fugitive slaves. Since Canada was still under British rule, it could not extradite people to a jurisdiction that imposed harsher punishment than its own penalties. Canada's decision set a precedent for future runaway slave disputes and established Canada as the main stop on the Underground Railroad. The Blackburns' home became part of that system.

In 1837, Thornton Blackburn created the first taxicab business in Toronto when he had a carriage built, which he painted yellow and red. For many years, he monopolized the local cab business. When Thornton died on February 26, 1890, Lucie inherited a house, a small barn, and $17,000. The couple had no children. Lucie died five years later at age 90.

Canadian Genealogy Index, 1600s–1900s.

Census of Canada (1871, 1881).

Frost, Karolyn Smardz. *I've Got a Home in Glory Land: A Lost Tale of the Underground Railroad.* New York: Farrar, Straus & Giroux, 2007.

McRae, Norman. "Blacks in Detroit, 1736–1833: The Search for Freedom and Community and Its Implications for Educators." PhD diss., Univ. of Michigan, 1982.

Newspapers: "The Blackburns Have Left a Glorious, Green Legacy," *Toronto Star,* June 11, 1986, A6; "Untold Stories of the Underground Railroad: Slaves Met Tricksters, Spies on Freedom's Trail," *Detroit News,* February 8, 2000, 1C; "Two Nations Pay Tribute to Slaves' Flight from Louisville to Canada," *LCJ,* April 26, 2002, 1A.

Ontario, Canada Deaths, 1869–1934.

—*Sallie L. Powell*

BLACKBURN, WILLIAM (b. 1848, Kentucky; d. April 2, 1880, Covington, KY), pastor of the First Baptist Church in Covington, KY. Kentucky native William Blackburn arrived in Covington in 1869 and became pastor of the **First Baptist Church** in 1870, replacing **Jacob Price,** the church's first pastor. The First Baptist Church had been actively involved in providing space for one of the city's private African American schools, and the practice continued under Blackburn as pastor. In 1869, Blackburn, **Isaac Black,** and Jacob Price were members of a delegation representing Covington at the **Freedmen's Bureau** for Education convention in Louisville. In October 1872, Blackburn and the other Covington delegates drew on what they had heard at the convention and began to organize a board of trustees for the city's proposed public African American schools. The result was a board that eventually oversaw the city's two African American public schools, one at First Baptist Church and the other at the Methodist church.

Blackburn was apparently a Civil War Union army veteran; if so, he may have been one of the large number of African American Civil War veterans living in Covington who filed claims against the government for back pay and bounty. In December 1869, an effort was made to organize Covington's African American soldiers into a post under the banner of the **Grand Army of the Republic** (GAR). In September 1875, Blackburn was installed as the past noble grand in the Grand Lodge of the United Order of Odd Fellows, No. 1650. The installation took place at Greer's Block in Covington, opposite the site of John G. Carlisle School. On April 2, 1880, Blackburn died and was buried in Linden Grove Cemetery in Covington. On January 3, 1898, the William B. Blackburn Post 43 of the GAR, named in his honor, opened, and the first officers were installed.

"Grand Army Officers," *KP,* January 4, 1898, 1.

—*Theodore H. H. Harris*

BLACK COFFEY (Jason Coffey, b. 1979, Clay Coffey, b. 1981, Lexington, KY), musician brothers. Compared with performers Rick James and George Clinton, Lexington brothers Jason and Clay Coffey combined soul with rhythm and blues and country at the core. They signed with Motown in 2002 and debuted their single, "Country Boyz," in the funk genre. Some of their other recordings include "Rocket Love," "Spill," and "Hard to Get." On October 26, 2002, they appeared on *Soul Train.*

Known for being "well-mannered" and "down-to-earth," the brothers were raised in a musical family milieu and developed their harmonious craft by performing in church and school choirs. Former University of Kentucky basketball player and forward for the Boston Celtics Walter McCarty provided the duo an entrance into the music profession when he invited them to record in Boston. They honed their songwriting and their vocal arrangements there.

Jason equated Kentucky's music industry with the **Underground Railroad** because there had not been an extensive music outlet for new musicians. When asked about the name of their band, Clay answered, "In our family, we always say that coffee grinds down fine and brews deep." He believed that their music did the same: "It grinds down to the essence of soul music and it brews deep, rich and flavorful."

"Kentucky's Hottest R&B and Hip Hop: Black Coffey." http://kyfinest .tripod.com/blackcoffey.html (accessed April 6, 2009).
Rogers, Charles E. "Black Coffey Checks In: RS-One Demands Pay," *New York Amsterdam News,* August 15–August 21, 2002, 27.

—*Sallie L. Powell*

BLACK EXPOS, community entertainment and entrepreneurial fairs held in Owensboro and Louisville. Black expos grew on the national scene in the 1970s, particularly in larger cities like Chicago and Indianapolis. Politicians, athletes, and show-business people were among those who attended. Although these events offered a sense of community, they also provided evidence of African American economic expansion.

In 1937, the ***Louisville Defender*** newspaper originated Kentucky's likely first black expo with a cooking show. The founder of the expo and publisher of the newspaper, **Frank Leslie Stanley Sr.,** died of a heart attack at Louisville's Black Expo in 1974. However, the celebration continued to grow. Business exhibits, auto shows, job fairs, nationally known performers, a talent show, and a gospel show have provided entertainment for more recent expos.

Owensboro began its event in 1973 as a means to soothe racial tensions and help all citizens "reach a new level of sensitivity." In the early years, civil rights activists Rev. Ralph Abernathy and Dick Gregory spoke at Owensboro's Black Expo. Activities currently include a parade, games, music, dances, food, beauty pageants, and Sunday evening worship services. Owensboro's 1989 Black Expo program announced: "We are here celebrating our progress, which is the result of the toil of generations of blacks and their determined fight for equality as citizens of this community."

"Black Expo." *Jet,* December 1971, 64–65.
Newspapers: "Expo Focuses on Heritage of Blacks," *OMI,* August 12, 1989, 1B; "Growing Black Expo Has Unity Heritage," *LCJ,* November 12, 1999, 1B; "A Hot Time Gospel Singing Kicks Off 29th Annual Black Expo," *OMI,* July 9, 2001, 1.

—*Sallie L. Powell*

BLACK SIX, group of African Americans from Louisville indicted for conspiracy to destroy public property, including oil refineries, during a 1968 riot. In 1968, Louisville saw some of its worst race-related violence of the twentieth century. For weeks, tensions had been mounting since the April assassination of Martin Luther King Jr. An incident of police brutality against a black man on May 8 sparked a wave of citywide violence on May 27. Black churches and businesses were bombed, unarmed blacks were beaten and shot (including two black teenagers who

died), white-owned stores were looted and vandalized, and the National Guard was sent to restore order.

After the violence subsided, six black individuals were arrested and charged with conspiracy to blow up oil refineries along the Ohio River and the actual destruction of a cab company and a dry cleaner. Louisville's civil rights community immediately rallied in support of the "Black Six"—Robert Sims, Sam Hawkins, James Cortez, Manfred Reid, Walter "Pete" Crosby, and Ruth Bryant. The West End Community Council (WECC) raised money for their legal defense, and an interracial Ad Hoc Committee for Justice was formed to protest "violations of Constitutional rights in the handling of the case."

After two years of legal delay, the trial finally began in June 1970. During the court proceedings, demonstrations and rallies were held daily, and a black flag was placed on the statue of Thomas Jefferson outside the courthouse. The prosecution initially offered the Black Six a last-minute deal that would have reduced the charges and issued a $50 fine, but all six rejected the deal. The evidence against them was slim. Reid was suspected because he was one of the first African Americans to confront the police after the May incident that triggered the riots, and Cortez publicly promised "trouble" if the abusive officer was not fired. The most egregious charges were against Bryant, who was suspected simply because she donated money to organizations like the WECC. She did not even participate in the riots because she was celebrating her daughter's birthday. It became apparent that there was no conspiracy among the six to damage public property during or after the May riot. After the prosecution rested its case on July 7, 1970, Judge S. Rush Nicholson directed the verdict of not guilty for lack of evidence.

"'Black Six' Freed of Charges; Denounce Witnesses." *Jet,* July 23, 1970, 16.
K'Meyer, Tracy E. *Civil Rights in the Gateway to the South: Louisville, Kentucky, 1945–1980.* Lexington: Univ. Press of Kentucky, 2009.
Newspapers: "6 Blacks Acquitted in Conspiracy Trial," *NYT,* July 8, 1970, 28; "Exhibit Shows Tumult, Success of Open-Housing Movement," *LCJ,* April 1, 2000, 1B; "Inauguration Day: Kentucky Civil-Rights Timeline," *LCJ,* January 20, 2009, 2K; "Unity Dinner to Honor Ruth and Roscoe Bryant," *LCJ,* November 6, 2011, B3.
Williams, Kenneth H. "'Oh Baby . . . It's Really Happening': The Louisville Race Riot of 1968." *Kentucky History Journal* 3 (1988): 48–64.

—*Joshua D. Farrington*

BLUE, THOMAS FOUNTAIN, SR. (b. 1866, Farmville, VA; d. 1935, Louisville, KY), librarian. Born on March 6, 1866, in Farmville, VA, and trained as both a theologian and a librarian, Thomas Fountain Blue established himself as a notable public figure in Kentucky, becoming well respected in civic, religious, and educational circles among blacks. After graduating from Hampton Normal and Agricultural Institute in 1888, Blue briefly taught in his native Virginia before he moved on to earn a bachelor of divinity degree from Richmond Theological Seminary in 1898.

Blue was a pioneer librarian. In 1908, he joined the **Western Colored Branch Library** (WCBL) of Louisville (established in 1905, three years later it became the first Carnegie colored library branch in the country) as its first librarian. He was placed in

Thomas Blue (center, top row) and staff at Louisville Free Public Library Western Branch in Louisville, 1927.

charge of the **Eastern Colored Branch Library** established in Louisville in 1914 and headed the Colored Department of the Louisville Free Public Library, which was created in 1920. Blue established his place in history by being the first colored person to be appointed head of a department in a free public library, as well as the first African American to speak at a meeting of the American Library Association.

Inspired by his vision of training black librarians, Blue conducted annual apprenticeship classes for those willing to join library service. He designed and conducted a library training course for blacks in Louisville and Kentucky at the WCBL, in addition to introducing library science to trainees from Evansville, Houston, Memphis, and Cincinnati, among other cities. This was the first initiative of its kind in the country and represents one of Blue's far-reaching achievements. By introducing the professional field of library science to trainees from around the country, Blue helped shape a new generation of black librarians.

Blue, together with **Rachel Davis Harris,** a children's library specialist and the chief assistant in charge of school and extension work, established the Western and Eastern Colored Branches as community social centers. By 1935, when Blue died, the Louisville Colored Department under his leadership had initiated and administered extension library services in two junior high schools, 15 deposit stations, and 80 classroom collections. This form of outreach service became a model for other libraries in the South and eloquently testifies to Blue's foresight.

Dawson, Alma. "Celebrating African American Librarians and Librarianship." *Library Trends* 49, no. 1 (Summer 2000): 49–87.

Fultz, Michael. "Black Public Libraries in the South in the Era of De Jure Segregation." *Libraries and the Cultural Records* 41, no. 3 (Summer 2006): 337–59.

Van Jackson, W. "Negro Library Workers." *Library Quarterly* 10 (January 1940): 95–108.

—*Ogechi Anyanwu*

BLUES, African American music that indicated an emotional mood and musical style. The blues emerged in mainstream culture in the 1920s. Although it was related to **ragtime** and **jazz,** the blues had its roots in nineteenth-century field songs, church music, and folk expressions of African Americans from the South. The blues is a state of mind through musical expression by melancholy instrumental or vocal performances. By the early twentieth century, the blues spread northward as African Americans from the Deep South migrated to Kentucky and other states, generally to urban settings.

W. C. Handy (1873–1958), known as the Father of the Blues, lived in Henderson, KY, in the 1890s. Otto Zimmerman and Son of Cincinnati printed one of his first blues songs, "Memphis Blues," in 1912. In 1920, Handy published another blues tune, "Long Gone," with lyrics by Chris Smith. It was based on a Kentucky folk song about John Dean, who escaped from a Bowling Green, KY, jail. Arnold Shultz (1886–1931) of western Kentucky influenced a syncopated thumb-picking guitar style that later inspired Bill Monroe, Merle Travis, and other country musicians.

Kentucky urban blues was first documented in audio recordings of the 1920s and 1930s in both Louisville and Cincinnati, more often by songsters and **jug bands** performing a blend of blues, ragtime, and jazz. The Ohio River region of Louisville and northern Kentucky/Cincinnati created a sophisticated blues sound leaning toward urban ensemble performances rather than rural solo blues tradition. Beginning in the 1920s, **Walnut St.** in Louisville replicated the blues-infused Beale St. of Memphis with local artists such as singer **Sarah Martin** (1884–1955) and guitarist **Sylvester Weaver** (1896–1960). On October 24, 1923, Weaver made history when he and Martin recorded "Longing for Daddy Blues" and "I've Got to Go and Leave My Daddy Behind." Weaver became the first blues guitarist to have achieved the distinction of accompanying a singer and recording solo. Martin's popularity peaked nationally during the 1920s when she toured with W. C. Handy and Fats Waller. Weaver and Martin recorded many records together. Weaver was among the earliest black guitarists to record a blues guitar instrumental, titled "Guitar Rag" (1923). Weaver also discovered Louisville native **Helen Humes** (1913–1981), who sang the blues as well as other styles from big band to pop standards. After World War II, the Morgan Brothers Band and singer **Mary Ann Fisher** (1923–2004) performed blues at the Orchard Bar on Ninth St. in Louisville.

Many Cincinnati blues artists either were born in northern Kentucky or performed on both sides of the river. They included Jesse James, who resided in northern Kentucky and performed blues numbers such as "Southern Casey Jones" and "Lonesome Day Blues." Northern Kentucky also served as a performing venue for some renowned rhythm and blues (R&B) artists of King Records in Cincinnati. In 1948, sophisticated blues guitarist Lonnie Johnson (1900–1970) recorded his instrumental "Tomorrow Night," while that same year R&B singer Wynonie Harris (1915–1969) recorded "Good Rocking Tonight" at King Records, considered by some the birth of rock and roll. Other King Records blues artists included Bull Moose Jackson, Roy Brown, Little Willie John, Bill Doggett, Earl Bostic, and the legendary James Brown.

As rock music fans of the 1970s rediscovered the blues, Albert Washington, James "Pigmeat" Jarrett, and Ed Conley (all born or raised in northern Kentucky) performed the blues in the Cincinnati region. Big Joe Duskin (1921–2007), famous for his boogie-woogie piano blues numbers, such as "Cincinnati Stomp," got his start performing in both Newport and Cincinnati in his youth and gained international fame later.

Live blues performances resonated frequently in Louisville at Joe's Palm Room and annually at the Garvin Gate Blues Festival. The Southgate House and Chez Nora music clubs in northern Kentucky offer an eclectic blend of music, including blues.

Kentucky hosts several blues festivals. The W. C. Handy Blues Barbecue Festival in Henderson, the Garvin Gate Blues Festival in downtown Louisville, and the Hot August Blues Festival near Lake Kentucky at the Kenlake State Resort Park have all attracted large followings.

Bastin, Bruce. *Red River Blues: The Blues Tradition in the Southeast.* Urbana: Univ. of Illinois Press, 1986.

Cohn, Lawrence. *Nothing but the Blues: The Music and the Musicians.* New York: Abbeville Press, 1993.

Oliver, Paul. *Songsters and Saints: Vocal Traditions on Race Records.* Cambridge: Cambridge Univ. Press, 1984.

Russell, Tony. *The Blues—From Robert Johnson to Robert Cray.* New York: Schirmer Books, 1997.

"Sylvester Weaver—First Person to Record Blues Guitar." http://www.kentuckybluessociety.com/kentucky-blues-history/sylvester-weaver-first-person-to-record-blues-guitar/ (accessed August 15, 2013).

Tracy, Steven C. *Going to Cincinnati: A History of the Blues in the Queen City.* Urbana: Univ. of Illinois Press, 1993.

Wolfe, Charles K. *Kentucky Country: Folk and Country Music of Kentucky.* Lexington: Univ. Press of Kentucky, 1996.

—*John Schlipp*

BLYEW V. UNITED STATES (1871), **case in which the U.S. Supreme Court upheld a state's right to forbid African Americans to testify against whites.** On August 29, 1868, white men John Blyew and George Kennard entered the family home of Jack and Sallie Foster, African Americans in Lewis Co., KY. An argument ensued when the Foster family refused to house "a female kept by Kennard and Blyew." Blyew first struck the Fosters' 16-year-old son, Richard, with an ax. With multiple ax blows, the enraged Blyew and Kennard killed Jack, Sallie, and a blind nonagenarian family member, Lucy Armstrong, and seriously injured the couple's two young daughters, Laura and Amelia. After regaining consciousness, Richard managed to seek help from a neighbor. He provided a sworn and signed statement charging Blyew and Kennard with the massacre before he died of his injuries. The older daughter, Laura, suffering from a head gash, also identified the attackers. On the basis of the testimonies and the hard evidence of boot prints and the bloody ax, John Blyew and George Kennard were arrested for the murders of the four Foster family members.

Kentucky law, however, forbade African Americans and Native Americans to testify against white defendants. The case was then moved to federal court, where both men were found guilty and sentenced to hang. Some Kentucky Democrats opposed federal intervention in the case; therefore, in January 1869, Governor John W. Stevenson, a Democrat, requested that Kentucky's General Assembly provide financial appropriations to take the case to the U.S. Supreme Court. The Supreme Court first had to determine whether the federal court had jurisdiction in the case. Claiming that the **Civil Rights Act of 1866** was "not to be considered as 'affecting' mere witnesses in the case, nor any person not in existence," the Supreme Court resolved that only living persons could have requested the change of venue. After deliberating for almost a year, in April 1872, with Justices Noah Swayne and Joseph Bradley dissenting, the Supreme Court reversed the lower federal court's decision and required the state of Kentucky to judge the indictment of Blyew and Kennard. *Blyew v. United States* has been viewed as drastically weakening any prospect of a successful Reconstruction and "the first blow to the use of the Thirteenth Amendment for ending centuries of racial intolerance."

Blyew v. United States, 80 U.S. 581 (1871). http://supreme.justia.com/cases/federal/us/80/581/ (accessed April 17, 2009).

Howard, Victor B. "The Black Testimony Controversy in Kentucky, 1866–1872." *JNH* 58, no. 2 (April 1973): 140–65.

Newspapers: "Civil Rights Case in Kentucky," *NYT,* October 12, 1868, 2; "Five Men in Jail under Conviction for Murder," *NYT,* April 28, 1869, 11; "After Twenty-Two Years," *NYT,* December 14, 1890, 1.

Tsesis, Alexander. *The Thirteenth Amendment and American Freedom.* New York: New York Univ. Press, 2004, 64–67.

Ubertaccio, Peter N., III. *Learned in the Law and Politics: The Office of the Solicitor General and Executive Power.* New York: LFB Scholarly Publishing, 2005, 31–32.

—*Sallie L. Powell*

BOBTOWN, African American community in Madison Co., KY. Originally known as Joe Lick, the Madison Co. community of Bobtown was founded 12 miles south of Richmond, KY, around 1769. When African Americans were able to buy land after the Civil War, the neighborhood was renamed Bobtown in honor of an African American resident named "Uncle" Bob Fitch. Like many similar communities, a church, a school, and a store offered an important connection between the residents and the institutions that served them. Bobtown also had "a fair-sized cemetery" by the late nineteenth century.

The New Liberty Baptist Church was established in 1866. Born a slave to a white Baptist preacher, Rev. Thomas H. Broaddus pastored this church along with several other area churches. Broaddus was known as a gifted speaker and singer. In July 1904, Bobtown's Sunday school joined other area Sunday schools for a Grand Sunday School Rally and Children's Day celebration. Nearly 500 people attended the gathering to enjoy children reciting scripture verses.

Bobtown residents often had box suppers in order to raise funds for the church's Sunday school and for the public school, a one-room building built about 1865. On one occasion in December 1902, they earned enough money to buy a Christmas tree for the Sunday school even though they were harassed by "bushwhackers" who damaged "harness and bridles" while people were enjoying the food and fun. Decades later, the New Liberty Baptist Church held these "basket rallies" on the second Sunday in August, when people "brought bushel baskets" of food.

In the early 1950s, the Ladies Aid Club of the New Liberty Baptist Church helped raise money by having a baby contest. William "Hap" Baxter, the Sunday school superintendent and church janitor, was the only male member of the club. He drove the women to various homes for their meetings.

Bobtown's African American and white elementary schools were located across the street from each other. With school merging in the 1930s, African American students were bused to Middletown Consolidated School and Richmond High School. The white children were bused to a grade school and high school in Kingston.

Bobtown provided opportunities for entrepreneurs. The railroad industry was the biggest employer of African Americans. Agriculture also played a major role in the community. African American and white farmers often helped one another in tough times. Tobacco, pigs, and cattle provided major income sources.

The Bobtown influence spread from the local to the international level in World War II. Fount Mundy and his cousin, Sam Cornelison, not only served in the same military unit but also survived the war. These men and their families were active members of the New Liberty Baptist Church.

This rural hamlet initially experienced community through near isolation because of difficult traveling options, which limited access to other businesses and towns. The life of the citizens centered on the Bobtown institutions. This community offered various opportunities for social and cultural interaction between the races.

Burnside, Jacqueline Grisby. *Berea and Madison County.* Charleston, SC: Arcadia, 2007.
Engle, Fred A., and Robert N. Grise. *Madison's Heritage.* Richmond, KY: AA Printing Co., 1985.
Newspapers: "Kingston," *Richmond Climax,* December 3, 1902, 2; "Berea and Vicinity," *Berea Citizen,* July 21, 1904, 6.

—*Sallie L. Powell*

BOND, FREDERICK F. "FRED" (b. 1930, Louisville, KY; d. 1986, Louisville, KY), artist. Described as a thin man with an elegant goatee and perpetual cigarette smoking, Frederick F. Bond was born the third son of Thomas and Louise Bond. His father worked as a public school teacher in Louisville. Bond believed that Louisville African American artists like himself were like "the Good Fairy" because they "would run around and do good things and then disappear." Following his mentor, **Gloucester Caliman "G. C." Coxe,** Bond worked to assist African American artists in locating places to display their work. Bond joined with other artisans in launching Louisville's St. James Court Art Festival in the mid-1950s. In 1966, Bond, Coxe, an abstract painter, and sculptor **Edward Hamilton Jr.** established the Louisville Art Workshop, located on Main St. This organization offered the Louisville downtown community a vibrant and engaging cultural venue. Bond directed the Louisville Art Workshop from 1965 to 1973 and frequently supported it financially.

Bond initially contacted the Cincinnati Arts Consortium on 1515 Linn St. to show his own work. He ultimately served as its executive director from 1976 to 1983. In this capacity, he aspired to take the former Kroger Store building to an appealing conception that would meet the community's cultural needs and present the unheard voices of African Americans. In a 1977 interview, he posited that African American artists sought healthy competition and battled for serious respect in the creative media. His own experiences had taught him that his skills as a ceramic sculptor had to be revamped so he could become a painter for the conservative Louisville audience. Since he felt forced to compromise his artistic preferences, he maintained that the art world forced African American artists into working as "gallery slaves," and he compared their lives to "sharecropping." After his death in 1986, the Cincinnati Arts Consortium memorialized Bond by naming a gallery in his honor.

"Bonding Together." *Cincinnati Magazine,* June 1977, 59–61.
Dunnigan, Alice Allison, comp. and ed. *The Fascinating Story of Black Kentuckians: Their Heritage and Traditions.* Washington, DC: Associated Publishers, 1982.
Newspapers: "Neo-ancestralists Open Renamed Fred Bond Gallery," *CP,* February 6, 1995, 3B; "Legacy Isn't in His Work but in How He Nurtured," *LCJ,* July 27, 1999, 1C.

—*Sallie L. Powell*

BOND, HENRY (b. 1865, Anderson Co., KY; d. 1929, Williamsburg, KY), educator and law specialist. Henry Bond was a member of the second generation of the Bond family, an African American family committed to education. The matriarch was Aunt Jane, a former slave of mixed-blood ancestry. The father of her two sons, James and Henry, was Rev. Preston Bond, a white Methodist minister. Henry, the youngest, was born a free person in 1865. His formal education began at an all-black school in Anderson Co. Then, like his older brother, **James M. Bond,** Henry left home with his mother's approval and walked along the Old Wilderness Road to attend high school and college at **Berea College.**

In 1881, Bond arrived at Berea and enrolled in the Normal Preparatory division; however, he did not graduate from the college. During his tenure at Berea, his mother, aunt, and uncle moved to Williamsburg, KY, in Whitley Co. Henry left Berea College and joined the family. In Williamsburg, he met and married Anna Lee Gibson, a former resident of Berea. In order to better support his and Anna's family of nine children, Bond left Williamsburg for other opportunities, but he always returned.

Bond had two occupations: "reading law" and teaching. He did not graduate from college; thus he could not earn a law degree. However, in accordance with the practice of the time, he read the law for a local judge and eventually opened a law office. Although Bond was respected by local whites, he was still an African American living in the **Jim Crow** era in a southern state. Any major cases were submitted to white attorneys to avoid offending the sensibilities of whites.

Bond was more successful as an educator. He was the principal and only teacher at Williamsburg's Colored Academy. Despite his two professions, money was a constant problem for Henry and Anna and their nine children; still, they made tremendous sacrifices to help the children achieve their educational goals. All nine earned degrees: "Five of them went on to earn M.A.s, and two became physicians."

Henry Bond died of tuberculosis on January 6, 1929. He was buried in Williamsburg's Briar Creek Cemetery. Ironically, James, his older brother, died nine days later in Louisville of a heart attack while reading the newspaper.

Kentucky Commission on Human Rights. *Kentucky's Black Heritage: The Role of the Black People in the History of Kentucky from Pioneer Days to the Present.* Frankfort: Kentucky Commission on Human Rights, 1971.
Kentucky Death Records, 1852–1953.
Williams, Roger M. *The Bonds: An American Family.* New York: Atheneum, 1971.

—*Andrew Baskin*

BOND, HORACE MANN (b. 1904, Nashville, TN; d. 1972, DeKalb Co., GA), educator. The influence of Horace Mann Bond, a member of the third generation of the Bond family, transcended the borders of Kentucky. The youngest male of **James M. Bond** and Jane Bond's six children continued the legacy of the family matriarch, his grandmother, Aunt Jane, a former slave of mixed-blood ancestry who instilled the importance of education in her descendants.

Bond was a prodigy. He could read at age 3, entered high school at age 9, and graduated at the age of 14 from **Lincoln Institute** in Shelby Co., KY. He graduated cum laude with a BA degree from Lincoln University in Pennsylvania in 1923. Bond worked as an administrator at different colleges while pursuing graduate work at the University of Chicago. He earned an MA in 1926 and a PhD in sociology in 1936. His dissertation won the prestigious Rosenberger Prize as the outstanding work in the division of social sciences at the University of Chicago in 1936.

Bond was an excellent scholar. He used empirical evidence to reveal the effects of political disfranchisement and economic exploitation on academic performance in order to counter the accepted theory that intelligence testing demonstrated the innate racial inferiority of African Americans. Like W. E. B. DuBois, Bond was a vanguard in challenging the conventional interpretation of Reconstruction and the behavior of the Ku Klux Klan and other "redeemers" of the South.

As president of Fort Valley State College in Ft. Valley, GA (1939–1945), and Lincoln University in Pennsylvania (1945–1957), Bond faced the task of keeping white politicians and philanthropists happy while attacking segregation indirectly. He did not recommend abolishing segregation; he advocated equal funding. At both institutions, he was successful. In 1939, Fort Valley was a junior college but had evolved into a baccalaureate college 10 years later. At Lincoln, he pursued the development of African studies, increased the number of African American faculty, hired a Jewish faculty member, and improved the curriculum and physical facilities. He also provided assistance to the legal team that argued the *Brown v. Board of Education* case. Nonetheless, Bond was forced out of office in 1957. This action was believed to have occurred because of Bond's activism and the unwillingness of many whites (faculty, staff, and trustees) to accept an African American as president.

From 1957 to 1971, Bond was the dean of the School of Education at Atlanta University in Atlanta, GA. Bond married Julia Agnes Washington in 1929. They had three children: Jane Margaret, Horace Julian, and James. He died in Atlanta on December 21, 1972. Horace Julian Bond is better known as Julian Bond, a civil rights activist and politician of the late twentieth and early twenty-first centuries.

Bond, Horace M., and Julia W. Bond. *The Star Creek Papers.* Edited by Adam Fairclough. Athens: Univ. of Georgia Press, 1992.
Kentucky's Black Heritage: The Role of the Black People in the History of Kentucky from Pioneer Days to the Present. Frankfort: Kentucky Commission on Human Rights, 1971.
Urban, Wayne J. *Black Scholar: Horace Mann Bond, 1904–1972.* Athens: Univ. of Georgia Press, 1992.
Williams, Roger M. *The Bonds: An American Family.* New York: Atheneum, 1971.

—*Andrew Baskin*

BOND, J. (JAMES) MAX, JR. (b. 1935, Louisville, KY; d. 2009, New York, NY), architect and educator. Internationally known architect J. Max Bond Jr. entered Harvard University at age 16 and soon encountered the racist act of a cross burned in his dormitory's yard. A Harvard white professor met his decision to enter the architecture profession with the recommendation that he enter another vocation. His parents wanted him to be a doctor and had secured him a job as a hospital orderly in Louisville. Despite various challenges, Bond could not deny his interest in architecture, which began when he was a child living in Tuskegee, where his father, **J. Max Bond Sr.,** taught at the Tuskegee Institute. After earning his master's degree in architecture at Harvard in 1958, Bond furthered his skills abroad, particularly in Tunisia, France, and Ghana. His first creation, the Bolgatanga Regional Library in Ghana, was designed to incorporate natural ventilation, thus eliminating the need for air conditioning.

When Bond returned to the United States in the late 1960s, he led the Architects Renewal Committee of Harlem. One of its programs, Architecture in the Neighborhoods, taught technical skills to precollege African American and Puerto Rican students who expressed interest in architecture. As a partner in various architecture firms throughout the years, Bond developed designs for projects such as the Martin Luther King Jr. Center for Nonviolent Social Change in Atlanta, including King's crypt; the Schomburg Center for Research in Black Culture in Harlem; the Birmingham Civil Rights Institute in Alabama; and the **Kentucky Center for African American Heritage** in Louisville.

From 1980 to 1986, Bond worked on the New York City Planning Commission and was chairperson of the architecture division at the Columbia University Graduate School of Architecture and Planning from 1980 to 1984. He served from 1985 to 1992 as the dean of the School of Architecture and Environmental Studies at City College of the City University of New York. In 2003, the Lower Manhattan Development Corporation selected the architecture firm Davis Brody Bond, led by J. Max Bond Jr., for the World Trade Center memorial project.

Bond asserted that "architecture is power to transmit a culture's symbols, its politics." After a battle with cancer, he died on February 18, 2009. He was survived by his wife, Jean Carey Bond, and their children, Ruth M. Bond and Carey Julian Bond.

Newspapers: "Negro Architects Helping Harlem Plan Its Future," *NYT,* March 16, 1969, 57; "Breaking Molds, and Then Designing New Ones," *NYT,* April 21, 2004, B2; "Blueprint of a Life: Architect J. Max Bond Jr. Has Had to Build Bridges to Reach Ground Zero," *WP,* July 1, 2004, C1; "J. Max Bond Jr., Architect, Dies at 73," *NYT,* February 19, 2009, A20.

—*Sallie L. Powell*

BOND, J. MAX, SR. (b. 1902, Nashville, TN; d. 1991, Washington, DC), founder and president of the first state university of Liberia, West Africa. Born Maxwell Henry Bond to Rev. **James M. Bond** and Jane Bond, J. Max, as he later became known, served as the director of the Kentucky Interracial Commission from 1928 to 1931. As an active participant in the **Kentucky Negro Educational Association,** he pressed for legislation pertinent to Kentucky African American education. In 1930, as the president of the Kentucky Athletic Association, he worked to organize sponsorship of a statewide basketball tournament and track meet for Kentucky African American schools.

In 1936, Bond received a PhD in sociology from the University of Southern California with his thesis, "The Negro in Los Angeles." He served as dean of Dillard University, New Orleans, LA (1938–1940), dean of the School of Education, Tuskegee Institute, Alabama (1940–1944), U.S. State Department representative to the Inter-American Education Foundation and director of a teaching project in Port-au-Prince, Haiti (1944–1947), and dean of the School of Education at Atlanta University, Georgia (1947–1950). In 1950, he returned to work for the State Department and was sent to Monrovia, Liberia, where he helped establish and served as president of the first state university in Liberia until

1954. He then joined the International Cooperation Administration and worked as an adviser on international education missions in Afghanistan, Tunisia, Sierra Leone, and Malawi until his retirement in 1966.

Bond wrote a myriad of articles on African American education and particularly challenged the education system "to free the minds of children and adults from the American psychosis of racial hate and all of its attendant evils." He died of cancer on December 15, 1991, and was survived by his wife, Ruth Elizabeth Clement Bond, and his children, Jane Emma Bond, **J. Max Bond, Jr.,** and George Clement Bond.

Bond, J. Max. "Educational Programs for the Improvement of Race Relations: The Schools." *Journal of Negro Education* 13, no. 3 (Summer 1944): 390–97.
Dunnigan, Alice Allison, comp. and ed. *The Fascinating Story of Black Kentuckians: Their Heritage and Traditions.* Washington, DC: Associated Publishers, 1982.
Fleming, G. James, and Christian E. Burckel, eds. *Who's Who in Colored America.* 7th ed. *Supplement.* Yonkers-on Hudson, NY: Christian E. Burckel & Associates, 1950.
"K.N.E.A. Officers, April 1930 to April 1931." *KNEAJ* 1, no. 1 (October 1930): 2.
Newspapers: "Letters to the Times—Liberia's Government," *NYT,* July 1, 1951, 96; "J. Max Bond Sr., 89, an American Who Headed Liberian University," *NYT,* December 18, 1991, D23; "J. Max Bond Sr., 89, Dies—Helped Found U. of Liberia," *WP,* December 18, 1991, C13.

—*Sallie L. Powell*

BOND, JAMES M. (b. 1863, Lawrenceburg, KY; d. 1929, Louisville, KY), educator and minister. James M. Bond was born into slavery in Lawrenceburg, KY, on September 5, 1863. His mother, Jane, a younger brother, **Henry Bond,** and he were owned by Preston Bond. Shortly after the Bonds' emancipation in 1865, they moved to Barbourville, KY, where James was raised. In the early 1880s, he enrolled in **Berea College,** paying for his tuition with money from selling a young steer that he led for 75 miles from home. At Berea, he was employed as a bell ringer and janitor. When he graduated in 1892, Bond was one of only 2,000 blacks in the United States to have a college diploma. Three years later, he completed a divinity degree at Oberlin College in Ohio. At Oberlin, he met and married Jane Brown; they had four children. The Bonds moved to Birmingham, AL, and then to Nashville, TN; in Nashville, Bond served as pastor of the Howard Congregational Church. In 1896, Bond was elected a trustee of Berea College and received a doctor of divinity degree from Berea in 1901.

When Kentucky's 1904 **Day Law** compelled Berea to separate black and white students, the college established **Lincoln Institute** for blacks near Simpsonville. In 1906, Berea hired Bond to raise funds for the new school. Bond also was a member of the first governing board of the institute. Despite Bond's difficulties in working with Berea's president, William Goodell Frost (he once asserted to Frost that the president did not understand Negroes), he and another black Berea alumnus, Kirke Smith, conducted a successful fund-raising campaign, and Lincoln Institute

James M. Bond.

opened in 1912. Shortly thereafter, Bond took his family to Atlanta but eventually settled in Louisville.

Bond attempted to volunteer for the army but was rejected because of his age. During the war, he was YMCA service director at Camp Zachary Taylor near Louisville; afterward, he was the first director of the Kentucky YMCA for blacks. In 1926, he was the Kentucky delegate to the YMCA convention in Finland. Also, he was the first director of the newly formed Kentucky Commission on Interracial Cooperation, later the **Kentucky Council on Human Relations.** He traveled the state widely, promoting civil rights for blacks and encouraging interracial harmony. He facilitated a compromise in Louisville that established Chickasaw Park for blacks and Shawnee Park for whites. Bond died on January 15, 1929, and was buried in the Louisville Cemetery.

Williams, Roger M. *The Bonds: An American Family.* New York: Atheneum, 1971.
Wilson, Shannon H. *Berea College: An Illustrated History.* Lexington: Univ. Press of Kentucky, 2006.

—*Paul David Nelson*

BOND-WASHINGTON SCHOOL, elementary and high school in Elizabethtown, KY. In 1869, the trustees of the African School of Elizabethtown purchased land for $150. The new school opened in 1888. On June 2, 1920, the Elizabethtown Board of Education authorized a nine-month-term school for African Americans in a three-room building. The principal, A. L. Poole, was paid $85 a month; the first assistant, Mrs. A. L. Poole, received $75 a month; and the second assistant, Miss Nannie Board, earned $75 a month. In 1923, after moving to a new building funded by the local African American community and the Julius Rosenwald Fund, the school was named East Side High School. Black students trekked to this school from Hardin and Larue Counties because there were no African American schools in their communities. One former student, Carlton Best, remembered paying $3.96 a month for a round-trip train fare to the school.

In 1925, **Robert L. Dowery Sr.,** former Taylor County Training and High School principal and later president of the **Kentucky Negro Education Association,** became principal of East Side High School. In 1928, he proposed renaming the school Bond-Washington Graded and High School in honor of Dr. **James M. Bond,** minister, fund-raiser for the **Lincoln Institute,** and secretary of the Kentucky African American YMCA, and Booker T. Washington, the founder of Tuskegee Institute.

By 1935, the school also offered adult education classes and a nursery school. George W. Adams served as principal from 1935 to 1937. In November 1936, he made an appeal to the local white board of education to use the white high school's (Elizabethtown) gymnasium since the Bond-Washington girls' and boys' basketball teams were playing on a dirt court. The board agreed on the following conditions: only African American people were admitted into the games, Bond-Washington School would furnish all its own equipment, and the players had to dress at Bond-Washington School.

The school served as a major resource in the community. It sheltered some Louisville residents during the flood of 1937. Children of African American World War II military personnel were educated at Bond-Washington School since the all-white school on the Ft. Knox post did not admit them; and the school was used as a center for entertainment for African American troops.

Bond-Washington was a high school until 1956 and remained an elementary school until 1959, when the local schools were integrated. The school building served as a community center and then was closed.

Kentucky Historical Markers. "Bond-Washington School." http://www.waymarking.com/waymarks/WM917 (accessed April 23, 2009).
Robinson, Lottie Offett. *The Bond-Washington Story: The Education of Black People, Elizabethtown, Kentucky.* N.p.: Self-published, 1983.

—*Sallie L. Powell*

BOOKER T. WASHINGTON SCHOOLS, educational institutions established in several Kentucky cities in honor of the noted African American educator. Born a slave in Virginia, Booker T. Washington became a prominent educator and fund-raiser, as well as the leading African American spokesperson on various issues pertaining to the black race. As president of Tuskegee Institute in Alabama in the late nineteenth and early twentieth centuries, he conversed with U.S. presidents, white philanthropists, and business leaders of both races to promote African American interests. By the time he died in 1915, he had left an indelible mark on American history.

Throughout the South, a number of elementary and high schools were named in honor of Washington before and after he died. In Kentucky, schools named after Washington were erected in Ashland, Hopkinsville, Lexington, Louisville, and Winchester. The Booker T. Washington School in Ashland opened in 1903. As of 1931, this school included grades 1 through 12 and enrolled 186 students. Although the high school department was not yet accredited, the school housed a variety of extracurricular activities that included football and basketball teams, a Boys Hi-Y Club, and a Girls Reserve Club.

On September 11, 1916, a school named for Washington was opened in Lexington on Georgetown St. Out of a large number of entries, the board of education selected sign painter and songwriter Edward Clifton's suggestion to name the school for Washington. The school began with 216 students, but this number increased to 385 by 1954. The first principal was Paul Vernon Smith (1916–1935). He was followed by his wife, **Lucy Harth Smith,** who eventually served a term as president of the **Kentucky Negro Educational Association** and was active in the promotion of African American history.

Like other segregated schools, Booker T. Washington schools served as symbols of black pride, progress, and achievement. They were beacons in the African American community that encouraged black students to strive for excellence in education. The name of the school itself gave African American children an example of African American leadership. After the ***Brown v. Board of Education*** decision of 1954, most of these schools were closed as a result of desegregation. The Booker T. Washington School in Lexington was eventually relocated not far from its original site. It has served as a Montessori magnet school and more recently was designated an academy.

"Blue Grass of Kentucky." *IF,* May 6, 1916, 4.
"The Booker T. Washington School at Ashland." *KNEAJ* 1, no. 4 (April 1931): 21.
Kentucky Education Collection. Series I, folder Booker T. Washington. Univ. of Kentucky Special Collections.

—*Gerald L. Smith*

BOSWELL, ARNITA YOUNG (b. 1920, Detroit, MI; d. 2002, Los Angeles, CA), civil rights activist and professor of social work at the University of Chicago. Born into one of Kentucky's premier African American families, Arnita Young grew up in a home that valued education. Her father, **Whitney M. Young Sr.,** was president of **Lincoln Institute,** and her mother, **Laura Ray Young,** was the first Kentucky African American postmaster. Her younger siblings were civil rights advocate **Whitney M. Young Jr.** and educator **Eleanor Young Love.** Young earned her bachelor's degree in home economics from Kentucky State College (later named **Kentucky State University**) and a master's in social work from Atlanta University. She joined the American Red Cross and served as a recreation director for soldiers stationed in Germany during World War II. When she returned stateside, she worked as a social worker with the Red Cross, and a member of the **Tuskegee Airmen** at Fisk University in Tennessee trained her to fly.

In 1953, Young married dermatologist Dr. Paul Boswell, who died in 1982. She was a social work professor at the University of Chicago from 1961 to 1980. In 1966, she directed the women's division of a large civil rights demonstration in Chicago led by Dr. Martin Luther King Jr.

During the fourth Congressional Black Caucus Legislative Weekend in 1974, she founded the National Hook-up of Black Women, which was a support base for African American female activists. She continued her service to others in the 1980s as manager of social services for families with special-needs children at the University of Illinois at Chicago and the director of the Family Resource Center in Chicago's Department of Human Services. She founded the Chicago League of Black Women and the Woman's Board of the Chicago Urban League and was the first national director of Project Head Start.

Two years after Boswell's death, Chicago renamed Chokeberry Park Arnita Young Boswell Park in her honor. Through National Hook-up of Black Women, Brooklyn Technical High School bestows five $1,000 awards on accomplished African American students with the Arnita Young Boswell Scholarship Program.

Dunnigan, Alice Allison, comp. and ed. *The Fascinating Story of Black Kentuckians: Their Heritage and Traditions.* Washington, DC: Associated Publishers, 1982.
National Hook-up of Black Women, Inc. http://www.nhbwinc.com /history.htm (accessed April 27, 2009).
Newspapers: "Woman Who Helped King Lead March to Talk at Lunch," *Chicago Tribune,* January 14, 1996, 2; "Arnita Young Boswell, 82—Civil Rights Activist, Social Worker," *Chicago Tribune,* July 11, 2002, 9.

—*Sallie L. Powell*

BOTTS, HENRY (b. 1859, Bath Co., KY; d. 1946, Mt. Sterling, KY), city council representative and undertaker. According to his death certificate, Henry Botts was the son of Joseph Sunthimer and Caroline Botts. His mother was a free mulatto in Bath Co. as early as 1850. Thirty years later, Botts was literate, worked as a farmer, was married to Lucy, and had two daughters. His younger brother, Robert, lived with them, while his mother lived with a granddaughter nearby.

By 1890, Botts had moved to Mt. Sterling in Montgomery Co., KY. Seven years later, he had married his second wife, Sarah, a teacher. By 1900, he operated Montgomery Grocery Company with his partner, Peter Hensley. The grocery was noted for its superior coffee, along with seasonal fruits.

In November 1901, Botts and James E. Bean became Mt. Sterling's first African American officeholders when they were elected to the city council. However, in 1893, Walter Banks, a teacher, had been elected to the city council but had not been allowed to hold the position because he had been declared an unqualified voter. Botts's wife, Sarah, died one year after the election. In 1904, he married his third wife, Emma.

In August 1905, Montgomery Co. Republicans nominated Botts for coroner, which resulted in public outrage. The *Clay City Times* proclaimed that "the negro question" had "killed the Republican party" and that Montgomery Co.'s straight-party Republican voters faced a dilemma with Botts on the ticket. Botts immediately declined the nomination in a letter in the local newspaper. The *Clay City Times* quickly praised Botts for his decision.

The news of Botts's refusal reached as far as Spokane, WA. Nevertheless, he continued to serve on the city council.

Botts then joined Aquilla Marshall, a cabinetmaker, in the funeral business. In August 1907, he was elected sergeant-at-arms of the Colored Undertakers' Association of Kentucky. The organization in that meeting agreed to appeal to the white Falls City Undertakers Association not to provide burial arrangements for any African Americans since African American undertakers were not allowed to bury white people.

Botts continued to be reelected to the Mt. Sterling City Council and at times was unopposed. In December 1919, he retired from public office. Four years later, one of his legs was amputated below the knee. However, he continued to work in the funeral business as Botts and Son. He also served as an election officer for Mt. Sterling's Third Ward. He died at age 87 in 1946. His son, Gunoa Hensley Botts, and later his grandson, Gunoa H. Botts, also became undertakers.

Boyd, Carl B., Jr., and Hazel Mason Boyd. *A History of Mt. Sterling, Kentucky, 1792–1918*. Mt. Sterling, KY: C. B. Boyd, Jr., 1984.

Civil War Pension Index: General Index to Pension Files, 1861–1934.

Kentucky Death Records, 1852–1953.

Newspapers: untitled article, *Mt. Sterling Advocate,* November 5, 1901, 2; "Republicans in Convention" and "Notice," *Mt. Sterling Advocate,* August 30, 1905, 1, 3; "The Negro and Politics," *Clay City Times,* August 31, 1905, 2; untitled article, *Clay City Times,* September 7, 1905, 2; "Want All Negro Funerals," *IF,* August 10, 1907, 1; "Retired Councilmen," *Mt. Sterling Advocate,* December 22, 1919, 17.

U.S. Civil War Soldier Records and Profiles.

U.S. Federal Census (1860, 1870, 1880, 1900, 1910, 1920, 1930, 1940).

—*Sallie L. Powell*

BOURGARD, CAROLINE B. (b. 1862, Cannelton, IN; d. 1928, Louisville, KY), music teacher. Caroline B. Bourgard was born on June 23, 1862. After graduation from Louisville Girls High School in 1879, she continued her studies at colleges of music in Louisville, Cincinnati, Chicago, and New York City.

Bourgard was connected to Louisville's public schools for nearly 40 years. She started her career as a music teacher and in 1892 became the first public school supervisor of music. In 1908, she founded the first Louisville Music Teachers' Association and in 1916 the State Music Teachers' Association. In 1921, Bourgard established the first Louisville Women's Chorus and was a chairman of the Music Week programs held in Louisville under Mayor Huston Quin from 1921 to 1925. In 1923, she was appointed state director of music and held the post until her resignation because of ill health. Bourgard initiated a bill in the General Assembly making singing a required subject in public schools.

In 1927, Bourgard helped found the first art college in Louisville for African American children at the **Phillis Wheatley YWCA.** She personally supervised the work there and secured good instructors for talented black students, who were able to study various art disciplines. In 1928, that college of music and art, which bears Bourgard's name, moved to a new location at 2503 W. **Walnut St.** (now **Muhammad Ali** Blvd.). She left the college an endowment.

Bourgard was an organist at Highland Presbyterian Church. She was the author of *Woman's Song Reader, Child's Song Reader No. 1, A Manual of Music and Outlines for Teachers*, and *Book of Health Songs*, which she dedicated to the children of Kentucky. Bourgard died on August 3, 1928, and is buried in Cave Hill Cemetery.

Louisville Library Collections. Vol. 3. Louisville, KY: 1940.

Newspapers: *LCJ,* August 4, 1928; *LCJ,* August 5, 1928; *LCJ,* August 8, 1928.

Who's Who in Louisville. Louisville, KY: Standard Printing Company, 1926.

BOWLING GREEN ACADEMY, African American school in Bowling Green, KY. Bowling Green Academy was a small private high school offering multilevel African American education in Bowling Green, KY. The Kentucky Synod of the Cumberland Presbyterian Church (Colored) directed the school. As early as the school year of 1888–1889, the Synod operated the "Bowling Green Colored School." In October 1902, the Bowling Green Academy under the supervision of the Synod started with one student; its stated mission was the education of Kentucky's African American children, especially young men who wished to become ministers. It was incorporated in 1904. The Rev. R. L. Hyde, a graduate of the Agricultural and Mechanical College of Alabama (now Alabama A & M University), was the first president. The classes were held in the local church, where Hyde preached.

However, enrollment by the third year soon grew to 130, and a new building was purchased through interracial cooperation in the community. The two-story, nine-room brick building was located at 229 State St. The school was praised for its "prosperous condition and safe, conservative management." The academy offered rigorous training in theology, industrial arts, college preparation, and intermediate, primary, and normal education, as well as music instruction, both vocal and instrumental. The faculty consisted of eight teachers who believed that the mission of the school was "threefold, (1) education in general of all Negro children, especially in Kentucky, (2) education along special lines which shall fit our young men to fill more efficiently the pulpits of our churches, (3) to develop the Negro youth into good Christian citizens by educating the head, heart and hand."

Many of the students worked for their room and board as domestic help for local families, with their days starting at 5:30 a.m. and ending at 10:00 p.m. They worked in this manner for over 10 years as they went through the entire program of study. In 1904, the room, board, and tuition fee was set at $7.00 per month, and housing was provided for the female students of the academy in a 14-room home across the street that at one time had belonged to a prominent Bowling Green family. Very strict standards of moral conduct were required of the students; profanity, betting, gambling, and the use of any intoxicants were forbidden. In 1918, ownership of the school was transferred to the Board of Missions for Freedmen, Presbyterian Church in the U.S.A. The academy was renamed the Presbyterian Negro Academy, Bowling Green, and continued in operation on the college level until it closed in 1933.

Cumberland Presbyterian Church in America. "Bowling Green Academy." Cordova, TN, 2009. http://www.cumberland.org/hfcpc//cpca/bgacadem.htm (accessed April 22, 2009).

Gibson, H. A. "First Annual Report of the Bowling Green Colored School." Annual Report of the Board of Mission as found in the Minutes of the General Assembly of the Cumberland Presbyterian Church, 1889, 62–63.

Gore, Matthew Henry. *A History of the Cumberland Presbyterian Church in Kentucky to 1988.* Memphis, TN Joint Heritage Committee of Covenant and Cumberland Presbyteries, 2000.

Wolfe, Mrs. H. M. *Mission Schools and Their Value.* Bowling Green, KY: 1918.

—*Nancy Richey*

BOYD, BEN (b. ca. 1866, Texas; d. 1924, Paducah, KY), baseball owner, manager, and player. Ben Boyd, son of Henry and Lettie Boyd, worked at a Paducah steamery as a teenager in the late 1880s. By March 1899 (and possibly earlier), he had organized an African American baseball team called the Paducah Nationals. Until 1910, different organized "colored" teams of Boyd's competed frequently before large crowds across the Midwest and South, including St. Louis, Nashville, New Orleans, and Atlanta. The team played Kentucky teams in Mayfield, Danville, Fulton, Owensboro, and Louisville. It also competed against a white team in Quincy, IL. A July 1904 game in Macon, GA, proved to be a unique challenge for Boyd's team. The *Paducah Evening Sun* reported that among the 2,000 African American and white fans in attendance, some people had provided weapons to the opposing team to intimidate the Paducah players and the umpires.

Boyd was determined to play the best white and African American teams he could. In August 1904, he challenged the white K.I.T. (Kentucky, Illinois, and Tennessee) League (a.k.a. the Kitty League) pennant champion from Cairo, IL, to play a three-game series. He announced that he would wager $500 that his team could win two of the three games. He even attended one of its games and, with his "loud shrill voice," rattled Paducah's white pitcher.

Boyd recruited players from various states, and some of his players advanced to more elite teams of the Negro League. For example, Felix "Dick" Wallace from Owensboro, KY, played for the St. Louis Giants, and the Chicago Giants secured Pearl Head and Louis Thomas, both from Cairo, IL. Paducah newspapers noted that Boyd's teams had "crack" talent and that his players were "the fastest." Boyd sometimes pitched and also played left field. His sons, George and Frank, also played, and Ben Boyd Jr. was the team mascot. Boyd organized his teams in February and played through October. The home games were generally at Paducah's Wallace Park, but the team also played at Eureka Park in Rowlandtown. He promoted the baseball games to Paducah's white community by offering reserved seating in half of the grandstand and promising that "the best of order will be strictly maintained."

By 1910, Ben Boyd supported his sister, three children, and two nephews by working as a boiler washer for a railroad company. In 1920, he worked as a railroad company watchman, a position he held until his death on May 4, 1924. He was buried in Paducah's Oak Grove Cemetery.

Kentucky Death Records, 1852–1953.

Newspapers: "Baseball," *PES*, June 8, 1904, 5; "No Chance," *PES*, July 27, 1904, 4; "Wants to Play K.I.T. Winners," *PES*, August 18, 1904, 2; "Ball Notes," *PES*, August 20, 1904, 2; "Goes North," *PES*, April 21, 1905, 3; "Arnold Leaves," *PES*, July 29, 1907, 8.

U.S. Federal Census (1880, 1900, 1910, 1920).

—*Sallie L. Powell*

BOYD, CHARLES WESLEY (b. 1865, Mt. Sterling, KY; d. 1951, Charleston, WV), religious educator and supervisor of colored schools of Charleston, WV. Charles Wesley Boyd, eldest son of John and Ella (Steele) Boyd, learned early the importance of education and religion. In 1891, he graduated from Ohio's Wilberforce University and shortly afterward married Kate Jarrison. He joined the West Virginia Teachers' Association and encouraged the passage of a compulsory school law. Boyd spent his entire career as an educator in the public schools of West Virginia. In 1900, he organized Charleston's Garnet High School and served as its principal for four years. He was later appointed the supervisor of African American schools in the city.

For 18 years, Boyd served as the director of religious education at Charleston's First Baptist Church. Under his leadership, First Baptist established the first African American Sunday school in West Virginia to be recognized as having a "Standard Sunday School." A specialist in Sunday school organization, Boyd served as treasurer of the State Sunday School Convention. He also joined other African American leaders in Charleston, WV, in protesting the showing of the film *The Birth of a Nation*.

Boyd died in Charleston, WV, on February 1, 1951. He was 85 years old.

Caldwell, A. B. *History of the American Negro.* Vol. 7, *West Virginia Edition.* Atlanta, GA: A. B. Caldwell, 1923.

Mather, Frank Lincoln, ed. *Who's Who of the Colored Race: A General Biographical Dictionary of Men and Women of African Descent.* Vol. 1. Chicago: Memento Edition, 1915.

Newspapers: "Birth of a Nation," *Washington Bee,* December 25, 1915, 1; "Garnet High School 2000 Reunion Slated This Weekend," *Charleston (WV) Gazette,* August 10, 2000, P7.

West Virginia Deaths Index, 1853–1973.

Woodson, Carter G., ed. "Early Negro Education in West Virginia." *JNH* 7 (1922): 23–63.

—*Sallie L. Powell*

BOYD, HENRY (b. 1802, Kentucky; d. 1866, Cincinnati, OH), inventor and furniture manufacturer. Born a slave, Henry Boyd apprenticed as a cabinetmaker and learned the skills of a carpenter and joiner as a young boy. He negotiated his freedom from his master by working two jobs: chopping wood during the day and tending boiling salt kettles at Ohio's Kenhawa salt works in the evening. He earned enough money to purchase his freedom and then moved to Cincinnati in 1826. Despite his muscular physique, racial discrimination initially prevented him from finding employment. He eventually found work as a stevedore on Cincinnati's riverfront. After he built a counter for one white merchant, his skills opened up work in home building, which enabled him to purchase his brother and sister out of slavery.

In the mid-1830s, Boyd created what became known as the Boyd bedstead. The bed frame incorporated a doweled design that did not use any nails and thus established a strong structure. The debate continues whether he was able to obtain a patent or whether a white man patented his model. However, one federal document listed "cabinet patent" under his business. Boyd later stamped his beds with his name in order for customers to know that they had purchased his superior product. In 1836, he established H. Boyd Company, a furniture store. In 1842, he opened a furniture factory on Eighth and Broadway Sts. using steam-powered machinery and employed a multitude of African American and white men. In 1850, the census reported the value of his real estate as $20,000.

Although he never received a formal education, Boyd was a student of history, geography, mathematics, and politics. He assisted abolitionist Calvin Fairbank and William Casey, a Cincinnati freeman, in the **Underground Railroad** by helping a family of 14 travel safely to Lawrenceburg, IN. In contrast, one newspaper writer claimed that he believed that Boyd did not take any "active part among the colored people." Either his involvement in the Underground Railroad or his business success or both created animosity among the townspeople, which resulted in his business being burned down several times. He closed his business in 1863. He was buried in an unmarked grave in Spring Grove Cemetery, Cincinnati, OH, in 1866.

"Cincinnati, May 20, 1948," *Rochester (NY) North Star,* June 9, 1948, 2.

Levine, Robert S., ed. *Martin R. Delany: A Documentary Reader.* Chapel Hill: Univ. of North Carolina Press, 2003.

Lucas, Marion B. *The History of Blacks in Kentucky: From Slavery to Segregation, 1760–1891.* 2nd ed. Lexington: Univ. Press of Kentucky, 2003.

Nell, William Cooper. *The Colored Patriots of the American Revolution, with Sketches of Several Distinguished Colored Persons: To Which Is Added a Brief Survey of the Condition and Prospects of Colored Americans.* Boston: Robert F. Wallcut, 1855.

Selected U.S. Federal Census Non-population Schedules, 1850–1880.

Sinclair, Bruce, ed. *Technology and the African-American Experience: Needs and Opportunities for Studies.* Cambridge: MIT Press, 2004.

Sluby, Patricia Carter. *The Inventive Spirit of African Americans: Patented Ingenuity.* Westport, CT: Praeger, 2004.

U.S. Federal Census (1850, 1860, 1870, 1880).

—*Sallie L. Powell*

BRACKTOWN, African American community northwest of Lexington, KY. Before the Civil War, James H. Henderson, the Martin family, and Fredrick Braxton owned the land northwest of Lexington that would eventually constitute the community of Bracktown, located on Highway 421/Leestown Rd. After the war, however, a series of real estate transactions reshaped the area. The Henderson family sold 21 acres to William Parr, who sold them to Robert Stone. In 1887, Stone divided the land into lots and sold it to freedmen who could afford the $100 per acre he demanded. The Martins' land was also subdivided and sold, with black residents constituting the bulk of the population. Although Stone tended to call the area Stonetown, local blacks preferred the moniker Bracktown in honor of Fredrick Braxton, a former slave and the first pastor of the Main Street Missionary Baptist Church, who owned land in the southern part of the community and was a leader in the creation of Bracktown.

Although Bracktown was never a large settlement, it featured a few small businesses, including a grocery and a blacksmith's shop. It also had its own one-room frame schoolhouse that taught black students through the eighth grade. Although the school suffered from the usual limitations due to segregation, locals remembered it fondly for its excellent teachers. In addition to local businesses, several residents worked at E. R. Bradley's Idle Hour Farm, which was adjacent to the community.

Perhaps no institution was more essential to the development of Bracktown than First Baptist Church. Founded in 1880, the

A teacher and a group of Bracktown students, 1901.

church originated from a revival meeting where 12 people were converted. Four years later, Rufus and Mary M. Lisle sold one acre of land to the trustees of the Bracktown Baptist Church for $100 down and $100 to be paid in a year at 6 percent interest for a church house, followed by the construction of a sanctuary in 1890. After additional growth and a generous donation from E. R. Bradley, a new sanctuary was completed in 1931. First Baptist Church stood at the heart of community life, both as a religious institution and as a recreational center. In the late twentieth century, the membership of the church surged under the pastorship of Reverend C. B. Akins Sr., prompting the construction of another new building that would seat 900.

Although Bracktown has maintained its distinct rural character, several developments, including the creation of Masterson Station Park, have affected the community since its inception. In 1935, the federal government constructed the United States Narcotic Farm to treat drug addicts. In 1974, the institution, which had become infamous for allowing the CIA to use its subjects for LSD research, closed and became the Federal Correctional Institution, although it was later converted to a medical complex for prisoners, the Federal Medical Center. More influential in transforming the community has been industrial development along Leestown Rd. that has increased traffic to the area. In response, the community has adopted a Small Area Plan that has allowed for development while still maintaining the region's local culture.

Akins, C. B., Sr. *From Burden to Blessing: Herein Lies the History of a Small Rural Church with Portable Biblical Principles That Propelled It from 65 to over 700 Members.* Naperville, IL: Storybook, 2001.

Anderson, Virginia. Interview by Emily Parker, August 22, 1986. Blacks in Lexington Oral History Project, Louie B. Nunn Center for Oral History, Univ. of Kentucky Libraries.

Carter, Grace. Interview by Emily Parker, August 25, 1986. Blacks in Lexington Oral History Project, Louie B. Nunn Center for Oral History, Univ. of Kentucky Libraries.

Lexington–Fayette Urban County Government. *Bracktown Small Area Plan.* Lexington, KY: Lexington–Fayette Urban County Government, 1998.

Newspapers: "The Road More Traveled: Development Moves into Northwest Lexington," *LHL,* April 10, 1994, A1; "Keeping City's History in Plans for Its Future," *LHL,* February 23, 1998, B1; "Bracktown Church Keeps Growing," *LHL,* October 16, 2004, H1.

—*Stephen Pickering and Paul Wallen*

BRADDOCK, GENERAL (b. unknown; d. Meade Co., KY), the first freed slave in Hardin Co. Although little is known of the early life of General Braddock, he was the slave of famed British general Edward Braddock. He fought beside his owner during the French and Indian War, including the battle at Ft. Duquesne (1755). After Edward Braddock was killed during the war, rumor has it that the slave, General Braddock, was given to other military figures, including George Washington and Col. John Smith. Although evidence does not support the legend that he was given to George Washington, after the French and Indian War ended, a Virginian, Jacob Van Meter, purchased Braddock.

In 1779, Van Meter took General Braddock to frontier Kentucky, where he settled in the Otter Creek and Mill Creek areas of what would become Hardin and Meade Counties. During a time of particularly hostile relations between white settlers and the region's American Indians, Braddock emerged as one of central Kentucky's best-known "Indian killers." Braddock was particularly lethal with a tomahawk, which he could supposedly throw into an oak tree from over 50 yards away. During the 1788 Salt River massacre, when a party of frontiersmen was attacked, Braddock risked his own life to rescue a wounded man named Henry Crist. Crist later became a congressman in the early 1800s and frequently retold stories of General Braddock's heroics. Braddock also reportedly fought Indians with Thomas Lincoln, father of future president Abraham Lincoln.

After Braddock became established as one of the region's most able and virile fighters, Van Meter promised him freedom if he killed 10 Indians. After promptly accomplishing this task, Braddock became Hardin County's first freed slave in March 1797. Within less than a month, on April 9, 1797, he married a woman by the name of Becky Swan. Together, they purchased small plots of land in present-day Meade and Hardin Counties. One of these, it is speculated, later became known as **Free Negro Farm,** one of the few pre–Civil War free black communities in the county. Braddock also worshipped alongside whites as an active member of Mill Creek Baptist Church.

Although research has yet to determine much about General Braddock's death, some believed that he lived to be almost 100 years old. Some accounts suggest that he was buried near the old farm of Jacob Van Meter in the Otter Creek Baptist Church cemetery. Others argue that he was buried in an unmarked grave in a cemetery at Free Negro Farm. Although many events and details of General Braddock's life remain a mystery, the stories that do exist are evidence of the importance of African Americans to the development and history of Kentucky since its origins as frontier terrain. General Braddock Creek, part of the Freeman Lake Trail in Elizabethtown, KY, was named in his honor.

Adams, Evelyn Crady. "Goodin's Fort (1780) in Nelson County, Kentucky." *FCHQ* 27, no. 1 (January 1953): 3–28.

Kempf, Gary. *A History of Fort Knox: Battles, Extinct Communities, Churches, Schools, and Historic Vignettes.* Vine Grove, KY: Ancestral Trails Historical Society, 1998.

Simon, F. Kevin, ed. *The WPA Guide to Kentucky.* Lexington: Univ. Press of Kentucky, 1996.

Smith, Harvey H. *Lincoln and the Lincolns.* New York: Pioneer Publications, 1931.

Urbahns, Paul. "More Moremans—Pleasant Moreman: The Free Negro of Meade County." *Ancestral News* 19, no. 3 (Fall 1994): 101–4.

—*Joshua D. Farrington*

BRADFORD, BILL "BILLY" (b. 1935, Covington, KY), first African American mayor in northern Kentucky. Bill Bradford was born on March 4, 1935, the son of Thomas and Sarah White Bradford. His father worked at a factory in Newport for many years. Billy spent most of his days laboring on a dairy and tobacco farm in Boone Co. owned by his maternal grandparents, John W. and Sarah Fisher. During those years, he attended one of Boone Co.'s colored schools through the 8th grade and then was transferred to the **Lincoln-Grant School** in Covington; he left school after completing the 10th grade.

As a youth, Bradford did not foresee a life in public service. However, as a church steward at **Barnes Temple A.M.E. Church** in **Elsmere** and an admirer of Dr. Martin Luther King's integration and nonviolent philosophies, young Bradford began to take on more leadership roles within his community (Bradford was able to meet King in 1964 at an A.M.E. church convention at the Cincinnati Gardens in Cincinnati). For example, in 1974, he became the first African American elected to the Elsmere City Council; he held that office until 1980. Bradford returned to the council in 1982 and in 1994 was elected vice mayor of Elsmere. At that time, he also was one of the founding members of the Elsmere Fire District Board, a group that helped acquire much-needed equipment for the local fire department. Bradford also was elected to the Elsmere Housing Authority Board. Asked about these accomplishments, Bradford replied, "As a farm kid from Boone County . . . I never imagined a life in politics. I have always enjoyed helping people."

In 1998, Billy Bradford was elected mayor of Elsmere, the first African American to hold such a position in northern Kentucky. He lists the completion of the Garvey Rd. connector and the Industrial Rd. project, as well as the construction of the Elsmere Senior Center, as some of the important ventures of his tenure as mayor. More important, however, Mayor Bradford has proclaimed that his spirituality, a dedicated staff, and a diligent city council are the main reasons for his success as mayor; he is also proud that he has been able to help foster a community where African Americans and whites can work and live together harmoniously. Having served as mayor, Bradford continued to serve his community in the office of councilman.

Bradford, Bill "Billy." Interviews by Eric R. Jackson, Elsmere, KY, June 15 and 19, 2006.
"First Annual Northern Kentucky African-American Heritage Festival—1995." Northern Kentucky African American Heritage Task Force Collection, W. Frank Steely Library, Northern Kentucky Univ.
Newspapers: "Folks View Bradford as Listener, Leader," *KP*, October 24, 1998, 7K; "Northern Kentucky's First Black Mayor," *KP*, October 24, 1998, 1K.

—*Eric R. Jackson*

BRADLEY, JAMES (b. ca. 1800, Africa), slave who purchased his freedom. James Bradley, a slave who became an abolitionist, was born into slavery in Africa and as an infant was taken to South Carolina. He was sold to a slave trader who sold him to the owner of the Bradley Plantation in Pendleton Co., KY, from which Bradley derived his surname. As a teenager, he moved to Arkansas with his owner, performing normal duties by day. By night, with permission from his master, he did odd jobs for other plantation owners and received wages. On many days, Bradley was able to muster only a few hours of sleep. After five years, he had saved $700, which he used to purchase his freedom.

Once free, he briefly returned to northern Kentucky before entering into free territory in Ohio, crossing the Ohio River at Covington. Soon afterward, Bradley was admitted to the Lane Theological Seminary in Cincinnati. As the first African American student there, he joined in the seminary's abolitionist movement, participating in the famous Lane Debates of 1834. He later attended the Sheffield Manual Labor Institute, a branch of Oberlin College in northern Ohio, for one year. From then on, Bradley appears to be lost to history.

A statue of Bradley was placed along Riverside Dr. in Covington, marking roughly where he crossed the Ohio River into Ohio. Created by sculptor George Danhires, the bronze statue has dimensions 49 by 29 by 53 inches, with a base of 28 by 8 by 17 inches. Bradley is depicted sitting on a park bench reading a book, a tribute to a man who, in difficult circumstances, taught himself to read.

"Former Slave Receives Honor 153 Years Late." *CE*, November 2, 1987, D1.
Lesick, Lawrence Thomas. *The Lane Rebels: Evangelicalism and Antislavery in Antebellum America.* Metuchen, NJ: Scarecrow Press, 1980.
Weaver, Randall. "Confronting the Soul Destroyers: James Bradley and the Abolitionist Movement's Origin." *Journal of Unconventional History* 11, no. 2 (Winter 2000): 1–13.

—*Kareem A. Simpson*

BRADY, ST. ELMO (b. 1884, Louisville, KY; d. 1966, Washington, DC), first African American to earn a PhD in chemistry in the United States. In June 1903, graduating senior St. Elmo Brady delivered one of the class orations at Louisville's **Central High School** commencement services. Brady continued his education at Fisk University in Nashville and graduated with a degree in chemistry. After teaching science for a few years at Tuskegee Institute, he matriculated at the University of Illinois and in 1916 became the first African American to earn a PhD in chemistry in the United States with his dissertation, "The Divalent Oxygen Atom." As a student at the University of Illinois, he was the first African American admitted to the chemistry honor society, Phi Lambda Upsilon.

Brady published various scholarly articles that generally focused on the characterization of organic acids. Following the prototype of George Washington Carver, he researched plants native to the southern United States for their useful chemical products. Brady was an excellent scientist but was primarily known for his educational skills. At the University of Illinois, he created a faculty training program in infrared spectroscopy, which was used to identify chemical compounds. He served on the faculty and as the head of the science departments at Tuskegee Institute, Howard University, and Fisk University (where white students from Vanderbilt and other Nashville colleges enrolled in his classes). After his retirement in 1952, he helped Mississippi's Tougaloo College develop a chemistry department and facilities.

Brady died on Christmas Day, 1966, in Washington, DC.

Department of Chemistry at the University of Illinois, "St. Elmo Brady (1884–1966)," 2011. http://www.chemistry.illinois.edu/about/illini_chemists/brady.html (accessed September 21, 2009).
Newspapers: "The High School Commencement," *AB*, June 26, 1903, 2; "D. O. W. Holmes Elected by University Trustees to Fill Place of Dean Moore," *Washington Bee,* October 11, 1920, 4.
Parsons, Charles L. "The American Chemical Society." *Science* 44, no. 1130 (August 25, 1916): 288.

Titcomb, Caldwell. "The Earliest Ph.D. Awards to Blacks in the Natural Sciences." *Journal of Blacks in Higher Education,* no. 15 (Spring 1997): 92–99.

—*Sallie L. Powell*

BRANSFORD FAMILY, influential explorers, guides, and interpreters at Mammoth Cave. By the late nineteenth century, Mammoth Cave, located in western Kentucky, had become one of the leading tourist attractions in the nation. With more than 350 miles of explored passageways and another 600 miles of unexplored paths, Mammoth Cave is the largest cave system in the world. The cave has attracted the interest of scientists, poets, writers, ministers, and photographers from around the world.

African Americans began working in the cave in 1838. **Stephen Bishop** was a slave whose owner leased him to serve as an explorer and guide when he was a teenager. Masterson (Mat) Bransford, a son and slave of Thomas Bransford, a wealthy white farmer, was leased to work at the cave. He was joined by another slave named Nick who was not related to Mat but chose to adopt the Bransford last name. The early slave guides worked under extremely difficult circumstances. They relied on ropes, candles, and oil-burning lanterns to navigate the dark and dangerous cliffs and caverns of the cave. Over the years, Mat guided scholars

Mat Bransford.

through the cave and became knowledgeable about science and geology. An 1863 Louisville newspaper article compared him to a famous Yale scientist named Silliman. He was described as the "colored guide . . . who is familiar with the geological and chemical formations peculiar to the cave, and discourses of all its wonders with an apparent knowledge of his subjects that would do credit to Professor Silliman." By 1860, Mat had walked 50,000 miles in the cave. He was 37 years old at that time.

Other generations of Bransfords descended from Mat. From 1872 to 1894, Mat's son Henry worked in the cave as a guide. One traveler described him as the "walking thesaurus of the cave." Mat's grandson, Will, the third generation of Bransfords to serve as a guide, represented the cave at the 1893 World's Columbian Exposition in Chicago. Along with his wife, Zemmie, he owned and operated the Bransford Resort, which they established to provide food and lodging to African Americans visiting the cave. Mat even traveled to Niagara Falls and passed out postcards inviting African Americans to visit the cave.

By 1931, there were 20 guides, eight of whom were Bransfords—Will, Matt, Louis, Clifton, Arthur, Eddie, Elzie, and George. When the cave became a national park in 1941, no African Americans were working as guides. Victims of racial discrimination, some took jobs with the **Civilian Conservation Corps** or migrated to northern cities in search of employment. More than 60 years later, Jerry Bransford, a fifth-generation Bransford, began giving tours. His family stories and memories have allowed tourists to have a personal encounter with the Bransfords of Mammoth Cave.

"Black History at Mammoth Cave." http://www.nps.gov/maca/history culture/black-history.html (accessed August 21, 2013).

Lyons, Joy. *Making Their Mark: The Signature of Slavery at Mammoth Cave.* Fort Washington, PA: Eastern National, 2006.

Ohlson, Kristin. "The Bransfords of Mammoth Cave." *American Legacy* 17 (Spring 2006). https://www.google.com/#fp=2885013f9be 7e5c9&q=The+Bransfords+of+Mammoth+Cave (accessed August 21, 2013).

Thompson, Bob, and Judi Thompson. *Images of America: Mammoth Cave and the Kentucky Cave Region.* Charleston, SC: Arcadia, 2003.

—*Gerald L. Smith*

BRASHEAR, CARL MAXIE (b. 1931, Tonieville, KY; d. 2006, Portsmouth, VA), U.S. master diver. Shortly after his birth in Tonieville, KY, in Larue Co., Carl Maxie Brashear, the son of McDonald and Gonzella Brashear, moved to Sonora, KY, in Hardin Co. Growing up on a farm, Brashear dreamed of one day living a life full of adventure. He dropped out of school. At the age of 17, he failed the entrance exam for the army, but he had more luck with a supportive recruiter for the navy, which he joined in 1948.

After serving as a boatswain's mate, Brashear attended diving school in Bayonne, NJ. He almost dropped out after racist students attempted to intimidate him, but with the aid of some supportive staff and his own determination, he persevered, graduating 16th in a class of 17. By this time, Brashear—already the first black salvage diver—decided that he would try to become the Navy's first black master diver. He pursued this goal by attending first-class diving school, where he graduated third in a class of 17 in 1963.

On March 25, 1966, an incident aboard the USS *Hoist* devastated Brashear's plans. During a salvage operation to recover an atomic bomb off the coast of Spain, a loose pipe struck him below the knee, causing multiple compound fractures and eventually the amputation of the lower part of his leg. However, he refused to give up on his dream of becoming a master diver. After presenting officers with several pictures of himself diving while using an artificial leg, he was allowed to enter second-class diving school, where he graduated as the first black master diver in 1970.

In 1979, Brashear retired after numerous struggles with alcoholism. In 2000, his life was depicted in the film *Men of Honor,* and he was inducted into the Gallery of Great Black Kentuckians two years later. He died at the Naval Medical Center in Portsmouth, VA, on July 25, 2006.

Brashear, Carl M., with Paul Stillwell. *The Reminiscences of Master Chief Boatswain's Mate Carl M. Brashear, U.S. Navy (Retired).* Annapolis, MD: U.S. Naval Institute, 1998.
Newspapers: "Ex-Navy Diver Refused to Abandon His Dream," *KP,* February 28, 2002, 13A; "First Black Navy Diver Dies at 75," *LHL,* July 26, 2006, B5.
"Nothing Can Stop the Chief." *Ebony* 23 (April 1968): 40–46.
Williams, Albert. *Black Warriors: Unique Units and Individuals in African American Military History.* Haverford, PA: Infinity, 2003.

—*Stephen Pickering*

BREAN, DAVID (b. 1925, Neptune, NJ; d. 2004, New York City, NY), visual artist. David Brean, the son of Rev. William L. and Bessie E. Brean, born on April 12, 1925, was a renowned African American artist and educator. Brean graduated from William Grant High School in Covington in 1943. During his senior year, he prepared an art piece that was part of an exhibit at the Cincinnati Art Museum in September 1943. He enlisted in the U.S. Army on June 19, 1943, to serve in World War II. After the war, Brean earned a BA and a BS in education from the University of Cincinnati in 1955. In September 1956, he enrolled in Columbia University, New York City, pursuing a master of fine arts degree. That same year, he was one of 51 students from throughout the nation to receive a John Hay Whitney Foundation scholarship. He graduated with an MFA on June 4, 1957.

Brean became a director and later director emeritus of the Visual Arts Department of the Harlem School of the Arts in New York and a friend of its founder, Dorothy Maynor. He taught at the school from its very beginning. Brean exhibited at the Cincinnati Art Museum, the Cincinnati Modern Art Society, and the Alms Gallery at the University of Cincinnati. His other shows were in New York City, at the Art Students League Gallery and at the Macy Art Gallery at the Teachers College and East Hall Gallery, both at Columbia University.

The Brean family attended the **Ninth St. Methodist Episcopal Church** in Covington. Brean crafted several pieces of art that he donated to the church. Brean died on October 12, 2004, in New York City and was cremated. His ashes were returned to Covington and buried with his mother in Linden Grove Cemetery.

Murray, Wendy. "Kids' Art Brings Poems to Life—Harlem School of the Arts Students." *Instructor,* January–February 1995.

Newspapers: "Gets Fellowship," *KTS,* June 12, 1956, 2A; "Scholarship," *KTS,* October 11, 1956, 4A.

—*Theodore H. H. Harris*

BRIDGEMAN, ULYSSES LEE "JUNIOR" (b. 1953, East Chicago, IN), professional basketball player and entrepreneur. Ulysses Lee "Junior" Bridgeman led his East Chicago Washington High School basketball team to the Indiana state championship his senior year. From 1971 to 1975, he was a legendary basketball player for the University of Louisville. The six-feet-five forward and guard played a critical role in leading Coach Denny Crum's Cardinals to the NCAA Final Four in 1975. Bridgeman earned a bachelor's degree in psychology and played basketball for 10 years in the National Basketball Association (NBA) with the Milwaukee Bucks and 2 years with the Los Angeles Clippers. He was considered one of the best players as the sixth man coming off the bench.

While playing professional basketball, Bridgeman developed his leadership skills as a player representative and negotiations liaison, treasurer, and president of the NBA Players Association. When his basketball career ended in 1987, Bridgeman became a restaurant entrepreneur because "people were always going to eat." Bridgeman owned 153 restaurants in five states by 2004 and became one of Wendy's five most productive franchisers. He employed over 5,320 people. Described as soft spoken and diplomatic, Bridgeman characterized himself as "a servant-leader," meaning that he helped others be better. He has served on various boards, including the University of Louisville's Board of Trustees; cochaired the capital campaign for the African American Heritage Foundation; and helped establish the Cardinal Degree Completion Program, known as the Bridgeman Scholarship, to help former University of Louisville athletes complete their education.

Bradby, Marie. "Junior Bridgeman's Cardinal Rule." *Louisville Magazine,* August 2005, 39–42.
Newspapers: "Bridgeman Delivers as Bucks' Swingman," *NYT,* March 8, 1981, S9; "Bridgeman Still Taking a Hands-on Approach," *NYT,* January 25, 2004, SP2.
Passing the Torch: Lessons Learned—Wisdom Shared; Conversations with Louisville Leaders about Life, Leadership and Service. Louisville, KY: Butler Books, 2005.

—*Sallie L. Powell*

BRITTON, MARY ELLEN (b. 1855, Lexington, KY; d. 1925, Lexington, KY), medical doctor, educator, club leader, and writer. The first woman to practice medicine in Lexington, KY, Mary Ellen Britton, the daughter of Henry Harrison Britton and Laura Marshall, was born on April 16, 1855. Henry, who was of Spanish and Indian heritage, was a free carpenter and barber, while Laura was the daughter of Mary, a slave woman, and the Honorable Thomas Francis Marshall, a renowned Kentucky statesman from a very prominent family. Laura was freed by her mistress at the age of 16 in 1848. Mary was the third of 10 children, who included a brother, well-known jockey **Tommy Britton,** and a sister, **Julia Britton Hooks,** social reformer and accomplished musician.

In 1871, the Britton family moved to newly founded Berea, where most of the children attended school. Mary Britton's education was tragically interrupted when both her parents died

Dr. Mary Britton.

within a few months of each other in 1874. Soon she began a career teaching in segregated schools sponsored by the **American Missionary Association** in Lexington and surrounding areas. In 1897, she publicly announced her intention to abandon teaching and train as a physician. She studied at the Sanatorium in Battle Creek, MI, and at the American Missionary College of Medicine in Chicago, where she received her medical degree. In 1902, she was licensed as a doctor in Lexington. From her home at 545 N. Limestone, she practiced her specialties, physiotherapy and hydrotherapy. She retired in 1923.

Throughout her life, Dr. Britton was a prolific journalist, publishing in newspapers in Kentucky, Indiana, and Ohio and even as far away as Maryland. She usually addressed subjects of social reform: education, women's suffrage, and social equality among the races. She argued vehemently against racial segregation laws and organized rallies supporting desegregation. At a historic demonstration in Frankfort on April 15, 1892, Britton spoke before the joint Railroad Committee of the Kentucky Senate and House of Representatives in protest of Kentucky's separate railroad coach laws. Mary Britton was the coauthor of a pamphlet titled *President Frost's Betrayal of the Colored People in His Administration of Berea College,* a resounding denunciation of William Goodell Frost's policies after the passage of the **Day Law.** She

was a founding director of **Lexington's Colored Orphan Industrial Home** and president of the Women's Improvement Club. In 1925, she died at the age of 70 and was buried in Lexington's Cove Haven Cemetery.

Dunnigan, Alice Allison, comp. and ed. *The Fascinating Story of Black Kentuckians: Their Heritage and Traditions.* Washington, DC: Associated Publishers, 1982.

Sears, Richard D. *A Utopian Experiment in Kentucky: Integration and Social Equality at Berea, 1866–1904.* Westport, CT: Greenwood Press, 1996.

—*Richard D. Sears*

BRITTON, THOMAS M. "TOMMY" (b. ca. 1873, Berea, KY; d. 1901, Cincinnati, OH), jockey. Thomas Britton, brother of Dr. **Mary E. Britton** and **Julia B. Hooks,** lived with various relatives when his parents, Henry and Laura Britton, died shortly after his birth. At the age of 14, he began his turf career as a stable boy for James Williams in Louisville and soon progressed to riding. In 1891, legendary jockey **Isaac Murphy,** along with many other Lexington African Americans, as well as a few white residents, attended Britton's wedding to Pearl Jackson. His sister Julia played the organ, his brother-in-law and local barber **Benjamin Franklin** played the violin, and noted jockey **Will Alfred "Monk" Overton** of Chicago was one of the ushers. A floral horseshoe with the last names of the bride and groom adorned the altar. Shortly after his marriage, Britton's sister Lucy married his jockey friend, Will Overton.

Well known in racing circles as an honorable and very successful jockey, Britton triumphed in five Lexington races during his marriage week. He then won the Kentucky Oaks in Louisville, the American Derby in Chicago, and the Tennessee Derby two consecutive years. In 1892, only three horses raced in the **Kentucky Derby,** Huron, Phil Dwyer, and Azra. Ed Corrigan owned Huron and Phil Dwyer and planned for Britton to sprint Huron ahead of **Alonzo "Lonnie" Clayton** on Azra in hopes of tiring the horse. Will Overton was to then win the race on Phil Dwyer. Near the finish line, Britton and Clayton were so close that neither could use their whips. Britton's horse, Huron, lost by a nose.

Despite the defeat, that was Britton's most successful racing year. He finished first in 81 out of 350 contests. The next year, Britton nearly died after falling off his horse, Miss Dixie, at Washington Park. His fractured skull left him with "insane spells" and "mentally unbalanced." He became a reckless rider and lost his jockey license for two seasons. He was arrested for spousal abuse, and he and his wife divorced in 1895. Five years later, they remarried in Cincinnati, and he won Latonia by a neck when he quickly recovered after his horse had thrown him.

In 1901, Thomas Britton committed suicide in Cincinnati via carbolic acid. Some reported that unemployment and financial stress caused his death. Others believed that the death of his only child, Tommie, eight years old, run over by a hemp wagon affected Britton's emotional disposition. He had left a note for his sister, Susan Franklin, that he wished to be buried in Lexington.

Hotaling, Edward. *The Great Black Jockeys: The Lives and Times of the Men Who Dominated America's First National Sport.* Rocklin, CA: Forum, 1999.

Newspapers: "Under a Horseshoe," *LL,* May 6, 1891, 2; "Azra Won the Derby," *NYT,* May 12, 1892, 2; "Jockey Tom Britton," *LL,* January 29, 1893, 6; "Tom Britton a Suicide," *LH,* May 10, 1901, 1.
                                                        —Sallie L. Powell

BROOKS, CHARLES H. (b. ca. 1860, Paducah, KY; d. ca. 1951, Philadelphia, PA), businessman and author. Beginning at age 17, Charles H. Brooks taught for 13 years in his hometown, Paducah. When he was 21, he married Matilda Mansfield, a Paducah schoolteacher and graduate of Roger Williams University. The next year he joined Paducah's Independent Order of Odd Fellows, a fraternal organization, and promptly became the lodge's permanent secretary. He soon was elected a delegate to the Kentucky Grand Lodge and later to the Biennial Moveable Committee of the Odd Fellows National Convention.

In 1889, Brooks was appointed clerk in the Pension Office at Washington, DC. In Washington, he completed a business course at Spencerian College, followed by his graduation in law from Howard University. In 1892, he resigned his government position and moved to Philadelphia when he was elected the grand secretary of the Grand United Order of Odd Fellows. The following year, he wrote the official history of the Odd Fellows organization. He later traveled to Europe to attend the International Conference of Odd Fellows. In 1903, Brooks entered the real estate and insurance businesses. He chartered the Reliable Mutual Aid Society and the Cherry Building and Loan Association. He served as the second vice president of the National Negro Business League and on various hospital boards. Through Brooks's real estate brokerage business, he was a successful investor for various corporations.

Active in his local church, Brooks wrote the *Official History of the First African Baptist Church,* Philadelphia, PA, in 1922. He continued to work in the insurance business in his older years and died when he was in his early 90s.

Moore, Jacqueline M. *Leading the Race: The Transformation of the Black Elite in the Nation's Capital, 1880–1920.* Charlottesville: Univ. Press of Virginia, 1999.
Simms, James N. *Simms' Blue Book and National Negro Business and Professional Directory.* Chicago: James N. Simms, 1923.
White, Charles Frederick. *Who's Who in Philadelphia.* Philadelphia: A.M.E. Book Concern, 1912.
                                                        —Sallie L. Powell

BROOKS, ROBERT HAROLD (b. 1915, Sadieville, KY; d. 1941, Philippines), World War II soldier. The son of sharecroppers, Robert Brooks worked as a sales clerk before his enlistment in the military on March 15, 1941. Brooks was five feet tall, weighed 115 pounds, and was fair skinned. Because his race was listed as white on his application, Brooks passed for white.

In the segregated U.S. Army, Brooks served in the maintenance department with D Company, 192nd Tank Battalion, and trained at Ft. Knox, qualifying as a half-track and tank driver. His unit transferred to the Philippines to become part of General Douglas MacArthur's forces in the Pacific. On December 8, 1941, the day after the bombing of Pearl Harbor, the Japanese attacked Clark Field near Ft. Stotsenburg, Philippines. Brooks reportedly had attempted to get into his half-track to fire his .50 caliber machine gun when he was killed at age 26. He was officially declared the first U.S. armed forces casualty of World War II.

Brooks's race was not discovered until the military invited his parents to a memorial ceremony at Ft. Knox. On December 23, 1941, the main parade ground at Ft. Knox was named Brooks Field in his honor. A year later, a Louisville **Central High School** teacher, **George L. Bullock,** wrote the words proclaiming Brooks as a martyr in the song "Private Robert Harold Brooks," which was published by W. C. Handy Brothers Music Company. Brooks was awarded the Purple Heart posthumously and is buried in the Manila American Cemetery and Memorial in Ft. Bonifacio (formerly Ft. William McKinley), Philippines.

Handy, W. C. *Unsung Americans Sung.* New York: Handy Brothers Music Co., 1944.
Proviso East High School Bataan Commemorative Research Project. http://www.proviso.k12.il.us/bataan%20web/brooks.htm (accessed May 6, 2009).
U.S. World War II Army Enlistment Records, 1938–1946.
World War II and Korean Conflict Veterans Interred Overseas.
                                                        —Sallie L. Powell

BROOKS MEMORIAL HOSPITAL (HOPKINSVILLE), the only African American hospital in Hopkinsville, KY. Brooks Memorial Hospital defied racial and cultural norms by accepting both black and white patients during the **Jim Crow** era. Located in Hopkinsville, KY, the private facility was built by Phillip Carruthers Brooks Sr., a local black surgeon and physician. Brooks, who received his undergraduate and medical degrees from Howard University in Washington, DC, built the hospital with private funds and accepted nothing from state or local governments. He named the hospital for his parents, Henry L. and Carrie Haynes Brooks.

Construction of Brooks Memorial Hospital commenced in 1941. Shortages due to World War II delayed the project, but the facility opened its doors at 201½ S. Virginia St. on July 9, 1944. The hospital's opening filled a void created by Hopkinsville's Jennie Stuart Hospital, which treated whites only. It also kept local blacks from driving the 75 miles to the nearest clinic that accepted black patients. Beyond Hopkinsville residents, the 30-bed facility also drew patients from throughout Kentucky and surrounding states and even from as far away as Chicago.

In 1958, Brooks Memorial Hospital garnered statewide attention when Dr. Phillip Carruthers Brooks Sr. treated a white race-car driver who had been refused care by the nearby Jennie Stuart Hospital, a whites-only facility. The driver, Clinton Reynolds, lay unattended for over an hour at Jennie Stuart. Dr. Brooks treated Reynolds at Brooks Memorial for cracked ribs, multiple lacerations, and cuts in considerably less time. Both the ineffectiveness of doctors at Jennie Stuart and the quality of care provided at Brooks Memorial were reported to the Kentucky Medical Association. In 1975, Dr. Brooks received the General Practitioner of the Year Award from the National Medical Association for his work at Brooks Memorial Hospital and in the medical field. The hospital closed in 1976.

"Brooks, Phillip C." Notable Kentucky African Americans Database. http://www.uky.edu/Libraries/NKAA/subject.php?sub_id=145 (accessed June 20, 2012).

Cobb, W. Montague. "Brooks Receives 1975 General Practitioner of the Year Award." *Journal of the National Medical Association* 67, no. 6 (1975): 449, 477–80. http://www.ncbi.nlm.nih.gov/pmc/articles /PMC2609445/pdf/jnma00484-0067.pdf (accessed June 25, 2012).

Horton, John Benjamin. *Profiles of Contemporary Black Achievers of Kentucky.* Louisville, KY: J. Benjamin Horton & Associates, 1983.

Turner, William T., and Donna K. Stone. *Hopkinsville.* Charleston, SC: Arcadia, 2006.

"White Medics Refuse Racer Aid, Negro Responds." *Jet Magazine* 14, no. 20 (1958): 26. books.google.com/books?id=6rcDAAAAMBAJ &printsec=frontcover&source=gbs_summary_r&cad=0_0#v =onepage&q&f=false (accessed Jun 25, 2012).

                                                              —*LeDatta Grimes*

BROWN, EDWARD DUDLEY "BROWN DICK" (b. 1850, Lexington, KY; d. 1906, Lexington, KY), jockey and horse trainer.

Born into slavery in Lexington, KY, in 1850, Edward Dudley Brown was an acclaimed African American jockey and horse trainer. At age seven, he was sold to Woodburn Stud Farm, owned by Robert A. Alexander of Midway, KY. Initially trained as a stable boy, Brown was later given the opportunity to be an exercise boy, working horses into shape through conditioning gallops and timed drills.

Brown did well as an exercise boy. In 1864, Robert Alexander and his horse trainer, **Ansel Williamson,** also a slave, decided on Brown as the jockey for the farm's promising horse, Asteroid, in a St. Louis race. Brown won this race and went on to win the next eight races as the jockey of Asteroid. However, he did not race under his own name. According to early race records, he raced as Dick, Alexander's Dick, or Dick Alexander. Williamson called him Brown Dick after his fastest racehorse with that name. Later, when the Civil War crossed into Kentucky, Confederate soldiers swept through the area and made off with Asteroid. Alexander was later forced to pay a large ransom for the return of his horse. This event unnerved the owner, who took both his horses and his slaves and settled in Illinois until the end of the war.

In 1867, Robert Alexander died, and Brown began working with his nephew, Daniel Swigert. Three years later, they made racing history. Riding Kingfisher in the 1870 Belmont Stakes, Brown became the first African American to win the stakes. However, he was unable to maintain the required weight to remain a jockey and rode his last official race in 1874. Undeterred by this development and having gained vast knowledge of horses and horse racing, he became a horse trainer.

Brown became a tremendously successful trainer, known nationwide. Three years after his training debut, Baden Baden, a horse he trained, won the 1877 Kentucky Derby. Brown trained two more Kentucky Derby winners, Ben Brush (1896) and Plaudit (1898). He used his profits to begin his own stable, Ed Brown and Co., and became one of the wealthiest African Americans in Kentucky.

Brown died of tuberculosis in Lexington, KY, on May 11, 1906. He was buried in an unmarked grave in Midway, KY. His legacy and contribution were recognized when he was inducted into the National Museum of Racing and Hall of Fame in 1984.

Hotaling, Edward. *The Great Black Jockeys: The Lives and Times of the Men Who Dominated America's First National Sport.* Rocklin, CA: Forum, 1999.

Kentucky Death Records, 1852–1953.

Kentucky Historical Society. "Kentucky Historical Marker Database: Edward Dudley Brown." Frankfort, 2009. http://migration.ken tucky.gov/kyhs/hmdb/MarkerSearch.aspx?mode=All (accessed July 26, 2014).

National Museum of Racing and Hall of Fame. "Edward D. Brown." Saratoga Springs, NY, 2004. http://www.racingmuseum.org/hall /trainer.asp?ID=236 (accessed September 8, 2009).

Renau, Lynn S. *Racing around Kentucky.* Louisville, KY: Lynn S. Renau, 1995.

Smith, Gene. "The Winner." *American Legacy,* Summer 2001, 11–12.

                                                              —*Benjamin Rawlins*

BROWN, EDWARD HALL (b. 1861, Henderson Co., KY; d. 1946, Henderson, KY), blacksmith.

Born on May 8, 1861, the eldest son of Michael (Mike) Brown and his wife, Susan, Edward Hall Brown followed his father's career path as a blacksmith. Mike arrived in Henderson in 1860 as a slave of the mayor's wife. He was allowed to keep his blacksmith earnings and soon purchased his wife for $1,000. After the Civil War, he opened his blacksmith shop on First St. Edward worked closely with his father, particularly learning how to handle skittish horses. In 1898, he went into business for himself.

Brown's blacksmith skills led to his business accomplishments of owning several homes, his shop, and stock in mercantile interests. He served as a juror in the U.S. district court and was a member of the National Horseshoers' Association and the Henderson Blacksmiths' Association. By 1905, he and other African American community leaders had established (**Frederick**) **Douglass High School,** an African American high school in Henderson.

Brown, his wife, and his five children lived at 935 Clay St., and his shop was located at 422 First St. His son, Sneed, began working with him as a teenager and plied the family trade for 51 years, retiring in 1959. In his later years, Edward Brown continued to work as a blacksmith but also worked in the coal mines and took in boarders. The three generations of blacksmiths extended for over 93 years and had the oldest business in Henderson operating under its original name, Brown's Blacksmith Shop. In an interview, Brown noted how things changed, but he claimed, "There is no way of shoeing a horse by steam or electricity. It must be done by plain hand and muscle." Brown was buried in Fernwood Cemetery, Henderson, KY.

Arnett, Maralea. *The Annals and Scandals of Henderson County, Kentucky, 1775–1975.* Corydon, KY: Fremar, 1976.

Dannheiser, Frieda J., ed. *History of Henderson County, Kentucky.* Henderson County Genealogical and Historical Society, 1980.

Mather, Frank Lincoln, ed. *Who's Who of the Colored Race: A General Biographical Dictionary of Men and Women of African Descent.* Vol. 1. Chicago: Memento Edition, 1915.

Newspapers: "No Business like Shoe Business for Local Smiths," *Henderson (KY) Gleaner,* October 13, 2002; "Everyday People," *Henderson (KY) Gleaner,* July 11, 2006.

U.S. Federal Census (1910, 1920).

                                                              —*Sallie L. Powell*

BROWN, JESSE EVERETT "DOC" (b. 1856, Bedford, VA; 1951, Louisville, KY), businessman.

Jesse Everett Brown came

to Kentucky from Virginia when he was in his early 30s. He attended **Louisville National Medical College** and practiced medicine until the creation of the Board of Medical Examiners. "Doc" Brown was forced to quit his medical profession because he had not taken his final medical examination, which was required by the board.

In 1924, the same year his wife, Ella, died, Brown purchased the Lawless Tobacco Company. The business was quite successful until the Great Depression, when it lost a substantial number of customers. Some have classified Brown as Louisville's first African American businessman and insurance agent. He was an avid supporter of the YMCA and enjoyed extensive popularity among prominent political officials. At his death in 1951, the 94-year-old Brown was working as a paper salesman.

Dunnigan, Alice Allison, comp. and ed. *The Fascinating Story of Black Kentuckians: Their Heritage and Traditions.* Washington, DC: Associated Publishers, 1982.
Kentucky Death Records, 1852–1953.

—*Sallie L. Powell*

BROWN, JOHN WILLIAM "SCOOP" (b. 1922, Lexington, KY; d. 2002, Lexington, KY), athlete and sports official. Lexington native John William Brown (frequently called John Will "Scoop" Brown) was the son of Hiram and Anna Mae Brown. His father was one of the first African American owners of a moving company in Lexington, and his mother worked as a maid at the the Lafayette Hotel. His parents sold the land of his childhood home on Patterson St. for Carver School.

At **Dunbar High School,** Brown was an all-state athlete in basketball and football and also an all-national basketball player. He earned his nickname, Scoop, because of his baseball ability as a first baseman. He played for the Winchester White Sox and then played and managed the **Lexington Hustlers** (1945–1949), a semiprofessional team. One of his teammates was **William E. "Bunny" Davis,** and they played against future superstars like Satchel Paige, Willie Mays, and Hank Aaron. Brown invited his friend Bobby Flynn, a white baseball player, to try out for the team. When Flynn made the team, the Lexington Hustlers became the first integrated baseball team in the South.

Brown worked for Lexington's parks and recreation system and became the district recreational supervisor responsible for all of Lexington's African American parks. In this role, he formed the Push Mobile Derby (a Soap Box Derby contest), organized the Lexington **Dirt Bowl,** and helped integrate Small Fry football. He developed his sports officiating skills through his job.

Brown worked eight basketball championships for the Kentucky High School Athletic League, the all-black high school athletic association. After the white organization, the Kentucky High School Athletic Association (KHSAA), integrated in 1958, Brown became the first African American to officiate the boys' state basketball tournament in 1963. By the end of his officiating career in 1985, he had officiated the boys' state basketball tournament four times and the state football finals three times and had become the first African American referee to work the National Association of Intercollegiate Athletics tournament, the

first African American to officiate in the University of Kentucky's Memorial Coliseum, and a top official in the Ohio Valley Conference. He also introduced officiating to **Brenda Lee Garner Hughes,** the first African American woman to officiate Kentucky's girls' high school state basketball tournament.

In 1994, Brown was inducted into the Dawahares/KHSAA Hall of Fame. He died of cancer on June 27, 2002, and was buried in **Camp Nelson** National Cemetery. In April 2010, Scoop Brown Ln., located between Georgetown St. and Douglass Park, was named in his honor.

Kelley, Brent. *"I Will Never Forget": Interviews with 39 Former Negro League Players.* Jefferson, NC: McFarland, 2003.
Newspapers: "Kentucky High School Cage Tourney Has 1st Tan Referee," *BAA,* March 23, 1963, 14; "19 State Sports Figures Join High School Hall of Fame," *LHL,* March 23, 1994, C4; "'Scoop' Brown Knows the Score," *LHL,* November 26, 2000, K1; "Athletic Standout Played, Integrated and Officiated," *LHL,* June 28, 2002, D1; "Street Named for 'Scoop' Brown," *LHL,* April 30, 2010, A6.

—*Wardell Johnson*

BROWN, LEE LOWELL (b. 1879, Spring Station, KY; d. unknown), newspaper correspondent, educator, and politician. While Lee Lowell Brown was still an infant, his parents, Edward and Lucy, moved the family from Spring Station in Woodford Co. to Louisville. After graduating from **Eckstein Norton Institute** in 1901, Brown taught at the school for the next six years. He then served as an assistant principal at Henderson's (**Frederick) Douglass High School** for two years.

Brown returned to Louisville and worked as a news correspondent for the *Louisville News,* a newspaper that he helped organize. In 1913, he ran for the Kentucky state legislature seat from Louisville's 10th Ward. The Republican Party never thought that an African American candidate had a chance of winning the primary, so it ignored Brown. He won by 31 votes but lost to the Democratic candidate even though the district was primarily African American. Disappointed by the loss, Brown blamed his defeat on the Republican Party's opposition and "the failure of blacks to vote a straight Republican ticket."

As a businessman and civil leader, Brown owned Brown's Letter Shoppe and had served as principal of a stenography school named Brown's Commercial School. He was a member of the National Negro Press Association and executive secretary of the Louisville branch of the **National Association for the Advancement of Colored People** (NAACP) in the early 1920s. He helped organize NAACP branches in 10 Kentucky cities and visited white-owned businesses and industries to persuade them to hire African Americans. In 1930, he served as a Jefferson Co. deputy sheriff. He and his wife, Etta, lived at 1012 W. Chestnut St. in Louisville with his mother, Lucy.

Mather, Frank Lincoln, ed. *Who's Who of the Colored Race: A General Biographical Dictionary of Men and Women of African Descent.* Vol. 1. Chicago: Memento Edition, 1915.
Wright, George C. *Life Behind a Veil: Blacks in Louisville, Kentucky, 1865–1930.* Baton Rouge: Louisiana State Univ. Press, 1985.
Yenser, Thomas, ed. *Who's Who in Colored America, 1941–1944.* 6th ed. Brooklyn, NY: Thomas Yenser, 1942.

—*Sallie L. Powell*

BROWN, MARIE SPRATT "MAUDE" (b. 1869, Kentucky; d. ca. 1959, Louisville, KY), educator. In 1898, Marie Spratt Brown, known as Maude, was the first female elected president of the **Kentucky Negro Educational Association** (KNEA). She began her teaching career in the Louisville public schools. She attended classes at the University of Chicago for seven consecutive summers, specializing in home economics, and then worked briefly at a YWCA in St. Louis.

After returning to Kentucky, Brown taught in various school systems across the state, including Bowling Green, Mayfield's **Dunbar High School,** Paducah's West Kentucky Industrial College for Colored Persons (later known as **Western Kentucky Community & Technical College**), and Hyden in Leslie Co. In 1931, while teaching in Mayfield, she attended and graduated magna cum laude from Tennessee A&I State College. She later attended Fisk University to work on a master of arts degree and completed her MA degree at Western Reserve University in Cleveland, OH. She also served as the supreme basileus of **Alpha Kappa Alpha Sorority.**

Brown was devoted to the KNEA and held nearly every office in the organization. She served on the Research Committee in the late 1930s. After her marriage to Rev. Henry P. Porter, Maude Brown Porter represented Louisville on the KNEA's Resolutions Committee in 1948. In her poem "The K.N.E.A.," she encouraged teachers to join the association and praised the abilities of **Atwood S. Wilson,** the KNEA secretary-treasurer from 1922 to 1942. In 1953, Tennessee's Lane College awarded her an honorary degree of doctor of humanities for her contributions to social work and education.

Dunnigan, Alice Allison, comp. and ed. *The Fascinating Story of Black Kentuckians: Their Heritage and Traditions.* Washington, DC: Associated Publishers, 1982.
"Hold Commencement at Lane College in Tenn." *PD,* January 5, 1953, 4.
"Editorial Comment, Marie Spratt Brown," *KNEAJ* 6, no. 2 (February–March 1936): 2.

—*Sallie L. Powell*

BROWN, RUSSELL S., SR. (b. 1889, London, KY; d. 1981, Chicago, IL), clergyman and community activist. Russell S. Brown, the son of Bartlett and Alice Brown, moved from Kentucky to Kansas with his family when he was young. He graduated from Topeka High School and later earned his bachelor of divinity degree at Ohio's Payne Theological Seminary in 1915, the same year he married his wife, Floy.

Brown pastored churches in several states. He was also a political and civic activist. In Memphis, he guided the construction of the South's First Community House for Soldiers. He served as chaplain at the Fulton County Jail, conducted services at Atlanta's federal prison, and served for two years as chairman of the Committee on Race Relations. During World War I, he was the pastor at Camp Funston, KS.

In 1929, Brown was the first minister and second African American elected to the Cleveland, OH, City Council. He immediately took a stand on the established color lines of Cleveland's City Hospital, which refused to hire African American interns and nurses. Brown joined two other African American council-men in opposition to the city's proposal to build an East Side Hospital, not because the African American community did not need a hospital, but because the City Hospital remained closed to African Americans.

After moving to Denver, Brown was the first African American to receive its local newspaper's Hall of Fame award for active city citizenship. In 1948, he was elected chief secretary of the African Methodist Episcopal (A.M.E.) General Conference and served as financial officer of the organization until 1976.

Boris, Joseph J., ed. *Who's Who in Colored America, 1927.* New York: Who's Who in Colored America Corp., 1927.
Griffin, William Wayne. *African Americans and the Color Line in Ohio, 1915–1930.* Columbus: Ohio State Univ. Press, 2005.
Wright, Richard Robert, Jr. *Encyclopaedia of the African Methodist Episcopal Church.* 2nd ed. Philadelphia: Book Concern of the A.M.E. Church, 1947.

—*Sallie L. Powell*

BROWN, WILLIAM WELLS (b. 1814, Montgomery Co., KY; d. 1884, Chelsea, MA), former slave and author. William Wells Brown, novelist and historian, was born a slave in 1814 on the farm of Dr. John Young in Montgomery Co. His mother, Elizabeth, is said to have been the daughter of Simon Lee, a slave soldier in the Revolutionary War, and his father may have been a cousin of his owner. At an early age, Brown moved to a farm near St. Louis with his owners' household. In 1834, Brown escaped to Ohio from the job he held on a river steamboat. He was aided by a Quaker named Wells Brown, and in gratitude he adopted the Quaker's name as his own.

Brown made his way to Cleveland, where he worked at a variety of jobs, from barber to banker. As a steward on a Lake Erie steamboat, he was able to ferry 69 fugitive slaves to freedom. Brown became lecturer for the Western New York Anti-Slavery Society in 1843. Four years later he moved to Boston and launched his writing career.

Brown wrote *Narrative of William Wells Brown, a Fugitive Slave, Written by Himself* (1847). His reputation as an abolitionist spokesman grew, along with fears that fugitive-slave bounty hunters would carry him back to slavery. In 1849, he represented the American Peace Society at the world Peace Conference in Paris. He remained in Europe in voluntary exile for five years. During that time, he was a regular speaker at abolition meetings and published his first novel, *Clotel; or, The President's Daughter: A Narrative of Slave Life in the United States, with a Sketch of the Author's Life* (1853). This book was a fictional account of Thomas Jefferson's alleged long-term relationship with his slave mistress, Sally Hemmings, portraying the dehumanizing effects slavery had on her and their children. Considered too controversial for publication in the United States, the book was first published in England and went through several printings and a number of changes before being published in the United States in 1864 with all references to Jefferson removed. Over the next 30 years, Brown wrote on the history of slavery, the black experience in America, and the role of black soldiers in the Civil War. He published a collection of slave songs and a five-act play based on his own escape from slavery. His writings, though not literary masterpieces, are significant because Brown was among the country's first and best-known black historians, authors, and playwrights.

Brown was married twice, first in 1834 to Elizabeth Schooner of Cleveland and then to Annie Elizabeth Gray of Cambridgeport, MA. He was survived by two daughters, Clarissa and Josephine. He died on November 6, 1884, and was buried in the Cambridge (MA) Cemetery.

Eblen, Tom. "Black History Month: Scholar's Research on Author William Wells Brown Finds New Truths about His Life." *LHL,* February 19, 2013.
"Ex-Slave Author from Lexington Deserves Prominence." *LHL,* March, 12, 2003.
Farrison, William Edward. *William Wells Brown: Author and Reformer.* Chicago: Univ. of Chicago Press, 1969.
Heermance, J. Noel. *William Wells Brown and Clotelle: A Portrait of the Artist in the First Negro Novel.* Hamden, CT: Archon Books, 1969.
"William Wells Brown, 1814?–1884, Narrative of William W. Brown, a Fugitive Slave. Written by Himself." Boston: The Antislavery Office, 1847; Documenting the American South, the University of North Carolina at Chapel Hill, University Library, 2004. http://docsouth .unc.edu/neh/brown47/summary.html (accessed July 26, 2014).

BROWNE, BIRDIUS WILLIAM (b. 1906, Warsaw, KY; d. 1986, Paducah, KY), educator and Tennessee Valley Authority agent. Birdius William Browne moved from Warsaw, KY, to Decatur, IL, when he was young. He was an outstanding athlete in school and was awarded a medal by the government of Decatur. He graduated from Kentucky State College (later known as **Kentucky State University**) in 1926. He immediately started teaching at Mt. Olivet, Kentucky. Two years later, Rev. William Taylor of the Ninth Street Baptist Church in Covington married Browne to Florida native Jessie Davis. The couple established a home in Melbourne, FL, where Birdius served as the principal of Melbourne High and Vocational School.

Browne left teaching and Florida in the 1930s when he joined the Tennessee Valley Authority (TVA). While working for the training staff section, he collaborated with five other authors on *Labor Relations in TVA.* In October 1935, he transferred to the relocation department and became the only African American reservoir removal agent in Alabama's Wilson-Wheeler Dam area. His excessive caseload prevented him from providing quality care to every affected black family, but he did create distinctive methods for assisting families. For example, when one family refused to move because their landlord held their six mules in mortgage, Browne negotiated a settlement between the landlord and the family where the landlord kept four of the mules, leaving the family with two so they could start farming in another location. He pushed for the TVA to build a community recreation ground that included a baseball diamond in the newly formed community of Orrsville.

Browne returned to Kentucky in the 1940s and worked at Paducah's West Kentucky Vocational Training School, which was built on the grounds of the former West Kentucky Industrial College. In the 1960s, he taught and was later a principal at Lincoln Junior High School. He later became a counselor with the Paducah Board of Education and in the mid-1970s served as vice president of Draughons Business College. Retired by 1986, Browne died

at the Parkview Convalescent Center, and Paducah's Hamock Funeral Home handled the funeral arrangements.

"Birdius Browne." *PS,* November 9, 1986, 4.
Grant, Nancy L. *TVA and Black Americans: Planning for the Status Quo.* Philadelphia: Temple Univ. Press, 1990.
Yenser, Thomas, ed. *Who's Who in Colored America, 1930–1932.* 3rd ed. Brooklyn, NY: Thomas Yenser, 1933.

—*Sallie L. Powell*

BROWN MEMORIAL C.M.E. CHURCH, first African American C.M.E. church in Louisville, KY, to move from an undesirable location. The current edifice housing the Brown Memorial C.M.E. Church, located at 813 W. Chestnut St., is the last known work of noted Louisville architect Gideon Shryock, who also designed the Jefferson County Courthouse and the Old Kentucky State Capitol. The church is a blend of two distinct nineteenth-century styles: Greek Revival and Romanesque Revival. It was built as the Chestnut Street Methodist Church. Construction began in 1863 and was completed in 1864; the formal dedication took place on Sunday, September 17, 1865.

The building was purchased in 1907 by the Center Street C.M.E. Church, then located on Center St. between Green and **Walnut.** The Christian Methodist Episcopal Church grew out of the Methodist Church South. Originally established in 1854, the Center Street C.M.E. Church was the first church of that denomination to be organized in Louisville, in 1870. The third general conference of the C.M.E. Church was held in Louisville at the Center Street Church in 1874. Later the congregation, under the leadership of Dr. L. H. Brown, became the first black church in Louisville to move from an undesirable location. The Jefferson County Jail was built in front of the Center Street Church on Green St. at Sixth. It was then that Dr. Brown purchased the Chestnut St. property and moved the congregation to the new location.

The first service in the renamed Chestnut Street C.M.E. Church was held on the second Sunday in May 1907. In May 1954, the congregation changed the name to Brown Memorial as a tribute to Dr. Brown. Three of its pastors became bishops: **W. H. Miles** (the first bishop of the C.M.E. Church), C. H. Phillips, and C. L. Russell. The church was rededicated on Sunday, April 1, 1990, after extensive restoration. The building was listed on the National Register of Historic Places in July 1979.

"Celebrating Our History, Brown Memorial CME Church Celebrates 160th Anniversary." Martha Elson. http://www.courier-journal .com/story/news/history/river-city-retro/2014/05/16/celebrating -history-brown-memorial-cme-church-celebrates-th-anniversary /9189789/ (accessed July 26, 2014).

—*Evelyn L. Waldrop*

BROWNSTOWN, African American community in Louisville, KY. Brownstown, a little-known African American community in part of what is now Old Louisville, developed shortly after the Civil War with the influx of former slaves into Louisville. The community was centered on Second and Magnolia Sts. when this area was some distance from the built-up parts of the city. It was named for a man named Brown. The *Globe,* a short-lived newspaper, noted on September 3, 1875, that "the original Brown, a brown-skinned, gray-haired old man, for whom this place is named, is still located out here. He is growing old now and looks very much as one would suppose that 'old black Joe' looks."

That person may have been Henry Brown, a laborer who lived on the west side of Third St. between Bloom St. and Cardinal Blvd., originally B and C Sts. He is the only Brown shown in that area in city directories of the period. By 1875, the Little Flock African (Baptist) Church had been established on Second St. near Shipp Ave., an area now within the Belknap Campus of the University of Louisville. By the early 1880s, there were two additional black churches: Zion Methodist on Second St. near Magnolia and Washington Chapel (Methodist) on Second near Shipp.

Apparently, as in **Smoketown** to the northeast, the residents built shotgun cottages on leased land. The cottages were still in place on Second in the early 1890s between Magnolia and Bloom Sts., but during that decade they were replaced with substantial brick homes as middle-class white suburbanization spread to the area and property values rose.

As old Brownstown vanished under the suburban tide, the black churches vanished too. The Little Flock Church had moved to E. Broadway as early as 1886, and Zion Methodist to 15th St. by 1893. Washington Chapel vanished from the record even earlier. The African American residents scattered to various parts of the city, some perhaps to the black community of **Ft. Hill** directly to the east, which was named for a Civil War fort in the vicinity.

Caron's Louisville City Directories, 1884–1892.
Sanborn Atlas: Louisville, 1892.

—George H. Yater

BROWN V. BOARD OF EDUCATION, 1954 U.S. Supreme Court decision that ruled against racial segregation in public schools. *Brown v. Board of Education* is one of the most important cases involving racial segregation ever decided by the Supreme Court of the United States. In *Plessy v. Ferguson* (1896), the court had promulgated the separate-but-equal doctrine. For over half a century, that doctrine had authorized racial segregation in the nation's public schools. Most courts failed to insist on true equality when they upheld local school practices. However, starting in 1938, a series of Supreme Court cases signaled that egregious discrimination might no longer be tolerated, especially in higher education.

In 1950 and 1951, four cases about public school segregation were tried in the lower courts and appealed to the Supreme Court: Segregated facilities in Topeka, KS, were held to be socially and psychologically damaging even though they were equal, but the district court said that under stare decisis it could do nothing. The NAACP Legal Defense Fund proved that African American schools in Clarendon Co., SC, were inferior and the court ordered that equal facilities be provided. However, the district court refused to declare segregation illegal per se. A district court in Virginia found that African American schools in Prince Edward Co. were inferior and ordered that equal facilities be provided but refused to order that black students be admitted to white schools. The Delaware Supreme Court ordered that black students be admitted to white schools until such time as the African American

schools were made equal to the white schools. The four cases were combined and argued before the Supreme Court of the United States, which rendered a unanimous verdict on May 17, 1954, that in the field of public education the doctrine of separate but equal has no place. Separate educational facilities are inherently unequal. The cases were restored to the docket for further argument on the question of appropriate remedies. All parties were invited to participate.

The implementation decision, commonly known as *Brown II*, was announced by a unanimous court on May 31, 1955. The cases were remanded to lower courts with the instruction that said courts require school authorities to make a prompt and reasonable start toward full compliance with the ruling. The inferior courts might consider a myriad of problems related to the transition to a racially nondiscriminatory system, but the Supreme Court stated that the validity of these constitutional principles could not be allowed to yield simply because of disagreement with them.

Before the *Brown* decision, black and white leaders in Kentucky were preparing for school desegregation on all levels. The 1949 **Lyman T. Johnson** case against the University of Kentucky opened graduate and professional schools to blacks. In 1950, the Kentucky General Assembly permitted equal access to undergraduate colleges with the repeal of the **Day Law. Berea College,** the University of Louisville, Nazareth, and Ursuline responded quickly to the law, and other institutions soon followed.

After the *Brown* decision, some school districts, including Williamsburg Independent Schools, quickly integrated their schools in 1955. Seventy-five percent of Kentucky's school districts had adopted plans to desegregate by the fall of 1956. Shortly afterward, almost 50 percent of the state's black school-age students were attending integrated schools. Several school districts, such as Sturgis High School, tried various means to avoid compliance with the law. Approximately a dozen lawsuits were filed in the federal courts requiring various schools to integrate. In the 1955–1956 school year, the Louisville Public Schools desegregated through a "freedom of choice" plan without major resistance. In 1969, the Supreme Court ruled that the policy of allowing "all deliberate speed" for desegregation was no longer constitutionally permissible. The court stated that "the obligation of every school district is to terminate dual school systems at once and to operate now and henceforth only unitary schools."

Louisville's desegregation plan met public and legal resistance after the Louisville Public Schools and Jefferson County Schools were merged in 1975. After extensive litigation through the 1990s and the first years of the twenty-first century, the U.S. Supreme Court ruled in 2008 that the Jefferson County Public School system had fulfilled the mandate of integrated schools required by *Brown v. Board of Education.*

Alexander v. Holmes, 396 U.S. 19 (1969).
Brown v. Board of Education, 347 U.S. 483 (1954).
Brown v. Board of Education, 349 U.S. 294 (1955).
Hardin, John A. *Fifty Years of Segregation: Black Higher Education, 1904–1954.* Lexington: Univ. Press of Kentucky, 1997, 109–10.
Johnson v. Board of Trustees, 625 Civ. E.D. Ky. (1948).
Kleber, John E., ed. *The Kentucky Encyclopedia.* Lexington: Univ. Press of Kentucky, 1992, 263, 264.

Plessy v. Ferguson, 163 U.S. 537 (1896).

Whitley County History Book Committee. *Whitley County, Kentucky, History and Families, 1818–1993.* Paducah, KY: Turner, 1994.

—*Charles F. Faber*

BRUCETOWN, African American community in Lexington, KY. Originally called Bruce's Addition, Brucetown was formed in 1865 when landowner William W. Bruce joined other prominent Lexington businessmen in dividing low-elevation property for freedmen to build homes. Bruce operated a hemp factory on N. Limestone St. near Seventh St. Brucetown was located near the factory for Bruce's African American employees to live. The community was bordered on the south by Seventh St., on the east by N. Limestone St., on the west by Broadway, and on the north by the Belt Line railroad.

Brucetown made national news in January 1878 when seven white men killed three African American men, Tom Turner, Edward Claxton, and John Davis, who were suspected of having information about a previous murder of a white man by an African American named Stiver. Stiver had been immediately lynched two weeks before the assault in Brucetown. The white men first attacked Turner in his residence. When he refused to leave his home, he was shot four times in the presence of his wife. Claxton and Davis were hanged in adjacent woods.

In 1880, Brucetown consisted of 513 African American homes. Brucetown, along with **Pralltown** and Adamstown, contained "the highest percentage of farm laborers" of all the Lexington **African American hamlets.** In the early 1900s, residents organized a baseball team that played other Lexington African American teams. Brucetown, along with some other local African American communities, suffered greatly in March 1909 when a rainstorm completely submerged the neighborhood.

Evergreen Baptist Church has served as a cornerstone of Brucetown since the congregation organized in 1869. Brucetown Park has provided recreational opportunities for the inhabitants.

Residents of Brucetown remain proud of their historical roots and identity. The Brucetown Neighborhood Association holds its annual festival, Brucetown Day, in early August. The event is free and open to the public.

Kellogg, John. "The Formation of Black Residential Areas in Lexington, Kentucky, 1865–1887." *Journal of Southern History* 48, no. 1 (February 1982): 21–52.

———. "Negro Urban Clusters in the Postbellum South." *Geographical Review* 67, no. 3 (July 1977): 310–21.

Newspapers: "Mob Violence in Kentucky," *NYT,* January 18, 1878, 1; "Colored," *LL,* May 3, 1908, 9; "Last Week's Storm in Kentucky," *Hazel Green Herald,* March 4, 1909, 4; "The Eight Little Towns in Lexington," *LL,* February 1, 1914, 3; "Smith to Be Honored at Evergreen Baptist," *LHL,* June 4, 1983, C2; "Brucetown Plans Annual Festival," *LHL,* August 8, 2001, 2.

—*Sallie L. Powell*

BRUNER, PETER (b. 1845, Winchester, KY; d. 1938, Oxford, OH), escaped slave and soldier. Peter Bruner, a slave who escaped to fight in the Civil War, was born at Winchester, Clark Co., KY, in 1845. As a lad, he labored under harsh conditions in his owner's tannery and on occasion was hired out to others. His numerous failed escape attempts usually resulted in severe punishment. In July 1864, Bruner finally made good his escape, fleeing 41 miles to **Camp Nelson,** KY, the largest black recruiting center in the commonwealth. There he enrolled in Company C, 12th Regiment, Heavy Artillery, U.S. Colored Troops. Bruner served primarily garrison duty in central and western Kentucky. Mustered out of service in 1866, he moved to Oxford, OH, where in 1868 he married Fannie Procton. The couple had five children.

After struggling for several years as a farm laborer, handyman, and watchman, Bruner became the janitor and messenger at Miami University in Oxford. His memoirs, published in 1918, depict the difficulties bondsmen faced in fleeing slavery and contain one of the best accounts of black soldier life in Kentucky during the Civil War. Bruner died on April 6, 1938, and was buried in Woodside Cemetery, Oxford.

Blassingame, John W., ed. *Slave Testimony: Two Centuries of Letters, Speeches, Interviews, and Autobiographies.* Baton Rouge: Louisiana State Univ. Press, 1977.

Bruner, Peter. *A Slave's Adventures toward Freedom: Not Fiction, but the True Story of a Struggle.* Oxford, OH: 1918, Documenting the American South, the University of North Carolina at Chapel Hill, University Library, 2004. http://docsouth.unc.edu/neh/bruner/summary.html (accessed July 27, 2014).

—*Marion B. Lucas*

***BUCHANAN V. WARLEY,* 1917 U.S. Supreme Court decision.** The U.S. Supreme Court's decision in *Buchanan v. Warley* on November 5, 1917, held unconstitutional a 1914 Louisville ordinance prohibiting a person from moving into a block where a majority of the residents were of another race. **William Warley,** a black who headed the Louisville branch of the **National Association for the Advancement of Colored People,** tested the ordinance when he contracted to buy a lot on a predominantly white street from Charles Buchanan, a white realty agent sympathetic to the NAACP. Warley claimed that the ordinance invalidated their contract, and Buchanan sued for specific performance, arguing that the ordinance unconstitutionally deprived him of property. In doing so, both men worked together in seeking to abolish the ordinance. When the state courts upheld the ordinance in *Harris v. City of Louisville* (1915), Buchanan appealed to the U.S. Supreme Court.

The Supreme Court held that the ordinance denied members of both races the right to own and dispose of property as they saw fit and thus violated the due process clause of the U.S. Constitution, as well as the **Civil Rights Act of 1866.** States and municipalities, the court conceded, should be accorded wide latitude in meeting the asserted objectives of the ordinance—protecting racial purity, preserving racial peace, and maintaining property values. However, such objectives could "not be promoted by depriving citizens of their constitutional rights and privileges." Nor, upon analysis, was the ordinance found to be reasonably related to the attainment of its stated objectives.

The court distinguished the *Buchanan* case from precedents like ***Plessy v. Ferguson*** (1896) and *Berea College v. Kentucky* (1908), which had upheld state segregation laws. The laws upheld in these cases merely limited the enjoyment of a right by "reasonable rules in regard to the separation of races." By contrast, the court asserted, the Louisville ordinance imposed absolute limitations on the disposal of property and thus amounted to an unconstitutional taking. Although the *Buchanan* case did not overturn the precedents, its affirmation of federal civil rights laws and amendments and its recognition of limits on segregation were one of the first judicial steps away from **Jim Crow.**

Freund, Paul A., and Stanley N. Katz, eds. *History of the Supreme Court of the United States.* New York: Macmillan, 1984.

Wright, George C. "The NAACP and Residential Segregation in Louisville, Kentucky, 1914–1917." *RKHS* 78 (Winter 1980): 39–54.

—*Daniel G. Stroup*

BUCKNER, GEORGE WASHINGTON (b. 1855, Green Co., KY; d. 1943, Evansville, IN), physician and minister and consul general to Liberia. George Washington Buckner, physician and diplomat, was born into slavery on the Stanton Buckner plantation in Green Co., KY, on December 1, 1855. Freed at the age of 10, he was educated in a freedmen's school and a private school in Greensburg. In 1870, he lived briefly in Louisville with an aunt and was a household servant for a white family. He became one of the first black teachers in Green Co. in 1871 and later moved to Indianapolis to reside with another aunt; there he attended public school and eventually graduated from Terre Haute State Normal School. After teaching for several years in Indiana in Vincennes, Washington, and Evansville, he returned to Indianapolis to receive his medical degree from Eclectic Medical College. In 1890, he moved to Evansville and, except for a brief time out of the country, was a practicing physician there for 53 years.

Buckner, a member of the Democratic Party, was interested in public affairs, and in 1913 President Woodrow Wilson appointed him minister and consul general to Liberia. Known as the "Elder Statesman of Indiana Blacks," he resigned the position in 1915 because of persistent bouts of African fever caused by the tropical climate and returned to Evansville.

In 1879, Buckner married Estella White, who died of tuberculosis in 1889. In 1896, he married Anna Cowan; they had five children. Buckner died in Evansville on February 16, 1943. His son, Zack, donated many of the memorabilia Buckner had acquired in Liberia to the Evansville Museum. The G. W. Tower at 710 Oak Street was constructed on the site of his residence.

"Dr. George Washington Buckner." http://web.usi.edu/boneyard /buckner.htm (accessed August 13, 2014).

Sides, Patricia. "History Lesson: Dr. George Washington Buckner, March 1, 2011. Evansville Courier & Press." http://www.courier press.com/lifestyle/history-lesson_20140612130501642 (accessed August 13, 2014).

BUCKNER, HARRY E. (b. unknown, Hopkinsville, KY; d. ca. 1938, Milwaukee, WI), baseball pitcher. A giant among baseball pitchers, Harry Buckner played for a myriad of teams named Giants. He began his career with the Chicago Unions in 1896, but like many baseball players of his era, he moved from team to team. He played for the Columbia Giants for a couple of seasons (1899–1901), the Philadelphia Giants (1903), the Cuban X-Giants (1904–1905), the Quaker Giants, the Brooklyn Royal Giants (1909–1910), the New York Lincoln Giants (1911–1912), the Smart

Set (1912), and the Schenectady Mohawk Giants (1913) and ended his playing career with the Chicago Giants (1914–1918). Buckner was one of the few American baseball players to play in Cuba in the early twentieth century when he pitched for Almendares in the 1907 Cuban winter league. According to teammate Sol White, who managed and played shortstop for the Philadelphia Giants, Buckner's pitching skills were equal to those of Andrew "Rube" Foster, one of the leaders of the Negro Baseball League, and they both could easily have pitched for the white leagues. Buckner and Foster dominated opponents when they were part of the pitching rotation of the 1909 Brooklyn Royal Giants.

In 1916, Buckner returned to "his old home" in Hopkinsville. He was considered "a once-famous" ballplayer. His athletic skills had enabled him to play infield, outfield, and catcher, but his pitching expertise landed him the trainer position for the white Milwaukee Brewers. His lotions and rubdowns facilitated the quick return of injured pitchers. In his playing days, Buckner was known as the Crutch and the Cyclone. Once he became a trainer, he was known simply as Doc.

Under the leadership of Coach Red Smith, the Milwaukee Brewers "ordered" Buckner home because of poor health in the late 1930s, and he died soon thereafter.

Cottrell, Robert Charles. *The Best Pitcher in Baseball: The Life of Rube Foster, Negro League Giant.* New York: New York Univ. Press, 2004.

Negro Leagues Baseball eMuseum. http://www.coe.ksu.edu/nlbemu seum/history/players/buckner.html (accessed August 27, 2008).

Newspapers: " 'Giants' in Baseball," *NYT*, May 28, 1907, 6; "Sparks from the Diamond," *IF*, September 21, 1907, 7; "Hopkinsville Negro," *HK*, April 4, 1916, 1.

Podoll, Brian A. *The Minor League Milwaukee Brewers, 1859–1952.* Jefferson, NC: McFarland, 2003.

White, Sol, and Jerry Malloy. *Sol White's History of Colored Base Ball with Other Documents on the Early Black Game, 1886–1936.* Lincoln: Univ. of Nebraska Press, 1996.

—*Sallie L. Powell*

BUCKTOWN, African American community in Winchester, KY. Although the official name may be Poynterville, Winchester residents know this African American neighborhood as Bucktown. Winchester's white newspaper, along with other area white newspapers, represented Bucktown primarily in a negative light in the early twentieth century. Stories about the neighborhood included robberies, drunkenness, murder, dueling, chicken stealing, crap games, and bootlegging. Even in a 1909 account of a flood where the water stood three feet deep and caused extensive property damage, the local newspaper quoted a citizen claiming that the flood "cleaned" Bucktown, and it was hoped that it would remain that way. Winchester's mayor, J. A. Hughes, issued an order to the police department to arrest any man in the community who did not work and was loafing in the area.

Occasionally articles included prominent African American establishments and leaders. Curry's Eating House, Birl Turner's livery business, Oren Bates's store, and a carriage drummer provided services to the community. Rev. J. W. Hutchens had remodeled Clarke's Methodist Episcopal Church in the early 1900s, and D. R. Taylor sold dry goods and notions from his department store.

Decades later, Bucktown was home to a massive Labor Day weekend celebration. Hundreds of people from nearby communities and areas such as Chicago, Cleveland, and California jammed the neighborhood. The roots festival featured beauty queens, scholastic achievers, musicians, and the local African American motorcycle club, the Ebony Riders. The gala ended with a parade on Labor Day. In 2008, Heritage Park was dedicated as not only a green space for Winchester's African American citizens but also a demonstration of a revival of the Bucktown area.

Alvey, R. Gerald. *Kentucky Bluegrass Country.* Jackson: Univ. Press of Mississippi, 1992.
Newspapers: "Flood in Bucktown," *WN,* February 24, 1909, 1; "Colored Column," *WN,* February 27, 1909, 3; "Loafers Must Go to Work," *Mt. Sterling Advocate,* September 15, 1909, 8; "Heritage Park Dedicated," *Winchester Sun,* October 29, 2008, A10; "Labor Day Celebration, Parade a Winchester Tradition," *Winchester Sun,* August 31, 2011.

—Sallie L. Powell

BUFFALO SOLDIERS, African American troops assembled after the Civil War. On July 28, 1866, Radical Republicans passed a bill through Congress authorizing the creation of six regiments of black troops. The regiments, consisting of the 9th and 10th Cavalry and the 38th, 39th, 40th, and 41st Infantry, would primarily be deployed as part of the numerous wars and skirmishes with Native Americans in the West. In 1868, the infantry units were combined into two regiments, the 24th and 25th Infantry. The troops collectively earned the nickname "buffalo soldiers" from their Native American opponents. The origin of the name is a matter of debate; some claim that it was a tribute to their ferocity in combat, while others have suggested that it was in reference to the soldiers' "wooly heads."

Initial recruitment efforts primarily centered on Louisiana but eventually spread to other states. In late 1866, officers opened a recruiting depot in Louisville, to immediate success. In January 1867, all 115 soldiers that joined the 9th Cavalry were recruited in Louisville, and another recruitment center was opened in Lexington in an attempt to capitalize on the influx of Kentuckians. Between 1868 and 1877, roughly 40 percent of the new recruits to the 9th Cavalry were Kentuckians.

Several prominent buffalo soldiers hailed from Kentucky. In 1881, **Brent Woods,** born into slavery in Pulaski Co., led his unit to victory after his commanding officer was killed in battle; he received the Medal of Honor for his actions 13 years later. In 1886, **Allen Allensworth,** a native of Louisville, was commissioned as a chaplain of the 24th Infantry. Highly regarded for his efforts in education within the army, Allensworth became the highest-ranking black officer in the history of the army when he was promoted to lieutenant colonel in 1906. **Thomas Shaw** received the Medal of Honor for his heroic actions at Carrizo Canyon in New Mexico on August 12, 1881, and was buried in Arlington National Cemetery in 1895. **Charles Young,** the third black graduate of West Point, was born in May's Lick, KY. He led the 10th Cavalry during the celebrated charge up San Juan Hill during the Spanish-American War.

Although most historians use the term "buffalo soldiers" to refer to black troops from the end of the Civil War to the Spanish-

American War, various units that descended from the original regiments remained active until integration of the armed forces after World War II. Mistreated in the service and often ignored afterward, buffalo soldiers received more attention after historians emphasized the importance of their service. In 2000, members of the 9th and 10th Cavalry were honored with a stone memorial erected next to the army post's main flagpole at Ft. Knox.

Craig, Berry. *Hidden History of Kentucky Soldiers.* Charleston, SC: History Press, 2011.
Johnson, Harry. "Buffalo Soldiers: The Formation of the Ninth Cavalry Regiment, July 1866–March 1867." MMAS thesis, U.S. Military Academy, West Point, 1978.
Kenner, Charles L. *Buffalo Soldiers and Officers of the Ninth Cavalry, 1867–1898: Black and White Together.* Norman: Univ. of Oklahoma Press, 1999.
Leckie, William H., with Shirley A. Leckie. *The Buffalo Soldiers: A Narrative of the Black Cavalry in the West.* Rev. ed. Norman: Univ. of Oklahoma Press, 2003.
Newspapers: "Kentucky Negro: Capt. Charles Young, Ninth Cavalry, May Be Promoted to Major," *LL,* January 6, 1912, 4; "Black Hero Given Formal Military Burial," *LHL,* October 29, 1984, A1; "Buffalo Soldiers Get Memorial at Fort Knox," *LHL,* February 25, 2000, B3.
Trowbridge, John. "How Two Kentucky 'Buffalo Soldiers' Earned the Medal of Honor." http://kentuckyguard.wordpress.com/2013/02/22/17632/ (accessed May 22, 2013).

—Stephen Pickering

BULLOCK, GEORGE L. (b. ca. 1892, Tennessee; d. unknown), lyricist and teacher. George L. Bullock had a passion for design, poetry, and music. He taught mechanical drawing at Louisville's **Central High School** for more than two decades. As an active member of the **Kentucky Negro Educational Association** from the 1920s into the 1940s, he gave presentations at the annual meetings titled "Graphic Thoughts" and "The Industrial Language." He served on the Committee to Arrange Exhibits and as the Industrial Arts Department secretary. He chaired the Committee on Industrial Exhibits and served as secretary of the Vocational Education Department.

Bullock played the violin and directed Central High School's Girls' Drum and Bugle Corps. In 1940, his poem "My Ambition" was selected for publication in the *World's Fair: Anthology of Verse.* As a biographical lyricist, he wrote songs on Booker T. Washington, Frederick Douglass, and Pearl Harbor hero Dorice "Dorie" Miller for W. C. Handy's publishing company. His song "Private **Robert Harold Brooks,**" about a Kentucky African American soldier who died fighting the Japanese in the Philippines, exemplified his descriptive style.

Dunnigan, Alice Allison, comp. and ed. *The Fascinating Story of Black Kentuckians: Their Heritage and Traditions.* Washington, DC: Associated Publishers, 1982.
Handy, W. C. *Unsung Americans Sung.* New York: Handy Brothers Music Co., 1944.
KNEAJ 1, no. 1 (October 1930): 5, 18; 4, no. 1 (October–November 1933): 9; nos. 1–3 (October–November 1939): 9, 17; 13, no. 1 (November–December 1942): 7.
Proceedings of the Kentucky Negro Educational Association, April 18–21, 1923; April 23–26, 1924; April 22–25, 1925; April 18–21, 1928.

—Sallie L. Powell

BURDETT, GABRIEL (b. 1829, Garrard Co., KY; d. 1914, Leavenworth, KS), educator and minister. Gabriel Burdett was born a slave (probably owned by Hiram Burdett) in Garrard Co., KY, and remained enslaved, along with his wife and children, until he joined the Union army at the age of 35. In his 20s, Burdett began serving as the minister of a segregated black congregation in the Baptist church at Forks of Dix River, where white Burdetts were prominent members. On January 22, 1855, Burdett married Lucinda Hoffman in Garrard Co.; they had 12 children, including Maggie, Smith, John G. (named after Rev. John G. Fee), Charles W., Gertrude, and Cora, but only three of Burdett's children outlived their father.

Burdett enlisted in the Union army at **Camp Nelson** on July 15, 1864, as a private in Company I, 114th U.S. Colored Infantry Volunteers; he was honorably discharged on September 15, 1866. While he was stationed at Camp Nelson, Burdett met Rev. John G. Fee, who became his teacher, mentor, and sponsor, and with Fee, he labored to help the families of Camp Nelson soldiers. Fee was impressed with Burdett's preaching and invited the younger man to become the first black trustee of **Berea College,** a position he held for 12 years. After a brief military excursion into Texas, Burdett settled at Camp Nelson, where he became minister of a free church Fee had founded and took charge of a school (also founded by Fee) known as **Ariel Academy.** Under the sponsorship of the **American Missionary Association,** for nearly a decade, Burdett continued his religious and educational ministry at Camp Nelson among the freed slaves. His political interests grew during this time, and he became well known in the Republican Party, attending conventions and serving as a presidential elector. In 1877, deeply disillusioned about prospects for racial equality in Kentucky, he became the leader of a group of African Americans from central Kentucky who migrated to Kansas among the **Exodusters.** He and his family first settled in Pottawatomie Co. and later in Cloud Co., but he had left Kansas by 1910, when he resided in Logan Co., OK. By then, he no longer listed his occupation as minister; he was an 80-year-old mail carrier. On November 17, 1914, he died in Leavenworth, KS, in the hospital of the National Military Home, and was buried near that facility.

Burdett, Gabriel. Pension records. National Archives; copies in Gabriel Burdett File, Berea College Archives.

Lucas, Marion B. "Gabriel Burdett." In *The Kentucky Encyclopedia,* edited by John E. Kleber, 142. Lexington: Univ. Press of Kentucky, 1992.

Sears, Richard D. *A Utopian Experiment in Kentucky: Integration and Social Equality at Berea, 1866–1904.* Westport, CT: Greenwood Press, 1996.

—*Richard D. Sears*

BURKS, ISHMON FARLEY, JR. (b. 1945, Louisville, KY), first African American Kentucky state police commissioner. The parents of Ishmon Burks guided him into a productive life. He was named for his father, a chemical operator, who had joined six other complainants when the Louisville, KY, branch of the **National Association for the Advancement of Colored People** filed a racial discrimination lawsuit against Du Pont Chemical Company in 1963. The suit requested the pay difference from when the employees should have been promoted. A $14-million settlement resulted nearly three decades later. Burks's mother, **Juanita Pauline Farley Burks,** was president and CEO of J. P. Burks Construction in Louisville.

After earning his diploma from Shawnee High School, Burks graduated as the distinguished military graduate at Lincoln University in Jefferson City, MO, and was commissioned a 2nd lieutenant in the army. He was awarded the Bronze Star in Vietnam in 1970. Among other positions in his extensive military career, he was an instructor at the U.S. Military Academy at West Point and chief of personnel for military police at the Pentagon. He retired as a colonel in 1993.

Burks earned a master's degree in education from Indiana University and a master's in criminology from the City University of New York. After he returned to Kentucky in 1995, he served as executive vice president and chief operating officer of Louisville's Spalding University. Governor Paul Patton appointed him commissioner of the Kentucky State Police on August 22, 2000; he was the first African American to hold that position.

The 55-year-old Burks announced his goals as diversifying the state's police force and improving the training and education of officers. At the time of his appointment, only 43 sworn officers were minorities and only 33 were female out of the 977 newly deputized Kentucky State Police law enforcers. In 2002, Governor Patton selected Burks as Justice Cabinet secretary in addition to his position as state police commissioner. One of his main goals in this new position was to develop legislation that would toughen Kentucky's prescription drug laws. Burks resigned at the end of Governor Patton's administration.

For a short time, Burks worked as executive vice president of communications for DHB Industries, which manufactured protective body armor. In 2006, he assumed the position of program coordinator for the Criminal Justice Program at Jefferson Community and Technical College in Louisville. Burks has been recognized as a Distinguished Alumnus at Historically Black Universities and as a Louisville Distinguished Citizen.

"Biographies: Justice Cabinet Executive Staff." http://ky.gov/agencies/justice/html/bios.htm (accessed November 17, 2009).

Jefferson Community College. http://www.jefferson.kctcs.edu/administration/provost/WholeCampus22609.pdf (accessed November 17, 2009).

Kentucky State Police. "Official Kentucky State Police Press Release." http://kentuckystatepolice.org/text/topress/pr_4_16_02.htm (accessed November 17, 2009).

Newspapers: "Burks New Chief of State Police; Administrative Skills, Ability with People Cited," *LHL,* August 23, 2000, A1; "Retired Army Officer First Black KSP Chief," *KP,* August 23, 2000, 1K.

Sanders, Donna Burks. E-mail, January 27, 2010, to KAAE Office.

—*Sallie L. Powell*

BURKS, JUANITA PAULINE FARLEY (b. 1920, Marion, KY), African American female entrepreneur. Born in Crittenden Co. to Allen Farley, a farmer and World War I veteran, and Donna Farley, a cook, Juanita Farley was taught the importance of education. Her mother had to quit school when she was in the sixth grade because of Juanita's grandmother's death. This made Donna determined that her children would be educated. Juanita attended

Kentucky State College (later **Kentucky State University**) for two years and then married Ishmon Burks Sr. in Louisville. Ishmon, a chemical operator, joined six other complainants when the Louisville, KY, branch of the **National Association for the Advancement of Colored People** filed a racial discrimination lawsuit against Du Pont Chemical Company in 1963. The suit requested the pay difference from when the employees should have been promoted. A $14-million settlement resulted nearly three decades later.

The couple raised their three children, **Ishmon Jr.,** Donna, and Robert, in Louisville's West End. Burks worked as a night-shift custodian at South Central Bell and a nurse at Central State Hospital but wanted to operate her own business. After all three of her children graduated from college, she took some business courses at the University of Louisville. In 1974, at age 54, she and her husband mortgaged their home, and she obtained a federal small-business loan to open her first business, City Plaza, a personnel recruitment service that matched minority workers with Fortune 500 companies. Her later business ventures included a nursing business, an alcoholic beverage distributorship, a stop-smoking center, and a shoe store.

In 1980, Burks established J. P. Burks Construction, a construction and glass company, after receiving a promise of government contracts via affirmative action. Over 20 years later, she continued to work 12-hour days. Her company supplied glass for the expansion of the south wing of the Kentucky Fair and Exposition Center and was awarded a $193,000 contract to supply sprinklers for the renovation of Churchill Downs.

Burks served her community in various arenas. Even though she never learned to drive and knew Governor Julian Carroll only by his newspaper photographs, Burks was appointed by the governor in the late 1970s to President Jimmy Carter's energy board. In 1983, she received the Woman of Achievement award from the Business and Professional Women of River City and also became a member of the Prichard Committee for Academic Excellence. Governor Brereton Jones later named her to the University of Louisville's Board of Trustees. In 2006, the Actors Theatre of Louisville ended its season with *Crowns: Portraits of Black Women in Church Hats* and honored Burks, dubbed Louisville's Hat Queen. She owned 29 hats, including one specially made for her by Frank Olive, the famous **Kentucky Derby** hat designer.

In her mid-80s, Burks claimed, "As long as I got breath in my body I'm going to be doing something." The death of her youngest son, Robert, from diabetes led her to educate the African American community about the disease.

Newspapers: "Prichard Committee Changing Its Focus," *LHL,* September 8, 1983, A1; "83-Year-Old Loves Business," *LCJ,* October 1, 2003, F1; "Faith and Fashion," *LCJ,* April 16, 2006, 11.

Sanders, Donna Burks. E-mail, January 27, 2010, to KAAE Office.

"She Made Sure I Had an Education." *Today's Woman,* February 1, 2004.

—*Sallie L. Powell*

BURKS CHAPEL A.M.E. CHURCH, African Methodist Episcopal Church in Paducah, KY. At the wooden home of Dinah Jarrett, located at 635 Ohio St. in Paducah, KY, Burks Cha-

Burks Chapel A.M.E. Church.

pel A.M.E. Church was organized with 12 members in 1858. Paducah's second-oldest African American church was named for its founder and first pastor, Moses Burks. A frame church was built a little over a decade later, and the church established the first organized school for Paducah's African American children. In 1873, Kentucky's African Methodist Episcopal Church held its sixth annual conference at the church.

The church was a central point for community interests. In the early 1900s, nearly a thousand people attended Burks Chapel's annual Sunday school picnics. After Kentucky's **Day Law** prevented African Americans from matriculating at **Berea College,** J. W. Dinsmore, a Berea College dean, along with two African American Berea College graduates, traveled to Paducah to raise funds for the construction of the future **Lincoln Institute.** The first meeting was held at Burks Chapel, and the second one was convened at **Washington Street Baptist Church.**

Various speakers have lectured at Burks Chapel. In the early 1900s, bishops from across the nation spoke at the church, including Bishop C. T. Schaffear, whose presentation was "What I Saw in Africa." A large crowd attended missionary E. Marie Carter's oration. When the expanding church membership of almost 700 people had outgrown its building, Rev. G. W. Robinson conceived a fund-raising method that divided the membership into 13 groups and sent them throughout the community to raise no less than $100 each. They raised $1,525 and built their current edifice in 1911.

Surviving three major floods, Burks Chapel A.M.E. Church still stands on the corner of Ohio St. and Seventh St. in Paducah. In 2008, the members celebrated their 150th anniversary with various guest speakers, including Rev. Charlene Boone, who spoke at the service honoring women in ministry.

Kentucky Historical Marker Database. http://migration.kentucky.gov /kyhs/hmdb/MarkerSearch.aspx?mode=All (accessed November 11, 2009).

Newspapers: "Colored Conference," *PSD,* October 6, 1903, 4; "Local Lines," *PS,* August 12, 1905, 5; "Raised $1,525," *PES,* June 10, 1907, 5; "Colored School," *PES,* December 14, 1908, 4; "Burks Chapel's 150th Anniversary Celebration Kicks Off This Weekend," *PS,* May 2, 2008.
—*Sallie L. Powell*

BURLEIGH, ANGUS AUGUSTUS (b. 1845, unknown; d. 1938, Los Angeles, CA), one of the first African Americans to graduate from Berea College. The origins and early life of Angus Augustus Burleigh are shrouded in mystery. His death certificate (copy in his file in the Berea College Archives) states that he was born "on the high seas Atlantic Ocean" in April 1845 (day unknown), a son of Charles A. Burleigh, a native of London, England, and Carlotta De Dasco, born in St. Augustine, FL. But Burleigh himself left many different versions of his parentage, his birthplace, his parents' birthplaces, and his mother's ethnicity in public records over the years. Censuses (1880, 1900, 1910, 1930) record his birthplace as Kentucky, Mexico, "at sea," and Virginia, in that order; his parents' birthplaces are similarly varied. According to medical records, Burleigh claimed that his mother was from Granada, Spain—a doctor's annotation says that he was "very dark, possibly Moorish." Apparently, he was born on a ship because his father was the captain, while his mother was an American slave woman; he may have been born free, but he and his family were (perhaps) sold into slavery in Virginia after his father died.

Angus Augustus Burleigh.

On August 22, 1864, Angus A. Burleigh enlisted as a private at **Camp Nelson,** KY, in Company G, 12th U.S. Colored Heavy Artillery, and was given the rank of corporal the next day. On November 2, 1865, he was promoted to the rank of sergeant and was discharged at that rank in Louisville on April 24, 1866. He had first met Rev. John G. Fee at Camp Nelson. Fee invited him to come to Berea as a student. Burleigh's arrival in a classroom at the Berea school precipitated a walkout of most of the white students present, but he persisted and in 1875 became one of the first men of color to graduate from **Berea College.**

Burleigh married Louisa E. Shaffer in Greene Co., OH, on November 25, 1875. They had two sons, Otto F. and Cornelius H., and a daughter, Benitta. Burleigh became a minister in the African Methodist Episcopal Church and briefly served as chaplain of the Illinois State Senate; his chaplaincy in the U.S. Army lasted from about 1874 to 1906, according to his own account. But he had many different residences (Brooklyn, NY; Quincy, IL; Milwaukee, WI; Bloomington, IN; Redondo, CA) and many different occupations, including schoolteacher, salesman on the railway, and farmer.

Burleigh lived to be honored as Berea's oldest living graduate, dying at age 93 on May 24, 1938, in the National Military Home in the Veterans Administration Facility in Los Angeles, where he was buried. In the late twentieth century, Hasan Davis, a talented African American graduate of Berea College, played Angus A. Burleigh in a one-man dramatic monologue, *The Long Climb to Freedom,* which was staged very successfully across Kentucky and in many other states.

Angus Augustus Burleigh File, Berea College Archives.
Sears, Richard D. *A Utopian Experiment in Kentucky: Integration and Social Equality at Berea, 1866–1904.* Westport, CT: Greenwood Press, 1996.

—*Richard D. Sears*

BURLEY, DANIEL GARDNER (b. 1907, Lexington, KY; d. 1962, Chicago, IL), journalist, sportswriter, editor, musician, composer, and disc jockey. Born in 1907 in Lexington, KY, Daniel G. Burley was the son of James Burley, a Baptist preacher, and Anna V. Burley. After his father's death, Burley's mother remarried and later settled in Chicago, IL, where Burley attended Wendell Phillips High School.

Daniel Burley began his long and respected career as a journalist when he joined the staff at the *Chicago Defender* in 1928. He worked for three years with the *Defender* as a sports editor, columnist, and reporter. In 1932, he became the city editor, columnist, and sports and theatrical editor for the *Chicago Sunday Bee* while also writing pieces for the Associated Negro Press. He spent two more years with the *Chicago Defender,* from 1935 through 1937, before moving to New York, where he became managing editor as well as sports editor, city editor, theatrical editor, and reporter for the *New York Amsterdam News.* He later managed or wrote for the *Southside Civic Telegram,* the *New York Age,* and *Ebony* and was also the founder of *Jet* magazine.

Burley's reporting on the nightlife of Harlem while he was in New York also gave him the opportunity to explore his musical interests. Often writing about the emerging jive and **jazz** scene in the city, he later authored *Daniel Burley's Original Handbook of Harlem Jive* in 1944. Capturing the complexities of African American culture and linguistics, Burley's jive handbook helped popularize this new form of music beyond the jazz community. An accomplished piano player himself, he tried his hand at musical composition and created the group Dan Burley and the Skiffle Boys, which influenced future generations of jazz, **blues,** and rock-and-roll bands. He was a member of the American Federation of Musicians and served as a disc jockey for WWRL and WLIB in New York City.

Burley's role as sports editor also allowed him to address issues surrounding racial discrimination in American sports. Although he reported on sports ranging from golf to football, his most spirited coverage was of African American Jackie Robinson's entrance into the baseball major leagues in 1947. Frustrated by obstacles faced by black leagues because of segregation, he argued in 1943 that "colored baseball is but a poor shadow of the major league—the real thing." He believed that integration of the leagues not only would break barriers but also would allow black players the opportunity to showcase their undeniable talent. During the 1950s, he again used his columns to campaign for the young Willie Mays, who eventually played center field for the New York Giants. Burley moved back to Chicago in the early 1950s and died there in October 1962. He was buried in Burr Oak Cemetery.

"Burley, Daniel G." Notable Kentucky African Americans Database, Univ. of Kentucky. http://www.uky.edu/Libraries/NKAA/record.php?note_id=688 (accessed December 14, 2009).

Fleming, G. James, and Christian E. Burckel, eds. *Who's Who in Colored America.* 7th ed. *Supplement,* 77–78. Yonkers-on-Hudson, NY: Christian E. Burckel & Associates, 1950.

Goldstein, Warren. "Before You Could Say Jackie Robinson." *NYT,* May 16, 2004.

Hamm, Theodore. "Dan Burley's Original Handbook of Harlem Jive (1944)." *Brooklyn Rail,* December 2008–January 2009. http://www.brooklynrail.org/2008/12/express/dan-burleys-original-handbook-of-harlem-jive-1944 (accessed December 14, 2009).

Klima, John. "When the Yankees Were Not Ready for Willie Mays." *NYT,* September 13, 2009.

Lanctot, Neil. *Negro League Baseball: The Rise and Ruin of a Black Institution.* Philadelphia: Univ. of Pennsylvania Press, 2004.

—*Stephanie M. Lang*

BURNS, HARVEY (b. 1884, Louisville, KY; d. 1931, Louisville, KY), Louisville undertaker. The son of George and Mary (Scott) Burns, Harvey Burns was primarily raised by his grandparents, Sam and Harriet McDaniel, in Louisville, KY. He obtained only an eighth-grade education. As a young man in his 20s, Burns worked as a steamer in a tobacco factory. He later operated a saloon, ice cream businesses, and soft-drink stands.

By 1920, the 35-year-old Burns owned a funeral home and had become the chairman of the 9th and 10th Ward Republican Club. Additionally, the Board of Safety had appointed him Louisville's official city undertaker for African Americans. Burns had earned the reputation of an underworld figure who provided the black vote to the Republican Party. In June 1920, white police officer Miles Pounds and others raided a crap game on W. **Walnut St.**

Burns was among those arrested. He provided a fake name, Luke Jones, at the police station. Prosecuting Attorney Robert Lucas, also a prominent Republican who knew Burns, never questioned Burns for using the false name. According to a white newspaper, the *Kentucky Irish American,* policeman Pounds was "fired" for arresting Burns.

Identified as "the Republican negro boss," Burns pushed for accessibility to Shawnee Park for African Americans, helped the needy find jobs and housing, and intervened with police to get African Americans released from jail. However, he was also accused of controlling several gambling places to such an extent that such businesses were not allowed to open unless "King Harvey" gave "his royal permission." In the November 1921 election, another Louisville undertaker, **Arthur D. Porter Sr.**, announced his candidacy for mayor on the newly created **Lincoln Independent Party** (LIP) ticket, which formed for the purpose of opening political doors for Louisville's African Americans. Some local black leaders, including Harvey Burns, who had benefited from Republicans, immediately besieged Porter. Some ruffians associated with Burns attacked Porter and other LIP members with rocks and eggs, and Porter's Funeral Home suffered several incidents of vandalism, including gunshots.

Burns clearly went to great lengths to retain his political and financial power, which included expensive clothing and cars. In 1930, his home was valued at $10,000. He died the next year of acute gastritis. His funeral was well attended, and he was buried in Greenwood Cemetery. He was survived by his wife, Annie, his 17-year-old daughter, Harvetta, who later became a funeral director, and his 10-year-old son, Harvey R. Burns.

Kentucky Death Records, 1852–1953.

Newspapers: "Caught Simmons' 'Jack,'" *Cleveland Gazette,* March 20, 1920, 2; "Democrats," *Kentucky Irish American,* July 3, 1920, 1; "Republicans," *Kentucky Irish American,* April 16, 1921, 1; "Republicans," *Kentucky Irish American,* September 10, 1921, 1.

Smith, Suzanne E. *To Serve the Living: Funeral Directors and the American Way of Death.* Cambridge, MA: Belknap Press of Harvard Univ. Press, 2010.

U.S. Federal Census (1900, 1910, 1920, 1930).

Wright, George C. *Life Behind a Veil: Blacks in Louisville, Kentucky, 1865–1930.* Baton Rouge: Louisiana State Univ. Press, 1985.

—*Sallie L. Powell*

BURNS, THOMAS "TOMMIE," JR. (b. 1933, Mississippi), entrepreneur. Raised on a Mississippi farm, Thomas "Tommie" Burns Jr. left with his parents' blessings for Louisville, KY, when he was 18. He stayed with a relative, worked as a molder for the American Standard plant, and soon married his wife, Barbara. Believing that he should take advantage of every opportunity offered to him, Burns accepted a friend's invitation to clean Bacon's Department Store in Shively in the evenings after working his day job. His strong work ethic led to him cleaning all Bacon's Department Stores in Louisville and establishing Burns Janitor Services, which became incorporated in 1975. A year later, his daughter urged him to open Broadway Roller Rink since Louisville's West End had virtually no recreational options for young people.

Burns maintained, "I never had anybody give me anything but a chance." He believed that contributing to the community was more important than money. He was involved in the Boy Scouts of America, the Louisville Chamber of Commerce, the March of Dimes, and Spalding University.

With no formal education, Burns parlayed his janitorial business into Burns Enterprises, which included not only the skating rink but also Burns Chemical and Supply, B-Line food marts, Burns Rigging, and Burns Packaging. In 1995, Burns Janitor Service was the 12th-largest minority business in the United States. Burns then founded T & WA Inc., a tire and wheel assembly company, expanding plants into Indiana, Michigan, Mississippi, South Carolina, and Alabama that serviced Mercedes, Honda, and Hyundai. Less than a decade later, the corporation had annual sales of $500 million and more than 200 employees.

In 2002, Governor Paul Patton appointed Burns to the University of Louisville's Board of Trustees. A year later, he was selected a finalist for the Ernst and Young Entrepreneur of the Year award. In 2007, Burns partially sold the company to some Cincinnati businessmen and remained a part-time consultant for at least five years. Burns turned over his janitorial business to his youngest daughter, Shea, in 2009. Burns acted on his business philosophy: "I was born with zero and I will die with zero." He willingly and successfully took chances in his entrepreneurial enterprises.

Biz Journals. http://louisville.bizjournals.com/louisville/stories/2003 /05/05/daily41.html (accessed December 2, 2009).

Burns Janitor Service. http://www.burnsjanitor.com/bjslegacy.htm (accessed November 30, 2009).

Newspapers: "Sensible Chance Paid Off," *LHL,* April 3, 1994, 3; "Even Hard Work Requires Being Given a Chance," *LHL,* April 10, 1994, 2; "Patton Replaces Reid Critic as Member of KSU Regents," *LHL,* June 6, 2002, B5; "Minority Business to Supply Hyundai," *LHL,* June 12, 2003, C6.

—*Sallie L. Powell*

BURROUGHS, NANNIE HELEN (b. 1879, Orange, VA; d. 1961, Washington, DC), religious leader, educator, political organizer, and civil rights activist. Born in Orange, VA, in 1879, Nannie Helen Burroughs graduated from Business High School in Washington, DC, with honors in 1896. As a stenographer and typist, she worked on Philadelphia's *Christian Banner* with Rev. Lewis G. Jordan, a prominent Baptist minister, and the Foreign Mission Board of the National Baptist Convention (NBC). In 1901, she moved to Louisville, KY, to continue her work with the board and became its editorial secretary. Along with seven other employees, she boarded with Jordan and his mother until 1913.

In Kentucky, Burroughs joined others, such as **Mary Cook Parrish,** in 1904 to stress the need for an African American hospital. Recognized for her organizational skill, she established the Women's Industrial Club, which emphasized education for young women, and later the Women's Auxiliary of the NBC, the largest black women's organization in the United States. She was elected secretary and later president of the organization. Her tireless efforts promoting equal justice and education for women culminated in her establishing the National Baptist Woman's Convention (WC), a national forum for black Baptist women of which she was elected corresponding secretary and, in 1948, president.

In 1907, Burroughs received an honorary master's degree from **Eckstein Norton Institute.** A year later, she conceived and promoted a National Woman's Day as a way of promoting cohesion among black women and as a fund-raiser for the WC. The *Louisville Courier-Journal* covered her 1908 speech to the Baptist Women's Missionary Society of Kentucky, where she stressed cleanliness in homes and missions. As a speaker, she traveled to other parts of the state, including the **Hopkinsville Male and Female College.**

Burroughs published a handbook on business operations, *What to Do and How to Do It.* In 1909, she founded the National Training School for Women and Girls in Washington, DC, which educated women from the United States, Africa, and the Caribbean. In public forums, she expressed her concern about the European influence on Africa. She advocated for the eradication of lynching and discrimination based on racial differences and for employment and voting rights for women.

"Work, Support Thyself, to Thine Own Powers Appeal" was Nannie Helen Burroughs's motto. She died in Washington, DC, on May 20, 1961, at the age of 82. In 1964, her former training school was posthumously renamed the Nannie Helen Burroughs School in her honor.

Gregory, Shelia T. "Educators, Modern." In *Black Women in America,* edited by Darlene Clark Hine. Oxford Univ. Press, 2005. http:// www.oxfordreference.com/views/ENTRY.html?subview=Main &entry=t252.e0124 (accessed February 2, 2009).

Higginbotham, Evelyn Brooks. "Burroughs, Nannie Helen." In *Black Women in America,* edited by Darlene Clark Hine. Oxford Univ. Press, 2005. http://www.oxfordreference.com/views/ENTRY.html ?subview=Main&entry=t252.e0051 (accessed February 2, 2009).

Newspapers: "William J. Simmon's Business Institute," *AB,* November 13, 1903, 3; "Notes of Local Interest," *AB,* September 16, 1904, 2; "Nannie H. Burroughs Addresses Words of Cheer," *LCJ,* May 27, 1908, 8; "M & F College," *HK,* November 7, 1908, 2.

Roefs, Wim. "Civil Rights Movement." In *Black Women in America,* edited by Darlene Clark Hine. Oxford Univ. Press, 2005. http:// www.oxfordreference.com/views/ENTRY.html?subview=Main &entry=t252.e0069 (accessed February 2, 2009).

U.S. City Directories, 1821–1989 (1901–1913).

U.S. Federal Census (1910).

—*Norma E. Threadgill-Goldson*

BURSE, KIM M. HATCH (b. 1954, U.S. Air Force base in Germany), state revenue secretary and bank president and CEO. Early in her life, Kim Hatch moved among various military bases. When her parents divorced, she and her mother went to live with her grandmother in Louisville. Her mother graduated at the top of her class with a biology degree from the University of Louisville, but she was unable to find a job. Letters from social workers explained the problem: Kim's mother was black and had diabetes. The family survived on welfare and child-support payments and lived in public housing.

Through federal grants, Kim earned an accounting degree in 1976 from the University of Kentucky and then worked for a Louisville accounting firm. She and her husband, **Raymond Burse,** married in 1980, and five years later, she earned her master's degree in business administration from the University of Kentucky.

When her third son was only six months old, Burse was appointed secretary of the Revenue Cabinet by Governor Brereton Jones; she was the first African American woman to hold a cabinet position in Kentucky and the fourth African American to hold a cabinet-level post in Kentucky's history. During her tenure (1991–1995), she dramatically changed the state's tax-collecting agency. She established training programs, updated technology, created better planning and efficiency methods, prosecuted tax cheats, consolidated the cabinet's scattered offices, and improved confusing taxpayer paperwork. Her redirection of the revenue agency resulted in an additional $24 million in 1994. One of her key goals was to hire more minorities, and she used a creative method to accomplish that goal. She sent letters to Lexington and Louisville ministers of black churches that included employment opportunities, job qualifications, and steps to get those jobs. She also compiled information packets with job descriptions and explanations of the process required to get each job. In two years, she increased the number of minorities in her cabinet 58 percent, the largest increase among Kentucky's cabinets.

After leaving the Revenue Cabinet, Burse became the founding president and CEO of Louisville Development Bancorp, the holding company of the Louisville Community Development Bank; she was the first woman and African American CEO of a Louisville bank. Her position allowed her to accomplish one of her main goals, improving the quality of life for others, as she oversaw the demolition of the housing project where she had once lived and the transformation of the property into a development where former project tenants were able to be homeowners. She earned the Martha Layne Collins Leadership Award, was inducted into the University of Kentucky's Gatton College of Business and Economics Alumni Hall of Fame, and received the Kentucky Society of CPAs in Government Award. In 2009, she served as vice president of corporate services for Goodwill Industries of Kentucky, one of the largest Goodwill operations in the world.

Newspapers: "Burse Is First Black Woman to Join Cabinet," *KP,* December 7, 1991, 16K; "Revenue Secretary Praised for Focus," *LHL,* January 2, 1994; "Revenue Secretary Shows How to Find, Hire More Minorities," *LHL,* August 28, 1994, A1; "Efficient Burse Polishes Reputation of Tax Cabinet," *LHL,* August 21, 1995, B1; "Commitment to Helping Earns Kim Burse Award," *LHL,* August 17, 2001, B5.
Who's Who in Black Louisville. 3rd ed. Columbus, OH: Who's Who Publishing Co., 2009.

—*Sallie L. Powell*

BURSE, LUTHER, SR. (b. 1937, Hopkinsville, KY), college president and Forest Service official. Born in Christian Co., Luther Burse Sr. earned degrees at Kentucky State College (later **Kentucky State University**), Indiana University, and the University of Maryland. He began his education career in the Chicago public schools in the late 1950s. After earning his doctorate in education, he was an industrial arts professor at Cheyney State College in Pennsylvania, where he was elected a director of the National Education Association Board and in 1981 became the college's interim president. He served as president of Fort Valley State College, a predominantly African American school in Georgia, from 1983 to 1989.

Burse then left the education profession to work for the Forest Service and served as the acting associate director of the U.S. Department of Agriculture. In 1992, he was named the Forest Service's director of civil rights. Burse maintained that minorities were negatively affected by the National Forest Service's reorganization of personnel and consolidation of districts. He argued that the problems also hindered people with disabilities from equal access to buildings, programs, and facilities; and extensive travel distances encumbered employees with disabilities and those caring for family members with disabilities. In 1998, he joined a committee that drafted the "Memorandum of Understanding between the National Black Farmers Association, the USDA Forest Service, and the USDA Coalition of Minority Employees."

Along with his job as the Forest Service's director of civil rights, Burse has served as the president of Kentucky State University's National Alumni Association. He and his wife, Mamie, have two children, Luther Jr. and Elizabeth.

"People," *Jet,* June 10, 1976, 29; "Education," September 5, 1983, 53; "People," January 25, 1993, 20.
Kazi, Kuumba Ferrouill. "The Forest Service Is Growing Diversity." *Black Collegian* 24, no. 2 (November / December 1993): 72–76.
Newspapers: "Reinstatement of College Chief Denied," *Atlanta Journal-Constitution,* September 14, 1988, B4; "Report: National Forest Violated Civil Rights," *New Hampshire Union Leader* (Manchester), March 22, 1997, A4.
Who's Who among African Americans. 14th ed. New York: Gale Research, 2001.

—*Sallie L. Powell*

BURSE, RAYMOND MALCOLM (b. 1951, Hopkinsville, KY), former president of Kentucky State University. Academically astute and a gifted athlete, Raymond Malcolm Burse turned down several football scholarships to attend Centre College in Danville, KY, and graduated with a bachelor of science degree in chemistry and mathematics in 1973. His initial plan was medical school, but as a Rhodes scholar at Oxford, he changed his career to law. He won his first of three Oxford blues, an athletic award for the highest competitor, when he scored in his rugby debut against Cambridge, becoming the first African American and only the sixth American to receive that honor. He earned his law degree at Harvard Law School in 1978 and became a partner in the Louisville law firm Wyatt, Tarrant, and Combs.

With no experience as a teacher or college administrator, but with a stellar academic background and membership in Kentucky's Council on Higher Education, Burse became one of the youngest college presidents in the United States when he was appointed **Kentucky State University**'s president in 1982. He focused on the school's perceived second-rate image by challenging the institution's community to strive for academic excellence and promoting the school's visibility throughout the state. He created the **Whitney M. Young** College for Leadership Studies, which targeted top-ranking high school students. When he left Kentucky State University in 1989, he was praised for revitalizing a stagnant university even though some viewed him as an abrasive manager.

Burse returned to Wyatt, Tarrant, and Combs, working in corporate, tax, and securities law. He has also worked as general

Raymond Burse.

counsel for Louisville-based General Electric Consumer and Industrial. Active in his community, he has served as vice chair of the Louisville Community Foundation, chair of the Louisville Free Public Library Advisory Commission, a board member of the Greater Louisville Chestnut Street YMCA, vice chair of the African American Heritage Foundation, and chair of the National Collegiate Athletic Association Council subcommittee to review minority opportunities in intercollegiate athletics.

On July 1, 2014, Burse returned to Kentucky State University as the interim president. He made national news because of his decision to give $90,000 of his salary to the institution's lowest paid workers. Because of his "executive management skills" Burse was hired as the school's president on October 24, 2014. Upon the announcement Burse said, "I am probably smarter, better equipped to be able to fulfill the role. I've learned a lot. I have learned a lot from corporate America."

He and his wife, **Kim Burse**, have three sons.

Who's Who in Black Louisville. 3rd ed. Columbus, OH: Who's Who Publishing Co., 2009.

Centre College. http://www.centre.edu/web/news/2007/1/mlkburse .html (accessed December 1, 2009).

Newspapers: "Dark Calls Finley 'Best Friend,'" *NYT,* December 3, 1974, 52; "President Urges Staff to Start," *LHL,* January 11, 1983, B1; "Burse Bids KSU Farewell, Says He Feels 'Very Good,'" *LHL,* April 19, 1989, A1; "Former KSU President Burse Returning to Kentucky Law Firm," *LHL,* July 1, 1989, C2; "Centre's MLK Day to Feature Raymond Burse," *LHL,* January 10, 2007, E3; "Kentucky State University, Interim Hired as President, Contract Extended until June 30, 2018," *LHL,* October 25, 2014, A1.

—*Sallie L. Powell*

BURTON, NELSON (b. 1922, Covington, KY; d. 2010, Cincinnati, OH), jazz musician. Nelson Burton, born on September 12, 1922, a musician, **jazz** historian, speaker, and author, was the son of James R. and Ardell Coleman Burton. He graduated from **Lincoln-Grant High School** in 1939 and attended Kentucky State College (later known as **Kentucky State University**) in Frankfort, receiving a football scholarship. He was not able to serve in World War II because of a medical condition (a double hernia) that caused him to be classified 4-F. Like many young African American men at the time, Burton believed that serving his country would be a way to become accepted as a full citizen of the United States, thereby helping break down segregation laws. Because he was not able to become a soldier, he chose to work at the foundry of the Wright Aeronautical factory just north of Cincinnati in Evendale, OH. He also volunteered to play drums for the USO groups that entertained the troops, thus beginning his 50-year career as a rhythm drummer. Burton was a house musician for Cincinnati's famed black Cotton Club in the 1940s and 1950s and a studio musician in the 1950s for legendary King Records of Cincinnati. During his career, Burton backed up or had jam sessions with some of the most popular entertainers in the United States: Pearl Bailey, Count Basie, Cab Calloway, Nat King Cole, Duke Ellington, Harry James, and Maybelle Smith.

In the 1970s, with Lisa Ledin, a public-radio announcer and producer, Burton started recording his memoirs, which were published in 2000 as *Nelson Burton: My Life in Jazz.* Even in his 80s, he was still willing to perform on his drums or speak to young people about jazz music. He believed that jazz music was an important element of American culture that must be kept alive. Burton died in July 2010.

Burton, Nelson. *Nelson Burton: My Life in Jazz.* Cincinnati: Clifton Hills Press, 2000.

—*Jessica Knox-Perkins*

BURTON, THOMAS WILLIAM (b. 1860, Madison Co., KY; d. 1939, Springfield, OH), physician and businessman. Born in a log cabin of slave parents and the youngest of 15 children, Thomas Burton was illiterate until his conversion to Christianity motivated him to obtain an education. At age 21, he walked 15 miles to Berea, KY, with only $9.75 in his pocket. He graduated from **Berea College** and taught school for one year at Waco, KY. In 1892, he earned his medical degree from Indianapolis's Eclectic College of Physicians and Surgeons and immediately started his practice in Springfield, OH. He married Hattie B. Taylor from Cynthiana, KY, the following year. Shortly after his marriage, Ohio governor William McKinley commissioned Burton assistant surgeon of the 9th Battalion Infantry in Ohio's National Guard with the rank of captain.

In 1897, Burton joined Dr. H. R. Hawkins, of Xenia, OH, and formed the Ohio Mutual Medical Association, Ohio's African American medical society. The organization existed for only two years because most African American physicians and surgeons belonged to white associations. Burton then joined the National Medical Association and became vice president of the Ohio branch in a meeting in Lexington, KY, in 1904.

Burton operated several businesses, including the first drugstore owned and operated by an African American man in Springfield, OH. He attempted to open a hospital and later became head of a sanatorium in Mt. Clemens, MI. Not all of his businesses were in the medical field. He bought a shoe store and operated the *Loyal Legion of Honor,* the first African American newspaper in Springfield. In 1901, he attended the National Negro Business League in Chicago as Springfield's Business League representative.

Burton demonstrated his poetry talents in his 1910 autobiography. He served as a leader in various community organizations, including the Freemasons and the Elks. He was a major and surgeon in the 1st Regiment of the Uniformed Rank Knights of Pythias. Active in his church, Burton served as trustee and superintendent of the Trinity A.M.E. Church Sunday School for 30 years. He died almost exactly 47 years after he arrived in Springfield.

African American National Biography. http://keepmedia.org/a /African-American-National-Biography/Burton-Thomas/9465582/ (accessed December 14, 2009).
Burton, Thomas William. *What Experience Has Taught Me: An Autobiography of Thomas William Burton.* Cincinnati: Press of Jennings and Graham, 1910.

—*Sallie L. Powell*

BUSH V. KENTUCKY (1883), U.S. Supreme Court case regarding jury selection. John Bush, a former slave, worked for the prominent white Van Meter family of Fayette Co., KY. In 1879, a disagreement between Bush and the family resulted in the accidental shooting of Annie Van Meter, one of the family's adolescent daughters. Because both Annie Van Meter's father and Bush fired their weapons at the same time, no one was certain which bullet injured the girl. She died a week later from either blood poisoning or scarlet fever.

Bush was arrested for murder, but the confusion regarding the cause of death and who inflicted the original wound resulted in a hung jury that prompted a second trial. The second trial's all-white jury found Bush guilty and sentenced him to death. In 1880, Bush appealed the decision. The jury, he claimed, was not informed of the difference between involuntary manslaughter and murder, or whether the death was caused by scarlet fever or infection from the wound. The central point of contention, however, focused on the court's selection process for Bush's all-white jury. Kentucky law at the time of Bush's second trial excluded all African Americans from serving on juries, which was unconstitutional.

After a series of appeals and retrials, *Bush v. Kentucky* reached the U.S. Supreme Court. In January 1883, the court reversed Bush's conviction on the grounds that he was denied his rights as a citizen granted in the Fourteenth Amendment. At the same time, the court also ruled that Bush had no grounds to move his case to the U.S. circuit court, meaning that his new trial would once again be in the Fayette Co. court system.

By the time Bush's new trial began in early 1884, the Kentucky statute excluding African Americans from jury pools was no longer in effect, and officers were instructed to compile their juries regardless of race. Bush's jury, however, was once again all white and once again found him guilty and sentenced him to death. Although Bush appealed the decision, he could not get the verdict overturned. The U.S. Supreme Court refused to hear the case again, claiming that because the Kentucky statute was null and void, there was no evidence that Bush's Fourteenth Amendment rights had been violated again. The jurors, they claimed, could have been excluded for reasons other than race, so Bush's all-white jury could have been a coincidence. Despite at least one escape attempt, Bush was hanged on November 21, 1884, after giving a 10-minute speech maintaining his innocence.

Bush v. Kentucky, 107 U.S. 110 (1883). http://www.law.cornell.edu /supremecourt/text/107/1100 (accessed June 12, 2013).
Newspapers: "A Dark Crime Expiated," *DEB,* November 22, 1883, 1; "Supreme Court Work," *NYT,* January 30, 1883, 3; "Death Accidental and Suicidal," *LCJ,* February 6, 1884, 4; *DEB,* August 14, 1884, 2; "Two Murderers Hanged," *NYT,* November 22, 1884, 1.
Section 1, Chapter 62, General Statutes of Kentucky. In *The General Statutes of Kentucky. . . . .* Frankfort, KY: Major, Johnston & Barrett, 1881.

—*Dana Caldemeyer*

BUSINESS. From Kentucky's beginning as a county of Virginia in the 1700s, most African Americans were treated as property in the context of slavery. Despite this, some blacks in Kentucky who gained their freedom adopted an entrepreneurial spirit and used it to benefit themselves and others. Kentucky's free blacks engaged in small businesses in the state's urban areas. Among these were Louisville free blacks Shelton Morris, a barbershop and bathhouse owner in the 1830s, and **Washington Spradling,** who operated a barbershop and speculated in real estate. Spradling used his wealth to assist over 30 slaves to escape. In 1851, free blacks Henry and **Elizabeth "Eliza" Tevis** used their funds to purchase 40 acres in southeastern Jefferson Co. This property became the basis of the Newburg/Petersburg community.

After the Civil War and the ratification of the Thirteenth Amendment formally ended slavery in Kentucky, more blacks engaged in small businesses to serve their communities and generally did not compete with whites. Barber and beauty shops, restaurants, and blacksmiths, undertakers, and other skilled craftsmen with black clientele were usually the offerings. However, some provided a different type of service. In the mid-1800s, former slave **Nancy Anderson** earned a living as a ragpicker in Lexington. Professional service businesses such as lawyers and doctors operated as early as 1871, when **Nathanial Harper** became the first black lawyer in the state. To care for black patients, Louisville's **Henry Fitzbutler** opened his medical practice in 1872, and Manchester, KY, native **Artishia Gilbert** opened her practice in 1893. Black physicians and nurses found it difficult to receive medical privileges at white hospitals. Consequently, black hospitals and private clinics were created to meet this need. Among these was the **Red Cross Hospital** in Louisville, established in 1899 as well as smaller facilities such as Frankfort's **Winnie A. Scott Memorial Hospital.**

Some black entrepreneurs served multiple needs in their communities. Covington's **Horace Sudduth** operated a real estate agency, owned the Manse Hotel in Cincinnati, and was president of Covington's Industrial Federal Savings and Loan. Likewise, Lexington's **Jordan Carlisle Jackson Jr.** owned a fruit and confectionary shop before becoming the co-owner of an undertaking business and a livery stable. Jackson was also one of many

Elite Cab Company on South Second Street in the African American business district in Danville, KY.

Kentuckians involved in Booker T. Washington's National Negro Business League. Along with Dr. **Thomas Tyler Wendell** and many others, he participated in the Colored Congress of Farmers and Businessmen at Scott Co.'s **New Zion.**

At the turn of the century, black Kentuckians formed various other business organizations, including Louisville's Progressive Mechanic Association (1896) and Jessamine Co.'s United Order of Industry (1907). The Progressive Mechanic Association formed for the benefit of all Kentucky African Americans with plans to equip the black community with the best modern machinery, offer young African Americans training and employment opportunities, and "foster and encourage industry among our people." Nicholasville native Alfred Britton organized the United Order of Industry for black workers to contract their labor to hemp growers. Further into the twentieth century, the Medical Society of Negro Physicians, the Kentucky Congress of Barbers and Beauticians, the Lexington Colored A&M Fair Association (1869–1940s), the **African American Businessmen's Association of Covington,** and the Kentucky Colored Embalmers and Undertakers Association enabled Kentucky black businesses to function more effectively. Although women participated in some of these organizations, it was also common for them to own and operate individual ventures. **Elizabeth Slaughter** and **Leanna Snowden** ran their own millinery businesses.

At one point, there were nearly 50 black weekly newspapers in the state. Among the most successful were those in Louisville (the *Louisville Leader,* the *Louisville Defender,* and the *Louisville News*) and Lexington (the *Kentucky Standard*). Most had a limited subscriber and advertiser base, and by 1951, the *Louisville Defender* was the only functioning black weekly after the closure of the *Louisville Leader.* Beginning in 1879, the *American Baptist* of the **General Association of Baptists in Kentucky** discussed religious and social issues affecting blacks. Other black newspapers that were not well known included the *Richmond Climax,* the *Richmond Enquirer,* the *Ohio Falls Express,* the *Frankfort Tribune,* and countless other weeklies that later terminated.

In Kentucky's black communities and neighborhoods, small consumer-oriented businesses became integral to black survival. In the era of de jure or legal racial segregation, black businesses served communities that were often located along specific streets,

such as Louisville's **Walnut St.** and Lexington's **Deweese St.** A black-owned insurance company, movie theaters, and taxicab services served their customers. Black-owned taverns operated in wet counties where spirits and beer could be sold legally after 1935. Some of these operations were small joints where blacks could drink, secretly gamble, or, in some instances, procure female accompaniment. Not surprisingly, bars that sold more than alcohol and entertainment were not located in these same blocks. Because they were located in so-called red-light districts, working-class and middle- to upper-class blacks could avoid the problems associated with these establishments. Many African American businesses were found in black neighborhoods, such as Frankfort's **Crawfish Bottom,** Louisville's **Little Africa** and **Smoketown,** Bowling Green's **Shake Rag,** and Paducah's **Uppertown.**

These operations survived because racial segregation practices and laws denied African Americans accommodation at white businesses. However, black entrepreneurs were not always guaranteed continued success. In some businesses, black consumers had no choice. For example, African American travelers in the state were not welcomed at most white hotels. Instead, travelers could use only black establishments, such as Louisville's Allen Hotel and the **Chestnut Street YMCA,** Bowling Green's Southern Queen Hotel, or Paducah's Hotel Metropolitan, owned and operated by **Maggie Steed,** to secure reasonable lodging for the night.

During the **civil rights movement** era from 1945 to 1964, a growing middle class among Kentucky black businesses sought to expand their opportunities. **Mammoth Life and Accident Insurance,** based in Louisville, continued to develop until it was absorbed by Supreme Life Insurance Company of Chicago, another black-owned firm. Ownership and purchase of the rhythm and blues radio station WLOU in Louisville by Rev. **William E. Summers III** marked another step forward.

By the late 1980s, Kentucky blacks **Cornelius Martin,** Winston Pittman, and Henry Shaw were listed by *Black Enterprise* magazine among the 100 leading black automobile dealers in the United States. Other blacks served as upper-level executives with Kentucky-based Ashland Oil, the General Electric Company offices in Louisville, the General Motors plant in Bowling Green, and other major corporations. **Rohena Miller** established her own advertising agency in Louisville.

By 2000, Kentucky blacks moved from operating small mom-and-pop businesses to a variety of businesses, including car transportation services (Charlie W. Johnson in Louisville), garbage removal services (Dan Taylor, Bowling Green), funeral homes (**Woodford Porter** in Louisville and others), construction and human resources (**Juanita Farley Burks** in Louisville), mall developer (**Lenny Lyles** in Louisville), contractor and building supply (McKinley Walker in Mt. Sterling), convenience stores (**Ulysses Lee "Junior" Bridgeman** in Louisville), and many others. Kentucky businesses and entrepreneurs had the same challenges as their white counterparts with the additional impediment of racial limitations on credit from banks. Black businesses in Kentucky survived during segregation, but prosperity meant continued operation and not necessarily vast wealth accumulation. Well-to-do blacks often kept their prosperity private and rarely flaunted their success. Benefactors of their prosperity were often churches, fraternal and civic organizations, and a few private institutions that served blacks before desegregation. Some of these are Simmons University (later known as **Simmons College of Kentucky**) in Louisville, **Lincoln Institute** near Simpsonville, Chandler Normal School in Lexington, and **Eckstein Norton Institute** in Cane Springs.

Kentucky blacks established both banks and savings and loan associations (Continental National Bank, **First Standard Bank, Freedman's Savings and Trust Company, American Mutual Savings Bank,** and **Progressive Building and Loan Association**) and created investment banks to redevelop blighted urban neighborhoods in the larger metropolitan areas. However, these efforts were not pervasive. Widespread economic empowerment among Kentucky black entrepreneurs and businesses remained an ongoing work in progress as the twenty-first century began.

Kleber, John E., ed. *Encyclopedia of Louisville*. Lexington: Univ. Press of Kentucky, 2001.
Newspapers: "Colored Conference at New Zion," *LL,* November 19, 1905, 2; "Negro Workmen," *LL,* July 20, 1907, 8.
Smith, Gerald. *Lexington, Kentucky*. Black America. Charleston, SC: Arcadia, 2002.
Tenkotte, Paul A., and James C. Claypool, eds. *The Encyclopedia of Northern Kentucky*. Lexington: Univ. Press of Kentucky, 2009.
Weeden, H. C. *Weeden's History of the Colored People of Louisville*. Louisville, KY: H. C. Weeden, 1897.

—*John A. Hardin*

BUSING, controversial method for the desegregation of public education. The multifaceted debate over school busing to integrate public education combined societal and legal conflicts, including the role of courts, the concerns of African Americans and whites, and competition among governmental branches. In 1954, the U.S. Supreme Court in **Brown v. Board of Education** nullified racially segregated public education, and Louisville boasted of its integrated schools two years later. However, the battle over mandatory school busing for integration purposes burst the myth of Louisville's peaceful race relations.

A 1972 **Kentucky Commission on Human Rights** report proclaimed the failure of the Louisville Board of Education's 1956 plan for never adapting to shifting circumstances. Racial isolation of students had reached an extreme level, as demonstrated by the highest percentage of segregation among elementary students since total segregation was abolished in 1956. Although the number of Louisville African American teachers had increased overall, it had decreased in predominantly white schools. The report warned against the "rapid shift to resegregation in Louisville."

In contrast to Louisville, Lexington's school system had systematically closed black schools while upgrading white schools; therefore, the two communities varied in their response to court-ordered busing. Along with the Lexington–Fayette County Human Relations Committee, the Kentucky Civil Liberties Union filed a desegregation suit against the Fayette County School District in 1971. Some Lexington citizens signed petitions and attended school board meetings en masse. As part of Black Unity Day on August 28, 1972, approximately 200 demonstrators peacefully marched from Duncan Park to the Fayette County Courthouse "protesting the closing of inner city schools and the busing of black children to suburban schools."

Kentucky was not the only state dealing with the busing issue. The Supreme Court addressed a myriad of school-busing questions in various cases, including *Green v. County School Board* (New Kent Co., VA, 1968), *Swann v. Charlotte-Mecklenburg School District* (Charlotte, NC, 1971), *Keyes v. School District No. 1* (Denver, CO, 1973), and *Milliken v. Bradley* (Detroit, MI, 1974). In 1974, after a federal court mandated a busing program to integrate Boston's public schools, violence erupted in the Massachusetts city in which rocks and racial epithets were hurled at African American students bused to a predominantly white school.

That same year, Louisville exhibited a similar behavioral pattern when the U.S. Court of Appeals for the Sixth Circuit in Cincinnati, OH, ordered federal district court judge James F. Gordon to desegregate Louisville and Jefferson Co. schools. Gordon's plan required that roughly 22,000 students be bused in the first year in order that African Americans would constitute 10 to 35 percent of each school's student body. The plan used an alphabetic selection method. While white students would be bused for 2 of their 11 years of education, African American students would be bused for 8 or 9 of their 11 years; thus African Americans bore the heavier burden of busing.

Antibusing groups countered with school boycotts, sanctions against probusing businesses, petitions, demonstrations, and violence. Hostile behavior included arson, vandalism, racial slurs, lynching threats, cross burning, and sniper fire on buses carrying children and on African American homes. The Kentucky Taxpayers' Association, a conservative organization, invited the Ku Klux Klan to hold a rally at a local Holiday Inn. State police officers rode school buses, and the Kentucky National Guard helped restore order. However, some local police officers displayed antibusing stickers on their vehicles.

Some citizens exhibited their animosity toward busing with white flight. They either moved to nearby counties or sent their children to private schools. Several sent their children to stay with relatives, and a few lived in mobile homes beyond Jefferson Co.'s border. This behavior connected school integration with housing integration.

Not everyone was against busing. On the pro-integration side, Progress in Education, formed by African American and white activists, not only backed school desegregation but also supported busing as a plan to accomplish it. The **National Association for the Advancement of Colored People** and the predominantly white Kentucky Civil Liberties Union displayed biracial cooperation. Various religious communities provided "white support for peaceful school desegregation."

Bused students experienced occasional antagonistic treatment from bus drivers and frequent overcrowded conditions. One African American student, Rodney Swain, told of his lengthy, congested bus ride. The driver required three people to a seat, but students were still standing. The full bus passed students waiting at the next stop. The lack of transportation left nearly 200 students waiting at their stops, forcing African American students to miss classes and risk failure. Some students reported one-sided discipline, with more African American students receiving suspension.

On the political side, President Richard Nixon had "strongly opposed forced school busing to achieve racial balance." The *Louisville Courier-Journal* warned that President Gerald Ford apparently "embrace[d] the Nixonian view that equal rights are good unless they might cost an election." State politics followed a similar pattern. Governor Julian Carroll filed a suit questioning the constitutionality of mandatory busing. In the Kentucky General Assembly, Representative Dottie Priddy introduced an antibusing amendment to the Kentucky Constitution.

The busing deliberations did not end in the 1970s and continued to divide Americans in subsequent decades. In 1992, Louisville elementary schools adopted a voluntary busing plan but kept the mandatory busing plan for middle and high schools. African Americans and whites sued for free school choices in the twenty-first century. Georgia Eugene, a community activist, observed in a 2005 interview: "I think that school busing was set up to bring about dispersal. It was to make people move. I call it white flight and black pursuit. They fly and we follow, and they fly and we follow." In 2007, by a 5–4 vote, the U.S. Supreme Court in *Meredith v. Jefferson County Board of Education* rejected a race-based school-assignment plan as unconstitutional.

Douglas, Davison, ed. *School Busing: Constitutional and Political Developments*. Vol. 1, *The Development of School Busing as a Desegregation Remedy*. New York: Garland, 1994.

Kentucky Commission on Human Rights. *Louisville School System Retreats to Segregation*. 1972. Education Resources Information Center. http://www.eric.ed.gov/ERICDocs/data/ericdocs2sql/content _storage_01/0000019b/80/3b/25/39.pdf (accessed January 27, 2010).

K'Meyer, Tracy E. *From Brown to Meredith: The Long Struggle for School Desegregation in Louisville, Kentucky, 1954–2007*. Chapel Hill: The Univ. of North Carolina Press, 2013, 156.

———. *Civil Rights in the Gateway to the South: Louisville, Kentucky, 1945–1980*. Lexington: Univ. Press of Kentucky, 2009.

McAndrews, Lawrence J. "The Politics of Principle: Richard Nixon and School Desegregation." *JNH* 83, no. 3 (Summer 1998): 187–200.

Wright, George C. *A History of Blacks in Kentucky*. Vol. 2, *In Pursuit of Equality, 1890–1980*. Frankfort: Kentucky Historical Society, 1992.

—*Sallie L. Powell*

BUTLER ROSS, TRACEY (b. 1966, Kittery, ME), first woman African American dentist in northern Kentucky. Tracey Butler Ross, the first woman African American dentist in northern Kentucky, was born on June 5. 1966, the daughter of George T. Butler and Beverly Dickerson Butler. As a U.S. Air Force brat, Butler lived in California, North Carolina, and Florida before moving in 1975 to Covington, KY, the childhood home of her parents. She attended the Covington public schools, graduating at the age of 16 from Holmes High School in 1983.

Two teachers at the Sixth District Elementary School in Covington provided the support that launched her on to the road of success. At age 9, she was encouraged by her fourth-grade teacher, Mrs. Gebhart, to be an obstetrician-gynecologist instead of an obstetric nurse. At age 11, at the insistence of Mr. William Gray, she was promoted into the eighth grade and was thus enabled to enter Holmes High School the next year, where she later graduated with honors. During those early years, she already had the goal of becoming a medical doctor, and she excelled scholastically as a result of encouragement by her mentors.

Butler attended **Kentucky State University** (KSU) in Frankfort on a full four-year presidential scholarship. In 1987, she graduated from KSU with a BS degree in biology, but she inadvertently missed the application deadline for entry into the University of Louisville Medical School. On the advice of her mentor, Dr. Kathy Peale, a local Frankfort attorney, Butler decided to apply to the UL Dental School for her first year, intending to apply to the Medical School to begin her second year. It was this pivotal decision that introduced Butler to her lifelong calling as a dentist. She obtained her DMD in 1991.

Wanting to give back to her community, Butler returned to Covington immediately after graduation. She began employment with the Northern Kentucky Family Health Center and stayed there for more than 12 years. Butler married Covington resident Richard Ross in 1996, and they reside in the Main Strasse neighborhood of Covington. In 2001, she and her husband cofounded New Horizons Christian Ministries, and currently they serve as its pastors. With the ever-present desire to bring excellence to a waning community, Dr. Butler Ross began her private practice in 2003 at 1044 Scott St. in Covington. At the close of her first year in practice, she proudly boasted a clientele of more than 1,000 patients, a number that continues to grow. She continues with her desire of "changing lives, one smile at a time."

Butler Ross, Tracey. Interview by Theodore H. H. Harris, Covington, KY, July 2006.

"Dentist to Serve Hometown." *KP*, April 20, 1991, 25K.

—*Theodore H. H. Harris*

C

CABELL, AARON HALL (b. 1855, Henderson, KY; d. 1915, Henderson, KY), merchant and the first African American to run for public office in Henderson, and CABELL, GEORGE CLARENCE (b. 1860, Henderson, KY; d. unknown, Henderson, KY), merchant. Aaron Hall Cabell and George Clarence Cabell were born in slavery to Civil War veteran James Cabell and Harriet Cabell. Aaron married Amanda Rucker and opened a grocery business while he was in his early 20s in Henderson, KY. The couple had only one child, Viola. They later sent her to Haven High School in Missouri, where she was the only African American student and graduated with honors, afterward becoming a music teacher. Aaron's younger brother, George, joined him in the mercantile trade as a grocery wagon driver. One of the challenges Aaron faced was the failure of two previous African American groceries in the community. In 1880, Aaron's business success produced the need for a larger building and led to other real estate investments.

The following year, Aaron ran for the Henderson City Council, becoming the first African American to run for public office in the town. He faced two white opponents, R. E. Cook and Kennedy (first name unknown) for the Third Ward seat. Kennedy withdrew from the race on election day and gave his support to Cabell but still received 23 votes. Cook narrowly beat Cabell by 22 votes. Cabell continued his political involvement as a delegate to the Republican National Convention in Chicago in 1888 and the Progressive National Convention in 1912.

Aaron inspired other African American men, including his younger brother, George, to explore business opportunities. In 1895, George went into the grocery business for himself. His first marriage to Emma produced five children. He had two children with his second wife, Lovenia (Lavenia).

In the 1899 *Henderson City Directory,* Aaron Cabell's name was listed in large print with a description of his business as a "Dealer in Staple and Fancy Groceries, Canned and Bottled Goods." The following year, he attended the first meeting of the National Negro Business League in Boston, MA. Booker T. Washington was president of the League. Aaron was recognized for his commercial expertise because he owned not only a grocery store but also other businesses and residences. After returning from Boston, Aaron and 11 other white grocers were indicted for forming a trust. The charge claimed that all the men agreed to sell the flour purchased from an Evansville, IN, firm for the same price, gaining a 10-cent profit on each barrel. Seven months later, Kentucky governor John Crepps Wickliffe Beckham pardoned the men before the trial was held.

In 1904, Aaron purchased for $5,000 about six acres on Clay St., known as Held's Park, and renamed it Cabell Park; he was the only African American in Kentucky to own and control a park. He also served as a trustee of Mount Zion Cemetery, president of the Fraternal Hall Association, Cemetery and Burial Company, and a state officer in Sons of Veterans. George was

the director of the Cemetery and Burial Company and also a Sons of Veterans member. Their 44-year-old father, James, had enlisted from Owensboro, KY, in the U.S. Colored Troops in 1864. As a Civil War veteran, James was provided a headstone when he died in 1881 and was buried in Henderson's Fernwood Cemetery.

In 1915, Aaron retired from the grocery business with plans to attend to his real estate interests, but he died in November of heart disease, only eight months after his daughter died of tuberculosis. He was buried near his father at Fernwood Cemetery. Information regarding George's death remains unknown; however, in 1930, his widow, Lovenia (Lavenia) Dixon Cabell, was still offering laundry service from her home, and their 19-year-old son, Aaron, worked as a porter at a local clothing store. Their daughter, Thelma, was 11 years old.

Arnett, Maralea. *The Annals and Scandals of Henderson County, Kentucky, 1775–1975.* Corydon, KY: Fremar, 1976.
Henderson City Directory, 1899.
Kentucky Death Records, 1852–1953.
Mather, Frank Lincoln, ed. *Who's Who of the Colored Race: A General Biographical Dictionary of Men and Women of African Descent.* Vol. 1. Chicago: Memento Edition, 1915.
Newspapers: "They Hold Good Positions," *IF,* July 5, 1890, 4; "Pardoned before Trial," *Hickman Courier,* May 3, 1901, 3; "Mr. Aaron H. Cabell," *Colored American* (Washington, DC), November 1, 1902, 5; untitled article, *IF,* July 16, 1904, 3; "First Black Candidate Ran Close," *Henderson (KY) Gleaner,* August 12, 2001.
Proceedings of the National Negro Business League, Its First Meeting Held in Boston, Massachusetts, August 23 and 24, 1900. Boston: J. R. Hamm.
U.S. Federal Census (1870, 1880, 1900, 1910, 1930).

—*Sallie L. Powell*

CABELL, DELMO BARTELL (b. 1894, Madisonville, KY; d. 1977, Detroit, MI), pharmacist, CABELL, NEWELL ATWOOD (b. 1890, Nashville, TN; d. unknown), pharmacist, and CABELL, ROGER W. "DOC" (b. 1893, Madisonville, KY; d. 1972, Henderson, KY), pharmacist. Sons of Peter R. and Lucy Cabell, Newell, Roger, and Delmo Cabell entered the pharmaceutical field. Their father was a teacher and later became a grocer. The oldest sister, Daisy, also became a teacher. All three brothers earned their degrees from Louisville's **Simmons University** (later known as **Simmons College of Kentucky**). In addition, Delmo graduated from Atkinson Institute in 1912. He and Roger graduated with their degrees in pharmacy from Meharry Medical College in Nashville, TN.

When the brothers registered for the military in World War I, Newell, living in Madisonville, KY, became one of 4 registered pharmacists out of a class of 17 students in July 1917. He then moved to Washington, DC, to work at Douglas Pharmacy. Roger was working as an insurance agent for **Mammoth Life and Accident Insurance Company** in Madisonville, KY. He rose to the rank of sergeant in the U.S. Army. Delmo, a single man, lived in Madisonville and worked as a pharmacist for R. E. White in Owensboro, KY.

By 1920, Newell had returned to Henderson, KY, from Washington, and he and his older sister, Daisy, boarded there while he worked at a local pharmacy. Ten years later, he was married to Virginia and owned his own drugstore in Bowling Green, KY. After the war, Roger worked at his father's grocery store in Madisonville. By 1930, he was married to Alice, a teacher, and owned a drugstore in Louisville. At the same time, Delmo owned his home and a drugstore in Providence, KY. He had one employee, Maney Alexander, a prescriptionist. Delmo, active in the community, joined others in obtaining noted orator Roscoe Conkling Simmons to speak in Providence, KY, to an interracial audience in 1937.

Several years later, Roger joined Delmo in his Providence business. About that same time, Newell had returned to Henderson. By the mid-1950s, Roger owned Acme Drug Store on Dixon St. in Henderson, and his two brothers, Newell and Delmo, worked with him. Roger also taught at Alves School, and Newell was married to his second wife, Josephine. Delmo later owned and operated Cabell Drug Store in Evansville, IN, while still living in Henderson.

Roger had been an active member of Madisonville's Merriweather Lodge No. 43 of the Prince Hall Free and Accepted Masons and served on Henderson's Board of Housing and Building Appeal, the Human Rights Committee, and the Chamber of Commerce. In 1969, he retired and died three years later. He was survived by his second wife, Claudine, and his son, Jerry, and was buried in Fernwood Cemetery, Henderson, KY.

In 1977, Delmo died in Detroit, MI, nine years after his wife, Louellia. He was buried beside his wife and near his brother, Roger, at Henderson's Fernwood Cemetery. Newell's death information has not been located.

Arnett, Maralea. *The Annals and Scandals of Henderson County, Kentucky, 1775–1975.* Corydon, KY: Fremar, 1976.
Boris, Joseph J., ed. *Who's Who in Colored America, 1927.* New York: Who's Who in Colored America Corp., 1927.
Henderson, Kentucky, City Directory, 1959.
Kentucky Death Index, 1911–2000.
The Mullin-Kille and Gleaner & Journal Henderson Kentucky Con Survey City Directory, 1953.
"Kentucky Board of Pharmacy." *The National Druggist* 47, no. 8 (August 1917): 318.
Newspapers: "Madisonville, Ky.," *IF*, March 27, 1915, 8; "Roscoe Simmons Speaks in Ky.," *PD*, December 10, 1937, 6; "Death Claims 'Doc' Cabell," *Henderson (KY) Gleaner*, December 19, 1972, 2; "Deaths," *Henderson (KY) Gleaner*, August 4, 1977, 2.
Report of the Kentucky Board of Pharmacy, 1943.
Tennessee City Birth Records, 1881–1915.
U.S. Federal Census (1900, 1910, 1930, 1940).
World War I Draft Registration Cards, 1917–1918.
—*Sallie L. Powell*

CADENTOWN, African American community in Fayette Co.
In 1869, Irish entrepreneur Owen Caden sold one-half- to five-acre tracts of land at $100 per acre to African American freedmen. The 43-acre property was triangular-wedge shaped and located in the southeastern section of Fayette Co. near a railroad, which facilitated transportation of people and products. Like other **African American hamlets** of the era, the community of Cadentown was named after the land developer.

In a short time, Cadentown consisted of homes for 24 families, a school, three churches, two general stores (Caudill's Grocery Store and Mr. Bryan's Grocery Store), a benevolent society, and a cemetery. Two of Cadentown's churches of different denominations followed a practice common in smaller communities, that of alternating services so that the congregations could share the building and attend each other's services on alternate weeks. The Baptist and Methodist members held their baptisms in a nearby pond. Later, Mollie Strider and Emma Allen organized the building of Haven Methodist Church.

In 1914, the Cadentown school, along with some other local African American schools, created a penny lunch system. The Cadentown teachers used oil stoves to provide lunch once a week for their students. The school provided $2.30 worth of food in two weeks to its children. In 1922–1923, a **Rosenwald school** was built behind the Baptist Church through the Rosenwald Fund. It served grades one through six until its closure in the fall of 1946. Famed architect Frank Lloyd Wright designed the building.

Although many Cadentown citizens worked outside the community, they subsidized their economy by farming, including raising animals such as pigs and chickens, producing various fruits and vegetables, and growing tobacco and hemp. They also fished and hunted. The churches, the school, and the stores provided community for Cadentown's residents. These institutions filled social, political, educational, and economic needs. People also enjoyed entertainment through sports. The townspeople frequently gathered to watch their Hamburg Players play baseball.

Unlike many Kentucky African American hamlets, Cadentown has kept some of its original buildings and its initial size of 43 acres. Urban development surrounds the community, but the Cadentown Neighborhood Association has fought to keep its historic neighborhood. In 1999, Cadentown became the first rural black hamlet within Fayette Co. to request a designation as a historic zone. Cadentown School was added to the National Register of Historic Places on April 5, 2006. The school and the neighboring Cadentown Baptist Church have been renovated, and there are plans to open the school as a museum.

Finney, Céline. "A Place to Call Their Own: The Cultural and Historic Landscape of Cadentown, Kentucky." MA thesis, Univ. of Kentucky, 2003.
Newspapers: "County Colored Schools," *LL*, February 8, 1914, 2; "Holding On to History," *LHL*, August 4, 1999; "Cadentown Leads Effort Saving Black Settlements," *LHL*, February 24, 2001, A1.
—*Fiona Young-Brown*

CAESAR (b. ca. 1758, Chesterfield Co., VA; d. 1836, Fayette Co., KY), artificer. Caesar was born a slave on the plantation of William Robertson. In 1773, Robertson's son, James, inherited Caesar and decided to migrate to the Natchez District on the Mississippi River. He took Caesar with him, and they arrived at Holston River, where they and about 150 other settlers and their slaves built boats and embarked on a long and perilous voyage down the Tennessee, Ohio, and Mississippi Rivers to Natchez. After reaching the settlement that summer, Robertson, a carpenter, settled on 250 acres and made a living building houses for settlers and merchants in the area.

In the spring of 1778, Capt. James Willing led an expedition down the Mississippi River to raid British settlements in West Florida (which included Natchez) and to keep the river open as a supply route from New Orleans to George Rogers Clark's forces in the Illinois country. When Willing secured Natchez for the Americans in March, Robertson joined his forces, under the command of Capt. Robert George, and sailed up the Mississippi River to Ft. Clark (Kaskaskia, IL), taking Caesar with him. In March 1779, Robertson was commissioned a lieutenant, and Caesar was made an artificer in Captain George's artillery company.

Artificers were skilled carpenters, sawyers, coopers, and blacksmiths who constructed most of the forts, wagons, and boats that were used by the Americans in the Illinois country. Caesar, a carpenter, was one of the artificers who rebuilt Ft. Clark in the spring of 1779. That summer, Captain George's company was ordered to Louisville. After spending the bitterly cold winter of 1779–1780 there, the company went down the Ohio River and built Ft. Jefferson, just south of present-day Wickliffe, KY. The artificers built the stockade fence, blockhouses, boats, gun carriages, and storehouses. Caesar was the only known African American who served as an artificer at Ft. Jefferson, enduring Indian attacks and lack of food and other supplies until the fort was evacuated in June 1781.

Caesar and the rest of Captain George's company sailed up the Ohio River to Ft. Nelson, and Caesar spent the next two years repairing the fort and building boats, including a large armed galley that patrolled the Ohio River. In 1782, James Robertson, who had been on detached duty on the Mississippi River throughout the war, died in Natchez, and Caesar came into the possession of Philip Barbour, a Virginia merchant and trader. Barbour sold Caesar to John Campbell, whose slave he remained until Campbell's death in 1799. By 1807, Caesar had been taken to Lexington, KY, by William Beard, one of Campbell's heirs. Caesar lived on the Beard farm for the rest of his life and died there.

Estate Inventory of James Robinson, July 1, 1782. Jefferson County Order and Minute Book, 45.

George Rogers Clark Papers, 1779–84 (photostats of original papers), Special Collections Department, Filson Club Historical Society, Louisville, KY.

James Robinson Heirs v. Philip C. S. Barbour, Old Chancery Court (Jefferson Co.) Case 1738 (1818).

—*Cornelius Bogert*

CALVARY BAPTIST CHURCH (LOUISVILLE), African American Baptist church in Louisville, KY.

In 1829, free and enslaved African Americans formed their own congregation separate from the racially mixed Walnut Street Baptist Church in Louisville. The First Baptist Church, led by Reverend **Henry Adams,** initially worshiped in a building on Market St. Four years later, Benjamin Stansberry, a white man, deeded a plot of land on Fifth St. near York to Henry Smith, a free African American Baptist preacher. Stansberry also donated a dollar to assist Smith in devoting his time to the ministry instead of domestic work.

The **Fifth Street Baptist Church** was established. A little over a decade later, division among the members occurred, and the York Street Baptist Church was established. Reverend W. W. Taylor directed an industrial arts program at Polytechnic Preparatory School for orphans and pastored the church from 1845 until his death in 1882. Reverend C. S. Dinkins succeeded him as the senior pastor. Under his leadership, the church changed its name to Calvary Baptist Church and began its association with State Colored Baptist University (later known as **Simmons College of Kentucky**). In 1886, **Charles Henry Parrish Sr.,** a recent graduate and professor of State University, began his pastorate. The church property was in debt $5,200, and the church had 111 members. Within a decade, Parrish increased the church's membership to over 1,000, and the church owned its location property and a mission at 28th and **Walnut** Sts. Parrish pastored the church until 1931. Calvary Baptist Church purchased its current site at 1368 S. 28th St. in 1958.

Kentucky Historical Society Markers Database. http://migration .kentucky.gov/kyhs/hmdb/MarkerSearch.aspx?mode=All (accessed April 5, 2010).

Lucas, Marion B. *A History of Blacks in Kentucky: From Slavery to Segregation, 1760–1891.* 2nd ed. Frankfort: Kentucky Historical Society, 2003.

Newspapers: "Children's Corner," *Afro-American Mission Herald,* January 1, 1901, 3; "Faith in Action," *LCJ,* April 23, 2005, B2.

Parrish, C. H. *Golden Jubilee of the General Association of Colored Baptists in Kentucky: From 1865–1915.* Louisville, KY: Mayes Printing Co., 1915.

—*Sallie L. Powell*

CAMPBELL, ISRAEL S. (b. 1815, Russellville, KY; d. 1898, La Marque, TX), preacher.

Israel S. Campbell rose from humble beginnings in slavery to become known as an instrumental figure in the black Baptist church in Texas. Born on a western Kentucky farm, Campbell endured numerous dislocations as a youth, moving from master to master after being purchased and sold several times before his 12th birthday. His experiences in slavery, which he recounted in his autobiography, persuaded him to seek his freedom. After multiple failed attempts to flee from masters in Kentucky, Tennessee, and Mississippi, he finally succeeded in reaching Canada in 1849.

While Campbell was a slave, he witnessed a vision that inspired him to become a preacher. He followed this calling after arriving in Canada, where he was ordained and eventually preached at various churches in both the North and South, including six years at Sandusky City Baptist Church in Ohio. In 1865, he arrived in Houston, TX, where he served as the pastor of Antioch Baptist Church before initiating work at the First Regular Missionary Baptist Church of Galveston, the first independent black Baptist church in Texas. The church was established in the community of Settlement, which local African Americans called Campbellville in his honor.

Campbell served for 24 years as pastor before passing away on June 13, 1898, in La Marque, TX. He was buried in Lakeview Cemetery in Galveston.

Campbell, Israel. *An Autobiography: Bond and Free; or, Yearnings for Freedom, from My Green Brier House; Being the Story of My Life in Bondage, and My Life in Freedom.* Philadelphia: C. E. P. Brinckloe & Co., 1861.

Cathcart, William. *The Baptist Encyclopedia.* Philadelphia: Louis H. Everts, 1881.

Early, Joe, Jr. "Israel S. Campbell: 'The Father of Black Texas Baptists.'" *Baptist History and Heritage* 39 (2004): 98–102.

Pegues, A. W. *Our Baptist Ministers and Schools.* Springfield, MA: Willey & Co., 1892.

—*Stephen Pickering*

CAMPBELL, MADISON (MAT) (b. 1823, Madison Co., KY; d. 1896, Madison Co., KY), clergyman. Madison (Mat) Campbell was born into slavery to Jackson and Lucy. His owner, Audley or Edly Campbell, had purchased Lucy when she was 16 years old. In his autobiography, Campbell noted his family genealogy over three previous generations. He wanted to be a Baptist preacher in the early 1840s, but his Methodist slave master directed him to be a Methodist preacher. Slaves were not allowed to preach unless their white owners gave permission. Campbell preached at the interracial Bethlehem Methodist Church for about a decade even though he disagreed with three of its principles. He believed that the only form of baptism was immersion and that infants could not receive baptism, and he questioned the doctrine of falling from grace. When his owner died, the owner's wife allowed Campbell to preach for the Baptist denomination. In 1857, he was ordained by the white Baptists of the Tates Creek Association in Lincoln Co. and began preaching the following year at the United Colored Baptist Church in Richmond, KY. Even though some whites feared that his preaching was "running the negroes crazy," others allowed him to preach to their slaves.

The death of Campbell's slaveholder created financial difficulties, and his widow sold many of her slaves, including Campbell's mother, brothers, one sister, and three of his sister's children. Only Campbell, his father, and a sister remained in the widow's possession. Campbell negotiated a deal with the widow to hire himself out as a laborer. In return, he paid her $100 a year for the next eight years. She also allowed him to purchase a horse so that he could travel throughout the county to preach.

In 1843, Campbell married Polly Woods Ballard, a slave owned by Madison Co. sheriff Palestine Ballard. The owners of Campbell and Polly allowed him to visit her two times a week. Campbell hired himself out to Ballard in order to be close to his family, which included 14 children. In 1863, he bought himself out of slavery for $233 and hired his wife. They worked at a government post in Nicholasville. Half of his wife's earnings went to her slaveholder. In 14 months, between their wages and his wife's profits from selling cakes and pies to soldiers, they acquired $616. After the Civil War, they purchased a home.

Campbell organized churches throughout the county: New Liberty, Kirksville, Mt. Pleasant, Otter Creek, Mt. Nebo, and Goodloe Chapel. He helped establish the Baptist Church's South Elkhorn District and a few years later organized the Mt. Pleasant District Association. In 1870, the **General Association of Baptists in Kentucky** met in Paris, KY, to discuss a school to educate preachers and teachers. In 1892, State Colored Baptist University (later known as **Simmons College of Kentucky**) awarded him a doctor of divinity degree.

Shortly after his wife's death in 1894, the 72-year-old Campbell married Roxana Moberly, a 37-year-old widow from his church. The unhappy union ended with her desire for a divorce and locking him out of their house. He sought shelter with his children.

Campbell served several times as a delegate to Republican conventions and traveled across the state preaching to various churches. He ministered to Richmond's United Colored Baptist Church for almost four decades until his death in 1896.

Campbell, Madison. *Autobiography of Elder Madison Campbell: Pastor of the United Colored Baptist Church.* Richmond, KY: Pantagraph Job Rooms, 1895.
Engle, Fred A., and Robert N. Grise. *Madison's Heritage.* Richmond, KY: AA Printing Co., 1985.
Kentucky Death Records, 1852–1953.

—*Sallie L. Powell*

CAMP BRECKINRIDGE, site of a demonstration by African American women during World War II. Built in 1942 in northwestern Kentucky between Morganfield and Henderson, Camp Breckinridge served as a training site and internment camp for prisoners of war during World War II. During the 1940s and 1950s, many African Americans passed through its gates, including Lionel Hampton and Joe Louis, who entertained troops serving at the encampment. One of the army installation's most famous soldiers was Jackie Robinson, who was stationed there in 1944 and played baseball for the camp's team. However, as in the experience of many black men and women who served in World War II, racism was a fact of life at the base. One African American soldier recalled an officer ordering him to stop reading a poetry book containing the works of Langston Hughes because it "might cause some trouble."

One of the most significant events that occurred at the base during World War II was a series of protests by a group of African American women. In 1943, 175 black women affiliated with the Women's Army Corps (WAC) were transferred from boot camp to Camp Breckinridge, the first group of black women enlistees ever to be stationed in Kentucky. Upon arrival, these well-educated women, many of whom had previously worked as schoolteachers and administrative assistants, were assigned menial jobs like sweeping and scrubbing floors, folding laundry, and cleaning warehouses. Despite their complaints to superior officers that the chores were improper assignments for WACs, they continued to be assigned to menial labor. In another instance, a group of white soldiers entered the barracks of the young black women and harassed them. The soldiers were later protected by their white officers from punishment.

A report issued by the War Department stated that the black WACs "were not given proper assignments," and the camp's newly installed brigadier general ordered that the women were to be given assignments "commensurate with their skills." Like other protests during World War II, the protest of the black WACs at Camp Breckinridge was part of a larger struggle by African Americans to seek full freedom and equality at home while they were fighting for it abroad.

Heady, Peyton. *History of Camp Breckinridge.* Morganfield, KY: Hites' International Printing, 1987.
McGuire, Phillip, ed. *Taps for a Jim Crow Army: Letters from Black Soldiers in World War II.* Lexington: Univ. Press of Kentucky, 1993.
Sadler, Georgia Clark. "From Women's Services to Service Women." In *Gender Camouflage: Women and the U.S. Military,* edited by Francine D'Amico and Laurie Weinstein. New York: New York Univ. Press, 1999.

"6 WACs Resign: WAC Clerks Decline to Scrub Floors." *Philadelphia Afro-American*, July 10, 1943, 1.

—*Joshua D. Farrington*

CAMP NELSON, Civil War military garrison for African Americans. Camp Nelson, located south of Nicholasville in Jessamine Co., high on the palisades of the Kentucky River, was established in 1863 and named in honor of Maj. Gen. William Nelson. By August 1863, thousands of slaves from central Kentucky, impounded to build railroads for the Union army, were stationed there. When drafting of blacks began in Kentucky on March 10, 1864, Camp Nelson immediately became the most important recruiting station and training camp for blacks.

Many regiments formed at Camp Nelson, including the 5th and 6th U.S. Colored Cavalries and the 114th and 116th U.S. Colored Heavy Artilleries. As the number of soldiers increased, so did the number of refugees from slavery. But since Kentucky was a slaveholding state, Camp Nelson was not a legal refuge for the dependents of black soldiers who had been slaves. In November 1864, 400 women and children were ordered from the camp and driven out by armed soldiers; many of them, undernourished and ill clad for the subfreezing weather, died of exposure. The order was reversed and some refugees returned to camp, but 102 died within a few weeks.

Abolitionist minister John G. Fee, who arrived at Camp Nelson as a volunteer missionary in July 1864, founded schools for blacks, recruited workers from missionary societies, established a church that remained active at Camp Nelson for decades, and proposed and administered an official refugee home. Unfortunately, there were many deaths. Of 3,060 refugees who entered the camp, 1,300 died. Nevertheless, many men and women considered Camp Nelson their cradle of freedom because, when dependents of Kentucky's black soldiers were finally emancipated, Camp Nelson became the chief center issuing emancipation papers to former slaves. Designated a U.S. cemetery for Union dead in 1867, Camp Nelson has remained a military cemetery. In 2014, it was designated a national historic landmark.

Sears, Richard D. *A Practical Recognition of the Brotherhood of Man: John G. Fee and the Camp Nelson Experience.* Berea, KY: Berea College Press, 1986.

—*Richard D. Sears*

CAMP NELSON REFUGEE CAMP, federal camp for African American refugees of the Civil War. Camp Nelson Refugee Camp was located in southern Jessamine Co. along the Kentucky River. During the Civil War, **Camp Nelson** originally served as a supply camp for Union operations in eastern Tennessee and later as a recruiting station for African American soldiers. Camp Nelson developed into a refugee camp as the families of enlisted black soldiers and slaves from central Kentucky fled their owners and sought refuge at the federal encampment. Their number in the spring of 1864 was estimated to be anywhere from 500 to 1,500.

Although some refugees were permitted to remain at Camp Nelson as servants or laborers, in many instances they were forcibly expelled. The camp's commander, Brig. Gen. Speed S. Fry, refused to provide food and shelter for black women and children, as well as the sick and elderly who were related to the soldiers or had been forced off the property of their owners. At times, refugees who were escaped slaves were returned to their owners, while others were forced to leave because of supply shortages. After the tragic deaths of women and children who were expelled from the camp in frigid conditions in November 1864, the federal government changed its policy thanks to the efforts of John G. Fee and other humanitarian and religious spokespersons.

With Capt. T. E. Hall serving as the superintendent, a refugee camp was eventually constructed that included individual buildings. In March 1866, an estimated 300 refugees, nearly 50 percent of the refugee population, had died over the previous 15 months.

Camp Nelson.

Despite the appalling death rate, nearly 1,000 women and children remained at Camp Nelson. After the war, many refugees stayed in the area. Kentucky abolitionist John G. Fee, along with a small group of northern white missionaries, supported the community's development by collecting donations for supplies, caring for the needy, attempting to buy land that could be sold to black farmers, and encouraging the establishment of black churches and schools.

Their efforts at helping establish a permanent settlement were thwarted by whites who were alarmed by the presence of a black community. These attackers robbed and threatened the black families and white missionaries who remained at Camp Nelson. For more than a week in November 1866, residents set up watch and guarded their homes from attack. Although soldiers from the **Freedmen's Bureau** arrested two suspects during the altercation, no reinforcements were sent, and the area continued to suffer from periodic attacks. Today there is no longer a significant black community residing in the area.

Berlin, Ira, ed. *Freedom: A Documentary History of Emancipation, 1861–1867.* Ser. I, Vol. 1. *The Destruction of Slavery.* Cambridge: Cambridge University Press, 1985, 626–32.
Lucas, Marion B. "Camp Nelson, Kentucky, during the Civil War: Cradle of Liberty or Refugee Death Camp?" *FCHQ* 63, no. 4 (October 1989): 439–52.
———. *A History of Blacks in Kentucky: From Slavery to Segregation, 1760–1891.* 2nd ed. Frankfort: Kentucky Historical Society, 2003.
—*Selena Sanderfer*

CANAAN MISSIONARY BAPTIST CHURCH (LOUISVILLE), African American Baptist megachurch in Louisville, KY.

On March 16, 1983, almost 100 people, including Rev. Walter Malone Jr., met in the basement of Louisville's Little Flock Baptist Church on Hancock St. to form Canaan Missionary Baptist Church. The group worshipped in a shared building with Magazine Street Seventh Day Adventist Church while it raised funds to purchase a $1-million facility on Dixie Hwy. The acquisition included a parsonage and a gym.

Nashville, TN, native Walter Malone Jr. has been the church's only pastor. Malone earned his degrees from Fisk University, American Baptist College, and Louisville's Southern Baptist Theological Seminary and his doctorate of ministry from United Theological Seminary in Dayton, OH. He has written two books, *An Operative Faith for an Oppressed People* and *From Holy Power to Holy Profits.*

Under Malone's leadership and the practice of "holistic" ministry, the church's membership grew. In 1996, it bought the Southeastern Christian Church complex on Hikes Ln. for $7.3 million. The property included 22 acres, a 2,200-seat sanctuary, educational facilities, a fellowship hall, and a family-life center. Now known as the Canaan Christian Church, its membership has grown to over 4,000 through its philosophy, "We're builders, not beggars."

As one of only two African American megachurches in Kentucky, Canaan specializes in community outreach through its various programs that incorporate its beliefs in self-help and teamwork. The church has established the Canaan Community Development Corporation, a nonprofit conglomerate for the purpose of community economic empowerment. Under this umbrella, programs consist of education and computer literacy, employment, housing, the Performing Arts Center, and the Child Development Center. The Family Life Center comprises family recreation, the Imani Fellowship focused on children of single parents, the Drama Ministry, and the Library Ministry. Other programs include Rites of Passage, "an intense 10-month program of instruction, attitude, and skill development" for young people, and Sons of Issachar, an after-school program.

Under a 2004 federal spending bill, Republican U.S. representative Anne Northup, along with 210 other Kentucky-specific earmarks, distributed "nearly $1.5 million for 24 after-school, job training and social services programs, many of them run by African-American churches." Canaan Church was one of five African American recipients.

Billingsley, Andrew. *Mighty like a River: The Black Church and Social Reform.* New York: Oxford Univ. Press, 1999.
Canaan Missionary Baptist Church. http://www.canaanchristian.com/ (accessed April 13, 2010).
Newspapers: "Kentucky Report," *KP,* January 9, 1996, 13A; "Louisville Projects Net $36 Million," *LCJ,* January 23, 2004, A1; "Recreation to Go: Taking It on the Road," *LCJ,* October 25, 2005, A1.
—*Sallie L. Powell*

CAPERS, EUGENIA (JEAN) MURRELL (b. 1913, Georgetown, KY), first African American assistant police prosecutor in Cleveland and first African American city council person of any major U.S. city.

Jean Murrell's parents, Edward Murrell and Dolly Ferguson Murrell, met at State Normal School for Colored Persons (later known as **Kentucky State University**) and were married in 1900. Edward's educational experience of Kentucky's segregated schools inspired him to move his family to his wife's home state of Ohio in 1919 so his children would have an integrated education. As teachers, Jean's parents emphasized education by giving a book to each of their children every Christmas. Jean attended Western Reserve University on an athletic / scholastic scholarship. After graduating with a physical education degree, she taught elementary and high school physical education for several years in Cleveland before she entered law school in 1941.

In 1943, Jean married Clifford Capers and continued to attend law school by taking night classes. Upon graduation from Cleveland Law School, known today as Cleveland-Marshall College of Law, she immediately began her practice of law in 1945.

Capers, a Democrat, served as the first African American assistant police prosecutor for three years. She ran for the Cleveland City Council in 1945 and 1947 in a traditionally Republican ward but lost both races. However, in 1949, she won, becoming the first African American city council person of any major U.S. city. Active in the community, Capers sponsored block parties with no admission charge. These street festivals allowed political candidates to meet voters. Block parties involved entire families and were particularly valuable in reaching young voters. Since white newspapers mostly ignored Capers, her father, an independent printer, supported her campaigns through his paper, the *Informer.*

As a city councilwoman, Capers located city jobs for African Americans and protested Cleveland's taxicab segregation. From

1960 to 1964, she served as an assistant attorney general. She believed that the time was right to increase African American governmental positions, organized a small group of interracial activists, and developed a political strategy for electing an African American mayor.

Carl B. Stokes was chosen as the candidate. He described Capers as "one of the brightest politicians ever to come out of Cleveland." Stokes lost his bid to become the city's first African American mayor in 1965, but the foundation had been laid for his victory two years later. Stokes, a grandson of slaves, beat Seth Taft, the grandson of a U.S. president.

Capers held the post of special counsel to the Ohio attorney general in the mid-1960s and served as a Cleveland municipal judge from 1977 to 1985, when state law forced her to retire. She believed that lawyers should "defend those least capable of defending themselves." Before her retirement, she founded the Ohio State Council of Democratic Women and helped launch the National Association of Black Women Attorneys in 1972. Her alma mater bestowed an honorary doctor of laws degree on her when she was 96 years old. She continued to practice senior law until she retired at age 98 in 2011. In January 2013, she reached her 100th birthday, but much to her chagrin, she spent it at Judson Manor care facility since the Cuyahoga County Probate Court had appointed a guardian for her.

Benjamin Rose Institute. "Caring for Older Adults and Those Who Care for Them." http://www.benrose.org/MythBusters/MB_Capers _Rose.cfm (accessed April 19, 2010).

Hazzard-Gordon, Katrina. *Jookin': The Rise of Social Dance Formations in African-American Culture.* Philadelphia: Temple Univ. Press, 1990.

Newspapers: "Carl Stokes Embodied the Dream," *Akron Beacon Journal,* April 4, 1996, A5; "Sisters in Their 90s, Hugs for the Ages," *Cleveland Plain Dealer,* May 19, 2009, B1; "At 100 Years Old, Judge Jean Murrell Capers Is Still Trying to Do It Her Way," *Cleveland Plain Dealer,* January 13, 2013.

Stokes, Carl B. *Promises of Power: A Political Autobiography.* New York: Simon & Schuster, 1973.

—*Sallie L. Powell*

CARPENTER, OLEONA (OLIE) ATKINS (b. 1902, Winston-Salem, NC; d. 1993, St. Louis, MO), first college-trained African American librarian in Kentucky. Named for her mother, Oleona, who was also a teacher, Olie Atkins was nurtured in an educational environment. Her father, Simon Green Atkins, founded and served as president of Slater Industrial Academy, which later became Winston-Salem State University. Olie earned her library degree from Virginia's Hampton Institute Library School in 1927 and worked as an assistant librarian at Tuskegee Institute for two years.

In 1928, the Rosenwald Fund proposed to the Kentucky State Industrial College (later known as **Kentucky State University**) that it would donate "one dollar for every two dollars the school spent on a book, if the school would hire a trained librarian." The following year, shortly after she married Joseph C. Carpenter, Olie was hired as the school's librarian, becoming the first college-trained African American librarian in Kentucky. She transferred to the newly opened **Louisville Municipal College** for

Negroes in 1931 to become its head librarian; her sister, Eliza V. Atkins (**Eliza Valeria Atkins Gleason**), became the assistant librarian.

Carpenter left after only one year at the college, and her sister became the school's head librarian. She continued her education, earning a degree in English at Bradley University and a degree in medical library science at the University of Denver. She worked as a medical librarian at Homer G. Phillips Hospital in St. Louis for 10 years before becoming Maryland State College's head librarian in 1952.

A few years later, Carpenter traveled overseas with her sister, Eliza, her brother-in-law, Dr. Maurice Gleason, and her niece, Joyce Gleason. Besides touring Europe and visiting the Brussels Fair, she journeyed to the Near East, including Turkey and Egypt.

Carpenter died in St. Louis, MO, in 1993.

Ash, Lee, ed. *Who's Who in Library Service: A Biographical Directory of Professional Librarians in the United States and Canada.* Hamden, CT: Shoe String Press, 1966.

BAA, July 29, 1958, 6.

A Directory of Negro Graduates of Accredited Library Schools, 1900–1936. Washington, DC: Columbia Civic Library Association, 1937.

"Society," *Jet,* July 24, 1958, 40.

Jones, Reinette F. *Library Service to African Americans in Kentucky, from the Reconstruction Era to the 1960s.* Jefferson, NC: McFarland, 2002.

—*Sallie L. Powell*

CARROLL, ALFRED MILTON (b. 1912, Louisville, KY; d. 1966, Louisville, KY), attorney. Alfred Milton Carroll, son of Jeremiah and Minnie Carroll, was born in Louisville, KY, on July 1, 1912. After attending the local public schools, he completed a two-year program at **Louisville Municipal College** and then graduated from Ohio's Wilberforce University. In 1937, he enrolled in Howard University's School of Law.

In the process of completing his law degree, he sought admission to the University of Kentucky's Law School in 1939 but was denied admission on the grounds that the state's 1904 school segregation statute (commonly called the **Day Law**) prohibited his enrollment and that Wilberforce was at that time unaccredited. However, Kentucky governor A. B. Chandler found $1,600 from his emergency funds to support Carroll's law school education at Howard University. These funds were allocated under the 1936 **Anderson-Mayer State Aid Act** because Kentucky granted special scholarships to blacks for out-of-state professional and graduate schools in order to maintain racial segregation in the state's professional and graduate schools.

Upon completing his degree in 1940, Carroll returned to Louisville to establish his law practice. Before passing the bar exam in 1945, he served as a carpentry teacher at **Central High School** and supervisor at the Hoosier Ordinance Plant in southern Indiana. From 1945 to 1947, he served as president of the Louisville branch of the **National Association for the Advancement of Colored People** (NAACP). In 1948, he sought election to the U.S. House of Representatives on the Progressive Party ticket but lost to Republican Thruston B. Morton. He served as legal counsel in several important Kentucky civil rights cases. The most notable were *Johnson v. Board of Trustees of University of Kentucky* (1949), which ended black student exclusion at the University of Kentucky, and *Sweeny v. City of Louisville* (1952), which desegregated Louisville's city parks.

A lifelong member of Louisville's **Quinn Chapel A.M.E. Church,** Carroll served as an ordained minister in the African Methodist Episcopal Church. From 1952 to 1966, he was the pastor of Louisville's St. Paul A.M.E. Church and cocounsel for the West Kentucky Conference of the A.M.E. Church. He held memberships in the NAACP, Sword and Shield Honorary Fraternity, and **Alpha Phi Alpha Fraternity.** He was married to Mary Frances Hodges and had four children: Mona C. Murphy, Constance Hughes, Milton A. Carroll, and Alfred G. Carroll. He died of pancreatic cancer on November 21, 1966, in Louisville.

Newspapers: "Minister of the Week," *LD,* March 17, 1959, 4; "Alfred Carroll, Minister Lawyer, Dies," *LCJ,* November 23, 1966; "Alfred M. Carroll, Minister and Attorney Gets Last Rites as Crowd Overflows Church," *Louisville Defender,* December 1, 1966, 1, 11.

—*John A. Hardin*

CARSON, JULIA MAY PORTER (b. 1938, Louisville, KY; d. 2007, Indianapolis, IN), first African American and woman elected to the U.S. Congress from Indiana and first woman to lie in state at the State Capitol rotunda in Indianapolis, IN. The daughter of a single teenage mother who was a housekeeper, Julia May Porter Carson moved from Kentucky when she was a child. She graduated from Crispus Attucks High School in Indianapolis, IN, and attended Martin University and Indiana University–Purdue University. After a divorce, she raised her two children on a United Auto Workers' secretary's salary. She worked from 1965 to 1972 as a staff assistant for Representative Andrew Jacobs Jr. of Indiana.

With Jacobs's encouragement, Carson ran for the Indiana State House of Representatives and won her first of over two dozen undefeated elections. Among her political offices, she served in the Indiana State Senate (1976–1990) and as Center Township trustee (1990–1996). The following year, she became the first African American woman from Indiana to serve in the U.S. Congress.

Carson, a Democrat, championed children's and women's rights, actively advocated for the homeless, and staunchly opposed the 2003 invasion of Iraq. She stated at an Indianapolis rally that the Iraq War was an aggressive act "to protect U.S. oil interests" and that the country had not learned the lessons of the Vietnam War. She assisted the historical restoration of Lyles Station, IN, an African American settlement and **Underground Railroad** stopover, and authored legislation for Rosa Parks to receive the Congressional Gold Medal in 1999.

Carson was known for her sense of humor and friendly relationships even with opponents. She fought "for those without a voice." After her death from lung cancer, she became the first woman in Indiana history to lie in state in the Indiana State Capitol rotunda. Carson was buried in Crown Hill Cemetery in Indianapolis. Her grandson, André Carson, filled her congressional seat after a special election.

Biographical Directory of the United States Congress, 1774–2005.
The Black Past: Remembered and Reclaimed. "Carson, Julia May Porter" and "Carson, André." http://www.blackpast.org/?q=aah/carson-julia-1938-2007 and http://www.blackpast.org/?q=aah/carson-andre-1974 (accessed April 26, 2010).
Newspapers: "First Black Woman Is Elected to Congress from Hoosier State," *Evansville Courier,* November 6, 1996, D1; "Cancer Claims Indiana Congresswoman—Rep. Julia Carson, 69, Hailed for 'Advocacy' for 7th District," *Ft. Wayne Journal Gazette,* December 16, 2007, 1C; "Rep. Julia Carson: Indiana Democrat Opposed Iraq War," *WP,* December 16, 2007; "Carson's Love of History Helped Lyles Station Grow," *Evansville Courier-Press,* December 18, 2007, B3; "Mourners Remember Carson," *Evansville Courier-Press,* December 22, 2007, A1.

—*Sallie L. Powell*

CARTER, LEON JOHN, III (b. 1944, Bowling Green, KY; d. 1984, Toledo, OH), and CARTER, LILLIE MAE BLAND (b. 1919, Bowling Green, KY; d. 1982, Toledo, OH), poets. Lillie Mae Bland Carter, the daughter of poorly educated parents, John and Maude Bland, graduated valedictorian from State Street High School in Bowling Green, KY. She earned her BS and MA degrees from Tennessee State University in Nashville. She worked as a stenographer for the Veterans Administration in Washington, DC, and later incorporated the experience into her poem "Black America."

In 1968, Carter began teaching at Martin Luther King School, Toledo, OH. In 1972, she traveled with two other educators on a 23-day tour of five African nations for a comparative study of the African education system and the American school system. Her later poetry, such as "A Pharaoh's Companion," reflected this trip.

Her literature appeared in various publications, and Langston Hughes placed some of her work in the Schomburg Collection in New York City. In 1971, 42 of her poems were published in *Black Thoughts.* This compilation demonstrated her often pithy insights on the African American experience in addition to her usage of religious verse and prose. In 1975, she compiled 15 of her poems along with poetry from various members of her family, including her husband, some of her children, grandchildren, and other relatives. Because few African American writers had been included in anthologies, Carter assembled the three-generation anthology, *Doing It . . . Our Way.*

One of the poignant sections of the book was a poetic correspondence between mother and son. Leon John Carter III followed in his mother's poetic footsteps. In 1966, he graduated from Tennessee State University. He joined the air force and became an officer. After returning to Toledo, OH, in 1970, he served as director of Upward Bound, a minority-affairs program at the University of Toledo. His literary work appeared in several periodicals. In 1973, *Black Windsongs* was published. Along with limericks about seasons and the weather, he integrated his military experience and questioned his purpose in life and the role of the nation.

Lillie Mae Carter retired in 1981 after 30 years as a teacher and reading specialist. She died the following year. Because she was a member of three different sororities, sorority rites were administered at her funeral. Her son, Leon J. Carter III, followed her in death only two years later at the age of 39 of a heart attack.

Carter, Leon J., III. *Black Windsongs.* London: Mitre Press, 1973.
Carter, Lillie Mae. *Black Thoughts.* London: Mitre Press, 1971.
———, comp. *Doing It . . . Our Way.* London: Mitre Press, 1975.

Dunnigan, Alice Allison, comp. and ed. *The Fascinating Story of Black Kentuckians: Their Heritage and Traditions.* Washington, DC: Associated Publishers, 1982.

Newspapers: "B.G. Native Authors Book," *BGDN,* August 1, 1972, 46; "Program in Honor of Leader," *Toledo (OH) Blade,* January 13, 1979, 18; "Lillie Carter," *Toledo (OH) Blade,* June 16, 1982, 5.

Townsend, Dorothy Edwards, comp. and ed. *Kentucky in American Letters.* Vol. 3, *1913–1975.* Georgetown, KY: Georgetown College Press, 1976.

—*Sallie L. Powell*

CASEY, DWANE (b. 1957, Morganfield, KY), basketball coach.
Union Co. native Dwane Casey was a four-sport high school star. He earned athletic letters in basketball, baseball, cross country, and football. Casey, known to be "tremendously quick" and "a team leader in hustle and hard work," played basketball for the University of Kentucky from 1976 to 1979. In his junior year, the team won the NCAA championship. After graduating from the university with a degree in business administration, he was hired as an assistant coach at Bowling Green's Western Kentucky University under Coach Clem Haskins.

Shortly after his 29th birthday, Casey began working as an assistant coach for Eddie Sutton at the University of Kentucky. He was only the third former player to be hired as an assistant coach at the university. Many considered Casey a "rising star" in the profession, but a 1988 recruiting scandal nearly ended his dreams of becoming a head basketball coach. An overnight mail package sent by Casey to the parent of a basketball recruit included a videotape and $1,000. Casey claimed that he had not put any money in the envelope and had placed the open package on a secretary's desk for her to mail. The NCAA investigated. Casey filed a $6.9-million defamation lawsuit against the delivery service. The suit was later settled out of court. On March 20, 1989, Casey resigned one day after Coach Eddie Sutton resigned.

After leaving Kentucky, Casey coached Japan's National Team and led it to its first world championship appearance in over 30 years. He became an assistant coach for the Seattle SuperSonics in 1994 and was promoted to associate head coach of the team in 2000. Five years later, he was hired as head coach of the Minnesota Timberwolves with the expectations of returning the team to the National Basketball Association (NBA) playoffs. When Casey was unsuccessful in improving the Timberwolves, he was fired after only a season and a half. He then became an assistant coach for the Dallas Mavericks. In 2011, he was named head coach of the Toronto Raptors.

Newspapers: "Casey Viewed as Rising Star in World of Coaching," *LHL,* April 15, 1988, A9; "Great Expectations—Casey's Job: Return Wolves to Playoffs," *St. Paul (MN) Pioneer Press,* June 18, 2005, D1; "Raptors Name Former Mavs Assistant Casey as Coach," Reuters (Canada), June 21, 2011.

University of Kentucky. Explore UK. http://exploreuk.uky.edu/images /kukuarp/2009ua007/2009ua007_013b.jpg (accessed May 4, 2010.

—*Sallie L. Powell*

CATHOLIC COLORED HIGH SCHOOL, only African American Catholic high school in Louisville, KY. Louisville's only Catholic high school exclusively for African Americans opened in 1921 when St. Augustine Catholic Elementary School at **St. Augustine Catholic Church,** 1310 W. Broadway, added high school classes. In 1929, the name was changed from St. Augustine High School to Catholic Colored High School when the Archdiocese of Louisville took over the school and moved it to the St. Mary's (Immaculate Conception) Catholic School building at 428 S. Eighth St. near Cedar. By 1931, Sister Frances Louise was listed as the principal.

The black parish elementary schools in Louisville, St. Augustine and St. Peter Claver at 522 Lampton St., sent their graduates to Catholic Colored High School. However, because of the small number of black Catholics in Louisville, the classes at the high school remained small. The school's sense of community was heightened by kinship among the students, many of whom had come from Bardstown and nearby Springfield, KY.

The size of the student population did not deter the Sisters of Charity of Nazareth from offering pupils an education grounded in classical studies. The nuns taught classes in mathematics, chemistry, English, Latin, algebra, and economics, accompanied by strict discipline. As in other high schools, dances, plays, and sports were also a part of school life. The pastor of St. Augustine Church drove the basketball team throughout the state to play other black schools. When integration made all-black schools no longer necessary, the archdiocese closed the facility in 1958.

LCJ, February 28, 1999.

CENTER OF EXCELLENCE FOR THE STUDY OF KENTUCKY AFRICAN AMERICANS (CESKAA), research center for African American history. Located at **Kentucky State University** (KSU) in Frankfort, the Center of Excellence for the Study of Kentucky African Americans (CESKAA) was established "to serve as the primary vehicle for researching, collecting, preserving, and distributing information and materials about Kentucky African Americans and African heritage." It has functioned as a research and service center, providing materials for museum collections and archival research, as well as programs geared toward community outreach and public education.

CESKAA originated as part of an 11-point plan of direction, called KSU Visions, released in April 1992. The original mission of the institution, according to KSU president **Mary Levi Smith,** was "to encompass teaching, research, a cultural component, as well as one that looked at the preservation of artifacts related to Kentucky African Americans." The university also cited five goals for the center: the establishment of an archive, increased awareness of the contributions of Kentucky African Americans, publications on relevant issues, enhancement of the liberal studies mission of the university, and service as a "clearing-house for information and research regarding issues that relate to the life and lifestyles of African Americans." Budgetary projections stated a need for $5 million initially, with an eventual need for $11 million overall, most of which was sought through donations from major corporations.

In 1993, the university selected James Joseph Gordon, formerly senior historian at the Afro-American Historical and Cultural Museum in Philadelphia, as its first director. The following year, it increased its fund-raising drive through a Celebrity and

VIP Weekend, which included singer Robert Guillaume and Cincinnati Reds player Joe Morgan. In 1996, Anne Butler took over as director of CESKAA. Through her dedicated leadership, the center contributed to a series of documentaries, including Kentucky Educational Television programs on the **Underground Railroad** and the **civil rights movement** in Kentucky, and initiated a series of popular programs like the annual Many Cultures–One Art Quilt Show. CESKAA was located in Jackson Hall, the first permanent building on Kentucky State University's campus and a historical starting point for collegiate education for Kentucky African Americans.

Appleton, Thomas H., Jr., Melba Porter Hay, James C. Klotter, and Thomas E. Stephens, eds. *Kentucky: Land of Tomorrow.* Frankfort: Kentucky Historical Society Foundation, 1998.
Kentucky State University. *Kentucky State University Catalogue, 2011–2012.* http://www.kysu.edu/NR/rdonlyres/A3FAA8E1-89AE-4591-BC91-A80857E069EF/0/KSUCatalogue2011_2012.pdf (accessed August 21, 2012).
Newspapers: "Q&A: Dr. Mary L. Smith, KSU President," *Frankfort State-Journal,* October 25, 1992, E1; "KSU to Push for Black History Center," *LHL,* February 10, 1994, B3.

—*Stephen Pickering*

CENTRAL COLORED/MARY D. HILL SCHOOL, first public school for African Americans in Kentucky. Although public schools were first established in Louisville in 1829, African American students were not provided with a free education until after the Civil War. On October 7, 1873, the first public school building in Kentucky for those students was dedicated in Louisville. The choir of **Fifth Street Baptist Church** opened the program with a setting of Psalm 40, appropriately titled "I Waited Patiently."

Built by the city for $23,000, the Central Colored School was erected on the southeast corner of Sixth and Kentucky Sts. J. B. McElfatrick and Son, the architects of this Renaissance Revival building, also designed Macauley's Theatre, which opened six days later. Taxes from all black-owned property in Louisville were allocated for the support of the school. Within three years, more than 1,000 children attended classes at the school, which significantly upgraded local African American education.

The school continued to teach grades one through eight until 1882, when junior and senior classes were added. Part of the building then became Central Colored High School (later **Central High School**). In 1893, another year was added, making it a three-year high school. Because of overcrowding, Central moved to Ninth and Magazine Sts. in 1895. The original building was then named Sixth Street School and was used as an elementary school for white children only. In 1917, the name was changed to Mary D. Hill School in honor of the supervisor of public school kindergartens, who had died the previous year. The school closed in 1970 and became the Hill Adult Learning Laboratory. In 1981, the building was sold to a graphic design firm.

Mary D. Hill School: Landmark and Landmark Site Designation Report. Louisville, KY: The Commission, 1975.
Newspapers: *Louisville Commerical,* October 8, 1873; *LCJ,* December 15, 1916; *Louisville Herald,* April 17, 1921; *LCJ,* April 14, 1954; *LCJ,* December 6, 1982.

—*Robert Bruce French*

CENTRAL HIGH SCHOOL, first high school for African Americans in Louisville. Central High School, originally called Central Colored High School, was Louisville's first African American high school. It was opened in September 1882 on the corner of Sixth and Kentucky Sts., with 27 students, a principal, and one teacher. In 1895, Central moved to Ninth and Magazine Sts.

Until 1907, the school was exclusively an academic institution, but under the prodding of Booker T. Washington and other black national leaders, a case was made for manual training. Central's curriculum was then geared toward both academic and vocational skills; the latter included dressmaking, cosmetology, automobile mechanics, plumbing, electricity, home economics, blueprinting, and machine shop.

In 1912, Central moved to Ninth and Chestnut Sts. However, in order to accommodate the growing interest in vocational education, the manual training department remained at Ninth and Magazine Sts. until 1952, when it also moved to Chestnut St.

By 1932, Central Colored High School had 900 students and 30 teachers and was still expanding. The school improved both in size and quality so that in 1932 it was accredited by the Southern Association of Colleges and Secondary Schools. In 1945, the name was changed to Central High School in response to students' and parents' protests about the use of the word "colored." By 1950, the school had nearly 1,300 students and 52 teachers.

Because of rapid growth, Central High School moved to its fourth location at 12th and Chestnut Sts. in September 1952. Its new facilities were unsurpassed in the Louisville school system.

At Central High School, athletics were important, especially basketball. Central won several state and national championships, most notably under the head coaching of **William L. Kean** (1923–1958) and Robert Graves (1965–1984). Although boxing was not included in the school curriculum, a number of boys participated in it in private gymnasiums. Most notable was Cassius Clay (**Muhammad Ali**), class of 1960, who won the world heavyweight championship three times.

In 1963, **Atwood Wilson** retired after serving 29 years as principal. His retirement ushered in a period of many changes. In 1964, the Louisville Board of Education initiated a plan of token integration by transferring a few of Central's teachers to East End schools and East End teachers to Central. Despite these efforts, Central remained Louisville's only predominantly African American high school until September 1975, when court-ordered **busing** began. This led to tension between old and new students. The desegregation of Central was met with protests from alumni, teachers, parents, and students who believed that the school would lose its tradition, spirit, and excellence. By 1982, what had once been Louisville's only all–African American high school was about 70 percent white.

In 1986, Central High School began offering magnet courses in order to draw the area's top African American students. In 1991, the Jefferson County School Board voted to adopt a new plan, Project Renaissance, which replaced the busing plan in which a student's assignment was decided by the first letter of his or her last name. The plan required each school to be at least 15 but not more than 50 percent African American. Magnet career programs were used in schools throughout the county to encourage integration. That same year, Central became a county-wide magnet school with programs in law, medicine, and other areas. Its name was changed to Central High School Magnet Career Academy, and it offered a four-year precollegiate program, an advanced program, and an honors program. In 1997, a new issue arose over quotas. Although the student body at Central was nearly 50 percent African American in the 1996–1997 school year, there were at least 600 vacancies in the school because of the inability to attract white students. At the same time, large numbers of African American students were turned away, and citizens asked that an exception be made at Central by increasing the 50 percent limit. The school board refused, saying that making an exception for Central would poke a hole in the desegregation dike.

In the late 1990s, Central students began receiving national attention as Merit Scholars, and the school has continued to develop its role as an important magnet school for the area.

"Central to the Debate," *Louisville,* August 1997, 36.

CHAPPELL, ROY MARTIS (b. 1921, Williamsburg, KY; d. 2002, Chicago, IL), Tuskegee Airman. Roy Chappell was born to Lionel and Flora Chappell in Williamsburg, KY. He spent most of his early years in Monroe, MI, where he was the only African American in his high school's graduating class. He then returned to the state of his birth and attended Kentucky State College (later named **Kentucky State University**).

In 1944, during his junior year, Chappell was drafted and served as a bombardier and navigator with the **Tuskegee Airmen** of the 477th Bombardment Group. While he was stationed outside Seymour, IN, Chappell participated in the famous 1945 Freeman Field mutiny, in which he and almost 100 other African American officers were arrested after trying to integrate a segregated officers' club in a protest against unequal treatment in the military. This protest was one of many African American demonstrations that eventually prompted President Harry S. Truman to call for the end of military segregation.

After the war, Chappell moved to Chicago, studied at Roosevelt College, and taught elementary school for 30 years. Until his death in 2002, Chappell served as president of the Chicago chapter of Tuskegee Airmen, where he became the only person ever to win the organization's two highest honors, the National President's Award and the Brigadier General Noel Parrish Award. He also worked with the Experimental Aircraft Association Young Eagles Program. In 2001, he was awarded the Phillips 66 Aviation Leadership award, one of the most prestigious awards for civilian aviators. After his death, an honorary historical highway marker was unveiled at Briar Creek Park in Williamsburg, KY, and a city street was renamed to bear his name. In 2003, Kentucky State University honored its prestigious alumnus with the Roy M. Chappell Community Education Center.

"Census." *Jet* 102, no. 18 (October 21, 2002): 54.
"Roy Martis Chappell Honored with Historical Highway Marker." *Konnection Employee Newsletter,* Kentucky Transportation Cabinet, February 2006, 16.

—*Joshua D. Farrington*

CHAPPELL, WILLA BROWN (b. 1906, Glasgow, KY; d. 1992, Chicago, IL), first African American female to receive a pilot's license in the United States. Willa Brown Chappell was born on January 22, 1906, in Glasgow, KY, to Eric B. Brown, a minister, and Hallie Mae Carpenter Brown. When Willa was six, her family moved to Indianapolis, IN, and later to Terre Haute, IN, where she received her primary education. It was in primary school that she developed her passion for aviation. She was greatly influenced by Bessie Coleman, an African American female from Chicago who went to France to receive her pilot's license.

Chappell worked as a teacher until her dream of being a pilot was realized on June 22, 1938, when she received her license. The following year, she became a cofounder of the National Airmen's

Willa Brown Chappell.

Association of America. On its behalf, she lobbied the U.S. government to include African Americans in the U.S. Army Air Corps and the Civilian Pilot Training Program (CPTP). In 1940, Congress authorized the use of African Americans in the CPTP and commissioned Chappell as an African American coordinator in Chicago. Through her training, she became the first African American officer, at the rank of lieutenant, in the Civil Air Patrol. Some of the people she trained went on to become part of the 99th Pursuit Squadron at Tuskegee Institute, better known as the **Tuskegee Airmen.**

Chappell was a fixture in the Chicago African American community until her death from a stroke on July 18, 1992.

"Kentucky: Kentucky Commission on Human Rights—Great Black Kentuckians." February 23, 2009. http://kchr.ky.gov/gallergreat black.htm (accessed January 16, 2010).

Minderovic, Christine. "Brown, Willa Beatrice, 1906–1992." In *Contemporary Black Biography.* Gale Research, 2004. Encyclopedia .com. http://www.encyclopedia.com/doc/1G2-2874200022.html.

—*Vincent Gonzalez*

CHEANEY, HENRY ELLIS (b. 1912, Henderson, KY; d. 2006, Frankfort, KY), educator and historian. Henry Ellis Cheaney, the son of Steven Ellis and Magnolia Radford McGuire Cheaney, was born in Henderson, KY, on July 1, 1912. He attended Henderson's **(Frederick) Douglass High School,** where he played football, baseball, and basketball and ran track. After graduation, he attended Kentucky State Industrial College for Colored Persons (later known as **Kentucky State University**), where he continued his athletics in track and football, being part of the first national Negro Football Championship team in 1934. He also established and coached the college's boxing program and graduated in 1936. The college's president, **Rufus B. Atwood,** immediately hired him to teach English and history. In addition to teaching, Cheaney coached the college's debate and boxing teams and worked as the director of college publicity, the supervisor of the college YMCA, the college alumni agent, and the college chaplain. He received his master's degree in history from the University of Michigan (1941) and his PhD in history from the University of Chicago (1961).

Dr. Henry Ellis Cheaney receiving an honorary doctorate from Berea College, pictured with his wife Ora Mae.

During his 46-year tenure, Cheaney became an excellent historical witness to the changes in the institution as it underwent the process of moving from Kentucky State Industrial College for Colored Persons (1926) to Kentucky State College for Negroes (1938) to Kentucky State College (1952) to Kentucky State University (KSU) (1972). He was one of the original 12 members who founded the college's chapter of the **Phi Beta Sigma Fraternity,** was later inducted into the Distinguished Service Chapter of the fraternity, and became the first recipient of the A. [Asa] Philip Randolph Award, one of the fraternity's highest honors.

Cheaney made his greatest impact in the classroom. He became a legend at KSU and at other state institutions as an outstanding professor and mentor to legions of African American students. Those he taught and those who met him believed that he was "deserving of every superlative" and simply "the best teacher anytime and anywhere." He became a lasting influence on African American students in Kentucky. One of the foremost authorities on African American history in the state, he amassed much of the research on Kentucky African American history. His personal collection was used for the writing of *A History of Blacks in Kentucky,* a two-volume work by Marion B. Lucas and George C. Wright. He authored the article on Kentucky in the *International Encyclopedia* and a series of newspaper biographies on outstanding Kentucky African Americans. He also coauthored the text *Kentucky's Black Heritage,* which was widely used in the Kentucky public school system.

Kentucky State University honored him with the Henry E. Cheaney Endowed Scholarship for full-time undergraduate students majoring in history or political science. In 2001, the Henderson County Sports Hall of Fame recognized his athletic achievements. On July 18, 2006, Cheaney died at the Frankfort Regional Medical Center. His body was interred at Fernwood Cemetery in Henderson, KY.

"Dr. Henry E. Cheaney-Portrait of Dedication." http://www.angelfire .com/ky/juggernaut/cheaney.html (accessed July 28, 2014).

"In Memoriam." *Journal of Blacks in Higher Education, JBHE Weekly Bulletin,* August 3, 2006. http://www.jbhe.com/latest/news/8-3-06 /memoriam.html.

"Kentucky State University." http://www.kysu.edu/ (accessed July 28, 2014).

Lexington Herald-Leader. "African American News and Genealogy." http://africanamericangenealogy.blogspot.com/2006_07_01_archive .html.

Newspapers: Ron Jenkins, "'A Legend': Cheaney Excelled in Sports Academia," *Evansville Courier and Press,* July 21, 2006, n.p.; "Dr. Henry E. Cheaney–Portrait of Dedication: KSU History Professor Remembered as a Legend," *LHL,* July 21, 2006, C1; Charlie White, "Historian Henry E. Cheaney Dies at 94: Collected Data on African Americans," *LCJ,* July 21, 2006, 6B.

Written for the "Brotherhood" by Warren S. Galloway, Jr. on December 16, 2008. http://bluephi.net/blog/2008/12/16/noted-history -professor-dr-henry-e-cheaney/.

—*Aingred G. Dunston-Coleman*

CHENAULT, MARCUS WAYNE (b. 1951, Winchester, KY; d. 1995, Riverdale, GA), assassin of Martin Luther King Jr.'s mother, Alberta. Born in Winchester, KY, to Marcus H. and Henda Lee Chenault, Marcus Wayne Chenault was described by his neighbors as a "nice boy" who delivered newspapers and regularly attended church with his parents. During his junior year at Ohio State University, however, Chenault became increasingly eccentric and withdrawn. Disillusioned with Christianity, Chenault began exploring different religions. According to a neighbor in Columbus, "One week he was eating this because he wanted to be a Jew; then one week he wouldn't eat this because he wanted to be a Muslim."

During a Sunday service on the morning of June 30, 1974, Chenault entered Martin Luther King Sr.'s Ebenezer Baptist Church in Atlanta, where he shot and killed Alberta Williams King (mother of Martin Luther King Jr. and the church's organist) and a deacon, Edward Boykin. After the killings, Chenault proclaimed, "I am a Hebrew," and that his real name was "Servant Jacob." Despite the testimony of two psychiatrists who stated that he suffered from schizophrenia, Chenault was sentenced to death. After the protests of the King family, who opposed capital punishment, the sentence was reduced to life in prison, where Chenault died of a stroke at age 44. Haggard and Son Funeral Home in Winchester handled the burial arrangements, and he was interred at Hillcrest Cemetery.

"M. W. Chenault, 44, Gunman Who Killed Mother of Dr. King." *NYT,* August 22, 1995, D20.
"The Third King Tragedy." *Time,* July 15, 1974.

—*Joshua D. Farrington*

CHEROKEE STATE PARK, state park for blacks in western Kentucky.

Established in 1951 by the State Parks Department, Cherokee State Park was the only state park for African Americans in Kentucky. Located in Aurora near Kentucky Lake State Park, which was reserved for whites, Cherokee was described by a Kentucky State Highway map as "the finest 'colored' vacation site in the South." The park spread out over more than 300 acres. It offered picnic tables, 12 cottages, a boathouse, a restaurant, and a beach. There were more than 15 persons on staff. The surrounding hickory, oak, and ash trees, along with opportunities for fishing and swimming, provided a refreshing and relaxing atmosphere away from the perils of discrimination. The park was a very popular vacation spot that attracted African Americans from the Midwest and the South and from as far north as New York.

With the gradual desegregation of public accommodations in Kentucky, the state closed Cherokee State Park as a segregated facility reserved for blacks in 1964. However, the park gave all its African American visitors lifelong memories. Jacob White, a former manager at the park, remembered it "as a great thing. A lot of us had no place to go, and we could go and feel just like everyone else and enjoy this very scenic place." Gladman Humbles looked forward to enjoying the park's leisure environment: "When you had to go to a low-paying job, working long hours probably, no overtime was available in those days. You had a family to take care of and it was a struggle just to make ends meet. And you can imagine back then what a treat it would be to take a drive up to the park."

After the park closed, the bathhouse was razed and some of the cottages were relocated to nearby Kenlake State Park. Murray State University used one of the buildings for storage. In 2009, the park

was placed on the National Register of Historic Places. The Friends of Cherokee State Park led a successful campaign to encourage the state to restore the park. On September 15, 2010, Governor Steve Beshear participated in a ceremony to celebrate the renovation of the park's dining hall, which would serve as part of Kenlake State Resort Park. "This project preserves an important aspect of African American history, an important part of state park history and an important part of Kentucky history, "said Beshear.

Governor Steve Beshear's Communication Office. "Gov. Beshear Celebrates Re-opening of Former Cherokee State Park Facility." September 15, 2010. http://migration.kentucky.gov/newsroom/governor/20100915cherokee.htm (accessed December 9, 2013).
Hatton, Angela. WKMS 91.3 FM. "Cherokee State Park." http://wkms.org/post/cherokee-state-park (accessed December 9, 2013).
Newspapers: "Fun in the Fifties; Cherokee Was Kentucky's Only State Park Designated for Blacks," *LHL,* February 27, 2008, E1; "Rare Segregated Park Heads toward New Life—Western Ky. Site Was for Blacks Only in the 1950's," *LHL,* August 24, 2009, B3.

—*Gerald L. Smith*

CHESTNUT STREET YMCA and KNIGHTS OF PYTHIAS, branches of African American organizations in Louisville, KY.

The six-story building at 930 W. Chestnut St. has been the home of both the Pythian Temple and the Young Men's Christian Association (YMCA), two organizations that have played an important role in Louisville's African American community.

The Order of the Knights of Pythias, originally a whites-only organization, was founded in 1864 in Washington, DC, by Justus Henry H. Rathbone. Its principles were friendship, charity, and benevolence. Although the first white Pythian lodge was organized in Louisville in 1869, very little is known about the formation of black lodges. By 1893, two were listed in the Louisville city directory. By 1915, there were 11 African American Pythian lodges in the city, all meeting at 419 S. Sixth St. In addition to charity work, the organization served as a source of social entertainment. Members were generally the better-educated and most prominent and successful leaders of the black community, who served as role models for black youth. In 1925, the national convention for African American Pythians was held in Louisville and drew 25,000 delegates.

In 1915, a new building was completed at 930 W. Chestnut St. that served as the state headquarters for African American Pythian lodges. The architect was Henry Wolters, who was born in Germany and moved to Louisville in 1872. The six-story structure is built of buff brick with limestone trim and entrances. At one time the building housed a drugstore, a movie theater, a restaurant, a photography studio, an ice cream parlor, and doctors' offices. It also included hotel rooms for men, rooms for lodge meetings, and a ballroom on the sixth floor that led up to a roof garden. The Pythian lodge became inactive in the 1930s because of the Great Depression, but the building continued to be used for offices and apartments. During World War II, it was used as a USO for black soldiers, with dances held regularly. After the war, a portion of it housed the Davis Trade School for African Americans.

One of the first YMCA branches in the city was the branch for African Americans. In 1885, Albert Mack began a one-man campaign to establish the organization. With the assistance of others, such as **Thomas F. Blue,** first librarian of the **Western Colored Branch Library,** the first facility opened in 1892 at 942 W. **Walnut St.** In 1906, the western branch bought the former John P. Byrne house at 920 W. Chestnut St., adjacent to the site of the future Pythian building. At this point, the branch adopted the name Chestnut Street Branch YMCA.

The YMCA served as an alternative to pool halls and other hangouts of black youth. It functioned as a recreational center with reading rooms and Bible study classes. It also organized baseball and basketball teams. This branch closed in 1932, also because of the Depression, but was reorganized in 1946. In 1953, a citywide YMCA capital funds campaign goal of $1.5 million was completed. The Chestnut Street Branch's allocation was used to purchase and renovate the Pythian building at a cost of $550,000. The structure provided lodging for men, meeting and conference rooms, and space for various youth and adult activities. The YMCA of Greater Louisville organized another capital funds drive in 1976. Of the $5 million raised, the Chestnut Street Branch used $500,000 for construction of a gymnasium at 920 W. Chestnut. An additional $150,000 was made available through a grant from the City Community Development Fund to upgrade the facility in the Pythian building and the extension unit at Market and 38th Sts. In 1978, another grant was secured to renovate the sixth floor for a teen center and ballroom.

Wright, George C. *Life Behind a Veil: Blacks in Louisville, Kentucky, 1865–1930.* Baton Rouge: Louisiana State Univ. Press, 1985.

CHILDERS, LULU VERE (b. 1870, Dry Ridge, KY; d. 1946, Howell, MI), first director of Howard University's School of Music. Lulu Vere Childers was born to former slaves Alexander Childers and Eliza Butler in Dry Ridge, KY, in 1870. Her family moved to Howell, MI, when Childers was five. She lived there until she graduated from high school and then attended the Oberlin Conservatory of Music in Ohio. After obtaining a degree in music, she taught at public schools in Ulrichsville, OH (1896–1898), and Wiley College in Marshall, TX (1898–1900). From 1900 to 1905, she served as director of the Music Department at Knoxville College in Tennessee.

In 1905, Childers was appointed instructor of methods and music at Howard University, and the following year she was named director of music of the newly established Music Department. As director, she developed a college-level curriculum, hired instructors, and formed the University Choral Society. Her diligent efforts led the school to upgrade the department to a conservatory in 1912 and to the School of Music in 1918.

Childers also started an annual concert series that brought famous musicians to Howard. Childers invited Marian Anderson to participate in the 1939 series. It was this invitation that launched the infamous serious of events in which Anderson was prohibited from singing in Washington's segregated facilities. She eventually sang at the Lincoln Memorial after the intervention of Eleanor Roosevelt and Interior Secretary Harold Ickes.

Childers retired in 1940. Two years later, Howard University bestowed an honorary doctor of music degree on her. She died at her home in 1946. A portrait of Childers hangs in the Lulu Vere Childers Hall of the Fine Arts Building at Howard University.

Logan, Rayford. *Howard University: The First Hundred Years, 1867–1967.* New York: New York Univ. Press, 1969.
Logan, Rayford, and Michael Winston, eds. *Dictionary of American Negro Biography.* New York: Norton, 1982.
Patterson, DeAnna Rose. "A History of Three African-American Women Who Made Important Contributions to Music Education between 1903 and 1960." M.A. thesis, Bowling Green State Univ., 2007.

—Joshua D. Farrington

CHILDRESS, WILLIAM HOBBS, JR. (b. 1911, Washington, DC; d. 1993, Lexington, KY), state legislator. William Hobbs Childress Jr. was born in Washington, DC, in 1911 but moved to Nashville as a young child, where he attended middle and high school at Fisk University training schools. In 1929, he continued his education at Fisk when he enrolled at the university, and four years later, he earned his bachelor's degree in economics.

In 1936, after struggling to make a living as an insurance agent in Nashville, Childress moved to Louisville to live with his cousin, Dr. Franklin Belver Beck, a dentist. After two more years on a small income selling insurance, Childress was appointed a probation officer in 1938. He served in the army during World War II and received two Bronze Stars, the EAME Theatre Ribbon, and the Good Conduct Ribbon. After the war, Childress returned to Louisville and served as the deputy circuit court clerk of Jefferson Co. from 1952 until his retirement in 1981. He was also active in Kentucky branches of the **National Association for the Advancement of Colored People** and the **National Urban League.**

Childress's major accomplishment came after he was elected to the state legislature in 1960 when he sponsored House Bill 163, which created the **Kentucky Commission on Human Rights.** Although he served only one term, the passage of his bill was one of the milestones in Kentucky legislative history. In 1993, William Childress died at Lexington's Veterans Administration Hospital and was buried in **Camp Nelson** National Cemetery.

Childress, William. Interview by Ann Grundy, July 25, 1986. Blacks in Lexington Oral History Project, Special Collections and Digital Programs, Univ. of Kentucky.
Kentucky's Black Heritage: The Role of the Black People in the History of Kentucky from Pioneer Days to the Present. Frankfort: Kentucky Commission on Human Rights, 1971.
Robinson, Ann R. Taylor. *Childress Touched Many One Man.* Lexington, KY: Heart to Heart & Associates, 1998.

—Joshua D. Farrington

CHILES, JAMES ALEXANDER (b. 1860, Richmond, VA; d. 1930, Richmond, VA), prominent Lexington attorney during the early twentieth century. Born to Richard and Martha Chiles, J. Alexander Chiles first attended the Freedmen's School in Richmond, VA, before he and his twin brother, John, had to leave school to go to work and earn money to help the family. While working in a tobacco factory and as a porter and bellboy in a hotel, Chiles maintained his interest in acquiring an education. In 1882, he enrolled in Lincoln University in Chester Co., PA, and graduated five years later. Between 1887 and 1889, he

James Alexander Chiles, 1895.

attended the Law Department at the University of Michigan. The following year, he began practicing law in Richmond, VA. After practicing law for a few months there, he moved to Lexington, KY, at the urging of his friend Dr. **John E. Hunter.** On July 23, 1891, he married Fannie J. Baines of Philadelphia, who became a schoolteacher in Lexington.

Chiles used his legal skills to challenge separate-but-equal laws on railroad transportation. As early as 1903, he battled with the Chesapeake and Ohio Railroad for violation of his rights as an interstate traveler. In 1907, he won damages in the amount of $100 because he had to transfer to the accommodations reserved for "colored," which were not equal to those reserved for whites. In 1910, Chiles argued his own case against the Chesapeake and Ohio Railroad Company before the U.S. Supreme Court, claiming that he had to sit in a **Jim Crow** car as he made his way from Washington to Lexington. The case challenged Kentucky's **Separate Coach Law,** but the court upheld Kentucky's law and affirmed the right of railroad companies to enforce the segregation of interstate passengers. Chiles's case was dismissed.

Chiles remained a visible and active member of the African American community. He spoke out against the Kentucky General Assembly's discussion of a bill to disfranchise black voters in 1904. He also lobbied for a black school truant officer and a physician in black schools in Lexington. In 1913, Governor James McCreary appointed him to serve as a delegate to the 50th-anniversary observance of the Emancipation Proclamation in Philadelphia.

Attorney Chiles died in Richmond, VA, in April 1930. The Lexington Bar Association wrote a tribute in his memory.

Newspapers: *Maysville (KY) Daily Public Ledger,* October 29, 1903; "Jim Crow Law," *HK,* April 15, 1905, 4; "Atty Chiles," *LL,* April 19, 1910, 7; "The 'Jim Crow' Decision," *NYT,* June 2, 1910, 8.

—*Gerald L. Smith*

CHINN, JULIA (b. unknown; d. 1833, Scott Co., KY), mistress of Richard Mentor Johnson, ninth vice president of the United States. Julia Chinn, a slave held by a pioneer and legislator in Kentucky, was bequeathed to Richard Mentor Johnson when her former owner died in 1814. Johnson, a member of the U.S. House of Representatives and a prominent resident of Scott Co., KY, openly took her as his mistress and gave her exceptional control of his affairs. While he worked in Washington, she lived in his house and ran the farm, and when they were together, he allowed her to host his parties. He also readily supported two children produced by the relationship, providing his daughters with land and money and arranging marriages for them with white husbands.

In 1833, a cholera outbreak swept through Scott Co., and Chinn caught the disease and died. When Johnson campaigned for the vice presidency a few years later, newspapers ridiculed his flouting of the color line, and Chinn was the subject of a derogatory song titled "Johnson's Wife of Old Kentucky." Nevertheless, Johnson was elected on a ticket with Martin Van Buren, and he issued no apologies for his behavior. The scandal gradually faded away after Johnson withdrew from public life, but in 2005, over 100 of Johnson and Chinn's descendants gathered in Georgetown, KY, to recognize their biracial heritage.

Brown, Thomas. "The Miscegenation of Richard Mentor Johnson as an Issue in the National Election of 1835–1836." *Civil War History* 39 (1993): 5–30.

Meyer, Leland Winfield. *The Life and Times of Colonel Richard M. Johnson of Kentucky.* New York: s.n., 1932.

"Unearthing Their Roots—Sharing Uncommon Ancestors, a Diverse Kentucky Family Reunites." *LHL,* July 23, 2005, A1.

—*Stephen Pickering*

CHITTISON, HERMAN (b. 1908, Flemingsburg, KY; d. 1967, Cleveland, OH), pianist. Born on October 8, 1908, to Charles Chittison, a carpenter, and Sarah Chittison, a laundress, Herman "Ivory" Chittison, a Flemingsburg native, started playing piano at the age of 8. By age 19, he was playing with the Kentucky Derbies, a Louisville, KY, **jazz** band. His powerful style of stride piano was influenced by James P. Johnson and Fats Waller. In 1928, his career skyrocketed when he joined the popular Zack Whyte orchestra.

Throughout the early 1930s, Chittison accompanied Clarence Williams, Stepin Fetchit, Adelaide Hall, and Ethel Waters. In 1934, he traveled to Europe with Louis Armstrong. He soon after called Paris, France, home and played alongside the Willie Lewis band. During his four-year stay in Paris, Chittison also recorded numerous piano solos. He played with the Harlem Rhythmakers in Egypt with fellow Kentuckian **William G. "Bill" Coleman.** He returned to the United States the following year and could frequently be seen playing in New York's Greenwich Village nightclubs, Ruban Bleu and the Blue Angel, throughout the 1940s. During this time, Chittison was also the pianist for eight years for the popular live radio show *Casey, Crime Photographer.* Throughout the 1950s and 1960s, after settling in Cleveland, OH, Chittison continued to play with his band, the Herman Chittison Trio, until his death from lung cancer in 1967. He was interred in Cleveland's Highland Park Cemetery.

Doran, James. *Herman Chittison: A Bio-Discography.* Bel Air, MD: International Association of Jazz Record Collectors, 1993.
"Herman Chittison." In *Swing: Great Musicians, Influential Groups, 1500 Recordings Reviewed and Rated.* San Francisco: Miller Freeman Books, 2000.
"Herman Chittison, Jazz Pianist, Dies." *NYT,* March 16, 1967, 47.

—*Joshua D. Farrington*

CHRISTIAN, CHAUNCEY LEWIS (b. 1896, New York, NY; d. 1991, Teaneck, NJ), certified public accountant and business executive. Born on May 17, 1896, in New York City, Chauncey Lewis Christian lived his early years in Virginia with his mother, Clara Cross Christian, a dressmaker, and his grandmother, Silvia Cross, a washerwoman. He graduated from Armstrong High School in Richmond, VA, and shortly thereafter worked as cashier, field agent, and secretary for the Southern Aid Society of Virginia in Charlottesville. In 1919, he joined the **Samuel M. Plato** Construction Company in Marion, IN, which later expanded to Louisville, KY. Christian, a cost accountant, was responsible for purchasing and labor contracts.

Even though African Americans were not allowed to take the Kentucky certified public accountancy examination, Plato encouraged the light-skinned Christian to take the test. In 1926, out of 50 testers, he was 1 of 7 who passed, becoming the first African American certified public accountant in Kentucky and the third in the country. By 1930, Christian and his wife, Lillian (a.k.a. Opal) Terry, had two children. Their son, Chauncey Lewis Christian Jr., was born in Louisville and later became a mechanical engineer with Polaroid.

In 1944, Christian left Plato Construction Company as a junior partner and worked at the Gale Agency, a supplier of performing artists such as the Ink Spots and Ella Fitzgerald, in New York City until 1958. The Gale Agency then became the Circle Artist Corporation, making Christian the only African American partner in a prominent Broadway talent agency. He later formed his own business, Christian and Christian Certified Public Accountants, and retired in 1985. He died at age 94.

Hammond, Theresa. *A White-Collar Profession: African American Certified Public Accountants since 1921.* Chapel Hill: Univ. of North Carolina Press, 2007.
Newspapers: "Ex–Southern Aid Cashier Is Juror No. One in Carbo Case," *BAA,* October 27, 1959, 4; "Obituaries," *Record* (NJ), January 18, 1991, c07.
"New York Beat." *Jet,* July 10, 1958, 63.
U.S. Federal Census (1900, 1910, 1930).
U.S. World War I Draft Registration Cards, 1917–1918.

—*John A. Hardin*

CHURCH OF OUR MERCIFUL SAVIOR (LOUISVILLE), oldest African American Episcopal Church in Louisville, KY. The oldest African American Episcopal Church in Louisville, the Church of Our Merciful Savior traces its origin to 1861. At that time, Rev. William I. Waller, a missionary, started St. Mark's Episcopal Mission as a "separate and distinct congregation" for Louisville blacks. It purchased the German Lutheran church building on Green and Preston Sts. and by 1867 was led by the talented preacher Rev. Joseph Atwell. The church thrived under Atwell's leadership but ceased to exist after he left the state in 1868.

In 1870, a black Episcopal presence reemerged in the form of a mission on Eighth near Cedar St. The church became an official mission of the Episcopal Diocese in May 1872 and was recognized as the Church of Our Merciful Savior. In 1873, an endowment by Rev. John Norton allowed the church to move to Grayson and Ninth Sts. Rapid growth made it necessary to secure a larger sanctuary, and in April 1891, the church again moved to a Gothic structure built by plow magnate B. F. Avery around 1854. The building on the site had been gutted by fire, but the congregation was able to preserve the structure until another fire leveled the building in January 1912. One of its influential pastors was Rev. LeRoy Ferguson. His close association with blacks and whites contributed to his high regard in philanthropic circles. His efforts resulted in several contributions from steel magnate Andrew Carnegie's foundation.

A new church was built in 1912 under the leadership of Bishop Charles Woodcock at the present site at 11th and **Walnut** Sts. It was designed by Louisville architect George Herbert Gray. When the federal government completed the Beecher Terrace Housing Project in 1940, the church was allowed to remain, and the new development was built around it; it was reported that the church was so well respected in the community that local gambling houses would not open their doors to customers until after church services were finished.

During World War II, the church worked in cooperation with other area churches to support United Service Organization clubs for GIs, with Dudley Hall of the church serving as an officer's lounge and the parish house serving as a military police battalion headquarters. The church is currently located at 473 South 11th Street in Louisville.

Lucas, Marion B. *A History of Blacks in Kentucky.* Vol. 1, *From Slavery to Segregation, 1760–1891.* Frankfort: Kentucky Historical Society, 1992.

CIVILIAN CONSERVATION CORPS (MAMMOTH CAVE), program that provided the opportunity for young African American men to participate in the development of Mammoth Cave National Park. The Civilian Conservation Corps (CCC) was a New Deal program created during President Franklin Delano Roosevelt's first 100 days in office. Intended to alleviate unemployment among young men, it included an amendment that allowed African Americans to participate in the program. On May 22, 1933, two months after Roosevelt signed the bill creating the CCC, the first CCC camp in Kentucky was established at Mammoth Cave. Known as both Camp 510 and NP-1, it was initially composed of both whites and African Americans living in segregated quarters that had originally been constructed for the Bluegrass Country Club. In less than a year, all the white men had been transferred to one of three white-only camps in the Mammoth Cave vicinity.

In 1926, Mammoth Cave National Park was officially authorized by the U.S. Congress, but little work had been done at the site until the CCC arrived. The men of Camp 510 were the first arrivals, but the camp was fraught with problems relating to discrimination. By 1934, the camp had already had 10 different commanders and was viewed as the worst camp in the V Corps region, which encompassed Indiana, Kentucky, Ohio, and West Virginia. Under the leadership of Capt. Paul Mitchell and later Lt. Paul Cullen, Camp 510 became a model camp nationally. The camp was recognized as the best camp in Region V in 1938 and held that distinction for three years.

Above ground, African Americans helped plant approximately one million trees, built roads and buildings, worked on water and sewer systems, and helped create the park's fire-detection infrastructure. Within the Mammoth Cave system, they removed large rocks and helped build miles of footpaths for tourists. In 1935, African Americans ingeniously created a hoisting system that freed the corpse of a Native American who came to be known as Lost John from a massive slab of limestone. Secretary of the Interior Harold Ickes personally commended this achievement by the men of Camp 510 later the same year. In addition to the construction skills the men learned while working, the CCC also provided the men of Camp 510 an opportunity to be educated. Classes were provided three nights a week in subjects such as mathematics, reading, and writing. The educational endeavors were supplemented by the camp's library. African American CCC camps were located in Ft. Knox and Russellville.

In 1937, President Roosevelt attempted to make the CCC a permanent agency. The effort failed, so the CCC was disbanded in 1942. Over the nine years the CCC was active at Mammoth Cave, the men of all the camps accomplished so much infrastructure work that the national park was able to be dedicated in 1946. The men of Camp 510 helped make accessible a natural treasure that now more than 1.5 million people enjoy each year. Mammoth Cave has become so well known that it was designated a world heritage site and part of the United Nations' International Biosphere Reserves program in 1981.

Cole, Olen. *The African-American Experience in the Civilian Conservation Corps.* Gainesville: Univ. Press of Florida, 1999.

Mack, Dwayne. "Kentucky." In *Black America: A State-by-State Historical Encyclopedia,* edited by Alton Hornsby, 317. Santa Barbara, CA: ABC-CLIO, 2011.

Maher, Neil M. *Nature's New Deal: The Civilian Conservation Corps and the Roots of the American Environmental Movement.* New York: Oxford Univ. Press, 2008.

Mammoth Cave National Park, National Park Service, and Western Kentucky University. "Civilian Conservation Corps at Mammoth Cave National Park." Bowling Green, KY, 2003. http://www.wku.edu/library/nps/ccc/ (accessed June 25, 2011).

Schmitzer, Jeanne Cannella. "Black Experience at Mammoth Cave, Edmonson County, Kentucky, 1838–1942." MA thesis, Univ. of Central Florida, Orlando, 1996.

———. "CCC Camp 510: Black Participation in the Creation of Mammoth Cave National Park." *RKHS* 93, no. 4 (Autumn 1995): 446–64.

—*John R. Burch Jr.*

CIVIL RIGHTS ACT (1866), federal legislation granting equality for male citizens. On April 9, 1866, the 39th Congress approved the Civil Rights Act of 1866. The opening line of the law defined it as "an act to protect all Persons in the United States in their Civil Rights and furnish the means of their vindication." Additionally, the law granted citizenship and the same rights enjoyed by white males to all male persons in the United States "without distinction of race or color, or previous condition of slavery or involuntary servitude."

Kentucky African Americans soon discovered that some white Kentuckians ignored many provisions of the law and in many cases violated the law without punishment from law enforcement or agents of the courts. Violations included the denial of their testimony in cases where whites were accused of theft or brutality or in many cases of lynchings of accused black lawbreakers. Demonstrated hostility toward blacks seeking to use their rights has been found in various sources, including **Freedmen's Bureau** records and local newspapers. One 1866 report noted over two dozen whippings of black men and women, 3 rapes, 8 attempted murders, 9 murders, and 1 case of burning a black person alive. In an 1866–1867 Freedmen's Bureau report, 20 murders, 18 shootings, and 11 rapes were found in 319 incidents of white maltreatment of blacks despite the protections defined by the 1866 Civil Rights Act.

Since black Kentuckians were not affected by the 1863 Emancipation Proclamation and the legislature refused to ratify the Thirteenth Amendment to the U.S. Constitution, many white Kentuckians, in open defiance, continued to practice slavery-era traditions of treating all blacks as inferior and punished those who dared to assume that they were equal to whites. The Kentucky legislature passed multiple racial segregation measures affecting schools and marriages, among other laws that contravened the federal law. Rarely were whites arrested for any crimes against black men and women since state law prohibited black testimony in state courts until 1872.

In the midst of these uncertain conditions, the U.S. Congress approved and the states subsequently ratified the Fourteenth Amendment to the U.S. Constitution, which permitted all males aged 21 or older the right to vote regardless of race. It added four provisions not included in the Civil Rights Act of 1866 (including the right of naturalized immigrants and African Americans to vote). This amendment constitutionally defined civil rights, but opponents of civil rights daily denied black men the exercise of the rights, privileges, and immunities enjoyed by white males in many instances. Moreover, the state's legal system continued to selectively deny many of these rights to blacks by ignoring this federal law in the commonwealth's city and county courts.

Civil Rights Act of 1866, 14 Stat.27 (1866). 39th Congress of the United States, CRA 1866, 14th Statutes-at-Large, 27–30.

Lucas, Marion B. *A History of Blacks in Kentucky.* Vol. 1, *From Slavery to Segregation, 1760–1891.* Frankfort: Kentucky Historical Society, 1992.

—*John A. Hardin*

CIVIL RIGHTS ACT (1964), federal legislation against discriminatory practices. On June 11, 1963, President John F. Kennedy, responding to recent episodes of racial violence across the South, declared that he would ask Congress "to enact legislation giving all Americans the right to be served in facilities which are open to the public." Over the next five months, debates began in Congress over the proper form of a civil rights bill, but Kennedy's assassination on November 22 left the fate of the bill in Lyndon B. Johnson's hands. However, Johnson promised to stay true to Kennedy's legislative agenda; in a speech to Congress on November 27, 1963, he declared that "no memorial oration or eulogy could more eloquently honor President Kennedy's memory than the earliest possible passage of the civil rights bill for which he fought so long."

In this statement, President Johnson had the support of Kentucky's African American population, which had been heavily involved in the movement for civil rights legislation for the previous decade. In the late 1950s and early 1960s, the struggle had primarily been local. In 1963, activists in Louisville had succeeded in attaining an ordinance banning discrimination in public places, one of the first of its kind in a southern city. Similar efforts toward voluntary desegregation and legal remedies had existed in other cities in the state but had received less publicity. In Lexington, the *Herald* and the *Leader* both refrained from reporting on civil rights activities within the city.

Kentuckians' efforts to secure civil rights at home translated into a broader movement for state and federal legislation. In his 1964 State of the Commonwealth Message shortly after taking office, Governor Edward Breathitt appeared to back civil rights, stating, "The right of all citizens to equal treatment in places of public accommodation, regardless of race or color, is one which must find vindication through legislative action." In other areas of the state, activists rallied in favor of the federal legislation, supporters engaged in a letter-writing campaign to members of Congress, and an interracial delegation of seven Kentuckians traveled to Washington to express their support. However, civil rights leaders were often frustrated by the state government's refusal to push for state legislation—Breathitt admitted that he would prefer to wait for the final passage of a federal bill first—and began a series of demonstrations that culminated in the **March on Frankfort** on March 5, 1964. Activists were disappointed by Breathitt's lukewarm reception of the demonstration, but he backed a resolution encouraging Congress to pass a civil rights bill at the National Governors' Conference.

On February 10, 1964, the House of Representatives passed the final version of its civil rights legislation. Delaying tactics by southern politicians postponed passage in the Senate, but on June 19, 1964, it was adopted by a vote of 73 to 27 and was signed into law on July 2, 1964. The Civil Rights Act of 1964—supported by both Kentucky senators and one representative—prohibited discrimination on the basis of race, color, religion, sex, or national origin. In an effort to enforce the law, the **Kentucky Commission on Human Rights** sent out copies of the text of the public-accommodations title and requested reports on any companies that failed to comply. The federal bill put additional pressure on Kentucky's General Assembly to adopt a state law, but in the immediate aftermath of its passage, a majority of lawmakers admitted that they would not support a special session to adopt a civil rights bill in Kentucky. Only after an additional 18 months of

pressure did the legislature enact the **Civil Rights Act of 1966,** which in many ways provided stronger protection of civil rights in Kentucky.

Adams, Luther. *Way Up North in Louisville: African American Migration in the Urban South, 1930–1970.* Chapel Hill: Univ. of North Carolina Press, 2010.
Harrell, Kenneth E., ed. *The Public Papers of Governor Edward T. Breathitt, 1963–1967.* Lexington: Univ. Press of Kentucky, 1984.
Kentucky Commission on Human Rights. *Federal Law and State Legislation: Keys to Advancing Human Rights.* Frankfort: Commission on Human Rights, 1964.
K'Meyer, Tracy E. *Civil Rights in the Gateway to the South: Louisville, Kentucky, 1945–1980.* Lexington: Univ. Press of Kentucky, 2009.
Loevy, Robert D., ed. *The Civil Rights Act of 1964: The Passage of the Law That Ended Racial Segregation.* Albany: State Univ. of New York Press, 1997.
Newspapers: "Civil Rights Bill Now before Congress," *LD,* April 16, 1964, 1; "Local NAACP Maps Plans for Civil Rights Law Test," *LD,* July 9, 1964, 1; "The Making of a Civil Rights Bill in 1964," *LD,* July 9, 1964, 9; "Front-Page News, Back-Page Coverage," *LHL,* July 4, 2004, A1.
Smith, Gerald L. "Blacks in Lexington, Kentucky: The Struggle for Civil Rights, 1945–1980." MA thesis, Univ. of Kentucky, 1983.

—*Stephen Pickering*

CIVIL RIGHTS ACT (1966), first significant civil rights law passed in the South. The Kentucky Civil Rights Act of 1966 was both the high-water mark of the **civil rights movement** in Kentucky and, as Martin Luther King Jr. described it, "the strongest and most comprehensive civil rights bill passed by a southern state."

A precursor to the act, a bill banning discrimination in public accommodations, was introduced in the General Assembly in 1964 by Rep. Norbert Blume of Louisville. Drafted by the **Kentucky Commission on Human Rights** (KCHR), a state agency established in 1960 with limited powers to promote improvements in the racial climate, the Blume bill had the support of the **Allied Organizations for Civil Rights** (AOCR), a statewide coalition. The head of the coalition was **Frank Stanley Jr.,** the son of the publisher of the *Louisville Defender* and a prominent student leader during protests against segregation in downtown Louisville in 1959 and the early 1960s.

At the start of the 1964 session, Governor Edward T. Breathitt (1963–1967) had called for passage of a strong public-accommodations bill. Breathitt indicated, however, that he preferred to wait for enactment of the federal civil rights statute then making its way through Congress and in any case would not work actively for the cause until the last 15 days of the session. In late February, with the Blume proposal locked in the House Rules Committee and the session drawing to a close, Breathitt announced his support of a less comprehensive measure introduced in the Senate by Shelby Kinkead of Lexington.

Disappointed with the governor's belated support of the weaker Kinkead bill, AOCR leaders organized a march on the State Capitol. Late on a rainy Friday morning, March 5, 1964, 10,000 demonstrators demanded passage of a tough public-accommodations measure. Several leaders of the march, including Martin Luther King Jr., criticized Breathitt, both in speeches to the crowd and later in a private meeting with the governor.

Breathitt reiterated his commitment to civil rights and the next day joined with AOCR and KCHR members to hammer out a compromise bill that exempted barbershops and beauty parlors, taverns, and bowling alleys, as the Kinkead bill had done, but incorporated the stronger enforcement provisions of the Blume bill. The compromise bill ultimately received only 21 of the 29 votes needed to move out of committee and onto the floor, despite Breathitt's dramatic personal appeals before both the House and the Rules Committee and a hunger strike in the House gallery by 32 AOCR members throughout the session's last week.

After the defeat of the public-accommodations bill, Breathitt pledged to call a special session of the General Assembly if he could be assured of legislative support. In May, at a conference of Kentucky mayors, the governor received a unanimous resolution for a strong civil rights bill. But in a spirited meeting with legislators in July, just weeks after President Lyndon Johnson signed the **Civil Rights Act of 1964,** only 35 of the 103 lawmakers present indicated that they would support an administration-drafted public-accommodations measure in a special session.

Over the next 18 months, Breathitt consolidated his administration's power over the legislative leadership and mended fences with state civil rights leaders. On December 16, 1965, at a major conference on civil rights in Louisville, where he shared the platform with King, Breathitt pledged that a forthright new civil rights bill that addressed fair employment as well as public accommodations would be a centerpiece of the upcoming legislative session.

Introduced as House Bill 2 on January 4, the session's first day, the civil rights bill remained for nearly two weeks in the Rules Committee, where 12 amendments, most designed to preempt resistance from western Kentucky legislators, were attached. Once introduced on the House floor on January 17, the amended bill was substituted for the original by a voice vote. After a plea by Democratic floor leader John Y. Brown, a move to call the "previous question" passed 57–25, preventing the addition of further amendments. After only two hours of debate, HB 2 itself passed by a resounding bipartisan vote of 76–12. On January 25, as Democratic factions and Republicans competed for the mantle of most ardent defender of civil rights, the Senate endorsed the measure 36–1, with George Brand of Mayfield casting the only dissenting vote. Soon after the Senate vote, in a little-noticed but symbolically important action, Rep. **Jesse Warders,** a Louisville Republican who was the General Assembly's only black member, introduced legislation that purged from the statutes all the "dead-letter" segregation laws that had once authorized racial discrimination.

Signed by Governor Breathitt beneath the Lincoln statue in the Capitol rotunda on January 27, 1966, the Kentucky Civil Rights Act of 1966 was stronger in some respects than the federal Civil Rights Act of 1964. Whereas the equal-employment provisions of the federal law applied only to interstate commerce and initially only to firms with 100 or more employees, the Kentucky statute prohibited racial discrimination in all businesses with 8 or more workers and also applied to labor organizations and employment agencies. The accommodations section of the Kentucky law guaranteed "full and equal" access to public services except for barbershops, beauty parlors, and small, family-owned boardinghouses. The legislation significantly strengthened the

KCHR, granting it extensive authority to address complaints and issue regulations, and it gave cities and counties broad power to adopt and enforce civil rights ordinances.

The Civil Rights Act of 1966 provided criminal penalties only in cases of retaliation against individuals seeking protection under the law, and it explicitly rejected preferential hiring as a means of correcting racial imbalances in employment. The act did not address residential segregation, which became the focal point of the Louisville open-housing demonstrations in 1967 and a new state civil rights act in 1968. Nor did it address educational inequities, the issue at the heart of the Louisville **busing** controversy of the mid-1970s. Full equality for blacks remained a dream deferred. The Civil Rights Act of 1966 nonetheless stands as a major blow against the legal foundations of discrimination in Kentucky life and the first significant civil rights law passed by a state south of the Ohio River.

Harrell, Kenneth E., ed. *The Public Papers of Governor Edward T. Breathitt, 1963–1967.* Lexington: Univ. Press of Kentucky, 1984.

—*Anthony Newberry*

CIVIL RIGHTS MOVEMENT, activities, organizations, and persons involved in the efforts to gain civil rights in public accommodations, employment, and housing for Kentucky African Americans. The civil rights movement in Kentucky was a struggle by black and white citizens to overcome the segregation, discrimination, and inequality that constrained African American life. Between the 1940s and the 1970s, Kentucky civil rights activists fought **Jim Crow**—the system of legal racially discriminatory practices—in three main areas: public accommodations, employment, and housing. Efforts to address civil rights in education are addressed in this volume in the essay on **education.**

Public Accommodations

The struggle for equal access to public accommodations began before the dawn of the twentieth century in the area of transportation. In 1870, a group of black men employed direct action, a lawsuit, and negotiations with city officials to secure the desegregation of Louisville's streetcars. Twenty years later, African Americans organized and similarly attempted to stop racial segregation on railroads in the state through the Kentucky **Anti–Separate Coach Movement.**

Although in the 1920s and 1930s most black leaders concentrated on improving the conditions of African American life within the framework of segregation, immediately after World War II agitation against Jim Crow itself increased. In 1947, the Louisville branch of the **National Association for the Advancement of Colored People** (NAACP) sued to open the facilities at the city's parks to blacks on an equal basis. As a result, in January 1952, a federal district court ordered the city to open the golf courses. More important, in 1955, following a Supreme Court precedent, the Kentucky Court of Appeals ruled against all segregation in public parks, a decision that opened 24 state parks to African Americans. In 1951, the statewide Interracial Hospital Movement lobbied the governor and succeeded in getting publicly financed facilities to admit black patients. In the early 1950s, Kentuckians returned to the issue of transportation but now

Civil rights demonstration in downtown Lexington, 1960.

1960 sit-in demonstration in Lexington.

focused on opening waiting rooms and lunch counters in the terminals. As part of that effort, in December 1953 Bishop **C. Ewbank Tucker** and members of the Kentucky Bureau for Negro Affairs refused to move from the white waiting room of the Greyhound interstate bus terminal in Louisville. Although Greyhound did not yet change its policy, the incident was part of growing pressure by local organizations on individual businesses to open their facilities on an equal basis.

The major push for the end of discrimination in public accommodations began at the end of the 1950s and climaxed in the early 1960s. The NAACP Youth Council in Louisville sponsored sporadic weekend demonstrations at drugstore lunch counters in the late 1950s and in 1959 led a "stand-in" demonstration against the Brown Theater. Meanwhile, the **Congress of Racial Equality** (CORE) formed affiliates in Louisville, Lexington, Richmond, Covington, and Frankfort. When African American students launched sit-ins in Greensboro, NC, triggering a region-wide wave of demonstrations, young people in Kentucky followed their example by staging selected protests in both large and small Kentucky towns.

The first and most disruptive incident involved Kentucky State College (later known as **Kentucky State University**) students, who protested both downtown segregation and on-campus conditions. When college officials tried to restrain the activism by

expelling 12 students, campus unrest escalated, leading to the torching of the school's gymnasium. The disorder and crackdown by authorities slowed the Frankfort movement, but meanwhile CORE and the NAACP Youth Council stepped up their efforts in Lexington and Louisville. In Lexington, by October 1960, six months of demonstrations succeeded in opening drugstores, dime stores, and lunch counters. By May 1961, the movie theaters desegregated as well. The Louisville battle was more protracted. A spring 1961 sit-in campaign and fall 1961 election put pressure on local government and led to the seating of a new board of aldermen, which created a Human Relations Commission but failed to pass open-accommodations legislation. After two more years of negotiations, demonstrations, and mass arrests, in May 1963 the Louisville Board of Aldermen adopted an ordinance against segregation in public accommodations.

Civil rights leaders followed up on the passage of Louisville's law with an effort to gain similar legislation on the state level. Some groundwork had already been laid. In 1960, under the leadership of Governor Bert Combs, the state legislature adopted a policy of nondiscrimination and established the **Kentucky Commission on Human Rights** (KCHR). In 1963, the commission drafted a statewide public-accommodations measure, which was introduced in the legislature in January 1964. To demonstrate public support for the measure, a new statewide civil rights group, the **Allied Organizations for Civil Rights** (AOCR), headed by **Frank Stanley Jr.** of Louisville, organized a mass march on Frankfort. On March 5, 1964, 10,000 citizens gathered at the State Capitol to hear addresses by Jackie Robinson, Rev. Ralph Abernathy, and Rev. Martin Luther King Jr. Despite this show of mass support and a short-lived hunger strike of 25 activists, the legislature rejected the bill. Two years later, after the federal **Civil Rights Act of 1964** was adopted, Kentucky's civil rights leaders tried again, introducing a new antidiscrimination measure in the 1966 session and this time succeeding. The Kentucky **Civil Rights Act of 1966**—the first such bill passed in the South—required that public accommodations, with a few exceptions, be open to all races.

Employment

The 1966 Kentucky Civil Rights Act also outlawed discrimination by employers of 8 or more people, climaxing a long battle for

Civil rights demonstration in Lexington, 1963.

equal employment opportunity for African Americans and demonstrating the link in the Kentucky movement, as elsewhere, between "jobs and freedom." During and after World War II, attention focused on employment in the defense industry and for black veterans. Immediately after the war, Kentuckians joined the nationwide but ultimately unsuccessful movement for a permanent Fair Employment Practices Commission (FEPC). Despite the failure of the FEPC, the NAACP, the **National Urban League,** the Negro Labor Council, and the interracial Congress of Industrial Organizations unions continued to push employers to hire on a nondiscriminatory basis and local governments to adopt fair-employment legislation. In the early 1960s, the issue was joined with public accommodations when sit-in demonstrations and boycotts called for jobs in local businesses. In Louisville, CORE launched boycotts against Sealtest and Coca-Cola, and the NAACP targeted chain grocery stores, while in Lexington young activists picketed downtown department stores.

In response to this agitation, in 1960 the legislature created the State Merit System, which prohibited employment discrimination in state government jobs. In 1963, Governor Bert Combs issued the Code of Fair Practice, which expanded the proscription on discrimination in state employment to include businesses that held contracts with the state. These measures were important symbolically but did not affect the majority of African Americans, who worked for private businesses. When civil rights leaders reintroduced the state civil rights bill in 1966, it included not just public accommodations but also employment. When the law passed, it made employment discrimination illegal and included some of the most complete enforcement provisions in the nation at that time. The KCHR, which had the responsibility for enforcement, began receiving complaints of discrimination within a week of the law's adoption. Although the legislation created a procedure for pursuing grievances through the KCHR, often local people still had to use demonstrations, boycotts, and lawsuits to open particular businesses or guarantee equality on the job. Responding to these pressures, by the mid-1970s a number of communities had adopted city affirmative-action policies. Despite these policies on the state and local levels, however, throughout the decade the KCHR documented persistent employment discrimination and economic inequality between whites and blacks.

Housing

Housing segregation was both one of the first targets of activists in the state and one of the last civil rights issues addressed by the General Assembly. In 1914, the city of Louisville adopted an ordinance restricting black and white residents to different streets. The new local branch of the NAACP almost immediately challenged the law, which resulted in the Supreme Court ruling in ***Buchanan v. Warley*** (1917) that such ordinances were unconstitutional. Although cities could no longer require segregation by law, however, the actions of builders, bankers, real estate professionals, and white homeowners created rigid housing segregation. In an early challenge to the barriers restricting African Americans' housing options, Andrew and Charlotte Wade desegregated a Louisville suburb in 1954 with the help of a white activist couple, Carl and Anne Braden, who bought the house on the Wades' behalf. When the Wades moved in, their presence in the neighborhood triggered a wave of opposition that included dynamiting the home and resulted in a sensationalized sedition trial that forced the Wades out and stalled any movement for changes in residential segregation.

A decade later, after the passage of the city's open-accommodations ordinance, Louisville activists pressed for a similar measure outlawing discrimination in the sale or rental of residential property. For three years, the open-housing movement pressured local officials with negotiations, mass demonstrations, a boycott, and threats to the Kentucky Derby, which were greeted by intransigence in city hall and violence by white opponents of open housing. In the meantime, the KCHR drafted a model open-housing ordinance, which in July 1966 became the basis of a measure adopted by Bardstown and Nelson Co. Finally, after an election campaign in which African Americans voted as a bloc and replaced almost the entire board of aldermen, in December 1967 Louisville adopted its own open-housing law.

As other smaller communities adopted the KCHR model ordinance, momentum grew for a state measure. In 1968, Senator **Georgia Davis Powers** introduced a state fair-housing bill in the Kentucky Senate, while Representatives **Mae Street Kidd** and **Hughes McGill** did the same in the House. The 1968 Kentucky Fair Housing Act was adopted late in the legislative session and made it illegal to discriminate in housing sales and rentals. Enforcement once again fell to the KCHR, which opened housing opportunity centers in Louisville and Lexington in 1969 to help black families find homes in previously white areas. In the wake of the state law, other cities, including Bowling Green and Hopkinsville, adopted their own ordinances. The KCHR continued to monitor residential segregation, however, and throughout the 1970s reported ongoing discrimination against minorities in housing.

By the end of the 1960s, Kentucky had adopted legislation prohibiting discrimination in each of the areas targeted by civil rights activists: public accommodations, employment, and housing. But the civil rights movement was more than a struggle for laws; it was an effort to overcome racism. By the late 1960s, the ideals of black community empowerment and consciousness began to influence Kentuckians, producing such diverse results as black arts and culture programs, African and African American history in school curricula, community self-defense against the drug trade, and the marshaling of the black vote for real political power. The most significant impact was on college campuses, where African American students formed black student unions and fought for the hiring of black faculty, recruitment of black students, changes in the curriculum, and more outreach to black communities.

This black power movement was never as separatist or violent as its popular media image depicted. Instead, it consisted of an additional set of strategies for achieving racial equality, and its most important legacy was increased appreciation for grassroots activism and empowerment and for the multicultural character of Kentucky society. Neither new laws nor new ideas and strategies finished the job of ending racism in the commonwealth; that is an ongoing project. The civil rights movement in Kentucky, however, was a time of concentrated activism that yielded new legislation and mechanisms for fighting discrimination, as well as new ways of relating, living, and thinking about race in the state.

Fosl, Catherine, and Tracy E. K'Meyer. *Freedom on the Border: An Oral History of the Civil Rights Movement in Kentucky.* Lexington: Univ. Press of Kentucky, 2009.

Kentucky's Black Heritage: The Role of the Black People in the History of Kentucky from Pioneer Days to the Present. Frankfort: Kentucky Commission on Human Rights, 1971.

Lucas, Marion B. *A History of Blacks in Kentucky.* Vol. 1, *From Slavery to Segregation, 1760–1891.* Frankfort: Kentucky Historical Society, 1992.

Smith, Gerald L. "Direct Action Protests in the Upper South: Kentucky Chapters of the Congress of Racial Equality." *Register of the Kentucky Historical Society* 109, nos. 3 and 4 (Summer/Autumn 2011): 351–93.

Wright, George C. *A History of Blacks in Kentucky.* Vol. 2, *In Pursuit of Equality, 1890–1980.* Frankfort: Kentucky Historical Society, 1992.

—*Tracy E. K'Meyer*

CLAIR, MATTHEW WESLEY (b. 1865, Union, WV; d. 1943, Washington, DC), Methodist Episcopal bishop. Matthew Wesley Clair, who became a Methodist Episcopal bishop, was born on October 21, 1865, the son of Anthony and Ollie Green Clair. He graduated from Morgan College (now Morgan State University) in Baltimore, MD, and earned a doctorate from Bennett College in North Carolina, a divinity degree from Howard University in Washington, DC, and another degree from Wilberforce College in Ohio. In 1889, he was ordained a minister in the Methodist Episcopal Church. He served churches at Harper's Ferry, WV, and Staunton, VA, and was eventually assigned to the Ebenezer and then the Asbury Methodist Church, both in Washington, DC. He worked for several years in Washington for various Methodist national organizations. In 1920, he was one of the first two African Americans elected bishops within the Methodist Episcopal Church; he was made the bishop of Africa and assigned to Monrovia, Republic of Liberia. His missionary groups took motion picture equipment and films to Africa to use in teaching morality and religion.

In 1924, Clair was assigned to Covington, KY, in charge of a territory including the states of Kentucky and Tennessee. In Covington, he and his wife, Eva Wilson Clair, resided at 1040 Russell St. It is believed that he was stationed in Covington because there were three African American Methodist Episcopal churches in Covington and one in Newport. His preaching often included examples from, and discussions about, his experiences in Africa. In 1926, he was selected as one of eight northern Kentuckians to appear in that year's *Who's Who.* In 1936, he retired and remained in Covington.

On June 28, 1943, Clair died while he was in Washington, DC, to conduct funeral services for his brother-in-law, Edward Gray, a Cincinnati medical doctor. Clair's funeral was conducted at the Asbury Methodist Church in Washington, and he was buried in Harmony Cemetery on the east side of Washington. Bishop Clair's oldest son, Matthew Wesley Clair Jr., became the Methodist bishop of St. Louis and in 1964 participated in protests against the segregation of congregations within his denomination.

Newspapers: "Taking Films to Heathens: Eighty-Six Methodist Missionaries to Sail This Week," *NYT,* January 27, 1926, 21; "Eight Northern Kentuckians in 1926 Edition of *Who's Who,*" *KP,* October 8, 1926, 5; "Methodists Raise Six to Episcopate," *NYT,* May 18, 1936, 15; "Bishop Is Dead," *KTS,* June 28, 1943, 1; "Death Notice," *KP,* June 29, 1943, 4; "Matthew Clair a Link to History," *KP,* January 16, 1995, 4K.

—*Michael R. Sweeney*

CLARK, CHARLES HENRY (b. 1855, Christian Co., KY; d. unknown), minister, banker, president of the National Baptist Sunday School Congress, and cofounder of the National Baptist Publishing House. Charles Henry Clark was born into slavery in Christian Co., KY, on October 15, 1855. His enslaved mother was Mary Clark, and he never knew his father, Washington Clark, who escaped north when Clark was an infant. Enslaved for nine years, Clark became a servant to his master's wife at the age of seven. Against the law, the master's wife initiated Clark's long path toward education by teaching him to read. At the outbreak of the Civil War, Clark's stepfather, Jerry Clark, who demanded that his children "think like revolutionaries," fought with a black division of the Union army. After the Civil War, ingrained with a sense of greater purpose from his stepfather and having received a rudimentary education from his master's wife, Charles Clark enrolled at a local school in Hopkinsville.

He quickly graduated, earned a teaching certificate, and taught at the city's Mount Zion Baptist Church.

While teaching, Clark became involved in Hopkinsville's African American church community. He eventually earned a doctor of divinity degree from Kentucky's Cadiz Normal and Theological College. In 1880, he was ordained by Canton Baptist Church, and he simultaneously served multiple churches in the city for the next four years. For the rest of the 1880s, Clark held various pastorates shepherding churches in Princeton and Owensboro. In 1892, he was named pastor of Mt. Olive Missionary Baptist Church in Nashville, TN. Within five years of Clark's arrival, the church had expanded its congregation from 200 members to 1,800. While he was building his reputation in Nashville, Clark cofounded the National Baptist Publishing House, served as president of the Tennessee Baptist Convention, was appointed by the governor to the Educational Convention of Negro Leaders, and became a director of the Penny Savings Bank.

In 1920, Clark became pastor of Chicago's Ebenezer Baptist Church. As he had in Nashville, Clark increased the church's membership exponentially during his tenure. He also served as director of the Binga State Bank, the first African American bank in Chicago. According to the 1940 U.S. census, Clark, at age 85, was still serving as a pastor and lived with his second wife, Irma Mae, a 35-year-old schoolteacher, and three female boarders.

Bacote, Samuel William. *Who's Who among the Colored Baptists of the United States.* Kansas City, MO: Franklin Hudson, 1913.

"Charles Henry Clark." In *African American National Biography,* edited by Henry Louis Gates Jr. and Evelyn Brooks Higginbotham, vol. 2. New York: Oxford Univ. Press, 2008.

Lovett, Bobby. *How It Came to Be: The Boyd Family's Contribution to African American Religious Publishing from the 19th to the 21st Century.* Lavergne, TN: Lightning Source Press, 2007.

Simms, James N. *Simms' Blue Book and National Negro Business and Professional Directory.* Chicago: James N. Simms, 1923.

U.S. Federal Census (1940).

—*Joshua D. Farrington*

CLARKE, ANNA MAC (b. 1919, Lawrenceburg, KY; d. 1944, Douglas, AZ), first African American woman to become an officer and command an all-white regiment. Anna Mac Clarke was born in Lawrenceburg, KY, on June 20, 1919. Her maternal grandmother, Lucy Medley, raised her to observe high moral standards and to overcome any limitations that society would try to place on her because of race. Clarke's brief life reveals that she applied the advice.

Clarke graduated from Kentucky State College (later named **Kentucky State University**) in Frankfort with a degree in sociology and economics in 1941. During her tenure at Kentucky State College, Clarke participated in sports, the school's newspaper, and the **Delta Sigma Theta Sorority.** She returned to Lawrenceburg after graduation but could find employment only as a domestic. After thoughtful consideration, she enlisted in the all-volunteer Women's Army Auxiliary Corps (WAAC) on June 20, 1942.

After completing basic training in Des Moines, IA, Clarke was one of three African Americans to enter Officer Candidate School; she was the only one to graduate. Like other African Americans in the military at that time, she too experienced racial segrega-

tion and discrimination. African Americans could not use the swimming pool except for one hour on Friday evenings, "after which the water was immediately purified." The Officer's Club was also off limits to African Americans. In 1943, Clarke overcame the indignities and was commissioned a 1st lieutenant, becoming the first African American WAAC to command white troops.

That same year, the WAAC became the Women's Army Corps and part of the regular military. Clarke, along with other African American officers, protested the formation of an all-black regiment at Ft. Des Moines. To protest the section marked "Reserved for Negroes" at the theater at Douglas Field in Arizona, Clarke sat in a seat outside the area; the commanding officer issued an order to ban segregation at the theater. The sit-in was one of the steps on the road to the desegregation of the armed forces.

In March 1944, her appendix ruptured, and gangrene developed soon afterward. A brilliant life was cut short on April 19, 1944. Her brother, Sgt. Robert Franklin James, served as the escort officer to return her body to Kentucky. Clarke's funeral was held at the Evergreen Baptist Church in Lawrenceburg, KY. She was buried in segregated Woodlawn Cemetery in Stringtown, outside Lawrenceburg. On September 28, 1945, her grandmother, Lucy Medley, applied for a headstone or marker from the military for Clarke's unmarked grave. A historical marker stands in her honor in Lawrenceburg.

"Clarke, Anna Mac" Notable Kentucky African American Database, Univ. of Kentucky Libraries. http://uky.edu/Libraries/NKAA/all .php?sort_by=C.

Historical marker, Anderson County Courthouse, Lawrenceburg, KY.

"Lt. Anna Mac Clarke." Women in Kentucky Military. http://www .womeninkentucky.com/site/military/clarke.html.

Trowbridge, John M. "Anna Mac Clarke: A Pioneer in Military Leadership." *Cochise Quarterly* 26 (Winter 1996).

———. "Anna Mac Clarke Death." In *Lest We Forget: African American Military History by Historian, Author, and Veteran Bennie McRae, Jr.* Hampton University. http://lestweforget.hamptonu.edu/page .cfm?uuid=9FEC43DB-BF88-B46BA702EBD29CF07D11 (accessed March 7, 2013).

—*Andrew Baskin*

CLARKE, JOHN MILTON (b. ca. 1820, Madison Co., KY; d. 1902, Cambridge, MA), escaped slave and abolitionist. Born in Madison Co., KY, John Milton Clarke was auctioned off as a slave at the age of six despite appearing white to most observers. His master, Joseph Logan, was actually the husband of Clarke's white aunt, but he treated his slaves cruelly and sold Clarke's sister south, where she married a Frenchman and inherited a small fortune. She left a good deal of her fortune to her brother upon her sudden death, but his master refused to accept $1,000 for his freedom.

Unable to gain his emancipation through financial means, Clarke decided to escape. Around 1840, he joined a band of musicians that performed at a ball across the Ohio River in Cincinnati. He then escaped to Oberlin, OH, where he lived for several years while aiding, as he put it, a "goodly number" of his "former acquaintances and fellow-sufferers." In Oberlin, he also reunited with his brother, **Lewis George Clarke,** a fellow escaped slave and abolitionist. He was almost recaptured when a Kentucky slave-catcher seized him, but he escaped with the support of a mob of antislavery sympathizers.

Along with his brother, Milton Clarke began a career as an abolitionist speaker in the North, publishing his recollections with the aid of Rev. J. C. Lovejoy in 1846. He moved to Cambridge, MA, where he served as a member of the 4th Massachusetts in the Civil War. In 1870, he became the first African American elected to public office in Cambridge with a stint on the Common Council before resigning to work as a messenger for the U.S. Subtreasury.

In the last years of his life, he issued a statement intended to set straight the story of his life, including a declaration that if he and his brother had not been born, "***Uncle Tom's Cabin*** would never have been written." He died in 1902.

Cambridge Historical Commission. *Cambridge Historical Commission: Black History Month—African American Trailblazers.* http://www2.cambridgema.gov/Historic/aahmonth.html (accessed November 12, 2012).

Clarke, Lewis, and Milton Clarke. *Narrative of the Sufferings of Lewis and Milton Clarke, Sons of a Soldier of the Revolution, during a Captivity of More than Twenty Years among the Slaveholders of Kentucky, One of the So-Called Christian States.* New York: Arno Press, Reprint, 1969.

Michaud, Denise, and the Madison Historical Society. *Madison.* Images of America. Charleston, SC: Arcadia, 2010.

"Story of a Slave," *Dubuque Herald,* December 21, 1900, 6.

—Stephen Pickering

CLARKE, LEWIS GEORGE (b. 1815, Madison Co., KY; d. 1897, Lexington, KY), escaped slave and abolitionist.

Born to a half-white slave and a weaver from Scotland, Lewis George Clarke toiled as a slave in Madison Co., KY, despite being regarded as a "white slave" by most observers. Passed from master to master, he finally decided to strike out for freedom after hearing a report that he was to be sold down the river to Louisiana. After one false start, he set out in August 1841 and eventually reached Cleveland, OH, where he stayed for several days before crossing into Chatham, Ontario, Canada. He worked briefly there before returning to Oberlin, OH, where he reunited with his brother, **John Milton Clarke,** who had also escaped.

In 1846, Clarke, with the assistance of J. C. Lovejoy, published *Narrative of the Sufferings of Lewis Clarke.* The work was later expanded to include his brother's recollection of his own escape. Impressed with the quality of his work, author Harriet Beecher Stowe arranged to meet him in the late 1840s. In *The Key to Uncle Tom's Cabin,* she noted that she based various aspects of her character George Harris, many of which readers found difficult to believe, on details from Clarke's life.

Clarke enjoyed some fame on account of his role in the creation of ***Uncle Tom's Cabin,*** and he gave speeches against slavery in several free states. After living with his wife and children in Oberlin for several years, he moved to Lexington, KY, where he died in poverty in 1897. In honor of his role in history, the governor ordered that his body lie in state in the City Auditorium; he was the first African American to have that honor. His tomb-stone, located in Westwood Cemetery in Oberlin, OH, includes the title "The Original George Harris of Harriet Beecher Stowe's Book *Uncle Tom's Cabin.*"

Clarke, Lewis, and Milton Clarke. *Narrative of the Sufferings of Lewis and Milton Clarke, Sons of a Soldier of the Revolution, during a Captivity of More than Twenty Years among the Slaveholders of Kentucky, One of the So-Called Christian States of North America.* Boston: Bela Marsh, 1846.

Documenting the American South, University of North Carolina at Chapel Hill, University Library. http://docsouth.unc.edu/neh/clarkes/summary.html (accessed July 28, 2014).

Newspapers: "Uncle Tom's Cabin," *LCJ,* May 16, 1881; "Uncle Tom's Cabin," *LH,* December 17, 1897, 1.

Oberlin Historical and Improvement Organization. *Westwood: A Historical and Interpretive View of Oberlin's Cemetery.* Oberlin, OH: Oberlin Historical and Improvement Organization, 1997.

Stowe, Harriet Beecher. *The Key to Uncle Tom's Cabin.* London: Clarke, Beeton, & Co., 1853.

—Stephen Pickering

CLAY-ASHLAND, community of freed Kentucky slaves in Liberia.

Clay-Ashland was founded by emigrants from Kentucky in 1847. Clay-Ashland served as the capital of a settlement known as Kentucky in Africa. The town was named after Kentucky senator and congressman Henry Clay, an advocate of colonization; his last name was combined with the name of his home in Lexington, KY. Many slave owners in Kentucky were interested in the colonization movement, and they often freed slaves in their wills with the stipulation that they be sent to Liberia. The Kentucky in Africa settlement was the result of efforts by the **Kentucky Colonization Society,** a state affiliate of the American Colonization Society.

In 1821, the national society founded the colony of Liberia. Formed in 1828, the Kentucky affiliate began to raise funds in order to purchase 40 miles of territory along the Liberian coast. This land was to be set aside for occupancy by Kentucky emigrants who would live "under the government and laws of Liberia" and were "entitled to all its privileges and immunities." The Kentucky campaign, led by Alexander Cowan, raised $5,000 for the purchase of this land from the American Colonization Society. The settlement included approximately 40 square miles of land north and west of the St. Paul River.

Cowan traveled to Kentucky in Africa with 36 emigrants in 1846. Upon their arrival, they were greeted by J. J. Roberts, the governor of Liberia, who had established a small, temporary housing settlement for purposes of acclimation. After six months, the new emigrants were permitted to settle permanently on separate farms or in one of the communities constructed in the Kentucky-owned portion of the colony. The largest of these, the community of Clay-Ashland, was established along the St. Paul River, 15 miles inland from Monrovia, in Montserrado Co. Each family and single adult received a deed for five acres of land in Clay-Ashland, with additional land granted to large families.

By 1878, the town had grown to an estimated population of 1,000. In 1858, Clay-Ashland was proposed as an alternative to Monrovia, the nation's capital, as a site for a national college. Although this proposal was eventually rejected, Clay-Ashland was again the center of national attention when it became the birthplace of the True Whig Party in Liberia in 1869. **William David Coleman,** a member of the party, had been a resident of Fayette Co., KY, before emigrating to Clay-Ashland in 1853. He served as president of Liberia from 1896 to 1900. Although years of civil war destroyed much of the original town, the entire region known initially as Kentucky in Africa began to be referred to as Clay-Ashland in the twentieth century.

Bennett, Charles Raymond. "All Things to All People: The American Colonization Society in Kentucky, 1829–1860." PhD diss., Univ. of Kentucky, 1980.

Burrowes, Carl Patrick. *Power and Press Freedom in Liberia, 1830–1970.* Trenton, NJ: Africa World Press, 2004.

Cowan, Alexander. *Liberia, as I Found It in 1858.* Frankfort, KY: A. G. Hodges, 1858.

Newspapers: "From Liberia," *NYT,* May 9, 1859, 2; "Liberian County Is Up for 'Adoption,'" *LHL,* June 19, 2004, B1.

Shick, Tom W. *Behold the Promised Land: A History of Afro-American Settler Society in Nineteenth-Century Liberia.* Baltimore: Johns Hopkins Univ. Press, 1980.

—*Elizabeth Schaller*

CLAYBROOK V. OWENSBORO, 1884 suit that challenged separate school funding systems. *Claybrook v. Owensboro,* a suit brought by black citizens of Owensboro in 1883, challenged the 1866 Kentucky law setting aside taxes collected from "negroes and mulattoes" for the support of black schools. The suit was touched off when the General Assembly in 1880 authorized the establishment of a black school in Owensboro to serve the 500 black children of that town. A group of black parents, citing the equal protection clause of the Fourteenth Amendment to the U.S. Constitution, contended that the black school was inferior and thus denied equal educational opportunity to their children. The suit claimed that the black school operated for only "about three months each year," with "only one inferior school-house," and "facilities of every kind very inferior to those of the white children." Judge John W. Barr of the Federal District Court for Western Kentucky agreed with the plaintiffs and enjoined the Owensboro school board from paying out the percentage of money in the common school fund equal to the percentage of black children in the system, thus threatening to shut down the white schools. Since many other towns in Kentucky had a similar arrangement, the decision threatened the entire state school system. In response, the General Assembly, on March 18, 1884, repealed the act establishing the separate funding system and placed all tax money in the hands of the public school board. This law was an important step toward advancing black education in Kentucky and the pursuit of full equality.

Dew, Lee A., and Aloma W. Dew. *Owensboro: The City on the Yellow Banks.* Bowling Green, KY: Rivendell Publications, 1988.

Howard, Victor B. *Black Liberation in Kentucky: Emancipation and Freedom, 1862–1884.* Lexington: Univ. Press of Kentucky, 1983.

—*Lee A. Dew*

CLAYSVILLE, African American suburb of Paris, KY, in Bourbon Co. After President Abraham Lincoln's **Emancipation Proclamation,** several slave owners in the area of Paris, KY, drove away their slaves, who sought protection in Paris. Many of these freed people rented a stable for $10.00 a month. With the support of white landowner Samuel H. Clay and Bourbon Co. native and Baptist minister **Elisha W. Green,** a multitude of free African Americans established the community of Claysville on the southeast border of Paris. Clay had originally planned to create a shipping pen out of his property near some railroad tracks, but the city leaders were opposed to his idea. He then divided the land into lots of 75 by 60 feet and coordinated the sale of the property with Reverend Green to African Americans. Clay agreed to build on each lot a cottage, with one door and a chimney, for the price of $500 cash or $100 down payment with the remainder of the loan at 6 percent interest; thus began the first opportunity for African Americans in Paris to purchase land.

Freedmen's Bureau agents initially assisted these African Americans with the transition from slavery to freedom, but violence, labor disputes, and opposition to the education of African Americans still emerged. The local newspaper perpetually publicized negative racial stereotypes in the form of stories of various crimes, mostly related to alcohol or associated with gambling, and called the Paris suburb "wicked" or "notorious."

Despite the proliferation of negative media coverage, Claysville was the birthplace of **Garrett Augustus Morgan,** who invented the tricolor traffic signal and a gas mask that became the prototype for the one used in World War I. In 1897, two African American members of the Salvation Army evangelized in Claysville and then held religious services on Paris's courthouse square. The community was served by Jackson's Grocery, and many of its citizens worked for the Louisville and Nashville Railroad or in agriculture. Some of the citizens, like Ben Combs, were Union veterans. In 1903, the funeral of Claysville's Elizabeth Erin was the first African American funeral ever held in the Paris Catholic Church. A year later, the community had installed electric lights.

Claysville struggled against numerous obstacles. In 1900, the local board of health issued arrest warrants for two Claysville citizens for harboring smallpox sufferers and not reporting them. The penalty for such an offense was not less than $100 and not more than $500. In addition, the guilty party could be imprisoned for not more than six months. A person who had not been vaccinated against smallpox could receive the same fine. By 1908, the Bourbon County Health Board funded these vaccinations. The community cared for itself and organized a grand celebration for the opening of the lodge for the **United Brothers of Friendship** and the **Sisters of the Mysterious Ten.** Among other events, the Claysville baseball team played the Clintonville team for the championship of Bourbon Co. The winner's purse was $20.00.

Even in 1920, Claysville citizens were still not counted in the Paris census. They had no water services. The next year, a catastrophic fire that originated in Mud Macon's Pool Room raced through the community, destroying nine homes. African American firefighters tried to battle the blaze but failed because of the lack of water service.

In 1972, because of a local public housing project, the last remaining slum house in Claysville was demolished.

Everman, H. E. *Bourbon County since 1865.* Richmond, KY: H. E. Everman, 1999.

Green, Elisha W. *Life of the Rev. Elisha W. Green.* Maysville, KY: Republican Printing Office, 1888.

Newspapers: "Board of Health Warning," *Bourbon News* (Paris, KY), April 20, 1900, 5; "What? Yes! The Best Time Ever," *Bourbon News* (Paris, KY), August 13, 1907, 3.

—*Sallie L. Powell*

CLAYTON, ALONZO "LONNIE" (b. 1876, Kansas City, KS; d. 1917, Los Angeles, CA), jockey. Born to Robert and Evaline Clayton in Kansas City, KS, Alonzo "Lonnie" Clayton moved as a young boy with his family to North Little Rock, AR. When he was 12, he ran away from home and joined his 16-year-old brother, Albertus, who was a jockey in Chicago. Clayton began his career as an exercise boy for Elias J. "Lucky" Baldwin. In 1890, in Clifton, NJ, he rode in his first race and later that year won his first victory.

In 1892, at the age of 15, Clayton rode Azra and became the youngest winner of the **Kentucky Derby.** The 1892 Kentucky Derby consisted of only two other entries besides Azra: the horses ridden by **Will Alfred "Monk" Overton** and **Thomas "Tommie" Britton** from Lexington, KY. Louisville industrialist George J. Long, who founded Bashford Manor Stud, owned Azra. Ed Corrigan owned the other two horses, Huron and Phil Dwyer. Because of the rain-soaked track and only three entries, little was expected from the race. Corrigan's strategy sent Tommie Britton on Huron to establish an accelerated pace and exhaust Azra so Monk Overton could win with Phil Dwyer. The plan initially seemed to work as Huron jetted five lengths ahead of Azra. The teenaged Clayton maintained his composure and stayed within striking distance as Overton's horse could not keep the pace and fell further behind the leaders. As they neared the finish line, Clayton's Azra and Britton's Huron were neck and neck exchanging the lead position. Before a crowd of 10,000 fans, Azra won by a nose.

Widely known in the New York racing circuit, Clayton competed and won across the country, including the Kentucky Oaks, the Latonia Oaks, the Tennessee Oaks, and various other races. He raced three more times in the Kentucky Derby. He placed second in 1893 and 1897 and finished third in 1895. That same year, he built a Queen Anne house on his parents' farm that he had bought them in Arkansas. Two years later, he constructed a two-story commercial building on Main St. in North Little Rock. In 1899, the family left Arkansas. In the home's attic, someone had written in pencil, among other things, all the names of the family, "Mama and Papa Clayton," "1899," and "Goodbye."

Clayton's jockey career ended with his last race in Memphis, TN, in 1904. In 1917, he died of chronic pulmonary tuberculosis and was buried in Los Angeles at Evergreen Cemetery.

Bradburn, Cary, *The Encyclopedia of Arkansas History and Culture.* http://www.encyclopediaofarkansas.net/encyclopedia/entry-detail.aspx?entryID=5300 (accessed June 2, 2010).

"Day of Colored Jockey Seems to Have Passed." *NYT,* April 11, 1903, 82.

Hotaling, Edward. *The Great Black Jockeys: The Lives and Times of the Men Who Dominated America's First National Sport.* Rocklin, CA: Forum, 1999.

Saunders, James Robert, and Monica Renae Saunders. *Black Winning Jockeys in the Kentucky Derby.* Jefferson, NC: McFarland, 2003.

—*Sallie L. Powell*

Alonzo Clayton (right).

CLAYTON, DENISE (b. 1952, Louisville, KY), first black woman judge on the Kentucky Circuit Court and the Court of Appeals. A native of Louisville, KY, Denise Clayton knew from an early age that she had a knack for defending others. After earning a bachelor's degree from Defiance College in Ohio, she decided to put this skill into practice by enrolling in the Brandeis School of Law at the University of Louisville. In 1973, she received an early break when Charles Lunderman, a prominent African American attorney, offered her a job as a clerk in his office despite her minimal experience. She earned her JD and was admitted to the bar in 1976.

Clayton served in a variety of roles during her early career. She began her legal profession as an estate and gift tax attorney for the Internal Revenue Service before starting her own private practice. She also operated a student legal services program for the University of Louisville and was the associate director of Louisville's Legal Aid Society before moving to the position of Jefferson County District Court judge in 1996.

In 2000, Clayton became the first African American woman to be appointed a circuit judge when Governor Paul Patton named her to that office for the 30th Judicial Circuit, Division 7. Governor Patton pointed to her service record as the reason for his selection, noting that she had "shown ability, a sense of fairness, and an exceptional aptitude that made her a clear choice for this position." While fulfilling her role as a judge, Clayton also served as the chair of the Kentucky Commission on Racial Fairness, which studied discriminatory practices in courts and fought against the higher removal rate for black jurors in trials. She also participated in the county's truancy program and volunteered her time to speak to at-risk students. In October 2007, she became the first African American woman in Kentucky to be named to the Court of Appeals after Governor Ernie Fletcher selected her for the appointment.

During her tenure as a judge, Clayton has received numerous honors and awards, including the Distinguished Alumna Award from the Brandeis School of Law, the Community Service Award from the Optimist Club of Louisville, and the Public Advocate Award from Kentucky's Department of Public Advocacy.

"Judge Denise Clayton." *Kentucky: Court of Justice.* http://courts.ky.gov/courtofappeals/judges/clayton.htm (accessed August 29, 2012).
Newspapers: "Governor Patton Appoints the First African American Woman to the 30th Circuit Judgeship," *LD,* October 19, 2000, 1; "Clayton First Black Woman on Ky. Appeals Court," *LCJ,* October 19, 2007, A1.
Price, Melynda J. "Policing the Borders of Democracy: The Continuing Role of *Batson* in Protecting the Citizenship Rights of the Excluded." *Iowa Law Review* 97 (2012): 1635–44.
Who's Who in Black Louisville. 2nd ed. Columbus, OH: Who's Who, 2008.

—*Stephen Pickering*

CLAYTON, EDWARD T. (b. 1921, Louisville, KY; d. 1966, Atlanta, GA), Louisville newspaperman, editor of *Ebony* and *Jet* magazines. Edward T. Clayton was born in Louisville, KY, to a prominent middle-class African American family in 1921. His father, **Eugene Clayton,** was the first black alderman of the city and among the first black politicians in the South. As a young man during World War II, Ed Clayton was the sports editor for the Tuskegee Air Field GI newspaper, the *Hawks Cry.* Upon his return home in 1945, Clayton became the sports editor of the *Louisville Defender.* In addition to his love of sports, Clayton also had a more serious journalistic side. In 1947, he won the Wilkie Award for his investigation of illegal taxicab services in Louisville.

Clayton's talent caught the eye of black publishing mogul John H. Johnson, who named Clayton the first editor of his new publication, *Jet* magazine, in 1951. Under Clayton's leadership as executive editor, *Jet* became one of the most important black publications during the civil rights era. During the 1950s and early 1960s, Clayton also served as coeditor of Johnson's other publications, *Ebony* and *Negro Digest.*

Clayton's influence with the publishing community appealed to Martin Luther King Jr., who wanted someone to handle public relations for the Southern Christian Leadership Conference (SCLC). Although the job paid less money than his current position, Clayton moved to Atlanta to work for King and the SCLC during the height of the **civil rights movement** in 1963. He wrote speeches and conducted research for King, put together SCLC press releases and handled the organization's public relations, and served as editor of the SCLC's monthly bulletin.

On September 11, 1966, Clayton died of a heart attack. Always seeking new projects, a few months before his death he had started his own newspaper, the *Atlanta Voice.* When asked in a 2010 interview if she had any comments on the life and legacy of her late husband, Clayton's wife, Xernona, replied: "Let me quote what journalist after journalist said at his funeral: 'Every black journalist who has a good job today owes it to Edward Clayton.' That was because Edward insisted on holding himself and others to the highest standards. He wanted his journalists to be as good, or better, as any journalist at the *New York Times* or *Chicago Tribune.*"

Clayton, Xernona. Telephone interview by the author, September 20, 2010.
Clayton, Xernona, with Hal Gulliver. *I've Been Marching All the Time: An Autobiography.* Atlanta: Longstreet Press, 1991.
Fleming, G. James, and Christian E. Burckel, eds. *Who's Who in Colored America.* 7th ed. Yonkers-on-Hudson, NY: Christian E. Burckel & Associates, 1950.

—*Joshua D. Farrington*

CLAYTON, EUGENE (b. 1895, Louisville, KY; d. 1960, Louisville, KY), first African American elected to the Louisville Board of Aldermen. Eugene Clayton was born in Louisville, KY, to Susan and Scott Clayton in August 1895. As a teenager, Clayton began working at the city's Radiator and Standard Sanitary Corporation. He eventually worked his way up to foreman, a prestigious position for an African American in the **Jim Crow** era, and served the company for almost 50 years until his retirement in 1958.

In 1945, Clayton, a Republican, ran for alderman of Louisville's predominantly black 12th Ward against Democrat **William Beckett.** Upon his victory, Clayton became the first African American alderman in the history of Louisville and the first black elected to a city government in the South since Reconstruction. His victory was touted by national Republicans, who pointed to Louisville's Eugene Clayton and **Charles Anderson** as examples of African American support. In 1946, Clayton was invited to sit beside leading Republican congressmen as a head table guest at a Republican National Committee Lincoln Day Dinner in Washington DC, where he was asked to recite the Gettysburg Address.

Although Clayton served only one two-year term, his legacy extended past his brief stint in politics. His son, **Edward,** became editor of the influential *Jet* magazine and was a close associate of Martin Luther King Jr. After Clayton's death of a stroke in 1960, his daughter-in-law, Xernona Clayton, attempted to buy a hat for the funeral at Louisville's Stewart's Department Store. She was initially denied service because she was black. However, when it was revealed that she was related to Eugene Clayton, the clerk exclaimed, "Oh, my goodness, Mr. Eugene Clayton," apologized, and promptly gave her service. Living his entire life in a segregated city, Eugene Clayton had earned not only the trust of the black community who voted him into office but also the respect of Louisville's white citizens.

Clayton, Xernona. *I've Been Marching All the Time: An Autobiography.* Atlanta: Longstreet Press, 1991.
Dunnigan, Alice Allison, comp. and ed. *The Fascinating Story of Black Kentuckians: Their Heritage and Traditions.* Washington, DC: Associated Publishers, 1982.

"Eugene Clayton, Ex–Louisville Alderman, Dies at 66." *Jet,* April 7, 1960, 8.

—*Joshua D. Farrington*

CLAY V. UNITED STATES, Muhammad Ali draft case. The **Muhammad Ali** draft case is historically significant because it promoted public debate on the Vietnam War nationally as well as locally. Ali's draft status first became controversial in 1964 when he was classified 1-Y (exempted) because he did not pass intelligence standards at the age of 22. That was the same year he became heavyweight boxing champion of the world and it was first reported that he had joined the Nation of Islam. The federal government tried to suppress public debate on Vietnam, but Ali's fame and draft exemption created acrimonious discussion of the war and Ali's exemption from military service. The government lowered the mental-aptitude requirement for conscription, and Ali was reclassified 1-A (eligible) in 1966. The champ filed for conscientious objector (CO) status, and his case quickly created a public debate. Ali based his CO claim on his Muslim religion and being a minister. He believed that Vietnam was an "unholy war" in Islamic teaching, and he concluded that the Vietnamese were another dark-skinned people struggling for their freedom. Despite the fact that the Justice Department's hearing examiner recommended CO status for Ali, the department itself nonetheless advised the draft board to reject his claim. The rejection was based on three conclusions: first, Ali's beliefs did not bar military service in the U.S. Army; second, the teaching of the Nation of Islam was defined as racial and political rather than religious; and last, Ali's claims were not consistent since they appeared only when he faced military service. He was indicted and stripped of his heavyweight title and license, forced out of boxing in his prime. In 1971, upon appeal, the Supreme Court ruled in Ali's favor; he returned to boxing and regained his heavyweight title.

Clay v. United States 397.F2D 901 (5th) cir. 1968.

—*Benjamin T. Harrison*

CLEMENT, EMMA CLARISSA (b. 1874, Providence, RI; d. 1952, Louisville, KY), church leader and first black woman named American Mother of the Year. Born Emma Clarissa Williams to John and Abby Early Williams of Providence, RI, Emma was the only black in her 1894 high school graduating class. She then enrolled in Livingstone College, a college of the African Methodist Episcopal Zion (A.M.E.Z.) Church in Salisbury, NC. There she met and married Rev. **George Clinton Clement** in 1898.

Initially, Emma worked as an assistant teacher at Livingstone College. However, after the birth of the first of seven children, family and church responsibilities soon replaced her full-time teaching career. Emma, an accomplished pianist and vocalist, supplemented her husband's preacher's salary by teaching music. She characterized herself as an old-fashioned mother: she was very strict, yet affectionate, supportive, and kind. In 1900, the Clement family migrated to Louisville, KY, when Rev. Clement became pastor of the Twelfth Street A.M.E.Z. Church.

Emma Clement gained national prominence through her church work as a member of the Council of Churchwomen and as national president of the Women's Missionary Society of the A.M.E.Z. Church. In 1918, she became a charter member of the Southern Commission on Interracial Cooperation. Locally, she served as secretary of the Kentucky (Negro) Division of the American Field Army Cancer Society, as parliamentarian of the **Kentucky Association of Colored Women's Clubs,** and as president of Louisville's Charity Pity Literary Club. Her other memberships included the Tuberculosis and the Heart Associations, **Alpha Kappa Alpha Sorority,** and the American Red Cross.

Despite a national practice of **Jim Crow**–sanctioned racism, the American Mothers Committee of the Golden Rule Foundation named 71-year-old Emma C. Clement the American Mother of the Year for 1946. The committee recognized her "great personal qualities as a mother of children who are devotedly serving their country and their people, as a partner in her husband's ministry in his life time, and as a social and community worker in her own right." It added that she embodied "the great spirit of America." Her acceptance speech was broadcast nationwide by radio.

After that honor, Clement received more than 1,200 invitations to speak at various churches, luncheons, civic meetings, and other functions nationwide. These speaking engagements gave her numerous opportunities to address the topic of racial equality and issues relating to equitable funding for black education and health care facilities. She was one of 18 people named to the 1946 Honor Roll of Race Relations for "improving race relations in terms of real democracy."

Clement died on December 26, 1952, having attended Christmas Eve services only two days earlier. Her family buried her in Louisville Cemetery.

"American Mother." *Time* 47 (May 13, 1946): 25.

Fleming, G. James, and Christian E. Burckel, eds. *Who's Who in Colored America.* 7th ed. Yonkers-on-Hudson, NY: Christian E. Burckel & Associates, 1950.

Johnson, Dorothy Sharpe, and Lula Goolsby Williams. *Pioneering Women of the African Methodist Episcopal Zion Church.* Charlotte, NC: A.M.E. Zion Publishing House, 1996.

McDaniel, Karen Cotton. "Emma C. Clement." In *Notable Black American Women,* vol. 2, edited by Jessie Carney Smith, 103–5. Detroit: Gale Research, 1996.

McKean, Else. *Up Hill.* New York: Shady Hill Press, 1947.

Newspapers: "Louisville Negro Is Chosen American Mother of 1946," *LCJ,* May 2, 1946, 1; Lucy Greenbaum, "Mothers Extolled in Day of Tributes: 2,000 in Central Park Hear Guest of Honor Plead Cause of Starving Children," *NYT,* May 13, 1946.

"People: The Mother." *Newsweek,* May 13, 1946, 28.

"Requiescat in Pace: Mrs. Emma Clarissa Clement." *Atlanta University Bulletin,* ser. 3 (December 1952), 38.

—*Karen Cotton McDaniel*

CLEMENT, GEORGE CLINTON (b. 1871, Mocksville, NC; d. 1935, Louisville, KY), African Methodist Episcopal Zion bishop, activist, and author. George C. Clement, born to Rev. Albert Turner and Eveleanor (Carter) Clement in Mocksville, NC, followed in his father's footsteps. He was licensed to preach before his 17th birthday. By 1893, he was an ordained minister of the African Methodist Episcopal Zion (A.M.E.Z.) Church. From 1894 until 1900, he was pastor of various North Carolina A.M.E.Z.

churches. While attending Livingstone College, an A.M.E.Z. institution, he met Emma Clarissa Williams, whom he married on their college commencement day, May 25, 1898. The marriage produced seven children, all of whom graduated from Livingstone College. His wife, **Emma C. Clement,** became the first black woman named American Mother of the Year in 1946.

In 1900, Clement became the pastor of Twelfth Street A.M.E.Z. Church in Louisville, KY. Under his leadership, the church prospered and moved to the corner of 13th and Broadway, where it became known as Broadway Temple A.M.E. Zion Church. From 1904 until 1916, he served as editor of the *Star of Zion,* the A.M.E.Z. publication, in which he encouraged his readers to find ways to elevate black people and their communities. He also managed the A.M.E. Zion Publication House in Charlotte, NC.

In May 1916, at the General Conference in Louisville, Clement was consecrated bishop of the A.M.E. Zion Church in Louisville and the Third District, which included Kentucky, Indiana, and a portion of North Carolina. He served as chairman of the Committee on Church and Race Relations of the Federal Council of Churches of Christ in America for 13 years, frequently speaking at national and international conferences. His professional affiliations crossed racial boundaries as he worked with such groups as the executive committee of the Methodist Ecumenical Council and the Historical Commission of World Methodism. He maintained membership in the Association for the Study of Negro Life and History, the Masons, and **Kappa Alpha Psi Fraternity.** In 1924, he published a collection of his many speeches as *Boards for Life's Building.*

Within Louisville, Bishop Clement served as president of the Board of Directors of the Reform and Manual Training School for Colored Youth and as vice president and director of Louisville's **First Standard Bank.** He was also a member of the Commission on Interracial Cooperation, which was dedicated to resolving civil rights issues. In 1920, he and other black Louisville leaders led a successful campaign to defeat a University of Louisville bond issue that excluded black educational opportunities. Through those efforts, the University of Louisville made a commitment to provide a college education for blacks in 1925.

Clement died in Louisville on October 23, 1935. He was buried in Louisville Cemetery.

Mather, Frank Lincoln, ed. *Who's Who of the Colored Race: A General Biographical Dictionary of Men and Women of African Descent.* Vol. 1. Chicago: Mather, 1915.

The National Cyclopedia of American Biography. New York: J. T. White, 1950.

Smith, Jessie Carney, ed. *Notable Black American Men.* Detroit: Gale Research, 1998.

Yenser, Thomas, ed. *Who's Who in Colored America: A Biographical Dictionary of Notable Living Persons of African Descent in America.* Brooklyn, NY: Thomas Yenser, 1933.

—*Karen Cotton McDaniel*

CLEMENT, RUFUS EARLY (b. 1900, Salisbury, NC; d. 1967, Manhattan, NY), first dean of Louisville Municipal College and former president of Atlanta University. In 1940, after being told by a white police officer that he would be shot if he entered a whites-only area in Atlanta, Rufus Early Clement replied,

"If I get shot, I'll get shot in the back." Such tenacity and courage were characteristic of Clement's career as an educator. Unlike university presidents of previous decades, Clement refused to bow to the demands and expectations of white society by limiting black higher education to vocational training.

Although he was born in Salisbury, NC, to Bishop **George C. Clement** and **Emma Clement,** Rufus spent his formative years growing up in Louisville. He returned to Salisbury to attend Livingstone College, where, at the age of 25, he became one of the youngest deans in the school's history. Clement had other plans in mind, and within five years he had obtained his MA and PhD in history from Northwestern University. The following year, **Louisville Municipal College** (LMC) was opened, and Clement was named the school's first dean.

During his six-year tenure at LMC, Clement made it a point to hire credentialed faculty and directed the school's curriculum to emphasize liberal arts and science degree programs over vocational skills. In 1936, Clement and **Rufus B. Atwood** of **Kentucky State College** (later known as **Kentucky State University**) formed the Negro State Coordinating Committee, which advocated the hiring of blacks in state jobs and federal projects, the appointment of blacks to the Kentucky Board of Education, the establishment of a black history curriculum for public schools, and an increase in funding for Kentucky's black colleges.

In 1937, Clement became the president of the Atlanta University System, which also included Spelman College and Morehouse College. In addition to his academic career at Atlanta University, where he published numerous articles on black education, sports, and history, Clement became the first African American elected to public office in Atlanta since Reconstruction when he became the city's first black member of the board of education in 1953. Serving from 1937 to 1957 and again from 1966 to his death of a heart attack in Manhattan, NY, in 1967, Clement was the longest-serving president of Atlanta University.

"Dr. Rufus Clement Wins in Atlanta." *Washington Afro-American,* May 19, 1953, 4.

"Education: Clement to Atlanta." *Time,* May 10, 1937.

Hardin, John A. *Fifty Years of Segregation: Black Higher Education in Kentucky, 1904–1954.* Lexington: Univ. Press of Kentucky, 1997, 53, 59.

"Milestones." *Time,* November 17, 1967.

Smith, Gerald L. *A Black Educator in the Segregated South: Kentucky's Rufus B. Atwood.* Lexington: Univ. Press of Kentucky, 1994, 117.

—*Joshua D. Farrington*

COE RIDGE, African American community in Cumberland Co., KY. Coe Ridge was a tiny black community in the foothills of southern Cumberland Co., KY, just north of Clay Co., TN, founded by former slaves. After the Civil War, Ezekiel and Patsy Ann Coe received from their former owner 1,200 to 1,500 acres of hill country at the rear of his plantation, where they lived with their children and extended family. An island of black culture, the Coe settlement withstood for almost a century the attempts of antagonistic white neighbors to remove this racial "scar" from their midst.

Coe Ridge, sometimes referred to as Zeketown, produced a group of residents whose defense of their homes made them legendary by the time the community died in the late 1950s. By then, it had become a refuge for white women rejected by their families. Moonshining in Zeketown during the first half of the twentieth century eventually brought the downfall of the Coe enclave. After years of raids, arrests, and skirmishes, revenue agents won out. The residents of Coe Ridge headed for the industrial centers north of the Ohio River. Only a cemetery marks the site of the settlement.

Montell, William Lynwood. *The Saga of Coe Ridge: A Study in Oral History.* Knoxville: Univ. of Tennessee Press, 1970.

—*William Lynwood Montell*

COGGS, PAULINE REDMOND (b. 1912, Paris, KY; d. 2005, Milwaukee, WI), social worker, professor, and first black woman director of the Washington, DC, Urban League. Pauline Redmond was born in Paris, KY, to Rev. John B. Redmond, a Methodist Episcopal minister, and Josephine Redmond. During her formative years, the Redmond family moved to Chicago. She eventually graduated from the University of Chicago and received a master's degree in social work from the University of Pittsburgh. After college, she married Theodore W. Coggs, a graduate of Howard University.

Pauline Coggs then served as director of the youth activities department of the Chicago Urban League from 1936 to 1940. In 1942, she became the first African American woman director of the Washington, DC, Urban League. During her stay in Washington, Coggs also served as a part-time instructor of social work at Howard University and an aide to Mary McLeod Bethune. Her work with Bethune provided her entrance into Franklin Roosevelt's famous "Black Cabinet," and Coggs quickly became a personal friend of Eleanor Roosevelt.

In the late 1940s, Coggs moved to Milwaukee and immediately became involved in the Wisconsin Welfare Council, where she served as assistant executive secretary. In the subsequent decades, Coggs became a major player in Milwaukee society. She was appointed by the state's governor to serve on the Wisconsin Civil Rights Commission and was a professor of social work at the University of Wisconsin–Milwaukee. In 1999, the **Alpha Kappa Alpha Sorority** formed the Pauline Redmond Coggs Foundation and named a prestigious sorority award in her honor. Coggs died at age 93 on July 29, 2005. She was buried in Forest Home Cemetery in Milwaukee, WI.

Geenen, Paul. *Milwaukee's Bronzeville, 1900–1950.* Charleston, SC: Arcadia, 2006.
"The Month." *Crisis,* November 1942, 344.
Newspapers: "Striving to Combat Myths and Ignorance Never Goes out of Style," *Milwaukee Journal Sentinel,* December 4, 2002, 2B; "Coggs 'Silent Strength' behind Political Dynasty," *Milwaukee Journal Sentinel,* July 28, 2005, 7.
"Tape U.S.A." *Jet,* April 9, 1959, 11.

—*Joshua D. Farrington*

COLE, I. WILLIS (b. 1887, Memphis, TN; d. 1950, Louisville, KY), publisher of the *Louisville Leader*. The son of James Henry and Roberta Cole, I. Willis Cole was born on January 22, 1887, and graduated from LeMoyne College in Memphis at the age of 19. From there he moved to Chicago and entered the Garrett

Bible Institute. On a trip to Louisville to sell Bibles, Cole decided to quit school and settle there.

Shortly thereafter, in 1917, he founded the I. Willis Cole Publishing Company and produced the inaugural issue of the *Louisville Leader,* a weekly newspaper for African Americans. In his editorials, Cole adamantly condemned racial discrimination, stressed the importance of black pride, and often encouraged blacks to withhold their patronage from businesses owned or operated by whites. The *Leader* soon became Louisville's foremost black newspaper, and Cole continued as its publisher until his death.

Cole was actively involved in a number of community and business activities. He was a board member of the **Mammoth Life and Accident Insurance Company,** president of the Mammoth Realty Company, and president of the Falls City Chamber of Commerce. He was also involved in the **Louisville Urban League** and served for a time as president of the Louisville branch of the **National Association for the Advancement of Colored People.** He was the first African American to sit on the advisory board of the Kentucky National Youth Administration, one of the agencies established by the federal government during the presidency of Franklin D. Roosevelt.

Cole and his first wife, Katherine Walker, had four children: I. Willis Jr., Ruthlyn, Katherine, and Anna. After Mrs. Cole's death in 1921, he married Rosa Long. Their children were Lattimore and Tella. Cole died on February 19, 1950, and is buried in Louisville Cemetery.

Wright, George C. *Life Behind a Veil: Blacks in Louisville, Kentucky, 1865–1930.* Baton Rouge: Louisiana State Univ. Press, 1985.

—*John A. Hardin*

COLE, WILLIAM (b. ca. 1820, Jefferson Co., KY; d. 1881, Louisville, KY), musician. William Cole, who was born a free African American, joined **James C. Cunningham**'s popular band as a violinist in the late 1840s. In 1855, Cole, who lived near Seventh and Green Sts. in Louisville, organized his own string band. Cole's Cotillion Band became very popular and played for a wide variety of functions, including cotillions, balls, picnics, barbecues, parades, political rallies, and steamboat excursions. His band was in great demand by trade groups and social organizations such as firemen, butchers, carpenters, and Odd Fellows. He was best remembered for his dance music at picnics and barbecues. He and his wife, Anna Graves, had two children, Ida and Lizzie. He died on April 6, 1881, and is buried on a small farm he owned in Jefferson Co.

—*Cornelius Bogert*

COLEMAN, JOHN H. (b. 1868, Covington, KY; d. 1943, Cincinnati, OH), owner of an African American real estate firm. Black businessman John Coleman, the son of David and Mary C. Coleman, was born on January 31, 1868, and moved to Cincinnati in 1882. In 1884, he took a position as the head bellman at the Palace Hotel, where he continued working for 12 years. He resided at 730 Barr St. in the city's West End. In 1911, Coleman became an elevator operator at the Methodist Book Concern, a position he held for 30 years. During this time, he began pursuing a career in real estate sales. In 1918, he moved from Barr St. to 1214 Lincoln Ave. in the Walnut Hills neighborhood of Cincinnati, where he opened the Coleman Real Estate Company, the first African American real estate firm in the area. Later, he moved his real estate office to Richmond St. in Cincinnati's West End.

Coleman was a 32nd-degree Mason; politically, he was a Republican. Coleman was also active in the Methodist Episcopal Church. He served as president of the United Order of Good Shepherds, for 10 years was a member of the Walnut Hills Welfare Association, and belonged to both the Negro Protective Association and the Queen City Fountain No. 853. In the 1940s, Coleman served as secretary of the Colored Waiter Alliance Local No. 541 of the American Federation of Labor, located in downtown Cincinnati on Plum St. He died at his home in Walnut Hills on September 14, 1943, and was buried in Union Baptist Cemetery in Cincinnati.

Dabney, Wendell P. *Cincinnati's Colored Citizens: Historical, Sociological and Biographical.* Cincinnati: Dabney, 1926.
Newspapers: "Death Notices," *Cincinnati Times-Star,* September 15, 1943, 26; Obituary, *Cincinnati Times-Star,* September 16, 1943, 36.
Williams' Cincinnati Directory, 1884–1944.
—*Theodore H. H. Harris*

COLEMAN, LOUIS HENRY, JR. (b. 1943, Louisville, KY; d. 2008, Louisville, KY), minister and community and civil rights activist. Community leader and civil rights activist Louis Henry Coleman Jr., son of Louis and Dorothy Coleman, was born and raised in **Smoketown,** an African American community in Louisville, KY. He attended **Central High School,** where he ran track with Cassius Clay (later known as **Muhammad Ali**). In 1963, he attended Kentucky State College (later named **Kentucky State University**), where he lettered for two years in football as a defensive end and three years in baseball as a third baseman. He graduated with a degree in health and physical education and later returned to the university to serve as both an assistant baseball coach (1987–1988) and the football team's wide receiver and defensive coach (1988–1991). After college, Coleman signed with the Pittsburgh Pirates' AA farm club, where he played for one season before returning to school. He earned a master's degree in community development from the University of Louisville and then completed a divinity degree from Louisville Presbyterian Theological Seminary in 1974. Coleman served as pastor of Shelbyville Congregational Methodist Church for 20 years before becoming pastor of First Congregational Methodist Church in Louisville in 1992.

Coleman became the **Louisville Urban League**'s director of housing and urban affairs in 1974, a position he held for 12 years. He had begun working with the Urban League a few years earlier when he was put in charge of its New Thrust program, a grassroots initiative. He was interested in improving police-community relations. While working with the Urban League, he was drawn to examine issues of police brutality, as well as minority hiring practices within the Louisville police department. This interest in advocacy and social justice led Coleman to found the Justice Resource Center in Louisville in 1975. Through Coleman's efforts, the Justice Resource Center worked to reduce street violence and combat drug abuse.

Coleman was frequently characterized as a 1960s-vintage activist, and he was identified by Rev. Walter Malone Jr. as "a necessary irritant to Kentucky." In 1973, for instance, he began work on a class-action lawsuit brought against Du Pont, his father's former employer, regarding racial discrimination within its seniority system. He was also instrumental in winning a lawsuit challenging the lack of diversity among Kentucky high school coaches. Coleman drew attention to the racial exclusivity of Idle Hour Country Club and other prominent social clubs, and his protests at Valhalla Golf Club during the 1996 PGA Championship had a national impact on the role of minorities in the organization.

In 2000, Coleman was inducted into the Kentucky Civil Rights Hall of Fame. He was also recognized for his athletic career at Kentucky State University during a Hall of Fame induction ceremony in 2007. Coleman died on July 5, 2008, and was buried in Calvary Cemetery in Shelbyville, KY. He was posthumously awarded the Louisville Urban League's Martin Luther King Jr. Citizenship Award in 2009.

Kleber, John E., ed. *The Encyclopedia of Louisville.* Lexington: Univ. Press of Kentucky, 2001.
K'Meyer, Tracy E. *Civil Rights in the Gateway to the South: Louisville, Kentucky, 1945–1980.* Lexington: Univ. Press of Kentucky, 2009.
Newspapers: "Activist Louis Coleman, 64, Dies—Outspoken Leader Fought for Equality for Minorities," *LHL,* July 6, 2008, B1; "Activist Was a 'Tireless Fighter,'" *LCJ,* July 6, 2008, A1; "Kentucky's Activist Fought Many Battles," *Franklin State Journal,* July 10, 2008; "Louisville Civil Rights Activist and Pastor Dies Unexpectedly," *New York Beacon,* July 10, 2008, 16; "Funeral Held for Activist—1,000 Celebrate Man Who 'Made People Uncomfortable' and 'Opened Doors,'" *LHL,* July 12, 2008, D1.
—*Elizabeth Schaller*

COLEMAN, WILLIAM DAVID (b. 1842, Fayette Co., KY; d. 1908, Clay-Ashland, Liberia), president of Liberia. William David Coleman was born in Fayette Co., KY, and migrated at age 11 to **Clay-Ashland,** Liberia, with his widowed mother. Too poor to afford an education, Coleman worked as a farmer and carpenter. He eventually developed a successful career as a merchant. At age 35, he entered politics, first being elected to the Liberian House of Representatives in 1877, where he swiftly rose through the ranks and became Speaker of the House. From 1879 to 1892, Coleman served his country as an influential senator.

In 1892, Coleman became the True Whig Party's candidate for vice president and served two terms alongside President Joseph James Cheeseman. In 1896, Cheeseman died in office, and Coleman became the second Kentucky-born Liberian president, the other being **Alfred Russell.**

As a self-described progressive president, Coleman increased government revenue through bonded warehouses at six major ports, reopened Liberia College, and was reelected twice. However, his policy of expansion into Liberia's tribal lands eventually led to the massacre of an extralegal military force sanctioned by Coleman. This scandal forced Coleman to resign from office. He ran three additional unsuccessful bids for president before his death in 1908.

Burrowes, Carl Patrick. *Power and Press Freedom in Liberia, 1830–1970: The Impact of Globalization and Civil Society on Media-Government Relations.* Trenton, NJ: Africa World Press, 2004.

Dunnigan, Alice Allison, comp. and ed. *The Fascinating Story of Black Kentuckians: Their Heritage and Traditions.* Washington, DC: Associated Publishers, 1982.

Kraaij, Fred P. M. Van Der. "President William David Coleman, 1896–1900." Liberia: Past and Present of Africa's Oldest Republic. Liberia, 2010. http://www.liberiapastandpresent.org/ColemanWilliam David.htm (accessed June 8, 2010).

—*Joshua D. Farrington*

COLEMAN, WILLIAM G. "BILL" (b. 1904, Centerville, KY; d. 1981, Toulouse, France), trumpeter. Renowned **jazz** musician William G. "Bill" Coleman was born in Centerville, KY, to Robert and Roberta Johnson Coleman in 1904. At the age of five, he moved with his family to Cincinnati, where he taught himself to read music and to play the trumpet.

In December 1927, Coleman moved to New York City, where he played alongside Cecil and Lloyd Scott, Mary Lou Williams, Andy Kirk, and Don Redman's orchestra. Throughout the 1930s, he toured across Europe, where he grew particularly fond of Paris, France, which at the time was home to other jazz greats like Coleman Hawkins and Benny Carter. From 1938 to 1940, Coleman performed in Egypt as a member of the Harlem Rhythm Makers alongside fellow Kentuckian **Herman Chittison.**

In 1948, Coleman permanently moved to Paris, where he played with the Edward's Jazz Band. During the remaining decades of his life, Coleman toured the United States, Europe, West Africa, and Asia, playing with jazz legends Fats Waller, Stephane Grappelli, and Teddy Wilson. His album *Bill Coleman in Paris* captures his musical style of elegant, fluid phrasing in his melodic ideas. His book *Trumpet Story* was originally published in French in 1981 and with Northeastern University Press in 1991.

Barnhart, Scotty. *The World of Jazz Trumpet: A Comprehensive History and Practical Philosophy.* Milwaukee, WI: Hal Leonard, 2005.

Coleman, Bill. *Trumpet Story.* Boston: Northeastern Univ. Press, 1991.

—*Joshua D. Farrington*

COLETOWN, African American settlement in Fayette Co. According to the 1830 U.S. federal census, white landowner Horatio Johnson had three other white people living with him and owned eight slaves. One of those slaves was Milly Cole. Five years later, in his will, Johnson emancipated Cole and left his land to his brother and his sister, Sarah. Sarah died in 1843; her will gave 10 acres to Milly Cole (sometimes spelled Milley or Millie) and "her heirs forever."

Around those acres, the community of Coletown formed in southeastern Fayette Co. on Walnut Hill Rd. In 1850, 50-year-old Milly Cole lived with her husband, Benjamin, a woodchopper, and her three children, Rosanna, Mary J., and David, eight grandchildren, and 92-year-old Hannah Cole. Their property was valued at $400. In 1868, Milly died, and the property was subdivided among her three children. By 1870, at least one of her grandchildren still lived in Coletown.

In 1910, the citizens of Coletown decided to extend their school term by two months. They organized themselves as the

"Aunt Bell Elmore of Coletown, Fayette County" is inscribed on the back of this photo.

Coletown Pay School and hoped to inspire other African American communities also to extend their school terms through subscription. In 1920–1921, a two-teacher school was built in Coletown via Rosenwald Funds. The total construction cost was $3,800.

Women played a major role in the farming community of Coletown. The local newspaper particularly praised two female farmers, Mamie Williams and Lucy Clarke, as "industrious" and "prosperous and respected." In 1931, in her role as chairperson of a state committee for colored citizens, Mrs. Olive Sasportas Hunter, wife of Dr. John E. Hunter, promoted a "better-homes week" where the public was invited to view homes that had been "modernized." Mr. and Mrs. J. D. Keene's home in Coletown was one that had been remodeled.

Even though Coletown, KY, no longer appears on a map, many Fayette Co. citizens recognize it as an African American community that provided stability and opportunity for its citizens.

Newspapers: "Colored Notes," *LL*, March 4, 1910, 4; March 11, 1912, 9; August 6, 1912, 11; April 27, 1931, 11.

Smith, Peter Craig. "Negro Hamlets and Gentlemen Farms: A Dichotomous Rural Settlement Pattern in Kentucky's Bluegrass Region." PhD diss., Univ. of Kentucky, 1972.

Turley-Adams, Alicestyne. *Rosenwald Schools in Kentucky, 1917–1932.* Frankfort: Kentucky Heritage Council, 1997.

U.S. Federal Census (1830, 1840, 1850, 1870).

—*Sallie L. Powell*

COLLINS, ALFRED "SONNY" (b. 1953, Madisonville, KY), football player. Madisonville, KY, native Alfred "Sonny" Collins led the Madisonville Maroons to back-to-back Class 2A state runner-up finishes in football. He rushed for 6,200 yards and scored 76 touchdowns from 1968 to 1971. He was also a four-time first-team all-state player in football and a state champion sprinter.

Collins idolized Chicago Bears running back Gale Sayers and took Sayers's jersey number 40 for his own when he played at the University of Kentucky. Described as "unusually gregarious" and "unusually self-confident," Collins wore flamboyant clothing and covered his bald head with an Afro wig when he was not playing football. On the field, he emulated his idol's running style. As an explosive running back, he set an unbroken school record of 3,835 yards. He scored 26 career touchdowns and rushed for 100 or more yards in 18 games. In 1973, he accumulated 1,213 yards, a single-season rushing record at the university that Owensboro native **Mark Higgs** broke in 1987. He was a three-time All–Southeastern Conference player, and the Atlanta Falcons drafted him in the second round in 1976.

Collins's professional football career ended after one season. In 1989, he returned to the University of Kentucky to complete his undergraduate degree in communications. In 1991, he formed the Sonny's Pals program to provide role models for emotionally and behaviorally disabled Fayette Co. students. Living near Fayetteville, GA, and after retiring from Delta Airlines, he spent most of his time riding motorcycles. He was inducted into the Kentucky Athletic Hall of Fame in 2002 and the Kentucky High School Athletic Association Hall of Fame in 2013.

Newspapers: "Kentucky's Collins a Big Fan of Sayers," *Lakeland (FL) Ledger,* August 31, 1974, 9A; "Sonny Collins Is Back at UK to Work on Unfinished Business," *LHL,* July 20, 1989, C2; "Troubled Children Get New Pals," *LHL,* September 24, 1991, B1; "Collins Still a Speed Demon on Two Wheels," *LHL,* July 27, 2012, B1; "Herald-Leader's Fields among 11 Inductees," *LHL,* June 3, 2013, C1.

—*Wardell Johnson*

COLORED FAIRS, major county-wide social events organized by African Americans for African Americans to promote agricultural products and entertainment in their communities. In 1816, Kentucky held its first recorded fair in Lexington on the

Board of directors and officers of the Lexington Colored A&M Fair Association in 1899.

farm of Lewis Sanders, who lived on Georgetown Rd. The fair was a showcase for local livestock. Within 20 years, other agricultural products were displayed, and several counties in the state held fairs. Before the Civil War, Louisville hosted a regional and industrial fair. Soon after the war, African Americans began organizing their own fairs. The Colored Agricultural and Mechanical Association held the first such fair in Lexington in October 1869. About 10,000 African Americans attended. The association consisted of a board of directors, officers, and stockholders who had invested in the fair. Each year the fair continued to grow in popularity.

In 1872, 25 acres were leased on Georgetown Pike, and an amphitheater was constructed to hold more than 2,000 people. Later, a half-mile track was formed on the grounds for horse races. The association spent several months planning the event. It hired watchmen to observe fences and cooks to feed members of the association. Omnibuses and hacks were contracted to carry passengers to and from the fairgrounds. In 1887, the Lexington Colored Fair was moved to the white fairgrounds on S. Broadway because of transportation issues and increased crowds. In 1908, Booker T. Washington was the headlined guest and gave an address.

The Lexington Colored Fair continued to serve as a major source of entertainment into the 1940s. There were a variety of exhibits and activities: farm animals, displays of agricultural products, horse and mule races, bicycle races, and foot races, as well as baby contests and oratorical competitions. There was plenty of food and music, and patrons could see "the flying Dutchmen," "the giant and the pigmy," or the horned frog. The Lexington Colored Fair became so popular that the "best white classes" patronized the event.

The Lexington Colored Fair was clearly the most popular and probably the longest-running fair, but African Americans in other counties organized similar events. The Shelby County Colored Fair was established in 1872, and the Bourbon County Colored Fair opened in 1873. In 1879, colored fairs were held in Stamping Ground and Midway, KY. Fairs were also organized in Washington Co. and Danville, Columbia, and Stanford, KY. Colored fairs were held either in August or September, but not every year. The Scott County Colored Fair Association announced that its event would be held on the Elks Fair Ground in 1906. There was even a discussion among African American fair promoters to organize a Colored State Fair Association. Fairs contributed to the social, cultural, and economic life of African Americans. The 1909 Colored Fair in Louisville included a speech by Maggie L. Walker, described as the "only colored female and banker and editor." These fair events had all but disappeared before the period of desegregation.

Betts, Raymond F. "Fairs." In *The Kentucky Encyclopedia,* edited by John E. Kleber, 303. Lexington: Univ. Press of Kentucky, 1992.
Darst, Stephanie. *One Hundred Kentucky State Fairs: A Pictorial History.* Louisville: Kentucky State Fair Board, n.d.
"Land and Stock." *Semi-weekly Interior Journal* (Stanford, KY), March 15, 1898, 2.
"Negro Fair to Follow One for White People." *CJ,* September 7, 1909, 12.
—*Gerald L. Smith*

COLORED ORPHANS' HOME (LOUISVILLE), first Louisville welfare institution for African Americans. An orphanage formed in 1877 by a coalition of African American churches in Louisville to offer education and a stable social environment for children, the Colored Orphans' Home was also the first welfare institution opened in the city for people of color. Originally founded at Taylor Barracks at 3rd and Oak Sts., the home moved to a larger facility at 18th and Dumesnil in 1878. The site was donated by the **American Missionary Association.** The home received financial and material support from black churches and civic groups throughout the city. The Ladies Sewing Circle made the home its special project, donating furniture, blankets, sheets, and clothing. Other women's groups held annual fund-raising events at the home, baking cakes and pies for residents and for sale.

Larger churches, notably the **Fifth Street Baptist Church,** and fraternal organizations such as the **United Brothers of Friendship** gave annual contributions and helped with the home's upkeep. At its peak, the home supported around 70 children and operated on a budget of less than $5,000 annually.

For three decades, the Colored Orphans' Home was supported only by contributions from the city's black community. In 1909, Rev. Elijah Harris was elected president with the goal of attracting white benefactors. One of his first supporters was James B. Speed, who gave $500 in 1910, an amount greater than the total from all other white contributors. It soon became fashionable for wealthy whites to support the home. Soon the board of directors was dominated by this group. Eventually, a yearly grant from the Louisville Welfare League was established that provided 90 percent of the home's funds.

In 1921, the annual report of the Louisville Welfare League described the home as "unsanitary and totally unfit for any use. Yet this building continues to house children. . . . This is the only colored orphanage in the city, and the conditions are so wretched that it should either acquire a new building or cease to operate." But children were still living in the home two years later, with 67 children housed in a facility with a capacity for 25, often with 3 children to a bed. The home moved to larger facilities at 1224 Dixie Hwy. in 1928 and closed in 1935.

Wright, George C. "Blacks in Louisville, 1890–1930." PhD diss., Duke Univ., 1977.
———. *Life Behind a Veil: Blacks in Louisville, Kentucky, 1865–1930.* Baton Rouge: Louisiana State Univ. Press, 1985.

COLORED PEOPLE'S UNION BENEVOLENT SOCIETY OF LEXINGTON, organization formed by slaves to bury the dead, care for the sick, and provide support to orphans and widows. In the 1840s and 1850s, free blacks across the South, particularly in the upper and border states, began organizing benevolent societies. Among the most renowned of these societies were Lexington's Colored People's Union Benevolent Society No. 1 and No. 2, formed in 1843 and 1852, respectively. According to their original bylaws, the organizations' stated purpose was "to promote the happiness of our fellow beings; to disseminate, support and sustain moral principles, to foster and encourage civilization." One of their primary roles was to take care of the dead. Upon the death of a male member, the societies provided a burial and gave financial assistance to his family.

Many whites in Lexington supported No. 2 with financial and moral support and in 1852 even allowed the society to create a lodge in the city organized by enslaved blacks. Despite the benign pretenses of the group, however, what the white supporters did not know was that the Union Benevolent Society also encouraged education among free blacks and trained its members in skilled labor—a subversive act for the time. Moreover, the group also actively participated in the **Underground Railroad** network, cooperated with underground agents throughout the state, and encouraged slaves to run away.

After the Civil War, the Union Benevolent Society No. 2 remained active within the black community of Lexington. In 1866, for example, it helped organize the city's first major black convention, which lobbied for black political rights and encouraged its members to educate themselves about national events. During the 1870s, numerous other union benevolent societies were organized throughout Kentucky, and all patterned themselves after the model of the Lexington group.

The Lexington organization also continued to maintain the support of whites by publicly emphasizing only its less subversive goal of caring for the dead; the *Lexington Leader* called it "a most excellent colored organization." Under the leadership of James Harvey, **Jordan Jackson,** Henry King, and Leonard Fish, the society was incorporated by the Kentucky General Assembly in 1870. It now had the power to buy and sell burial plots and purchased the first four acres of land that formed Lexington's **African Cemetery No. 2.** The cemetery has since become a significant geographic landmark in documenting the history and heritage of Lexington's African American community.

From its very inception, the organization served both benign and subversive functions in Lexington as it publicly engaged in acts of charity and privately worked to subvert the racial order of the nineteenth century. The purpose of the Union Benevolent Society No. 1 and No. 2 is best summed up in a statement issued by the organization in 1877: "Come then and join us, and we will do you good, and afford you an opportunity of exercising the highest happiness of human life, doing good to others."

Brown, Tamara, Gregory Parks, and Clarenda Phillips, eds. *African American Fraternities and Sororities: The Legacy and the Vision.* Lexington: Univ. Press of Kentucky, 2005.

Hollingsworth, Randolph. *Lexington: Queen of the Bluegrass.* Charleston, SC: Arcadia, 2004.

Malone, Jacqui. *Steppin' on the Blues: The Visible Rhythms of African American Dance.* Urbana: Univ. of Illinois Press, 1996.

McCulloch, James, ed. *Democracy in Earnest: Southern Sociological Congress, 1916–1918.* Washington DC: Southern Sociological Congress, 1918.

"A Prosperous Society." *LL,* February 3, 1892, 2.

Union Benevolent Society No. 1 of Lexington, Kentucky. *Constitution and By-laws of the Colored People's Union Benevolent Society No. 1 of Lexington, Kentucky.* Lexington: W. M. Purnell, 1877.

—*Joshua D. Farrington*

COLORED SOLDIERS MONUMENT, the only monument in Kentucky honoring African American veterans of the Civil War. On July 4, 1924, Kentucky's Colored Soldiers Monument was unveiled in honor of African American soldiers who fought during the Civil War. Despite a ban on recruiting blacks until after 1864, over 23,000 African Americans from Kentucky served the Union and constituted almost one-third of all Kentuckians who fought in Union regiments. Only Louisiana provided more African American soldiers during the war.

The monument was erected by the Women's Relief Corps No. 8, an auxiliary of the **Grand Army of the Republic,** and was placed in Frankfort's Green Hill Cemetery. According to a Frankfort newspaper at the time, the monument, a simple 10-foot, four-sided limestone pillar, cost "several hundred dollars" and was funded by contributions from "patriotic and public spirited citizens of both races." The front features the symbol of the Grand Army of the Republic and the inscription "In Memory of the Colored Soldiers Franklin County, Kentucky Who Fought in the Civil War 1861–1865." The names of 142 African American soldiers are inscribed on the other three sides. Although the front inscription implies that the soldiers were from Franklin Co., subsequent research has revealed that the men came from various places across the state.

The Colored Soldiers Monument was rededicated to Kentucky's African American Civil War soldiers on October 11, 1997. The monument is the only one in Kentucky that honors African Americans who fought in the Civil War, and one of only four in the entire nation.

"Colored Soldiers' Monument to Be Unveiled." *Frankfort State Journal,* July 3, 1924.

Trowbridge, John. "Union African American Soldiers Honored in Green Hill Cemetery, Franklin County." *Kentucky Ancestors* 36, no. 3 (Spring 2001): 125–29.

—*Joshua D. Farrington*

COMMONWEALTH OF KENTUCKY V. ELLIS, landmark 1882 federal court case declaring that funding for black public schools in Kentucky must be equal to that for white schools. In February 1873, a group of concerned African American citizens formed the Colored Men's State Educational Union, which pressured the General Assembly to provide "equal school privileges" to all children, regardless of race or color. It argued that the recently adopted Fourteenth Amendment required that Kentucky not only construct black schools but also provide equal funding to those schools. If the state could not provide equal funding, the organization argued that all schools would have to be integrated in order to remain within the constitutional boundaries of the Fourteenth Amendment.

On February 23, 1874, the Kentucky General Assembly responded to this pressure from black citizens and established a separate school system for black children. Funding for the system, however, was not equal to that of white public schools. The system was to be entirely funded by taxes from black-owned property and fines and forfeitures paid by African Americans. The Education Act of 1874 also authorized the creation of the Negro Teachers' State Educational Association. Although it was an official organization of the state, its members immediately began to voice their opposition to the unequal funding of black schools.

After years of ignored requests, in 1881, the group filed a federal lawsuit to secure equal allotment of funds. The case was brought before the court by Emmet W. Bagby, a white lawyer from Paducah and a well-connected Republican official, who argued that racially separate taxes were in direct violation of the Fourteenth Amendment's equal protection clause. On April 4, 1882, Judge John Baxter of the federal circuit court in Paducah agreed with Bagby and black activists that the Fourteenth Amendment required that "any fund created by the state for educational purposes must be equally and uniformly distributed among both classes, and neither in the raising of the fund by taxation, nor in the distribution of it, must there be any inequality or any discrimination on account of race or color." The judge further warned the state that if these funds could not be provided equally, the state would have to either integrate or close public schools.

The General Assembly immediately responded to the court's demands. On April 11, Republican James Breathitt introduced a bill that called for equal funding. Similarly, after seeing Republican support for the decision, the Democratic caucus, held on April 20, agreed not to oppose the court order. Although a vocal minority of Democrats walked out in protest of their party's support of an equalization bill, the legislation was passed soon after.

Although, at the time, this case was seen as a victory for Kentucky's African Americans, implicit in the decision was the validation of the right of the state to create separate but equal school districts for black and white students. This case helped set a legal pattern to be followed by other southern states for creating segregated school systems without violating the federal court's interpretation of the Fourteenth Amendment. In 1896, the U.S. Supreme Court upheld the precedent of separate but equal spelled out in lower-court decisions like *Commonwealth v. Ellis.*

Howard, Victor. *Black Liberation in Kentucky: Emancipation and Freedom, 1862–1884.* Lexington: Univ. Press of Kentucky, 1983.

——. "The Struggle for Equal Education in Kentucky, 1866–1884." *Journal of Negro Education* 46, no. 3 (Summer 1977): 305–38.

Kousser, J. Morgan. "Making Separate Equal: Integration of Black and White School Funds in Kentucky." *Journal of Interdisciplinary History* 10, no. 3 (Winter 1980): 399–428.

Wright, George C. *Life Behind a Veil: Blacks in Louisville, Kentucky, 1865–1930.* Baton Rouge: Louisiana State Univ. Press, 1985.

—*Joshua D. Farrington*

CONGRESS OF RACIAL EQUALITY, national civil rights organization consisting of local chapters. The Congress of Racial Equality (CORE) was founded in Chicago, IL, in 1942. It was an interracial organization that practiced and promoted nonviolent direct-action protests as a means of eliminating segregation in public accommodations. The organization gradually garnered national attention. Five years after it was formed, CORE organized an interracial bus tour or freedom ride of the Upper South to test the region's response to a Supreme Court decision to outlaw segregation in interstate travel. This freedom ride traveled through the state of Kentucky.

By the early 1960s, CORE had expanded beyond its original northern boundaries. The first Kentucky chapter was formed in Lexington in 1959. National Field Secretary Gordon Carey believed that nonviolent direct action would be a successful method for resolving "racial problems and conflicts" in the state. On July 11, 1959, the Lexington CORE held its first sit-in at Varsity Village, a restaurant near the University of Kentucky campus. By the spring of 1960, the chapter was leading demonstrations at lunch counters at local McCrory's, Kresge, and Woolworth's department stores. Meanwhile, CORE chapters had formed in Louisville, Frankfort, Richmond, and Covington by the end of the year.

Louisville had a "small chapter." Its members protested segregation at Stewart's Dry Goods Company, organized pickets at the Bell Telephone Company to gain black employment opportunities, and successfully joined with the local chapter of the **National Association for the Advancement of Colored People** and the local Human Relations Committee in support of the passage of a local public-accommodations ordinance.

The Frankfort chapter was organized by faculty and staff at Kentucky State College (later named **Kentucky State University**) and began to challenge segregation in the city's restaurants but abruptly disbanded when several students were expelled from the college because of unrelated incidents on campus.

In Richmond, white Eastern Kentucky State College faculty were instrumental in founding the Madison League for Racial Equality, which was a chapter of CORE. The interracial group faced harassment and violence but joined forces with the Lexington chapter to challenge segregation in local drugstores in 1961.

The Covington chapter challenged segregation in the Madison and Liberty Theatres. In 1961, the Covington chapter became part of the northern Kentucky chapter, which included Campbell, Kenton, and Boone Counties. The chapter actively waged demonstrations against segregated public facilities and successfully gained employment for African Americans in grocery stores (A&P and Kroger) and the Sears, Roebuck department store.

In 1964, the federal government passed the **Civil Rights Act of 1964** outlawing segregation in public accommodations. CORE members contributed significantly to making this act possible. By the late 1960s, Lexington had the only active chapter in the state. On a national level, CORE weakened as a result of ideological and financial issues. The Lexington chapter eventually dissolved in the early 1980s.

Smith, Gerald L. "Direct-Action Protests in the Upper South: Kentucky Chapters of the Congress of Racial Equality." *RKHS* 109, nos. 3–4 (Summer/Autumn 2011): 351–93.

—*Gerald L. Smith*

CONWILL, HOUSTON E. (b. 1947, Louisville, KY), sculptor and painter. Houston Conwill, the son of Mary Herndon and Adolph Conwill, was born on Louisville's West Side in 1947. After attending Louisville's Flaget High School and graduating from St. Meinrad High, in Indiana, he joined the air force and served in Vietnam. In 1973, Conwill graduated from Howard University and received a master's degree in fine arts three years later from the University of Southern California. Before moving to California, Conwill was commissioned to do a series of stained-glass windows and murals at Louisville's **St. Augustine Catholic Church.**

African culture and rituals heavily influenced Conwill's art. Many of his exhibitions also blend his sculptures and paintings with dance, music, and other performances to form site-specific conceptions. His *Cakewalk* (1983) installation piece, for instance, featured performances of the traditional African American dance. In 1993, Conwill collaborated with his sister, poet and artist **Estella Conwill Májozo,** and architect Joseph DePace to create the Martin Luther King Jr. Memorial at the San Francisco Museum of Modern Art. The trio continued their partnership with other pieces, including *The New Ring Shout* (1995), which was installed in the floor of the central rotunda of the Federal Office Building in New York City. It commemorated the uncovering of a nearby eighteenth-century African burial ground and relied heavily on African language and markings. In 2010, Conwill again joined his sister and DePace to create *DuSable's Journey* for Chicago's Harold Washington Library Center. The cosmogram depicted the water routes used by Haitian-born Jean Baptiste DuSable to reach Chicago.

As a public artist, Conwill has received numerous awards, including the Guggenheim Memorial Foundation Fellowship, two National Endowment for the Arts Fellowships, and the Prix de Rome. Along with his sister, Estella, he has been among the most accomplished African American artists of the twentieth century from Kentucky.

Dunnigan, Alice Allison, comp. and ed. *The Fascinating Story of Black Kentuckians: Their Heritage and Traditions.* Washington, DC: Associated Publishers, 1982.

Gazda, Elaine, ed. *The Ancient Art of Emulation: Studies in Artistic Originality and Tradition from the Present to Classical Antiquity.* Ann Arbor: Univ. of Michigan Press, 2002.

"The Harold Washington Library Center, Part 4: The Lower Level Complex." *Chicago Examiner,* November 24, 2010, n.p.

Riggs, Thomas, ed. *St. James Guide to Black Artists.* Detroit: St. James Press, 1997.

—*Joshua D. Farrington*

COOKSEY, SOLOMON (b. 1833, Logan Co., KY; d. 1926, Russellville, KY), builder. Solomon Cooksey was born into slavery, but sources vary on his birth year, with ranges from the 1830s to the 1840s. According to his death certificate, he was born on February 27, 1833, and his father was Sid Cooksey. One source indicates that Solomon bought his freedom. However, another source reports that on May 27, 1850, the will of Dorcas Cooksey freed Solomon, along with his mother, Caroline, and his siblings, Miranda Elizabeth, James, Eliza, Harriet, and Mary Jane. By 1860, Caroline and these children, along with two additional children, lived in the Russellville area. She worked as a laundress, Solomon as a farm laborer, and two daughters as house servants.

Cooksey married his wife, Susan, on June 9, 1866. By 1870, the family had grown to include three children: Harriet, Sallie, and George. Cooksey, who was illiterate, farmed and purchased land. In 1875, he built a two-story brick Victorian home in Russellville. In 1880, the family included three additional children: Magie, Charles, and Corah. By 1920, Cooksey was widowed, and two of his adult children, Harriet and Charles, both teachers, lived with him.

Solomon Cooksey died at age 93 on September 4, 1926, and was buried in Maple Grove Cemetery in Russellville. His son Charles continued to live in the brick house and taught school for 40 years until his death in 1939. The home, from the time it was constructed, remained in the family for 70 years. The house was later restored to its 1870s form and became part of the West Kentucky African American Heritage Center in Russellville, KY, in 2005.

Kentucky Death Records, 1852–1953.

"Task Force to Preserve African American History in Western Kentucky." *News-Democrat Leader* (Russellville, KY), August 26, 2005. http://www.newsdemocratleader.com/view/full_story/1595871/article-Task-force-to-preserve-African-American-history-in-Western-Kentucky?instance=search_results (accessed August 14, 2013).

U.S. Federal Census (1860, 1870, 1880, 1920).

Vanderpool, Montgomery. *Colored Marriage Bonds, Logan County, Kentucky, to 1900.* Russellville, KY: M. Vanderpool, 1985.

"West KY African American Heritage Center." http://www.historicrussellville.com?West_Ky_African_American.html (accessed February 21, 2013).

—*Sallie L. Powell*

COPELAND, MAYME L. BROOKS (b. 1884, Paducah, KY; d. 1962, Hopkinsville, KY), rural supervisor in the Kentucky State Department of Education. Born in Paducah, KY, to Milton Brooks, a brick mason, and Mattie Brooks, Mayme L. Brooks demonstrated an enthusiasm for education at a young age when she earned a place on the sixth-grade honor roll at Paducah's Lincoln School in May 1898. Nevertheless, in 1904, before completing her collegiate education, she married Rev. Dr. Thomas H. Copeland, a Colored Methodist Episcopal minister, and started a family. In 1910, the Copeland family, including Mayme's parents, lived in Louisville, where Thomas served a local church and Mayme worked as a milliner. By 1920, Thomas, Mayme, and their only surviving child, Mattie, lived in Hopkinsville, where Thomas served a local church and Mayme worked as the church's stenographer. According to one source, she led the Colored Women's Division of Kentucky's Republican Party in the 1920s.

Copeland graduated from Kentucky State Industrial College for Negroes (later known as **Kentucky State University**) in 1933. She then taught in various schools and later became supervisor of Christian and Todd County African American schools. In addition to her valuable contributions to state education, Copeland also aided the local black community. In 1935, she joined Hop-

kinsville city councilman and prominent mortician **Edward W. Glass** in a mass Red Cross fund-raising drive for Hopkinsville's African American community.

The Jeanes Foundation (a.k.a. the Negro Rural School Fund), which trained African American teachers and employed African American teaching supervisors, awarded a fellowship to Copeland to attend Columbia University in New York. In 1937, Copeland earned her master's degree in rural education. After graduation, Copeland, as state supervisor of African American elementary schools, became 1 of only 10 African Americans employed in the South in state departments of education. Of those 10, she was 1 of only 2 to receive part of her salary from the Southern Education Foundation. She was also active in the **Kentucky Negro Educational Association,** where she served as the head of the Rural Department for 15 years. In Frankfort, she also taught rural education part-time at Kentucky State College. She additionally was appointed the head of the Rural Department of the American Teachers Association.

In July 1947, Copeland retired from the state education system and joined her minister husband in devoting her time to rural church work. She served as supervisor of rural churches of the Colored Methodist Episcopal Church. In 1955, she received an honorary doctor of humanities degree from Mississippi Industrial College. She died in 1962 and was buried in Hopkinsville's Cave Spring Cemetery.

Collier-Thomas, Betty. *Jesus, Jobs, and Justice: African American Women and Religion.* New York: Random House, 2010.

Daniel, Walter. "Current Trends and Events of National Importance in Negro Education." *Journal of Negro Education* 7, no. 2 (April 1938): 220–24.

Dunnigan, Alice Allison, comp. and ed. *The Fascinating Story of Black Kentuckians: Their Heritage and Traditions.* Washington DC: Associated Publishers, 1982.

Kentucky, Marriage Records, 1852–1914.

KNEAJ 9, no. 3 (March–April 1940); 23, no. 2 (April 1952).

Newspapers: "Colored Department," *Paducah Daily Sun,* May 21, 1898, 3; "Mass Meet to Be Held on Monday," *KNE,* November 15, 1935, 4; "Fellowship Is Awarded Here," *KNE,* April 27, 1937, 6; "Kentuckian Gets High Post," *Capital Plaindealer* (Topeka, KS), September 11, 1937, 3; "Prominent Kentucky School Teacher Will Retire July 1," *PD,* June 20, 1947, 3.

U.S. Federal Census (1900, 1910, 1920, 1940).

—*Joshua D. Farrington*

CORBIN RIOT (1919), the expulsion of the majority of African Americans from a rural Kentucky community. On November 1, 1919, the *Lexington Herald* headlined "Negroes Driven from Corbin by Mob of Whites." Sources vary on the cause and details, but they basically agree that on October 31, Halloween, a white mob of approximately 150 gun-toting men herded over 200 African Americans onto a Louisville and Nashville (L&N) Railroad train at 2:15 a.m. and banished them to Knoxville, TN, almost 90 miles south. The small town of Corbin, KY, in southeastern Kentucky consequently joined other communities nationwide in what became known as the Red Summer of 1919 because of the many bloody interracial encounters. The social upheaval occurred in the midst of the rise of **Jim Crow,** the

Great Migration of African Americans, urbanization, and economic stress with the return of World War I veterans.

Corbin experienced a taste of change when it became a railroad hub in the early 1900s, but the L&N Railroad Company had hired African Americans as early as 1886. Four African American families had lived in Corbin for years, according to the 1910 census. White citizens became fearful with the increase in the black population when the railroad hired several hundred African American workers in 1919. Many of Corbin's white citizens viewed recent crimes of robbery, gambling, prostitution, and bootlegging as a result of that population growth.

On October 30, 1919, A. F. Thompson, a white railroad night watchman, reported that he had been robbed and stabbed by two black men. Some sources questioned whether the two men had been white but had worn blackface paint, and others suspected that Thompson had lost the money through gambling with some blacks. In any case, this event resulted in a mob commandeering a municipal band that had played at a Republican political rally for Congressmen John M. Robsion Sr. and King Swope at the local school. As the band played "There'll Be a Hot Time in the Old Town Tonight," many of the African Americans in the town were marched to the depot in "the first musical racial cleansing." Some blacks escaped by running out of town. Initially, there were rumors of injuries and killings, which turned out to be false. The mob discussed removing all blacks from Corbin, including longtime residents, but decided to leave them alone. However, although the 1910 census recorded 60 African Americans in Corbin, there were only 3 blacks in 1920.

The local authorities did little to prevent this expulsion. Patrolman C. S. Browning, who had attended the political rally, attempted to stop the mob, but to no avail. He urged the crowd not to hurt anyone. Some white citizens hid some blacks in their homes. Days later, some white residents editorialized in the local newspaper their disgust at the mob's actions, claiming that the Corbin name had "gone out over the nation with a black spot that can never be removed" and that the deed would destroy future business. One writer maintained that "Corbin must hang her head in shame."

As a result of these types of 1919 riots, African Americans and whites formed the Commission on Interracial Cooperation. Under the leadership of the organization's director, **James M. Bond,** Steve "Pistol Pete" Rogers, a mob ringleader, served a two-year prison sentence, and 29 others were indicted. Until the 1960s, Corbin still exhibited the sundown-town mentality with the sign "Niggers Don't Be Here When the Sun Goes Down."

Griggs, Kristy Owens. "The Removal of Blacks from Corbin in 1919: Memory, Perspective, and Legacy of Racism." *RKHS* 100, no. 3 (Summer 2002): 293–310.

Henson, Robby. *Trouble Behind: A Film about History and Forgetting.* Cicada Films, 1990.

Jaspin, Elliot. *Buried in the Bitter Waters: The Hidden History of Racial Cleansing in America.* New York: Basic Books, 2007.

Newspapers: "Stabbed and Robbed on Way from Work," *Corbin Times,* October 31, 1919, 1; "Negroes Driven from Corbin by Mob of Whites," *LH,* November 1, 1919, 1.

Wright, George C. *Racial Violence in Kentucky, 1865–1940: Lynchings, Mob Rule, and "Legal Lynchings."* Baton Rouge: Louisiana State Univ. Press, 1990.

—*Sallie L. Powell*

CORINTHIAN BAPTIST CHURCH (NEWPORT), oldest African American church in Campbell Co., KY. The Corinthian Baptist Church is the oldest African American church in Campbell Co. On February 24, 1869, the African American community in Newport, having established what was at the time known as Zion Baptist Church, was meeting on Eglantine St. near Cabot St. In July, the congregation purchased a house for its worship services. It attempted to raise $1,000 by requesting donations from area Christians. In November 1872, Zion Baptist Church changed its name to Corinthian Baptist Church, and Mr. B. Jones became its first pastor. In 1873, the church moved to a location on Roberts St. in Newport, with Dennis S. Lightfoot as pastor.

On October 24, 1882, the Corinthian Baptist Church purchased the First German Baptist Church building at Columbia and Jefferson Sts. In 1885, Lightfoot was replaced as pastor by J. W. Hawkins, and in February 1892, John W. Clark became pastor. After the George Wiedemann Brewery purchased the property of Corinthian Baptist Church on Columbia St. for $2,000 in 1892, the congregation bought the church building that had formerly belonged to the First Presbyterian Church on Columbia St. near Fifth St. From July 1899 until 1902, C. P. M. Bigbee served as pastor. During that period, the District Convention of Kentucky Baptists and the National Baptist Convention were both convened at the church. A traditionalist, Bigbee regularly took new converts to the nearby Ohio River to be baptized, sometimes even when the river's waters were icy.

The flood of 1937 did extensive damage to the Corinthian Baptist Church's building, which the church members later restored. In 1956, the Newport Board of Education sought to purchase the church's property in order to build a new school. The church fought the proposed purchase but lost the subsequent lawsuit, in which the court decided that the church had to sell the property to the Newport Board of Education for $23,000 and that the premises must be vacated immediately. The church eventually found a suitable new location at the northwest corner of Seventh and Saratoga Sts., and on April 2, 1958, the Corinthian Baptist Church's new building was dedicated.

Newspapers: *Cincinnati Daily Gazette,* February 25 and July 1, 1869; *Cincinnati Daily Gazette,* November 25 and 29, 1872; *Cincinnati Daily Gazette,* May 2, 1873; *KTS,* December 19, 1956, 4A.

—*Theodore H. H. Harris*

COTTER, JOSEPH SEAMON (b. 1861, Nelson Co., KY; d. 1949, Louisville, KY), poet and educator. The son of Martha Vaughn, a freed slave of the Rowan family of Federal Hill (of **"My Old Kentucky Home"** fame), Cotter was born into poverty in a log cabin near Bardstown, KY, on February 2, 1861. Eight years later, he and his mother moved to a farmhouse at 36th St. and Virginia Ave. in Louisville. Cotter's early education was limited and was derived mainly from the songs sung and stories told by his mother, who taught him to read by the age of four.

His early schooling ended when he was forced to quit the third grade to help support his family. He went to work as a manual laborer at a local brickyard and later became a teamster. At 22, he entered night school and, upon graduation, began a 50-year career as an educator in Louisville's public schools.

From 1889 to 1893, Cotter taught at Western Colored School, and from 1893 to 1911 he was principal of **Dunbar School.** He was then appointed principal of Samuel Coleridge Taylor School, where he served until his retirement in 1942. As an educator, Cotter was credited with winning approval for the practice of naming schools in African American neighborhoods after famous African Americans.

Cotter discovered a talent for storytelling as a child, and as an adult he published several books of poetry, folktales, drama, and songs, achieving local and national recognition as one of Louisville's most accomplished and significant African American writers. Cotter's writing was generally solemn in tone, with a deep spiritual base. His stories of African American life were straightforward and bold, and many of his poems paid tribute to local civic leaders.

His first book, *A Rhyming,* was published in 1895. His other works include *Links of Friendship* (1898), *A White Song and a Black One* (1909), *Negro Tales* (1912), *Collected Poems* (1938), *Sequel to the "Pied Piper of Hamlin" and Other Poems* (1939), and *Caleb the Degenerate: A Play in Four Acts—A Study of the Types, Customs and Needs of the American Negro* (1940). Cotter was a strong supporter of libraries for African Americans and organized storytelling contests in those libraries. He was also a member of the National Storyteller's League, the **National Association for the Advancement of Colored People,** and the Authors League of America.

Cotter married Maria F. Cox in 1891, and they had three children. Their son, Joseph S. Cotter Jr., was also a promising poet until his untimely death at the age of 24. Cotter Sr. was remembered for his dedication to education and his pride in his African American heritage. The Cotter Homes housing project and the Joseph S. Cotter Elementary School were named in his memory in 1956. Cotter died on March 14, 1949, and is buried in Greenwood Cemetery.

Cotter, Joseph S., Sr. *Twenty-Fifth Anniversary of the Founding of Colored Parkland or "Little Africa," Louisville, Kentucky, 1891–1916.* Louisville, KY: I. W. Cole Publishing Co., 1934, 1.
Shockley, Ann Allen. "Joseph S. Cotter, Sr.: Biographical Sketch of a Black Louisville Bard." *CLA Journal* 18 (March 1975): 327–40.

—*J. Blaine Hudson*

COTTON, JOHN ADAMS (b. 1865, Manchester, KY; d. 1943, Henderson, NC), minister and president of the Henderson Institute and Knoxville College. John Adams Cotton was born just after the Civil War to his freeborn parents, Nelson and Zelpha Cotton, in Manchester, KY. Having no money, Cotton worked to pay for his education at **Berea College** from 1887 to 1891 and received two bachelor's degrees from Knoxville College in Tennessee in 1891 and 1893. He then turned his focus to the Presbyterian Church, studied at the Pittsburgh Theological Seminary in Pennsylvania, and received his doctor of divinity degree from the National Training School at Durham, NC.

After initially preaching in Cleveland, TN, Cotton was transferred by the Presbyterian Church to Henderson, NC. In addition to his duties with the church, Cotton became the second African American president of the Henderson Institute, which he ran from 1903 to 1940. During Cotton's tenure at the school, the Henderson Institute established a hospital and nearly doubled the size of its faculty and student body.

In 1940, Cotton became the first African American president of Knoxville College. His church in Henderson, which continues to serve the Henderson community, was later renamed the Cotton Memorial Presbyterian Church. Cotton died in Henderson, NC, on June 15, 1943. His wife, Maude, a music teacher and the writer of the Federation of Negro Women's Clubs' song "We Are Lifting as We Climb," died two years later.

Caldwell, Arthur Bunyan. *History of the American Negro and His Institutions.* Vol. 4, *North Carolina Edition.* Atlanta: A. B. Caldwell, 1921.
"College and School News." *Crisis,* December 1940, 371.
North Carolina Death Certificates, 1909–1975.
Vann, Andre. *Vance County, North Carolina.* Charleston, SC: Arcadia, 2000.

—*Joshua D. Farrington*

COWAN, BRENDA DENISE (b. Sturgis, KY, 1963; d. Lexington, KY, 2004), Lexington's first black female firefighter. Brenda Denise Cowan was born to Rev. Tabb Frank Scott Cowan and Irene Cowan of Union Co. on May 9, 1963. She was a basketball standout for the Union County High School Bravettes and was named Most Valuable Player in 1979 and 1981. Her brother, Fred Cowan, was a member of the University of Kentucky's 1978 national championship team. After moving to Lexington, Brenda served as the team's "little sister" as a teenager, according to friends "helping team members with things like laundry and baking the occasional cookies."

Despite her brother's athletic success, Brenda earned her own place in Lexington's history when she became the city's first black female firefighter in 1992. Interviewed after first receiving the job, Cowan told the *Lexington Herald-Leader* that her career goal was "always to move up." One fellow firefighter remarked that "she would go anywhere and do anything," and Fire Chief Robert Hendricks said, "She was the top of the line, the best at everything she did." Her tenacity and dedication to her job led to her promotion to lieutenant in 2004.

On February 13, 2004, less than a week after her promotion, Cowan was shot and killed when she responded to a domestic violence injury. After a six-hour standoff, police arrested Pat Hutchinson, who had also killed his wife and wounded three other emergency personnel. Cowan was Lexington's third firefighter to die in the line of duty and was believed to be the first African American female career firefighter ever to die in the line of duty, according to the International Association of Women in Fire and Emergency Services. The day after her death, she was awarded the Medal of Valor from the Association of Black Professional Firefighters. Her body was interred at New Salem Baptist Cemetery in Sturgis.

Even more important to her than her career was Cowan's spirituality. She was a devout Christian and a member of Consoli-

COXE, GLOUCESTER CALIMAN "G. C." 125

dated Baptist Church, where she served on the greeting and culinary ministries and hosted the church's mother/daughter luncheon planning committee in her home. According to her pastor, Rev. Richard Gaines, "You can't tell her story without saying she loved her God. . . . Everything else in her life was a byproduct of that; she touched lives."

Brenda Cowan's legacy has continued to touch lives through the Brenda D. Cowan Coalition for Kentucky. The organization was formed through a partnership with her family, fire, and police departments to protect and serve victims of domestic violence. The coalition provides legal services, child care, supportive housing, clothing, and youth services to victims across the Bluegrass State.

Brenda D. Cowan Coalition for Kentucky. "Brenda Cowan Center." http://www.cowancoalition.org/BCCCenter (accessed July 16, 2010).

International Association of Women in Fire and Emergency Services. "Lt. Brenda Cowan." http://www.i-women.org/in_memoriam.php?person=28 (accessed July 16, 2010).

Lexington Fraternal Order of Firefighters. "Remembering Our Brothers and Sisters." http://www.lfdfof.org/remember (accessed July 16, 2010).

Newspapers: "Brenda Cowan Never Had to Prove Herself," LHL, February 14, 2004, A1; Obituary of Brenda Cowan, Evansville (IN) Gleaner, February 17, 2004; "Slain Firefighter Buried in Hometown; Many at Graveside Service Knew Brenda Cowan Growing Up," LHL, February 20, 2004, A1.

—*Joshua D. Farrington*

COX, WESLEY J. (b. Louisville, KY, 1955), basketball player. A standout forward and center in high school and college basketball, Wesley Cox was born in Louisville, KY, on January 27, 1955. He drew attention for his athletic ability and strength during four years at Louisville Male High School, where he led the basketball team to an overall record of 83–17 and the Kentucky state championship in 1971. During his senior year, he averaged 19.5 points per game and was named Kentucky Mr. Basketball, a title awarded to the top high school senior in the state. He then led a combined team of all-stars from Kentucky and Indiana against stars from across the United States in the inaugural Kentucky Derby Festival Basketball Classic, where he earned Most Valuable Player honors for his team with 20 points, 15 rebounds, and 6 blocked shots. Several Indiana all-stars described Cox as "the best kid in the country."

After graduating in 1973, Cox attended the University of Louisville. He made a similar impression on the university's basketball team, earning the award for Missouri Valley Conference Newcomer of the Year for a freshman season in which he averaged 14.1 points and 8.1 rebounds per game. In four seasons with the team, he helped it compile a 90–25 record and was a key part of the squad that made it to the Final Four in 1975. In 1977, he received All-American honors before entering the National Basketball Association (NBA) draft after graduation.

On June 11, 1977, the Golden State Warriors selected Cox as the 18th pick in the first round of the draft. Cox, who admitted that he had doubted that he would be selected in the first round, suffered through injuries and poor conditioning in his first year with the Warriors, although he finished the season with a run of better performances. He failed to improve substantially in his second season, however, and his NBA career ended after only two years. He then returned to Louisville, where he worked in sporting goods and as a teacher. In 2001, Cox was inducted into the Kentucky Athletic Hall of Fame.

Brown, Russ. *Cardinals Handbook: Stories, Stats and Stuff about Louisville Basketball.* Wichita, KS: Wichita Eagle and Beacon Pub., 1996.

Dunnigan, Alice Allison, comp. and ed. *The Fascinating Story of Black Kentuckians: Their Heritage and Traditions.* Washington, DC: Associated Publishers, 1982.

Newspapers: "Kentucky-Indiana Outduel U.S. Stars," KNE, "Louisville, Indiana Cage Stars to Meet Tonight," *Harlan Daily Enterprise,* June 17, 1973, 2; "Cox Joins Benson in 1st Round," LCJ, June 11, 1977, C1.

—*Stephen Pickering*

COXE, GLOUCESTER CALIMAN "G. C." (b. 1907, Carlisle, PA; d. 1999, Louisville, KY), artist. For four decades, G. C. Coxe was the dean of Louisville's African American artists, a founder of significant art organizations, a mentor to a constellation of young artists, and a daringly experimental abstract painter.

Coxe was born to Della (Caliman) and P. J. A. Coxe, a Presbyterian minister, on May 7, 1907. The family moved to a mission post in Louisville in 1924, where Coxe attended Central Colored High School (later named **Central High School**) and contributed to founding the Bourgard School of Music and Art at 27th and **Walnut** Sts.

At age 44, Coxe enrolled at the University of Louisville, becoming the first African American to receive an Allen R. Hite Art Scholarship and the university's first black fine arts graduate. In 1959, he helped found Gallery Enterprises and later the Louisville Art Workshop, which provided exhibition and studio space for artists of all races from the mid-1960s to the mid-1970s. In 1999, he was honored at the annual African American Invitational Art Exhibition for his impact on the Louisville art scene and for nurturing generations of artists, who called him "G. C."

Although Coxe was admired by artists, he was often frustrated by the lack of local support and sales and periodically held bonfires of his inventory to make way for new work. In 1999, he wrote, "I have thought many times of quitting. [But] how can I, when at the finish of a piece there comes another image. I hope that with each finished piece, the viewer will look beyond the surface, the form and color and see and understand the indescribable—the other part of me—of all of us. God? Spirit?"

Coxe's enigmatic paintings suggest the pulsating rhythms and mystery of life. His radical use of nontraditional materials began with the *Minimal Series* (1968–1970), in which he used wire woven through monochromatic canvas. Continuing to discover the extraordinary in the ordinary and the spiritual in the mundane, Coxe later incorporated molded cardboard, carpet remnants, upholstery fabric, and even pantyhose into his dynamic abstractions.

At the time of his death, Coxe had almost completed writing an autobiography. With his wife, the former Jodie Brown, he attended **Grace Hope Presbyterian Church.** He is buried in

Highland Memory Gardens in Mount Washington, KY. After his death on July 24, 1999, a *Louisville Courier-Journal* editorial praised Coxe as one who "never stopped stretching and straining the boundaries of artistic convention."

Gloucester Caliman Coxe, a Retrospective: Rags and Wires, Sticks and Pantyhose Too. Louisville, KY: Allen R. Hite Art Institute, Univ. of Louisville, 1995.
LCJ, July 27, 1999.

—*John Franklin Martin*

CRAFT, REBECCA (b. 1887, Versailles, KY; d. 1945, San Diego, CA), president of the San Diego NAACP and founder of the Women's Civic League. Rebecca Brown Wilson was born in Versailles, KY, on June 4, 1887. After graduating from Kentucky Normal and Industrial Institute for Colored Persons (later named **Kentucky State University**), she taught for a brief period at various schools in central Kentucky. In 1910, she moved with her husband, John E. Craft, to San Diego, CA. Although she had experience, the public school system of the city denied her a teaching position because of her race. Her husband was initially employed as a janitor but eventually found success in real estate and as the owner of Crafty Cleaning Company.

In 1932, John Craft became the president of the San Diego branch of the **National Association for the Advancement of Colored People.** Two years later, Rebecca Craft founded the Women's Civic League, a civil rights organization that quickly grew to 200 members. In addition to leading the league until her death, Craft also succeeded her husband as president of the city's NAACP during the late 1930s and early 1940s. As the leader of two of San Diego's most active civil rights organizations, Craft created a scholarship program and successfully lobbied city of-ficials to hire the first black police officer and black teacher. Active in the Democratic Party, she also hosted numerous fund-raisers at her home for Helen Gahagan Douglas and other influential politicians. She died of cancer in a San Diego hospital on December 6, 1945.

Fikes, Robert, Jr. *The Struggle for Equality in "America's Finest City": A History of the San Diego NAACP.* San Diego: San Diego Branch of the National Association for the Advancement of Colored People, 2012.
Madyun, Gail. "'In the Midst of Things': Rebecca Craft and the Woman's Civic League." *San Diego Historical Society Quarterly* 34, no. 1 (Winter 1988): 29–37.
"Woman Power Works for Civic Group." *San Diego Union,* June 9, 1975, D1.

—*Joshua D. Farrington*

CRAWFISH BOTTOM, former African American community in Frankfort, KY. Crawfish Bottom was a small neighborhood along the Kentucky River in northern Frankfort, KY, that was destroyed during urban-renewal efforts of the 1960s and 1970s. Some people called the community the Craw or just Craw, while others later called it the Bottom or simply Bottom. Each nickname derives from Crawfish Bottom, an earlier name allegedly recalling the presence of crayfish along the river.

Neighborhood residents were, for the most part, poor. Although the neighborhood was known as an African American neighborhood, it always contained some percentages of white residents as well. As early as the 1870s, the neighborhood developed a reputation among outsiders for being the "bad part of town," playing host to the city's drinking and gambling establishments, as well as being the focal point of prostitution in Frankfort. This reputation, perpetuated by journalists and historians,

Crawfish Bottom. Photo of the neighborhood from the "Civic League" series.

Mayo-Underwood School, 1930.

became ingrained in public memory and was eventually used to justify the urban-renewal efforts to destroy the neighborhood in the 1960s and 1970s.

In an oral history project conducted in the 1990s by James E. Wallace, neighborhood residents recalled a close-knit African American community brought together by recurrent flooding and rebuilding; exemplary schools, such as the Mayo-Underwood School at the corner of Mero and Wilkinson Sts.; and community institutions, such as the American Legion Building and the Corinthian Baptist Church. The memory and history of this neighborhood have been well documented in a range of archived resources—the oral history project, a series of 1913 photographs taken to document Frankfort's "slums," numerous newspaper accounts, maps such as the Sanborn Insurance Maps, and, finally, the preservation of documentation inherently involved in the urban-renewal process. Although very little physical evidence remains of Craw, Bottom, or Crawfish Bottom, the neighborhood remains very active in the contemporary memory of Frankfort.

Boyd, Douglas A. *Crawfish Bottom: Recovering a Lost Kentucky Community.* Lexington: Univ. Press of Kentucky, 2011.

—*Douglas A. Boyd*

CRENSHAW, JESSE (b. Knob Lick, KY, 1946), first African American assistant U.S. attorney for the Eastern District of Kentucky and Lexington's first black state legislator. Jesse Crenshaw was born on September 23, 1946, the son of O. C. and Magdalene Brewer Crenshaw, in Knob Lick, a hamlet outside Glasgow. He grew up on his parents' and grandparents' large farm in Barren and Metcalfe Counties, where he helped with the tobacco and corn crops.

Although Crenshaw never participated in the civil rights demonstrations of his generation, he was politically aware even at a young age. The Crenshaw family was deeply involved in Glasgow Democratic politics and actively worked in almost every local race in the city. As a teenager in 1963, Jesse worked as a janitor at T. J. Sampson Community Hospital. After complaints that he was using the all-white bathroom, Crenshaw quit and told his boss, "If I was not good enough to use the white men's restroom, then I was certainly not good enough to clean it up."

After graduating from Ralph Bunche High School in Glasgow and attending **Kentucky State University,** Crenshaw joined the first generation of African Americans to attend law school at the University of Kentucky. During his final year in 1973, while serving as vice president of the Black American Law Students Association, he helped pressure the dean of the law school into hiring the school's first black law professor, William James.

Just four years after graduation, at the age of 31, Crenshaw became the first African American to be appointed assistant U.S. attorney for the Eastern District of Kentucky. In this position, whose jurisdiction included Lexington, Covington, Pikeville, and Catlettsburg, he oversaw civil and criminal cases that involved the federal government.

Following in his family's footsteps, Crenshaw became active in Lexington Democratic politics. After his election in 1992 as Fayette Co.'s Seventy-Seventh District member of the Kentucky House of Representatives, he became Lexington's first African American legislator. He also taught law and politics at Kentucky State. Crenshaw has perpetually advocated for reform in voting provisions that have disenfranchised over 186,000 Kentuckians.

Jesse Crenshaw has expressed his political philosophy as "through the use of the law and a law degree and its impact, you can improve society, you can change society."

Fosl, Catherine, and Tracy E. K'Meyer. *Freedom on the Border: An Oral History of the Civil Rights Movement in Kentucky.* Lexington: Univ. Press of Kentucky, 2009.
Miller, Penny. *Kentucky Politics and Government: Do We Stand United?* Lincoln: Univ. of Nebraska Press, 1994.
"Non-violent Felons Seek the Right to Vote Again." *LHL,* November 29, 2009, C1.

—*Joshua D. Farrington*

CROSBY V. RUCKER (1897), interracial boxing match. A year after the U.S. Supreme Court sanctioned segregation in *Plessy v. Ferguson* (1896), Louisville, KY, native Steve Crosby, an African American pugilist, fought Edmund "Kid" Rucker, a white boxer. Interracial boxing matches were not allowed in Kentucky because of the fear of "race excitement." Publicity about the fight spread not only throughout Kentucky but also into Indiana and Tennessee. Despite city and state officials' attempts to stop the fight, on September 17, 1897, the interracial contest was held on Six-Mile Island (six miles from Louisville on the Ohio River). The fighters were told of the time and place only four hours before the contest. One hundred and fifty African American and white fans boarded four tugboats about 10:00 p.m. to travel to the island. One of those fans was a young white woman disguised as a male. She later became Rucker's wife.

Already a professional fighter, Crosby possessed "a wicked left" punch. Rucker, still an amateur boxer, trained at the Young Men's Hebrew Association near his home in Louisville. A 24-foot ring was assembled on the island's sand, and kerosene lamps were suspended from the trees for visibility. White and black spectators stood on opposite sides of the ring. According to the *Louisville Courier-Journal* report, Crosby had the lead in the 11th and 12th rounds because of his powerful hits. However, decades later, Rucker claimed that up to the 13th round, Crosby had not hit him effectively. According to him, Crosby's "terrible strength" pushed him against the ropes; then Crosby hooked his jaw in "an obvious foul." Crosby knocked Rucker down four times, causing him to sustain a bloody face. During a break, some of Rucker's supporters gave him "nitrate of amyl pearls," which revived him. After 20 rounds, the referee called a draw.

Although no other newspaper accounts have been located, Rucker claimed that he and Crosby later had a rematch. They met at 8:00 p.m. at the Southern Railroad station and rode a special train to a picnic area in Crossroads. Rucker maintained that he beat Crosby in this battle.

Crosby began his fighting career in 1896. He had his best win average in 1899 and fought the most battles in 1904. In February 1912, the *Indianapolis Freeman* described him as "old Steve Crosby, the former star lightweight boxer." His last recorded fight was in April 1912.

BoxRec.   http://boxrec.com/list_bouts.php?human_id=10983&cat=boxer (accessed September 13, 2013).
Newspapers: "The Bout a Draw," *LCJ*, September 18, 1897, 8; "Negro Fights Six Men One Round Each," *IF*, February 17, 1912, 7.
Rucker, Edmund. "A Prize Fighter in the Nineties." *Harpers Magazine* 179 (August 1939).

—*Wardell Johnson*

CROSSWHITE, ADAM (b. 1799, Bourbon Co., KY; d. 1878, Marshall, MI), escaped slave. Adam Crosswhite was a fair-skinned mulatto slave born on October 17, 1799, who successfully escaped from his owner in Bourbon Co. His father was a white slave owner named Powers who was a half brother of Miss Frances Crosswhite. Ownership of Adam shifted to Frances Crosswhite through the will of her father, Isaac Crosthwaite (later spelled Crosswhite), on January 28, 1811. Frances married Ned Stone, who sold Adam Crosswhite for $200, and in 1819 Adam was traded to Francis Giltner, a planter in Bourbon Co. There, Adam married Sarah in a slave ceremony and raised four children, John Anthony, Benjamin Franklin, Cyrus Jackson, and Lucretia. Before 1830, Giltner moved the entire family and his slaves to Hunters Bottom in Carroll Co. along the Ohio River.

In August 1843, Adam Crosswhite learned that Giltner planned to sell part of Crosswhite's family. Crosswhite sought help from the **Underground Railroad** organization in Madison, IN. As runaway slaves, and after two narrow escapes while using the newly organized safe routes through Indiana, the Crosswhites managed to escape to Marshall, a town in south central Michigan. There, Adam maintained a low profile. He worked, built a cabin, and became accepted in the village.

In response to the increasing number of runaway slaves during the 1840s, slave owners in the north central river counties and the Bluegrass region of Kentucky sought to recover their financial investments. In 1846, a coalition of slave owners met in Covington and hired a spy to ferret out runaway slaves in southern Michigan. In the late fall of 1846, this spy, who called himself Carpenter, arrived in Marshall and in Cass Co. Masquerading as an abolitionist from Worcester, MA, he visited the homes of free people of color. The information he gathered led to two major raids by Kentuckians, the first at Marshall in Calhoun Co. and the second in Cass Co.

In December 1846, acting on intelligence gathered by the spy, Francis Troutman, the grandson of the former owner of Adam Crosswhite and a nephew of Francis Giltner, went to Calhoun Co.,

MI, posing as a schoolteacher seeking a place to settle. He hired local deputy sheriff Harvey Dixon to pose as a census taker to scout the Crosswhite family. On January 20, 1847, Troutman reappeared at Marshall with three other Kentuckians, William Franklin Ford, David Giltner, and James S. Lee, and, accompanied by Deputy Sheriff Dixon, went to the Crosswhite cabin. There they attempted to capture Adam, but he and his son Johnson fled through a cornfield. Crosswhite was able to secure counsel. Troutman stayed in the Crosswhite cabin with drawn pistol as several neighbors attempted to enter the house, one of whom, a Mr. Hackett, was assaulted by Troutman.

When Dixon returned, he charged Troutman with assault and battery on Hackett and with trespassing and housebreaking. Troutman paid $100 in fines the next day in the local court before Judge Randall Hobart. Meanwhile, the townspeople hid the Crosswhite family in the attic of George Ingersoll's mill. Isaac Jacobs, the hostler at the Marshall House, hired a team and covered wagon, and on the night of January 27, Ingersoll and Asa B. Cook drove the Crosswhite family to Jackson, where they boarded a train to Detroit. George De Baptiste, the former Underground Railroad leader at Madison, IN, met the Crosswhites in Detroit and took them into Canada.

The Kentuckians were furious, and several meetings of slave owners were held. Citizens of Trimble and Carroll Counties, led by Moses Hoagland of Hunters Bottom, met at Kings Tavern on February 10 and drew up three resolutions demanding that the Kentucky legislature call on its U.S. senators and congressmen to pass federal legislation giving slave owners redress and imprisoning and fining those who enticed, harbored, or aided runaway slaves.

By June 1847, Michigan newspapers along the southern tier were equally outraged that Kentucky posses were seizing fugitives in a free state whose citizens detested slavery. In August 1847, a large Kentucky raid led by Boone Co., KY, slave owners George W. Brazier and Benjamin Stevens was repulsed from Cass Co. after attempting to recapture several former slaves.

The legislative wheels were set in motion. Joseph Underwood's report and resolutions from the Kentucky legislature were sent to the U.S. Senate on December 20, 1847, and in May 1848, Senator Andrew P. Butler of South Carolina printed his report favoring strong federal sanctions against persons who aided runaway slaves; 10,000 copies were distributed. Momentum built for passage of the 1850 Fugitive Slave Act, which made it mandatory for U.S. marshals to seize runaway slaves, for representatives of the slave owner to identify the runaways, and for severe fines to be levied on all those aiding and harboring fugitive slaves. Henry Clay, a personal friend of Francis Giltner, proposed a clause mandating restitution of property to southerners reclaiming runaway slaves.

Attorney Francis Troutman returned to Michigan in May 1848 to gather evidence and press charges against those who had aided the Crosswhite family. On June 1, 1848, in Detroit, Justice McLane of the federal bench heard *Giltner v. Gorham*. McLane instructed the jury to ignore their attitudes toward slavery and decide the case only on the basis of the plaintiffs' right to the services of the fugitives and therefore the right to obtain financial redress. The first trial jury was hung and was discharged on

June 12. A second trial was held, and the jury awarded Giltner $1,926 in damages and heavy court costs, for a total of about $4,500. Zachariah Chandler, a leading antislavery Whig in Detroit, paid the greater part of the fine. Juryman Philo Dibble, a resident of Marshall, was publicly chastised from the pulpit by his Presbyterian minister for his participation in the verdict.

Northern reaction to passage of the 1850 Fugitive Slave Act was swift. By 1854, Indiana, Michigan, and Ohio had formed significant Republican parties that were obtaining antislavery majorities in their state legislative bodies, sending antislavery congressmen and senators to Washington, and, by 1860, giving Abraham Lincoln the presidential candidacy.

The Crosswhite family, with a new daughter, Frances, born in 1848 in Canada, returned to Marshall, MI, after the Civil War. Adam Crosswhite died on January 23, 1878, and was buried in Oakridge Cemetery in Marshall. In 1923, Michigan erected a bronze marker set in a stone boulder near the old Crosswhite cabin. The marker commemorates the runaway slave from Carroll Co., KY, and the role of the people of Marshall in repulsing the Kentucky posse.

Crosthwaite, Isaac. Will. Clark Co., KY, Will Book 3:54.

Crosswhite File, Marshall District Public Library, Marshall, MI.

Fuller, George N., ed. *Michigan: A Centennial History of the State and Its People.* Chicago: Lewis, 1939.

Gara, Larry. *The Liberty Line.* Lexington: Univ. of Kentucky Press, 1961.

Gardner, Washington. *History of Calhoun County, Michigan.* Chicago: Lewis, 1913.

Giltner v. Gorham, Case No. 5,453, Circuit Court D. Mich. (1848) (114 McLean 402; 6 West Law J. 491).

History, Arts, and Libraries. Adam Crosswhite Deposition (edited transcription). State of Michigan. http://www.michigan.gov/hal/0,7 -160-17451_18670_44390-160647-,00.html (accessed March 26, 2007).

History of Calhoun County, Michigan. Philadelphia: L. H. Everts, 1877.

Journal of the House of Representatives, Kentucky, February 13, 1847, 338–41.

Newspapers: *Battle Creek Tribune,* January 20, 1847; *Frankfort Weekly Commonwealth,* February 23, 1847; *Battle Creek Enquirer,* July 14, 1907; January 28, 1929; July 3, 1930; April 1960; *Enquirer and Evening News of Battle Creek, Michigan,* February 18, 1923; February 11, 1945; February 17, 1974.

—*Diane Perrine Coon*

CROWDUS, REUBEN ERNEST (b. 1865 ca., Bowling Green, KY; d. 1909, New York, NY), known as the Father of Ragtime. Comedian, singer, songwriter, actor, producer, playwright, and pianist, Reuben Ernest Crowdus (Crowders or Crowder) was born in the historic **Shake Rag** district in Bowling Green, KY. By the 1890s, he was using the stage name Ernest Hogan to capitalize on the popularity of Irish minstrel men and gaining national attention.

The details of his early life are sparse. His parents were Reuben Crowdus, a bricklayer and Civil War veteran, and Louise Crowdus, a cook. He was one of five children. Self-educated, as a juvenile, he began to travel with the tent and minstrelsy shows that toured the South, performing first as a pickaninny in a low-rent version of *Uncle Tom's Cabin.*

Hogan believed that his salvation and that of his race lay in the arts and worked toward breaking down the ever-present barriers that he met. He was the first African American star on Broadway, in Will Marion Cook's *Clorindy* (1898), and the first black star to reside in Harlem. He performed in Australia and Hawaii. By 1900, Hogan was earning over $300 per week, the highest pay for any black vaudeville entertainer of his time, and calling himself "the Unbleached American." He also produced and starred in such shows as *Rufus Rastus* and *The Oyster Man;* these and others provided many record-breaking performances.

Vaudeville entertainer Bert Williams overshadowed Hogan's talent, and Hogan's legacy was dominated by the effects of his best-selling song "All Coons Look Alike to Me." He published over 35 songs in his career, but none was as popular or as hated as this one. This song included the first use of "rag" on a song sheet, and Hogan was also credited with staging the first "syncopated-music" concert in history in 1905. Hence Hogan was sometimes called the Father of **Ragtime.** It should be noted that "Hogan came to regret having been responsible for bringing this 'coon' song before the public, a song he actually did not originate, but had appropriated from a Chicago saloon pianist." His influence, however, along with other nameless African American composers, led to the development of **jazz.**

Hogan, sick with tuberculosis, ruined his health with the strains of producing and staging *The Oyster Man,* and he was forced to give up performing. Although he needed no financial assistance himself, he was also a founding member of the Colored Actors Beneficial Association in 1905. He was married twice, first to Louise Hogan and then to a costar, Mattie Wilkes. He died on May 20, 1909, and was buried in **Mt. Moriah Cemetery** in Bowling Green, KY.

Berlin, Edward A. *Ragtime: A Musical and Cultural History.* Berkeley: Univ. of California Press, 1980.

"Ernest Hogan Sleeps His Final Sleep." *IF,* May 29, 1909, 5.

Jasen, David A., and Gene Jones. *Spreadin Rhythm Around*: *Black Popular Songwriters, 1880–1930.* London: Schirmer Books, 1998.

Southern, Eileen. *Biographical Dictionary of Afro-American and African Musicians.* Westport, CT: Greenwood Press, 1982.

U.S. Civil War Pension Index: General Index to Pension Files, 1861–1934.

—*Nancy Richey Marshall*

CRUMLIN, JAMES A., SR. (b. 1914, Spartanburg, SC; d. 2004, Louisville, KY), lawyer, minister, and civil rights activist. Known in Louisville as Mr. Civil Rights, James Crumlin spent the majority of his adult life striving for civil rights and equality for the city's African American community. Born in Spartanburg, SC, Crumlin moved to Washington, DC, with his young wife as a teenager in the early 1930s. After completing high school in 1934, he attended Howard University and received a law degree from the Robert H. Terrell Law School. Taking the advice of a professor to move to a city where African Americans had room for advancement, Crumlin and his wife settled in Louisville in 1944. Almost immediately after their move, Crumlin was drafted into the army and served a tour of duty in Europe.

After his brief stint in the military, Crumlin returned to Louisville, established a law practice, and immediately began what became a career of civil rights activism. He quickly became the president of the city's branch of the **National Association for the Advancement of Colored People** and served as legal counsel for the Kentucky State Conference of the NAACP. He also further advocated civil rights as a member of the **Kentucky Commission on Human Rights.** In 1948, Crumlin successfully appealed to the General Assembly to allow black doctors and nurses to train at state hospitals. He also was a leading attorney in suits against the city of Louisville that led to the desegregation of public golf courses, fishing ponds, and amphitheaters.

Crumlin was a major figure in the efforts to integrate education throughout the state. He represented **Lyman T. Johnson** in his successful lawsuit to integrate the graduate school of the University of Kentucky in 1948–1949. After the 1954 Supreme Court decision in *Brown v. Board of Education* ruled school segregation unconstitutional, Crumlin and other black attorneys filed lawsuits against segregated school systems across the state. By 1956, these efforts led to the desegregation of school systems in Clay, Sturgis, Scott Co., Fulton Co., McCracken Co., Hopkins, Owen, Richmond, Madison, Jessamine Co., Mayfield, Frankfort, Bowling Green, Warren, Co., and Knott Co.

Although he was forced to resign from the presidency of the Louisville NAACP chapter in 1960 by a competing faction, Crumlin remained active throughout the 1960s and 1970s. During this time, he served as an assistant commonwealth's attorney, prosecutor in the traffic court, commissioner of the Jefferson County Quarterly Court, and a Jefferson Co. judge. Throughout his career in civil rights and politics, Crumlin also served as the minister of Brown Temple A.M.E. Zion Church and seven other A.M.E. Zion churches throughout the city from the 1960s to the early years of the twenty-first century. In August 2004, James Crumlin Sr. died at the age of 90 in Louisville's Veterans Administration Medical Center.

Crumlin, James. Interview by Tracy K'Meyer, August 30, 1999. Courtesy of Oral History Center, University Archives and Records Center, Univ. of Louisville.
Kentucky's Black Heritage: The Role of the Black People in the History of Kentucky from Pioneer Days to the Present. Frankfort: Kentucky Commission on Human Rights, 1971.
"Rev. James A. Crumlin Sr. Dies." *LCJ,* August 28, 2004, B.7.
Wright, George C. *A History of Blacks in Kentucky.* Vol. 2, *In Pursuit of Equality, 1890–1980.* Frankfort: Kentucky Historical Society, 1992.

—*Joshua D. Farrington*

CUNNINGHAM, JAMES C. (b. 1787, St. George, Bermuda; d. 1877, Louisville, KY), violinist, bandleader, and dancing teacher. James C. Cunningham was born in Bermuda on May 3, 1787. He came to Louisville around 1835 and joined a band led by Henry Williams, an early free African American violinist. In 1847, Cunningham formed his own band, which included other free African Americans and German immigrants and quickly became the most popular band in the city. It played at fancy balls and cotillions, as well as for various trade groups, such as carpenters, mechanics, and firemen. In 1849, the band was selected to perform at the ball honoring President-elect Zachary Taylor, and in 1850 it played at a famous masquerade ball hosted by Sallie

Ward. Cunningham's band was also in great demand during the summers at watering places such as Paroquet Springs and Drennon Springs.

Cunningham was active in the **Underground Railroad.** He was implicated in an attempt by Rev. Calvin Fairbank to help a slave escape to Indiana in 1851 but was not arrested. The next year, Cunningham traveled to Pittsburgh to hear Frederick Douglass speak at a Free Soil Convention, and in 1855 he was accused of helping five slaves escape.

He married Lucinda B. Steele, and their children played important roles in Louisville's African American community. Their daughter, Mary V. Cunningham (1842–1919), was a well-known organist, and their son, **James R. Cunningham** (1853–1943), led his own brass band. James C. Cunningham died on June 18, 1877, and is buried in Eastern Cemetery.

—*Cornelius Bogert*

CUNNINGHAM, JAMES R. (b. 1853, Louisville, KY; d. 1943, Louisville, KY), cornetist and bandleader. James R. Cunningham was born on July 10, 1853, the son of **James C. Cunningham** and Lucinda B. Steele. His father led one of the most popular bands in Louisville. The younger Cunningham was working as a full-time musician by the time he was 17.

About 1874, he founded the Falls City Cornet Band, which quickly became one of the city's most popular bands. The group, which later became the Falls City Brass Band, played regularly on steamboats. It also performed for St. John's Day parades, festivals organized by the **Louisville Colored Musical Association,** train excursions, and the Louisville Colored Fair and even gave concerts on the frozen Ohio River. In 1895, Cunningham's "famous brass band" was selected to play for a huge barbecue in Wilder Park during the **Grand Army of the Republic** Encampment.

Cunningham counted among his many admirers songwriter Will S. Hays and newspaperman Henry Watterson. In the 1890s, Cunningham toured England, where he performed for Queen Victoria. His band was one of the first African American brass bands to tour Japan. Around 1900, the Falls City Brass Band began to play what was then known as "syncopated music"— **ragtime**-influenced dance music. Cunningham remained active in music as a teacher through the 1920s. He died on November 10, 1943, and is buried in Eastern Cemetery.

—*Cornelius Bogert*

CUNNINGHAM, RAOUL (b. 1943, Louisville, KY), civil rights activist. Born on May 13, 1943, in Louisville, KY, Raoul Cunningham began his activism for racial equality at the age of 14 when he joined the **National Association for the Advancement of Colored People** (NAACP). He attended integrated Male High School, which he called "a horrible experience." By his senior year, he was the first of many students arrested for participating in various sit-ins to desegregate Louisville's public places. His activism resulted in educators lowering grades, public taunts, and arrests. Louisville attorney **Benjamin Shobe** defended the arrested teens.

Cunningham studied government at Howard University in Washington, DC, where he organized a chapter of the Young Democrats of America. He became president of the District of

Columbia Federation of College Young Democrats. After his college graduation in 1965, he returned to Louisville and worked as campaign manager for **Georgia Davis Powers,** the first woman elected to the Kentucky State Senate. Speaker of the House (and later Kentucky governor) Julian Carroll hired Cunningham as a reading clerk; he was the first African American to hold that position. When he first reported to work, the Senate's chief doorkeeper would not allow him to enter until Carroll spoke on his behalf.

For 12 years, Cunningham was the senior assistant for legislation and community relations for U.S. senator Walter D. Huddleston. He worked on civil rights legislation and the Martin Luther King Jr. Holiday bill. Later, he served eight years as a deputy state personnel commissioner in the administrations of Democratic governors Martha Layne Collins and Wallace Wilkinson. He was inducted into the Kentucky Civil Rights Hall of Fame in 2003. Two years later, he was elected president of the Louisville branch of the NAACP. In 2006, the city of Louisville awarded him the Dr. Martin Luther King Jr. Freedom Award. The Martin Luther King Jr. State Commission awarded him its 2011 citizenship award. Cunningham, as president of the Louisville NAACP and a consummate political activist, continued to promote voter registration.

Cunningham, Raoul. Interview by Tracey E. K'Meyer August 24, 1999. Oral History Center, Univ. of Louisville, 2002.
Newspapers: "Activist Raoul Cunningham Honored," *LCJ,* January 13, 2006, B3; "Raoul Cunningham Gets King Citizenship Award," *LCJ,* January 13, 2011; "Raoul Cunningham: NAACP Presses for Voter Registration," *LCJ,* October 7, 2012; "50 Years Ago, It Was Teens Who Spearheaded Effort to Desegregate Louisville," *LCJ,* May 11, 2013, A1.
Powers, Georgia Davis. *I Shared The Dream: The Pride, Passion and Politics of the First Black Woman Senator from Kentucky.* Far Hills, NJ: New Horizon Press, 1995.
Who's Who in Black Louisville. 3rd ed. Columbus, OH: Who's Who, 2009.

—*Sallie L. Powell*

CURD, KIRKSEY L. (b. 1888, Fulton, KY; d. 1967, Philadelphia, PA), physician. Kirksey Curd was born to Ida and Curtis Curd in Fulton, KY, on February 25, 1888. When he was young, his family moved to Perry, OK. He graduated from Langston University in Oklahoma in 1907 and continued his education at Kansas Agricultural College from 1909 to 1910. As an African American in the Midwest, he found his talent relegated to segregated education and limited opportunities for advancement. After completing his college education in Kansas, Curd moved to New York to attend prestigious Cornell University, obtaining a degree in veterinary medicine in 1912. He then attended and received his medical degree from the University of Pennsylvania in 1917.

After becoming a medical doctor, Curd served as a 1st lieutenant in the U.S. Army Reserves during World War I. After his tour of duty, he established a permanent home in Philadelphia with his wife, Ursula. A talented musician, Ursula studied at the Curtis Institute and performed numerous solos with the Philadelphia Concert Orchestra.

After Kirksey Curd became a chief doctor at Frederick Douglass Memorial Hospital, he and his wife became a leading couple in Philadelphia's black community and were involved in local chapters of Masons, Odd Fellows, and Elks until his death in April 1967.

"Frederick Douglass Memorial Hospital, Philadelphia." *Journal of the National Medical Association* XXV, 3 (August 1933): 134.
Obituary of Ursula Curd, *Philadelphia Daily News,* June 23, 1988.
Yenser, Thomas, ed. *Who's Who in Colored America, 1941–1944.* 6th ed. Brooklyn, NY: Thomas Yenser, 1942.

—*Joshua D. Farrington*

D

DALY, RICHARD (b. unknown; d. unknown), active in the Underground Railroad. Although Richard Daly's birth and death dates, like those of many Kentucky slaves, are unknown, he was still alive in 1894 in Windsor, Canada, when he was interviewed by a reporter for a Detroit, MI, newspaper. Daly's four children were born between 1840 and 1850 in Hunter's Bottom, Carroll Co., KY. His oldest daughter, Mary, was listed as being age 17 in the 1860 Detroit census.

In the 1850s, Richard Daly, his brother Joe Daly, and Tom Owen were slaves owned by Samuel Fearn Sr. in Hunter's Bottom. The Fearn family came to Kentucky from Buckingham Co., VA. Samuel Fearn (1766–1828) (the father of Samuel Sr.) and his oldest son, George (1796–1869), arrived in 1803 in Hunter's Bottom, a 10-mile stretch of Ohio River bottomland between Canip and Locust Creeks. Samuel Fearn Sr., the family's fourth child, was born in Hunter's Bottom in 1806 and married Elizabeth Own in 1826. George and Samuel Fearn together owned about 1,000 acres along the banks of the Ohio River, straddling the Carroll and Trimble county line, but Samuel Sr.'s main income came from his gristmill and packet steamship businesses in Milton, on the Kentucky side of the Ohio River opposite Madison, IN. He also purchased timberland in Jackson Co., IN, on the White River. George Fearn speculated in land along the wharf area in Madison and along the Indiana shoreline on the east side of Madison. The two Fearn brothers were quite wealthy. Samuel Fearn had three slaves; George, a bachelor, owned four or five slaves. The Fearn family history states that George Fearn had become an ardent Methodist and emancipated all his slaves in his will. George was so pro-Union and so openly opposed to slavery that horses were stolen from his farm in a targeted attack by Confederate raiders during the Civil War.

In his 1894 interview, Richard Daly referred to Samuel and George Fearn as "kind," and it appeared that Daly had many advantages over other slaves in the region. He lived in a brick house behind the main Samuel Fearn homestead and was permitted to take produce to market in Madison, IN, in order to earn money to purchase his freedom. Furthermore, Samuel Fearn had set an extremely low purchase price, $100, for Daly's freedom, although comparable prices for slaves of his age and ability were well above $800 to $900. Daly claimed that by 1856 he had already saved $100 "in his pocket." Fearn, like many of Hunter's Bottom slave owners, allowed Richard to make frequent conjugal visits to his wife, Kitty, a house servant owned by Moses Hoagland, who lived east of the Fearns along the Ohio River toward Carrollton. Richard and Kitty had four living children, who by law and custom were owned by Moses Hoagland.

But the most unusual fact about Richard Daly was that he had worked actively in the **Underground Railroad** (UGRR) for some years. He stated that he had ferried 30 fugitive slaves across the Ohio River before 1856. He would meet the slaves two miles above Milton and row them across in his small boat. During the 1850s,

this route through Eagle Hollow in Carroll Co., KY, was one of the most active crossing points on the Ohio River between Cincinnati and Louisville. Daly's method of signaling his friend, a white leader of the UGRR (probably John Carr), was also highly unusual. Daly said that he would row into the middle of the Ohio River and shoot a revolver into the air. The UGRR agent would then shoot his revolver in response. By the time Daly arrived at the Indiana shore, his white friend would be ready and would take charge of the runaways.

It was well known that Samuel Fearn enjoyed hunting and had several hunting dogs always running through the house and farm, but for a slave to have access to a revolver and ammunition was remarkable. Moreover, the sound of gunshots in the middle of the Ohio River at night would have carried to both shores. If the Indiana UGRR agent heard it, the Fearns would have heard it also. Therefore, it has been suggested locally that the Fearn brothers tacitly, if not actively, approved of Daly's aiding runaway slaves.

Daly said that he was happy in his circumstances and had no plans to escape, but then his wife, Kitty, unexpectedly died. Richard was concerned about his children and asked Mrs. Hoagland to keep them in Hunter's Bottom, and she agreed. However, a short time later, the Hoaglands' daughter married a doctor and moved to Louisville. She asked that Mary, the oldest Daly daughter, go with her permanently. When Richard Daly learned that his family was to be separated, he went to pick up all four children. They crossed the Ohio River and took the Madison UGRR route north through Indiana. Daly said that they rode horses northward, accompanied successively by two sets of UGRR agents, one from twilight to midnight and another from midnight to dawn. The family members slept in various farmhouses until they reached Michigan. There, they boarded the Michigan Central Railroad to Detroit and crossed over the ferry to Windsor, Canada.

In Canada, Daly worked feeding cattle for a man named Hiram Walker, who exported livestock to Great Britain from a farm located along the Detroit River. Daly said that he had crossed the Atlantic Ocean several times with these shipments. At some point, he married a second time. In 1894, three of the children who escaped with him were living in Detroit, and one child had died in Windsor.

Apparently Joe Daly and Tom Owen continued to live with Samuel Fearn at Hunter's Bottom even after the Thirteenth Amendment to the U.S. Constitution freed all slaves. When George Fearn died in 1869, he left Fearn Hill, his antebellum home, to his nephew, George Fearn. The emancipation clause was still in George's will, but it was moot since his slaves were already free by law.

Blassingame, John W., ed. *Slave Testimony.* Baton Rouge: Louisiana State Univ. Press, 1977.

Coon, Diane Perrine. "Southeastern Indiana's Underground Railroad Routes and Operations." Unpublished technical report, U.S. Park Service and Indiana Department of Natural Resources, Indiana Department of Historic Preservation and Archaeology, Indianapolis, 1999.

Emma McClaran Fearn family Bible. In possession of Larry Douglas Smith, Louisville, KY.

Smith, Larry Douglas. "The Fearns of Hunter's Bottom, Kentucky." Louisville, KY: Orders to L. D. Smith, 1992.

—*Diane Perrine Coon*

DANIEL, WILBUR N. (b. 1918, Louisville, KY; d. 1999, Chicago, IL), Chicago preacher, activist, and NAACP leader who integrated Austin Peay State University. On January 2, 1918, Wilbur Daniel was born to Fannie and Nathan Daniel in Louisville, KY. He received his early education at West Point, KY, and Louisville's **Central High School.** He then obtained a bachelor of science degree from Tennessee State University and a bachelor of theology degree at the American Baptist Theological Seminary. After serving briefly as a pastor in Garrett, IN, Daniel became the first African American to be accepted into graduate school at Austin Peay State College (later known as Austin Peay State University) in Clarksville, TN, from which he graduated with a master's degree in 1957. During his time in graduate school, Daniel also managed to pastor Clarksville's St. John Baptist Church.

Immediately after graduation, Daniel accepted a position as pastor of Chicago's Antioch Baptist Church. Within 10 years, Daniel expanded the church to almost 5,000 members. In 1966, the church purchased a 21-acre lot and, with the help of the Federal Housing Administration, constructed a $6-million apartment complex that provided low-cost housing to those in need.

In 1962, Daniel became president of the Chicago branch of the **National Association for the Advancement of Colored People** (NAACP), the organization's largest and oldest branch. Two years later, he stepped down from the post when he won the Republican primary congressional nomination for Illinois's First District. His opponent was the incumbent, William Dawson, who easily won the race in the overwhelmingly Democratic district. Throughout the 1970s, Daniel continued to lead his church, served on the NAACP's Executive Board, and headed the Adult Department of the National Baptist Sunday School Congress. In 1979, he was appointed chairman of the Chicago Police Board.

Daniel died in Chicago on October 26, 1999. Austin Peay State University named the Wilbur N. Daniel African-American Cultural Center in his honor.

"Biography of Dr. Wilbur N. Daniel." http://www.apsu.edu/aacc /biography (accessed March 26, 2013).

Dunnigan, Alice Allison, comp. and ed. *The Fascinating Story of Black Kentuckians: Their Heritage and Traditions.* Washington, DC: Associated Publishers, 1982.

Newspapers: Bob Hunter, "New NAACP President Follows 'Four Precepts' in Daily Life," *Tri-State Defender* (Memphis), January 26, 1963, 7; "Negro Church Plans Housing in Chicago," May 22, 1966; *NYT,* May 22, 1966, 43; Jack Houston, "Black Leader Exults in 'Spiritual Power,'" *Chicago Tribune,* April 10, 1980, A2; "University Names Center after African American Pastor," *Tennessee Tribune,* February 1, 2007, A5.

—*Joshua D. Farrington*

DANIELS, C. MACKEY (b. 1937, South Carolina), minister and civil rights leader. C. Mackey Daniels's political activism began in his home state of South Carolina. He reportedly led the "Sumter 26," who supposedly were the subjects of "the first student arrests of the civil rights era." He earned his degree from Morris College, Sumter's historically black college.

In 1978, Daniels began his ministry in Kentucky at Louisville's West Chestnut Street Baptist Church. Five years later, when Louisville debated whether the city and Jefferson Co. should merge, he joined other African American leaders to oppose the merger on the grounds that it would lead to loss of African American political power due to low African American population in the county. He asserted, "We are tired of other people carving out our turf for us." When he was vice chairman of the Jefferson County School Board, he pushed for a boycott of the schools because of discrimination in the schools and in the election of the board's chairperson.

As a leader of the Louisville branch of the **National Association for the Advancement of Colored People** (NAACP), Daniels pushed for increased involvement of African Americans in voting and argued that school desegregation had influenced black-on-black homicides because youths had lost African American teachers as role models. He served on Louisville–Jefferson County's Human Rights Commission and was the Kentucky Bar Association's first African American arbitrator in the county courts. Jefferson Co. honored him in 1997 with its Martin Luther King Jr. Award for his role in an interracial partnership between his predominantly black church and the mostly white Highland Presbyterian Church. In 1998, the Progressive National Baptist Convention, with 2.5 million members, unanimously elected Daniels to a four-year term as its president.

Daniels's tenure as the organization's president was filled with political and social conflicts. He revived activism through the fight against AIDS with compassion and prevention, addressed youth violence, stressed evangelism, and supported historically black colleges. He pushed for boycotts against South Carolina's usage of the Confederate flag and against prisons because of their enormous incarceration and deaths of young African Americans.

Daniels urged the end of President William "Bill" Clinton's impeachment trial and pleaded for the nation to forgive him. He maintained that there was a difference between a sin and a crime. In 2001, he advocated that Rev. Jesse Jackson be forgiven for his sin of adultery. That same year, Daniels joined other NAACP leaders in opposing President George W. Bush's faith-based initiative, governmental funding of religious social services, on the basis of separation of church and state. He equated this plan with Judas accepting money for the betrayal of Jesus and said that this action would muffle the African American voice of political opposition.

The Progressive National Baptist Convention met that year in Miami, but the organization left the Marriott Waterside hotel abruptly after the so-called punch-bowl incident (a white waiter was accused of spitting into the punch bowl before dinner). Daniels told the 800 delegates that refunds from the hotel were demanded. The organization's legal team in this situation included the former attorney of O. J. Simpson, Johnnie Cochran.

Daniels ended his presidential term in 2002 but continued his ministry and civic activism. He encouraged Louisville citizens to participate in the 2010 U.S. census.

Newspapers: "KY Pastor Wins National Post," *LHL,* August 16, 1998, B3; "Baptists Urge Help for Blacks' 'Survival'; Progressive Convention Outlines 10 Steps to Take," *LHL,* August 2, 2000, C12.

—*Sallie L. Powell*

DANNER, MARGARET (b. 1910, Pryorsburg, KY; d. 1984, Chicago, IL), poet.

Margaret Esse Danner was born to Caleb and Naomi Esse in Pryorsburg, KY. Her literary talent was evident from a young age. She won a local poetry contest in the eighth grade for her poem "The Violin." During Danner's first year of high school, her family moved to Chicago, a city that would become the perfect venue for an emerging poet. After graduation, Danner attended two of Chicago's most prestigious schools, Loyola and Northwestern Universities.

In 1951, *Poetry: A Magazine of Verse* published Danner's "Far from Africa: Four Poems," a work that propelled her into the upper echelons of black poets of the 1950s. Ahead of its time, Danner's "Far from Africa" encouraged African Americans to celebrate their cultural roots in Africa. Five years later, Danner became the first black woman assistant editor of *Poetry,* the publication that had launched her career. Her first collection of poetry was printed in 1960, and in 1961, she became poet-in-residence at Wayne State University. She later served in the same position at Miles College, Virginia Union University, and LeMoyne–Owen College. Additionally, she was an artist-in-residence in Detroit, Memphis, and Richmond, VA. During the 1960s, Danner founded the Boone House in Detroit, which served as a gathering place for aspiring poets and artists. In 1964, Danner and famed poet Langston Hughes recorded a poetry-reading session at the Boone House.

In total, Danner published five books. She died in Chicago, IL, on January 1, 1984. Her poems can be found in numerous anthologies and are well known for their theme of celebrating her African heritage.

Danner, Margaret. "Far from Africa: Four Poems." In *The Poetry of Black America: Anthology of the 20th Century,* edited by Arnold Adoff, 134–37. NY: HarperTeen, 1973.

Page, Yolanda, ed. *Encyclopedia of African American Women Writers.* Vol. 2. Westport, CT: Greenwood Press, 2007.

—*Joshua D. Farrington*

DARBY, THEODORE ROOSEVELT "BLIND TEDDY" (b. 1906, Henderson, KY; d. 1975, East St. Louis, IL), musician.

Taught to play guitar by his mother, **blues** singer and guitarist Theodore Roosevelt Darby frequently encountered trouble with authorities when he was a teenager. He spent a year in a reformatory and a year in a city workhouse for illegal moonshine transportation. After the family moved to St. Louis, Darby lost his eyesight to glaucoma, and he turned to music.

Darby performed under various pseudonyms, such as Blind Blues Darby and Blind Squire Turner, but he predominantly used "Blind Teddy" Darby. He worked with guitarist Peetie Wheatstraw, and his cousin Tom Webb usually accompanied him on piano. Between 1929 and 1937, Darby worked with four different recording labels and produced 24 songs, including "Lose Your Mind," "Lawdy Lawdy Worried Blues," and "Bootleggin' Ain't Good No More." During the Depression, in his song, "Meat and Bread Blues (Relief Blues)," Darby identified governmental assistance programs as a means to get food and keep his girlfriend. Darby apparently doubted whether he would collect relief funds and warned that if he did not receive financial aid, he would resort to violence.

Darby quit the music business in 1937 after his cousin and pianist Tom Webb was murdered. He started a new career as an ordained minister at the King Solomon Holy House of Prayer in East St. Louis, IL. In the early 1960s, he returned to music but did not release the recordings. He died in December 1975.

"Blind Teddy Darby Biography." http://www.artistdirect.com/artist /bio/blind-teddy-darby/569733 (accessed November 10, 2010).

Larkin, Colin, ed. *The Guinness Encyclopedia of Popular Music.* Vol. 1. Chester, CT: New England Pub. Associates, 1992.

Lawson, R. A. *Jim Crow's Counterculture: The Blues and Black Southerners, 1890–1945.* Baton Rouge: Lousiana State Univ. Press, 2010.

Library of Congress. *Blind Teddy Darby: Complete Recorded Works in Chronological Order, 1929–1937.*

Social Security Death Index.

Van Rijn, Guido. *Roosevelt's Blues: African-American Blues and Gospel Songs on FDR.*

—*Sallie L. Powell*

DAVID, GEORGE FRANKLIN (b. 1862, Leesburg, KY; d. 1937, Lexington, KY), minister and delegate to the Republican National Convention.

One of 12 children of Baldwin, a farmer, and Hannah David, George Franklin David joined the African Methodist Episcopal Church in 1881 and was licensed to preach at Covington, KY, in 1886. He served six church appointments in Kentucky and two in Columbus, OH. He was responsible for the building of Kentucky African Methodist Episcopal churches in Hickman, Sulphur Wells, and Leesburg. In 1904, he became a presiding elder. In 1911, Ohio's Wilberforce University awarded David an honorary doctor of divinity degree, and he graduated from Payne Theological Seminary in Wilberforce the following year.

David was a member of the Masons, the Odd Fellows, **Kappa Alpha Psi,** and the **United Brothers of Friendship.** He served as treasurer of Wilberforce University and as a delegate to the African Methodist Episcopal Church's General Conference in 1912, 1920, and 1924. He also represented Kentucky as an alternate delegate to the Republican National Convention in 1920 and was a delegate-at-large to the convention in 1924. In 1932, he reportedly claimed, "God Almighty is a Republican."

His wife, Rhoda, was also active in the church as a Sunday school teacher and served as a delegate from Kentucky to the national Women's Methodist Missionary Society in 1911, 1915, 1919, and 1923. The Davids had two biological sons, Charles W. A. and George Franklin Jr., and an adopted son, Minor Sterling. Their birth sons graduated from Wilberforce University and earned doctorates in business from the University of Chicago. Charles became principal of Russell School in Lexington, KY, and George Jr. was a professor at Wilberforce University. When George Jr. became grand polemarch of Kappa Alpha Psi, he used his father's idea and divided the fraternity into supervisory districts. Minor Sterling remained in Lexington.

Rhoda died in their home in Lexington in 1928. George Franklin David died of influenza almost 10 years later.

Crump, William L., and C. Rodger Wilson. *The Story of Kappa Alpha Psi: A History of the Beginning and Development of a College Greek Letter Organization, 1911–1971*. Philadelphia: Kappa Alpha Psi Fraternity, 1972.

Kentucky Death Records, 1852–1953.

Newspapers: "Pick Kentucky Delegates," *NYT,* March 4, 1920, 17; "Kentucky's Big Four," *Hartford Republican,* March 5, 1920, 4; "Republican State Convention," *Adair County News,* March 10, 1920, 4.

U.S. Federal Census (1800, 1880, 1900, 1910).

Wright, Richard Robert, Jr. *Centennial Encyclopaedia of the African Methodist Episcopal Church.* Philadelphia: Book Concern of the A.M.E. Church, 1916.

———. *Who's Who in the General Conference.* Philadelphia: A.M.E. Book Concern, 1924.

—*Sallie L. Powell*

DAVIDS, TICE (b. unknown; d. unknown), escaped slave. What are the origins of the **Underground Railroad?** The tale of Tice Davids has beguiled many scholars. In 1895, Ohio historian Wilbur Henry Siebert maintained that the organization that transferred enslaved people to freedom initially was known as the Underground Road. According to a story by Rush R. Sloane, a Sandusky, OH, mayor, abolitionist, and Underground Railroad activist, that name resulted from Kentucky's Tice Davids's escape from his master.

Reportedly, in 1831, Davids's unnamed master chased him to the edge of the Ohio River and almost caught him there, but the slave jumped into the water and began to swim to the Ohio side, near the small community of Ripley. With a constant watchful eye on his property, the slave owner obtained a small rowboat and continued his pursuit of Davids. Once ashore, the master was unable to find any signs of the dripping wet runaway slave and explained the mystery by claiming that Davids "must have gone off on an underground road." Siebert stated that Rev. W. M. Mitchell, an African American resident of southern Ohio, recounted nearly the same version. Another account claimed that the escape occurred in Columbia, PA. Siebert asserted that traditional anecdotes such as this one could not "be trusted in the details of time, place and occasion." In a 1937 *New York Times* article, Sloan said that the account was "as reliable as any."

The location of Ripley, OH, supports the possible truth of this narrative. Even though this portion of the Ohio River was extremely deep, it was also especially narrow, which made Ripley a valuable freedom portal for escaping slaves. On the Kentucky side, the rural region was between the small towns of Augusta and Maysville. Rev. John Rankin, a former minister in Kentucky, was living in Ripley. He was a leading abolitionist, and his home was a well-known stop on the Underground Railroad and possibly Davids's hideaway.

Although research has yet to locate documented evidence of Tice Davids, he allegedly settled near Sandusky, OH.

"Old Slave 'Depot' Found in Ohio Home," *NYT,* March 21, 1937, 52.

Rankin House. http://www.ripleyohio.net/htm/rankin.htm (accessed January 25, 2011).

Siebert, Wilbur H. "The Underground Railroad in Ohio." *Ohio History: The Scholarly Journal of the Ohio Historical Society* 4 (1895): 44–63. http://publications.ohiohistory.org/ohstemplate.cfm?action =detail&Page=000457.html&StartPage=44&EndPage=63 &volume=4&newtitle=Volume%204%20Page%2044 (accessed January 25, 2011).

Siebert, Wilbur Henry. *The Underground Railroad from Slavery to Freedom.* New York: Macmillan, 1898.

Touring Ohio. http://www.touring-ohio.com/southwest/ripley/ripley .html (accessed January 24, 2011).

—*Sallie L. Powell*

DAVIDSON, SHELBY JEAMES (b. 1868, Lexington, KY; d. 1931, Washington, DC), inventor, attorney, and businessman. The son of Shelby Davidson, a carriage driver, and Willie Davidson, a laundress (one source lists his mother as Amelia Scott Davidson), Shelby Jeames Davidson was educated in Lexington and Louisville. While attending Howard University in Washington, DC, Davidson obtained employment with the Treasury Department in 1893 through the assistance of Kentucky congressman William C. P. Breckinridge. In 1896, he graduated from Howard. The Kentucky state bar admitted him in 1899, and he became a member of the bar of the District of Columbia the following year. The District of Columbia Court of Appeals admitted him to practice law in 1903.

While continuing to work in the Post Office Division of the Treasury Department, Davidson became the resident adding-machine expert. He increased work efficiency and productivity with his 1908 patent of a paper-rewind mechanism for adding machines that included an alarm system to warn the operator of paper-loading problems. He later invented an automated machine that would add postal fees. His last invention attempt was to create a coin-counting machine. While working in the Post Office Division, he started the House of Davidson, a real estate business. He resigned from the Treasury Department in 1912 and was admitted to practice law before the U.S. Supreme Court.

In 1923, as executive secretary of the District of Columbia branch of the **National Association for the Advancement of Colored People,** Davidson led the organization in making a formal protest to President Calvin Coolidge over his appointment of Virginia's C. Bascom Slemp as secretary to the president. Their objections to Slemp's appointment were based on his vote against the Dyer antilynching bill and his preference that the Republican Party be all white.

Davidson died two months short of his 63rd birthday. He was survived by his wife, Leonora Coates Davidson, and two children, Eugene and Ophelia.

Fouché, Rayvon. *Black Inventors in the Age of Segregation: Granville T. Woods, Lewis H. Latimer, and Shelby J. Davidson.* Baltimore: Johns Hopkins Univ. Press, 2003.

Mather, Frank Lincoln, ed. *Who's Who of the Colored Race: A General Biographical Dictionary of Men and Women of African Descent.* Vol. 1. Chicago: Memento Edition, 1915.

Newspapers: "Colored Column," *WN,* April 10, 1909, 2; "The Great Conference," *Washington Bee,* April 1, 1911, 1; "Negroes Protest Naming of Slemp," *NYT,* August 17, 1923, 2.

Work, Monroe N., ed. *Negro Year Book, 1931–1932.* Tuskegee Institute, AL: Negro Book Publishing Co., 1931.

—*Sallie L. Powell*

DAVIS, BENJAMIN OLIVER, JR. (b. 1912, Washington, DC; d. 2002, Washington, DC), first African American brigadier general in the U.S. Air Force and lt. general in any branch. Born on December 18, 1912, in Washington, DC, Benjamin Oliver Davis Jr. followed in the military footsteps of his father, Benjamin Oliver Davis Sr., who was the first African American general in the U.S. Army. After attending the University of Chicago, Davis Jr. entered the U.S. Military Academy in 1932. Although he was shunned by his classmates and treated as a pariah, he graduated 35th in a class of 276 in 1936. He was the fourth black graduate of the academy. During World War II, he won his wings, was promoted to lieutenant colonel, and served with the **Tuskegee Airmen** in Italy as commander of the first all-black air unit, the 99th Pursuit Squadron, and then as commander of the outstanding 332nd Fighter Group. He was awarded the Silver Star and the Distinguished Flying Cross for bravery in action.

After the war, Davis commanded the all-black 477th Bombardment Group at Godman Field, part of Ft. Knox, KY. He helped draft plans to integrate the air force in 1948. He commanded the 51st Fighter-Interceptor Wing during the Korean War, flying an F-86 jet fighter. He was promoted to lieutenant general in 1965, after long service in the Pentagon and overseas. He retired from the air force in 1970.

In 1991, he published his autobiography, *Benjamin O. Davis, Jr., American: An Autobiography.* He was advanced to general on December 9, 1998. He died on July 4, 2002. When he was buried in Arlington National Cemetery on July 17, President William Jefferson Clinton eulogized him.

Applegate, Katherine. *The Story of Two American Generals: Benjamin O. Davis, Jr. and Colin L. Powell.* Milwaukee, WI: Gareth Stevens, 1995.
Davis, Benjamin O., Jr. *Benjamin O. Davis, Jr., American: An Autobiography.* Washington, DC: Smithsonian Institution Press, 1991.
"General Benjamin Oliver Davis Jr." U.S. Air Force. http://www.af.mil/AboutUs/Biographies/Display/tabid/225/Article/107298/general-benjamin-oliver-davis-jr.aspx (accessed July 29, 2014).

—Paul David Nelson

DAVIS, BETTY (BETTIE) WEBB (b. 1879, Scott Co., KY; d. unknown, New York), and **DAVIS, EDWARD BENJAMIN** (b. 1875, Scott Co., KY; d. 1934, Georgetown, KY), educators. Both born in Scott Co., KY, Betty and Edward Davis married on December 30, 1896, and became devoted educators in Georgetown, KY. Betty earned her BS degree from State Normal School for Colored Persons (later named **Kentucky State University**) in Frankfort and obtained her library science training at Morehouse-Spelman Library Institute for Negro Librarians. Edward was educated at Walden College in Nashville, TN, and graduated with his AB degree from **State Colored Baptist University** (later known as **Simmons College of Kentucky**) in Louisville, KY. Betty and Edward taught at Chambers Avenue School in Georgetown, KY.

Edward served as the school's principal from 1908 until his death in 1934. He was president of the **Kentucky Negro Educational Association** from 1925 to 1927. In 1924, he established a four-year high school program for African Americans in Georgetown and pushed for Kentucky to create a state university for African Americans. Chambers Avenue School was renamed Ed Davis High School five years later.

Betty taught domestic science from 1918 to 1934. In 1923, she initiated the first African American library in Georgetown, located in the school. Ten years later, the library was named the Charles Steele Branch after a former principal of the Georgetown Public Colored School. After Edward's death, Betty became the school's principal. She created the Betty Webb Davis Scholarship Loan Fund to assist underprivileged children to attend college. She retired in 1940 and moved to live with their only child, Kate Mae Davis Moore, in New York City.

In 2003, on the site of the former Ed Davis High School, the Ed Davis Learning Center was opened in Ed Davis Park.

"Georgetown High School, Georgetown, Kentucky." http://classic schools.com/Kentucky/Georgetown/Georgetown_High_School/ (accessed November 15, 2010).
Jones, Reinette F. *Library Service to African Americans in Kentucky, from the Reconstruction Era to the 1960s.* Jefferson, NC: McFarland, 2001.
Kentucky Death Records, 1852–1953.
"Departments of Industrial Education." *KNEAJ* 6, no. 1 (October–November 1935): 6; 6, no. 2 (February–March 1936): 8; 9, no. 3 (March–April 1940): 22.
U.S. Federal Census (1900, 1910, 1920, 1930).
Yenser, Thomas. *Who's Who in Colored America.* 4th ed., *1933–1937,* and 6th ed., *1941–1944.* Brooklyn, NY: Thomas Yenser, 1937 and 1942.

—Sallie L. Powell

DAVIS, VAN D., JR. (b. 1929, Louisville, KY; d. 1991, Los Angeles, CA), firefighter. Van Davis Sr. and his wife, Nancy, also known as Nannie, were living in Louisville, KY, with his parents, Charles and Lucy Davis, when their first son, Van Jr., was born. The family soon moved to California, and Davis attended high school in Willowbrook. He joined the navy when he was 17. In 1953, he became the first African American firefighter at the Los Angeles County Fire Department.

In the following year, African American firefighters from the Los Angeles City and County Fire Departments formed the Stentorians for the purpose of addressing issues of discrimination and segregation in the departments. Davis was the first member from the county fire department to become president of the Stentorians. He was also the first and only African American director of Local 1014 of the International Association of Firefighters. Davis actively recruited African Americans and other minorities to join the Los Angeles County Fire Department. In December 1978, Davis was the leading plaintiff in a discrimination lawsuit against Los Angeles Co. that went to the U.S. Supreme Court.

In Davis's 20-year career, no African American firefighters were promoted. His son, Aquil Basheer, followed his father into the firefighter career.

County of Los Angeles v. Davis. http://ftp.resource.org/courts.gov/c/US/440/440.US.625.77-1553.html (accessed December 7, 2010).
Kentucky Birth Index, 1911–1999.

"Behind the Scenes, Vand Davis, Jr." Los Angeles County Fire Department. http://www.fire.lacounty.gov/Behind/StentVanDavisJr.asp (accessed December 6, 2010).

U.S. Federal Census (1920, 1930).

—Sallie L. Powell

DAVIS, WILLIAM E. "BUNNY" (b. 1917, Perryville, KY; d. 2001, Danville, KY), athlete, businessman, civic leader, and mayor pro tem.

Considered one of the superior athletes of Danville's Bate High School, William E. "Bunny" Davis, son of horse trainer Lloyd Davis and Hester Davis, competed in track and field, football, basketball, and baseball. He ran the 100-yard dash in 9.7 seconds. He earned his nickname through his quick, zigzag sprints as a football running back and also became an all-conference tailback. In his senior year of high school, 1936, he became an all-state basketball forward and played on the All-American Negro High School Basketball Team in Roanoke, VA.

After graduation, Davis worked as a recreational director in Danville while he played shortstop for the Danville Yankees, an African American baseball team. He later played right field for the **Lexington Hustlers,** the first integrated baseball team in the South. He led the team in home runs. He also coached boys' and girls' basketball at his alma mater. In 1942, he married one of his former female players, Lillian Beasley.

After Davis retired from competitive athletics, he continued in sports by officiating basketball and becoming the first African American umpire of integrated Kentucky high school baseball. He officiated four state baseball tournaments and umpired college baseball for the Kentucky Southeastern Conference.

Besides officiating, Davis started a moving-van company, Bunny's Moving Service, in Danville. In 1982, he retired and became more active in community service. He was the first African American businessman on several Danville boards, including the Police and Firefighters' Merit Board and the boards of the local hospital, the United Way, the Selective Service, the Kiwanis Club, and the Chamber of Commerce. Beginning in 1992, Davis served for five years as Danville's mayor pro tem, the first African American to hold such a high government position in the town. He also served for 13 years on the Danville City Commission. He held the position of chief doorkeeper for the Kentucky House of Representatives for 28 years.

In 1991, Davis was inducted into the Kentucky High School Athletic Association Sports Hall of Fame. The community of Danville honored him with the William E. "Bunny" Davis Recreation Complex in 1997. Davis died a few months after his 84th birthday and was buried in Danville, KY. Two years later, the **Kentucky Commission on Human Rights** posthumously honored Davis in its Gallery of Great Black Kentuckians poster series.

Kelley, Brent. *"I Will Never Forget": Interviews with 39 Former Negro League Players.* Jefferson, NC: McFarland, 2003.

Kentucky Commission on Human Rights. http://kchr.ky.gov/about/gallergreatblack.htm?&pageorder=3&selectedpic=35 (accessed December 11, 2008).

Kentucky High School Athletic Association Sports Hall of Fame Inductees. http://www.khsaa.org/hallfame/1991.pdf (accessed December 8, 2010).

Newspapers: "William 'Bunny' Davis, Athlete, Commissioner," *LHL,* October 14, 2001, B2; "State Panel Honors Danville Man," *LHL,* March 19, 2003, E14.

Stout, Louis. *Shadows of the Past: A History of the Kentucky High School Athletic League.* Lexington, KY: Host Communications, 2006.

U.S. Federal Census (1920, 1930, 1940).

—Sallie L. Powell

DAVIS, WILLIAM HENRY (b. 1872, Louisville, KY; d. unknown, Washington, DC), businessman, educator, and stenographer.

Son of former slaves Jerry and Susan Davis, William Henry Davis graduated salutatorian of Louisville Colored High School (later known as **Central High School**) in 1888. He attempted to register at Louisville's Bryant and Stratton Business College but was refused enrollment because of his race. He was hired there as a janitor and proceeded to teach himself shorthand, typewriting, and bookkeeping through textbooks and the white students' assignments on the blackboards that he cleaned.

Davis soon found a job working at a law firm, Cary and Spindle. He took his lunch breaks in the law library and later became the first African American stenographer in a Kentucky court. At 21, he worked as a stenographer for a financial institution, Germania Safety Vault and Trust Company. He also taught African American students stenographer skills.

In 1896, Davis actively campaigned in the African American community for the Republican Party and was rewarded with the position of private secretary of Louisville mayor George Davidson Todd. He married Julia Louise Hubbard that same year. Three years later, Davis moved his family to Washington, DC, and earned a doctorate in pharmacology at Howard University Medical Department in 1902. He opened Mott Night Business High School and later became the principal of Armstrong High School.

Davis held many governmental positions, including in the Treasury Department, and in 1917, he served as the secretary of Dr. Emmett Scott, special assistant to the secretary of war. Davis was responsible for addressing complaints by African American soldiers and ensuring that they and their families received military benefits. He soon ascertained that more African Americans were drafted than whites in the South and notified the authorities, to no avail. He also pushed for the acceptance of African American women in the military and persuaded Secretary of War Newton D. Baker to establish the first navy office staffed by African American women. Davis's daughter, Sarah, was one of 16 African American Yeomanettes.

In the 1920s, Davis worked as the secretary of the presidential commission that investigated economic conditions in the Virgin Islands. In 1934, in his early 60s, he was a special adviser on compliance and enforcement for the National Recovery Administration. Two years later, his son, John Preston Davis, a journalist and civil rights advocate, helped establish the National Negro Congress.

Hartshorn, William Newton, and George W. Penniman. *An Era of Progress and Promise, 1863–1910: The Religious, Moral, and Educational Development of the American Negro since His Emancipation.* Boston: Priscilla Publishing Co., 1910.

John P. Davis Collection. http://www.johnpdaviscollection.org (accessed December 8, 2010).

U.S. Federal Census (1880, 1900, 1920).

—Sallie L. Powell

DAVISTOWN, African American communities in Garrard, Woodford, and Fayette Cos. African American communities in three different Kentucky counties have used the name Davistown. Garrard Co.'s Davistown was located near the Dix River a short distance from Bryantsville, Lancaster, and Danville. Woodford Co.'s Davistown was established near Midway, KY, about 12 miles from Lexington. Fayette Co.'s Davistown was formed southwest of downtown Lexington.

These Davistown hamlets exemplified post–Civil War community establishment by African Americans. Many of these settlements were formed by the estate owner's sale or gift of the land. Davistown in Garrard Co. was named for the owner of the acreage, W. M. Davis. Woodford Co.'s Davistown reportedly originated when a prominent white landowner, a Mrs. Davis, gave Lou Guy, an African American woman, a tract of land, which she divided among other African Americans. In 1865, an attorney, Willard Davis, sold narrow lots to African Americans in Lexington. These villages created a foundation through institutions such as churches and schools. They also formed community through recreation and work.

In the 1890s, citizens of Garrard Co.'s Davistown entertained themselves through brass bands, picnics, and dances. In 1896, they established a school under the tutelage of C. F. Anderson and his assistant, Miss S. B. Kincaid. Two years later, the district raised over $130 for a new school building that was estimated to cost $430. The students petitioned the school board to name it the Anderson School House in honor of their teacher.

In these early years, many African Americans worked on hemp farms. They were also active in their local churches. In 1903, the Green River Sunday School Convention, the Western Green Valley Sunday School Convention, the Howard Creek Association, and the South District Sunday School Convention held their meetings in Garrard Co.'s Davistown. In 1914, the Davistown Baptist Church obtained a new minister, Rev. William Hocker, from Hodgenville, KY. The local newspaper reported that the community had not experienced "such a spiritual awakening" since the 1870s. The baptisms were performed in the Dix River and witnessed by both African Americans and whites. The hamlet was also active in raising money for the Red Cross.

In the 1920s, Woodford Co.'s Davistown operated a school for five months a year, then later seven months, followed by nine months. The school generally had only two or three teachers. By the early 1970s, the average family size was three, and the average length of residence was almost 43 years.

Fayette Co.'s Davistown was originally known as Davis Bottoms because it was located in the bottom of steep valleys near the railroad tracks. By 1880, 30 African American households lived in the area. There were no churches or schools in this Davistown. It became one of the oldest and poorest areas of Lexington. Although talk of urban development spanned decades, the community, located just a short distance from Rupp Arena, which hosted the University of Kentucky men's basketball games, as well as many other entertainment events, remained neglected. The Fayette Co. community has since witnessed a transformation with the construction of new homes and road development.

Hewlett, Jennifer. "Davistown's Historic Undertaking: New Homes Part of Redevelopment," *Herald-Leader*, December 16, 2007, A1.

Kellogg, John. "The Formation of Black Residential Areas in Lexington, Kentucky, 1865–1887." *Journal of Southern History* 48, no. 1 (February 1982): 21–52.

Newspapers: "One More Spiritual Land Slide," *Lancaster (KY) Central Record,* January 16, 1914, 4; "Davistown School," *Lancaster (KY) Central Record,* March 11, 1898, 3.

Proceedings of the Kentucky Negro Educational Association, April 21–24, 1926.

Rennick, Robert M. *Kentucky Place Names.* Lexington: Univ. Press of Kentucky, 1988.

Smith, Peter Craig. "Negro Hamlets and Gentlemen Farms: A Dichotomous Rural Settlement Pattern in Kentucky's Bluegrass Region." PhD diss., Univ. of Kentucky, 1972.

—Sallie L. Powell

DAWSON, DERMONTTI FARRA (b. 1965, Lexington, KY), football player and first Lexington, KY, native to be inducted into a major professional sports hall of fame. One sports columnist described Dermontti Farra Dawson as "the strongest player in the history of Kentucky football." As a tackle at Bryan Station High School, he was also nationally ranked in the discus and shot. When he played at the University of Kentucky (UK), he stood 6 feet, 2 inches tall, weighed 265 pounds, bench-pressed 415 pounds, cleaned 385 pounds, and squatted over 700 pounds. He played guard for two years prior to playing the center position. Several scouts rated him as the top center in the 1987–1988 season. He graduated with a degree in education. In 1988, the

Dermontti Dawson.

Pittsburgh Steelers drafted him in the second round. During his years with the Steelers, he played in 170 consecutive games and was selected seven consecutive times for the AFC Pro Bowl (1992–1998).

Considered "the best center in pro football," Dawson, age 36, retired from the only team he ever played for, the Pittsburgh Steelers, in 2000. He returned to Kentucky and lived with his family in Nicholasville. He founded the not-for-profit PRO Foundation to help disadvantaged children, became a commercial realtor, and served on UK's Board of Trustees. He was inducted into UK's Hall of Fame (2005) and the Kentucky High School Athletic Association Hall of Fame (2007). In 2010, the Cincinnati Bengals offered him a coaching internship.

In 2012, Dawson was inducted into the National Football League Hall of Fame. Of the six inductees, he was the only one who had played in a Super Bowl. In 2013, he, along with several other Pittsburgh Steelers players, held his fifth youth football camp at Robert Morris University in Pittsburgh.

Newspapers: "Dawson Is Coming on Strong," *LHL,* August 24, 1984, C1; "Steelers Pick EKU's Jones 1st, Dawson 2nd," *LHL,* April 25, 1988, C1; "Dawson 'Having a Ball' as Mr. Mom," *LHL,* July 29, 2001, C2; "UK Hall of Fame Inductees," *LHL,* September 9, 2004, C3; "Dawson Finds a New Line of Work," *LHL,* August 3, 2010, C1; "Pro Football Hall of Fame," *LHL,* August 5, 2012, A1.

—*Wardell Johnson*

DAWSON, OSCEOLA ALEESE (b. 1906, Roaring Springs, KY; d. 1963, Paducah, KY), author, civil rights activist, and soprano. Born in Trigg Co., KY, two-year-old Osceola Dawson and her mother moved to Christian Co. after the death of her father to live with her paternal grandparents. She graduated from high school at age 16 as valedictorian of her class. In 1929, she attended Paducah's West Kentucky Industrial College (now **West Kentucky Community and Technical College**) and worked as the school's registrar.

Along with becoming a New York–trained soprano, Dawson wrote a collection of short stories, *Of Human Miseries,* in 1941. Eighteen years later, she completed a documentary, *The Timberlake Story,* on Clarence Timberlake, a president of Paducah's vocational school. Her other literary works include *Love Thy Creed* and *The Racial Problem as I See It.*

In 1951, while active in the **National Association for the Advancement of Colored People** (NAACP), Dawson was responsible for a discrimination complaint against Paducah's atomic energy plant that led to a court order regarding its hiring policies in regard to African Americans. She served as Paducah's and Kentucky's NAACP secretary and regularly traveled on speaking tours. In 1957, she traveled to Baltimore to attend the National Christian Missionary Convention, Disciples of Christ. The following year, she was recognized as one of 10 Kentucky African American Women of Achievement.

A quiet woman, Dawson was known for handling race issues in a low-key but firm manner. She was regarded as "a symbol of hope" for Kentucky's African Americans. She advised students to accomplish their goals on their own merits and not to use race as a justification for mediocrity. She died in Paducah at age 57.

Crisis, April 1952 and March 1953.

Dunnigan, Alice Allison, comp. and ed. *The Fascinating Story of Black Kentuckians: Their Heritage and Traditions.* Washington, DC: Associated Publishers, 1982.

Hull, Debra Beery. *Christian Church Women: Shapers of a Movement.* St. Louis: Chalice Press, 1994.

Newspapers: "At Convention," *Washington Afro-American,* August 27, 1957, 17; "Office Cat," *HK,* December 8, 1959, 4.

"Osceola A. Dawson," Notable Kentucky African Americans Database, Univ. of Kentucky. http://nkaa.uky.edu/record.php?note_id=110 (accessed January 25, 2011).

—*Sallie L. Powell*

DAY LAW, Kentucky law prohibiting integrated education. The Day Law, proposed by Representative Carl Day of Breathitt Co., KY, on January 12, 1904, was overwhelmingly enacted six months later by both houses of the state legislature. The law made it illegal for any college or school in the state to be integrated, or for any private institution to establish an integrated branch within 25 miles of the mother institution. Substantial fines were levied on any school that violated the law. This legislation was specifically aimed at **Berea College,** which had been established in the late 1850s as the state's first integrated institution. The law was a manifestation of Kentucky's continual de jure and de facto racial discrimination against African Americans in the late nineteenth century. On October 8, 1904, a Madison Co. grand jury indicted the college for violating the law's provisions, and the case, titled *Commonwealth v. Berea College,* went to court.

Although the president of Berea College, William Goodell Frost, opposed the Day Law, his arguments against it were ambivalent. He pointed out that since he had become president in 1892, the college had been effectively segregated and that the ratio of white to black students had been altered from about 50-50 to about 7 to 1. Nevertheless, he opposed the Day Law, arguing that the legislation was an impediment to Berea College's liberty of contract and the practice of a lawful calling and, therefore, a violation of the federal constitution's right of due process.

In 1906, the Kentucky Court of Appeals ruled against the college, and the case was appealed to the Supreme Court of the United States. Two years later, the court ruled against the college, declaring that a state's power to incorporate a private institution included the power to alter or repeal the charter. More important, the court held that the Day Law did not destroy the college's ability to educate both African American and Caucasian students, but this process just could not occur simultaneously or in the same building. Justice **John Marshall Harlan,** a Kentuckian, wrote an impassioned dissent against this interpretation of the law.

The Day Law remained in effect until 1948, when the legislature amended it to allow black physicians and nurses to pursue a postgraduate seminar in Louisville's public hospitals. A further amendment in 1950 allowed white colleges and universities to enroll blacks if the governing board of a white institution determined that Kentucky State College for Negroes (later named **Kentucky State University**) in Frankfort offered no comparable programs or courses. Berea College, under the leadership of President Francis S. Hutchins, was the first institution to integrate, followed shortly thereafter by the University of Kentucky, the

University of Louisville, and others. In 1954, the U.S. Supreme Court ruling in **Brown v. Board of Education** made the Day Law unenforceable by declaring all "separate but equal" state school legislation unconstitutional.

Blakeman, Scott. "Night Comes to Berea College: The Day Law and the African-American Reaction." *FCHQ* 70 (January 1996): 3–26.

Heckman, Richard Allen, and Betty Jean Hall. "Berea College and the Day Law." *RKHS* 59 (1968): 35–62.

Nelson, Paul David. "Experiment in Interracial Education at Berea College, 1858–1906." *JNH* 59 (1974): 13–27.

Peck, Elisabeth S. *Berea's First 125 Years, 1855–1980.* Lexington: Univ. Press of Kentucky, 1982.

Wilson, Shannon H. *Berea College: An Illustrated History.* Lexington: Univ. Press of Kentucky, 2006.

—*Paul David Nelson and Eric R. Jackson*

DEARING, J. EARL (b. 1921, Vinton, VA; d. 1969, Louisville, KY), attorney and civil rights activist. J. Earl Dearing, born in Virginia on March 29, 1921, was raised on a farm. In the days of segregation, he walked three miles each way to attend the local grade school because school bus service was for whites only. He attended the closest African American high school, the Lucy Addison High School, in Roanoke, VA, an eight-mile bicycle ride. In 1942, he graduated from Virginia Union University in Richmond, a black Baptist college, and entered the army. After four years of military service, he enrolled in law school under the GI Bill at Western Reserve University in Cleveland. He moved to Louisville in 1950.

A tall, soft-spoken man with a penchant for bow ties, Dearing was both an attorney for and president of the local and state chapters of the **National Association for the Advancement of Colored People** (NAACP). In this capacity, he advocated, for five years, a local ordinance outlawing discrimination in public accommodations that passed in 1963. Dearing had been upset when he was prevented from taking his son to see *Bambi* in a downtown theater. That event resulted in his campaign to integrate all public facilities.

Locally, Dearing was the first African American to be appointed to the position of deputy clerk of the police court in Jefferson Co. He was also appointed to the positions of assistant police court prosecutor and municipal court judge. In 1965, Dearing was the first black to be elected police court prosecutor. In 1969, he was also the first black nominated by the voters in a primary election for a circuit court judgeship (the 4th Division of Common Pleas Court), but he died before the general election. A Republican, he served on the party's national advisory committee on crime and law enforcement and a national task force on crime and delinquency.

Dearing married Mary Alice Hambleton of Louisville, and they had two children, David Earl and Frances Penn. He died on August 22, 1969, and is buried in Cave Hill Cemetery.

Newspapers: *Louisville Courier-Journal and Times,* August 24, 1969; *LD,* August 28, 1969.

DELANEY, ELIZABETH BERRY (b. 1882, Fayette Co., KY; d. 1964, Cincinnati, OH), owner of a funeral home. Elizabeth Berry Delaney, a funeral home owner and operator and an organization leader and clubwoman, was born in Fayette Co. on September 13, 1882. Orphaned at a young age, Elizabeth was raised by her grandmother in an environment that promoted self-reliance, religion, education, and community service. She attended public schools in Lexington and completed the normal course at **Berea College** in Berea. On April 28, 1898, she married John W. Delaney. They made their home in Covington, where John operated the Delaney Funeral Home. **John W. Delaney Jr.,** their only child, was born in 1912. Elizabeth acquired a mortician's license in 1919 and joined her husband in operating the family's funeral business. After John Delaney's death eight years later, she became the sole owner of the establishment and continued its operation for nearly 40 years. When her son later joined her in the business, the firm was renamed E. B. Delaney and Son Funeral Home and expanded to include a second funeral establishment in Cincinnati. As a businesswoman, Elizabeth was one of the first women to serve on the Board of Directors of the National Negro Business League, founded in 1900 by Booker T. Washington. She was also an active member of the National Association of Black Funeral Home Directors.

She was an active member of the **First Baptist Church of Covington** and served in many roles, including 12 years as the church's treasurer. Another area of commitment for Delaney was the State and Local Federation of Colored Women's Clubs. She was elected president of the Ladies Improvement Club in Covington and in 1926 became the 11th president of the Kentucky Association of Colored Women's Clubs. Delaney's interest in youth led her to promote the establishment of junior clubs for young girls in affiliation with the federation.

Delaney's executive ability and eloquence in public speaking, coupled with her interest in civic affairs and women's suffrage, positioned her for numerous leadership roles. She was the first African American chairwoman of the Colored Women Voters of Kenton Co. and used her influence to stake a claim for African American women voters within the Republican Party. Moreover, she became a member of the Kentucky Commission on Interracial Cooperation and attended the first Southern Women and Race Cooperation Conference, held in 1920 in Memphis, TN.

Delaney was instrumental in establishing several chapters of the Order of the Eastern Star and other civic organizations throughout northern Kentucky. She was an active member and served in multiple roles in each organization of which she established a chapter. After a brief illness, Delaney died at age 82 on February 17, 1964, and was buried in Mary E. Smith Cemetery in **Elsmere.**

Newspapers: "Colored Notes and News," *LL,* February 18, 1964, 14; "Elizabeth Delaney," *KP,* February 20, 1964, 14K.

"Our President." *Kentucky Club Woman* 8, no. 3 (July 1926). John and Elizabeth Delaney Collection, Center of Excellence for the Study of Kentucky African Americans, Kentucky State Univ.

—*Anne S. Butler*

DELANEY, JOHN W. "JACK," JR. (b. 1912, Latonia, KY; d. 1991, Cincinnati, OH), judge and owner of a funeral home. Judge and businessman Jack Delaney was the only child of John W. and Elizabeth B. Delaney. Born on September 5, 1912, he attended Covington's Lincoln-Grant School, commonly known as the Seventh St. School, and graduated from William Grant High School in 1929. He was a classmate of World War II hero Maj. Melvin W. Walker. Delaney became active in his mother's funeral business, E. B. Delaney and Son Funeral Home, in Covington. Later he earned a bachelor's degree at the University of Cincinnati; he also graduated from the Salmon P. Chase College of Law in Cincinnati, from the Cincinnati College of Embalming, and from Cincinnati's Cosmopolitan School of Music.

In 1966, Delaney was named the first African American judge pro tem in Kenton Co. Seventeen years later, the job title was changed to deputy judge executive, making Delaney Kenton Co.'s second-highest-ranking official. He wrote the articles of incorporation of the Northern Kentucky Community Council, which evolved into the Northern Kentucky Community Center. In conjunction with Macedonia Missionary Baptist Church and **St. James A.M.E. Church,** both in Covington, he helped develop the Geisler Garden apartments as low-income housing units.

Delaney was the historian of his Masonic Order lodge and later became a 33rd-degree Mason, at which level he served as a member of the Supreme Council. He was a grand master of Prince Hall Masonic Grand Lodge, president of the National Funeral Directors Association, and eastern vice president of Epsilon Nu Delta mortuary fraternity. He was a member of the **First Baptist Church of Covington,** where he served on the board of trustees as treasurer for many years and as organist for the senior choir. On May 17, 1991, Delaney died in Cincinnati and was buried in Mary E. Smith Cemetery in **Elsmere.**

Newspapers: "Pass Bar Examination," *KTS,* April 17, 1958, 1A; "New Attorneys," *KTS,* April 24, 1958, 15A; "Kenton County's No. 2 Man Shuns the Limelight," *KP,* February 7, 1983, 1K; "John Delaney, Funeral Director, Public Servant," *CP,* May 18, 1991, 9A.

—*Theodore H. H. Harris*

DELTA SIGMA THETA SORORITY, INCORPORATED, historically African American service and social collegiate sorority with extensive Kentucky membership. Founded on January 13, 1913, by 22 collegiate women at Howard University, Delta Sigma Theta Sorority, Incorporated, is a predominantly black sisterhood of college-educated women committed to a lifetime of public service.

The founders of the sorority were Winona Cargile Alexander, Madree Penn White, Wertie Blackwell Weaver, Vashti Turley Murphy, Ethel Cuff Black, Frederica Chase Dodd, Osceola Macarthy Adams, Pauline Oberdorfer Minor, Edna Brown Coleman, Edith Mott Young, Marguerite Young Alexander, Naomi Sewell Richardson, Eliza Pearl Shippen, Zephyr Chisom Carter, Myra Davis Hemmings, Mamie Reddy Rose, Bertha Pitts Campbell, Florence Letcher Toms, Olive Jones, Jessie McGuire Dent, Jimmie Bugg Middleton, and Ethel Carr Watson. With over 200,000 members, the sorority provides an impressive list of public service initiatives through its Five-Point Program Thrust of Economic Development, Educational Development, International Awareness and Involvement, Physical and Mental Health, and Political Awareness and Involvement. On January 13, 2013, Delta

Sigma Theta Sorority celebrated 100 years of sisterhood and public service.

Today, there are over 900 chapters of the sorority located throughout the United States and internationally. In Kentucky, eight collegiate chapters and seven alumnae chapters have been created:

- Xi Chapter, the oldest chapter of any Greek-letter organization in the state of Kentucky, was chartered on April 15, 1922, at Simmons University (later known as **Simmons College of Kentucky**) in Louisville. In 1931, the liberal arts programs and student organizations of Simmons University were assumed by **Louisville Municipal College.** When Louisville Municipal College was closed in 1951 and its programs merged with the University of Louisville, Xi Chapter continued to function at the University of Louisville.
- In 1932, the first alumnae chapter of Kentucky was chartered in Lexington, KY, as Chi Sigma. The name was later changed to the Lexington Alumnae Chapter.
- The Louisville Alumnae Chapter was chartered as Alpha Alpha Sigma in April 1933 and became the largest chapter of Delta Sigma Theta in Kentucky.
- The Frankfort Alumnae Chapter was established as Beta Upsilon Sigma graduate chapter in January 1945. Before 1945, the graduate and undergraduate members of the sorority in Frankfort were also members of Alpha Pi Chapter, chartered in 1934 at Kentucky State College, which is known today as **Kentucky State University.**
- The Paducah Alumnae Chapter was established in 1970 in Paducah, KY.
- Eta Zeta Chapter (Western Kentucky University) was founded on March 14, 1970.
- On May 9, 1970, Eta Rho Chapter (Eastern Kentucky University) and Eta Omicron Chapter (Morehead State University) were founded.
- Eta Upsilon Chapter (Murray State University) was established on May 22, 1970, and became MSU's first historically African American sorority chapter.
- Mu Epsilon Chapter was established at the University of Kentucky in 1975 in Lexington.
- The Hopkinsville Alumnae Chapter was established on May 20, 1978, in Hopkinsville.
- The Ft. Knox Alumnae Chapter was established in 1981 in Ft. Knox, KY.
- The Bowling Green Alumnae Chapter was established on May 15, 1993, in Bowling Green.
- Sigma Zeta Chapter (Northern Kentucky University) was chartered on March 11, 1995.

Giddings, Paula. *In Search of Sisterhood: Delta Sigma Theta Sorority and the Challenge of the Black Sorority Movement.* New York: Morrow, 1988.

—*Shannon M. Drane*

DEWEESE STREET (LEXINGTON), hub of African American businesses in Lexington. Named for a local cashier in the mid-1800s, Dewees Street originated as a small side road connected to Main St. in Lexington, KY. Over time, the name shifted to its modern spelling of Deweese Street, although locals attempted to keep the original intact. Located in Lexington's East End, the half-mile stretch of road was at the center of a business boom that culminated in the 1940s, primarily among African American businesses.

Deweese Street, known colloquially as "do as you please street," became a central hub of the African American community in Lexington. In addition to barber shops, funeral homes, insurance agencies, and other local businesses, it featured a wide array of entertainment venues. Perhaps most prominent was the **Lyric Theatre,** a 924-seat white-owned theater that allowed open seating to people of all races. Several nightclubs in the area, including Club Hurricane and the Derby, advertised live music and promoted some of the more popular **jazz** musicians of the time. The vibrant nightlife on Deweese Street also attracted visitors, and some locals recalled children leaving the streets before dark to avoid the times when the area became "very adult."

In the 1960s, however, Deweese Street entered into a period of rapid decline. Desegregation allowed African American consumers to shop at white-owned businesses that offered lower prices and greater selection. The Lyric Theatre shuttered its doors in April 1963, and most major venues followed suit in the years thereafter. Although several local businesses remained in place, Deweese Street's status as the central hub of black businesses had disappeared.

Several projects materialized in the decades after the region's collapse to revitalize the area for both economic and historical reasons. In 1986, the Urban City Council approved the use of $8 million to add a shopping center and housing to Deweese Street, although locals expressed mixed feelings about the nature of the revitalization, and efforts to push the development through stalled over the next few years. A building project in the 1990s furthered the decline, cutting the street to less than half its original length. In 1999, the Lexington **Urban League** moved its headquarters to Deweese Street, initiating a new array of attempts to reinvigorate the area's economy and community. Although disagreement over the future of the East End continued to hinder concentrated action, the reopening of the Lyric Theatre in 2010 after a $6-million overhaul marked a victory for those who hoped to restore Deweese Street to its original prominence in the black community.

Newspapers: "Name Misspelled," *LL,* August 28, 1907, 2; "City Officials Working on Project to Revive Deweese Street," *LHL,* April 21, 1985, B1; "Remembering Kentucky's 'Black Business Capital,'" *LHL,* February 21, 2000, 13.
Schein, Richard H. "Acknowledging and Addressing Sites of Segregation." *Forum Journal* 19 (2005): 34–40.

—*Stephen Pickering*

DICKINSON, BLANCHE TAYLOR (b. 1896, Franklin, KY; d. 1972, Franklin, KY), poet, author, and journalist. The only child of Thomas Taylor, a prosperous farmer, and Laura Taylor, Blanche Taylor was born on a farm in Franklin, KY, on April 15, 1896. One writer described Blanche, when she was quite young, as "an intelligent child" and reported her saying, "Tell the world we are rising." She attended the local public schools, **Bowling Green Academy,** and Simmons University (later known as **Simmons College of Kentucky**) in Louisville. She did not receive a

degree, but she was able to make a living as a schoolteacher. She married Verdell Dickinson, a truck driver who was born in Trenton, Todd Co., KY, in 1898.

Dickinson's early success as a poet was evident in her publications in her hometown paper, the *Franklin Favorite,* and then in the **Louisville Leader,** the *Chicago Defender,* the *Pittsburgh Courier,* and *Crisis.* In 1926, while living in Sewickley, PA, outside Pittsburgh, Dickinson earned honorable mention in the *Crisis* contest for her poem "That Hill." A year later, she won the Buckner Award for "conspicuous promise." In December 1928, she wrote a short story, "Lured by a Brown Siren," for the *Atlanta Independent.*

On February 23, 1929, in the *Baltimore Afro-American,* Dickinson wrote a story about meeting and interviewing Amelia Earhart. She expressed her thrill at meeting the female aviator and described her "captivating personality." Dickinson questioned Earhart about her opinions on race, particularly whether African Americans were capable of flying. Earhart responded, "The capability of the individual only should be considered."

Dickinson's poetry possesses a haunting quality that showcases the aloneness and vulnerability of an African American woman in a white world. One poem, "The Walls of Jericho," echoes this in its lines "We want in, the dark ones cried," and "There is no room for us all." These titles and others, such as "To an Icicle" and "Four Walls," were her initiation as a Harlem Renaissance poet.

In March 1930, after an apparent move to Pittsburgh, Dickinson performed as the guest speaker for the local YMCA. The title of her speech was "Cultural Values of Negro Poetry." From the lack of sources, she apparently ended her writing during this time. In April 1931, one newspaper reported her as "Mrs. Verdell Dickinson, honored guest" at a bridge luncheon. Research has yet to locate any more precise information on her. A "Blanche Taylor" died in Franklin, KY, in January 1972. Dickinson's husband, Verdell, died in Pittsburgh in April 1978. It seems that Blanche Taylor Dickinson disappeared into the aloneness about which she had written so eloquently.

Buck, D. D. *The Progression of the Race in the United States and Canada: Treating of the Great Advancement of the Colored Race.* Chicago: Atwell Printing and Binding Co., 1907.
Cullen, Countee, ed. *Caroling Dusk: An Anthology of Verse by Negro Poets.* New York: Harper & Brothers, 1927.
Honey, Maureen, ed. *Shadowed Dreams: Women's Poetry of the Harlem Renaissance.* New Brunswick, NJ: Rutgers Univ. Press, 2006.
"The Horizon." *Crisis,* February 1927, 206.
Newspapers: "Negroes Get Prizes for Literary Work," *NYT,* May 8, 1927, 19; "Lured by a Brown Siren," *Atlanta Independent,* December 1, 1928, 2; "Amelia Earhart Discusses the Negro: Transatlantic Woman Flier Believes in Race's Ability," *BAA,* February 23, 1929, 2, 5; "Pennsylvania: Pittsburgh," *BAA,* March 22, 1930, 19; "Pittsburgh," *BAA,* April 25, 1931, 5.
Social Security Death Index.
U.S. Federal Census (1910, 1920, 1930).

—*Nancy Richey*

DIGGS, ELDER WATSON (b. 1883, Christian Co., KY; d. 1947, Indianapolis, IN), one of the founders of Kappa Alpha Psi

Fraternity. Born to Cornelia Diggs on December 23, 1883, Elder Watson Diggs was one of three children. He was a 1908 graduate of Indiana State Normal School (now known as Indiana State University) in Terre Haute. The following year, he enrolled in Howard University. There he met fellow student Byron K. Armstrong, also from Indiana. The two men chose to enroll in Indiana University in the fall of 1910. Feeling the distant and cold experience of being black male students on the Indiana campus, they, along with eight other African American students, formed Kappa Alpha Nu Fraternity in 1911. The name was officially changed to **Kappa Alpha Psi** on April 15, 1915. The organization was established as a national fraternity, and Diggs was selected to hold the office of grand polemarch. He held this position for six consecutive years. In 1916, he became the first African American to graduate from the Indiana University School of Education.

Diggs began his career in education in Indiana, but when World War I began, he joined the officer's training camp at Ft. Des Moines, IA. Commissioned as a lieutenant, Diggs was a member of the 368th Infantry in Europe. He also became a captain in the Reserve Officers' Training Corps.

Diggs's first wife, Clara Bell Smith, who was from Lexington, died in 1913 and he married Elizabeth Byrd in 1916. After the end of World War I, Diggs returned to Indianapolis and became the principal of the city's Public School 42. According to one student, he was a stern disciplinarian. "I remember him being out on the sidewalk at the schoolhouse every morning rushing us kids to get to class saying, 'Get to class! Get to class,'" recalled Ross Morrison.

In 1924, Kappa Alpha Psi recognized Diggs as the first recipient of the Laurel Wreath, the fraternity's highest award. After Diggs's death in 1947, the school in which he had served as principal was named Elder Watson Diggs IPS School 42. Diggs was buried in Crown Hill Cemetery in Indianapolis.

"Brother Ross Morrison Remembers Founder Elder Watson Diggs." *Kappa Journal.* http://kappajournal.com/?p=407 (accessed August 6, 2013).

Crump, William L. *The Story of Kappa Alpha Psi: A History of the Beginning and Development of a College Greek Letter Organization, 1911–1971.* Philadelphia: Kappa Alpha Psi Fraternity, 1972.

Elder Watson Diggs School 42. "History of Our School." http://42.ips.k12.in.us/category/general-information/ (accessed August 6, 2013).

—Gerald L. Smith

DILLARD, WILLIAM "BILL" OTIS, SR. (b. 1938, Hopkinsville, KY; d. unknown), first African American sheriff in Kentucky. William "Bill" Dillard's athletic skills at Hopkinsville's Attucks High School led to a football scholarship at Kentucky State College (later known as **Kentucky State University**). In 1957, a knee injury ended his college career, and he returned to his hometown. He worked as a counselor in a maximum-security ward at Western State Hospital, a mental institution, and later served as a youth counselor at Camp Breckinridge Job Corps Center in Morganfield. In 1968, he became the first African American deputy sheriff in Christian Co., KY. He then worked as an undercover agent in drug control for Montgomery Co., TN, and, in 1975, became a Hopkinsville city police officer and obtained his law-enforcement training at Eastern Kentucky University.

Dillard returned to work at Christian Co.'s sheriff's department three years later. In a four-man primary in 1981, he was elected the first African American sheriff in Kentucky. He announced plans for a strong antidrug program. He successfully lobbied for the sheriff's succession amendment. In November 1988, a grand jury questioned his methods of dealing with drug trafficking and bootlegging. He denounced its investigation as politically motivated.

After serving two terms, Dillard lost his reelection bid for sheriff. Just a few weeks after leaving office, in January 1990, he and three other men, including two former deputies, were arrested in an FBI drug sting. They were indicted on drug-related charges, including conspiracy to sell cocaine, paid protection for a drug dealer, and theft of $12,000 in government money. Dillard pleaded innocent, joked with the media about the publicity surrounding the case, and questioned them whether the University of Louisville had won its ball game. He claimed that he was working undercover to investigate the drug dealings of George Art Davis, who he later learned was an FBI undercover agent.

Along with the three other men, Dillard was convicted. He served part of his sentence at a federal prison in Terre Haute, IN, and the rest of it at the Federal Correctional Institute at Beckley, WV. After serving his time, Dillard returned to Hopkinsville.

Newspapers: "Hopkinsville Could Have State's 1st Black Sheriff," *BGDN,* July 27, 1981, 2; "Ex-Sheriff Is Convicted in US Court," *KNE,* June 23, 1990, 1A, 2A.

—Sallie L. Powell

DILS CEMETERY (PIKE COUNTY), considered the first integrated cemetery in eastern Kentucky. In the 1840s, Colonel John R. Dils settled in Pikeville and became a wealthy businessman through his dry goods store, tannery, and investments in coal and timber. Dils opposed slavery and hired free blacks for his enterprises. He also provided grave sites for his employees and their descendants. More than 500 graves are located on two acres overlooking Pikeville. Over 150 African American graves have been found in Dils Cemetery, but only 49 have been conclusively identified.

Some of those identified include Frank and Alvindia Waller and former slave Aggie Justice and her son, Jim. Frank Waller served as Thomas "Stonewall" Jackson's aide. Jim Justice was the first African American to own property in the area. Along with African Americans, whites were buried in the cemetery, including some of Dils's descendants and members of the infamous McCoy family.

Appalachian Quarterly, June 1998, 99.

Kentucky Genealogical Society. http://www.kygs.org/archives/pike_dils/008.htm and http://www.kygs.org/archives/pike_dils/009.htm (accessed February 4, 2011).

Torok, George D. *A Guide to Historic Coal Towns of the Big Sandy River Valley.* Knoxville: Univ. of Tennessee Press, 2004.

—Sallie L. Powell

DINWIDDIE, WILLIAM THOMAS (b. 1865, Danville, KY; d. 1928, Lexington, KY), dentist and carpenter. William Thomas Dinwiddie was born in Danville, KY, on May 2, 1865. His mother died when he was 4 years old, and at the age of 13, he dropped out of school to apprentice for his father, who was a carpenter. Four years later, his father died, and the orphaned Dinwiddie left Danville to attend Knoxville College in Tennessee. After two years, however, Dinwiddie returned to Danville to further his carpentry skills. After quickly becoming one of the finest carpenters in the city, he moved to Lexington, a bigger market for his finely tuned skills. According to W. D. Johnson, a contemporary who wrote about Dinwiddie in 1897, much of the extravagant and artistic woodwork found in the upper-class homes of Lexington in the era was completed by Dinwiddie.

William Dinwiddie had grander plans than settling as one of Lexington's finest carpenters. In 1893, he entered Meharry Medical College in Nashville, TN, where he studied dentistry. After graduating in three years, he returned to Lexington and opened his own office. He was among the first black dentists not only in Lexington but also in the entire state of Kentucky. His practice was so successful that he was recruited by Meharry Medical College to become the chair of the Department of Prosthetic Dentistry. Life in Nashville away from his friends and life in Lexington, however, was too difficult, and Dinwiddie returned to his practice in Kentucky after his first semester on the job. Throughout the first two decades of the twentieth century, Dinwiddie's practice flourished, and he became one of Lexington's most respected African American citizens. His grave is located among those of other prominent black Lexingtonians at Cove Haven Cemetery.

Davis, Merlene. "100-Year-Old Cemetery Restored to Dignity." *LHL,* May 18, 2008, D1.
Johnson, W. D. *Biographical Sketches of Prominent Negro Men and Women of Kentucky.* Lexington, KY: s.n., 1897.
Lucas, Marion B. *A History of Blacks in Kentucky: From Slavery to Segregation, 1760–1891.* 2nd ed. Frankfort: Kentucky Historical Society, 2003.
Richings, G. F. *Evidences of Progress among Colored People.* 8th edition. Philadelphia: Geo. S. and Co., 1902.

—*Joshua D. Farrington*

DIRT BOWL, summer basketball competition in Lexington and Louisville. Considerable debate has existed about both when the Dirt Bowl summer basketball league began and whether it was first played in Lexington or in Louisville. In one account, the Dirt Bowl began at Douglass Park in Lexington, KY, on an earthen court in 1962. Others contend that the Dirt Bowl started in Lexington in 1967 and was initially played on a clay tennis court with basketball goals. However, some suggest that the Dirt Bowl began in Louisville in 1968, although the Louisville Parks Department officially hosted the summer league in 1970. In any case, it is clear that the Dirt Bowl has existed largely because of the work of men like Herb Washington, who helped organize the event in Lexington since the early 1970s. No matter when or where the Dirt Bowl began, it enhanced the high level of competition and the love of basketball in black communities across Kentucky and has been home to some of the best basketball games played anywhere in the nation.

During its heyday in the late 1970s and early 1980s, the Dirt Bowl was ranked as one of the best summer basketball leagues in the nation. In Louisville, the Dirt Bowl benefited from a potent mix of playground legends and high school and collegiate players. Sanctioned by the National Collegiate Athletic Association, players tested their skill against the best competition, including **Clem Haskins,** Jim Rose, and **Jim McDaniels** of Western Kentucky University; Henry Bacon, **Darrell Griffith,** Jim Price, and Ron Thomas of the University of Louisville; and Claude Virdon, Goose Ligon, **George Tinsley,** and Dan Issel of the American Basketball Association's Kentucky Colonels. In Lexington, National Basketball Association players **Jack Givens** matched up against James Lee. **Brenda Lee Garner Hughes**, the first African American woman to officiate the Kentucky High School Athletic Association's "Sweet Sixteen" Girls' State Basketball Tournament, obtained some of her officiating training there.

Louisville's Dirt Bowl, held at Shawnee Park on "Super Sunday" in July, was canceled in 2005. Complaints of violence and noise stopped the contest, but it returned a year later with only 10 teams registered. In Lexington, the days of the Dirt Bowl competition culminated on "Super Bowl Sunday" in July at Herb Washington Arena, a recently built half-million-dollar stadium, and as many as 8,000 people attended. In 2007, Lexington's center court was named Ethan Jenkins Center Court in honor of a 26-year-old man who collapsed and died of a heart condition while playing. In addition to the high caliber of play, vendors, concessions, live entertainment, a dunk contest, and the all-star game played in the evening offer energetic amusements for the Lexington and Louisville communities.

Ballard, Chris. *Hoops Nation: A Guide to America's Best Pickup Basketball.* Lincoln: Univ. of Nebraska Press, 2004.
Carr, Keiara. "Dirt Bowl Draws Crowd to Shawnee Park." *LCJ,* August 13, 2012, B3.
Mendes, Guy, Nancy Carpente, David Brinkley, Otis Ballard, and Chuck Burgess. *World of Our Own Kentucky Folkways.* Vols. 3–4. Lexington: Kentucky Educational Television, 1998. VHS video.
Newberry, Mayor Jim, Fayette Urban County Government, Division of Government Communications. July 18, 2008. http://209.85.173.104/search?q=cache:c9IT9_d_9MAJ:www.lfucg.com/news_releases/08july/dirtbowl080718.pdf+Dirt+Bowl+Lexington&hl=en&ct=clnk&cd=2&gl=us&client=firefox-a.

—*Luther Adams*

DOMESTIC LIFE AND ACCIDENT INSURANCE COMPANY, long-standing early to mid-twentieth-century insurance business located in Louisville. In June 1920, three former employees of Louisville's **Mammoth Life and Accident Insurance Company—Green Percy Hughes, James E. Smith,** and W. F. Turner—organized the Domestic Life and Accident Insurance Company, which was chartered to sell insurance in September 1921. Its headquarters were initially located in the **Knights of Pythias** building on Chestnut St., but in 1924, it moved into its own building at 601 W. **Walnut St.,** located directly across the street from Mammoth Life. By the time of the move, it had issued over 50,000 policies totaling almost $6 million worth of insurance. At its height in the mid-1920s, Domestic Life employed over 300 African Americans and had active field agents in Lexington, Paducah, Bowling Green, Glasgow, and numerous other towns across Kentucky and in cities from Cincinnati to

Cleveland in Ohio. The company's executives also played a central role in the establishment of numerous other business ventures, including **First Standard Bank,** Standard Building and Loan Association, and Parkway Building and Loan Association. Although the Great Depression slowed Domestic Life's growth and contributed to the 1930 suicide of its president, Green Percy Hughes, it remained fiscally solvent and debt free throughout the 1930s and 1940s under the leadership of its new president, **William Wallace Spradling,** and vice presidents **Mary Virginia Cook Parrish,** Reverend R. D. Stoner, M. B. Lanier, and W. F. Turner.

In 1961, the white-owned Kentucky Central Life and Accident Insurance Agency purchased Domestic Life and resold it that same year for almost $2 million to one of the nation's largest insurance businesses, Chicago's Supreme Life Insurance Company of America. In 1973, Lawrence Cole, grandson of **I. Willis Cole,** became manager of Supreme Life's Louisville branch.

"A Banker, a Builder, and a Town of Thrifty Negroes." *Opportunity,* October 1923, 311–12.

Dunnigan, Alice Allison, comp. and ed. *The Fascinating Story of Black Kentuckians: Their Heritage and Traditions.* Washington, DC: Associated Publishers, 1982.

"Kincaid Has Parlayed Loan into an Empire," *Park City Daily News* (Bowling Green), November 19, 1961, 12.

Stuart, M. S. *An Economic Detour: A History of Insurance in the Lives of American Negroes.* New York: Wendell, Malliet & Co., 1940.

Wright, George C. *Life Behind a Veil: Blacks in Louisville, Kentucky, 1865–1930.* Baton Rouge: Louisiana State Univ. Press, 1985.

—*Joshua D. Farrington*

DOMESTIC WORKERS, primarily African American female servants working for white families. As Kentucky's black women transitioned from slave labor to free labor, they found themselves working in the same domestic positions as before freedom or in similar ones. Because whites barred black women from all other employment, they accepted these positions to support their families or supplement their husbands' meager earnings. Occupations included cook, maid, laundress, waitress, day worker, general servant, and children's nurse. Although some black men worked in white households as gardeners, coachmen, chauffeurs, or general servants, most domestic workers were women.

Domestic workers often began their careers between the ages of 10 and 16, caring for young children. Those who lived with their employers complained of long work days and weeks, poor pay, sexual harassment, and deplorable living conditions for servants on the job. To distance themselves from slavery, most domestics preferred to live outside their workplace if possible, travel to their employers daily, perform their "day work," and return home each evening. Significant benefits of this arrangement were their ability to tend to their family's needs and to participate in the activities of the black community, particularly church services. Of the domestic positions, laundress or washerwoman was the most preferred occupation. A washerwoman picked up or received dirty clothing from her employers on Monday and worked on it in her own home throughout the week. She could care for her family members, prepare their meals, complete her own household chores, and involve herself in community and church work while performing her laundry jobs.

Disagreements between domestics and their employers often arose over wages for the long work days, which sometimes lasted 12 hours. The women were always poorly compensated for their rigorous work, and employers often substituted used clothing and leftover food for the agreed-on cash wages, thus swindling the women of their rightful earnings. However, some employers and workers consented to "pan-toting" or taking leftover food and pastries as a supplement to paid wages. In the 1880s, black domestics worked 60 hours per week for as little as $3. Others earned between $25 and $125 annually, scarcely enough to survive. Conflicts between domestics and their employers sometimes resulted in the women either quitting or being fired. Through their lodges and support groups, women were able to survive between jobs and blacklisted problem employers.

In 1902, the Lexington Board of Health discussed passing an ordinance to prohibit washerwomen from carrying soiled clothes on streetcars. In 1919, in response to Louisville's streetcar strike, African American washerwomen presented the possibility of also striking for a 10-cent increase in wages because of the rise of transportation costs. **Margaret Pryor,** who later became a wealthy heiress; church and civic leader Gertrude Boulder, who died in police custody after a false arrest; and the mother of the legendary jockey **Isaac Murphy** exemplified Kentucky female domestic servants. These women went daily into white employers' homes to earn a livelihood for their own families.

Clark-Lewis, Elizabeth. *Living In, Living Out: African American Domestics and the Great Migration.* New York: Kodansha America, 1994.

Lucas, Marion B. *A History of Blacks in Kentucky.* Vol. 1, *From Slavery to Segregation, 1760–1891.* Frankfort: Kentucky Historical Society, 1992.

Newspapers: "Board of Health," *LL,* February 8, 1902, 4; "Tubs May Strike Next," *Hartford Herald,* October 8, 1919, 3.

Wright, George C. *Life Behind a Veil: Blacks in Louisville, Kentucky, 1865–1930.* Baton Rouge: Louisiana State Univ. Press, 1985.

—*Karen Cotton McDaniel*

DONEGHY, JOSEPH EDMUND (b. 1914, Louisville, KY; d. 1993, Washington DC), member of numerous state and federal parole boards and of the appeals council of the Social Security Administration. Joseph Doneghy was born in Louisville to John and Maggie Doneghy, who moved to Toledo, OH, when Joseph was a small boy. By the age of 20, Joseph had graduated from the University of Toledo. He furthered his studies at the University of Toledo School of Law and the University of Chicago School of Social Work. From 1937 to 1959, he held various positions in Toledo, serving as probation counselor, Boys' Club worker for the Frederick Douglass Community Association, and playground director of Toledo's Division of Recreation. He also served as the juvenile court's boy referee. In 1950, he was named Toledo's "outstanding young man" by the Junior Chamber of Commerce for his successful rehabilitation of countless troubled juveniles. In 1959, Doneghy was appointed chairman of the Ohio Pardon and Parole Commission, which held the ultimate power in deciding whether prisoners were to be pardoned or paroled.

In 1966, Doneghy moved to Washington, DC, after he was appointed to a position as a hearing examiner on the Federal Parole Board. In 1971, he was named chief hearing examiner, and a year later he was appointed to the appeals council of the Social Security Administration. He held this position until his retirement in 1972 and continued to live in Washington until his death from a heart attack in 1993.

Newspapers: "Negro Honored for Aiding Boys," *NYT*, March 4, 1951, 61; Joseph E. Doneghy obituary, *WP*, April 26, 1993.
"Ohio Parole Chairman Joins Federal Parole Board." *Jet*, August 18, 1966, 4.
"Toledo Man Heads $12,000 a Year Parole Post." *Jet*, October 22, 1959, 5.

—*Joshua D. Farrington*

DORAM, CATHERINE "KITTY" (b. unknown, Danville, KY; d. unknown, Cincinnati, OH), businesswoman active in the Underground Railroad. Catherine "Kitty" Doram appears to be quite a conundrum, but as an African American woman aggressively involved in the **Underground Railroad,** she had to be concealed. In 1889, Laura Haviland wrote about an emotional "Kitty Dorun" when she heard news of a recaptured slave girl. The following year, Rev. Calvin Fairbank, a white abolitionist, told a story of "Kitty Dorum." She had escaped slavery at age 13 with only 36 cents and had used that money to start her seamstress business. By 1864, she was a "rich" property owner in Cincinnati, OH. He described her as "a large, tall old black woman" with the dignity of Sojourner Truth. During one of Fairbank's church services, Doram, sitting in the back of the sanctuary, raised a handkerchief and challenged the congregation to make a financial contribution. After several attempts at passing the collection plate, she was not satisfied with the results. She then waved a $10 bill, threw it on the table, and proclaimed that others should copy her. Over $100 was raised.

Doram reportedly was a member of the Underground Railroad from the 1840s, before white abolitionist Levi Coffin. She was known as "Cincinnati's most accomplished female operative," and her home sheltered many runaway slaves. When Fairbank was imprisoned for his role in assisting escaped slaves, Doram not only was on the committee to raise money for his release but also was the largest contributor.

Doram family genealogist Viola Gross maintained that Catherine Doram of Cincinnati was the unmarried sister of Thomas Anderson Doram, son of free, prominent landowners **Dennis** and **Diademia Doram** of Danville, KY. Catherine was a property owner whose 1866 will authorized the sale of her landholdings, with the proceeds going to her daughter, Mary Buckner, the Cincinnati Colored Orphan's Asylum, and two other women. Levi Coffin, a "good friend," was the executor of her will. If this Catherine Dorum was involved in the Underground Railroad, she could not have been an escaped slave because her parents were free people. She possibly told the tale of being an escaped slave to connect more easily with the people she was assisting.

In 1870, a mulatto dressmaker, Catherine Doran, lived in Cincinnati. She was 33 years old.

Fairbank, Calvin. *Rev. Calvin Fairbank during Slavery Times.* Chicago: R. R. McCabe & Company, 1890.
Griffler, Keith P. *Front Line of Freedom: African Americans and the Forging of the Underground Railroad in the Ohio Valley.* Lexington: Univ. Press of Kentucky, 2004.
Gross, Viola. *Two Hundred Years of Freedom: A Genealogy and History of the Doram, Rowe, Barbee and Allied Families.* N.p.: Kinnersley Press, 2003.
Haviland, Laura S. *A Woman's Life-Work: Labors and Experiences.* 4th ed. Chicago: Publishing Association of Friends, 1889.
U.S. Federal Census (1870).

—*Sallie L. Powell*

DORAM, DENNIS, JR. (b. 1796, Danville, KY; d. 1870, Danville, KY), and DORAM, DIADEMIA (DIADAMIA) (b. 1810, Harrodsburg, KY; d. 1883, Danville, KY), former slaves and business owners. In 1995, the discovery in an old barn of two severely damaged oil portraits of an antebellum African American couple uncovered the prominence of free, educated landowners in Kentucky. Dennis Doram and his wife, Diademia, were born in slavery. Dennis's father, Dennis Doram Sr., was purportedly an American Indian, and his mother, Lydia, was the daughter of her slave master, Gen. Thomas Barbee, and a slave woman. When Doram was only two months old, his grandfather and owner freed his slaves in his will and stipulated that the children receive an education in reading and writing and the boys in mathematics. When Diademia was four years old, her father, Gibson Taylor, a freeman, bought the freedom of his wife, Cloe, and their children for $700 from Moses O. Bledsoe of St. Louis, MO. Dennis and Diademia were married on February 15, 1830, in Boyle Co., and they had 12 children.

As an educated freeman, Doram meticulously recorded his business dealings in buying and selling property. His property consisted of land acreage in Kentucky and Indiana, lots in Danville, livestock, and slaves. One of those Danville lots included a brick house in which Kentucky's first constitution had been ratified. He possibly purchased slaves to free them because documents indicate that he emancipated Mary, a 23-year-old slave, in 1846, and the following year, he freed Lydia, a slave woman. By 1850, he had acquired 215 acres and was able to pay tuition for the education of four of his children costing $20. Ten years later, his property had increased to 300 acres on the Dix River, more livestock, and a 56-year-old male slave.

In 1866, Doram was a member of the First Convention of Colored Men of Kentucky and was elected to the Committee on Finance. He participated in the debate on a resolution claiming citizen rights for African Americans. He warned that even though the resolution was willing to forgo voting rights, it could still enrage whites.

At his death in 1870, Doram's will bequeathed a Danville lot, a horse, and a bed to each of his children. In 1873, Diademia owned 40 acres on the Dix River valued at $450. She died 10 years later. Dennis and Diademia were buried in Hilldale Cemetery in Danville, KY.

One year after Diademia's death, her daughter, Sarah Doram Faulkner, a graduate of **Berea College,** purchased the Doram property on Main and Second Sts. in Danville from her mother's estate for $1,800. She planned to modernize the building and have a store in front. Her other siblings were also influential. Gibson, considered "a highly respected" Danville citizen, operated a grocery and confectionery. Thomas Anderson Doram was a prominent farmer. Joshua served as a first sergeant in the 114th U.S. Colored Infantry at **Camp Nelson.** Robert Cassius Clay Doram fought as a buffalo soldier. In 1898, younger sister Sue opened a rock quarry.

"Current Events." *Semi-Weekly Interior Journal* (Stanford), December 7, 1883, 2.

Gross, Viola. *Two Hundred Years of Freedom: A Genealogy and History of the Doram, Rowe, Barbee and Allied Families.* N.p.: Kinnersley Press, 2003.

"Inventory of the Doram-Rowe Family Collection, 1829–1975." Special Collections Kentucky Historical Society.

Proceedings of the First Convention of Colored Men of Kentucky. Louisville: Civill & Calvert, Printers, 1866.

U.S. Federal Census (1840, 1860).

U.S. Federal Census Mortality Schedules (1850–1885).

U.S. Federal Census Slave Schedules (1860).

—*Sallie L. Powell*

DORAM, THOMAS MADISON (b. 1871, Danville, KY; d. 1941, Danville, KY), Kentucky's first black veterinarian. The child of a farmer and tradesman, Thomas Madison Doram developed an admiration for horses and other farm animals while he was growing up on an extensive stretch of land in Danville, KY, with his parents, Thomas and Susan Doram. He also learned the usefulness of a good trade from his father, practicing his abilities at woodworking while he was in public school and pursuing a career in carpentry at **Eckstein Norton Institute** in Cane Springs, KY. While he was at the institute, he helped rebuild one of the buildings that had been destroyed in a fire.

In 1896, Doram returned to his first love, entering McKillip Veterinary College in Chicago, IL. The only black student to enter the program, he excelled in his training, leading the class in various courses during his first two years. In his third year, he was appointed senior assistant instructor in pharmacology. In 1899, he graduated from the college with a doctorate in veterinary medicine. Contemporaries differed on whether he was the first or second African American to receive that honor, but more recent evidence suggests that he was probably the third black graduate from a veterinary program.

Doram practiced briefly in Evanston, IL, before returning to Danville in 1902. For the next few decades, he enjoyed a successful and celebrated practice as the state's first black veterinarian. An account published in numerous African American newspapers lauded him as "the leading veterinary surgeon" in Danville, and he was respected enough to be used as a source of testimony in a lawsuit regarding the deaths of several mules due to negligence on the part of a railroad. Occasionally, he offered veterinary advice on the care of horses in the pages of the *Danville Advocate.*

On November 20, 1941, Doram died of pneumonia in his hometown. He was buried in Hilldale Cemetery.

Cincinnati, New Orleans, and Texas Pacific R.R. Co. v. Gregg. Kentucky Law Reporter 25 (1904): 2329–2333.

Newspapers: "Indications of Much Progress," *Cleveland Gazette,* January 10, 1914, 1; "Horses Have Grip," *Maysville Public Ledger,* January 15, 1916, 2; "Funeral Tuesday for Negro Veterinarian," *Danville Advocate-Messenger,* November 23, 1941, 1.

Richardson, Clement. *National Cyclopedia of the Colored Race.* Montgomery, AL: National Publishing Company, 1919.

Richings, G. F. *Evidences of Progress among Colored People.* 8th edition. Philadelphia: G. S. Ferguson, 1902.

—*Stephen Pickering*

DOUGHERTY, CHARLES "PAT" DOUGLASS (b. 1879, Summer Shade, KY; d. 1939, Chicago, IL), baseball pitcher. Born in Summer Shade, a small town in Metcalfe Co., KY, Charles "Pat" Dougherty was one of the most talented baseball players of his era. He began his pitching career in the early 1900s with the Indianapolis Unions and the Vincennes, IN, Idaho Stars.

In addition to his talent, he was one of the few left-handed pitchers in the Negro leagues, which made him a highly recruited athlete. In 1909, he signed with Chicago's Leland Giants as a major player on a star-studded team that included Rube Foster and "Pete" Hill. With Dougherty's help, the Giants went on to an unheard-of 123–6 record in the 1910 season. The following year, after an impressive performance against the Chicago Giants, Dougherty obtained the nickname "the Black Marquard" after the white star pitcher Rube Marquard of the Chicago Cubs. He ultimately joined the Giants from 1914 to 1917, where he continued to be one of the most dominant pitchers in the league. He remained in Chicago until his death in 1939.

Pat Dougherty, alongside **Clinton Thomas,** ranks as one of the most successful baseball players in the Negro leagues to come from Kentucky.

Debono, Paul. *The Indianapolis ABCs: History of a Premier Team in the Negro Leagues.* Jefferson, NC: McFarland, 2007.

Heaphy, Leslie, ed. *Black Baseball and Chicago: Essays on Players, Teams, and Games.* Jefferson, NC: McFarland, 2006.

Porter, David L. *Biographical Dictionary of American Sports, Baseball, Revised and Expanded Edition A–F.* Westport, CT: Greenwood Press, 2000.

—*Joshua D. Farrington*

DOUGLAS, LAURA (b. 1949, Louisville, KY), business executive and attorney. Louisville native Laura Green was one of 10 children of George W. and Mamie Lee Green. She later married Robert L. Douglas. She graduated with a degree in political science from the University of Louisville in 1969. Five years later, she earned her JD from the University of Louisville's Brandeis School of Law and then became an attorney for Chevron USA in Louisville until 1977.

In 1979, Douglas began working in Iowa. She held various positions, including director of affirmative action at the University of Iowa. From 1984 to 1985, she was an instructor of Afro-American studies at Ohio University. She then returned to Kentucky and worked as an attorney and manager of the Louisville Legal Aid Society for five years. In 1995, after her job as legal counsel at Louisville's Metropolitan Sewer District, Kentucky governor-elect Paul Patton appointed Douglas to his cabinet as secretary of the Public Protection Cabinet. She was only the second African American woman to head a state cabinet.

In 1999, Douglas resigned her cabinet position and joined the Louisville Water Company as vice president and general counsel. The next year, Governor Patton appointed her to the **Kentucky State University** Board of Regents. She later became chairperson of the board. In 2003, Louisville mayor Jerry Abramson requested that Douglas chair the Citizens Commission on Police Accountability. In October of that year, she joined Louisville Gas and Electric and Kentucky Utilities as director of communications. She became the company's vice president of corporate responsibility and community affairs in November 2007.

Douglas has three children with her husband, Robert, an emeritus professor of the University of Louisville's Pan-African Studies Department, and five stepchildren from his previous marriage. She has served on various civic and professional boards, including those of Louisville's Actors Theatre and Republic Bank and Trust Company.

Kentucky Birth Index, 1911–1999.
"Laura Douglass." Louisville Gas and Electric and Kentucky Utilities. http://lge-ku.com/douglas_bio.asp (accessed June 22, 2012).
Newspapers: "Patton Names 4 More to Cabinet Positions," *LHL,* December 7, 1995; "Chairwoman Comes with Range of Experiences," *CJ,* March 7, 2003, A1; "Mamie Lee Green," *CJ,* June 28, 2005, obituaries.

—*Sallie L. Powell*

DOWERY, ROBERT L., SR. (b. 1893, Shelbyville, KY; d. 1952, Shelbyville, KY), educator. Described as tall and slender, Robert L. Dowery Sr. grew up in Shelbyville, KY, and started his teaching career there in 1916. Initially, an additional job as an insurance agent supplemented his teaching salary. His teaching career was also briefly interrupted by his military service in World War I.

Dowery became principal at **Franklin High School** in 1920. Two years later, he served as principal at Taylor County Training and High School in Campbellsville. Beginning in 1925, as principal, he and his three teachers successfully enhanced Elizabethtown's East Side High School, a four-room building, by broadening the curriculum and adding activities. These improvements included college preparatory courses, spelling bees, a glee club, field trips to places like Mammoth Cave, and sports such as girls' and boys' basketball. He also changed the name of the school to **Bond-Washington Grade and High School.**

In his 10 years in Elizabethtown, as a member of the **Kentucky Negro Educational Association** (KNEA), Dowery organized and became president of the Fourth District Teachers Association. He pushed for African American supervisors in the state's segregated Department of Education. His colleagues viewed him as "one of our most progressive young educators."

Dowery earned his AB degree from Kentucky State Industrial College for Negroes (later named **Kentucky State University**) in 1931 and his MA degree from Atlanta University in 1942. While holding principal positions in Manchester, Columbia, Franklin, and Shelbyville, he climbed the education profession's ladder through his diligent work in the KNEA and reached the rank of president of the organization in 1950. In his campaign

platform, some of his goals included amendments to Kentucky's **Day Law** (which segregated education by race), federal aid for education, a minimum yearly salary of $2,400 for teachers, and equal education for every child. He often signed his presidential messages to the KNEA with phrases such as "Yours for an aggressive and progressive K.N.E.A." or "Yours for an equal educational opportunity for every Kentucky child."

Dowery and his wife, Melinda, had two children: Robert L. Jr. and Mary Amy. Robert Jr. earned his BS from Kentucky State College in 1949, and Mary earned her degree from Knoxville College in 1950. Robert Jr. became a coach and teacher in Drakesboro, KY, until he was recruited by the Harlem Globetrotters in 1951. After his playing days, he returned to the education profession in Maryland.

In 1952, Dowery retired as KNEA president because of personal and family illnesses. He died eight months later. He was buried in Zachary Taylor National Cemetery in Louisville, KY.

"District Organizers,"*KNEAJ* 1, no. 1 (October 1930), 2; "Announcements," 21, no. 2 (March 1950), 4; "The President's Letter," 22, no. 1 (December 1950), 4; "Letter On Salary," 23, no. 1 (February-March 1935), 30.
Proceedings of the Kentucky Negro Educational Association, April 17–20, 1929.
Robinson, Lottie Offett. *The Bond-Washington Story: The Education of Black People, Elizabethtown, Kentucky.* N.p.: Self-published, 1983.
Yenser, Thomas, ed. *Who's Who in Colored America, 1930–1932.* 3rd ed. Brooklyn, NY: Thomas Yenser, 1933.

—*Sallie L. Powell*

DRANE, JOHN FRANKLIN (b. 1866, Washington Co., KY; d. 1931, Hopkinsville, KY), Baptist minister. John Franklin Drane struggled in poverty to become a minister. He graduated from Louisville's **Central High School** but was unable to afford formal classes in theology. Instead, he took correspondence courses from McKinley Extension University of Oak Park, IL. In 1898, at age 30, he became a minister, serving Louisville's Church of the Good Shepherd. He later moved to Covington to work in the purchasing of Ninth Street Baptist Church.

In 1905, while living in Covington, Drane acted as the treasurer of the 26th Annual Session of the Ministers and Messengers at the Consolidated District Convention of Negro Baptists in Kentucky. After his work in Covington, he moved to Mays Lick and created a building fund there. He was then appointed to the Committee on Finance of the Consolidated Baptist Association. In 1907, he was called to the pastorate of the Plymouth Baptist Church in Maysville.

-Franklin traveled the country during his ministry. He attended the **General Association of Baptists in Kentucky** in Hopkinsville in 1908 and the 1909 National Baptist Convention in Columbus, OH. He was a Mason, an Odd Fellow, and a Good Samaritan. In religious bodies, he served on the Baptist Foreign Mission Board of the National Convention and as chairperson of the Union District Association and Sunday School Convention. He was also grand chaplain of the Free and Accepted Masons. He founded and was elected president of the Taft Republican Club, which met in his Maysville church to encourage African American voters to support Republican candidates. He publicly invited whites to attend his Sunday services. On January 1, 1915, Franklin took charge of Bowling Green's State Street Baptist Church, which had a seating capacity of 1,100 and cost $20,000. He also edited Bowling Green's weekly newspaper, *Blaze*. He was married twice and had three children. He later moved to Hopkinsville, where he died in 1931.

Kentucky Death Records, 1852–1953.
Newspapers: "Women's Work," *AB*, December 9, 1904, 1; "Our Colored Citizens," *Daily Public Ledger* (Maysville), July 14, 1909, 3.
Richardson, Clement. *The National Cyclopedia of the Colored Race.* Montgomery, AL: National Publishing Company, 1919.
U.S. Federal Census (1930).

—*Sallie L. Powell*

DRURY, THEODORE (b. ca. 1867, Kentucky; d. ca. 1943, Philadelphia, PA), founder of one of the first and most successful black-operated opera companies during the early twentieth century. Although little is known of Theodore Drury's early life, he was one of the most important cultural African American figures of his era. According to a 1900 edition of *Colored American* magazine, Drury was born in Kentucky to a "musical family." Beyond this scarce information, Drury formed one of the first and most successful black opera troupes, the Theodore Drury Opera Company, in New York City in 1889. Although he typically used white orchestras, the casts and leading roles were almost exclusively black. Early reviews were mixed, but after he completed his studies as one of the few black students at the National Conservatory of Music, his company became enormously popular by the early 1900s. Between 1900 and 1908, the company presented Bizet's *Carmen,* Gounod's *Faust,* and Verdi's *Aida,* among many other works. to black and white audiences at the Lexington Avenue Opera House in New York City.

After a period of study abroad in the 1910s, Drury settled in Boston, where he established a music studio and taught voice, piano, elocution, and French conversation. He even published a book on music theory. He later relocated his studio to Philadelphia, where he revived the Drury Opera Company and presented *Faust* at a 1928 Republican Party event that featured the governor of Rhode Island. He also produced a well-received version of *Carmen* in 1938.

According to the 1940 U.S. federal census, Drury, in his mid-70s, lived with his wife, Tiny, at Wyalusing Ave. in Philadelphia. He worked as a private music teacher, and his wife worked as a maid. After his death, his wife still lived in the same home in 1950.

During an era in which minstrel shows and vaudeville were immensely popular, Theodore Drury defied popular stereotypes. In 1906, a white reviewer for the *New York Times* raved about the 100 talented black men and women who made up the cast of Drury's production of *Aida.* Drury's lasting legacy was that in an era steeped with racism, he demonstrated that African Americans could appear on the stage not just as comedic caricatures but as serious and talented actors and vocalists.

Logan, Rayford W., and Michael Winston. *Dictionary of American Negro Biography.* New York: Norton, 1982.

Newspapers: "Colored Opera Stars Produce Verdi's 'Aida,'" *NYT,* May 29, 1906, 11; "'Faust' Presented by Colored Company," *Evening Tribune* (Rhode Island), October 31, 1928, 11.
Scheurer, Timothy, ed. *American Popular Music: The Nineteenth Century and Tin Pan Alley.* Madison, WI: Popular Press, 1989.
U.S. City Directories, 1821–1989.
U.S. Federal Census (1940).

—*Joshua D. Farrington*

DUDLEY, THOMAS UNDERWOOD (b. 1837, Richmond, VA; d. 1904, New York, NY), Episcopal bishop. Thomas Underwood Dudley, Episcopal bishop of Kentucky, was born in Richmond, VA, on September 26, 1837, to Thomas and Maria (Friend) Dudley. He graduated from the University of Virginia in 1858. After serving as a major in the Confederate army, Dudley graduated from the Seminary of Virginia in Alexandria in 1867. He served the church in Virginia and Maryland, was made assistant bishop of Kentucky in 1875, and became the second bishop of Kentucky in 1884. Dudley was widely respected for his vigor and piety and held various community and national offices, including chancellor of the University of the South in Sewanee, TN (1894–1904), and chairman of the House of Bishops (1901–1904). His three principal interests were missionary expansion of the church among all the economic classes of Kentucky, education, and the free and unrestricted rights of black Americans. In *How Shall We Help the Negro?,* Dudley, who was characterized by the bishop of South Carolina as "too much reconstructed," wrote that "the negro is a man and a citizen; that the conditions of our life are all changed; that old things are passed away, and that the new things which are come to us demand . . . the uplifting of the negro."

Dudley married Fanny B. Cochran in July 1859, and they had four daughters before her death. In 1869, he married Virginia F. Rowland, with whom he had two sons and a daughter; his second wife died in 1877. In June 1881, he married Mary E. Aldrich, who survived him. Dudley died in New York City on January 27, 1904, and was buried in Louisville's Cave Hill Cemetery.

Lee, Rebecca Smith, and Frances Keller Swinford. *The Great Elm Tree: The Heritage of the Episcopal Diocese of Lexington.* Lexington, KY: Faith House Press, 1969.
Wynes, Charles E. "Bishop Thomas U. Dudley and the Uplift of the Negro." *RKHS* 65 (July 1967): 230–38.

—*Rick Kennedy*

DUFFY, WILLIAM M., JR. (b. 1953, Louisville, KY), sculptor. Born and raised in Louisville, William Duffy graduated from the Louisville School of Art in 1976. Although he studied painting and sculpting with wood and metal, it was by a fluke that he discovered his "first love": stone. While he was driving home from his job at the Louisville Museum of History and Science, he came across a car accident that had just occurred. A car had smashed into a bank building's column, sending chucks of marble into the street. Duffy asked if he could take a piece home and immediately began constructing a sculpture. He knew immediately that he discovered his "destiny."

Teaching himself the skills needed to sculpt stone, Duffy ultimately left his job at the museum to focus exclusively on his art.

His sculptures have won over 30 awards and can be found in numerous locations throughout Louisville, including Phillip Morris USA, YUM! Brands, and the J. B. Speed Art Museum. He also served on the Kentucky Art Council's marketing program, Kentucky Crafted, and was commissioned by the council to create the award presented to the winners of the Governor's Awards in the Arts in 2008.

Duffy has additionally contributed generously to educating Louisville's youth by frequently teaching his skills and appreciation of sculpture to students across the city. In 1997, he received a commendation from the board of education for 25 years of "sharing his outstanding artistic gifts with students and staff in the Jefferson County Public Schools."

His sculptures often focus on the themes of family and love and are inspired by African, Oceanic, and Eskimo tribal sculptures. Despite these distinct styles, his pieces attempt to show the universal experiences of family and love, regardless of culture. According to Duffy, "My subject matter is also universal with the intent of portraying the human bond that exists between us all."

Duffy, Lindsey A. "William M. Duffy, Sculptor." Louisville, KY, 2010. http://www.wmduffy.com (accessed November 15, 2010).
Newspapers: "Painting Inspires Stamp, Greeting Card," *LCJ,* December 5, 1999, 61; "Jefferson Celebrates Black History," *LCJ,* February 26, 2002, 1B.

—*Joshua D. Farrington*

DUKA, VERONICA MARIE (b. 1977, Campbellsville, KY), Miss Kentucky winner and Miss America contestant.

Campbellsville, KY, native Janet L. Johnson went to New York City to become a model and met and married Scott Duka, who was white. Their daughter, Veronica Marie Duka, was born on February 11, 1977.

In 1992, as a student at Campbellsville's Durham High School, Duka competed in the 200-meter dash at the Class A state high school track-and-field competition. She was raised by a single mother, and beauty pageants helped fund her college education. She attended Campbellsville College with a theater major and a music minor. In 1995, as Miss South Central Kentucky, she was second runner-up in the Miss Kentucky contest. The next year, Duka won the Miss Kentucky crown, becoming only the second African American to win the competition. **Lydia Lewis** was first in 1973.

At 19, Duka was also one of the youngest winners. She identified herself as biracial, and her platform emphasized multicultural education. She was 10th runner-up in the Miss America contest. In her role as Miss Kentucky, Duka took a year off from college and earned her $20,000 scholarship funds by giving numerous speeches. The Kentucky Department of Agriculture hired her to speak at schools, sharing the message that underage tobacco usage was illegal. Critics attacked this message, claiming that tobacco's health risks should also be included.

After Duka's reign as Miss Kentucky, a local Lexington television station hired her. Afterward, she moved to New York City. In 2000, she performed in the play *Dracula*. She later married Sean Cort.

Veronica Duka.

Newspapers: "State High School Track and Field Results," *KP,* June 1, 1992, 7K; "A Cause beyond Pageantry," *LHL,* July 18, 1996, 3; "Miss KY Paid to Tell Youths about Tobacco Law," *LHL,* July 18, 1996, C1; "Triumph over Adversity Is Pageant Refrain," *Newark (NJ) Star-Ledger,* September 11, 1996, 15; "Critics: Miss Kentucky Soft on Tobacco," *KP,* November 21, 1996, 12A; "A Reign That Poured: Year Was Busy for Miss Kentucky," *LHL,* June 15, 1997, J1; "The Heather Channel," *LHL,* October 3, 1997, 2.
Willis, John. *Theatre World, 1999–2000.* New York: Applause Theatre & Cinema Books, 2003.

—*Sallie L. Powell*

DUNBAR, JOSHUA (b. ca. 1822, Garrard Co., KY; d. 1885, Dayton, OH), slave, soldier, and father of poet Paul Laurence Dunbar.

Birth information on Joshua Dunbar, a Kentucky slave, has remained scarce, and sources disagree. According to the U.S. Colored Troops Military Service Records, 1861–1865, Dunbar was born about 1822, but according to the U.S. National Homes for Disabled Volunteer Soldiers, 1866–1938, his birth would have been around 1817. Both records have his birth location as Garrett Co., KY. Since there is no county of that name in Kentucky, it has been assumed that he was born in Garrard Co.

During slavery, Dunbar was trained as a plasterer. He escaped slavery via the **Underground Railroad** to Canada but then returned to the United States to enlist in the military during the Civil War. On June 2, 1863, Dunbar signed with the U.S. Colored

Troops in the 55th Massachusetts Infantry. Because of varicose veins, he was discharged on October 22, 1863. On January 9, 1864, Dunbar enlisted in the 5th Massachusetts Cavalry and was honorably discharged with the rank of sergeant on October 31, 1865.

Dunbar married **Matilda Murphy** on December 24, 1871. They settled in Dayton, OH, and had two children, Elizabeth, who died in early childhood, and Paul Laurence, who later became a famous poet. A few years later, the Dunbars separated and then were granted a divorce on January 9, 1877. The Dayton city directory of that year listed Matilda as a widow.

Although Paul Laurence Dunbar did not live with his father during most of his childhood, he nevertheless may have used the life experiences of his father as a model for some of his works, such as the poem "The Colored Soldiers." One of Dunbar's stories may provide clues to Joshua Dunbar's escape. "The Ingrate," first published in *The Strength of Gideon* in 1900, tells the story of a Kentucky slave named Josh whose owner hires him out as a plasterer to an employer in Lexington. Josh's owner decides to teach him to read and write so that he will not be cheated out of his wages, but he is shocked when his slave forges a pass and escapes to Canada.

Joshua Dunbar died of pneumonia at the National Home for Disabled Soldiers in Dayton, OH, on August 16, 1885. He was buried in Dayton National Cemetery. A few years later, the Dayton city directory listed Matilda as the "widow of Joshua." On June 13, 1917, she filed for his Civil War pension.

Dunbar, Joshua. Military records (courtesy of Mr. Paul LaRue, Washington Courthouse, Ohio), including muster rolls and discharge papers; Matilda Dunbar's widow's pension application (also in the possession of Paul LaRue).

Dunbar, Paul Laurence. *Works of Paul Laurence Dunbar.* The Perfect Library, 2013.

Jarrett, Gene Andrew, and Thomas Lewis Morgan, ed. *The Complete Stories of Paul Laurence Dunbar.* Athens: Ohio Univ. Press, 2005.

National Park Service. http://www.nps.gov/history/Nr/twhp/wwwlps/lessons/115dayton/115putting.htm and http://www.nps.gov/daav/historyculture/joshuadunbarsfamilytree.htm.

U.S. City Directories, 1821–1989.

U.S. Civil War Pension Index: General Index to Pension Files, 1861–1934.

U.S. Colored Troops Military Service Records, 1861–1865.

U.S. National Homes for Disabled Volunteer Soldiers, 1866–1938.

—*Joanna Lile*

DUNBAR, MATILDA MURPHY (b. ca. 1846, Lexington or Shelby Co., KY; d. 1934, Dayton, OH), mother of poet Paul Laurence Dunbar. Matilda was born into slavery but was not certain of her exact birth date. Sources also disagree on her birthplace. In her earliest memories, she was about seven years old when she was sold to David Glass near Lexington, KY. Some narratives maintained that a "cultured" man in Lexington owned her. The slave owner read aloud to his wife as Matilda sat at his feet, and this act perpetuated her love of poetry. However, later in life, Matilda told an interviewer about serving a myriad of masters in the Louisville area. One was Dr. Cary, an uncle of poets Alice and Phoebe Cary. Matilda said that their poetry

prompted her to encourage her son, Paul Laurence Dunbar, to write poetry.

Matilda and Wilson Murphy were married while both were slaves. They had two sons, William and Robert. Shortly after the **Emancipation Proclamation,** Wilson died. Matilda left Louisville to be with her mother and grandmother in Dayton, OH. She met the much older **Joshua Dunbar,** a plasterer and former Kentucky slave who had fled to Canada but had returned to fight in the 55th Massachusetts Infantry, an all–African American unit. They married in 1871, and Paul Laurence Dunbar was born the next year. The couple divorced a few years later.

As a single, illiterate mother, Matilda learned to read and write from schoolchildren and worked in her home as a laundress. Paul helped her with preparing the fire and carrying the hot water. One of her greatest joys was when he graduated from high school.

Matilda, without a doubt, influenced her son. He dedicated his first publication, *Oak and Ivy*, in 1892, to her. His poem "When Malindy Sings" honored her vocal skills. Her stories of slave days reportedly influenced his poetry. She was known for her wit and told one reporter that she had forbidden her son to travel into the South until he was a grown man.

After her son's death in 1906, she dedicated their home to his memory. She was known to give personal tours of his library even in her older years. Matilda died 28 years after her son. In 1936, the Dunbar House became the first state African American memorial.

Brown, Hallie Quinn. *Homespun Heroines and Other Women of Distinction.* Xenia, OH: Aldine, 1926.

Gentry, Tony. *Paul Laurence Dunbar: Poet.* New York: Chelsea House, 1989.

Newspapers: "Mother of Dunbar, Famous Poet, Dies in Dayton," *BAA,* March 3, 1934, 22; "When Mrs. Matilda Dunbar Was a Little Girl," *BAA,* March 3, 1934, 5.

U.S. Federal Census (1880).

Wiggins, Lida Keck. *The Life and Works of Paul Laurence Dunbar.* New York: Dodd, Mead, 1907.

—*Sallie L. Powell*

DUNBAR SCHOOLS, more than a dozen African American schools across the state of Kentucky named in honor of the noted poet. Paul Laurence Dunbar (1872–1906), a poet and novelist**,** became one of the first widely known and well-regarded African American writers. Late in his career, and particularly after his death, it became common to name African American schools in his honor. In the first decade of the twentieth century, at least four schools, located throughout Kentucky, were named after Dunbar. By 1936, over a dozen Kentucky elementary and high schools bore the name of the esteemed poet.

In 1894, Louisville educator and poet **Joseph Cotter** founded Ormsby Avenue Colored School, which was renamed the Eighth Street Colored School when it relocated to Eighth and Kentucky Sts. in 1897. In 1910, Cotter renamed it Dunbar School in honor of his friend and fellow poet **George Marion McClellan** served as principal of the school from 1911 to 1919. In 1916, the school relocated to the vacant **Central High School** building, where it remained open until 1965.

Lexington Dunbar High School.

The opening of other Dunbar schools followed, most in the early 1900s. In 1899, the three-room building of Somerset's Dunbar School was constructed. Its first high school class graduated in 1925. In 1942, the school was rebuilt, and the new building functioned as a high school until 1956. In 1964, the Dunbar School consolidated with Somerset High School, and the building was closed. Another African American Dunbar school was opened in **Elsmere,** KY, around 1900. Located at 421 Spring St., the Elsmere Dunbar School taught elementary grades. A new, larger building, renamed the Wilkins Heights School, replaced the Elsmere Dunbar School in 1948. Additionally, the Dunbar High School in Mayfield, KY, became part of the Mayfield Independent City School District when it was founded in 1908. In 1921, a new building was constructed, and the school expanded to include a high school. The Mayfield Dunbar School closed when the school district desegregated in 1958.

In the following decades, many more schools adopted the writer's name. The Dunbar School in Cadiz, KY, was organized in 1916. The school, housed in a four-room frame building, eventually consolidated with Dotson High School in Princeton, KY. In 1920, the Dunbar School in Nicholasville, KY, moved into a four-room brick structure. By 1930, the school had expanded to include a four-year high school and was renamed Rosenwald-Dunbar in recognition of Rosenwald funding. The school closed in 1963; it later reopened as a desegregated elementary school. The Dunbar High School building in Owensboro, KY, was completed in 1923. The school began as a grade school, having replaced the Upper Ward Colored School. In 1958, the Owensboro Public School District was desegregated, although Dunbar High School remained open as an alternative for African American students until 1963. Organized in 1936, the Palmer-Dunbar Colored High School served the African American population in Wheelwright, KY. The school was named in part for the district superintendent, Palmer Hall, in addition to honoring Dunbar's memory.

The Dunbar High School in Morganfield, KY, was established in 1930 to serve the entire African American population of Union Co., KY. In 1956, the Morganfield school became part of a nationally publicized controversy. On August 31, eight students from Dunbar High School enrolled in the all-white Sturgis High School. On the first day of class, the students were prevented from entering the school by a large mob; city officials and school board members refused to intervene on their behalf. Governor Albert Chandler sent state police and the Kentucky National Guard to Sturgis in order to prevent the situation from escalating to violence. On September 6, the students were escorted into the school by 200 guardsmen. They attended Sturgis High School for a week while over half of the school's white students boycotted. Finally, after a ruling by the state attorney general that prohibited the students from attending Sturgis until a definitive integration plan was implemented in Union Co., the students were refused admission to the school on September 19. A year later, the board of education closed Dunbar High School, and the students were transferred to Sturgis High School.

Two other Dunbar schools taught African American students in Kentucky in the early part of the twentieth century, although little has been written about either. In Paducah, KY, the Dunbar School was one of seven public schools for African Americans in the city. In Carrollton, KY, a brick building housed the Dunbar Colored School, which was opened before 1900.

The best-known Kentucky Dunbar school, Paul Laurence Dunbar High School in Lexington, was built on Upper St. in 1922. The school served grades 9 through 12 and became the first African American high school in Kentucky to be accredited by the Southern Association of Colleges and Secondary Schools in 1930. Professor **William Fouse** served as the first principal of Dunbar High School until his retirement in 1938. The school remained open until the district desegregated in 1967, and it then served as a junior high school until 1972. Most of the original building was demolished in 1974. Because of the proud tradition of Dunbar High School in Lexington, the Fayette County School Board agreed to name the next high school built in the district after the famous poet. The new school, located in southeastern Fayette Co., was completed in 1990. Although few ties to the old school were maintained, the design of the new Paul Laurence Dunbar High School did include a room of memorabilia associated with the old Dunbar school.

The list of schools named in honor of Dunbar has served as an inspiration to students and a tremendous testament to the influential legacy of a great African American poet.

Jefferson County Public Schools Archives and Records Center. "Jefferson County Public School History." Louisville, KY, 2008. http://media.jefferson.k12.ky.us/groups/jcpshistory/ (accessed September 11, 2012).

Jessamine County Historical Society. *History of Jessamine County, Kentucky.* Dallas: Taylor, 1993.

Newspapers: "Colored Notes," *L-L,* February 1, 1932, 10; "Lexington's Black Community Found Magic at Dunbar," *LHL,* February 16, 1986, B1; "Ground Broken for Dunbar High School," *LHL,* November 15, 1988, B1; "School's Name Evokes Mixed Emotions," *LHL,* January 24, 1990, B1; "Schools of Distinction," *KP,* January 19, 1998, 4K; "Dunbar School to Hold Reunion This Weekend," *(Somerset, KY) Commonwealth Journal,* August 14, 2008.

Potter, Hugh O. *A History of Owensboro and Daviess County, Kentucky.* Owensboro, KY: Daviess County Historical Society, 1974.

Wright, George C. *A History of Blacks in Kentucky.* Vol. 2, *In Pursuit of Equality, 1890–1980.* Frankfort: Kentucky Historical Society, 1992.

—*Elizabeth Schaller*

DUNCAN, LA VAL TODD (b. 1907, Louisville, KY; d. 1979, Louisville, KY), businessman and insurance executive. The only child of Henry and Cora McClasky Duncan, La Val Duncan moved in his youth from Louisville to Nelson Co., KY. While he attended school, his father held various jobs, including farmer, shoemaker, and barber. Duncan graduated from Louisville's Simmons University (later known as **Simmons College of Kentucky**) in 1927 and earned his business administration degree from Ohio State University in 1933. In the following year, he became an insurance agent for the **Mammoth Life and Accident Insurance Company.**

Duncan advanced through the organization, holding positions of field auditor, cashier, treasurer, and vice president. He belonged to numerous civic organizations and fraternities, such as the Downtown Kiwanis Club of Louisville, the National Association of Housing and Redevelopment, the National Insurance Association, and the National Conference of Christians and Jews. In 1969, he was elected chairman of Louisville's Housing Authority and was reelected to the position in 1975. He served on the boards of various businesses, including Saints Mary and Elizabeth Hospital and the formerly known **Red Cross Hospital,** which had been created by some Louisville African American doctors in 1899.

Duncan married De Jarnette Pate of Christiansburg, VA, in 1937. They had two children: a son, La Val Jr., and a daughter, DeVon. At his death, he was married to Julia Duncan. In Duncan's honor, the family requested donations to the United Negro College Fund.

"Biography." LaVal T. Duncan Papers, 1958–1965. University Archives and Records Center, Louisville, KY. Viewed through the Kentucky Virtual Library Archival Finding Aids. http://kdl.kyvl.org/cgi/f/findaid/findaid-idx?c=kyead;cc=kyead;q1=duncan;rgn=main;view=text;didno=1976-106 (accessed February 16, 2011).

Kentucky Birth Records, 1852–1910.

Kentucky Death Index, 1911–2000.

"La Val Duncan, Former Housing Board Chief, Dies." *LCJ*, May 6, 1979, B4.

U.S. Federal Census (1910, 1920, 1930).

—*Sallie L. Powell*

DUNCAN, ROBERT TODD (b. 1903, Danville, KY; d. 1998, Washington, DC), baritone singer. Born in Danville, KY, to John Charles Duncan and Letitia "Lettie" (Cooper) Duncan, Robert Todd Duncan spent most of his youth in Somerset, KY, where he attended **Dunbar School.** Duncan's musical aptitude was evident at age six when his mother discovered him playing the music of Bach by ear on their piano. He graduated from the high school department at Simmons University (later known as **Simmons College of Kentucky**) in Louisville in 1922. That same year, he entered Butler University in Indianapolis and graduated in 1925. Subsequently, Duncan returned to Louisville, where he taught music classes at Simmons University. In 1929, he undertook graduate studies at Columbia University Teachers College. Soon he taught music and voice as a faculty member at Howard University.

Besides teaching, Duncan made his New York opera debut with the Aeolian Opera (an all-black opera company) in Mascagni's *Cavalleria Rusticana* in 1934, where one of George Gershwin's friends heard him perform. This led to Duncan's lead role in *Porgy and Bess* on Broadway in 1935. In 1936, Duncan successfully led a protest movement of the cast of the on-tour Washington, DC, run of *Porgy and Bess* until the National Theatre audience was fully integrated. As the first black singer to perform in a major New York City opera company in 1945, he played a crucial role in desegregation.

Duncan's additional Broadway credits include the musicals *Cabin in the Sky* (1940) and *Lost in the Stars* (1949), for which he won a Tony Award. He appeared in the feature film *Unchained* (1955), in which he introduced one of the most popular recorded songs of the twentieth century, "Unchained Melody."

Paul Laurence Dunbar High School, Domestic Art and Science class, Lexington, KY, 1929.

In 1934, Duncan married Gladys Jackson and had one son, Charles. He taught into his 90s. He died at the age of 95 in Washington, DC, on February 28, 1998. In 2005, Todd Duncan was inducted into the Kentucky Civil Rights Hall of Fame in Frankfort and the Kentucky Music Hall of Fame in Renfro Valley and in 2006 into the Gallery of Great Black Kentuckians.

Kozinn, Allan. "Todd Duncan, 95; Sang Porgy and Helped Desegregate Opera." *NYT*, March 2, 1998, A15.
Robinson-Oturu, Gail M. "The Life and Legacy of Todd Duncan: A Biographical Study." PhD diss., New York Univ., 2000.
Schick, Elizabeth A., ed. *Current Biography Yearbook, 1998.* New York: H. W. Wilson Company, 640.
Vallance, Tom. "Obituary: Todd Duncan." *Independent,* March 3, 1998, Features 18.

—*John Schlipp*

DUNHAM, NORMAN EARLE (b. 1890, Lexington or Scott Co., KY; d. unknown), physician. Norman Earle Dunham, the second son of Levi and Louise (Lulu) Scott Dunham, attended and graduated from Fayette Co. schools. After graduating from Clark University in Worchester, MA, he took premedical courses at Fisk University from 1914 to 1917. The tall, slender Dunham then returned to Kentucky. Most likely to earn money for medical school, he farmed in partnership with others near Louisville.

In 1921, Dunham earned his medical degree from historically black Meharry Medical College in Nashville, TN. He married Sadie Lyerson of Nashville a few months after graduation. The couple then moved to Covington, KY, where they purchased a home at 1222 Russell St. He started his medical practice while Sadie taught school in Cincinnati, OH.

Dunham was active in the Baptist church, a Mason, and a member of the **Kappa Alpha Psi Fraternity**'s executive committee. As a general surgeon and member of the Tri-City Medical Association, he served at Cincinnati's Mercy Hospital and was the medical examiner for the **United Brothers of Friendship,** an organization that had been formed in 1861 in Louisville, KY.

Dabney, Wendell P. *Cincinnati's Colored Citizens: Historical, Sociological and Biographical.* Cincinnati: Dabney, 1926.
Kentucky Death Records, 1852–1953.
U.S. Federal Census (1900, 1930).
World War I Draft Registration Cards, 1917–1918.

—*Sallie L. Powell*

DUNLAP, MOLLIE ERNESTINE (b. 1898, Paducah, KY; d. 1977, Ann Arbor, MI), librarian, editor, bibliographer, and activist. The first child of Robert H. and Emma M. (Donavan) Dunlap, Mollie Ernestine Dunlap received her early education in Paducah, KY. Beginning in 1918, she earned degrees from Wilberforce University, Ohio State University, and the University of Michigan, where in 1932 she received her MA in library science as a recipient of a fellowship from the Julius Rosenwald Fund. While she was a student at Wilberforce, she served as an instructor for five years. In 1925, she became a librarian at Winston-Salem Teachers College in North Carolina. She returned to Wilberforce in 1934 as its librarian.

Dunlap launched a survey of the reading habits of African American students at various colleges and universities. She used freshmen and seniors in an effort to determine their reading habits as they entered and departed each institution. Although her survey determined that students read little outside required assignments, it concluded that students did not need encouragement to read newspapers. Many students liked fiction, and their second choice was poetry. Dunlap concluded in a 1933 publication that college libraries not only had an educational responsibility to students but also should provide recreational reading.

In her 1935 *Journal of Negro Education* essay "Special Collections of Negro Literature in the United States," Dunlap demonstrated the need for bibliographical African American literature. She collected data from numerous African American educational institutions. On the basis of her research, she suggested the need for an extensive, detailed account of the myriad of African American archival collections.

Dunlap belonged to various library organizations. As a member of the American Library Association's (ALA) Committee on Racial Discrimination, she drafted a resolution for the equal treatment of African American librarians not only in the ALA but also in all libraries. After retiring in 1966, she returned to Central State University to create and organize the African American archival collection at the Hallie Q. Brown Memorial Library. She became the university archivist in 1968.

Living in an Ann Arbor, MI, retirement home, Dunlap died in 1977, and her body was buried in Wilberforce, OH.

Dunlap, Mollie E. "Recreational Reading of Negro College Students." *Journal of Negro Education* 2, no. 4 (October 1933): 448–59.
———. "Special Collections of Negro Literature in the United States." *Journal of Negro Education* 4, no. 4 (October 1935): 482–89.
Fleming, G. James, and Christian E. Burckel, eds. *Who's Who in Colored America.* 7th ed. *Supplement.* Yonkers-on-Hudson, NY: Christian E. Burckel & Associates, 1950.
Jordan, Casper Leroy. "Mollie Ernestine Dunlap." In *Notable Black American Women,* vol. 2, edited by Jessie Carney Smith, 194–95. Detroit: Gale Research, 1996.
Social Security Death Index.
U.S. Federal Census (1900, 1910, 1920, 1930).
Washington, Dorothy Ann. In *Dictionary of American Library Biography,* vol. 3, edited by Donald G. Davis, 85–88. Westport, CT: Libraries Unlimited, 2003.

—*Sallie L. Powell*

DUNNIGAN, ALICE ALLISON (b. 1906, Logan Co., KY; d. 1983, Washington, DC), journalist and civil rights activist. Born in 1906 in Logan Co., near Russellville, KY, Alice Allison Dunnigan was the daughter of Lena Pittman and Willie Allison, a laundress and a tobacco tenant farmer. She attended rural segregated schools, began writing for the *Owensboro Enterprise* at the age of 13, and graduated from Knob City High School in Russellville. In 1926, she received a teaching certificate from Kentucky State College (later named **Kentucky State University**) in Frankfort, and she also attended West Kentucky Industrial College (later known as **West Kentucky Community and Technical College**) in Paducah.

From 1924 to 1942, Dunnigan taught at Mt. Pisgah, a rural segregated school in Todd Co. She continued writing African American news for area and state newspapers, which included the

DUPEE, GEORGE WASHINGTON   155

Alice Dunnigan.

Hopkinsville Globe. Twice married and divorced, she had one son. When her school closed in 1942, she moved to Washington, DC, where she worked as a federal employee and took classes at Howard University.

In 1946, Dunnigan became the Washington correspondent of the *Chicago Defender* and a member of the Associated Negro Press, which she headed from 1947 to 1961. In 1946, she became the first African American woman to gain press passes to cover both houses of Congress, and in 1948, she became the first African American White House correspondent and a member of the Women's National Press Club. Although she suffered racial indignities on more than one occasion, she did not falter and earned a reputation as a tough reporter who asked hard questions and expected, and received, answers.

In 1948, Dunnigan accompanied President Harry Truman on the campaign trail and made several speeches on his behalf in Kentucky. Both John F. Kennedy and Lyndon B. Johnson recognized her ability and placed her on committees in their administrations. She served as education consultant for the Equal Employment Opportunity Committee from 1961 to 1965. In 1966–1967, she was an information specialist for the Department of Labor and then the editorial assistant for the President's Council on Youth Opportunity from 1967 to 1970, when she retired. She also traveled with Lady Bird Johnson on a cross-country education observation tour of America.

Dunnigan wrote her autobiography, *A Black Woman's Experience: From Schoolhouse to White House* (1974), and *The Fascinating Story of Black Kentuckians: Their Heritage and Traditions* (1982). During her lifetime of public service, she traveled extensively in the United States and abroad and received more than 50

national and international awards and an honorary doctorate from Colorado State Christian College. In 1982, she was inducted into the Kentucky Journalism Hall of Fame.

On May 6, 1983, Dunnigan died in Washington, DC, and was buried in Maryland National Memorial Park, Laurel, MD.

Crowe-Carraco, Carol. *Women Who Made a Difference.* Lexington: Univ. Press of Kentucky, 1989.
Dunnigan, Alice Allison. *A Black Woman's Experience: From Schoolhouse to White House.* Philadelphia: Dorrance and Company, 1974.
———, comp. and ed. *The Fascinating Story of Black Kentuckians: Their Heritage and Traditions.* Washington, DC: Associated Publishers, 1982.
Kleber, John E., ed. *The Kentucky Encyclopedia.* Lexington: Univ. Press of Kentucky, 1992.

—Carol Crowe Carraco

DUPEE, GEORGE WASHINGTON (b. 1826, Gallatin Co., KY; d. 1897, Kansas City, MO), minister. The son of Cuthbert and Rachael Dupee, slaves of a Baptist minister, George Washington Dupee was born on July 24, 1826, in Gallatin Co., KY. His mother died when he was only two weeks old, and her last wish was that others would "raise him right." He worked a variety of assigned tasks before being converted by the teachings of a Baptist preacher in 1842. Two years later, he claimed to have experienced a miracle when he read

Rev. George Dupee.

the third chapter of the book of John despite previously being illiterate. After some initial resistance, he took this as a sign that he should become a preacher, and he received ordination from the president of Georgetown College in 1851.

Dupee's career in the ministry began at a black church in Georgetown, where he preached for a few years before leaving to organize and establish several other churches in the region. In 1855, he became pastor of Lexington's **Historic Pleasant Green Missionary Baptist Church,** but his owner decided at this time to put him up for auction in January of the following year. His congregation, mostly composed of slaves and former slaves, lacked the funds to buy his freedom, but they successfully petitioned members of the Lexington First Baptist Church for aid. Parishioners at Pleasant Green repaid the debt by sending money tied in a handkerchief to the home of First Baptist Church's white preacher every week.

Now a freeman, Dupee decided to preach to slaves in western Kentucky, moved to Paducah, and became pastor of historic **Washington Street Missionary Baptist Church.** In 1861, he organized the first ministers' and deacons' meeting for blacks in the state, and in 1867, he helped create the First District Baptist Association. He also served as moderator of the state's General

Association of Colored Baptists in Kentucky (later known as the **General Association of Baptists in Kentucky**) between 1869 and 1881. As part of that organization, he founded the *Baptist Herald* and served as managing editor and owner; in 1879, the journal was renamed the ***American Baptist,*** and ownership shifted to **William H. Steward.**

By the end of his long career in the ministry, Dupee was reputed to have baptized over 10,000 converts, married over 15,000 couples, and preached over 15,000 funerals. After his death in Kansas City, MO, on September 5, 1897, reports stated that over 1,000 people attended the funeral at Washington Street Baptist Church. He was buried in Oak Grove Cemetery in Paducah.

Newspapers: "Rev. G. W. Dupee," *Paducah Daily Sun,* July 27, 1897, 1; "Last Respects," *Paducah Daily Sun,* September 9, 1897, 4; "Kentucky Preacher Helped Found African-American Baptists," *KNE,* February 12, 1996, 1B.

Parrish, C. H. *Golden Jubilee of the General Association of Colored Baptists in Kentucky: From 1865–1915.* Louisville, KY: Mayes Printing Co., 1915.

Pegues, A. W. *Our Baptist Ministers and Schools.* Springfield, MA: Willey & Co., 1892.

Peoples, T. H., Jr. *Essence of a Saga: A Complete History of the Oldest Black Baptist Congregation West of the Allegheny Mountains, Historic Pleasant Green Missionary Baptist Church.* Lexington, KY: s.n., 1990.

—*Stephen Pickering*

DURRETT, PETER "OLD CAPTAIN" (b. ca. 1733, Caroline Co., VA; d. 1823, Lexington, KY), recognized as the founder of First African and Historic Pleasant Green Missionary Baptist Churches in Kentucky. Born into slavery as the property of Captain Durrett in Caroline Co., VA, Peter Durrett (spellings of his last name vary) was called Old Captain. At age 25, he was converted to Christianity as a Baptist. He then began to proselytize other slaves. When the owner of Durrett's wife decided to move to Kentucky, the slaveholder exchanged another slave for Durrett in order to keep the couple together. Durrett arrived in Kentucky, about eight miles east of Lexington, in 1785. He was connected with a white Baptist church at the head of Boone Creek.

After the church dissolved, Durrett and his wife "hired themselves of their master," which meant that they were able to live away from their master but had to surrender their wages to their owner. John Maxwell, a white Lexington pioneer, offered land, helped build their cabin, and allowed Durrett to hold religious meetings on his property. As converts increased, many wanted to be baptized, but Durrett was not ordained and therefore was not allowed to baptize members. Durrett, along with 50 followers, approached the South Kentucky Baptist Association for ordination. The organization denied his ordination but still encouraged Durrett in his ministry. He took its encouragement and baptized converts. These evangelistic efforts launched the historical origins of both **First African** and **Historic Pleasant Green Missionary Baptist** Churches. Even though church organizational records were not kept, church historians believe that Durrett founded these churches in 1801 or sometime in the last decade of the eighteenth century. He continued his ministry until his death. In 1823, he died at age 90 in his small cabin near Lexington.

Bishop, Robert H., collector and arranger. *An Outline of the History of the Church in the State of Kentucky, during a Period of Forty Years. . . .* Lexington, KY: Thomas T. Skillman, 1824. Reprinted in *Essence of a Saga: A Complete History of the Oldest Black Baptist Congregation West of the Allegheny Mountains, Historic Pleasant Green Missionary Baptist Church (Formerly African Baptist Church),* edited by T. H. Peoples Jr. Lexington, KY: s.n., 1990.

McIntyre, L. H. *One Grain of the Salt: The First African Baptist Church West of the Allegheny Mountains.* Lexington, KY: L. H. McIntyre, 1986.

Parrish, C. H. *Golden Jubilee of the General Association of Colored Baptists in Kentucky: From 1865–1915.* Louisville, KY: Mayes Printing Co., 1915.

Spencer, John H., and Burrilla B. Spencer. *A History of Kentucky Baptists: From 1769 to 1885.* Cincinnati: J. R. Baumes, 1886.

—*Sallie L. Powell*

DUVALLE, LUCIE N. (b. 1868, Louisville, KY; d. 1928, Louisville, KY), educator. The child of Peter and Ann DuValle, Lucie DuValle was born on August 16, 1868, the eldest of four daughters. She received her education in Louisville's public schools and, though still only a girl herself, in 1878 began her teaching career at the Eastern Colored School at the corner of Breckinridge and Jackson Sts. Five years later, DuValle transferred to the Western Colored School. In 1890, she became the first female principal in the Louisville public school system when she was appointed to head the California Colored School, later renamed Phillis Wheatley School. During her 38-year tenure there, she was credited with instituting the first "parents meetings," which were precursors to the Parent-Teacher Association, and with establishing a number of programs at Wheatley, such as health and vocational training.

In honor of DuValle's contributions to education, the Lucie N. DuValle Junior High School was opened at Ninth and Chestnut Sts. in September 1952 in the old **Central High School** facility. In 1956, DuValle Junior High was moved to 3500 Bohne Ave. in a structure it shared with Joseph S. Cotter Elementary School. Thirty years later, DuValle Junior High was renamed the DuValle Education Center, which offered various opportunities to the surrounding community, such as GED courses, vocational training, and a Head Start program.

Lucie DuValle died of a heart attack on December 1, 1928, and is buried in Eastern Cemetery.

E

EASTERN COLORED BRANCH LIBRARY (LOUISVILLE), early African American library. In 1908, the first Carnegie-endowed library building for African Americans was opened in Louisville. Named the **Western Colored Branch Library,** it opened its doors to the city's black community, which had been denied entrance into the city's other public libraries. Because of the success of the West End library, many African Americans in Louisville's East End almost immediately began demanding a library of their own.

After raising $1,000 from black residents of the East End, **Albert Meyzeek,** who had been instrumental in bringing the Western Colored Branch Library to Louisville, and Rev. C. C. Bates appeared before the city's library board to petition the construction of another Carnegie library. The pair was given $4,000 to buy land for what would become the Eastern Colored Branch Library. By the time of its grand opening on January 28, 1914, the library had been built, with considerable assistance from the Carnegie Foundation, at a total cost of almost $45,000. The building was designed by famed Kentucky architect Brinton B. Davis. At the time of its completion, Louisville became the only city in the United States with two African American libraries.

Located at the corner of Hancock and Lampton Sts., the Eastern Colored Branch Library was an instant success. Demonstrating African Americans' hunger for knowledge in a city where they had been denied library service their entire lives, the library served over 14,000 patrons in its first seven months.

Like the Western Branch, its Eastern counterpart was supervised by **Thomas F. Blue,** who was made director of the newly created Colored Department of the Library Board. Blue launched an extensive program that trained the female staff for both libraries. One of his most successful students was **Rachel Harris,** who eventually took charge as head librarian of the Eastern Colored Branch in the 1920s, with a salary of $55 per month. Because of the enormous success at training librarians at both branches, Louisville became the center of librarian training for African American women throughout the South. Blue's staff was also frequently sent to other states to help train librarians for newly established colored branch libraries.

The remarkable success of the Eastern Colored Branch Library is a testament to the persistent demand for equal access to books and education by blacks in a segregated city. The library not only became vital to the community of Louisville but also trained and educated African Americans throughout the entire South.

"Blue, Thomas Fountain," "Carnegie Libraries," and "Harris, Rachel Davis." In *The Encyclopedia of Louisville,* edited by John E. Kleber, 97–98, 160–61, 370. Lexington: Univ. Press of Kentucky, 2001.

Jones, Reinette F. *Library Service to African Americans in Kentucky, from the Reconstruction Era to the 1960s.* Jefferson, NC: McFarland, 2001.

Wright, George C. *Life Behind a Veil: Blacks in Louisville, Kentucky, 1865–1930.* Baton Rouge: Louisiana State Univ. Press, 1985.

—*Joshua D. Farrington*

EASTERN KENTUCKY COALFIELDS, workplace and home for many Kentucky African Americans. Despite the stereotypical image of a sooty-faced, slumped-back white miner shown walking the railroad tracks toward a coal camp house filled with sad-eyed white children, something else permeated the color of coal in eastern Kentucky—black people. And although they have been ignored generally, as well as in African American literature, popular culture, and social science, they have been in the region for a very long time.

Lynch Colored Public School marching band, 1957.

Harlan coal miners, Arch Minerals of Kentucky.

Although there were small numbers of African Americans in the area during slavery, a critical mass of them found their way deep into Kentucky's Appalachian Mountains in the late 1800s, when King Coal started to fuel the Industrial Revolution. Between 1900 and 1950, their numbers grew rapidly in Barbourville, Benham, Black Mountain, Cumberland, Evarts, Fleming, Harlan, Haymond, Hazard, Jenkins, Kenvir, Lynch, Manchester, McRoberts, Middlesboro, Pikeville, Pineville, and Redd Foxx. Jobs in the coal industry and the building of rail lines provided matchless breaks for the first generation of blacks coming to Kentucky's Appalachian frontier, mainly recruited by coal companies from central Alabama.

The impact of the mechanization of the coal industry beginning immediately after World War II adversely affected all miners, but because black miners held the jobs that were hardest hit by automation—unskilled hand loading—its effect was toughest on them. Just as had occurred a half century earlier when their grandparents left the South for the improved life that the coal industry in Appalachian Kentucky offered, the black Appalachian exodus began anew, this time for cities in the midwestern, north central, and East Coast states.

Over the years since 1920, Harlan Co. has had the highest concentration of African Americans in Kentucky's 55 Appalachian counties, just less than half of the 120 counties in the state. Predictably, by 1960, as miners were displaced by machines and mine closures restructured the area's economy, Harlan came to represent the pattern of blacks' outmigration throughout the region. Of 72,200 counted in the 1940 census of population in Harlan Co., 7,900 were black. Forty years later, they numbered fewer than 2,000. In 2010, only 643 blacks lived in Harlan Co. That pattern of outmigration has been replicated in each of the major coal counties in eastern Kentucky: Bell, Clay, Floyd, Harlan, Letcher, Perry, and Pike.

Throughout Kentucky, for blacks, mountain life and mining work were "no crystal stair" during the era of legal segregation that lasted through the mid-1960s. Racial and economic disparities were pervasive in education, job-promotion opportunities, and private enterprise. In company towns like Benham (International Harvester), Lynch (United States Steel), and Jenkins (Elkhorn Coal Corporation), housing was regulated by the corporations because they owned it. They provided relatively equal housing for blacks and whites. All-black or all-white sections of coal towns existed until fairly recently; and until 1970, when black miners in Lynch sued U.S. Steel, the supervisors and company administrative officials' jobs were held solely by whites. The food-serving counters at the company stores and the country clubs were racially exclusive venues, as were bars, dance halls, schools, and most other social gathering places, such as churches. The only racially integrated organization from its beginning (1890) was the United Mine Workers of America.

In the boom times between World War I and World War II and through the mid-1960s, the daily lives of most black coal-mining families and the communities in which they lived throughout central Appalachia were not significantly different in socioeconomic dynamics from those of their black counterparts in other parts of Kentucky and nationwide. The vast majority of these poorly educated black people who came to the coalfields held what were essentially manufacturing jobs for just under a century, as was the case in most of the nation.

In the period between World War II and the decision in **Brown v. Board of Education** in 1954, it was not uncommon for nationally known entertainers such as Cab Callaway, B. B. King, and Bessie Smith to do shows in Harlan Co. Teams such as the Birmingham Black Barons from the Negro Baseball League played in the black coal camps. Semiprofessional baseball teams, black and white, organized and sponsored by coal companies, played on a highly competitive level in eastern Kentucky up through the 1950s; the circuit ran through coal towns from Bluefield, Beckley, and Gary in southern West Virginia to Appalachia, Big Stone Gap, Norton, and Stonega in southwest Virginia and through Middlesboro, Lynch, and Benham to Hazard, a 100-mile radius from Harlan Co. in southeastern Kentucky.

Harlan **Rosenwald,** Lincoln in Middlesboro, **Dunbar** in Jenkins, Liberty in Hazard, and the Benham and Lynch Colored Schools were striking for their excellent faculties, most of whom were graduates of Kentucky State College (later known as **Kentucky State University**). High school graduation and college-going rates for schools like these were extraordinarily high, greater than rates for the general population. Together with churches that formed the London District Baptist Missionary and Educational Association, these schools were renowned, at least in Kentucky, for producing excellent students and athletic teams.

A critical mass of these working-class black people in the coal camps of eastern Kentucky—and the only black professionals, the schoolteachers and administrators—belonged to self-help benevolent societies, such as the **Freemasons,** the Elks, the Knights of

Lynch Colored School football team, 1924.

Pythias, the Court of Calanthe, and the Order of the Eastern Star. Twice a year through the mid-1970s, extravagant observations were held where lodge brothers and their affiliated women's groups would parade through the black sections of town in colorful dress. These public affirmations of a living sense of community validated the ethic that lay beneath their collective missions: "Friendship, Benevolence and Charity." Since the late 1960s, the **Eastern Kentucky Social Club,** beginning in Cleveland, OH, has held annual gatherings on Labor Day weekend, drawing thousands of former coal-town residents, families, and friends to locations where they settled and has formed chapters of the club in Atlanta, California, Chicago, Cleveland, Dayton, Detroit, Houston, Indianapolis, Lexington, New York City, Washington, DC, and Nashville.

Dozens of blacks from eastern Kentucky have made stellar accomplishments in the military, business, education, law, and public service. Harlan Co. is the only spot in the world that can claim three native sons—two from Benham and one from Lynch—who played for the Harlem Globetrotters: Willis "Bunny" Thomas, **Paul "Showtime" Gaffney,** and **Bernard "Bernie" Bickerstaff.** A four-decade National Basketball Association coach with five head coaching positions under his belt, Bickerstaff has served as an assistant for the Cleveland Cavaliers. Harlan Rosenwald graduate Larry Kirksey, who coached National Football League Hall of Famer Jerry Rice, has been the receivers coach for the Houston Texans. **Greg Page** of Middlesboro, who died of injuries suffered in a practice session while he was a freshman on the University of Kentucky football team in 1967, was among the first black football players in the Southeastern Conference. Carolyn Mitchell-Sundy has served in a number of influential positions, including vice president for diversity at Southeast Community College in her native Harlan Co. Karl D. Turner, a Lynch native who has made a home in New Orleans for the past three decades and holds a philosophy degree and a master's in international economics, worked as a CEO of the only black-owned seafood import/export company in the United States. Like dozens of other notables from the area, Harlan High graduate Georgenna Riley, from a family of 11, stood out as medical director of radiology for the Ohio region of health care giant Kaiser Permanente. David Olinger, a Hazard native and **Berea College** graduate, has served for three decades in the U.S. Attorney Office, while **Porter "P. G." Peeples** of Lynch has been the longest-serving chief officer of a **National Urban League** office in Lexington, KY. Many others have crossed the mountains from the coalfields of eastern Kentucky to reach the summit of their chosen professions.

The coal seams in Kentucky's Appalachian Highlands became the source of enormous wealth over the past century for the whites who owned and managed the mines, but most who worked in the mines during that time were economically hard pressed. On most quality-of-life measures, Kentucky has been one of the nation's poorest and sickest states, and mountain residents have been poorer than people in other parts of the Bluegrass State. Indeed, a case can be made that being black in Appalachian Kentucky makes one even worse off than the white majority. Not only are the jobs that brought them to the region going fast and not likely to return, but also the few blacks who remain in coalfield towns face other profound challenges: welfare and drug dependency and their role in a future not dependent on coal-mining jobs. Those blacks in eastern Kentucky who choose to remain or return have a rich history on which to rely and a past deeply rooted in a dogged determination to stay alive and thrive despite the odds and to pass on courage, faith, and hope to the coming generations.

Condon, Mable Green. *A History of Harlan County.* Nashville, TN: Parthenon Press, 1962, 74–83.

Cornett, Pearl. "The Mountain Negro of Hazard, Kentucky." In *Our Appalachia: An Oral History,* edited by Bill Weinberg and Laurel Shackleford, 123–27. New York: Hill & Wang, 1977.

Eller, Ronald D. *Uneven Ground: Appalachia since 1945.* Lexington: Univ. Press of Kentucky, 2008, 214–21.

Guillebeaux, Jack. "Not Just Whites in Appalachia." *South Today* 3, no. 10 (June 1972): 27–32.

Hall, C. Ray "The Hillbilly's Burden." *Courier-Journal Scene,* September 9, 1995, 14–15.

Hayden, Wilburn, Jr. "African-American Appalachians: Barriers to Equality." In *Social Work in Rural Communities,* 2nd ed., edited by Leon H. Ginsberg, 227–46. Alexandria, VA: Council on Social Work Education, 1993.

Hill, Bob. "Black Home in Appalachia—A Return to Roots Deep in Eastern Kentucky." *Courier-Journal Magazine,* June 28, 1987, 8–13.

Lewis, Ronald L. *Black Coal Miners in America: Race, Class, and Community Conflict.* Lexington: Univ. Press of Kentucky, 1985, 88–95.

Turner, William H. "Engaging Minorities in Community Building." *LHL,* December 9, 2013, A11.

Wagner, Thomas E. and Phillip J. Obermiller. *African-American Miners and Migrants: The Eastern Kentucky Social Club.* Urbana: Univ. of Illinois Press, 2004, 1–15.

—*William H. Turner*

EASTERN KENTUCKY SOCIAL CLUB, organization of coal-mining families and their friends living in eastern Kentucky. The end of the 1940s witnessed a decline in the use of manual labor in the coal mines of eastern Kentucky. Automated machinery displaced large numbers of both black and white coal miners, who began migrating out of the area. Unemployed black miners, along with their families, relocated to northern cities for employment opportunities. Members of black families who had grown up in the mining towns of eastern Kentucky wanted to retain the friendships and memories they had all shared before this migration movement.

In 1967, seven friends met at the home of Armelia Moss in Cleveland, OH, and began discussing plans to organize a reunion of black families who had once lived in Benham and Lynch. They continued their discussions for two years before deciding that they "needed an official place of meeting." They decided to meet at the Red Satin Lounge in Cleveland. Early members included Moss, Della and Willie Watts, Roland Motley, James Meadows, and Clarence and Betty Rogers. They held various fund-raising events to help pay expenses for a reunion. Former Harlan Co. residents who had migrated to Atlanta, Detroit, and Chicago, as well as those still living in Benham and Lynch, learned about the plans for a reunion. "It was just friends telling friends and families telling families," recalled Della Watts. After several years of meetings and plans, a reunion for black migrant families was held on the East Side of Cleveland at the Shakerlee Hall in 1970. "The first reunion was just hugging and kissing and reminiscing," recalled Willie Watts. But support for the organization grew rapidly. It was originally named the Southeastern Kentucky Social Club but was renamed the Eastern Kentucky Social Club to include persons from Barbourville, Cumberland, Harlan, Hazard, Jenkins, Middlesboro, Pine Mountain, Pikeville, and Whitesburg who wanted to participate in the reunions. The annual reunions were scheduled for Labor Day weekend. Andrea Massey, a member of the Lynch chapter, noted that "the purpose of the EKSC is to keep the families together, keep them coming together."

Some reunions attracted more than 3,000 persons. Chapters of the club were organized in Atlanta, Chicago, Detroit, Lynch, and Washington, DC, among other cities. Local chapters raise funds throughout the year in order to attend the reunions, as well as to support organizations such as the **National Association for the Advancement of Colored People** and other charities. **Porter G. Peeples,** a native of Harlan Co., KY, spoke at the reunion banquet in Lexington in 2011. He emphasized the importance of encouraging younger generations to get involved: "The reason is because we want to be assured that the legacies established by our parents and forebears are kept alive. And that the future generations would know about the contributions of African-Americans who lived in the coal mining towns of Eastern Kentucky."

Davis, Merlene. "Merlene Davis: Ties That Bind Social Club Grew out of Eastern Kentucky Coal Country." http://www.kentucky.com/2011/08/28/1859669/merlene-davis-ties-that-bind-social.html (accessed May 29, 2014).

Wagner, Thomas E., and Phillip J. Obermiller. *African American Miners and Migrants: The Eastern Kentucky Social Club.* Urbana: Univ. of Illinois Press, 2004.

—*Gerald L. Smith*

EAVES, JERRY LEE (b. 1959, Louisville, KY), basketball player and coach. Jerry Lee Eaves was born on February 8, 1959, in Louisville. As a talented basketball player in high school, Eaves decided to play at the newly built Ballard High School near his home in Louisville's East End rather than at the traditional powerhouse, Male High School. In 1976, with Eaves leading the way, Ballard shocked Male in a surprising upset, and the following year he led his team to a state championship.

As a highly recruited six-feet-four McDonalds' All-American guard, Eaves remained in his home city and attended the University of Louisville. In his four years with the Cardinals, Eaves averaged 9.7 points, 2.6 assists, and 1.8 rebounds. During his tenure at Louisville, the Cardinals won the 1980 NCAA Championship, and Eaves was named All-Metro Conference for the 1980–1981 season. After graduating from Louisville, Eaves was selected in the 1982 National Basketball Association (NBA) draft by the Utah Jazz. In his five seasons in the NBA, Eaves played with the Jazz and the Sacramento Kings and had 1,132 points and 414 assists in his 168 played games.

After his career as a player, Eaves began coaching at both college and professional levels. From 1990 through 2003, Eaves served as an assistant coach at Howard University and the University of Louisville, as well as an NBA assistant coach with the New Jersey Nets, the Charlotte Hornets, and the Cleveland Cavaliers. From 2003–2012 he was the head coach of North Carolina A&T in Greensboro.

"NC A&T Names Eaves as New Basketball Coach." *Winston-Salem Journal,* May 2, 2003.

"Eaves Removed as Aggies Head Coach." Official Site of Aggie Athletics North Carolina A&T. http://www.ncataggies.com/ViewArticle.dbml?DB_OEM_ID=24500&ATCLID=205397194 (accessed April 1, 2013).

Terhune, Jim. *Tales from the 1980 Louisville Cardinals.* Champaign, IL: Sports Publishing, 2004.

—*Joshua D. Farrington*

ECKSTEIN NORTON INSTITUTE, industrial training school in Cane Springs, KY. In 1890, Dr. **William J. Simmons** resigned as president of Kentucky Normal and Theological Institute (later known as **Simmons College of Kentucky**) in Louisville to establish the Eckstein Norton Institute, a school specializing in the industrial training of African Americans. With funding from prominent Louisville businessmen such as Louisville and Nashville Railroad (L&N) executives Eckstein Norton and Milton Smith, Simmons purchased 75 acres of land across the Bullitt Co. line near the L&N rail line in Cane Springs. In mid-September, the school, consisting of one central brick building surrounded by six additional frame structures, opened with 24 students and 16 teachers, many of whom had followed Simmons from State University. Although the institute, with its motto "Education of the hands, head, heart, and mind," offered business classes such as bookkeeping, the pride of the school was its industrial department, which offered training in carpentry, blacksmithing, farming, painting, cooking, tailoring, and dressmaking. Simmons believed that after firmly establishing Eckstein Norton, he would be able to open a branch closer to Louisville and train competent domestic servants. However, Simmons died at the end of October later that year. Undaunted, Louisville businessmen continued to fund the school and persuaded Simmons's assistant, Dr. **Charles Parrish Sr.,** to assume the presidency, a post he held until the school's closing. After donations from the Louisville benefactors slowed, the Eckstein Norton Institute merged with the **Lincoln Institute** in Simpsonville in 1912. By that time, it reportedly had provided aid to 1,794 students while graduating 189.

Wright, George C. *Life Behind a Veil: Blacks in Louisville, Kentucky, 1865–1930.* Baton Rouge: Louisiana State Univ. Press, 1985.

ECLIPSE HALL, building owned and used by the Grand United Order of Odd Fellows in Louisville, KY. Located at 1230 W. **Walnut St.** in Louisville, Eclipse Hall was opened in 1872 as a market and saloon under the ownership of Henry Koch. By 1876, part of the building was rented to African American groups for dances and balls, and the Grand United Order of Odd Fellows (GUOOF) began to hold meetings there. In 1885, the GUOOF bought the building and renamed it Odd Fellows Hall. The building was destroyed by the 1890 tornado but was rebuilt and enlarged. In 1908 the Bijou Theater, the first black-owned theater in Louisville, opened in the rear of the building under the management of Edward D. Lee. The theater offered vaudeville acts by both white and black artists and operated under several different names before it closed its doors in 1921. The building remained under the ownership of the GUOOF until it was razed in the 1960s.

Weeden, H. C. *Weeden's History of the Colored People of Louisville.* Louisville, KY: H. C. Weeden, 1897.

—*Cornelius Bogert*

ECTON, GEORGE FRENCH (b. 1846, Winchester, KY; d. 1929, Chicago, IL), runaway slave and state legislator in Illinois. George French Ecton, the son of Anonia and Martha Ecton, was born into slavery in Winchester, KY, in 1846. As a young child, he was forced to weed crops, and as a teenager he became a full hand at the plow. Since Kentucky was a Union state during the Civil War, the **Emancipation Proclamation** did not apply to slaves like Ecton. Thus, in 1865, George and a fellow slave decided to "make way for liberty" and escape. The two young men received forged freedom papers from a white abolitionist, walked 18 miles to Paris, and boarded a train to Cincinnati.

In Cincinnati, Ecton worked as a deckhand for a steamship named *Sherman* that traveled between southern Ohio and Wheeling, WV. After making just one laborious round trip, Ecton sought odd jobs around the city while he attended night school taught by Luella Brown. In 1873, Ecton left Cincinnati and moved to Chicago, where he was immediately hired to manage the Hotel Woodruff dining room, a prestigious job for an African American during this era. He married Patti R. Allen, also from Winchester, in 1877.

Ecton also established ties with the city's Republican machine. During the 1880s, he became the first African American elected to the Illinois General Assembly, where he served as the representative from Chicago's Third Senatorial District. After a single term in office, Ecton returned to his career as one of Chicago's preeminent caterers. He remained active in local Republican politics until his death in 1929.

"First Negro Member of State Legislature Dead." *Chicago Daily Tribune,* September 21, 1929, 24.
Reed, Christopher Robert. *Black Chicago's First Century.* Vol. 1, *1833–1900.* Columbia: Univ. of Missouri Press, 2005.
Simmons, William. *Men of Mark: Eminent, Progressive and Rising.* Cleveland: George M. Rewell, 1887.

—*Joshua D. Farrington*

EDISON, HARRY EDWARD "SWEETS" (b. 1915, Beaver Dam, KY; d. 1999, Columbus, OH), jazz musician. Most biographies claim that Harry Edward "Sweets" Edison was born in Columbus, OH. However, the 1920 and 1930 U.S. federal censuses determined his birth state as Kentucky. Edison's father, Wayne, apparently deserted the family, and by the time Sweets was four years old, he and his mother, Katherine "Kitty" Meryl Borah Edison, lived with his maternal grandmother, Mizlar Borah, in Columbus, OH. Stories vary on how he first learned to play the trumpet, but as a young man, he joined the Count Basie band in 1937 and stayed until 1950. Saxophonist Lester Young nicknamed Edison Sweetie Pie because of his easy tones, but Basie reportedly shortened it to Sweets.

Edison's trumpet style was described as a variation of two methods: "a crisp, tightly muted attack and open-horn playing." His solos provided a musical narrative in a minimalist approach, but with light humor. As he aged, he played shorter notes in softer tones. In his lengthy career, Edison performed with renowned musicians, such as Buddy Rich, Quincy Jones, Frank Sinatra, Billie Holiday, and Ella Fitzgerald. In 1983, the Los Angeles Jazz Society awarded him its first tribute award, and in 1993, he was named an American Jazz Master.

Even though he fought prostate cancer for 14 years, he frequently toured, playing in various **jazz** venues. A few months before his death, he returned to Columbus, OH. He was buried in Glen Rest Memorial Estate in Reynoldsburg, OH.

Carnes, Mark Christopher, ed. *American National Biography: Supplement 2.* Vol. 26. Oxford: Oxford Univ. Press, 2005.
Newspapers: *NYT,* August 26, 1976, 39; July 18, 1982, 46; July 29, 1999, C25; *Chicago Sun Times,* July 28, 1999, 46.

Ohio Deaths, 1908–1932, 1938–1944, and 1958–2007.
U.S. Federal Census (1920, 1930).

—*Sallie L. Powell*

EDUCATION, Kentucky African American institutions, movements, and persons. The roots of black education in Kentucky are found in early nineteenth-century black churches, such as First Colored Baptist Church (**Fifth Street Baptist Church**) of Louisville under Reverend **Henry Adams** in 1829, and abolitionist outposts, such as **Berea College** in 1866, both of which offered classes to persons of color. Other persons, white and black, found that although educating African Americans was not illegal, it was dangerous. Only after 1865 did the threat of violence against privately supported education of blacks end. Private African American education continued at churches or various Christian denominational associations.

In an 1866 state law, the General Assembly required that "all taxes derived from the property of negroes and mulattoes were set aside to be used to provide for taking care of their paupers and the education of the children." The taxation rate at that time was 5 cents per $100 worth of taxable property. The voters had to approve the purchase of the site, repairing and refurbishing a building, and "better payment" of teachers. Moreover, the black schools were to be under white trustees, and the teachers of these schools had to hold teaching certificates. This was problematic since a Kentucky normal school for black teachers did not exist, and local white teachers did not want to teach blacks.

The funds raised for these schools apparently were insufficient. By 1874, state laws required that funds for these schools be obtained from additional sources: taxes on dogs owned by blacks and state taxes on suits, deeds, or any license collected from blacks "with the exception of the amount collected from commonwealth's attorneys." The same law required each black male over 21 to pay a poll tax of $1.00. All these laws complied with Section 187 of the 1866 state constitution, which mandated that blacks and whites could not be educated in the same school.

Not all African Americans accepted the sparse funds for their schools generated from these racially specific taxes after "black paupers were cared for." With the help of Emmett Bagby, a white Paducah lawyer, Jesse Ellis sued the state in federal circuit court in late 1881, arguing that his Fourteenth Amendment rights and certain rights under the 1875 Civil Rights Act were violated. The judge in the case, John Baxter, noted that he had no specific remedy for Ellis, but that he had ruled in the Ohio case *United States v. Buntin* that the state must equalize black school funding, integrate the schools, or dismantle the entire system. On August 6, 1882, Kentucky's electorate approved a measure equalizing the school funds by increasing the property tax rate. The measure also required that "the common school fund of the state shall hereafter be united and become one fund, to which the white and colored pupils shall be entitled in the same proportion." Not all school districts complied with this change.

In one case, a group of African American citizens chaired by Edward Claybrook filed a suit, ***Claybrook v. Owensboro,*** to force the Daviess Co. school commissioner and the Owensboro city schools to provide adequate public schools for the citizens. Although the Owensboro city school district finally provided improved funding for its black schools, the district still supported its white schools with more money.

The commonwealth's ambivalence toward public education was rooted in an aversion to spending scarce tax dollars on unnecessary training of farmers, miners, or others who allegedly did not need it. As late as 1889, members of the General Assembly supported a "fair English education" (grades 1–3) for all but thought that any more than this was wasteful. Blacks, traditionally limited to farm work, domestic service, and other semiskilled occupations, should not demand any more education than whites.

Louisville Courier-Journal editorial writer "Marse" Henry Watterson argued that blacks educated in certain semiskilled and service occupations would help whites become more prosperous and thus improve all of society. Watterson supported the existence of industrial training schools such as Bullitt Co.'s **Eckstein Norton Institute** at which blacks were given vocational training. Breathitt Co. legislator Carl Day obtained passage in 1904 of a law requiring racial segregation in the state's private schools. The legislation, called the **Day Law** in his honor, was aimed at privately operated **Berea College,** which had a tradition of racially integrated classes for "Appalachian youth" after the end of the Civil War. After Berea College was found guilty of violating the law, both the conviction and racially segregated Kentucky schools were upheld by a U.S. Supreme Court ruling in 1908.

During this era, black communities in Louisville, Lexington, Paducah, Bowling Green, Hopkinsville, and elsewhere struggled with limited resources to maintain elementary and secondary schools. An important movement to improve black education was the joint effort by Kentucky African American communities, the **Kentucky Negro Education Association,** the Kentucky Department of Education, the Tuskegee Institute, the Julius Rosenwald Fund, and other out-of-state private philanthropies. Collectively, these organizations provided resources for 158 facilities broadly called **Rosenwald schools** from 1917 to 1932. Although most were located in rural and less urbanized counties, some were found even in more urbanized counties, such as Fayette and Jefferson.

When smaller counties could not afford to create and operate segregated secondary schools, African Americans were advised—and in some counties required—to go to distant counties that operated all-black secondary schools. Fifty-five black high schools eventually were created throughout the state's 120 counties. Many of these secondary schools—such as State Street High School in Bowling Green, **Lincoln-Grant School** in Covington, **Bond-Washington High School** in Elizabethtown, (**Frederick**) **Douglass High School** in Henderson, Lynch Colored High School in Lynch, **Dunbar High School** in Lexington, and **Central High School** in Louisville—became centers of community pride and academic excellence. If a county could not afford an all-black high school, it would send its African American secondary students to the privately supported, all-black **Lincoln Institute** in Simpsonville, created in 1904 after blacks were excluded from Berea College.

After the ***Brown v. Board of Education*** rulings in 1954 and 1955 and the subsequent desegregation of Wayne Co. schools in 1955 and Louisville public schools in the fall of 1956, African American elementary and secondary schools were either closed or merged with white schools. The 55 black high schools that African American communities had supported under segregation were gradually transformed into different facilities or, in some cases, destroyed by neglect. Some black teachers were gradually reassigned from their segregated environments into integrated settings. Within most of these settings, African American teachers were no longer visible to black students and in many circumstances not even to white students. Despite violent resistance to desegregation in the Clay and Sturgis communities in 1956, largely peaceful but slow desegregation became the rule in Kentucky districts in the 1950s and 1960s.

Jefferson Co. was the largest Kentucky system to address desegregation. Other communities closed their black schools during the 1950s and 1960s. Integration took place slowly, but not before all-black Louisville Central High won the state basketball tournament in 1969 and African Americans were gradually recruited to the major state universities' athletic teams.

Despite these events, larger districts, such as Louisville, discovered that complete desegregation was far more difficult. In 1975, whites in southwestern Jefferson Co. visibly (and violently) opposed court-ordered **busing** to achieve racial balance. Their hostility came from the realization that white students would be required to travel to black neighborhood schools instead of a few blacks attending mostly white schools.

Ironically, some whites now bitterly felt the same frustration that black parents had experienced for decades when black students were bused past all-white schools closer to their home or were required to move to an area miles distant that had an all-black high school. These events occurred when the largely black Louisville public school system merged with the largely white Jefferson Co. system in 1975. This merger and subsequent battles by some white parents to avoid enrolling their children in integrated schools led to violent upheavals in mostly white areas of Jefferson Co.

Court-ordered busing led to a multiyear effort to end federal court control of the Jefferson Co. public school system. In June 2007, the U.S. Supreme Court ruled in *Meredith v. Jefferson County Board of Education* that the use of race in assigning students purely to achieve integration was not allowable. This ruling, which affected a similar case involving the public schools of Seattle, WA, held that the desegregation plans in both districts violated constitutional guarantees of equal protection and that a student's race could not be the only factor to consider. In 2008, the Jefferson County public school system amended its plan to consider the income, education, and minority status of parents in two geographic areas of the county; the plan was later amended to use data from the 2010 census tracts.

Postsecondary education for blacks was equally uneven and challenging. African Americans who migrated from the state found collegiate education in states beyond its borders. However, black student matriculation at Kentucky's public and private colleges became a persistent challenge. Formal postsecondary education for blacks in Kentucky began in 1879 with the establishment in Louisville of Kentucky Normal and Theological Institute by the **General Association of Baptists in Kentucky.** By 1900, the institution changed its name to State Colored Baptist University of Louisville and offered bachelor's, master's, and professional degrees in theology, law, and medicine. In 1930, financial difficulties forced it to close its various divisions and operate only its theological department under the name Simmons University (later known as **Simmons College of Kentucky**). By 2013, the institution had expanded its theological traditions to include a new liberal arts focus.

In 1886, Kentucky State Normal School for Colored Persons (now **Kentucky State University**) was created by the state legislature and located in Frankfort to provide teachers for all-black public elementary and secondary schools. This institution was funded poorly and, because of its location in the state capital, became enmeshed in partisan politics by some of its presidents until 1929. At this point, President **Rufus Atwood** removed the political connections from the college's management, required the faculty—including himself—to hold earned graduate degrees, and introduced a high level of academic rigor. Under his firm hand, an academically strengthened Kentucky State was desegregated in 1954 and gradually enabled his successors to attract a quality, racially integrated faculty, staff, and student body.

By 1918, Paducah was the site of West Kentucky Industrial College (now **West Kentucky Community and Technical College**). This institution was created by the Kentucky General Assembly to provide "industrial training similar to the Tuskegee school" in the western part of the state. In 1938, this institution was reorganized as the West Kentucky Vocational School for Negroes, and its liberal arts courses shifted to Kentucky State College (now **Kentucky State University**) in Frankfort.

Integration of white colleges and universities was not accepted until 1949. This change followed the court-ordered desegregation of the University of Kentucky's (UK) graduate school in 1949 as the result of a lawsuit brought by **Lyman T. Johnson,** a black Louisville school teacher and **National Association for the Advancement of Colored People** branch president. Federal judge H. Church Ford ruled that Johnson had been denied equal treatment under federal and state laws and required UK to admit Johnson and others similarly situated until the state established an institution and courses of study equal to those offered by UK. Despite on-campus cross burnings and other harassments, 31 other blacks followed Johnson to the Lexington campus to enroll in summer graduate classes.

Within a year of Johnson's summer 1949 classes, three white private colleges in Louisville and **Berea College** allowed black enrollments under a 1950 amendment to the Day Law that permitted these colleges to admit blacks since they offered classes not available at Kentucky State University. In 1951, the University of Louisville closed **Louisville Municipal College for Negroes,** an all-black division of the university created in 1931. It subsequently permitted black students to enroll at the University of Louisville as equals.

In 1952, Paducah Junior College refused to allow black admissions, claiming that West Kentucky Vocational School for Negroes was a separate but equal equivalent to it. A successful 1953 federal court case pressured the college to admit three black students without incident. By 1955, Kentucky's all-white state teachers' colleges—Western, Eastern, Morehead, and Murray—began enrolling black undergraduates.

As a result of national litigation in the 1960s and 1970s in other states that had not fully desegregated, Kentucky's public colleges and universities came under federal scrutiny. In an effort to end the appearance of segregation, some critics even suggested closing Kentucky State University. Instead, these events led to the creation of several Kentucky Plans for Equal Opportunities (1982–1987, 1990–1997) and a U.S. Department of Education Office of Civil Rights Partnership Agreement (2003). In each of these agreements, the Kentucky Council on Postsecondary Education (CPE) was mandated to make and enforce civil rights goals in Kentucky. One of these tasks was increasing the numbers of African American faculty, staff, and students in Kentucky. The CPE monitored the number of African American faculty, staff, and students in Kentucky's colleges and universities and completed a massive statewide diversity study to help it to determine future policies.

Acts of the Commonwealth of Kentucky, 1865–1866, February 16, 1866; *Acts,* 1881–1882, 1:130.

Adams, Alicestyne. *Rosenwald Schools in Kentucky 1917–1932.* Georgetown, KY: Georgetown College, 2007.

Claybrook v. City of Owensboro, D. Kentucky 16 F. 297 (1883).

Dew, Lee A. "*Claybrook v. Owensboro:* An Early Victory for Equal Educational Opportunity in Kentucky." *Daviess County Historical Quarterly* 8, no.1 (January 1990): 2–15.

Ellis, William E. *A History of Education in Kentucky.* Lexington: Univ. Press of Kentucky, 2011.

Hardin, John A. *Fifty Years of Segregation: Black Higher Education in Kentucky, 1904–1954.* Lexington: Univ. Press of Kentucky, 1997.

Kousser, J. Morgan. "Making Separate Equal: Integration of Black and White School Funds in Kentucky." *Journal of Interdisciplinary History* 10, no. 3 (Winter 1980): 399–428.

Smith, Gerald L. *A Black Educator in the Segregated South: Kentucky's Rufus B. Atwood.* Lexington: Univ. Press of Kentucky, 1994.

Tilford-Weathers, Thelma Cayne. *A History of Louisville Central High School.* Louisville, KY: Thelma Cayne Tilford-Weathers, 1982.

—*John A. Hardin*

ELLIOTT, CYNTHIA ELAINE (b. 1958, Detroit, MI), attorney.

A Michigan native, Cynthia Elaine Elliott earned her undergraduate and law degrees from Detroit's Wayne State University. After graduation in 1980, she worked as a staff attorney for union auto workers and then as a Detroit Legal Aid attorney. She later moved to Louisville to become a field investigator for the **Kentucky Commission on Human Rights.**

In 1990, Elliott began her tenure in Jackson, KY, with the Appalachian Research and Defense Fund of Kentucky (AppalRed), which provided low-income clients legal assistance regarding family law, public aid, and unemployment. Four years later, while Elliott and her two children were away from home, an arsonist destroyed her home at 1 a.m. by placing accelerant at two doors. Elliot voiced the possibility that the felon thought that she and her daughters, ages 9 and 13, were home because her car was in the driveway. Because of the early morning time and their blocked means of escape if the family had been present, Elliott believed that they would have assuredly died. The FBI investigated the attack as a racial hatred crime because Elliott had been dating a white man. The next year, she married Paul M. Tolson.

In 1997, Kentucky governor Paul Patton appointed Elliott special justice on the Kentucky Supreme Court; she was the first African American woman to hold that position. Four years later, she left AppalRed to work for the Kentucky Department of Public Advocacy. She later moved to Ohio to serve as managing attorney for Advocates for Basic Legal Equality, a multicounty legal services program. In 2007, Elliott returned to eastern Kentucky as AppalRed's executive director in Prestonsburg, becoming the first African American in that position.

Elliott served on the Prichard Committee for Academic Excellence, as a board member of the Kentucky High School Athletic Association, and a member of the Eastern Kentucky University Board of Regents. In February 2011, the board of AppalRed fired Elliott on the basis of a whistleblower's accusation of overspending the organization's budget. Even though she was locked out of her office and blocked from obtaining records for her defense, Elliott's attorney claimed that the dismissal was a fraud. In October 2011, Elliott countersued, contending that she had been fired because of her gender and race. She maintained that her dismissal was retaliation for her firing of white employees.

Involved in the Kentucky Plus America Pageant since 1999, Elliott became Kentucky state director of the pageant and coached many contestants. She pursued her charity interests as founder of Save Our Children and Keep Them Safe, an organization that provided support and guidance for youth. As a foster mother, Elliott served on the Foster Care Review Board.

Kentucky Marriage Index, 1973–1999.

Newspapers: "Arson Destroyed Breathitt Home," *LHL,* June 30, 1994, A1; "Business People," *LCJ,* June 28, 2007, 2D; "Legal Aid Agency Fires Its Director," *LHL,* February 3, 2011, A3; "Former Director of Legal-Aid Agency Sues over Her Firing," *LHL,* October 13, 2011, A3.

Office of Governor Paul Patton. Press release. http://www.e-archives .ky.gov/_govpatton/search/pressreleases/1997/aasupcrt.htm (accessed May 22, 2008).

The Miss Plus America Pageant: Kentucky Plus America Pageant. http://www.missplusamerica.com/ (accessed August 19, 2013).

—*Sallie L. Powell*

ELLIOTT, WILLIE MAE (b. 1917, Madisonville, KY; d. 2004, Madisonville, KY), funeral home director and civil rights activist.

Willie Mae Elliott was the first daughter of Sanders Elliott, a coal miner, and Mary Bell Lewis Elliott. In 1929, she graduated from Madisonville's **Rosenwald High School.** While her older brothers Otis and James B. followed their father into the mining industry and her brother Durwood worked with cars, Elliott graduated from Gupton-Jones College of Embalming and Mortuary Science in Nashville, TN. In 1941, she purchased property in Madisonville and opened Elliott Funeral Home. Another brother, Edward, and her only sister, Elizabeth Elliott Vanleer, joined her in the business.

In 1972, Elliott built a new funeral home, Elliott Mortuary. Licensed in Kentucky, Tennessee, and Indiana, she served as president of the Embalmers and Funeral Directors Association of Kentucky. She started the first funeral limousine service, owned and operated the first private EMT ambulance service in Hopkins Co., and opened a cemetery, Elliott Memorial Gardens.

Elliott, a lifelong member of the **National Association for the Advancement of Colored People,** was involved in local school integration. As a funeral home director, she was the first African American to integrate Madisonville's Odd Fellows Cemetery. She ran for Hopkins Co. judge executive and Hopkins Co. coroner in the 1980s. In 1988, she was responsible for the funeral arrangements of three-year-old Tabatha Foster, who was the world's longest survivor of a five-organ transplant.

The last surviving member of her immediate family, Elliott was interred in Elliott Memorial Gardens on April 17, 2004.

Funeral Program: "Celebration of the Life: Willie Mae Elliott, 1917–2004."

Kentucky Birth Index, 1911–1999.

Newspapers: "Our Door Is Open," *Madisonville (KY) Messenger,* June 24, 1967, 2; "Give Them Flowers while They Can Smell," *Madisonville (KY) Messenger,* January 2, 1974, 6; "Tabatha's Good Times Recalled," *KNE,* May 14, 1988, 10B.

U.S. Federal Census (1920, 1930).

U.S. Social Security Death Index, 1935–Current.

—*Sallie L. Powell*

ELLIS, JAMES "JIMMY" (b. 1940, Louisville, KY; d. 2014, Louisville, KY), winner of the World Boxing Association heavyweight championship. A sparring partner of **Muhammad Ali** who went on to win the World Boxing Association (WBA) heavyweight championship, Jimmy Ellis was born on February 24, 1940, in Louisville, the son of Walter and Elizabeth (Roe) Ellis. Originally a middleweight trained by Angelo Dundee, Ellis won his first professional fight with a third-round knockout on April 19, 1961. Later he served as a sparring partner of Ali for two years. After moving up in weight class, Ellis won the WBA heavyweight crown on April 27, 1968, with a 15-round decision over Jerry Quarry. In an effort to unify the heavyweight title, he faced World Boxing Council champion "Smokin'" Joe Frazier on February 16, 1970; Frazier knocked Ellis out in the fifth round. In 1987, Ellis made a comeback in the sport, but as a trainer, not a fighter. Ellis and his wife, Mary Etta, have seven children. Ellis had Alzheimer's disease. He passed away on May 6, 2014.

Goldstein Richard. "Jimmy Ellis, a Boxer Long in Ali's Shadow, Dies at 74," *NYT,* May 6, 2014.

ELMORE, RONN (b. 1957, Louisville, KY), popular Christian relationship therapist and author. Ronn Elmore, known widely as the Relationship Doctor, has established himself as the most influential black relationship expert and has written extensively on the topics of marriage, family, and friendship from a distinctly African American and Christian perspective. Born in Louisville in 1957, Elmore came from a long line of ministers. He left Kentucky as a teenager to pursue his dream of becoming an actor and dancer. He studied at the Dance Theatre of Harlem and traveled throughout much of Europe. He even performed at Paris's infamous Moulin Rouge.

Elmore soon grew tired of traveling, returned to the United States, and obtained a degree in public relations and journalism from Antioch University of Los Angeles in 1981. While he was searching for jobs, he took a temporary position at a local church, where he felt a calling to enter the ministry. He enrolled at Fuller Theological Seminary in Pasadena, CA, where he concentrated his studies on psychology and family counseling. After graduating in 1989, he persuaded Faithful Central Church, in Los Angeles, to establish the Relationship Center, which he would head. After a series of successful seminars on relationships, Elmore wrote his first book, *How to Love a Black Man,* in 1996. Since its extraordinary success, Elmore has written numerous subsequent books on the topic of relationships, such as *How to Love a Black Woman* and *No-Nonsense Dating.* During the 1990s and the early years of the twenty-first century, Elmore began his own radio show and appeared on numerous television talk shows. His advice has been featured in *Ebony, Essence, Jet, Newsweek,* and *USA Today.*

Aaseng, Nathan. *African-American Religious Leaders.* New York: Infobase Publishing, 2003.

Elmore, Ronn. *How to Love a Black Woman.* New York: Warner Books, 1999.

Phelps, Shirelle, ed. *Contemporary Black Biography.* Detroit: Gale Group, 1999.

—*Joshua D. Farrington*

ELSMERE, community in Kentucky. The city of Elsmere is located on land originally granted by the Commonwealth of Virginia to John D. Watkins and Robert Johnson in 1785. The Watkins-Johnson property was located on Dry Ridge Trace, a natural high point that runs from near the Ohio River to central Kentucky. The tract was divided by a buffalo trail used in 1793 to build the Georgetown Rd., which became the primary route to central Kentucky. This road ran near the western boundary of today's city of Elsmere.

According to legend, the first settlers arrived at the site that became Elsmere about 1820. The first house was built near present-day Shaw Ave. In 1834, the Commonwealth of Kentucky legislated improvements to the Georgetown Rd. by chartering the Covington and Lexington Turnpike and requiring the use of stone, gravel, wood, and other materials in its construction. By 1839, the first 10 miles of the turnpike from Covington were finished, including the section that passes through present-day Elsmere. At a cost of $7,800 per mile, it was the most expensive highway built in Kentucky up to that time. Toll booths situated every five miles charged 10 cents for a horse and cart.

The end of the Civil War initiated an economic revitalization in Cincinnati and northern Kentucky. As the urban areas grew, traffic on the turnpike increased. A railroad from Cincinnati into the South was needed to give developing industries better access to agricultural products. In 1874, the city of Ludlow outbid Covington and Newport for the railroad bridge from Cincinnati. The bridge's location at Ludlow meant that the most direct route to the South went through what later became Erlanger and Elsmere. To encourage selection of this route, property owners contributed funds and property for the railroad right-of-way. Laying of track began in 1876, and the first train rolled down the tracks on April 20, 1877, reaching Lexington in 2 hours and 45 minutes. Passenger service was inaugurated on July 23, 1877. A station was established south of Erlanger and named Woodside Station. After the opening of the railroad, a trip from that station to Covington or Cincinnati that took hours on the turnpike could be made in minutes on the train. Developers worked with the railroad company to hold Sunday excursions stopping at Woodside Park in order to introduce potential residents to the area. Lots were sold by the Woodside Land Syndicate with such enticements as railroad passes.

Additional development in this area occurred rapidly during the 1890s. The first church, St. Henry Catholic Church, was built in 1890, and a volunteer fire department was organized. On May 11, 1896, the area that had become known as South Erlanger was incorporated as the city of Elsmere. The city was named by developer Lou Nolan for a street in Norwood, OH; the name was said to mean "by the lake." Less than a year later, on January 25, 1897, the neighboring city of Erlanger was also chartered. Elsmere's first government included a town marshal and a jail, built in 1903 at the corner of Garvey and Ash Aves. Elsmere built its first school in 1899 on Central Row.

One aspect of the growth that occurred during this period was the migration of black families to the area. By 1900, at least 17 black families had settled in Elsmere and had established **Dunbar School** for the education of their children. This school burned, but the black families rebuilt; they continued to maintain the new school until the Erlanger-Elsmere Schools built Wilkins Heights Elementary School in 1951 on Capital St. Black residents also established the A.M.E. Church in Elsmere about 1905.

As usage of the railroad waned and automobiles became more prevalent, highway improvements assisted in the development of Elsmere. In 1913, Kenton Co. condemned and purchased the Covington-Lexington Turnpike so that tolls could be discontinued. Begun in 1915 and completed in 1921, the Dixie Highway was created by covering the old turnpike with concrete. The new highway encouraged development of the old farms around the cities, which resulted in a building boom in the Erlanger-Elsmere area in the 1920s. More than 400 homes were constructed in Erlanger and Elsmere, school systems were consolidated, and a new high school was completed in 1928. The first sewers in Elsmere were constructed in 1930; most of the work on the sewers was completed by the Works Progress Administration in the late 1930s. The city's fire department was organized, and a fire chief was appointed. The center of this business district was Dixie Hwy. at Garvey Ave. This intersection became known as Shankers Corner, named for a dry goods store there. Also located on Garvey was a movie house that doubled as a basketball floor. The Joyland Corner Building on Garvey hosted parties. For a time, the Erlanger-Elsmere Library was also located on Garvey near Dixie Hwy.

In 1952, Elsmere had grown enough that it was declared a fourth-class city by the Kentucky legislature. The old board of trustees became the town council. Construction of I-75 nearby in 1961 changed traffic patterns. Most travelers now bypassed Elsmere; however, the new highway provided more opportunities for suburban growth because it made Elsmere more convenient for residents of the larger cities.

In the 1970s, discussion of a merger between Erlanger and Elsmere resulted in a ballot initiative to merge the neighboring cities, but the measure was soundly defeated in both cities. After this decision, Elsmere undertook a major rebuilding of streets from 1971 to 1978 at a cost of $1 million. In the 1980s, under the leadership of longtime mayor Al Wermeling, Elsmere annexed land for industrial development and residential expansion, enabling development of an identity separate from that of Erlanger. Elsmere benefited substantially from industrial development in the 1980s and 1990s.

Building on its tradition of diversity, Elsmere elected **Billy Bradford,** a longtime councilman, as mayor in 1998. Mayor Bradford was the first African American to hold such a position in northern Kentucky.

With its advantageous location, excellent transportation to other cities, the availability of industrial land, a strong tax base, and the potential for residential expansion, Elsmere is in an excellent position for future growth. In 2010 Elsmere had a population of 8,451.

"2010 Census Population of Elsmere, Ky," Census Viewer (accessed August 1, 2014).
City of Elsmere Centennial Celebration, 1896–1996. Elsmere, KY: Centennial Committee of 1996, 1996.
Newman, Mary. *The Bicentennial Story of Elsmere, Kentucky, 1776–1976.* Elsmere, KY: Elsmere Volunteer Fire Department Ladies Auxiliary, 1976.
Newspapers: Caden Blincoe, "Small Community Enjoys 'Mainstream of Progress,'" *CE,* February 5, 1979, 2K; Janice Kathman, "Elsmere: A Tale of Two Cities," *Erlanger Dixie News,* May 5, 1988, 21.

—*Wayne Onkst*

ELY NORMAL SCHOOL, Louisville school for training African American teachers. In January 1866, Gen. Clinton B. Fisk ordered that the work of the Bureau of Refugees, Freedmen, and Abandoned Lands (the **Freedmen's Bureau**) be extended from Tennessee into the Commonwealth of Kentucky, even though the bureau's authority was supposed to extend only to former Confederate states. Fisk, who was the bureau's assistant commissioner for Tennessee and Kentucky, extended the bureau's activities into Kentucky in response to widespread racial violence and the state's refusal to ratify the Thirteenth Amendment and rescind its antebellum slave code. By March 1866, Gen. John Ely, bureau superintendent for Kentucky, divided the state into three subdistricts, with Louisville as the state headquarters. In the field of education, the Freedmen's Bureau, although despised by many whites, had its most lasting impact as a catalyst in the creation of educational opportunities for African Americans. This impact was particularly significant in urban areas such as Louisville, where U.S. Army units could protect school property, personnel, and students until public funds for and public acceptance of the education of African Americans could be secured.

An important example of the work of the bureau was Ely Normal School, which opened in April 1868 on the northeast corner of 14th and Broadway. The eight-room, two-story brick school was named in honor of General Ely, who was considered a strong advocate of black education and who had resigned from the army in November 1867. The Ely School was jointly financed by the bureau and the **American Missionary Association** at a total construction cost of $25,000. Its purpose was the training of African American teachers, both to extend educational opportunities to larger numbers of African American children and to replace white northern teachers in increasingly segregated schools for blacks.

As the only public school for African Americans in Louisville, Ely could not restrict its role to teacher training and enrolled 396 students initially, only 40 of whom were enrolled in its normal department. John Hamilton and O. H. Robins, white graduates of Oberlin College, served as the first two principals, and the school employed up to seven teachers, only one of whom was African American. However, although Ely's enrollment was large, its capacity was far from sufficient to accommodate the number of African Americans seeking an education.

On September 22, 1870, the Louisville Board of Education responded to repeated petitions from the local African American community and established public schools for African American children. In July 1871, it appointed a Colored Board of Visitors to advise the board on matters related to the staffing and operation of these schools. Because the public schools available to African Americans were still inadequate and too few, **Horace Morris,** secretary of the Board of Visitors, negotiated a lease of Ely Normal School at an annual cost of $900, and the building was used as a public school in 1872 and 1873. However, after the Freedmen's Bureau was discontinued in 1872 and additional public school facilities were made available in Louisville, the Ely Normal School building was abandoned and allowed to deteriorate.

Bentley, George R. *A History of the Freedmen's Bureau.* Philadelphia: Univ. of Pennsylvania Press, 1955.

Dunnigan, Alice Allison, comp. and ed. *The Fascinating Story of Black Kentuckians: Their Heritage and Traditions.* Washington, DC: Associated Publishers, 1982.

Louisville City Directory, 1872, 1873.

Lucas, Marion B. *A History of Blacks in Kentucky.* Vol. 1, *From Slavery to Segregation, 1760–1891.* Frankfort: Kentucky Historical Society, 1992.

Nieman, Donald G. *The Freedmen's Bureau and Black Freedom.* New York: Garland Pub., 1994.

Wilson, George D. *A Century of Negro Education in Louisville, Kentucky.* Louisville, KY: Louisville Municipal College, 1941.

—*J. Blaine Hudson*

ELZY, ROBERT JAMES (b. 1884, Lexington, KY; d. 1972, New York, NY), founder and executive secretary of New York City's Urban League. Born and raised in Lexington, KY, to James Henry and Margaret Elzy, Robert Elzy left Kentucky as a teenager to attend Fisk University. After graduation in 1909, he furthered his education by completing graduate work in education and social work at Columbia University and New York University. After a brief stint as a principal at North Carolina's Joseph K. Brick School, he returned to Kentucky for a teaching position at State Normal School for Colored Persons (later known as **Kentucky State University**).

In 1917, he joined the **National Urban League** and was given the responsibility of organizing a new branch in Brooklyn, NY. At the time of its founding, the Brooklyn Urban League had an annual budget of $1,800. Within 25 years, under Elzy's direction, the Brooklyn and Manhattan Urban Leagues had merged and operated with an annual budget of over $75,000. Under Elzy's leadership, the Brooklyn Urban League sent over 15,000 children to summer camps and found jobs for thousands of black men and women during the Great Depression. In 1930, President Herbert Hoover invited him to participate in the White House Conference on Child Health and Protection.

Except for three years (1938–1941), when Elzy was named assistant administrator in charge of Negro affairs for the National Youth Administration, he remained the director and executive secretary of the Brooklyn Urban League until his retirement in 1950. Even after retiring, he remained active in the New York community, serving on the boards of directors of the Brooklyn Council of Boy Scouts, the city Welfare and Health Council, and the city Youth Board. He died at the Harlem Hospital Center at the age of 87 in 1972.

Fleming, G. James, and Christian E. Burckel, eds. *Who's Who in Colored America.* 7th ed. Yonkers-on-Hudson, NY: Christian E. Burckel & Associates, 1950.

Newspapers: "Many Experts for White House Meet," *BAA,* November 15, 1930, 3; "Robert Elzy of Urban League, Champion of Black Welfare, Dies," *NYT,* February 20, 1972, 68.

—*Joshua D. Farrington*

EMANCIPATION DAY, celebration of the signing of the Emancipation Proclamation. On January 1, 1863, the telegraphed announcement that President Abraham Lincoln had signed the **Emancipation Proclamation** was sent across the nation. Even though the executive order did not apply to Kentucky, a border state, many of its black population celebrated Emancipation Day; some also called it Jubilee Day. However, African Americans did not have a consensus on an official observance date. As in other states, Kentucky's commemoration day of emancipation varied. Some areas recognized January 1 as Emancipation Day; others celebrated on **August 8,** September 22, or Juneteenth (June 19). Reasons for the August 8 emancipation remembrance vary among sources and include honoring the British West Indies' abolition of slavery in 1834. On September 22, President Lincoln signed his "preliminary proclamation," which set 100 days for seceding states to return to the Union. Juneteenth recognized the last notification of slaves of their freedom in Texas on June 19, 1865.

Louisville and Lexington initially held the largest events, with Louisville's emancipation observance enveloped in a political tone. After the January 1, 1866, festivities, between 4,000 and 5,000 Louisville participants unanimously petitioned the Kentucky legislature for full civil rights. Lexington's January 1, 1866, events included patriotic songs, uniformed soldiers, political speeches, and well-dressed spectators. Years later, **Historic Pleasant Green Missionary Baptist Church** hosted events. Danville, Lancaster, and Hopkins Co. also memorialized Emancipation Day on January 1. Paducah initially celebrated on January 1 but later changed to August 8.

On August 8, 1883, Owensboro's **United Brothers of Friendship** sponsored Emancipation Day events at the local fairgrounds. Other communities, including Paducah, Hopkinsville, Russellville, Allensville, Henderson, and Marion, celebrated with August 8 emancipation galas. Henderson and Hopkinsville later changed their Emancipation Day to September 22. Maysville, Hartford, Beaver Dam, Fulton, and Columbia also recognized that date. In 1899, Hartford's African American organizers advertised in the local paper that "white friends" were invited, and admission was 10 cents.

At the turn of the twentieth century, while many of Kentucky's black citizens enjoyed Emancipation Day fairs with various contests, the majority of the state's celebrations included a parade, music, speakers, games, and food. Speakers included African American leaders like attorney **William Clarence Hueston Sr.** and **Dr. William Henry Ballard Sr.,** owner of Ballard Pharmacy. **Elizabeth "Lizzie" Fouse** read the Emancipation Proclamation at the celebration in Lexington on January 1, 1914. Baseball was the major sporting competition, and barbeque was a favorite food. Some communities included dances and beauty queen contests. Schools closed, and railroads offered special trains at reduced fares.

Jenkins, KY, in Letcher Co., near the border with Virginia, honored Emancipation Day on August 8. In 1924, three horseback riders led a throng of participants up a mountainous town road. A brass band with its members in white coats followed the riders as automobiles and pedestrians joined the parade.

Lexington held its first celebration of Juneteenth, a daylong event, in 1999. The activities began at **African Cemetery No. 2** with a history presentation and continued with a march to the Dunbar Center. The celebration continued with food, music, and academic contests. In 2005, thanks to Louisville representative Reginald Meeks, brother of artist **Renelda Meeks Higgins Walker,** Kentucky acknowledged Juneteenth National Freedom Day on June 19 as a state holiday. In 2012, Russellville and Logan Co. remembered Emancipation Day on August 8 with festivities at Hampton Park, including basketball, softball, and golf tournaments.

No matter which day African Americans observe as Emancipation Day, these events celebrate freedom from slavery. The gatherings offer a sense of community to their participants and are filled with pageantry and excitement.

Lucas, Marion B. *A History of Blacks in Kentucky: From Slavery to Segregation, 1760–1891.* 2nd ed. Frankfort: Kentucky Historical Society, 2003.

Marshall, Anne E. *Creating a Confederate Kentucky: The Lost Cause and Civil War Memory in a Border State.* Chapel Hill: Univ. of North Carolina Press, 2010.

National Juneteenth Observance Foundation: Kentucky. http://nationaljuneteenth.com/Kentucky.html (accessed October 9, 2013).

Newspapers: "Fatal Shooting Affair among Negroes at Owensboro," *Breckinridge News* (Cloverport, KY), August 8, 1883, 3; "Emancipation Celebration," *Earlington (KY) Bee,* January 6, 1898, 4; "Fair Ground, Hartford, Ky.," *Hartford Herald,* September 13, 1899, 3; "Clarence Hueston's Address," *LL,* December 28, 1906, 2; "The Emancipation Celebration," *Adair County News* (Columbia, KY), September 27, 1911, 1; "Lexington to Mark Day of Freedom from Slavery," *LHL,* June 17, 1999, B1; "Russellville Commemorates 8th of August," *Russellville (KY) News-Democrat and Leader,* August 14, 2012, A1.

Taber, Dave. "August 8 Is Emancipation Day. But Not Everywhere." *Appalachian History.* http://www.appalachianhistory.net/2012/08/august-8-is-emancipation-day-but-not.html (accessed October 9, 2013).

Wiggins, William H., Jr. *O Freedom! Afro-American Emancipation Celebrations.* Knoxville: Univ. of Tennessee Press, 1987.

Wright, George C. *A History of Blacks in Kentucky.* Vol. 2, *In Pursuit of Equality, 1890–1980.* Frankfort: Kentucky Historical Society, 1992.

—*Sallie L. Powell*

EMANCIPATION PROCLAMATION, famous document signed by Abraham Lincoln that did not free slaves in Kentucky. At the outbreak of the Civil War, many white Kentuckians trusted Abraham Lincoln's promises not to abolish slavery. Throughout 1862, fugitive slaves of both pro-Union and pro-Confederate masters were frequently returned to their owners by the Union army, and Lincoln's numerous attempts to create a system of voluntary compensated emancipation were rejected by the state.

By late 1862, as the Union's casualty numbers continued to rise, Lincoln came to believe that by recognizing the freedom of the South's slaves, he could severely weaken the Confederate forces. On January 1, 1863, Lincoln issued the Emancipation Proclamation, in which he declared that "I do order and declare that all persons held as slaves . . . are, and henceforward shall be free," and that the Union army would "recognize and maintain the freedom of said persons."

Although the declaration applied only to Confederate states, many white Kentuckians, who correctly believed that it signaled the eventual demise of slavery, met it with intense opposition. The *Lexington Observer and Reporter,* a pro-Union paper, called the executive order unconstitutional and noted: "Be assured that a large majority of the people of the United States are for the Union as it was and the Constitution as it is, and are resolved to preserve them against the continued assaults of abolitionists and secessionists." The *Louisville Daily Democrat* wrote, "We scarcely know how to express our indignation at this flagrant outrage of all constitutional law, all human justice, all Christian feeling." By January 10, Kentucky governor James F. Robinson had denounced the order, and the legislature passed a resolution rejecting its constitutionality.

The fears of slave owners were justified because the Emancipation Proclamation transformed the Civil War into a war of black liberation. Although the order did not free slaves in Kentucky, once the proclamation was generally known, they became increasingly willing to flee their masters, and thousands of enslaved Kentuckians did so, correctly believing that they would find freedom under the Union banner. Similarly, beginning in 1863, Union troops became more welcoming of fugitive slaves in the state and were indifferent to the requests of pro-Union slave owners who demanded the return of their slaves. By 1864, thousands of Kentucky blacks had fled to **Camp Nelson** and other Union recruiting posts throughout the state.

By the end of the war in 1865, Kentucky and Delaware remained the only two slaveholding states. Kentucky, however, with an estimated 100,000 men and women still enslaved, far outpaced Delaware's 900 men and women enslaved. Slavery in Kentucky continued to exist until the Thirteenth Amendment was ratified on December 18, 1865. Although the amendment became law, in a final act of defiance, Kentucky refused to ratify its passage.

Beginning in 1866 and continuing through the twenty-first century, African Americans throughout Kentucky marked emancipation by holding **Emancipation Day** celebrations on January 1, the date Lincoln signed his order. Although the Emancipation Proclamation did not directly apply to slaves in Kentucky, African Americans throughout the state and nation celebrated its symbolism. For the first time, the federal government promised to protect the interests and human rights of black men and women.

Guelzo, Allen. *Lincoln's Emancipation Proclamation: The End of Slavery in America.* New York: Simon & Schuster, 2004.
Harrison, Lowell H., and James C. Klotter. *A New History of Kentucky.* Lexington: Univ. Press of Kentucky, 1997.
"Important from Kentucky: Gov. Robinson's Message to the Legislature." *NYT,* January 10, 1863, 1.
Lucas, Marion B. *A History of Blacks in Kentucky: From Slavery to Segregation.* 2nd ed. Frankfort: Kentucky Historical Society, 2003.
Wright, George C. *Life Behind a Veil: Blacks in Louisville, Kentucky, 1865–1930.* Baton Rouge: Louisiana State Univ. Press, 1985.

—*Joshua D. Farrington*

ESTILL, MONK (b. unknown; d. 1835, Madison Co., KY), one of the first freed slaves in Kentucky history. Monk Estill, a slave belonging to Capt. James Estill, arrived in Kentucky during the 1770s and in 1779 planted and maintained a nursery of apple trees in Boonesborough. In 1780, Monk moved to Estill's Station, established by Captain Estill southeast of present-day Richmond. On March 20, 1782, Wyandot Indians tomahawked 14-year-old Jennie Gass at Estill's Station and captured Monk Estill, whom they interrogated. By exaggerating the strength of the garrison, the slave persuaded the Indians to postpone their planned assault. Two days later, the Indians were attacked by James Estill and 25 Kentuckians at Little Mountain (now Mt. Sterling, KY).

During the bloody conflict, known as the Battle of Little Mountain or Estill's Defeat, Capt. James Estill was stabbed to death, and 13 of his men were either killed or gravely wounded. While the battle raged, Monk Estill escaped and carried James Berry, one of the wounded, nearly 25 miles back to Estill's Station. He later distinguished himself by manufacturing gunpowder for Boonesborough and Estill's Station. It is thought that he mined saltpeter (potassium nitrate crystals) for the black powder mixture at Peyton Cave in Madison Co.

Monk Estill was five feet, five inches tall and weighed 200 pounds. He had three wives, by whom he had 30 children. One of his sons, Jerry, was the first black child born in Boonesborough. In 1782, in recognition of his services, Monk Estill was given his freedom by James Estill's son Wallace, who provided for Monk until his death in Madison Co. in 1835. Monk Estill, who became a Baptist minister and lived in Shelbyville, is considered the first freed slave in Kentucky history.

Cotterill, Robert S. *History of Pioneer Kentucky.* Cincinnati: Johnson and Hardin, 1917.

—*Ted Franklin Belue*

***EUBANKS V. UNIVERSITY OF KENTUCKY* (1941), lawsuit challenging the segregated admissions policy at the University of Kentucky.** On September 10, 1941, Charles Lamont Eubanks, a recent graduate of Louisville's **Central High School,** filed suit against the University of Kentucky (UK) and its leadership to se-

cure admission to its school of engineering. Members of the **National Association for the Advancement of Colored People** Legal Defense Fund and its local team supported his lawsuit (called *Eubanks v. Donovan* in the early stages of the lawsuit); this legal action was their first Kentucky education case. Within two months, Thurgood Marshall joined the team and filed a new complaint asking for $3,000 in damages and an injunction to force UK to admit African Americans.

UK argued that the 1904 **Day Law** prohibited black students such as Eubanks (who had graduated with honors) from engaging in an integrated educational setting in the state. Moreover, in less than a month, the State Board of Education created a two-year civil engineering curriculum of one teacher, two students, and inadequate engineering equipment at Frankfort's Kentucky State College (later known as **Kentucky State University**) with the purpose of fulfilling the separate-but-equal mythology. The lawsuit meant that Eubanks and his NAACP counsel were challenging a state segregation law that had been supported by several Supreme Court rulings.

The lawsuit followed the 1938 Supreme Court ruling (*Missouri ex. rel. Gaines v. Canada*) requiring states like Kentucky that sustained racial segregation to demonstrate that their racially segregated educational programs were truly equal to each other. To avoid this problem, Kentucky blacks, wanting truly equivalent programs, were offered out-of-state scholarships through the 1936 **Anderson-Mayer State Aid Act.** However, Eubanks wanted to go only to the University of Kentucky.

Attorneys for the university met the lawsuit with multiple legal maneuvers. Motions delaying the actual prosecution of the case moved from local courts to the federal District Court for the Eastern District of Kentucky in Lexington. With each legal motion, plaintiff Eubanks grew less enthusiastic about the outcome. As he sought employment in various jobs in Louisville, local blacks grew uncomfortable about his challenge to the racial status quo. Additionally, Eubanks's personal adversities of divorce and army entrance rejection reportedly caused him to suffer from depression. In January 1945, the district court in Lexington dismissed the case because, according to court rules, it was not prosecuted (actually argued) through two terms of the court. UK remained racially segregated until **Lyman T. Johnson** succeeded in a similar lawsuit in 1949.

Eubanks did not continue his quest for an engineering degree. He remained in Louisville and worked in various jobs in local businesses. On March 11, 1964, he died of a "malignant neoplasm of kidney" at age 40.

Eubanks, Charles. Commonwealth of Kentucky death certificate, March 11, 1964, Department of Vital Statistics, Kentucky Cabinet for Health and Family Services, Frankfort, KY.
Eubanks v. Donovan, Civil Action File No. 215, 1941, District Court of the United States of the Eastern District of Kentucky, Lexington.
NAACP Papers. Pt. 3, The Campaign for Educational Equality: Legal Department and Central Office Records, 1913–1950. Microfilm, Univ. of Kentucky, Lexington.
Newspapers: *LCJ,* September 10, 1941; *LD,* January 13, 1945.
Tushnet, Mark V. *Making Civil Rights Law: Thurgood Marshall and the Supreme Court, 1936–1961.* New York: Oxford Univ. Press, 1994.

—*John A. Hardin*

EVANS, EUGENE (b. 1855, Louisville, KY; d. unknown), Baptist minister, political activist, editor, and author. Born to an enslaved father and a free mother, Eugene Evans and his younger sister, Marcella, were reared in Louisville, KY. In 1869, their father died, leaving the family financially impoverished. Evans worked in a brickyard to help support the family and was licensed to preach at age 18. He served his first church in Brandenburg, KY, for three years, undeterred by death threats from the Ku Klux Klan. In 1876, he moved to Rockford, IN, where he initiated his political activism through candidate support. He also established and published the *Baptist Banner.*

Three years later, Evans moved back to Kentucky to serve Elizabethtown's First Church. While he was there, he published the *Christian Pilot.* In 1882, he moved to Lexington to serve Main Street Baptist Church, at the time the largest African American church in Kentucky. He unified the various factions in the church and liquidated much of the church's debt. He additionally published the paper *Fair Play.* In Lexington, he crossed denominational lines and attended the Colored Methodist Conference.

In 1884, Evans's next appointment was serving Bowling Green's State Street Baptist Church, where he organized the Baptist Union District Association, the Sunday School Convention, and the Ministers' and Deacons' Meeting. He also continued his newspaper editing with the *Bowling Green Watchman,* a Republican Party paper. In the *Watchman,* he praised **William J. Simmons** for his educational work at Louisville's State Colored Baptist University (later known as **Simmons College of Kentucky**). Evans later served as a trustee at the university.

Three years later, Evans transferred to Frankfort's black **First Baptist Church** on Clinton St., which was deeply divided. In a letter to the editor of the *Frankfort Roundabout,* Evans blamed poor leadership and not only challenged the African American community but also requested support from white citizens to help the church prosper. He signed his letter, "I remain, for the elevation of my race." Two months after his arrival, Evans baptized 124 converts in less than an hour in the Ohio River.

In Frankfort, the state's capital, Evans increased his political activism as a delegate to the Republican State Convention. After his defeat as a candidate for registrar of the Land Office, he asserted, "Kentucky Republicans have plenty of taffy for the Germans and Irish, but not even a cold potato for the Negro." He declared that he was risking his life to participate in politics and claimed that he had not received votes because of his race. Evans warned the Republican Party not to take the black vote for granted. He joined other African American delegates in an effort to have their voices heard. One delegate shouted, "You want our votes, but you also want all the offices."

Considered an excellent writer, Evans wrote several pamphlets and attempted authorship of a book, *Some Arrows from My Quiver.* He used the local newspaper's "Letters to the Editor" section to express his opinions on religion and politics. He responded to one man's attack by claiming that he was "too well known in Kentucky to pay much attention to every little pop-gun that jumps up for notoriety."

In 1891, Evans was elected spokesman of an African American delegation of the **Anti–Separate Coach Movement** of Kentucky. Two years later, he reportedly left the state, "called to other fields of labor." Sources indicate that he moved to Philadelphia.

Newspapers: "Editor Roundabout," *Frankfort Roundabout,* April 2, 1887, 8; "Hot Shot," *Maysville (KY) Daily Evening Bulletin,* June 10, 1887, 2.

Pegues, A. W. *Our Baptist Ministers and Schools.* Springfield, MA: Willey & Co., 1892.

Underwood, Elsworth E. *A Brief History of the Colored Churches of Frankfort, Kentucky.* Frankfort, KY: Elsworth E. Underwood, 1906.

—*Sallie L. Powell*

EVANS, WILLIAM LEONARD, JR. (b. 1914, Louisville, KY; d. 2007, Tucson, AZ), publisher of *Tuesday* magazine. W. Leonard Evans, as he preferred to be called, was the son of renowned architect and Urban League secretary **William L. Evans Sr.** and Beatrice Evans, who, in 1919, became the first African American insurance saleswoman in Louisville. Born in Louisville in 1914, Evans moved to Chicago with his parents in 1919. Four years later, his parents returned to Louisville, where they lived until they moved to Buffalo, NY, in 1927.

During the 1930s, Evans attended Fisk University for two years before transferring and receiving a business degree from the University of Illinois. After graduation, he worked as an advertising executive with the Chicago firm owned by famed white advertiser Arthur Meyerhoff, but he soon left for New York to form his own agency that targeted African Americans. In 1953, Evans organized a network of 40 national radio stations that targeted African American communities with shows like *The Story of Ruby Valentine.* The stations enjoyed enormous success in the mid-1950s and even garnered a large white audience because of the quality of the programming.

In 1965, Evans formed Tuesday Publications, which published a weekly newspaper insert, *Tuesday* magazine, that featured positive stories on African American life, politics, and culture. The magazine's name referred to the day on which black newspapers were traditionally printed in the North so that they could reach southern African Americans by the weekend. In its first printing, *Tuesday* reached over 1.3 million homes and could be found in the Sunday editions of major newspapers throughout the country, such as the *Philadelphia Bulletin,* the *Milwaukee Journal-Sentinel,* the *Chicago Sun-Times,* and the *Cleveland Plain Dealer.* The publication was so successful that Evans published a secondary magazine, *Tuesday at Home,* in 1970. By 1973, the two magazines were inserted into the Sunday editions of 23 major newspapers, including the *Chicago Tribune,* and reached over 4.5 million subscribers. At its peak in the early 1970s, Tuesday Publications was the 29th-largest black-owned business in the United States, based on gross revenues, and the second largest of the nine devoted to communications.

Evans eventually retired in Arizona after Tuesday Publications did not survive the economic downturn of the late 1970s. In 1975, he received an Illini Achievement Award from the University of Illinois Alumni Association. He died after suffering a stroke in Tucson, Arizona, in 2007.

Newspapers: "Advertising: Dialogue for Negro and White," *NYT,* April 15, 1965, 54; "W. Leonard Evans Jr.," *Chicago Tribune,* June 27, 2007, 9.

Pride, Armistead, and Clint Wilson II. *A History of the Black Press.* Washington, DC: Howard Univ. Press, 1997.

EVANS, WILLIAM LEONARD, SR. (b. 1883, Louisville, KY; d. 1966, Buffalo, NY), teacher, architect, and social activist. Born and raised in Louisville, William L. Evans graduated from Fisk University in 1909. He then studied engineering and architecture at Columbia University from 1910 to 1911. He returned to Louisville after completing his studies and taught drawing and design at Louisville **Central High School** until 1916. For the next three years, he served as a partner in one of the city's few black architectural firms.

In 1919, he was named industrial work secretary for the Chicago Urban League, the first industrial work secretary of any **National Urban League** branch. He returned to Louisville in 1923, where he partnered with renowned architect **Samuel M. Plato** to form the Plato and Evans Architectural Firm. Evans designed churches, lodges, and schools that were built throughout Kentucky, Indiana, and Ohio.

Evans left the firm in 1927 after he was appointed executive secretary of the Buffalo Urban League in New York. During his tenure, which lasted well into the 1950s, Evans fought for jobs, political representation, and affordable housing for Buffalo's black community. According to another resident of the city, Evans "was one of two individuals who had contributed most to the African American community of Buffalo." In addition to his service with the Urban League, Evans served on the Mayor's Committee on Stabilization during the Great Depression and was appointed to numerous other positions within the city, including serving on the city's planning commission. He was also one of the most influential members of the Buffalo Commission in the New York State Commission against Discrimination. During the 1930s, he also taught classes at Buffalo State Teachers College and developed courses on African Americans, which he subsequently taught, at the University of Buffalo.

William L. Evans Sr. was the father of **W. Leonard Evans Jr.**, an important African American businessman and publisher. Evans Sr. died in Buffalo in 1966. After the deaths of Evans and National Urban League director **Whitney Young Jr.**, the Buffalo Urban League memorialized the two leaders with the creation of the annual William L. Evans/Whitney M. Young Humanitarian Award.

Canaan, Gareth. "'Part of the Loaf': Economic Conditions of Chicago's African-American Working Class during the 1920's." *Journal of Social History* 35, no. 1 (2001): 147–74.
Williams, Lillian Serece. *Strangers in the Land of Paradise: The Creation of an African American Community, Buffalo, New York, 1900–1940.* Bloomington: Indiana Univ. Press, 1999.
Yenser, Thomas, ed. *Who's Who in Colored America, 1933–1937.* 4th ed. New York: Thomas Yenser, 1937.

—Joshua D. Farrington

EWING, THOMAS H. (b. 1856, Kentucky; d. 1930, Leavenworth, KS), medical doctor, minister, and investor. Little is known about Thomas H. Ewing's early life, but by the time of his death, he was one of Kansas City's most important and wealthiest African Americans. According to census data and a brief 1913 biography, he was born in Kentucky, presumably near Paducah, just before the outbreak of the Civil War. After hearing about the opportunities out West, T. H. Ewing, as he was known, joined thousands of postwar Americans in westward expansion. As a young man without means, he walked from Paducah to Kansas City, MO, and eventually settled in Nebraska. A self-educated man, Ewing attended a medical college in Nebraska and eventually opened a medical practice and pastored a church in Lincoln.

In 1887, Ewing was called to take over Vine Street Baptist Church in Kansas City, MO. At the time of his arrival, it was a small church that served an impoverished community. Only three of its members, for instance, owned their own house. Ewing started three financial clubs in Kansas City and taught his parishioners the importance of owning property, spending frugally, and saving—things he practiced with remarkable success in his own life. By 1912, Vine Street was one of the three largest black Baptist churches in the city, and over 100 of its 600 members owned their own house and property.

By the time of his death in 1930, Ewing had become, in the words of a contemporary, "the wealthiest colored Baptist minister in the entire West." He owned farms in Oklahoma and Kansas, had various properties in Kansas City, MO, and South Park, KS, and owned his own homestead in Leavenworth. According to historian Charles Coulter, because of T. H. Ewing's position as an influential minister, as well as his wealth, he was one of the most important men who "helped shape Kansas City's African American community before World War I."

Bacote, Samuel William. *Who's Who among the Colored Baptists of the United States.* Kansas City, MO: Franklin Hundson, 1913.
Coulter, Charles. *"Take Up the Black Man's Burden": Kansas City's African American Communities, 1865–1939.* Columbia: Univ. of Missouri Press, 2006.

—Joshua D. Farrington

EXODUSTERS, formerly enslaved African American southerners who organized migration movements to Kansas after the Civil War. Kentucky African Americans began to leave the state for Kansas during the 1860s and 1870s. In 1880, of the 43,000 blacks living in Kansas, almost 7,000 claimed Kentucky as their state of birth. Emigrant groups from Fayette, Garrard, Scott, Boyle, Ohio, Jessamine, and Jefferson Counties in central and northern Kentucky participated in large numbers. Exodusters founded all-black settlements, such as Dunlap Colony in Morris and Lyon Counties, Singleton Colony in Cherokee Co., and **Nicodemus** Colony in Graham Co.

Some historians suggest that the Exoduster movement was sparked by dishonest land speculators who sought to profit from land sales to African American farmers, while others emphasize the role of corrupt politicians who needed the support of African American voters in order to win close elections. Immediate strains, such as cotton crop failures and yellow fever epidemics, were also important motivating factors. The most significant cause was the combination of political, economic, and violent repression that African American southerners experienced during

Reconstruction. Grassroots leaders such as Henry Adams of Louisiana and Benjamin "Pap" Singleton of Tennessee believed that emigration would improve the African American condition and encouraged many to leave the South. Former slaves, many of whom were engaged in sharecropping or crop lien arrangements, reasoned that if they could become independent farmers in Kansas, they could secure economic and political self-determination.

In 1877, **Gabriel Burdett,** a former slave and minister, became disillusioned because of Kentucky's racial inequality. He left **Camp Nelson,** where he had worked with the **American Missionary Association,** and led a group of African Americans to Kansas. That same year, 30 African Americans from Lexington, KY, become part of the founding of Nicodemus Colony. A few months later, 150 people from Scott Co., KY, joined the community. Two years later, Green Co., KY, native **Junius G. Groves** settled in Edwardsville, KS, and became known as the Potato King for his farming skills.

The Exoduster movement reached its height in 1879, during the aftermath of the economic crisis of 1873 and the withdrawal of federal forces from the South in 1877. In 1879, more than 15,000 African American southerners immigrated to Kansas. The states that contributed the most participants were located along the Mississippi River, including Tennessee, Kentucky, Louisiana, Arkansas, Missouri, and Mississippi. Some families were unable to reach Kansas because of financial difficulties and were forced to settle in cities en route, such as St. Louis, MO, or Louisville, KY. Agencies such as the Kansas Freedman's Relief Association provided some assistance but generally were not equipped to provide substantial help to such a large number of emigrants.

Today, most Exoduster towns have been abandoned. The lack of railroads isolated the all-black settlements, and many Exodusters eventually relocated to more developed towns and cities. Nicodemus is located in northwest Kansas in Graham Co. It has a population of fewer than 100 residents.

Cohen, William. *At Freedom's Edge: Black Mobility and the Southern White Quest for Racial Control.* Baton Rouge: Louisiana State Univ. Press, 1991.

Lucas, Marion B. *A History of Blacks in Kentucky.* Vol. 1, *From Slavery to Segregation, 1760–1891.* Frankfort: Kentucky Historical Society, 1992.

Painter, Nell Irvin. *Exodusters: Black Migration to Kansas after Reconstruction.* New York: Norton, 1992.

—Selena Sanderfer

EXUM, WILLIAM (b. 1910, Carbondale, IL; d. 1988, Lexington, KY), educator, athlete, college coach, and university athletic director. William Exum was born in Carbondale, IL, on May 10, 1910. His parents, William and Ruth Exum, later moved to Gary, IN, where young William graduated from the local schools in 1928. Next, he attended the University of Wisconsin, where he excelled in track, cross-country, football, basketball, and baseball. He competed in track against 1936 Olympic champion Jesse Owens. He was the first African American varsity football player and the second African American intercollegiate athlete at Wisconsin. His academic achievements were also notable: bachelor's and master's degrees from the University of Wisconsin and a doctorate in physical education from New York University in the 1950s. He worked at Bethune-Cookman University, Morehouse College, and Lincoln University in Missouri. He served for three years in the U.S. Army during World War II.

In addition to serving in several administrative roles for athletics, including athletic director, at Kentucky State College (later known as **Kentucky State University**) from 1949 to 1980, he served as a manager of U.S. track teams at the 1972 and 1976 Olympics and the 1971 Pan American Games. He coached the Kentucky State cross-country team to its first NCAA national championship in 1964 and served on various NCAA national committees.

Exum continued to reside in Frankfort after his retirement in 1980. He died at Lexington's Veterans Administration Medical Center on August 1, 1988. In 1994, Kentucky State University honored him with the William Exum Athletic Center.

Newspapers: "Retired KSU Athletic Director, Coach William Exum Dies," *LHL,* August 11, 1988, C7; "Exum a Great Athlete and Coach," *Merrillville (IN) Post-Tribune,* February 6, 2003, B2.

"Celebrating Black History, William Exum '36," University of Wisconsin Badgers. http://www.uwbadgers.com/history/black-history-exum.html (accessed April 1, 2013).

—John A. Hardin

F

FARMINGTON HISTORIC HOME, plantation home owned by John and Lucy Speed. The Farmington Historic Home, located at Bardstown Rd. and the Watterson Expressway, was built for John and Lucy Gilmer (Fry) Speed and was the center of a sprawling, 500-acre hemp plantation. The house may have been designed from a plan by Thomas Jefferson.

John Speed was a 36-year-old widower with two young daughters when he met and married 29-year-old Lucy Gilmer Fry. Both had come across the Wilderness Road from Virginia at the age of 10, along with their respective families and slaves. Sometime after his 1808 marriage to Lucy, John, together with David Ward and William Pope Jr., purchased over 2,000 acres of fertile land along Beargrass Creek in Jefferson Co. The land was divided among them; and John, his young bride, and his two daughters settled into log cabins on his portion of the property in 1809.

The 14-room Federal-style house was begun in 1815 and completed in 1816. A contract (discovered in 1998) for construction of the house identified Robert Nicholson as the builder and Paul Skidmore as the individual who drew up the plan for the Speeds, quite possibly based on a plan for a house by Thomas Jefferson. Close similarities between the Farmington plan and the plan by Jefferson, which both include octagonal rooms and enclosed staircases in the same locations, have led scholars to suggest the Jefferson connection with Farmington. Family associations between Lucy Fry's family and Jefferson provide additional circumstantial evidence for this idea. Lucy's maternal grandfather, Thomas Walker, was a guardian of Thomas Jefferson, and her aunt's house in Charlottesville, also named Farmington, received an addition designed by Jefferson in 1802.

John Speed developed into a successful hemp planter, though he sought to diversify with other crops at Farmington. Livestock, apple orchards for cider production, a small dairy, corn, wheat, and tobacco rounded out the plantation's production.

Enslaved African Americans were involved in every aspect of the plantation's operation, from probably firing and laying bricks for the house and its dependencies to tending the dairy and livestock, maintaining the house, serving the family, weaving, spinning, gardening, and creating income from their hire-out status. At the death of John Speed in 1840, 57 slaves were listed in the inventory of the property. Among them was 41-year-old Morocco, who sometimes functioned as a courier, and Rose, who, along with Morocco, frequently traveled to market with farm goods to sell.

John and Lucy Speed saw 11 children reach adulthood from his two marriages—five sons and six daughters. All the children played prominent roles in the growing young river city. The Speed daughters, with the exception of Mary and Eliza, married and became leading matrons of Louisville. Susan Speed Davis contributed to the establishment of the Home for Friendless Women. Mary became a noted pianist and lived with Eliza all her life. Sons Joshua and James had significant influence in both local and national politics.

In 1835, Joshua Speed moved to Springfield, IL, to open a mercantile store. After two years in business, Speed met another young man, Abraham Lincoln, who was beginning his own career. Lincoln sought credit at the store. He received both credit and an offer to share quarters with Speed in his room above the store. Over the next three years, Speed and Lincoln became political allies and intimate friends, entertaining the rising young men who congregated in the store after hours to sort out the latest political developments in the region. They remained roommates until 1841, when Speed returned to Louisville after the death of his father.

In August 1841, Lincoln, suffering from depression after a break in his relationship with Lexington-born Mary Todd, traveled to Louisville at the request of Joshua to regain his spirits. Joshua was clearly disturbed by his friend's state of mind and felt that a few weeks at Farmington would be beneficial. Lincoln spent an undetermined amount of time, probably about three weeks, visiting with the Speeds and aiding young Speed's courtship of Fanny Henning. Both men spoke at length about their relationships with women. This bond continued throughout Lincoln's life.

During this 1841 trip, Lincoln frequently traveled into Louisville to visit with fellow lawyer James Speed, who remembered Lincoln's often ribald joking. In 1864, Lincoln asked James Speed to serve as attorney general in his cabinet. Speed served beyond Lincoln's death but resigned in 1866.

In 1845, widow Lucy Speed moved into town to live with various of her children, while another daughter, Peachy, along with her husband, Austin L. Peay, operated the plantation. Much of it had been subdivided and sold both to family members and to others. After the 1849 death of Austin Peay in a cholera epidemic, Peachy ran Farmington herself along with her slaves. These included David Spencer, reported to be a master bricklayer, and Martha, a young girl who later married David and served as a cook for Peachy Peay. In 1865, the Civil War was over, slavery had been abolished, and Peachy sold Farmington to German farmers.

In 1959, Farmington Historic Home became the flagship house of Historic Homes Foundation and opened for tours. Farmington is listed on the National Register of Historic Places.

Construction contract. Bullitt Papers, microfilm reel 7, Filson Club Historical Society.

Ottesen, Ann I. "A Reconstruction of the Activities and Outbuildings at Farmington, an Early Nineteenth Century Hemp Farm." *FCHQ* 59 (October 1985): 395–425.

—Deborah Spearing

FARRIS, ELAINE (b. 1955, Clark Co., KY), first full-time African American school superintendent in Kentucky. Born and raised in Clark Co., Elaine Farris graduated from Eastern Kentucky University with a degree in secondary health and physical education in 1977 and received her MA in health education from the same school in 1981. For the next seven years, she worked as a physical education teacher in Clark Co. She began her meteoric rise in 1993 when she was appointed assistant principal at George Rogers Clark High School. In 1998, she became the principal of Shearer Elementary School in Winchester, and she was named the elementary director for Fayette County Public Schools in 2001.

Elaine Farris.

In 2004, 50 years after the U.S. Supreme Court decision in *Brown v. Board of Education,* Elaine Farris became the first permanent superintendent in any of Kentucky's 176 school districts. In a tight 3–2 vote, the Shelby County School Board named Farris the county's new superintendent. At the time of her appointment, Shelby Co. had more than 5,400 students, 700 employees working in 10 schools, and an annual budget of $39 million.

In 2007, she left that post when she was named a deputy commissioner with the Kentucky Department of Education. Less than two years later, in January 2009, Farris was named interim education commissioner for the Kentucky Board of Education while the board searched nationwide for a new director. In April 2009, Farris resigned from her interim post and returned to her native Clark Co., where she had just been appointed the county's new superintendent of public schools.

Reflecting on her historic appointment in 2004, Farris said, "I feel like that I've opened some doors for minority candidates and superintendents. . . . I just want to be a good role model. . . . And I would like to see all the students look at me as an individual and judge me by the content of my character and not so much by the color of my skin."

Newspapers: "I've Opened Some Doors," *CE,* June 23, 2004; "A Kentucky First," *LHL,* June 23, 2004, A1.

—*Joshua D. Farrington*

FARRISTOWN, one of several historic African American communities throughout the state of Kentucky. Immediately after the Civil War, large numbers of African Americans migrated to Berea, a town founded by Rev. John G. Fee. Fee advocated Christian brotherhood and sought to create an integrated community. According to Rev. John A. R. Rogers, superintendent at **Berea College** in 1866, African Americans were attracted to Berea because it was "the land of promise, and to reach it with all they had on their backs, or at best in a rickety old cart, was the fulfillment of their hopes."

Farristown was named for three African American members of the Farris family, Charlie, Arthur, and Henry. Arthur was a student at Berea College in 1903. Located about a mile from Berea College in Madison Co., Farristown was considered part of the area called Black Valley because of the dense population of African Americans. It was a rural neighborhood located in the southern part of the county that consisted of both black and white farm families.

In the close-knit community, Farristown Baptist Church was established in 1883, and sometime during the early to mid-twentieth century, Arthur "A. J." Baxter opened the Farristown General Store. Baxter, who had attended Berea College and graduated from Wilberforce University in Ohio, was a successful farmer, and his wife, Joella White, was a schoolteacher. Farristown Baptist Church baptisms were held in Baxter's pond. Groups of children played throughout the area, and traveling baseball teams entertained spectators in games in the open field. Among the families in the community were the Ballards, the Bennetts, the Blythes, the Broaduses, the Chenaults, the Dunsons, the Martins, the Walkers, and the Whites. Sgt. Anderson White was a Union soldier who served in Company K of the 13th Colored Artillery, **Grand Army of the Republic**.

By the end of the twentieth century, the community was no longer as populated as it had been because family members had died or moved away. However, the community received new life with the construction of the Farristown Middle School, which opened in 2011.

Burnside, Jacueline Grisby. *Berea and Madison County.* Black America. Charleston, SC: Arcadia, 2007.
Newspapers: "Ground Broken for Farristown Middle School." *Berea Citizen,* June 7, 2010, A-1, A-8; "Dunson, 81, Shares Her Memories of Farristown," *Berea Citizen,* February 24, 2011, A-1, A-8.
Sears, Richard D. *A Utopian Experiment in Kentucky: Integration and Social Equality at Berea, 1866–1904.* Westport, CT: Greenwood Press, 1996.

—*Gerald L. Smith*

FEDRIC, FRANCIS (b. ca. 1805, Fauquier Co., VA; d. ca. 1882, Baltimore, MD), slave and minister. Born in Fauquier Co., VA, Frances Fedric grew up a slave on a plantation near the Cedar Run River. At a young age, he was moved with his family to Mason Co., KY. His cleverness earned him the affection of his mistress, who used him as a house slave and gave him various domestic tasks. He was less popular, however, with his master's son, who beat him relentlessly in drunken rages after the old master died.

After being flogged for attending a prayer meeting, Fedric made his first attempt at escaping, hiding in a cavern in a swamp named Bear's Wallow before hunger forced him to return. He received 107 lashes for his attempt. In 1854, a second effort was more successful. With the aid of the **Underground Railroad,** he traveled to Canada, where he adopted the last name Fedric before journeying to Europe. In Great Britain, Fedric, who had experienced a religious conversion as a slave, began a career as a lecturer and preacher, delivering several speeches on the evils of slavery. After the Civil War, he returned to the United States and lived in Baltimore with his wife. He continued to preach across the United States, including several trips across the South and into the states where he had once toiled in bondage. Having learned to read and write while he was a slave, he recounted his story in three different narratives. His last name varied among sources: Fedric, Frederick, and Fredericks. Although his exact birth and death years remain uncertain, it can be surmised from the lack of information on him after 1882 that he died sometime around that year.

Frederick, Francis. *Autobiography of Rev. Francis Frederick, of Virginia.* Baltimore: J. W. Woods, Printer, 1869.

Innes, C. L., ed. *Slave Life in Virginia and Kentucky: A Narrative by Francis Fedric, Escaped Slave.* Baton Rouge: Louisiana State Univ. Press, 2010.

—*Stephen Pickering*

FERRILL, LONDON (b. ca. 1789, Hanover Co., VA; d. 1854, Kentucky), Baptist minister. London Ferrill was born into slavery in Hanover Co., VA, around 1789, and was apprenticed to a carpenter as a child. Converted at age 20, he decided to become a Baptist minister despite a Virginia law forbidding slaves to be baptized or ordained. Although he possessed little formal education, he soon demonstrated an unusual gift for preaching. Awarded his freedom at his owner's death, Ferrill moved with his wife to Lexington, KY, around 1815. There his exemplary lifestyle and conservative nature quickly won support among the white power structure. Invited to join **First African Baptist Church,** the oldest black church in Kentucky, Ferrill refused, citing its irregular relationship with white Baptists. Eventually called as pastor of First African Baptist and encouraged by white Baptists to accept the position, Ferrill received official ordination in 1821, and in 1824 his church entered the Elkhorn Baptist Association.

Over the next 30 years, Ferrill became the dominant black minister in central Kentucky as First African Baptist grew to be the largest black congregation in the commonwealth, with 1,820 members. During his ministry, Ferrill baptized more than 5,000 people. He started a school for children of church members in the early 1830s. The Ferrills set examples for the entire community, adopting two children to whom the couple eventually left their estate. During the famous 1833 cholera epidemic, of which his wife became one of the victims, Ferrill selflessly nursed the sick of both races. He became known for his phrasing in conducting the marriage ceremony: realizing the tenuousness of slave marriages, Ferrill pronounced couples wedded until parted by "death or distance." Ferrill died on October 12, 1854.

Spencer, J. H., and Burilla B. Spencer. *A History of Kentucky Baptists: From 1769 to 1885.* Cincinnati: J. R. Brumes, 1886.

—*Marion B. Lucas*

FIFTH STREET BAPTIST CHURCH (Louisville), second African American church founded in Kentucky. Originally known in 1829 as First African Baptist Church, it was on Market St. between Seventh and Eighth Sts. Around 1835, a slave owner dedicated the ground at Fifth and York Sts. as a place of worship for his slaves. A meeting house was erected beyond the city limits in a place described as swampy and difficult to reach. In 1839, the church, which had become Fifth Street Baptist Church, was organized as a house of worship for the slaves of white parishioners of the First Baptist Church. Under the leadership of pastor **Henry Adams,** who came to preach in 1839, black members were taken out of the white Baptist church three years later. At the time of separation from First Baptist, the church had a charter membership of 475 members. The church also holds the distinction of being the first piece of real estate owned by blacks in the city. In 1848, it established itself on Fifth St. south of **Walnut St.**

Although the church was not free from the influence of the white standing committee, it largely controlled its own affairs. In 1866, it began a movement for a hospital for freed slaves. In the 1870s, the church revolutionized the concept of social welfare by assigning a deacon to supervise visitation in each of the city's wards. It provided boxes of clothing for poor members and gave financial support to destitute members during the 1873 depression. By June 1876, the church was able to give three dollars a week to the poor, comparable to a laborer's weekly wage. The church gave annual financial support to and held fund-raising drives for the **Colored Orphans' Home** and St. James Home for the elderly. In addition, it awarded a college scholarship. The church also sponsored missionary work in Africa. It established several branch missions, some of which became churches. The church is at 1901 W. Jefferson St., its fourth location.

General Association of Colored Baptists in Kentucky Yearbook. Louisville, KY: General Association of Colored Baptists in Kentucky, 1943.

Lucas, Marion B. *A History of Blacks in Kentucky.* Vol. 1, *From Slavery to Segregation, 1760–1891.* Frankfort: Kentucky Historical Society, 1992.

Spencer, John H., and Burrilla B. Spencer. *A History of Kentucky Baptists: From 1769 to 1885.* Cincinnati: J. R. Baumes, 1886.

Wright, George C. *Life Behind a Veil: Blacks in Louisville, Kentucky, 1865–1930.* Baton Rouge: Louisiana State Univ. Press, 1985.

FIGGS, UKARI OKIEN (b. 1977, Fayette Co., KY), first African American woman from the Bluegrass region to play in the Women's National Basketball Association. Born on March 31, 1977, in Fayette Co., Ukari Okien Figgs started playing basketball at age six. She honed her skills on a dirt court at the family home in Scott Co.'s **New Zion,** an **African American hamlet** on the border of the two counties. Her paternal grandfather, Winston Figgs, farmed there. Her parents, Gregory, a Scott County High School principal, and her mother, Gail, supported their youngest child's athletic ambitions. Her Nigerian godparents named her Ukari Okien, which means "Unto us, God has given grace."

In 1995, Figgs, along with her teammate Camille Cooper, led Georgetown's Scott County High School to the Kentucky High School State Basketball Championship. Figgs was selected as Kentucky's Miss Basketball. After graduation that year, she and Cooper attended Purdue University in WestLafayette, IN, and helped the school win the NCAA championship in 1999. Figgs

Ukari Figgs at the induction for the Dawahares Kentucky High School Hall of Fame, alongside Commissioner Julian Tackett (left) and her father Greg Figgs (right).

was named Most Valuable Player. She then joined the Los Angeles Sparks and the five-feet-nine point guard guided the team to the Women's National Basketball Association championship in 2001.

Figgs retired from playing professional basketball in 2004. With her mechanical engineering degree from Purdue University, she worked as a production engineer specialist at Georgetown's Toyota Motor Manufacturing and was assistant coach for the Scott County High School boys' basketball team. In 2007, her college alma mater inducted her into the Purdue Intercollegiate Athletics Hall of Fame. Two years later, Purdue hired her as assistant coach for its women's basketball team. In 2011, the University of Kentucky appointed her assistant athletics director for women's basketball. In November 2013, she resigned from the University of Kentucky to become an assembly engineering specialist at Toyota in Georgetown, KY. She was named to the Dawahares/Kentucky High School Athletic Association Hall of Fame for the Class of 2014.

"Figgs Names Assistant AD for UK Hoops," University of Kentucky Athletics. http://www.ukathletics.com/sports/w-baskbl/spec-rel /060811aaa.html (accessed April 3, 2013).
"Former Boilermaker Ukari Figgs Named Assistant Coach," Purdue Sports. http://www.purduesports.com/sports/w-baskbl/spec-rel /041309aaa.html (accessed March 2, 2011).
Kentucky Birth Index, 1911–1999.
Newspapers: "Fame, but Not Success, Eludes Her," *LHL,* November 4, 2001, J1; "What's Up With . . . ? Ukari Figgs; Retired as Player but Chasing Titles Still," *LCJ,* February 23, 2004, E1; "Herald-Leader's Mike Fields among 11 Inductees to KHSAA Hall of Fame," *LHL,* June 2, 2013; "Kentucky Assistant AD Ukari Figgs Steps Down," *LHL,* November 1, 2013.

—*Sallie L. Powell*

FINN, MARVIN (b. ca. 1913, Clio, AL; d. 2007, Louisville, KY), folk artist. While sources disagree about his birth year, Marvin Finn was born to Alabama sharecroppers in the 1910s. Although he never finished first grade, Marvin noted that he was always "pretty sharp" and was taught the intricacies of woodworking by

his father, who whittled homemade toys for his 13 children. Finn used the knowledge he gained from his father to become one of Kentucky's most recognizable folk artists during the late twentieth century.

In 1952, Finn followed an older brother to Louisville and worked in the city for the next 26 years at various odd jobs in construction, pumping gas, and loading barges. Finn was first recognized in the 1970s when local residents expressed interest in the complex toys—three-level dollhouses and trucks with doors that opened—that he made for his five children. In 1982, Finn experienced his earliest art shows at the Kentucky School of Art after its director was impressed by pieces Finn sold in a yard sale. Two years later, his work was featured in the opening show of the Kentucky Crafts Foundation gallery. Throughout the rest of the 1980s and 1990s, his art was sold throughout the country, including New York City's Bloomingdale's.

Finn's most recognizable works are his colorfully painted and fancifully patterned wood cutouts of chickens and other birds. His Flock of Finns, a public art display of 24 colorfully painted giant steel birds, was displayed throughout Louisville and was placed on permanent display at Waterfront Park in 2002. After Finn's death in 2007, a local art dealer commented on Finn's artistic legacy in Louisville: "I think he was an icon. . . . I think he's probably not replaceable. . . . I never saw any work like his. He was known all over the region and the country."

Newspapers: "Fans Flocked to His Work," *LCJ,* January 31, 2007, B1; "Flock of Finns Return to Park," *LCJ,* February 13, 2009, B3.

—*Joshua D. Farrington*

FINNEY, NIKKY (b. 1957, Conway, SC), poet, educator, and Affrilachian writer. Lynn Carol Finney was born to civil rights activists Frances (née Davenport) and Ernest A. Finney Jr. on August 26, 1957. She adopted the name Nikky while she was in high school. Her undergraduate education was completed at Talladega College in Alabama, where she graduated with a BS in English in 1979. Finney then began graduate studies in African American literature at Atlanta University but eventually left the program.

Nikky Finney.

Her first book of poetry, *On Wings Made of Gauze,* was published in 1985. A decade later, *Rice* was published. It was honored with the Pen Open Book Award. In the early 1990s, she accepted a position teaching creative writing at the University of Kentucky and completed *Heartwood.* Soon after her arrival in Kentucky, she joined with **Frank X Walker, Crystal Wilkinson,** and other noted writers in founding the Affrilachian Poets. Her third book of poetry, titled *The World Is Round,* was published in 2002. In 2011, her book of poetry *Head Off & Split* won the National Book Award for poetry. Actor John Lithgow called her acceptance speech "the best acceptance speech for anything I've ever heard in my life."

Finney has served as professor of English and Provost's Distinguished Service Professor at the University of Kentucky. In 2013, she announced that she would leave Kentucky and return to her home state of South Carolina. The University of South Carolina in Columbia offered her the John H. Bennett Jr. Chair in Creative Writing and Southern Literature, a joint appointment in the Departments of English and Literature and the African American Studies program.

Finney, Nikky. *Head Off & Split.* Evanston, IL: TriQuarterly, 2011.
———. *Heartwood.* Lexington: Univ. Press of Kentucky, 1997.
———. *On Wings Made of Gauze.* New York: William Morrow, 1985.
———. *Rice.* Toronto: Sister Vision, 1995.
———. *The World Is Round.* Atlanta, GA: InnerLight, 2002.
Gretlund, Jan Nordby. "Finney, Nikky." In *The New Encyclopedia of Southern Culture,* vol. 9, *Literature,* edited by M. Thomas Inge. Chapel Hill: Univ. of North Carolina Press, 2008.
Newspapers: "Poetry in Emotion—Finney Basks in Literary Award, Hopes It Boosts Arts at UK," *LHL,* November 19, 2011, A1; "Renowned Poet Finney Is Leaving UK—She's Going to S.C. for a Job at 'Home,'" *LHL,* January 8, 2013, A1.

—*John R. Burch Jr.*

FIRMANTOWN (Woodford Co.), African American community near Versailles. The origins of Woodford Co.'s small **African American hamlet** Firmantown are elusive. According to J. Winston Coleman, a white historian writing in the 1940s, the community was first formed by "'kindly masters' leaving plots of ground for their old and faithful servants." Although little documentary evidence exists to support it, according to this theory, the freedmen later subdivided the land among their children and relatives.

However, Erving Smith, who lived in Firmantown for over 76 years and was the son of one of the community's first documented residents, recalled a different origin of the community. Smith believed that the town was formed in the 1870s after a black man with the last name Furman won 18 acres of land in a lottery with a 10-cent ticket. The first documented evidence regarding Firmantown reveals that in 1877, there was indeed a Mr. Furman who owned a plot of land and a house. Additionally, there were three other small properties in Firmantown at the time, which were owned by "R. Peters, R. Brown, and H. Smith."

Regardless of its origins, during the early 1890s, a one-room log-cabin schoolhouse was established to serve the small community. By 1900, Firmantown had a population of about 150 residents. The community remained small, however, throughout the twentieth century, and most of its inhabitants worked as agricultural laborers or domestic servants. By the 1960s, Firmantown residents included a number of white families. Firmantown is located off Paynes Mill Rd. between Versailles and Pisgah.

Asher, Brad. *Kentucky.* Northampton, MA: Interlink Books, 2006.
Coleman, J. Winston. *Slavery Times in Kentucky.* Chapel Hill: Univ. of North Carolina Press, 1940.
Smith, Peter Craig. "Negro Hamlets and Gentleman Farms: A Dichotomous Rural Settlement Pattern in Kentucky's Bluegrass Region." PhD diss., Univ. of Kentucky, 1972.
Smith, Peter Craig, and Karl B. Raitz. "Negro Hamlets and Agricultural Estates in Kentucky's Inner Bluegrass." *Geographical Review* 64, no. 2 (April 1974): 217–34.

—*Joshua D. Farrington*

FIRST AFRICAN BAPTIST CHURCH (LEXINGTON), early African American church in Lexington, KY. Around 1785, **Peter "Old Captain" ("Brother Captain"** or **"Rev. Captain") Durrett,** a slave from Virginia, arrived in Fayette Co., KY, where he attended church services with a small separate Baptist gathering at the head of Boone's Creek. After he and his wife moved to Lexington with their master, he initiated church services of his own in a cabin on the property of John Maxwell. His ministry to local blacks established the foundation of First African Baptist Church around 1790, although Durrett was denied ordination after applying to the South Kentucky Baptist Association. During his tenure as pastor of the church, he led as many as 300 members in worship.

In the late 1810s and early 1820s, the congregation split into two churches, one of which chose to continue under the name of First African Baptist, while the other eventually assumed the name Pleasant Green Baptist Church (later **Historic Pleasant Green Missionary Baptist Church**). Leadership of the former church devolved to **London Ferrill,** a freed slave from Virginia. He worked with white leaders in the city to legitimate the position of First African Baptist, joining the church to the Elkhorn Baptist Association, and increased the congregation to over 1,800 members. In 1833, the church purchased land at the corner of present-day Short and **Deweese** Sts., where an Italianate-style building was completed in 1856. First African Baptist Church remained at this location for the next 131 years, surviving another split in 1862 that led to the establishment of Main Street Baptist Church.

During the remaining years of the nineteenth century, the church witnessed the arrival and departure of several preachers, including **William J. Simmons,** eventual president and namesake of **Simmons University.** By the 1920s, the church building had grown to include a pipe organ and a Sunday School Annex Building that was considered one of the finest of its time. In 1926, Rev. Homer Nutter assumed leadership of the church, beginning a career that spanned nearly five decades. During his pastorate, he worked to improve the church building, renovating it several times, and quietly fought behind the scenes on behalf of the **civil rights movement** in Lexington.

In 1987, the congregation, under the leadership of Rev. Leon McIntyre, moved to a new building on Price Rd. The original

First African Baptist Church at its location on Short and Deweese Streets.

building was sold to Central Christian Church, which used it as a child-care center. In 2012, the First African Foundation announced plans to purchase the site, which had been listed on the National Register of Historic Places in 1986, as the foundation for a concert hall, cultural center, and museum.

Bishop, Robert H. *Outline of the History of the Church in the State of Kentucky, during a Period of Forty Years.* Lexington, KY: Thomas T. Skillman, 1824.

McIntyre, L. H. *One Grain of the Salt: The First African Baptist Church West of the Allegheny Mountains.* Lexington, KY: L. H. McIntyre, 1986.

Newspapers: "Church's Members Celebrate New Home," *LHL,* July 13, 1987, B1; "Honoring a Pioneer: Nutter Remembered for Civil Rights, Religious Leadership," *LHL,* July 13, 1989, B1; "Black Churches' Rich Legacy Explored," *LHL,* February 16, 2008, F1; "A Humble Beginning, a Promising Future," *LHL,* February 29, 2012, B1.

Spencer, John H., and Burrilla B. Spencer. *A History of Kentucky Baptists: From 1769 to 1885.* Cincinnati: J. R. Baumes, 1886.

—*Stephen Pickering*

FIRST BAPTIST CHURCH (COVINGTON), oldest African American congregation in northern Kentucky. In August 1864, Rev. George W. Dupee, along with 22 charter members, organized the First Baptist Church of Covington, which was first known as the Bremen St. Baptist Church. It is the oldest African American congregation in northern Kentucky. The church's first building was located on Bremen St., and **Jacob Price** was its first pastor. From its earliest days, the church has been involved in community activities, including education and civil rights. Under Price's leadership, the church hosted a number of rallies and organizational meetings to prepare the way for local African American private schools. In April 1866, the first private school opened at the church, directed by the Freedmen's Aid Commission and the **Freedmen's Bureau.** In late 1866, the **Ninth St. Methodist Episcopal Church** was formed out of the Bremen St. Baptist Church.

In 1869 the church on Bremen St. moved to Third St. and changed its name to Third St. Baptist Church; the school remained on Bremen St. It was after this move that Jacob Price and a small group of parishioners left the congregation because of a disagreement with other members. In 1870, the Third St. Baptist Church called **William Blackburn** as pastor. When citizens of Covington were asked to select delegates to attend the first statewide African American political convention in Frankfort, the delegate-selection meeting was held at the Third St. Baptist Church. During the ensuing years, the church grew and became more involved in the struggles of the African American community.

In 1874, the Third St. Baptist Church moved from Third to Robbins St. and erected a building at the new location; the congregation moved again in 1877 to a site on W. 13th St., where another church building was built. At that time, it changed its name to the First Colored Baptist Church of Covington. Placed in the cornerstone, laid on May 20, 1877, were copies of the Bible, several religious periodicals, Covington's 1877 city directory, a list of prominent city officials, and copies of that day's newspapers: the *Ticket,* the *Enquirer,* the *Volkesblatt,* the *Volksfreund,* and the *Commercial Gazette.* After the move to 13th St., Price and his splinter group returned, and Price succeeded in uniting the congregations briefly. A second separation resulted in establishment of the Ninth St. Baptist Church by departing members.

A number of pastors followed Blackburn at the First Baptist Church. In 1911, Rev. F. C. Locust became pastor. On July 7, 1915, a tornado destroyed the church building. In 1916, the church purchased a site on E. Ninth St., and construction began. One of the guest speakers at the new church dedication, April 7, 1917, was Mrs. **Elizabeth Beatrice Fouse** of Lexington. The new structure included beautiful stained-glass windows, financed by some of the oldest African American families of Covington and by the auxiliaries of the church. On August 30, 1941, Reverend Locust and First Baptist Church celebrated his 30th and the church's 77th anniversary. In 1947, when Locust was suffering from a serious illness, William P. Halbert was called to serve as his assistant. Halbert officially became pastor in July 1948, after Locust's death, and the congregation prospered under his leadership. He organized new auxiliaries and led a progressive program of development and advancement, encouraging community and civic involvement. The L. B. Fouse Civic League's leadership drew much of its membership from the First Baptist Church. Halbert retired in 1971, and A. B. Moore was called to serve as pastor in 1972. Moore resigned after serving for two years; he later founded Crucifixion Baptist Church on E. 10th St. On October 26, 1975, Willie R. Barbour became pastor of the First Baptist Church and served until 2001. On June 22, 2003, the First Baptist Church appointed Adam P. Crews Sr. its new full-time minister.

125th Anniversary Booklet. Covington, KY: First Baptist Church, 1989.
Newspapers: *Covington Ticket,* May 19, 1877, 1; *Covington Ticket,* May 21, 1877, 3; *Newport Local,* May 22, 1877, 2; "New Church to Be Erected," *KP,* January 9, 1915, 1; "Colored Baptists to Dedicate Church," *KP,* April 7, 1917, 1; "Two Anniversaries for Negro Baptist Church," *KP,* August 30, 1941, 1; "Black Past Often Unsung," *KP,* February 5, 1996, 4K; "Black Churches Offered Stability in Troubled Times," *KP,* January 20, 1997, 4K.

—*Theodore H. H. Harris*

FIRST BAPTIST CHURCH (FRANKFORT), African American Baptist church in Frankfort, KY. Before 1833, Frankfort's First Baptist Church was an integrated institution. Under the leadership of John Ward and Ziah Black, the African American membership formed a separate church that met in various homes for over a decade. Rev. Henderson Williams (1838–1843) served as the church's first minister. John Ward donated land for a church building in 1844. Through the leadership of the next pastor, Rev. James Monroe (1845–1864) organized a statewide meeting between Kentucky black ministers and their respective deacons in neighboring Versailles. Subsequently, Monroe became one of the founding members of the General Association of Colored Baptists in Kentucky. In 1866, First Baptist Church hosted the second State Convention of Colored Baptists, and Monroe presented the keynote address.

Rev. Robert Martin (1864–1884) reportedly baptized more members into the congregation than any other minister. One of those members was **William H. Steward,** the founder of the *American Baptist* newspaper. Beginning in 1885, the church suffered from divisions over various issues, including debts and lawsuits. Rev. Eugene Evans (1887–1894) helped rebuild the congregation by asking for assistance from not only the African American members but also the white community and by baptizing 124 converts in less than an hour.

The church's growth necessitated a new building. In 1903, under the pastorate of Robert Mitchell (1898–1903), a lot was purchased on Clinton and High Sts. When the city ignored the church's petition for a building permit, the decision was made to construct the building without permission. The city council arrested and fined the involved parties.

The church's trustees obtained a temporary injunction to block the city's assault. However, Judge James E. Cantrill suspended the ruling with the claim that the church was a "nuisance." The trustees then presented the case to the Court of Appeals. In 1904, in *Boyd v. Board of Councilmen of the City of Frankfort,* Judge W. E. Settle ruled against the previous court, maintaining that the judgment had been "largely based upon race prejudice." In 1905, construction of First Baptist Church, sometimes known as Big Bethel, continued under the pastoral leadership of Rev. W. T. Silvey (1905–1919). The local white-owned newspaper asserted that the abundant raised funds proved "what even these humble and despised people can do in the cause to which they have given their hearts. It is an object lesson for those who are more fortunately situated in life."

Rev. Kidd Leon Moore Jr. (1960–2006) served the church's longest pastorate, 46 years. He was active in the community and marched with Rev. Martin Luther King Jr. for civil rights. Rev. Robert Earl Houston Sr. became the church's 16th pastor in 2009. Under his leadership, the church has grown in membership and financial contributions.

Boyd v. Board of Councilmen of the City of Frankfort, 25 L.R. KY (1904), 1311–19.
First Baptist Church (Frankfort). http://www.firstbaptistfrankfort.com /FBC/History.html (accessed June 1, 2011).
Kentucky's Black Heritage: The Role of the Black People in the History of Kentucky from Pioneer Days to the Present. Frankfort: Kentucky Commission on Human Rights, 1971.
Legislative Research Commission. http://www.lrc.ky.gov/record/07rs /HR60/bill.doc (accessed June 1, 2011).
Lucas, Marion B. *A History of Blacks in Kentucky: From Slavery to Segregation, 1760–1891.* 2nd ed. Frankfort: Kentucky Historical Society, 2003.
Newspapers: *Frankfort Roundabout,* December 25, 1886, 2; April 2, 1887, 8; April 30, 1887, 1; May 26, 1906, 4.
Parrish, C. H. *Golden Jubilee of the General Association of Colored Baptists in Kentucky: From 1865–1915.* Louisville, KY: Mayes Printing Co., 1915.

—*Sallie L. Powell*

FIRST STANDARD BANK (LOUISVILLE), first African American bank in Kentucky. The evolution of African American businesses in Louisville unfolded in several stages, beginning with the establishment of small shops and service enterprises in the 1830s. By World War I, larger-scale businesses emerged with the opening of Mammoth Mutual Co. (later **Mammoth Life and Accident Insurance Co.**) in July 1915. **Domestic Life and Accident Insurance Co.** followed in June 1920, and its executives, while awaiting their charter, immediately began soliciting capital subscriptions for a bank to create both a depository for its funds and an engine to drive community economic development.

On January 17, 1921, the banking commissioner of Kentucky authorized the First Standard Bank to conduct regular banking operations. Touted as the "million dollar bank," First Standard became the first African American bank in Kentucky when it opened on February 5, 1921, with **Wilson Lovett** as president, **W. W. Spradling** as vice president and chairman of the board, and Dr. L. R. Johnson and Bishop **G. C. Clement** as vice presidents. Lovett resigned in July 1929 to assume the treasurership

First Standard Bank.

of Supreme Life Insurance Co. and was succeeded as president by longtime First Standard cashier J. R. Ray.

Located first at Seventh and eventually at Sixth and **Walnut** Sts., First Standard served both as a symbol of community pride and a source of working capital for African American businesses, which could not borrow at reasonable rates, if at all, from local white-owned financial institutions. By the mid-1920s, First Standard boasted $375,000 in total deposits, $500,000 in total assets, and more than $300,000 loaned to local African American entrepreneurs. Building on the success of Domestic Life and First Standard, Lovett and his partners also established other companies, for example, the Standard Building and Loan Association and the Parkway Building and Loan Association.

Despite their many accomplishments, African American businesses, even in this "Golden Age" of the 1920s, were fragile institutions marginal to the larger national economy and dependent on the limited earning (and purchasing) capacity of African Americans in a racially segregated society. This fragility was exposed most graphically with the onset of the Great Depression. When their depository institution, the Louisville Trust Co., closed after the failure of the National Bank of Kentucky, First Standard and the American Mutual Savings Bank, an extension of Mammoth Mutual, failed to open on November 17, 1930.

In an effort to salvage these key financial institutions, First Standard and American Mutual merged in January 1931 under the leadership of W. W. Spradling to form the Mutual Standard Bank. With strong community support, Mutual Standard opened briefly in April 1931. However, while factors external to the African American community caused the failure of First Standard, the economic weakness of that community in the throes of the Great Depression undermined Mutual Standard from its inception. Mutual Standard closed on May 7, 1931, and was subsequently liquidated by the Kentucky Banking Commission. More than 40 years passed before another African American bank was established in Louisville.

Newspapers: *Louisville Leader,* January 12, 1921; July 6, 1929; September 14, 1929; September 21, 1929; November 22, 1930; December 6, 1930; January 10, 1931; February 7, 1931; February 14, 1931; February 28, 1931; April 4, 1931; May 9, 1931; May 16, 1931; May 14, 1932; September 23, 1932; October 15, 1932.
The Crisis Magazine, 20 (July 1920): 148.
The Crisis Magazine, 20 (February 1, 1921): 175.
Wright, George C. *Life Behind a Veil: Blacks in Louisville, Kentucky, 1865–1930.* Baton Rouge: Louisiana State Univ. Press, 1985.

—*J. Blaine Hudson*

FISHER, ISAAC (b. 1871, Danville, KY; d. unknown), and Lillie A. Sinkler (b. 1874, Charleston, SC; d. unknown), educators. Isaac Fisher's mother, Polly Davis, was one of the founding members of New Mission Baptist Church in Danville, KY. The church's first pastor was **Wallace Fisher,** who may have been related to Isaac. In 1898, Rev. Wallace Fisher incorporated the Danville Polytechnic Seminary Company, and Isaac became its leader the following year.

Only two years before his management position at Polytechnic Seminary, Isaac Fisher graduated from Louisville's State University (later known as **Simmons College of Kentucky**) and taught for one year there. He was an active member of the Colored Teachers' Association and presented "The Importance of Arithmetic as a Discipliner of the Mind" for the organization's program at Hanging Fork in 1896.

A year later, Fisher married Lillie A. Sinkler, a graduate of Alabama's Selma University who had taught at State University. While Isaac acted as Polytechnic Seminary's principal, Lillie served as its vice principal. She later taught graded classes and music at the institution. By 1900, Lillie's sister, Ethel, and brother, Joseph, lived with the Fishers while Ethel attended school and Joseph worked at a hotel.

Under the leadership of the Fishers, the school not only was active in its community through concerts and football games but also was known in other states. One Washington, DC, newspaper identified Isaac Fisher as the founder and supervisor of Polytechnic Seminary. Fisher traveled in Kentucky and to other states to raise funds for the educational institution. James A. Shuttleworth, a white Louisville philanthropist, donated $2,500 for a steam laundry plant in 1902. Traveling in Ohio and Michigan, Fisher accumulated $10,000 in donations in 1909. Dora E. Johnson, a single woman from Norwalk, OH, acted as one of four financial agents who worked to raise funds for the school. In 1911, Danville's Polytechnic Seminary consisted of 2 male teachers, 7 female teachers, 93 male students, and 85 female students.

Isaac and Lillie Fisher worked together in their teaching profession and frequently attended the State Teachers' Association meetings. In one program, Isaac presented a lecture, "Industrial Education in Rural Schools." He additionally performed the secretarial duties of the Executive Board of the South District Sunday School Convention. Lillie was very active in various organizations and held several positions, including state secretary of the Endowment Bureau of Samaritans, state secretary of the Baptist Women's Missionary Convention, assistant secretary of the State Federation of Women's Clubs of Kentucky, and member of the Executive Board of the City Federation of Women's Clubs in Danville.

Information on the deaths of this influential couple is currently unknown.

"Current Events." *Semi-Weekly Interior Journal,* October 23, 1896, 1.
Parrish, C. H. *Golden Jubilee of the General Association of Colored Baptists in Kentucky: From 1865–1915.* Louisville, KY: Mayes Printing Co., 1915.
"Shreds and Patches." *Colored American,* February 8, 1902, 7.
U.S. Federal Census (1880, 1900, 1910).

—*Sallie L. Powell*

FISHER, MARY ANN (b. 1923, Henderson, KY; d. 2004, Louisville, KY), blues singer and backup vocalist for Ray Charles. Known as the Queen of the Blues, Mary Ann Fisher was born in Henderson in 1923. When she was four years old, her father was murdered, and her impoverished mother sent Mary Ann to the Kentucky Home Society for Colored Children in Louisville. Although she stayed at the orphanage for only one year until her adoption by a couple from Russellville, the institution proved to be a major source of inspiration for the rest of her life. The orphanage, known throughout the city for its famed marching band, was also home to music legends **Robert Elliott "Jonah" Jones**, **William "Dicky" Wells,** and **Helen Humes.** Fisher recalled that hearing the band practice was her earliest introduction to the power of music.

In the 1950s, Fisher returned to Louisville to pursue her music career; her only training came from singing gospel in church. She washed dishes at the Boston Cafe during the day and sang at various clubs throughout Louisville and Ft. Knox at night. During a 1955 tour in Kentucky, Ray Charles heard about Fisher's talent from a promoter. After hearing her sing, Charles, who at that point had no female backup vocalists, decided to "try out a little experiment" and asked Fisher to join his already popular band.

Within a matter of days, the two became lovers (she was unaware that Charles had been married for less than a month), and Fisher was given a segment of the show to sing solo **blues** ballads. She continued to tour with Charles for the next three years. In 1958, he added three more female backup vocalists to his routine, calling the four women the Raeletts. Jealousy of the new additions compounded Fisher's growing disillusionment with Charles that began with his increased drug abuse and sexual misconduct. That same year, she dropped out of the band and pursued independent work.

Fisher moved to New York, where she performed with Dinah Washington at Carnegie Hall and with Billie Holiday before her 1959 death. She also lived with fellow singer Jimmy Scott. During the early 1960s, she moved to Los Angeles and performed with such legends as James Brown, B. B. King, Jackie Wilson, Percy Mayfield, and Bobby Bland.

In 1967, she returned to Louisville and had difficulty finding music work. In 1972, after a series of various jobs, she found a full-time position at General Electric, where she worked for almost a decade. As she had done in her early life, she worked manual labor during the day and performed at night. By 1984, she had returned to full-time music work, playing regular performances at the Savoy. Throughout the rest of the 1980s and the 1990s, she performed at numerous venues and events across the city. Although she worked for decades alongside the country's top performers, Fisher did not release her first solo album, *Songbird of the South,* until 2003. She died in Louisville the following year.

According to Ray Charles, Mary Ann Fisher was the subject of three of his songs: "Mary Ann," "What Would I Do without You?," and "Leave My Woman Alone." In 2004, she was played by Aunjanue Ellis in the blockbuster movie *Ray.* After her death, she was inducted into the Kentucky Music Hall of Fame and was the subject of a documentary, *Queen of the Blues.*

Charles, Ray, and David Ritz. *Brother Ray: Ray Charles' Own Story.* Cambridge, MA: Da Capo Press, 2003.
"Fisher, Louisville's 'Queen of Blues,' Dies." *LCJ,* March 13, 2004, B1.
Lydon, Michael. *Ray Charles: Man and Music.* New York: Routledge, 2004.

—*Joshua D. Farrington*

FISHER, WALLACE (b. 1848, Danville, KY; d. unknown, Danville, KY), Baptist minister and educator. Born into slavery to owner John J. Craig, Wallace Craig, at age 16, fought for his freedom in the 116th U.S. Colored Infantry stationed at **Camp Nelson,** KY. He served for three years in the military. By 1870, he had taken the last name Fisher and worked on Craig's farm in Boyle Co. Two years later, he organized a Baptist church in Junction City. Services were originally held under a tree because his log cabin was too dark.

One local newspaper reported that during a revival, Fisher baptized 119 people near the Hanging Fork Bridge. He later publicly expressed his gratitude to black and white contributors. Considered a state evangelist, Fisher served other churches in Perryville and Mt. Salem. In 1892, he and 14 members established New Mission Baptist Church in Danville, KY.

In 1898, Fisher, as the chief incorporator, filed articles of incorporation with the secretary of state for the Danville Polytechnic Seminary Company. The next year, **Isaac Fisher** headed the educational institution. Isaac, the son of Polly Davis, who was a founding member of New Mission Baptist Church, may have been related to Wallace Fisher.

In almost 50 years of pastorate, Fisher baptized nearly 3,500 people. In 1912, he spoke to an integrated crowd at Danville's "colored school house." He taught school for seven years and was acknowledged as a supporter of **Lincoln Institute.** He served for two years as a Danville councilman. The specific dates of Fisher's teaching and political service and his death information seem lost to history.

"Bright, Lincoln County." *Semi-Weekly Interior Journal*, June 18, 1886.
Civil War Pension Index: General Index to Pension Files, 1861–1934.
"Here and There." *Daily Public Ledger* (Maysville), November 18, 1898.
Parrish, C. H. *Golden Jubilee of the General Association of Colored Baptists in Kentucky: From 1865–1915.* Louisville, KY: Mayes Printing Co., 1915.
U.S. Civil War Soldiers, 1861–1865.
U.S. Federal Census (1870, 1880, 1900, 1910).

—*Sallie L. Powell*

FITZBUTLER, HENRY (b. 1837, Canada; d. 1901, Louisville, KY), physician, publisher, and civil rights activist. Born in December 1837 to slave parents who had escaped north to Canada, Henry Fitzbutler became the first black graduate of the University of Michigan's medical school in 1872. That summer, Fitzbutler moved his family from Ontario to Louisville and opened a small office. Although Fitzbutler's practice struggled for the first few years, it served a vital role in assisting the city's 15,000 African Americans, who were turned away from white physicians and hospitals.

After the passage of the Civil Rights Acts of 1875, which prohibited discrimination in hotels, restaurants, public transportation, and public amusement places, Fitzbutler became a vehement advocate for the equal use of these facilities. He was considered outspoken by more conservative African Americans who desired the use of these places only when white leaders felt it was possible. Fitzbutler took a more demanding position and claimed that each citizen had a right to public facilities, although he too disapproved of the use of force. To publicize his and other African Americans' opinions on political issues, Fitzbutler established a weekly newspaper, the *Ohio Falls Express,* in 1879. It condemned segregation and discrimination and was published until 1904. Fitzbutler's continued interest in politics, coupled with his desire to improve African American education, prompted him to run without success for the school board several times during the 1880s. In so doing, he was the first African American to campaign for an elective post in Louisville. He continued his participation in politics when he formed the R. B. Elliott Club in 1894. Named for the prominent African American politician from South Carolina, the club lobbied to get equal-rights Republicans into office.

In 1886, Fitzbutler joined several local African American physicians who had recently moved to the city, including Drs. W. A. Burney, Rufus Conrad, E. S. Porter, W. O. Vance, and B. F. Porter, and one white physician, John A. Octerlony, to establish a medical college and free infirmary. In the fall of 1886, **Louisville National Medical College** opened its doors to all races. With receipt of its state charter in 1888, it became one of five medical schools in the nation to offer degrees to African Americans. The school, which held classes for the first year in a fraternal lodge building, had four teachers (Fitzbutler, Burney, Vance, and Conrad) who taught bacteriology, histology, and pathology. The school graduated six students in its first class, who had been studying under Fitzbutler, in the spring of 1889. Later that year, the school purchased the Louisville College of Pharmacy building on Green St., between First and Second Sts., and reopened with an expanded faculty. In 1891, it became affiliated with State University, which later became Simmons University, and initiated a nurse-training program a year later. The three-year physician program attracted approximately 30 students per year, mainly men and women from Kentucky, Indiana, and Tennessee, and had graduated 175 students by the time its doors closed in 1912.

Fitzbutler married Sarah McCurdy (**Sarah Helen McCurdy Fitzbutler**) in 1866. They had five children: Prima, Mary, James, Myra, and William. Fitzbutler died on December 27, 1901, and is buried in Greenwood Cemetery.

Lucas, Marion. *A History of Blacks in Kentucky.* Vol. 1, *From Slavery to Segregation, 1760–1891.* Frankfort: Kentucky Historical Society, 1992.
Wright, George C. *Life Behind a Veil: Blacks in Louisville, Kentucky, 1865–1930.* Baton Rouge: Louisiana State Univ. Press, 1985.

FITZBUTLER, SARAH HELEN MCCURDY (b. 1847, Pennsylvania; d. 1923, Chicago, IL), first African American woman to graduate from medical school in Kentucky. Sarah Helen McCurdy was born in Pennsylvania on October 13, 1847. Her father, William H. McCurdy, a prosperous cattle and horse farmer, later moved the family to southern Ontario. In 1866, she married **Henry Fitzbutler.** During the first years of their marriage, the young couple resided in New Canaan and Amherstburg, Ontario. In 1871, Henry attended the Detroit Medical School. After one year, he transferred to the University of Michigan, where in 1872 he became the first African American to earn a medical degree. Sarah and their two children remained in Amherstburg until the family moved to Louisville after Henry's graduation. For the next two decades, Sarah raised their family, five of whom survived to maturity, and supported Henry in his efforts to advance the status of blacks in Louisville.

After her children were older, Sarah entered the **Louisville National Medical College.** She presented a paper, "Inflammation," at her graduation commencement in 1892. She then joined her husband's practice. Sarah also served as the primary nursing instructor at the medical college and as the superintendent of its teaching hospital. She was noted for her work in obstetrics and pediatrics. After Henry's death in 1901, Sarah continued to practice medicine in Louisville. In the last years of her life, she moved to Chicago, where several of her children were pursuing their careers. She died in Chicago on January 13, 1923, and was buried alongside her husband at Greenwood Cemetery in Louisville. A memorial to the Fitzbutlers and their work is located in Louisville at the **Church of Our Merciful Savior,** 473 S. 11th St.

"College Commencement," *IF,* April 23, 1892, 6.

Davis, Elizabeth Lindsay. *Lifting as They Climb.* Washington, DC: National Association of Colored Women, 1933.

Hanawalt, Leslie L. "Henry Fitzbutler: Detroit's First Black Medical Student." *Detroit in Perspective: A Journal of Regional History* 1 (Winter 1973): 126–40.

Illinois, Deaths and Stillbirths Index, 1916–1947.

Kletzing, Henry F., and William Henry Crogman. *Progress of a Race; or, The Remarkable Advancement of the Afro-American.* Atlanta, GA: J. L. Nichols & Company, 1903.

Louisville, Kentucky, City Directory, 1893.

U.S. City Directories, 1821–1989.

FONTAINE FERRY PARK, segregated amusement park that was a cultural mainstay of Louisville from the early 1900s to the 1960s. Described by the *Louisville Courier-Journal* as a "staple of fun for many Louisville families" and a "cultural capital of the region," the privately owned Fontaine Ferry Park was an all-white institution from its opening in 1905 through the 1960s. The 64-acre park, often pronounced "Fountain Ferry" by locals, was situated alongside the Ohio River in Louisville's West End. It featured more than 50 rides, including its iconic wooden roller coasters; swimming pools; a skating rink; and a funhouse. Entertainers like Will Rogers and Frank Sinatra frequently appeared on the park's stages.

Although it was immensely popular with the city's white citizens, Fontaine Ferry was a symbol of **Jim Crow** to African Americans. **Eleanor Jordan,** who would later become active in the city's **civil rights movement,** recalled "riding past that amusement park and hearing the sounds of children laughing and screaming on the roller coaster," and that she could daily see the green lights atop the Ferris wheel. When she asked her parents if she could go, her mother's "eyes would fill up with tears, and my father would just kind of look away." The answer was always a somber no. C. L. Jeffries, a student at an integrated school in New Albany, IN, remembered the excitement of an elementary school class field trip to the park in the early 1960s. As the children were unloaded, the black students were asked to remain behind. They were then told that they could not ride the rides, but they could sit and play in the picnic area. While his white classmates enjoyed the thrills of the Wooden Beast and other rides, Jeffries noted that "on that day, a group of young black boys and girls learned about the real world of racism. . . . Mine was not a happy time; and its owner was the person who taught my friends and me the meaning of hate."

As more black families moved into Louisville's West End, Fontaine Ferry became a target of young African Americans during the civil rights movement. In May 1961, **Frank Stanley Jr.** and Louisville's chapter of the **Congress of Racial Equality** initiated a summer-long protest of the park. Although the **National Association for the Advancement of Colored People** refused to support the stand-ins and pickets, the protests of Fontaine Ferry became some of the largest of the year. On June 15, 9 adults, including Frank Stanley Jr., and 19 teenagers were arrested during a protest. Because of previous arrests for demonstrations, Stanley was initially sentenced to three months in prison. Although his sentence was eventually overturned, his arrest only emboldened activists. Thirty-five black students and 2 white adults resumed picketing the day after his arrest, and protesters reached almost 60 a day by the end of the week.

Picketing Fontaine Ferry was particularly dangerous because protests were conducted at night, when the park was most active. When protesters were walking through the white neighborhood adjacent to the park, they were frequently struck with glass bottles and bricks. During one protest, they were met with a counterprotest of hundreds of white citizens who carried signs stating "Tickets Back to Africa" and "2-4-6-8 We Don't Want to Integrate." Cups of rocks and flashbulbs were thrown at demonstrators, and cars bearing the Confederate flag frequently whizzed by the picket line.

Postcard of the entrance to Fontaine Ferry Park.

Despite the protests of 1961, the park did not integrate until it was forced to by law, after the passage of the **Civil Rights Act of 1964.** Although the park was integrated, many African Americans did not feel welcome and continued to argue for equal treatment, without success. During the Louisville riots of May 4, 1969, Fontaine Ferry became a primary target of angry and embittered African Americans, who vandalized and burned many rides and buildings. To them, Fontaine Ferry remained a symbol of the discrimination and prejudice that plagued the rest of the city. The park was shut down the very next day and, despite failed attempts to reopen under different names in the 1970s, officially closed in 1975.

Adams, Luther. *Way Up North in Louisville: African American Migration in the Urban South, 1930–1970.* Chapel Hill: Univ. of North Carolina Press, 2010.

Dockery, Robert. Interview, September 12, 1999. Univ. of Louisville Oral History Center.

K'Meyer, Tracy E. *Civil Rights in the Gateway to the South: Louisville, Kentucky, 1945–1980.* Lexington: Univ. Press of Kentucky, 2009.

Newspapers: C. L. Jeffries, letter to the editor, *LCJ,* June 27, 2004, D2; "Fontaine Ferry Days," *LCJ.* May 10, 2009; "Black History Month. June 17, 1961: Fontaine Ferry Park," *LCJ,* February 12, 2010.

—*Joshua D. Farrington*

FOREMAN, EDGAR STEWARD (b. 1866, Ohio Co., KY; d. 1929, Hopkinsville, KY), attorney, educator, and coal company operator. Son of Jacob Foreman, a farmer, and Ann Foreman, Edgar Steward Foreman came from a family of older twin sisters, two older brothers, a younger sister, and a younger brother. In 1893, at an Ohio Co., KY, teachers' assemblage, the multiskilled Foreman presented lectures on government, history, English, spelling, and science. In one of his presentations, he argued that the rules of the home were comparable to the rules of government. In 1898, he graduated from Central Tennessee College. In 1902, he earned his law degree from Tennessee's Walden University Law School and was admitted to the Tennessee bar that same year. The next year, he was admitted to the Kentucky bar and started his law practice in Hopkinsville while simultaneously teaching school.

In 1904, Foreman married Esther Sanders, and they had two children, Annie and Henry. In the year of his marriage, he served as a reserve delegate for the Lexington, KY, district at the Twenty-Fourth General Conference of the Methodist Episcopal Church, held in Los Angeles, CA. For a short time, he was an assistant editor and part owner of Hopkinsville's *Colored Teacher,* a monthly educational journal that cost subscribers 15 cents per paper. In 1909, he became a member of E. S. Foreman Company, a coal firm. That same year, he surprised the Hopkinsville community by running for representative against Hiram Brown, an attorney whose father and grandfather had previously represented the county in the legislature. He lost to Brown with only 672 votes against Brown's 1,152 votes.

Foreman served as secretary of the Christian County Committee of the Progressive Party and was a member of the Knights of Pythias. He died on November 6, 1929, just 17 days shy of turning 63. His death certificate listed his occupation as teacher.

Hingeley, Rev. Joseph B., D.D. *Journal of the Twenty-Fourth Delegated General Conference of the Methodist Episcopal Church.* New York: Eaton & Mains, 1904.

Kentucky Death Records, 1852–1953.

Newspapers: "Colored Teachers," *Hartford Republican,* September 29, 1893, 1–2; "Only Three Strong Fights," *HK,* March 30, 1909, 1.

Smith, J. Clay, Jr. *Emancipation: The Making of the Black Lawyer, 1844–1944.* Philadelphia: Univ. of Pennsylvania Press, 1993.

U.S. Federal Census (1870, 1880, 1910, 1920).

—*Sallie L. Powell*

FT. HILL, African American community in Louisville, KY. The neighborhood known traditionally as Ft. Hill (but dubbed Meriwether by the city of Louisville about 1975) takes its name from the Civil War Ft. Horton that occupied a large area of elevated land in the southwest angle of the junction of Meriwether Ave. and Shelby St. This was one of a series of fortifications surrounding Louisville to protect the city from possible Confederate attack. Much of the hill on which the fort stood has been graded away, although it was more or less intact as late as 1905.

The neighborhood is bounded by Shelby St. and the Schnitzelburg area of the Germantown neighborhood to the east and by Preston St. to the west. It extends north to about Ormsby Ave. and south to about Eastern Pkwy. Meriwether Ave. cuts through the neighborhood on an east-west axis. Little is known about the development of the area in the years immediately after the Civil War. By the mid-1880s, however, farmland was being slowly converted to residential and commercial use. Industrial operations sprang up along the railroad opened through the area in 1871. Mule-drawn streetcars on Shelby St. had reached the northern edge of Ft. Hill by the late 1870s, but much open land remained, and small dairy farms persisted until early in the twentieth century.

The sparse early population was mixed black and white, but by the end of the nineteenth century there were few white residents west of Shelby St. That area west to Preston was practically all African Americans, most of whom lived on Meriwether and on north-south Bland St. Most are listed in the city directories as laborers. They found employment in the factories along the railroad, the sand and clay quarry that stretched north from Bergman (part of the street was dug away), the Gernert Lumber Yard, and two brick manufacturers. One brickyard was operated by J. H. Egelhoff, who also had a park on Preston St. at the railroad crossing. The park was used by black workingmen for the annual labor celebration held on May 1.

In 1894, the Shelby Street Colored School, a small frame building, was opened at Shelby and Burnett Ave. During that decade, black churches made their appearance. Both the Bland Street Baptist Church and Miles Chapel A.M.E. Church, also on Bland St., were founded in the 1890s. In 1905, **Red Cross Hospital** (no connection to the American Red Cross), the only private medical institution that treated African Americans, moved from downtown Sixth St. to the Ft. Hill area at 1436 Shelby St. Red Cross was a two-story frame dwelling that stood almost alone. With the closure of the Louisville National Medical College in 1912, it operated the only nurse-training program in Kentucky for African Americans. The hospital was later expanded, and in 1951 a new brick building was erected. With the end of segregation in Louisville hospitals, this pioneering institution closed in 1975. The building later housed several programs of the Volunteers of America in Kentucky.

Another institution that closed with the end of segregation in schools in 1956 was the Lincoln Colored School on Bland St. at Morgan Ave. The two-story brick structure had been opened in 1912 to replace the inadequate Shelby St. Colored School. It was located within what is now Lincoln-Preston Park, which memorializes the school in its name.

Bergmann, G. T. "Map of Jefferson County." 1858.
Louisville Post, April 9, 1891.
Sanborn Insurance Atlas, 1892 and 1905 editions.
"Street Directory." *Caron's Louisville City Directory,* 1884–1915 editions.
U.S. Engineer Corps. "Map of Louisville and Its Defenses," 1865. Reproduced in *Courier-Journal Magazine,* September 30, 1956.
U.S. Geological Survey topographical map, Eastern Louisville, surveyed 1904–1905.

—*George H. Yater*

FT. SPRING, possibly the only African American community in Fayette Co. founded by slaves before the Civil War. Located in Fayette Co., midway between Lexington and Versailles, KY, Ft. Spring was a primarily **African American hamlet** identified by several names. Each name included an anecdotal explanation of its origin. Many accounts have not been authenticated. In 1826, Lewis O'Neal reportedly erected a stone tavern, and the village of Slickaway grew around it. During the Civil War, Union troops commandeered the structure. A spring arose directly beneath the building and led to the name Ft. Spring. A later occupant of the house remembered the spring running underneath the kitchen and reported that after opening a trap door, one could touch the water.

One version alleged that the location was named Slipperyway or Slippery Way after a horse slipped on the icy road at the site and its rider died after a fall into the South Fork of Elkhorn Creek. Another account claimed that Maj. Thomas Sthreshly gave land to three of his slaves, who established a settlement called Reform. There was a post office with that name from 1854 to 1857. In 1859, the Ft. Spring Church was organized in an old mill building. During the antebellum era, slaves reportedly slipped away to this area for evening social gatherings. The site became known as Slipaway and then Slickaway. The Slickaway post office was established in 1872.

Scholar Peter Craig Smith located the land deeds and debated the theory of the hamlet's creation. He noted that Sthreshley did not give the land to the freed slaves, but he and his wife, Patty, sold one and a half acres to a freeman, Henry Clark, for $197.25 in 1826. Some lifelong residents told Smith that their families had acquired their property after the Civil War from landowner Harvey Worley. Smith also argued that since the village had been founded by white settlers and was not primarily African American until after the Civil War, it would have been unlikely that slaves would have "slipped away" to the site.

In 1886, embarrassed post office patrons supposedly requested that the name Slickaway be changed to Ft. Spring, the name of Worley's home. Other sources alleged that this occurred in 1890. Lewis O'Neal's stone tavern may have been Worley's home.

One 1901 newspaper account claimed that the village's name of Slickaway originated when a saloon owner named Morgan dropped a barrel of whiskey. When it slid down the hillside, he yelled, "Slick-a-way!" The paper noted that the name was changed to Reform in 1862. The name was later changed and pluralized to Ft. Springs, according to this account, in the early 1890s.

The Slickaway tavern lodged stagecoach patrons in its red stone structure. In 1901, Frank Allen, an African American businessman, used the two ground floors for his restaurant and shaving parlor. An unnamed African American family occupied the upper rooms. By that time, Ft. Spring's school was the first in the county to inaugurate a 10-month term, but the school closed in 1910. Most of the residents attended Ft. Spring Baptist Church, and their dead were buried in Ft. Spring Cemetery. In 1905, Ft. Spring citizens witnessed electricians preparing trolley wires for a connection between Lexington and Louisville.

In 1914, all Kentucky troops and one company of the 29th U.S. Infantry planned to camp for 10 days at Ft. Spring. One newspaper account claimed that the camp site was "an amusement park with all the attractions of a modern city play ground." Ft. Spring had become the annual encampment for the Kentucky National Guard.

By 1971, Ft. Spring had a population of about 70 people. It struggled financially, and most of its citizens still used outdoor privies. In 1975, the New Vine Baptist Church in Ft. Spring celebrated the 100th anniversary of its formation with guest preachers for two services.

Newspapers: "Fort Springs," *LH,* September 15, 1901, 10; "Trolley Wires Go Up," *LL,* December 10, 1905, 6; "Fort Spring School," *LL,* March 8, 1910, 9; "Annual Encampment," *Hartford Republican,* June 26, 1914, 1; "How Bluegrass Towns Received Their Names," *LL,* August 15, 1931, 12; "Slickaway and Donerail—Why Those Names?," *LL,* January 15, 1950, 90; "Fort Spring Looks Ahead," *LL,* July 19, 1971, 4; "100th Anniversary," *LL,* October 25, 1975, C4; "A Living History of Racial Segregation," *LHL,* February 16, 2005, D1.
Rennick, Robert M. *Kentucky Place Names.* Lexington: Univ. Press of Kentucky, 1988.
Smith, Peter Craig. "Negro Hamlets and Gentlemen Farms: A Dichotomous Rural Settlement Pattern in Kentucky's Bluegrass Region." PhD. diss., Univ. of Kentucky, 1972.

—*Sallie L. Powell*

FOUSE, ELIZABETH BEATRICE COOK "LIZZIE" (b. 1875, Lancaster, KY; d. 1952, Lexington, KY), educator, clubwoman, and activist. Born in Lancaster, KY, on May 14, 1875, Elizabeth Beatrice Cook was the daughter of William and Mary (Kennedy) Cook. Affectionately known as Lizzie, she attended both State Colored Baptist University (later known as **Simmons College of Kentucky**) and **Eckstein Norton Institute** in Cane Springs, Bullitt Co. After graduation, she taught at Lexington's Constitution Street School and joined the National Teachers Association and the **Kentucky Negro Educational Association.**

On August 10, 1898, Lizzie married **William Henry Fouse,** a teacher in the Corydon Colored High School in Corydon, IN. She

Lizzie Fouse.

joined him as a teacher in that school system until 1904, when she quit teaching, dedicated her time to community activism, and participated in a myriad of organizations. Although she was living in Indiana, Fouse continued her membership in such Kentucky groups as the Baptist Women's Education Convention and became a charter member of the **Kentucky Association of Colored Women's Clubs** (KACW) in 1903. In 1908, the Fouses moved to Covington, and Lizzie joined both the Ladies Improvement and the Ladies Union Clubs. Before returning to Lexington in 1913, she was elected president of the KACW and launched the Scholarship Loan Fund to assist black students with college funding.

On the national level, beginning in 1914, Fouse held a variety of offices in the National Association of Colored Women's Clubs. Many of her organizational commitments were with interracial groups, such as the United Council of Church Women, the Southern Regional Council, and the **Kentucky Commission on Negro Affairs.**

In addition to women's clubs, Fouse was an active member of the First Baptist Church, for which she purchased an organ. When the Lexington branch of the **National Association for the Advancement of Colored People** was established in 1919, the Fouses were among the 100 charter members, and Lizzie was elected corresponding secretary. She was among the founders of Lexington's **Phillis Wheatley YWCA** in 1920. She also served as the chair of the City Federation of Women's Clubs in Lexington, which protested police mistreatment of black citizens, such as Gertrude Boulder, who was mistakenly arrested for public drunkenness and then died while in police custody.

Internationally, Fouse served as a delegate to the 1933 International Congress of Women, which convened in Chicago. She represented the United States in England and Ireland at Women's Christian Temperance Union meetings in 1947, where she was the guest speaker at a banquet in Belfast Castle, Ireland.

Fouse died on October 22, 1952, and was buried in Greenwood Cemetery (later named Cove Haven Cemetery) in Lexington. In 1953, her work was recognized through the L. B. Fouse Civic Center in Covington.

Fouse Family Papers. Special Collections, M. I. King Library, Univ. of Kentucky Libraries, Lexington, 1998.

"Lizzie Beatrice Fouse." In *Who's Who in Colored America: An Illustrated Biographical Directory of Notable Living Persons of African Descent in the United States,* edited by G. James Fleming and Christian E. Burckel. 7th ed. Yonkers-on-Hudson, NY: Christian E. Burckel & Associates, 1950.

McDaniel, Karen Cotton. "Altruistic Activism: The Life Work of Elizabeth 'Lizzie' Fouse." In *Kentucky Women: Their Lives and Times,* edited by Melissa A. McEuen and Thomas H. Appleton. Athens: Univ. of Georgia Press, forthcoming.

Williams, Lillian Serece, and Randolph Boehm. *Records of the National Association of Colored Women's Clubs, 1895–1992.* Bethesda, MD: Univ. Publications of America, 1993.

—Karen Cotton McDaniel

FOUSE, WILLIAM HENRY (b. 1868, Westerville, OH; d. 1944, Lexington, KY), educator. In 1868, William Henry Fouse was born in Westerville, OH, to Squire and Sarah Fouse, illiterate slaves who had been freed by their North Carolina master only three years earlier. In 1884, Fouse became the first black graduate of Westerville's two-year high school. He spent the next seven years cleaning boots, waiting tables in Columbus, and working various other jobs to pay for his education at Westerville's Otterbein College. In 1893, he became the school's first African American graduate and shortly thereafter began his lifelong career as an educator.

Upon graduation, he founded Corydon Colored High School in Indiana. He remained at the school until he was named the principal of Lincoln School in Gallipolis, OH, in 1904. Four years later, Fouse became principal of Covington, KY's, William Grant High School, part of **Lincoln-Grant School.** In 1913, Fouse became the principal of Russell School in Lexington, where he lived for the rest of his life. That same year, he became supervisor of all African American schools in the city. He married Lexington native **Elizabeth B. Cook Fouse,** and the couple had a profound impact on black education in the city and the state through the 1940s. William Fouse was instrumental in the foundation of the Bluegrass Oratorical Association, the Bluegrass Athletic Association, and the Pennies Savings Bank.

In 1920, Fayette Co. approved a bond issue that created a new black high school. After (Paul Laurence) **Dunbar High School** opened in 1923, William Fouse was appointed its first principal. He served in this position until his retirement in 1938. During

William Henry Fouse (standing), teaching in an outdoor classroom, ca. 1900–1910.

Fouse's 15-year tenure, Dunbar became the first black high school in Kentucky to qualify for admission to the Southern Association of Colleges and Secondary Schools.

Fouse also became president of the **Kentucky Negro Educational Association.** As president, he publicly opposed the proposed merger of Kentucky State College (later named **Kentucky State University**) and West Kentucky Industrial College and spoke out against the perceived accommodationist stances of **Whitney Young Sr.** and Kentucky State's **Rufus Atwood.** Fouse argued that higher education opportunities for blacks in Kentucky were already severely limited, and that the merger would only worsen the problem. He believed that Atwood and others should push for integration of certain programs at the University of Kentucky, and he called for "absolute equality in educational opportunity" at the college level in the state.

In 1944, Fouse died at his home at 219 N. Upper St. in Lexington. Recognized even by a white journalist in the 1910s as "one of the most progressive colored school men of the State," Fouse, alongside his wife, Elizabeth, was a leading proponent of equal education in Lexington and throughout the state for over 30 years.

Guide to the Fouse Family Papers. Margaret I. King Library, Special Collections. Univ. of Kentucky.

Hardin, John A. *Fifty Years of Segregation: Black Higher Education in Kentucky, 1904–1954.* Lexington: Univ. Press of Kentucky, 1997.

Mather, Frank Lincoln, ed. *Who's Who of the Colored Race: A General Biographical Dictionary of Men and Women of African Descent.* Vol. 1. Chicago: Memento Edition, 1915.

Newspapers: "Colored Notes," *LL,* August 11, 1913, 7; obituary, *LH,* June 2, 1944, 24.

—*Joshua D. Farrington*

FOX V. CENTRAL PASSENGER RAILROAD CO., case involving a legal challenge to discriminatory practices in Louisville's streetcars. On October 30, 1870, Robert Fox, his brother Samuel, and Horace Pearce—all African American men—boarded a Central Passenger streetcar at the corner of 10th and **Walnut** in Louisville, KY. The driver, following company rules that allowed only black women to ride inside the car, ordered the men to leave. The three men refused, noting that they had the right to travel on public transportation and that they were willing to test that right. Other drivers arrived and expelled the passengers from the streetcar by force.

By this time, the streetcar had been surrounded by a crowd composed primarily of African Americans, most of whom were part of this movement to challenge segregation in transportation. Some individuals threw various missiles at the car, and others shouted encouragement to the three men, who reboarded the streetcar and took their seats. This time, the superintendent of the Central Passenger Company arrived and offered a refund, which was refused. With traffic at a standstill, local police appeared on the scene, arrested the three protesters, and charged them with disorderly conduct.

The conflict was clearly being used as a test case for practices of segregation of public transportation when it went to court in the days following. The *Louisville Courier-Journal*'s early reports on the demonstration noted that it "bears every appearance of being a preconcerted attempt to test the legal right of the city railway corporations to forbid the riding of negroes or colored men upon their cars," and articles on the trial bore the headline "The Test Case." The local court, however, decided firmly in favor of the prosecution, fining the men for disorderly conduct and agreeing with the principle that the streetcar companies had a right to regulate their clientele. The Fox brothers appealed to the U.S. district court. Through a fluke of timing, the case could not be heard for several months, so local African Americans attempted to keep pressure on streetcar companies through petitions and boycotts.

In May 1871, *Fox v. Central Passenger Railroad Co.* was finally heard before the circuit court. Fox's lawyer made a simple appeal to the Thirteenth and Fifteenth Amendments in his argument, and Judge Bland Ballard was receptive to the message. He ruled that chartered companies "could not designate what class or race of citizens they should transport," and "applicants of all colors must be carried, or the companies suffer the consequences in damages." Louisville African Americans responded by immediately boarding streetcars across the city. Although most of the activity was peaceful, in some areas the demonstrations almost erupted into racial violence.

As these "ride-ins" continued for several days, tensions heightened in Louisville, culminating in a mayor's meeting designed to remedy the situation. Although the streetcar companies' owners were resistant to ending their policy of segregation, they finally relented after recognizing the hazards of continued conflict and eventual governmental involvement. *Fox v. Central Passenger Railroad Co.* effectively struck a blow at segregation in public transportation in Louisville, but it was only a partial victory because segregation remained present in almost every aspect of life for African Americans in the city.

Newspapers: "Almost a Riot," *LCJ*, October 31, 1870, 4; "'Riding on a Rail,'" *LCJ*, May 12, 1871, 4.
Norris, Marjorie M. "An Early Instance of Nonviolence: The Louisville Demonstrations of 1870–1871." *Journal of Southern History* 32 (1996): 487–504.
Wright, George C. *Life Behind a Veil: Blacks in Louisville, Kentucky, 1865–1930.* Baton Rouge: Louisiana State Univ. Press, 1985.

—*Stephen Pickering*

FRANCIS, LELIA ILES (b. 1903, Salt Lick, KY; d. 1999, Dayton, OH), first black realtor in Ohio. Lelia Iles Francis was born in Salt Lick, KY, in 1903. Growing up during the era of **Jim Crow,** she had to walk eight miles a day to go to school. She attended Kentucky State College (later named **Kentucky State University**) and taught in rural schools in Bath Co. for nine years. In the 1940s, not wanting her children to have to walk to the distant black public schools (the closest black high school was 25 miles away), Lelia and her husband, Charles Francis, moved their family to Dayton, OH, where her brother already lived.

Although her husband became the president of the Dayton and Ohio chapters of the **National Association for the Advancement of Colored People** (NAACP), Lelia Francis was successful in her own right. In 1947, she became the first black realtor in Ohio and the second in the country. For over 50 years, Francis Realty owned and sold property in West Dayton and was an instrumental force in integrating white neighborhoods in Dayton View. Although the business experienced financial and legal trouble in the 1990s, with the elderly Francis still in charge, she still managed over 100 units and donated a 10-room house for the city's homeless in 1992.

Throughout her life, Francis publicly fought for open housing, jobs, training programs, and better schools. During the 1960s, she was arrested while protesting against a downtown department store that refused to hire more African Americans and later joined a march on the local courthouse to demand more black public employees. A lifelong Republican, Francis ran an unsuccessful bid for the state legislature in 1968.

Even as late as 1991, she led a drive against a proposed landfill close to the homes of many African Americans in Dayton. That same year, she was given the Miley O. Williamson Award of Distinction by the NAACP. She died in Dayton after a fall in 1999. Her granddaughter accurately summed up Lelia Francis's life: "Grandma was an entrepreneur, a social and civic leader in an age when women didn't work. . . . She was Dayton's own Rosa Parks."

Newspapers: "Defeating Racism Ongoing Crusade," *Dayton Daily News*, January 20, 1992, 1A; "Lelia Iles Francis Dies," *Dayton Daily News*, July 26, 1999, 3B.

—*Joshua D. Farrington*

FRANK, JOHN H. (b. 1859, Louisville, KY; d. 1941, Louisville, KY), Baptist clergyman and activist. Born in Louisville, KY, John H. Frank was baptized at **Fifth Street Baptist Church** in March 1877. He became a licensed minister seven years later. He first served as an assistant minister at his home church; one year later, he began his lifelong service as its senior pastor. His annual salary beginning in 1886 was $1,200.

Frank worked in various capacities as the church's minister. He simultaneously headed Louisville's South Publishing Company and served as a member of the state executive committee of the **Anti–Separate Coach Movement.** Frank favored an immediate fight against the proposed bill instead of waiting until it became law. He was part of management for the **Colored Orphans' Home** and was active in the YMCA. In the 1890s, he edited and published the Fifth Street Baptist Church's religious journal, *Messenger*. He had no problem asking for assistance from the white community. He asserted, "I think white people owe us something more than a word of commendation." He argued that neither religious faith nor political affiliation should determine the amount of assistance provided.

As the pastor of one of the largest churches in Kentucky, with a membership of nearly 2,000, Frank served as a moderator of the **General Association of Baptists in Kentucky,** as a representative to the National Baptist Convention, and as president of the Foreign Mission Board. He was also involved in the Kentucky State Teachers Association. A doctor of medicine, Frank joined other leading African American men to form the Cave Dwellers Life Association, a life insurance company, in 1906.

Frank reportedly had "one of the best homes in the city" of Louisville. He and his wife, Clara, had four children. Census records indicate that his mother-in-law, his four adult children, two grandchildren, and several boarders lived in the house for numerous years. He served Louisville's Fifth Street Baptist Church for five decades and for a few years as minister emeritus. On March 24, 1941, he died a widower of Parkinson's disease.

Kentucky Death Records, 1852–1953.

Newspapers: "The General Association," *AB,* August 21, 1903, 1–2; "Pastor of One Church for Twenty-Three Years," *LCJ,* November 7, 1909, 44.

Parrish, C. H. *Golden Jubilee of the General Association of Colored Baptists in Kentucky: From 1865–1915.* Louisville, KY: Mayes Printing Co., 1915.

Pegues, A. W. *Our Baptist Ministers and Schools.* Springfield, MA: Willey & Co., 1892.

Smith, S. E., ed. *History of the Anti–Separate Coach Movement in Kentucky.* Evansville, IN: National Afro-American Press, 1895.

U.S. Federal Census (1900, 1910, 1920, 1930).

Wright, George C. *Life Behind a Veil: Blacks in Louisville, Kentucky, 1865–1930.* Baton Rouge: Louisiana State Univ. Press, 1985.

—*Sallie L. Powell*

FRANKLIN, BENJAMIN (b. 1849, Lexington, KY; d. 1935, Lexington, KY), businessman and chiropodist. With a Horatio Alger biography, Benjamin Franklin was born into slavery but prospered as a prominent businessman and chiropodist in Lexington, KY. Franklin named himself when he was christened around the age of 10. At 16, he enlisted in the 18th U.S. Colored Infantry. He returned to Lexington a freeman to work for his former master, Judge George Robertson, chief justice of Kentucky. Franklin's mother, Emma Washington, had remained with Robertson.

Franklin stayed for a short time in Robertson's employment before traveling to England and other foreign countries with a Louisville man named Newcomb who had health problems. When Franklin returned to Lexington, he assisted Chief Justice Robertson, who had suffered a paralytic stroke. On February 3, 1871, Franklin physically supported Robertson as he gave a speech at the inauguration of Governor Preston Leslie.

In that same year, Franklin became a self-employed barber in Lexington. During years of working as a barber, he held various other jobs. He worked at a brickyard in Midway, as a house servant in Louisville, and as an attendant in the Negro Department of the Eastern Kentucky Insane Asylum. On September 18, 1879, he married Susan Britton, the daughter of Henry and Laura Britton and sister of Dr. **Mary E. Britton** and jockey **Tommy Britton.** Several years later, Franklin played the violin at Tommy's wedding.

Active in his community, Franklin traveled to Baltimore, MD, with five other Lexington African American businessmen to attend the National Negro Business League's meeting in August 1908. A year later, the *Lexington Leader* reported one of Franklin's investments. He had displayed in his business window a steel engraving titled *The First Reading of the Emancipation Proclamation before the Cabinet.* Dr. L. B. Todd, a relative of Mary Todd Lincoln, had owned the engraving before his death. Franklin's business interests also included his work as a chiropodist. He cared for the feet of many Lexington citizens.

On February 8, 1914, Franklin's wife, Susan, died. Benjamin Franklin died 21 years later. He had practiced chiropody for 40 years. He was buried in Lexington's Greenwood Cemetery (now Cove Haven Cemetery).

Hamilton, G. P. *Biographical Sketches of Prominent Negro Men and Women of Kentucky.* Memphis: E. H. Clarke and Brother, 1911.

Kentucky Death Records, 1852–1953.

Newspapers: "Todd Picture," *LL,* February 12, 1909, 11; "Colored Notes," *LL,* March 19, 1935, 11.

U.S. Colored Troops Military Service Records, 1861–1865.

U.S. Federal Census (1880, 1900, 1910, 1930).

Wright, John D., Jr. *Lexington: Heart of the Bluegrass.* Lexington, KY: Lexington–Fayette County Historic Commission, 1982.

—*Sallie L. Powell*

FRANKLIN D. ROOSEVELT INDEPENDENT VOTERS LEAGUE, organization active in Louisville politics in the mid-1940s. Organized by African Americans, the Franklin D. Roosevelt Independent Voters League briefly emerged as a distinct voice in Louisville politics in 1946 and 1947. In 1946, African Americans throughout the country, led by A. Philip Randolph, demanded that President Harry Truman and the Democratic Party create a permanent Fair Employment Practices Committee (FEPC). In Louisville, the FDR Independent Voters League joined forces with the **National Urban League** and the **National Association for the Advancement of Colored People** in pressing Kentucky's representatives to support the pending national legislation. In February 1946, the Independent Voters League was active in mass meetings throughout the city and circulated petitions in 105 precincts in support of a national FEPC. Although Senator Alben Barkley ultimately supported the legislation, Louisville's Democratic representative, Emmet O'Neal, opposed it.

O'Neal's opposition to the FEPC angered many of the city's black voters, who felt betrayed by the party they had supported throughout the presidency of Franklin D. Roosevelt. Further contributing to their frustration, Democratic mayor Leland Taylor refused to include a single African American on his slate of aldermanic candidates for the 1947 election. During that year's elections, the FDR Independent Voters League demonstrated the political independence of Louisville's black voters and led a campaign against the city's Democratic establishment. However, Charles L. Scott, the organization's leader, was careful to note that the lack of support for the local Democratic Party in that year's election "does not mean we have changed our party affiliation." He continued that "it is only an alternative in the effort to prevent . . . the election of a political set-up that would hinder rather than help the Negro politically."

By November 1947, the league endorsed Eldon Dummit, the Republican nominee for governor, over Earle Clements, and the entire Republican ticket for the board of aldermen. Scott explained that the reason behind the Republican endorsements was that "the Democratic party in Kentucky has not made an appreciable bid for the Negro vote" and had taken their support for granted in previous elections. Although their slate of aldermanic candidates failed in the election, an African American Republican, **Dennis Henderson,** defeated the Democratic candidate, **William Childress,** for state representative in Kentucky's 42nd Legislative District. Henderson's victory, partially attributed to the Independent Voters League, gave the city its second African American representative in the General Assembly.

K'Meyer, Tracy E. *Civil Rights in the Gateway to the South: Louisville, Kentucky, 1945–1980.* Lexington: Univ. Press of Kentucky, 2009.

Newspapers: "R. C. Black Heads Unit to Plan F.E.P.C. Here," *LCJ*, January 30, 1945; "Senator Barkley Is Commended," *Louisville Leader*, February 2, 1946; "Board to Continue Local Campaign for F.E.P.C. Bill," *LCJ*, February 24, 1946; "FDR Independent Voters League Neutral on Childress and Henderson," *Louisville Leader*, November 1, 1947.

—*Joshua D. Farrington*

FRANKLIN GRADE AND HIGH SCHOOL, educational and social institution in Franklin, KY. In 1867, Franklin Public School served the African American community in Simpson Co., KY. Classes were held in the Little Methodist Episcopal Church located on John J. Johnson St. in the Harristown neighborhood of Franklin. Children and adults attended. In 1870, the school moved to Williams Hall on W. Madison St. and became Franklin Grade School. In 1896, 106 students were enrolled. Beginning in 1926, Principal T. C. Burford formed a plan to add a grade each year. The first high school graduating class was in 1931. Four years later, Katherine Ryan Douthitt organized an alumni association that financially assisted the school.

G. Briscoe Houston was the last principal at the W. Madison St. location before the school's move to a new, two-story, brick building on Walker Ave. The old school building was sold for $600. The new school was renamed Lincoln High School. Government funds aided the erection of the $40,000 building, which was dedicated in 1940. The alumni association purchased playground equipment. **Robert L. Dowery Sr.** served twice as principal of the school (1920–1922 and 1942–1949). He later became president of the **Kentucky Negro Educational Association.**

With the new school building, various activities blossomed, including music and athletics. The alumni association purchased a piano for the chorus, which won first prize at Fisk University on April 21, 1932. In 1948, Douthitt, the catalyst of the alumni association, was also one of the coordinators of the Lincoln Band, which won first-place honors in Bowling Green in 1961. Girls' and boys' basketball teams were organized in 1941. George L. Douthitt coached the last girls' basketball team in 1947. The school's football team materialized in 1919, and the Pirates football squad was district champion in 1949. The Sportsman Club formed in 1946. Years later, when girls were allowed to join the club, it was renamed the Sportsman and Industrial Club.

The school building was more than just an educational institution; it also provided a place for social activities and community events. In 1965, the integration of Simpson Co. schools ended the communal richness of Lincoln High School for the county's black residents. Sports, musical programs, and the alumni association stopped their endeavors. Only the Sportsman and Industrial Club continued to serve the community through recreational opportunities for youth and adults.

In September 2003, the Franklin Grade and High School building on W. Madison St. was listed on Preservation Kentucky's Most Endangered List. A month later, the Franklin City Commission approved about $25,000 toward the purchase of the building. Franklin's African American Heritage Committee and the Simpson County Tourism Commission joined in helping buy the building.

Beach, Mrs. James, Sr., and James Henry Snider, comps. *Franklin and Simpson County: A Picture of Progress, 1819–1975.* Thompkinsville, KY: Monroe County Press, 1976.
"Editorial Comment: Our Front Cover." *KNEAJ*, March–April 1941.
"K.N.E.A. Kullings." *KNEAJ*, November–December 1942.
Newspapers: "Historic Site 'Endangered,'" *Franklin Favorite*, September 25, 2003, A1; "City to Help Buy Historic Building," *Franklin Favorite*, October 2, 2003.
Stout, Louis. *Shadows of the Past: A History of the Kentucky High School Athletic League.* Lexington, KY: Host Communications, 2006.
U.S. Department of the Interior. National Park Service. National Register of Historic Places Registration Form. http://pdfhost.focus.nps.gov/docs/NRHP/Text/95001515.pdf (accessed August 20, 2013).

—*Andrew Baskin*

FREDERICK DOUGLASS SCHOOLS, four African American schools across the state of Kentucky named in honor of the writer and abolitionist. Frederick Douglass (ca. 1818–1895), author, abolitionist, and diplomat, was regarded as a great orator. He fought for rights for immigrants, women, and minority groups and traveled across the United States to speak about equal rights and social equality. In the early twentieth century, it became common to name African American schools in honor of Douglass. Kentucky had four such schools: Douglass School in Louisville (1910–1961), Douglass Elementary and High School in Lexington (1929–1971), Frederick Douglass High School in Henderson (1932–1965), and Douglass High School in Murray (ca. 1930–1967).

Douglass School in Louisville, also referred to as Banneker-Douglass School, was named in honor of the abolitionist in 1910. Founded in 1887, the school was originally named the Main Street Colored School. In 1906, the school was moved, and the name was changed to Pearl Street Colored School. Douglass School merged with the Morris School and was renamed Omer Carmichael Elementary in 1961. The Pearl St. building was torn down shortly thereafter as part of urban-renewal efforts, in particular the construction of Interstate 65 in Louisville, in the 1960s.

Rosenwald funding aided in the construction of the Douglass School in Lexington, which opened under the leadership of Principal C. H. Bonner in 1929. A new Douglass High School building was completed in 1948. In 1951, the old Douglass Elementary School building was moved onto the new high school property, and new rooms, including an auditorium, were added to the building in the new location. By 1954, the Douglass campus was the only African American school serving grades 1 through 12 in Fayette Co., KY. In 1955, a Douglass School student became the first African American to attend a white school in the county, having enrolled in the summer school program at Lafayette High School. The school was temporarily closed because of the integration of the school system in 1964. It was later reopened as an integrated elementary school and remained in operation until 1971.

The Frederick Douglass High School building in Henderson was completed in 1932. Before that, classes for African American high school students had been held on the top floor of the Alves St. Elementary School building. In 1924, the high school classes moved to a separate rented building before Rosenwald funding was received to construct the new building in 1931. Henderson

Douglass High School in Lexington, 1948.

Francis Jones served as the first principal of Frederick Douglass High School. The school was designed to educate students from the city of Henderson, although it also accepted students from the surrounding county. The last principal of the school, Herbert Kirkwood, served until the high school was closed after integration of the school district in 1965. The building was added to the National Register of Historic Places in 1980.

Also referred to as Murray-Douglass School, Douglass High School in Murray, KY, was the alma mater of several people who made significant contributions to African American history in Kentucky. Graduates Geneva Arnold, Bobby Brandon, Arlene Keyes, and Willie Earl Perry enrolled in the first integrated class of students at Murray State University in 1955. **Dennis Jackson,** a star football player in high school, became the first African American varsity athlete at Murray State University in 1960. The school was closed as part of desegregating the Calloway Co. schools in 1967. Students from Douglass were brought into the Murray Independent School System. Although the school was closed, the building retained the spirit of the abolitionist for which it was named when it served as the scene of a civil rights march in honor of Martin Luther King Jr. in 1968.

Arnett, Maralea. *The Annals and Scandals of Henderson County, Kentucky, 1775–1975.* Corydon, KY: Fremar, 1976.

Jefferson County Public Schools Archives and Records Center. "Jefferson County Public School History." Louisville, KY, 2008. http://media.jefferson.k12.ky.us/groups/jcpshistory/ (accessed September 25, 2012).

Jennings, Dorothy, and Kerby Jennings. *The Story of Calloway County, 1822–1976.* Murray, KY: Murray Democrat Publishing Company, 1980.

Newspapers: "School Moving," *LHL,* October 7, 1951, 2; "The Old, and Where the New Will Be," *LHL,* June 3, 1953, 14; "Douglass Student to Study at Lafayette," *LHL,* June 7, 1955, 1; "Douglass High Building Makes National Register," *Evansville Press,* September 15, 1980; "Douglass Reunion Set," *Murray Ledger and Times,* July 25, 2012.
—Elizabeth Schaller

FREEDMAN'S SAVINGS AND TRUST COMPANY, banking institution established by Congress in 1865 that had branches in Louisville and Lexington, KY. In 1865, Congress created the Freedman's Savings and Trust Company to serve as a major banking institution for the thousands of recently freed slaves throughout the South. Louisville's branch opened in September 1865 and was initially run by prominent white citizens; a black man, **William H. Gibson Sr.,** served as an assistant cashier. Within three months, the bank's deposits totaled over $300,000, which demonstrated the determination of newly freed black men and women to save money for education and property.

After moving four times, the Louisville branch found its permanent location in the city's white business district. In December 1868, **Horace Morris,** a black man who had been deeply involved in the **Underground Railroad,** became the bank's first hired cashier. Under Morris's direction, the bank flourished and became one of the most prosperous branches in the country. Depositors increased from 709 in 1868 to 1,166 in 1870. By 1874, the total number of depositors was almost 3,000.

Although the *Lexington Daily Press* described the Lexington branch of the bank as "very prosperous" during its first year, it never enjoyed the success of the branch in Louisville. Plans for the bank began in 1865, but it did not officially open until 1870.

White men dominated the branch's leadership, although three African Americans, W. L. Taylor, Henry King, and James Turner, served on the board. Many of the bank's problems could be traced to its inept administrator, J. G. Hamilton, the white cashier who was already burdened with administering the city's **American Missionary Association**-run schools. A later investigation of the bank's records traced shortages directly to Hamilton.

Both branches served a wide variety of clients. Accounts ranged from around $5 to over $900, and the average depositor had around $74 in the bank. The majority of its accounts were from members of the working class, who deposited only a few cents at a time. Some of the largest accounts were from Kentucky's black soldiers. Between 1865 and 1867, army officers were encouraged to collect money from soldiers in the field to be deposited directly into the Louisville branch. The Louisville branch was seen as such a stable institution by the city's citizens that 11 percent of its depositors were white. Local black organizations also invested in the bank. In Louisville, numerous Reconstruction-era self-help groups, like the Sanitary Commission, used the bank's services. Lexington's branch helped finance improvements to the Independent Baptist Church.

In 1874, despite the success of the Louisville branch, the national bank collapsed from fraud and incompetent administration in its Washington headquarters. To no avail, African Americans in Louisville and Lexington petitioned Congress to compensate them for their lost bank accounts. Kentucky senator James Beck, however, led the drive to oppose government involvement in providing aid to the bank's depositors. In the 1880s, Congress provided some financial assistance, giving patrons no more than 60 percent of their original balances. Although it was a small relief, many African Americans were left with a deep distrust of financial institutions and the federal government.

"Freedman's Savings and Trust Company." *Lexington Daily Press,* December 19, 1871, 4.

Gilbert, Abby L. "The Comptroller of the Currency and the Freedman's Savings Bank." *JNH* 57, no. 2 (April 1972): 125–43.

Lucas, Marion B. *A History of Blacks in Kentucky: From Slavery to Segregation, 1760–1891.* 2nd ed. Frankfort: Kentucky Historical Society, 2003.

Wright, George C. *Life Behind a Veil: Blacks in Louisville, Kentucky, 1865–1930.* Baton Rouge: Louisiana State Univ. Press, 1985.

—*Joshua D. Farrington*

FREEDMEN'S BUREAU, federal agency to assist freed slaves. On March 3, 1865, the U.S. Congress established the Bureau of Refugees, Freedmen, and Abandoned Lands (better known as the Freedmen's Bureau) for the benefit of freed slaves in former Confederate states. Since Kentucky had been loyal to the Union, this new federal organization ostensibly had no legal jurisdiction there, but on December 26, 1865, Gen. Oliver O. Howard, commander of the bureau, officially incorporated Kentucky into the Tennessee District, under the command of Maj. Gen. Clinton B. Fisk.

The justification for applying Reconstruction laws to Kentucky was clear: when the Civil War ended, the state had refused to ratify the Thirteenth Amendment, and violence against freed black people soon escalated to the level of atrocity. From July 1866 to January 1869, Rev. T. K. Noble, chaplain and chief superintendent of the bureau's Kentucky schools, reported to his Washington supervisor, Rev. J. W. Alvord, over 100 incidents and outrages in which Freedmen's Bureau schools and churches not connected with it were openly burned, teachers were harassed, and freedmen were assaulted or murdered.

During its very brief tenure of three years, the Kentucky bureau was underfunded, understaffed (57 officials for the entire state), and underprotected, since most federal troops had already been withdrawn from the region. But in some ways, the Freedmen's Bureau achieved a great deal in many areas. It set up special courts in major cities and towns, trying to ensure justice for former slaves.

The most urgent problems, however, were neither legal nor political, since black people were starving to death. Clothing, shoes, and fuel were in short supply among the African American population; they urgently needed medical attention; orphans, the disabled, the aged, and the mentally ill required care. In addition, some black people were still enslaved in Kentucky, even after the Freedmen's Bureau was established. Obviously, these problems were huge and not amenable to easy or quick solutions—and time was short. The bureau supplied rations to freed people, mainly in population centers, such as the cities of Louisville, Lexington, Paducah, Bowling Green, and **Camp Nelson.** Only one hospital, which operated for two years—Refugee's and Freedmen's Hospital in Louisville—provided medical care, but dispensaries where blacks could receive treatment were located in several cities.

The most effective actions of the Freedmen's Bureau in Kentucky were in the field of education. By 1869, the bureau sponsored 267 schools with 284 teachers (80 percent of whom were black) and 13,000 students. These numbers are astounding since the schools were maintained in spite of constant threats and incidents of vandalism, arson, and terrorism. Students and teachers were beaten, tortured, and murdered as white Kentuckians became more determined to stop the operations of the Freedmen's Bureau by any means and more opposed to any signs of progress for African Americans. "Kentucky," according to one study, "had the dubious distinction of being in the forefront in its violent opposition to the activities of the Freedmen's Bureau." In September 1868, Maj. Benjamin P. Runkle, who was also a prominent Republican attorney and politician, received orders to close down most of the Freedmen's Bureau offices in the commonwealth. Staff members who had organized and supervised the agency's schools were gradually eased out and therefore closed many of the schools. By January 1, 1869, all the bureau's offices in Kentucky except one in Louisville were closed. This remaining office closed in 1872.

The years 1870 through 1874 were the low point of education for blacks in the state, but the consequences of what was basically a withdrawal of all federal supervision from Kentucky went far beyond the condition of schools. A white population that had already expressed a widely held desire to keep the black population enslaved by "murders and outrages" was greatly enabled during this nadir of social justice in the commonwealth.

Harrison, Lowell H., and James C. Klotter. *A New History of Kentucky.* Lexington: Univ. Press of Kentucky, 1997.

Lucas, Marion B. *A History of Blacks in Kentucky.* Vol. 1, *From Slavery to Segregation, 1760–1891.* Frankfort: Kentucky Historical Society, 1992.

Sears, Richard D. *Camp Nelson, Kentucky: A Civil War History.* Lexington: Univ. Press of Kentucky, 2002.

Webb, Ross. "Benjamin P. Runkle and the Freedmen's Bureau in Kentucky, 1866–1870." In *The Freedmen's Bureau and Black Freedom,* edited by Donald G. Nieman. New York: Garland, 1994.

—*Richard D. Sears*

FREEDMEN'S PLEASURE GARDEN, **park and recreation facility for African Americans in Louisville, KY.** Although after 1865 African Americans in Louisville were no longer prohibited from gathering for public and private occasions, such as parades, picnics, and steamboat excursions, they were denied access to the city's popular parks and gardens, such as Woodland Garden and Lion Garden. Consequently, there was no single location where African Americans could gather on a regular basis to hear speakers, listen to summer band concerts, or enjoy other activities.

In 1870 John McCarthy, a 60-year-old, Irish-born lawyer, purchased about four acres in the California neighborhood on 15th St. between Gallagher and O'Hara Sts. for the development of a "complete pleasure resort for the colored population of the city." The new "pleasure resort" was named Freedmen's Pleasure Garden, although it was sometimes called California Garden. It opened under black management on May 21, 1870, and featured speakers and Sunday night sacred concerts by **William Cole**'s Brass Band. The Freedmen's Pleasure Garden included a dancing hall, a roller-skating rink, a speaker's stand, and a baseball field. It closed after the 1871 season, and the property was sold to the Martin Seen and Bro. brewery.

—*Cornelius Bogert*

FREEDMEN'S SCHOOLS, schools created to educate former slaves. Established in 1866 under the Bureau of Refugees, Freedmen, and Abandoned Lands (the **Freedmen's Bureau**), freedmen's schools sought to educate former slaves with the hope of making them productive, contributing citizens. The Freedmen's Bureau Educational Division in Kentucky, under the leadership of army chaplain Thomas K. Noble, was able to establish schools with 10,422 students by 1870. State aid for these schools, however, was quite limited. An act of the Kentucky General Assembly on February 16, 1866, provided for revenues from taxes on blacks to be used for freedmen's schools. On March 9, 1867, the legislature allocated a small per student payment to black schools from black tax revenue. Because of the impoverished condition of most Kentucky blacks, these measures realized very little for the schools.

White hostility toward blacks found a target in the freedmen's schools. In Paducah, Mt. Sterling, and Glasgow, whites broke up black school sessions, and in Crab Orchard the freedmen's school was burned down. Many black schools served as a focal point for the continuing feud between Union and Confederate sympathizers. Despite these adversities, the freedmen's schools prevailed. On February 23, 1874, after the Freedmen's Bureau was dissolved, Kentucky created a uniform school system for blacks and allocated to it all administrative duties except funding, which still came from taxes on blacks and was controlled by the state.

On April 24, 1882, the Kentucky legislature allocated money for black schools to come from the same fund as that for white institutions on a pro rata basis. This measure ensured the continuation of education for blacks in Kentucky.

Kimball, Philip Clyde. "Freedom's Harvest: Freedmen's Schools in Kentucky after the Civil War." *FCHQ* 54 (July 1980): 272–88.

Webb, Ross A. *Kentucky in the Reconstruction Era.* Lexington: Univ. Press of Kentucky, 1979.

FREEMASONS, one of the largest black fraternal organizations in Kentucky after the Civil War. Prince Hall Freemasonry, the black fraternal organization affiliated with the Scottish Rite, first appeared in America during the revolutionary era. Kentucky's Masons, however, were exclusively white until 1850, when Bird Parker, the pastor of **Quinn Chapel A.M.E. Church, Jesse Meriwether,** and other prominent freed blacks in Louisville sought to form their own branch of Prince Hall Freemasonry after observing black Masons in Ohio. However, out of fear of white backlash and "black laws" that limited the ability of freedmen in Kentucky to assemble, the men established the Mt. Moriah Lodge No. 1, F. & A.M., in nearby New Albany, IN.

After three years of making the dangerous journey across the Ohio River and a five-mile walk into New Albany, the group decided to move the Mt. Moriah Lodge into Louisville. Their first meetings were held at a home owned by **Washington Spradling Sr.** on **Walnut St.** Despite breaking the city's black laws, many of Louisville's leading African Americans were members of the lodge, including Jesse Meriwether, **William H. Gibson Sr.,** William Butcher, and Berry Evans. In 1859, the police raided a lodge meeting and arrested its 21 members. However, the jailor, a Mason, refused to admit the men to jail, and the judge, also a Mason, dropped the case. After this sympathetic reaction by the jailor and the judge, police left the lodge alone during its subsequent meetings.

By 1865, Mt. Moriah had over 100 members, and three additional lodges were created: Meriwether Lodge No. 13, David Smith Lodge No. 15, and St. Thomas Lodge No. 20. The following year, leaders in Ohio granted the state's lodges permission to form the Grand Lodge of Kentucky. Jesse Meriwether was shortly thereafter elected grand master, and Andrew Shafer was named

Freemasons.

grand secretary. In 1875, the Grand Lodge of Kentucky was officially given state sovereignty and broke all remaining ties with the Grand Lodge of Ohio. By the early 1880s, there were over 15 black Masonic lodges throughout Louisville. Prince Hall Freemasonry also grew exponentially in the state's other large cities, like Paducah and Lexington, after the end of the Civil War. By the turn of the century, Kentucky had 41 lodges and over 1,200 members and had established Royal Arch Chapters, Knights Templars, and Ladies' Chapters throughout the state. Many of Kentucky's leading African Americans were Masons, including **William H. Steward,** editor of the *American Baptist,* who served as the Worshipful Master of the Grand Lodge of Kentucky and High Priest of Enterprise No. 4.

Membership in a lodge provided many benefits for African Americans, who faced intense economic and social discrimination throughout the late 1800s. Lodges provided financial assistance to members in need, cared for sick members, and supported the families of deceased members. In Louisville, Masons purchased small pieces of land to build recreational centers. Lodges, which were purchased by members, represented African American financial success and served as status symbols in black communities. By the turn of the century, African American Masons owned approximately $40,000 worth of real estate property throughout the state.

Although Prince Hall Masonry diminished in numbers during the mid-twentieth century, it remained a vital part of many black communities throughout the state. Founded in 1921, the Lexington chapter of Prince Hall Shriners remained active in promoting various charities in the city into the twenty-first century. As of 2011, the Grand Lodge of Kentucky represented 69 lodges spread throughout the state and five Prince Hall Affiliated Temples located in Paducah, Louisville, Covington, Hopkinsville, and Lexington.

DuBois, W. E. B. *Economic Co-operation among Negro Americans.* Atlanta: Atlanta Univ. Publications, 1907.
Most Worshipful Prince Hall Grand Lodge of Kentucky, Inc. "History of Prince Hall Masonry in Kentucky." http://www.phglky.com (accessed September 6, 2011).
Muraskin, William A. *Middle-Class Blacks in a White Society: Prince Hall Freemasonry in America.* Berkeley: Univ. of California Press, 1975.
"Noble Cause: Bring Black, White Shriners Together." *LHL,* April 16, 2006, B1.
Wright, George C. *Life Behind a Veil: Blacks in Louisville, Kentucky, 1865–1930.* Baton Rouge: Louisiana State Univ. Press, 1985.

—*Joshua D. Farrington*

FREE NEGRO FARM (MEADE CO.), pre–Civil War African American community. There are three major accounts that describe the origins of Free Negro Farm, a 300-acre farm located in Meade Co. just north of Vine Grove, Hardin Co., KY. The traditional account described by white authors notes that the community was first formed by Hardin Co.'s first freed slave, **General Braddock,** who had a reputation as a skilled "Indian killer." The story goes that his owner promised Braddock freedom if he killed 10 Native Americans. After completing this task, Braddock was granted his freedom in March 1797. Braddock later purchased

several plots of land on Valley Creek. One of those tracts of land was believed to have been the area of Free Negro or Freed Negroes in Meade Co. The location of Braddock's grave remains a mystery, but many believe that he was buried in an unmarked grave located in Free Negro Cemetery.

The second account of Free Negro Farm's origin asserts that a former slave owner, Martha Patricia Hynes, granted freedom to two female slaves and one male slave near the end of the Civil War. She also reportedly gave them 10 acres of land near what was generally believed to be Free Negro Farm. This account was supported by one of Hynes's descendants in the 1980s, as well as a lifelong African American resident of the area surrounding Free Negro Farm, Hagan Hinton.

The third and probably most accurate account suggests that Free Negro Farm was first formed by a freed slave by the name of Pleasant Moreman. Although there are many unmarked graves in the community's cemetery, the only two inscribed stones are those of Pleasant Moreman and his wife, Jemima. The first legal deed relating to Free Negro Farm shows that Pleasant Moreman bought 269 acres for $225 on February 24, 1847, from the estate of a deceased land speculator. Although other families also lived on the land, the farm remained in the possession of Moreman's descendants until 1931, when it was sold outside the family. The other stories may have elements of truth, but existing records indicate that Pleasant Moreman was the first property owner, at least legally, of Free Negro Farm.

Very few known written records trace the history of Free Negro Farm after the Civil War, although it was known throughout Meade Co. as a place where many African American families lived. In 1918, at the height of World War I, construction began on Ft. Knox. The closest town to the construction site was Stithton, a segregated community that was eventually subsumed by the military base. Many African Americans knew the town by a sign in its train station that warned blacks: "Do not let the sun set on you in Stithton!" During the construction at Ft. Knox, a group of black laborers from Louisville who had just arrived in Stithton was greeted by a white mob armed with shotguns and rifles. The laborers were then instructed that they could not stay in town, and they were forced to stay at Free Negro Farm until permanent accommodations that were approved by whites could be provided.

Little remains on the site that was Free Negro Farm. Besides a small cemetery, there are a number of small cabins and one large, two-story log cabin on the property.

Kempf, Gary. *A History of Fort Knox: Battles, Extinct Communities, Churches, Schools, and Historic Vignettes.* Vine Grove, KY: Ancestral Trails Historical Society, 1998.
Smith, Harvey H. *Lincoln and the Lincolns.* New York: Pioneer Publications, 1931.
Urbahns, Paul. "Local Slave Was Indian Fighter." *Inside the Turret,* February 5, 1984, 148.
———. "More Moremans, Pleasant Moreman: The Free Negro of Meade County." *Ancestral News* 19, no. 3 (Fall 1994): 101–4.

—*Joshua D. Farrington*

FRYE, HELEN FISHER (b. 1918, Danville, KY; d. 2014, Danville, KY), civil rights activist and first African American graduate of the University of Kentucky Library School. Helen

Fisher and her twin brother, Matthew, were born to Lydia Moran and George Fisher of Danville, KY, on June 24, 1918. Helen completed elementary and high school at the segregated Bate School in the city and was valedictorian of the 1938 graduating class. Upon graduation, she enrolled at what is now **Kentucky State University,** graduating in 1942 with a degree in education. She taught school in three county schools before returning to Bate School, where she was a sixth-grade teacher and later school librarian.

Frye attended Indiana University, where she completed her master's degree in education. With the gradual end of Kentucky's segregated higher education in the 1950s, she was allowed finally to attend graduate school at the University of Kentucky. She faced further discrimination in the classroom from her teachers. However, in 1963, she graduated with a second master's degree in library science, becoming one of the first African Americans to graduate from the university's College of Library and Information Sciences. She later became the first African American to enroll in classes at Centre College. In Danville, she was the first black to be president of the local teachers' association.

Frye's community involvement began in groups such as the Ladies Domestic Economy Club, the Busy Sunshine Club, the **Kentucky Association of Colored Women's Clubs,** and **Alpha Kappa Alpha Sorority,** as well as the First Baptist Church. She described herself as an integrationist and resented separation of people because of skin color. In 1951 and before her enrollment at Centre College, she helped organize its first integrated production, *Porgy and Bess,* showcasing Danville native **Robert Todd Duncan.**

Frye began an effort to revive the local Danville branch of the **National Association for the Advancement of Colored People** and served as the branch's president until 1968. In this position, she led citizens of Danville in numerous sit-ins, demonstrations, and boycotts protesting segregated facilities. She also organized a junior chapter of Danville's NAACP branch. During her administration, the Danville NAACP branch secured the integration of public housing and helped an African American get elected to the city council. She served as the chairman of the Public Housing Commission, as president of the Danville–Boyle County Human Rights Commission, and as a member of the Kentucky African American Heritage Commission, among many other appointments. She married John Goodwin Frye in 1975 and retired in 1980.

In 2006, the University of Kentucky School of Library and Information Science honored her with the **Lyman T. Johnson** Award for her many years of service as a librarian, teacher, and civil rights activist. In 2012, Helen Fisher Frye received the Kentucky Assisted Living Facilities Association's Resident Lifetime Achievement Award for her many accomplishments. She died on Wednesday, November 26, 2014. Her funeral was held at First Baptist Church, Second and Walnut streets in Danville.

The Advocate Messenger, December 3, 2014.

"Danville Woman Honored for Decades of Volunteer Work." Ephraim McDowell Health, 2012. http://www.emhealth.org/index.php/about us/emh-news/729-danville-woman-honored-for-decades-of -volunteer-work (accessed August 8, 2013).

Fifty Years of the University of Kentucky African-American Legacy, 1949–1999. Lexington: Univ. of Kentucky, 1999.

Fosl, Catherine, and Tracy E. K'Meyer. *Freedom on the Border: An Oral History of the Civil Rights Movement in Kentucky.* Lexington: Univ. Press of Kentucky, 2009.

Frye, Helen Fisher. Interviews by Betsy Brinson, 1999 and 2000. Kentucky Oral History Commission.

Jones, Reinette F. *Library Service to African Americans in Kentucky, from the Reconstruction Era to the 1960s.* Jefferson, NC: McFarland, 2001.

—*Karen Cotton McDaniel*

FRYE, JOHN HENRY (b. 1875, Danville, KY; d. 1949, Danville, KY), physician. A lifelong Boyle Co., KY, physician, John Henry Frye was the son of Orange Tinsley Frye Sr. and Mary Eliza Green Frye. His father farmed and bred prize-winning Berkshire hogs. In 1900, in order to fund his education, Frye worked as a servant for Louisville white attorney Edmund Trabue. Frye and his father, Orange, graduated that same year from Louisville's State Colored Baptist University. Five years later, Frye earned his medical degree from **Louisville National Medical College,** which became the Medical Department of State Colored Baptist University (later known as **Simmons College of Kentucky**).

By age 34, Frye had an established medical practice and lived with his wife, Florence, and his sons, John G. and James E., in Boyle Co. He raised tobacco in order to supplement his income. His sister, Lucile, age 25, later worked for him in his office. In 1915, Frye attended the Eleventh Annual Meeting of the Volunteer State Medical Association of Tennessee in Nashville. On the second day of the conference, he offered the "Welcome on Behalf of Negro M.D.'s of Danville."

Nine years after his 91-year-old mother was killed by an automobile, Frye died in the hospital. He was buried in Hilldale Cemetery.

"Deaths," *Journal of the American Medical Association,* http://jama .ama-assn.org/content/142/5/352.full.pdf (accessed May 2, 2011).

"Society and Personal," *Journal of the National Medical Association* 7, no. 3 (July–September, 1915). http://www.ncbi.nlm.nih.gov/pmc /articles/PMC2622148/pdf/jnma00842-0083.pdf (accessed May 2, 2011).

Kentucky Death Records, 1852–1953.

Newspapers: "Sweep Stakes," *Springfield Sun (KY),* August 22, 1906, 8; "Tobacco Brings $24.50 per Hundred over Danville Breaks," *Crisis,* December 19, 1913, 7.

Parrish, C. H. *Golden Jubilee of the General Association of Colored Baptists in Kentucky: From 1865–1915.* Louisville, KY: Mayes Printing Co., 1915.

U.S. Federal Census (1900, 1910, 1920).

World War I Draft Registration Cards, 1917–1918.

—*Sallie L. Powell*

FULLER, ALEXANDER (b. 1824, Stamping Ground, Scott Co., KY; d. 1898, Worthville, Carroll Co., KY), and Fuller, Duncan (b. 1823, Kentucky; d. 1865, Gallatin Co., KY), brothers active in the Underground Railroad. Alexander Fuller and his brother, Duncan Fuller, were active in the **Underground Railroad.** They lived in Gallatin Co. in the 1840s and 1850s and later moved to Carroll Co. in the Sanders Precinct near Worthville. The Fuller brothers were Unionists; Duncan served with Union Company B, 7th Kentucky Cavalry, was captured at Dalton, GA, in 1864, and was a prisoner of war until he was mustered out at Edgefield, TN, on July 4, 1865.

Significantly, Duncan and Alexander Fuller were closely related to members of the New Liberty Baptist Church near Quercus Grove, IN, a known station on the Underground Railroad routes leading from Patriot, Markland, Florence, Vevay, and Lamb, IN. Rev. Alexander Sebastian, the founding preacher of that church, spent time in the Warsaw, Gallatin Co., area.

According to family historians, Alexander and Duncan Fuller voted Republican in the heavily Democratic precinct of Worthville-Sanders. This was a strongly Confederate-leaning portion of Carroll Co., and voting Republican was not only dangerous but foolhardy during the 1860–1880 period. Only the most dedicated Unionists would brave the nearby Ku Klux Klan activities along the Kentucky River and in Owen Co.

Ephraim Fuller, the father of Alexander and Duncan, had settled at Stamping Ground, Scott Co., KY, before 1830. Ephraim and both sons gravitated to Warsaw, Gallatin Co., in the 1840s, and the two brothers married sisters: Alexander married Amanda Melvina Knox on October 12, 1845, at Warsaw, and Duncan married Angelina Knox on August 14, 1846, also at Warsaw. They were daughters of Robert Knox and Mildred Ann Bohanan, who moved to Warsaw from Franklin Co., KY, during the early 1840s and were probably associated with the short-lived Presbyterian Church at Warsaw (1837–1867).

Two daughters of Ephraim Fuller, Sarah Ann and Mercy Fuller, married brothers, Enos and David Ellis, respectively, settled in Switzerland Co., IN, and were associated with the Separate Baptist Church at East Enterprise, which merged with the Freewill Baptist Church nearby, forming the New Liberty Baptist Church near Quercus Grove, Switzerland Co. Members of this congregation formed a significant Underground Railroad station, providing safe houses and conductors from Patriot, Markland, Vevay, and Lamb.

The Underground Railroad was active from 1840 to 1861 along the Ohio River between Gallatin Co., KY, and Switzerland Co., IN. There were at least five crossing points where runaway slaves from Gallatin and eastern Carroll Counties were aided, or at least sighted, by Underground Railroad activists on the Indiana side of the Ohio River: from Sugar Creek, KY, to Patriot and Florence, IN; from Warsaw, KY, to Markland, IN; from Warsaw or Ghent, KY, to Vevay, IN; from Carrollton, KY, to Lamb, IN; and from Prestonville, KY, to Brooksburg, IN.

Precisely what role Alexander and Duncan Fuller played in these operations is not clear, but the two represent a substantial number of white yeomen who, together with numerous free people of color, enabled runaway slaves to reach places of safety in southern Indiana.

Coon, Diane Perrine. "Southeastern Indiana's Underground Railroad Routes and Operations." Unpublished technical report, U.S. Park Service and Indiana Department of Natural Resources, Indiana Dept. of Historic Preservation and Archaeology, Indianapolis, 1999.

Duvall, Jeffery. E-mail correspondence with Diane Perrine Coon regarding family history and genealogy, June–July 2006.

—Diane Perrine Coon

G

Simmons, William. *Men of Mark: Eminent, Progressive and Rising.* Cleveland: George M. Rewell, 1887.

Wright, George C. *Life Behind a Veil: Blacks in Louisville, Kentucky, 1865–1930.* Baton Rouge: Louisiana State Univ. Press, 1985.

—*Joshua D. Farrington*

GADDIE, DANIEL ABRAHAM, SR. (b. 1833, Hart Co., KY; d. 1911, Louisville, KY), influential minister of numerous churches throughout Kentucky. Described by a contemporary as "one of the great towers of the Baptist cause in Kentucky," Daniel Abraham Gaddie was born the son of a slave owner in Hart Co., KY, on May 21, 1833. After he was freed, Daniel changed his last name from Jamison, the surname of his biological father, to Gaddie.

Gaddie spent his formative years as a blacksmith but was converted to Christianity in the 1860s by a white man named Robert Gardner. In 1865, he was ordained a minister by **Green Street Baptist Church** in Louisville, of which he was a member. Over the next seven years, he pastored several churches across the state in Elizabethtown, Campbellsville, Glendale, and Hardin Co.

In 1872, he was called to return to Green Street Baptist to become its head pastor. During his tenure, which lasted until his death in 1911, Gaddie married over 500 couples, and the church added more than 2,000 new members to its rolls. **William J. Simmons** estimated that 1,500 of those new members were recent converts to Christianity, many of whom were attracted to Gaddie's dynamic preaching style.

Gaddie was also heavily involved in the state and national Baptist associations. After years of representing his state at national conventions, he was elected treasurer of the National American Baptist Convention in 1886. He additionally served as the vice president of the American Consolidated Baptist Convention and was a major force within the **General Association of Baptists in Kentucky.**

Although he never received a formal education because of the constraints of slavery, Gaddie was a vocal advocate of increased educational opportunities for the state's African Americans. As early as 1869, he was a leading participant in Kentucky's Colored Education Convention. He also directed large portions of donations at Green Street Baptist Church to fund various educational institutions throughout Louisville. Gaddie was particularly involved in State University (later known as **Simmons College of Kentucky**) at Louisville, serving on the board of trustees for 7 years and the executive board for 16. Because of his service, Gaddie was given an honorary doctor of divinity degree by the school in 1887.

Gaddie died on November 13, 1911. Prominent Louisville undertaker **James H. Hathaway** handled the funeral arrangements. Gaddie was buried in Eastern Cemetery.

Kentucky Death Records, 1852–1953.

Lucas, Marion B. *A History of Blacks in Kentucky.* Vol 1, *From Slavery to Segregation, 1760–1891.* Frankfort: Kentucky Historical Society, 1992.

Parrish, C. H. *Golden Jubilee of the General Association of Colored Baptists in Kentucky: From 1865–1915.* Louisville, KY: Mayes Printing Co., 1915.

Pegues, A. W. *Our Baptist Ministers and Schools.* Springfield, MA: Willey & Co., 1892.

GAFFNEY, PAUL "SHOWTIME" (b. 1968, Benham, KY), "clown prince" of the Harlem Globetrotters. Despite a difficult childhood in the coalmining area of Harlan Co., Paul "Showtime" Gaffney never lost his smile and desire to make people laugh. After the death of his mother when he was an infant and the death of his adopted mother when he was two, Gaffney was raised in Lynch by his adopted father, Ellis Gaffney. Gaffney describes his adopted father as the biggest influence in his life and once said that "they say where you come from doesn't matter, but it really does matter. . . . Who works harder than people in the coal mines? It was just bred in you to work hard."

It was this work ethic that led Gaffney to become an All-District star at Cumberland High School. As a star forward for Tennessee Wesleyan University, Gaffney led the team in scoring and made All-Conference. His talent and colorful personality caught the eye of the Harlem Globetrotters. In 1996, Gaffney became the youngest "clown prince," or lead showman, in the famed team's history.

Describing Gaffney's talent and sense of humor, one reporter noted that "his smile and Kentucky drawl remind me of Magic Johnson's country cousin." The Globetrotters' vice president said that the reason Gaffney was selected to the esteemed position of clown prince was that in addition to being "a great basketball player . . . when people see his smile, it lights up the crowd." In addition to his trademark half-court hook shot, Showtime, as he was known to thousands of fans, could be seen throwing shoes at opponents while they took foul shots, faking a humorous injury, or throwing a bucket of water into the crowd during a game. Hooked up to a live microphone throughout the game, Gaffney also drew thunderous laughter for comments about opponents' foul-smelling armpits or referees' bad calls. Making people laugh, in addition to displaying his talents, was one of Gaffney's favorite aspects of his career. He once remarked that "when people come in here, they forget their troubles. . . . Everybody just becomes a kid." For almost a decade, during the 15-minute autograph session before games, Showtime was consistently the most popular team member demanded by fans.

After playing in over 2,250 games in 80 countries, Gaffney retired from the Globetrotters in 2008. In his 14-year career with the team, Gaffney played in faraway places from Lebanon to Croatia and in front of world leaders like British royalty and South African president Nelson Mandela. After traveling the globe, Paul Gaffney retired to his home in Houston, TX, where he owns a custom clothing shop.

"The Clown Prince of Basketball." *Boys Life,* February 1997, 10–12

Green, Ben. *Spinning the Globe: The Rise, Fall, and Return to Greatness of the Harlem Globetrotters.* New York: HarperCollins, 2005.

Newspapers: "Globetrotter Shoots for Home," *LHL,* January 15, 1999, 3; "Harlan Boasts Globetrotters Connections," *LCJ,* May 8, 2005, B1.

"Tears of the Clowns." *Vibe,* October 1996, 104–5.

—*Joshua D. Farrington*

GAINES, CLARENCE EDWARD "BIG HOUSE," SR. (b. 1923, Paducah, KY; d. 2005, Winston-Salem, NC), basketball coach. Born in Paducah, KY, on May 21, 1923, Clarence Edward Gaines was the only child of Olivia Bolen and Lester Gaines. At Paducah's Lincoln High School, Gaines played basketball and football and graduated as salutatorian in 1941. He attended Morgan State College on a football scholarship, where his 6-feet-4, 250-pound size earned him the nickname "Big House."

After graduating with a degree in chemistry, Gaines became head football and basketball coach at Winston-Salem University, a historically black college. After coaching football for four years, he concentrated on coaching basketball. His 1967 basketball team won the NCAA Division II national championship, and he was named Division II coach of the year. In 1968, he was inducted into the Helms Hall of Fame. In 1978, Winston-Salem State University opened the C. E. Gaines Center in his honor, and he was inducted into the Naismith Hall of Fame in 1982. At the time of his retirement, after coaching from 1946 to 1993, Gaines's 828 victories were the second highest by any coach in NCAA history. Twice he served on the U.S. Olympic Committee. He was active in numerous community and philanthropic organizations.

In 1950, Gaines earned a master's degree in education from Columbia University and married Clara Berry. The couple had two children: Clarence Edward Gaines Jr. and Lisa Gaines McDonald. On April 18, 2005, "Big House" Gaines died of complications from a stroke. His remains were cremated.

Gaines, Clarence E., with Clint Johnson. *They Call Me Big House.* Winston-Salem, NC: John F. Blair, 2004.
Newspapers: Viv Bernstein, "Big House Gaines, 81, Basketball Coach, Dies," *NYT,* April 20, 2005, C19; John Dell, "Loss of a Giant," *Winston-Salem Journal,* April 21, 2005; Paul Nowell, "Final Respects Paid to 'Big House' Gaines," *USA Today,* April 22, 2005.

—*Charles F. Faber*

GAINES, HARRIS BARNETT (b. 1888, Henderson, KY; d. 1964, Chicago, IL), assistant state's attorney in Cook Co., IL, and member of the Illinois state legislature. Born in Henderson, KY, to William and Mamie Gaines, Harris Barnett Gaines moved with his family to Chicago during his childhood. As a teenager, he worked for his father's construction business, which had become one of the most successful African American plastering companies in the city. Gaines remained in Chicago for the rest of his life and eventually obtained a law degree from DePaul University.

Harris Gaines married Irene McCoy Gaines, who later became the president of the National Association of Colored Women, and he and his wife were one of the preeminent political couples in Chicago's black community from the 1920s through the 1950s. Working through the Republican political machine, Gaines served as assistant state's attorney in Cook Co. from 1925 to 1928. In 1928, he was elected to the Illinois state legislature, where he represented Chicago's First District for seven years. In 1935, he authored and sponsored the Illinois Civil Rights Act, which banned discrimination in any public locations. During his tenure, he also sponsored bills to guarantee jury trials and other constitutional protections to defendants and led the drive during the Great Depression for laws that provided unemployment insurance and old-age pensions.

Both Gaines and his wife died in Chicago in 1964. He was the father of future Illinois state representative Charles E. Gaines.

Alexander, Sadie. *Who's Who among Negro Lawyers.* Washington, DC: National Bar Association, 1945.
Materson, Lisa G. *For the Freedom of Her Race: Black Women and Electoral Politics in Illinois, 1877–1932.* Chapel Hill: Univ. of North Carolina Press, 2009.
Styles, Fitzhugh Lee. *Negroes and the Law in the Race's Battle for Liberty, Equality and Justice.* Boston: Christopher Publishing House, 1937.
Williams, Erma Brooks. *Political Empowerment of Illinois' African-American State Lawmakers from 1877 to 2005.* Washington, DC: Univ. Press of America, 2008.

—*Joshua D. Farrington*

GAINES, WALLACE ARKANSAS (b. 1865, Dayton, OH; d. 1940, Evansville, IN), businessman and grand supreme master of the United Brothers of Friendship. African American businessman and civic leader Wallace Gaines was born on April 15, 1865, and came to Covington with his parents about 1875. He began working for his uncle in Ottoway Burton's barbershop at 706 Washington St., shining shoes; he continued as a bootblack until he found other employment in the handling of furniture and feathers.

By 1880, Gaines was serving as president of the "colored" Garfield First Voters Club, which supported James Garfield of Ohio for president in the 1880 election. He rose quickly within the Republican Party and received an appointment in 1881 as a storekeeper in the Federal Revenue's collection department. During the administration of President Benjamin Harrison (1889–1893), he was appointed a U.S. gauger; the duties of a gauger included inspecting scales and other measuring devices used to determine the official weight of grains and other supplies. When the Republican Party was out of power, Gaines became a hauling contractor by serving grain and whiskey distilleries. During this period, he joined the **United Brothers of Friendship,** which by the late 1890s had become the largest African American civic association in the country. Gaines rose through that organization's ranks and by 1897 was the grand supreme master. This position placed him at the head of an estimated 300,000 African American voters nationwide. With such backing and political connections, Gaines was mentioned as a candidate for the post of registrar of the U.S. Treasury. He traveled to Washington, DC, to lobby for the job but did not receive it; instead, he returned home to resume his job as a federal gauger, which he kept only briefly. In May 1898, he was appointed a federal court bailiff but resigned the same day after it was determined that the job would interfere with his support of the renomination of his personal friend Walter Evans, a Republican congressman.

In 1904, while doing his job as a special revenue agent for the U.S. Treasury Department, Gaines discovered that the wholesale whiskey house of Crigler and Crigler, located on Pike St. in Covington, was moving untaxed whiskey barrels. His report to the tax collector and revenue agent led to action in the U.S. district court.

Gaines was a founding member, president, and director of the **Progressive Building and Loan Association,** which was created for the African American community of Covington. The association, which operated from 1906 to 1910, was located at the corner of Seventh and Scott Sts. adjacent to the W. A. Gaines Funeral Home.

For a number of years, Gaines owned the W. A. Gaines Funeral Home at 633 Scott St. He was the first African American funeral director in Covington. In 1908, he started a funeral home in Evansville, IN. In 1912, he expanded his funeral home businesses to include Henderson, KY; in 1913, he sold his Covington business to **Charles E. Jones.** In July 1913, Gaines married Tillie Young, a teacher at **Lincoln-Grant School** and a former treasurer of the Progressive Building and Loan Association, and the couple moved to Evansville, IN. He died in August 1940 in Evansville and was buried in Highland Cemetery, Ft. Mitchell. At the time of his death, he was a 33rd-degree Mason.

Newspapers: "The Colored Garfield First Voters' Club," *(Frankfort, KY) Daily Commonwealth,* October 25, 1880, 1; "Colored Man, Who Is Said to Be Booked for High Position," *KP,* July 24, 1897, 8; "Building Association Will Be Organized," *KP,* May 31, 1906, 2; "When History Is Overlooked," *KP,* February 8, 1999, 4K; "Blacks at Turn of Century Persevered to Improve Lives," *KP,* January 17, 2000, 4K; "Wallace Gaines Achieved Success in a Difficult Era for African-Americans," *KP,* February 2, 2004, 4K.

—*Theodore H. H. Harris*

GAITHER, WILLIAM (b. 1910, Belmont, KY; d. 1970, Indianapolis, IN), guitarist and blues singer. The son of Samuel Gaither and Bertha Kennison, William Gaither was born on April 21, 1910, and moved to Louisville in 1920. He made his first recordings for Victor Records in December 1931. In 1932, he moved to Indianapolis and from 1935 to 1941 enjoyed success recording for Decca and Okeh Records under the names Little Bill and Leroy's Buddy (a reference to pianist Leroy Carr). He returned to Louisville in 1940 and operated a radio repair shop on Seventh St. In 1942, he was drafted into the army, was assigned to the all-black 24th Infantry Regiment, and saw active duty in the Solomon Islands. He was discharged in 1945 and moved back to Indianapolis in 1948, where he died on October 30, 1970. He is buried in New Crown Cemetery.

—*Brenda K. Bogert*

GARNER, MARGARET (b. 1833, Boone Co., KY; d. 1858, Mississippi), runaway and recaptured slave. An African American fugitive who escaped from slavery in northern Kentucky, called Peggy by her owner, became one of the most infamous, tragic, and complex figures in the history of American slavery because of what occurred in the winter of 1856. Born on June 4, 1833, on the Maplewood plantation in Boone Co., KY, young Margaret was the property of John P. Gaines, a local farmer. In 1849, at the age of 16, she married Robert Garner, who lived nearby and was owned by John Marshall. By the fall of that year, Margaret was pregnant with her first child. Simultaneously, because of his close ties with President Zachary Taylor, whom he had befriended during their military service in the Mexican War, Gaines was offered and subsequently accepted the governorship of the Oregon Territory. Almost immediately Gaines arranged for his brother, Archibald, who owned a plantation in Arkansas, to purchase the Maplewood property, including all the accompanying enslaved African Americans.

With the possible change in ownership, Margaret's life became extremely difficult and harsh. In addition to her giving birth to four children between 1850 and 1855 (Thomas, 1850; Samuel, 1852; Mary, 1854; and Priscilla or Cilla, 1855), it appears that she was abused sexually. Also, it seems that Robert Garner may not have been the biological father of all her children.

On January 27, 1856, the Garner family escaped in a stolen sleigh, headed to Covington, KY, and eventually traveled across the frozen Ohio River to Cincinnati. They hid overnight in the home of Margaret's cousin, Elijah Kite, but quickly were discovered by a large group of whites who included several slave-catchers and a few members of both the Gaines and the Marshall families, as well as several law-enforcement officials. After hearing some noise outside, Robert Garner, who was armed, fired a shot that wounded one man. In response, several men from outside the house rushed in, but what they witnessed shocked them for years. Gripping a knife covered with blood and standing over the nearly decapitated body of her daughter, Mary, 23-year-old Margaret Garner shouted that she would rather see her children dead than returned to slavery at the Maplewood plantation. However, before she could kill another child, Margaret was surrounded and overpowered.

The entire Garner family was arrested and jailed immediately. The family's trial in Cincinnati lasted two weeks and generated crowds of hundreds of people daily. In the end, however, the judge ruled that the Garner family must be returned to slavery in Kentucky. Subsequently, both the Gaines and Marshall families sent the Garners to a plantation in Arkansas. Eventually, they became the property of a Mississippi judge. However, the true whereabouts of Margaret soon became unknown until her husband revealed in an interview in 1870 that she had died of typhoid in the fall of 1858. Author Toni Morrison based her novel *Beloved* on Margaret Garner's rebellious act.

Bordewich, Fergus M. *Bound for Canaan: The Underground Railroad and the War for the Soul of America.* New York: Amistad-HarperCollins, 2005.
Hudson, Blaine J. *Encyclopedia of the Underground Railroad.* Jefferson, NC: McFarland, 2006.
Weisenburger, Steven. *Modern Medea: A Family Story of Slavery and Child-Murder from the Old South.* New York: Hill & Wang, 1998.
Yanuck, Julius. "The Garner Fugitive Slave Case." *Mississippi Valley Historical Review* 40 (1953): 47–66.

—*Eric R. Jackson*

GARRISON-CORBIN, PATRICIA (b. 1947, Louisville, KY; d. 2009, Philadelphia, PA), successful businesswoman and financial adviser. Born and raised in Louisville, Patricia Garrison graduated from Western Kentucky University in 1969. The year before, she chartered and became president of the college's first black Greek-letter organization, **Alpha Kappa Alpha Sorority.** She then obtained a master's degree in urban studies from the University of Louisville. In 1971, she became the first African American female Sloan Fellow at the Massachusetts Institute of Technology, from which she graduated with a degree in finance.

After years of being a social worker in Florida during the 1970s, Patricia and her husband, James Corbin, moved to Philadelphia, where she served as a financial adviser to Mayors William J.

Green and W. Wilson Goode throughout the 1980s. In 1985, she moved briefly to New York City to become the vice president of Drexel Burnham Lambert, a Wall Street investment banking firm. Within two years, she had returned to Philadelphia and started her own business, P. G. Corbin and Company. P. G. Corbin, the first Wall Street financial services corporation owned by an African American woman, became the third-biggest company in the financial services industry by 1993. The multibillion-dollar consulting firm specialized in providing financial advice to municipal governments across the country.

As CEO of a major financial institution, Garrison-Corbin was asked to serve on numerous government committees. In 1986, President Ronald Reagan appointed her to the advisory panel to the secretary of housing and urban development, and she served on a commission of the Environmental Protection Agency in 1994. In 1995, she was named the Revlon Business Woman of the Year; a year later, she was inducted into the Distinguished Hall of Alumni at Western Kentucky University. In 1998, she served on the Visiting Committee of the University of Louisville Business School. In 2000, in Philadelphia, she helped negotiate the building of a new baseball stadium for the Phillies and was appointed to the Tax Reform Commission in 2003. Patricia Garrison-Corbin died of breast cancer in Philadelphia in October 2009.

"Patricia Garrison-Corbin." WKU Hall of Distinguished Alumni. http://www.wku.edu/tradition/hoda96.html (accessed April 28, 2011).

"Patricia G. Corbin, Financial Whiz, Dies at 62." *Philadelphia Daily News*, October 21, 2009.

P. G. Corbin & Co. "Press Release: African American Wall Street Pioneer Dies." October 2009. http://www.nasphq.org/pdf/PRESS _RELEASE_DEATH_OF_ PATRICIA_GARRISON_CORBIN_. pdf (accessed April 28, 2011).

—*Joshua D. Farrington*

GAUNT, WHEELING (b. ca. 1813, Carrollton, KY; d. 1894, Yellow Springs, OH), benefactor of Wilberforce College. Wheeling Gaunt, described as a mulatto, was born into abject poverty as a slave, but over his lifetime he amassed a large fortune and gave most of it away to philanthropic projects. To this day, the poor families of Yellow Springs, OH, receive a Christmas gift of 25 pounds of flour and 10 pounds of sugar from the foundation Gaunt established. The funds for these donations came from a gift to the community of nine acres that the former slave owned next to Antioch College. In 1884, Wheeling Gaunt gave a $5,000 financial contribution to enable Wilberforce College in Wilberforce, OH, to become one of the leading traditionally black colleges in the United States. Gaunt was a friend and benefactor of Daniel A. Payne, the presiding bishop and an evangelist for the African Methodist Episcopal Church and the first president of Wilberforce College.

Wheeling Gaunt's slave owner during the 1840s was John R. Gaunt, an attorney at Carrollton. Wheeling's father was a white man, a leading merchant, who sold Wheeling's mother to a slave trader when Wheeling was very young. In later years, Wheeling claimed that he inherited his knowledge of how to make and save money from that first slave owner-father. Wheeling married his first wife, Amanda, also a mulatto slave, in 1838 in a typical slave wedding.

John R. Gaunt permitted Wheeling to earn his freedom, as a few other Carroll Co. slave owners did for their slaves. Wheeling Gaunt earned money for his emancipation by picking apples and shining shoes over and above his regular chores. When John Gaunt died in 1841, his inventory of properties listed "One Negro Man, Wheeling," worth $600. Wheeling and another slave, Louisa, were willed to John's wife, Nancy, and their children. The emancipation bond of $500, dated May 5, 1845, at the Carroll Co. Courthouse, among Nancy, Alfred R., and John E. Gaunt, William Root, and George Hinkley, witnessed by several justices of the peace of Carroll Co., stated that on that day they emancipated their slave, Wheeling.

Two years later, Wheeling Gaunt, a free person of color, purchased a house and two lots in Carrollton. He then purchased for $200 Nick, a slave owned by M. D. Smith; the contract stated that Nick was to be free on reaching the age of 21. There is speculation that this boy, born in 1841, was Wheeling's son. In 1849, Wheeling purchased in-lots 138 and 139 at the corner of Fourth and High Sts. in Carrollton.

Wheeling purchased Amanda, his wife, for $500 and then emancipated her sometime before the 1850 federal census, which listed the family together as free people of color living in Carrollton. Wheeling Gaunt, then 35, had $1,000 in real estate and was listed as a farmer. His wife, Amanda, was aged 29, and Nicholas Gaunt was 9 years old. In 1858 and 1859, Wheeling purchased in-lots 189 at Fifth and Sycamore Sts.; 287 on Seventh St.; 135 at Fourth and Main Sts., a large lot along the Ohio River; and 136 on the southeast corner of Fourth and Main Sts. in Carrollton.

Ten years later, Wheeling Gaunt, age 45, remained in Carrollton, and his occupation was listed as teamster. He had $1,500 in real estate and $3,000 in personal property. His wife was 38 years old, and their son, Nicholas, was no longer living with them. In 1860, Wheeling cashed out his Carrollton properties for $2,800 and headed for Yellow Springs, OH. Greene Co. historians in Ohio speculate that he may have heard about Moncure Conway's emancipated slave colony at Yellow Springs, founded in 1862, or he may have followed Bishop Daniel A. Payne to Wilberforce College. There may be an even better link with Kentucky. The most famous **Underground Railroad** conductor between Louisville and Cincinnati, **Elijah Anderson,** would have known Wheeling Gaunt very well, since it was Anderson who established the Carrollton and Kentucky River route for escaping slaves. Anderson often took groups of runaway slaves up from Kentucky through northwestern Ohio to Sandusky, and he would have known about the abolitionists, black and white, at Yellow Springs.

Although the 1870 census of Greene Co., OH, listed Wheeling Gaunt, worth $4,000 in real estate and $6,000 personal property, as just a day laborer, he proved to be an excellent real estate speculator, buying and selling town lots near Antioch College between 1864 and 1890. For his residence, Gaunt built a substantial two-story Greek Revival building near the corner of N. Walnut and Dayton Sts. and four small cottages he called "Gaunt cottages." In 1887, the first year of racial integration at Yellow Springs, Gaunt ran for the city school board.

Although Gaunt never received any formal education, he was very interested in Bishop Daniel A. Payne's concepts of education for black citizens. Gaunt's gifts to Wilberforce College began with his donation of a sizable brick house and property that he owned at 131 N. Walnut St., on the north side of Yellow Springs. At that time, it was valued at $1,650. In 1884, he gave $5,000 in endowment funds to support Wilberforce University and the Payne Theological Seminary at Wilberforce.

The Gaunt holdings on the south side of Yellow Springs, originally nine acres, became a gift to the community of Yellow Springs and the financial source of the Christmas gifts to the poor. Named in his honor, Gaunt Park now contains Gaunt Pool, baseball fields, and a sledding hill. Wheeling Gaunt was also a major contributor to his church, the Central Chapel, an A.M.E. church at the corner of High and Davis Sts. in Yellow Springs. He donated a bell, the vestibule, and the belfry.

When his wife, Amanda, died in 1889, Wheeling erected a large, ornate marble tombstone in the Glen Forest Cemetery at Yellow Springs. He was married a second time, to Mrs. Elizabeth Nichols of Xenia, OH, on July 2, 1890. Elizabeth received a bequest of $7,000 when Wheeling died of Bright's disease on May 10, 1894, and she was asked to care for Wheeling's sister, Louise Chandler, during her lifetime. Gaunt willed the remainder of his property to Wilberforce University and the Payne Theological Seminary. The *Yellow Springs Weekly Citizen* asserted that Wheeling Gaunt was the "richest colored man in Ohio" and stated that he was "known to every distinguished man of his race, from Fred Douglass to Bishop Payne." On May 18, 1894, both blacks and whites from Wilberforce, Springfield, Xenia, and Yellow Springs, OH, packed the church and lined the funeral procession for Wheeling Gaunt, the former Carroll Co., KY, slave. He was buried next to his first wife, Amanda, in the Glen Forest Cemetery.

In addition to more than 15 Virginia black families whom Moncure Conway led to Yellow Springs in 1862, a number of families from northern Kentucky resettled at Yellow Springs. The 1870 U.S. census lists the following resettled Kentucky families as residents of Yellow Springs: Tolbert Baker, Alfred Benning, Andrew Benning, Francis Botts, John Cloak, Jackson Coffee, Henry Ford, Mack Ford, Peter Ford, Benjamin Grimes, Alfred Henry, Allen Jones, Eliza Lee, Charles Morgan, Anderson Ramsey, Vincent Smith, William Talber, Charles Webster, Charles Willis, and Harrison Wilson.

Deal, Steve. "Wheeling Gaunt: Our Remarkable Patron: What We Know. What We Think." http://www.yshistory.org/Gaunt.pdf (accessed July 25, 2006).

"Emancipated Gaunt Slave Prospered as a Free Man," *Carrollton News Democrat,* February 2, 2004, 4.

Emancipation papers, May 5, 1845, Carroll Co. Courthouse, Carrollton, KY.

Freedom from Religion Foundation. "Moncure Conway House Designated Underground Railroad Network to Freedom Sites." http://www.ffrf.org (accessed July 25, 2006).

—*Karen Claiborne and Diane Perrine Coon*

GAY, TYSON (b. 1982, Lexington, KY), world champion sprinter. The son of Daisy Gay Lowe and Greg Mitchell, Tyson Gay grew up with one sister and two half siblings. He graduated from Lafayette High School in Lexington, KY, where he broke the state championship record with a time of 10.46 seconds in the 100 meters. He attended Barton Community College in Great Bend, KS, followed by the University of Arkansas, where he studied sociology and marketing.

Gay ran the 60-, 100-, and 200-meter races in college and won the NCAA championship in the 100 meters with a time of 10.06 seconds in 2004. In 2005, he turned professional, set his personal best time of 6.55 seconds in the 60 meters, and had his first international gold medal finish with a time of 19.96 seconds in the 200 meters at the International Association of Athletics Federations (IAAF) World Athletics Final. At the 2007 World Championships in Athletics, Gay won gold medals in the 100 and 200 meters and the 4×100-meter relay. He ran the 100 meters at the 2008 Beijing Olympics but did not make the final round. In 2009, he ran the second-fastest 100 meters and third-fastest 200 meters ever, with times of 9.69 and 19.58 seconds, respectively. Altogether, he has won four gold medals in IAAF competitions and three at the World Championships.

Plagued by injuries, including hamstring and groin problems, Gay had hip surgery just a few months before the 2012 London Olympics. He still competed and crossed the finish line of the 100-meter dash in fourth place, which meant no Olympic medal for him. In 2013, he announced that despite being in "the twilight of his career" at age 30, he was training for the 2016 Summer Olympic Games in Rio de Janeiro.

Newspapers: "Catch Him If You Can," *LHL,* March 4, 2007, A1; "Tyson Gay Back on Track and Healthy Again," *Rutland (VT) Herald,* February 23, 2013.

"Tyson Gay." International Association of Athletics Federations. http://www.iaaf.org/athletes/biographies/letter=0/athcode=185464/index.html (accessed December 28, 2010).

"Tyson Gay." USA Track and Field. http://www.usatf.org/athletes/bios/gay_tyson.asp (accessed December 28, 2010).

—*Kevin Hogg*

GENERAL ASSOCIATION OF BAPTISTS IN KENTUCKY, historic statewide organization of African American Baptists. On August 15, 1865, Rev. **Henry Adams** led the organization of the State Convention of Colored Baptists at the **Fifth Street Baptist Church** in Louisville, KY. Before this meeting, a group of African American Baptists had already purchased property to establish a Baptist college in Frankfort. This property was transferred to the convention in 1866. In 1869, the convention was renamed the General Association of Colored Baptists of Kentucky during a meeting at the First Baptist Church in Lexington. Members present at this meeting also voted to establish the Baptist college in Louisville instead of Frankfort.

The association was committed to sharing the gospel and establishing an institution of learning. Fund-raising among individuals and churches was strongly encouraged to meet those objectives. Each year the number of churches affiliated with the association increased. In 1877, Rev. John G. Fee was a guest speaker on education. On November 25, 1879, the association founded Kentucky Normal and Theological Institute (KNTI) on Seventh and Kentucky Sts. in Louisville. The school changed names through the years, ultimately being named **Simmons**

College of Kentucky. In September 1883, the Baptist Women's Missionary Convention was organized to assist in raising funds for KNTI. The **American Baptist** newspaper was also founded to support the association's mission and publicize programs.

By the turn of the century, the association focused on state, home, and foreign missions. The body had created a motto: "More Baptists, and more Baptists enlisted for service." The association was also politically active and, in 1899, endorsed the Republican Party during the upcoming November election. A committee that had examined the candidates declared, "All the great measures leading to the preservation of the Union, the abolition of slavery, the establishment of the highest public credit . . . have been the works of the Republican party."

Since its founding, the General Association of Baptists of Kentucky has grown to include 650 Missionary Baptist churches and over 170,000 members. Although predominantly African American, "colored" was not used by the last half of the twentieth century. The Needs of the Race Committee, the State Mission Board, the *American Baptist* newspaper, and several other auxiliaries remain integral components of the association, which strives to carry out the Great Commission.

"Colored Voters, Heed." *Earlington (KY) Bee,* October 5, 1899, 4.

General Association of Baptists in Kentucky Website. http://www .gabnky.org/index.html (accessed October 16, 2013).

Steward, William H. "History of the General Association Colored Baptist in Kentucky." In *Golden Jubilee of the General Association of Colored Baptists in Kentucky: From 1865–1915,* C. H. Parrish. Louisville, KY: Mayes Printing Co., 1915.

—Gerald L. Smith

GEX LANDING INCIDENT, conflict between Confederate soldiers and a unit of the U.S. Colored Troops at Ghent, KY. Resentment against the U.S. Colored Troops (USCT) established by President Abraham Lincoln in the spring of 1863 dominated Kentucky politics into 1864, and it festered particularly in the north central counties, where Confederate sympathies were most pronounced. The Union forces were thinly stretched across Kentucky. Confederate colonel George Jesse had been ordered to collect the scattered remnants of Gen. John Hunt Morgan's cavalry after Morgan's forces were routed in June 1864 at Cynthiana, KY. Jesse stationed himself in familiar territory at New Castle in Henry Co. As his now relatively independent forces strengthened, Jesse harassed supply lines and targeted Union supporters throughout the area.

Recently promoted Lt. Frederick D. Seward led a detachment of Company C of the 117th USCT, mustered at Covington in July 1864, into this hostile territory in August 1864. This squad of untrained infantry was sent to protect recruits obtained for the 5th U.S. Colored Cavalry (USCC) among slaves and free people of color in Carroll, Gallatin, Grant, and Owen Counties. The officers of USCT and USCC units were white. Indiana native Frederick Seward had completed two years of service with Company E, 9th Minnesota Regiment, before his promotion to lieutenant. About August 22, the USCT squad arrested James Southard, a leading Confederate sympathizer and ferryman at Ghent, Gallatin Co. Southard owned land along the Ohio River that formed the Ghent landing. His brother notified Colonel Jesse, who was

in Henry Co., that James Southard had been taken by USCT troops.

Jesse's cavalry caught up with the USCT squad at the plantation of Lucien C. Gex, just outside Ghent, on August 29, 1864. According to eyewitness Virginia Craig, that night the USCT unit had been separated into two groups of six each; one group was fed dinner at the farm of her father, Albert Craig, and the other group was fed at an unspecified nearby farm. Jesse's men surprised and captured the USCT soldiers, and in their first engagement with the enemy, the Union troops were scattered across the farms of Albert and John A. Craig. The Confederate States of America (CSA) troops rescued Southard at John A. Craig's farm. There were casualties among the USCT troops, but the exact number of them is unknown. Over the next day or so, several different accounts of the incident were recorded, and thus the tale of the Gex Landing Massacre was established.

On August 30, 1864, Union lieutenant colonel Thomas B. Fairleigh, at Louisville, requested aid from J. Bates Dickson, assistant adjutant at Lexington: "Last evening [Confederate colonel] Jesse with 150 men captured a squad of eight or ten colored troops at Ghent and murdered them. Other squads are in the country where he is hunting. Can't you send some men there?"

Virginia Craig recorded in her diary of August 30, 1864, that six of the USCT soldiers were fed at her house and were surprised and captured by rebel soldiers who had searched the house. She said that Southard was being held at her cousin John's house and was rescued. According to her diary, one USCT soldier had been killed and subsequently buried on Albert Craig's lower farm, two wounded USCT soldiers had been put on the packet steamer *Rowena* bound for Cincinnati, and the rest had been captured, including a white recruiter.

A Cincinnati newspaper, the *Commercial Dispatch,* carried the story within the week, claiming that one of the two wounded USCT soldiers had died in transit on the *Rowena.* This story further claimed that there had been 60 USCT and 100 CSA soldiers involved in the incident at Ghent.

A highly partisan version of the "massacre" was carried in the August 31, 1864, issue of the *Louisville Daily Journal,* generally a pro-Union newspaper. There it was stated that Jesse's troops had massacred unarmed Negro troops, "shooting them like wild beasts." The next day, the *Louisville Daily Journal* reported that Jesse's troops had destroyed Lock No. 1 on the Kentucky River and had "proclaimed vengeance against all Negro soldiers and recruits. It will be [Jesse's] policy to murder all that may fall into his hands. His recent massacre of the blacks at Ghent shows that his words [are] not simple idle bombast."

Two days later, the newspaper corrected its earlier story: "Jesse did not murder negroes at Ghent—none killed except in attack. His men urged him to murder entire party but he refused the barbarous act." On September 5, the newspaper reported that "seven of the colored soldiers reached Owenton [KY] from Port Royal [KY] on Wednesday last where released . . . one a Sgt., two wounded, fifteen captured, eight remained with rebels voluntarily . . . no bad treatment by Jesse."

As if the story were not confused enough by the presence of two different black units at the skirmish, in November 1864, elements of the 5th USCC were assigned to patrol duty at Ghent and

Warsaw. Local citizens apparently made no distinction between the USCT and USCC units.

In December 1864, the 117th USCT, stationed at **Camp Nelson** in Jessamine Co., was folded into the 25th Union Brigade, and white regiments in the brigade were transferred. The 117th Regiment under the 25th Corps saw action at Richmond and Appomattox in Virginia and in the final Texas campaign. Compared with these other battles, the Gex landing skirmish was insignificant. The official regimental records of the 5th USCC state that at the Ghent skirmish one soldier was killed, six were captured but later escaped, and five returned to their unit.

The story was embellished further during the early 1900s when A. L. Gex, the son of Lucien Gex, found three graves churned up by a cyclone (tornado) and reported seeing "foot bones in perfectly preserved shoes."

The wide discrepancies concerning the numbers involved in the Ghent incident can be attributed to wartime hysteria and to newspaper reporting that was dependent on local sources for its news coverage. The presence of both cavalry and infantry units among the black troops and recent recruits of slaves from the region added to confusion about the number of deaths and about those who were released or remained with the Confederates.

From the family letters exchanged during the Civil War, it appears that the Gex and Craig families originally supported Kentucky's neutrality but were bitterly opposed to the formation of USCT units and the military draft. By 1865, these families had affiliated themselves totally with the Conservative Democrats, a political faction that tipped the balance in the Kentucky legislature toward a pro-southern position after the Civil War.

Abbett, H. J., Warsaw, to A. G. Craig, July 18, 1865. Craig Papers, King Library, Univ. of Kentucky, Lexington.

Carroll Co. Deed Book 2:157, 196; 17:119; 20:2, Carroll Co. Court House, Carrollton, KY.

Cincinnati newspaper clippings, September 1864, made by Lucien Gex. Craig Papers. Craig Co., VA.

Craig, Virginia. Diary excerpt. King Library, Univ. of Kentucky, Lexington.

Gex, A. L., son of Lucien Gex. Embellished narrative, ca. 1900. Craig Papers, Craig Co., VA.

Harrison, Lowell H., and James C. Klotter. *A New History of Kentucky.* Lexington: Univ. Press of Kentucky, 1997.

Newspapers: *Louisville Daily Journal,* August 31 and September 1, 3, and 5, 1864.

Prichard, James. "Colonel Jesse." Typed manuscript, Kentucky Libraries and Archives, Frankfort.

—*Diane Perrine Coon*

GIBBS, CLINTON (b. 1891, Petersburg, KY; d. 1970, Cincinnati, OH), musician and organist of the African American First Baptist Church in Walnut Hills, OH. Organist Clinton Gibbs was the son of Frances Gibbs, born on August 8, 1891, in Petersburg, KY. By 1900, the Gibbs family was living along Wayne St. in the Walnut Hills neighborhood of Cincinnati. In 1926, Clinton Gibbs became the organist of the African American First Baptist Church in Walnut Hills, located just to the east and behind the former Lane Seminary complex along Gilbert Ave. Gibbs had studied music theory at Holderbach College with Prower Symon,

once an instructor at the Cincinnati College Conservatory of Music. Gibbs also served at Carmel Presbyterian Church and St. Andrew's Episcopal Church in Cincinnati. He was the director of the Queen City Glee Club and was on the faculty of the local Lillian Aldrich Settlement School of Music. He became the vice president of the Cincinnati branch of the National Association of Negro Musicians and was a member of the Masonic Order. He was affectionately called "the Professor."

Gibbs, who never married, died at his home at 2819 Preston St. in Walnut Hills on May 1, 1970, and after services at his beloved First Baptist Church, he was buried in United American Cemetery in the nearby Evanston neighborhood of Cincinnati.

Newspapers: "Clinton Gibbs," *CE,* May 5, 1970, 18; "Clinton Gibbs Services Tomorrow," *CP,* May 6, 1970, 50.

Warner, Jennifer S. *Boone County: From Mastodons to the Millennium.* Burlington, KY: Boone Co. Bicentennial Book Committee, 1998.

GIBSON, CLIFFORD (b. 1901, Louisville, KY; d. 1963, St. Louis, MO), blues singer and guitarist. Although Clifford Gibson became a well-known **blues** guitarist in St. Louis, MO, little is known of his early life. Scholars believe that he was born in Louisville or possibly Henderson, but many of his contemporaries claimed that he was from various places across the South, ranging from Arkansas to Mississippi to Alabama. Nonetheless, Gibson spent considerable time refining his musical skills in Louisville until he moved to his permanent home in St. Louis during the 1920s.

By the time he recorded most of his 20 titles for ORS and Victor in 1929, Gibson had established himself as one of the most talented blues guitarists in Missouri. In 1931, he also accompanied Jimmie Rodgers on a Victor single. Influenced by Lonnie Johnson, Gibson's work is noted for its extended guitar treble runs and his "original, moralizing lyrics," as seen in his "Whiskey Moan Blues." Outside the studio, Gibson spent most of his time during the 1920s and 1930s playing on the streets of St. Louis. He continued to work as a street musician, often accompanied by a performing dog, during the next two decades. In 1960, he reappeared on recordings as Grandpappy Gibson. In total, Gibson recorded over 40 titles during his 40-year career.

Larkin, Colin, ed. *The Encyclopedia of Popular Music.* 4th ed. New York: Oxford Univ. Press, 2006.

Oliver, Paul. *The Story of the Blues.* London: Cresset Press, 1969.

Titon, Jeff Todd. *Early Downhome Blues: A Musical and Cultural Analysis.* Chapel Hill: Univ. of North Carolina Press, 1977.

—*Joshua D. Farrington*

GIBSON, WILLIAM H., SR. (b. 1829, Baltimore, MD; d. 1906, Louisville, KY), educator and politician. William H. Gibson Sr. was born in 1829 in Baltimore, the son of free blacks Philip and Amelia Gibson. Precocious, he studied with Baltimore's best-known black teachers and soon demonstrated talent in instrumental and vocal music. At age 18, answering a call from black Methodists to establish a school for their children, Gibson moved to Louisville. His school emphasized the three Rs, music, and vocational training. By the late 1850s, Gibson's older students were studying algebra, geometry, and Latin, and on the eve of the Civil War he opened grammar schools in Lexington and Frankfort, only to see them closed because of the conflict. During the Civil War, when harassment of free blacks increased in Louisville, Gibson moved to Indianapolis, where he began recruiting black troops. In 1866, Gibson returned to Louisville and resumed his teaching career.

Gibson was a leader in the post–Civil War black educational conventions, an untiring advocate of public schools for blacks, and eventually a principal in Louisville's black school system. In 1868, he became an assistant to the cashier at the **Freedman's Savings and Trust Company.** His status among black Republicans resulted in a number of patronage appointments; in 1870, he was appointed mail agent on the Louisville and Nashville Railroad (now part of CSX Transportation). Harassment by whites along the line forced Gibson to resign in favor of a position in the U.S. Revenue Department in 1874. He was a delegate to numerous Republican Party conventions at the state and national levels but failed in attempts at elective office. With the decline of Republican Party support of Kentucky blacks, Gibson was reduced by the turn of the century to accepting a position as night janitor at a Louisville bank.

Gibson was an early member of the Masons and one of the founders of the Louisville-based **United Brothers of Friendship.** He was a founder or officer of most of Louisville's black cultural organizations, including the Mozart Society and the Colored Music Association, and of social programs, such as the black YMCA, the **Colored Orphans' Home,** and the Louisville Colored Cemetery Company. Gibson died in 1906 and was buried in the Louisville Cemetery.

Gibson, W. H., Sr. *Historical Sketch of the Progress of the Colored Race, in Louisville, Ky., as Noted by the Writer during a Period of Fifty Years.* Louisville, KY: Bradley & Gilbert, 1897.

Simmons, William. *Men of Mark: Eminent, Progressive and Rising.* Cleveland: George M. Rewell, 1887.

—Marion B. Lucas

GILBERT (WILKERSON), ARTISHIA GARCIA (b. 1868, Manchester, KY; d. 1904, Louisville, KY), educator and the first African American female Kentucky native to pass the Kentucky State Medical Boards and practice medicine in Kentucky.

Artishia Garcia Gilbert, the only child of William and Amanda Gilbert, earned the nickname "little teacher" as a preschool-age child when she learned to spell and read by traveling daily with a teacher to school in Clay Co., KY. In 1878, the family moved to Louisville. She graduated as the valedictorian from State University (later known as **Simmons College of Kentucky)** in 1889. She first worked as editor of the magazine *Women and Children* and then returned to State University to teach English and Greek. On July 1, 1890, the 12th annual meeting of the **Kentucky Negro Educational Association** was held in Hopkinsville, KY. Gilbert was elected secretary of the organization.

Gilbert, active in various religious organizations and women's clubs, served as Kentucky's agent and later as president of the **Baptist Women's Educational Convention of Kentucky** and on the board of directors of the **Colored Orphans' Home.** She then entered the medical field and graduated with a medical degree from **Louisville National Medical College** in 1893. She opened her practice at 938 Dumesnil St. in Louisville.

In 1896, Gilbert extended her medical education at Howard University in Washington, DC, where she met and married attorney Bernard Orange "B. O." Wilkerson. According to a 1900 Howard University publication, she worked as an assistant to the professor of obstetrics at State University's Medical Department and served as superintendent of Louisville's Red Cross Sanitarium (also known as **Red Cross Hospital).** However, the 1900 U.S. federal census did not list her as having employment.

Gilbert died a few weeks after the birth of her third child in 1904. Her middle child, Artishia Gilbert Wilkerson, was two and a half years old when her mother died. She later attended Howard University and graduated from the University of Chicago, majoring in mathematics in 1923. She married Rev. Frederick Douglass Jordan and became an active religious leader and clubwoman. Living in California, she became the first African American elected director of the Los Angeles chapter of the American Mission to Lepers.

"In Memoriam," *AB*, April 8, 1904, 3.

Lamb, Daniel Smith. *Howard University Medical Department, Washington, D.C.: A Historical, Biographical, and Statistical Souvenir.* Washington, DC: Medical Faculty of Howard University, 1900.

Scruggs, L. A. *Women of Distinction: Remarkable in Works and Invincible in Character.* Raleigh, NC: L. A. Scruggs, 1893.

U.S. Federal Census (1900).

Wright, Richard Robert, Jr. *Encyclopaedia of the African Methodist Episcopal Church.* 2nd ed. Philadelphia: Book Concern of the A.M.E. Church, 1947.

—Sallie L. Powell

GILLIAM, SAM (b. 1933, Tupelo, MS), one of the most acclaimed African American artists of the twentieth century.

Born in Tupelo, MS, in 1933, Sam Gilliam moved with his family to Louisville when he was eight years old. After graduating from **Central High School** in 1951, Gilliam entered the University of Louisville, graduating four years later with a BA in fine arts. After a two-year stint in the army, Gilliam returned to Louisville, where he taught art at Jackson Junior High School while working on his master's degree at the University of Louisville. While he was there, Gilliam worked closely with some of the city's most influential black artists, including **Edward Hamilton Jr.** and **G. C. Coxe.**

After graduating in 1961, Gilliam and his wife, Dorothy, who would become an influential reporter and author in her own right, moved to Washington, DC. During his subsequent 40-year career, Gilliam was the recipient of dozens of national awards and grants, including a National Endowment of the Arts Fellowship and a Solomon Guggenheim Foundation Fellowship. His works have been displayed in over 50 cities around the world, including the Washington Gallery of Modern Art and the prestigious Venice Biennale.

Although his work ranges from watercolors to sculptures, Gilliam's most recognized pieces are his draped canvases, which are colorful works of abstract expressionism. Rather than being confined within a frame, his often room-sized painted cloths are "molded by continuous folding and modeling" and draped across enormous walls. They often are accompanied by jarring titles like *Firefly Blacktop* and *All Cats Are Grey at Night.*

In 2006, some of Sam Gilliam's most acclaimed pieces were on temporary display in a retrospective exhibition at Louisville's Speed Art Museum.

Binstock, Jonathan. *Sam Gilliam: A Retrospective.* Berkeley: Univ. of California Press, 2005.
McCready, Eric. "Tanner and Gilliam: Two American Black Painters." *Negro American Literature Forum* 8, no. 4 (Winter 1974): 279–81.
"Sam Gilliam Looking Back," *LCJ,* June 4, 2006, 11.

—*Joshua D. Farrington*

GILMORE, ARTIS (b. 1949, Chipley, FL), professional basketball player. Artis Gilmore grew up in rural Florida before moving during his senior year in high school to Dothan, AL. A third-team All-American in high school, Gilmore spent two years at then Gardner-Webb Junior College in North Carolina before transferring to Jacksonville University in Florida. Although he played only two years at Jacksonville, the seven-feet-two center immediately transformed the team. During his collegiate senior year, the All-American led the Dolphins to a 27–2 season. After a stunning victory against a University of Kentucky team that starred Dan Issel, Gilmore brought Jacksonville University to the NCAA championship game, where it was defeated by powerhouse UCLA.

A-Train, as he was popularly known, averaged 20 points and 20 rebounds during his two years at Jacksonville and was drafted by both the National Basketball Association's (NBA) Chicago Bulls and the American Basketball Association's (ABA) Kentucky Colonels in 1971. He chose to play for the Colonels, who signed him for $1.5 million over 10 years. During his first year playing for the Louisville-based team, Gilmore was named the ABA's Rookie of the Year and Most Valuable Player and led the team to a 68–14 record. In 1975, after having taken his team to two previous ABA finals, Gilmore led the Colonels to victory in the ABA championship against Indiana.

A year after the championship, the ABA folded, and Gilmore was the number one pick by the Chicago Bulls in the NBA's dispersal draft. In 1978, he was given a $4.5-million contract for seven years with the Bulls, the largest salary package in the NBA and one of the 10 largest in all international sports. Over the course of the next 12 years, he played for the Bulls, the San Antonio Spurs, and the Boston Celtics.

At the end of his 16-year professional career in 1988, which included playing in a staggering 670 consecutive games, Gilmore had amassed 24,941 points, 16,330 rebounds, and 2,497 blocks in the ABA and the NBA. Additionally, he was a five-time ABA All-Star and a six-time NBA all-star. His career .599 field-goal percentage remains the highest in NBA history. Additionally, he was the 3rd-highest shot blocker, 4th-highest rebounder, and 14th-highest scorer in professional basketball history.

After playing the 1989 season for a team in Italy, A-Train returned to Florida, where he worked as a representative of W. W. Gay Construction and joined the staff at Jacksonville University. In 2011, Gilmore was inducted into the Naismith Memorial Basketball Hall of Fame and the Kentucky Athletic Hall of Fame.

Carey, Mike, and Michael McClellan. *Boston Celtics: Where Have You Gone?* Champaign, IL: Sports Publishing, 2005.
"Gilmore Deal Gives Blacks 8 of Sports Top 10 Pacts." *Jet,* October 8, 1978.
"It's Still a Big Man's Game." *Ebony,* January 1973.
Newspapers: "Gilmore Is Signed to Colonels' Pact Worth $1.5 Million," *NYT,* March 17, 1971, 53; "Artis Gilmore Earned Call from Hall of Fame," *LHL,* April 10, 2011, C2.
Pluto, Terry. *Loose Balls: The Short, Wild Life of the American Basketball Association.* New York: Simon & Schuster, 1990.

—*Joshua D. Farrington*

GIVENS, JACK "GOOSE" (b. 1956, Lexington, KY), outstanding men's basketball player at the University of Kentucky. Born in Lexington, KY, on September 21, 1956, Jack "Goose" Givens emerged as one of the most talented basketball players in the country while he was at Bryan Station High School. The three-time All-State forward helped lead the Defenders to two state tournaments in the early 1970s. In 1974, he was named Kentucky's Mr. Basketball.

Recruited by teams across the country, including UCLA, Givens and James Lee of Lexington's Henry Clay became the first highly recruited black players ever to sign with the University of Kentucky (UK). Despite some criticisms by white fans, Givens became one of the team's premier players during his four-year career. In 1975, as an important freshman reserve, Givens helped bring UK to a national championship game against UCLA. During his sophomore and junior years, Givens became the team's leading scorer and led UK to the 1976 NIT championship and the NCAA tournament's Elite Eight in 1977.

As the team's main scorer and senior leader, Givens sealed his status as a legendary player during his senior year. In what has been described as "one golden moment forever enshrined . . . in

Jack Givens.

the state's sports lore," Givens scored 41 points to lead Kentucky to a 94–88 win over Duke in the 1978 NCAA championship game, giving the school its fifth national title. At UK, Givens's field-goal percentage was an impressive .514 from the floor, and his free-throw percentage was .803 from the line. As of 2010, the three-time All–Southeastern Conference forward remained the number three all-time scorer in UK men's basketball history, amassing a total of 2,038 points.

Although he was the 16th pick in the 1978 National Basket-ball Association (NBA) draft, Givens's professional career lasted only two seasons with the Atlanta Hawks. During the 1980s and 1990s, Givens became a popular television color commentator for the NBA's Orlando Magic. He also worked as a basketball analyst for numerous television networks, such as Turner Sports, NBC, and ESPN. In 1992, Jack "Goose" Givens's UK jersey was retired, and he was inducted into the Kentucky High School Athletic Association Hall of Fame in 2001.

Givens, Jack "Goose." Interview by Anthony Wright, August 16, 1978. Blacks in Lexington Oral History Project, Louie B. Nunn Center for Oral History, Univ. of Kentucky.
Newspapers: "'The Goose' Capped Stellar UK Career with 41-Point Gem in Title Win over Duke," *LHL,* July 25, 1999, 13; "Givens among 12 New Inductees," *LHL,* June 20, 2001, D3.

—*Joshua D. Farrington*

GLASS, EDWARD W. (b. 1859, Hopkinsville, KY; d. 1941, Hopkinsville, KY), prominent undertaker and Hopkinsville city councilman. A slave in Christian Co. and later an employee of Western State Mental Hospital, Benjamin Glass and his wife, Louisa, had eight children. Their eldest son, Edward W. Glass, entered the business world as a saloon keeper but soon became an undertaker. He married Sallie Sharp in 1881. They had nine children, including their eldest son, Dr. **James Garfield Glass,** a Henderson, KY, physician, who initially worked with his father in the funeral business.

Edward W. Glass actively engaged in civic organizations and politics. In 1884, he was elected grand treasurer and later grand master of the **United Brothers of Friendship** and the **Sisters of the Mysterious Ten.** According to journalist and author **John Benjamin Horton,** Glass, as a delegate to the Republican National Convention, cast the first vote for Frederick Douglass as the Republican Party nominee for U.S. president in 1888. In 1892, along with two other Hopkinsville men, Glass established the *Indicator,* a newspaper that lasted a few years. He was one of five elected delegates to attend the Cotton States Exposition of 1895 (the Atlanta Exposition), where Booker T. Washington presented his Atlanta Compromise speech. The next year, he won a city council seat representing Hopkinsville's "Bloody Fifth" Ward dominated by about 400 African American citizens. In all likelihood, he was among the first African Americans elected to political office in Kentucky. He was qualified for the job because of his previous experience as a schoolteacher, Internal Revenue Service employee, city constable, and deputy sheriff. The local newspaper described him as "light mulatto" and "well educated"; he operated his funeral business near the railroad depot and was "comfortably fixed" because he owned his home and other property.

In 1904, considered one of the most prominent Kentucky African American Republicans, Glass served as a delegate-at-large to the National Republican Convention in Chicago. A few months later, he and another Hopkinsville undertaker applied for membership in the Funeral Directors' Association of Kentucky but were denied. This resulted in the formation of the Colored Funeral Directors of Kentucky, and Glass was elected president. A few years later, he served as president of Hopkinsville's Negro Business League.

On October 26, 1911, after 15 years on the Hopkinsville City Council, Glass wrote a nearly full-page letter in the local newspaper describing his accomplishments and explaining his plans for withdrawal from the upcoming city council election. He believed that his ability to work across party lines and with African Americans and whites had enriched Hopkinsville. Not only had streets been improved, but so had schools, the police, and fire protection. He had pushed for the law to be enforced equally. Although he believed that he could win another election, he thought that the cost was too great on his business and his family.

However, Glass continued his community and political involvement. In 1915, he contracted for a new brick, two-story building to house his undertaking business. The next year, a few months after his wife died, he participated in the celebration of the laying of the cornerstone for Attucks High School. In 1936, he served as first vice president of the newly reorganized Hopkinsville branch of the **National Association for the Advancement of Colored People.** From 1939 to 1941, he was a member of the **Kentucky Negro Educational Association**'s advisory committee. He died of pneumonia on March 10, 1941, and was buried beside his wife in Hopkinsville's Cave Springs Cemetery.

Horton, John Benjamin. *Not without Struggle.* New York: Vantage Press, 1979.
Newspapers: *Maysville (KY) Evening Bulletin,* March 1, 1895, 3; "A Colored Councilman," *HK,* November 10, 1896, 1; "E. W. Glass," *HK,* August 6, 1897, 14; "News and Notes," *AB,* March 4, 1904, 2; "Negroes Excluded," *HK,* August 12, 1904, 8; "Ed W. Glass Withdraws," *HK,* October 26, 1911, 8.
Wright, George C. *A History of Blacks in Kentucky.* Vol. 2, *In Pursuit of Equality, 1890–1980.* Frankfort: Kentucky Historical Society, 1992.

—*Sallie L. Powell*

GLASS, JAMES GARFIELD (b. 1882, Hopkinsville, KY; d. 1962, Henderson, KY), doctor who practiced medicine for 50 years in Henderson, KY. According to his World War I draft registration card and his gravestone, James Garfield Glass was born in Hopkinsville, KY, on November 12, 1882. The son of undertaker **Edward Glass** and Sallie Glass, Glass followed in his father's footsteps by graduating from Cincinnati's Clark Embalming School. He then earned his MD from Nashville's Meharry Medical College, then a part of Walden University, in 1908. After an internship at Hubbard Hospital and a brief stint working with his father as an undertaker, Glass moved to Henderson, KY, to begin a medical practice that would span five decades.

In Henderson, Glass met Ora Kennedy (**Ora Kennedy Glass**), a local teacher, and the two were married on November 6, 1913.

Together, they figured prominently in local affairs. Glass participated in several community organizations, including the Knights of Pythias and the **United Brothers of Friendship,** and served as chairman of the Board of Trustees of the A.M.E. Zion Church. Ora, meanwhile, served as president of the Henderson PTA for 10 years and led fund-raising efforts for a new high school building.

At the conclusion of a career marked by continual service to the residents of Henderson, Glass received numerous awards and honors in appreciation of his work. In August 1953, the National Medical Association presented him with a certificate of award in recognition of his service, and Meharry Medical College presented him with the President's Award to mark his five decades spent practicing medicine in 1958. The city of Henderson observed Dr. James G. Glass Day at the Washington and Elm First Baptist Church on December 13, 1959. Although Glass was unable to attend because of illness, residents—including the mayor, the county judge, and numerous representatives of the medical profession—celebrated his career through speeches, a choral performance, and a financial award. Three years later, at the age of 80, Glass died at his home. He was buried in Henderson's Fernwood Cemetery.

Mather, Frank Lincoln, ed. *Who's Who of the Colored Race: A General Biographical Dictionary of Men and Women of African Descent.* Vol. 1. Chicago: Memento Edition, 1915.
Newspapers: "In Honor of a Community Servant," *Hopkinsville Gleaner and Journal,* December 15, 1959; "Dr. Glass, Prominent Negro Physician, Dies," *Hopkinsville Gleaner and Journal,* September 8, 1962, 1.
U.S. World War I Draft Registration Cards, 1917–1918.

—*Stephen Pickering*

GLASS, ORA KENNEDY (b. 1893, Henderson, KY; d. 1971, Henderson, KY), founder of the Kentucky State Colored PTA and women's club leader.   Ora Kennedy was born in Henderson, KY, to Rev. Paul H. and Virginia (Harris) Kennedy on May 30, 1893. Her father was a minister and founder of the oldest black Baptist church in Henderson. She supported her church as the piano player at services and was the president of the Junior Missionary Society. During her lifetime, she served in all departments of the church. She attended Henderson's colored schools and later graduated from Simmons University (later known as **Simmons College of Kentucky**) in Louisville. After graduation, she taught school in Henderson until she married Dr. **James Garfield Glass.** The Glasses had two children, Edward and Dorothy.

Ora Glass worked diligently in Henderson's black community through her club activities and was elected state president of the **Kentucky Association of Colored Women's Club** from 1932 to 1933, during which time the state group comprised 74 clubs. Her involvement in the church continued, and she was appointed the permanent national chairperson of the Baptist Woman's Day in 1942. In 1943, she was one of three Kentucky women selected by the **National Association for the Advancement of Colored People**'s *Crisis* magazine as a First Lady of Colored America. Glass founded the state colored PTA and served as the organization's president for six years. She was also the president of the

Henderson PTA for 10 years and served as second vice president of the National Congress of Colored Parents and Teachers. During her term as state president, she established a priority of obtaining college scholarships for Kentucky's black high school graduates through the United Negro College Fund. Glass headed a successful campaign to raise money to build a colored high school in Henderson and established a library for blacks. She also served as the state Republican Party chairman for eight years.

Glass was active in groups connected to her husband's medical profession. Locally, she served as president of the Bluegrass Auxiliary of the National Medical Association (NMA) and nationally was the first vice president of the Women's Auxiliary of the NMA, which promotes the interest of African American doctors. Her community involvement was far reaching, and she provided her expertise and passion to such other groups as the Henderson United Fund, the Mayor's Summer Recreation Committee, the Community Relations Council of the Breckinridge Job Corps Center, and the HUW Council. She chaired the Health Committee of Henderson County, the Red Cross board, and the Negro Division of Bookmobile of Kentucky. She belonged to many organizations, including the Frederick Douglass Historical Society, Washington, DC, and the Evansville College Women's Club, the Order of the Eastern Star, the R. G. Shaw Circle, and the Daughters of Elks.

Glass was appointed to serve on the National White House Conference on Children and Youth and the **Kentucky Commission on Human Rights.** She contributed a great deal to her community and excelled in her work and efforts to uplift her race and provide a better life for her people. Ora Kennedy Glass died in December 1971 and was buried next to her husband in Henderson's Fernwood Cemetery.

"First Ladies of Colored America." *Crisis,* January 1943, 17.
Johnson, Mrs. J. E. "Statistical Report of the National Association of Colored Women Incorporated, 1933." Records of the National Association of Colored Women, reel 20, frame 635.
"Services for Mrs. Glass Scheduled Wednesday." *Henderson Gleaner,* December 14, 1971, 1.
Fleming, G. James, and Christian E. Burckel, eds. *Who's Who in Colored America.* 7th ed. Yonkers-on-Hudson, NY: Christian E. Burckel & Associates, 1950, 213.

—*Karen Cotton McDaniel*

GLEASON, ELIZA VALERIA ATKINS (b. 1909, Winston-Salem, NC; d. 2009, Louisville, KY), first African American to earn a PhD in library science and first African American to become a dean of a library school.   Born the ninth child of professional educators Simon Green and Oleona Pegram Atkins in Winston-Salem, NC, Eliza Valeria Atkins learned early the importance of education. Her father founded Slater Industrial Academy (later Winston-Salem State University) in 1892. Her mother served as a teacher and later assistant principal at the school. Her older sister, **Oleona (Olie) Atkins Carpenter,** became the first college-trained African American librarian in Kentucky.

In 1930, Eliza graduated from her mother's alma mater, Fisk University. The next year, she earned her BS in library science from the University of Illinois. She began her first library job as assistant librarian that summer at **Louisville Municipal College** (a racially segregated college of the University of Louisville). In less than a year, she replaced her sister, Olie, as the institution's head librarian. Eliza not only managed the library but also taught library classes. For almost two decades, this library department, together with Louisville's **Western Colored Branch Library,** provided the only library classes for African Americans in Kentucky.

In 1935, Eliza left Kentucky. She earned her master's degree the following year at the University of California, Berkeley. In 1937, she married Maurice F. Gleason, a physician, and completed her PhD in 1940 at the University of Chicago. Gleason's dissertation, "The Government and Administration of Public Library Service to Negroes in the South," was published as a book, *The Southern Negro and the Public Library,* which included information on Kentucky African American library service.

After earning her doctorate, Gleason became dean of Atlanta University, where she organized a library school, becoming the first African American dean of a library school. She left Atlanta University for Chicago to join her husband when he set up his medical practice in 1946. She continued her profession in the Chicago area.

In the 1990s, Gleason returned to Kentucky to live with her daughter, Joy Gleason Carew, a professor of pan-African studies at the University of Louisville. She died on her 100th birthday. At her request, her remains were cremated and interred with those of her family in Winston-Salem, NC.

Hine, Darlene Clark, Elsa Barkley Brown, and Rosalyn Terborg-Penn, eds. *Black Women in America: An Historical Encyclopedia.* Brooklyn, NY: Carlson, 1993.

Jones, Reinette F. *Library Service to African Americans in Kentucky, from the Reconstruction Era to the 1960s.* Jefferson, NC: McFarland, 2001.

Obituary, *LCJ,* December 21, 2009.

College of Arts and Sciences, Hall of Honor Inductees, University of Louisville. http://louisville.edu/artsandsciences/hallofhonor /inductees/eliza-atkins-gleason-1909-2009 (accessed June 3, 2011).
—*Sallie L. Powell*

GLOVER, JAMES MONROE "JUICY" (b. 1931, Sawmill Hollow, KY), football player for Kentucky State University and the first black center in the National Football League. James Monroe Glover was born near Cumberland, KY, in the small community of Sawmill Hollow and played high school football at Benham Colored High in Benham, KY. Glover recalled that after graduating from high school, he wanted "to get an education and get out of the coal mines" of eastern Kentucky. He was accepted at Kentucky State College (later named **Kentucky State University**) and continued his football career there.

As a freshman in 1952, Glover, known as Juicy on the playing field, was Kentucky State's starting fullback. That same year, he participated in the school's first interracial football game, scoring the first touchdown in Kentucky State's 39–0 victory over Taylor University. In 1953, he was drafted into the army but returned to Kentucky State in 1956. Over the next few years at the school, he was named an All-American and emerged as one of the greatest linebackers in the school's history.

After graduating, he was drafted as the National Football League's first black center. Although he never was placed on an active roster, Juicy was affiliated with the Baltimore Colts and the Chicago Bears before ending his brief career with the Hamilton Tiger Cats in the Canadian Football League. In 1973, he was inducted into the Kentucky State University Hall of Fame, and he served as an assistant football coach for his alma mater in the 1990s.

Newspapers: "KSC Defeats Taylor in Homecoming Game," *LD,* November 5, 1952; "Football Runs Deep on the Country Gridiron," *Harlan Daily Enterprise,* August 19, 1983, 23; "Coal Country's 'Common Bond,'" *LHL,* August 31, 1997, B1.

Stout, Louis. *Shadows of the Past: A History of the Kentucky High School Athletic League.* Lexington, KY: Host Communications, 2006.
—*Joshua D. Farrington*

GOODLOE, DON SPEED SMITH (b. 1878, Lowell, KY; d. 1959, Washington, DC), first president of Maryland Normal and Industrial School. Don Speed Smith Goodloe was born to Don and Amanda Goodloe in Lowell, KY, in 1878. From 1892 to 1898, he attended **Berea College** at the same time as the historian **Carter G. Woodson,** who would become his lifelong friend. After spending a year at Knoxville College and serving as principal of a school in Newport, TN, Goodloe returned to Lowell, where he taught until 1903. He then moved to Pennsylvania and simultaneously graduated from both Allegheny College and Meadville Theological School in 1906. Although Goodloe was the first black graduate of Meadville, a school affiliated with the Unitarian Universalist denomination, he had to abandon his ministerial ambitions after he was informed that no congregation would ever accept him as its minister because of his race.

Goodloe returned to Kentucky and refocused his career on education. From 1906 to 1910, he served as superintendent of Danville Polytechnic Institute and the head of a local Bible school. In 1911, after serving briefly as the vice principal of Manassas Industrial School in Virginia, Goodloe was named the first president of Maryland Normal and Industrial School (later known as Bowie State University), the state's first black college.

Although most of the records of his 10-year tenure as the school's president were burned in a fire in 1920, Goodloe oversaw the school at a time when it was significantly underfunded by the state. He even used his own home to provide housing to many students. In 1988, the house was listed on the National Register of Historic Places. Among the famous visitors to the 14-room house during Goodloe's years as president were Carter G. Woodson, Kelly Miller, and Alain Locke.

After leaving the college, Goodloe moved to Baltimore, where he became president of the Standard Benefit Life Insurance Company. He eventually moved to Washington, DC, where he died in 1959. In 2005, the Bowie Unitarian Universalist Fellowship in Bowie, MD, changed its name to Goodloe Memorial Unitarian Universalist Congregation in honor of Don Speed Smith Goodloe.

Floyd-Thomas, Juan M. *The Origins of Black Humanism in America: Reverend Ethelred Brown and the Unitarian Church.* New York: Palgrave Macmillan, 2008.

"Historical News." *JNH* 44, no. 4 (October 1959): 385–87.

Morrison-Reed, Mark. *Black Pioneers in a White Denomination.* 3rd ed. Boston: Unitarian Universalist Association, 1994.

"News from the Alumni." *Meadville Theological School Quarterly Bulletin* 1, no. 1 (December 1906): 33.

"Reviving the Memory of an Obscure Educator." *WP,* February 26, 1987, M1.

—*Joshua D. Farrington*

GOODLOETOWN, largest African American residential area in Fayette Co. Lexington's Limestone St. and Winchester Rd. formed the borders of Goodloetown, also known as Goodlowtown and sometimes simply called Goodloe. White citizens considered the bottomlands of this area nearly uninhabitable and used it for mule stalls during the Civil War. By 1871, the community was settled near a railroad and named for Cassius Clay's nephew, William Cassius Goodloe. In the 1880s, Gunntown and Bradley Street Bottoms merged with Goodloetown, making it the largest African American community in Fayette Co.

The neighborhood comprised churches, schools, and businesses. A church building had existed on the corner of Short and **Deweese** Sts. since 1789. In 1833 the **First African Baptist Church** purchased the property. Roxey Turner led the Power Church movement in the city until her death in 1901. Goodloetown's Colored Normal School prospered under the leadership of Professor A. Hatch, an Oberlin College graduate, who served as the principal from 1885 to 1889. Over the years, the community lost four schools, including Constitution School, which was located on the corner of Race and Second Sts. Various businesses were located in the district, including **Mammoth Life and Accident Insurance Company** on Deweese St. This business not only provided employment opportunities but also supplied fair insurance rates to African Americans.

Prominent African Americans lived in Goodloetown, including famous **Kentucky Derby**–winning jockey **Isaac Murphy.** The Colston family was also in the horse business. Some were trainers, one was a jockey, and another was the owner of Colston, the third-place finisher in the 1911 Kentucky Derby. In 1917, Dr. John Knox Polk and his wife, Anna, purchased a home on Deweese St. and established **Polk Infirmary** on the lower level. After Polk's death, Dr. J. R. Dalton operated the medical facility. In 1998, the Lexington–Fayette County Urban League purchased the building. For almost a quarter century, Goodloetown resident Dr. **Thomas T. Wendell** served as staff physician at Lexington's Eastern State Mental Hospital.

Goodloetown enjoyed numerous forms of entertainment and recreation. In 1935, the Charles Young Park and Community Center became the first community center and second public park opened to Lexington's African Americans. From 1948 to 1963, the **Lyric Theatre,** an Art Deco–style structure, hosted first-run movies, fashion shows, and live entertainment. It was restored and reopened in 2010. The **Roots and Heritage Festival** was launched in 1989. Beginning as a street fair, the monthlong entertainment offered various activities, such as art exhibits, parades, stage performances, vendors, and sports.

African American Heritage Guide. Lexington, KY: Isaac Scott Hathaway Museum, 2009.

Bolin, James Duane. *Bossism and Reform in a Southern City: Lexington, Kentucky, 1880–1940.* Lexington: Univ. Press of Kentucky, 2000.

Hobgood, Patrick. "Constructing Community: An Exhibition of the Voices of Goodloetown." *Kaleidoscope: University of Kentucky Journal of Undergraduate Scholarship* 4 (2006): 39–44. http://www.uky.edu/Kaleidoscope/fall2005/page39.html (accessed June 15, 2011).

Kellogg, John. "The Formation of Black Residential Areas in Lexington, Kentucky, 1865–1887." *Journal of Southern History* 48, no. 1 (February 1982): 21–52.

Kentucky Historical Society. Historical Marker Database Search. http://migration.kentucky.gov/kyhs/hmdb/MarkerSearch.aspx?mode=All (accessed June 15, 2011).

Lucas, Marion B. *A History of Blacks in Kentucky: From Slavery to Segregation, 1760–1891.* 2nd ed. Frankfort: Kentucky Historical Society, 2003.

Newspapers: "Death of Prof. A. Hatch," *LL,* January 1, 1889, 1; "A Place in History Guide Highlights City's African-American Sites," *LHL,* March 22, 2000, 19.

Roots and Heritage Festival. http://ns12.webmasters.com/*rootsandheritagefestival.com/httpdocs/about.html (accessed June 16, 2011).

—*Sallie L. Powell*

GOODWINE, PAMELA RENEÉ (b. 1960, Youngstown, OH), first African American female judge in Lexington, KY. A native of Youngstown, OH, Pamela Reneé Goodwine was born in 1960 and was adopted by Willie and Ophelia Goodwine. She was a member of Youngstown's South High School debate team, and her senior classmates elected her "Most Likely to Succeed." She graduated with honors, including a valedictorian scholarship, in 1978.

Goodwine had planned to attend Carnegie Mellon University in Pittsburgh, PA, where she was offered a four-year scholarship, but she forfeited her scholarship to care for her father, who had been diagnosed with lung cancer. After her father's death, Goodwine, at age 19, moved to Lexington, KY, enrolled at the University of Kentucky, and launched the first step toward her dream of becoming a judge by working as a court reporter to finance her education. Within six months of coming to Lexington, however, her uncle, Thomas Robinson, was charged with the murder of Goodwine's mother, and within the following year, Goodwine was diagnosed with Crohn's disease. Her education came to a halt.

After several surgeries, Goodwine recuperated. She returned to the University of Kentucky and completed her undergraduate education, graduating with honors with a bachelor's degree in business administration in May 1991. She was accepted into the University of Kentucky's College of Law and received her JD degree in 1994. After law school, she remained in Kentucky and accepted a position at the law firm of Wyatt, Tarrent and Combs. In 1999, Governor Paul Patton appointed her interim judge in the Fayette District Court. In 2003, Goodwine was elected circuit court judge and ran again unopposed in 2006.

Goodwine has received numerous honors and awards, including the 2001 Fayette County Bar Association Outstanding Young Lawyer Award, and she was inducted into the Carol Martin

Gatton College of Business and Economics Alumni Hall of Fame. She has also served as chairperson and commissioner of the **Kentucky Commission on Human Rights.**

Goodwine, Pamela. Interview by Jessica Bryant, Lexington, KY, February 17, 2009.

Goodwine, Pamela. Interview by Renee Shaw, *Connections with Renee Shaw*, KET2, April 27, 2008.

Medical Leader Staff. "Lecture Series Features Goodwine." *Medical Leader,* March 3, 2007. http://www.medicalleader.org/pmc_news .html?id=1952 (accessed March 3, 2009).

Newspapers: "South High Graduates Get Awards," *Youngstown (OH) Daily Vindicator,* June 9, 1978, 9; "Mr. Robinson Dies; Accused in 2 Deaths," *Youngstown (OH) Daily Vindicator,* June 2, 1983, 32; "Goodwine Appointed Interim Judge," *LHL,* August 20, 1999, B1.

—*Jessica Bryant*

GORDON, ROBERT L. (b. 1941, Lexington, KY; d. 2007, Inkster, MI), business executive, city manager, and grand polemarch of Kappa Alpha Psi Fraternity. The son of Roscoe Demus and Alice Gordon-Williams, Robert L. Gordon was born in Lexington, KY, and was a graduate of (Paul Laurence) **Dunbar High School.** He was baptized at the **Maddoxtown** Baptist Church. He completed his undergraduate education at Edward Waters College in Jacksonville, FL, and pursued graduate study at Florida A&M and the College of Finger Lake in New York. He taught high school before working as an international executive with Ford Motor Company. He was also employed as the human resource director for the cities of Highland Park and Inkster, MI. He eventually became the city manager of Inkster.

In 1982, Gordon became the 24th grand polemarch of **Kappa Alpha Psi Fraternity** during the organization's conclave in Detroit, MI. He came to this office with a wealth of experience. He led the formation of the Ann Arbor–Ypsilanti–Inkster Alumni Chapter's Silhouettes Organization in 1973. Gordon was also an authority on parliamentary procedure. There were 80,000 members of the organization during Gordon's term in office. In 1984, the Kappas passed a resolution that the U.S. government should abolish military aid to South Africa. The resolution also criticized President Ronald Reagan's Task Force on Food Assistance as a "national disgrace."

Gordon served as grand polemarch for three years. The Ann Arbor–Ypsilanti–Inkster Alumni Chapter established the Robert L. Gordon Achievement Award. Gordon died on June 9, 2007 surrounded by his family. He was cremated, but members of Kappa Alpha Psi held a public burial ceremony.

"Kappas Blast Reagan's U.S. Overseas Policies." *Jet,* July 13, 1984, 24.

"Robert L. Gordon." http://www.legacy.com/Obituaries.asp?Page=Life Story&n=Robert-L-Gordon&personID=89078733 (accessed October 14, 2013).

—*Gerald L. Smith*

GOWENS, HENRY LYTLE, JR. (b. 1884, Lexington, KY; d. 1953, Philadelphia, PA), ophthalmologist. Henry Lytle Gowens Jr. was born in Lexington, KY, to Henry and Amanda Gowens on September 1, 1884. In 1903, he graduated from Howard University after only three years there. He then attended Hahnemann Medical School in Philadelphia, from which he graduated in 1908. Over the course of the next 20 years, he continued to work at various hospitals throughout the city, including Hahnemann Hospital, where he served as the chief of its eye department. During this time, he also focused on research and published "The Advantage of Atropine in Refraction" in the *Journal of Ophthalmology, Otology and Laryngology* and the *Hahnemannian Monthly.*

In the early 1940s, he became the center of a Philadelphia lawsuit after he moved into a previously all-white neighborhood. The suit was ultimately rejected by Judge Curtis Bok, who noted that Gowens had a right to live in the neighborhood because he was "a doctor in good standing, and by no stretch of the imagination could be held to be . . . a common nuisance."

In 1942, Gowens was named chief of the eye department at Mercy-Douglass Hospital. The following year, he was also hired as an assistant surgeon at Philadelphia General Hospital. He served in both positions through the early 1950s. He was a member of the Philadelphia County Medical Society and a fellow of the American Academy of Ophthalmology and Otolaryngology. Henry Gowens Jr. died at Hahnemann Hospital in 1953.

Bontemps, Arna Wendell, and Jack Conroy. *Anyplace But Here.* Columbia: Univ. of Missouri Press, 1997.

"Dr. Henry L. Gowens Jr." *NYT,* January 4, 1953, 78.

Fleming, G. James, and Christian E. Burckel, eds. *Who's Who in Colored America.* 7th ed. Yonkers-on-Hudson, NY: Christian E. Burckel & Associates, 1950.

Gowens, Henry L. "Atropine in Refraction,"*Hahnemannian Monthly* 56 (June 1921): 390–91.

Rogers, Naomi. *An Alternative Path: The Making and Remaking of Hahnemann Medical College and Hospital of Philadelphia.* New Brunswick, NJ: Rutgers Univ. Press, 1998.

—*Joshua D. Farrington*

GRACE HOPE PRESBYTERIAN CHURCH, African American church and community center in Louisville. In 1898, six students from Louisville Presbyterian Seminary—E. V. Dickey, H. McDowell, E. P. Piller, **John Little,** E. H. Mosley, and D. D. Little—decided to establish a mission among African Americans. The downtown area south of Broadway, which was called **Smoketown,** and north of Broadway, called Uptown (east of the central business district), constituted the city's largest and poorest black settlements. These areas harbored saloons, gambling houses, and prostitutes. Student missionaries wanted to address the problems caused by their presence and bring hope to these long-neglected areas.

In 1898, they opened a Sunday school in a small house on Preston St. near Pearl St. with 23 people in attendance. This was the founding of Hope Mission in Uptown. The following year, the second Sunday school was opened at the corner of Jackson and Lampton Sts. with 30 people present. This school was the beginning of Grace Mission in Smoketown. Under the leadership of the young students, with help from the seminary and local residents, the two missions grew rapidly to about 100 attendees during the first year.

In the fall of 1899, the Presbytery of Louisville decided that the missions should be permanently maintained. John Little, one of the founders and a graduate of Presbyterian Seminary, became the first director of the missions. Both missions expanded and moved to new sites. Grace Mission moved to the corner of Rose-lane and Hancock Sts. in 1902. Hope Mission purchased the building at 314 S. Hancock St. in 1911. The missions became important parts of the community. Attendance and interest in the services increased rapidly, and by 1907 both missions had more than 500 members. In 1910, the Sunday school of Grace Mission organized as Grace Presbyterian Church, part of the Presbyterian Church in the USA, with Dr. **William Sheppard** as its pastor. In 1935, the Hope Mission became the Hope Presbyterian Church, with Dr. Charles Allen as pastor. Urban renewal and construction in the Uptown area forced many residents to move eastward in the 1950s and 1960s. This led to a drop in attendance at Hope Church. In 1964, the Grace and Hope Churches merged as Grace Hope Presbyterian Church at the corner of Hancock and Rosel-ane Sts.

The executive directors and many staff members of Grace and Hope community centers had always been white. In the mid-1950s and 1960s, there was a gradual increase in the number of black staff members. In 1966, Rev. Irvin S. Moxley became the first black executive director of the community center at Grace Hope Presbyterian Church. In 1977, Grace Hope Church moved to a brick building at 702 E. Breckinridge St. Rev. Keith O. Paige began his service in 1991. In 1998, Grace Hope Presbyterian Church celebrated 100 years of ministry.

Richardson, Charles E. *Grace Hope Presbyterian Church.* Louisville, KY: 1998.

GRAGSTON, ARNOLD (b. 1840, Mason Co., KY; d. 1938, Detroit, MI), a conductor on the Underground Railroad. Born on Christmas Day, 1840, Arnold Gragston grew up a slave on Col. John Tabb's farm in Mason Co., KY. Although he was subject to the typical abuse and mistreatment inflicted on slaves in antebellum Kentucky, his experience was atypical in the unusual amount of personal freedom granted him by his master and the education he received from a fellow slave.

Gragston eventually used this personal freedom to participate extensively in the **Underground Railroad.** Over the course of four years, he rowed over 100 slaves across the Ohio River to Ripley, OH, where there was a station for escaped slaves on their way farther north. After nearly being caught in 1863, Gragston finally took his own trip to freedom, along with his wife. Concerned about remaining in Ripley, so close to his former master, he moved farther north to Detroit, where he lived with 10 children and 31 grandchildren.

In 1938, shortly before Gragston's death, he was interviewed as part of the Federal Writers' Project. His account has become a vital piece of several exhibits on the Underground Railroad, most recently with the opening of the National Underground Railroad Freedom Center in Cincinnati, OH. In Germantown, KY, near where Gragston originally toiled on Tabb's farm, a historical marker memorializes his heroic efforts.

"Black Family Reunion Especially Special This Year." *CE,* August 20, 2004.
National Humanities Council. "Narrative of Arnold Gragston." Research Triangle Park, NC, 2007. http://nationalhumanitiescenter

.org/pds/maai/community/text7/gragstonwpanarrative.pdf (accessed June 14, 2011).
Wagner, Tricia Martineau. *It Happened on the Underground Railroad.* Guilford, CT: Pequot Press, 2007.

—*Stephen Pickering*

GRAHAM, DERRICK (b. 1958, Frankfort, KY), educator and state legislator from Frankfort. Derrick Graham, son of Paul V. and Delores Metcalf Graham and a descendant of George Metcalf, a **buffalo soldier,** was born and raised in Frankfort, KY. He graduated from **Kentucky State University** in 1980. After obtaining a master's degree in political science from Ohio State University in 1982, Graham returned to Frankfort, where he taught social studies at Frankfort High School.

In 1992, Graham was elected commissioner of Frankfort and served the city in that position for the next eight years. In 2002, he was endorsed by the Kentucky Education Association and was elected state representative of Kentucky's 57th District. Even during the statewide Republican electoral victories of 2010, Graham, a Democrat, defeated his Republican opponent by a margin of two to one. Throughout his entire political career, he remained loyal to his roots as an educator and continued in his position as a social studies teacher.

As an African American state legislator, Graham has called for greater diversity at the University of Kentucky and has sponsored prison reform bills. In 2007, during the investigation of unethical behavior by Kentucky governor Ernie Fletcher and other state lawmakers, Graham led the drive for ethics reform, noting that "on both sides, we have abused the system."

Given his background as an educator, Graham was named a member of the Board of Regents of Kentucky State University and served as chairman of the Subcommittee of Budget Review on Primary and Secondary Education in the General Assembly. In 2012, he retired from teaching at Frankfort High School and was inducted into its Hall of Fame but continued to serve in the Kentucky legislature.

Glasser, Paul. "Democrats Hold on to Seats in State House." Frankfort State-Journal.com, November 3, 2010/. http://www.state-journal .com/news/printer_friendly/4925465 (accessed May 4, 2011).
Harrod, Kay. "PBS Series Puts Buffalo Soldiers in Derrick Graham's Life." Frankfort State-Journal.com. http://www.state-journal.com /local%20news/2009/09/27/pbs-series-puts-buffalo-soldiers-in -derrick-graham-s-life (accessed April 15, 2013).
Newspapers: "A Way with Words," *LHL,* April 1, 2007, D1; "Governor Will Not Push Jail Bills in '08," *LHL,* February 9, 2008, A1; "Candidate Bios," *LHL,* November 2, 2008, D7.
Wheatley, Kevin. "Graham Retires from FHS after Nearly 3 Decades." Frankfort State-Journal.com. http://www.state-journal.com/local %20news/2012/06/10/graham-retires-from-fhs-after-nearly-3 -decades (accessed April 15, 2013).

—*Joshua D. Farrington*

GRAND ARMY OF THE REPUBLIC POSTS, local fraternal organizations that offered benefits to white and black Union veterans. Founded in Illinois in 1866, the Grand Army of the Republic (GAR) originated as an outgrowth of a movement to provide fraternal organizations for former Union soldiers who had fought during the Civil War. Viewed as a tool of the Republican

Party, the GAR had few initial successes in the South, but a provisional department was formed in Kentucky in 1866. This initial attempt to create a GAR branch failed, but a second attempt succeeded in 1883. This new GAR Department incorporated 12 local posts from across the state, including 4 "colored" posts. The *Louisville Courier-Journal* later named the Warner Post from Louisville, KY, a colored post that originated in Chicago, as the oldest local organization in the state.

By the 1890s, tensions had increased nationally regarding the color line in the GAR. In 1891, the Louisiana and Mississippi Departments attempted to force the national organization to ban African American posts. In response, one delegate from Kentucky answered that his state now included 27 black posts, and that "it was the colored man that came to [the nation's] assistance" during the Civil War. The drive to disband black posts in the GAR failed. Kentucky members of the Woman's Relief Corps, the female auxiliary of the GAR, attempted for several years to achieve a division of black and white corps into separate organizations and were finally successful in 1901.

The most public display of concern over the proper roles of black and white members emerged before the 29th Annual Encampment of the Grand Army of the Republic, hosted in Louisville in 1895. Several newspapers reported that black veterans were to be refused accommodations at the gathering. Although the claims seemed to be mostly unfounded, and African Americans constituted a "large percentage" of the 5,000 marchers in the parade through the city, the state organization continued to deal with demands for racial restrictions from its members.

Kentucky's GAR Department acted ambivalently toward racial discrimination after the conclusion of the national encampment in Louisville. In 1899, an attempt to pass a resolution denouncing recent lynchings in Georgia was rejected because it "savored of politics," even though one leading member of the organization stated that "it was the duty of this body to condemn lynching law, whether the victim was white or black." In 1907, one of the state's officers responded to complaints regarding the "race question" by commenting that "the amendments to our constitution should have forever stopped that so far as our order is concerned," and the department commander stated even more bluntly that "the colored comrades are in our department to stay" during the encampment the following year. The commander also praised a "half dozen posts which, while chiefly white, admit on equal terms the few colored soldiers who live in the neighborhood." There is no indication that any formal action was taken to separate organizations for black and white members of the GAR in Kentucky.

Davies, Wallace E. "The Problem of Race Segregation in the Grand Army of the Republic." *Journal of Southern History* 13 (1947): 354–72.

Gannon, Barbara. *The Won Cause: Black and White Comradeship in the Grand Army of the Republic.* Chapel Hill: Univ. of North Carolina Press, 2011.

Grand Army of the Republic. *Kentucky G.A.R. Year Book, 1907–1908.* Berea, KY: Berea College Printing Department, 1908.

"Louisville's Posts," *LCJ*, September 11, 1895.

Marshall, Anne E. *Creating a Confederate Kentucky: The Lost Cause and Civil War Memory in a Border State.* Chapel Hill: Univ. of North Carolina Press, 2010.

O'Leary, Cecilia Elizabeth. *To Die For: The Paradox of American Patriotism.* Princeton, NJ: Princeton Univ. Press, 1999.

—*Stephen Pickering*

GRANT, TRAVIS "THE MACHINE" (b. 1950, Clayton, AL), professional basketball player. Travis ("the Machine") Grant, born on January 1, 1950, in Clayton, AL, arrived on the campus of **Kentucky State University** (KSU) in Frankfort for the 1968–1969 basketball season. Under new coach Lucias Mitchell, the team posted a 10–15 record. The next season, Grant scored 75 points against Northwood Institute in Michigan and led the nation in scoring with 35 points per game. He helped KSU win its first National Association of Intercollegiate Athletics (NAIA) championship, which it won again in 1971 and 1972. Grant, a six-feet-eight swingman, led the nation in scoring in 1971–1972, averaging nearly 40 points a game and finishing with 4,045 career points, a collegiate record. He was the first choice of the Los Angeles Lakers in the 1972 National Basketball Association draft, but in 1973 he jumped to the San Diego Conquistadors of the American Basketball Association. He played the 1975–1976 season with the Kentucky Colonels and the Indiana Pacers before a knee injury ended his career. After returning to KSU and earning a BS degree in 1979, Grant became the boys' basketball coach at Walker High School near Atlanta, GA. In March 1987, the three-time All-American, 1970–1972, was named to the NAIA Golden Anniversary All-Star team.

GRAY, LEONARD W. (b. 1942, Louisville, KY; d. 2005, Louisville, KY), Democratic Party activist, state legislator, and adviser to Governor Paul Patton. Born and raised in Louisville's West End, Leonard Gray graduated from **Central High School** alongside his neighborhood friend, Cassius Clay (later known as **Muhammad Ali**), in 1960. After establishing a successful consulting business, he became deeply involved in the Jefferson County Democratic Party as an adviser to various candidates in the 1970s. In the 1980s, he joined Joseph McMillan, **Gerald Neal,** and other influential African Americans in PAC-10, an organization that raised money and supported candidates who advanced the interests of Louisville's black community.

After losses in state legislature races in 1973, 1981, and 1986, Gray defeated incumbent Democrat Ben Handy in the 1988 primary and thus was ensured a spot in the General Assembly. Gray served in the House from 1989 until 1995, spending three of those years as the chairman of the Jefferson Co. delegation. In 1990, he was the primary sponsor of the bill that established Martin Luther King's birthday as an official state holiday.

In 1995, he served as the minority chairman of Paul Patton's campaign for governor. Many credited Gray with delivering critical votes in Louisville that led Patton to a narrow victory over Republican Larry Forgy. The following year, he became Patton's first African American appointee, serving as legislative liaison. In 1997, Gray was called to testify before a grand jury after allegations of voter fraud emerged in the wake of Patton's narrow electoral victory. Although two other Patton aides were found guilty, and Gray's personnel records were subpoenaed, he was never indicted.

In 1999, he was named Patton's director of minority affairs. In this position, Gray was responsible for ensuring that the African American community was aware of open government jobs, and he helped black businesses obtain government contracts. He also was in charge of identifying black workers who were eligible for promotion to midlevel management jobs inside state government. "It's going to give hope to a lot of people who feel they've been shut out of the system," Gray recalled.

Leonard Gray retired from politics after Patton's term expired in 2003. In April 2005, his younger sister, Anita Louise Gray, who had served as a delegate to the 2004 Democratic Convention, died. Gray died three months later. **A. D. Porter** and Sons Funeral Home handled the arrangements, and he was buried in Calvary Cemetery.

Fosl, Catherine, and Tracy E. K'Meyer. *Freedom on the Border: An Oral History of the Civil Rights Movement in Kentucky.* Lexington: Univ. Press of Kentucky, 2009.

Newspapers: "House OKs King Birthday as State Holiday," *LHL,* January 13, 1990, C3; "Patton Picks Legislator as His House Liaison," *LHL,* November 22, 1995, B3; "Headline: Ex-Legislator, Democratic Activist Leonard Gray Sr. Dies," *LCJ,* July 19, 2005, B1.

—*Joshua D. Farrington*

GREEN, ELISHA WINFIELD (b. ca. 1818, Bourbon Co., KY; d. 1893, Maysville, KY), founder of Kentucky Normal and Theological Institute. Elisha W. Green, founder and pastor of African American Baptist churches in Maysville, Flemingsburg, and Paris, KY, and one of the foremost African American leaders in post–Civil War Kentucky, was born into slavery. His short autobiography, printed in 1888, indicates in its subtitle what Green himself saw as his accomplishments—*One of the Founders of the Kentucky Normal and Theological Institute—Now the State University at Louisville, Kentucky; Eleven Years Moderator of the Mount Zion Baptist Association; Five Years Moderator of the Consolidated Baptist Educational Association and over Thirty Years Pastor of the Colored Baptist Churches of Maysville and Paris.* Those achievements and more were earned in the context of slavery and racism, conditions that Green faced with dignity and courage.

As a youth in Bourbon Co., he barely escaped a group of patrollers who broke up a religious service of slaves with whips. Around age 10, Green was moved to Mays Lick in Mason Co. On many occasions over the years, he had contact with "negro traders" and remembered particularly a group of 50 slaves who came through the community during his youth. Observing them brought him, and at least one white witness, to tears and led him to write, "The stain of slavery and its degrading impressions will long linger in the minds of generations yet unborn."

Green went through a succession of owners and was put up for auction on the square at Washington, KY. In the early 1830s, he was converted while plowing a field and was baptized six months later in the north fork of the Licking River. In 1835, Green married Susan Young, who was also a slave. In 1838, he moved to Maysville, 12 miles away, and often had to walk that distance to visit his wife, being questioned along the way by skeptical whites about why he was alone.

Green became a sexton for the white First Baptist Church in Maysville and was allowed to attend services. The leaders of that church recognized his devout nature and his singing ability. He was permitted to hold services for the African American community in 1844. On May 10, 1845, the Baptist Church licensed Reverend Green to preach, and he organized the Bethel Baptist Church in Maysville that year. He founded the Mount Zion Baptist Church in Flemingsburg in 1853 and the First Baptist Church in Paris for African Americans in 1855.

Although Green had contact with operators of the **Underground Railroad** and had many opportunities to escape while he was traveling in Ohio to perform religious services, he did not. After buying his freedom, he was able to purchase freedom for his wife and three of his children in 1858. He and his wife saw the removal of their son John in Maysville and watched him being sold in Paris. They never had contact with him again.

After the Civil War, Green was elected vice president of the Kentucky **Negro Republican Party** at its convention in Lexington in 1867. In 1875, he and his congregation built a brick structure for the Bethel Baptist Church in Maysville that served the congregation for a century. He continued to pastor his churches, worked for the education of freedmen, and lobbied against discriminatory laws, such as those that prevented blacks from testifying against whites in judicial proceedings.

During the period of emancipation, many freed slaves left their former masters or were ejected from their former homes. In Paris, a group of such freedmen was housed in a stable for $10 a month. Its chimney was a hole in the roof. Because Green believed that it was "as much my duty to look out after the interests of my people as to preach the gospel," he persuaded his Paris congregation to buy houses in a development from Samuel Clay. The lots measured 60 × 75 feet, and on each was built a cottage with a door and a chimney. This led to a community of home-owning African Americans.

On June 8, 1883, while riding the Maysville and Lexington Railroad from Paris to Maysville, Green was attacked by two white professors of the Female Millersburg Institute in Kentucky for refusing to give up his seat. Green brought charges against Professors Gould and Bristow in Paris and was awarded damages in the amount of $24. In the controversy that followed, many newspapers in Kentucky commented on the case, favoring Green. The *Maysville Bulletin* called Green a man respected by his own race and "by the white population of Maysville."

Rev. Green baptized some 6,000 individuals, many in the Ohio River. He died at his home on November 1, 1893. His funeral was a community event, and the church overflowed with mourners. Green was buried in the Maysville Cemetery, which was segregated at the time.

Green, Elisha. *Life of the Rev. Elisha W. Green.* Maysville, KY: Republican Printing Office, 1888. Documenting the American South. http://docsouth.unc.edu/neh/greenew/greenew.html (accessed April 2, 2006).

Kentucky Gateway Museum files, Maysville.

—*George Vaughn and John Klee*

GREEN, EMMA CASON (b. 1886, North Middletown, KY; d. 1983, Chicago, IL), self-employed dressmaker and poet. Born in North Middletown on May 11, 1886, according to the Social Security Death Index, Emma Cason, daughter of James and Rebecca Cason, spent the first half of her life in the state of Kentucky.

In 1905, she married Charles Henry Green, a Bourbon Co. farmer, and she attended Kentucky Classical and Business College in her hometown. Emma Cason Green engaged in a variety of professional and personal activities, participated in church choirs and youth groups with the Disciples of Christ, worked as a self-employed dressmaker, and wrote poetry in her spare time.

Green and her family moved to Anderson, IN, in the 1940s. Some of her poetry appeared in a book by Jimmie Curtis entitled *Attempting to Express My Thoughts.* Her poem "These Youngsters of Today" expressed typical concerns over the state of the world and the opportunities left for future generations. In another poem, "The End," she reflected on her life with her husband, who had died in 1957. She also wrote several speeches and other forms of creative writing, including *History of the Second Christian Church, North Middletown, Ky.* These writings and other papers have been collected in the Emma Cason Green Papers as part of the Black Women in the Middle West Project, housed at the Indiana Historical Society.

After her husband's death, Green moved to Chicago, IL, to be near her daughter, Lucille. Surviving all her family and living nearly to age 100, she was a patient in Chicago's Hearthside Nursing Home until her death in January 1983. She was buried in Prescott Cemetery in North Middletown, KY.

"Emma Cason Green Papers, 1939–1983." Finding aid at the William Henry Smith Memorial Library, Indiana Historical Society, Indianapolis, 2004. http://www.indianahistory.org/our-collections/collection-guides/emma-cason-green-papers-1939-1983.pdf (accessed April 16, 2013).

Newspapers: "Celebrating Women's History," *Indianapolis Star,* March 4, 2000, N1; "Poem Shows Some Things Never Change," *Indianapolis Star,* March 4, 2000, N2.

Social Security Death Index.

Sue, Jacqueline Annette. *Black Seeds in the Blue Grass.* Corte Madera, CA: Khedcanron Press, 1983.

U.S. Federal Census (1910, 1940).

—Stephen Pickering

GREEN, HARRY S. (b. 1855, Kentucky; d. 1922, Owensboro, KY), operator of the first commercial barbecue stand in Owensboro, KY.

Born on October 7, 1855, Harry S. Green lived at the corner of Ninth and Hall Sts. in the eastern part of Owensboro, KY. In 1890, he began selling barbecue from his home. Although his barbecue pit was "simply a hole dug in the ground," his decision to sell the product established his business as the first barbecue stand in the city. Most of the details of his enterprise have been lost, but according to residents of Owensboro at the time, he was successful, selling as much as 1,000 pounds of barbecue during each year's county fair.

Census records document Harry Green as a tobacco laborer, and his wife, Harriet, worked as a laundress. The couple married in 1879. One of their sons, Pearl, later worked as a policeman in 1940.

Green's small barbeque business ended at his death on October 7, 1922. He was buried in **Greenwood Cemetery,** a graveyard started 16 years earlier for the burial of African American residents of the city.

Despite the relative lack of information on Green, historians of Owensboro have mentioned the small business he ran out of his home as initiating a long tradition of barbecue businesses in the city. After several local restaurants began selling barbecue following Green's success, Owensboro styled itself "the Bar-B-Q Capital of the World." In 1979, the city began holding an annual International Barbecue Festival in celebration of its culinary heritage.

Egerton, John. *Southern Food: At Home, on the Road, in History.* New York: Alfred A. Knopf, 1987.

Kentucky Death Records, 1852–1953.

Potter, Hugh O. *History of Owensboro and Daviess County, Kentucky.* Owensboro, KY: Daviess County Historical Society, 1974.

U.S. Federal Census (1900, 1910, 1920, 1940).

—Stephen Pickering

GREEN, JACOB D. (b. 1813, Queen Anne's Co., MD; d. unknown, England), runaway slave.

Jacob D. Green was born a slave in Maryland and worked as an errand boy on a plantation owned by Judge Charles Earle, who sold Green's mother when he was 12 years old. Green ran away after his wife and children were sold in 1838. He made it to Philadelphia, where he worked until 1842, when he was captured by a slave hunter. He was then sold to a new master in Memphis, TN. He escaped again in 1846 and made it to New York but was recaptured in Utica.

On the trip back to his former master, Green escaped again and managed to elude captors for over four months in Ohio. In Zanesville, OH, Green was arrested for breaking a store window. While he was in jail, a Kentuckian claimed to be Green's owner, paid his fine, and brought him to Louisville in 1847. He was then sold to Silas Wheelbanks and worked in Louisville as a coachman and waiter. In 1848, while driving Wheelbanks's daughter to Centreville, he pulled the stagecoach to the side of the road and tied her to a tree. He then fled to Louisville and stowed himself aboard a boat bound for Cincinnati. When he reached his destination, he was recognized by his master's nephew, whom he fended off with a large rock. He eventually found connections to the **Underground Railroad,** which guided him to Toronto, Canada.

In 1851, Green moved to England, where he worked as an antislavery lecturer. In 1864, he published a book, *Narrative of the Life of J. D. Green, a Runaway Slave, from Kentucky.* Around 8,000 copies were printed. The 43-page narrative detailed his various experiences as a slave in America and his numerous attempts to escape. No record remains of his life after the book's publication.

Andrews, William L. *To Tell a Free Story: The First Century of Afro-American Autobiography, 1760–1865.* Urbana: Univ. of Illinois Press, 1988.

Andrews, William L., and Henry Louis Gates, eds. *Slave Narratives.* New York: Library of America, 2000.

Green, Jacob D. *Narrative of the Life of J. D. Green, a Runaway Slave, from Kentucky, Containing an Account of His Three Escapes, in 1838, 1846, and 1848.* Huddersfield, England: Henry Fielding, Pack Horse Yard, 1864.

Lucas, Marion B. *A History of Blacks in Kentucky.* Vol. 1, *From Slavery to Segregation, 1760–1891.* Frankfort: Kentucky Historical Society, 1992.

—Joshua D. Farrington

GREEN, JIM (b. 1949, Eminence, KY), world-class track athlete and two-time NCAA champion at the University of Kentucky. The son of a sharecropper in the small community of Eminence, KY, Jim Green, an all-around athlete in football, basketball, baseball, and track, spent much of his youth training for an athletic career by running on local railroad tracks. Although his high school did not have a track team, Green entered state meets on his own, winning the state championship in track in the 100- and 220-yard dash events during his sophomore, junior, and senior years. During these meets, he set state records for the 100- and 220-yard dashes with times of 9.6 and 21.2 seconds, respectively. He attracted additional attention for his football skills and once scored 10 touchdowns in a single game. When several top-tier schools recruited him at the conclusion of his high school career, he accepted a track scholarship at the University of Kentucky (UK) to, in his words, "open up the doors for other kids that may have wanted to go to the University of Kentucky but always said [it] was a big, white, racist institution."

The first African American on UK's track team, Green gained immediate success, winning the NCAA 60-yard dash indoors as a freshman in 1968. He won the same event again in 1971, capping an impressive college career that included eight victories in Southeastern Conference individual events. During that time, he also earned six All-America honors and was considered a contender in world-class competitions, although hamstring injuries in 1968 and 1972 kept him from participating in the Olympic trials in both years. Green later noted that his experience at the University of Kentucky was marred at times by overt racism in competition and everyday life, but he remained committed to his education. In 1971, he became the first African American varsity athlete to graduate from the University of Kentucky.

In 1973, Green briefly entered on a professional track career, running in several events in multiple countries for the next four years, before moving to Louisville and beginning a career as a sales representative for a pharmaceutical company. He has been recognized on numerous occasions for his contributions to athletics, including induction into the Kentucky Athletic Hall of Fame in 1997, the Mason-Dixon Hall of Fame in 2005, and the UK Athletics Hall of Fame in 2007. The Kentucky Black Sports Hall of Fame announced him as an inductee for 2011. The Theta Omega Chapter of **Omega Psi Phi Fraternity** honored Green for his leadership in the organization with the Jim Green Golf Classic in 2012.

Newspapers: "Jayhawks Score in Houston Track," *NYT,* June 9, 1968, S3; "Green's Sprinting Helped Pave Way," *LHL,* February 20, 1998, C1; "Sprinter Leads Mason-Dixon Hall's First Class—Green's Legacy Began at Games," *LHL,* March 3, 2005, B8; "UK Announces Inductees for Athletics Hall of Fame," *LHL,* April 26, 2007, D8.

Omega Psi Phi Fraternity, Theta Omega Chapter. http://ques-theta omega.org/content/wp-content/uploads/2012/04/OmegaGolf Classicw.pdf (accessed April 16, 2013).

—*Stephen Pickering*

GREEN, NANCY "AUNT JEMIMA" (b. 1834, Montgomery Co., KY; d. 1923, Chicago, IL), the first model for "Aunt Jemima." Born on March 4, 1834, in Montgomery Co., KY, Nancy Green grew up as a slave, an experience that she often re- counted in stories and anecdotes after gaining her freedom. She later moved to Chicago, IL, where she began work as a cook and nurse for a local judge and his family. It was here that she gained a reputation for both her excellent cooking and her outgoing personality.

Both characteristics attracted the attention of the R. T. Davis Milling Company, which was engaged in a search for a person to act as the personification of "Aunt Jemima," the company's manufactured image for its pancake mix. In 1893, Green signed a lifelong contract for her new role and performed the part at Chicago's Columbian Exposition, where she served pancakes while regaling the crowd with stories and songs. Such was her popularity that the image of Aunt Jemima was inextricably linked to the pancake mix and led Green to a host of appearances at expositions in support of the product.

Green additionally helped organize the Olivet Baptist Church, one of Chicago's largest African American churches, and was one of its first missionary workers. On September 1, 1923, while Green was standing on a sidewalk in Chicago, an automobile, after colliding with another car, struck and killed her. She was buried in Chicago's Oak Woods Cemetery. Her image lived on in advertisements and packaging for years thereafter. Eventually, the model was changed, but the classic—and frequently controversial—image of Aunt Jemima remains an indelible part of the history of mass marketing.

Kern-Foxworth, Marilyn. *Aunt Jemima, Uncle Ben, and Rastus: Blacks in Advertising Yesterday, Today, and Tomorrow.* Westport, CT: Praeger, 1994.

Manring, M. M. *Slave in a Box: The Strange Career of Aunt Jemima.* Charlottesville: Univ. of Virginia Press, 1998.

"The Story of Aunt Jemima." *St. Joseph (MO) News-Press,* February 15, 1950, 6.

Wallace-Sanders, Kimberly. *Mammy: A Century of Race, Gender, and Southern Memory.* Ann Arbor: Univ. of Michigan Press, 2008.

—*Stephen Pickering*

GREENE, HORACE HENRY (b. 1907, Louisville, KY; d. 1986, Lexington, KY), prominent Methodist minister. Horace Henry Greene, known throughout his life as H. H., was born in Louisville, KY, to George Isaac and Eva Greene on April 12, 1907. After graduating from **Central High School,** he attended the Gammon Theological Seminary in Atlanta, from which he graduated in 1929. That same year, he returned to Kentucky and pastored small Methodist churches in Irvington and New Zion for most of the 1930s. In 1939, he was named pastor of Gunn Methodist Church in Lexington and became active in the city's political life. He was a charter member of the board of directors of the city's YMCA and made two unsuccessful runs for Lexington city commissioner. In 1948, he was appointed the superintendent of the Louisville District of the Lexington Conference, an organization that represented the state's black Methodist churches. He left Kentucky briefly in 1952 to serve at Cincinnati, OH's, Calvary Church but returned to the state the following year to pastor R. E. Jones Temple in Louisville.

During his tenure at Jones Temple, H. H. Greene furthered his reputation as one of the most influential black ministers in Kentucky. In 1961, he became the first African American president of the Louisville Ministerial Association. Throughout the remainder of the 1960s, Greene also served as chairman of the black division of the Blue Grass Council of the Boy Scouts of America and a member of the board of directors at Union College and the Wesley Foundation at **Kentucky State University.** In 1971, he was awarded an honorary doctorate from Union College.

During the mid-1960s, Greene returned to Lexington and became the region's district superintendent of the United Methodist Church. In this position, he was deeply involved in the merging of black and white United Methodist churches throughout Kentucky and Tennessee. In 1966, he became the second African American appointed to the Lexington Board of Education, filling the vacated seat of the first black board member, Carl Lynem. He was appointed to fill another vacated seat on the newly formed Fayette County Board of Education in 1973.

Throughout the rest of the 1970s and the early 1980s, Greene remained active in Lexington's civic life, serving as an assistant chaplain and a member of the Board of Directors of Good Samaritan Hospital. He died of cancer at his Lexington home on August 22, 1986, and was buried in Lexington's Cove Haven Cemetery. At the time of his death, he was the pastor of Wesley Chapel United Methodist in Chaplin, Allen Chapel United Methodist in Finchville, and St. John United Methodist Church in Shelbyville. In 1991, the H. H. Greene Child Development Center was named in his honor at Lexington's Bluegrass-Aspendale housing project.

Newspapers: "Louisville Negro Breaks Vote Pattern," *Christian Science Monitor,* May 19, 1961, 3; "Local Minister Named to City School Board," *LH,* April 21, 1966, 1; "Minister, Civic Leader H. H. Greene Dies," *LHL,* August 23, 1986, B1.
Williams, Ethel. *Biographical Directory of Negro Ministers.* New York: Scarecrow Press, 1965.

—*Joshua D. Farrington*

GREEN STREET BAPTIST CHURCH (LOUISVILLE), church that hosted the first National Convention of Colored Baptists in 1879. First known as Second African Church, the Green Street Baptist Church originated at First and Market Sts. on September 29, 1844, and moved to Green (Liberty) St. and took its current name in 1860. The first deacons were elected in 1845 under church organizer George Wells, who served until his death, possibly from cholera, in 1850. At the time of his death, the congregation numbered 280. During the Civil War, the church organized a Soldiers' Aid Society to support black troops enlisting in the Union army. By April 1865, the end of hostilities was imminent, and the church organized a day school to educate soon-to-be-freed slaves.

From its founding, the church worked to instill moral values in the congregation. On May 10, 1846, the church voted to discipline members "for acts such as disorderly conduct; Sabbath breaking; nonattendance of church; attending a carnival or circus; failure to speak to one another; wife beating; cursing; drunkenness; dancing; playing cards, checkers, or dominoes; adultery; fornication; lying; fighting; fussing; gambling; malicious gossip; having to appear in court; and shooting marbles on Sunday." The church later required members to receive a marriage license from the state within 90 days of marriage, ending the old informal cer-

emony from slavery times that required only that a bride and groom jump over a broom to be considered united. Any members failing to comply would be excluded from the church.

In 1879, the first National Convention of Colored Baptists was held at the church. In 1886, the church took a bold step forward in seeking equal recourse under the law in Kentucky by circulating a petition for the state legislature to pass a civil rights bill. On September 29, 1930, the church moved to 519 E. Gray St. On August 3, 1967, Martin Luther King Jr. preached at Green Street in support of a black voter-registration drive. This was his last visit to Louisville. The church's membership lists include the names of many who are descendants of the church's original charter members.

General Association of Colored Baptists in Kentucky. Louisville: The American Baptist, 1943.
Spencer, J. H. *History of Kentucky Baptists.* Cincinnati: 1885.

GREENWOOD CEMETERY, cemetery in Owensboro, KY, that from 1906 to 1976 served as the final resting place for over 2,000 citizens, including Civil War, World War I, and World War II veterans. In February 1906, a group of 34 African Americans in Owensboro, led by attorney Edward Arnold Watts, purchased a 16-acre plot of land and formed the Greenwood Cemetery Association. The Greenwood Cemetery continued to serve the city's black community for the following 70 years.

The two oldest monuments in the cemetery predate its incorporation. Although their gravestones are at Greenwood, the obituaries for Kittie Ann Jones (died on January 13, 1905) and Benedict A. Hayden (died on August 13, 1905) indicate that they were buried elsewhere. It is unknown when their tombs were moved. Gravestones of many members of the military are located in the cemetery. Four of these (Richard Hardesty, George W. Robertson, Henry Michion Taylor, and Robert Woodard) were Civil War veterans; 48 were World War I veterans; and 14 fought in World War II. Many of Owensboro's most influential African Americans were also buried in the cemetery, including medical doctors, ministers, and teachers. Felix Wallace, an Owensboro native who was the owner and manager of the St. Louis Giants Negro League baseball team, was also buried at Greenwood.

In 1957, the Greenwood Cemetery Association was dissolved, but the **United Brothers of Friendship,** a fraternal organization, continued to maintain the cemetery until it dissolved in 1972. During the 1970s, Greenwood fell into a state of disrepair, and its last documented burial was in February 1976. The cemetery remained in poor shape, the victim of overgrown brush and vandals, throughout the 1980s and early 1990s. Some family members even removed their loved ones' gravestones to protect them, and others were unable to locate family members' graves because of the tangled brush and tall weeds that had taken over the cemetery's grounds.

In 1996, Wesley Acton and Emily Holloway formed the Greenwood Cemetery Restoration Committee. Together, they promoted the historical importance of the cemetery and organized over 200 volunteers to engage in a massive two-year restoration project. Around the same time, a local genealogist, Jerry Long, pored through thousands of burial certificates for Daviess Co.

and discovered that over 2,000 people had been buried at Greenwood, although only about 300 gravestones existed. He later compiled an exhaustive list of all known men and women buried in the cemetery.

In 2001, continued care of the cemetery was ensured after the Daviess County Fiscal Court purchased the property. Throughout the rest of the decade, Greenwood Cemetery, located on 1821 Leitchfield Rd., joined other cemeteries in Owensboro as the site of Memorial Day observances that featured a military honor guard, a 15-gun salute, and the playing of taps.

Long, Jerry. *Greenwood Cemetery: 1821 Leitchfield Road, Owensboro, Kentucky.* Utica, KY: McDowell Publications, 2006.
Newspapers: "Greenwood Cemetery Association Formed to Provide Burial Ground for Colored People," *Owensboro Inquirer,* February 20, 1906, 1; "Greenwood Cemetery Is More Crowded Than Thought," *OMI,* March 3, 2005, C1; "Cemetery Project in the Works," *OMI,* December 28, 2005, B1; "Services Honor Veterans, Others," *OMI,* May 29, 2011, C1.

—*Joshua D. Farrington*

GREVIOUS, AUDREY LOUISE ROSS (b. 1930, Lexington, KY), civil rights advocate and educator. Born on September 3, 1930, to a single mother, Martha Ross, Audrey Louise Ross Grevious grew up on Race St. in Lexington. She attended Constitution Elementary School and later graduated from (Paul Laurence) **Dunbar High School.** In 1948, she attended Kentucky State College (later known as **Kentucky State University**) but was forced to quit school to help support her mother. After working as a secretary at a Lexington black newspaper, the *Town Crier,* she eventually returned to Kentucky State to complete her degree in elementary education in 1955. In Frankfort, she joined the **National Association for the Advancement of Colored People,** an organization in which she would become even more deeply involved as the 1950s progressed.

In 1957, just out of college, Grevious was elected president of the Lexington NAACP and was hired as a teacher at Kentucky Village, a reformatory school for delinquent children. At the time of her hiring, Kentucky Village was a segregated institution, and white faculty members ate separately in a private dining room. After teaching for only six months, Grevious decided to protest, walked into the white faculty dining room, sat down, and ate her lunch. The white faculty responded by throwing their food in trashcans or on the floor and walking out of the cafeteria. Although they complained to the superintendent, Grevious remained at the job and later became the school's principal in the 1960s.

As the Lexington NAACP president, she was deeply involved in the city's **civil rights movement.** One of her first projects was protesting the lack of African American clerks in local grocery stores. Although she was once arrested while picketing the Strand Theater, Grevious also worked closely with Lexington's police chief, E. C. Hale, to prevent police brutality and mass arrests of demonstrators. This relationship is often credited for making the movement in Lexington more peaceful than in Louisville and other segregated cities in the South.

Violence did not fully elude Grevious, however. During a sit-in at the lunch counter of H. L. Green, a waitress dumped a pitcher of tea on her clothes. The following week, the manager of the store was prepared for protesters and guarded the front door with a chain. When Grevious led a line of protesters outside the store, the manager repeatedly beat her leg with the chain. Although she suffered nerve damage that would last the rest of her life, Grevious simply responded to the attack by singing "Yield Not to Temptation."

She was also close friends with **Julia Lewis,** president of the Lexington chapter of the **Congress of Racial Equality** (CORE). In fact, while Grevious headed the NAACP, Lewis served as vice president of the organization. At the same time, Grevious served as vice president of CORE. Unlike the civil rights movement in other cities, these two major organizations in Lexington worked hand in hand and were both led by women.

After Kentucky Village closed its doors in 1971, Grevious eventually became a teacher at Maxwell Elementary, where she worked until her retirement in the late 1980s. In the 1990s, she remained active, fighting for fair employment in city jobs and promoting community activism as the president of St. Martin's Village Neighborhood Association. The **Kentucky Commission on Human Rights** inducted her into its Civil Rights Hall of Fame in 2012.

Fosl, Catherine, and Tracy E. K'Meyer. *Freedom on the Border: An Oral History of the Civil Rights Movement in Kentucky.* Lexington: Univ. Press of Kentucky, 2009.
Grevious, Audrey. Interview by Arthur Graham, February 19, 1985. Louie B. Nunn Center for Oral History, Univ. of Kentucky, 1985 OH045 KH 306.
Grevious Audrey. Interview by Boyd Shearer Jr. and Harold Barker, April 23, 1997. Louie B. Nunn Center for Oral History, Univ. of Kentucky, 1997OH035 KH 614.
Kentucky Commission on Human Rights. Kentucky Civil Rights Hall of Fame 2012. http://kchr.ky.gov/hof/hoff12.htm?&pageOrder=0&selectedPic=8 (accessed April 17, 2013).
Newspapers: "Former Adversaries Recall the Struggle for Civil Rights," *LHL,* August 5, 1984, A16; "Besides Teaching, Educator Was Force for Unity against Racism," *LHL,* February 18, 2004, B1.

—*Joshua D. Farrington*

GRIFFEY, WOLFORD LESLIE (b. 1916, Gatliff, KY; d. 1982, Benham, KY), first African American mine foreman for International Harvester. The son of a barber in a Whitley Co. coal camp, Wolford Griffey grew up playing baseball with his brothers, Robert and Donald. With practice and a few pointers from former Negro League players in nearby Packard, the three eventually caught the eye of the International Harvester Company, which fielded a team that competed in a league with teams from other camps. International Harvester hired the trio, and in 1940, they joined the Harvester Sluggers in the small town of Benham, KY. The Griffeys balanced their work in the mines with fiercely contested baseball games against some of the best African American teams in the region, and some of the more contentious games ended because of the threat of violence.

International Harvester, like many coal companies in the 1940s, attempted to use race relations as a mechanism for control of its workforce, and Griffey endured several reminders of this fact throughout his 33 years in the mines. The town of Benham was segregated, and black families lived in smaller company-owned houses on the east side. His own path toward advancement in the company was also hindered despite his desire to take the test for the foreman position. He also suffered from the dangers common to all coal miners of the time, but he survived an explosion that embedded coal particles in his neck. Another miner involved in the incident later said that Griffey saved his life.

In the 1970s, Griffey finally persuaded his superiors to let him take the test for the foreman position, and when he successfully completed it, he became International Harvester's first black foreman. As a 32nd-degree Mason, he served as Deputy Grand Master of the Mountain District of the Jurisdiction of Kentucky. He remained in Benham for the rest of his life alongside his wife, Lacey, who also established herself as a civic leader by her membership on the city council. Weakened by black lung disease that he contracted in the mines, Griffey died at the age of 66 in 1982. He was buried in Benham Cemetery.

Newspapers: "Wolford Griffey Sr.,"*Harlan Daily Enterprise,* November 6, 1982, 10; "Benham's Black Miners Had Tough Time Moving Up," *LCJ,* January 31, 1999, M8.

Sutter, L. M. *Ball, Bat, and Bitumen: A History of Coalfield Baseball in the Appalachian South.* Jefferson, NC: McFarland, 2009.

—*Stephen Pickering*

GRIFFITH, DARRELL ANTHONY (b. 1958, Louisville, KY), basketball player and recipient of the John Wooden Award. Darrell Anthony Griffith, college basketball's Dr. Dunkinstein, was born on June 16, 1958, in Louisville, the son of Monroe and Maxine Griffith. As a youngster, he practiced with the Kentucky Colonels of the American Basketball Association. After leading Louisville's Male High School to the 1976 state basketball championship, he was named a high school All-American. Later that year, Griffith entered the University of Louisville and was the only high school player invited to the 1976 Olympic trials. After the 1977 World University Games, he was an All-American guard at Louisville in 1979–1980. Griffith led the "Doctors of Dunk" to the 1980 National Collegiate Athletic Association national championship and received the John Wooden Award as the nation's top player. He finished as the career leading scorer at the University of Louisville with 2,333 points. After graduating with a BA in mass communications, he was chosen in the first round of the 1980 National Basketball Association draft by the Utah Jazz. After an outstanding first season, Griffith was named the NBA Rookie of the Year. He played his entire professional career with the Utah Jazz and retired in 1991. He was inducted into the College Basketball Hall of Fame in 2014.

Embry, Mike. *Basketball in the Bluegrass State.* New York: Leisure Press, 1984.

GRIFFITH, GEORGE A. (b. ca. 1841, Owensboro, KY; d. unknown, Wyandotte, KS), first Kentucky-born African American attorney. George A. Griffith, born in Owensboro, KY, joined the 14th U.S. Colored Infantry in Gallatin, TN, when he was 22 years old. At five-feet-five, he was described as having a white complexion. He worked as a barber at the time of his enlistment in 1863.

By 1870, Griffith was a teacher and had married Anna Jones, whose mother, Eliza Jones, lived with them. In that same year, the Fifteenth Amendment to the U.S. Constitution, which permitted African American men to vote, was ratified. Griffith, active in Kentucky's Republican Party, spoke to African American and white audiences in Owensboro clarifying the amendment. On May 4, 1870, a committee of Griffith, Louisville's J. B. Stansberry, and Frankfort's Henry Marrs traveled the state explaining the newly acquired rights and duties of African American men.

On November 23, 1871, Louisville judges Henry J. Stites and Horatio W. Bruce tested Griffith along with Indiana native **Nathaniel R. Harper.** They became the first African Americans to be admitted to the Kentucky bar. The *Louisville Courier-Journal* announced that the men were "found well qualified," and the reporter expressed approval of their accomplishment. Harper later established Harper Law School in Louisville, and Griffith, "a fluent and logical speaker," continued his political involvement in Owensboro.

In March 1872, Kentucky's Republican Convention included African American delegates for the first time. Griffith was one of eight. Along with other delegates, he fervently argued for equal representation for African Americans on the Republican ticket. He incorporated his military experience of eight battles and twice having been wounded into his justification for equal representation, stating, "No man freed me, but myself." He warned that Kentucky had 42,000 African American voters who should not be disenfranchised. He maintained that African American support of the Republican Party should be rewarded by placing qualified men in political offices.

Griffith continued his political involvement and less than a decade later joined two white Republicans in disapproval of the party's support for Ulysses S. Grant's presidential third-term race. After Grant lost this race, Griffith seemingly vanished from the political scene. By 1900, he and his wife, Anna, had moved to Wyandotte, KS, where he served as a minister.

Freedman's Bank. Heritage Quest Online.

Howard, Victor B. *Black Liberation in Kentucky: Emancipation and Freedom, 1862–1884.* Lexington: Univ. Press of Kentucky, 1983.

Kansas State Census Collection, 1855–1925.

Newspapers: "Negro Lawyers," *LCJ,* November 24, 1871, 1; *Hickman (KY) Courier,* "Negro Lawyers," *Hickman (KY) Courier,* December 2, 1871, 1; untitled article, *Kentucky Statesmen,* March 19, 1872, 3.

Smith, J. Clay, Jr. *Emancipation: The Making of the Black Lawyer, 1844–1944.* Philadelphia: Univ. of Pennsylvania Press, 1993.

U.S. Colored Troops Military Service Records, 1861–1865, 1870, 1880.

U.S. Federal Census (1900).

—*Sallie L. Powell*

GRIFFYTOWN, African American neighborhood in Jefferson Co., KY. Griffytown is an African American neighborhood between the cities of Anchorage and Middletown. The community has its origins in the post–Civil War Reconstruction era, a time of changing settlement patterns in rural Jefferson Co.

The community appears to have been settled by Dan Griffy, who purchased a single isolated lot from Silas O. Witherbee of Middletown in 1879. According to property records, Griffy, who was black, had been living on the land before his purchase. Local tradition holds that Griffy purchased a log cabin that had once belonged to early Middletown settler Minor White and moved it to his lot. Witherbee filed a plat to create Calloway's Addition in 1892, including the lot where Dan Griffy lived. It appears that by the 1890s the community was being referred to as Griffithtown and later Griffytown. Witherbee sold lots to African Americans into the early 1900s. The original lots were further subdivided and sold throughout the twentieth century. The community underwent an urban-renewal project in the 1960s.

Hallenberg, Leone W. *Anchorage*. Anchorage, KY: Anchorage Press, 1959.

Louisville and Jefferson County Planning Commission. *Griffytown Redevelopment Plan*. Louisville, KY: 1976.

—*Donna M. Neary*

GROVES, JUNIUS GEORGE (b. 1859, Green Co., KY; d. 1925, Edwardsville, KS), entrepreneur and agriculturalist. Junius George Groves, the son of Martin and Mary Anderson Groves, was born enslaved in Green Co., KY, on April 12, 1859. As a freedman possessing little money, he walked to Kansas City amid the **Exoduster** movement, arriving there in 1879. In 1880, he married Matilda E. Stewart of Kansas City, MO. Twelve of their 14 children survived into adulthood.

Groves's agricultural career began in sharecropping near Edwardsville, KS. In 1884, he and Matilda began purchasing farmland nearby, increasing their holdings from 80 to 500 acres by 1905. Their enterprises also included purchasing and shipping produce throughout North America; operating and owning a general merchandise store; and possessing mining and banking stock in Indian Territory, Mexico, and Kansas. Groves cofounded the State Negro Business League, the Pleasant Hill Baptist Church Society, the Kaw Valley Potato Association, and the Sunflower State Agricultural Association.

As a successful, self-educated landowner and entrepreneur, Groves, described as the richest African American man in Kansas, became one of the most prosperous African American men at the turn of the twentieth century. Descriptions of his wealth ranged from a net worth of $80,000 to being a millionaire. Among his most noteworthy accomplishments were earning the title of Potato King and founding the community of Groves Center, both in the early 1900s.

Groves died of a heart attack on August 17, 1925. One newspaper declared his funeral, which was held on his estate, "the largest funeral ever in Edwardsville." He was believed to have been buried in Groves Cemetery, Groves Center. His will included all his children, and he planned the land to pass on to future generations, but that was not the case. In August, five years after his death, the Knights of Pythias of Missouri purchased the property because of delinquent taxes and other money owed by the Groves family. Members of the family blamed bad weather and a poor potato market for their financial troubles. Groves's widow died a few weeks later.

Anders, Tisa M. "Junius G. Groves." http://www.blackpast.org (posted January 2008).

Hawkins, Anne. "Hoeing Their Own Row: Black Agriculture and the Agrarian Ideal in Kansas, 1880–1930." *Kansas History* 22 (Autumn 1999): 200–213.

Newspapers: "Colored Potato King Dies of Heart Disease," *Kansas City Advocate,* August 21, 1925, 1; "J. G. Groves Funeral," *Kansas City Advocate,* August 28, 1925, 1; "Potato King's Farm Goes under Hammer," *PD,* August 8, 1930, 4; "Potato King's Widow Dies," *PD,* August 29, 1930, 1.

Radicia, Angela Doyle. "Junius Groves and the Community of Groves Center." Paper delivered at the Mid-America Conference on History, Tulsa, OK, September 2007.

Washington, Booker T. *The Negro in Business.* Tuskegee, AL: Hertel, Jenkins, & Co., 1907. Reprint, Chicago: Afro-Am Press, 1969.

—*Tisa M. Anders*

GRUBBS, ALBERT, SR. (b. 1832, Lexington, KY; d. 1901, Sacramento, CA), pioneer in California in 1854. Born a slave in Lexington, KY, Albert Grubbs claimed in his later life to have been one of Henry Clay's most trusted servants, traveling with him across the country and closing his eyes after he died. Although little evidence remains to corroborate this claim, more information exists about his later life after he joined the westward migration to California in 1854. In Sacramento, Grubbs established himself as a leading African American member of the community and pursued several political and business ventures throughout the rest of his life.

In his early years in Sacramento, Grubbs operated a laundry business and eventually moved into teaming or hauling service. He took an active role in city politics, participating in several meetings of the Colored Central Republican Club and receiving an endorsement for the position of city porter in 1896. He also sought and attained election to the position of city scavenger, the nineteenth-century equivalent of a sanitation worker. In 1901, Grubbs, already confined to bed because of a long illness, suffered severe burns when his lamp exploded. He died a little over a week later, on October 30, 1901. His obituary named him "one of the oldest and most highly-respected colored citizens of Sacramento."

Beasley, Delilah L. *The Negro Trail Blazers of California.* Los Angeles: s.n., 1919.

Newspapers: "New Scavenger Elected," *Sacramento Record-Union,* May 24, 1892, 3; Obituary, *Los Angeles Times,* October 31, 1901, 5.

—*Stephen Pickering*

GUNNER, BYRON (b. 1857, Marion, AL; d. 1922, Reading, PA), minister and activist. Born in Marion, AL, Byron Gunner was the son of Joseph Gunner, a carpenter, and Caroline Gunner. He received his early education in a church-sponsored school and graduated from Talladega College with a degree in theology in 1880. He then taught school for the next four years in Paris, TX, under the auspices of the **American Missionary Association** and published a weekly newspaper, the *People's Informer*. In 1884, he was ordained a minister in New Orleans, LA, and served as pastor of St. Paul Congregational Church in New Iberia, LA, for five years.

In 1890, Gunner moved to Lexington, KY, and served as minister of the newly formed First Congregational Church. He worked to raise building funds. Three years after moving to Lexington, he married Cicely Savery, the daughter of William Savery, one of the founders of Talladega College. They had four children, including their oldest, **Mary Frances Gunner,** a playwright and YWCA secretary.

In Lexington, Gunner became very active against the proposed separate coach legislation. He raised funds as he lectured across the state with speeches such as "Devil on Wheels" and "How to Smash the Devil." In 1892, he joined three other Lexington representatives to Frankfort to address Kentucky's General Assembly against the separate car bill. In 1895, Gunner ended his ministry in Lexington. In September, he returned and delivered an address, "The Stimulation of Higher Education," to a crowd at the Lexington Opera House.

Gunner moved to the Northeast and served in various churches while also vigorously fighting racial injustice. In 1914, as president of the National Independence Equal Rights League, he joined other delegates and challenged President Woodrow Wilson over the newly formed segregation system of black and white civil service employees in governmental departments. Two years later, he proposed a National Race Congress.

In 1922, as pastor of Washington Street Presbyterian Church in Reading, PA, Gunner briefly suffered from intestinal problems. He died while his wife was attending her mother's funeral in Alabama.

Mather, Frank Lincoln, ed. *Who's Who of the Colored Race: A General Biographical Dictionary of Men and Women of African Descent.* Vol. 1. Chicago: Memento Edition, 1915.

Newspapers: "They Oppose the Bill," *LL,* March 22, 1892; "President Resents Negro's Criticism," *NYT,* November 13, 1914, 1; "Byron Gunner's Call," *Cleveland Advocate,* August 12, 1916, 460–61; "Deaths," *Reading (PA) Eagle,* February 9, 1922, 2.

Smith, S. E. *History of the Anti–Separate Coach Movement in Kentucky.* Evansville, IN: National Afro-American Press, 1895.

U.S. Federal Census (1870, 1900, 1910, 1920).

—*Sallie L. Powell*

GUNNER, MARY FRANCES (b. 1895, Lexington, KY; d. unknown), playwright and YWCA secretary.

Born in Lexington, KY, Mary Frances Gunner was the first child of Rev. **Byron Gunner** and Cicely Gunner. Her family taught her community involvement. Her father served as president of the National Independence Equal Rights League, and her mother was the president of the New York State Federation of Women's Clubs. Her maternal grandfather, William Savery, was one of the founders of Alabama's Talladega College. As the only African American student at New York's Suffern High School, Gunner academically led her class. She then attended Howard University, becoming vice president of the Howard chapter of the **National Association for the Advancement of Colored People** and the **Delta Sigma Theta Sorority** delegate to the Intercollegiate Socialist Society Conference in 1913. Two years later, she earned her AB degree. She taught school for a few years before becoming the general secretary of the YWCA in Montclair, NJ, in 1918. She served in that same capacity in Brooklyn in the 1920s.

In 1930, Gunner wrote *Light of the Women,* a play for high school girls that combined historical African American women Sojourner Truth, Harriet Tubman, and Phillis Wheatley with modern female roles of teacher, doctor, and minister. She earned her MA from Columbia University the same year with her thesis, "Employment Problems among Negro Women in Brooklyn." She also presented a 30-minute program on a New York radio station about the issues that African Americans faced. In 1932, she publicly condemned lynching as not "a Negro question" but "a national question."

From 1938 to 1950, Gunner worked as branch manager of the New York State Employment Service. She married Jerry Van Dunk of Hillburn, NY, in 1946.

"Men of the Month," *Crisis,* October 1911, 235.

Fleming, G. James, and Christian E. Burckel, eds. *Who's Who in Colored America.* 7th ed. *Supplement.* Yonkers-on-Hudson, NY: Christian E. Burckel & Associates, 1950.

Giddings, Paula. *In Search of Sisterhood: Delta Sigma Theta and the Challenge of the Black Sorority Movement.* New York: Morrow, 1988.

Richardson, Willis, ed. *Plays and Pageants from the Life of the Negro.* Jackson: Univ. Press of Mississippi, 1993.

—*Sallie L. Powell*

GUTHRIE, ROBERT VAL (b. 1930, Chicago, IL; d. 2005, San Diego, CA), psychology educator.

After the birth of Robert Val Guthrie and his twin brother, Paul Lawrence Guthrie Jr., their family moved to Richmond, KY. Guthrie's father, Paul Lawrence Sr., accepted the position of school principal at the Richmond Colored School. Several years later, he became principal of (Paul Laurence) **Dunbar High School** in Lexington, KY. Robert Guthrie graduated from the high school in 1947. He and his twin brother then attended Florida A&M University. The Korean War interrupted Guthrie's collegiate education when he registered for the draft in 1950. He served in the U.S. Air Force and returned to college under the GI Bill in 1953. He earned his BA from Florida A&M University in 1955.

Guthrie then enrolled at the University of Kentucky as the only African American in the psychology master's program, receiving his MA in 1960. Because of the racism he experienced, he stated that his primary goal was to get his degree and "get the hell off campus." He then became the first and only African American faculty member at San Diego Mesa College. In 1970, he obtained his PhD from United States International University in San Diego.

Guthrie worked in various psychology fields, including research, teaching, government service, and private practice. His seminal, divisive 1976 book *Even the Rat Was White: A Historical View of Psychology* not only revealed the contributions of early African American psychologists but also challenged the psychology profession's questionable research and its exploitation of African Americans.

In 2001, Guthrie became the first African American psychologist to donate his papers to the National Archives of American Psychology in Akron, OH. He died four years later of brain cancer and was buried in Mount Hope Cemetery in San Diego, CA.

O'Connor, Eileen M. "An 'American Psychologist.'" *Monitor on Psychology* 32, no. 10 (November 2001). American Psychological Association. http://www.apa.org/monitor/nov01/american.aspx (accessed June 29, 2011).

"Robert V. Guthrie, 75; Noted Psychology Educator." *San Diego Union-Tribune,* November 12, 2005. http://www.signonsandiego

.com/uniontrib/20051112/news_1m12guthrie.html (accessed June 24, 2011).

Williams, Robert L. *History of the Association of Black Psychologists: Profiles of Outstanding Black Psychologists.* Bloomington, IN: AuthorHouse, 2008.

—Sallie L. Powell

GWYNN, JOHN AUSTIN (b. 1853, Caswell Co., NC; d. 1917, Richmond, KY), medical doctor and newspaper editor. Born in slavery in North Carolina, John Austin Gwynn worked in the tobacco industry and attended public school in Danville, VA, in 1875. He graduated from Hampton Institute in 1879. He taught school near Petersburg, VA, and later served as principal for one year. In 1883, he entered Howard University and earned his MD in 1889. He stated that he had struggled through "a hard time financially, but kind friends" had helped him.

After furthering his education at Bellevue Hospital Medical College in New York City, Gwynn began practicing medicine in Ashland, KY, on January 5, 1891. He served both black and white patients. The next year, he moved his practice to Richmond, KY, where he met and married Fanny S. Miller, a schoolteacher.

In 1898, Gwynn was appointed a member of the Board of Pension Examining Surgeons and then elected secretary of the board. He also served on the Board of Control of the Knights of Pythias. In 1909, he established and operated as editor of the *Richmond Sentinel,* considered by one white newspaper "one of the leading papers in the state for colored people—owned and edited by them." The newspaper covered central Kentucky.

Gwynn additionally sang in a quartet for area funerals. He and his wife had two children. Both died from tuberculosis in their teen years. Gwynn died on January 18, 1917, and was buried in Richmond's Maple Grove Cemetery.

Kentucky, Death Records, 1852–1953.

Lamb, Daniel Smith. *Howard University Medical Department, Washington, D.C.: A Historical, Biographical, and Statistical Souvenir.* Washington, DC: Medical Faculty of Howard University, 1900.

Newspapers: "Colored Column," *WN,* February 13, 1909, 7; "A Hustler," *Richmond (KY) Climax,* August 2, 1911, 5.

Twenty-Two Years Work of the Hampton Normal and Agricultural Institute at Hampton, Virginia. Hampton, VA: Normal School Press, 1891.

—Sallie L. Powell

H

HAGGARD, CHARLES (b. 1896, Lexington, KY; d. 1986, Lexington, KY), owner and operator of an African American funeral home for over 40 years. Born on a farm in the Lexington area on September 4, 1896, Charles Haggard grew up as one of 14 children with his parents, James and Kate Haggard. After brief service in World War I, he began work as a chauffeur, a job he held for several years. Shortly thereafter, he completed work at the **Lincoln Institute** and graduated from the Cincinnati College of Embalming in 1939. During this time, he served apprenticeships with Crittenden and Cunningham in Lexington and B. Crittenden in Cincinnati. In 1940, he passed the state board of examiners and received his certification for embalming and funeral directing. Haggard then briefly worked at the John T. Hawkins Funeral Home in Lexington.

On June 2, 1940, Haggard announced the opening of his own funeral home, located on E. Second St. in Lexington. He advertised the Haggard Funeral Home in local newspapers, mentioning the business's specialization in plastic surgery and capacity for complete funeral home service. By 1950, his business was successful enough to fund a large construction project that increased capacity and installed new features, including an electric organ and a pulpit. His wife, Lula Haggard, also a licensed funeral director, aided him in these endeavors until her death in 1969.

In 1982, the Cincinnati Foundation for Mortuary Education inducted Haggard into its Century Club, and the Kentucky Association of Morticians selected him as its Man of the Year in 1985. He operated the funeral home until his death on March 6, 1986. One of the state's oldest funeral directors at the time of his death, he had also become a local icon of Lexington's African American community. His obituary noted that he was a leader in the movement to get black funeral directors recognized by the state Board of Embalmers and Funeral Directors, and according to the executive secretary of the Kentucky Association of Morticians, "Of all the old members who started the fight and never gave up, only Mr. Haggard survived to see it become a reality."

Newspapers: "Colored Notes," *LHL*, June 2, 1940, 16; "Charles Haggard Funeral Home Finishes Construction Project," *LHL*, January 8, 1950, 24; "Charlie Haggard, Funeral Director, Dies," *LHL*, March 8, 1986, C10.
Smith, Gerald L. *Lexington, Kentucky.* Charleston, SC: Arcadia, 2002.
—*Stephen Pickering*

HALE V. KENTUCKY, U.S. Supreme Court case that dealt with African Americans' constitutional right to jury representation. The U.S. Supreme Court decision in the case *Hale v. Kentucky* (1938) held that blacks had been denied their constitutional rights to representation on a jury. The defendant in the original case, Joe Hale, a 19-year-old black, was convicted in 1936 of murdering a white who was "stopping colored women

and asking them to get in his car." The jury in the case, selected from a pool that contained no blacks, convicted Hale, and he was sentenced to die in the electric chair. When the Kentucky Court of Appeals in May 1937 denied Hale's request for a reversal, the **National Association for the Advancement of Colored People** took the case to the U.S. Supreme Court. The appeal showed that no blacks had served on state juries in McCracken Co., where Hale was convicted, from 1906 to 1936, although blacks had been represented on federal juries in Paducah in McCracken Co. during the same period. The Supreme Court held that this violated equal protection under the laws guaranteed under the Fourteenth Amendment to the U.S. Constitution and ordered a new trial. Hale appeared in circuit court in Paducah on April 25, 1939, was allowed to plead guilty to a lesser charge, and was sentenced to life imprisonment. He was paroled in 1947.

Hale v. Kentucky, 303 U.S. 613 (1938).

—*John E. L. Robertson*

HALEY, SISTER PATRICIA, SCN (b. 1945, Columbus, GA), first African American Sister of Charity of Nazareth, first African American Catholic nun to serve in the Archdiocese of Louisville, and founding member of the National Black Sisters' Conference. Sister Patricia Haley, SCN, was born on August 22, 1945, in Columbus, GA, to Blanche (née Miles) Haley, a native of

Sister Patricia Haley, ca. 1950s.

Phenix City, AL, and an alumna of the Tuskegee Institute. After her mother's marriage to Julius Haley, Patricia was legally adopted by her stepfather and was given his surname. A cradle Catholic, Haley was baptized into the church in Birmingham, AL, in 1945 and attended Catholic elementary and secondary schools in Columbus, GA, as well as in Montgomery, Phenix City, and Birmingham, AL.

During her senior year at Birmingham's all-black Holy Family High School (administered by the all-white Sisters of Charity of Nazareth [SCN]), Haley became active in the **civil rights movement.** As student council president, she helped organize her classmates, who professed a commitment to nonviolent, direct action against segregation. In early May 1963, Haley and several Holy Family students were arrested and jailed for participating in the pivotal Birmingham youth marches for black civil rights.

In September 1963, Haley made history when she entered the novitiate of the Sisters of Charity of Nazareth, headquartered in Nazareth, KY, as the congregation's first African American postulant. In 1964, Haley professed her first vows as a sister and took the religious name of Ann Barbara. In the same year, Haley entered her congregation's Nazareth College (now Spalding University), where she earned a BS in elementary education and a minor in sociology in 1968. In 1967, the SCN assigned Haley to teach in Louisville, and as a result, Haley became the first black nun to serve in the 159-year-old archdiocese.

From August 17 to August 24, 1968, Haley, along with 154 of the nation's approximately 1,000 black Catholic sisters, gathered at Mount Mercy College (later Carlow University) in Pittsburgh, PA, to establish the National Black Sisters' Conference (NBSC), a permanent federation of nuns committed to black liberation and eradicating racism in the Catholic Church and society at large. Elected to the NBSC's first executive board in 1968, Haley emerged as a formidable voice in the black Catholic movement in the late 1960s and 1970s. In 1972, she professed her perpetual vows as a sister. In 2005, Haley was elected to the NBSC presidency and served until 2007.

Copeland, M. Shawn. "A Cadre of Women Religious Committed to Black Liberation: The National Black Sisters' Conference." *U.S. Catholic Historian* 14, no. 1 (1996): 121–44.

Green, Nathaniel. "The Making of Black Catholics: A History of the Black Experience in the Catholic Archdiocese of Louisville, Kentucky; A Report to the West End Catholic Council from the Archdiocesan CCD Office." Unpublished manuscript, ca. 1980. Brother Joseph Davis Papers, Univ. of Notre Dame Archives, Notre Dame, IN.

Haley, Sister Patricia, SCN. Interview by Shannen Dee Williams, March 30, 2013.

Williams, Shannen Dee. "Black Nuns and the Struggle to Desegregate Catholic America after World War I." PhD diss., Rutgers Univ., 2013.

—*Shannen Dee Williams*

HALL, GEORGE EDGAR (b. 1889, Greenville, KY; d. 1931, New York, NY), lawyer, government worker, and fraternal and civic leader. George Edgar Hall was born in Greenville, KY, on January 10, 1889. The son of a coal miner, James Henderson

Hall, and Elizabeth (Elliott) Hall, he attended Howard Academy in Washington, DC. In 1916, he earned a BA degree from Howard University and then enrolled in the Howard University School of Law, from which he graduated with a law degree in 1920.

During his time at Howard, he became president of several groups, including the college chapter of the **National Association for the Advancement of Colored People** and the debating society, where he competed as a varsity debater for two years. Hall also became president of his 1916 graduating class and his senior law class of 1918. In the fall of 1918, he obtained a passport and served as YMCA secretary in France until 1919.

In 1920, Hall moved to New York City to practice law and later enrolled at New York University, from which he graduated in 1925 with the doctor of juridical science, the first African American to earn that degree at the school. He also worked as the Democratic Party's New York State organizer of the black vote in 1928. He had a distinguished career as a jurist and eventually received an appointment as assistant district attorney for New York County on January 17, 1929.

Hall was a member of several fraternal and professional associations, including **Omega Psi Phi,** of which he became the fourth grand basileus (1915–1916); the Elks; the Harlem Lawyers Association; the New York County Lawyers Association; and the Board of Managers of the 135th Street Branch of the YMCA in New York. He married Flora E. Pearce on August 11, 1928. In 1931, Hall died and was buried in Gouldtown Memorial Park in New Jersey.

Boris, Joseph J. *Who's Who in Colored America, 1928–1929.* New York: Who's Who in Colored America Corp., 1929.

Omega Psi Phi Fraternity, Incorporated. Official International Website. http://www.omegapsiphifraternity.org/about.asp (accessed July 1, 2011).

—*David H. Jackson, Jr.*

HALL, HENRY ELLIOTT (b. 1875, Henderson, KY; d. 1944, Louisville, KY), founder and longtime president of Kentucky's largest black-owned business, Mammoth Life and Accident Insurance Company.

Henry Elliott Hall, son of Burrell and Millie (Glass) Hall, was born in Henderson, KY, on November 22, 1875. As a teenager, when he was not in school, he worked in tobacco factories to help support his family. When he was 17, he moved to Virginia to attend Hampton Institute. After graduating in 1896, he returned to Henderson Co., where

Henry Elliott Hall.

he taught for three years at a rural schoolhouse and continued to work in tobacco factories.

In 1900, H. E. Hall, as he was often called, became a Kentucky agent for the Virginia-based Benevolent Insurance Company. Over the next four years, he worked his way up to become the state manager. In 1904, the company withdrew from Kentucky, and Hall formed his own insurance company, the National Benevolent Union of Kentucky. The company survived for over five years but was plagued by legal trouble because it was not officially licensed by the state. In 1911, after Hall had been threatened with arrest for operating without a license, he persuaded Atlanta Mutual to acquire the business. It was able to meet the legal requirements for an insurance company and retained Hall as state manager. Within less than three years, he also simultaneously became state manager of the Standard Life Insurance Company of Atlanta.

In 1914, the accident department of Standard Life withdrew from Kentucky. This prompted Hall to join with another insurance man in the state, **W. H. Wright,** and try again to form his own insurance agency. After initially being refused a license by the state insurance department, Hall and Wright were granted a license after a favorable ruling by the Kentucky Court of Appeals. They opened **Mammoth Life and Accident Insurance Company** in Louisville on July 12, 1915. That same year, **Charles H. Parrish Sr.** wrote that Mammoth "is destined to be one of the greatest Negro companies in the country." During Hall's tenure as president, which lasted from 1915 until his death in 1944, the company became the largest black-owned business in Kentucky and one of the largest in the country, expanding to seven states as far away as Wisconsin. Hall was interred in Louisville's Greenwood Cemetery.

Parrish, C. H. *Golden Jubilee of the General Association of Colored Baptists in Kentucky: From 1865–1915.* Louisville, KY: Mayes Printing Co., 1915.

Stuart, Merah Steven. *An Economic Detour: A History of Insurance in the Lives of American Negroes.* New York: Wendell, Malliet & Co., 1940.

Wright, George C. *Life Behind a Veil: Blacks in Louisville, Kentucky, 1865–1930.* Baton Rouge: Louisiana State Univ. Press, 1985.

—*Joshua D. Farrington*

HALL, LILLIAN HAYDON CHILDRESS (b. 1890, Louisville, KY; d. 1958, Indianapolis, IN), first African American to graduate from the Indiana Public Library Commission Summer School for Librarians. Born on February 24, 1890, in Louisville, KY, Lillian Haydon Childress Hall was the daughter of George and Elizabeth Wintersmith Haydon. In 1910, she married William Hobbs Childress, whom she met at Fisk University. In June 1915, she was admitted to the Indiana Public Library Commission Summer School for Librarians (now the Indiana University School of Library and Information Science) and was the first African American to graduate from the school, receiving her librarian's certificate on July 24, 1915.

After graduation, Hall became manager of the Cherry Street Branch Library (1915–1921) of the Evansville–Vanderburgh County Public Library in Indiana. Her husband died in 1919. She later worked for the Indianapolis–Marion County Public Library, heading two of its Negro branches, the Paul Laurence Dun-

bar Branch (1921–1927) and the Crispus Attucks Branch (1927–1956). In June 1929, she married John Wesley Hall. She retired in 1956. On April 23, 1958, she died and was buried in Crown Hill Cemetery in Indianapolis.

"Along the Color Line: Social Uplift." *Crisis* 11, no. 1 (1915): 8.

Fenton, Michele. "A Great Day in Indiana: The Legend of Lillian Childress Hall." *Black Caucus of the American Library Association, Inc. Newsletter* 39, no. 2 (November / December 2010): 5–6.

McPheeters, Annie L. *Library Service in Black and White: Some Personal Recollections, 1921–1980.* Metuchen, NJ: Scarecrow, 1988, 11.

—*Michele Fenton*

HALLIBURTON, CECIL DURELLE (b. 1900, Hickman, KY; d. 1956, Nashville, TN), dean of St. Augustine's College and president of Voorhees School and Junior College. A native of Hickman, KY, Cecil Durelle Halliburton, the son of a teacher, George T. Halliburton, and Mattie Halliburton, devoted most of his life to education, both for himself and others. A graduate of Pennsylvania's Lincoln University, where he participated in the school newspaper and headed the glee club, Halliburton went on to earn several more degrees, graduating from the New York School of Social Work in 1930 and earning his MA from the University of Pittsburgh in 1933.

He supported his educational pursuits by teaching others, engaging in a variety of high school teaching jobs during the 1920s. In 1930, he joined the faculty of St. Augustine's College in North Carolina, where he taught in the Social Science Department for 20 years. During his tenure at St. Augustine's, he also wrote a history of the school, titled *A History of St. Augustine's College, 1867–1937.* From 1943 to 1949, Halliburton served as dean of the college. He then continued his work in administration as president of Voorhees School and Junior College in 1950. After leaving that position for a job as registrar and director of admissions at Fisk University, Halliburton died of a heart attack at the age of 55 in Nashville, TN.

Foster, Laurence, ed. *The Alumni Directory of Lincoln University.* Oxford, PA: Lincoln University, 1946.

Newspapers: "St. Augustine's Dean," *BAA,* October 10, 1942, 14; "Halliburton Dies at Fisk," *BAA,* September 1, 1956, 19.

—*Stephen Pickering*

HAMILTON, ANTHONY "TONY" (b. ca. 1869, Columbia, SC; d. 1904, Menton, France), jockey. Known by some as the Black Demon and sometimes called Andy, Anthony "Tony" Hamilton earned world-renowned success through his racing skills. In 1887, he won the American Derby in Arlington Heights, IL, and the St. Louis Derby the following year, but finished only sixth in the 1888 **Kentucky Derby.** Hamilton dominated the New York racing scene from 1887 to 1896. He began by winning at Gravesend on the 1886 Kentucky Derby winner Ben Ali, owned by Kentucky's James Ben Ali Haggin, later owner of Elmendorf Farm in Fayette Co. His last New York win was at the Metropolitan Handicap at Belmont Park in 1896. His best racing year was 1890, with five New York race wins, when he earned $20,000 and placed third best overall with 113 wins.

Anthony Hamilton.

In a ceremony described as "one of the most elaborate affairs in St. Louis," Hamilton married Annie L. Messley, the stepdaughter of Frank Estell, a wealthy African American businessman, in January 1891. The newlyweds traveled to Lexington, KY, for a lavish reception at the home of jockey **Isaac Murphy.** A few months later, Hamilton, identified as "the cleverest" of the African American jockeys, miraculously survived, without injury, a somersault fall of his horse and him at New York's Sheepshead Bay track.

In 1896, the *New York Times* attacked Hamilton's character in several articles that accused him of cheating with bookmakers by restraining one mount in a race and then pushing the same horse to win in the next race. The New York racing association revoked Hamilton's jockey license but reinstated it a month later. Some claimed that he lacked the intelligence to have concocted such a scheme.

By the early 1900s, racing moguls preferred white jockeys. Some African American jockeys raced in other countries, including Hamilton, who raced in Austria in 1901. In his early 30s, he raced in Russia for several years. In 1904, his career ended at the Moscow Central Hippodrome in the All-Russia Derby when his mount, Crossing, fell. Some horses trampled the five-feet-two Hamilton, causing the loss of one eye. Sources vary on where and when he died, but all accounts agree that tuberculosis caused his death. According to the Reports of Deaths of American Citizens Abroad, Anthony Hamilton died in Menton, France, on the French Riviera, on February 21, 1904. One report maintained that he died in a private railroad car wearing sable and rings on each finger. Another account stated that his friends reclaimed the body from a pauper's grave to give him a proper burial. According to one account, he had earned around $100,000 in 10 years, but he "never had the slightest appreciation of the value of money" and had given away most of his wealth.

Hotaling, Edward. *The Great Black Jockeys: The Lives and Times of the Men Who Dominated America's First National Sport.* Rocklin, CA: Forum, 1999.

———. *Wink: The Incredible Life and Epic Journey of Jimmy Winkfield.* New York: McGraw-Hill, 2005.

Newspapers: "Tests for the Suburban," *NYT,* June 15, 1887, 2; "Jockey Hamilton," *LL,* January 12, 1891, 5; "Hamilton's Bad Trouble," *NYT,* June 27, 1891, 2; "Hamilton Is All Right," *NYT,* August 1, 1896, 6; "Yankee Jockeys Abroad," *NYT,* February 25, 1901, 8; "Gossip of the Turf," *DRF,* January 2, 1903, 1; "Passing of the Negro Rider," *DRF,* February 22, 1917, 3.

Renau, Lynn S. *Racing around Kentucky.* Louisville, KY: L. S. Renau, 1995.

Reports of Deaths of American Citizens Abroad, 1835–1974.

Saunders, James Robert, and Monica Renae Saunders. *Black Winning Jockeys in the Kentucky Derby.* Jefferson, NC: McFarland, 2003.

—*Sallie L. Powell*

HAMILTON, EDWARD, JR. (b. 1947, Cincinnati, OH), sculptor. Born in Cincinnati in 1947, Edward Hamilton Jr. was brought to Louisville as a small child by his adoptive parents, Amy Jane and Edward Hamilton Sr., who owned a barbershop and laundry business on **Walnut St.** Hamilton's artistic talent was first noticed by a teacher at Parkland Junior High School, who encouraged him to further develop his natural abilities. A few years later, while he was at Shawnee High School, a white art teacher again noticed his potential and helped him prepare a portfolio to send with college applications. Hamilton received a four-year scholarship to the Art Center School at the University of Louisville.

After graduating from college, Hamilton worked at various part-time jobs before finding work as an art teacher at Iroquois High School in 1970. Three years later, in an event that would radically alter the course of his life, Hamilton met famed sculptor Barney Bright while picking up art supplies for his class. That same day, Bright invited Hamilton to his studio, and the two became close friends. The meeting prompted Hamilton to quit his teaching job and focus on becoming a full-time artist.

To make money, he assisted Barney with sculptures like the acclaimed and publicly displayed *Louisville Clock* and was commissioned by numerous Catholic churches throughout the city to create liturgical pieces to be used in services. In 1978, he created a 20-inch bronze racehorse that was put on permanent display at Louisville Downs. The figure would become the trophy given to winners of the track's annual $200,000 Pacing Race.

In 1983, Ed Hamilton's big break on the national scene came when he was commissioned by the Hampton Institute in Virginia to construct a statue of Booker T. Washington. Two years later, he created a sculpture of famed boxer Joe Louis for Detroit's Cobo Center. In 1997, he created the Amistad Memorial, honoring the slaves who revolted on the infamous ship, which was permanently placed in the New Haven, CT, City Hall. In 1998, his 3,000-pound bronze sculpture *The Spirit of Freedom* was permanently installed in Washington, DC. Also referred to as the African American Civil War Soldiers Memorial, it was the first memorial designed by a black artist and displayed on federal land in the nation's capital. In 2000, Hamilton designed a bust of civil rights martyr

Medgar Evers that was unveiled at the **National Association for the Advancement of Colored People** National Convention in Baltimore.

Working from his Louisville-based studio, Hamilton also designed numerous works and memorials displayed throughout Louisville and Kentucky. His plaque honoring Thomas Clark was permanently exhibited at the Kentucky History Center; his bronze statue of **Whitney Young Jr.** was prominently displayed on the campus of **Kentucky State University;** and a sculpture of famed football player **Lenny Lyles** sits on the grounds of the University of Louisville's Cardinal Park complex. In 2001, he designed Louisville's **York** Memorial, honoring the slave and frontiersman who accompanied Lewis and Clark. In 2008, he was commissioned to construct a statue of Abraham Lincoln that became one of the most noteworthy installations at Louisville's Waterfront Park.

Hamilton, Ed. *The Birth of an Artist: A Journey of Discovery.* Louisville, KY: Chicago Spectrum Press, 2006.

Newspapers: "A Struggle for Justice Receives Its Due," *NYT,* September 20, 1992, CN19; "Lunch with . . . Ed Hamilton," *LCJ,* June 13, 2008, A8.

"This Week in Black History," *Jet,* July 21, 2008, 13.

—*Joshua D. Farrington*

HAMMOND, JOSEPH B. (b. 1916, Bardstown, KY; d. 1997, Louisville, KY), Louisville businessman and owner of the esteemed nightclub Joe's Palm Room. Born in 1916 in Bardstown, KY, to Walter and Mary Hammond, Joseph Hammond, as a small child, moved with his parents to Louisville. After serving in the navy during World War II, Joe, as he was popularly known, returned to Louisville and worked as the manager of a nightclub named Dave's Palm Room.

In 1954, Hammond had saved enough money to purchase the club from its owner, Dave Snyder. Hammond renamed the lounge, located at 13th and Magazine Sts., Joe's Palm Room. Under his leadership, it became one of the most successful black businesses in Louisville, second only to **Mammoth Life and Accident Insurance Company,** and one of the most renowned nightclubs in the country.

Joe's Palm Room grew in popularity with both white and black patrons throughout the 1960s and 1970s, in large part because it hosted some of the biggest names in **jazz.** Hazel Miller, Bobby Ledford, Pete Peterson, and other well-known classical jazz musicians were regular guests of the club. The club, decorated with improvisational artwork, elegant decor, and plush couches, was also frequented by **Muhammad Ali,** local politicians, and hundreds of annual **Kentucky Derby** guests.

Hammond, a vocal critic of urban renewal, was forced to relocate his club in the late 1960s. Unlike most black businesses from the old **Walnut St.** corridor of Louisville's West End, Joe's Palm Room continued to thrive at its new location on W. Jefferson St. The new Joe's Palm Room doubled its previous square footage and featured two outdoor patios, three dance floors, black leather banquet seating, and an elegant dark-wood interior. Although it initially received opposition from a local neighborhood that was skeptical of having a nightclub nearby, the new location

became even more prosperous. In 1979, Hammond sold the club; however, its name remained Joe's Palm Room, and it continued to prosper through the early years of the twenty-first century.

In addition to the nightclub, Hammond was deeply involved in other business ventures in Louisville. He also owned a dry cleaners and a real estate business, Hammond Realty Company, and was the first African American salesperson for the Falls City Brewing Company. In the late 1970s, he served on PNC Bank's Board of Directors and as the chairman of the board of the Continental National Bank of Kentucky. He was also an original founder of PAC-10, a black political organization that advocated on behalf of Louisville's black community throughout the 1980s, and served as an economic adviser for Martha Layne Collins's campaign for governor in 1983. After his death in 1997, the Kentucky General Assembly passed a resolution recognizing "the determination, the passion, and the conviction that Joseph B. Hammond displayed while striving to better his community."

Black Business in Louisville. Frankfort: Kentucky Commission on Human Rights, 1969.

Hudson, J. Blaine. "African-American Culture and Folklife in Louisville, Kentucky." Kentucky Folkweb. Kentucky Folklife Program at the Kentucky Historical Society. http://www.wku.edu/kentucky folkweb/KYFolklife_African.html (accessed June 28, 2001).

"Kentucky Politics: Collins Group Concentrating on Jefferson Economy." *Harlan Daily Enterprise,* September 14, 1983, 13.

Kinnard, William, and Stephen Messner. *Effective Business Relocation: A Guide to Workable Approaches for Relocating Displaced Businesses.* Lexington, MA: D. C. Heath, 1970.

State Senate of Kentucky. 98 RS BR 1408. 1998 Regular Session.

—*Joshua D. Farrington*

HAMPTON, KYM MICHELLE (b. 1962, Louisville, KY), professional basketball player. Louisville native Kym Michelle Hampton, a high school track and basketball star, graduated from Iroquois High School in 1980. At six-feet-three, she dominated the center position at Arizona State University, where she was the only basketball player, male or female, in the school's history to score over 2,000 points and grab over 1,000 rebounds. In 1984, she graduated with a theater degree and five years later was inducted into the university's Hall of Fame. Since the United States did not have a women's professional basketball league when she graduated from college, Hampton played professional basketball for over a decade overseas in Spain, Italy, France, and Japan.

The Women's National Basketball Association (WNBA) formed in 1996. Hampton became the first Kentucky African American woman to play in the WNBA when she participated in the organization's ceremonial first tip-off between the Los Angeles Sparks and the New York Liberty on June 21, 1997. She scored the New York Liberty's first basket and started every game for the next three seasons. Her destroyed right knee forced her to retire at age 38 in 2000.

After her retirement, Hampton pursued careers in singing, acting, modeling, and public speaking. She was inducted into the Dawahares/Kentucky High School Athletic Association Hall of

Fame in 2005. As the New York Liberty's fan development leader, Hampton started a video blog to promote the team in 2009. She has helped market the team through various community programs. In 2011, the New York Liberty formed a Ring of Honor to commemorate the franchise's biggest contributors, and Hampton was one of five awarded that tribute.

Eger, Bob. *Maroon & Gold: A History of Sun Devil Athletics.* Champaign, IL: Sports Publishing LLC, 2001.
Newspapers: "Hampton Wants One Title for the Road," *Greensboro News and Record,* September 1, 1999; "Hall of Famer Hampton Finds There's a Spotlight after Basketball," *CJ,* March 16, 2005.
Women's National Basketball Association. "New York Liberty: Kym Hampton, Fan Development Leader." http://www.wnba.com /liberty/news/kym_hampton.html (accessed July 14, 2011).

—*Sallie L. Powell*

HAMPTON, LIONEL LEO (b. 1908, Louisville, KY; d. 2002, New York, NY), jazz vibraphonist and bandleader. Charles Edward Hampton Jr. married Gertrude Morgan in Louisville, KY, on December 15, 1906. Their son, Lionel Leo Hampton, was born on April 20, 1908. Hampton later noted in his autobiography that his father, a railroad worker, was frequently not at home, and his mother chose to move back to her hometown of Birmingham, AL. He also recounted that during World War I his father was declared missing and that he was the son of a war hero. Many years later, Hamilton met an elderly man who he believed was his estranged father because of their similar appearances. Nevertheless, Kentucky death records document a Charles Hampton, an African American laborer, who died from tuberculosis in Louisville on March 17, 1909.

By 1910, Lionel Hampton and his mother were living in Birmingham, AL, with her parents, James Richard and Louvenia Morgan. Hampton's grandfather worked as a railroad fireman, and his grandmother was an evangelist. Church music influenced Hampton's musicality. By 1920, the family was living in Chicago, where Hampton received much of his early music education on drums. After high school, he moved to Los Angeles, CA, and played in several bands.

In a 1930 recording session with Louis Armstrong, Hampton was the first **jazz** musician to be recorded playing vibraphone. In 1936, Hampton joined the Benny Goodman Orchestra, breaking the color barrier in jazz music. He was instrumental in the Goodman's band success during the late 1930s, including the famous 1938 Carnegie Hall concert. In 1940, Hampton formed his own big band. The band was an instant success, known for its first-class musicians, showmanship, and high-energy performances. In 1942, he recorded his biggest hit, "Flying Home," still considered a classic of the big-band genre.

Hampton remained active in music throughout his life, touring overseas, serving on the Board of Directors of the Kennedy Center, and helping establish the University of Idaho's annual jazz festival. In 1987, the university's school of music was named the Lionel Hampton School of Music, the only music school named for a jazz musician. The flamboyant master of the vibraphone died at Manhattan's Mount Sinai Medical Center on August 31, 2002.

Hampton, Lionel, with James Haskins. *Hamp: An Autobiography.* New York: Amistad, 1993.
Kentucky Death Records, 1852–1953.
Kentucky, Marriage Records, 1852–1914.
"Lionel Hampton, Who Put Swing in the Vibraphone, Is Dead at 94." *NYT,* September 1, 2002, 1.
Schuller, Gunther. *The Swing Era: The Development of Jazz, 1930–1945.* New York: Oxford Univ. Press, 1989.
Simon, George T. *The Big Bands.* 3rd ed. New York: Macmillan, 1973.
U.S. Federal Census (1900, 1910, 1920, 1940).

—*Michael A. Richardson*

HAMPTON, PETER GEORGE (b. 1871, Bowling Green, KY; d. 1916, New York, NY), most recorded African American of the early 1900s. Peter George Hampton, a native of Bowling Green, KY, was born on August 7, 1871. In his teenage years, he began performing as a musician and vaudeville entertainer, playing the harmonica and the banjo. In the late 1890s, he toured with several minstrel companies, including P. T. Wright's Nashville Students and John W. Isham's Octoroons, where he was part of Hampton and Johnson banjo duettists. In 1900, he used a newspaper advertisement, "$500.00 Reward for P. G. Hampton," in a self-promotion of his talents on numerous musical instruments and the sale of his collection of novelty musical equipment.

In 1902, Hampton joined the *In Dahomey* troupe, where he met his common-law wife, Laura Bowman, who was a popular actress and entertainer in her own right. The two made several tours across Europe, where they were immensely popular. Hampton recorded over 150 flat discs and cylinders during his tours; he was the most recorded African American in the United States or Europe, as well as the first African American recorded playing the harmonica. He was also the first African American to appear in a British film.

In 1908, Hampton and Bowman presented "Down in Kentucky," a vocal duet, at the Hippodrome. They also delighted King Edward VII at Buckingham Palace. Besides entertaining in Europe, they also performed in Africa, Asia, Russia, and India. The impending outbreak of World War I in 1914 forced them to abandon their tour, and they fled to the United States. On the trip home, Hampton grew ill. He died two years later at his home at 129 West 136th St. in New York City.

Lotz, Rainer E. *Black People: Entertainers of African Descent in Europe and Germany.* Bonn: Birgit Lotz, 1997.
Newspapers: "The Stage," *IF,* March 4, 1899, 4; "$500.00 Reward for P. G. Hampton," *IF,* January 27, 1900, 5; "Pete Hampton and Bauman Make Big Hit," *IF,* June 20, 1908, 5; "New York News," *IF,* March 25, 1916, 5.
U.S. Passport Applications, 1795–1925.
Wynn, Neil A., ed. *Cross the Water Blues: African American Music in Europe.* Jackson: Univ. Press of Mississippi, 2007.

—*Stephen Pickering*

HARBUT, WILLIAM LUTHER (b. 1885, Lexington, KY; d. 1947, Lexington, KY), horse-racing groom. Born on Parker Mills Rd. in Lexington, KY, to Sam and Sue Ella Harbut, William Luther Harbut grew up in the heart of horse country. After moving to **Maddoxtown,** where he built a house for his wife and 12

William Harbut and Man o' War, 1934.

children, he worked for a series of local horsemen, including Colonel Phil T. Chinn and J. W. Bailey. Eventually, he served as stud man on Harry B. Scott Sr.'s farm on Russell Cave Pike. When Scott accepted a position at Sam Riddle and Walt Jeffords's Faraway Farm, he decided to take Harbut along to work as a groom.

At Faraway Farm, Harbut met and befriended the famous racehorse Man o' War. For the next 17 years, he served as Man o' War's groom and unofficial publicist. Despite never having seen the horse race, he researched his career in detail and crafted a narrative of his victories—and one loss, which Harbut angrily claimed was the product of an inept starter—on which he would expound to the crowds that gathered to see the former champion. Eventually, tourists came to consider him an integral part of the experience of a visit to Faraway Farm. According to one story, British ambassador Lord Halifax, after hearing several tales during a visit, claimed that it was "worth coming halfway 'round the world to hear."

By 1941, Harbut's and Man o' War's careers had become so inextricably linked that the two appeared together on the cover of the *Saturday Evening Post* in September. Harbut's fame, however, did not entirely transcend racial barriers. Segregation was still practiced on the farm, and when Man o' War's birthdays were celebrated, he was required to sit at his own table away from the white participants. He also worked 16 hours a day for little pay, although his family recalled that he would stay extra hours to answer questions simply because he "loved his job."

In March 1946, Harbut suffered a stroke that forced him to retire. He continued to ask visitors about the welfare of Man o' War until he died at his home on Huffman Mill Rd. in Lexington on October 3, 1947. Less than a month later, Man o' War—"the mostest horse in the world," in Harbut's words—died as well. Many contemporaries paid tribute to the relationship of the man and the horse by suggesting that Man o' War's death was the product of heartbreak. Harbut was buried in the Maddoxtown Baptist Church Cemetery.

Ardery, Philip. *Heroes and Horses: Tales of the Bluegrass.* Lexington: Univ. Press of Kentucky, 1996.
Bowen, Edward L. *Man o' War.* Lexington, KY: Eclipse Press, 2000.
Kentucky, Death Records, 1852–1953.
Newspapers: "Will Harbut, Man o' War's Groom, Dies," *LH,* October 4, 1947, 1; "Will Harbut Is Dead; Man o' War's Groom," *NYT,* October 5, 1947; "For One Man, Racing's Glory Days Live On," *LHL,* October 8, 1985, A1; "'A Living Flame,'" *LHL,* July 27, 1997, C1; "A Man, a Horse, a Love Story," *LHL,* October 2, 2010, B3.

—*Stephen Pickering*

HARDIN, BONIFACE (b. 1933, Louisville, KY; d. 2012, Indianapolis, IN), civil rights activist and founder of Martin University. Born into a deeply religious family in 1933 as James Dwight Randolph Hardin, the son of Albert A. and Elizabeth Hansbro Hardin, he attended Catholic elementary schools in Bardstown and Louisville. At age 13, he joined St. Meinrad Archabbey in Indiana, where he began an education in languages and theology. Prior to his ordination as a priest in 1959, he adopted the religious name Boniface. Hardin also received training in business at the Notre Dame School of Commerce. After being assigned to Holy Angels Church in Indianapolis in 1965, he participated in the **civil rights movement,** befriending Dr. Martin Luther King Jr. and calling attention to the need for affirmative action.

In 1969, Rev. Fr. Boniface Hardin and Sr. Jane Schilling opened the Martin Center Institute for Afro-American Studies, which was designed to address the needs of the African American community, as well as medical concerns. In 1977, Hardin converted the Martin Center into a college based on the liberal arts model, and it was fully accredited in 1978. Hardin served as president of Martin University for thirty years, retiring in 2007 from a school that had increased from an initial population of 7 students to an enrollment of nearly 1,300. His service was rewarded by several awards and honors, including International Citizen of the Year and Indiana Living Legend.

On March 24, 2012, Hardin died of complications from a stroke he had suffered in September 2011. He was buried in St. Meinrad Archabbey Cemetery.

Ax, Ethan. "Rev. Fr. Boniface Hardin, Founder of Martin University, Retires." *Black Collegian* 37 (2007): 73–77.

Bodenhamer, David J., and Robert Graham Barrows, eds. *The Encyclopedia of Indianapolis.* Bloomington: Indiana Univ. Press, 1994.

Goodall, Hurley. "Seeing a Dream Come to Fruition." *Diverse: Issues in Higher Education* 24 (2007): 16–17.

"Hardin Remembered for Life of Service." *Indianapolis Recorder,* March 29, 2012. http://www.indianapolisrecorder.com/religion/article_eb893faa-79a3-11e1-bd36-0019bb2963f4.html (accessed April 26, 2013).

—*Stephen Pickering*

HARDIN, WILLIAM JEFFERSON (b. ca. 1830, Russellville, KY; d. 1889, Park City, UT), Wyoming's first African American legislator. William Jefferson Hardin was born free in Russellville, KY, around 1830. His mother was a free black woman, and his father was white—allegedly the brother of U.S. representative Benjamin Hardin. William was educated at a school for free blacks. According to the *Topeka Tribune,* he taught school in Louisville in the 1850s.

Hardin then moved to several states and settled in Denver, CO, in 1863. There he earned his living as a barber and became a leader in the city's black community, advocating for the right to vote for African American men. He was a delegate to the Republican National Convention in 1872. The next year, he moved to Cheyenne, WY, where he continued barbering and engaging in political activism. He was twice elected to the Wyoming Territorial House of Representatives. Because of a change in dates of election and service, Hardin's legislative tenure extended from shortly after his first election in November 1879 until his successor took office in January 1884. As a legislator, Hardin opposed a ban on interracial marriages and supported property rights for married women. He was elected mayor of Park City, UT, in 1884. Despondent over a failed marriage and deteriorating health, he committed suicide on September 13, 1889.

Berwanger, Eugene H. "William J. Hardin: Colorado Spokesman for Racial Justice, 1863–1873." *Colorado Magazine* 52 (1975): 52–65.

Brown, Larry K. "Wyoming's First Black Legislator: William Jefferson Hardin." *True West,* April 1999, 44–49.

Hardaway, Roger D. "William Jefferson Hardin: Wyoming's Nineteenth-Century Black Legislator." *Annals of Wyoming* 63 (Winter 1991): 2–13.

Topeka Tribune, June 27, 1885, 4.

—*Roger D. Hardaway*

HARGRAVES, WILLIAM FREDERICK "BILLY," COLONEL (b. 1932, Cincinnati, OH), first African American from Covington to become both a U.S. Air Force pilot and a Rhodes Scholar candidate. William Frederick Hargraves II, a U.S. Air Force colonel who was raised in Covington, is the son of William and Annie Leona Thomas Hargraves, both of whom were educa-

tors at Covington's **Lincoln-Grant School.** Hargraves was the first African American from Covington to become a U.S. Air Force pilot and a Rhodes Scholar candidate. He attended Lincoln-Grant Grade School and graduated with honors from Miami University of Ohio with a BS in education. At Miami University, he was a member of the Air Force ROTC and was commissioned a 2nd lieutenant upon graduation. He entered the U.S. Air Force in 1955 after receiving his MA in physics. Later that year, Hargraves entered the U.S. Air Force pilot-training program. In 1956, he earned his silver wings at Goodfellow Air Force Base, San Angelo, TX. In Texas, Hargraves married Maurine Collins of San Angelo on July 5, 1957.

During his distinguished career in the air force, Hargraves served as commander of the 10th Military Airlift Squadron, as an air liaison officer research scientist at the air force's Weapons Research Center, as an instructor pilot with the 22nd Military Airlift Command, and as an air liaison officer with the 1st Army of the Republic of Vietnam (ARVN) Division. He returned to Miami University to serve as an assistant professor of aerospace science with the Air Force ROTC program from 1971 through 1974. From 1978 to 1982, he was chief of flight deck development in the Research and Development section at Wright-Patterson Air Force Base, Dayton, OH; he then became deputy division chief at the Pentagon. He retired from the air force in 1982 after 30 years of distinguished service. Colonel Hargraves has received numerous military medals and commendations, including the Distinguished Flying Cross, the Air Medal, an Air Force Commendation Medal with two oak leaf clusters, the Vietnam Service Medal with five bronze stars, and the National Defense Service Medal.

After Hargraves retired from the air force, he became an assistant professor and assistant dean of arts and sciences at Central State University, Wilberforce, OH. In 1992 he was named to the Black Hall of Fame in Covington. At Central State University, Hargraves received two awards from students: in 1997 the Teacher of the Year Award and in 2001–2002 and 2002–2003 the Most Inspirational Teaching Award. Colonel Hargraves resides in Oxford, OH, with his wife.

Newspapers: "Praise God. Viet Hero Returns," *KP,* February 17, 1971, 2K; "Military Notes," *KTS,* August 15, 1956, 6A; "Silver Wings," *KTS,* August 22, 1956, 6A; "Major William Hargraves Earns Air Force Honors," *Oxford (OH) Press,* November 11, 1971, 3; "Center's Event Salute Black History," *KP,* February 22, 1992, 11K; "Tests of Character," *Dayton Daily News,* June 8, 1997, E1.

—*Theodore H. H. Harris*

HARLAN, JOHN MARSHALL (b. 1833, Boyle Co., KY; d. 1911, Washington, DC), U.S. Supreme Court justice known for defending the civil rights of African Americans. John Marshall Harlan moved to Louisville in 1861 and, except for a few years, lived there until he left for Washington to take up his seat on the Supreme Court in 1877. Harlan was the son of James Harlan, a lawyer and politician, and Eliza Shannon (Davenport) Harlan and was educated at Centre College in Danville and at Transylvania Law School in Lexington. After graduation in 1852, he joined his father's Frankfort law practice and plunged into politics. He began his career as a Whig follower of Henry Clay and then made brief alliances with many other parties before settling down as a Republican in 1868.

Elected county judge of Franklin Co. in 1858, Harlan resigned in 1861 and moved to Louisville. He set up a law practice, but at the outbreak of the Civil War he entered military service. A firm supporter of the Union, he raised a regiment in Louisville and served with distinction as a colonel in the Union cavalry. He left the army in early 1863 after the death of his father and returned to Frankfort. Later that year, he was elected Kentucky attorney general. After his term expired in 1867, he moved back to Louisville, residing at Brook and Jacob Sts. and then on Broadway between First and Second Sts. He practiced law out of offices on Jefferson St. between Fifth and Sixth Sts. and spent much time campaigning. Harlan was the Republican candidate for governor in 1871 and 1875. He lost both times but is credited with putting the party on the map in Kentucky. In 1876, he delivered the Kentucky delegation to Rutherford B. Hayes at the national nominating convention. Shortly after Hayes became president in 1877, he appointed Harlan to the Supreme Court.

Harlan's reputation rests on his Supreme Court opinions, especially those defending the civil rights of African Americans. Harlan grew up in a slaveholding family and had owned slaves himself. Like many Kentuckians, he defended slavery while fighting for the Union in the Civil War. But when he joined the Republican Party, which stood for black rights, Harlan said that he had changed his mind, and his nearly 34 years on the Supreme Court (1877–1911) proved that he had. He wrote 1,161 opinions. The most famous are his dissents in civil rights cases. His masterpiece was an eloquent protest against the court's approval of separate but equal status for blacks in *Plessy v. Ferguson* (1896). "Our constitution is colorblind," he wrote. "All citizens are equal before the law." He was vindicated almost 60 years later when the court struck down the separate-but-equal doctrine in *Brown v. Board of Education* (1954). A quiet southern gentleman in private life, Harlan was a passionate jurist, and many of his views were ahead of their time. He has been included on some modern lists of the court's greatest justices.

Harlan married Malvina French Shanklin of Evansville, IN, on December 23, 1856. The marriage produced six children. One of their grandchildren, also named John Marshall Harlan, was appointed to the Supreme Court in 1955. Harlan died at his home in Washington, DC. He is buried in that city's Rock Creek Cemetery.

Beth, Loren P. *John Marshall Harlan: The Last Whig Justice.* Lexington: Univ. Press of Kentucky, 1992.

Friedman, Leon, and Fred L. Israel. *The Justices of the United States Supreme Court, 1789–1969.* Vol. 2. New York: Chelsea House, 1969.

John Marshall Harlan Papers. Univ. of Louisville, Louis D. Brandeis School of Law, and Library of Congress, Washington, DC.

Westin, Alan F. "John Marshall Harlan and the Constitutional Rights of Negroes: The Transformation of a Southerner." *Yale Law Journal* 66 (1957): 637–710.

Yarbrough, Tinsley E. *Judicial Enigma: The First Justice Harlan.* New York: Oxford Univ. Press, 1955.

—*Charles Thompson*

HARLAN, ROBERT JAMES (b. ca. 1816, unknown; d. 1897), businessman, civil rights activist, and legislator. Robert James Harlan was reared by James Harlan, a Kentucky representative, slave owner, and the father of U.S. Supreme Court justice **John Marshall Harlan.** A slave by law, Robert Harlan experienced atypical freedom in education, business opportunities, and travel, according to some sources because of his questionable paternity. One of James Harlan's sons educated Robert, and he was allowed to learn the barber's trade in Louisville. He later operated a barbershop in Harrodsburg and then a grocery in Lexington.

In 1848, with his owner's consent, Harlan traveled to California and profited from the gold rush when he accrued $45,000 in gold. He moved to Cincinnati, OH, and invested in property and business, including a photography and daguerreotype gallery. He also earned money buying and selling racehorses. He traveled throughout the United States, into Canada, and to the World's Fair in London in 1851. After purchasing his freedom for $500, he moved to London in 1858.

Harlan returned to Cincinnati 10 years later and became active in the community. He served as trustee of the local black schools and the Colored Orphan Asylum. He became the first and only African American member of Ohio's Republican State Central Committee. In 1872, President Ulysses S. Grant introduced Harlan, a delegate-at-large to the Republican National Convention, as one of the convention's speakers. Known for his oratorical skills, he fought throughout his political career for the rights of African Americans, including the abolition of Ohio's "black laws," which required African Americans to prove their free status. He was a delegate to the National Civil Rights Convention that met with President Grant, and Grant later asked Harlan for a private meeting. In 1875, then Governor Rutherford B. Hayes commissioned Harlan as a colonel of a battalion of 400 men, a title he frequently used. He served as a special agent in various federal departments under Presidents Grant and Chester A. Arthur.

Beth, Loren P. *John Marshall Harlan: The Last Whig Justice.* Lexington: Univ. Press of Kentucky, 1992.

Gordon, James W. "Did the First Justice Harlan Have a Black Brother?" In *Critical Race Theory: The Cutting Edge,* edited by Richard Delgado and Jean Stefancic. Philadelphia: Temple Univ. Press, 2000, 118–25.

Simmons, William. *Men of Mark: Eminent, Progressive and Rising.* Cleveland: George M. Rewell, 1887.

—*Sallie L. Powell*

HARNEY, BENJAMIN ROBERTSON "BEN" (b. 1871, Louisville, KY; d. 1938, Philadelphia, PA), ragtime musician and composer. Benjamin Robertson "Ben" Harney was the son of Benjamin and Margaret (Draffen) Harney and the grandson of John Hopkins Harney, editor of the *Louisville Democrat.* Although he promoted himself as the "inventor of **ragtime**" music, Harney almost certainly was not. However, he was in the forefront of that turn-of-the-century musical style, and music historians credit him with two very important distinctions. His "You've Been a Good Old Wagon, but You've Done Broke Down" (Louisville: Greenup Music Co., 1895) was the first published ragtime song, and his popularity as a performer in New York City took the nation's music-publishing capital by storm the following year, contributing significantly to the ragtime craze that soon swept the country.

According to Jessie Boyce Harney, his wife and stage partner, Harney composed "Good Old Wagon" and another staple of the Harneys' act, "Mister Johnson, Turn Me Loose," while he was living in Middlesboro, KY, in the early 1890s. (Jessie Harney, also a Kentuckian, performed under the stage name Jessie Haynes.)

After returning to Louisville, Harney performed his songs in minstrel shows before persuading Greenup to publish "Good Old Wagon" in 1895. John Biller, conductor of the Macauley's Theatre orchestra, helped Harney transcribe the song for piano and received equal billing as composer on the original sheet music. Isidore Witmark, the New York publisher who reissued both Harney songs in 1896, was dubious that Harney actually had composed the pieces, so he took a train to Louisville to verify that Harney was the composer.

Starting in 1896, Harney performed at several New York vaudeville houses, but appearances at Tony Pastor's Fourteenth Street Theatre sealed his fame. Isidore Witmark recalled later: "Harney . . . quickly became a New York fad. . . . Those who remember the sensation caused by the earliest **jazz** pianists will imagine the furor created by Ben Harney's ragging the scale. . . . Ben Harney had the huskiest voice most people had ever heard in a human being, and this quality made his voice just right for ragtime singing." Harney's dexterity as a pianist and stick dancer was a source of amazement. Harney used stick dancing to accompany his song "You've Been a Good Old Wagon, but You've Done Broke Down." While he was sitting at the piano with a cane in one hand, he tap-danced with one or both feet and the cane during the rests of the stop-time section.

Because of his dark complexion, his ability to imitate the African American style of music, and his use of black players in his act, Harney's racial roots have been debated by some ragtime commentators. However, the historical evidence strongly suggests that he was white and not of mixed race.

Harney's vaudeville performances took him all over the United States and to Europe and the Pacific, including visits to Australia and the Fiji Islands. He composed more than two dozen songs, including "The Cake-Walk in the Sky" (1899), and wrote *Ben Harney's Rag Time Instructor* (1897), a 10-page manual explaining how to "rag" other music.

Jazz and other musical forms supplanted ragtime after World War I, and Harney's career was cut short by a heart attack in 1923. He died 15 years later in impoverished circumstances. He is buried in Philadelphia's Fernwood Cemetery. Funds were raised for a grave marker, which Harney's widow had inscribed "In Memory of My Beloved Husband / Ben R. Harney / Creator of Ragtime."

Berlin, Edward A. *Ragtime: A Musical and Cultural History.* Berkeley: Univ. of California Press, 1980.

Blesh, Rudi, and Harriet Janis. *They All Played Ragtime.* New York: Oak Publications, 1971.

Tallmade, William H. "Ben Harney: The Middlesborough Years, 1890–93." *American Music* 13 (Summer 1995), 167–94.

Witmark, Isidore, and Isaac Goldberg. *The Story of the House of Witmark: From Ragtime to Swingtime.* New York: Lee Furman Inc., 1939.

—*William L. Ellison Jr.*

HARPER, NATHANIEL R. (b. 1846, Indianapolis, IN; d. 1921, Louisville, KY), one of the first two blacks to practice law in the Louisville court system and Kentucky's first appointed African American judge. Nathaniel R. Harper was the eldest son of Hezekiah and Elizabeth Harper. As a child, he moved to Detroit, where he was educated, and he migrated to Louisville in 1869 with his wife, Drusilla. He was one of the first two African Americans (the other was **George A. Griffith**) admitted to the Kentucky bar (November 23, 1871) and quickly became Kentucky's best-known black lawyer.

During the era of segregation, Harper, like most African American attorneys, was dependent on predominantly poor black clients and was often treated disrespectfully in open court by white lawyers. Although he often found it difficult to make a living as a practicing attorney, Harper's basic conservatism made him an attractive candidate for numerous political patronage positions. In 1878, he became the first black notary public in the state and in 1888 Kentucky's first black judge. In the 1890s, he was instrumental in founding Central Law School, which became affiliated with black-controlled State University (later known as **Simmons College in Kentucky**) in Louisville.

In 1895, Harper was nominated for the Kentucky General Assembly but withdrew, to the consternation of his black supporters, under pressure from Republican officials. In recognition of his loyalty to the "Party of Lincoln," he was appointed commissioner of the Bureau of Agriculture, Labor, and Statistics of the Colored People of Kentucky by Gov. William O. Bradley (1895–1899). Harper was a choirmaster and a playwright and was active in civic and church affairs. He was the father of six children and a longtime resident at 1302 W. Madison St. He is buried in Louisville Cemetery.

Dunnigan, Alice Allison, comp. and ed. *The Fascinating Story of Black Kentuckians: Their Heritage and Traditions.* Washington, DC: Associated Publishers, 1982.

Louisville Leader, February 5, 1921.

Lucas, Marion B. *A History of Blacks in Kentucky.* Vol. 1, *From Slavery to Segregation, 1760–1891.* Frankfort: Kentucky Historical Society, 1992.

Wright, George C. *Life Behind a Veil: Blacks in Louisville, 1865–1930.* Baton Rouge: Louisiana State Univ. Press, 1985.

—*J. Blaine Hudson*

HARRIET BEECHER STOWE SLAVERY TO FREEDOM MUSEUM, museum in Washington, Mason Co., KY. The Harriet Beecher Stowe Slavery to Freedom Museum occupies a brick townhouse in Washington, Mason Co., that dates from 1807. In 1833, it was owned by Marshall Key, a nephew of Chief Justice John Marshall and a brother of Col. Thomas Marshall, who served as a staff officer under Gen. George Washington. That year, Key's daughter became a pupil of Harriet Beecher Stowe (1811–1896), author of ***Uncle Tom's Cabin*** (1852). After a visit to the house, Stowe received the inspiration for the book's characters Uncle Tom and Topsy. The real-life name of the person who inspired Topsy was Jane, and she later married Isham Anderson. Behind the museum is a small brick structure, known as the Indian Fort, which settlers used to ward off American Indians who sometimes crossed the Ohio River at nearby Maysville. Included in this museum are the original mantels, woodworking, floor, and doors; slavery artifacts, including slave leg irons; period furnishings; and Civil War artifacts. The museum is included on **Underground Railroad** tours.

Newspapers: Melinda Myers Vaughn, "A Stop on Freedom Road," *KP*, September 17, 1997, 1KK; Karin Admiraal, "Festival Great Way to Learn History," *KP*, September 17, 2005, 6K.
Safe Passage. http://www.safepassageohio.org (accessed June 10, 2006).
Washingtonkentucky.com. "Washington, Ky." http://washingtonken tucky.com (accessed June 10, 2006).

—*Kareem A. Simpson*

HARRIS, EVERETT G. (b. 1867, Amelia Court House, VA; d. 1936, Louisville, KY), minister and founder of the Plymouth Settlement House in Louisville. After Everett G. Harris graduated from Howard University's School of Religion, the **American Missionary Association** sent him to Louisville in 1893 to shepherd the small assembly that would become the **Plymouth Congregational United Church of Christ.** At the time of Harris's arrival, the church was meeting at Ninth and Broadway, but by 1902 a new meeting place had been built at 1630 W. Chestnut St., on the edge of African Americans' westward expansion. The church's present structure was erected at the same location in 1929.

Although Harris concentrated his early efforts on increasing the membership of his congregation, he also became especially concerned with the needs of the area's children and **domestic workers.** By 1911, he had conceived of the need for an arm of the church directed specifically at social ministry, in particular, a settlement house. It took six years for the plan to come to fruition, but in the fall of 1917, the Plymouth Settlement House opened at 1624–26 W. Chestnut, next door to the church. The settlement house, which featured a large auditorium, classrooms, and dormitory rooms for black female servants, stressed both religious and domestic training and provided a number of youth programs for the community's children. One of the more notable services Harris offered at the settlement house was an employment bureau that found placement for black female domestics. In 1919, Plymouth Settlement House became a member of the Louisville Welfare League. Harris continued as the settlement house's superintendent and pastor of Plymouth Congregational until his death in 1936. The house is now called the Plymouth Community Renewal Center.

In addition to his ministerial duties, Harris was active in the civic affairs of Louisville. He was a board member of the Commission on Interracial Cooperation, a moderate organization that sought to "improve race relations and elevate the status of blacks." Harris also served on the Interdenominational Ministerial Alliance and was, for a time, a member of the Board of Directors of the Louisville **Colored Orphans' Home.**

Not long after coming to Louisville, Harris married **Rachel Davis Harris,** known for her work at the **Western Colored Branch Library.** Both his wife and a son, J. Everett Harris, survived Harris, who is buried in Louisville Cemetery.

Berry, Benjamin Donaldson, Jr. "Plymouth Settlement House and the Development of Black Louisville, 1900–1930." PhD diss., Case Western Reserve Univ., 1977.

Wright, George C. *Life Behind a Veil: Blacks in Louisville, Kentucky, 1865–1930.* Baton Rouge: Louisiana State Univ. Press, 1985.

HARRIS, LARNELLE STEWARD (b. 1947, Danville, KY), Christian vocalist. Born in Danville, KY, Larnelle Steward Harris moved to Louisville as a young child. After graduating with a degree in voice from Western Kentucky University, he toured as a drummer with a band named the Spurrlows from 1970 to 1972. In the mid-1970s, after a brief stint with a Christian rock band named First Gear, Harris embarked on what would become a highly successful solo career. Rather than recording in the genre of black gospel, Harris, often credited as helping speed integration in the traditionally white-dominated branch of inspirational music, was one of the first black vocalists to be accepted in the emerging genre of contemporary Christian music. His first major solo album, *Tell It to Jesus*, was released in 1975. It was followed by over a dozen more during the next 30 years. Except for a three-year tour in the mid-1980s with Bill Gaither and the Gaither Vocal Band, Harris remained an independent solo artist for most of his career.

In 1983, Harris won a Grammy for a duet with Sandi Patti in the song "More than Wonderful." He won three more Grammys as a solo artist and 11 Dove Awards for albums such as *Give Me More Love in My Heart* (1981), *The Father Hath Provided* (1988), and *Unbelievable Love* (1996). Additionally, the Gospel Music Association named Harris the Male Vocalist of the Year in 1983, 1986, and 1988 and the Songwriter of the Year in 1988.

In addition to his best-selling albums, Harris toured with Billy Graham's evangelism crusades and appeared on numerous television programs, including *Life with Regis and Kathie Lee* and *The 700 Club.* In 1992, his song "Mighty Spirit" was featured in a public-service announcement by the Points of Light Foundation. The song won that year's Silver Bell Award for Distinguished Public Service, and Harris was invited to the White House by President George H. W. Bush. He was also the first American Christian artist to perform inside the Kremlin after the fall of the Soviet Union.

Although he has toured extensively throughout the United States and the world, Harris and his wife, Mitzy, have lived in Louisville throughout his long career. During that time, he has served as treasurer and later as deacon at Maple Grove Baptist Church. He was a 2007 inductee into the Gospel Music Association Hall of Fame and a 2011 inductee into the Kentucky Music Hall of Fame.

Carpenter, Bill. *Uncloudy Days: The Gospel Music Encyclopedia.* San Francisco: Backbeat Books, 2005.
Cusic, Don, ed. *Encyclopedia of Contemporary Christian Music: Pop, Rock, and Worship.* Santa Barbara, CA: ABC-CLIO, 2010.
"Harris Gives Voice to His Love of Gospel." *LHL*, October 19, 1986, K1.
Kentucky General Assembly. Resolution 98 RS BR 2691. 1998 Regular Session, March 31, 1998.

—*Joshua D. Farrington*

HARRIS, LAWRENCE (b. 1879, Lexington, KY; d. 1911, Lexington, KY), church leader, author, and proponent of African American businesses. Born in 1879, in Lexington, KY, to Walker and Easter Harris, Lawrence Harris became deeply involved in

Main Street Baptist Church as a teenager. By the turn of the century, he had served in the church's choir, as superintendent of its Sunday school, and as a general field missionary for the Baptist Sunday school association in Kentucky. He was also the manager of the *Kentucky Baptist* newspaper and the secretary of the Lexington chapter of the black Elks.

In addition to his religious activities, Harris was an author. In 1902, the *Lexington Leader* published an article on Harris, "who was making a name for himself as a writer of poetry," and his poem "Uncle Si's Fox Chase." The poem, written in dialect that supposedly resembled that of an old slave, was reminiscent of the tales of Brer Rabbit and other black folklore. In 1907, he published a short book titled *The Negro Population of Lexington in the Professions, Business, Education, and Religion,* one of the few works of the era that focused exclusively on Lexington's black community. One of the primary purposes of the book was to highlight the city's black-owned businesses and to encourage both black and white patrons to conduct business with the various stores, barbers, doctors' offices, lawyers, and real estate agents listed in its pages. Because of his religious background, Harris also suggested that by supporting black businesses and describing the virtues of Lexington's prominent religious and civic leaders, the book would help reduce crime within the black community.

Although he showed promise of an even more successful literary career, Harris tragically died at the age of 32 after he contracted pulmonary tuberculosis. He was survived by his wife, Lizzie, and his five-year-old son, Lawrence Harris Jr., and was buried in Greenwood Cemetery (later named Cove Haven Cemetery). The *Lexington Leader* reflected on his life, remarking that he "was one of the most prominent and highly respected young colored men in Central Kentucky. He enjoyed the confidence and respect of the many citizens, both white and colored."

Harris, Lawrence. *The Negro Population of Lexington in the Professions, Business, Education, and Religion.* Lexington, KY: s.n., 1907.
Newspapers: "Lawrence Harris," *LL,* December 28, 1902, 2; "Colored Notes," *LL,* April 11, 1911, 11.
Wright, George C. *A History of Blacks in Kentucky.* Vol. 2, *In Pursuit of Equality, 1890–1980.* Frankfort: Kentucky Historical Society, 1992.

—*Joshua D. Farrington*

HARRIS, RACHEL DAVIS (b. 1869, Louisville, KY; d. 1969), teacher and librarian at the Western Colored Branch Library in Louisville. After graduating from **Central High School** in Louisville in 1885, Rachel Davis Harris began her career as a teacher in the public schools at a time when teaching was one of the best-salaried professions open to black women. She soon became a children's librarian in an effort to help African American children develop an interest in reading. As a librarian at the **Western Colored Branch Library** in Louisville, she succeeded in a profession in which black women were virtually nonexistent. In the 1920s, Harris worked at the **Eastern Colored Branch Library** and became a senior assistant there.

Although Harris never had formal training and education as a librarian, she gained experience while working with **Thomas Blue,** the head of the first Colored Department of the Louisville Free Public Library. They became close friends and professional partners. Together Blue and Harris developed a standard training course that educated black librarians from across the South.

Recognizing the significance of a public library in the lives of black children, Harris and Blue also collaborated to make libraries both community centers and important gathering places for young blacks. They enlisted elementary school principals, teachers, and ministers to become actively involved in the library's programs for children. Wide-ranging discussions, lectures, and exhibitions were organized at library branches to entice children to become involved in reading. In 1923, Harris created 58 classroom library collections in the 30 African American schools of Louisville and Jefferson Co. In 1935, she succeeded Blue as head of the Colored Department of the library.

She was married to Rev. **Everett G. Harris,** pastor of **Plymouth Congregational United Church of Christ.** She participated in many church activities and sometimes preached there. In 1954, the Harris Recreational Center, located at 1723 S. 34th St. in the Cotter Homes housing project, was dedicated and named for Reverend Harris, and the library it housed was named for Rachel Harris.

Harris was a member of the American Library Association and the Woman's Missionary Union.

Louisville Times, March 22, 1954.
Malone, Cheryl Knott. "Louisville Free Public Library's Racially Segregated Branches, 1905–35." *RKHS* 93 (Spring 1995): 159–79.
U.S. Work Projects Administration. *Libraries and Lotteries: A History of the Louisville Free Public Library.* Cynthiana, KY: Hobson Book Press, 1944.

HARRISON, LISA DARLENE (b. 1971, Mt. Washington, KY), professional basketball player. A native of Mt. Washington, KY, Lisa Darlene Harrison attended nearby Louisville Southern High School. Around six feet tall, she led her team to the 1988 Kentucky State Basketball Championship and earned Most Valuable Player honors. In 1989, her senior year, Harrison, considered the best player in the nation, was named Kentucky's Miss Basketball, the Naismith Trophy winner, and *USA Today* Player of the Year honoree. A strong inside player, she scored 3,361 points, the fifth-highest number of points scored in Kentucky girls' high school basketball. She also played volleyball and competed in track.

After graduating from high school, Harrison played basketball at the University of Tennessee under legendary coach Pat Summitt. At the end of her collegiate career, she was named a member of the Kodak Women's Basketball All-American team. She ranked 13th on the University of Tennessee's all-time scoring list (1,135 points) and 7th all-time in rebounding (814).

When Harrison graduated from college, no professional women's basketball leagues existed. She used her communications and broadcasting degree to work as marketing director for the Bike Athletic Company in Knoxville, TN. In 1996, with the formation of the American Basketball League (ABL), Harrison joined the Portland Power and later the Columbus Quest. As the ABL declined, the Phoenix Mercury of the Women's National Basketball Association (WNBA) recruited Harrison in 1999. That same year, she was inducted into the Dawahares/Kentucky High School Athletic Association Hall of Fame. Harrison played 161 games, scored 452 field goals, and grabbed 634 rebounds for the

Mercury. In 2004, she retired and joined the Mercury's coaching staff.

Kentucky High School Athletic Association. http://www.khsaa.org (accessed July 1, 2011).
Newspapers: "Southern Star Potentially Best Girl Ever in State," *LHL,* December 15, 1987, C3; "Harrison Becomes 12th Lady Vol Kodak All-American," *Knoxville News-Sentinel,* April 3, 1993, C1.
—*Sallie L. Powell*

HARRODS CREEK, Jefferson Co. community. The area of Harrods Creek is bordered roughly by the Ohio River on the west, U.S. 42 on the east, Lime Kiln Ln. on the south, and the area near Hays Kennedy Park on the north. Formerly known as the Seminary Land, the area was first laid out by the Transylvania Company, a frontier firm that also established Transylvania Seminary (now Transylvania University) in Lexington. The company sold lots, but the planned town never developed. The Harrods Creek area developed as an important depot for goods making their way to inland Kentucky or south to Louisville via the Louisville-Westport Pike, which later became River Rd.

The area was named for either James Harrod, the founder of Ft. Harrod (modern-day Harrodsburg), or Capt. William Harrod, the commander of the first fort in Louisville. Flat-bottomed cargo boats frequently stopped at the mouth of Harrods Creek in the late eighteenth century to avoid going as far as the dangerous falls of the Ohio River and to visit the famous Harrod's Tavern, the site of the modern-day Captains Quarters Restaurant.

Although many cargo boats began bypassing Harrods Creek by the beginning of the nineteenth century, the overland ferry to Utica, IN, was still popular. Farmers began to populate the fertile soils surrounding the Harrods Creek area and nearby Goose Creek and Little Goose Creek and shipped their well-known ground flour and cornmeal to Louisville. Transportation into town became easier after 1877 with the completion of the narrow-gauge Louisville, Harrods Creek, and Westport Railroad. In 1904, the interurban line was adapted to electric service, which opened the area to suburbanization. Wealthy families such as the Browns and the Hilliards constructed summer houses and weekend retreats that eventually became permanent residences.

African Americans have also played an important role in that area. After emancipation, many Harrods Creek slaves moved into the region known as the Neck near present-day Hoskins Beach Rd. The racial mixture of the district was solidified in the 1920s when farmer and developer James Taylor purchased a large tract of land north of the creek and sold the subdivided lots solely to other African Americans.

In the 1990s, citizens of the Harrods Creek area fought a proposal that would have bisected their community by building a bridge to the Indiana side of the Ohio River.

History of the Ohio Falls Cities and Their Counties. Vol. 2. Cleveland: L. A. Williams Company, 1882.
A Place in Time: The Story of Louisville's Neighborhoods. Louisville, KY: Courier-Journal, 1989.

HARRODS CREEK BAPTIST CHURCH, one of the oldest African American Baptist churches in Louisville. Founded in 1797 and originally known as the Regular Baptist Church near **Harrods Creek,** the Harrods Creek Baptist Church is one of the oldest African American Baptist churches in the Louisville metropolitan area. The church's first minister was Rev. William Keller, a Virginia carpenter who was known for his skill as both a hunter and a brewer. During its early life, the church was affiliated with several local Baptist organizations, such as the Salem Association, which it joined in 1797. The church then switched to the Long Run Association in 1803 and finally to the Sulphur Fork Association in 1855. In 1822, the church constructed a modest stone sanctuary at Brownsboro that still exists as one of Oldham Co.'s oldest church buildings.

After the death of Keller in 1817 (according to legend, killed by a bear), Rev. Benjamin Allen built the church to well over 200 members. However, while serving as the church's minister, Allen came under the influence of reformer Alexander Campbell, who advocated a departure from the elaborate doctrines of existing denominations and a return to simple Biblicism. Allen converted to the teachings of Campbell and in 1831 took all but 17 members of the Harrods Creek congregation with him to found what would become the Brownsboro Christian Church.

In 1966, a modern brick worship facility was built on the property next to the original stone edifice at 7610 Upper River Rd. In 1976, the old sanctuary was added to the National Register of Historic Places. Nevertheless, because of the expense of maintenance, considerable controversy existed during the early 1980s concerning the fate of the previous building. In 1981, however, the church voted to undertake a restoration project, an effort that occupied it well into the 1990s.

Masters, Frank M. *A History of Baptists in Kentucky.* Louisville: Kentucky Baptist Historical Society, 1953.
Newspapers: *LCJ,* November 1, 1989; *LCJ,* August 8, 1997.
Norris, Kenneth Ray. "The Impact of Interpersonal Conflict on Koinonia within the Harrods Creek Baptist Church, Brownsboro, Kentucky." DMin diss., Southern Baptist Theological Seminary, 1983.
—*Timothy Wood*

HART, JACK (b. unknown; d. unknown), early pioneer in Kentucky. Apart from occasional mentions in letters and archival records, little is known of the life of Jack Hart, one of the first African Americans to explore Kentucky's frontier. Often referred to as Captain Jack Hart, he was the slave and bodyguard of pioneer Nathaniel Hart. He first entered Kentucky with his master in 1774 and was present the following year at the signing of the Sycamore Shoals Treaty in Tennessee, which resulted in the purchase of "Kaintucke" from the Cherokees. Scholar Anne Butler speculates that he "may have been the first African American to reach the lands lying on the south side of the Kentucky River" during his explorations with Nathaniel Hart and Daniel Boone in the mid-1770s. The sparse historical record even indicates that Jack Hart may have served as Boone's "pilot" or guide as Boone explored Kentucky's wilderness. Hart may also have helped discover the site where Ft. Boonesborough was built, and he was present at the time of its construction.

During his travels, Hart was given a gun by his master's brother. In 1782, he lent the gun to a traveler headed to fight at the battle of Blue Licks, where it was subsequently forever lost.

Emancipation documents indicate that Hart was freed in 1803, but he continued to live with the Hart family for the subsequent four decades. An 1845 letter by Nathaniel Hart referred to Jack as "an aged Negro man of clear intellect and memory" and said that he was at the reinterment of Daniel Boone in Frankfort. Although he was supposedly freed in the early 1800s, an 1846 declaration by the Kentucky General Assembly referred to Hart as a slave. The declaration honoring Hart proposed that the state replace his lost rifle because he "endured the perils, privations and hardships incident to the pioneers." The law would also have made him exempt from state laws banning slaves from carrying arms. The resolution failed to pass after being submitted three times on the floor of the House.

Although the resolution failed, a legend circulated among Nathaniel Hart's descendants that claimed that Jack was reissued a rifle before his death. This rifle allegedly disappeared after the family estate was raided during the Civil War. The legend also claims that a portrait of him was prominently displayed in the family home and was loaned for an exhibit in Chicago at the 1893 World's Columbian Exposition. It was subsequently destroyed during a house fire in 1902.

In 2004, the Kentucky General Assembly finally passed a declaration honoring the life of Captain Jack Hart and ordered the purchase of a flintlock-design Kentucky long rifle to be presented to the Kentucky Historical Society on behalf of Hart.

Butler, Anne S. "Duty, Courage, and Indomitable Spirit: African Americans in the Military." In *Joining the Ranks: African Americans in the Military.* Frankfort: Kentucky Historical Society, 2003.
McKinney, Helen E. "Bonds of Trust: Honoring Jack Hart, Kentucky African American Pioneer." *Pioneer Times: An Online Journal of Living History,* 2010. http://www.graphicenterprises.net/html/hart_rifle.html (accessed May 3, 2012).
"Thursday, February 4, 1846." *Journal of the Representatives of the Commonwealth of Kentucky.* Frankfort: A. G. Hodges, 1847, 266–67.

—*Joshua D. Farrington*

HARVEY, WARDELLE GREEN, SR. (b. 1926, Boonville, IN), civil rights leader in Paducah, KY. Born in the small town of Boonville, IN, on June 12, 1926, Wardelle Green Harvey Sr. would later recall his youth as being relatively free of the segregation and racism that were common at the time. After feeling called to the ministry and moving to Evansville, IN, however, Harvey experienced firsthand the culture of segregation in bus stations and swimming pools. Under the tutelage of another minister, he became involved in politics and civic work, beginning a struggle for civil rights that would endure for the rest of his life.

In 1962, Harvey moved to Paducah, KY, to take over the leadership of the Harrison Street Baptist Church. Unhappy with the opportunities afforded African Americans in the community and displeased with the activity of the local branch of the **National Association for the Advancement of Colored People,** he organized the Non-partisan League, which devoted itself to integrating various institutions in the city, including restaurants and theaters. In 1968, Harvey also engaged in community outreach of a broader nature, running for city commissioner and campaigning in white neighborhoods and other areas that former black candidates had avoided. Although he lost the election, he was appointed to the position on an interim basis after the elected candidate died suddenly. After his 90-day term expired, he was elected in his own right and was reelected for two more terms.

After he completed his career as city commissioner, Harvey attained some local notoriety for attending a Ku Klux Klan rally in Paducah in 1975. The Klan had applied for and received a permit to hold a meeting in the city, but the mayor allowed it to do so only if it declared it to be public. As a statement of principle, Harvey decided to attend, even after he witnessed examples of violence against African Americans before the meeting. Klan members later tried to intimidate him by driving past his house several times, but no more violence occurred.

Harvey continued to preach and work for civil rights after the 1970s, moving to Paducah's New Greater Love Missionary Baptist Church in 1987. He became the first African American on Paducah's housing board and "initiated the first African American state-approved day care center." In honor of his contributions to the city and the state, the **Kentucky Commission on Human Rights** named him an inaugural member of the Kentucky Civil Rights Hall of Fame on July 18, 2000.

Harvey, Wardelle G., Sr. Interview by Betsy Brinson, August 16, 2000. Civil Rights in Kentucky: Oral History Project, Kentucky Historical Society.
Newspapers: "Human Rights Inductees," *LHL,* July 19, 2000, B5; "Harvey Grateful, but Work Not Finished," *Paducah Sun,* July 20, 2000, 1A.

—*Stephen Pickering*

HASKINS, CLEM (b. 1943, Campbellsville, KY), basketball player and coach. Clem Haskins, basketball player and coach, was born in Campbellsville, KY, on August 11, 1943, the son of Columbus and Lucy (Smith) Haskins. He attended Campbellsville's Durham High School and Taylor County High School, graduating in 1963. He was named to Kentucky's high school all-state team and played in the state's Sweet Sixteen tournament in 1962. Haskins attended Western Kentucky University from 1963 to 1967. He was named the Ohio Valley Conference's most valuable player three years in a row (1965, 1966, and 1967) and was named All-American in the 1965–1966 and 1966–1967 seasons. In 1967, he was the first-round draft choice of the Chicago Bulls and the third draft choice overall. He played with the Chicago Bulls (1967–1970), the Phoenix Suns (1970–1974), and the Washington Bullets (1974–1976). In 1977, he joined the coaching staff at Western Kentucky University and became the head coach of the Hilltoppers in 1979. He was named Rookie Coach of the Year in 1979 by NBC. In 1986, he became head coach of the University of Minnesota Golden Gophers.

Haskins married Yevette Penick in 1965. They have three children: Clemette, Lori, and Brent.

—*Stephen V. Wise*

HATCH, JOHN WESLEY (b. 1928, Louisville, KY), educator. John Wesley Hatch, son of John W. and Grace Hatch, was born in Louisville, KY, in 1928. After completing his elementary and secondary education, he wanted to pursue a law degree at the University of Kentucky (UK). However, Kentucky's statute mandating racial segregation of education (the **Day Law**) prohibited him from attending UK in 1948. Instead, the university sent four law-yers to Kentucky State College (later known as **Kentucky State University**) to teach him. When UK did desegregate under court order in 1949, he continued to take law classes at UK, albeit still in a segregated status on the campus.

After two semesters at Kentucky State and one at UK, Hatch gave up the legal career path. Instead, he pursued a successful teaching and consulting career in public health. He earned de-grees at Knoxville College (BA in sociology), Atlanta University (master's in social work), and the University of North Carolina at Chapel Hill (doctor of public health education). An army vet-eran (1952–1955), he served as an international consultant on public health in Massachusetts, Mississippi, Cameroon, South Africa, North Carolina, and many other sites. He worked with various religious denominations (including the A.M.E. Zion Church, the United Methodist Church, and the World Council of Churches) on improving health for underserved populations. In 1995, he retired from the University of North Carolina at Chapel Hill as the Kenan Professor of Public Health.

John W. Hatch Papers, 1967–1995. http://www.lib.unc.edu/mss/inv/h/Hatch,John_W.html (accessed April 30, 2013).
Newspapers: "First Black Law Student at UK Recalls Loneliness," *LHL,* May 3, 1994, A1; "UK Integrator: 'You've Got to Walk the Walk,'" *LHL,* February 27, 2002, 14.

—*John A. Hardin*

HATCHER, E. PORTER, JR. (b. 1936, Louisville, KY; d. 2012, Louisville, KY), representative in the Kentucky General As-sembly. Born in September 1936 in Louisville, KY, E. Porter Hatcher Jr., the son of a U.S. mail carrier, graduated from the University of Louisville. He established a practice, the Hatcher Company, as an insurance agent and real estate broker in Louis-ville on 20th St. and W. Broadway. He served on the Board of Trustees of Spalding University and briefly served on the board of directors of the Louisville Branch of the **National Association for the Advancement of Colored People.** In 1975, he decided to run for the office of alderman in Louisville as a Democrat, citing his desire to "improve schools, transportation, public safety, [and] sanitation." He succeeded in defeating incumbent Lois Morris. As alderman, he was primarily known for his role in a contested elec-tion for chairman of the Louisville Board of Aldermen, dead-locking a vote with the support of the new mayor, William Stansbury. He eventually lost the bid, but only after 70 ballots and a debate that lasted through the night.

In 1978, he was elected to the Kentucky General Assembly as the representative of the 43rd District, a position he held for over 20 years. During his tenure, he took an active interest in finan-cial matters, opposing ethics reforms that required lawmakers to report sources of income and expressing interest in the leader-ship of the House Banking and Insurance Committee. In 1999, however, Hatcher's insurance license was suspended after he was accused of stealing customers' premiums. After pleading guilty to insurance fraud and a charge of illegally using campaign con-tributions, he resigned from the General Assembly on December 4, 1999. As part of a plea agreement, Hatcher was given only five years' probation. He was ordered to pay almost $45,000 in restitution.

On December 26, 2012, Hatcher died at age 76. Hathaway and Clark Funeral Home managed the burial arrangements.

Newspapers: "Louisville Voters to Elect 12 to the Board of Aldermen," *LCJ,* November 1, 1975; "Legislator's Insurance License Is Sus-pended," *LHL,* January 22, 1999, B3; "Louisville Legislator Hatcher Resigns," *LHL,* December 4, 1999, C7; "Former Represen-tative Pleads Guilty to Fraud," *BGDN,* December 11, 1999, 6A; "For-mer State Representative E. Porter Hatcher Jr. Dies at Age 76," *LCJ,* December 29, 2012.

—*Stephen Pickering*

HATCHETT, HILLIARY RICE, JR. (b. 1918, Lexington, KY; d. 1985, Columbus, OH), chairman of the Department of Fine Arts at Savannah State College. Hilliary Rice Hatchett Jr. was born in Lexington, KY, on June 27, 1918. After his mother, Gen-evieve, died while he was a small child, he was raised by his father, Hilliary Hatchett Sr., who worked as a porter at a Lexington rail-road transfer station. In 1940, Hatchett graduated from Ohio's Capital University with a bachelor's degree in music. From 1942 to 1945, he served in the U.S. Army and was stationed in Italy, France, and Germany. In 1943, he directed a concert of the Negro soldier chorus that was featured in the main opera theater of Palermo, Sicily.

After returning to the United States, he obtained a master's degree in music from Ohio State University in 1946. He also received training at the Juilliard School of Music during the summers of 1947 and 1949. In 1946, he was appointed superin-tendent of music for black schools in Greenville, SC. He served in that position for two years before he was named the chairman of the Department of Fine Arts at Georgia's Savannah State College in 1948. During his tenure at Savannah State, Hatchett served as the chairman of the Georgia State Music Festival and coauthored the school's anthem, the "Savannah State College Hymn."

Hilliary Hatchett died in Columbus, OH, on July 5, 1985, and was buried in Long Island National Cemetery in New York.

Fleming, G. James, and Christian E. Burckel, eds. *Who's Who in Colored America.* 7th ed. Yonkers-on-Hudson, NY: Christian E. Burckel & Associates, 1950.
Mize, J. T. H., ed. *The International Who Is Who in Music.* 5th ed. Chi-cago: Who Is Who in Music, 1951.
Obituary. *LHL,* July 8, 1985, C11.

—*Joshua D. Farrington*

HATHAWAY, ISAAC SCOTT (b. 1872, Lexington, KY; d. 1967, Montgomery, AL), first African American commissioned to de-sign a U.S. Mint coin. Born on April 4, 1872, to Rev. Robert Elijah and Rachel Hathaway, in Lexington, KY, Isaac Scott Hatha-way showed an interest in the art of sculpting at an early age. Dur-ing a visit to a Cincinnati museum at the age of nine, Hathaway noticed that there were no busts of prominent black figures, and he then promised to rectify that problem when he was older. Growing up in a small frame house in a poor neighborhood, Ha-thaway made the most of his limited opportunities, practicing sculpting when he had supplies and selling painted portraits of horses from the local tracks. His successes with his portraits funded an education that included Chandler College in Lexington, the New England Conservatory in Boston, MA, and the Cincinnati Art Academy in Ohio.

In 1891, Hathaway began teaching in Jessamine Co., a career he would continue for the rest of his life. He supplemented this occupation by opening a studio in the chicken coop behind his birth home on Lexington's Pine St. in the Davis Bottom neighborhood. According to the 1900 U.S. federal census, he lived in Cincinnati and worked as an artist. Throughout the early 1900s, his skill landed him a series of odd but rewarding commissions. After the Bath Furnace meteorite landed in Kentucky in 1902, the Smithsonian hired him to make a cast to be displayed in the museum. In 1904, he gained additional notoriety with his plaster model for a litigation case regarding the death of businessman Robert C. Whayne. Hathaway sculpted a 16-by-7.5-foot section of the land where Whayne's body was found, as well as a 6-foot section of a tree trunk.

Hathaway became especially well known for crafting death masks and life masks, which captured the features of important figures like **R. C. O. Benjamin,** Mary McLeod Bethune, George Washington Carver, **Benjamin Davis,** Frederick Douglass, Paul Laurence Dunbar, and **Carter G. Woodson.** In 1907, he moved to Washington, DC, and founded the Afro-Art Company, where he produced miniature busts of influential African American figures. Hathaway and his company later moved to Pine Bluff, AR, where he established a ceramics program at Arkansas State College. He also helped establish ceramics programs at the Tuskegee Institute, Alabama Polytechnic Institute, and Alabama State College, earning the informal title of "the dean of Negro ceramists." In 1947, the U.S. Mint asked him to create a commemorative coin for Booker T. Washington; he was the first African American commissioned to design a coin for that institution.

Hathaway died in Tuskegee, AL, on March 12, 1967. In 2002, a nonprofit committee called the Isaac Scott Hathaway Museum organized to promote his memory and art. The organization later moved to the Robert H. Williams Cultural Center in Lexington, KY.

Alabama Deaths and Burials Index, 1881–1974.
Fleming, G. James, and Christian E. Burckel, eds. *Who's Who in Colored America.* 7th ed. *Supplement.* Yonkers-on-Hudson, NY: Christian E. Burckel & Associates, 1950.
Newspapers: "Shifting Scenes," *IF,* May 7, 1904, 1; "Casting Light on Art History," *LHL,* March 5, 2003, B1; "Black History Museum Gets New Home—Will Move into History Center," *LHL,* December 25, 2006, A1.
U.S. Federal Census (1900).

—*Stephen Pickering*

HATHAWAY, JAMES HARRIS (b. ca. 1863, Mt. Sterling, KY; d. ca. 1950, Louisville, KY), businessman. Born the eldest child of Perry Hathaway, a farm hand, and his wife, Eliza, in Mt. Sterling, KY, James Harris Hathaway began his business career in his hometown. With limited education, he operated a profitable grocery venture. He then sold the business and moved to Louisville, where he acquired a wagon and started a transfer operation in the 1880s. Because of his success, his white competitor, Smith and Nixon, sold its wagons and horses to him and also contracted its business to him.

In 1892, Hathaway married Louisville native Columbia Gray, and that union produced six children. As his family grew, so did his business ventures. His transportation company provided vehicles for funerals, which led him to activate Falls City Undertaking and Embalming Company on Burnett Ave. in the Ft. Hill area in 1901. He advertised that he sold the best funeral supplies at the lowest cost. He also invested in over 100 acres of land in Jefferson Co., where he raised Thoroughbred horses, sheep, hogs, and cattle.

Hathaway managed his funeral business until his death. His middle daughter, Columbia, and her husband, Chester Clark, assumed ownership. In 2002, the U.S. Senate paid tribute to the renamed Hathaway and Clark Funeral Home, the oldest African American–owned and operated funeral home in Louisville, for its over 100 years of service to the community.

Congressional Record: Proceedings and Debates of the 107th Congress, Second Session, June 5, 2002.
Kentucky Death Records, 1852–1953.
Louisville, Kentucky, City Directory, 1890.
"New Firms." *LCJ,* December 31, 1901, 6.
Richardson, Clement. *The National Cyclopedia of the Colored Race.* Montgomery, AL: National Publishing Company, 1919.
U.S. Federal Census (1870, 1880, 1900, 1910, 1920, 1930).
U.S. Indexed County Land Ownership Maps, 1860–1918.

—*Sallie L. Powell*

HATHAWAY, JAMES SHELTON (b. 1859, Mt. Sterling, KY; d. 1930, Richmond, KY), educator. James S. Hathaway, son of Lewis and Ann Hathaway, was born into slavery in Mt. Sterling, Kentucky, on March 29, 1859. In 1875, he enrolled at **Berea College** and joined Union Church the following year. He graduated with honors in Berea's classical AB course in 1884. That year, Berea's president, E. Henry Fairchild, hired him to teach mathematics and Latin. He was one of two African American faculty members (the other was **Julia Britton Hooks**) at the college during Fairchild's administration. On July 21, 1887, he married Celia Anderson. He served as clerk of town for Berea and edited a newspaper, the *Lexington Standard.* He received a master's degree from Berea in 1891. In 1893, he angrily resigned his faculty position when President William Goodell Frost, Fairchild's replacement, charged him with incompetence and refused to promote him to a professorship. Hathaway and other African American alumni, in a pamphlet titled "Save Berea College for Christ and Humanity," maintained that Frost was marginalizing black Bereans in an effort to increase white Appalachian enrollments and segregate the college campus. Frost denied the charges but continued to implement his program.

Hathaway joined the faculty of the State Normal School for Colored Persons (later known as **Kentucky State University**), Frankfort, as an agriculture teacher in 1893. He became a respected member of the faculty and was appointed president of the institution in 1900. In 1902, the school became Kentucky Normal and Industrial Institute. According to the *Mt. Sterling Reporter,* Hathaway was a graduate not only of Berea College but also of Louisville National Medical College. He also served several years as president of the State Colored Teachers' Association.

Hathaway accepted the efficacy of separate industrial education for blacks rather than liberal arts and argued that it was the only hope for black youth to receive any higher education at all. In 1907, he was forced to resign the presidency of the institute for political reasons but returned, after serving as principal of Maysville Colored High School, on September 29, 1910. Two years later, after having achieved significant progress in academics and improvements in the school's physical plant, he resigned for the final time. Uncorroborated speculations hinted at fiscal irregularities.

Hathaway and his wife, Celia, had two children, James and Elizabeth. By 1920, he was principal of Richmond High School in Richmond, KY, and his daughter was a teacher. On February 18, 1930, Hathaway died of a cerebral hemorrhage.

Burnside, Jacqueline G. "Suspicion versus Faith: Negro Criticisms of Berea College in the Nineteenth Century." *RKHS* 83 (1985): 237–66.

Dunnigan, Alice Allison, comp. and ed. *The Fascinating Story of Black Kentuckians: Their Heritage and Traditions.* Washington, DC: Associated Publishers, 1982.

Hardin, John A. *Onward and Upward: A Centennial History of Kentucky State University, 1886–1986.* Frankfort: Kentucky State Univ., 1987.

"James Hathaway, A.M., M.D.," *Mt. Sterling (KY) Reporter,* April 14, 1906, 9.

Kentucky Death Records, 1852–1953.

Nelson, Paul David. "Experiment in Interracial Education at Berea College, 1858–1906." *JNH* 59 (1974): 13–27.

U.S. Federal Census (1920).

—*Paul David Nelson*

HATHAWAY, JOHN (b. ca. 1877, unknown; d. 1905, Winchester, KY), jockey. John Hathaway was an accomplished rider in his teen years. In 1892, he rode Notus on a rain-soaked track in Chicago's Garfield Derby but lost to **Tommy Britton,** who rode Yo Tambien. All the riders and their horses were covered in mud at the finish of the race.

The well-known jockey gained more notoriety for the way his life ended than for his racing accomplishments. After Hathaway retired from racing, he worked as a waiter at a hotel in Jackson, KY, where he lived with his girlfriend, Etta Thomas. For unknown reasons, she announced her plans to leave him and move to Winchester. Hathaway became enraged and tore her clothes; she still left him. In January 1904, Hathaway found Thomas at a Winchester brothel owned by Alice Bean. He persuaded the women to let him in and that he was only there to reimburse Thomas for the clothes he had ripped. When Hathaway was not able to persuade Thomas to leave with him, he shot her several times, killing her instantly, before trying unsuccessfully to kill himself.

Initially, Hathaway pleaded guilty. The first trial ended in a hung jury because one juror argued for a life sentence instead of the death penalty. The second trial in May 1894 rendered the "quickest verdict on record with a death penalty attached" in Winchester, KY. In less than 10 minutes, Hathaway was found guilty.

His attorneys unsuccessfully fought the verdict through the Court of Appeals in *Hathaway v. Commonwealth.* Kentucky governor John Crepps Wickliffe Beckham refused to commute his sentence to life imprisonment. Hathaway was baptized in a bathtub at the jail. Along with celebrated jockey **Jimmy "Wink" Winkfield,** who had just returned from racing in Russia, Hathaway's mother, Mary, and his sister visited him before the execution. On January 3, 1905, after drinking a cup of coffee and showing amazing courage, John Hathaway marched in a procession, including five African American ministers, to the scaffold in a blinding snowstorm in Winchester, KY. Hathaway's mother collapsed after her son's hanging and died shortly afterward. It was reported that Hathaway was "the first jockey of note to be hanged," and his execution was the first legal hanging in Clark Co. in over 50 years.

Hathaway v. Commonwealth of Kentucky, Ky. L. Rptr. 630 (July 15, 1904), 630–34.

Newspapers: *Earlington (KY) Bee,* July 21, 1904, 6; *Lexington (KY) Blue-grass Blade,* December 12, 1904, 4; *Bourbon News* (Paris, KY), January 3, 1905, 5; *Berea (KY) Citizen,* May 19, 1904; October 13, 1904, 6, and January 5, 1905, 6; *Clay City Times,* May 26, 1904, 3, and January 5, 1905, 3; *Maysville (KY) Daily Public Ledger,* May 23, 1904; *LL,* December 31, 1904, 4, and January 8, 1905, 1; *Lexington Morning Herald,* January 5, 1904; *Mt. Sterling Advocate,* May 25, 1904, 3; *Paducah Sun,* May 10, 1904, and January 3, 1905, 1; *Richmond Climax,* May 19, 1904, and December 28, 1904, 3; *Semi-weekly Interior Journal* (Springfield, KY), May 13, 1904, May 24 1904, 1, and October 14, 1904.

Southwestern Reporter 82 (August 17–December 7, 1904): 400–401.

—*Sallie L. Powell*

HAYDEN, ANDERSON "ANDREW" (b. 1852, Bourbon Co., KY; d. 1911, Lexington, KY), businessman. Anderson Hayden was born in slavery to Anderson and Cynthia Sherman Hayden of Bourbon Co., KY. Sometimes called Andrew, Hayden received little education, but he could read and write. He prospered in the blacksmith trade and was considered "one of the most proficient horseshoers" in the state. He and his wife, Anna, lived in a brick home in an otherwise all-white, prominent neighborhood in Cynthiana, KY. At times, they had a live-in cook and a servant. The Hayden children did not survive into adulthood, so Anna concentrated on the home. She was known for her "very large and fine collection of house plants." Her younger sister, Emma David, a chiropractor, lived with the Haydens for about 20 years. Anna's younger brother, Rev. **George Franklin David,** served several Kentucky African Methodist Episcopal churches and was a Kentucky delegate-at-large to the Republican National Convention in 1924.

The *Lexington Leader* described Hayden as "one of the most successful and enterprising colored citizens of Kentucky." He purchased rental property, and at his death, his estimated worth was between $30,000 and $40,000. He died at age 59 in Lexington's Eastern Kentucky Asylum for the Insane. He was buried in Cynthiana, where his wife died at age 92 in 1948.

"Colored Notes." *LL,* May 7, 1911, sec. 2, 10.

Kentucky Death Records, 1852–1953.

Richings, G. F. *Evidences of Progress among Colored People,* 10th ed. Philadelphia: George S. Ferguson Co., 1903.

U.S. Federal Census (1900, 1910, 1920, 1930).

—*Sallie L. Powell*

HAYDEN, LEWIS GRANT (b. ca. 1811, Lexington, KY; d. 1889, Boston, MA), escaped slave and antislavery activist. The slave of a Presbyterian minister in Lexington, KY, Lewis Grant had an epiphany at the age of 13 after the Marquis de Lafayette bowed his head to him during a trip through the countryside. Animated by a "hatred of slavery from that day," Grant experienced great personal tragedy as a slave in a border state, including having his first wife and child sold to Henry Clay and then farther south. He, too, was bought and sold on several occasions before he finally managed to escape to freedom with the help of **Delia Webster** and the **Underground Railroad.** After this escape, he changed his name to Lewis Hayden.

After brief stints in Canada and Detroit, Hayden moved to Boston, MA, where he became a leader in the abolitionist movement. After the passage of the Fugitive Slave Law, he actively supported the Boston Vigilance Committee and offered his house as a station for escaped slaves. At the outbreak of the Civil War, he recruited for the 54th Regiment, and he was elected to the Massachusetts legislature in 1873.

Lewis Hayden died on April 7, 1889. The *New York Times* reported that probably "no colored man who has passed away in Boston has been honored with a more imposing demonstration or greater evidence of esteem."

Collison, Gary. "'This Flagitious Offense': Daniel Webster and the Shadrach Rescue Cases, 1851–1862." *New England Quarterly* 68 (1995): 609–625.

Newspapers: "Lewis Hayden," *Rochester (NY) North Star,* July 21, 1848, 2; "Lewis Hayden Dead," *NYT,* April 8, 1889, 1; "Honors to a Colored Man," *NYT,* April 12, 1889, 2.

Robboy, Stanley J., and Anita W. Robboy. "Lewis Hayden: From Fugitive Slave to Statesman." *New England Quarterly* 46 (1973): 591–613.

Strangis, Joel. *Lewis Hayden and the War Against Slavery.* North Haven, CT: Linnet Books, 1999.

—Stephen Pickering

HAYDEN, WILLIAM (b. 1785, Bell-Plains, VA; d. unknown), slave-narrative author. Born in Bell-Plains, VA, in 1785, William Hayden was separated from his mother at the age of five when he was sold to an owner from Kentucky. He spent the next three decades with various masters throughout central Kentucky. Some masters were crueler than others. One promised him freedom after the wedding of her daughter but sold him soon after the marriage. Another master, Thomas Phillips of Georgetown, allowed Hayden the freedom to work for additional wages outside his duties as a slave.

Hayden proceeded to amass a large amount of personal savings by selling fish caught in the Kentucky River to local innkeepers, cleaning boots, chopping wood, washing dishes, and playing the tambourine at parties. He also worked for Elijah Craig, the owner of a Georgetown rope-making factory, where he eventually rose to the position of foreman. He later learned the barber trade and was so talented that his master built him his own barbershop in Georgetown.

Like many slaves, Hayden had a deep desire to learn to read and write. In 1804, while serving as a wagon maker in Lexington, he spent a portion of his earned wages to pay for evening literacy classes. He first practiced writing with a stick in the dirt and later with homemade ink on discarded paper he picked up on the Fayette County Courthouse floor. Within three years, he joined another slave from Lexington named Ned and taught a class of about 30 students at the night school.

In 1824, Hayden had saved enough money from his various endeavors to purchase his freedom. He eventually settled in Cincinnati, where he wrote a 154-page book, *Narrative of William Hayden: Containing a Faithful Account of His Travels for a Number of Years, Whilst a Slave, in the South,* describing his experiences as a slave in Kentucky. According to modern scholars, the work remains one of the more unusual slave narratives written during the antebellum era because Hayden focuses more on spiritual liberation than on the brutalities of slavery.

Bland, Sterling Lecater, Jr., ed. *African American Slave Narratives: An Anthology.* Vol. 1. Westport, CT: Greenwood Press, 2001.

Hayden, William. *Narrative of William Hayden: Containing a Faithful Account of His Travels for a Number of Years, Whilst a Slave, in the South.* Cincinnati: s.n., 1846.

Lucas, Marion B. *A History of Blacks in Kentucky.* Vol. 1, *From Slavery to Segregation, 1760–1891.* Frankfort: Kentucky Historical Society, 1992.

—Joshua D. Farrington

HAYES, CLIFFORD (b. 1895, near Glasgow, KY; d. 1957, Ohio), jug band, blues, and jazz fiddler. Born into a family of talented African American musicians, Hayes learned to play the fiddle at an early age and performed with his brothers in a string band. About 1914, the family moved to Louisville, where Hayes became an integral part of Earl McDonald's Louisville **Jug Band,** playing **blues** and popular tunes. From 1915 to 1927, he traveled with McDonald, visiting New York, Chicago, and Atlanta for recording sessions and performances. By 1927, he was fronting his own band, playing more **jazz** and blues and fewer jug band standards. He continued playing music until his death.

—Brenda K. Bogert

HAYES, EDGAR JUNIUS (b. 1904, Lexington, KY; d. 1979, San Bernardino, CA), pianist, composer, and bandleader. Edgar Junius Hayes, the son of Edward and Fanny Hayes, was born in Lexington, KY, on May 23, 1904. He started playing the piano at age six. He studied at Fisk University and graduated from Wilberforce University with a degree in music in the early 1920s. After graduation, instead of accepting a scholarship at Oberlin to acquire his master's degree, he played professionally and led several bands.

In 1931, Hayes joined the Mills Blue Rhythm Band in New York City as an arranger, pianist, and part-time musical director. Hayes was instrumental in the band's high-quality recordings and performances and stayed with the band until 1937. He then formed his own band. The Edgar Hayes Orchestra was highly regarded, often mentioned as slightly below the level of the very best big bands of that era, led by Duke Ellington, Jimmie Lunceford, and Count Basie. The band's only commercial hit, recorded in February 1938, was "Stardust," featuring Hayes on the piano. The flip side of "Stardust" was the song "In the Mood." Glenn Miller liked "In the Mood" and recorded it at a slower tempo. With a few other minor changes, it became the biggest-selling record of 1940, and arguably the most recognized song of the big-band era, but Edgar Hayes's band recorded it first and in a much more swinging version.

Despite its touring success, the band never had another hit record. Hayes broke up the band and moved to Southern California in 1942. He performed regularly into the 1970s, primarily as a solo pianist at clubs, bars, and restaurants. He died in San Bernardino, CA, on June 28, 1979.

"Edgar Hayes, Jazz Pianist, Longs for the Concert Stage." *BAA*, March 2, 1935, 9.

Schuller, Gunther. *The Swing Era: The Development of Jazz, 1930–1945.* New York: Oxford Univ. Press, 1989.

Simon, George T. *The Big Bands.* 3rd ed. New York, Macmillan, 1973.

—*Michael A. Richardson*

HAYES, EDYTHE LARSENIA JONES (b. 1933, Selma, AL; d. 1999, Lexington, KY), educator. Born on August 3, 1933, in Selma, AL, Edythe Larsenia Jones earned a bachelor's degree from West Virginia State University in 1952. The following year, she received her master's from the University of Kentucky and began her career as a teacher at Lexington's Carver Elementary School. For the next 43 years, she served the school system in a variety of positions, including principal, supervisor of federal programs, supervisor of special education, adult education department head, special projects assistant, assistant superintendent, and deputy superintendent for administration. In 1972, she was the first African American woman to serve as an assistant superintendent in Fayette Co. She designed and guided the implementation of the school improvement councils, a forerunner of the school-based decision-making councils established under the Kentucky Education Reform Act. With the Lexington Chamber of Commerce, she helped establish a successful school/business partnership. She developed programs for at-risk children to ensure that strategies were in place to help children with special needs. She provided leadership to the school district's Task Force on Excellence and the Equity Task Force.

In 1980, she became the first African American woman to be named to the University of Kentucky Board of Trustees, where she served as secretary and acting chairwoman. She also served on the **Kentucky State University** Board of Regents, the Lexington Community College advisory board, and the Kentucky Edu-

cational Television, Bluegrass Airport, Lexington Salvation Army, and Urban League boards. Among the awards she received were a Community Achiever Award from the YMCA Black Achievers program, the Optimist Cup, and a YWCA Women of Achievement Award.

After her retirement in 1992, the Fayette County Board of Education named the Edythe J. Hayes Middle School in her honor. Her husband, Arthur Eugene Hayes, a retired army lieutenant colonel, Veterans Affairs Medical Center physical therapist, and owner and operator of H-Lawn Acres farm, died on February 4, 1997. Edythe Hayes died on February 22, 1999. Both were buried in Lexington Cemetery. Edythe Hayes was survived by her mother, Lucy Jones, two sons, Eric and Rodney, and six grandchildren.

Newspapers: "High-Ranking Black Administrator Gets No. 2 Spot in Fayette Schools," *LHL*, March 17, 1987, B1; "Obituaries—Lexington and State," *LHL*, February 6, 1997, C2; "Edythe Jones Hayes, 1933–1999: Longtime Assistant Fayette Schools Chief," *LHL*, February 24, 1999, B1.

—*Charles F. Faber*

HAYES, ROLAND WILTSIE (b. 1887, near Curryville, GA; d. 1977, Boston, MA), African American tenor. Roland Wiltsie Hayes was one of seven children of William and Fannie (Mann) Hayes, a former slave. He studied voice in Chattanooga with Arthur Calhoun and later attended Fisk University in Nashville. Moving to Louisville in 1910, he became a waiter at the Pendennis Club. There he attracted the attention of the city's business and musical elite, who arranged for him to study in Boston. He made his debut there on November 11, 1915, at Jordan Hall.

During his career of almost 60 years, Hayes sang hundreds of recitals in America and Europe. Between 1918 and 1961, he presented 16 programs in Louisville halls that included **Quinn Chapel A.M.E. Church;** Macauley's, Brown, and National Theaters; Louisville Memorial Auditorium; and **Central High School.** To acknowledge his status as an artist and role model for succeeding generations of African American singers, the University of Louisville awarded him an honorary doctor of humanities degree in 1972.

In 1932, Hayes married Helen Alzada Mann, his first cousin, in California, where he was appearing at the Hollywood Bowl. One daughter, Afrika Fanzada Hayes, was born in 1935. On January 1, 1977, Hayes died of pneumonia and is buried in Mt. Hope Cemetery in Mattapan, MA.

Carter, Marva Griffin. "In Retrospect: Roland Hayes—Expressor of the Soul in Song." *Black Perspective in Music* 5 (Fall 1977): 189–220.

Helm, MacKinley. *Angel Mo' and Her Son, Roland Hayes.* Boston: Little, Brown and Company, 1942.

LCJ, February 19, 1990.

Marr, Warren II. "Conversation with Roland Hayes." *Black Perspective in Music* 2 (Fall 1974): 186–90.

Woolsey, F. W. "Conversation with Roland Hayes." *Black Perspective in Music* 2 (Fall 1974): 179–85.

—*Robert Bruce French*

HELEM, CARL C. "KINGFISH" (b. 1925, Horse Cave, KY; d. 2001, Ashland, KY), basketball player who played for the Harlem Globetrotters from 1948 to 1955. A native of Horse

Edythe Hayes, being sworn in as a board of trustees member, 1980.

Cave, KY, Carl C. Helem played center for Horse Cave Colored High School's basketball team. He had to deal with the usual hindrances faced by the attendees of an impoverished, neglected school. The coach of the basketball team, Newton Thomas, had little knowledge of the sport before Helem's arrival, and the team was forced to practice outside on a clay court because the school had no money for a gym. In 1944, however, Helem led the team to an undefeated season and the state championship of the all-black Kentucky High School Athletic League. Named the tournament's most valuable player, he then repeated the feat the next year, giving the Horse Cave Tigers back-to-back state championships.

After high school, Helem joined the Tennessee State University Tigers, beginning another productive run as a basketball player. Helem led the team in scoring his freshman year, was twice named an All-Midwest player, and was part of a team that lost only eight games between 1945 and 1949. Helem left before his senior year to marry Jacquelyn Coleman, but his speed and scoring ability drew attention. In 1948, he left Kentucky for Chicago, hoping to continue his basketball career professionally.

In Chicago, Helem tried out for the Harlem Globetrotters, although he later admitted that he thought he had little chance of making the squad. To his surprise, the team chose him from about 80 other players, and he was soon traveling across the country with a new team and a new nickname, Kingfish. Helem played for the Globetrotters for eight years. During his tenure with the team, the Globetrotters twice beat the defending National Basketball Association champion Minnesota Lakers, and the team played overseas for the first time in 1950.

In 1999, Helem received several honors at a luncheon held at the Metropolitan Club in Covington, KY. The Globetrotters named him a Legend, an award given to only 13 previous Globetrotters before Helem's selection. On the same night, Ashland Inc. also honored Helem for 35 years of service in maintenance and security at its Catlettsburg refinery, a job he had held since retiring from the Globetrotters in 1955. Two years later, Helem died of congestive heart failure in Ashland at the age of 75. In 2006, his daughter, Carla Cecilia Helem, a Vietnam War navy veteran, died.

Burdette, Dick. *Jump, Johnny, Jump!* Bloomington, IN: AuthorHouse, 2007.

Newspapers: "50 Years Later, Tigers Recall Times They Roared," *LHL,* September 27, 1996, B1; "Ky. Globetrotter Honored Living Legend from Horse Cave," *LHL,* December 31, 1999, C1; "Ex–Horse Cave Standout Legendary Globetrotter 'Kingfish' Helped Harlem Conquer Lakers," *LHL,* February 20, 2001, C4.

—*Stephen Pickering*

HELM, MARLENE M. (b. 1949, Buffalo, NY), first African American female superintendent of a school district in Kentucky. A longtime supporter of education in Kentucky, Marlene M. Helm, after completing high school in Buffalo, NY, earned a bachelor's degree in elementary education from **Kentucky State University** in 1971. In 1976, she received a master's degree from the University of Kentucky, and she earned a doctoral degree in education from the same institution in 1990. During this time, she worked for the Scott Co. school system and as a Lexington schoolteacher.

Helm also served in a variety of roles in administration for both education and local government. In 1999, Kentucky governor Paul Patton pulled her from the Council on Postsecondary Education, a position to which he had appointed her in 1997, and asked her to work as secretary of the Education, Arts, and Humanities Cabinet. In 2004, the Fayette County Board of Education unanimously selected her as the interim superintendent of Fayette Co. schools, the first African American superintendent of a school district on either an interim or a full-time basis. After her three-month stint as superintendent, Helm joined Eastern Kentucky University's staff as interim dean of college education. She served there for a year before Lexington mayor-elect Jim Newberry selected her as his commissioner of social services.

In recognition of her work in Kentucky, Helm has received several awards and honors. In 2005, the University of Kentucky **Lyman T. Johnson** Alumni Club awarded her its Torch of Excellence, and in the same year the YMCA of Central Kentucky Black Achievers named her its winner of the Community Achiever of the Year award. The Kentucky Governor's School for the Arts has also named an award in her honor, granting the Marlene M. Helm Award to alumni of the GSA program who contribute to the arts in their community.

In 2011, Helm became the chair of the Graduate Teacher Education Program at Midway College in Midway, KY. The next year, she was appointed vice president for academic affairs, Midway College's top academic post.

Newspapers: "Governor Appoints 2 Cabinet Secretaries," *LHL,* March 11, 1999, B1; "Interim Leader for Schools Is Selected—Black Woman Is First to Hold Post in Kentucky," *LHL,* March 18, 2004, A1; "Black Achievers Presents '05 Awards," *LHL,* May 3, 2005, B3; "New Mayor's Leadership Team Has Familiar Faces—Threat of Veto Clouds Beatty's Appointment," *LHL,* December 22, 2006, A1; "Midway College Promotes Helm," *LHL,* May 2, 2012, C2.

—*Stephen Pickering*

HENDERSON, CHARLES L. (b. 1893, Paris, KY; d. 1918, France), first African American from Covington to die in France during World War I. Charles L. Henderson, the son of Harriet Lee, was the first African American from Covington to be killed in action while serving in France during World War I. On April 1, 1918, Henderson was among the first African Americans to depart Covington for Camp Zachary Taylor in Louisville. He was with the 325th Field Signal Battalion, 92nd Infantry Division. These African Americans, drafted into the U.S. Army by the Covington Selective Service Board, were given a grand send-off by the community, family, and friends, as demonstrated by the brass band that accompanied them to their train. When Henderson died, the military authorities had a difficult time locating his nearest relative, even though his mother, his brother, and a nephew were living in Covington. Henderson was buried in the Oise-Aisne American Cemetery, Fère-en-Tardenois, France.

On September 1, 1919, World War I veterans in Covington decided to honor their fallen comrades by organizing an American Legion post. Henderson was honored by the naming of the Charles L. Henderson American Legion Post No. 166. William H. Martin Jr., a veteran of World War I, was selected as its first commander. In May 1932, Charles H. Bishop became the new commander at an installation held at the Knights of Pythias Hall. In July of that year, a minstrel show was presented under the sponsorship of Post No. 166 at its post home at Prospect and Wheeler Sts. In December 1941, Post No. 166 was reactivated just before Pearl Harbor. The Charles L. Henderson American Legion Post No. 166 remains an active part of the community.

Newspapers: "Selects Start Soldier Life," *KP*, April 1, 1918, 1; "To Form Negro Post," *KP*, September 1, 1919, 2; "Seeking Kin of Dead Soldier," *KTS*, November 4, 1919, 28; "Soldier's Kin Sought," *KP*, November 4, 1919, 1; "Legion to Install," *KP*, May 6, 1932, 7; "Officers Installed," *KP*, May 10, 1932, 2; "Plan Minstrel Show," *KP*, July 19, 1932, 1; "To Give Minstrel Show," *KP*, July 24, 1932, 8; Jim Reis, "All Quiet on the Home-Front Then Came Pearl Harbor," *KP*, December 7, 1998, 4K.

—*Theodore H. H. Harris*

HENDERSON, DENNIS (b. 1896, Grenada, MS; d. 1979, Louisville, KY), second African American representative elected to the Kentucky General Assembly. Dennis Henderson was born to Augustus H. and Rosa Henderson on January 20, 1896. Although his parents were farmers in rural Mississippi, Henderson attended Talladega College and received his law degree from Howard University in 1923. The following year, he moved to Louisville and eventually became a partner in the Ray and Henderson Law Agency.

In 1947, Louisville's only black representative, **Charles W. Anderson,** declined to run for another term, and Henderson won the Republican Party's nomination in the primary. That November, he defeated **William Childress** in the race for state representative of Kentucky's 42nd Legislative District. In winning, he became the second African American elected to the General Assembly.

Even though he served only one term, Henderson introduced numerous civil rights bills in his two years in Frankfort. In 1948, he sought to amend the **Day Law** to permit blacks to attend graduate and professional schools in the state, thus integrating them. He also introduced legislation that would have allowed African Americans to try on clothing in stores without being required to buy it (which was a private code practiced by stores throughout the state). Despite their moderate nature, both bills were rejected. His major accomplishment was sponsoring and pushing through the assembly a bill that allowed black nurses to train alongside white nurses at hospitals per their governing boards' approval. Although it was a modest bill, for the first time since the Day Law was passed in 1904, a form of integrated education was legal in Kentucky.

Henderson continued to practice law into the 1950s and became a major stockholder and director of **Domestic Life and Accident Insurance Company** in the late 1950s and early 1960s. He died in Louisville in 1979.

"FDR Independent Voters League Neutral on Childress and Henderson." *Louisville Leader*, November 1, 1947.
Fleming, G. James, and Christian E. Burckel, eds. *Who's Who in Colored America.* 7th ed. Yonkers-on-Hudson, NY: Christian E. Burckel & Associates, 1950.

Hardin, John A. *Fifty Years of Segregation: Black Higher Education in Kentucky, 1904–1954.* Lexington: Univ. Press of Kentucky, 1997.
"Risk Stockholders May Get Big Sums for Shares," *Jet*, February 9, 1961, 49.

—*Joshua D. Farrington*

HENDERSON, ERSKINE "BABE" (b. ca. 1864, unknown; d. 1913, Versailles, KY), jockey. Erskine "Babe" Henderson rode in the **Kentucky Derby** three times. In 1882, when he was 18 years old, Henderson placed sixth aboard Pat Malloy behind the winner, Apollo, ridden by African American jockey **"Babe" Hurd.** The next year, his horse, Chatter, started the race with the lead pack but fell to the rear. The 21-year-old's racing experience proved beneficial when he rode Joe Cotton, owned by Capt. Jim T. Williams and conditioned by African American trainer Abe Perry, in the 1885 Kentucky Derby.

Favored to win, Henderson and Joe Cotton received rousing applause from the 16,000 spectators when they entered the track. He controlled his horse in the race with a firm hand, and his knees kept Joe Cotton on the outside of the middle pack of 10 Thoroughbreds. Henderson at the three-quarter post made his move and started passing the leaders. In the homestretch, he used the whip and spurs on Joe Cotton to barely beat Bersan, the runner-up, and came within a half second of the fastest Kentucky Derby track speed. The winning stake was worth about $4,500. A month later, Henderson rode Joe Cotton to win the Tennessee Derby. Some scholars believe that Henderson also rode Joe Cotton that same year in winning his third derby in New York, but the 1885 *New York Times* and the *Chicago Tribune* listed James "Jimmy" McLaughlin as the jockey who won the Coney Island Derby on Joe Cotton.

Henderson disappeared from the public arena after his derby wins. In 1913, nearly 50 years old, he reportedly revisited the Kentucky Derby as a trainer who was "still small enough to gallop his own horses." Henderson died in Versailles, KY, a few months later around Thanksgiving Day.

Leach, George B. *The Kentucky Derby Diamond Jubilee.* Louisville, KY: Gibbs-Inman Co., 1949.
Newspapers: "Crowding the Record," *LCJ*, May 15, 1885, 6; "Joe Cotton Beats Tyrant," *NYT*, June 21, 1885, 5; "Colored Notes," *LL*, November 26, 1913, 5.
Renau, Lynn S. *Racing around Kentucky.* Louisville, KY: L. S. Renau, 1995.
Saunders, James Robert, and Monica Renae Saunders. *Black Winning Jockeys in the Kentucky Derby.* Jefferson, NC: McFarland, 2003.

—*Sallie L. Powell*

HENDERSON, JENNIE KATHERINE EDMONIA (b. 1900, Jefferson Co., KY; d. 1947, Louisville, KY), blues singer and evangelist. Between 1924 and 1926, Jennie Katherine Edmonia Henderson traveled to Chicago to make **blues** records for Paramount, Okeh, and Vocalion. Her accompanists included top **jazz** musicians such as Jelly Roll Morton, Tommy Ladnier, and Johnny Dodds. By 1928, she was teaching music and giving gospel concerts at the Griffith Conservatory of Music at 1412 W. Chestnut St. in Louisville. By 1932, she had married and had become the

Reverend Edmonia Buckner, pastor of the Church of the Living God at 1821 W. **Walnut St.** (**Muhammad Ali** Blvd.). She is buried in Louisville Cemetery.

—Brenda K. Bogert

HENDERSON PUBLIC LIBRARY, the first library structure built specifically for African Americans in 1904. The product of a grant from Andrew Carnegie and years of activism on the part of Edward Asher Jonas, a local newspaper publisher, the Henderson Public Library opened on August 1, 1904. Headed by local archivist and historian Susan Towles, the library held an initial offering of 500 books that would be available to any resident of the city of Henderson.

The Henderson Public Library was particularly novel in that it also opened a branch for the African American population, which was located in a single-room annex at the back of the Eight Street Colored School. The result of "the intelligent and fair action of the public school board," the annex served a dual purpose, answering the demands of African Americans for library access while maintaining the main branch for white patrons. The accommodations were far from equal. The main branch of the library held 500 books and received roughly $3,000 over the space of five years, whereas the branch for the city's black citizens contained only 100 books with a budget for the same period of $234. The two branches even held separate opening ceremonies; a newspaper noted that the opening of the main branch garnered the attention of a "large crowd of Henderson's best people," while a "large crowd of the colored citizens" performed similar procedures at the annex.

During the next few decades after opening, the annex increased its collection to over 1,500 books and was moved to a new location to handle increased patronage. In 1942, the library increased the clientele of the branches even further by opening lending privileges to residents of the county, who had previously been unable to check out books. In 1954, the library marked an end to segregation by merging the two branches into one location. Despite its closing, the African American branch of the Henderson Public Library marked a turning point in the history of libraries nationally because it was the first structure of its type built specifically to serve African Americans in the community.

Arnett, Maralea. *The Annals and Scandals of Henderson County, Kentucky, 1775–1975.* Corydon, KY: Fremar, 1976.

Jones, Reinette F. *Library Service to African Americans in Kentucky, from the Reconstruction Era to the 1960s.* Jefferson, NC: McFarland, 2001.

"Public Library Opened Last Night." *Henderson Daily Gleaner,* August 4, 1904, 1.

Wright, George C. *A History of Blacks in Kentucky.* Vol. 2, *In Pursuit of Equality, 1890–1980.* Frankfort: Kentucky Historical Society, 1992.

—Stephen Pickering

HENRY BAIN SAUCE, barbeque sauce. The recipe for Henry Bain Sauce, created and served at the Pendennis Club, 218 W. **Muhammad Ali** Blvd. and heralded as a "delightful concoction which seems to make even the finest cut of beef taste just a little

better," is a closely guarded secret. It was named after its originator, an African American who was a 40-year employee of the club. He began work as an elevator operator in the 1880s and later became the headwaiter of the club's dining room. Bain, who died on May 1, 1928, was also the uncle of famed singer **Roland Hayes.**

Centennial of the Pendennis Club. Louisville, KY: The Pendennis Club 1981.

HENSON, JOSIAH (b. 1789, Charles Co., MD; d. 1883, Dresden, Ontario), runaway slave and abolitionist spokesman. Josiah Henson, born on June 15, 1789, in Charles Co., MD, was a runaway slave from Kentucky who wrote an autobiography said to have influenced Harriet Beecher Stowe's **Uncle Tom's Cabin** (1852). Advocates of this view say that Stowe read Henson's book, first published in 1849 and later in half a dozen editions and adaptations, and used him as the model for her Uncle Tom. Although these claims are debatable, Kentucky has placed a historical marker east of Owensboro in Daviess Co. on U.S. 60 near the spot where Henson, or "Uncle Tom," had a cabin. In 1825, Henson led 18 slaves from Maryland to relocate on the Amos Riley farm in Daviess Co., where he became an overseer. The next five years proved crucial for him. For one thing, he became a preacher, which gave him a sense of mission. For another, in spite of dedicated service to the Rileys, he narrowly avoided being sold, an experience that prompted him in 1830 to escape to Canada with his wife and four children. During his years there, Henson founded a community for runaway slaves and became a popular abolitionist speaker. Henson died on May 5, 1883, and was buried by the black community of Dresden, Ontario.

Lobb, John ed. *An Autobiography of the Rev. Josiah Henson ("Uncle Tom") from 1789 to 1881.* London, Ontario: Schuyler Smith and Co., 1881.

—Dan Bradshaw

HERNDON, JAMES R. "SWEET EVENING BREEZE" (b. 1892, Scott Co., KY; d. 1983, Lexington, KY), early African American cross-dresser. Lexington has had many colorful characters in its history, including James Herndon, better known as Sweet Evening Breeze or Sweets. He was born in Scott Co., the seventh child of John and Kate Herndon, on July 2, 1892. Stories abound about the eccentric, cross-dressing performer, including one that Herndon told in an interview. At a young age, he suffered an eye injury. An uncle took him to Lexington's Good Samaritan Hospital and abandoned him for some unknown reason. Many at the hospital, including Lake Johnson, the hospital administrator, befriended Herndon. Growing up in the hospital, he learned to entertain patients with a ukulele and to deliver the mail.

Although elements of the story may be true, census files document Herndon living with his family, including his younger brother, Eugene, in Georgetown, KY, in 1900 and 1910. The records list his age as 5 and 16. By 1920, he lived with his uncle, Andrew Smith, and worked as a hospital orderly, a position he held for over 40 years. This employment brought in a high income, which was very unusual for an African American at this time of segregation. Herndon eventually bought and moved into a house at 186 Prall St., in an African American neighborhood over 100 years old.

Herndon was one of the key figures of early gay rights in Lexington. He frequently wore a gown or tailored suit, applied makeup, and walked the city streets with long strides. In an era when this was unacceptable, he somehow seemed to make it work. As people passed him on the street, they would shout a greeting to him, wave, or honk their car horns, and he would respond with a smile and a wave. He was seen on many occasions visiting the Phoenix Hotel and the Gilded Cage Bar. Whenever the hospital held a doctor/nurse basketball game, he was their cheerleader. In his drag-queen regalia, he danced "The Dance of the Bongo Bangoes" at Woodland Park Auditorium. During World War II and after, he would meet the troop trains that came into town and would offer the soldiers his famous homemade "sweet cakes," which earned him the name Sweets. He had a very deep faith and attended the **Historic Pleasant Green Missionary Baptist Church** on W. Maxwell St.

On February 19, 1969, a young African American, Leigh Angelique, was arrested for violating Lexington's ordinance against cross-dressing except on Halloween. Attorney Harry Miller took the case, and Herndon testified on behalf of the "girl" and proceeded to persuade Judge James Amato to dismiss the case by pointing to a woman in the courtroom and saying that if Angelique was to be arrested for wearing makeup, the woman should be, too. In the end, Lexington's ordinance against public drag was apparently overturned, and gays for years celebrated that day as Bastille Day.

James Herndon moved to the Homestead Nursing Center for his final years and died on Friday, December 16, 1983. He was buried in the Lexington Cemetery. After his death, the Royal Sovereign Imperial Court of Kentucky, a drag-queen group, created the James Herndon Award as its highest award. The Lexington Men's Chorus named a small ensemble group Sweet Evening Breeze.

Edwards, Don. "Cross-Dresser of Yesteryear Was a Test of Tolerance." *LHL,* July 8, 1999, B-1.

Hewlett, Jennifer. "Retired Orderly Sweet Evening Breeze, Dies." *LHL,* December 18, 1983, B-9.

Holland, Jeffrey Scott. "Sweet Evening Breeze." In *Weird Kentucky.* New York: Sterling, 2008, 101.

Jones, Jeff. "A Sweet Evening Breeze in Lexington." *Chevy Chaser Magazine* (Lexington, KY), September 2002.

U.S. Federal Census (1900, 1910, 1920).

—*Kris Clark*

HICKMAN, DANIEL (b. 1841, Scott Co., KY; d. 1917, Topeka, KS), colonizer and religious leader of the African American community in Nicodemus, KS. One of the first **Exodusters** to abandon the Upper South for Kansas in the 1870s, Daniel Hickman was born into slavery in Scott Co., KY, in 1841. While he was a slave, Hickman challenged authority by secretly learning to read and write, and he became a Christian in 1862. After the conclusion of the Civil War and the end of slavery in Kentucky, he pursued a career as a minister, preaching at several churches before settling at Mount Olive Baptist Church in Dry Run, KY. In an

attempt to find a better life for his family and followers, he then assembled an expedition west that eventually reached **Nicodemus,** KS, in 1878.

In Nicodemus, Hickman established himself as a civic and religious leader. In 1879, he and a few of his followers built a church with a sod edifice—the first building constructed for worship in the county—that they named Mount Olive after their former place of worship. Hickman also dabbled in local politics, participating in a contentious feud over the location of the county seat and earning election as county coroner and chairman of the Graham County Commissioners during the 1880s and 1890s. He continued to work as a minister and briefly as a custodian at the state capitol before his death on November 17, 1917. He was buried in Mount Olive Cemetery in Nicodemus, KS, next to the church that he had helped build.

"Daniel Hickman." In *The African American National Biography,* edited by Henry Louis Gates Jr. and Evelyn Brooks Higginbotham, 4. New York: Oxford Univ. Press, 2008.

Hamilton, Kenneth Marvin. *Black Towns and Profit: Promotion and Development in the Trans-Appalachian West, 1877–1915.* Urbana: Univ. of Illinois Press, 1991.

U.S. Department of the Interior. *Promised Land on the Solomon: Black Settlement at Nicodemus, Kansas.* Washington, DC: Government Printing Office, 1986.

—*Stephen Pickering*

HIGGINS, CHESTER A., JR. (b. 1946, Lexington, KY), staff photographer at the *New York Times* and creator of several photography exhibitions and books. Born in Lexington, KY, Chester A. Higgins Jr., the son of prominent journalist and magazine editor **Chester A. Higgins Sr.,** grew up in New Brockton, AL, a small town south of Montgomery. He displayed early interests in biology and electronics and briefly worked as an electrician and plumber in a nearby town. In 1967, while attending Tuskegee University as a business administration major, he became interested in photography during a stint with the school newspaper. A year later, he bought his own camera and took pictures across the country to expose the problems facing black students and the conflicts over Vietnam.

After working with the American Society of Magazine Photographers and several years of freelance photography, Higgins signed on as a staff photographer for the *New York Times* in 1975, becoming the first person to be hired as a staff photographer by the *Times* without any experience as a news photographer. Higgins and his wife, Louisville native **Renelda Meeks Higgins Walker,** also worked together for the *Crisis.* He has since become a world-renowned photographer, a "cultural anthropologist with a camera," as he calls himself, whose photographs have appeared in *Life, Time, Newsweek,* and other magazines. He has also created numerous significant art exhibitions centered on his photography and has published several books celebrating the dignity, decency, and character of the experience of people of color.

Newspapers: "Chester Higgins: Hunter of Images," *Indianapolis Recorder,* October 29, 1994, A1; "Feeling the Spirit: Works by Photographer Chester Higgins Jr. Reflect 26-Year-Old Search for 'His People' across the Globe," *Tri-State Defender,* May 20, 1998, 1B.

Rupp, Carla Marie. "People-Watching Pastime Pays Off for Photographer." *Editor and Publisher* 111 (1978): 36–38.

—*Stephen Pickering*

HIGGINS, CHESTER A., SR. (b. 1917, Chicago, IL; d. 2000, Washington, DC), writer and editor for numerous newspapers and magazines, including the *Louisville Defender* and *Jet* magazine. After moving with his family from Chicago to Lexington at an early age, Chester A. Higgins Sr. received his education at several Kentucky institutions, including **Dunbar High School,** Kentucky State College (later known as **Kentucky State University**), **Louisville Municipal College,** and the University of Louisville. In 1941, Higgins enlisted in the 758th Tank Battalion, which was stationed at Ft. Knox. During his service in the army, Higgins endured virulent racism and harsh living conditions because of the unit's segregation, under which he and his fellow black soldiers were confined to the worst temporary housing in Ft. Knox in a corner called Tent City.

His experiences with racial tension in the war and elsewhere fed into an activism for African American rights that manifested itself in a prolonged and significant career in journalism and print media. Beginning with a position as a reporter and feature writer for the *Louisville Defender,* Higgins went on to perform a variety of roles for nearly as many newspapers and magazines, including stints as an editor of the Detroit edition of the *Pittsburgh Courier,* contributing editor of *Ebony* and *Tan* magazines, and senior editor of *Jet* magazine. He supplemented his time in journalism with other jobs as well, teaching at Malcolm X College in Chicago and serving as an adjunct professor at Howard University. He also contributed to several larger organizations, taking a job in 1976 as assistant chief in the Public Affairs Office of the Department of the Army and supporting the **National Association for the Advancement of Colored People** by editing its *Crisis* magazine from 1981 to 1983.

In 2000, Chester Higgins Sr. died at age 83 in Washington, DC, and was buried in Arlington National Cemetery. Two months before his death, the Kentucky House of Representatives adjourned in his honor, passing several resolutions acknowledging "his immeasurable contributions to the Commonwealth of Kentucky." He was the father of **Chester A. Higgins Jr.,** a renowned photographer for the *New York Times.*

"Chester A. Higgins, Sr.; Writer and Editor." *WP,* May 30, 2000.
Higgins, Chester A., Sr. Review of *Hit Hard,* by David Williams. *Crisis* 90 (1983): 45–47.
Kentucky House of Representatives. HR168. Frankfort, KY, March 20, 2000.

—*Stephen Pickering*

HIGGS, KENNETH "KENNY," JR. (b. 1955, Owensboro, KY), basketball player inducted into the Louisiana Basketball Hall of Fame. Kenny Higgs was an All-American point guard who played for Owensboro High School. He led the school to a state basketball championship in 1972. He finished his high school career with more than 2,200 points, averaging 27.1 points and 6.1 assists a game. He was also runner-up for the state's Mr. Basketball title when he graduated in 1974. Recruited by a number of major programs, Higgs signed with the Louisiana State University bas-

ketball program under Coach Dale Brown. "I was looking for more than basketball," recalled Higgs. "I was looking to build a foundation and a life after basketball." Higgs became known as the "most prolific assist-maker" in the school's history. He set both Southeastern Conference and school records with 645 career assists. During one game, he scored 44 points. At LSU, Higgs gained honorable mention All-American honors twice and was selected to the All–Southeastern Conference second team three times.

In 1978, Higgs was drafted 13th in the third round by the National Basketball Association's Cleveland Cavaliers where he played during the 1978–1979 season. He played two years (1980–1982) with the Denver Nuggets. After three years in the NBA, Higgs played basketball overseas. He eventually returned to Owensboro to lead the Kenny Higgs School of Professional Basketball with a focus on enhancing the skills of elementary and middle school students. His younger half brother, **Mark Higgs,** signed to play football with the University of Kentucky in 1984 and later played running back for four National Football League teams.

In 1997, Kenny Higgs was recognized as one of the 50 greatest players to play in the Dust Bowl at Kendall-Perkins Park in Owensboro. In 2011, Higgs was inducted into the Louisiana Basketball Hall of Fame. "Every player wants to be inducted or be remembered for something they've done in life. LSU was the beginning of the whole start of life for me," said Higgs.

LSUsports. May 6, 2011. http://www.lsusports.net/ViewArticle.dbml?DB_OEM_ID=52–&A (accessed December 13, 2012).
Newspapers: "Higgs Says He'll Sign with Cats Wednesday," *LHL,* February 7, 1984, C1; "Dust Bowl Names Top 50 Players of All Time," *OMI,* July 23, 1997, 1B; "Young Players Attempt to Follow Higgs Path," *OMI,* July 18, 1998, 1A.

—*Gerald L. Smith*

HIGGS, MARK DEYON (b. 1966, Owensboro, KY), professional football player. Born on April 11, 1966, in Owensboro, KY, Mark Deyon Higgs, half brother of professional basketball player **Kenneth "Kenny" Higgs Jr.,** led Owensboro High School in rushing yards as a football running back. In 1984, his senior season, he ran for 2,858 yards and scored 32 touchdowns, becoming a senior All-American and a two-time all-stater. At 5-feet-8 and 185 pounds, he ran for 6,721 yards in his four-year high school career, surpassing **Alfred "Sonny" Collins**'s record set in Madisonville, KY, in 1971.

Even though some people questioned his size for playing football, Higgs signed with the University of Kentucky (UK). From 1984 to 1987, despite a knee injury, he scored 26 touchdowns and rushed for 2,982 yards, second to Collins's rushing record at UK. In 1988, the Dallas Cowboys drafted him in the eighth round and he played one season for them. He then played one season for the Philadelphia Eagles. He spent four years with the Miami Dolphins and was the team's leading rusher for three consecutive seasons. In 1994, the Dolphins released him even though he had a career-high 915 yards that season. He then played one year for the Arizona Cardinals before leaving professional football.

In 1996, Higgs established M&T Transportation, a firm that managed shuttle-bus drivers at Ft. Lauderdale–Hollywood International Airport. In 2005, he was inducted into the newly created

UK Athletics Hall of Fame. In 2009, he was voted into the Dawahares/Kentucky High School Athletic Association Hall of Fame. In a 2012 interview, after experiencing some economic challenges, Higgs expressed the reality of playing professional football when he declared, "NFL stands for Not for Long. Trust me, it's not for long."

"Hall of Fame." University of Kentucky Athletics. http://www.ukath letics.com/genrel/042705aaa.html (accessed August 22, 2013).
Kentucky High School Athletic Association. http://khsaa.org/hallfame /2009.pdf (accessed August 21, 2013).
Newspapers: "Higgs Says He'll Sign with Cats Wednesday," *LHL*, February 7, 1984, C1; "Dolphins Release RB Higgs," *Orlando Sentinel*, November 16, 1994, C3; "Devils' Higgs 'The Best' Owensboro Running Back Became a Legend on Football Field," *OMI*, September 26, 2010, B1; "When the Cheering Stops, Real Life Begins," *Ft. Lauderdale (FL) Sun Sentinel*, September 23, 2012, A1.
—*Sallie L. Powell*

HILL, CARL MCCLELLAN (b. Norfolk, VA, 1907; d. 1995, Hampton, VA), president of Kentucky State University from 1962 to 1975. The fourth of eight children, Carl McClellan Hill was born in Norfolk, VA, on July 27, 1907. In his youth, Hill devoted himself to work in the church, a passion that later earned him the nickname Deacon. Attending Hampton Institute for his undergraduate work, he also developed a passion for chemistry, which he taught at George P. Phenix Laboratory School. He later earned his master's and doctorate degrees at Cornell University and embarked on a career in science.

Hill taught at North Carolina AT&T University and headed the chemistry department at Tennessee State University from 1944 to 1951. His wife, Mary Elliott Hill, then took over for a year because of his work with the Tennessee Valley Authority. He did continuous research in addition to his teaching duties, producing over 52 research papers during his career. In 1962, Hill—then considered one of the top six chemistry professors in the nation and the dean of the School of Arts and Sciences—accepted the position of president at Kentucky State College (later known as **Kentucky State University**).

During his 13-year tenure at Kentucky State University, Hill oversaw several changes that elevated the school to university status in 1972. He also pushed for increased integration of the traditionally black school, doubling white enrollment in two years. When he retired in 1975, he had served for the second-longest time as the school's president, exceeded only by his predecessor, **Rufus Atwood.**

Hill's retirement was short lived. He moved back to Hampton, VA, with his second wife, Helen Ware Hill, and served as interim president of Hampton University in 1976 and full-time president from 1977 to 1978. He then retired for good and focused more on his work with the First Presbyterian Church of Hampton. He died at the age of 87 on April 4, 1995.

Newspapers: "Busy Scholar to Head K.S.C.," *LCJ*, August 21, 1962, Sec. 2.1; "TSU's Dean Hill Inaugurated as the President of Kentucky State," *Tri-State Defender*, October 19, 1963, 11; "Carl McClellan Hill, Former HU President," *Daily Press* (Hampton Roads, VA), April 7, 1995, B4.

Smith, Gerald L. *A Black Educator in the Segregated South: Kentucky's Rufus B. Atwood.* Lexington: Univ. Press of Kentucky, 1994.
—*Stephen Pickering*

HILL, WILLIAM H. (b. 1880, Warsaw, KY; d. unknown, Cincinnati, OH), undertaker. Born on April 4, 1880, William H. Hill was the first child of Daniel Hill, a farm worker, and Nettie (Johnson) Hill. His father died when he was 12 years old. According to census records, Nettie, Hill's mother, had married Thomas Moody, a farmer, by 1900. Besides the 20-year-old Hill, who worked as a waiter, the family included four other children and Nettie's mother. The 1910 U.S. federal census did not include William Hill or Thomas Moody, but Nettie lived with her four children, a son-in-law, a grandson, and her mother in Warsaw. She and her mother worked as washerwomen in the home. She and some of the children were labeled white, but others, including her mother, were recorded as mulatto.

In contrast, Wendell P. Dabney, author of *Cincinnati's Colored Citizens,* related the story that the 12-year-old Hill left school and "went to work like a man" to support his family after the death of his father and brought his family to Cincinnati with him. When he was 39, Hill went to Cincinnati and married Gladys McGee in 1919. He started his funeral business that same year. According to the 1920 U.S. federal census, the couple had four lodgers living with them, but no family members. Dabney reported that after Hill's business prospered, he purchased the Warsaw homestead for his family. By 1930, Hill and his wife were listed as proprietors of his funeral business, and their one lodger worked as chauffeur for the company.

Hill belonged to various organizations, including the Masons, the Knights of Tabor, and the Cincinnati Colored Civic Club. He served as president of the Ohio State Association of Elks. His business was located at 630 W. Fifth St., and he and his wife lived on W. Eighth St. in Cincinnati. He had retired by 1942.

Boris, Joseph J., ed. *Who's Who in Colored America, 1928–1929.* New York: Who's Who in Colored America Corp., 1929.
Dabney, Wendell P. *Cincinnati's Colored Citizens: Historical, Sociological and Biographical.* Cincinnati: Dabney, 1926.
U.S. Federal Census (1880, 1900, 1910, 1920).
U.S. World War II Draft Registration Cards, 1942.
—*Sallie L. Powell*

HINES, CARL R. (b. 1931, Louisville, KY), member of the Louisville Board of Education and state representative from 1977 to 1986. Born to Frederick Hines, an insurance agent, and Ruth Hines in Louisville, KY, Carl R. Hines graduated from **Central High School** in 1949. After two years at the University of Illinois, he joined the air force during the Korean War in 1951 and earned the Air Force Distinguished Flying Cross for his service in Korea. Hines resumed his studies at the University of Illinois in the mid-1950s before transferring to the University of Louisville. After attending law school at the University of Louisville, he opened a real estate business, Carl R. Hines Realty, located at 1300 W. Broadway. Throughout the rest of the 1960s and the 1970s, Hines was deeply involved in Louisville's African American community, serving as a board member of the city's **National Associa-**

tion for the Advancement of Colored People branch, chairman of the Shawnee District Boy Scouts of America, president of Just Men's Civic and Social Club, and executive secretary of the Louisville and Jefferson County Community Action Committee.

In August 1968, Hines was appointed to fill a vacancy on the Louisville Board of Education and was elected outright to the same position in that year's election. In 1972, he was reelected and became a member of the Jefferson County Board of Education when the city and county school systems merged in 1975. The following year, he was instrumental in overseeing the desegregation of Louisville's public schools that accompanied the merger.

In November 1977, he became the first black state representative elected from Louisville's 43rd District. During his almost decadelong tenure in the General Assembly, Hines sponsored many important pieces of legislation, including a bill that raised Kentucky's minimum wage and another that substituted contemporary language for the offensive line referring to "darkies" in the song "My Old Kentucky Home." Governor Martha Layne Collins also appointed him to serve on the Medicaid Program Review Team and as a Kentucky delegate to the 1985 Education Commission of the States. During his time as representative, he was a member of the Executive Committee of the National Black Caucus of Black Legislators.

Hines lost his seat to fellow Democrat and popular member of the board of alderman E. Porter Hatcher, in 1986. After the loss, Hines remained active in the city, serving as the executive director of the Housing Opportunity Center and a board member of the Louisville Housing Commission. His real estate business continued to thrive through the early years of the twenty-first century.

Hines, Carl. Interview by Catherine Herdman, June 28, 2006. Kentucky Legislative Oral History Project, Louie B. Nunn Center for Oral History, Univ. of Kentucky.
"House Passes Bill to Increase State Minimum Wage to $3.35." *LHL,* March 31, 1986, A11.
Kentucky Commission on Human Rights. *1982 Kentucky Directory of Black Elected Officials.* Frankfort: Commonwealth of Kentucky, 1982.
Mallegg, Kristin, ed. *Who's Who among African Americans.* 22nd ed. Detroit: Gale, 2008.

—*Joshua D. Farrington*

HINTON, CLARENCE DAVID (b. 1916, Sharpsburg, KY; d. 2008, Silver Spring, MD), otolaryngologist. Clarence David Hinton was born on October 10, 1916, in Sharpsburg, KY, and was raised by his single father in Peoria, IL, after his mother died when he was three years old. He attended Northwestern University on an academic scholarship and also played halfback on the school's football team, including the 1936 Big Ten championship team. In 1938, he graduated with a bachelor's degree; four years later, he obtained his medical degree from Howard University.

During World War II, he served as a medical officer in the army and was assigned to the all-black 335th Station Hospital in Burma. From 1946 to 1949, he practiced family medicine in Washington, DC, until he decided to specialize in otolaryngology, the study of the ear, nose, and throat. He furthered his stud-

ies in Philadelphia at the University of Pennsylvania and Temple University and worked briefly at Philadelphia General Hospital.

In the early 1960s, he returned to Washington, DC, where he was the chairman of Howard University Hospital's Otolaryngology Department from 1963 to 1979. From 1978 to 1980, he chaired the ear, nose, and throat division at Children's National Medical Center and became the first African American chairman of the DC Medical Society's otolaryngology section. He later returned to Howard University, and although he officially retired in 1990, he remained a visible presence at the school's hospital through 2001.

In addition to being named to Northwestern University's Athletics Hall of Fame, Clarence Hinton was given a lifetime achievement award by the National Medical Association in 1993. He was married to ViCurtis Hinton, who helped raise millions of dollars as the coordinator for the Legal Defense Fund of the National Association for the Advancement of Colored People. He died on September 23, 2008, at Holy Cross Hospital in Silver Spring, MD.

"Ear, Nose, Throat Doctor Clarence David Hinton, 91." *WP,* October 4, 2008, B6.
Fleming, G. James, and Christian E. Burckel, eds. *Who's Who in Colored America.* 7th ed. Yonkers-on-Hudson, NY: Christian E. Burckel and Associates, 1950.

—*Joshua D. Farrington*

HISTORIC PLEASANT GREEN MISSIONARY BAPTIST CHURCH, one of the oldest African American churches in the United States. Located at 540 W. Maxwell St. in Lexington, KY, the Historic Pleasant Green Missionary Baptist Church claims to be the fourth-oldest black Baptist church in the United States and the oldest African American congregation west of the Allegheny Mountains. The church was founded by Peter Durrett, also known as Brother Captain, a slave in Virginia who, after discovering that his wife was intended to be sold to a slave owner in Kentucky, requested to be traded. The slave owner agreed to the trade, and in 1781, Durrett became the property of a prominent Kentucky slave owner, John Maxwell, who built a cabin for Durrett where he held the first worship services in what he named the African Baptist Church.

At this time, the tenor of the nation reflected the three-fifths compromise in which blacks were not considered to be fully represented as individuals; thus, in Kentucky, slaves were not granted religious independence and were usually required to attend the same church as their white owners. The white Baptist Association did not officially ordain Durrett to the ministry but granted him permission to start his own black church. In 1822, Durrett's congregation purchased land from a white doctor, Frederick Ridgely, and built the African Baptist Church. The Pleasant Green congregation continues to worship on this site today.

After Durrett died in 1823, at the age of 90, the church was led by several other pastors, including George Washington Dupee, who became the church's fourth pastor in 1855. When Pleasant Green Baptist Church's congregation discovered that Dupee, a slave, was about to be sold, it borrowed $850 from the white Baptist Church to purchase Dupee's freedom. The church members

*Historic Pleasant Green Missionary
Baptist Church.*

eventually repaid the loan. In 1858, Dupee left Lexington and became pastor of the Washington Street Missionary Baptist Church
in Paducah, KY, and he became the organizer of the First Association of Black Churches in the state in 1867. Dupee died in 1897.

The church at times has housed schools, Boy Scout troops, and
other community-service organizations. During the 1960s, Pleasant Green, under the leadership of Rev. **William A. Jones Sr.**,
became one of the most politically active black churches in
America, serving as the organizational hub of boycotts, pickets,
stand-ins, and other demonstrations. The church has been
home to religious and political figures of distinction, including
Rev. Dr. **William A. Jones Jr., Julia E. Lewis, William Childress,
Harry Sykes,** and John Wigginton. At one time, the church
housed an impressive music program, dedicating the city's only
organ with a rank of chimes in 1931.

Affiliated with the Progressive National Baptist Convention,
the church has worshipped at Maxwell and Patterson Sts. in
downtown Lexington since 1822. The current building, erected
in 1930, was listed on the Blue Grass Trust for Historic Preservation in 2001. Only 17 senior pastors have served the church since
1790. Since the 1950s, Pleasant Green has been among the largest black congregations in Lexington, ordinarily numbering between 1,500 and 1,800 members.

Today the Historic Pleasant Green Missionary Baptist Church
still heralds its rich history of slavery and liberation. As a re-
minder, the church designed a garden and symbolically buried
Brother Captain on the church property. The church has contributed much to the African American community in Lexington
and surrounding areas and holds a prominent place in Kentucky
African American history.

"Congregation's Dream Culminates in Commodious $75,000 Church
     Edifice." *LL*, August 16, 1931.

Curtis, Nancy C. *Black Heritage Sites: An African American Odyssey and
     Finder's Guide.* Chicago: American Library Association, 1996, 103–4.
Lucas, Marion B. *A History of Blacks in Kentucky: From Slavery to Seg-
     regation, 1760–1891.* 2nd ed. Lexington: Univ. Press of Kentucky,
     2003, 122–23.
Woodson, Carter G. *The History of the Negro Church.* 2nd ed. Wash-
     ington, DC: Associated Publishers, 1921, 85–86. http://docsouth
     .unc.edu/church/woodson/woodson.html.
Wright, John D. *Lexington: Heart of the Bluegrass; An Illustrated His-
     tory.* Lexington: Univ. Press of Kentucky, 1994, 66–67.
                                            —*Jessica Bryant and Rev. LaMont Jones Jr.*

**HODGE, WILLIAM J. (b. 1920, Groesbeck, TX; d. 2000, Louis-
ville, KY), minister and civil rights activist.** Born to tenant
farmers in rural Texas, William J. Hodge was the oldest of nine
boys. After graduating from Groesbeck's segregated high school,
he briefly attended Samuel Houston College in Austin until the
economic strains of the Great Depression made it impossible for
him to continue.

By the mid-1940s, he had saved enough money to finish his
college education, graduating from Southern University in Baton
Rouge, LA. He then studied at Oberlin College in Ohio, where he
received his doctor of divinity degree. In 1950, almost immediately after graduating from Oberlin, he was named the head pastor of Diamond Hill Street Baptist Church in Lynchburg, VA. In
Lynchburg, he established a friendship with another young Baptist minister, Martin Luther King Jr., and became active in the
city's branch of the **National Association for the Advancement
of Colored People** (NAACP).

In 1957, he left Lynchburg to become the pastor of Louisville's
Fifth Street Baptist Church, one of the most influential and prestigious black churches in Kentucky. His civil rights activism began almost immediately after he arrived in Louisville when he

was refused a cup of coffee at a segregated lunch counter. Within less than two years, he had risen to the top of the city's most active civil rights organization, becoming president of the Louisville NAACP branch. In 1962, he was elected president of the Kentucky Conference of the NAACP and served as both Louisville and state NAACP president throughout the rest of the decade. In 1975, he was elected as a Democrat to the Louisville Board of Alderman, where he served as chairman of the Housing and Community Development Committee and the Rules Committee. In 1977, he was reelected as 10th Ward Alderman, and in 1978, he became the first black president of the Louisville Board of Alderman. In 1982, he resigned from the board after he was named president of Simmons Bible College (later known as **Simmons College of Kentucky**), a position in which he served until his retirement in 1996.

Throughout his time as a civil rights activist, Hodge never lost his focus on his pastoral calling and was an active member of the Progressive National Baptist Convention. From the early 1960s through the 1970s, he also served as dean, director, vice president, and eventually president of the Progressive National Baptist Congress of Christian Education. In Kentucky, he served as the vice moderator of the **General Association of Baptists in Kentucky** and was the founder of Louisville's Interdenominational Ministerial Coalition. In 1995, after 38 years as the pastor of Fifth Street Baptist Church, he retired and was replaced by his son, Phillip L. Hodge Sr.

In 1990, Louisville's S. 21st St. was renamed Dr. W. J. Hodge Street in honor of Hodge's prominent role in shaping the city's history. Hodge died of complications related to kidney failure on December 27, 2000, and was buried in Louisville's Cave Hill Cemetery.

Adams, Luther. *Way Up North in Louisville: African American Migration in the Urban South, 1930–1970.* Chapel Hill: Univ. of North Carolina Press, 2010.
Hodge, W. J. Interview by Chuck Staiger, December 14, 1977. Oral History Series, tapes 422 and 423. Univ. of Louisville.
K'Meyer, Tracy E. *Civil Rights in the Gateway to the South: Louisville, Kentucky, 1945–1980.* Lexington: Univ. Press of Kentucky, 2009.
—*Joshua D. Farrington*

HOLLAND, JAMES PHILLIPS (b. 1934, Bowling Green, KY; d. 1998, Bloomington, IN), first African American from Kentucky to be named to West Point. Born in Bowling Green, KY, on December 31, 1934, James Phillips Holland pursued a career in science early in his life. Despite being nominated for appointment to West Point by Senator John Sherman Cooper in 1954, the first African American from Kentucky to receive that honor, Holland chose to finish his BS at Kentucky State College (later known as **Kentucky State University**), graduating magna cum laude in 1956. He pursued advanced degrees in endocrinology, earning an MA from Indiana University in 1958 and a PhD in 1961.

After briefly joining the faculty of Howard University, Holland returned to Indiana University in 1967, where he worked in the biology department for 30 years. During his tenure at the university, Holland gained a reputation as a sterling researcher and teacher. He pushed for action on behalf of minority students on

campus and "earned every major teaching award on the Bloomington campus." In 1997, he became the first recipient of the Chancellor's Medallion, which was created to recognize those distinguished for their service on campus. A year later, Holland died on March 24, 1998, after a long battle with cancer. In his honor, Indiana University established the James P. Holland Memorial Lecture Series.

"Holland's Love for Biology Contagious." *Bloomington Herald-Times,* February 23, 2008.
Indiana University. "Dr. James P. Holland." Hudson and Holland Scholars Program. http://www.indiana.edu/~hhsp/about/history /holland.html (accessed July 18, 2011).
"Senator Names First Kentucky Negro to West Point." *Jet,* March 25, 1954, 6.
Young, Herman A., and Barbara H. Young. *Scientists in the Black Perspective.* Louisville, KY: Lincoln Foundation, 1974.
—*Stephen Pickering*

HOLMES, HELEN FAIRFAX (b. 1902, Williamsport, PA; d. 1995, Frankfort, KY), civil rights leader, teacher, and community organizer. Helen Fairfax was born on October 17, 1902, in Williamsport, PA, to John W. Fairfax and Isabella Tanner Fairfax. She became the first African American salutatorian at Williamsport Area High School, an integrated school. After graduation, she accepted a full scholarship to Bucknell University in Lewisburg, PA, where she was the college's only black student during most of her academic career there. She later completed her master's degree from Columbia University and married Booker Taliaferro Holmes. After graduating with a degree in English from Bucknell, she taught high school in Durham, NC, which had a significant effect on her racial perspective. She found it difficult "to remember not to sit in the first vacant seat I saw on the bus."

Consequently, Holmes felt compelled to challenge segregation laws and policies when she moved to Frankfort, KY, in 1943 and became the head of the English Department at Kentucky State College (later known as **Kentucky State University**). She brought enthusiasm and new ideas to the English Department, establishing a broader curriculum that included drama at the college. One of her many programs included some outstanding personalities, such as Langston Hughes.

Holmes also participated in various organizations in the community, including the Beta Upsilon Sigma graduate chapter of **Delta Sigma Theta Sorority,** the Women's Progressive Club, and others. She served as a Girl Scout leader for 20 years and expanded the black girls' program in Frankfort from 2 troops to 12 troops. At Frankfort's St. John A.M.E. Church, she was a trustee and steward.

In 1948, Holmes became president of the Frankfort branch of the **National Association for the Advancement of Colored People** (NAACP) and served in that position for 20 years, coordinating every aspect of local protest activities during the **civil rights movement.** Under her leadership, segregated establishments in Frankfort witnessed countless boycotts, picketings, and sit-ins. By the end of 1961, her involvement in Frankfort's community led to the integration of some eating establishments, the public library, the YMCA, two hotels, and the cafeteria facilities of Frankfort's King's Daughters Hospital and the employment of blacks on the local police force and in city offices.

During Holmes's NAACP tenure, two major civil rights marches occurred in Frankfort. The first took place in December 1961, and the second was the more widely publicized 1964 **March on Frankfort** led by Martin Luther King Jr. with 10,000 participants from across the state. Holmes included a diverse population in her activism, using college students, campus faculty and staff, **Congress of Racial Equality** workers, and especially local townspeople. Her strategic attacks on segregated local establishments were the catalysts for changes in state and local policies that led to civil rights for black Kentuckians.

On June 5, 1995, Holmes died at age 92. She was interred in Sunset Memorial Gardens in Versailles, KY.

Holmes, Helen. Interview by Dr. Gerald Smith, Frankfort, KY, June 27, 1988.
———. Interview by James Wallace, July 25, 1991. Kentucky Historical Society, Frankfort.
Kentucky Thorobred Newspaper (Kentucky State University), January 1949.
Smith, Gerald L. *A Black Educator in the Segregated South: Kentucky's Rufus B. Atwood.* Lexington: Univ. Press of Kentucky, 1994.

—*Karen Cotton McDaniel*

HOOKS, BELL [GLORIA JEAN WATKINS] (b. 1952, Hopkinsville, KY), feminist writer and theorist. Bell hooks wrote that at the moment of her birth, "two factors determined my destiny, my having been born black and my having been born female." Originally named Gloria Jean Watkins, hooks was the child of a janitor and a stay-at-home mother and grew up in segregated Hopkinsville, KY, where she first encountered the forces of racism and patriarchy that would shape her career as a writer. She attended all-black schools, including Hopkinsville's Crispus Attucks High School. She considered her educational experience positive because of the strong support from her teachers. When she was forced to join integrated Hopkinsville High School, however, she remembered her teachers regarding her with contempt.

Despite this treatment, hooks continued to pursue her dream of becoming a writer. After receiving a degree in English from Stanford University in 1973, she earned a master's degree at the University of Wisconsin–Madison and began teaching at the University of Southern California. In 1978, she released *And There We Wept* under the pseudonym bell hooks, chosen as a tribute to her great-grandmother and written in lowercase to keep readers' focus on the message and not on the author. Meanwhile, she continued to polish a manuscript that she had written when she was 19 years old.

In 1981, hooks published the final product, *Ain't I a Woman? Black Women and Feminism,* which challenged theorists who considered sexism and racism separately. Her extensive defense of the idea that "the two issues were inseparable," despite some initial criticism, eventually made the book a classic in feminist theory. In 1992, *Publishers Weekly* named it one of the "twenty most influential women's books of the previous twenty years." Hooks continued to write at a prolific rate, producing over 30 books that featured critical essays on race and gender, as well as autobiographical accounts of her struggles as a child and as a writer.

Hooks had similar success in her teaching career. After earning a PhD at the University of California–Santa Cruz, she taught at several institutions of higher education, including Yale University, Oberlin College, and City College of New York. In 2004, she returned to Kentucky after accepting a position as Distinguished Professor in Residence in Appalachian studies at **Berea College.** Despite having earlier expressed misgivings about returning to her home state, she concluded an essay on her decision by writing, "Coming back to my native place I embrace with true love the reality that 'Kentucky is my fate'—my sublime home."

Griffiths, Sian, ed. *Beyond the Glass Ceiling: Forty Women Whose Ideas Shaped the Modern World.* Manchester: Manchester Univ. Press, 1996.
hooks, bell. *Ain't I a Woman? Black Women and Feminism.* Boston: South End Press, 1981.
———. *Belonging: A Culture of Place.* New York: Routledge, 2009.
———. *Remembered Rapture: The Writer at Work.* New York: Henry Holt, 1999.
Newspapers: "City Native 'Talks Back' on Issues for Blacks," *KNE*, February 27, 1992, 7A; "A Voice for Black Feminists," *LHL*, October 17, 1993, J1; "Native Daughter," *NYT*, December 15, 1996, BR32; "The Eye of the Storm," *NYT*, November 13, 1997, F1; "Writer Says State Inherently Racist," *LHL*, March 3, 1999, A1.

—*Stephen Pickering*

HOOKS, JULIA BRITTON (b. 1852, Frankfort, KY; d. 1942, Memphis, TN), Berea College's first African American teacher. Julia Britton, a child music prodigy later known as the Angel of

Julia Britton Hooks.

Beale Street, was born free to Henry Harrison and Laura Marshall Britton in Frankfort, KY, on May 4, 1852. She was a sister of Dr. **Mary Ellen Britton** and **Kentucky Derby** jockey **Thomas "Tommy" Britton.** Raised in Lexington, KY, she attended **Berea College** and became an instructor there in instrumental music from 1870 to 1872, teaching black and white students. She taught in Greenville, MS, from 1872 to 1876. Then she settled in Memphis, TN, and served as a public school teacher and principal of the Virginia Avenue School. She married Charles F. Hooks in 1880.

Julia Hooks became a leader in black cultural and educational affairs and helped start the Liszt-Mullard Club to promote classical music. She also founded the integrated Hooks School of Music (where she taught W. C. Handy), the Hooks Cottage School for black children, the Colored Old Folks Home, the Orphan Home Club, and a home for juvenile offenders. In 1895, she wrote the essay "Duty of the Hour" for the *Afro-American Encyclopaedia*.

In 1917, Hooks's husband, Charles, a juvenile-detention officer, was murdered by a 15-year-old inmate. Hooks continued her social work with the institution and other club work for several more years. On March 9, 1942, she died nearly two months before her 90th birthday at the Colored Old Folks Home that she had helped establish. She was the grandmother of Benjamin J. Hooks, executive director of the **National Association for the Advancement of Colored People.**

Haley, James T. *Afro-American Encyclopaedia; or, The Thoughts, Doings, and Sayings of the Race.* Nashville: Haley and Florida, 1895.

Lewis, Selma. "Julia Britton Hooks, 1852–1942." In *The Tennessee Encyclopedia of History and Culture,* edited by Caroll Van West. Nashville: Tennessee Historical Society, 1968.

Wilson, Shannon H. *Berea College: An Illustrated History.* Lexington: Univ. Press of Kentucky, 2006.

—*Paul David Nelson*

HOOPER, ERNEST JACKSON (b. 1900, Philadelphia, PA; d. 1983, Cincinnati, OH), coach and educator. Born on January 19, 1900, Ernest Jackson Hooper was raised in Philadelphia by his mother, Louisa Hooper, his aunt, Mary E. Holland, a dressmaker, and his grandmother, Georgianne Jackson. When Hooper registered for the World War I draft, he was an 18-year-old student at Cheney Training School in Philadelphia.

By 1923, Hooper lived at 127 W. Broadway St. in Winchester, KY. He taught and coached at Winchester's Oliver High School and was a member of the **Kentucky Negro Educational Association** (KNEA). During one of its business sessions on April 18–21, 1923, he presented an address, "The Educational Content of an Industrial Subject." He also coached the girls' and boys' basketball teams and the football team in that same year. Even though he was small in stature, Hooper was an excellent coach. All three teams were successful. The two basketball teams won the Bluegrass championship, and the football team played the eminent Lexington **Dunbar High School** team to a scoreless tie. The next year, Hooper again addressed the KNEA in his presentation "Educational Values."

By 1928, Hooper taught shop at Crispus Attucks High School in Indianapolis, IN. He graduated from Bradley Polytechnic Institute in Peoria, IL, in 1930. He later moved to Cincinnati, OH, and lived at 116 Ehrman Ave. He died on October 1, 1983.

Proceedings of the Kentucky Negro Educational Association, April 18–23, 1923, and April 23–26, 1924. Kentucky State University Archives and Special Collections, Frankfort, KY.

Stout, Louis, *Shadows of the Past: A History of the Kentucky High School Athletic League.* Lexington, KY: Host Communications, 2006.

U.S. Federal Census (1910 and 1930).

World War I Draft Registration Cards, 1917–1918.

—*Sallie L. Powell*

Ernest Jackson Hooper (center, second row), with the African American women's basketball team at Oliver High School in Winchester, KY, 1922.

HOPKINS, TELMA (b. 1948, Louisville, KY), singer with Tony Orlando and Dawn and popular television actress. Born in Louisville, KY, and raised near Detroit, MI, Telma Hopkins knew from an early age that she wanted to be a singer. Detroit's music scene, centered on Motown, gave her numerous opportunities, and she began her career singing backup for other performers, including the Jackson Five and the Supremes. In 1970, she and Joyce Vincent Wilson joined Tony Orlando to form the group Tony Orlando and Dawn. In 1971, the group had a hit with "Knock Three Times," and it followed up this success with the Grammy-nominated single "Tie a Yellow Ribbon round the Ole Oak Tree," which was the best-selling single of 1973.

After Tony Orlando and Dawn disbanded following a few short-lived variety shows, Hopkins pursued a career in acting. In 1980, she joined the cast of *Bosom Buddies* as the character Isabelle, and she followed that performance with a five-year stint on *Gimme a Break!* In 1989, she attained her best-known role as Aunt Rachel on *Family Matters,* a character she played over a span of nine years. Afterward, she continued to act on numerous other television shows, and she has been active in organizations in support of African American women and underprivileged children.

"Hopkins, Telma." In *Encyclopedia of African American Actresses in Film and Television,* edited by Bob McCann. Jefferson, NC: McFarland, 2010.

Newspapers: "With an Eye On: Telma Hopkins, the Accidental Actress with a Message to Tell," *Los Angeles Times,* January 23, 1994; "A Dedicated Role Model: Entertainment Veteran Telma Hopkins Serves Children, Needy in Hands-On Manner," *Sacramento Observer,* November 20, 2002, E3; "Accolades for Detroit's Own Telma Hopkins," *Michigan Chronicle,* May 7, 2008, D1.

—*Stephen Pickering*

HOPKINSVILLE MALE AND FEMALE COLLEGE, educational institution for African Americans. In 1883, the First District Baptist Association at the Green Valley Baptist Church in Clinton, KY, founded the Hopkinsville Male and Female College (later named the South Western Kentucky Institute). The privately funded boarding school offered courses at elementary through college levels for the purpose of educating African Americans, particularly teachers and preachers. In 1890, the board of directors purchased land on Hopkinsville's Vine St. Five years later, a board of trustees replaced the directors. In 1899, the articles of incorporation were drafted, thereby formally creating Hopkinsville Male and Female College, and the construction of the main building was finished. The first floor housed four classrooms, an office, a kitchen, a hall, and a combined auditorium and chapel. The second floor contained a dormitory divided by a hall, 7 male rooms, and 10 female rooms. The building had many windows, at least six chimneys, and a cupola.

Classes began in the spring of 1900. In the fall, Patterson Tilford Frazer became president and served for over a decade. During Frazer's term, the college flourished as a respectable institution. Frazer's many accomplishments included bringing Booker T. Washington to speak at the college on several occasions and organizing a theological department. During its existence, the college enrolled anywhere between 50 and over 100 students.

The school offered its students rigorous coursework. In the four years of the Model School Department, some of the classes included reading, arithmetic, geography, writing, and history. The Preparatory Department taught Kentucky history, rhetoric, political science, English, classical languages, algebra, geometry, psychology, and botany. During the final four college years, a student would take over 17 classes. A sampling includes trigonometry, French, philosophical history, zoology, biology, chemistry, geology, astronomy, and logic. Also offered were music, business, theology, and dressmaking and plain sewing departments and even a summer course for teacher exam preparation.

Despite its early successes, the Male and Female College underwent several difficult experiences. The college temporarily closed because of legal issues. In 1914, there was a court battle between Frazer and the board of directors. Frazer claimed that the board of directors owed him $2,000 in back salary, whereas the directors questioned the validity of his work contract. Frazer lost the case. By 1917, Rev. E. Williams served as president of the school. The college then went through a series of presidents, lost sufficient funding, and temporarily had to close its doors in the late 1920s. Furthermore, class sizes shrunk during the Great Depression, and a tornado destroyed the main building in 1935.

The college continued to operate during the 1940s and 1950s, but its focus shifted from general education to theological studies. On November 4, 1965, this shift led the board of directors to rename the school Hopkinsville College of the Bible, with the primary mission of training students for the ministry.

Annual Catalogue of the Hopkinsville M. & F. College. Hopkinsville, KY: New Era Print, 1902.

Dunnigan, Alice Allison, comp. and ed. *The Fascinating Story of Black Kentuckians: Their Heritage and Traditions.* Washington, DC: Associated Publishers, 1982, 154 and 190.

Hauke, Kathleen A., ed. *The Dark Side of Hopkinsville: Stories by Ted Poston.* Athens: Univ. of Georgia Press, 1991, xviii and 30.

Jones, Thomas Jesse. *Negro Education: A Study of the Private and Higher Schools for Colored People in the United States.* Vol. 2. Washington, DC: Government Printing Office, 1917, 277.

Newspapers: "Booker Is Coming," *HK,* February 26, 1907, 4; "Negro Orator Made a Hit," *HK,* November 25, 1909, 1; "In Circuit Court," *HK,* November 5, 1914, 1; "Colored College," *HK,* September 27, 1917, 8.

Turner, William T. "The History of Higher Education in Hopkinsville, Kentucky, 1849 to the Present." PhD diss., Austin Peay State Univ., 1973. Black History / Male & Female College folder, Pennyrile Area Museum, Hopkinsville, KY.

—*Jonathan McClintock*

HORNER, CHARLES D. (b. 1859, Tennessee; d. unknown), high school principal. Charles Horner was the principal of Newport's African American **Southgate Street School** from 1897 to 1904. He married Rebecca Day Minnes, and the couple had six children, including **Charles E. Horner,** who became a medical doctor in Newport. The family resided in the Cincinnati neighborhood of Cumminsville until Charles D. Horner became principal of the Southgate Street School in 1897. Horner was active in the Newport community; for example, in June 1899 he was elected an officer of the Colored Four Hundred Society of Newport. The Horners resided at 152 Van Voast Ave. in Bellevue in 1900 and later moved to 404 W. Fourth St. in Newport. In August 1902, Horner helped organize and was a speaker at the Kentucky State Colored Chautauqua, which was held at Electric Gardens at 11th and Brighton Sts. in Newport.

While Horner was principal of Southgate, he requested that the high school's program be expanded from three to four years to match the program of Newport High School. His proposal was accepted and implemented, and the Southgate Street High School continued to offer its African American student body four years of high school until it closed in 1921. In June 1905, Horner was asked by the Newport Board of Education to resign as principal and was given until the July board meeting to reply to its demand. The board minutes do not indicate the reason for the board's request. He resigned before the July board meeting, and from that time on, no further information about Horner is available.

Newport Board of Education. *Fifty-Third Annual Report of the Public Schools of Newport.* Newport, KY: Campbell Co. Printing, 1901.
Newspapers: "Newport," *CE,* July 18, 1899, 3; "Newport News," *KTS,* August 15, 1902, 3; "Horner Must Go," *KP,* June 22, 1905, 5; Jim Reis, "Educator's Son Worked Hard to Be Called 'Doctor,'" *KP,* February 4, 2002, 4K.

—*Theodore H. H. Harris*

HORNER, CHARLES E. (b. 1882, Cincinnati, OH; d. 1948, Cincinnati, OH), first African American medical doctor in Newport, KY. Charles E. Horner, the son of **Charles D. Horner** and Rebecca Day Minnes Horner, became the first African American medical doctor in Newport. He attended public schools up to the eighth grade, leaving school at age 15. At age 16, he went to work in a restaurant as a cook and a pantry man. In 1899, at age 17, Horner moved from Ohio to Newport and began working as a janitor at the **Southgate Street School,** where his father was the principal; he also waited tables at evening parties. He later held janitorial jobs at two churches and worked as a window washer, a porter in stores, and a waiter at nighttime poker parties.

In 1903, with $300 in his bank account, Horner entered the Eclectic Medical College in Cincinnati, attending classes during the day and working as a waiter at night. He graduated with a degree in medicine from the college in 1907. In 1908, he worked as a Pullman porter stationed in Chicago, traveling throughout the United States, Canada, and parts of Mexico. In 1910, he took the Kentucky Medical Board examination and passed with an average score of 79. In May 1911, Horner married Emma Walker. He began his medical practice in Newport, where he lived, and treated mostly white patients.

In February 1918, Horner almost lost his life while trying to visit patients in a flooded area of Newport. He was in the floodwaters in a flatboat with a man named George Wooding when the vessel capsized at Fourth and Isabella Sts. Wooding drowned, but Horner was rescued and recovered.

Horner was active in St. Andrew's Episcopal Church in Cincinnati. He was a 32nd-degree Mason. In the 1930s, Horner was married a second time, to Katharine Berry. In 1943, he retired from medical practice and moved to a farm he owned in Williamsburg, OH. He died in 1948, and his remains were cremated at the Cincinnati Crematory.

Dabney, Wendall P. *Cincinnati's Colored Citizens: Historical, Sociological and Biographical.* Cincinnati: Dabney, 1926.
Newspapers: "Man Drowned When Flatboat Capsized on Flooded Street," *KTS,* February 12, 1918, 11; "Death Notices," *KE,* October 13, 1938, 32; "Newport Physician to Face Grand Jury," *KP,* August 8, 1940, 1; "Dr. Charles E. Horner," *KTS,* October 13, 1948, 4; Jim Reis, "Educator's Son Worked Hard to Be Called 'Doctor'," *KP,* February 4, 2002, 4K.

—*Theodore H. H. Harris*

HORTON, JOHN BENJAMIN (b. 1904, Lumpkin, GA; d. 1997, Louisville, KY), journalist and author. Born in 1904 in Lumpkin, GA, to John Henry and Duckey Louvenia Horton, John Benjamin Horton moved to Omaha, NE, as a teenager. After graduating from Omaha High School, he attended Omaha Presbyterian University and Omaha Law School. After graduation, he began his career as a newspaperman by opening two African American papers in Omaha.

In 1940, Horton moved to Louisville, KY, to work for the ***Louisville Defender,*** where he served as a columnist and advertising director for 14 years. During the 1950s, he opened J. Benjamin Horton and Associates in the old **Mammoth Life** building at Sixth and Walnut Sts. and published his own magazines, including the *Louisville Buyers Guide* and *News Digest.* His most popular publication, the *Kentucky Negro Journal,* was one of the most important chronicles of the **civil rights movement** and black life in the state.

Horton was active in the city and state's Republican Party, even running for Congress in 1964. He served on numerous committees in the local branch of the **National Association for the Advancement of Colored People** and was national director of public relations for **Phi Beta Sigma Fraternity** and the National Pan-Hellenic Council.

Horton was also the author of numerous books, such as *Old War Horses of Kentucky, Profiles of Contemporary Black Achievers in Kentucky,* and *Flights from Doom,* his autobiography. His most influential book, *Not without Struggle,* was published in 1979 and remains one of the few book-length works that documents the African American struggle for civil rights in Kentucky. In his eloquent epilogue, Horton remained hopeful, writing, "It was not without struggle that we came this far; and not without struggle shall we achieve freedom's goal. . . . In a state darkened by hate, fear and prejudice, Kentucky as we know it may yet provide a beacon that will guide all Americans to social peace, justice and freedom."

"Black History Month." *LCJ,* February 10, 2009, B3.
Horton, J. Benjamin. *Flights from Doom: The Autobiography of the Life, Observations, Experiences and Involvements in America of an African-American Journalist, Author and Publicist.* Louisville, KY: J. Benjamin Horton & Associates, 1990.
———. *Not without Struggle.* New York: Vantage Press, 1979.

—*Joshua D. Farrington*

HOUSTON, ALLAN WADE, JR. (b. 1971, Louisville, KY), professional basketball player and philanthropist. Allan Wade Houston Jr. is a member of a family that has made historic contributions to the history of basketball in Kentucky. His grandfather,

Allan Wade Houston Sr.

William Lee Kean, coached at **Simmons College of Kentucky** and Louisville's **Central High School**. His father, **Allan Wade Houston Sr.,** was the first African American to serve as an assistant coach at the University of Louisville and later became the head coach at the University of Tennessee. A six-feet-six guard at Ballard High School, Allan Jr. played on the team that won the state basketball title his junior season in 1988. He began his senior high school season ranked among the top players in the state and finished the year averaging more than 22 points a game, first team all-state, member of the McDonald's All-American High School Basketball Team, and recipient of the title Mr. Kentucky Basketball.

Houston initially signed a national letter of intent to play for the University of Louisville but was released from the letter to play for his father, who was hired as the men's head basketball coach at the University of Tennessee. "I have always wanted to play for my dad," said Houston, "My father will go out of his way to help me, and I would be more comfortable playing for him." At Tennessee, Houston became a two-time All-American, the school's all-time leading scorer with 2,801 points, and the second all-time leading Southeastern Conference scorer.

In 1993, the Detroit Pistons drafted Houston. He signed as a free agent with the New York Knicks in 1996, where he played for the next nine years. He averaged 17 points per game and led the team to the 1999 National Basketball Association finals. He received an Olympic gold medal with the U.S. basketball team during the 2000 Summer Games in Sydney, Australia. In 2000 and 2001, he was selected to the NBA all-star team. After signing a multimillion-dollar contract in 2001, Houston experienced

chronic knee problems and missed several games. He retired in 2005 but attempted an unsuccessful comeback a couple of years later. He was later appointed an assistant general manager for the Knicks. He established Allan Houston Enterprises and the Legacy Foundation, which supports "The Father Knows Best" Basketball Retreat. In 2013, he was inducted into the Kentucky High School Basketball Hall of Fame, furthering the legacy of his father and grandfather, who had been earlier inductees.

"Allan Houston." *Hoopedia.* http://hoopedia.nba.com/index.php?title=Allan_Houston (accessed December 12, 2012).
"Allan Houston's No. 20 to Be Retired." *Tennessee Men's Basketball,* January 31, 2011. http://www.utsports.com/sports/m-baskbl/spec-rel/013111aab.html (accessed August 7, 2013).
Cloud, Olivia. "The Kean Brothers." *LCJ,* July 3, 2007. http://www.courier-journal.com/article/20070704/OPINION04/707041137/The-Kean-Brothers (accessed August 7, 2013).
Newspapers: "Ballard Player Houston Named All-American," *LHL,* March 7, 1989, C3; "Houston, Harrison Named State's Best," *LHL,* April 9, 1989, C8; "Houston Asks U of L to Release Him," *LHL,* May 10, 1989, D3.

—*Gerald L. Smith*

HOUSTON, ALLAN WADE, SR. (b. 1944, Alcoa, TN), basketball coach and entrepreneur. Alcoa, TN, native Allan Wade Houston Sr. could not play collegiate basketball at nearby segregated University of Tennessee in Knoxville when he graduated from Charles M. Hall High School in 1962. However, Houston (known as Wade) was the first African American basketball player to earn a scholarship at the University of Louisville. In 1964, as a sophomore, he, Eddie Whitehead, and **Sam Smith** broke the color barrier when they played varsity basketball for Louisville. He graduated from the university with a degree in health and physical education.

In 1968, Houston married Alice Kean, the daughter of **William L. Kean,** Louisville's **Central High School** coach who helped integrate the all-white Kentucky High School Athletic Association in the late 1950s. Houston earned his master's degree in educational psychology from the University of Louisville the same year he started coaching at Louisville's Male High School. He led the school to the 1974–1975 Kentucky state basketball championship. He then began his 13-year tenure as the first African American assistant coach at the University of Louisville. The school won national championships in 1980 and 1986. In 1987, he helped organize the Black Coaches Association.

Two years later, Houston returned to his home state as the first African American coach of a major sport in the Southeastern Conference when the University of Tennessee hired him as its men's basketball coach. Even though Houston was described as "a class person" who provided an excellent role model and diligently served in the community, his teams suffered record losses. In 1994, he left coaching and entered the business world.

Houston and his wife owned Houston-Johnson, Inc., an automotive warehousing, transportation, and logistics firm. In 2007, Houston and his wife cochaired Kentucky governor Steve Beshear's inauguration committee. He has served on the Kentucky Horse Racing Commission, the Kentucky Commission on Philanthropy, and the University of Louisville Athletic Association. In 2011, he was inducted into the Kentucky Black Sports Hall of Fame.

Kentucky Horse Racing Commission. http://www.khrc.ky.gov/NR /rdonlyres/612D35C1-4432-4FAF-93B7-F617903B295B/0 /CommissionHouston.pdf (accessed July 7, 2011).

Miller, Patrick B., and David K. Wiggins, eds. *Sport and the Color Line: Black Athletes and Race Relations in Twentieth-Century America.* New York: Routledge, 2004.

Newspapers: "Houston Resigns as Vols Coach Resignation during 5–19 Year Effective at End of Season," *LHL,* March 1, 1994, C1; "Kean Left Special Legacy for Houstons," *LHL,* February 2, 1999, D1.

—*Sallie L. Powell*

HOUSTON, WALTER SCOTT, JR. (b. 1918, Owensboro, KY; d. 1979, Cincinnati, OH), businessman and attorney. Shortly after his birth, Walter Scott Houston Jr., the only child of **Walter Scott Houston Sr.** and Anna Mae Houston, moved with his parents from his hometown, Owensboro, KY, to Lockland, OH, north of Cincinnati. Houston "exhibited great mental brilliancy" by age eight. His father died the following year. His mother, a Fisk graduate and Kentucky native, taught school to support the household, which included Houston, his grandmother, his aunt, and two funeral home janitors.

As an adult, Houston became a prominent undertaker in Cincinnati. Active in the **National Association for the Advancement of Colored People,** he protested one white doctor's policy of segregated waiting rooms in early 1946. In the summer of that year, he delivered the Cincinnati NAACP branch's welcome address at the 37th Annual Conference of the organization. By 1952, he had become an attorney and was influential in the desegregation of Cincinnati's Coney Island amusement park. At nearly 400 pounds, Houston presented an imposing figure when he provided free legal advice to African Americans arrested during Cincinnati's 1967 racial unrest. In 1973, arson destroyed his two funeral parlors, Cincinnati's Glenn Hall and Jordan Funeral Home and Lockland's Houston and Sons. Houston died six years later.

Dabney, Wendell P. *Cincinnati's Colored Citizens: Historical, Sociological and Biographical.* New York: Negro Univ. Press, 1970.

Kentucky Birth Index, 1911–1999.

Newspapers: "Undertaker Protests White Doc's Segregation," *BAA,* January 5, 1946; "Arson Suspected in Cincinnati," *Toledo Blade,* July 30, 1973.

Ohio Deaths, 1908–1932, 1938–1944, and 1958–2007.

U.S. Federal Census (1920, 1930).

—*Sallie L. Powell*

HOUSTON, WALTER SCOTT, SR. (b. 1888, Owensboro, KY; d. 1927, Cincinnati, OH), businessman. Walter Scott Houston Sr., the son of Robert and Maggie Houston of Owensboro, KY, demonstrated extensive financial judgment at the early age of 18. In 1906, one year before his father's death, Houston's economic astuteness created a sizable nest egg from his meager earnings. His thriftiness enabled him to purchase a home, and he finished the payments on it within six years. Later, he used the same procedure to procure another home.

In 1910, Houston married Owensboro native Grace Harding, who died five years later. His 1917 World War I draft registration card listed him as single and working as chief janitor for Owensboro's Masonic Temple. He was described as slender and bald. He soon married Kentucky native and Fisk graduate Anna Mae Lee, the mother of his son, **Walter Scott Houston Jr.,** who was born in Owensboro in 1918.

Shortly after his son's birth, Houston moved his family to Lockland, OH, near Cincinnati. He established a reputation for efficiency while working for the Philip Carey Company, an asbestos-mining company that sold insulation. He then started a cigar booth and later opened a grocery used by both African Americans and whites.

A few years before his death, Houston entered the funeral business. His property was valued at $50,000 in 1926. Nearly 40, he died the next year.

Dabney, Wendell P. *Cincinnati's Colored Citizens: Historical, Sociological and Biographical.* New York: Negro Univ. Press, 1970.

Ohio Deaths, 1908–1932, 1938–1944, and 1958–2007.

U.S. Federal Census (1900, 1920, 1930).

World War I Draft Registration Cards, 1917–1918.

—*Sallie L. Powell*

HOWARD, BENJAMIN FRANKLIN (b. 1860, Kentucky; d. 1918, Covington, KY), founder of the first African American Elks lodge in the United States. Benjamin Franklin Howard, who established Elks lodges for African Americans, was raised in Covington. After he obtained a copy of the Elks' initiation ritual—the organization was then all white—Howard rewrote the ritual for use by African Americans and copyrighted it. Because it was denied a charter in Kentucky, the first African American Elks lodge (**Improved Benevolent and Protective Order of Elks of the World**) was incorporated in Cincinnati. However, before the lodge was established in Cincinnati, Covington was home to its headquarters. Later, other African American lodges were created under Howard's leadership throughout the United States, laying the foundation for the establishment of an Elks grand lodge. In June 1899 the first Grand Lodge for the African American Elks met in Cincinnati, and Howard was elected the grand exalted ruler. A constitution for the new Grand Lodge was drawn up and approved. Howard served as the lodge's grand exalted ruler until July 28, 1910.

In 1916, the state of Kentucky finally permitted B. F. Howard to incorporate a lodge, called Ira Lodge No. 37, in Covington. Howard was its first exalted ruler. After he failed to become the new grand exalted ruler of the Southern Grand Lodge, however, Howard left the organization but continued his fraternal involvement by joining a new organization in Cincinnati, the Fraternal Mutual Benevolent Association. Howard, the founding father of the first African American Elks lodge in the United States, lived in Covington until his death in 1918 and was buried in Covington's Linden Grove Cemetery.

Harris, Theodore H. H. "The History of Afro-American Elkdom and Benjamin Franklin (B. F.) Howard in Covington, Kentucky,

1889–1918." *Northern Kentucky Heritage* 1, no. 2 (Spring–Summer 1994): 43–44.

Newspapers: Michelle Day, "Lodged in History, Elks to Host National Ceremony Here for Black Leader Ben Howard," *KP,* October 16, 1987, 7K; John C. K. Fisher, "Elks in Covington Honor Black Chapter's Founder," *KP,* October 19, 1987, 14K; "Black Elks Founder Honored with Marker," *KP,* November 27, 1995, 2K; "Park Honors Elks Group Founder," *CE,* December 2, 1995, C3; "Covington Officials Rededicate City Park," *CE,* August 30, 1998, C1B.

—*Theodore H. H. Harris*

HOWARD, JAMES LEONARD (b. 1942, Sturgis, KY; d. 2011, Choctaw, OK), participant in the integration of Sturgis High School in 1956. As a young African American resident of Sturgis, KY, a small town in the western part of the state, James Leonard Howard, son of Lawrence and Jettie Howard, was forced to take a bus to an all-black high school located 13 miles away despite the presence of a school for whites, Sturgis High School, only blocks from his home. In 1956, Howard and nine other young black students decided to enroll in the closer high school, testing the limits of the recent ***Brown v. Board of Education*** decision in Kentucky. Although he later recalled his first day at the school as being relatively benign, he was greeted by an angry mob the next time he tried to enter the school. In the following week, angry protesters burned a cross in a local park, and Kentucky governor Albert Benjamin Chandler called in the National Guard.

The decision to force integration at Sturgis High School initially failed. The attorney general of Kentucky, Jo M. Ferguson, ruled that only school boards, not parents and children, had the right to enact integration, and the local school board seized the opportunity to remove black students from white schools. The next year, Howard and other students tried again with more success. Although there was still an outcry against integration, a judicial order had granted the students the right to integrate, and he was able to graduate from the school in 1960.

After graduation, Howard joined the air force and stayed in the service for 20 years. Afterward, he moved to Oklahoma, where he served as assistant administrator of the Office of Personnel Management and as executive director of the Oklahoma Merit Protection Commission. Praised as a continual advocate for equal rights long after his endeavors in Sturgis, Howard died at the age of 68 on January 19, 2011.

Ellis, William E. *A History of Education in Kentucky.* Lexington: Univ. Press of Kentucky, 2011.

Fosl, Catherine, and Tracy E. K'Meyer. *Freedom on the Border: An Oral History of the Civil Rights Movement in Kentucky.* Lexington: Univ. Press of Kentucky, 2009.

Howard, James. Interview by Betsy Brinson undated. Living the Story Collection in Civil Rights in Kentucky: Oral History Project, Kentucky Historical Society.

"Taking Stand in Sturgis—School Was on Front Lines of Desegregation in State." *LHL,* May 17, 2004, A1.

—*Stephen Pickering*

HOWARD, JOHN DALPHIN (b. 1869, Shelbyville, KY; d. 1920, West Baden Springs, IN), editor and founder of the *Indianapolis Ledger*. John Dalphin Howard was born in Shelbyville, KY, on May 23, 1869. As a teenager, he moved to New Albany, IN,

with his parents, John and Delia Belle Howard. After graduating from high school, J. D., as he was frequently called, moved to Indianapolis. In 1895, he became a traveling representative for one of the premier black newspapers, the *Indianapolis Freeman,* and within less than 10 years had become the paper's advertising manager. Many credited Howard's efforts in raising thousands of dollars in advertising as a major factor in keeping the newspaper afloat during difficult economic times.

While selling ads, Howard also wrote crime serials and short stories that the *Freeman* often reprinted, and he formed his own publication, the *National Domestic Magazine* (1896–1898). In 1912, he left the *Freeman* and founded his own newspaper, the *Indianapolis Ledger.* During his eight years as editor, the paper grew to become one of the most influential black newspapers in the region.

Howard was also deeply involved in the early years of **African American baseball** as a promoter of the Indianapolis ABCs. He was one of the five known members of the drafting committee that wrote the constitution and charter of the Negro National League. He did not live to see the formation of the league, however, dying one month before its official creation on January 8, 1920, in West Baden Springs, IN. He was buried in Indianapolis.

Debono, Paul. *The Indianapolis ABCs: History of a Premier Team in the Negro Leagues.* Jefferson, NC: McFarland, 2007.

Mather, Frank Lincoln, ed. *Who's Who of the Colored Race: A General Biographical Dictionary of Men and Women of African Descent.* Vol. 1. Chicago: Memento Edition, 1915.

"Pencilings." *IF,* June 25, 1904, 7.

—*Joshua D. Farrington*

HOWARD, THEODORE ROOSEVELT MASON (b. 1908, Murray, KY; d. 1976, Chicago, IL), leading civil rights figure and medical doctor in Mississippi and Chicago during the 1950s and 1960s. Theodore Roosevelt Howard was born in Murray, KY, during one of the worst outbreaks of racial violence in the region's history, the Black Patch Wars. Throughout the rest of his life, T. R. M., as he preferred to be called, confronted similar episodes of racial violence. Born to unskilled tobacco laborers Arthur and Mary Chandler Howard in 1908, Howard attended the Murray Colored School (later known as [**Frederick**] **Douglass School**) as a small boy.

When he was 12 years old, a white Murray citizen hired Howard to care for his two-year-old son. The man's brother, Will Mason, was the head of the city's main hospital (and, in fact, had delivered Howard). Howard idealized Dr. Mason and was hired to perform various odd jobs around the hospital. Mason even taught Howard how to operate on animals. When Howard was 16, Mason provided him with a letter of recommendation and financial assistance to attend Oakwood Junior College in Huntsville, AL. After he graduated in 1927, Howard changed his legal name to Theodore Roosevelt Mason Howard in honor of his white mentor. Howard continued his education and received a BS degree from Union College in Barbourville, KY. He then attended the College of Medical Evangelists of Loma Linda (now Loma Linda University) in Loma Linda, CA. After receiving his medical degree, Howard found work at Nashville's Riverside Sanitarium and Hospital.

In 1947, Howard founded the Friendship Medical Clinic and Hospital in Mound Bayou, MS, and within a decade he was the chief surgeon in two of the state's largest black hospitals and was named president of the National Medical Association. In 1951, he founded the Regional Council of Negro Leadership (RCNL), which connected previously isolated civil rights activists like Medgar Evers and Amzie Moore. According to one scholar, by 1955, the RCNL was "the most significant mobilization of African Americans anywhere in the country." Howard received national notoriety for his nationwide protests after the lynching of Emmett Till in 1955. His activism quickly led to increased threats on his life, and out of fear for his life, he was smuggled out of the state inside a coffin. For his work in Mississippi, the *Chicago Defender* ranked Howard first in its annual honor roll for 1956. After hiding briefly in California, Howard eventually settled in Chicago, where he set up a controversial abortion clinic, ran unsuccessfully for Congress, and continued his civil rights activism. Amassing assets that at their peak numbered in the millions of dollars, Howard also held board positions at Memphis's Tri-State Bank and Universal Life Insurance Company.

T. R. M. Howard, one of the most important early leaders of the **civil rights movement,** helped Medgar Evers obtain his first job (and delivered the eulogy at his funeral), led voter-registration drives, raised money for the **National Association for the Advancement of Colored People** across the country, and introduced Fannie Lou Hamer to activism. Howard never ceased fighting for equality for African Americans. Even in his final years, he was finance chairman of Jesse Jackson's Operation PUSH, an organization that was initially headquartered in the basement of Howard's Chicago home.

Beito, David, and Linda Royster Beito. *Black Maverick: T. R. M. Howard's Fight for Civil Rights and Economic Power.* Urbana: Univ. of Illinois Press, 2009.

Houck, Davis, and David Dixon. *Rhetoric, Religion, and the Civil Rights Movement.* Waco, TX: Baylor Univ. Press, 2006.

"T. R. M. Howard: Mississippi Maverick." *Jackson Advocate,* September 24–September 30, 2009, 19A.

"T. R. M. Howard, Noted Physician, Dies at 68." *Jet,* May 20, 1976, 14.

—*Joshua D. Farrington*

HUDSON, JAMES BLAINE (b. 1949, Louisville, KY; d. 2013, Louisville, KY), educator, civil rights activist, and founder of the Saturday Academy, a community education program. James Blaine Hudson, as a student protester, occupied the University of Louisville's (U of L) dean's office; later, he held that same office. The only child of parents James and Lillian Hudson, J. Blaine Hudson, as he was known, spent much of his time with his maternal grandmother, Mabel Williamson, a retired schoolteacher, who influenced his appreciation of knowledge and creativity.

Hudson graduated from Louisville Male High School in 1967. Two years later, as a student member of the University of Louisville's Black Student Union, he joined other students in the occupation of the dean's office protesting the lack of African American faculty and board trustees and expressing the desire for a Pan-African Studies Department. He was jailed and summarily expelled for his activism. After returning to school, he received his BS degree with a double major in educational counseling and history in 1974 and his master of education in 1975. In 1981, he earned his doctor of education from the University of Kentucky.

For 10 years, Hudson worked in various capacities in the U of L's Preparatory Division. In 1992, he joined the Pan-African Studies Department faculty. From 1998 to 2003, he chaired the department and was associate dean of the university's College of Arts and Sciences from 1999 to 2004, when he was appointed its dean.

Hudson authored various works on the **Underground Railroad** and Louisville's African American history, including *Fugitive Slaves and the Underground Railroad in the Kentucky Borderland, Encyclopedia of the Underground Railroad,* and *Two Centuries of Black Louisville: A Photographic History,* coauthored with **Mervin Aubespin** and Kenneth Clay. To protest a statue of a Confederate soldier on the U of L campus, he directed the formation of Freedom Park. In 2002, he received the Martin Luther King Jr. Freedom Award from the city of Louisville. He chaired the Kentucky African American Heritage Commission and the Kentucky State Advisory Committee of the U.S. Commission on Civil Rights. He also founded the Saturday Academy, a community education program that taught African American history and world history from an African American perspective. The academy's sessions were free to the public, lasted three hours every Saturday, and were aimed at high school students and adults.

In 2012, Louisville mayor Greg Fischer appointed Hudson chairman of the Louisville Violence Prevention Work Group. Shortly after he had cranial surgery, Hudson resigned from the position. He died on January 5, 2013. **A. D. Porter** and Son Funeral Home handled the funeral arrangements. In May 2013, he was posthumously honored when the community-enrichment program he founded was renamed the J. Blaine Hudson Saturday Academy.

Newspapers: "J. Blaine Hudson, Educator," *LCJ,* February 12, 2012, E3; "J. Blaine Hudson, Ex–U of L Dean, Dies," *LCJ,* January 6, 2013, A1; "Community Sessions Will Be Renamed J. Blaine Hudson Saturday Academy," Targeted News Service (USA), May 14, 2013.

University of Louisville. "In Memoriam: Dean J. Blaine Hudson (1949–2013)." http://louisville.edu/facultysenate/documents/in-memorium/HUDSON.pdf/at_download/file (accessed July 26, 2013).

—*Sallie L. Powell*

HUDSON, JAMES E. (b. 1886, Frankfort, KY; d. 1964, Louisville, KY), first African American to address the Kentucky General Assembly. Frankfort, KY, native James E. Hudson lived with his wife, Callie, and son, Joseph, at 310 E. Third St. He held various manual labor jobs, including janitor and waiter in the Tulip Tea Room. He also served as a volunteer missionary at the state reformatory. He was the honorary vice president of the Christian Endeavor Society Bible School and honorary superintendent of the Corresponding Bible School.

Hudson, a devoutly religious man, always carried a Bible with him. While he was working as a Kentucky State Capitol elevator operator, some legislators borrowed his Bible when they were addressing an evolution bill. Scott Co.'s representative George C. Waggoner noticed Hudson's worn Bible and bought him a new one along with a Bible dictionary. On March 16, 1922, Hudson became the first African American to address Kentucky's General Assembly when he expressed his gratitude for the gifts.

Additionally, in 1922, Kentucky House of Representatives Resolution Number 16 addressed the issue that Hudson was compelled to work overtime, without compensation, late in the evenings to accommodate House and Senate members. Since there was no provision for reimbursement and the legislature viewed his service as beneficial, it was recommended that $180.00 be appropriated from the general fund to pay Hudson. The resolution was tabled.

Hudson's wife, Callie, died at age 50 in 1937. On October 9, 1964, Hudson died at age 78.

Caron's Directory of the City of Frankfort, Kentucky, 1921–1923 and *1928–1930.*

House Resolution No. 16. *Acts of the General Assembly of the Commonwealth of Kentucky,* 1922, 454–55.

Journal of the Kentucky Senate Regular 1926 Session. Vol. 1, 366–67.

Kentucky Death Index, 1911–2000.

United We Stand Minority Report. June 29, 2006, http://www.e-archives.ky.gov/pubs/sec_of_state/unitedwestandfinal.pdf (accessed July 15, 2011).

U.S. Federal Census (1920, 1930).

—*Sallie L. Powell*

HUESTON, WILLIAM CLARENCE, SR. (b. 1880, Lexington, KY; d. 1961, Washington, DC), judge, president of the Negro Baseball Association, and grand commissioner of education of the black Elks.

William C. Hueston was born to Sam and Bettie Hueston in Lexington, KY, on September 24, 1880. After graduating from Chandler Normal School, Hueston moved with his family to Kansas City, KS. In 1904, he graduated from the University of Kansas and moved to Illinois to study at the University of Chicago Law School, where he became the school's first African American graduate.

Hueston established a law firm in Kansas City and became active in city politics, running an unsuccessful campaign for city alderman in 1918. In 1924, he moved to Gary, IN, after he was appointed the city's first black judge. While serving as a magistrate judge, he also was instrumental in establishing the Central State Bank of Gary, the first black-owned state bank north of the Mason-Dixon line. During this period, Hueston also succeeded Rube Foster as the president of the Negro Baseball League, a position he held from 1927 through the early 1930s. In 1930, Judge Hueston was appointed an attorney on the staff of the solicitor of the U.S. Post Office Department and moved to Washington, DC. During subsequent decades, he established his own law firm in the city and was instrumental in creating the law library at Howard University.

Hueston was also an influential leader of the country's largest black fraternal organization, the **Improved Benevolent and Protective Order of the Elks of the World.** In 1925, he formed the organization's Department of Education and served as its grand commissioner through the 1950s. Under his leadership, hundreds of thousands of dollars in Elks' oratory scholarships were granted to help pay for young African Americans, including Martin Luther King Jr., to attend college. In 1952, Hueston, a devoted Republican, appeared on stage alongside Dwight Eisenhower during a presidential campaign stop in Harlem. Hueston died of a heart attack in his Washington, DC, home on November 25, 1961.

Coulter, Charles E. *"Take Up the Black Man's Burden": Kansas City's African American Communities, 1865–1939.* Columbia: Univ. of Missouri Press, 2006.

Hogan, Lawrence D. *Shades of Glory: The Negro Leagues and the Story of African-American Baseball.* Washington, DC: National Geographic, 2006.

Wesley, Charles. *History of the Improved Benevolent and Protective Order of Elks of the World, 1898–1954.* Washington, DC: Association for the Study of Negro Life and History, 1955.

"William C. Hueston, 81, Government Attorney." *WP,* November 26, 1961, B7.

—*Joshua D. Farrington*

HUGHES, BRENDA LEE GARNER (b. 1947, Lexington, KY; d. 1986, Lexington, KY), first African American female basketball official to referee the Kentucky Girls' State High School Basketball Tournament.

The only daughter of Mathew and Alice Alexander Garner, Brenda Lee Garner was born in Lexington, KY, on November 4, 1947. After graduating from Lexington's (Paul Laurence) **Dunbar High School** and attending the University of Kentucky, she married Gordon Hughes.

Later, as a divorced mother of two daughters, Monique and Lucy Lee, Hughes worked full-time for the U.S. Post Office and part-time for the Lexington Division of Parks and Recreation, where she obtained her referee training. **John William "Scoop" Brown,** former baseball player for the **Lexington Hustlers** and the first African American male to referee in the Kentucky Boys' High School State Basketball Tournament in 1963, introduced Hughes to officiating when he hired her as a part-time recreational director at Lexington's Charles Young Recreation Center in 1966. According to Brown, her responsibilities included organizing girls' basketball leagues, cheerleading squads, a girls' drill team, and girls' debate teams. Since racial segregation dominated African American girls' sports involvement, Hughes, through her own initiative, developed a citywide cheerleading organization for African American girls. In 1967, Lexington's Parks and Recreation Department named her one of two outstanding playground supervisors.

As a Parks and Recreation supervisor, her duties included refereeing in boys' and girls' basketball leagues. She officiated in recreational leagues, including the Senior **Dirt Bowl** Basketball Tournament. Held at Douglass Park on the third Sunday in July, this tournament, known as Super Sunday, demanded the best from coaches, players, and officials.

In the early years of Title IX and the return of girls' basketball to Kentucky, women officials were critical to the expansion of the game. Nonetheless, the male-dominated officiating milieu meant that the struggle for women included locating properly fitted uniforms. Brenda Hughes obtained a men's size small referee shirt that was large on her and initially wore ballet slippers, possibly because of inability to find referee shoes her size.

In 1972, shortly after the passage of Title IX, Hughes registered with the Kentucky High School Athletic Association. As the first African American female basketball official to work in the state

Brenda Hughes, 1973.

tournament, she refereed the Kentucky Girls' State High School Basketball Tournament in 1976, 1977, 1980, and 1981. Shortly after her 39th birthday, Hughes died of a brain illness on December 15, 1986. She was buried in Highland Cemetery, Lexington, KY. In 1995, the Kentucky High School Athletic Association posthumously elected Hughes to its Hall of Fame.

Powell, Sallie L. "'It Is Hard to Be What You Have Not Seen': Brenda Hughes and the Black and White of the Zebra Shirt—Race and Gender in Kentucky High School Basketball." *RKHS*, 109, nos. 3–4 (Summer and Autumn 2011): 433–65.

—*Sallie L. Powell*

HUGHES, GREEN PERCY (b. 1881, Bourbon Co., KY; d. 1930, Louisville, KY), founder and president of Louisville's Domestic Life and Accident Insurance Company. Green Percy Hughes was born outside Paris, KY, to William and Delphia Smith Hughes on January 27, 1881. He spent his formative years working on his father's Bourbon Co. farm. Although he only had a limited education, he moved to Louisville to attend State University (later known as **Simmons College of Kentucky**) in 1898.

After graduating with an AB degree in 1906, G. P. Hughes spent a number of years at various short-term jobs, including a "short time in Government service as a storekeeper." In 1912, he was hired as an insurance agent and district manager of the Lexington, KY, branch of Atlanta Life Insurance Company. During the late 1910s, he returned to Louisville and worked as an agent with **Mammoth Life and Accident Insurance Company.**

On May 17, 1921, he and two other Mammoth Life employees formed **Domestic Life and Accident Insurance Company.** The three divided their responsibilities, and Hughes was named president, **J. E. Smith** was named vice president, and W. F. Turner was named secretary and manager. Because Hughes had saved capital for over two years and brought with him many of his former clients, his business was one of the few black-owned insurance companies to have over $100,000 in fully paid capital stock before it officially opened on September 8, 1921. Originally located in a rented portion of the **Knights of Pythias** building on Chestnut St., Domestic Life purchased its own building at 610 W. **Walnut St.** in 1924. Although it never became as large as Mammoth Life, Louisville's largest black-owned insurance company, Domestic had signed over 50,000 policies, worth over $5 million, by the time it moved to its permanent location on Walnut Street.

Although Domestic Life survived long after the Great Depression, Hughes was among the numerous businessmen across the country who took their lives in the wake of the stock market crash, cutting his throat with a razor on August 7, 1930. G. P. Hughes was married to Sue Brannon Hughes, had four children, and lived at 2503 W. Walnut St. at the time of his tragic death.

Boris, Joseph J., ed. *Who's Who in Colored America, 1927.* New York: Who's Who in Colored America Corp., 1927.
Kentucky, Death Records, 1852–1953.
Stuart, Merah Steven. *An Economic Detour: A History of Insurance in the Lives of American Negroes.* New York: Wendell, Malliet, & Co., 1940.
Wright, George C. *Life Behind a Veil: Blacks in Louisville, Kentucky, 1865–1930.* Baton Rouge: Louisiana State Univ. Press, 1985.

—*Joshua D. Farrington*

HUGHES, SAMMY THOMAS (b. 1910, Louisville, KY; d. 1981, Los Angeles, CA), five-time all-star second baseman in the Negro Leagues. Known as a prodigious baseball talent in the ballparks of his hometown of Louisville, Kentucky, Sammy Thomas Hughes signed with the Louisville White Sox at age 18. A tall infielder at six-feet-four, Hughes played first base for the Washington Pilots before switching to second base, the position he played for the rest of his career. After the Pilots folded, Hughes joined the Nashville Elite Giants, who eventually ended up in Baltimore. While he was with the Elite Giants from 1933 to 1940, he established himself as an all-star second baseman, capable of excellent defense and high batting averages.

Hughes was selected to the East-West All-Star Game five times in his career, a record for second basemen. He hit for a career average of between .296 and .322—records for the period are questionable—with a high of .355 for the 1935 season. Regarded as the finest second baseman in the Negro leagues by many of his peers, Hughes supposedly received attention from the major leagues, along with fellow players Roy Campanella and Dave Barnhill, but a reported tryout with the Pittsburgh Pirates never materialized. His career, which was punctuated by a four-year stint in the army during World War II, ended in 1946 after one last run with the Elite Giants. After retiring from the game, Hughes worked for the Pillsbury Company and the Hughes Aircraft Company in Los Angeles, where he died on August 9, 1981.

McNeil, William. *Cool Papas and Double Duties: The All-Time Greats of the Negro Leagues.* Jefferson, NC: McFarland, 2001.

"Negro Baseball Stars Get Chance with Pittsburgh." *Florida Evening Independent,* July 27, 1942, 10.

Porter, David L. *Biographical Dictionary of American Sports: Baseball.* New York: Greenwood Press, 1987.

Riley, James A., ed. *The Biographical Encyclopedia of the Negro Baseball Leagues.* New York: Carroll & Graf, 1994.

—*Stephen Pickering*

HUMES, HELEN (b. 1913, Louisville, KY; d. 1981, Santa Monica, CA), jazz singer. Helen Humes was the daughter of John and Emma (Johnson) Humes. As a child she performed with **Bessie Allen**'s Booker T. Washington Community Center Band. She graduated from **Central High School** in 1926 and in 1927 traveled with guitarist Sylvester Weaver to St. Louis and New York City for her first recording sessions. From 1938 to 1942, she sang with the Count Basie band. Her hit records include "Be-Baba-Leba" (1945) and "Million Dollar Secret" (1950). In 1967, she retired from music and moved back to Louisville to care for her parents. In 1973, she came out of retirement to perform at the Newport **Jazz** Festival, which led to a successful comeback. In 1975, she was presented the key to the city of Louisville.

Dahl, Linda. *Stormy Weather: The Music and Lives of a Century of Jazzwomen.* New York: Limelight Editions, 1989.

Harris, Sheldon. *Blues Who's Who.* New York: Arlington House 1979.

O'Neal, Jim. "Helen Humes." *Living Blues* 52 (Spring 1982): 24.

—*Brenda K. Bogert*

HUMMONS, HENRY LYTLE, SR. (b. 1873, Lexington, KY; d. 1956, Indianapolis, IN), medical doctor. Henry Lytle Hummons Sr. was born to Thomas and Mary Ellen Hummons in Lexington, KY, on February 25, 1873. After graduating from Chandler Normal School in 1889, he left Kentucky to attend school at Knoxville College in Tennessee, from which he graduated in 1894. He then attended medical school at the Indiana School of Medicine in Indianapolis.

After graduating in 1902, he opened an office in Indianapolis, specializing in obstetrics. In 1911, he briefly left the city to conduct postgraduate work at Harvard Medical School. When he returned to Indianapolis, he helped establish the city's first free tuberculosis clinic, Flanner House, in 1919. In addition to serving Flanner House from its founding through 1931, he additionally served as the director of Lincoln Hospital.

Hummons was also deeply involved in the Indianapolis community. He was the founder of the city's YMCA branch and was an influential member of Witherspoon United Presbyterian Church, which later named a wing of its building in his honor. In 1953, he was named Man of the Year by **Omega Psi Phi Fraternity** and was commended by the Indiana Medical Association for his 50 years of medical service. He died in Indianapolis on April 5, 1956.

"Deaths." *Journal of the National Medical Association* 49, no. 1 (1957): 65.

Finding aid, H. L. (Henry Lytle) Hummons Papers, Indiana Historical Society. Indianapolis, IN.

Fleming, G. James, and Christian E. Burckel, eds. *Who's Who in Colored America.* 7th ed. Yonkers-on-Hudson, NY: Christian E. Burckel & Associates, 1950.

Nercessian, Nora N. *Against All Odds: The Legacy of Students of African Descent at Harvard Medical School before Affirmative Action, 1850–1968.* Cambridge, MA: Harvard Medical School, 2004.

—*Joshua D. Farrington*

HUMPHREY, WILLIAM (b. 1879, Mason Co., KY; d. 1958, Maysville, KY), teacher, principal, president of the Kentucky Negro Educational Association, and director of the Mason County Fund. William Humphrey, a well-known African American teacher, was the son of George and Annetta Berry Humphrey. Professor Humphrey, as he became known, began his academic career at age 13 while working as a school janitor at the colored school in Maysville. He finished 10 grades of school there in six years. He then attended **Berea College** in Berea for five years, working as a headwaiter at the same time. At Berea College, he completed his last two years of high school and three years of college, earning his BA in 1904. A year of graduate study at Harvard University in Cambridge, MA, followed, but health problems compelled him to return to Maysville for a period of rest. He later earned an MA from Ohio State University in Columbus and a BS at Tuskegee Institute in Tuskegee, AL.

At this time, Humphrey was asked to work with African Americans in Mason Co., and he helped rebuild the county's colored school at Mays Lick, which had burned. His teaching career began there. The following year, he took a teaching position at the old colored school in Maysville, where he served as principal from 1907 to 1930. In 1930, **John G. Fee Industrial High School** was built on E. Fourth St. in Maysville, and Humphrey served as an educator and principal in Maysville for a total of 42 years. Under his direction, Fee Industrial High School became a four-year high school for African Americans. Through his influence, the integration that took place in the late 1950s within the Maysville schools was accomplished more smoothly, even though he had retired in 1949.

In 1930, Humphrey was chosen as president of the **Kentucky Negro Educational Association.** Over the years, he served as a deacon and in every official lay position in Maysville's Bethel Baptist Church. From March 1950, when the Maysville Municipal Housing Commission was established to oversee the city's 100-unit low-cost housing program, until his death, Humphreys was part of the four-member governing body of the commission. In 1951, he became a director of the Mason County Fund, the forerunner of the United Appeal agency in the county.

Humphrey's wife, whom he married on June 16, 1920, was Allie Young from Bath Co., KY. They had two sons and also raised a foster daughter and three nephews. Humphrey died in Maysville at his home at 614 E. Third St. in 1958 and was buried in Washington Baptist Cemetery in Washington, KY.

Calvert, Jean, and John Klee. *Maysville, Kentucky: From Past to Present in Pictures.* Maysville, KY: Mason Co. Museum, 1983.

Newspapers: "William Humphrey an Honor to His Native City, Maysville, and Kentucky," *Maysville Public Daily Ledger,* June 15, 1904, 2; "Long Useful Life of City's Leading Colored Citizen Ends," *Maysville Public Ledger,* September 22, 1958, 1; "W. H. Humphrey,

Former Head at Fee, Dies," *Maysville Daily Independent,* September 22, 1958, 1.

Stout, Louis. *Shadows of the Past: A History of the Kentucky High School Athletic League.* Lexington, KY: Host Communications, 2006.

—*Mary Ellen Lucas*

HUNTER, BUSH A. (b. 1894, Lexington, KY; d. 1983, Lexington, KY), physician and first African American associate of the Fayette County Medical Society. Bush A. Hunter, physician, was born in Lexington on August 10, 1894, the son of **John E. Hunter,** MD. After attending Hampton Institute in Virginia, he enrolled at the Oberlin Conservatory in Ohio, where he studied voice and played cello. He graduated from Oberlin in 1915 and received a medical degree from Howard University a few years later. Hunter established his medical practice in Lexington in 1926. Health care was then rigidly segregated, and black physicians were excluded from hospital staffs. Despite these handicaps, Hunter ministered to patients in Lexington and surrounding communities for more than half a century.

Hunter was the first African American member of the Fayette County Medical Society and served as vice president of the Fayette County Cancer Society and medical adviser to the Selective Service System. In 1965, he was honored as Kentucky's Outstanding General Practitioner of the Year. Hunter and his wife, the former Mary W. Royster, had one son, Bush A. Hunter Jr. Hunter died in Lexington on November 30, 1983, and was buried in **Camp Nelson** National Cemetery in Jessamine Co., KY.

—*Doris Wilkinson*

HUNTER, JOHN E. (b. 1859, Mercer Co., VA; d. 1956, Lexington, KY), physician and first African American to practice surgery at St. Joseph Hospital in Lexington, KY. John E. Hunter, physician, was born in 1859 in Mercer Co., VA (now in West Virginia). Raised by a Quaker family who discovered him hidden in a wagon, Hunter graduated from Ohio's Oberlin College in 1887 and received a medical degree from Case Western Reserve University in Cleveland on May 2, 1890. After graduate work at Cleveland and Boston hospitals and at the Mayo Clinic, he and Perry D. Robinson opened a practice in Lexington, KY. Hunter later became the first African American physician to practice surgery at Lexington's St. Joseph's Hospital.

In 1904, Hunter was elected president of the National Medical Association. He also helped found the Florida A&M College Clinic Association in Tallahassee. Until 1950, when he was 90 years old, he taught clinics annually at the association's hospital. Hunter also played an active role in improving conditions for Kentuckians. He participated in the **Anti–Separate Coach Movement** and was one of the founders of Lexington's (Paul Laurence) **Dunbar High School.** The Hunter Medical Foundation, opened in 1973 and named in honor of his son, **Bush A. Hunter,** became part of Healthcare of Kentucky in 1982. Hunter died on November 14, 1956, and was buried in Lexington's Cove Haven Cemetery.

—*Doris Wilkinson*

HURD, "BABE" (b. 1867, Galveston, TX; d. 1928, Paris, KY), jockey. "Babe" Hurd's birth name may be lost to history, but his equestrian skills survive. He rode his first mount at age 13 for Maryland governor Oden Bowie. In 1881, Green B. Morris of Morris and Patton Stables bought his contract. The following year, in his first and only **Kentucky Derby,** Hurd jockeyed the stable's horse, Apollo, to the winner's circle.

This Kentucky Derby made history for three reasons: the first time bookmaking was used at Churchill Downs, the first real surprise win, and the first direct charge of corruption. The Dwyer Brothers' Runnymede was a 5-to-5 predicted winner, while Apollo only had a 10-to-1 chance. The *Louisville Courier-Journal* portrayed Hurd as possessing confidence and excellent rider's judgment for waiting in the sixth position in the race, thus "saving his horse for the punishing finish." To the casual fan, he appeared completely out of the competition. The crowd of 15,000 became vocal when Hurd dangerously weaved Apollo through the throng of horses into third position. Fifty yards farther, Apollo made a "cyclonic rush" and reached Runnymede's withers. Apollo beat Runnymede by half a length. Captain Sam Brown, a Pittsburgh millionaire turfman, charged that gamblers had bribed Runnymede's jockey, James "Jimmy" McLaughlin, to throw the race. However, Michael and Phillip Dwyer, owners of the runner-up, refuted Brown's claim and maintained that it was an honest race.

Thirty-five years later, Hurd described the race. He stated that McLaughlin had boasted before the race that he was going to teach the African American riders how to ride, but the African American jockeys **Erskine "Babe" Henderson,** John "Kid" Stovall, and Gibbs (first name unknown) decided "to show him a thing or two" and pinned him against the rail in the middle of the race. As Hurd passed McLaughlin, he shouted, "Jimmy, you're gone." Apollo's owner, Green B. Morris, assisted Hurd's dismount in the winner's circle, yelling, "My boy, you shall never want for a dollar as long as you live." Morris paid him the regular fee of $25 for the win. Hurd claimed that Morris paid him $10 when he lost a race and that he never received a regular salary.

Hurd ended his Thoroughbred jockey career after the Kentucky Derby because of his weight gain and became a steeplechase rider. He became a trainer in 1885. According to his 1892 voter's registration, he had lived in Chicago for at least a year and a half and worked at the Garfield Park Race Track. By 1900, he was training horses in St. Louis. In 1905, the *New York Daily Tribune* and the *St. Louis Republic* reported that "Babe" Hurd and his brother, Mitchell Hurd, had formed a racehorse partnership with Arthur Parker, which ended with Parker filing a lawsuit to liquidate the partnership. The 1870 U.S. federal census listed Mitchell Hurd living with his mother, Alice, and younger brother, Wilson, possibly an indication that Babe's first name was Wilson.

Hurd later returned to Kentucky and trained horses at Churchill Downs. He died after a short illness due to heart problems at Long Ridge Farm in Bourbon Co., KY, in December 1928. Edward W. Jackson Funeral Home handled the arrangements, and he was buried in Chicago, where his surviving daughter, Mrs. Alice Whitfield, lived.

Leach, George B. *The Kentucky Derby Diamond Jubilee.* Louisville, KY: Gibbs-Inman Co., 1949.

Newspapers: "Apollo Wins," *LCJ,* May 7, 1882, 6; "'Outlaw' Racetracks in Suit," *New York Daily Tribune,* January 6, 1905, 5; "Racing

Jennie V. Wendell (daughter of Dr. Thomas Wendell, left) and Dan Hunter (son of Dr. John Hunter, right) playing doctor, 1913.

Partners Disagree," *St. Louis Republic,* January 6, 1905, 3; "When Apollo Won the Kentucky Derby," *DRF,* April 10, 1917, 1; "First Upset in the Kentucky Derby," *DRF,* April 19, 1918, 2; "Colored Notes," *LL,* December 10, 1928, sec. 2, p. 10.

Renau, Lynn S. *Racing around Kentucky.* Louisville, KY: L. S. Renau, 1995.

Saunders, James Robert, and Monica Renae Saunders. *Black Winning Jockeys in the Kentucky Derby.* Jefferson, NC: McFarland, 2003.

U.S. Federal Census (1870).

—*Sallie L. Powell*

HUTCHINSON, CONRAD "HUTCH," JR. (b. 1919, Blooms-burg, PA; d. 1996, Grambling, LA), warrant officer and trend-setter of marching-band music. Conrad Hutchinson, an innovator in music for marching bands, was the son of Conrad and Helen Hutchinson. He earned his BA in music education from Tuskegee Institute (known today as Tuskegee University) in Macon Co., AL. During World War II, he served in the U.S. Army's Command Headquarters Band in Calcutta, India, and achieved the rank of warrant officer, junior grade. Hutchinson was awarded the Good Conduct Medal as well as the China, Burma, India Theater Medal with five battle stars. In 1945, he became music director for the **Lincoln-Grant Schools** in Covington.

It was while Hutchinson was at the Lincoln-Grant Schools that he initiated marching to contemporary music; the result was the distinctive step style of marching that is commonly performed by many African American marching bands today. Hutchinson would march the high school band around the schoolyard in this style, never missing any of the musical notes. Ever the creative mentor, Hutchinson developed a lasting relationship between his students and their music. He also developed popular school dance and **jazz** bands, and a number of his students went on to play professionally in clubs in and around Cincinnati. In Covington, Hutchinson resided at W. 10th St., on E. Bush St., and on Russell St.

When Hutchinson was not conducting the schools' bands, he worked for Cincinnati radio stations WSAI and WLW as staff organist, conducted theater bands and orchestras, and played the organ at churches. He was the staff arranger for Cincinnati's famed King Records and worked with the Three Music-Warner Brothers Publishers. He engaged in graduate study at the University of Cincinnati, Case Western Reserve University in Cleveland, OH, the New England Conservatory of Music, and Vandercook College of Music in Chicago, where he earned an MA in music education.

In 1952, Hutchinson left Covington and Lincoln-Grant Schools for a job at Grambling State University in Louisiana, where he served as music director for more than 40 years and received numerous awards. In 1996, he died in Grambling, LA, and was buried there.

"Celebration of Life, Conrad Hutchinson, Jr., March 9, 1996." Special Collections, A. C. Lewis Memorial Library, Grambling State Univ.
Grantonian, 1950 (William Grant High School yearbook). Collection of Theodore H. H. Harris.

—Theodore H. H. Harris

I

IMPROVED BENEVOLENT AND PROTECTIVE ORDER OF ELKS OF THE WORLD, organization founded by Kentuckians that became one of the largest and most prestigious African American fraternal orders in the United States. As a response to being denied entry into white fraternal organizations in the late nineteenth and early twentieth centuries, African Americans throughout Kentucky and the nation formed their own, autonomous societies. One of the largest of these organizations was the Improved Benevolent and Protective Order of Elks of the World (IBPOEW), modeled after the lily-white Benevolent and Protective Order of Elks of the World (BPOEW). Founded in 1899, the IBPOEW quickly developed a reputation as the most prestigious organization among the burgeoning black middle class and served an important role in promoting education throughout the country.

Kentuckians **Benjamin Franklin Howard** of Covington and Arthur J. Riggs of Shelbyville founded the IBPOEW. In 1898, Riggs obtained a copy of the BPOEW manual, which provided details on rituals, rites, and rules of order. How he secured the copy remains a mystery, although many African American Elks speculated that Riggs, a Pullman porter, took it from a white passenger on a train. Howard and Riggs brought the manuscript to an attorney, who determined that it was not copyrighted. The pair then had the document copyrighted in their name, printed duplicates, and began the process of forming their own organization. After being denied a charter in Covington, which remained the organization's unofficial headquarters, the first IBPOEW lodge met in Cincinnati, OH, in June 1899. Howard was named exalted ruler.

Over the next decade, African American Elks formed lodges across the country, but the state of Kentucky continued to refuse to incorporate any chapters. In 1916, after continued pressure from Howard, the Kentucky General Assembly finally granted the IBPOEW a charter. Soon after, Ira Lodge No. 37 was opened in Covington, and Benjamin Howard became its exalted ruler. By 1923, there were 8 IBPOEW chapters in Kentucky, and by 1955, there were 16 chapters in the state. In addition to the Covington lodge, there were three chapters in Louisville and lodges in Winchester, Richmond, Henderson, Danville, Ashland, Middlesboro, Lexington, Lynch, Hopkinsville, Guthrie, Bowling Green, and Owensboro. Throughout the 1950s, Lexington's Lodge No. 27 was the largest in the state and eighteenth largest in the nation, with over 120 members.

One of the most significant contributions by the national IBPOEW was its promotion of education. For example, an Elks scholarship paid for Martin Luther King Jr.'s college education. Lexington native and bank executive **William Clarence Hueston Sr.** was a driving force behind the IBPOEW's emphasis on education. Hueston was appointed the Grand Commissioner of Education at the organization's Grand Lodge of 1925, and he immediately established a Department of Education to focus on

educating African American youths. The Department of Education and Hueston's scholarship program became one of the most successful IBPOEW programs in the organization's history. Chapters throughout the country held youth oratorical contests, with college scholarships given as the grand prize. Elks in Kentucky also held annual oratorical contests. The 1934 contest, for example, held in Paducah at the height of the Great Depression, offered a $1,000 scholarship for the high school student who gave the best speech on the relationship between African Americans and the Constitution. Dean T. R. Dailey of West Kentucky Industrial College (later known as **West Kentucky Community and Technical College**), who also served as the educational director of the IBPOEW in Kentucky, ran the contest. Over 60 years later, national and Kentucky IBPOEW chapters were still holding oratorical contests and providing African American youths with scholarships. In 1997, over 35,000 black Elks flocked to Louisville to attend the national convention or Grand Lodge, where student finalists competed for thousands of dollars' worth of scholarships.

In 1987, the national IBPOEW hosted a ceremony in Covington to honor Benjamin Howard. Eugene Rice, exalted ruler of Ira Lodge No. 37, noted that Howard founded "the biggest black organization in the world," with more than 450,000 members. Hundreds of Elks from New York to California attended the ceremony. The Kentucky State Association of the Improved Benevolent and Protective Order of Elks of the World, which represents 8 Elks lodges, 10 Elks temples, and a number of women's auxiliaries, continues to have a strong presence in the state. In a 1990 interview, the state Elks president, Robert Gilbert of Richmond, succinctly summed up the ideals the organization had promoted since its inception almost 100 years earlier, promising that the IBPOEW would continue to stand for "charity, justice, brotherly love and civil liberty."

"Elks Announce Oratorical Contest." *KNEAJ* 4, no. 2 (February–March 1934): 7.

Harris, Theodore. "The History of Afro-American Elkdom and Benjamin Franklin (B. F.) Howard in Covington, Kentucky, 1889–1918." *Northern Kentucky Heritage* 1, no. 2 (Spring–Summer 1994): 43–44.

Newspapers: "Lodged in History," *KP*, October 16, 1987, 14K; "Elks Look toward Their Future at Convention in Lexington," *LHL*, June 22, 1990, C1; "Elks' Essay Contest Gives Chance at College Cash," *LHL*, January 28, 1997, 2.

Wesley, Charles. *History of the Improved Benevolent and Protective Order of Elks of the World, 1898–1954.* Washington DC: Association for the Study of Negro Life and History, 1955.

—*Joshua D. Farrington*

INTERRACIAL HOSPITAL MOVEMENT, organization that ended racial restrictions in Kentucky hospitals. On an autumn night in 1950, three young African Americans were taken to a hospital in Hardinsburg, KY, after being severely injured in a car accident. The hospital refused to admit black patients, so officials called for a black ambulance service in Louisville. While the ambulance drove the 70 miles to Hardinsburg, the men were given little medical attention, and they were forced to lie on a concrete floor. After newspapers reported the incident, which claimed the life of one of the three men, a biracial organization known as the Interracial Hospital Movement (IHM) was formed to demand desegregation of medical facilities across the state of Kentucky.

Led by Mary Agnes Barnett, an African American woman married to a leader of the Louisville Progressive Party, and Anne Braden, a white newspaper writer and also an activist in the Progressive Party, the IHM began an extensive petition drive in 1951. The movement eventually developed into a wide-ranging coalition that included both white and black members of civil rights organizations and labor unions. Additionally, Braden's door-to-door appeals garnered the support of important leaders in the religious community, such as J. C. Olden, who led the Militant Church Movement in Louisville, along with Rev. Albert Dalton of St. Stephen's Episcopal Church. Olden co-chaired the IHM after being impressed with Braden's commitment to the cause.

In January 1951, the IHM led a mass march on Frankfort, KY, where leaders presented Governor Lawrence Wetherby with the results of the petition drive. In total, the IHM collected around 11,000 signatures from residents across the state. The governor responded by ordering an immediate investigation of public hospitals. He then required all medical facilities receiving money from the state government to end practices of racial restriction.

The IHM sent a committee to Frankfort requesting legislative change in early 1952. The committee, led by J. A. Christian and William T. Byrd, asked that an amendment be attached to an impending Hospital Licensing Act that would rule "that no licensed hospital in the state may deny care to any person because of race, creed, or color." Supported by Senator C. W. A. McCann, the amendment passed the Kentucky Senate in February 1952. Shortly thereafter, the Kentucky State Medical Association issued a statement declaring that it was now in favor of barring discrimination in medical facilities. Although the House of Representatives modified the amendment to bar the denial of "emergency treatment" before the act was passed, the IHM had successfully initiated the process of desegregation of medical facilities in Kentucky.

Braden, Anne. Interview by Catherine Fosl, March 8–9, 1989. Anne Braden Oral History Project, Louis B. Nunn Center for Oral History, Univ. of Kentucky.

Fosl, Catherine. *Subversive Southerner: Anne Braden and the Struggle for Racial Justice in the Cold War South.* Lexington: Univ. Press of Kentucky, 2006.

K'Meyer, Tracy E. *Civil Rights in the Gateway to the South: Louisville, Kentucky, 1945–1980.* Lexington: Univ. Press of Kentucky, 2009.

Maund, Alfred. "New Day Dawning: The Negro and Medicine." *Nation* 196 (1953): 396–97.

"State Licensing Act Would Ban Race Discrimination." *LD,* February 16, 1952, 1.

—*Stephen Pickering*

IOTA PHI THETA FRATERNITY, INC., national fraternity founded by African American men. In the midst of the **civil rights movement,** Iota Phi Theta Fraternity, the nation's fifth-largest predominantly African American social service fraternity, was founded on September 19, 1963, on the steps of Hurt Gymnasium at Morgan State College (now Morgan State University) in Baltimore, MD, by 12 young men: Albert Hicks, Lonnie Spruill Jr., Charles Briscoe, Frank Coakley, John Slade, Barron Willis, Webster Lewis, Charles Brown, Louis Hudnell, Charles Gregory, Elias Dorsey Jr., and Michael Williams. These men established the fraternity's purpose as "the development and perpetuation of Scholarship, Leadership, Citizenship, Fidelity, and Brotherhood among Men." Additionally, they conceived the fraternity's motto, "Building a Tradition, Not Resting upon One!"

The fraternity's national governing body, the Grand Council, has responsibility for the group's governance. The grand polaris and other elected national officers head the national organization, while the executive secretary manages the national office. The regionally structured national body has regional polari who direct the Atlantic Coast, Gulf Coast, Ohio Valley, Eastern, Midwest, Southern, and Far West regions. Iota Phi Theta has over 300 chapters nationwide and around the world.

The fraternity's colors are charcoal brown and gilded gold; its symbol is the centaur; and the flower is the yellow rose. Members' nicknames include Iotas, Centaurs, Outlaws, and Thetamen. The *Centaur Magazine,* the official biannual publication of the fraternity, was initially issued as a newsletter. The fraternity's headquarters are located at Founders Hall on 1600 N. Calvert St. in Baltimore, MD. The fraternity holds membership in the National Pan-Hellenic Council and the North-American Interfraternity Conference.

The first Kentucky chapter of Iota Phi Theta Fraternity was Alpha Omicron Chapter, which was chartered on May 2, 1981, at **Kentucky State University** in Frankfort. Seven other undergraduate chapters have been chartered in the state since that time. The fraternity's graduate chapter, Beta Nu Omega, was founded at Ft. Knox, KY, in 2007.

Iota men continue to serve the country through their community-service initiatives, including the National Iota Foundation, the Iota Youth Alliance, Afya Njema, the Developing Better Fatherhood Project, Iota Minority Political Mobilization, the Community Reclamation Initiative, the Cultural Education Movement, Junior Achievement, and the INROADS Partnership. In August 2013, Iota Phi Theta held its 50th-anniversary celebration, "Living Our Dreams, Building on Our Traditions, Celebrating Our Success," in Baltimore, MD.

Iota Phi Theta® Fraternity Inc. http://www.iotaphitheta.org (accessed October 4, 2013).

Ross, Lawrence C., Jr. *The Divine Nine: The History of African American Fraternities and Sororities.* New York: Kensington, 2000.

—*Fenobia I. Dallas*

IRVIN, THEOPHILUS, JR. (b. 1915, Lexington, KY; d. 2009, Lexington, KY), horse trainer and first African American employed by the Kentucky Racing Commission. Theophilus Irvin Jr., born on August 22, 1915, was not expected to survive, but his grandmother, Matilda Morton, wrapped his feverish body in layers of clothing, warmed him by a stove, and applied ointment to him. Irvin, the son of a horse trainer, lived on Race St. adjacent to Lexington's first racetrack, the Kentucky Association Race Track, known as Chittlin' Switch. At age 15 and weighing 87 pounds, he started in the horse business by breaking yearlings with his father at Hickory Farm near Lexington.

In 1937, Irvin acquired his first license as an exercise boy. Ten years later, he followed his father's career path and obtained his first trainer's license. In 1977, the Kentucky Racing Commission hired him as assistant to the commission veterinarian, the first African American hired by the organization—"Not a popular decision at the time," Irvin noted in a 1999 interview. He encountered some hostility but chose not to dwell on any racist obstacles. His official duties included collecting horses' urine for drug tests, issuing licenses, and managing track equipment. In his youth, Irvin had desired to be a doctor. His position with the Kentucky Racing Commission allowed him to treat ailing horses, which he viewed as "the most enjoyable horse-related job he had."

Irvin died at age 93 on March 31, 2009. Lexington's Smith and Smith Funeral Home handled the burial arrangements. Irvin experienced some economic struggles. Once he traveled to New Orleans trying to find work but suffered hunger instead. When times were really tough, his wife, Olive Bell, worked at a clothing press, which burned her arms. These challenging periods affected Irwin so deeply that he could not tolerate seeing anyone hungry. His estate bequeathed thousands of dollars to Lexington's Hope Center, which provided food, clothing, and shelter to homeless people.

Kentucky Birth Index, 1911–1999.
Newspapers: "Winner of a Different Sort," *LHL,* April 28, 1999, A1; "Theophilus Irvin, 93, Dies—First African-American Employed by the KY Racing Commission," *LHL,* April 2, 2009, D5.
"Official Rulings," *Daily Racing Form,* May 11, 1977, 45.
U.S. Federal Census (1920).

—*Sallie L. Powell*

J

JACKSON, ABBIE CLEMENT (b. 1899, Salisbury, NC; d. 1986, Louisville, KY), missionary supervisor and A.M.E.Z. church and civic leader. Abbie Clement, daughter of Bishop **George C. Clement** and **Emma C. (Williams) Clement,** was born in Salisbury, NC, on March 13, 1899. She graduated from Livingstone College in Salisbury in 1916 and received additional education from Frankfort's Kentucky State College (later known as **Kentucky State University**) and New York City's Columbia University. She taught in the public school system in Louisville, KY, from 1920 to 1925. In 1925, Clement married Clarence P. Jackson and began to devote her full attention to church and civic activities.

From 1929 to 1943, Abbie Clement Jackson served as the missionary supervisor of the African Methodist Episcopal Zion (A.M.E.Z.) Church. In 1943, she became the executive secretary of the Women's Home and Overseas Missionary Society of the A.M.E.Z. Church. In 1945, Jackson was awarded the *Louisville Defender*'s citation as one of 10 outstanding citizens of Kentucky for her role on the National Board of the United Council of Church Women. Throughout her lifetime, she traveled extensively around the world representing the A.M.E.Z. Church at various international religious functions. She traveled to St. Thomas and St. Croix, Virgin Islands, because of her membership on the Denominational Committee in 1942. Beginning in 1948, she visited cities in Italy, Germany, England, France, Belgium, and Switzerland. That same year, she attended the First Assembly World Council of Churches meeting in Amsterdam, Holland, where she was an accredited visitor. She later represented her church in Georgetown, South America, and British Guiana.

In 1948, Jackson was selected as recording secretary of the United Council of Church Women. In 1950, she served as a fraternal delegate of the Methodist Women's Assembly in Cleveland, OH. She was a member of the Committee of Reference and Counsel and the Foreign Missions Conference of North America, served on the Executive Committee of the Home Missions Council of North America, and was also on the Board of Managers of the Missionary Education Movement of North America and Canada. While she was serving as president of the Women's Home and Overseas Missionary Society from 1955 to 1963, she visited all A.M.E.Z. foreign fields. After leaving office in 1963, she continued her service to the church and community. In Louisville, she served on the **Phillis Wheatley YWCA** committee of managers, the black branch of the Louisville Health Committee, the Louisville Family Services Board, the Louisville branch of the **National Association for the Advancement of Colored People,** and the Louisville Interracial Council. As vice president of the Louisville Council of Churches, she became the first woman to serve that body as an officer. She played a significant role in church groups in the United States and abroad with her unifying spirit and unbreakable dedication to Christian life. Shortly after her 87th birthday, she died at Louisville's Methodist Evangelical Hospital on April 8, 1986.

Dunnigan, Alice Allison, comp. and ed. *The Fascinating Story of Black Kentuckians: Their Heritage and Traditions.* Washington, DC: Associated Publishers, 1982.

Fleming, G. James, and Christian E. Burckel, eds. *Who's Who in Colored America.* 7th ed. Yonkers-on-Hudson, NY: Christian E. Burckel & Associates, 1950.

Johnson, Dorothy Sharpe, and Lula Goolsby Williams. *Pioneering Women of the African Methodist Episcopal Zion Church.* Charlotte, NC: A.M.E. Zion Publishing House, 1996.

Newspapers: "Ten Outstanding Kentuckians of 1945," *LD,* December 29, 1945, Souvenir edition; "Abbie Clement Jackson, 88, Dies; Held AME and Ecumenical Offices," *LCJ,* April 11, 1986, B6.

Walls, William Jacob. *The African Methodist Episcopal Zion Church: Reality of the Black Church.* Charlotte, NC: A.M.E. Zion Publishing House, 1974.

—*Karen Cotton McDaniel*

JACKSON, ANDREW (b. 1814, Bowling Green, KY; d. unknown), author of a slave narrative. The son of a slave and a free woman, Andrew Jackson was born on January 25, 1814. Although by birth he should have been legally free, Jackson spent the majority of his early life as a slave after his mother's master's heirs claimed that he had freed her only because of insanity. Jackson was passed from master to master for several years, plowing fields and cultivating tobacco. One master, however, told Jackson that he was required to "get married" to a female slave in order to produce children and create a "family of young slaves." If he refused, Jackson was to be sold to a slave trader who would sell him further south.

When he heard this ultimatum, Andrew Jackson decided to run away from his master and seek his fortune in the North. He first tried and failed to receive a certificate of freedom from a local clerk. After this failure, he slowly made his way north by escaping through woods, although he was pursued on several occasions by slave-catchers with guns and dogs. After several days of constant pursuit, Jackson stayed the night at the house of a doctor who gave him food and shelter, but he was recaptured the following morning and taken to prison, where he was abused for the jailers' amusement.

Later sold to a landlord in the Lexington area for the cost of his jail fees, Jackson then escaped again, traveling several miles north and working for almost a year to save up funds. He finally left Kentucky after this period and traveled to Wisconsin, where he stayed with a brother he had not seen for over nine years. After locals heard the story of his escape, some antislavery activists asked Jackson to speak in a meeting, which he did a few days later. After some success in that endeavor, he moved to New York and began participating in a lecture circuit on the issues of slavery and temperance.

In 1846 and 1847, Jackson delivered dozens of lectures and sermons on the evils of slavery. He also published several articles on the subject, as well as a handful of poems. In 1847, he compiled these writings and a narrative of his escape from Kentucky into one text, titled *Narrative and Writings of Andrew Jackson, of Kentucky,* which remains the primary source for information on his life.

Jackson, Andrew. *Narrative and Writings of Andrew Jackson, of Kentucky.* Syracuse, NY: Daily and Weekly Star Office, 1847. Miami, FL: Mnemosyne Reprint, 1969.

Lucas, Marion B. *A History of Blacks in Kentucky: From Slavery to Segregation, 1760–1891.* 2nd ed. Frankfort: Kentucky Historical Society, 2003.

—*Stephen Pickering*

JACKSON, BLYDEN E. (b. 1910, Paducah, KY; d. 2000, Durham, NC), educator. Blyden E. Jackson was born on October 10, 1910, in Paducah, KY. His father, George W. Jackson, was a school principal, and his mother, Julia R. Jackson, was a librarian. After earning a bachelor's degree from Wilberforce University in 1930, he began graduate work at Columbia University. After an interruption by the Great Depression, he finally secured a scholarship that enabled him to complete both his master's and doctoral degrees from the University of Michigan.

Jackson taught at a Louisville junior high school, followed by teaching stints at Fisk University in Nashville and Southern University in Louisiana. In 1969, he joined the faculty of the University of North Carolina (UNC) at Chapel Hill. During this appointment, he became one of the nation's preeminent scholars of African American literature and received tenure as the first black full professor on the campus and assignment as associate dean of the graduate school. He published many books and articles that generated national interest in African American literature. His 1955 article "The Case for American Negro Literature" made a major contribution to the introduction of black literature to American postsecondary campuses nationwide.

In 1992, UNC named the Office of Undergraduate Admissions for Jackson and his wife Roberta, the first building on the campus named for African Americans. Roberta Jackson, also a professor at UNC and the first black woman to earn tenure at UNC, died in July 1999, and Blyden Jackson died in Durham, NC, on May 1, 2000. The couple was survived by a stepson, James Hodges.

Newspapers: "Blyden Jackson, UNC's First Black Professor, Dies at 89," *Chapel Hill Herald,* May 6, 2000, 1; "Noted UNC Scholar Blyden Jackson Dies," *Chapel Hill News,* May 7, 2000, A9.

—*John A. Hardin*

JACKSON, BRENDA (b. 1946, Shelbyville, KY), first African American elected to the Shelby County Board of Education. A native of Shelbyville, KY, Brenda Jackson was among the first students to integrate Shelbyville High School, from which she graduated in 1964. She completed a bachelor's degree in business at **Kentucky State University** and took a job as a judicial auditor shortly thereafter. Her experiences with Kentucky's education system, however, led her to run for the school board in Shelby Co. After losing two elections where she received "hardly any votes at all," Jackson finally succeeded in becoming the first African American on the Shelby Co. school board in 1989.

During her more than 20 years of service on the board, Jackson was involved in several important moments in the history of blacks in education in Kentucky. In 2004, she made the motion to hire **Elaine Farris** as the superintendent of Shelby Co. public schools, the first black full-time superintendent in the state. Between 2005 and 2007, Jackson made history in her own right as the first female African American president of the Kentucky School Board Association.

As a member of the school board in Shelby Co., Jackson focused specifically on underprivileged children. She stated that her main goal was being "part of the team that reaches proficiency by 2014" and closes the "expectation gap" for children who were considered less able to learn than others. She also pushed for a "true alternative school" that would remove the stigma attached to children who did not attend the public high school. In 2010, Jackson retired from her position with the Administrative Office of the Courts but continued to serve on the Shelby Co. school board.

Newspapers: "A Kentucky First—Racial Barrier Broken, Shelby County Breaks Ground by Hiring Black Schools Chief," *LHL,* June 23, 2004, A1; "They Light Our Paths," *Shelbyville (KY) Sentinel-News,* February 7, 2011.
Shelby County Historical Society. *The New History of Shelby County, Kentucky.* Prospect, KY: Harmony House, 2003, 154.

—*Stephen Pickering*

JACKSON, DENNIS M. (b. 1940, Murray, KY), first black varsity athlete at Murray State University. Born to Roselle Blanton and raised in Murray, KY, Dennis Jackson was one of the city's finest high school athletes in the mid-1950s. A standout athlete for the segregated **Frederick Douglass High School**'s basketball and football teams, Jackson received a scholarship to Alcorn A&M. After less than a year at the Mississippi school, Jackson returned to Kentucky. At the start of the next semester in 1960, he joined the football team at Murray State University as a walk-on and became the school's first African American varsity athlete.

Jackson noted his initial difficulty in transitioning from an all-black high school to a school where he "would go all day without seeing another black person on campus." Murray State proved to be a good fit for Jackson, however, because the school's president frequently checked to ensure that "everything was going all right." By his second year, Jackson had received a scholarship and was a star halfback, receiver, tailback, and safety during the rest of his time at the school. He was named to the All–Ohio Valley Conference football team his senior year in 1964.

In addition to football, Jackson also ran track during his four years at Murray State. Since his high school did not have a track team, the sport had never interested Jackson until he was approached by Murray State's track coach, who encouraged him to join the team. Although his major athletic accomplishments were on the football field, Jackson participated in a 440-yard-relay team that tied an Ohio Valley Conference record, and he was one of the conference's elite track stars during the 1963 season.

In 1964, Jackson graduated from Murray State with a degree in physical education and returned to obtain his master's degree in secondary education administration in 1971. Over the next 30 years, Jackson worked as a high school teacher and later became assistant principal and athletic director at Paducah's Tilghman High School. During the early years of the twenty-first century, he served as the director of district personnel for the Paducah public school system.

During his 30 years as an educator, Jackson remained deeply involved in Murray State and Kentucky athletics. He served on the Board of Directors of the Murray State University Foundation, was co–grand marshal of the 2005 homecoming parade, and was named to the school's Athletics Hall of Fame in 2007. Jackson also served on the board of the Kentucky High School Athletic Association and was a high school basketball referee for over 25 years. He officiated 12 boys' and 3 girls' state tournaments. Because of his lifelong commitment to high school athletics, in addition to his success as a high school athlete, he was named to the Kentucky High School Athletic Association Hall of Fame in 1998. Dennis M. Jackson retired from the Paducah public school system in 2005.

Newspapers: "Study Highlights Shortage of Minority Educators," *LCJ,* December 12, 2002, B1; "Murray's First Black Student Is Honored," *LHL,* October 20, 2005, B3; "Jackson Only Wanted to Play," *PS,* January 27, 2007, B7.

—*Joshua D. Farrington*

JACKSON, ELIZA ISABEL "BELLE" (Mitchell) (b. 1848, Boyle Co., KY; d. 1942, Lexington, KY), educator and social activist. Eliza Isabel "Belle" Mitchell, daughter of Monroe and Mary Mitchell, slaves who had purchased their freedom, was born in Boyle Co., KY, on December 31, 1848. Her parents were devout Methodists, and Belle's entire life was characterized by her deep religious convictions and resulting commitment to community service. She spent her early childhood in Danville, KY, where she attended primary school; when she was 11, her parents moved to Xenia, OH, where she continued her education.

Eliza Jackson.

Mitchell became an ardent abolitionist, and in 1865, when she was still a teenager, Rev. John G. Fee hired her as the first African American teacher for the school at **Camp Nelson.** Her initial appearance in the dining hall prompted most of the white missionaries and teachers at the camp to protest the attempted integration. In spite of her youth, Belle Mitchell responded with courage and dignity in this deliberate test of civil rights in Kentucky. After being forced out of her work at Camp Nelson, she moved to Lexington, where she taught at a free school sponsored by the **First African Baptist Church** for the children of African American soldiers. In 1867, she taught at Howard School in Richmond, KY. In 1868, she enrolled at **Berea College** in the Normal Department; she did not finish her degree but was rehired by the school in Lexington. She became a prominent teacher in the Bluegrass region, working in Lexington, Frankfort, Louisville, Nicholasville, and Richmond.

On February 23, 1871, in Boyle Co., Mitchell married **Jordan C. Jackson,** a prominent African American businessman and undertaker in Lexington who was soon to become a trustee of Berea College. She supported her husband in all his political and professional activities and assisted him in his many business enterprises, but she also operated a millinery shop of her own in downtown Lexington. Her husband was "once quoted as saying that [his wife] was the best investment he ever made and that he owed much of his success to her," but she was never simply an adjunct of her husband. She continued her own community-minded, service-oriented activities.

In 1892, Jackson was a founder of Lexington's Colored Orphan Industrial Home (her husband was a trustee); she was active in the Colored Women's Club movement and "numerous other projects designed to benefit less fortunate blacks." She was elected president of the Ladies' Orphans' Home Society, a group of black women who managed the orphanage, and she served on the board of managers of the orphanage for almost 50 years. Jackson was president of the **Kentucky Association of Colored Women's Clubs,** which helped establish the **Phillis Wheatley YWCA** in Lexington. She was the mother of two adopted children, Minnie and Mitchell. Belle (Mitchell) Jackson died in Lexington on October 6, 1942. She was buried beside her husband in Greenwood (Cove Haven) Cemetery.

Burnside, Jacqueline G. "Black Symbols: Extraordinary Achievements by Ordinary Women." *Appalachian Heritage* 15 (Summer 1987): 11–16.

Notable Kentucky African American Database. Univ. of Kentucky Libraries, 2009. http://nkaa.uky.edu/.

Sears, Richard D. *A Utopian Experiment in Kentucky: Integration and Social Equality at Berea, 1866–1904.* Westport, CT: Greenwood Press, 1996.

Smith, Jessie Carney, ed. *Notable Black American Women.* Detroit: Gale Research, 1992.

—*Richard D. Sears*

JACKSON, IDA MAY JOYCE (b. 1863, Columbus, OH; d. 1927, Columbus, OH), teacher and ardent club leader who organized women's clubs and state associations in three states. The earliest connections of Kentucky women to the national club movement can be traced to Ida May Joyce Jackson and **Mary Cook**

Parrish, who attended the December 1895 Atlanta Congress of Colored Women. Born to James and Kate Joyce in Columbus, OH, on March 28, 1863, Ida May Joyce attended public schools and graduated from Columbus Central High School in 1882. She served as the first assistant to Professor W. H. Mayo in the public schools of Frankfort, KY, from 1885 until 1888. She accepted a position to teach at the State Normal School for Colored Persons (SNSCP), now **Kentucky State University,** also in Frankfort. SNSCP was headed by Professor **John H. Jackson,** whom she married on July 17, 1889. Interested in club work, she formed the Normal Reading Circle, which became one of the charter clubs of the **Kentucky Association of Colored Women's Clubs.**

In 1898, the Jacksons moved to Jefferson City, MO, where Ida Jackson organized local women's groups. On July 21, 1900, she and others established the Missouri Association of Colored Women's Clubs, and she was elected corresponding secretary. In 1901, the Jackson family moved to Colorado Springs, where again she worked diligently among the local women and became a charter member of a state federation with the founding of the Federation of Colored Women's Clubs of Colorado on June 13, 1904. Jackson was elected the first president of the Colorado group. She expanded her club activities to the National Association of Colored Women's Clubs in 1906 when she became national chairman of the Ways and Means Committee (1906–1908) and national treasurer (1910–1912).

In 1910, Ida and her husband retired in Columbus, OH. One of Kentucky's earliest and most prolific club organizers, Ida Joyce Jackson died on January 19, 1927. She was buried in Green Lawn Cemetery in Columbus, OH.

Davis, Elizabeth Lindsay. *Lifting as They Climb.* Washington, DC: National Association of Colored Women, 1933. Reprint, New York: Simon & Schuster, 1996.

Hardin, John A. *Onward and Upward: A Centennial History of Kentucky State University, 1886–1986.* Frankfort: Kentucky State Univ., 1987.

Mather, Frank Lincoln, ed. *Who's Who of the Colored Race: A General Biographical Dictionary of Men and Women of African Descent.* Vol. 1. Chicago: Memento Edition, 1915.

—*Karen Cotton McDaniel*

JACKSON, JOHN HENRY (b. 1850, Fayette Co., KY; d. 1919, Columbus, OH), educator. John Henry Jackson, son of Jordan C. Jackson Sr. and his wife, Ann, who were slaves in Fayette Co., KY, and brother of **Jordan C. Jackson Jr.,** was born in Lexington, KY, on October 31, 1850. He entered **Berea College** as a student in 1866 and joined Union Church on November 10, 1868; in 1874, he became the first black graduate of Berea and probably the first black college graduate in Kentucky. Years later, in 1893, he became president of the Berea College Alumni Association, and he taught briefly at Berea (1893–1894, teacher of pedagogics), the last African American professor hired at Berea College before the passage of the 1904 **Day Law.**

Like his brother Jordan, John H. was a Berea College trustee (1892–1896). Author of *History of Education: From the Greeks to the Present Time* (1903), Jackson enjoyed a long career as an educator in many different venues: he was both teacher and principal in public schools in Lexington (the first principal of Corall

Street School, 1875–1876). In 1881, he became president of the Lincoln High School in Kansas City, MO, where he held many other important positions: clerk of the Jury Commission, clerk of the Board of Police Commissioners, and member of the Board of Examiners, Kansas City. Returning to Kentucky, he became the first president of the State Association of Colored Teachers (later known as the **Kentucky Negro Educational Association**). He was the first president of the State Normal School for Colored Persons (now **Kentucky State University** in Frankfort) from 1887 to 1898 and again from 1907 to 1910. The first permanent building on the campus, now listed on the National Register of Historic Places, was named Jackson Hall in his honor. He went back to Missouri to be president of Lincoln Institute (now Lincoln University) in Jefferson City.

Jackson's work as a political and social activist included serving as a delegate-at-large from Kentucky to the Republican National Convention and in 1891–1893 as a leader in the **Anti-Separate Coach Movement,** opposing Kentucky's legislation establishing railroad car segregation. His first wife was Henrietta Stewart of Louisiana, whom he married in July 1877; she died in November 1887. On July 17, 1889, he married Ida May Joyce, whom he had met at the State Normal School in Frankfort when it opened in October 1887; she was one of the first teachers there, an instructor in the Domestic Economy Department. **Ida Joyce Jackson** (as she was always called) had a very distinguished career as an educator, political activist, and writer. Late in his life, John H. and Ida Joyce Jackson lived in Colorado, but they moved finally to Columbus, OH, her birthplace. John Henry Jackson died there at the age of 68 on June 30, 1919.

"Biographical Sketches." Cole County [MO] Historical Society. http://www.colecohistsoc.org/bios/bio_ij.html (accessed June 17, 2013).

Mather, Frank Lincoln, ed. *Who's Who of the Colored Race: A General Biographical Dictionary of Men and Women of African Descent.* Vol. 1. Chicago: Memento Edition, 1915.

Notable Kentucky African American Database. Univ. of Kentucky Libraries, 2009. http://nkaa.uky.edu/.

—*Richard D. Sears*

JACKSON, JORDAN CARLISLE, JR. (b. 1848, Lexington, KY; d. 1917, Lexington, KY), businessman and civic activist. Born on February 28, 1848, in Lexington, KY, Jordan Carlisle Jackson Jr. was a son of Jordan C. Jackson Sr., a hostler, and his wife, Ann, who were slaves in Fayette Co., KY. His brother **John Henry Jackson** was the first president of the State Normal School for Colored Persons (later known as **Kentucky State University**). Jordan served as a private in Company E, 5th U.S. Colored Cavalry, during the Civil War.

Jackson had almost no formal education but taught himself to read and write. In spite of his lack of schooling, he was successful in multifaceted careers and enterprises. He became editor of several newspapers in Lexington, including the *American Citizen.* One source praised his journalistic writing, stating that he combined "qualities that every man is not possessed of—literary talent and business qualifications." A list of his careers reveals his impressive combination of abilities: when he was a very young man, he worked on a farm in Kentucky; he used his savings to invest in a fruit and confectionery shop in Lexington; he

Jordan Carlisle Jackson Jr.

managed it so well that he impressed the Lexington branch of the Freedmen's Savings and Trust Company, which hired him as a teller; and he became a partner in an undertaking business in Lexington (the first black undertaker in the city), which grew, under his leadership, to be "considered by many to be the finest in central Kentucky," with a new building and "the best equipped livery stable in Lexington, with a capacity of one hundred horses."

Jackson's remarkable energy and enthusiasm appeared also in his public life, devoted to political activism and educational enterprises. He was a well-known African American Republican leader in Kentucky. A skillful politician, he won a seat as a delegate to the Republican National Convention in 1876 and again in 1892. He was chairman of the committee responsible for the creation of Douglass Park in Lexington. On July 1, 1892, a mass meeting at **St. Paul African Methodist Episcopal Church,** chaired by Jackson, was called to protest the Separate Coach Law for transportation vehicles. He was the spokesman of the committee that secured from the Kentucky legislature the enactment of the law establishing the State Normal School for Negroes at Frankfort (later known as **Kentucky State University**) and was an influential member of the Executive Committee of the National Negro Business League.

In addition, Jackson was a representative of his church in the General Conference of the A.M.E. Church. From 1879 through 1895, he served as a trustee of **Berea College** and as a trustee of Wilberforce University in Ohio. On February 23, 1871, in Boyle

Co., KY, Jordan C. Jackson married **Eliza Isabel ("Belle") Mitchell Jackson,** a social activist, reformer, teacher, and businesswoman whose useful and energetic contributions to the African American community in Kentucky paralleled those of her husband. This remarkable couple was buried in Cove Haven (now known as Greenwood) Cemetery in Lexington.

Notable Kentucky African American Database, 1831–1850. Univ. of Kentucky Libraries, 2009. http://nkaa.uky.edu/.

Richings, G. F. *Evidences of Progress among Colored People.* 12th ed. Philadelphia: George S. Ferguson Co., 1905.

Smith, Jessie Carney, ed. *Notable Black American Women.* Detroit: Gale Research, 1992, 317–20.

Washington, Booker T. *The Negro in Business.* Tuskegee, AL: Hertel, Jenkins & Co., 1907.

—*Richard D. Sears*

JACKSON, LEE ARTHUR (b. 1950, Lynch, KY), first black president of the Kentucky Association of State Employees. The son of Sylmon and Marie Jackson, Lee Arthur Jackson was born in Lynch, KY, on April 14, 1950. A longtime state worker, Jackson held a position at the state employment office in Lexington as an unemployment insurance program supervisor during the mid-1980s. Although he never publicly complained about his working conditions, other social workers for the state noted that Kentucky had fallen behind in building and maintaining facilities for its employees. Frustrated workers swelled the ranks of the Kentucky Association of State Employees, an eight-year-old union, and in 1990, the union named Jackson its first black president.

As president of the Kentucky Association of State Employees, Jackson took the lead in defending employees against several changes the union perceived as negative. In 1991, the association filed a lawsuit to prevent the firing of almost 50 employees as part of an attempt to reorganize the Department of Education. Jackson dropped the suit after most of the workers were either rehired or given jobs elsewhere within the state. He also filed lawsuits on behalf of the Kentucky Association of State Employees intended to equalize vocational school teachers' pay with that of their counterparts in public education and grant state workers the opportunity to "hold positions in political parties, manage campaigns and even become candidates for paid political offices."

On February 21, 2000, Jackson's role in the state increased when he was elected the first black vice president of the Kentucky AFL-CIO, a federation of labor unions responsible for more than 100,000 employees in the state. On July 31, 2006, he retired from his position with the state employment office, but he remained in his roles with the Kentucky Association of State Employees and the AFL-CIO. He has continued to petition for the rights of state employees through legal action and an occasional editorial in the *Lexington Herald-Leader.*

Mallegg, Kristin B. *Who's Who among African Americans.* 22nd ed. Detroit: Gale, 2008.

Newspapers: "State Employees Group Files Lawsuit over Education Jobs," *LHL,* June 12, 1991, B2; "Settlement Near for Ky. Retirees," *LCJ,* August 17, 2006, A1.

"People." *Jet,* October 15, 1990, 20.

—*Stephen Pickering*

JACKSON, LUTHER PORTER (b. 1892, Lexington, KY; d. 1950, Petersburg, VA), educator, author, and civil rights and civic leader. Born in Lexington, KY, on July 11, 1892, to Edward and Delilah (Culbertson) Jackson, Luther Porter Jackson earned his AB degree from Fisk University in 1914, his AM degree from Columbia University three years later, and a PhD in history from the University of Chicago in 1937. In 1922, he married Johnella Frazer of Shelbyville, KY, and they had four children. He taught at Voorhees Institute in Denmark, SC, and Kansas Industrial College in Topeka, KS, and then joined the faculty of Virginia State College in Petersburg, VA, in 1922.

A close acquaintance of popular historian **Carter G. Woodson,** Luther Jackson, a prolific scholar in his own right, became a full professor of history and head of the Department of History at Virginia State. He contributed scholarly historical articles to numerous newspapers and magazines and served as a columnist for the *Norfolk Journal and Guide.* He published at least six books that addressed the African American experience, especially in Virginia, including *Free Negro Labor and Property Holding in Virginia, 1830–1860,* which was published under the auspices of the American Historical Association in 1942.

Jackson worked to facilitate voting for blacks in Virginia and to eliminate the state's poll tax and the lily-white primary in the state. Among other organizations, he was founder and president of the Virginia Voters League of Petersburg, a group that encouraged African Americans to register and vote. He was also a member of the Virginia State Teachers Association, the **National Association for the Advancement of Colored People,** the Association for the Study of Negro Life and History, the Elks, and **Omega Psi Phi Fraternity.** He died just three months before his 58 birthday on April 12, 1950.

Fleming, G. James, and Christian E. Burckel, eds. *Who's Who in Colored America.* 7th ed. Yonkers-on-Hudson, NY: Christian E. Burckel & Associates, 1950.

Guzman, Jessie Parkhurst, ed. *Negro Year Book: A Review of Events Affecting Negro Life, 1941–1946.* Tuskegee, AL: Department of Records and Research, Tuskegee Institute, 1947.

Johnson, J. H. "Luther Porter Jackson." *JNH* 35, no. 3 (July 1950): 352–55.

Thorpe, Earl E. *Black Historians: A Critique.* New York: William Morrow, 1971.

—*David H. Jackson Jr.*

JACKSON, REID ETHELBERT, SR. (b. 1908, Paducah, KY; d. 1991, Baltimore, MD), prominent educator. As the son of an elementary school principal, Reid Ethelbert Jackson Sr., learned from an early age the value of education for blacks in Kentucky. Born on December 7, 1908, in Paducah, Jackson moved to Louisville with his parents after his father accepted a job as head of a local elementary school. After receiving his public education in Louisville, Jackson attended college at Wilberforce University in Ohio, from which he graduated with honors. He decided to focus on education in his graduate career and received a PhD from Ohio State University in that field in 1937.

After receiving his doctorate, Jackson taught at a number of historically black colleges, including Talladega, Alabama State, West Virginia State, and Central State. He also served in administration on several occasions, most notably as a dean and director of educational research at Wilberforce, and he published several articles in education journals. Many of these articles argued for improved methods for educating African Americans in the South, and he remained committed to establishing equal opportunities through education. In the last years of his life, he taught at Morgan State University while living in Baltimore, MD, where he died on June 29, 1991.

Jackson, Reid E. "The Development and Present Status of Secondary Education for Negroes in Kentucky." *Journal of Negro Education* 4 (1935): 185–91.

"Reid Jackson, Sr., Morgan Professor, Dies at 83." *Baltimore Sun,* July 2, 1991, 3D.

"Who's Who on the Convention Program." *KNEAJ* 18 (1947): 13–14.

—*Stephen Pickering*

JACKSON STREET METHODIST EPISCOPAL CHURCH, one of the oldest black churches in Louisville. In 1832, a small group of African Americans completed the construction of Jackson Street Methodist Episcopal Church in Louisville. Located in one of the city's swampy areas that attracted hundreds of croaking frogs, the church was also often referred to as the Frog Pond Church. By 1860, it had about 80 members and a Sabbath school that was attended by both slaves and free men.

In addition to its Sabbath school, the church formally opened a grade school for children in 1865. Taught by Henry Miller, the school had over 40 pupils by the end of the decade. In 1870, the city of Louisville declared that it would support black public schools through taxes largely paid by African Americans themselves. One of the three initial schools incorporated into Louisville's black public school system was Jackson Street Methodist. Mrs. E. Stansberry was named the school's principal, and Mary A. Johnson and Florence Murrow, a white woman, were hired as teachers. Despite promises of financial support, the school struggled through most of the decade because the city allocated less than $1,000 for all three black schools to share.

Jackson Street Methodist was also deeply involved in promoting black churches throughout the region. In 1869, the Lexington Conference of the Methodist Episcopal Church, one of the nation's first missionary conferences for African Americans, was formed in Harrodsburg, KY. The first Lexington Conference was held in 1870 at Jackson Street Methodist and was attended by delegates from Kentucky, Ohio, Illinois, Michigan, Wisconsin, and Minnesota. The church also served as the supervisor of one of Kentucky's two administrative districts of the Colored Missionary District of the Colored Methodist Episcopal Church. Moreover, through the early 1900s, Jackson Street Methodist also served as a frequent meeting place for Kentucky's branch of the Woman's Home Missionary Society.

In 1923, after its original building on Jackson St. became too dilapidated to repair, the congregation moved to a new building on the corner of Sixth and **Walnut Sts.** In addition to the relocation, members also changed the name of their church to R. E. Jones Temple after the Methodist Church's first black bishop, Robert Elijah Jones. The church remained active in the city's religious life throughout the 1920s and early 1930s, serving as the meeting place for organizations ranging from the **Kentucky Negro Educational Association** to the Boy Scouts.

By the 1940s, however, the church's membership had significantly dwindled, and it officially closed its doors in 1946. In 1949, David M. Jordan, a Methodist minister who had a reputation for successfully reinvigorating dying churches, was assigned to redevelop R. E. Jones Temple. Reestablishing the church in a new building on Jefferson St., Jordan enticed many of the church's old members back into the congregation. In 1961, **Horace Henry ("H. H.") Greene,** who had served as the church's pastor since the mid-1950s, became the first African American president of the Louisville Ministerial Association.

R. E. Jones Temple eventually relocated again to Algonquin Pkwy. and continued to serve Louisville's black community for the rest of the twentieth century. In 2003, it merged with several other churches to form Mosaic United Methodist Church on St. Andrews Church Rd.

Dunnigan, Alice Allison, comp. and ed. *The Fascinating Story of Black Kentuckians: Their Heritage and Traditions.* Washington, DC: Associated Publishers, 1982.

Hudson, J. Blaine. "African American Religion in Ante-bellum Louisville, Kentucky." *Griot* (Southern Conference on Afro-American Studies) 17, no. 2 (Fall 1998).

"Louisville Ministers Name First Negro President." *Jet,* May 18, 1961, 44.

Lucas, Marion B. *A History of Blacks in Kentucky: From Slavery to Segregation, 1760–1891.* 2nd ed. Frankfort: Kentucky Historical Society, 2003.

—Joshua D. Farrington

JACOBSON, HARRIET PRICE (b. 1879, Lexington, KY; d. 1961, Oklahoma City, OK), educator and poet. Harriet Price Johnson was born on October 20, 1879, in Lexington, KY, the daughter of Robert and Nannie Price Johnson. In 1902, she married Robert Jacobson of Alabama. She received a bachelor of science from Kansas State Teachers College in 1932.

Jacobson taught in the rural schools of Oklahoma from 1893 to 1896 and the rural schools of Kansas in 1897. She was an educator for Oklahoma City schools from 1898 to 1935 and an advisory teacher from 1935 to 1947. In 1941, Jacobson received an award for her 42 years of service.

Jacobson was a member of philanthropic organizations, such as the Oklahoma Association of Negro Teachers, the Oklahoma City Coordinating Council, the YWCA, the Big Sisters Organization, and the **National Association for the Advancement of Colored People.** Most notably, Jacobson was the founder and first president of the East Side Culture Club in 1907. Under her leadership, the club initiated the unification of local black women's clubs into a single state organization. On April 16, 1910, the East Side Culture Club, along with seven others, became the Oklahoma Federation of Colored Women Clubs, and she served as its first president from 1910 to 1915. As president, she influenced the establishment of the State Training School for Negro Boys and the State Training School for Negro Girls.

Jacobson was also a published poet. Her works were printed in various anthologies, such as *Anthology of Verse by Oklahoma Writers* (1939 edition) and *Outstanding Contemporary Poets* (1939). A book of her poems, *Songs in the Night,* was printed in 1947. She died in Oklahoma City on July 3, 1961.

Fleming, G. James, and Christian E. Burckel, eds. *Who's Who in Colored America.* 7th ed. Yonkers-on-Hudson, NY: Christian E. Burckel & Associates, 1950.

"Long Time City Teacher Is Dead." *Oklahoman,* July 4, 1961.

Wesley, Charles H. *The History of the National Association of Colored Women's Clubs: A Legacy of Service.* Washington DC: The Association, 1984.

—Anne Gray Perrin

JAMES, GRACE (b. 1924, Charleston, WV; d. 1989, Louisville, KY), physician, professor, and health care advocate. Grace Marilynn James was the fourth of seven children born to Edward L. James Sr., owner of a produce company, and Stella Grace (Shaw) James, postmistress of Institute, WV. James graduated from West Virginia State College in 1944 and did postgraduate work at the University of Chicago and West Virginia State College before entering Meharry Medical College in Nashville, TN. She graduated from Meharry in 1950. James worked during her internship and residency at Babies Hospital and Vanderbilt Clinic and in New York City at Columbia Presbyterian Hospital and Harlem Hospital, where she completed her studies. She was also a fellow in the care of handicapped children of the Children's Evaluation and Rehabilitation Clinic of the Albert Einstein College of Medicine at Yeshiva University's Jacobi Hospital.

James was one of the first two African Americans appointed to the faculty of the University of Louisville School of Medicine. She was assistant clinical professor of pediatrics and among the first African American women to gain membership in the Jefferson County Medical Society and be appointed a staff member of the old General Hospital.

In 1973, James founded a health care facility serving the poor in the West End. Located at 2209 W. Broadway, it was known as the West Louisville Medical Center and served people in the **Russell,** California, **Shawnee,** and Portland neighborhoods. By 1980, the project had failed financially. She also founded the Teen Awareness Project, designed to help reduce the teenage birthrate among blacks. James served in many medical and minority advancement groups, including the Falls City Medical Society and the Council on Urban Education, a citizens' group concerned with education problems facing black children. As president of the Louisville chapter of the **National Association for the Advancement of Colored People,** James was a vocal opponent of inadequacies in the education of African Americans in public schools.

James was married to Charles Carlisle O'Bannion of Madison, IN, from 1952 to 1957. After their divorce, James adopted a son, David. After her death of a heart attack at home, a scholarship fund in her name was created at Meharry Medical College in Nashville, TN.

Newspapers: *LCJ,* December 3, 1980; *LCJ,* January 25, 1989.

JAMES, THOMAS (b. unknown; d. unknown), minister responsible for freeing hundreds of slaves during the Civil War.

A freeman from New York, Rev. Thomas James came to Louisville during the Civil War to work among the city's African American refugees and soldiers. He was acting as an agent for the **American Missionary Association,** which had been founded in 1846 to promote the peaceful abolition of slavery and to further the belief that blacks deserved full and equal rights of citizens. In 1864, James took over as supervisor of a large refugee camp located on Broadway near the city limits. Plagued by rampant disease and substandard shelter, the refugee camp improved under James, who constructed a refugee home on the site and established the first school for the city's refugee children.

In 1865, in response to James's allegations that many blacks were being imprisoned in slave pens across Louisville, the Union military commander of Kentucky, Maj. Gen. John M. Palmer, gave James the authority to investigate the situation by attaching him to the office of the provost marshal. As a result, James was responsible for freeing hundreds of former slaves from the city's slave jails and from slave traders. During the time he spent in Louisville, James was a controversial figure who drew criticism from certain city leaders and ministers who believed that his tactics were too radical. Proslavery forces were particularly hostile toward him, and James often received death threats. James eventually left Louisville, and little is known of him afterward.

Lucas, Marion B. *A History of Blacks in Kentucky.* Vol. 1, *From Slavery to Segregation, 1760–1891.* Frankfort: Kentucky Historical Society, 1992.

JASMIN, ERNEST A. (b. 1934, Jacksonville, FL; d. 2004, Louisville, KY), Kentucky's first African American commonwealth's attorney. The son of a Catholic forklift driver and a Baptist tobacco worker, Ernest A. Jasmin later noted the heavy influence of religion in his early childhood after his birth on October 18, 1934. Years later, he developed a similar affinity for law during a speech class at Florida A&M University. After a stint in the army, which led to his transfer from his home state of Florida to Kentucky, Jasmin enrolled in night law school at the University of Louisville. In 1967, he earned his degree and was admitted to the bar.

After Jasmin worked in private practice and as a judge for several years, Dave Stengel, who was elected commonwealth's attorney in 1976, appointed him as an assistant. A relentless prosecutor, Jasmin pushed for the death penalty in all cases that met the legal requirement for it to be applied. In 1987, voters in Jefferson Co. elected him to the position of commonwealth's attorney in his own right with 70 percent of the vote; he was the state's first black commonwealth's attorney and one of the first blacks elected to a county-wide office in Jefferson Co.

As commonwealth's attorney, Jasmin earned the epithet "preacher for the prosecution" because of his use of both fiery rhetoric and appropriate Bible verses during his speeches. He also established a Narcotics Unit with four prosecutors dedicated to working drug cases, which made up a third of the potential cases in his department. In 1991, however, he gained some notoriety for failing to successfully prosecute Mel Ignatow for the murder of his girlfriend, although later evidence proved that he was guilty. Jasmin retired from his position as commonwealth's attorney

shortly thereafter and served as a circuit judge from 1992 to 1999. On April 30, 2004, only months after the Louisville Bar Association honored him for his contributions, he died at age 69 in Louisville, KY.

Hawkins, Walter L. *African American Biographies: Profiles of 558 Current Men and Women.* Jefferson, NC: McFarland, 1992.
Newsapapers: "Jasmin Wins in Bid to Be Jefferson's Top Prosecutor," *LCJ,* November 4, 1987, B1; "Prosecutor of Famed Murder Cases Dies," *LCJ,* May 1, 2004, A1.

—*Stephen Pickering*

JAY'S CAFETERIA, restaurant. Jay's Cafeteria was opened in April 1974 by owner-proprietor Frank Foster and his wife, Barbara Jean. Originally located at 504 S. 18th St., the cafeteria moved in 1994 half a block west to a larger facility at 1812 Muhammad Ali Blvd. The 100 percent black-owned and operated restaurant has grown from a 150-seat local eatery to a spacious 400-seat mauve and dark green dining and catering establishment worth an estimated $1.7 million. The name Jay's was derived from Foster, who is a junior, and his wife's name, Barbara Jean.

The cafeteria is part restaurant and part community center to the inhabitants of the west Louisville neighborhood. There are bulletin boards announcing activities and meetings, as well as several private rooms at the site that are often used for these meetings. Jay's has been a lunch mecca for employees of the U.S. Postal Service, Brown-Forman, Philip Morris, and Courtaulds Coatings. The clientele is a unique mixture of the city's population.

Jay's thriving business is based on big portions of homemade food served at reasonable prices. The menu fare is traditional American, with features such as liver and onions, pot roast, barbecued ribs, pork chops, a variety of vegetables, and its signature dessert, sweet potato pie. Catering is a large part of the business, and the restaurant has catered events for many of the city's largest corporations and civic celebrations.

Jay's has been a regular stop for many famous people, including Vice President Al Gore, **Muhammad Ali,** Don King, Wesley Snipes, Patti LaBelle, and the Temptations. The restaurant is also a popular stop for government employees, including Louisville mayors, county judges/executives, and Kentucky's governors.

LCJ, March 11, 1995.

JAZZ, genre of music. Although no single definition can be attached to jazz, this uniquely American art form traces its origins to the intermingling of African, European, and Creole musical cultures in New Orleans during the late 1800s. With the passing of each decade, jazz musicians developed a complex and expressive tonal language that emphasized rhythmic variation and syncopation, a sophisticated harmonic vocabulary, and a fluid melodic line whose bent notes and chromaticism echoed its roots in the **blues** and gospel tradition. Distinct musical styles emerged (**ragtime,** New Orleans and Chicago jazz, swing, bebop, progressive, avant-garde, fusion, and mainstream) that continue to evolve.

It is unclear how Kentuckians first became acquainted with these new, intoxicating sounds. Unquestionably the Ohio River and the railroads were two vital transportation avenues along which many jazz pioneers migrated. As early as 1909, Boston novelist Elliot Paul, writing in *My Old Kentucky Home,* noted that he was enthralled by a black musician in a "sporting house" at Seventh and Market Sts. and said, "Whatever else I remember about Louisville, my most poignant recollections have to do with hearing . . . jazz."

The *Island Queen* and other excursion boats on the Ohio River booked New Orleans–style jazz bands, such as Sidney Desvigne's Southern Syncopators. From the early 1900s until World War I, jazz was performed primarily in shady brothels and saloons. However, after the army shut down the red-light district and Prohibition forced the closure of the bars, the music moved to mainstream nightclubs and dance halls that featured local jazz ensembles. During the 1920s, Magnolia (later Rainbow) Gardens at Third and Avery Sts., Edgewater Garden on Upper River Rd., and the Madrid ballroom at Third and Guthrie Sts. were some of the favorite spots that hosted orchestras, such as Bernie Cummings's band. Before World War II, Louisville played host to the greatest practitioners of this fledgling art form. Louis Armstrong, George Gershwin, Duke Ellington, and Benny Goodman all demonstrated to Louisville audiences the virtuosity and elegance inherent in the musical genre.

The 1950s and early 1960s are generally considered to be the halcyon days of Louisville jazz, as attested by the popularity of area venues that showcased local talent. Encompassing all points of the city's geography—from the East End's Topaz (969 Baxter Ave.) and the Kentucky Tavern (Lexington Rd. and Grinstead Dr.) to the Idle Hour (545 15th St.) and the Top Hat (1210 **Walnut St.** [**Muhammad Ali** Blvd.]); from the South End's Iroquois Gardens (5306 New Cut Rd.) to downtown's Riney's (414 Walnut St.) and the Arts in Louisville (519 Zane St.)—small jazz combos entertained nightly. This was a period when many of the "white clubs" were strictly segregated. Not until 1967 did the white Musicians' Union (Local 11) and the black Musicians' Union (Local 637) merge to become Local 11-637.

After a decline of the jazz scene in the 1970s, a jazz renaissance of improvisational music occurred throughout the 1980s when such clubs as the Fig Tree and Othello's (both at Third and Broadway), Just Jazz (2901 Bardstown Rd.), and various downtown hotel lounges catered primarily to a jazz clientele. Formed originally in 1967 as the Louisville Jazz Council, the Louisville Jazz Society promotes jazz music through educational programs and monthly concerts featuring both local and national performers. The city and its active arts community have continued to attract outstanding jazz musicians to its major concert settings (the Brown Theatre and the Kentucky Center for the Arts) and outdoor music festivals, such as Jazz in Central Park, a series of concerts started in 1992 under the sponsorship of the Kentucky Center for the Arts and funded by the Lila Wallace–Reader's Digest National Jazz Network.

The future of jazz improvisation appears promising locally, in large part because of the efforts of jazz educators dedicated to guiding students' tonal imagination. James Aebersold, a New Albany, IN, saxophonist of international renown in the field of jazz education, has conducted a summer jazz workshop in Louisville annually since 1975. Bellarmine University and Indiana University Southeast include jazz courses in their curricula. The University of Louisville School of Music has offered a bachelor of arts degree in music with emphasis in jazz since 1996. WFPL / WFPK-FM has presented jazz as a staple of its broadcast format since 1980.

A listing of nationally known jazz performers born in Louisville chronicles the entire history of this improvisational medium: vocalist **Sara Martin** (1884–1955), vocalist and dancer **John "Bubbles" Sublett** (1902–1986), vibraphonist **Lionel Hampton** (1908–2002), trumpeter **Robert Elliott "Jonah" Jones** (1909–2000), vocalist **Helen Humes** (1913–1981), guitarist Jimmy Raney (1927–1995), pianist Rahn Burton (1934–), and saxophonist Don Braden (1963–), who moved to Louisville at age four.

Lionel Hampton, jazz musician and vibraphonist, was born on April 20, 1908, in Louisville. Hampton's parents, Charles Edward and Gertrude (Morgan) Hampton, moved there when his father went to work for the railroad. Since railroad work kept the elder Hampton away, the new mother returned to Birmingham, AL, her hometown. Hampton first recorded with Louis Armstrong in 1930, and by 1936 he was playing in the Benny Goodman Quartet. Hampton became one of the best-known jazz musicians, recording extensively and touring worldwide. "Flying Home" and "Hamp's Boogie Woogie" were his two indispensable trademarks. In 1936, Hampton married Gladys (Riddle) Neal.

Robert Elliott "Jonah" Jones, jazz trumpeter, was born in Louisville on December 31, 1909. A student of Bertha Ella Allen's Sunday school music class at the Booker T. Washington Community Center at Ninth and Magazine Sts., Jones began his music career at age 10. Many of Allen's child musicians later became active band members because they could read music. By age 14, Jones had started his professional career in the pit orchestra at the Palace Orchestra at 11th and **Walnut** (now **Muhammad Ali** Blvd.) Sts. At 17, he began playing on a riverboat. He joined Jimmie Lunceford's band in 1931 and moved through some of the best bands of the 1930s and 1940s, including McKinney's Cotton Pickers and the bands of Fletcher Henderson, Benny Carter, and Cab Calloway. In 1954, Jones toured Europe with a solo act and returned to form a quartet that maintained its popularity in New York City clubs throughout the 1960s. Making his home in New York City, Jones continued to perform and record mainstream jazz albums through the early 1990s.

Mattingly, Rick. "Jazz Educators Speak." *Louisville Music News,* February 1995.
Newspapers: *LCJ,* August 24, 1980; *LCJ,* January 27, 1984; *LCJ,* August 25, 1985; *LCJ,* February 9, 1992; *LCJ,* March 30, 1996.
Yater, George H. *Flappers, Prohibition and All That Jazz.* Louisville, KY: Museum of History and Science, 1984.

—Steve Crews

JEFFERSON COUNTY POORHOUSE, housing facility for the poor. About 1858, Jefferson Co. established a poorhouse in a log structure near Jeffersontown. About 20 years later, the log building was replaced with several one-story residences, a small hospital, a two-story dining hall, and housing for the superintendent, all built of frame and painted white. The facilities were used by men and women, young and old, and black and white in the hope of creating a caring family atmosphere in which the homeless poor could find relief.

In 1914, a new, beautifully designed two-story brick and stone facility replaced the worn frame buildings. The new poorhouse included a basement, electric lights, hot and cold running water, and steam heat. A separate one-story, 50-room facility housed African American residents, and a 1.5-million-gallon spring-fed reservoir supplied ample water. Later, the poorhouse ceased to operate as such and became the Jefferson County Home for the Aged. More recently the building housed the Jeffersontown Branch of the Louisville Free Public Library and then was used commercially.

Johnston, Tyler. *Jeffersontown, Kentucky—The First 200 Years.* Jeffersontown, KY: City of Jeffersontown, 1997.
Louisville Times, February 8, 1908.

—*Joellen Tyler Johnston*

JENNINGS, SAM (b. ca. 1893, Breckinridge Co., KY; d. Hardinsburg, KY, 1932), legally lynched in Breckinridge Co. in 1932. The illegitimate son of a Breckinridge Co. woman, Sam Jennings later reckoned that he was born around 1893, although he was unsure of his actual birth date. He attended school for a few years at a local all-black institution but left before completion. In 1914, his mother died of tuberculosis, and Jennings left Hardinsburg, KY, to enlist in the U.S. Army in 1917. He served for two years and received an honorable discharge in 1919. He returned to Kentucky and married a woman named Mary Ellen Morton shortly thereafter.

On October 6, 1930, a local white woman named Mabel Downs was sexually assaulted by a black man near some woods at the city limits. On the basis of her description of the attacker, police began a search for Sam Jennings and arrested him at a nearby railroad track. Jennings claimed that Downs was not able to positively identify him as her assaulter at the time, but she later stated that she was positive that he was the perpetrator. After his indictment, Jennings was moved to a jail in Louisville to lessen the threat of mob violence.

A trial ensued that lasted for most of the month of October. Jennings pled not guilty to the charge of rape, but the prosecution was able to demonstrate effectively that Jennings often traveled in the area where the rape occurred and that he matched the description of the attacker. Jennings was asked to testify in his own defense, and a witness for the defense testified that he saw another black man matching the attacker's description in the area at the time of the crime. But during the rebuttal, the prosecution assembled a dozen witnesses who all agreed that Jennings's reputation in the community was widely regarded as bad, which called his testimony into question.

On October 24, the jury found Jennings guilty of murder and sentenced him to death by hanging on December 15, 1930. His lawyers successfully stalled the date by appealing the decision, demanding a writ of habeas corpus, and trying to establish lunacy on the part of their client, but all their attempts to overturn the conviction ultimately failed. On June 17, 1932, a large crowd estimated at 6,000 people gathered in Hardinsburg to watch the execution. After declaring his innocence one last time, Jennings was hanged by the neck until dead. There were two more public hangings in 1934 in Smithland and 1936 in Owensboro, but Kentucky then abandoned the practice.

Newspapers: "Negro Indicted for Attacking White Girl," *Irvington Herald,* October 10, 1930, 1; "Jury Condemns Negro to Hang," *Irvington Herald,* October 31, 1930, 1.
Ryan, Perry T. *Legal Lynching: The Plight of Sam Jennings.* Lexington, KY: Alexandria Printing, 1989.

—*Stephen Pickering*

JESSE HAPPY CASE, legal proceedings for extradition of a Kentucky slave from Canada. In 1833, Jesse Happy, a slave in Fayette Co., KY, escaped when he procured a horse from his owner, Thomas Hickey, and rode it to the Niagara valley. He left the horse on the U.S. border along with written instructions for the return of the animal to Hickey and then crossed into Ontario, Canada.

In 1835, a full two years after Happy's escape, the grand jury of Fayette Co. indicted Happy for horse stealing. Two years after the Kentucky indictment, on August 14, 1837, Hickey offered an affidavit for the prosecution, but he gave a physical description of Happy, as well as his possible whereabouts, rather than recounting the alleged theft. Five days later, Kentucky governor James Clark wrote to the lieutenant governor of Upper Canada, Sir Francis Bond Head, to request the extradition of Jesse Happy to Kentucky. On September 7, 1837, David Castleman, a wealthy Kentucky horse breeder, appeared before Michael Aikman, the justice of the peace for the District of Gore, in order to take Happy into custody.

However, Happy was placed in Ontario's Hamilton Jail for his detainment. The next day, the attorney general of Gore, the Honorable Mr. Hagerman, said that there was adequate proof of guilt for horse stealing, and extradition was approved. Nevertheless, Sir Francis Bond Head received petitions from Canadian citizens of all ethnicities who protested the deliverance of Happy to Kentucky and back into slavery.

On September 9, 1837, the Executive Council of Upper Canada met to resolve whether it was legal to return escaped slaves accused of criminal acts to the United States. If Happy were to be returned to Kentucky, then he would be automatically punished for escaping slavery. The Executive Council asked for the support of England's Law Officers of the Crown. Meanwhile, Chief Justice John Beverlay Robinson ordered that time be given to gather affidavits in Happy's defense since the alleged offense had occurred four years before any effort at extradition by Kentucky and since no course of action had been taken in Kentucky to punish the alleged felony.

On October 12, 1837, the Executive Council refused the extradition request on the basis of insufficient evidence, and Happy was released on November 14, 1837. Canada received a response from the British government four months after Happy was released. In a joint opinion, dated February 25, 1838, Sir John Campbell and Sir Robert Mousey Rolfe concluded that there should be no reference to slave status in the accusation of a crime, that evidence for alleged offenses should be obtained in Canada according to Canadian laws, and that Canada did not have to extradite if there was no evidence of a crime.

Leask, J. MacKenzie. "Jesse Happy, a Fugitive Slave from Kentucky." *Ontario History* 54 (June 1962): 87–98.

Silverman, Jason H. "Kentucky, Canada, and Extradition: The Jesse Happy Case." *FCHQ* 54, no. 1 (1980): 50–60.

Woodson, Carter G., ed. *JNH* 5 (1920). Lancaster, PA: Association for the Study of Negro Life and History.

—*Anne Gray Perrin*

JIM CROW, historical term for the age of racial segregation. Jim Crow was the name of a minstrel performance put on by Thomas "Daddy" Rice in Louisville, KY, in the early 1830s. Rice was a performer from New York and supposedly portrayed "a Kentucky corn-field negro" as part of a racist song and dance routine. The act soon became a nationwide success. By the late nineteenth century, Rice's performance had become synonymous with the social, political, economic, and legal oppression African Americans faced on a daily basis.

Racial segregation was at the root of Jim Crow. After the Civil War, African Americans and whites were separated by both custom and law. Separate churches, schools, streetcars, and neighborhoods became more common. Inferior housing was a critical problem for blacks. Africans Americans were forced to live in the poorest environments and occupy homes on narrow lots that were not as well constructed as the housing options available to whites.

In 1874, the Kentucky legislature established a separate school system for blacks until legal pressure via the 1884 *Claybrook v. Owensboro* lawsuit forced the public education system to equalize school funding. The equalization of school funding did not significantly improve the funding of black schools. Well into the twentieth century, black schools lagged behind those of whites in books, supplies, equipment, and building construction.

Segregation in transportation, recreation, and public accommodations was firmly in place in Kentucky by the 1880s. African American railroad passengers encountered "white" and "colored" ticket windows and a "colored waiting room." Theaters, restaurants, baseball parks, and racetracks segregated the races. Jim Crow practices subjected African Americans to racial violence, second-class citizenship, and derogatory images of themselves. Kentucky and the South's racial patterns were cemented when the U.S. Supreme Court ruled in the historic 1896 case *Plessy v. Ferguson* that separate but equal was constitutional. In 1904, the Kentucky legislature passed the **Day Law,** which outlawed integrated higher education in Kentucky. Other measures were taken to further guarantee the separation of the races. The state segregated black and white mentally ill patients at Eastern State Hospital in Lexington. Orphanages, libraries, and hospitals were racially segregated. Madisonville and Louisville passed residential segregation ordinances. Water fountains and bathrooms were separate. Nancy Johnson lived in the small eastern Kentucky community of Baxter and recalled, "In Harlan they would have the nice water fountains for the whites, and then they'd have little fountains someplace else for blacks." But there were times and places where segregation was not rigidly enforced. For example, Booker T. Washington and delegates to the 1909 National Negro Business League conference in Louisville were given access to the city's public accommodations. The following year, Washington visited Hopkinsville and was not accorded the same privilege.

By the 1950s and 1960s, civil rights demonstrations nationwide led to the decline and death of Jim Crow. In the forefront of this

African American adolescents competing in a watermelon-eating contest at a baseball game at Parkway Field in Louisville, ca. 1940s. This image reflects the kind of racist stereotypes whites projected onto African Americans during the Jim Crow era.

movement in the Bluegrass State were chapters of the **Congress of Racial Equality** and **National Association for the Advancement of Colored People.** Kentucky passed the **Civil Rights Act of 1966,** which helped further eliminate the existence of racial segregation in the state.

Cockrell, Dale. *Demons of Disorder: Early Black Face Minstrels and Their World.* New York: Cambridge Univ. Press, 1997.

Fosl, Catherine, and Tracy E. K'Meyer. *Freedom on the Border: An Oral History of the Civil Rights Movement in Kentucky.* Lexington: Univ. Press of Kentucky, 2009.

Lucas, Marion B. *A History of Blacks in Kentucky.* Vol. 1, *From Slavery to Segregation, 1760–1891.* Frankfort: Kentucky Historical Society, 1992.

Wright, George C. *A History of Blacks in Kentucky.* Vol. 2, *In Pursuit of Equality, 1890–1980.* Frankfort: Kentucky Historical Society, 1992.

—*Gerald L. Smith*

JOHN G. FEE INDUSTRIAL HIGH SCHOOL, African American high school in Maysville, KY. In 1928, the voters of Maysville approved a bond issue to finance the creation of a black high school named for John Greg Fee, the famed abolitionist and founder of **Berea College,** who was born in nearby Bracken Co. Fee had once been a minister in Mason Co. Located on the south side of E. Fourth St., east of the city limits at that time, John G. Fee Industrial High School became noted for its quality academic and vocational training; many of its graduates went on to Kentucky State College (now **Kentucky State University**) at Frankfort. The school offered both high school and elementary school grades, and its students were drawn from the city and the county. It also had an excellent record in athletics. The 1933 and 1934 girls' basketball teams, coached by Miss E. M. Clement, were state champions; in 1952, the boys' basketball team, under coach John Fields, was the state runner-up, losing to Louisville Central in the finals. Professor **William Humphrey** (1879–1958), the first principal of John G. Fee Industrial High School (1929–1949), is remembered as the administrator who oversaw the institution's many achievements; the second and last principal was O. W. Whyte (1949–1957).

The integration of both the Maysville and the Mason Co. school systems began in 1956. That September, the Mason Co. system withdrew 78 students from John G. Fee Industrial, both at the high school and elementary levels, and enrolled them in previously all-white county schools; the Maysville city schools closed the 10th through 12th grades at the black school and enrolled 23 African American students at Maysville High. John G. Fee Industrial High School continued a few more years until the process of integration was completed in Mason Co. The school building was then leveled for construction of a parking lot.

Calvert, Jean, and John Klee. *Maysville, Kentucky: From Past to Present in Pictures.* Maysville, KY: Mason Co. Museum, 1983.

Caron's Maysville City Directory, 1934.

Newspapers: "Integration in Mason," *KTS,* February 16, 1956, 12A; "Maysville Schools to Integrate," *KTS,* September 3, 1956, 4A.

JOHNSON, ARTHUR LLOYD, JR. (b. 1914, Lawrence, KS; 2005, Louisville, KY), educator, state legislator, and tennis player. Born on December 5, 1914, in Lawrence, KS, Arthur Lloyd Johnson Jr. graduated from Lawrence Memorial High School in 1932. He then attended the University of Kansas for two years before transferring to the Hampton Institute in Virginia in 1934. After graduating from Hampton, A. L. Johnson, as he frequently was called, served in the U.S. Army during World War II. After the war, Johnson settled in Louisville, KY, where he taught at various schools throughout the Jefferson County Public Schools and coached tennis, football, and basketball for over 37 years.

In 1963, Johnson was elected to represent the 40th Legislative District, the second African American Democrat elected to the Kentucky General Assembly. Although he served for only two years, during his first month in office, he, along with two other representatives, cosponsored the Civil Rights Act of 1964, which would have banned discrimination in public accommodations. Despite support for the bill by Governor Ned Breathitt and influential white legislator Norbert Blume, it failed to pass the General Assembly. However, the ultimate passage of the **Civil Rights Act of 1966** was in large part due to the struggle of Johnson and others to pass the 1964 bill.

A. L. Johnson was also acclaimed for his skills on the tennis court. In 1955, he became the first African American to participate in the Louisville Public Parks Tennis League and spent the next 40 years training hundreds of teenagers in the sport. In 1991, he won the consolation bracket in the United States Tennis Association's National 75 Grass Court singles division and continued to participate in American Tennis Association national tournaments into his late 70s. He also served as the vice president of the Mid-western Tennis Association and was inducted into the Kentucky Tennis Hall of Fame in 1993. Early in the twenty-first century, the annual Arthur Lloyd Johnson Memorial Tennis Tournament was established in Louisville in his honor. On December 26, 2005, A. L. Johnson died in Louisville and was buried in Highland Memory Gardens in Mount Washington.

Kentucky House of Representatives. 06 RS BR 2517. 2006 Regular Session.

Newspapers: "Losing in Tennis Surely Spotlights Winning Attitude," *Richmond (VA) Times-Dispatch,* August 10, 1994, E7; "Arthur Lloyd Johnson Jr.," *LCJ,* Obituary, December 29, 2005.

—*Joshua D. Farrington*

JOHNSON, DONALD "GROUNDHOG" (b. 1926, Covington, KY), baseball player and coach. Five-feet-six, right-hand-hitting Donald "Groundhog" Johnson, the first African American from Covington to try out for the Cincinnati Reds baseball team, was the son of Howard Johnson and Margaret Battle. Johnson attended **Lincoln-Grant School** in Covington, which did not have a baseball team. He learned baseball by playing with the older kids in the neighborhood.

In 1947, Johnson was a member of a Covington baseball club named the Twenty Counts, which played most of its home games at the old Covington Ballpark along Ninth St. in the Willow Run section of town. Later that year, he tried out for the Cincinnati Reds. Ralph "Buzz" Boyle, the head scout for the Reds organization, had found Johnson. After signing a contract, Johnson was assigned to Ogden, UT, a Class C Reds farm team, but because of an altercation that occurred before he even got off the train, he returned to Covington and was released by the major-league club. In 1948, Johnson began a five-year stint in the Negro Baseball League (NBL). He was in the last group of players before the league folded during the 1950s. Johnson played the infield in both the National and American divisions of the NBL for the Philadelphia Stars and the Chicago American Giants, finishing his career with a respectable lifetime batting average of .335. Afterward, he played semipro ball with the Cincinnati Tigers.

When he returned to the area, Johnson was employed by Shillito's Department Store in Cincinnati. After his retirement from Shillito's, he was again active in baseball, this time coaching at Finneytown (OH) High School. During the 1980s, Johnson coached at Hughes High School in Cincinnati when former Covington Lincoln-Grant basketball coach James Brock was that school's athletic director. In 1996, Johnson was inducted into the Negro League Hall of Fame. Also, he worked at the Evanston Community Center and coached baseball at Walnut Hills High School in Cincinnati. Covington mayor Butch Callery renamed the old Randolph field at Ninth and Prospect Sts. in Johnson's honor on August 6, 2005.

Kenton Co. Public Library. *Covington.* Images of America. Charlestown, SC: Arcadia, 2003.

Little, Aiesha D. "Cincinnati Kid: Donald Johnson." *Cincinnati Magazine,* April 2005, 70–71.

Newspapers: Robert Alan Glover, "Play Ball! Negro Leagues' Players in the Spotlight on Opening Day," *KP,* March 29, 2003, 6K; Troy Lyle, "'Groundhog' Johnson Honored; Ballfield Named for Black Player," *KP,* July 23, 2005, 3K.

JOHNSON, GEORGE ANDERSON (b. 1890, Shelby Co., KY; d. unknown), educator. George Anderson Johnson was born in Shelby Co., KY, on April 22, 1890. He received adequate primary and secondary school training that prepared him to enroll at Indiana University in Bloomington, from which he graduated with a bachelor of arts degree in 1915. One year after he finished at Indiana University and at the age of 25, he married Edith Todd of Orleans, IN. George and Edith had four children: Margaret, Mary E., George L., and Fred T. Not fully satisfied with his educational attainments, Johnson completed a master of arts degree from Columbia University in 1925.

Johnson established himself as a leading black educator in the United States. After teaching school, he became a principal in Vincennes, IN, and supervising principal in Fort Smith, AR. He spent 35 years as principal of Howard High School in Wilmington, DE. Founded in 1867, Howard High School was the only high school for African Americans in Delaware for many years. In addition, Johnson served as a lecturer to Baltimore school principals in 1926.

In addition to his professional work, George Johnson was a member of several professional and fraternal organizations. He served as president of the Wilmington Principals Association and vice president of the Wilmington Suburban Principals Association and was a member of the National Education Association, the Delaware Education Association, the Odd Fellows, and **Kappa Alpha Psi Fraternity.**

"A Brief History of Howard." http://www.howard.nccvt.k12.de.us/PDF/About_History.pdf (accessed July 2, 2011).

Fleming, G. James, and Christian E. Burckel, eds. *Who's Who in Colored America.*7th ed. Yonkers-on-Hudson, NY: Christian E. Burckel & Associates, 1950.

Indiana Alumni Magazine 3, no. 2 (November 1940): 26. http://institutionalmemory.iu.edu/aim/bitstream/handle/10333/3191/IAM_November1940.pdf;jsessionid=3913BAE4C3F52F5654DC969174E9D2F9?sequence=1 (accessed July 2, 2011).

—*David H. Jackson Jr.*

JOHNSON, ISAAC (b. 1844, Elizabethtown, KY; d. 1905, Ogdensburg, NY), author of a slave narrative. In 1840, Isaac Johnson's paternal grandfather, Griffin Yeager, a Kentucky native, obtained a slave woman from Madagascar whom he named Jane. In his will, he bequeathed her, along with other farm property, to his son, Richard "Dick" Yeager. Richard Yeager took Jane as if she were his wife to a small farm on the Green River. They prospered agriculturally, primarily as tobacco growers. In 1844, Isaac Johnson was the second child born to this union.

When other people moved into the surrounding area, they expressed their disapproval of Yeager's relationship with his slave, Jane. In 1851, Yeager yielded to the social pressure and sold his farm and his family, which consisted of Jane, Louis, age nine, Isaac, age seven, Ambrose, age five, and Eddie, age two. Isaac Johnson was sold to William Mattingly for $700. Jane was sold without her children for $1,100. Johnson never saw his family again.

In his narrative, Johnson told of his experience of learning that his father had sold his family into the "Divine institution" of American slavery. He explained that this was why he chose his mother's maiden name for his last name. After various attempts to escape his enslavement, Johnson found freedom when he observed Company A, 8th Michigan Regiment, near his Kentucky home. He hired himself to a Captain Smith. His master attempted to retrieve him, but the unit's colonel refused to assist him in the search. Captain Smith then gave Johnson a revolver and ammunition to protect himself. Johnson wrote that in a short time he experienced two forms of freedom: work for wages and possession of a weapon.

In 1864, in Detroit, Johnson left his job with Smith and enlisted in the 1st Michigan Colored Infantry at age 20. After the Civil War, he moved to Canada and worked as a mason and stonecutter. In 1874, he married Theadocia Allen. He and his family settled in Ogdensburg, NY, where he completed his narrative in 1901. He died of a heart attack on December 5, 1905, and his widow received his Civil War pension.

Civil War Pension Index: General Index to Pension Files, 1861–1934.

Johnson, Isaac. *Slavery Days in Old Kentucky.* Ogdensburg, NY: Republican & Journal Print, 1901.

———. *Slavery Days in Old Kentucky.* Introduction by Cornel J. Reinhart. Canton, NY: Friends of the Owen D. Young Library and the St. Lawrence County Historical Association, 1994.

—*Sallie L. Powell*

JOHNSON, JAMES BARTLETT (b. 1830, Taylor Co., KY; d. 1900, Louisville, KY), preacher. Born in slavery in Taylor Co.,

KY, James Bartlett Johnson, at age 18, felt the call to preach at his conversion. He delayed preaching until he could learn to read. In 1853, he married Mary A. Buchanan, also from Taylor Co., who had been freed from slavery at age 3. Shortly afterward, Johnson was separated from his wife and child when he was sold and taken to Louisiana. He preached his first sermon and organized a church there in 1858. He continued to preach even though he was threatened with a whip for preaching to the slaves on the plantation.

After serving three years on the Union side in the Civil War, Johnson returned to Kentucky, found his family from which he had been separated, and settled in Louisville. He joined the African Methodist Episcopal Zion (A.M.E.Z.) Church and became part of its Conference in 1867. Staying no more than two years at any appointment, he pastored in Springfield, Russellville, Greenville, and two assignments in Indiana: New Albany and Indianapolis. In 1879, he returned to Kentucky and ministered at Louisville's Twelfth Street Church and a year later at Jacob Street Tabernacle. He served as presiding elder of the First and Second Districts of the church's Kentucky Conference toward the end of his career. In his ministry, he was selected four times as a local delegate to the national meeting of the A.M.E.Z. Church General Conference, twice in New York City, once in New Bern, NC, and finally in Pittsburgh, PA, in 1892.

Johnson and his wife, Mary, were married for around 40 years and had seven children, but only two reached adulthood. Johnson, a resident of Chapel St. in Louisville's Ward 10, died of paralysis on September 27, 1900.

Hood, James Walker. *One Hundred Years of the African Methodist Episcopal Zion Church; or, The Centennial of African Methodism.* New York: A.M.E. Zion Book Concern, 1895.

Kentucky Death Records, 1852–1953.

U.S. Federal Census (1870, 1880, 1900).

—*Sallie L. Powell*

JOHNSON, JOHN J. (b. 1945, Louisville, KY), **civil rights activist and NAACP leader.** Raised in Franklin, KY, John J. Johnson began developing his interest in government and civil rights at Lincoln High School. At 17, he became the youngest president of any Kentucky chapter of the **National Association for the Advancement of Colored People** (NAACP). He graduated from the all-black school one year before the **Civil Rights Act of 1964.** His high school principal was assigned the assistant principal position of the area's newly integrated school system. Johnson witnessed a school board meeting that dismissed his high school principal on false charges, which spurred his civil rights actions, including a fight to integrate Franklin's segregated swimming pool.

Johnson served as Kentucky state president of the NAACP for 14 years. He increased the number of branches from 4 to 42 and pushed for the hiring of African American state troopers. He remained active in various civil rights roles in Kentucky until he joined the national NAACP staff in Baltimore, MD, in 1986. He worked for two decades at promoting civil rights not only in the United States but also in various other countries. While he was in Baltimore, he graduated from Sojourner-Douglass College with a degree in community development and public adminis-

John J. Johnson.

tration. He ended his service for the national NAACP in the position of chief executive of operations in 2006.

In 2007, Johnson returned to Kentucky when he was unanimously appointed the executive director of the **Kentucky Commission on Human Rights.** In this capacity, he has pushed for the inclusion of Hispanics and other minorities in "building Kentucky's future"; the expansion of Kentucky's civil rights law to include children bullied for sexual orientation and gender identity; and the prevention of any specialty license plates that bear the Confederate flag or images supporting the institution of slavery.

Johnson has received numerous accolades, including a street named in his honor in Franklin, selection to the Kentucky Commission on Human Rights Hall of Fame, and the NAACP's Medgar Evers Award. On Martin Luther King Jr.'s birthday in 2005, Johnson spoke of the economic complexities that faced African Americans but praised the community for its work through the African American Heritage Center. Johnson's godmother, Lucille Brooks, had founded the center, which was located on the corner of Jefferson St. and John J. Johnson Ave.

"History Makers. John J. Johnson Biography." http://www.thehistory makers.com/biography/biography.asp?bioindex=1315&category =CivicMakers&name=John+J.+Johnson (accessed September 12, 2011).

Kentucky Commission on Human Rights. Biography of Executive Director John J. Johnson. http://kchr.ky.gov/aboutExecDir.htm (accessed September 12, 2011).

Newspapers: "Johnson Says Keep Dream Alive," *BGDN,* January 17, 2005; "Civil Rights Pioneer Chosen as Human Rights Commission Director," *KP* (Cincinnati, OH), August 24, 2007, A7.

Who's Who in Black Louisville. 3rd ed. Columbus: Who's Who Publishing Co., 2009.

—*Sallie L. Powell*

JOHNSON, LAURA "DOLLY" (b. ca. 1852, Kentucky; d. unknown), White House cook. Better known as Dolly, Laura Johnson reached the pinnacle of her culinary craft when she became the White House cook for President Benjamin Harrison and later for President Grover Cleveland. Various newspapers covered the story of how she replaced Madame Pelouard, whose elaborate French cooking did not delight President Harrison's "plain" palate. First Lady Caroline Harrison was credited with hiring Johnson.

Sources conflict over her birthplace (Louisville, Lexington, or Georgetown, KY) and also provide different origins of her presidential employment. Some portray Johnson as the longtime family cook for the Harrisons while they lived in Indianapolis, but the *Detroit Plaindealer* described another version in 1889. The article maintained that Johnson had cooked for many years for Lexington native and Louisville attorney Col. John Mason Brown. She had earned a comfortable living and at about 37 years of age had planned to retire in Lexington. Brown described her as one of the best cooks in the United States. After dining at the Browns' home, Theodore Roosevelt praised Johnson's cooking and, according to the newspaper writer, possibly recommended her to the Harrisons.

Johnson managed two kitchens in the White House—one below the private dining room and one under the serving room and butler's pantry. The first was used for state dinners, while the second was for the presidential family's dining. Johnson supervised Mary Robinson from Virginia. Robinson made the pies, baked the bread, and assisted Johnson. Johnson brewed the soups and cooked the meats. Both women wore Dutch blue calico dresses with white aprons.

In 1890, female photographer Frances Benjamin Johnston photographed Johnson holding a dish and standing in the middle of the main White House kitchen. Johnston was a distant cousin of First Lady Frances Cleveland, which might explain how the Clevelands kept Johnson as their cook when they returned to the White House in 1893. When Johnson worked for the Harrisons, she was paid $75 a month. Her pay increased to $150 a month under the Cleveland administration. The end of her employment term at the White House and her whereabouts after she left the White House remain a mystery.

Miller, Adrian. "Presidential Cooks: Cooking Truth to Power." In *American I Am Pass It Down Cookbook: Over 130 Soul-Filled Recipes,* edited by Jeff Henderson and Ramin Ganeshram, 73–75. NY: SmileyBooks, 2011.
Newspapers: "Will Cook for the President," *Detroit Plaindealer,* December 20, 1889, 1; "Keeping a Mansion," *Pittsburgh Dispatch,* June 1, 1890, 1; untitled article, *Maysville (KY) Evening Bulletin,* March 11, 1893, 3.

—*Sallie L. Powell*

JOHNSON, LOUIS BROWN "SWEET LOU" (b. 1934, Lexington, KY), first African American major-league baseball player from Lexington, KY. Born on September 22, 1934, in Lexington, KY, to Shirley and Sidney Johnson, Louis Brown Johnson was the oldest of five children who grew up in the African American community of **Pralltown,** where he became known throughout the neighborhood as an outstanding softball player. In spite of his talent with the ball and bat, no high school conference affiliations recognized blacks in baseball; consequently, football and basketball became the forefront of Johnson's interests at (Paul Laurence) **Dunbar High School,** and he became an All-Star player in both sports.

Johnson attended Kentucky State College (later known as **Kentucky State University**) for one year on a basketball scholarship, but in the summers and briefly after his time at Kentucky State, he played baseball for the **Lexington Hustlers,** an African American baseball team. In 1953, the minor-league affiliate of the New York Yankees recruited him as an outfielder; he later moved to various other teams, including the Kansas City Monarchs. With the Monarchs, Johnson had the opportunity to play with outstanding baseball legends, such as Buck O'Neal, who served as his mentor.

In 1960, Sweet Lou, as Johnson was often called, entered the major-league scene when he played for the Chicago Cubs; however, he achieved major-league fame in 1965, when he was traded to the Los Angeles Dodgers. During the World Series that year, Johnson demonstrated his talent by hitting a home run in the fifth game and in the seventh game that led the team to victory. After his time with the Dodgers, Johnson played briefly with the Chicago Cubs, the Cleveland Indians, and the California Angels before retiring in 1969.

Since 1981, Johnson has lived in Los Angeles and has worked for the Dodgers. He became involved in various community-service projects for both major- and minor-league baseball, including the Employment Assistance Program and the Baseball Assistant Team Program, and as an alcohol and drug counselor to baseball players. In spite of his work in Los Angeles, he frequently attended the annual **Pralltown** Day held in Lexington, KY, on the Saturday of Labor Day weekend at Lou Johnson Park, which was named in his honor in 1978. In 2004, Johnson was again honored with Lou Johnson Way, the street leading into the park.

Baseball Almanac. 2009. Miami (FL): Baseball Almanac. http://baseball-almanac.com/players (accessed March 25, 2009).
Johnson, Louis. Interview by Jessica Bryant, Lexington, KY, February 1, 2009.
Major League Baseball Louisville. 2009. New York (NY): Major League Baseball. http://losangeles.dodgers.mlb.com (accessed March 25, 2009).
Newspapers: "T-Ball League Honors Ex-Player from Lexington," *LHL,* June 7, 1998, B1; "Protecting Pralltown," *LHL,* September 2, 1998, 3; "'Sweet' Gets His Street—City's First Black Major Leaguer Has Road Named after Him," *LHL,* August 12, 2004, A1.

—*Jessica Bryant*

JOHNSON, LYMAN TEFFT (b. 1906, Columbia, TN; d. 1997, Louisville, KY), educator and civil rights activist. Born on June 12, 1906, in Columbia, TN, Lyman Tefft Johnson was the son of Mary Dew and Robert Graves Johnson. In 1926, he earned his high school diploma from Knoxville College's preparatory academy. He received his bachelor's degree from Virginia Union University in 1930 and his master's from the University of Michigan in 1931. From 1933 until 1966, he taught at Louisville's **Central High School.** Later, he served as an assistant principal in public schools and at Flaget High School in Louisville. From 1939 to 1941, he served as president of the Louisville Association of Teachers in Colored Schools and won a campaign to end racially based inequalities in the pay of the city's teachers. In 1949, he was the plaintiff in a lawsuit that opened the University of Kentucky's graduate programs to African American students. Although his admission was fiercely opposed at the time, the university later awarded him an honorary doctorate and now offers fellowship programs in his name. From 1978 to 1982, he served as a member of the Jefferson County Board of Education. The Lyman T. Johnson Middle School was named in his honor. A courageous civil rights leader, he led efforts to desegregate swimming pools, parks, hotels, restaurants, and other facilities. Active in several professional and civil rights organizations, including the Kentucky Civil Liberties Union and the Louisville Urban League, he served for six years as head of the Louisville branch of the **National Association for the Advancement of Colored People.** In 1936, he married Juanita Morrell, who died in 1977. They had two children: Yvonne Johnson Hutchins and Lyman Morrell Johnson. Lyman T. Johnson died in Louisville at the age of 91 on October 3, 1997. His body was donated to the University of Louisville School of Medicine.

Lyman Johnson.

Hall, Wade. "Johnson, Lyman Tefft." In *The Kentucky Encyclopedia,* edited by John E. Kleber, 474–75. Lexington: Univ. Press of Kentucky, 1992.

———, ed. *The Rest of the Dream: The Black Odyssey of Lyman Johnson.* Lexington: Univ. Press of Kentucky, 1988.

Stepp, Holly E. "Lyman T. Johnson—1906–1997, Teacher Is Mourned as Humanitarian." *LHL,* October 5, 1997.

—*Charles F. Faber*

JOHNSON, THELMA BANKS (b. 1909, Mt. Pleasant, FL; d. 2012, Henderson, KY), first African American extension agent in Kentucky and first African American elected official in Henderson Co. Born in Mount Pleasant, FL, on May 8, 1909, Thelma Banks Johnson was expected to contribute to her family's livelihood by working in the cotton fields after completing eighth grade. She moved to Georgia with her family early in her childhood, but although she toiled in the fields during the day, she continued to study in her spare time. A few years later, she departed for Savannah, GA, where she enrolled in Georgia State Industrial College. In 1929, she graduated and went on to earn a degree in home economics from Ohio State University.

For 34 years, Johnson served as an extension agent, first working for the University of Georgia and then for the University of Kentucky. In 1946, she moved to Henderson, KY, where she remained for the rest of her life. Johnson worked primarily with underprivileged and low-income families, teaching practical information about subjects like nutrition and child development. She later recalled struggling with racism throughout her career, with lower pay for black agents and difficulties in serving black clients effectively. In honor of her service, the National Association of Extension Home Economists awarded the Distinguished Service Award to Johnson, who was the first African American to receive the award in Kentucky. She retired from her job as an extension agent in 1970.

In 1979, Johnson became the first African American elected to public office in Henderson Co. when she was elected to the school board, where she served for eight years, six of them as chairperson. In 1984, she was named Distinguished Citizen of the Year by the Chamber of Commerce. She continued to work in the community after her retirement, volunteering at nursing homes and assisting with programs dedicated to early childhood development and education. On March 17, 2011, Johnson and a crowd of over 80 people gathered at the site of the old Seventh Street School to celebrate her life with the establishment of the Thelma Banks Johnson Early Learning Center. Johnson died at the age of 103 on October 26, 2012.

Johnson, Thelma. Interview by Maxine Ray, Kentucky Oral History Commission, Kentucky Historical Society, October 21, 2000.

Newspapers: "Thelma Johnson's 101 and Going Strong," *Henderson (KY) Gleaner,* June 14, 2010; "'Great Lady' Honored: Ground Is Broken for Learning Center," *Henderson (KY) Gleaner,* March 18, 2011, B1; "Her Legacy: A Passion for Teaching," *Henderson (KY) Gleaner,* October 28, 2012, 1.

—*Stephen Pickering*

JOHNSON, WENDELL LUCIAN, SR. (b. 1897, Lexington, KY; d. unknown, Kansas), educator and social worker. Wendell

Lucian Johnson was the only child of Morrison Churchill Johnson, a barber, and dressmaker Katie (Nelson) Johnson. The young family initially lived with Katie's mother, Amanda Nelson, in Lexington, KY. By 1910, Churchill's barber business supported them.

Johnson graduated from Russell High School in 1913. He received a scholarship at Hampton Normal Institute, Virginia, because of his outstanding academic record. As a member of the institute's 1919 graduating class, he presented a speech, "The Negro as a Patriotic American."

In 1921, Johnson married Thelma Virginia Dunning from Norfolk, VA. They returned to Lexington, KY, where Johnson worked in private business. Three years later, Johnson became an instructor at Kansas Vocational School in Topeka and vice principal for six years. He later was an instructor at Oklahoma's Langston University. In 1935, he served as a social worker for the Shawnee County Welfare Center in Topeka, KS. Active in the Baptist Church, he became the first president of the Kansas State Layman Movement in 1950.

Johnson and his wife had two sons, Wendell Lucian Jr. and William C. Johnson. Wendell Lucian Johnson Jr. earned his doctorate from Atlanta University in the late 1940s with his dissertation, "A Study of Selected Non-disabled Veterans Reporting for Revaluation to the Veterans Administration Guidance Center, Atlanta University, Atlanta, Georgia, from January 1, 1948, to February 1, 1949."

Fleming, G. James, and Christian E. Burckel, eds. *Who's Who in Colored America.* 7th ed. *Supplement.* Yonkers-on-Hudson, NY: Christian E. Burckel & Associates, 1950.
Newspapers: "Colored Department," *LL*, February 14, 1915, 6; "Interesting Addresses," *Broad Ax* (Chicago), May 10, 1919, 2.
U.S. Federal Census (1900, 1910, 1930).

—*Sallie L. Powell*

JOHNSON, WILLIAM DECKER "W. D." (b. 1860, England; d. unknown), newspaper founder and editor. Described as a "bold" man with a "fearless pen," William Decker "W. D." Johnson was born in England. His father worked as a wholesale druggist in Manchester, and his mother was a native of Bengal, India. An extensive traveler, Johnson fluently spoke several languages. He immigrated to the United States in 1889. Four years later, he married Martha Jessie Prewitt, the daughter of **Clifton B. Prewitt,** a prosperous farmer, and Harriet Prewitt of Scott Co., KY.

In 1892, Johnson founded the *Lexington Standard*, an African American newspaper in Lexington, KY. Politically active in civil rights, he traveled across the state and used the newspaper as a means to educate African Americans and debate African American life in the segregated state. In 1897, he edited and published *Biographical Sketches of Prominent Negro Men and Women of Kentucky.* He additionally sold the *Lexington Standard* to **Robert Charles O'Hara "R. C. O." Benjamin** and then moved to Louisville to found the *Kentucky Standard,* which was located at 708 12th St.

An editorial in a Washington, DC, newspaper portrayed "Prof. W. D. Johnson" as an accomplished writer who arranged his editorials in the manner of an attorney's case preparation. He forcefully attacked the crime of lynching. Praised for his influence on Kentucky African Americans' knowledge of public affairs, Johnson wrote numerous editorials not only for his own newspaper but also in letters-to-the-editor format in additional Kentucky newspapers and other states' newspapers.

After the murder of *Lexington Standard* editor R. C. O. Benjamin, Johnson returned to the paper in 1908. At the Republican National Convention that same year, he served as the single black Republican delegate-at-large from Kentucky, and heavily campaigned for William Howard Taft as president. In 1909, while aggressively fighting for African American rights in newspapers and on the political platform, Johnson battled in Fayette County Circuit Court for control of his Lexington newspaper against Wade H. Carter, owner of the building that housed the newspaper, and Daniel I. Reid, a schoolteacher. Johnson won that case, but three years later he sold the newspaper to three Lexington men, including Reid. He then worked in the Forestry Bureau of the Agricultural Department in Washington, DC.

Johnson remained active in the Republican Party at least until 1915. His later activities are unknown, but his wife died a widow in Carlisle, KY, in 1939.

Johnson, W. D. *Biographical Sketches of Prominent Negro Men and Women of Kentucky.* Lexington, KY: Author, 1897.
Kentucky Death Records, 1852–1953.
Lexington Standard. Chronicling America, Library of Congress. http://chroniclingamerica.loc.gov/lccn/sn83025729/ (accessed September 7, 2011).
Newspapers: "An Honor to the Craft," *Colored American* (Washington, DC), August 4, 1900, 1; *Colored American* (Washington, DC), May 31, 1902, 5.
Smith, Rev. S. E., ed. *History of the Anti–Separate Coach Movement of Kentucky.* Evansville, IN: National Afro-American Journal and Directory, 1895.
U.S. Federal Census (1880, 1900).

—*Sallie L. Powell*

JOHNSON, WINIFRED "BIG WINNIE" (b. 1839, Henry Co., KY; d. 1888, Baltimore, MD), circus professional. Winifred Johnson was born in Henry Co. in 1839. Little is known of her early life, including her maiden name or her parentage. When she was 15 or so, she married a man with the last name Johnson, and the couple went on to have 10 children. Three survived to adulthood. From the age of 20 on, Johnson began to gain weight at a staggering rate. By the time of her death, she weighed 849 pounds.

In 1882, Johnson's husband died. A widow in need of income, she began to tour the country as part of a traveling circus. Known as Big Winnie, she was too large to travel easily. Instead, she was carried in a train boxcar that was opened to the public at each destination.

Johnson died on September 14, 1888, shortly before she was due to become an exhibit at Johnson's Dime Museum in Baltimore, MD. The official cause of death was "fatty degeneration of the heart." Twenty pallbearers carried her special-ordered coffin to its final resting place in Laurel Cemetery, Baltimore, and hundreds of people lined the street to watch the funeral procession.

"Big Winnie's Burial: The Prize Fat Colored Woman Laid at Rest Yesterday." *Baltimore Herald,* September 15, 1888.

Hartzman, Mark. *American Sideshow: An Encyclopedia of History's Most Wondrous and Curiously Strange Performers.* New York: Jeremy P. Tarcher / Penguin, 2005.

—*Fiona Young-Brown*

JONES, ALBERTA ODELL (b. 1930, Louisville, KY; d. 1965, Louisville, KY), attorney and civil rights activist. Born on November 12, 1930, in Louisville, KY, to Odell and Sarah (Sadie) Crawford Jones, Alberta Odell Jones learned the value of hard work and an education. The word "can't" was not part of her philosophy. A graduate of Louisville's **Central High School,** she majored in accounting and graduated third in her class from the University of Louisville. In 1959, she graduated fourth in her class from Howard University School of Law in Washington, DC. That same year, she became Kentucky's first practicing African American female attorney when she was admitted to the Kentucky bar.

Jones operated her practice from 2018 W. Broadway, where she handled domestic violence cases and addressed civil rights issues. In March 1960, as the leader of the Independent Improvement Club, she argued that political power would influence integration. Later, as president of the Independent Voters Association, she promoted voter registration by teaching African Americans how to vote with rented voting machines.

Nearby neighbor Cassius Clay (better known as **Muhammad Ali**) hired the 27-year-old Jones as the sole negotiator of his first professional boxing contract. She drove a hard bargain to secure his future. She arranged for 12 prominent white businessmen, known as the Louisville Sponsoring Group, to promote Ali's boxing career. She also coordinated a trust fund that he could not access until he was 35 years old. Clay signed the contract on October 26, 1960.

In March 1965, Jones directed the James "Bucky" Welch Rehabilitation Trust Fund. The seven-year-old boy had lost both his arms up to the elbows in a train accident when he attempted to retrieve his puppy. In July 1965, the *Kentucky State Bar Journal* announced Jones's appointment as assistant prosecutor in Jefferson County's Domestic Relations Court; she was the first female prosecuting attorney, black or white, in the county.

On August 5, 1965, only a month after her appointment, Alberta Odell Jones was murdered. Her blood-soaked car indicated that she had fought for her life. Her unconscious body was thrown from a bridge into the Ohio River, where she drowned. Police investigated three possible motives: robbery, revenge based on one of her cases, or part of a chain of unsolved murders of Louisville women. Her family contended that her involvement in civil rights might have resulted in her death. No one was arrested for her murder. Louisville's **A. D. Porter** and Sons Funeral Home handled her funeral arrangements, and she was buried in Greenwood Cemetery.

In May 2010, the commonwealth attorney notified Jones's sister, Flora Shanklin, that even though the police believed that they had solved the cold case and had a suspect, there was insufficient evidence to obtain a conviction. Without a confession or the discovery of additional evidence, no prosecution would occur.

"News of the Profession," *Kentucky State Bar Journal* 29, no. 4 (July 1965): 55.

A Legacy of Leadership: African American Pioneers in Kentucky Law. Louisville: Univ. of Louisville School of Law, Kentucky Chapter, National Bar Association, 2009 (originally released in 1995). Video recording.

Newspapers: "Methods of Pro-integration Groups Differ," *CJ,* September 14, 1960, 5; "Alberta Jones' Funeral Rites Held; Unsolved Murders Alarm West Enders," *LD,* August 12, 1965, 1; "Finally, a Suspect—but No Trial," *CJ,* May 4, 2010, A1.

—*Sallie L. Powell*

JONES, CHARLES EDWARD (b. 1880, Covington, KY; d. 1947, Covington, KY), funeral director. Charles Edward Jones was the son of Edward L. and Amanda Jones. As a youth, Jones lived at 724½ Sanford St. in Covington. In 1908, he was working for the **Wallace A. Gaines** Funeral Home as an embalmer; in 1913, he purchased the business from Wallace Gaines and renamed it the C. E. Jones Funeral Home. He moved the enterprise from 633 Scott St., in the heart of the African American business district, to 29 E. Seventh St., adjacent to the original William Grant High School.

Jones was treasurer of the **Ninth St. Methodist Episcopal Church** and president of the local chapter of the **National Association for the Advancement of Colored People** (NAACP). He was a 33rd-degree Mason and a member of Kenton Masonic Lodge No. 16, the treasurer of the Prince Hall Grand Lodge of Kentucky, and a director of the National Funeral Directors Association. He promoted African American education as a member of the community committee designated by the Covington Board of Education to review the plans for the new **Lincoln-Grant School**. The high school later honored him for his efforts by naming its auditorium after him. Jones was involved in many community and fraternal activities. As a member of the African American Businessmen's Association, he helped sponsor an annual summer picnic in the country for the African American community.

In 1920, the C. E. Jones Funeral Home relocated from 29 E. Seventh St. back to 633–635 Scott St., the original location of the Wallace A. Gaines business. From the 1920s until Jones's death, this was the unofficial meeting place of the **African American Businessmen's Association.** Being **Horace Sudduth**'s brother-in-law (Jones's sister Melvina had married Sudduth) helped Jones encourage other African Americans to enter business. Jones died in 1947 and was buried in Covington's Linden Grove Cemetery. After his death, his widow, Anna Mae Watkins Jones, a former schoolteacher at the Lincoln-Grant School, operated the funeral home until 1961.

Newspapers: "School Board Given Bids by Architects," *KP,* January 24, 1931, 1–2; Jim Reis, "Funeral Directors Assumed Civic Roles," *KP,* February 2, 1987, 4K; Ted Harris, "Reader Recollection," *KP,* March 2, 1992, 4K.

—*Theodore H. H. Harris*

JONES, DELLA MAE LEWIS (b. 1903, Williamstown, KY; d. 2009, Williamstown, KY), educator, librarian, and centenarian. Daughter of Richard and Sarah Jackson Lewis, Della Mae Lewis received her initial education in a one-room schoolhouse for African Americans in Williamstown, KY. Since Grant County did not have a high school for blacks, Della lived with an aunt in Cincinnati to attend high school. She returned to Kentucky and graduated from Shelby Co.'s **Lincoln Institute** in 1923. She then taught school in Wayne Co. and later in Boone Co.

In September 1929, Della married Bradley Jones; the Great Depression struck a month later. Kentucky then passed a law that married women could not teach school. Jones maintained, "If I had known that, I wouldn't have gotten married." The couple adopted a daughter, and Jones also cared for her parents until their deaths. The need for men to serve in World War II changed Kentucky's law against married female teachers. In 1940, Jones returned to teaching in Owen Co.'s New Liberty School and, against her husband's wishes, also continued her education with summer and extension courses at Kentucky State College (now **Kentucky State University**). Under this method, she took 17 years to graduate with an elementary education degree from the institution in 1957. Martin Luther King Jr. was the commencement speaker, and Jones prized a copy of his speech.

After integration, Jones became librarian at Owen County High School. Her husband died in 1969 and her daughter in 1972. Jones retired in 1974. For journalists and historians, Jones became a "living library" with her memories of the past. Willard Scott featured her as a centenarian on NBC's *Today Show*. In 2009, Kentucky State University granted her an honorary doctorate in humane letters. She was the school's oldest alumna, the oldest resident of Grant Co., and the only African American living in Williamstown, which declared May 13, 2009, Della Jones Day.

Some months before her death, she watched on television the inauguration of the first African American president, Barack Obama. Wearing an Obama T-shirt, she dabbed her eyes and said, "Look how far we've come." Jones had "lived this country's history."

One week after her 106th birthday, Jones died in her hometown of Williamstown. She was buried in the Williamstown Cemetery. The Della Jones Memorial Scholarship Fund was established at Kentucky State University in her honor.

"104 Years of Memories: Oldest Living Grad Recalls Her KSU Days." Kentucky State University: Onward and Upward. http://www.kysu.edu/about_ksu/president/ksu_Onward_and_Upward_4-08.pdf (accessed September 15, 2008).
Newspapers: "Williamstown Woman Is Witness to Change," *Grant County News,* January 27, 2009; "Della Jones, 106," *Grant County News,* July 21, 2009.
Northern Kentucky Views Presents. "Della Jones: A Grant County Treasure." http://www.nkyviews.com/grant/pdf/grant_della_jones.pdf (accessed September 15, 2011).

—*Sallie L. Powell*

JONES, EUGENE KINCKLE (b. 1885, Richmond, VA; d. 1954, Queens, NY), educator, fraternity leader, and government worker. Eugene Kinckle Jones was born to Joseph Endom and Rosa Daniel (Kinckle) Jones in Richmond, VA, on July 30, 1885. Eugene attended Wayland Academy, a preparatory school, and later enrolled in Virginia Union University, where he earned an AB degree in sociology in 1906. He graduated from Cornell University in Ithaca, NY, two years later with an MA degree in social science and economics. At Cornell, he became instrumental in the founding of **Alpha Phi Alpha Fraternity,** the first national Greek-letter fraternity established for black college men, and is recognized as one of the organization's "Jewels."

Jones moved to Louisville, KY, and taught at the State University (later known as **Simmons College of Kentucky**), where he specialized in the social sciences from 1908 to 1909. He also taught English and mathematics. On March 11, 1909, he married Blanche Ruby Watson of Richmond, VA, and they had two children, Eugene Kinckle Jr., and Adele Rosa. Jones transferred to **Central High School** in Louisville, where he worked as the general assistant, taught English, and coached football, basketball, baseball, and track. Significantly, in April 1911, he assisted in the establishment of the Alpha Lambda Chapter of Alpha Phi Alpha in Louisville, the first graduate chapter of the fraternity.

In 1911, Jones left this teaching position and moved to New York City, where he became the field secretary of the Committee on Urban Conditions among Negroes. This organization evolved into the **National Urban League,** and Jones worked as its executive secretary for decades. Under his leadership, branches of the Urban League spread throughout the country, and the group became a national organization. When he took the job, the league's budget was $2,500; by 1926, the budget had increased to almost $500,000. On January 11, 1954, at age 68, Jones died at his home in Queens, NY, after a brief illness.

Hayne, Coe Smith. *Race Grit: Adventures on the Border-land of Liberty.* Philadelphia: Judson Press, 1922.
Mason, Herman, Jr. *The Talented Tenth: The Founders and Presidents of Alpha.* Winter Park, FL: Four-G, 1999
Wesley, Charles H. *The History of Alpha Phi Alpha: A Development in College Life.* Chicago: Foundation Publishers, 1981.
Yenser, Thomas, ed. *Who's Who in Colored America, 1941–1944.* 6th ed. Brooklyn, NY: Thomas Yenser, 1942.

—*David H. Jackson Jr.*

JONES, FREDERICK MCKINLEY (b. 1893, Cincinnati, OH; d. 1961, Minneapolis, MN), inventor mainly associated with refrigeration and air-conditioning. Frederick M. Jones, an inventor, was the son of an Irishman, John Jones, and an African American mother. Jones lived in rooming houses in Cincinnati with his father, who later placed him in the care of Rev. William B. Ryan, a Roman Catholic priest. Father Ryan was the pastor at St. Ann Church in West Covington from 1909 to 1917.

Father Ryan provided Jones with an upbringing that was more typical for an Irish or German Catholic child than for an African American child. It was Father Ryan's view that a child's skin color did not matter. Hence, with Father Ryan's help and guidance, Jones learned to read and write and developed the mathematical and reading skills necessary for a strong foundation in mechanics and science. He became an inventor, an engineer, and a "mechanical whiz" who had special talents in dealing with machinery.

One of Jones's most significant contributions in the early part of his career was the design of a system that enabled refrigerated trucks and trains to keep fresh produce and meats from spoiling as they were transported across the country. Jones also contributed importantly to U.S. efforts during both world wars. During World War I, he initially served in France with the U.S. Army's

809th Pioneer Infantry Regiment. Because of his mechanical skills, he became an army electrician and helped wire several of the army's military installations in France, where he also taught practical electricity in the army's technical schools. During World War II, while he was employed at the United States Thermo King Control Company, Jones designed refrigerators used by the U.S. Army Air Force, the Marine Corps, and the Quartermaster Corps. Machines that Jones designed were also used to cool the cockpits and engines of various aircraft. He also invented a refrigeration unit that allowed blood plasma to be moved throughout the war's Pacific theater.

In the 1930s, when motion pictures were making the transition from silent films to sound films, Jones developed and patented both an electronic-soundtrack system and a ticket dispenser for movie theaters. He sold his sound-system patents to Radio Corporation of America. However, Jones's main focus was the design of mechanical refrigeration in overland trucks and trains and of the air-conditioning of automobiles. Jones is credited with helping design the refrigeration and air-conditioning units that were marketed by his employer, the United States Thermo King Control Company in Minneapolis. Jones held dozens of patents for his designs and inventions; the ones pertaining to refrigeration and air-conditioning were the property of the United States Thermo King Control Company. He was a member of the American Society of Refrigerating Engineers.

Jones died in Minneapolis in 1961 at age 67. He was buried in Fort Snelling National Cemetery in Minneapolis.

Congregation of the Sisters of Divine Providence, St. Anne Convent, Melbourne, KY, to Theodore H. H. Harris, April 29, 2004.
Jones, Frederick McKinley. Birth record. Archives and Rare Books Department, Univ. of Cincinnati.
———. Military service records. Minnesota Historical Society, St. Paul.
Ott, Virginia, and Gloria Swanson. *Man with a Million Ideas: Fred Jones, Genius / Inventor.* Minneapolis: Lerner, 1977.

—*Theodore H. H. Harris*

JONES, GAYL A. (b. 1949, Lexington, KY), prominent black female writer. As a young girl, Gayl Jones, the daughter of Lucille and Franklin Jones, learned an appreciation for the art of storytelling that was passed on to her from her mother and grandmother in Lexington, KY. A shy but precocious child, Jones made an impression on several teachers at Henry Clay High School because of her writing ability and affinity for literature. One of her teachers helped Jones acquire a scholarship offer from Connecticut College, a small but prestigious women's school. After graduating, she moved to Brown University for her graduate career, where she received an MA in 1973 and a DA in 1975. Jones then began a visiting lectureship at the University of Michigan, where she was eventually hired full-time in the English Department, the only African American woman in the department's faculty.

In the midst of her academic career, she published her first book, *Corregidora,* in 1975. Praised by renowned authors, including Toni Morrison and John Updike, her book told the story of a female **blues** singer in Kentucky and her struggles while dealing with a violent husband. Jones's second book, *Eva's Man,* published in 1976, appeared thematically similar because it featured another black woman's abusive relationship with a lover. Although *Eva's Man* did not receive the universal praise of its predecessor, the two books established Jones as a prominent black female author of the 1970s.

Although she published several poems and a few longer works after her two major books, Jones retreated even further from public life during the 1980s. In large part, this was due to an ongoing relationship with Bob Higgins, an increasingly unbalanced radical who drew the attention of police after he brought a shotgun to a gay rights parade in Michigan. To escape legal action (a guilty verdict in absentia for a felonious assault), the two fled to Europe for five years, only to return quietly to Lexington thereafter. In 1998, Higgins drew attention to his past record after sending threatening letters to local officials, blaming a racist conspiracy for the death of Jones's mother from throat cancer. When he was raided by police, Higgins committed suicide by stabbing himself in the throat, and Jones was briefly institutionalized in a mental hospital.

Despite the tragedy of her later years, Jones remained an important part of the literary world. In the midst of the chaos involving her husband in 1998, she released *The Healing,* which received critical acclaim. Only a year later, another book, titled *Mosquito,* appeared, although reactions were more mixed. Both books, like her earlier work, maintained Jones's interest in what she called "the psychology of characters—and the way(s) in which they order their stories."

Evans, Mari. *Black Women Writers (1950–1980): A Critical Evaluation.* Garden City, NY: Anchor Books, 1984.
Hine, Darlene Clark, Elsa Barkley Brown, and Rosalyn Terborg-Penn, eds. *Black Women in America: An Historical Encyclopedia.* Brooklyn, NY: Carlson, 1993.
Newspapers: "Cops Didn't Know Gayl Jones Was Acclaimed Writer: Novelist Institutionalized after Husband Kills Himself," *Los Angeles Sentinel,* March 11, 1998, B7; "Chronicle of a Tragedy Foretold," *NYT,* July 19, 1998, SM32.

—*Stephen Pickering*

JONES, HENRY WISE, SR. (b. 1873, Knoxville, TN; d. 1954, Louisville, KY), Baptist minister. According to census records and Rev. **C. H. Parrish Sr.,** Henry Wise Jones Sr. was born in Knoxville, TN. By the age of seven, Jones lived in Louisville, KY, with his parents, Henry and Lucy, two sisters, and one brother. He attended Knoxville College and State University (later known as **Simmons College of Kentucky**) in Louisville. By trade a marble polisher, Jones was ordained in the Baptist denomination in 1892. He married Mary Roberts five years later.

Jones began his ministry building Owenton Second Baptist Church in Owenton, KY. In 1904, he moved to Shelbyville, KY, to pastor Clay Street Baptist Church. Three years later, he left Kentucky to minister in Shelbyville, IN, and worked on remodeling Second Baptist Church. In 1911, he returned to Kentucky and served Lexington's **Historic Pleasant Green Missionary Baptist Church** for one year.

In May 1912, Jones became the pastor of Louisville's historic **Green Street Baptist Church.** As a State University alumnus, he was elected chairman of the Joint Commission representing the Interdenominational Alliance and the Baptist Ministers' and

Deacons' Meeting in 1921. He later followed **William Henry Steward** as chairman of Simmons's board of trustees. In 1950, he retired as pastor emeritus and died on May 2, 1954. He was buried in Eastern Cemetery in Louisville.

Jones's son, **William Augustus Jones Sr.,** followed his father into the ministry and served at Lexington's Historic Pleasant Green Missionary Baptist Church. His grandsons, **William Augustus Jones Jr.** and Henry Wise Jones, also became Baptist ministers.

Kentucky Commission on Human Rights. Hall of Fame, 2007. http://kchr.ky.gov/hof/halloffame2007.htm?&pageOrder=0&selectedPic=4 (accessed September 28, 2011).

Kentucky Death Index, 1911–2000.

Parrish, C. H. *Golden Jubilee of the General Association of Colored Baptists in Kentucky: From 1865–1915.* Louisville, KY: Mayes Printing Co., 1915.

U.S. Federal Census (1880, 1900, 1920, 1930).

Williams, Lawrence. *Black Higher Education in Kentucky, 1879–1930: The History of Simmons University.* Lewiston, NY: Edwin Mellen Press, 1987.

World War I Draft Registration Cards, 1917–1918.

—*Sallie L. Powell*

JONES, MARGARET ELLEN BARNES (b. 1911, Oberlin, OH; d. 2000, Washington, DC), member of the only African American Women's Army Corps unit to serve overseas during World War II. Born to **Margaret Sallee Barnes** and James D. Barnes, a civil rights and community worker and a chef, respectively, in Oberlin, OH, Margaret Barnes entered the Women's Army Corps (WAC) in 1943. Her first post was as 2nd lieutenant of an African American Women's Army Corps unit at **Camp Breckinridge,** KY. She was the executive officer of a company of 175 African American women. Although the women in this unit were trained for administrative work, they were assigned to menial jobs of cleaning floors and latrines. They protested their job assignments, and as a result, six women in Barnes's unit resigned. This caused Barnes to work for better working conditions by lobbying her former commander, Brig. Gen. Don Faith, for assistance. As a result of her involving the brigadier general, conditions improved for the WAC members at Camp Breckinridge.

In 1945, Barnes's unit, the 6888th Central Postal Directory Battalion, became the only battalion of African American women to serve overseas when it traveled first to England and then to France. After World War II, Barnes graduated from Howard University and attended graduate school at the University of Minnesota in history before being recalled to duty in 1949. In 1953, she married Everette Wendell Jones Sr., a navy man. Both were stationed separately in France. She retired as a major in 1965. On April 11, 2000, she died at Walter Reed Medical Center in Washington, DC. Her husband died three years later. Both are buried in Arlington National Cemetery.

Moore, Brenda L. *To Serve My Country, to Serve My Race: The Story of the Only African American WACs Stationed Overseas during World War II.* New York: New York Univ. Press, 1996.

Newspapers: Maria Newman, "Margaret Jones, 89, Officer in Black Army Unit," *NYT,* April 27, 2000, B13; "Margaret Jones; Served with WWII Black Battalion," *Los Angeles Times,* April 28, 2000.

Putney, Martha S. *When the Nation Was in Need: Blacks in the Women's Army Corps during World War II.* Metuchen, NJ: Scarecrow Press, 1992.

Sadler, Georgia Clark. "From Women's Services to Servicewomen." In *Gender Camouflage: Women and the U.S. Military,* edited by Francine D'Amico and Laurie Weinstein. New York: New York Univ. Press, 1999.

—*Hannah Reliford*

JONES, PAUL WILLIAM LAWRENCE (b. 1878, Mt. Sterling, KY; d. 1953, Cincinnati, OH), professor and coach at Kentucky Normal and Industrial Institute (now Kentucky State University). William Lawrence Jones was born in Mt. Sterling, KY, to Daniel and Sue Jones in 1878. As a small child who loved history, particularly adventure stories involving John Paul Jones, he earned the nickname Paul, a name he carried for the rest of his life. In 1898, he graduated from Kentucky Normal and Industrial Institute (later known as **Kentucky State University**) and from Simmons University (later known as **Simmons College of Kentucky**) two years later. After briefly studying at the University of Pennsylvania, Jones returned to Kentucky and served as a school principal at various schools in Cadiz, Somerset, and Owingsville. In 1907, he became a teacher at Kentucky Normal and Industrial Institute and within two years was principal of the school's Preparatory Department.

In 1912, Jones published a short history of Kentucky Normal and Industrial Institute and was appointed a professor of history and sociology in 1914. Over the course of the next 10 years, he became one of the school's most important scholars and was eventually appointed the dean of the College in 1924. In addition to writing poetry, Jones focused on expanding African Americans' awareness of their history. As a keynote speaker at the annual meeting of the Association for the Study of Negro Life and History held in Louisville in 1923, he encouraged fellow black scholars to "do our part towards placing" important black historical figures "before the world, erecting in their honor monuments in song and in story to the end that coming generations may be inspired."

Known on Kentucky State's campus as the Father of Athletics, Jones was also a major figure in developing the school's early sports teams by serving as manager and coach of the baseball, football, and track teams during the 1910s and early 1920s. From 1922 to 1938, he served as a member of the Champion Aggregation of All Conferences, which was responsible for naming the unofficial national Negro football college champion. During his tenure on this committee, Kentucky State was declared national champion four times. In 1932, he joined **Rufus B. Atwood** to form the Mid-western Athletic Conference. Throughout the 1920s and 1930s, he also wrote football-related articles for various national publications, including the *Crisis, The Official Intercollegiate Football Guide,* and *All Sports Record Book.* From 1928 until his death in 1953, he wrote a column on black college football in Spalding's *Intercollegiate Football Guide.*

In 1928, Jones left Kentucky to become the superintendent of the Colored Industrial School of Cincinnati, where he served for the remainder of his life. After his death in 1953, his personal papers and massive library were donated to Kentucky State. The donation has since become a significant part of the school's

Paul W. L. Jones.

Special and Rare Book Collection, which rivals the New York Public Library's Schomburg Center's collection of materials relating to African American history.

Bancroft, Edwin Henderson. *The Negro in Sports.* Rev. ed. Washington, DC: Associated Publishers, 1939.

Dunnigan, Alice Allison, comp. and ed. *The Fascinating Story of Black Kentuckians: Their Heritage and Traditions.* Washington, DC: Associated Publishers, 1982.

Jones, Paul W. L. "Negro Biography." *JNH* 8, no. 2 (April 1923): 128–33.

"Paul W. L. Jones Papers." Finding Aid. Blazer Library, Kentucky State Univ., Frankfort.

—*Joshua D. Farrington*

JONES, ROBERT ELLIOTT "JONAH" (b. 1909, Louisville, KY; d. 2000, New York), trumpeter. Robert Elliott "Jonah" Jones, **jazz** trumpeter, was born in Louisville on December 31, 1909. He began his professional career playing on a Mississippi riverboat and performed with the bands of such greats as Jimmie Lunceford, Fletcher Henderson, Benny Carter, Cab Calloway, and Earl Hines before he began working as a soloist in 1955. At that time, he achieved international success with his recordings of show tunes and jazz standards, which featured him on muted trumpet as the leader of his own quartet. He also appeared frequently on national television. Jones is considered one of the great jazz swing trumpeters and his improvised solos have been cited as models, along with his extensive work with mutes.

"Robert Elliott 'Jonah' Jones." *The Kentucky Encyclopedia.* Lexington: Univ. Press of Kentucky, 1992, 480.

—*Lee Bash*

Robert "Jonah" Jones.

JONES, SILAS (b. 1940, Paris, KY), award-winning playwright. One of eight children raised in poverty by sharecroppers, Silas Jones was born in Paris, KY, on January 17, 1940. Jones followed a passion for writing into a career in literature, completing his BA in English at Washington State University. After moving to Los Angeles, Jones began a long and productive writing career focused primarily on plays and short stories.

Jones's first play was presented by the Negro Ensemble Company in the late 1970s. The play, a "nightmare comedy" titled *Waiting for Mongo*, told the story of a young man waiting to be lynched in the basement of a church before having a dream where he defeats the approaching mob. *Waiting for Mongo* established Jones as a writer willing to mix racial commentary with surrealist imagery and presentation. Although he was most known for his plays, Jones also wrote for television and penned several short stories, the first of which won a prize for fiction in 1972. But Jones remained devoted to his career as a playwright, finishing over half a dozen more plays over the following decades and winning the inaugural Theodore Ward Prize for Playwriting in 1987. In addition to his career as a writer, Jones also remained active in the Los Angeles community, teaching creative writing in elementary schools and theaters.

Hischak, Thomas S. *American Theatre: A Chronicle of Comedy and Drama, 1969–2000.* Oxford: Oxford Univ. Press, 2001.
Newspapers: "Writer's Award Is Seeing His Play Done Right," *Chicago Tribune,* March 13, 1987; "Back Stage with Successful Playwright Silas Jones," *Cleveland (OH) Call and Post,* June 16, 1994, 3.

—*Stephen Pickering*

JONES, SUSIE PEARL WILLIAMS (b. 1891, Danville, KY; d. 1984, Greensboro, NC), religious organization executive. Born in her maternal grandmother's home in Danville, KY, Susie Pearl Williams was surrounded by an emphasis on education. Her grandmother had learned to read as a slave of a Presbyterian minister. Her parents, Frank L. and Fannie B. Williams, graduated from **Berea College.** Her father was a leader of African Americans who protested Kentucky's **Day Law** that forced segregated education in the state and the end of integration at Berea College.

Frank Williams taught school in Louisville and then served as a principal in Covington, KY. Later, he became the first African American high school principal in St. Louis, MO. After graduating from Covington's William Grant High School, Susie earned a bachelor's degree from the University of Cincinnati. She also attended summer sessions at the University of Chicago, where she met and married her husband, David Dallas Jones, in 1915.

In 1926, the family of six moved to Greensboro, NC, when David Jones was appointed president of Bennett College. Active in the Methodist denomination, David and Susie made their first overseas trip to Europe in connection with the World Methodist Federation. In the mid-1940s, Susie served terms as a vice president and president of the National United Council of Church Women, chair of the Intercultural and Interracial Relations Committee of the Women's Division of Christian Service, and a national board member of the YWCA.

After David's death in 1954, Susie became a registrar at Bennett College and retired in 1964. Five years later, she was the first African American woman to be awarded life membership in the North Carolina Council of Church Women. She died and was cremated in 1984. Bennett College commemorated her service to the institution with the Susie W. Jones Award, given to Bennett alumnae.

Fleming, G. James, and Christian E. Burckel, eds. *Who's Who in Colored America.* 7th ed. *Supplement.* Yonkers-on-Hudson, NY: Christian E. Burckel & Associates, 1950.
Hill, Ruth Edmunds, ed. *The Black Women Oral History Project.* Vol. 6. Westport, CT: Meckler, 1991.
North Carolina Death Collection, 1908–2004.
U.S. Federal Census (1900, 1910, 1920, 1930).

—*Sallie L. Powell*

JONES, VIRGINIA MAE LACY (b. 1912, Cincinnati, OH; d. 1984, Atlanta, GA), library educator. Known as the Dean of Deans, Virginia Mae Lacy was born in Cincinnati, OH, to Edward and Ellen Louise Parker Lacy but was raised in Clarksburg, WV. After a move to St. Louis, MO, she graduated from Sumner High School in 1929. A librarian at the St. Louis Public Library influenced Lacy's career decision of librarianship. She matriculated at Virginia's Hampton Institute and earned her bachelor of library science degree in 1933.

Lacy immediately inaugurated her professional livelihood as an assistant librarian at **Louisville Municipal College** for Negroes (a component of the University of Louisville). Municipal College was the only educational institution in Kentucky to offer library classes to African Americans. In 1935, Lacy organized the Librarians' Conference. She promoted the improved status of librarians and pushed Municipal College director **Rufus E. Clement** to give librarians full faculty status. The next year, she earned a bachelor of science degree in education from Hampton Institute. In Louisville, she received her first General Education Board Fellowship, which allowed her to attend the University of Illinois, where she received her master of science degree in library service in 1938.

The next year, Lacy's former supervisor, Rufus E. Clement, who had become president of Atlanta University, offered her the position of catalog librarian at Trevor Arnett Library. She accepted the post. In 1941, she married Edward A. Jones, professor of French and chairman of the Department of Modern Languages at Morehouse College. That same year, she became instructor of library science. In 1945, she earned her doctorate in library science at the University of Chicago, becoming the second African American to reach that goal, and was appointed dean of the School of Library Science at Atlanta University.

In 1966, Jones was elected vice president and president-elect of the Association of American Library Schools, and President Lyndon B. Johnson appointed her a member of his Advisory Committee on Library Research and Training Projects. She actively contributed to the library literature with such works as *Problems in Negro Public High School Libraries in Selected Southern Cities, Library Education in the South,* and *Reminiscences in Librarianship and Library Education.* In 1981, she retired as dean and was appointed the first director of the Atlanta University Center, Robert W. Woodruff Library. She died in Atlanta three years later. The following year, the Atlanta University named the Virginia L. Jones Exhibition Hall in her honor.

Hine, Darlene Clark, Elsa Barkley Brown, and Rosalyn Terborg-Penn, eds. *Black Women in America: An Historical Encyclopedia.* Brooklyn, NY: Carlson, 1993.

Jones, Reinette F. *Library Service to African Americans in Kentucky, from the Reconstruction Era to the 1960s.* Jefferson, NC: McFarland, 2002.

Newspapers: "Library Association Elects Prexy at Meet," *BAA,* February 19, 1966, 15; "President Names Library Advisers," *NYT,* August 14, 1966, 9.

Virginia Lacy Jones Papers. Robert W. Woodruff Library, Atlanta University Center. http://www.auctr.edu/rwwl/FindingAids/Virginia LacyJonesPapers.pdf (accessed September 19, 2011).

Wedgeworth, Robert. *World Encyclopedia of Library and Information Services.* Chicago; ALA Editions, 1993.

—*Sallie L. Powell*

JONES, WILLIAM AUGUSTUS, JR. (b. 1934, Louisville, KY; d. 2006, New York, NY), minister and social activist. The son of **William Augustus Jones Sr.** and grandson of **Henry Wise Jones Sr.,** two of Kentucky's best-known black preachers, William Augustus Jones Jr. became one of the country's most influential black preachers from the 1960s through the early years of the twenty-first century. He was born in Louisville on February 24, 1934. In 1940, his family moved to Lexington after his father became pastor of the **Historic Pleasant Green Missionary Baptist Church.** After graduating from (Paul Laurence) **Dunbar High School,** Jones attended the University of Kentucky until he enlisted in the army in 1954. As a 1st lieutenant stationed at Ft. Knox, he began preaching at the motor pool and instantly knew his life's calling.

After leaving the army in 1956, Jones finished his bachelor's degree at the University of Kentucky, was ordained at Pleasant Green, and later studied at Pennsylvania's Crozer Theological Seminary. In 1962, a year after obtaining his divinity degree, he was named the pastor of Brooklyn's Bethany Baptist Church, which under his leadership grew to over 5,000 members, becoming one of the largest black churches in the country.

In addition, Jones made social activism one of the major foci of his church. He led a successful protest movement against discriminatory employment practices by the State University of New York's Health Science Center, directed successful boycotts against discrimination at A&P grocery stores, headed the city's Operation Breadbasket, and opened a multimillion-dollar cafeteria that continued to serve the poor residents of the Bedford-Stuyvesant neighborhood into the twenty-first century. His social activism continued during the 1980s and 1990s as he protested against discriminatory tactics used by Mayor Rudolph Guiliani and formed the Amadou Diallo Coalition after the fatal police shooting of an African immigrant. Jones was also the mentor of Rev. Al Sharpton, who grew up in Bethany Baptist, and controversially used the church to provide sanctuary to Tawana Brawley's mother during the 1988 scandal.

Jones retired in 2005. The next year, Simmons University's (later known as **Simmons College of Kentucky**) School of Theology in Louisville was renamed the William Augustus Jones Jr. School of Preaching in his honor. Less than a month after the school was officially christened, he died in his Brooklyn home on February 4, 2006. After memorial services were held at Bethany Baptist and Lexington's Pleasant Green Baptist, Jones was buried near his parents in Lexington Cemetery.

Booth, Charles E. *Bridging the Breach: Evangelical Thought and Liberation in the African-American Preaching Tradition.* Chicago: Urban Ministries, 2000.

Newspapers: "Renowned Preacher, Civil-Rights Leader," *LHL,* February 7, 2006, B1; "Rev. William A. Jones, Civil Rights Activist, Dies at 71," *NYT,* February 8, 2006, C16.

Pendergast, Sara, Tom Pendergast, and Pamela M. Kalte, eds. *Contemporary Black Biography.* Detroit: Gale, 2007.

—*Joshua D. Farrington*

JONES, WILLIAM AUGUSTUS, SR. (b. 1907, Shelbyville, IN; d. 1968, Lexington, KY), minister and civil rights activist. Born on May 29, 1907, in Shelbyville, IN, to Rev. **Henry Wise Jones Sr.** and his wife, Mary Roberts Jones, William Augustus Jones Sr. was reared in Louisville and attended Morehouse College in Atlanta before transferring to State University (later known as **Simmons College of Kentucky**) in Louisville, from which he graduated. He was the recipient of an honorary doctorate from Monrovia College in Liberia, West Africa.

Jones served in his early ministry as pastor of the Evergreen Baptist Church of Lawrenceburg, KY, and then of the First Baptist Church of Nicholasville. In 1940, he accepted the call to serve as the 15th pastor of the **Historic Pleasant Green Missionary Baptist Church** in Lexington. As pastor of Pleasant Green, Jones liquidated Depression-era debt on an impressive Arts and Crafts–style edifice housing one of the city's finest pipe organs. A noted evangelist who preached all over the country, Jones was instrumental in the founding of the Progressive National Baptist Convention in 1961. During his tenure at Pleasant Green, the church took strong stands in favor of the freedom movement, including housing the organization of the **Congress of Racial Equality** and hosting Rev. James Farmer at the height of the **civil rights movement.** Jones encouraged his congregation and other black ministers in bloc voting that eventually led to the election of one of his members, **Harry N. Sykes,** to the position of mayor pro tempore of Lexington.

Jones married Mary Elizabeth Gill (1914–1999) of Lawrenceburg in 1933. The two had seven children, including **William Augustus Jones Jr.** (1934–2006) and Louis Clayton Jones (1935–2006). A daughter died in infancy.

Rev. William Augustus Jones Sr. died in Lexington, KY, on March 19, 1968. In death, he integrated Lexington Cemetery; the only other black person buried there had been a Civil War veteran laid to rest before the implementation of **Jim Crow** segregationist policies in Lexington and Fayette Co. during the last decade of the nineteenth century. In 2001, Jones was inducted into the **Kentucky Commission on Human Rights** Hall of Fame.

Jones, Amos N. *Historical Abstract of the Henry Wise Jones Family, 2007.* Washington, DC: Xanthas Express Press, 2007.

Peoples, Thomas H., ed. *Essence of a Saga: A Complete History of the Oldest Black Baptist Congregation West of the Allegheny Mountains, Historic Pleasant Green Missionary Baptist Church Formerly African Baptist Church.* Lexington, KY: s.n., 1990, 92.

Staff Report and Photograph. "Congregation's Dream Culminates in Commodious $75,000 Church Edifice." *Lexington Leader,* August 16, 1931.

—*Holly Jones Clark*

JONES, ZACHARIA KEELE (b. 1883, Bowling Green, KY; d. 1977, Bowling Green, KY), prominent medical doctor in Bowling Green. Zacharia Keele Jones was born the son of a former slave in Bowling Green, KY, on October 22, 1883. After attending State Street School, he moved to Frankfort to finish high school at Kentucky Normal School, from which he graduated in 1903. Desiring to become a medical doctor, but with little money to afford further schooling, he spent the next two years as a chef for a railroad company and working at the Swift Packing Company. He then attended Tennessee's Meharry Medical College from which he graduated as valedictorian in 1909. After interning at Mercer Hospital in Nashville, he returned to Bowling Green and established an office at 217 Main St. in 1911. He later moved his office and home to a permanent location in the historic Underwood-Jones House on 506 State St.

The next 62 years of his life were dedicated to serving Bowling Green's sick and poor citizens. During this time, Jones delivered approximately 2,500 babies, 200 of which were white. He was well known throughout the city for his generosity as a doctor, never turning down even the poorest patients. When he was treating his poor patients, he would frequently write "Jones condition" in Latin on their prescriptions, and the pharmacist would instantly know to fill the prescription for half price. In another instance, he personally drove a patient with polio from Bowling Green to Louisville, which at the time was a three-hour drive through hills on narrow curvy roads because there were no hospitals in Bowling Green that would treat black patients.

Z. K. Jones, as he preferred to be called, remained active in the medical profession through the early 1970s, serving as Bowling Green's oldest living physician, white or black. In 1973, Western Kentucky University honored him for his 62 years of service. At the ceremony, Governor Wendell Ford also presented him with the Kentucky Colonel award.

Dr. Jones died in Bowling Green at the age of 95 in 1977. After his death, the building that housed his office and home on State St. was nominated numerous times to be placed on the National Register of Historic Places.

Baird, Nancy Disher. *Healing Kentucky: Medicine in the Bluegrass State.* Lexington: Univ. Press of Kentucky, 2007.
"Interview with Dr. Z. K. Jones." December 11, 1975. Kentucky Library Special Collections, Western Kentucky Univ., Bowling Green, KY.
Jones, J. E. *A Profile of Z. K. Jones.* Bowling Green, KY: Master Printers, 1974.

—*Joshua D. Farrington*

JONES V. VAN ZANDT, U.S. Supreme Court decision that upheld the Fugitive Slave Act of 1793. One of four important cases involving fugitive slaves heard by the U.S. Supreme Court between 1842 and 1861, *Jones v. Van Zandt* centered on a group of nine slaves from Kenton Co., KY, in 1842. After escaping from their master, the slaves crossed the border into Ohio, where they met a farmer named John Van Zandt who was driving his covered wagon to the market. Van Zandt, an opponent of slavery, offered the travelers a ride, although it is unclear whether he knew that they were runaways. A few miles down the road, two slave-catchers overtook the wagon and captured eight of the fugitive slaves; the ninth escaped at Van Zandt's urging.

The slaves' owner, Wharton Jones, sued Van Zandt for the value of the escaped slave, the fee he was forced to pay the slave-catchers under Kentucky law, and the penalty required under the Fugitive Slave Act of 1793. In circuit court, the case was decided in favor of the plaintiffs, but the decision was appealed to the U.S. Supreme Court. After several delays, the case was presented to the Supreme Court in 1846 and 1847, with Salmon P. Chase and William H. Seward—antislavery Whigs who would play a central role in the formation of the Republican Party—representing Van Zandt.

In a written brief, Chase offered several arguments in defense of Van Zandt and against the Fugitive Slave Act of 1793. Chase asserted that since Van Zandt had picked up the fugitive slaves in Ohio, where African Americans were by rights presumed free, his actions could not be construed as harboring or concealing slaves. More broadly, he constructed a wide-ranging argument against the constitutionality of the law under which the case was being tried. Although he acknowledged that a former case, *Prigg v. Pennsylvania* in 1842, had declared the Fugitive Slave Act of 1793 constitutional, Chase argued that the decision had not taken into account important features of the Bill of Rights that opposed it in principle. Seward also issued a written brief that contained variations on the same claims.

The Supreme Court rejected all these arguments and ruled in favor of Jones. In the opinion written by Justice Levi Woodbury, the fugitive slave clause in federal law was upheld as a vital part of the Constitution that was not subject to change. Although Chase and Seward lost the case, their arguments further established their credentials as antislavery leaders and contributed to the growing sectional conflict between northerners and southerners. Van Zandt, meanwhile, was ordered to pay the fees required by law, but he died before the matter was settled.

Chase, S. P. *Reclamation of Fugitives from Service.* Cincinnati: B. P. Donogh & Co., 1847.
Finkelman, Paul. *Slavery in the Courtroom: An Annotated Bibliography of American Cases.* Washington, DC: Library of Congress, 1985.
Maltz, Earl M. *Slavery and the Supreme Court, 1825–1861.* Lawrence: Univ. Press of Kansas, 2009.
Rodriguez, Junius P. *The Historical Encyclopedia of World Slavery.* Vol. 1. Santa Barbara, CA: ABC-CLIO, 1997.
Swisher, Carl B. *History of the Supreme Court of the United States.* Vol. 5, *The Taney Period, 1836–64.* New York: Macmillan, 1974.

—*Stephen Pickering*

JONESVILLE, African American community in Bowling Green, KY, 1871–1966. Believed to have been founded by freed slaves soon after the Civil War, around 1871, Jonesville, a small African American community in Bowling Green, KY, was named, according to local folklore, for Grandma Jones, the owner of some of the original property. By present-day landmarks, the interior of Jonesville was bordered to the west by the railroad tracks, to the north by Dogwood Dr., to the east by Downing University Center, and to the south by the train trestle that passes over U.S. Highway 68 / KY 80. The Jonesville community encompassed a large area, approximately 30 acres, of Western Kentucky University's present campus.

Jonesville was a prosperous, close-knit neighborhood with grocery stores, beauty shops, service stations, and privately owned eateries such as Hardin's Sandwich Shop, as well as the Jonesville School, Mt. Zion Baptist Church (organized in 1886), and Salters Chapel African Methodist Episcopal Church (built in 1909–1910). The zenith of the neighborhood life was in the 1930s, when the population reached almost 300. The community continued to expand and by 1955, there were nearly 70 homes in the community and close to 500 people. Many former residents in interviews recall the community as a "slice of heaven" or "God's Little Acre," and that it was a stable neighborhood infused with a sense of commitment, responsibility and cooperation among residents.

The growth of Western Kentucky University caused the demise of Jonesville. The last real symbol that expressed the disappearance of the community was the sale of Mt. Zion Baptist Church in 1966. Jonesville was lost completely to an urban-renewal program by 1968. African American author James Baldwin dubbed this controversial program of land development "negro removal." Government reports show that 43 families were relocated from Jonesville to private and municipal housing, and that as many as 65 homes in the area were destroyed.

On April 10, 2001, the Kentucky Historical Society dedicated a historical highway marker to commemorate the existence and importance of the community and its residents. It is located at the intersection of College Heights Blvd. and U.S. 68 / KY 80 on Western Kentucky University's campus.

Buford, Henrietta. Interview by Steve Hutchinson, Bowling Green, KY, May 7, 1980.
Butts, Marjorie. Interviews by Maxine Ray, Bowling Green, KY, April 1992 and May 1998.
Deed Book Number 38, Warren County Courthouse, Bowling Green, KY, 553.
Harrison, Lowell H. *Western Kentucky University.* Lexington: Univ. Press of Kentucky, 1994.
Loyal, Taylor. "Buried Dreams." *College Heights Herald,* February 19, 2002, 1.
Standley, Fred L., and Louis Pratt. *Conversations with James Baldwin.* Jackson: Univ. Press of Mississippi, 1989.
Taylor, Dan. Interview by Maxine Ray, Bowling Green, KY, April 1992.
Taylor, Maxie Hines. Interview by Maxine Ray, Bowling Green, KY, April 1982.
Warren County Public School Records, Bowling Green, KY.
—*Maxine Ray and Nancy Richey*

JORDAN, ELEANOR FRANKLIN ALLEN (b. 1953, Louisville, KY), politician and women and children's advocate. Daughter of Fay Haralton and Ruth Marion Lester Allen, Eleanor Franklin Allen was born in Louisville's **Red Cross Hospital.** After she graduated from **Central High School** in 1971, she immediately attended Western Kentucky University. Marriages, motherhood,

divorces, and a welfare experience influenced Eleanor Jordan's perspective on women's and children's issues.

In her youth, she took a school trip to see the Kentucky State Capitol in Frankfort and remarked that she "didn't see anyone who looked like me." In 1996, Jordan, a Democrat, won a special election to become the only black woman in Kentucky's General Assembly at that time. She became a strong advocate for women and children. When the Kentucky legislature voted on a bill to require a 24-hour waiting period before a woman could obtain an abortion, Jordan argued, "This is not a conscience issue. It's a white male issue. . . . We've been told for hundreds of years what to do with our lives and we want to choose."

In 2000, Jordan ran a close race for Congress against incumbent Third District U.S. representative Anne Northup, a Republican. She argued against abortion restrictions and for equal pay and same-sex marriages. She won the support of organized labor and teachers' unions. In her unsuccessful bid for office, she raised $1.5 million. Her opponent raised almost $2.5 million, making it "the second most expensive race for a U.S. House seat in Kentucky history." If Jordan had won, she would have been the first African American to represent Kentucky in Congress.

The next year, Kentucky governor Paul Patton appointed Jordan ombudsman of the Kentucky Cabinet for Families and Children to serve from 2001 to 2004. In 2008, Kentucky governor Steve Beshear appointed her executive director of the Kentucky Commission on Women. She became the first African American to hold the position.

Clayton, Dewey M. "African American Women and Their Quest for Congress." *Journal of Black Studies* 33, no. 3 (January 2003): 354–88.
Jordan, Eleanor. E-mail message to Sallie L. Powell, February 28, 2013.
Newspapers: "House Passes Abortion Bill," *Williamson (WV) Daily News,* March 16, 1996, 5; "Women Urged to Take Reins of Political Power," *KP,* October 2, 1999, 1K; "Patton Endorsement Launches Jordan Congressional Bid," *LCJ,* December 16, 1999, B1.
—*Sallie L. Powell*

JUG BANDS, instrumental groups that played a musical technique that originated in Louisville, KY. Although a common misconception exists that rural white Appalachian country musicians originated jug bands, in fact, urban African Americans of Louisville invented and introduced this musical tradition. Jug band music, a descendant of minstrel and **ragtime** with some preceding **jazz** influence, developed in Louisville in the early 1900s. Its popularity peaked in the 1920s and 1930s along the inland Ohio and Mississippi Rivers, especially from Cincinnati to Memphis. It resurged with the folk-music revival of the 1960s. Jug bands varied in the number of musicians and the instruments used. Ordinarily one musician played the melody on a harmonica or a kazoo, while other band members played homemade stringed instruments, percussion spoons, or a washboard backed by another artist with a low humming, rhythmic sound created by blowing through a whiskey jug or a stove pipe replicating a bass tuba sound.

Early jug musicians shared stories with Fred Cox (a researcher in the early 1970s) revealing the origins of jug music with the Tite Brothers String Band of Louisville in the late 1890s. One of the

Ballard Chefs Jug Band.

band members, B. D. Tite, is credited with being one of the earliest musicians to bring the jug sound to the mainstream. However, the earliest documentation cites Louisville jug blower Earl McDonald and fiddler **Clifford Hayes** of the Louisville Jug Band as responsible for its introduction in the early 1900s to **Kentucky Derby** crowds. The Louisville jug music style grew in popularity when McDonald and Hayes performed in Chicago and New York around 1915, while the earliest audio recordings of their Louisville sound date from their performance with **Sara Martin**'s Jug Band for Okeh Records in 1924. Two years later, McDonald and Hayes recorded together for Victor Records as the Dixieland Jug Blowers and then separately under various band names. During the late 1920s and early 1930s, regional listeners heard the Louisville Jug Band sound on WHAS-AM radio with the Ballard Chefs, featuring McDonald and fiddler **Henry Miles.** Churchill Downs and the streets of Louisville continued to showcase jug music bands throughout this period.

Memphis and Cincinnati also featured jug bands documented in audio recordings of the 1920s and 1930s. Although the famous Memphis Jug Band was infused with the **blues,** the Cincinnati Jug Band (featuring talented artists such as Stovepipe No. 1, also known as Sam Jones), was influenced by the Louisville sound with more minstrel and ragtime traditions. An early recorded song, "Newport Blues," referred to Kentucky's "wide-open" city of Newport, where the Cincinnati band frequently performed at parties.

There has been a contemporary resurgence of jug music since the folk-music revival of the 1960s. Today's jug bands consist of a diverse mix of musicians, for example, the Juggernaut Jug Band of Louisville that has performed at events such as the National Jug Band Jubilee held annually in Louisville.

Cox, Fred, John Randolph, and John Harris. *Jug Bands of Louisville.* Compiled by Laurie Wright. Chigwell, UK: Storyville Publications, 1993.

Ikenberg, Tamara. "Jug-Band Music Comes Home." *LCJ,* July 1, 2005, E1, E4.

Jones, Michael L. "That Crazy Sound: Louisville Jug Bands." Chapter 2 in *Second-Hand Stories.* Louisville, KY: Weeping Buddha Press, 2006,

—John Schlipp

JUSTICE, DAVID CHRISTOPHER (b. 1966, Cincinnati, OH), professional baseball player. Professional baseball player David Christopher Justice was only four years old when his father, Robert Justice, abandoned the family. David's mother, Netti Justice, took a job as a housekeeper in order to support her son. Growing up in the North Avondale section of Cincinnati, David spent his time playing sports with the other boys in his neighborhood. Football, basketball, and baseball were his life, and he had dreams of someday playing in the National Basketball Association. At age 12, Justice began attending Covington Latin School in northern Kentucky. He was a prime candidate for the school, which requires students to skip at least one grade. Skipping grades was no problem for Justice because he excelled in academics as well as in athletics, particularly basketball. As a senior, he averaged 25.9 points per game and made the Catholic All-American high school basketball team. Justice graduated from Covington Latin School in 1982, two years early (he had skipped the seventh and eighth grades). He attended college at Thomas More College in Crestview Hills on a basketball scholarship. During his years at Thomas More, his athletic ability was showcased not only in basketball but also in baseball; the college's legendary coach, Jim Connor,

294 JUSTICE, DAVID CHRISTOPHER

mentored him in both sports. When Justice was 18, he was a junior in college and a favorite prospect of many baseball scouts.

His professional baseball career began in 1985, when he was drafted in the fourth round by the Atlanta Braves. While he was in the minor leagues, he worked odd jobs during the off-season. He drove a shuttle bus at the Cincinnati/Northern Kentucky International Airport and worked as an orderly at University Hospital in Cincinnati. In 1990, he played his first full season in the major leagues and received the National League Rookie of the Year award while playing with the Braves.

On January 1, 1993, Justice made headlines off the field by marrying actress Halle Berry. Their marriage was brief, ending in divorce after three years. In 1994, he was voted one of *People* magazine's 50 Most Beautiful People.

During his 14-season major-league career, Justice played for the Braves in the National League and in the American League for the Cleveland Indians, the New York Yankees, and the Oakland Athletics. During that time, he reached the World Series six times and made the baseball playoffs ten times. Justice was a three-time all-star who won World Series titles with the Braves in 1995 and the Yankees in 2000. He also holds the major-league record for the most postseason games played. His career batting average was .279. After retirement from baseball in 1999, he served as a baseball commentator for ESPN and the YES Network of the New York Yankees.

Baseball Almanac. http://www.baseball-almanac.com (accessed June 30, 2006).

Bradley, John Ed. "Justice Prevails." *Sports Illustrated,* June 6, 1994, 66.

Newspapers: Bill Peterson, "Coming Home: Once Again, Justice Returns with a Winner," *CP,* June 6, 1998, 3B; Chuck Johnson, "Postseason Justice," *USA Today,* October 1, 2002, 1; "Baseball Notebook," *Toronto Star,* February 7, 2003; William Croyle, "Latin School a Head Start," *CE,* February 10, 2006, 1B.

—*Susan Patterson*

K

KAPPA ALPHA PSI FRATERNITY, INCORPORATED, national fraternity founded by African American men during the period of segregation. Kappa Alpha Psi Fraternity was organized by 10 African American men on the campus of Indiana University at Bloomington on January 5, 1911. One of the founders was **Elder Watson Diggs,** who was born in Christian Co., KY. The fraternity was first known as Kappa Alpha Nu when it was incorporated on May 15, 1911. The name was effectively changed to Kappa Alpha Psi on April 15, 1915. The fraternity's objectives include uniting "college men of culture, patriotism and honor in a bond of fraternity" and encouraging "the spiritual, social, intellectual and moral welfare of members." Soon after its founding, undergraduate chapters of the fraternity sprang up on the campuses of historically black colleges throughout the country. Eventually, alumni chapters were also formed in cities. These graduate chapters allowed brothers to remain active in the fraternity while continuing to serve the community. With the desegregation of southern white institutions of higher learning, Kappa chapters were established in many academic institutions.

This national fraternity consists of 12 provincial chapters, and chapters are also located in South Africa. Kentucky is part of the South Central Province. The Louisville Alumni Chapter was established by **A. E. Meyzeek,** Elmer Mosee, Nelson Willis, Richard L. Jones, and A. C. Cox on October 20, 1920. In 1935, the Alpha Upsilon undergraduate chapter at **Kentucky State University** became the fraternity's 43rd chapter. In 1937, Alpha Upsilon had the best academic average of the Greek-letter organizations on the Kentucky State campus. Other chapters were founded throughout the state: Western Kentucky University's Epsilon Rho was founded in 1969; Morehead State University's Zeta Lambda chapter formed in 1971; Eastern Kentucky University's Eta Alpha chapter and Murray State University's Eta Beta chapter were founded in 1973. **Bernie Biggerstaff, Robert L. Gordon, Allan Houston,** and **Darryl Owens** are among the distinguished African American Kentuckians who are members of this fraternity. Nationwide, Kappas continue to promote their founding principles and serve their communities through various outreach programs.

"Active Chapters of Kappa." http://www.cs.virginia.edu/~gam9r/kapsi/activechapters.htm (accessed October 11, 2013).
"Kappa Alpha Psi Fraternity, Incorporated." http://www.kappaalphapsi1911.com/ (accessed October 10, 2013).
"Kappa Alpha Psi Fraternity, Inc.: Louisville Alumni Chapter." http://www.kappa-loukyalumni.com (accessed October 11, 2013).

—Gerald L. Smith

KAUFMAN, MONICA (b. 1947, Louisville, KY), anchorwoman at WSB-TV in Atlanta, GA. Monica Kaufman, daughter of Hattie Wallace Jones Edmondson and Maurice Jones, was born in Louisville, KY, on October 20, 1947. Kaufman earned a degree in English from the University of Louisville and was awarded the Michelle Clark Fellowship at the Graduate School of Journalism at Columbia University in New York. She proceeded to work first in public relations for Brown-Forman Distillers and then for two years as a reporter for WHAS-TV in Louisville. She also spent four years as a reporter for the *Louisville Times.*

In 1975, Kaufman was hired over Oprah Winfrey to become the first African American and the first female to anchor an evening newscast in Atlanta at WSB-TV. She spent over 30 years at the station, anchoring the evening newscast and hosting several series, including *Monica Kaufman Closeups.* She received 30 local and regional Emmy awards over the course of her career. In 1986, she received an honorary doctorate from Atlanta University. In 1989, she was presented the Distinguished Service to Broadcasting Award by the DiGamma Kappa honorary society at the University of Georgia. She was inducted into the Kentucky Journalism Hall of Fame in 2001. Kaufman retired from her position as anchorwoman at WSB-TV in 2012.

Hawkins, Walter Lee. *African American Biographies: Profiles of 558 Current Men and Women.* Jefferson, NC: McFarland, 1992.
Newspapers: "5 Inducted into Kentucky Journalism hall of Fame," *LHL,* March 24, 2001, C4; "America's 'Other Oprah,'" *LaGrange (KY) Daily News,* June 22, 2012, 6; "Anchor Woman," *Atlanta Magazine,* July 1, 2012; "Monica Pearson," *Atlanta Journal-Constitution,* July 22, 2012, E1.

—Elizabeth Schaller

KEAN, HENRY ARTHUR, SR. (b. 1894, Louisville, KY; d. 1955, Nashville, TN), player, coach, and athletic director. Louisville native and son of William Thomas and Alice Kean, Henry Arthur Kean Sr. graduated from Fisk University with a degree in physical education. He lettered in four sports: football, basketball, baseball, and tennis. He taught mathematics and coached football for 10 years at Louisville's **Central High School.** While he was there, he joined some other sports leaders in attempting to organize the Kentucky Colored State High School Athletic Association and requested that the **Kentucky Negro Educational Association** manage the group in 1929. Two years later, he joined **Whitney Young Sr.** from the **Lincoln Institute** in organizing a coaching school. Twenty-one participants in the school enrolled at Frankfort's Kentucky State Industrial College (later known as **Kentucky State University**), and 17 people registered at Paducah's West Kentucky Industrial College (later known as **West Kentucky Community and Technical College**). The coaching school organizers were also asked to organize a class in basketball coaching for women.

In the fall of 1931, **Rufus B. Atwood,** president of Kentucky State College, hired Kean as athletic director, and he also coached football, basketball, and baseball. He immediately became one of the leaders in the formation of the Kentucky High School Athletic League and served as its executive secretary from 1931 to 1945. The college became the home of Kentucky's African American state tournaments. Kean's younger brother, **William Lee Kean,** coached the first state basketball champions from Central High School.

In 1935, Kean earned his master of arts degree in physical education from the University of Indiana. He also took football coaching classes from Notre Dame's Knute Rockne. His Thorobreds, as he named them, dominated African American football for a decade, winning the National Negro Championship four times and the Midwestern Athletic Association Championships for 10 straight years. **Joseph "Tarzan" Kendall** was one of his most famous players.

In 1943, Tennessee State College (later named Tennessee State University) hired Kean away from Kentucky State for $10,000. His salary at Kentucky State had been $3,300. He continued his successful coaching career at Tennessee State until his death on December 12, 1955. His body was returned to Kentucky, and he was buried in Louisville's Eastern Cemetery.

"Athletic Department." *Proceedings of the Kentucky Negro Educational Association,* April 17–20, 1929, 10–11. Kentucky State University Archives and Special Collections, Frankfort, KY.

"Coaching School, or Not for 1931." *KNEAJ* 1, no. 3 (February 1931): 81–82.

Dunnigan, Alice Allison, comp. and ed. *The Fascinating Story of Black Kentuckians: Their Heritage and Traditions.* Washington, DC: Associated Publishers, 1982.

"Kean Resigns from K.H.S.A.L." *KNEAJ* 12, no. 2 (April–May 1945): 14–17.

Kentucky's Black Heritage: The Role of the Black People in the History of Kentucky from Pioneer Days to the Present. Frankfort: Kentucky Commission on Human Rights, 1971.

Stout, Louis. *Shadows of the Past: A History of the Kentucky High School Athletic League.* Lexington, KY: Host Communications, 2006.

—*Sallie L. Powell*

KEAN, WILLIAM LEE "BILL" (b. 1899, Louisville, KY; d. 1958), educator and coach. William Lee "Bill" Kean won more games than any other coach in the history of high school sports in Kentucky. The son of Alice E. and William T. Kean, he was born in Louisville on October 12, 1899. He was captain of the baseball, basketball, and football teams at **Central High School.** Despite his small size (5-feet-7, 140 pounds), he earned letters in four sports at Howard University and was quarterback on the Negro All-American team in 1922. Returning to Louisville in 1923, he taught health and physical education, served as athletic director, and coached football, basketball, baseball, track, and tennis. He relinquished some of his duties in 1956 but continued working until his death in 1958. His football team Yellow Jackets attained a record of 225 wins against only 45 losses and 12 ties for a winning percentage of 81.9. Included were 20 straight Thanksgiving Day contests against some of the best teams from Illinois, Indiana, Missouri, Tennessee, and West Virginia. His basketball teams did even better, winning 856 games while losing 83 for a percentage of 91.2. His teams won five state championships in the Kentucky High School Athletic League and four National Negro High School titles. One of his best squads was the 1956 team, which was undefeated in 38 games.

Kean earned a master's degree from Indiana University. He taught at Kentucky State College (later known as **Kentucky State University**), Tennessee State College, and **Louisville Municipal College.** For a time, he served as athletic commissioner of Kentucky's Negro high schools. In 1939, he married Helen Anthony. The couple had two children—a son, William Anthony, and a daughter, Alice Carolyn. His daughter married **Allan Wade**

Houston Sr., a highly successful coach at the high school and university levels. Kean's grandson, **Allen Wade Houston Jr.,** starred in basketball in high school, at the University of Tennessee, and in the National Basketball Association.

On April 29, 1958, Bill Kean died and was buried in Louisville's Eastern Cemetery. He was named posthumously to the Kentucky High School Athletic Association Hall of Fame in 1988, to the National High School Sports Hall of Fame in 1993, and to the Afro-American Hall of Fame in 1995.

"Bill Kean, Coach of Central High's Championship Teams, Dies at 58." *LCJ,* April 30, 1958, sec. 2, p. 1.

Kleber, John E., ed. *The Encyclopedia of Louisville.* Lexington: Univ. Press of Kentucky, 2001.

Stout, Louis. *Shadows of the Past: A History of the Kentucky High School Athletic League.* Lexington, KY: Host Communications, 2006.

—*Charles F. Faber*

KELLY, ADAM DAVID (b. 1860, Carthage, NC; d. 1934, Covington, KY), physician. Physician Adam Kelly attended public schools in North Carolina and then entered Bennett College in Greensboro, NC, receiving his AB in 1892. He married Mary Wendell in Nashville, TN, and in 1896 graduated from Nashville's Meharry Medical College. That same year, he moved to Covington, KY, and established his practice of general medicine and surgery. Kelly became the second African American medical doctor in the city. He was well known throughout Kenton Co. In May 1912, Kelly was an organizer of the State Medical Society of Colored Physicians, Surgeons, Dentists, and Pharmacists, who had gathered in Covington. Kelly also presented a paper, "Progress of Medicine since the Civil War," at that meeting.

On July 23, 1919, tragedy struck Kelly and his family. An intruder shot Kelly and his son in their home at 514 Scott St. while they were sleeping. Kelly's four-year-old son, Garland, died on the operating table at St. Elizabeth Hospital. Dr. Kelly recovered from his wound and continued his medical practice. No one was ever charged with the shooting.

Kelly was a trustee of the **Ninth St. Methodist Episcopal Church** and an active member of the local Republican Party. He was also involved in various fraternal organizations: the **Freemasons,** the Eastern Star, the Knights of Pythias, and the Odd Fellows. He died at age 73 and was buried in Linden Grove Cemetery in Covington.

Dabney, Wendell P. *Cincinnati's Colored Citizens: Historical, Sociological and Biographical.* Cincinnati: Dabney, 1926.

Newspapers: "Colored Medical Men Meeting in Covington," *KP,* May 10, 1912, 11; "Negro Doctor and Son Shot by Intruder," *KP,* July 23, 1919, 1; "Physician and Son Were Shot as They Slept," *KTS,* July 23, 1919, 18; "Investigation into Slaying of Physician's Son," *KTS,* July 24, 1919, 24; "Death," *KTS,* March 1, 1934, 2.

—*Theodore H. H. Harris*

KELLY, JAMES "JIM" MILTON (b. 1946, Paris, KY; d. 2013, San Diego, CA), martial artist and actor. James "Jim" Milton Kelly was born on May 5, 1946, in Paris, KY. He drew attention in his youth for his all-around athletic skills, competing on the basketball, football, baseball, and track teams at Bourbon County High School. He was awarded a football scholarship to the University of Louisville but left in protest of a coach's racism. Kelly began training in martial arts with Parker Shelton in Lexington, KY, and eventually earned his black belt in karate after moving to San Diego. In 1971, he won the middleweight division title at the Long Beach International Karate Championships and drew the attention of filmmakers.

In 1973, after a brief appearance in an earlier film titled *Melinda,* Kelly appeared in *Enter the Dragon* alongside Bruce Lee. His portrayal of Williams, a smooth-talking karate instructor fighting against racist cops, established him as a marketable actor, and he appeared in a string of martial arts films in the late 1970s and early 1980s. When the genre's popularity waned, Kelly turned to athletics again, becoming a ranked professional player on the United States Tennis Association's senior men's circuit and opening his own karate studio. He retained a fan following from his acting days and continued to appear at conventions in honor of his roles in popular martial arts films.

Kelly died of cancer in San Diego, CA, on June 29, 2013.

Clary, David. "What Ever Happened to . . . Jim Kelly?" *Black Belt,* May 1992.
"DVD Set Is Devoted to '70s Martial Arts Star Jim Kelly." *Los Angeles Times,* January 10, 2010, 19–22.
"Jim Kelly, 'Enter the Dragon's Baddest Mother." Salon.com. April 13, 2010. http://www.salon.com/entertainment/movies/film_salon/2010/04/13/jim_kelly_dragon_interview_open2010 (accessed July 19, 2011).

—*Stephen Pickering*

KENDALL, JOSEPH NATHANIEL "TARZAN" (b. 1909, Owensboro, KY; d. 1965, Owensboro, KY), Hall of Fame football player, coach, teacher, and principal. Owensboro, KY, native Joseph Nathaniel Kendall played high school basketball and baseball, but he starred in football. Although his Western High School team barely lost the United States Negro High School championship game, Kendall made the 1933 Negro High School All-American team. He played his collegiate football career at Kentucky State Industrial College (later known as **Kentucky State University**). The ambidextrous, 6-feet-2, 200-pound Kendall earned the nickname Tarzan for his superb athletic ability. He played quarterback, halfback, and fullback. Celebrated for his "bullet passes," Kendall was one of the first running quarterbacks and used a run-and-shoot method. He was also known for his booming punts with either foot. In 1934, his athletic strengths led the Kentucky State Thorobreds to a national championship among black college football teams. The next year the team won the Alumni Bowl and the Orange Blossom Classic. Even though the racial ideology of the era prevented him from competing in the professional ranks, Kendall, as a member of an African American all-star team, was able to test his skills against the Chicago Bears in 1935. This was the first time a black team had played against a National Football League squad.

After graduating with a history degree, Kendall served for 11 years as a teacher and coach at Rosenwald High School in Harlan, KY. In 1946, he became the school's principal. Two years later, he returned to coach football at his alma mater, Western High School. Kendall's "wide-open" coaching philosophy led the Owensboro school to an undefeated season and its third consec-utive West Kentucky Conference title in 1955. The 1960s integration of Owensboro schools resulted in Kendall's demotion from head coach to assistant coach.

In 1965, he drove with his brother and son to Frankfort for Kentucky State's homecoming festivities. Near Hardinsburg, the car left the road, and all three suffered broken bones. Kendall spent six weeks in a hospital recovering from his broken leg, but on Thanksgiving Day, he died of a blood clot at age 56. He was buried in Owensboro's Rosehill Elmwood Cemetery.

Nearly forgotten by the sports world, Kendall was posthumously inducted into several halls of fame decades after his death, including the Kentucky State Hall of Fame (1975), the College Football Hall of Fame (2007), the Kentucky Athletic Hall of Fame (2008), the Owensboro High School Hall of Achievement (2009), and the Black College Football Hall of Fame (2011). He was the first Kentucky State University player to be received into the College Football Hall of Fame. Because of his active role in Owensboro's recreational system, Kendall-Perkins Park on W. Fifth St. was named in his honor.

College Football Hall of Fame. http://www.collegefootball.org/famer_selected.php?id=90126 (accessed July 25, 2011).
Newspapers: "'One of the Finest,'" *OMI,* July 16, 2007, C1; "A Long Run to Daylight," *CJ,* July 22, 2007, 1.
Stout, Louis. *Shadows of the Past: A History of the Kentucky High School Athletic League.* Lexington, KY: Host Communications, 2006.

—*Sallie L. Powell*

KENNEDY, PAUL HORACE (b. 1848, Elizabethtown, KY; d. 1921, Henderson, KY), minister and missionary. Born a slave in Elizabethtown, KY, Paul Horace Kennedy received his only education as a child from a white friend who gave him covert lessons after a request from Kennedy. At the outbreak of the Civil War, he made an initial attempt to break free from slavery, informing some soldiers for the Union that he desired to be taken with them. They hid him in a wagon, but he was soon returned to his master. In 1863, he seized the initiative on his own, walking 200 miles to Louisville, where he enlisted in the 109th Regiment of the U.S. Colored Troops.

After the war, Kennedy taught music before undergoing a religious conversion and deciding to serve in the ministry. After being ordained by the First Baptist Church in Clarksville, TN, he served as a missionary for the First District Association. He continued this path in life after an education at Roger Williams University in Nashville, TN, returning to Kentucky, where he was named state missionary.

Kennedy preached at several major churches in Kentucky and Indiana in addition to serving as a missionary for over 30 years. He also supported his ministry through the publication of the *Baptist Directory and Year Book* in 1894 and 1895. In 1896, he attended the Republican National Convention in St. Louis, MO, and in the following year, he was named one of two "colored Deputies" in western Kentucky for the U.S. Marshals. He resigned his position a few months later after being fined for narrowly missing a local woman during target practice with his pistol.

On April 9, 1921, Kennedy died of a cerebral hemorrhage in Henderson, KY. He was buried in Fernwood Cemetery.

Haley, James T. *Afro-American Encyclopaedia; or, The Thoughts, Doings, and Sayings of the Race.* Nashville: Haley and Florida, 1895.
"Journey to Freedom." *Bits and Pieces of Hardin County History* 26 (2007): 9.
Newspapers: *Maysville Evening Bulletin,* July 8, 1897, 3; "Dr. James' Man, Kennedy," *HK,* August 10, 1897, 1; "Colored News," *Earlington (KY) Bee,* February 7, 1911, 4.

—*Stephen Pickering*

KENTUCKY ABOLITION SOCIETY, alliance of churches that opposed slavery. An association predominantly of Baptist churches that opposed the existence of slavery, the Kentucky Abolition Society was founded in 1808. Seeking a legal end to the "moral evil," the society held its first meeting on September 27 under the leadership of Revs. Carter Torrant and David Barrow. It adopted a constitution that called on its members to (1) work toward the constitutional abolition of slavery and the domestic **slave trade;** (2) speak out publicly against slavery; (3) ameliorate the conditions of slaves; (4) protect the interests of freedmen; and (5) seek justice for any blacks held in bondage contrary to the laws of the state. Religious pressure also was used at an individual level as member churches refused to engage in fellowship with slaveholders. The society favored gradual emancipation rather than immediate freedom and believed that the state should compensate slave owners for the loss of slaves.

In 1815, perhaps the year of its apex in membership, the association asked the Kentucky General Assembly for an act of incorporation. Barrow also petitioned the U.S. House of Representatives to establish a territorial asylum within the United States for all emancipated blacks and to provide financial aid for settlement by freedmen.

Undeterred by its lack of success, the Abolition Society in May 1822 started the monthly newspaper *Abolition Intelligencer and Missionary Magazine,* published at Shelbyville. Lack of support ended the publication after the 12th issue in April 1823. The society itself ceased to exist after 1827. Many slaveholders withdrew from churches that became associated with the society, and the most radical members of the organization often moved north, where conditions for helping blacks were more favorable. The removal of blacks to Africa was favored by other groups, such as the American Colonization Society, which had more appeal to southern whites.

Harrison, Lowell H. *The Antislavery Movement in Kentucky.* Lexington: Univ. Press of Kentucky, 1978.
Martin, Asa E. *The Anti-slavery Movement in Kentucky prior to 1850.* Louisville, KY: Standard Print Co., 1918.

KENTUCKY AFRICAN AMERICAN HERITAGE COMMISSION, organization to promote awareness of African American history and culture in Kentucky. On February 10, 1994, Governor Brereton Jones signed an executive order creating the Kentucky African American Heritage Commission (KAAHC). Its mission was "to identify and promote awareness of significant African American influences upon the history and culture of Kentucky and to support and encourage the preservation of Kentucky African American heritage and historic sites." From its inception, the KAAHC, consisting of 19 of the state's leading historians, preservationists, and scholars, provided thousands of dollars in grants vital to preserving and promoting Kentucky's African American Heritage.

In the period from 1994 to 2011 the KAACH identified and provided funds to promote and protect over 25 African American heritage sites across the state. In 1999, for example, the organization provided a $5,000 grant to promote the Historic Black Berea project, and in 2008 it provided a grant to the Shelby County Historical Society to research, locate, and preserve a mass grave and burial ground of soldiers from the 5th U.S. Colored Calvary who died in an ambush during the Civil War. Other historic sites the organization identified and helped preserve included the **Lincoln-Grant School** in Covington, the Georgetown College Underground Railroad Institute, Lexington's **African Cemetery No. 2,** the Lynch Colored School, and the Whitney Young Birthplace and Boyhood Home. In 2002, it sponsored the state's first African-American Heritage Forum, designed as a gathering place for the state's leading scholars and preservationists to discuss strategies for identifying and protecting the state's African American heritage sites. During the early years of the twenty-first century, the organization was also a driving force behind a statewide endeavor to identify, preserve, and rehabilitate **Rosenwald schools** across the state.

"Forum Plans Black History Agenda." *LHL,* February 23, 2002, C5.
Hudson, J. Blaine Hudson. "About the KAAHC." November 27, 2007. http://heritage.ky.gov/kaahc (accessed September 28, 2011).
"Professor Receives Grant for Black History Project." *LHL,* October 6, 1999, Bluegrass Communities section, 4.

—*Joshua D. Farrington*

KENTUCKY ASSOCIATION OF BLACKS IN HIGHER EDUCATION, organization founded in 1984 to promote the needs of African American staff and faculty throughout the state's colleges and universities. Dr. **William C. Parker,** former vice chancellor of minority affairs at the University of Kentucky, organized the Kentucky Association of Blacks in Higher Education (KABHE), initially called the UK Colloquium, in 1984. The KABHE's mission has been "to promote the advancement of blacks in higher education by articulating needs and concerns; promoting unity and cooperation; and enhancing the personal and professional growth of its membership." Of particular interest to the KABHE has been assisting colleges across the state in recruiting and retaining African American faculty.

Since its inception, the KABHE has represented African American staff and faculty in 43 of Kentucky's public and private colleges and universities. Divided into four regions—the Southeast, Northeast, Northwest, and Southwest—the organization has represented faculty at schools as big as the University of Kentucky and University of Louisville, as well as smaller private and community colleges. In addition to an annual statewide conference, each region has sponsored its own periodic meetings, which focus on promoting unity within the ranks of black faculty across its region.

As of 2012, the KABHE had over 150 members. The organization also published a quarterly online newsletter and gave annual awards to the state's leading African American educators.

"Black Educators Urged to Encourage Black Perspective." *LHL*, April 21, 1995, B1.

Carthell Communications Management Group. "Kentucky Association of Blacks in Higher Education." http://www.kabhe1.org (accessed February 10, 2012).

—*Joshua D. Farrington*

KENTUCKY ASSOCIATION OF COLORED WOMEN'S CLUBS, organization that united women's clubs in their racial uplift efforts.

Historically, Kentucky's black women were involved in organizing efforts of national club movements beginning with the Atlanta Congress of Colored Women, held in December 1895. **Mary V. Cook Parrish** and **Ida Joyce Jackson** were among the women attending the Atlanta Congress of Colored Women, which eventually led to the founding of the National Association of Colored Women's Clubs (NACW) in 1896. Kentucky's women first affiliated with the NACW through local clubs, such as the Eckstein Daisy Club and Louisville's Woman's Improvement Club.

The State Federation of Women's Clubs of Kentucky, now the Kentucky Association of Colored Women's Clubs (KACWC), began in November 1903 when black women representing 13 clubs coalesced at Louisville's **Plymouth Congregational United Church.** The 13 charter clubs—10 in Louisville and 1 each in Frankfort, Danville, and Covington—represented 180 members. Louisville schoolteacher **Georgia A. Nugent** was elected the organization's first president. In 1906, the KACW joined the NACW, and interest in club work expanded rapidly across the state. By 1915, the KACW had amassed 150 clubs that by 1931 had a total membership of 2,000 women, including seven city federations and one county federation. Since its meager beginnings in 1903, over 290 local women's clubs have joined the KACW.

The association's motto, "Looking upward not downward, outward not inward, forward not backward," addressed the racial uplift ideology prominent in the early twentieth century among African Americans. Across the state, women's clubs promoted education through day care, libraries, and parent-teacher groups; created and advocated for recreational facilities, such as the **Phillis Wheatley YWCAs** and parks, and for youth programs; and promoted health care through old-folks homes and orphanages and by supporting the **Red Cross Hospital** and other community health campaigns. The clubs were politically aggressive, calling for the repeal of unjust laws, such as the **separate coach** legislation in the 1890s, and supporting **Charles W. Anderson**'s legislation for pensions for widows and health care for mentally retarded citizens. During the modern **civil rights movement** of the 1960s, clubwomen such as **Helen Fairfax Holmes** were involved in direct-action protests against unjust practices at local establishments, as well as state and local governments.

In addition to the countless local initiatives, the association annually supported two statewide programs, the Scholarship Loan Fund and Cancer Control. In 1913, Lexington's **Elizabeth B. Fouse** established the Scholarship Loan Fund as a means to support college-bound black students. By 1933, the KACW had raised over $10,000 for scholarships that assisted 42 black students in obtaining college degrees. Kentucky was the first state to have a scholarship loan fund, an idea that was soon adopted by the NACW, with Fouse eventually chairing the national loan committee.

The KACWC was also the first state association to publish a club newsletter, the *Kentucky Club Woman*, initially edited by **Daisy Saffell.** In 1910, the KACWC hosted the annual conference of the NACW in Louisville and twice hosted the Central Association of Colored Women, in 1934 and again in 1969. The Kentucky Association of Colored Women's Clubs has faithfully served the interests of African Americans for more than 100 years.

Davis, Elizabeth Lindsay. *Lifting as They Climb.* Washington, DC: National Association of Colored Women, 1933.

"Federation of Women's Clubs: Lifting as We Climb." *AB* 26, no. 11 (January 8, 1904): 1.

Records of the Kentucky Association of Colored Women's Clubs. Kentucky Historical Society, Kentucky State Univ., the Univ. of Kentucky, and the Univ. of Louisville.

"Reports from State Clubs." *National Association Notes* 18, no. 3 (December 1915): 1.

Wesley, Charles Harris. *The History of the National Association of Colored Women's Clubs: A Legacy of Service.* Washington, DC: National Association of Colored Women's Clubs, 1984.

—*Karen Cotton McDaniel*

KENTUCKY BUREAU FOR NEGRO AFFAIRS, organization founded to protest segregation.

In 1940, Bishop **Charles Ewbank Tucker,** who served as the principal and charismatic figurehead throughout the organization's intermittent and periodic existence, formed the Kentucky Bureau for Negro Affairs (KBNA). Membership included African Americans from across the state, but the organization's focus was almost exclusively on Louisville.

With the creation of the KBNA, Tucker named himself executive chairman and claimed that the organization's goal was "to protect the Negro in his social, economic, educational, political and constitutional life." The organization's headquarters were located in Louisville's Mutual Life Building at 614 W. **Walnut St.** Its first officers were Ruth Hill of Richmond (vice chairman), S. S. Burnley of Louisville (secretary), and Nannie McElroy of Louisville (treasurer). Other influential members in the KBNA's early years included **I. Willis Cole** and **Fletcher P. Martin.** Initially, the organization described itself as a "mutual auxiliary" to civil rights organizations like the **National Association for the Advancement of Colored People** (NAACP). In 1946, one of the KBNA's first public protests occurred when it joined with the NAACP in picketing Louisville's segregated Memorial Auditorium during a showing of the play *Carmen Jones,* which featured an all-black cast.

After the 1946 protests, the KBNA appears to have receded until Tucker revived it in the early 1950s. In contrast to his early cooperation with the NAACP, Tucker, a staunch Republican, argued in a January 1953 KBNA meeting in Greensboro, KY, that the NAACP had become a "third wheel of the Democratic party," more concerned with electing Democratic politicians than advancing the cause of African Americans. By the end of the month, the KBNA had approximately 100 members from across the state and soon thereafter swelled to a peak membership of 3,000. Partisanship and dissatisfaction with the Democratic Party played a large role in the KBNA's membership growth. **Harry S. McAlpin,** a former journalist and one of Louisville's most influential black lawyers, was among the new members of the organization. Upon joining the KBNA, McAlpin renounced his previous Democratic affiliation and joined the Republican Party. Similarly, in 1952, one of Louisville's highest-ranking black Republicans, **Charles J. Lunderman Jr.,** resigned from a leadership post in the state and local NAACP in protest of what he perceived as pro-Democratic partisanship. By 1953, he had also joined the KBNA.

The year 1953 represented the peak of the activity of the KBNA. Tucker launched a letter-writing campaign protesting segregated office buildings operated by Jefferson Co., and within weeks "white" and "colored" signs were removed from the buildings. The KBNA's most notable protests occurred at Louisville's bus depot. The Greyhound terminal featured a "whites-only" waiting room, but the city's chief of police pledged not to arrest blacks who sat in the area, claiming that the city had no law mandating segregation. To test public promises by the chief of police and pressure the terminal's owners, Tucker and a small number of KBNA members conducted a sit-in in the whites-only waiting room. Although the terminal's owners refused to change their segregation policy, Tucker and his companions were not arrested or harassed by company officials or the police during their 20-minute protest.

In 1954, despite its criticisms of the partisanship of other civil rights organizations, the KBNA joined with the NAACP, the Negro Labor Council, the Militant Church Movement, and the *Louisville Defender* in establishing the Wade Defense Committee to help fund Andrew Wade's legal efforts to own a house in the all-white Louisville suburb of Shively in what became known as the **Wade-Braden affair.** This was one of the last major activities of the KBNA. By the early 1960s, Tucker had abandoned the KBNA to assume leadership of Louisville's newly created chapter of the **Congress of Racial Equality.**

K'Meyer, Tracy E. *Civil Rights in the Gateway to the South: Louisville, Kentucky, 1945–1980.* Lexington: Univ. Press of Kentucky, 2009.
Newspapers: "Negro Affairs Bureau Program Discussed," *LCJ,* December 9, 1940, sec. 2, p. 1; "Organization Formed to Protect Negroes," *LCJ,* November 25, 1940, sec. 2, p. 1; "Picket Line Marches on Segregated Auditorium," *BAA,* November 26, 1946, 15; "Attorney Tucker Calls NAACP 'Partisan,'" *LD,* January 21, 1953, 3.

—*Joshua D. Farrington*

KENTUCKY CENTER FOR AFRICAN AMERICAN HERITAGE, foundation in Louisville to promote Kentucky's African American history and culture. In the mid-1990s, the Louisville and Jefferson County African American Heritage Committee first developed the idea of a Kentucky Center for African American Heritage with the "single unifying goal of promoting African American contributions and history in the state of Kentucky." By 2001, the committee had designed plans for a $23-million, 19,000-square-foot complex at 18th St. and **Muhammad Ali** Blvd. in Louisville.

Although it faced difficulties in obtaining funding from both private and public sources, the center officially opened to the public on March 9, 2010. Its first exhibition was *Tutankhamen: Wonderful Things from the Pharaoh's Tomb* and featured reproduced

and actual artifacts from King Tut's tomb and ancient Egypt. Over the course of the summer, the exhibition drew over 5,000 visitors. Since its opening, the center has held exhibitions featuring African American jockeys and a portrait exhibition of important civil rights leaders by artist Robert Shetterly. It also purchased an 1840 painting by Charles Vaughn that depicts slavery in a Versailles homestead. The center has hosted numerous special events, including a genealogy workshop led by Megan Smolenyak, star of the NBC television show *Who Do You Think You Are?* On February 23, 2012, First Lady Michelle Obama visited the center.

In 2011, Democrat Gerald Neal and Republican David Williams sponsored a bill that brought the Kentucky Center for African American Heritage under the jurisdiction of the state. The governor was given the authority to appoint board members representative of all regions of the state, and the center became affiliated with the Kentucky Tourism, Arts, and Heritage Cabinet, a connection that furthered its ability to promote its exhibitions throughout Kentucky.

Kentucky Center for African American Heritage. "Our Story." http://www.kcaah.org/our-story (accessed February 10, 2012).
Newspapers: "Heritage Center Takes Shape," *LCJ,* July 9, 2004, B1; "Center Wraps Up Tut, Plans More Exhibits," *LCJ,* August 29, 2010, B3.

—*Joshua D. Farrington*

KENTUCKY CHRISTIAN LEADERSHIP CONFERENCE, Kentucky's branch of the Southern Christian Leadership Conference. Founded on April 15, 1965, at Mount Lebanon Baptist Church in Louisville, the Kentucky Christian Leadership Conference (KCLC) quickly became one of the most important civil rights organizations in the state. An affiliate of Martin Luther King Jr.'s Southern Christian Leadership Conference (SCLC), the KCLC was initially organized by some of Louisville's most active religious leaders of both races, including Garland Offutt, **A. D. Williams King,** brother of Martin Luther King Jr. and pastor at Zion Baptist Church, and Henlee Hulix Barnette, a white professor at Southern Baptist Theological Seminary. During the organization's heyday from 1965 through 1968, A. D. King served as chairman of the executive board, while Frederick Sampson Jr. and Leo Lesser each served stints as president. Its offices were adjacent to King's church at 23rd and W. **Walnut St.**

Almost immediately after its founding, the KCLC became active in the **civil rights movement.** In 1965, it led efforts to desegregate a hospital in Georgetown and launched an intense lobbying campaign for a ban on segregated public accommodations. Its ceaseless protests to Governor Edward Breathitt and members of the General Assembly were an important factor that led to the passage of the Kentucky **Civil Rights Act of 1966.** It also spearheaded the SCLC's Operation Breadbasket in Kentucky, a project designed to place qualified black workers in skilled positions at businesses that had a reputation for discrimination. One of the KCLC's most extensive endeavors was its advocacy of a ban on racial discrimination in housing. In September 1966, the organization joined the **National Association for the Advancement of Colored People** and other civil rights organizations in proposing an open-housing ordinance to the Louisville Board of Aldermen, which initially refused to act. In the spring of 1967, King and the KCLC began a series of nightly marches into the city's exclusively white neighborhoods, where they frequently were targeted by thrown bottles, rocks, and bricks. As a result of continued pressure by the KCLC and other organizations, the city eventually passed an open-housing law in December 1967, and the General Assembly passed a statewide open-housing bill the following year.

The KCLC underwent a significant transformation in leadership during the fall of 1968. Rev. A. D. King moved to Atlanta to become associate minister at Ebenezer Baptist Church in Atlanta replacing his assassinated brother Rev. Martin Luther King Jr., and Lesser resigned to focus his attention on his service as head of the West End Community Council. In their stead, a young militant activist, **Raoul Cunningham,** became executive director, Rev. **William E. Summers III** became president, and Rev. Charles Elliott Jr. became chairman. Cunningham attempted to revitalize the KCLC with large-scale projects that included voter-registration drives, boycotts of businesses with low black employment, and a campaign against landlords who refused to fix dilapidated housing. Despite these efforts, the departure of King and Lesser severely weakened the organization. By 1969, many white members claimed that their support was no longer desired and left the organization, funding had almost evaporated, and the creation of a day nursery at Zion Baptist had forced the organization to relocate to a vacant first floor of **Georgia Powers**'s duplex. Led by Summers, a faction within the KCLC objected to the political activism of Powers, a Democratic state senator and secretary of the KCLC, and Cunningham, who ran for chairmanship of the Democratic Party in the 42nd Legislative District in 1968. Summers eventually resigned, believing that the organization had abandoned its traditional nonpartisanship. In the fall of 1969, Lesser returned to his former position as president in hopes of restoring unity, but the KCLC disbanded by the end of 1970.

In 1973, Rev. Charles Kirby of Southern Star Baptist Church revived the KCLC and focused on the creation of a Martin Luther King Jr. holiday, voter-registration drives, and pro-**busing** demonstrations. By the late 1970s, after failure to generate widespread financial and volunteer support, the KCLC ceased all activity.

Barnette, Henlee Hulix. *A Pilgrimage of Faith: My Story.* Macon, GA: Mercer Univ. Press, 2004.

K'Meyer, Tracy E. *Civil Rights in the Gateway to the South: Louisville, Kentucky, 1945–1980.* Lexington: Univ. Press of Kentucky, 2009.

Newspapers: "Drop in White Support for KCLC Is Reported," *LCJ,* September 20, 1968, B1; "Floundering KCLC Seeks to Reorganize," *LCJ,* January 30, 1969, A18; "Local Chapter of SCLC Reactivated," *LCJ,* August 3, 1973, B14.

—*Joshua D. Farrington*

KENTUCKY COLONIZATION SOCIETY, society that advocated for the removal of all free African Americans from Kentucky. The Kentucky Colonization Society was founded in 1828 as an affiliate of the American Colonization Society, established in 1817 for the purpose of ending slavery and ridding the country of freed blacks by deporting them to distant colonies. Although it favored emancipation, the Kentucky society, which

had five local chapters, placed greater emphasis on removing freedmen from the state than on doing away with slavery. The number of freed blacks in Kentucky was small (7,317 as late as 1840). Freed blacks were forbidden to associate with either whites or slaves. Transporting them to colonies in Africa or to some distant (but unspecified) location in North America, the society contended, would remove the threat that they might aid runaway slaves, promote abolition, and help foment slave revolts.

Following the lead of the national organization, which had bought land in Africa on December 11, 1821, and founded the colony of Liberia, the state chapter began to raise money to pay for the voyage to Africa. On March 22, 1833, the Kentucky Colonization Society sent approximately 100 freedmen to New Orleans, where they embarked for Liberia on April 20. Although the organization received some favorable reports from the new colonists, diseases such as cholera resulted in the deaths of many. Among other setbacks for the society were the high demand for slaves in the cotton states, opposition to the society's antislavery stance, and resistance to migration on the part of blacks born in America. By 1844, 11 years after the initial voyage, fewer than 100 additional blacks had been sent to Africa.

Nevertheless, the Kentucky chapter persevered. It raised $5,000 in 1845 to buy 40 square miles in Liberia. In November of that year, it chartered a ship to carry an estimated 200 former slaves to the new colony, called Kentucky in Liberia. The capital of this colony was named **Clay-Ashland** in honor of Henry Clay, one of the founders of the American Colonization Society. When the vessel departed in January 1846, it carried only 35 former Kentucky slaves. This poor showing at such a high cost nearly destroyed the organization. With hopes of salvaging the Kentucky society, the legislature passed an act on March 24, 1851, requiring all slaves, when emancipated, to leave the state and prohibiting freedmen of other states from moving to Kentucky. Further, on March 3, 1856, the General Assembly appropriated $5,000 a year to aid the society. The legislative aid made little difference, however, and the last sizable expedition, only 42 former slaves, left Kentucky in May 1857. With the African colony failing because of disease and mismanagement, the society could not pay the high costs of transporting freed blacks to Africa, and it ceased operating in 1859. In its 30-year history, the Kentucky Colonization Society dispatched an estimated 658 emigrants to Africa.

Coleman, J. Winston, Jr. "The Kentucky Colonization Society." *RKHS* 39 (January 1941): 1–9.

Harrison, Lowell H. *The Antislavery Movement in Kentucky.* Lexington: Univ. Press of Kentucky, 1978.

KENTUCKY COMMISSION ON HUMAN RIGHTS, agency established to end discriminatory practices in Kentucky. On March 21, 1960, Governor Bert T. Combs signed House Bill 163 into law. The bill, sponsored by representative **William Childress,** created the Kentucky Commission on Human Rights, intended "to encourage fair treatment for, to foster mutual understanding and respect among and to discourage discrimination against any racial or ethnic group or its members." After appointing 11 members to the commission, Combs explained that although it was "not given power to force anyone to do anything," it could still "have a significant influence on developments in Kentucky to the extent that you here at this meeting give it your support."

The biracial commission began work by encouraging businesses to voluntarily ban discriminatory practices, relying heavily on an economic argument that it was "good business to serve all Kentuckians." After the passage of the **Civil Rights Act of 1964,** it requested reports on discriminatory practices throughout the state, although it lacked the power to initiate legal action under the law. Two years later, the commission's power grew substantially with an increased role under Kentucky's **Civil Rights Act of 1966.** In remarks before the passage of the bill, Governor Edward T. Breathitt announced his intention that under the new act, the Kentucky Commission on Human Rights would "bring about compliance, where possible, and court enforcement where necessary." The final version of the civil rights bill charged the commission with implementing the new policies against discrimination and empowered it to enforce the law through legal proceedings.

With its new position as an official arbiter for civil rights in the state, the commission expanded beyond its earlier emphasis on public accommodations. It took the lead in efforts to achieve open housing in Kentucky, drafting a model ordinance for the Bardstown–Nelson Co. government and offering resources and support with the passage of the Kentucky Fair Housing Act in 1968. Members also aggressively pursued desegregation in public schools, issuing an especially strong critique of Louisville's failed attempts in 1972. The following year, they offered their own three-step plan to speed the process of desegregation in education.

In the following decades, the Kentucky Commission on Human Rights tackled a more diverse array of issues. In addition to its previous concerns with racial discrimination, it addressed more fully other areas of unequal opportunities; challenges to sex discrimination became a more significant part of its duties after an amendment to the Civil Rights Act in 1964. The commission also became involved in projects designed to reveal the state's civil rights heritage, creating the Gallery of Great Black Kentuckians in 1970 and publishing *Kentucky's Black Heritage*—a junior high textbook supplement that highlighted black contributions—in 1971. In 2000, it celebrated its 40th anniversary by instituting the Kentucky Civil Rights Hall of Fame.

In 2010, the state celebrated 50 years of the Kentucky Commission on Human Rights with a yearlong civil rights awareness campaign. The commission, headquartered in Louisville with an office in Covington, continues to expand its scope to fight discrimination in all forms.

Harrell, Kenneth E. *The Public Papers of Governor Edward T. Breathitt: 1963–1967.* Lexington: Univ. Press of Kentucky, 1984.

Kentucky Commission on Human Rights. *Federal Law and State Legislation: Keys to Advancing Human Rights.* Frankfort: Kentucky Commission on Human Rights, 1964.

———. *Human Rights News.* Frankfort: Kentucky Commission on Human Rights, 1961–1974.

K'Meyer, Tracy E. *Civil Rights in the Gateway to the South: Louisville, Kentucky, 1945–1980.* Lexington: Univ. Press of Kentucky, 2009.

Newspapers: "Combs Names Human-Rights Commission," *LCJ,* September 9, 1960, sec. 2, p. 1; "Little Authority, Lots of Influence," *LCJ,* September 15, 1960, 6; "State's Human Rights Commission Turns 40," *LHL,* July 17, 2000, B1; "Kentucky Human Rights Agency Marks 50 Years," *LCJ,* March 19, 2010, B1.

Robinson, George W., ed. *The Public Papers of Governor Bert T. Combs: 1959–1963.* Lexington: Univ. Press of Kentucky, 1979.

—*Stephen Pickering*

KENTUCKY COMMISSION ON NEGRO AFFAIRS, biracial committee formed in 1944 to study ways in which Kentucky could improve race relations.   Created through an executive order signed by Governor Simeon Willis on September 21, 1944, the Kentucky Commission on Negro Affairs (KCNA) was instructed "to obtain and to study all the facts and conditions relating to the economic, educational, housing, health, and other needs for the betterment of Negro citizens of Kentucky." A biracial committee, the KCNA was cochaired by J. M. Tydings, the white director of the Kentucky Interracial Council, and William H. Perry Jr. of the **Kentucky Negro Educational Association.** Other prominent members of the committee included Lexington clubwoman **Elizabeth Fouse;** Robert E. Black, executive director of the Louisville Urban League; state legislator **Charles W. Anderson; Louisville Municipal College** professor **Charles H. Parrish Jr.;** the president of Kentucky State College (later named Kentucky State University), **Rufus Atwood;** educator **Whitney M. Young Sr.;** and prominent Louisville civil rights activists **James A. Crumlin** and **C. Ewbank Tucker.** On the basis of their backgrounds, members divided themselves into specialized subcommittees that focused on education, economics, housing, social welfare, health, and civil affairs.

After a year of investigation, the KCNA issued a 39-page report on November 1, 1945. In addition to describing the inequalities blacks confronted on a daily basis, a rare admission from a government-sponsored organization, the report called for the end of a number of discriminatory practices. The subcommittee on civil affairs, chaired by Anderson, called on the government to "require non-discrimination in state contracts and other public projects," end segregation on railcars, and repeal the **Day Law** so that black students could attend graduate school at white universities. The subcommittee on education, which was headed by Perry and whose membership included Atwood and Young, suggested that Kentucky State College (later known as **Kentucky State University**) receive the same funding as the University of Kentucky and that funding for the **Lincoln Institute** and West Kentucky Vocational School (formerly West Kentucky Industrial College) be increased. Other subcommittees sought funding to train black workers in industrial skills, to create a health education program in black public schools, to improve conditions in black orphanages, and to encourage the employment of black doctors and nurses on county boards of health.

Despite the efforts of the committee to provide specific goals and recommendations to the state, the government ignored most of its proposals. However, the *New York Times* nationally covered the report, which was reprinted in a small booklet, *Let's Pull Together, Kentuckians!,* published by the Southern Regional Council and the Kentucky Interracial Council in 1946.

Kentucky Commission on Negro Affairs. *Let's Pull Together, Kentuckians! A Digest of the Report of the Kentucky Commission on Negro Affairs.* Atlanta: Southern Regional Council, 1946.

———. *The Report of the Kentucky Commission on Negro Affairs, November 1, 1945.* Frankfort: n.p., 1945.

Smith, Gerald L. *A Black Educator in the Segregated South: Kentucky's Rufus B. Atwood.* Lexington: Univ. Press of Kentucky, 1994.

"The Upper South." *NYT,* December 16, 1945, S7.

Wright, George C. *A History of Blacks in Kentucky.* Vol. 2, *In Pursuit of Equality, 1890–1980.* Frankfort: Kentucky Historical Society, 1992.

—*Joshua D. Farrington*

KENTUCKY COUNCIL ON HUMAN RELATIONS, organization formed to facilitate school desegregation in Kentucky during the 1950s. On April 8, 1955, less than a year after *Brown v. Board of Education,* the Kentucky Council on Human Relations (KCHR) filed papers with the secretary of state to become an incorporated organization whose expressed goal was to "assist private and public bodies in research and education for intelligent, planned, and constructive integration of the schools in Kentucky." Its original founders were Hugh A. Brimm, a white professor at the Carver School of Missions and Social Work in Louisville; **Charles H. Parrish Jr.,** the only black professor at the University of Louisville; **William H. Perry Sr.,** a black medical doctor from Louisville; and J. Mansir Tydings, a white Quaker from Anchorage. The KCHR was affiliated with the Southern Regional Council, who provided it with a $25,000 grant from the Ford Foundation, and was sustained by membership dues. By August 1955, the organization had 120 members.

During the KCHR's first year, Brimm was appointed chairman, and Margaret W. Dagen, a white civil rights activist, served as executive director. It was headquartered at 1319 Heyburn Building in Louisville. In April 1956, Galen A. Martin was recruited to replace Dagen as executive director. A West Virginia native and a white graduate of **Berea College,** Martin, who had worked on a similar human rights council in Knoxville, TN, moved the KCHR's headquarters from Louisville to 208 W. Main St. in Frankfort so that the organization could expand its scope statewide. Upon moving to Frankfort, Martin struck up a friendship with President **Rufus Atwood** of Kentucky State College (later known as **Kentucky State University**), whose major concern was "to see that black teachers don't become the victims of pupil desegregation." By 1959, Atwood was appointed chairman of the KCHR, serving alongside executive director Martin.

The central mission of the organization was to gather information and publish reports on the progress of school desegregation throughout the state. Many of its reports, although careful not to be overly critical of desegregation efforts, paid special attention to the number of black teachers hired and fired in desegregated school systems. Although many African American teachers were negatively affected by desegregation, one KCHR report argued that "Kentucky will use a far higher proportion of colored teachers in integrated schools than the Northern states." Other reports held public and private colleges and universities accountable to promises of integration by publishing information regarding their enrollment of African American students. Another KCHR report, whose results were reprinted in the *Journal of Negro Education* in 1960, advocated "merit employment," where high school graduates would be evaluated by employers on the basis of individual abilities rather than race.

In 1960, Governor Bert Combs appointed Martin executive director of the newly established **Kentucky Commission on Human Rights.** A state-sponsored institution, the commission assumed many of the research responsibilities and functions of the KCHR. Although the KCHR remained the state affiliate of the Southern Regional Council, it was largely overshadowed by the state commission. In 1965, white activist Dorcas Ruthenburg spearheaded one of the council's last major projects, the creation of Housing Clearance Inc. to help African Americans locate affordable housing.

Martin, Galen. Interview by Betsy Brinson, November 4, 1999. Kentucky Civil Rights Oral History Project, Kentucky Oral History Commission, Kentucky Historical Society.

K'Meyer, Tracy E. *Civil Rights in the Gateway to the South: Louisville, Kentucky, 1945–1980.* Lexington: Univ. Press of Kentucky, 2009.

Newspapers: "Council Set Up to Aid Integration," *LCJ,* April 9, 1955, 12; "Negro-Schools Desegregation Study Sought," *LCJ,* August 16, 1955, 1; "G. A. Martin to Direct Human-Relations Unit," *LCJ,* April 2, 1956, 8.

—*Joshua D. Farrington*

KENTUCKY DERBY, horse-racing event held in Louisville, KY. The Kentucky Derby is a one-and-one-quarter-mile stakes race for three-year-old Thoroughbred colts, geldings, and fillies. The derby and the Kentucky Oaks are the oldest continuously contested American sporting events and the only Thoroughbred stake races run annually at the same site since their inception in 1875. At that time, these events were innovative approaches to spring racing that showcased young stock competing over distances that old-time trainers considered too grueling for all but their fittest animals.

The derby and the Kentucky Oaks were the creation of Meriwether Lewis Clark Jr. (1846–1899), whom Louisville businessmen and bluegrass horse breeders sent abroad in 1873 to study successful racing ventures in England and France. Clark was the nephew and heir apparent of John and Henry Churchill, wealthy Louisville urbanites who owned and raced Thoroughbreds as a hobby. Clark's wife was John Churchill's teenage ward, Mary Martin Anderson (1854–1934). Her considerable fortune came not only from investments in Louisville enterprises but also from a plantation near Greenville, MS, where Clark's younger brother, George Rogers Clark, practiced law and raced horses. Her grandfather was the founding secretary of the Lexington Jockey Club. Anderson had been raised by her aunts, one of whom, Pattie Anderson Ten Broeck (d. 1873), was married to Richard Ten Broeck (1811–1892), a horseman and track owner of international reputation. In the late 1850s, he became the first American to race American Thoroughbreds successfully in England.

The Civil War took a heavy toll on bluegrass farms, particularly those belonging to Southern sympathizers. Louisville businesses, on the other hand, profited both from the conflict and the southern expansion of the Louisville and Nashville Railroad, whose postwar manipulation of rates, routes, and schedules all but shut bluegrass agriculture out of Louisville's lucrative river trade.

After Woodlawn, eastern Jefferson Co.'s ill-fated track, closed in 1870, Thoroughbred owners desperately needed an accessible urban racetrack complemented by hotels, restaurants, and theaters—amenities that attracted wealthy eastern buyers to meets. Lacking the means to showcase promising young stock, the bluegrass racing industry's future appeared bleak. Long-term stability lay in the plan to link central Kentucky with northern markets via the Cincinnati Southern Railway. Ground was broken in 1873, but completion of that system was years in the future. When the panic of 1873 depressed already rock-bottom yearling prices, Clark's mission, backed by Churchill money and Ten Broeck's name, became vital to bluegrass breeders' economic survival. It also signaled the Louisville and Nashville management's interest in wooing Lexington commerce back to Louisville.

As the guest of Adm. Henry John Rous (1795–1877), longtime president of the English Jockey Club, Clark studied all aspects of the sport, including the Oaks and the Epsom Derby, classic races then almost 100 years old. Edward Stanley, 12th Earl of Derby, had suggested a one-and-one-half-mile race for fillies to senior members of the English Jockey Club in 1778. Named the Oaks for Lord Derby's country retreat near Epsom, the race was run in June 1779. The success of the Oaks led to plans for a mile-long race—lengthened to one and one-half miles in 1784—at Epsom, open to three-year-old colts and fillies, to be run in the spring of 1780. Tradition has it that Lord Derby and fellow Jockey Club member Sir Charles Bunbury set the terms of the race, agreeing that the event should be named for one of them, and that the decision should be made by the toss of a coin. The coin fell to Derby. Bunbury's Diomed won the race and then faded into oblivion. Twenty years later, the aged stallion was sold to Colonel Seldon, a Virginia horse breeder. Diomed was the champion sire of 1803, the first year his offspring competed at Virginia tracks. Horsemen termed his death in 1808 "a great natural disaster." Diomed's offspring reflected their sire's worth for the next half century before the Civil War brought regularly scheduled meets to a halt. A decade later, when Kentucky racing was near ebb stage, a Diomed descendant made history again.

Clark returned from Europe late in 1873 to superintend the building of the racetrack on his uncle's property just south of the city limits. As president of the Louisville Jockey Club and Driving Park Association, he scheduled the Kentucky Derby as the track's inaugural event on Monday, May 17, 1875. The Oaks was to be run on Wednesday. Clark and his associates assumed that the track's big draw would be the Louisville Cup, a well-publicized handicap race for older, better-known horses, set for Thursday of Spring Meet week.

To boost first-day attendance, Clark opened the infield to the public free of charge. Thus a crowd estimated at 10,000 to 12,000 saw Diomed's descendant, Kentucky-bred Aristides, ridden by Kentucky African American jockey **Oliver Lewis,** outrun 14 other entrants and set a new American record for the one-and-one-half-mile distance, the same distance as the English Epsom Derby. The Kentucky Derby took on a prestige the Louisville Cup never achieved even though there was no trophy to accompany the $2,850 purse Clark handed to Aristides's owner, H. Price McGrath. By 1896 the race's length was changed to the current one-and-one quarter mile distance.

Flushed with success, Clark boasted that within a decade a derby winner would be worth more than the farm on which he was foaled. Clark did not envision fillies winning against colts. The Oaks, he emphasized, showcased the abilities of distaff runners.

For the next 15 years, derby winners subsequently proved themselves champions, and derby publicity grew apace. Then Clark's track, popularly known as Churchill Downs, became mired in feuds with bookmakers. In 1894, Clark turned his debt-ridden operation over to the New Louisville Jockey Club, an association of local bookmakers that leased the grounds from John Churchill, as had the original Louisville Jockey Club. By then, Clark was estranged from his wife, and relations with John Churchill, his surviving uncle, who controlled the family fortune, were cool at best. When Churchill's will was probated in 1897, Clark had been virtually disinherited. After living in greatly reduced circumstances for five years, acting as steward at tracks rife with corruption, Clark committed suicide in Memphis 13 days before the 1899 derby.

Under New Louisville Jockey Club ownership, Churchill Downs became an attraction fit only for the dregs of society. After the 1902 spring meet, which featured a four-house derby field, even the bookmakers wanted out. Rallying to save the Downs, Louisville clothier Matt Winn persuaded local businessmen to invest in a facelift for the failing track. Building on that success, Winn took over the track's management and systematically realigned national racing interests in Churchill Downs' favor. Although fields remained small for the next decade, four derbys put the Louisville race back in the spotlight.

Outflanking a religious coalition of antigambling advocates intent on closing the Downs, Winn reintroduced pari-mutuel wagering at the 1908 derby, where a $5 win ticket on Stone Street paid $123.50. Five years later, Donerail not only set a new track record (2:04 4/5) but returned $184.90 on a $2 pari-mutuel ticket. In 1914, the heavy favorite, Old Rosebud, clipped more than a second off Donerail's record-setting time with a time of 2:03 2/5. In 1915, H. P. Whitney's Regret became the first filly to win the race.

Winn courted New York racing writers and publicists, who milked derby stories for all they were worth. When Sir Barton won the Kentucky Derby, the Preakness, and the Belmont in 1919, turf writer Charlie Hatton, mimicking English ways, dubbed the sweep "the Triple Crown," coupling the derby with racing's moneyed strongholds in Maryland and New York. Winn's only significant public relations defeat came in 1920 when he failed to secure Man o' War as a derby entrant. Samuel Riddle, Man o' War's owner, was one of those horsemen who believed that a colt should not be sent the punishing one-and-one-quarter-mile distance so early in the spring.

The year 1921 marks the first time researchers have found newspaper accounts of derby attendees singing Stephen Collins Foster's **"My Old Kentucky Home"** before the race. It became the state song in 1928.

When Churchill Downs celebrated its 50th anniversary in 1924, Winn commissioned Lemon and Son Jewelers to create unique trophies for the Kentucky Derby and the Oaks. The derby trophy was a 14-karat-gold lidded cup topped by a statue of a horse and jockey. One of identical design has been presented to the winning owner every year since. Winn's valet, Andy Phillips, always had the dubious honor of draping a hand-stitched, satin-backed swag of roses across the sometimes-still-fractious winner's withers. The presentation of a "blanket of roses" has been standard practice since 1908.

Winn teamed with bluegrass horsemen, especially professional gambler and philanthropist E. R. Bradley, to fill derby fields during the Great Depression. Bradley named 1932 winner Burgoo King for famed Lexington caterer James T. Looney. The 1933 derby was spiced by a stretch scuffle between the jockeys riding Head Play and Bradley's Brokers Tip. Few spectators realized what had happened until the *Louisville Courier-Journal* printed a head-on shot of the race on its front page the next day. The "fighting finish" exemplified the depths of Depression desperation; newsreel reruns of the race appeared in movie theaters around the country. Man o' War's son, War Admiral, won the Derby and the Triple Crown in 1937, signaling better times to come. Ethel Mar's Milky Way Farm's Gallahadion paid a whopping $72.20 to win in 1940.

During World War II, Winn turned Churchill Downs into a patriotic mecca for war-weary civilians and armed forces personnel. Faced with a government-ordered ban on racing in 1945, Winn took derby nominations as usual and ran the race on June 9, a month after V-E Day. By 1949, the first year WAVE televised the derby, the race was America's best-known sporting event, celebrating its diamond jubilee. For the next 30 years, derby winners such as Swaps, Carry Back, and Northern Dancer were national stars. In 1968, stewards disqualified Dancer's Image after routine postrace testing identified a then-prohibited medication in the winning colt's urine. Owner Peter Fuller's appeals dragged on for several years until the Kentucky Racing Commission finally declared that, except for pari-mutuel wagering, Calumet's Forward Pass was the 1968 derby winner.

In 1970, Diane Crump became the derby's first female jockey, finishing 15th on W. L. Lyons Brown's colt Fathom. Crump and a handful of women riders have faced brickbats, boycotts, and court tests to gain the right to ride. Only three other women have ridden in the Derby since them: Patricia Cooksey (1984, So Vague, 11th), Julie A. Crone (1992, Ecstatic Ride, 14th), and Andrea Seefeldt (1991, Forty Something, 16th).

During the 1970s, three derby victors—Secretariat, Seattle Slew, and Affirmed—were added to the twentieth-century roster of Triple Crown winners. Fillies Genuine Risk and Winning Colors won the 1980 and 1988 derbies, respectively, in a race that worldwide viewing audiences had come to know as "the greatest two minutes in sports."

Those two minutes, however, no longer supported the track year-round. Beginning in 1984, Churchill Downs' Board of Directors made significant leadership shifts. Derby tradition bowed to the realities of survival. In short order, the best derby boxes were sold to corporate sponsors, leaving many Louisvillians who wanted to participate in the hoopla no choice but to party at home or attend the Oaks. In 1987, track management, ignoring public outcry, terminated its long-standing contract with local derby rose supplier Kingsley Walker Florist and awarded the floral contract to Kroger, a Cincinnati-based grocery chain.

The derby has attracted a crowd in excess of 100,000 every year since 1969, hitting a record 163,628 for the 100th running in 1974, before construction of the Matt Winn Turf Course considerably diminished the space available for infield partying. On May 1, 1999, what was probably a record per square foot 151,051 fans filled 48,447 seats, the infield, and the back side for the 125th derby.

Reflecting in part a communications trend, interest in the televised derby declined steadily throughout the 1990s. Early in 1998, Churchill Downs announced and the State Racing Commission subsequently approved an innovative approach to the centuries-old prerace ritual, the pit pill, which determines horses' post positions. For the 1998 and 1999 derbies, the pill pull determined the order in which trainers, after a maximum of one minute's consultation with their derby horse owners, picked their spot in the starting gate. The goal of this unprecedented change was to enhance the strategic factor of the race and lure viewing audiences back to "the most famous two minutes in sports."

Images of the Twin Spires and slogans long associated with the Kentucky Derby, such as track president Bill Corum's "Run for the Roses," are now copyrighted and trademarked by Churchill Downs Inc. and cannot be used for promotional purposes without permission. Following professional football's lead, the corporation licenses all derby souvenirs, from the "official" julep glass to the "official" country ham and bourbon balls. Long gone are the days of free infields and easy entrepreneurship on which the derby's fame was built.

In his heyday, Paducah-born country humorist and bon vivant Irvin S. Cobb was asked to explain the emotion the Kentucky Derby evoked in Americans. "If I could do that," he said, "I'd have a larynx of spun silver and the tongue of an anointed angel. Until you go to Kentucky and with your own eyes behold the Derby, you ain't been nowhere and you ain't never seen nothin'!"

Burke, Jackie C. *Equal to the Challenge: Pioneering Women of Horse Sports.* New York: Howell Book House, 1997.

Hirsch, Joe, and Jim Bolus. *Kentucky Derby: The Chance of a Lifetime.* New York: McGraw-Hill, 1988.

Jim Bolus Collection. Kentucky Derby Museum Archives, Louisville.

Renau, Lynn S. *Jockeys, Belles, and Bluegrass Kings.* Louisville, KY: Herr House, 1996.

———. *Racing around Kentucky.* Louisville, KY: Lynn S. Renau, 1995.

—*Lynn S. Renau*

KENTUCKY NEGRO EDUCATIONAL ASSOCIATION, association that fought for equality for African American teachers and students. The Colored Teachers State Association was organized in 1877 in Frankfort at a black teachers' convention called by the state superintendent of public instruction, H. A. M. Henderson. During this meeting, the association launched the movement to establish what later became **Kentucky State University.** Corporal punishment and industrial training were major concerns of the association during the late nineteenth century. In 1913, the association was reorganized and incorporated under a new state charter as the **Kentucky Negro Educational Association** (KNEA). The organization sponsored annual essay-writing and spelling contests for students, as well as industrial and fine arts exhibits of students' work.

As the twentieth century progressed, the KNEA contributed funds to the struggle to equalize teacher salaries and facilities in black schools. It encouraged the admission of black students to

Past presidents of the Kentucky Negro Educational Association.

the University of Kentucky's graduate schools and sought repeal of the **Day Law,** which prohibited enrollment of black and white students in the same institution. In 1953, the members of the KNEA voted to change the name to Kentucky Teachers Association. In 1956, the Kentucky Teachers Association was dissolved when it merged with the formerly all-white Kentucky Education Association.

Dunnigan, Alice Allison, comp. and ed. *The Fascinating Story of Black Kentuckians: Their Heritage and Traditions.* Washington, DC: Associated Publishers, 1982.

—*Gerald L. Smith*

KENTUCKY NEGRO EDUCATIONAL ASSOCIATION JOUR-NAL, official publication of Kentucky's African American educational teachers' association. The *Kentucky Negro Educational Association Journal,* published bimonthly during the October–April school year, was the official organ of the **Kentucky Negro Educational Association** (KNEA). In the October 1930 inaugural issue, it stated that it would contain organizational updates and "matter of general interest to teachers and friends of educators." This included not only pedagogy, health, and home economics but also race matters, especially but not exclusively in relation to public education.

Under KNEA executive secretary **Atwood S. Wilson,** managing editor during the Depression era, the journal's mission was "to improve the status of the Negro teacher and to urge better equipment, better school buildings and better opportunity for Negro youth," rather than direct political lobbying like that of the **National Association for the Advancement of Colored People.**

In a February 1931 article, Kentucky State College (later known as **Kentucky State University**) president **Rufus B. Atwood** observed that Kentucky spent 20 times more on training white teachers than on training black ones, which affected local black education. As the solution, he proposed increased funding for black teacher training rather than integrating white facilities. The *KNEA Journal* challenged notions of racial inferiority, arguing that IQ tests evaluated educational preparation more than intelligence and that socioeconomic conditions, not a genetic lack of aptitude, explained black children's lower scores. It also published articles by distinguished activists like W. E. B. Du Bois, Mary McLeod Bethune, and W. W. Alexander, linking local efforts to the national stage.

The journal took a more vocal stance against segregation during World War II and afterward. Atwood observed that "the expensive dual system" of segregated schools especially affected education in local rural communities, and he quoted a federal estimate that at least 700 local black children could not go to school because there were too few of them in local areas for school districts to build a separate school. In a December 1945 editorial, the journal observed that international perception of racism at home "impairs America's opportunity for leadership among the nations," and that one solution would be for state educational boards "to establish programs planned to foster and develop such normal and natural inter-minglings" for youth across racial lines. It also reported on the legislative campaign to modify the **Day Law,** which banned integrated educational facilities, so it would not apply to postgraduate education.

The journal nevertheless still insisted first on improving black education rather than integration. It pushed for salary equalization among teachers, increased funding for black schools, and vocational schools for returning black veterans. KNEA president **Whitney M. Young Sr.** wrote an opinion piece for the *KNEA Journal* stating that although he was not opposed to integration, "I do not want any group to have the final say about where, when, and what type of education our children will have." However, the push to desegregate school facilities ultimately determined the journal's fate. In 1953, when the KNEA became the Kentucky Teachers' Association (KTA), the journal changed its name to the *KTA Journal,* and it was also dissolved when the KTA merged with the previously all-white Kentucky Education Association in 1956.

Atwood, R. B. "Kentucky Faces the Problem of Training Colored Teachers." *KNEAJ* 1, no. 3 (February 1931): 21–26.
"Our Record of Achievement." *KNEAJ* 12, no. 2 (January–February 1942): 6–7.
"Race Relations: An Opportunity." *KNEAJ* 17, no. 2 (December 1945–January 1946): 3–4.
Wilson, Atwood S. "The Intelligence of the Negro." *KNEAJ* 5, no. 2 (February–March 1935): 14–15.
Young, Whitney M. "Integration." *KNEAJ* 22, no. 1 (December 1950): 7.
—*David Lai*

KENTUCKY NEGRO WRESTLING, popular athletic entertainment mostly from the 1930s to the 1950s. In the early 1930s, Jim Mitchell, known as the Black Panther of Kentucky, which was later shortened to the Black Panther, competed in every professional wrestling weight class. Some scholars believe that Mitchell, known as the Dean of Negro Wrestlers, was most likely the first African American in modern professional wrestling. Mitchell, a bald, muscular wrestler, was famous for his "flying mare" technique, and as a "mystery wrestler," he wore a mask until the late 1940s, but he wore kid gloves throughout his wrestling career.

Professional wrestling divided the opponents into two categories: "villain" or "heel" and "Puritan" or "babyface." African American and white contestants could fight one night as the good guy and the next night as the evil opponent. The event's scripts determined the outcome of the match. Mitchell initially was not allowed to fight white opponents, but he did wrestle against Japanese and Hindu challengers. In 1939, the National Wrestling Association forced "Babe" Small, a Polish man, to fight as the villain against "King Kong" Clayton, an Ohio African American newcomer. The *Eugene Register-Guard* reported a "bare-knuckle brawl" with Small kneeing Clayton in the groin and attempting to throw peanut shells in his eyes. On September 2, 1941, "Gentleman Jack" Claybourne defeated Ethiopian wrestler Hallie Samara for the Kentucky Negro wrestling title in Louisville, KY. The following year, "King Kong" Clayton took the title.

On August 24, 1949, in the Olympic Auditorium in Los Angeles, CA, Jim "Black Panther" Mitchell wrestled Gorgeous George, a platinum-blond white man who played the role of "heel" to Mitchell's "babyface." Both were about 5-feet-9 and weighed 210 pounds. When the referee declared Gorgeous George the winner, the interracial crowd erupted, with African American patrons believing that an injustice had occurred. Brawls ensued inside and outside the arena.

Men were not the only ones to compete on the professional wrestling circuit. In November 1952, Red Fassas, promoter of the Lexington Athletic Club, scheduled the first African American women's wrestling match in the area at Woodland Auditorium. Eighteen-year-old Ethel Brown, born in Atlanta and reared in Cincinnati, OH, would battle 19-year-old Kathleen Wimbley from Columbus, OH. Brown's photograph highlighted the upcoming match in a Lexington newspaper. The women were part of white promoter Billy Wolfe's female wrestling troupe.

"Black Panther" Mitchell, an all-around athlete who played tennis, golf, basketball, and baseball, ended his career with a wrestling match against heavyweight boxing champion Joe Louis in 1956. Unable to deal with his declining career, Kentucky's 1941 wrestling champion "Gentleman Jack" Claybourne committed suicide in Los Angeles in 1960.

Newspapers: "Negro Decisions Villain on Foul," *Eugene (OR) Register-Guard,* August 31, 1939, 8; "Claybourne Takes Crown from Samara," *LCJ,* September 3, 1941, sec. 2, p. 8; "Heavies, Girls Vie Thursday on Mat Card," *LL,* November 23, 1952, 22.
Shabazz, Julian L. D. *Black Stars of Professional Wrestling.* Clinton, SC: Awesome Records, 1999.
Smith, R. J. *The Great Black Way: L.A. in the 1940s and the Lost African-American Renaissance.* New York: Public Affairs, 2006.
Woodford, John N. "Why Negro Suicides Are Increasing." *Ebony,* July 1965, 98.
—*Sallie L. Powell*

KENTUCKY RAID (also known as the Cassopolis Outrage), event in which Kentucky slave-catchers attempted to capture runaway slaves. Two large groups of enslaved people, altogether numbering at least 35, escaped from Kenton and Boone Counties during the spring of 1847. The first party of 22 departed on Saturday night, April 24; the second group followed a couple of weeks later. Aided by conductors of the **Underground Railroad,** both groups traveled north through Ohio and Indiana and on into Michigan. There, in the southwestern part of the state, they found refuge in rural Cass Co.

The fugitives from slavery spent the summer in Cass Co., living and working on farms owned by Quakers. They joined a growing black pioneer population that included free African Americans who had migrated to this northern refuge site. Cass Co.'s abolitionist reputation also caught the attention of white Kentuckians, including several aggrieved slave owners in Boone and Kenton Counties.

The slaveholders hired a spy to pursue their missing human property. Around June 1847, the spy arrived in Michigan, posing as an abolitionist from Massachusetts seeking subscribers for antislavery periodicals. Under this guise, he traveled from farm to farm, talking with the locals and secretly creating a map detailing the fugitives' whereabouts, He then returned to Kentucky and issued his report. A posse was gathered, composed of 22 slave owners and their agents. Fully armed and with wagons equipped to transport captives back to Kentucky, the slave-catchers arrived in Cass Co. on August 20, 1847. In the early hours of that Friday morning, the posse split into smaller raiding parties and set out to capture fugitives simultaneously at four different farms. As dawn broke, slave-catchers pounded on cabin doors and began their roundup. At some farms, they captured entire families; at others, either a wife or a daughter escaped and sounded the alarm. As the alarm spread, the raiding parties attempted to rendezvous at the local mill with their 10 captives. The Kentuckians soon found themselves surrounded by a growing number of locals, both black and white, who were armed with guns, axes, hoes, straw-cutters, and even fence posts that they had hastily pulled out of the ground. The Kentuckians, in turn, brandished their guns and bowie knives. Violence was averted when the Kentuckians agreed to take their captives to the county courthouse and submit proof of their ownership claims to a judge.

The entourage of slave-hunters, captured fugitives, and determined locals marched off together to the courthouse in Cassopolis, the county seat. Word of the raid continued to spread as they made their five-mile trek, and the number of Michiganders in the crowd swelled to 200 or 300. When they all arrived in town, 14 of the Kentuckians were arrested for attempted kidnapping, trespassing, and assault and battery. They also were served with a writ of habeas corpus, requiring that they produce the people they had abducted before the court. The Kentuckians posted bail and awaited trial.

The county's judge was unavailable, so the neighboring Berry Co. commissioner presided over the habeas corpus trial. Unbeknownst to the white southerners, the commissioner was an abolitionist and a covert member of the Underground Railroad. When the Kentuckians appeared before him to prove their ownership claims, the commissioner refused each type of evidence they presented, such as bills of sale and power-of-attorney documents. Instead, he insisted that they produce Kentucky's statutes proving that slavery was legal in the state. Although the statutes clearly existed, the Kentuckians did not have them in their possession, and the commissioner denied them time to obtain them. Consequently, he ruled that the captives should go free.

As soon as the captives and their families had left the county, all charges against the Kentuckians for what Michiganders called "the Kentucky Raid" were dropped. The Kentuckians, however, returned home infuriated. They described their experience in the local newspapers as the "Cassopolis Outrage," in which northern abolitionists defied the nation's law to help slaves escape. The slave owners and their allies pressured the U.S. Congress to pass a new fugitive slave law that would increase the penalties for helping slaves attain freedom. They also filed six lawsuits against the white abolitionists in Michigan, charging them with violating the Fugitive Slave Law of 1793. One lawsuit eventually went to trial in Detroit in December 1850. Although the case ended with a hung jury, the defendants settled rather than face a second trial subjecting them to the new 1850 Fugitive Slave Act that had just been passed by Congress.

"The Cassopolis Outrage—The Rights of Slavery, Parts I–IV." *Licking Valley Covington (KY) Register,* October 15, 1847, 3; November 5, 1847, 1.

"Kidnapping by the Wholesale." *National Antislavery Standard,* November 4, 1847.

Rogers, Howard S. *History of Cass County, from 1825–1875.* Cassopolis, MI: Vigilant Book and Job Print, 1875.

Sanford, Joseph, and John Hatfield. Interviews in *The Refugee; or, The Narratives of Fugitive Slaves in Canada,* by Benjamin Drew. Boston: J. P. Jewett, 1856. Reprint, Toronto: Prospero, 2000.

Sanford, Perry. "Out of Bondage: How Perry Sanford Escaped from Slavery; Thrilling Experience on His Way to Michigan." *Heritage Creek: A Journal of Local History* 9 (Winter 1999): 78–81.

—*Debian Marty*

KENTUCKY STATE UNIVERSITY, historically black educational institution. On May 18, 1886, Governor J. Proctor Knott signed a law creating the State Normal School for Colored Persons, later known as Kentucky State University. The law followed an impassioned plea to the legislature for a public normal school for blacks by **William J. Simmons,** president of State Colored Baptist University in Louisville (later known as **Simmons College of Kentucky**).

The State Normal School was located in Frankfort after competition for the site by Owensboro, Knottsville, Hopkinsville, Bowling Green, Danville, and Lexington. Situated on a scenic bluff above downtown Frankfort, the school enrolled 55 students

Recitation Hall (now Jackson Hall) was the first building on what became the Kentucky State University campus. The front section was built in 1887, and an addition was built in 1897.

Kentucky State University baseball team, 1916.

Kentucky State Industrial College for Colored Persons Glee Club, 1931.

from 21 Kentucky counties seeking normal or public school teacher's certificates. In 1890, it received funding from the second federal Morrill Land Grant Act that allowed the school to operate a farm in addition to its teacher education curriculum. However, most of its financial support came from state allocations because many of the students could not afford large tuition fees.

In each decade of its existence, changes affected the Frankfort campus. In 1902, the school became Kentucky Normal and Industrial Institute for Colored Persons and required all students "to take an industry" [*sic*] or vocational skill classes. In subsequent decades, the state allocated funds to build additional instructional buildings and residence halls for students. The first building, Recitation Hall, was renamed Jackson Hall for the first president, **John H. Jackson** (1886–1898; 1907–1910). In subsequent years, Kentucky State president **James Shelton Hathaway** (1900–1907; 1910–1912) sought additional funding to hire more faculty, increase academic offerings, and make the school serve as a source of properly prepared black teachers for Kentucky's schools. Two short-term presidents were James Givens (1898–1900) and **Francis M. Wood** (1923–1924).

During the presidency of **Green Pinckney Russell** (1912–1923, 1924–1929), the campus experienced several changes. In March 1926, it became Kentucky State Industrial College. In December 1926, a tragic fire in the women's dormitory led to the death of three female students. In the remaining years of his second term, political issues led to Russell's replacement by **Rufus B. Atwood,** who served as Kentucky State's president from 1929 to 1962. President Atwood's leadership carried Kentucky State through its transition to a four-year institution granting bachelor's degrees as Kentucky State College for Negroes. In 1952, "for Negroes" was dropped from its name. Campus enrollments remained consistent from the 1940s through the 1950s despite the gradual desegregation of Kentucky's public and independent colleges and universities.

In 1962, Dr. **Carl M. Hill** succeeded Atwood. Hill sought to increase the level of integration of faculty, staff and students. Although the campus experienced some minor student turmoil in the 1960s, Hill was able to transform Kentucky State College into Kentucky State University (KSU) with the addition of a master's degree program in public affairs in 1972. Three years later, Hill retired as president, and Dr. William Butts succeeded him.

Butts's administration secured new buildings and obtained funds for needed renovation of existing campus structures. However, Kentucky State underwent intense external criticism by the Kentucky Council on Higher Education for excessive out-of-state student enrollments. In 1982, attorney **Raymond Burse** was named president. KSU was then redefined as the state's public liberal arts institution with the creation of the **Whitney Young** College of Leadership Studies. President Burse was succeeded by **Mary L. Smith** (1989–1990, 1991–1998), John T. Wolfe (1990–1991), George Reid (1998–2002), Paul Bibbins (2002–2003), interim president William H. Turner (2003–2004), Mary Evans Sias (2004–2014), and president Raymond Burse in 2014.

Hardin, John A. *Onward and Upward: A Centennial History of Kentucky State University, 1886–1986.* Frankfort: Kentucky State University, 1987.

"Timeline of KSU History." http://www.kysu.edu/about/heritage/timelineofksuhistory/default.htm (accessed July 7, 2011).

—*John A. Hardin*

***KENTUCKY V. DENNISON,* U.S. Supreme Court case that set a precedent for gubernatorial discretion.** The last of several important cases tried before the U.S. Supreme Court on the subject of fugitive slaves before the Civil War, *Kentucky v. Dennison* centered on the escape of a slave from Louisville, KY, on October 4, 1859. The slave, a girl named Charlotte, was the property of C. W. Nichols, who allowed her to visit her mother as she accompanied him on a business trip to Wheeling, VA. Upon finding Charlotte on her journey in Cincinnati, OH, abolitionists seized the girl and took her to a state court, where she was declared free under state law.

Governor Beriah Magoffin of Kentucky, a states' rights supporter and eventual Confederate sympathizer, demanded the extradition of a free black named Willis Lago, who had aided in the escape of Charlotte. In turn, Governor William Dennison Jr. of Ohio, an antislavery Whig and future Republican, rejected the demand by issuing an opinion on the subject from his attorney general. This opinion argued that Lago had not committed any acts that constituted "treason or felony by the common law" or "which are regarded as crimes by the usages and laws of all civilized nations," and thereby the necessity of extradition was eliminated. The representatives of Kentucky, unhappy with this response, petitioned the Supreme Court for a writ of mandamus that would compel Dennison to relinquish Lago.

When the case finally appeared before the Supreme Court in late February 1861, several southern states had already seceded from the Union in reaction to Abraham Lincoln's victory in the election of 1860, and the fate of states in the Upper South like Kentucky remained in the balance. Further complicating the situation was the presence of Chief Justice Roger B. Taney, a states' rights supporter with strong southern leanings. Taney recognized that an imposition of federal power on state governments was especially dangerous at the time of the decision, but he also had a long record of supporting the rights of slaveholders. His opinion in *Kentucky v. Dennison* established a middle position, declaring that the petitioners from Kentucky were right in principle but acknowledging that although "Congress may authorize a particular state officer to perform a particular duty," it "does not follow that he may be coerced, or punished for his refusal."

In the short term, Taney's decision angered both northerners and southerners. Although he had decided in favor of the abolitionists, he had also clearly sided with the slaveholders in principle. In the long term, however, the decision had the more substantial impact of establishing a principle for governing extradition between states. The principle Taney established in *Kentucky v. Dennison* remained in place until 1987, when the court reversed itself in *Puerto Rico v. Branstad.*

Kentucky v. Dennison, 65 U.S. 66 (1860).

Mikula, Mark, and L. Mpho Mabunda, eds. *Great American Court Cases.* Vol. 2, *Criminal Justice.* Detroit: Gale Group, 1999.

Swisher, Carl B. *History of the Supreme Court of the United States.* Vol. 5, *The Taney Period, 1836–64.* New York: Macmillan, 1974.

—*Stephen Pickering*

KEYS, MARTHA JAYNE (b. 1892, Mayfield, KY; d. 1975, Louisville, KY), A.M.E. minister and evangelist. Daughter of Thomas Jefferson and Elizabeth Ann Keys, devout members of St. James African Methodist Episcopal (A.M.E.) Church in Mayfield, KY, Martha Jayne Keys received the call to the ministry at a young age but did not become active in her ministry until a few years later. Sources differ on when she actually began her ministry. One source claims that she began as a traveling evangelist at the age of 12 and preached throughout the United States and Canada. Another source maintains that shortly after she turned 14, her pastor, Rev. Green Price, allowed her to preach a "trial sermon" at the church despite the fact that the A.M.E. denomination barred women from ordination as ministers.

Keys matriculated at Lane College in Jackson, TN, and graduated with a degree in English theology from Payne Theological Seminary in Wilberforce, OH, in 1916. The year before her graduation, according to one newspaper, she attended, possibly for the first time, the A.M.E. Kentucky Annual Conference. After graduation, she traveled extensively as an evangelist and led revivals with her sermons and music. In 1920, Bishop Archibald J. Carey appointed her pastor of Moore's Chapel A.M.E. Church in Clinton, KY, in Hickman Co. She was active in the Women's Parent Mite Missionary Society (WPMMS) and the Woman's Home and Foreign Missionary Society. In 1927, she was the first woman to preach the quadrennial sermon at the WPMMS Convention in Columbus, OH. In 1930, she received her doctorate of divinity from Payne Theological Seminary. In the mid-1930s, she married and divorced Willie K. Marshall, an A.M.E. minister.

Keys served as pastor of four Louisville churches: St. John, Trinity, St. James, and Young's Chapel. She was elected to three A.M.E. General Conferences: 1936, 1952, and 1956. She began promoting the ordination of women ministers at the 1936 General Conference. Her campaign for women's ordination grew when she was asked to preach at the 1956 General Conference in Miami, FL. Through the persistent work of people like Dr. Martha Jayne Keys, the A.M.E. Church voted to accept the full ordination of women ministers at the 1960 General Conference.

Kentucky women such as Etta Graham and Rosa Means benefited from Keys's efforts. In the mid-1960s, Keys organized the Martha J. Keys Evangelical A.M.E. Church in Louisville, which originally met in her home. In 1972, she retired from the ministry and died at Louisville's King's Daughters and Sons Home on December 24, 1975.

Dickerson, Dennis C. "Martha Jayne Keys and the Ordination of Women in the African Methodist Church." *AME Church Review* 118, no. 385 (January–March 2002): 72–83.

"Mayfield, KY," *Freeman*, October 16, 1914, 4.

Wright, Richard Robert, Jr. *Encyclopaedia of the African Methodist Episcopal Church*. 2nd ed. Philadelphia: Book Concern of the A.M.E. Church, 1947.

———. *Who's Who in the General Conference*. Philadelphia: A.M.E. Book Concern, 1924.

—*Sallie L. Powell*

KIDD, MINNIE MAE JONES STREET (b. 1904, Millersburg, KY; d. 1999, Louisville, KY), businesswoman, politician, and civic leader. The daughter of Anna Belle Leer and Charles Robert Jones, who never recognized her (nor did she him), Minnie Mae Jones, as she was known as a child, lived on the borders of white and African American society. Under Kentucky law, she was black, but her blond hair and light skin gave her access to another world if she chose to enter it, as she sometimes did when she was shopping for hats and clothing. She attended local schools in Millersburg. At age 15, she enrolled at the **Lincoln Institute** in Simpsonville for a two-year course of study. Returning home in 1921, she became an independent sales agent in Bourbon Co. for the Louisville-based **Mammoth Life and Accident Insurance Company.** At age 21, she moved to Louisville and worked as supervisor of policy issues. In 1930, she married her first husband, Horace Leon Street, a Mammoth executive, who died in 1942.

During World War II, Street served in England with the American Red Cross and immediately afterward worked with the United Seamen's Service in Portland, ME. Returning to Louisville, she rejoined Mammoth Life Insurance as the director of public relations, a position she held until she entered politics. In 1947, she married James Meredith Kidd III. He died in 1977.

Mae Street Kidd.

In 1968, Mae Street Kidd sought election to the House of Representatives as a Democrat from Louisville's 41st Legislative District. She won by a two-to-one majority and was reelected for eight additional terms. Known as the Lady of the House and for her hats, she became a spokesperson for civil rights and a champion of the disadvantaged poor.

During her years in the legislature, Kidd became the first woman to serve on the Rules Committee, the first woman elected secretary of the Democratic caucus, and the first woman elected chair of the Enrollment Committee. In 1968, she sponsored a statewide open-housing bill, and in 1970, she drafted the Mae Street Kidd Act, which created the Kentucky Housing Corporation to loan money at low interest rates to home buyers of modest means. She also championed the idea of having Dr. Martin Luther King's birthday declared a state holiday. Kidd often said that her proudest achievement was the unanimous ratification by Kentucky of the Thirteenth, Fourteenth, and Fifteenth Amendments to the U.S. Constitution in 1976. This effort garnered her the annual achievement award from *Esquire* magazine.

Defeated in the 1984 general election, Kidd resumed her philanthropic and civic work in Louisville. On October 20, 1999, Mae Street Kidd died and was buried in Zachary Taylor National Cemetery. In May 2003, Louisville city officials posthumously recognized her by naming Mae Street Kidd Avenue in the **Park**

DuValle neighborhood in her honor. In 2004, the Kentucky Historical Society paid tribute to her with a historical marker in her hometown of Millersburg.

Hall, Wade. *Passing for Black: The Life and Careers of Mae Street Kidd.* Lexington: Univ. Press of Kentucky, 1997.

Kidd, Mae Street. Interview by Ken Chumley, 1993. Mae Street Kidd Oral History Project, Kentucky Historical Society. 22 audiocassettes.

Kleber, John E., ed. *The Encyclopedia of Louisville.* Lexington: Univ. Press of Kentucky, 2001.

"Park DuValle's Street Names Honor Seven 'Vibrant' Black Leaders." *LCJ,* May 14, 2003, N1.

—*Carol Crowe Carraco*

KIMBLEY, GEORGE (b. 1896, Frankfort, KY; d. 1996, Frankfort, KY), steelworker and union activist in Gary, IN. The son of former slaves, George Kimbley was born in Frankfort, KY, on July 14, 1896. He was raised in a house directly across the street from the family that had owned his parents. With limited options for advancement available to a poor African American in Frankfort, Kimbley quit Clinton Street School before finishing the eighth grade and traveled north to find employment as a teenager. In 1917, after working in various factories in Indianapolis and Detroit, he was drafted into the U.S. Army and served in France during World War I. After returning home in 1919, Kimbley settled in Gary, IN, where he found work with the U.S. Steel Corporation. Throughout the 1920s, Kimbley became active in Gary's African American community, participating in the local branches of the **National Association for the Advancement of Colored People** and the Universal Negro Improvement Association.

Over the next two decades, Kimbley became one of the city's most active union supporters, helping break down traditional barriers against African Americans. Throughout the 1920s, he served as a major organizer and recruiter for the Congress of Industrial Organizations in Gary. On July 9, 1936, he became the first person in Gary to officially join the Steelworkers' Organizing Committee. The following year, he became the first black staff representative in District 31 of the Steelworkers Union, which covered the entire Calumet Region of Chicago and Northwestern Indiana. He served in this position for the next 21 years.

After his retirement in 1958, Kimbley returned to Frankfort, where he died on July 2, 1996, 12 days before his 100th birthday on July 14, 1996.

Dickerson, Dennis C. *Out of the Crucible: Black Steelworkers in Western Pennsylvania, 1875–1980.* Albany: State Univ. of New York Press, 1986.

Needleman, Ruth. *Black Freedom Fighters in Steel: The Struggle for Democratic Unionism.* Ithaca, NY: Cornell Univ. Press, 2003.

Obituary. *LHL,* July 4, 1996, C2.

—*Joshua D. Farrington*

KING, ALFRED DANIEL WILLIAMS "A. D." (b. 1930, Atlanta, GA; d. 1969, Atlanta, GA), preacher and civil rights activist. Alfred Daniel Williams "A. D." King was the son of Rev. Martin Luther King Sr. and Alberta (Williams) King. Born in 1930, he was the youngest of three children. After completing his education at Morehouse College's Interdenominational Theological Center in Atlanta and preaching at First Baptist Church in Birmingham, AL, King accepted the pastor's post at Louisville's Zion Baptist Church on 22nd and **Walnut** (now **Muhammad Ali** Blvd.) in late 1964.

Soon after assuming his post in early 1965, King founded a state chapter of his older brother Martin's Southern Christian Leadership Conference (SCLC), known as the **Kentucky Christian Leadership Conference.** After playing a minor role in Louisville's civil rights battle for nearly a year and a half, King took a vocal stance in 1967 on the community's discriminatory housing policies. In early summer, he and other leaders of the Committee for Open Housing organized nightly marches through the South End, at which time he was jailed for 30 hours and forced to pay a $30 fine after leading a protest during prohibited hours.

Although Martin Luther King Jr. attended a couple of the marches, the number of demonstrators dried up midway through the summer. However, the efforts were rewarded late in 1967 when the recently elected Democratic Louisville Board of Alderman passed a new open-housing ordinance. After his brother was assassinated in Memphis, A. D. stepped up his presence nationally in the civil rights movement. In June 1968, he announced his resignation from Zion Baptist Church, which had become the largest African American Baptist church in Kentucky, in order to succeed his brother at Ebenezer Baptist Church in Atlanta and play a larger role in the SCLC.

A. D. King and his wife, Naomi Barber King, had five children. On July 21, 1969, King was found dead in his backyard swimming pool, the victim of an apparent drowning.

Hall, Wade. *The Rest of the Dream: The Black Odyssey of Lyman Johnson.* Lexington: Univ. Press of Kentucky, 1988.

KING, GEORGE N., SR. (b. 1932, Louisville, KY; d. 2013, Louisville, KY), businessman. A Louisville native, George N. King learned his strong work ethic from his father, a Louisville and Nashville Railroad employee, and his uncle, who worked for the Brown Hotel. Neither man ever owned a car, but both daily walked to their jobs. At age 14, King quit school (his greatest regret) and worked for Fred Stoner, a barber and boxing trainer. Stoner taught King to box, but Stoner's most successful pupil was Cassius Clay (later known as **Muhammad Ali**).

At the same time that he worked for Stoner, King waited tables at the Pendennis Club, where he met people who gave him business advice and supported him in the business world. The Wood Mosaic Corporation, a hardwood/veneer company owned by a white family, soon hired King as a janitor. Fourteen years later, the company determined that it was more cost effective to help King establish his own janitorial services than to pay him as an individual employee. In 1964, King began Mr. Klean's Janitor and Maintenance Service with only three accounts and 7 employees. The company grew to have more than 1,300 employees and serviced seven states, becoming the largest business of its kind in the country and making King the most prominent black Kentucky business employer in 1978. Four years later, the Small Business Administration named King Kentucky's Small Businessman of the Year.

In 1995, King sold the company to Burns Enterprises, operated by African American businessman **Tommie Burns Jr.,** but remained the company's president and CEO. In that same year, he formed King's Management Group, a management consulting firm. Five years later, he partnered with **Junior Bridgeman** and A. J. Bosse to form King Bridgeman Bosse, a general contractor and construction manager of commercial and industrial property. King Bridgeman Bosse was involved in the construction of the Muhammad Ali Center.

King, a member of the Greater Louisville Inc., the city's chamber of commerce, served on various boards, including the Jewish Hospital Foundation Board, the Louisville–Jefferson County Economic Development Commission, and the boards of trustees of Murray State University and the University of Louisville. He was a founding member of the Louisville chapter of 100 Black Men.

King died on July 1, 2013. **A. D. Porter** and Sons Funeral Home handled the death arrangements. His memorial service was held at the Salvation Army (formerly Male High School).

Dunnigan, Alice Allison, comp. and ed. *The Fascinating Story of Black Kentuckians: Their Heritage and Traditions.* Washington, DC: Associated Publishers, 1982.

"George N. King, Sr." Obituary, *LCJ,* July 3, 2013.

Passing the Torch: Lessons Learned, Wisdom Shared; Conversations with Louisville Leaders about Life, Leadership and Service. Louisville, KY: Butler Books, 2005.

　　　　　　　　　　　　　　　　　　　　—Sallie L. Powell

KIRK, ANDREW DEWEY "ANDY" (b. 1898, Newport, KY; d. 1992, New York City, NY), bandleader.

Andrew Dewey Kirk was the last African American bandleader from the big-band era who was born in northern Kentucky. When he was a child, his family moved to Denver, where he studied music under Paul Whiteman's father, Wilberforce. He was a contemporary of nationally known bandleaders Duke Ellington, Count Basie, and Jimmy Lunceford. Kirk's Clouds of Joy Orchestra became renowned throughout the nation when, in November 1929, it made its debut recording for the Brunswick label. During Kirk's early years, he maintained his home base in Kansas City, MO, while he traveled throughout the United States. His band developed a Southeast **jazz** style similar to that of Count Basie, also based in Kansas City. After his Clouds of Joy Orchestra broke up in 1948, Kirk continued to tour. During the 1950s, he made several stops in the greater Cincinnati area. On one occasion, he added some local talent from Covington to his tour. According to **Nelson Burton,** "Andy Kirk came to Covington and picked up an outstanding left handed drummer named Hoppie and another fellow named Al Sears who lived down in the bottom of Bush Street." Al Sears later left Kirk and went to work with Duke Ellington.

Kirk continued to play occasionally as he began to take up hotel management. During the 1970s, he worked at the Theresa Hotel in Harlem, NY. He remained a figure in the New York musical scene through his membership in the city's branch of the American Federation of Musicians until he developed Alzheimer's disease. His only child, Andy Kirk Jr., died in 1967. Andy Kirk Sr. died on December 11, 1992, in New York City and was buried there; he had no direct survivors.

"Andy Kirk." In *Encyclopedia of Popular Music,* 3rd ed., vol. 4, edited by Colin Larkin. London: Muze, 1998.

Hitchcock, H. Wiley, and Stanley Sadie, eds. *The New Grove Dictionary of American Music.* New York: Macmillan, 1986.

Ledin, Lisa, and Simon Anderson. *Nelson Burton: My Life in Jazz.* Cincinnati: Clifton Hills Press, 2000.

Warous, Peter. "Andy Kirk, 94, Big-Band Leader Known for the Kansas City Sound." *NYT,* December 15, 1992, B15.

　　　　　　　　　　　　　　　　　　　—Theodore H. H. Harris

KNIGHT, DAVID L. (b. 1863, Bullitt Co., KY; d. ca. 1922, Louisville, KY), early business pioneer in Louisville.

Described by the *Colored American Magazine* as "one of the most substantial and successful businessmen" in Louisville, David L. Knight was born in poverty to his widowed mother on April 16, 1863. Knight never had a formal education but was self-taught and learned to read at Sunday school. When he was 14, he traveled from his home in Bullitt Co. to Louisville, where he found manual labor with various employers.

In 1887, while working in a brickyard, he was inspired to pursue his own career after seeing an old horse grazing in a nearby field. Knight purchased the horse and a dilapidated wagon and embarked on a new career selling vegetables as a street vender. Although he made only 75 cents during his first few weeks, he eventually saved enough money to purchase a coal wagon and began delivering coal to local businesses.

By the turn of the century, he expanded his business beyond coal and became the owner of Louisville's first black-owned transfer company, which serviced white businesses by moving their products quickly across town. Throughout the first decade of the 1900s, Knight's business earned as much as $12,000 per year. Operating out of three vacant lots that he purchased for his stables and wagon yard, he employed 12 drivers and a stableman and owned 20 horses and 17 wagons outfitted with "Lightning Transfer" on their sides. He also boasted of being the first employer in Louisville to hire a black woman as bookkeeper and stenographer. In 1908, he leased a farm outside the city that supplied feed for his horses and garnered hundreds of dollars in extra profit through the sale of vegetables. In addition to his transfer line, he was the owner of Falls City Realty Company and served as president of Louisville Blacksmith and Wagon Builders, which specialized in horseshoeing and creating custom-built wagons.

Following Booker T. Washington's lead in establishing the National Negro Business League (NNBL), Knight joined with two other black businessmen in Louisville and formed Louisville's NNBL branch in September 1901. When the NNBL chose Louisville as the site of its 1909 annual convention, Knight was selected as chairman of the General Committee of Arrangements. At the convention, he delivered the opening address and gave introductory speeches for many of the convention's most illustrious guest speakers, including Booker T. Washington, Kentucky governor August E. Willson, and Louisville mayor James Grinstead.

Despite his business successes in the early 1900s, growing racism in the 1910s eroded much of Knight's white clientele, and with the invention of the automobile and more efficient methods of transportation, Knight's horse-centered business closed its doors only a few years after the Louisville NNBL convention.

According to the 1920 U.S. federal census and a 1922 Louisville city directory, Knight and his daughter, Josephine, lived at 1501 Chestnut St. He worked as a "second hand dealer," and she was a clerk. He died around 1922.

"First Day's Session." Records of the National Negro Business League, part 1, Annual Conference Proceedings and Organizational Records, 1900–1919. Microfilm edition, reel 2, frames 160–66, August 18, 1909.

Hartshorn, William Newton. *An Era of Progress and Promise, 1863–1910.* Boston: Priscilla Publishing, 1910.

Knight, D. L. "Transfer Business." Records of the National Negro Business League, part 1, Annual Conference Proceedings and Organizational Records, 1900–1919. Microfilm edition, reel 1, frame 248. Date not listed.

Lewis, Cary B. "Louisville and Its Afro-American Citizens." *Colored American Magazine* 10, nos. 3–4 (April 1906): 259–65.

U.S. City Directories, 1821–1989 (Caron's Directory, 1922 and 1924).

U.S. Federal Census (1920).

—*Joshua D. Farrington*

KNIGHT, ETHERIDGE (b. 1931, Corinth, MS; d. 1991, Indianapolis, IN), poet. Born in Corinth, MS, but raised in Paducah, KY, Etheridge Knight grew disenchanted with the poverty and racism he witnessed in his childhood. After dropping out of school at age 14, Knight developed an addiction to narcotics that he tried to escape by joining the army in 1947. His plan backfired, however, after he was discharged for a shrapnel wound that drove him even deeper into a heroin addiction. Knight turned to robbery to support his drug habit, but a purse-snatching crime earned him a 10- to 25-year sentence in the Indiana State Prison in 1960.

During the eight years he served, Knight began to write poetry. In 1968, he published his first book of poems, *Poems from Prison,* to rave reviews, especially in the African American community. His work, marked by **jazz**-oriented meter and prison imagery, grew in popularity over the next decade, and he published several more books of poetry. Knight received several awards for his poetry, including an American Book Award, and was also appointed to several positions at prestigious schools, but his drug and alcohol addictions kept him close to poverty for most of his life. On March 10, 1991, Knight died of lung cancer in Indianapolis, IN. In 1992, the Etheridge Knight Festival was founded to celebrate his legacy.

"Adieu, Gentle Poet; The Memories Linger." *Memphis Commercial Appeal,* March 16, 1991, B1.

Magill, Frank N. *Masterpieces of African-American Literature.* New York: HarperCollins, 1992.

Vannatta, Renee. "Etheridge Knight." Tennessee Literary Project, Middle Tennessee State University. http://www.mtsu.edu/tnlitproj /TLP_Web_Layout_Etheridge_Knight.pdf (accessed July 19, 2011).

—*Stephen Pickering*

KNOX, FERMON WENDELL (b. 1923, Dime Box, TX; d. 2001, Erlanger, KY), civil rights leader. Civil rights leader Fermon Knox was the son of Albert and Carrie Lovings Knox. He was raised in Lee Co., TX. At Freeman High School there, he excelled in basketball and football. When he graduated, he received many athletic scholarships for college, but World War II began, and he was drafted into the U.S. Army. He served in the Philippines for four years and contracted malaria there. Returning to the states, he was treated at a military hospital in Lexington. When Knox recovered, he was able to attend nearby Kentucky State College (later known as **Kentucky State University**) in Frankfort on a football scholarship that had been offered to him earlier. Knox became more politically and socially conscious of the world around him during his college years. Like many other African Americans soldiers returning from World War II, he was no longer willing to accept second-class citizenship after fighting for his country.

After college, he worked for the Monmouth Life Insurance Company, and in 1958 he was transferred to Cincinnati to manage the company's Cincinnati–Northern Kentucky District. He lived in Covington. During the height of the **civil rights movement,** Knox served as the president of the Northern Kentucky branch of the **National Association for the Advancement of Colored People** and later was the president of its regional division. As he helped organize and participate in marches, protests, and freedom rides across the United States, he met and worked with such leaders as Rev. Anthony Deye, Medgar Evers, **Lyman T. Johnson**, **Mae Street Kidd**, Martin Luther King Jr., Fred Shuttlesworth, Roy Wilkins, and his college classmate and friend **Whitney M. Young Jr.**

Knox was instrumental in lobbying both the Kentucky legislature and the U.S. Congress for passage of the housing desegregation and other civil rights laws. He helped bring about the desegregation of the Covington public schools. He planned the state march on Frankfort in 1964 and served as one of the speakers on that occasion, coordinated efforts to increase hiring of African Americans in local businesses, became the first executive director of the Northern Kentucky Community Action Commission, and served as the executive of the Louisville Community Action Commission. After 31 years in executive management of nonprofit organizations, Knox retired in 1997 as the chief executive officer of the Emmanuel Community Center in Cincinnati.

Knox was a lifelong member of **Alpha Phi Alpha Fraternity.** He served as the Kentucky A.M.E. Church Conference's lay organization president and historiographer and was an active member of **St. James A.M.E. Church** in Covington for 43 years. He also served on the boards of many nonprofit organizations. Governor Louie B. Nunn (1967–1971) honored Knox as a Kentucky Colonel. Knox was also nominated to the **Kentucky Commission on Human Rights** Hall of Fame in 2000 and 2001. He died of a stroke at his home in 2001 and was buried in Forest Lawn Memorial Park in Erlanger.

Knox, Fermon, to Benny Butler, April 1999. Northern Kentucky African American Heritage Task Force Oral History, Archives, Northern Kentucky Univ., Highland Heights.

Newspapers: *KP,* June 28, 2001, 4K; "Veteran Rights Crusader Dies," *KP,* October 25, 2001, 1; "Civil Rights Pioneer Dies," *KE,* October 26, 2001, B1; *Sequim (TX) Gazette Enterprise,* January 31, 2001.

—*Jessica Knox-Perkins*

L

LACEY, EUGENE (b. 1888, Covington, KY; d. 1965, Covington, KY), businessman. Eugene F. Lacey, the son of Samuel and Emma Lacey, was a lifelong resident of Covington. His early education was at **Lincoln-Grant School** in Covington, and he graduated from Woodward High School on Sycamore St. in downtown Cincinnati. In 1918, he opened his first grocery store at 508 Scott St. in Covington (currently the site of the Kenton Co. Public Library) while residing at nearby 839 Craig St. In 1919, Lacey married Bessie Merritt of Falmouth, and together they opened a second store in Covington at 205 E. Robbins St., calling it the Gene and Bess Store; the building also served as their home.

Sometime during those years, Gene Lacey found time to attend the University of Cincinnati and the American Institute of Management. He graduated from Alexander Hamilton Business School, and later the Laceys formed two companies, the Lacey Sausage Company and the Lacey Paper Company. In 1924, Gene and Bess Lacey faced a major challenge to their business when the Great Atlantic and Pacific Tea Company (A&P) and another major grocery chain moved into the neighborhood less than a block away from their small grocery, then located on Greenup St. The Laceys remained competitive not by charging low prices but by the convenience of their store and by employing local people, thus keeping the money spent at their store in the community. In 1926, Lacey closed his store at 508 Scott St.; in 1933 he opened a grocery store at Court and John Sts. in Cincinnati.

Lacey was a 32nd-degree Mason and served on the Southern Jurisdiction of the Supreme Council of Masons, was a member of the Odd Fellow Lodge, and became exalted ruler of Ira Lodge No. 37 of the Elks. He was a member of the National Negro Business League, served on the executive committee of the Cincinnati branch of the **National Association for the Advancement of Colored People,** and was active in the **Ninth St. Methodist Episcopal Church,** serving as treasurer and a trustee for many years. In 1931, Lacey was a speaker for the new Covington City Manager League, which supported the city manager form of government for Covington. There were 300 new members at the time within the Negro Division. Lacey was also a founding member of Covington's **African American Businessmen's Association.**

A frequent visitor to the Lacey household during the summer months of the 1940s was their nephew, **John A. Merritt,** later a college football coach. Gene Lacey died in 1965 and was buried in Mary E. Smith Cemetery in **Elsmere.**

Dabney, Wendell P. *Cincinnati's Colored Citizens: Historical, Sociological and Biographical.* Cincinnati: Dabney, 1926.

Newspapers: "Enroll 300 New Members in Colored Division," *KTS,* July 7, 1931, 2; "Eugene Lacey, Businessman," *KP,* July 6, 1965, 3K; Theodore H. H. Harris, "Reader Recollection," *KP,* March 2, 1992, 4K.

—Theodore H. H. Harris

LAINE, HENRY ALLEN (b. 1870, College Hill, KY; d. 1955, Richmond, IN), poet and educator. Often referred to as Kentucky's black poet laureate, Henry Allen Laine was born in Madison Co. to former slaves. He attended school in a slave cabin that could provide students only with split log benches, writing slates, and a single edition of *Webster's Speller.* He did not complete the eighth grade until he was 18 years old because of his primary responsibilities to work on his parents' small farm. Determined to continue his education, he worked at a sawmill to fund his studies at **Berea College,** from which he graduated in 1896.

After graduating, Laine found work as a schoolteacher in Madison Co., where he continued to teach for over 20 years. From 1904 to 1906, he served as the president of the Colored State Teachers' Association and later was a frequent speaker at its annual conventions after the organization evolved into the **Kentucky Negro Educational Association** in the 1910s. In 1910, he founded the Madison County Colored Teachers Association and remained president through the 1930s. In 1917, he was appointed the supervisor of Madison County Colored Schools.

In addition to his career as an educator, Laine was also deeply involved in educating and promoting central Kentucky's African American farmers. In 1915, he organized a farmers' club for blacks in the Richmond area, and two years later he became Madison Co.'s first black county extension agent when he was appointed county farm demonstration agent for black farmers. Six years later, he was appointed to the same position in Jessamine Co.

James Bond praised Laine's poetry for its mastery "of the Negro dialect" and said that it had "the ability to express . . . the psychology and the soul yearnings of the Negro race." His poems covered a variety of topics, from the joys of food in "Chidlings" to his criticism of lynchings in "A Kentuckian's Appeal." As an advocate of his friend Booker T. Washington's self-help philosophy, and as reflected in his work as a farm agent, in many of his poems, Laine promoted the importance of earning respect from white Americans through hard labor and the importance of maintaining a close relationship with one's land and property. His most famous poetry compilation, *Foot Prints,* was first published in 1914 and was reprinted five times into the 1980s. Throughout the 1910s and 1920s, his writings were frequently reprinted in the *Voice of the Negro,* the *Louisville Post,* and the *Richmond Pantagraph,* and he even read a poem before Kentucky governor J. C. W. Beckham.

As a leading cultural figure of central Kentucky, Laine organized the first Colored Chautauqua in Madison Co. in 1916. The festival, designed to promote black culture and education, was attended by Booker T. Washington and George Washington Carver.

After his retirement in the 1940s, Laine remained in Madison Co. and was named Man of the Year by Richmond High School in 1947. In 1952, he moved with his wife, Florence, to Richmond, IN, where he died three years later. In 2003, Henry Allen Laine was inducted into the Kentucky Civil Rights Hall of Fame and was posthumously awarded the John G. Fee Award by Berea College in 2009.

Henry Allen Laine Papers. Finding aid. Special Collections and Archives, Eastern Kentucky Univ.

Laine, Henry Allen. *Foot Prints*. Richmond, KY: Daily Register Press, 1924.

"Remembering a Civil Rights Voice." *Richmond (IN) Palladium-Item*, February 22, 2009, A1.

Rush, Theresa Gunnels, Carol Fairbanks Myers, and Esther Spring Arata, eds. *Black American Writers Past and Present: A Biographical and Bibliographical Dictionary*. Vol. 2. Metuchen, NJ: Scarecrow Press, 1975.

—*Joshua D. Farrington*

LAINE, JOSEPH F. (b. 1881, Winchester, KY; d. 1967, Louisville, KY), physician. Educated at **Berea College,** Joseph F. Laine completed his medical training in 1906 at Meharry Medical College, an institution in Nashville, TN, that was established in 1876 for the education of African Americans. He did postgraduate work at Meharry and at the Tuskegee Institute and Talladega College, both in Alabama. A practicing physician for over 60 years, Laine spent the majority of his career in Kentucky.

At the request of Dr. **John E. Hunter,** Laine established an office in Lexington, where he practiced for approximately 18 years. He then moved to Louisville and in the late 1920s founded the Laine Medical Clinic at 1120 W. **Walnut St.** (now **Muhammad Ali** Blvd.). Laine, who was influential in bringing other African American doctors to practice in Kentucky, was a member and president of both the Falls City Medical Society of Louisville and the Bluegrass State Medical Association. He was also active in civic affairs as a member of the **National Association for the Advancement of Colored People** and the Louisville Urban League.

Laine, who was survived by his wife, Bruce (Simpson) Laine, a son, Joseph F. Jr., and a daughter, Pauline, is buried in the Louisville Cemetery.

LAMPTON, EDWARD WILKINSON (b. 1857, Hopkinsville, KY; d. 1910, Petoskey, MI), African Methodist Episcopal (A.M.E.) bishop. Born in slavery, Edward Wilkinson Lampton was named for his maternal grandfather, Rev. Edward Wilkinson. A 1910 publication claimed that Wilkinson was "the first preacher of the African Methodist Episcopal Church in Kentucky" and had been imprisoned for his efforts to organize the church in 1857, the year of Lampton's birth. Lampton's family left Kentucky for Louisiana when he was young. He first learned a trade from his father, Albert R. Lampton, a brick mason. In 1886, he was ordained into the ministry in Greenville, MS.

In the 1890s, Lampton became politically active and served as a delegate to the National Republican Convention in St. Louis, MO. Beginning in 1892, he also served as a delegate to the A.M.E. General Conference every year until his death. He earned his doctor of divinity degree from Shorter College in Little Rock, AR. He wrote two books, *An Analysis on Baptism* and *A Digest of the Rulings and Decisions of the Bishops of the African Methodist Episcopal Church, 1847 to 1907.*

Lampton's business skills enabled him to acquire personal wealth and unanimous election as financial secretary of the entire A.M.E. Church in 1902. He held that position for seven years. During that time, he also served as grand master of the Prince Hall Masonic Lodge of Mississippi. In 1908, he was elected bishop for the states of Mississippi and Louisiana.

In 1909, one year before his death, Lampton fought racism on two fronts. He joined four other A.M.E. bishops in a discrimination complaint against four southern railroads and the Pullman Company, but the Interstate Commerce Commission dismissed the case. Then, because of death threats after a controversy with the telephone company, whose operators refused to address African American customers by courtesy titles, Lampton was forced to move from Greenville, MS, to Chicago, IL. Lampton died in Petoskey, MI, and his body was transferred to Greenville, MS, for burial.

Adams, Revels A. *Cyclopedia of African Methodism in Mississippi*. Natchez, MS: n.p., 1902.

"Bishop Edward W. Lampton." *New York Daily Tribune*, July 18, 1910, 5.

Hartshorn, William Newton, and George W. Penniham. *An Era of Progress and Promise, 1863–1910*. Boston: Priscilla, 1910.

—*Sallie L. Powell*

LANDRUM, STEPHEN (b. 1846, Barren Co., KY; d. 1923, Glasgow, KY), businessman and philanthropist. According to the 1900 U.S. federal census, Stephen Landrum was born in October 1846. He was most likely born into slavery in Barren Co. to Jack Wells and Rachel Landrum. At age 23, he worked in a factory in Glasgow and married his wife, Jennie, also known as Jane, in 1871. By 1880, he was a farmer.

Even though Landrum could neither read nor write, he was a mathematical whiz and could mentally add, subtract, and multiply without the use of paper. By the early 1900s, he primarily earned his wealth through real estate with a $500 monthly income. He customarily collected his tenants' rent on Sundays with the assistance of a walking cane. Ed H. Smith, Landrum's white attorney for two decades, maintained that Landrum (whom he called Uncle Steve) could easily recall each year how much rent he collected and how much he spent on repairs and could figure in his head how much his taxes were before Smith could tally them.

According to Smith, Landrum never had a lawsuit brought against him or was involved in one. He would sacrifice his own rights in order to avoid one. He did not trust banks and preferred cash transactions. He paid $4,500 in bills no larger than a 10 for a Glasgow home. Landrum refused to live in ostentatious housing but willingly aided his relatives. When a niece in Louisville notified him of her poor living conditions, which were causing ill health for her and her children, Landrum sent his attorney, Smith, to purchase a home for them. After selling a Glasgow business property for $9,000, he divided the cash among his relatives for each to buy a home.

In 1901, Landrum donated land and built a two-story elementary African American school. He provided funds in his will to support the school. A year after his death, the school was named Glasgow Training Academy and several years later was renamed Ralph Bunche School.

The two main provisions in his will were that anyone who contested his will would receive nothing, and that he wanted a modest funeral. However, not knowing Landrum's wishes before his death, his relatives had purchased a casket for $1,200. He was buried in Barlow Cemetery in Glasgow, KY.

Kentucky Death Records, 1852–1953.

Smith, Ed H. "Stephen Landrum, My Client." *Kentucky State Bar Journal* 5, no. 1 (December 1940): 15–17.

U.S. Federal Census (1870, 1880, 1900, 1920).

—*Sallie L. Powell*

LANE, WILLIAM LEROY (b. 1897, New York, NY; d. 1968, Ft. Worth, TX), African American priest. William Lane, the son of James Robert Lane and Alberteena Martin, became the first African American priest to minister within the Roman Catholic Diocese of Covington. Lane served at **Our Savior Catholic Church,** located at 242 E. 10th St. in Covington. In 1917, when the United States entered World War I, Lane signed up to become a camp secretary with the Catholic Knights of Columbus organization. After basic training at Camp Zachary Taylor, near Louisville, KY, he was stationed in France. He was a graduate of Fordham University in New York City and attended St. Mary Seminary in Latrobe, PA. He was ordained in 1933 by Bishop John Swint in Wheeling, WV. Before he came to Covington, Lane served in the diocese of Port of Spain, Trinidad, and the British West Indies.

Bishop Francis W. Howard spearheaded an effort to form an African American church and school as a mission of the Cathedral Basilica of the Assumption in Covington, and in 1943 the decision was made to do so. At one time, this new parish, named **Our Savior Catholic Church,** had both a grade and a high school; most of the students were from Covington and Newport. In 1945, the parish priest at Our Savior was Rev. Henry Haacke, assisted by the newly arrived Rev. William Leroy Lane. At this time and throughout the 1940s, the parish school at Our Savior had 60 students enrolled in grades one through eight. Lane's primary mission was to work with people of the surrounding neighborhoods and to attract converts to the church. He was of great help to the African American children because he received clothing in the form of jackets for the boys at the school from the Eilerman Clothing Store. He sought the assistance of another African American priest from Cincinnati to teach diction in the school. However, Lane was very outspoken on the question of racial prejudice. His efforts had attracted many converts, but it was time for him to move on. Lane left Covington in late 1947.

Afterward, Lane secured temporary assignments in various cities throughout Wisconsin and Minnesota. In 1951, he arrived in the Diocese of Dallas, TX, after a two-year tour of duty as an assistant priest at Holy Cross Church in Austin, TX. Later, he was named assistant pastor of St. Charles Parish in Gainesville, TX. In 1961, Lane was appointed assistant pastor of Holy Cross Parish in Dallas and became pastor there in 1964. At that time, he was one of only two African Americans among about 300 priests in the Diocese of Dallas. His appointment as pastor of Holy Cross Parish made Lane the first African American to lead a congregation in the Dallas Diocese. Lane's ministry flourished in the racially mixed Holy Cross Parish, which in 1965 consisted of 400 families. He retired as pastor because of failing health in 1967 and served as the associate chaplain of St. Joseph Hospital in Ft. Worth, TX, until his death in 1968. He was buried in Calvary Hill Cemetery in Dallas.

Foley, Albert S. *God's Men of Color.* New York: Arno Press reprint, 1969.

Newspapers: Jim Reis, "Our Savior Fills Unique Niche," *KP,* January 17, 1994, 4K; Ted Harris, "School's Pioneer," *KP,* October 27, 2005, 6K.

The Official Catholic Directory. New York: P. J. Kennedy, 1946–1949.

"Rev. William LeRoy Lane." Archives, Diocese of Dallas, TX.

—*Theodore H. H. Harris*

LANGE, JOHN, JR. (b. 1840, Harrodsburg, KY; d. 1916, Kansas City, MO), businessman, philanthropist, and concert promoter. John Lange Jr. was the second of 16 children born to John Lange Sr., a Mexican-Creole freeman from Baton Rouge, LA, and Louisa, a slave born in Georgia. His master, James Shannon, was the president of Bacon College in Harrodsburg, KY, from 1840 to 1850, when he moved and founded what was later known as the University of Missouri in Columbia. After the Civil War ended, Lange worked as a butcher with his father, who operated a dairy and grocery in Columbia. Even though Lange could read, he could not write. He later worked in real estate and became a contractor. One newspaper claimed that Lange "built nearly every road" in Columbia. He helped establish a school for African American children and build some churches in the community.

In 1873, Lange married Ruth Helen Jones. The couple was unable to have children, but after hearing 15-year-old pianist John William "Blind Boone" in a church musical concert, they invited him to live with them and treated him as family. In 1879, Lange became Boone's manager and formed the Blind Boone Concert Company, which included Boone, Lange and his wife, and Lange's youngest sister, Eugenia, who later married Boone.

Lange pushed advertising for Boone's concerts. In 1906, he believed that a newspaper had not promoted his client enough, so he paid $5.00 to each local newspaper to publicize the upcoming concert, which resulted in a sold-out performance. Although there were some tough financial times, Lange and Boone frequently earned around $150 to $200 a night and occasionally made $600 or more a night. They traveled 10 months a year, with Boone performing six days a week.

In July 1916, a car bumped Lange's car, and the offender sped away. Lange chased the driver and demanded a settlement but collapsed and soon died, aged 75.

Boone's career declined after Lange's death. In Columbia, MO, the African American Knights of Pythias named its lodge in Lange's honor. Lange had been a strong financial supporter of the John Lange Hospital, which suffered economically after his death and closed in 1920. Lange was buried in Highland Cemetery in Kansas City, MO.

Bacote, Samuel William. *Who's Who among the Colored Baptists of the United States.* Kansas City, MO: Franklin Hudson, 1913.

Batterson, Jack A. *Blind Boone: Missouri's Ragtime Pioneer.* Columbia: Univ. of Missouri Press, 1998.

Newspapers: "He Wanted to Advertise," *Lawrence (KS) Weekly World,* September 13, 1906, 8; "John Lange Is Dead," *University Missourian,* July 23, 1916, 1; "His Death Was Due to Fright," *University Missourian,* July 24, 1916, 3.

—*Sallie L. Powell*

LANGE, LAURA J. VANCE (b. 1880, St. Matthews, KY; d. 1948, Louisville, KY), first African American woman ordained in the Methodist Episcopal Church. The daughter of Alford

Vance and Mary Humble Vance and the wife of Clarence Lange, Laura J. Vance Lange, in a 1950 publication, stated that she was born on May 11, 1880, in St. Matthews in Jefferson Co., KY. After attending a Jefferson Co. grade school and then a private school, Lange graduated from a three-year theological training program at Garrett Biblical Institute (later known as Garrett-Evangelical Theological Seminary), a Methodist school near Chicago, IL.

On April 18, 1926, in Cincinnati, OH, Bishop Theodore Henderson ordained Lange a deacon; she was the first African American woman ordained in the Methodist Episcopal Church. A decade later, in his retirement year, Bishop **Matthew Wesley Clair** of Covington, KY, ordained her an elder. Lange served several rural churches, such as Chaplin and New Haven in Nelson Co. and Camp Branch in nearby Spencer Co., KY. She also ministered to churches in Hardinsburg and Harned in Breckinridge Co., along with Eddyville, Smithland, and Leitchfield. Additionally, she pastored in New Albany, IN.

Near the end of her life, Lange lived on W. Madison St. in Louisville, KY. On March 28, 1948, she died of a diabetic coma at the black **Red Cross Hospital.** She was buried near Louisville in Anchorage, KY.

Kentucky Death Records, 1852–1953.

Skelton, David E. *History of the Lexington Conference.* Lexington, KY: Self-published, 1950.

—*Sallie L. Powell*

LANIER, SHELBY, JR. (b. 1936, Louisville, KY), **police officer and one of the organizers of the National Black Police Association.** Born in 1936 in Louisville's Limerick neighborhood, Shelby Lanier Jr., a football star for **Central High School** in the early 1950s, graduated from Ohio's Central State College. After a brief stint as a baseball player in the Negro American League in the late 1950s, he joined the air force.

When Lanier returned to Louisville in 1961, despite his college education and experience in the air force, GE and IBM turned him down for skilled positions. He then applied to Louisville's police force. Although he earned one of the 10 highest scores on the civil service exam and was among the few applicants to have a college degree, Lanier was assigned a walking beat in the city's majority black West End. Despite token integration in the police force, black officers could not ride in police cars and were advised to contact a white officer if an arrest of a white criminal had to be made. In 1964, Lanier and George Bell became Louisville's first African American two-wheel motorcycle officers. In 1968, Lanier became one of the first African Americans to attend the Southern Police Institute Homicide Investigation School and the national Crime Prevention Institute and was reassigned to the homicide division.

In 1971, Lanier founded Louisville's Black Police Officers Organization. Four years later, he helped organize the National Black Police Association. Both organizations were designed to combat police brutality and improve the relationship between police and black communities. He remained president of each organization through the early 1990s.

In 1972, Lanier wrote the mayor stating that the police force acted as "judge and executioner" in black neighborhoods. In re-

sponse, the police department charged him with making political statements without the permission of a superior, and he was suspended and transferred to a lower-ranking position on the force. Again in 1977, Lanier was removed from duty because he publicly expressed a political position while on duty. After the black community fiercely protested his firing, Police Chief Jon Higgins referred to Lanier during a television interview as "perhaps the biggest racist in the Louisville Division of Police." After a lawsuit, Lanier was reinstated to the force, and Higgins was ordered to pay $1,000 for defaming his character.

Attempts to suppress Lanier's voice only furthered his resolve to reform the department. In 1986, he was suspended for giving a speech at a meeting of the Ad Hoc Coalition against Racist Violence, where he claimed that Louisville police officers' racism was a legitimate threat to the black community. The following year, he sued the department for discriminating against black officers in hiring and promotions. The city government settled the suit for $3.5 million, and the funds were given to 98 qualified black applicants who had been rejected.

Before his retirement from the police force in 1991, Lanier was elected the president of Louisville's branch of the **National Association for the Advancement of Colored People.** As president, he openly protested the lack of black faculty at the University of Louisville and advocated for equal education for black children after **busing** for racial desegregation was declared unconstitutional. Although he lost his reelection bid for president in December 1992, he remained active in Louisville's political life through the first years of the twenty-first century. In 1996, he ran an unsuccessful campaign against Steve Beshear in the Democratic primary for U.S. Senate. At a 2003 Louisville Black Police Officers Organization benefit dinner honoring Lanier's 30 years of service, Nation of Islam minister Jerald Muhammad summed up Lanier's career, remarking, "In this life, if you fight for black people, it's going to be a struggle, and Shelby has struggled for us."

Childress, Morton O. *Louisville Division of Police: History and Personnel, 1806–2002.* Louisville, KY: Turner Publishing, 2005.

Fosl, Catherine, and Tracy E. K'Meyer. *Freedom on the Border: An Oral History of the Civil Rights Movement in Kentucky.* Lexington: Univ. Press of Kentucky, 2009.

K'Meyer, Tracy E. *Civil Rights in the Gateway to the South: Louisville, Kentucky, 1945–1980.* Lexington: Univ. Press of Kentucky, 2009.

Newspapers: "Black Police Group Fights Brutality by Law Officers," *LHL,* August 15, 1991, B2; "Event Honors Activist, Retired Officer Shelby Lanier Jr.," *LCJ,* October 27, 2003, 1.

—*Joshua D. Farrington*

LAWRENCE, JESSE H. (b. 1901, Anchorage, KY; d. 1966, Louisville, KY), **state legislator.** Born outside Louisville in Anchorage, KY, to Elias D. and Nancy Lawrence, Jesse H. Lawrence grew up in Middletown in eastern Jefferson Co. After graduating from **Central High School,** he obtained his bachelor's degree from Howard University in Washington, DC, and a master of science degree from Indiana University.

Lawrence then settled in Louisville and became active in the city's African American community during the 1930s. He became the owner of Fannie L. Hobbs Funeral Home and served alongside **Charles H. Parrish** as a coach for multiple sports at **Louisville Municipal College.** In 1932, he joined **Rufus B. Atwood** in organizing and promoting the Mid-western Athletic Association, which was composed of Louisville Municipal College, Kentucky State College (later known as **Kentucky State University**), and other colleges from West Virginia and Ohio.

In 1949, Lawrence successfully ran as a Republican for representative of Louisville's 42nd District and became the third African American elected to the Kentucky General Assembly. During his first year in office, as the only African American serving in the 1950 General Assembly, he sponsored an amendment to the **Day Law** that would allow black students to attend white colleges if they had a program or a degree that was not offered by Kentucky State. Almost immediately after the amendment was passed, Bellarmine College, Nazareth College, Ursuline College, Southern Baptist Theological Seminary, Louisville Presbyterian Seminary, and **Berea College** voluntarily integrated many of their programs. Additionally, by the end of the year, the University of Louisville had agreed to accept black applicants to its professional and graduate schools. In November 1951, Lawrence was reelected and continued to represent Louisville's black community through the end of his second two-year term.

Lawrence remained active in Louisville Republican politics for the rest of the 1950s and early 1960s. In 1952, he became the first black politician to ride on presidential candidate Dwight Eisenhower's campaign train and had a private lunch with Dwight and Mamie Eisenhower between campaign stops in Evansville, IN, and Louisville. In 1960, he served as an alternate delegate to the Republican National Convention in Chicago. During the early 1960s, he served as the vice chairman of Louisville's city-county Republican Party and worked alongside **Frank Stanley Jr.** and the Non-partisan Registration Committee in advocating black voter registration. As a leading African American Republican in Louisville, Lawrence oversaw the 1961 municipal election campaign that garnered significant African American support for the Republican landslide in that year's local elections.

Jesse H. Lawrence died in Louisville on January 30, 1966.

"Eisenhower Special Train Gets New Look in West," *BAA,* September 23, 1952, 1.
Farrington, Joshua D. "Standing in the Wings: Black Voters in Louisville, Kentucky, and the Elections of 1960 and 1961." M.A. thesis, Univ. of Kentucky, 2008.
Hardin, John A. *Fifty Years of Segregation: Black Higher Education in Kentucky, 1904–1954.* Lexington: Univ. Press of Kentucky, 1997.
Kavanaugh, Frank. *Kentucky Directory: For the Use of Courts, State and County Officials, and General Assembly of the State of Kentucky.* Frankfort, KY: Perry, 1952.

—Joshua D. Farrington

LAWSON, JAMES RAYMOND (b. 1915, Louisville, KY; d. 1996, Nashville, TN), educator, college president, and scientist. Born in Louisville, KY, on January 15, 1915, James Raymond Lawson was the son of Daniel LaMont and Daisy Harris Lawson. Daniel Lawson, a graduate of Fisk University in Nashville, TN, and a member of the Fisk Jubilee Singers, was dean of Louisville's State Colored Baptist University (later known as **Simmons College of Kentucky**). After James Lawson completed his elementary and secondary education, he enrolled at Fisk University. In 1935, he became the university's first student to graduate with a degree in physics. In 1939, he earned his PhD from the University of Michigan in Ann Arbor.

After the death of his Fisk mentor, Elmer Imes, Lawson returned to Fisk as professor of physics and chair of the department in 1942. By 1948, he enabled Fisk to construct an infrared spectrophotometer and recruited five senior students to remain to complete their MA theses in infrared spectroscopy. This led to the establishment of the Fisk University Infrared Research Laboratory. After working at nearby Tennessee State University from 1955 to 1957, he returned to Fisk in 1957, became vice president in 1966, and was elected Fisk's eighth president and its first alumnus president in 1967. During the tumultuous time of his presidency, Lawson faced student protests and a waning white philanthropist financial base. The financial crisis led to budget cuts, and ill health forced Lawson to resign in July 1975.

Subsequently, Lawson served in administrative positions in the forerunner agency to the U.S. Department of Energy and became director of the National Aeronautics and Space Administration's Office of University Affairs. After several illnesses, he retired fully and eventually returned to Nashville, where he died on December 20, 1996.

Mickens, Ronald E. "James Raymond Lawson." *Physics Today* 50 (October 1997): 128.
Newspapers: "Fisk University Appoints Physicist as 8th President," *NYT,* November 4, 1967, 25; "Fisk Trims Budget, Loses President," *Washington (DC) Afro-American,* July 29, 1975, 6; "The Tennessee Tribune Remembers Dr. James Raymond Lawson: A Fisk Son," *Tennessee Tribune,* February 18, 1997.
Profiles of African Americans in Tennessee: James Raymond Lawson (1915–1996). http://www.tnstate.edu/library/documents/James_Lawson.pdf (accessed December 4, 2013).

—John A. Hardin

LAWSON, RAYMOND AUGUSTUS (b. 1875, Shelbyville, KY; d. 1959, Hartford, CT), concert pianist. Raymond Augustus Lawson was born in Shelbyville, KY, to Lewis and Mary Lawson on March 23, 1875. A musical prodigy, he served as his church's organist by the age of 10. A Louisville minister, **George McClellan,** immediately recognized his talent and urged Lawson's parents to send him to Fisk Academy in Nashville to finish his junior and high school education. Training under Mary Chamberlin, he quickly emerged as the school's most talented classical pianist. He subsequently completed Fisk's college course in music in 1895 and graduated with a bachelor's degree the following year.

In 1895, before his graduation, Lawson was encouraged to perform a concert tour in New England. After one of his concerts, an audience member was so inspired that she offered him a scholarship to attend the Hartford Conservatory of Music in Connecticut. After graduating from the conservatory in 1901, Lawson began his nearly 60-year career as a piano teacher, eventually earning the nickname the Dean of Hartford Teachers of Piano.

In addition to his teaching, Lawson frequently toured across the country and the world. In 1911, he became the first black pianist to perform concertos with a symphony orchestra when he performed as a soloist with the Hartford Philharmonic Society. That same year, he conducted tours in Germany. After attending one of Lawson's concerts, famed Polish pianist Theodor Leschetizky remarked, "Americans generally have technique; Mr. Lawson has poetry." In 1913, he joined Bert Williams as one of the few musicians among the 100 Distinguished Freedmen honored at W. E. B. DuBois's National Emancipation Exposition in New York. Over the course of the following decades, Lawson toured throughout the country, playing alongside musical legends such as Marian Anderson, **Roland Hayes,** and Harry T. Burleigh. Until his death on February 8, 1959, Lawson taught thousands of students in Connecticut, most of whom were white.

Badger, Reid. *A Life in Ragtime: A Biography of James Reese Europe.* New York: Oxford Univ. Press, 1995.

Logan, Rayford W., and Michael R. Winston, eds. *Dictionary of American Negro Biography.* New York: Norton, 1982.

Southern, Eileen. *The Music of Black Americans: A History.* 3rd ed. New York: Norton, 1997.

—*Joshua D. Farrington*

LAWSON, WILLIAM H. (b. ca. 1840, Maysville, KY; d. 1913, Louisville, KY), photographer, artist, and cofounder of the United Brothers of Friendship. William H. Lawson was born in Maysville, KY, in the early 1840s to freed blacks Robert and Maria Lawson. Evidence suggests that his single mother, who worked as a "wash woman," raised Lawson during much of his young life. Because of the limited opportunities offered freed blacks in antebellum Kentucky, he was sent to Ripley, OH, to attend school. In 1859, he moved to Louisville, where he learned the painter's trade as an apprentice of another freed African American named Peter Lewis. Less than three years later, Lawson had enlisted in the 122nd regiment of the U.S. Colored Infantry and was given the rank of quartermaster sergeant during the Civil War.

After the war, Lawson returned to Louisville, where he started his career in "artistic painting and decorating." In 1879, he became the first African American photographer to appear in Louisville's city directory and opened his studio at 319 W. **Walnut St.** Although the studio closed in 1886, he continued to work as a photographer and artist throughout the next two decades.

During the late nineteenth century, Lawson was described as "quite a prominent man" by author **Henry C. Weeden.** In addition to his photography studio and work as a successful contract painter, Lawson was deeply involved in many aspects of the city's African American community. Before his enlistment in the Civil War, on August 1, 1861, he joined seven other black men in Louisville in organizing the **United Brothers of Friendship** benevolent society. In addition to writing the group's ritualistic work, Lawson later served as both state and national grand master of the organization. By 1875, the society had expanded to numerous states and had become one of the largest black fraternal organizations in the country. During the 1870s, Lawson was president of the **Louisville Colored Musical Association,** which hosted large musical events and festivals that drew talented artists from throughout the state and the country. In 1872, at a time when both the Democratic and Republican Parties refused to field black candidates, Lawson ran unsuccessfully for marshal of the city court. He also served for over three decades as superintendent of the Twelfth Street Sunday School.

After 1900, Lawson was employed by the U.S. government, where he served as a storekeeper gauger until his death in 1913.

Gibson, W. H., Sr. *History of the United Brothers of Friendship and Sisters of the Mysterious Ten: In Two Parts, a Negro Order.* Louisville, KY: Bradley & Gilbert Co., 1897.

Lucas, Marion B. *A History of Blacks in Kentucky: From Slavery to Segregation, 1760–1891.* 2nd ed. Frankfort: Kentucky Historical Society, 2003.

Stevens, Albert Clark, ed. *The Cyclopedia of Fraternities.* New York: Hamilton Printing and Publishing Co., 1899, 288.

Weeden, H. C. *Weeden's History of the Colored People of Louisville.* Louisville, KY: H. C. Weeden, 1897.

—*Joshua D. Farrington*

LEE, JAMES "JIMMY" (b. 1887, Raceland, LA; d. 1915, Raceland, LA), jockey. James "Jimmy" Lee began his racing career exercising horses in New Orleans when he was 14. By 1905, he had his jockey license and rode in four races, winning two, at the New Orleans City Park track. Considered one of the best jockeys of his generation, Lee aspired to be greater than **Isaac Murphy.**

His record year occurred in 1907 when he placed first 217 times. However, Walter Miller was his closest competitor with 340 wins that same year. Lee jockeyed under contract for Cincinnati, OH, businessman J. B. "Rome" Respess. On June 5, Respess did not have any horses riding at the Kentucky Oaks at Churchill Downs; therefore, Lee rode as a free agent and won six consecutive races, an exceptional accomplishment. One reporter claimed that if a person had bet $1 on the first race and then had placed each race's winnings on the following race, the earnings would have been $14,932. Another African American jockey, Dale Austin, also rode in the six races and placed second to Lee three times.

Jimmy Lee.

Although Lee was called the Black Demon, his newspaper photo presented a formal portrait of a well-dressed 20-year-old. He was described as quiet, fearless, and professional. Lee told a reporter that the sounds of the crowd were the sweetest sound he had ever heard. In the same year, Lee experienced victory at Latonia's Derby, Oaks, and Clipsetta Stakes. He had another successful racing year in 1908 and became the last African American jockey to win a major stakes race when he won Saratoga's Travers Stakes. He won the California Derby in 1909.

Lee competed unsuccessfully in the **Kentucky Derby** in 1907, 1908, and 1909. He died in his hometown on Kentucky Derby day, May 8, 1915, the day the first filly, Regret, won.

Leach, George B. *The Kentucky Derby Diamond Jubilee.* Louisville, KY: Gibbs-Inman Co., 1949.

Newspapers: *Daily Racing Form,* February 3, 1907, 3; January 5, 1910, 4; *LCJ,* June 4, 1907, 8; June 5, 1907, 8; June 6, 1907, 8; *Louisville Times,* June 6, 1907, 3; *NYT,* March 7, 1905, 7; June 2, 1996, 59; *Richmond (VA) Afro American,* August 23, 1947, 20.

Renau, Lynn S. *Racing around Kentucky.* Louisville, KY: L. S. Renau, 1995, 142–45.

Saunders, James Robert, and Monica Renae Saunders. *Black Winning Jockeys in the Kentucky Derby.* Jefferson, NC: McFarland, 2003.
—*Sallie L. Powell*

LEE, JOHNSON C. (b. 1904, Versailles, KY; d. 1993, Lexington, KY), dentist. Named after his father's employer, U.S. senator Johnson Camden Jr., Johnson C. Lee grew up in Versailles, KY. After receiving $100 from his namesake, Lee set out to receive a better education, attending Meharry Medical College in Nashville, TN, where he studied dentistry. After receiving his degree, he moved to Lexington, KY, where he began his practice on S. Broadway.

One of a handful of black dentists in the city, Lee struggled to make ends meet during the Great Depression. In 1942, he joined the army during World War II and worked as a regimental dental surgeon for three and a half years. After the war, he joined the U.S. Army Reserves, which helped supplement his income and offered additional educational opportunities that otherwise would have been unavailable to him. He served with the reserves for 22 years, retiring as a lieutenant colonel.

After returning to Lexington, Lee resumed his dental practice, working with both black and white patients. His few black counterparts in the city had either left or died by the 1940s, so he was the only black dentist in Lexington for nearly a decade. He was the first African American to join the Kentucky Dental Association in 1960.

In addition to his dental career, Lee participated in several activities to support the local community. He volunteered to serve on an advisory committee for urban renewal, as well as a human rights committee; he also headed a housing commission board for six years. He attempted to create a semiprofessional baseball team after buying a local park, but low interest forced him to sell the property. Perhaps his most visible contributions were as a leader in the University of Kentucky's dental extern program, in which dental school students received professional experience in the basic workings of a dental office.

In 1985, Lee retired after over 50 years in dentistry. Meharry Medical College and the Kentucky Dental Association both sent him awards in recognition of his extended service, and a banquet was given in his honor by associates and friends the following year. Asked for his thoughts on his career, he described his job as a means by which to "relieve people of pain and suffering."

On December 3, 1993, Lee died in Lexington and was buried in **Camp Nelson** National Cemetery in Nicholasville, KY.

Lee, Johnson C. Interview by Edward Owens, July 3, 1978. Blacks in Lexington Oral History Project, Louie B. Nunn Center for Oral History, Univ. of Kentucky Libraries, Lexington.

Newspapers: "Dentist Considers Slowing Down after 50 Years," *LHL,* September 26, 1983, B1; "Dentist Lauded for 5 Decades of Service," *LHL,* August 31, 1986, B2; "Lexington," *LHL,* December 5, 1993, C2.
—*Stephen Pickering*

LEE, MARY SMITH BUFORD (b. 1898, Paris, KY; d. 1975, Stilwell, OK), dean of women at historically black Langston University in Oklahoma. Born on May 13, 1898, to Jessie B. and Nannie (Brooks) Smith in Paris, KY, Mary Smith spent only a short time in her birth state. By 1900, she and her parents were living with her paternal grandparents in Columbus, OH. According to the U.S. federal census, her father and grandfather were both laborers.

Smith earned a bachelor's degree in education from Wilberforce University in 1920. After she married John E. Buford and had a daughter, Mary, she graduated with a master's degree from Colorado State College of Education in Greeley, CO, in 1939. John died in 1944. Mary then took additional classes at the University of Michigan until 1946. While she was furthering her education, she also taught high school science from 1924 to 1945. She then became the dean of women at Oklahoma's Langston University, a historically black institution.

Married in 1948 to Joseph Sidney Lee, Mary Smith Buford Lee continued her role as Langston's dean of women and wrote various journal articles, including "We Train Our Leaders" for the *Journal of Negro Education* in 1950. She received fellowships from the National Tuberculosis Association, the State Health Department, and the Oklahoma Tuberculosis Association. Very active in numerous organizations, including the American Public Health Association and the American Social Hygiene Association, she was also regional director and secretary-treasurer for **Delta Sigma Theta Sorority.** She died in Stilwell, OK, in June 1975.

"Deltas Buy $1,000 in U.S. Defense Bonds." *PD,* April 10, 1942, 1–2.

Fleming, G. James, and Christian E. Burckel, eds. *Who's Who in Colored America.* 7th ed. *Supplement.* Yonkers-on-Hudson, NY: Christian E. Burckel & Associates, 1950.

Lee, Mary Buford. "We Train Our Leaders." *Journal of Negro Education* 19, no. 4 (Autumn 1950), 555–56.

Social Security Death Index.

U.S. Federal Census (1900, 1930, 1940).
—*Sallie L. Powell*

LEWIS, GEORGE GARRETT (b. ca. 1862, Kentucky; d. 1880, Hutchinson Station, KY), jockey. In May 1880, J. S. Showhan's horse Fonso dashed to the front, literally leaving all his opponents in his dust, to win the **Kentucky Derby.** The local newspaper recorded the jockey only by his last name, Lewis. Some sources listed him as George Lewis, one as Garrett Lewis; most just documented him as G. Lewis. At the end of the race, Billy Lakeland, a white jockey, claimed foul, the first in the derby's history. He maintained that just as he was about to pass Fonso, Lewis jostled his horse, causing a loss of momentum. The judges rejected his allegation.

The enigma of Lewis has caused some to believe that he was the brother of **Oliver Lewis,** who won the inaugural Kentucky Derby in 1875. However, the 1870 and 1880 U.S. censuses registered Garrett Davis Lewis in Hutchinson, KY, as the brother of **Isaac Lewis,** who won the 1887 Kentucky Derby. Possibly the three Lewises who each won a Kentucky Derby were not related, but they may have been cousins, if not brothers.

Lewis competed a month after the Kentucky Derby in a race in St. Louis, MO. He fell and suffered internal injuries. Lewis, still a teenager, died the next month in Hutchinson Station in Bourbon Co., KY.

Leach, George B. *The Kentucky Derby Diamond Jubilee.* Louisville, KY: Gibbs-Inman Co., 1949.
Newspapers: "Fonso in Front," *LCJ,* May 19, 1880, 4; "History of Derby," *DRF,* May 19, 1923, 4; "Morgan's Fine Display of Sportsmanship," *BAA,* May 3, 1966, 15.
Renau, Lynn S. *Racing around Kentucky.* Louisville, KY: L. S. Renau, 1995.
Saunders, James Robert, and Monica Renae Saunders. *Black Winning Jockeys in the Kentucky Derby.* Jefferson, NC: McFarland, 2003.
—*Sallie L. Powell*

LEWIS, ISAAC (b. ca. 1867, Hutchinson Station, KY; d. 1919, Chicago, IL), jockey. Isaac Lewis, a native of Bourbon Co., KY, was known for his incredible fearlessness and quickness out of the gate in horse races. He reportedly won his first race when he was only 11 years old. African American trainer Byron McClelland mentored Lewis at the McGrathiana Stud Farm outside Lexington, KY. One of its horses, Montrose, was later sold to the Labold Brothers Stable in Cincinnati, OH, which hired Lewis to ride Montrose in the 1887 **Kentucky Derby.**

Montrose was projected to place sixth in the field of seven horses. In the 1886 Kentucky Derby, Lewis had finished in sixth place, but his experience and McClelland's tutelage jetted Lewis into the lead before the first turn. He won by two lengths. On the same day, Lewis won two separate heats of the Frank Fehr City Brewery Purse. Later in May, he placed third at Latonia, again riding Montrose. He also rode Montrose twice at Chicago's Washington Park, winning in 1888. In 1889, jockey Jimmy McLaughlin rode so close to Lewis that he had to shift his whip to his left land, but Montrose still lost the race.

Lewis competed in four consecutive Kentucky Derbys, 1886 to 1889. He continued his riding career into the 1890s, winning at Saratoga and Hyde Park. In his early 30s, Lewis worked as a groom for the Harlem Jockey Club in Chicago, IL, in 1900. He managed a Turkish bath 10 years later. After a 22-year absence, Lewis returned to Lexington, KY, in 1914, to attend the races at the Kentucky Association track. A year later, his 23-year-old son, Charles, died at St. Joseph Hospital in Lexington and was interred in Greenwood Cemetery. Lewis died five years after his son on March 10, 1919, in Chicago.

Kentucky Death Records, 1852–1953.
Leach, George B. *The Kentucky Derby Diamond Jubilee.* Louisville, KY: Gibbs-Inman Co., 1949.
Newspapers: "Montrose Wins the Derby," *NYT,* May 12, 1887, 2; "Struggles at the Wire," *Chicago Tribune,* July 7, 1889, 13; "Kentucky Endurance Stakes," *DRF,* October 25, 1912, 1; "Crack Racers Are Ready for Meeting," *LL,* September 4, 1914, 8; "Colored Notes," *LL,* March 1, 1915, 6.
Saunders, James Robert, and Monica Renae Saunders. *Black Winning Jockeys in the Kentucky Derby.* Jefferson, NC: McFarland, 2003.
U.S. Federal Census (1870, 1880, 1900, 1910).
—*Sallie L. Powell*

LEWIS, ISHAM AND LILBURNE, nephews of Thomas Jefferson who murdered a slave child. In 1811, in the frontier county of Livingston in western Kentucky, a boy slave was the victim of one of the most horrifying crimes in Kentucky history. On the night of December 16, plantation owner Lilburne Lewis and his younger brother Isham assembled their slaves in a meat house, where, in an insane rage of drunken anger, they used an ax to hack to death Lilburne's young slave, George, and then tried to burn his body. They accused George of trying to run away after breaking their mother's water pitcher. During the slaughter, the first shocks of the great New Madrid earthquake struck, collapsing the chimney of the meat house. That night, a dog carried off the head of the corpse. The head was found by a neighbor a few months later, and the brothers were indicted but were never tried. Lilburne shot and killed himself while he was free on bail shortly before his trial was scheduled to begin. Isham was then jailed but escaped to Louisiana, where he died three years later in the Battle of New Orleans (1815).

Before moving to western Kentucky in 1808, the Lewis family had been part of the Virginia landed gentry. Lucy (Jefferson) Lewis, the mother of Isham and Lilburne, was the sister of President Thomas Jefferson, whose home, Monticello, was close to the extensive Lewis plantations. The Lewis and Jefferson families had intermarried for at least three generations. After the Lewises lost their property in Virginia, most of the family moved to the wild new land on the Ohio River near the mouth of the Cumberland River. They took their old aristocratic pretensions with them, and their indebtedness as well. Amid the crude independent democracy of the frontier, they did not flourish.

After the murder of George, several of the Lewis adults left the area, Lilburne Lewis's children were let out to guardians by the court, and the family died out.

Merrill, Boynton, Jr. *Jefferson's Nephews: A Frontier Tragedy.* Lexington: Univ. Press of Kentucky, 1987.
—*Boynton Merrill Jr.*

LEWIS, JULIA ETTA (b. 1932, Lexington, KY; d. 1998, Lexington, KY), president of the Kentucky Congress of Racial Equality (CORE) in Lexington, KY. Born on March 6, 1932, Julia Etta Lewis lived her entire life on Robertson Ave. in Lexington, KY. Her father, Charles Lewis, labored as a garbage employee, and her mother, Lula (Piersol), worked as a maid in a private home. Julia was employed as a registered nurse.

First a member of the **National Association for the Advancement of Colored People** (NAACP), Lewis later joined Kentucky's **Congress of Racial Equality** (CORE) and became president of the organization. She and **Audrey Grevious,** Lexington's NAACP branch president, become lifelong friends and merged forces to battle segregation in Lexington. One of their initial joint ventures occurred on a rainy day when the two groups picketed an African American neighborhood grocery in an effort to obtain the employment of black store clerks. Later, they formed a sit-in at city hall for the governmental hiring of African Americans. Their combined front of CORE and the NAACP, a rarity compared with most cities, led to a meeting with Lexington's police chief, E. C. Hale. After receiving assurances of peaceful demonstrations, Hale agreed not to arrest protesters unless store owners obtained a warrant, and this helped keep Lexington's **civil rights movement** relatively calm.

A "committed and forceful leader" of marches and deliberation, Lewis was known for her voice and extemporaneous quotes from the Bible, Martin Luther King, the classics, and poetry. She focused on fighting segregation in restaurants, theaters, public transportation, shopping, and education with nonviolent sit-ins, stand-ins, economic boycotts, and demonstrations. In August 1960, Lewis emphasized the importance of the involvement of local ministers and was pleased when the Council of Christians and Jews expressed its support. She traveled the state lecturing on the importance of civil rights and counseled political leaders on the issues. In the winter of 1961, she joined other protesters at the Phoenix Hotel because it would not allow African Americans to register as guests.

Lewis died at age 66 on December 4, 1998. Her funeral services were held at the **Historic Pleasant Green Missionary Baptist Church,** one of the most politically active African American churches in the country. O. L. Hughes and Sons Mortuary was responsible for the burial arrangements.

Fosl, Catherine, and Tracy E. K'Meyer. *Freedom on the Border: An Oral History of the Civil Rights Movement in Kentucky.* Lexington: Univ. Press of Kentucky, 2009.
Kentucky Commission on Human Rights. Hall of Fame 2001. http:// kchr.ky.gov/hof/halloffame01.htm?&pageOrder=0&selectedPic =8 (accessed March 4, 2013).
Kentucky Department for Libraries and Archives. Kentucky Birth, Marriage, and Death Databases: Births 1911–1999. Frankfort: Kentucky Department for Libraries and Archives.
Newspapers: "Obituaries—Lexington and Kentucky," *LHL,* December 6, 1998, B2; "Civil Rights Time Line," *LHL,* July 4, 2004, A8.
Smith, Gerald L. "Direct-Action Protests in the Upper South: Kentucky Chapters of the Congress of Racial Equality." *RKHS* 109, nos. 3–4 (Summer / Autumn 2011), 351–93.
———. *Lexington, Kentucky.* Charleston, SC: Arcadia, 2002.

—Sallie L. Powell

LEWIS, LOCKWOOD (b. 1891, Kentucky; d. 1953, Louisville, KY), singer and bandleader. Little is known about the early life of Lockwood Lewis, an African American, but by 1912 he was living in Louisville and working as a musician. Around 1918, he joined the John Embry Band on alto sax. During the early 1920s, he led the Booker T. Washington Community Center Band and

performed regularly with Louisville's **jug bands.** In 1926, he left town to tour with the Fess Williams Orchestra. From 1927 to 1930, he led the Missourians, a **jazz** band from St. Louis that reputedly "could outswing anybody within earshot." In 1930, the Missourians became Cab Calloway's band, and Lewis returned to Louisville, where he performed with local bands and operated a music studio until his death.

Schuller, Gunther. *The Swing Era: The Development of Jazz, 1930–1945.* New York: Oxford Univ. Press, 1989.

—Brenda K. Bogert

LEWIS, LYDA FLORENCE (b. 1948, Maysville, KY), first African American to be named Miss Kentucky. Lyda Florence Lewis was the first African American to be named Miss Kentucky; she was the third African American and the first from the South to participate in the Miss America pageant. Lewis wanted others to view her for her talents and accomplishments, without race as a factor. Lyda Lewis's pioneering firsts in beauty competitions paved the way for other black women in the state and the nation. She is the daughter of Edward Holt Lewis and Alice Kirk Johnson Lewis and graduated in 1966 from Maysville High School, where she was one of the first African American cheerleaders in the recently integrated schools. She also won awards for her academic work. She attended Morehead State University (MSU) in Morehead, KY, and graduated in 1970. She was the MSU homecoming queen in 1967, the first African American so named from any of the Kentucky colleges that had previously been open only to whites. Since the MSU homecoming queen was selected by a vote of the student body, her selection was a testament to her popularity among her peers; it was also noted in *Jet* magazine. Lewis was the first African American to compete in Kentucky's Mountain Laurel Festival Pageant, where she was named Miss Congeniality. She was crowned Miss Jeffersontown in 1972 and Miss Louisville in 1973 and, competing as Louisville's representative in the state beauty pageant, became Miss Kentucky in 1973. In 1974, she toured with the Miss America United Service Organizations Far East troupe. Lewis signed with the Ford Agency and worked as a model and an actress in New York City during the 1970s and 1980s.

Lyda Lewis file. Kentucky Gateway Museum Center, Maysville, KY.
Newspapers: "She's First Black Miss Kentucky," *KP,* July 16, 1973, 2K; "Black Is Beautiful for Lyda," *KP,* September 4, 1973, 4K; "Lyda Lovely Loses," *KP,* September 10, 1973, 3K.

—John Klee

LEWIS, OLIVER (b. 1856, Fayette Co., KY; d. 1924, Cincinnati, OH), jockey who won the first Kentucky Derby. Oliver Lewis was born in Fayette Co., KY, to Goodson and Eleanor Lewis. On May 17, 1875, **Ansel Williamson,** an African American trainer of Aristides, selected Lewis to ride the horse. The horse's owner, H. Price McGrath, had instructed Lewis to ride fast at the beginning of the race to wear out the competition and then pull back to let his other horse finish first. However, Lewis was so far ahead of the other competitors that McGrath was said to have waved him on, and they crossed the line two lengths ahead of the second-place horse. An American record of 2 minutes 37.75 seconds was

Oliver Lewis.

set in the race, which was then one and one-half miles. Lewis also rode Aristides to second place in that year's Belmont Stakes, but most of the rest of his career was spent as a bookmaker, a legal activity at that time. He created a race-result form that was the precursor of the *Daily Racing Form* charts.

Lewis was married and the father of six children, but few details are known about his life. He is buried in Lexington, KY, in **African Cemetery No. 2.** In August 2010, Lexington posthumously honored Lewis with a street extension named Oliver Lewis Way.

Giles, Yvonne. E-mail about African Cemetery No. 2 in Lexington, September 4, 2009.
"Newtown Pike Extension to Be Renamed Oliver Lewis Way." *LHL,* August 31, 2010, A3.
Routledge, Chris. "Oliver Lewis" in Pamela L. Kalte, ed., *Contemporary Black Biography,* 56:70–71. Detroit: Thomson Gale, 2006.
Saunders, James Robert, and Monica Renae Saunders. *Black Winning Jockeys in the Kentucky Derby.* Jefferson, NC: McFarland, 2003, 13–18.

—*Alice Wasielewski*

LEXINGTON COLORED ORPHAN INDUSTRIAL HOME,

housing facility for homeless children. By 1870, more than one-half of Lexington's population consisted of African Americans,

many of whom were still struggling under a system of economic oppression that included a lack of adequate housing, food, and educational opportunities. Children were most affected by this oppression. Therefore, a number of African American women who were involved in the emerging reform movement of the late nineteenth and early twentieth centuries attempted to help African American children left orphaned, but their goals extended beyond orphans because these women reformers sought to uplift the entire African American race after emancipation.

In 1892, the Ladies Orphan Home Society, consisting entirely of African American women, was formed to address societal issues, which included an increased number of orphans on Lexington's streets. Members of the committee sought funds to establish a home for African American orphans and elderly women in Lexington. **Eliza Isabel "Belle" Mitchell Jackson** was elected the first president of the organization and was the "driving force" behind the creation of the home.

In 1894, the Lexington Colored Orphan Industrial Home opened its doors after the society purchased a brick house and two acres of land on what later became Georgetown St. In its first year of operation, 29 children were admitted. Boys younger than 9 and girls younger than 10 were allowed to occupy the home. Admission standards for elderly women were stricter. Elderly women who wanted admission to the home had to demonstrate need, and the facility served more as a refuge. The Colored Orphan Industrial Home Board, organized two years earlier, was composed entirely of women who governed the home. Women had roles within five committees: admissions, home finding, school purchasing, repairs, and visiting. The school committee was the most important among these organizational structures because education was a central focus in Lexington Colored Orphan Industrial Home's goal of racial uplift.

The educational program consisted of religious instruction, common school instruction, and industrial training. The home's managers and female board members "fully realized that teaching the children was essential to preparing them for future usefulness, thereby enhancing their status in life." The women operated within the parameters of a racially oppressive society to cultivate an educated youth that would be the future of the race, but they suffered a serious setback when a fire caused by a defective flue killed three young children on February 27, 1912.

Fund-raising efforts were initiated after the devastating fire, and a groundbreaking ceremony was held for the new building in the spring of 1912. Operation of the home recommenced in August 1913. Lexington Colored Orphan Industrial Home remained open until 1988, when a decline in the orphan population and societal changes shifted the home's mission toward community outreach. The home then became the Robert H. Williams Cultural Center, named after a generous donor. Williams gave the organization funds from the sale of his home, which led the center to shift its focus from providing education and housing to destitute orphans toward being a community-service agency that focused on educational, cultural, and societal needs of all citizens within the community.

Byars, Lauretta Flynn. *Lexington's Colored Orphan Industrial Home: Building for the Future.* Lexington, KY: I. B. Bold Publications, 1995.

Newspapers: "Three Children Die in Flames Which Destroy Colored Orphans' Home," *LL,* February 27, 1912, 1; "Bodies of Little Children in Ruins of Orphans' Home," *LH,* February 28, 1912.

—*Ashley Sorrell*

LEXINGTON HUSTLERS, baseball club that crossed racial boundaries. Although the origins of the Lexington Hustlers have yet to be determined, on February 26, 1911, the *Lexington Leader* reported that the Lexington Hustlers Baseball Club had met the previous week and elected four officers. The team played its home games at Belt Line Park. The next year, the club expanded, with the Lexington Junior Hustlers battling against the East End Cubs and Jonestown.

In the early years, the Lexington Hustlers competed mostly against Kentucky teams, such as the Mt. Sterling Halls, the Capital City Club, the Jeffersonville Cubs, the Nicholasville All-Stars, the Lancaster All-Stars, the Richmond Browns, and the Paris Quicksteps. The team additionally battled white teams: the Newport Heidelbergs, the Louisville I.C.S., and Cincinnati teams—the Maroons, the Willows, the Ludlow White Sox, the Browns, and the Climax. It lost by two runs to the Chippewa Indians, a Native American team, in June 1913.

A. W. Welch owned the team that year, Charles Benchman served as captain, and Sanford Turner managed the club. Three years later, H. D. McDonsell owned the team, and the *Indianapolis Freeman* described the squad as "one of the best teams south of the Mason and Dixon line." By 1925, the Hustlers played at Dixie Ball Park and Stivers Field against teams like the Moorefield Athletics and the Louisville Royal Giants. The team battled against Frankfort's M. W. L. Giants for a "little world's series."

By 1941, the Hustlers played at Blue Grass Athletic Park on Newtown Pike, and Carl "Butch" Glass managed the team. In April 1945, Ovan Haskins, an African American real estate developer, was one of the leaders of the Blue Grass Athletic Club, Incorporated, which sold stock that supported the Hustlers. About the same time at which Jackie Robinson crossed the color barrier of baseball, **John Will "Scoop" Brown,** the Lexington Hustlers' first baseman and one of its managers, asked his white

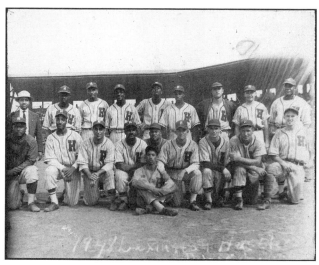

Lexington Hustlers.

friend, Bobby Flynn, to try out for the team. Flynn made the team, and by 1949, seven other white players joined the Hustlers. The *Chicago Defender* defined the squad as the "Team of Democracy." Along with Brown and Flynn, other noted Kentucky African American team members were **William E. "Bunny" Davis** and **Louis Brown "Sweet Lou" Johnson.** The interracial ball club played night games under lights before thousands of fans, and some of its games were broadcast on WLEX in 1949. Most of the players were paid $25 a game.

In July 1950, renowned LeRoy Robert "Satchel" Paige pitched for the Hustlers against the Homestead Grays, which included Walter "Buck" Leonard. Other Negro League teams, such as the Chicago American Giants and the Philadelphia Star, and legendary players Hank Aaron, Willie Mays, and Josh Gibson competed in Lexington against the Hustlers. The team disbanded sometime after the murder of its star pitcher, William "Willie" Swope, in 1952.

"Features of the Week." *Chicago Defender,* July 30, 1949, 13. Lexington Hustlers Baseball. http://lexingtonhustlers.wordpress.com/history/ (accessed September 27, 2013).

Heaphy, Leslie A. *The Negro Leagues, 1869–1960.* Jefferson, NC: McFarland, 2003.

Kelley, Brent P. *I Will Never Forget: Interviews with 39 Former Negro League Players.* Jefferson, NC: McFarland, 2003.

Newspapers: "Colored People," *LL,* July 19, 1903, 3; "Colored Notes," *LL,* February 26, 1911, 6; "Colored Notes," *LL,* June 2, 1912, sec. 2, p. 6; "Colored Notes," *LL,* June 16, 1913, 9; "Blue Grass Capital," *IF,* March 25, 1916, 1; "Lexington Hustlers Start Series Today with M.W.L. Giants," *LL,* September 20, 1925, 7; "Hustlers to Oppose White Sox Today," *LL,* August 10, 1941, 13; "Hustlers' Pitcher Is Slain on Street," *LL,* July 13, 1952, 15; "Local Baseball's Color Barrier," *LHL,* February 6, 2002, 3.

—*Sallie L. Powell*

LINCOLN FOUNDATION, foundation that helped serve the educational needs of students. In 1910, the Lincoln Foundation was established to oversee and manage the assets of the **Lincoln Institute,** a school for African Americans in Simpsonville, KY. After the 1954 U.S. Supreme Court ruling ordering the desegregation of schools, enrollment at the Lincoln Institute began to decline. In 1966, it closed; however, the Lincoln Foundation continued its work. It moved to Louisville and occupied different locations in the downtown area before the mid-1980s, when it moved to 233 W. Broadway. The foundation began to assist students and teachers to address the challenges of integrated education. The Youth Speaks program, developed under its executive director, J. Mansir Tydings, was crucial in promoting understanding of desegregation and other community issues. Students and representatives from all school systems held annual forums and regular discussions on WAVE-TV.

In the 1970s, the foundation began to explore other ways to serve the educational needs of students. Under the leadership of **Dr. Samuel Robinson,** who succeeded Tydings as executive director, the foundation offered various educational, cultural, and support programs to economically disadvantaged youth. It helped place gifted students in academic institutions by providing scholarships. The foundation developed several career-oriented training programs for high school students. It created workshops where, through the knowledge of arts and humanities, students could learn about African and African American culture and history. Because of its leadership in innovative educational programs, the foundation attracts financial support from corporate and governmental organizations.

LINCOLN-GRANT SCHOOL, African American public school in Covington. Lincoln-Grant School was the last in a succession of public African American schools opened in Covington. Until 1932, these schools were commonly known by either their street location or their church affiliation. In that year, after construction of the Lincoln-Grant School building at 844 Greenup St., the elementary school was named Lincoln-Grant School and the high school, located in the same building, was named William Grant High School. The building was commonly called Lincoln-Grant School.

The names of the schools honored William L. Grant, a white businessman and former member of the Covington City Council. When Grant decided to seek the Democratic nomination for Covington's seat in the Kentucky legislature, African American education received a boost. Recognizing the importance of the African American vote and aware of the poor conditions in black schools, he met with a few of the most prominent leaders of the African American Community: **Isaac Black,** a Mr. Dixon, George Durgin, and Rev. **Jacob Price.** Grant made a proposition: if African American voters supported him and if he was elected, he would have the city charter of Covington amended to include a new provision to establish an African American public school. Grant received the nomination, and, as promised, the city's revised charter created an African American school that opened one year later, in 1876.

In March 1876, the Kentucky legislature specifically mandated that the Covington Board of Education, "out of funds in their hand, derived by taxation under and by virtue of the City Ordinances of said City, be and are hereby authorized and empowered to establish and maintain schools for the colored children of the city in such numbers and localities as in their judgment will furnish sufficient educational facilities for the colored children of the city." It stipulated that "said schools shall be under the same control, rules and regulations as govern other schools of the city."

In response, the Covington Board of Education hired John S. McLeod, former principal at a private school for African Americans, as the first African American principal employed by the Covington board. In September 1876, the school housed in the Methodist church on Madison Ave. became known as the Madison Ave. School, with McLeod as principal and Arezelia Ross as the first assistant. By this time, the **First Baptist Church** had moved from Third St. to Robbins St., and this school became known as the Robbins St. School, with Constantia H. Taylor as teacher. In 1879, McLeod resigned and became a U.S. government gauger.

The Robbins St. School closed in 1880 and was replaced by one on land donated by William L. Grant. First called the Seventh St. School, it opened with 200 pupils and a new principal, Sam-

uel R. Singer; Darius Moffett was one of its teachers. Singer was still principal in 1888, when a new 12-year school opened. It included a high school on land donated by Grant, which the board of education named William Grant High School.

On June 21, 1889, William Grant High School held its first graduation exercise. The two graduates were Annie E. Price, daughter of prominent minister Jacob Price, and Mary E. Allen. In 1894, commencement was held at the Odd Fellows' Hall in Covington. This graduation attracted a large and enthusiastic audience. Board of education president James A. Averdick's address was well received, and board superintendent W. C. Warfield also spoke and presented diplomas.

The 1896 superintendent's annual report to the board of education recommended prompt action on the renting of schoolrooms as quickly as possible in the southeastern part of the city. This was done and relieved the crowded conditions at the Seventh St. School. A result was expansion of the elementary school into what was called the Sixth St. Annex. On August 23, 1900, Singer was asked to resign as the principal of William Grant High School and Seventh St. Elementary School, and in September the board hired Frank L. Williams, a native of Louisville, to replace Singer. Williams, who was actively involved in the community, was one of the founding members of the **Progressive Building and Loan Association.** On June 19, 1908, the high school's 19th annual commencement took place at the public library auditorium. In July, Williams resigned his position at the Seventh St. School and accepted a similar position in St. Louis, MO. The next principal was **William H. Fouse,** a native of Lexington. In May 1909, the name of the elementary school was changed from Seventh St. School to Lincoln School. A month later, Robert P. Johnson's one-teacher school in Latonia was merged into the Lincoln School. Johnson became a teacher at Lincoln School, and his students were picked up and transported there by car. William Fouse resigned as principal in 1913 and was replaced by Robert L. Yancey. In October 1914, a night school, serving African American adults who had missed their opportunity for an education earlier, opened at the then-merged Lincoln Elementary-Grant High School. Some Campbell Co. students began attending Lincoln-Grant School after the African American school in Southgate in Campbell Co. closed in 1921. The elementary students there were sent to an African American grade school in Newport, but the high school students were sent to Lincoln-Grant in Covington. The Newport school continued to pay $50 annually per student until the 1955–1956 academic year, when African American students from Campbell Co. began attending Newport High School.

In 1925, the Covington Board of Education decided to build a new Lincoln-Grant School. Lincoln-Grant's principal, Robert Yancey, attended a special board meeting to complain that only $100,000 would be spent on his new school, while $425,000 was earmarked for a white school. The board remained unchanged, and Yancey eventually resigned in 1926. He was replaced by a teacher, Henry R. Merry, who continued as principal until he retired in 1955.

In May 1929, during site selection for the new African American school, the Julius Rosenwald Foundation of Chicago, financer of several African American schools in rural Kentucky, became involved. The preferred building site, on Greenup St. between Ninth and Saratoga Sts., had seemed too expensive. However, the foundation said that it would help finance the purchase and also buy machine-shop and wood-shop equipment for the school. Several hundred citizens attended a special board meeting called to discuss site selection for the new school. Businessman **Charles E. Jones** presented a resolution from the Utopia Club showing that that organization favored the Ninth and Greenup location; the same view was expressed by the Covington Ministers Alliance and the William Grant Alumni Association, represented by **Horace Sudduth.** The board chose the site unanimously, and the new Lincoln-Grant School building, financed in part by the Julius Rosenwald Foundation and costing $250,000, was dedicated on March 31, 1932. At the dedication, the principal, Henry R. Merry, was the speaker of record; the former principal, Robert L. Yancey, extended his greetings as well.

In 1927, Paul Redden came to William Grant High School to teach physical education and to coach football and basketball. His football teams were undefeated and won the African American Kentucky State Football Championship in 1929 and 1932, but football was dropped that year because the school had no football field. Redden continued to coach basketball until he left to become head football coach at Knoxville College in Tennessee in 1952. He had started a winning tradition in athletics at Lincoln-Grant that was extended into the mid-1960s by coach James Brock.

Teachers at Lincoln-Grant stressed having a well-rounded education and fostered a variety of extracurricular activities. Dr. **Clarence Cameron White,** the world-renowned African American opera composer and director, visited Lincoln-Grant in November 1938 and conducted several institutes on music. To keep the community involved, a training session was held in the evening at **Ninth St. Baptist Church** and at the First Baptist Church. The training period resulted in a memorable public concert featuring students and adults performing African American spirituals.

Throughout the history of Lincoln-Grant School, the Parent-Teachers Association encouraged academic excellence and parental involvement, as did Lincoln-Grant faculty, whose qualifications were considered grade A within the state. Each teacher had at least a bachelor's degree, and most held a master's degree or were continuing their education through graduate study at leading universities. After 1932, the school's faculty continued to improve, as did graduation rates and the numbers of graduates attending college. In the 1950s, five high school faculty members held master's degrees or double master's degrees, and one had a PhD. The school always received high marks from the Southern Association of Schools.

The Covington Board of Education took note of the 1954 U.S. Supreme Court decision in ***Brown v. Board of Education*** at its July 1955 meeting. In May 1956, the local branch of the **National Association for the Advancement of Colored People** sent a letter to superintendent Glenn O. Swing concerning desegregation of the schools. In 1957, one African American student, Jessie

Moore, attended Holmes High School. Covington Independent Schools were divided into districts, with the exception of Lincoln-Grant School, and desegregation took place within the districts and on a district-by-district basis. In 1959, African American students living in Peaselburg (a section of Covington) began attending Seventh District School; other African Americans began attending their neighborhood schools in 1961. Some students were moved from Lincoln-Grant to John G. Carlisle School if they lived in the Russell St. area. The board of education never mandated that African American high school students attend Holmes High School until William Grant High School was closed in 1965. Lincoln-Grant School was integrated after it was renamed the Twelfth District School in 1967. In the 1970s, the integration of Covington Independent Schools was finally complete, with the U.S. Department of Health, Education, and Welfare's pressure through redistricting and **busing** of students.

The 1954 U.S. Supreme Court decision affected athletics also. William Grant High School, which fielded only a basketball team, was admitted to the Kentucky High School Athletic Association (KHSAA) in December 1956. For the remainder of that school year, the school was permitted to remain in the Kentucky Negro Basketball Conference, which became defunct when other African American teams were admitted to the KHSAA. In March 1957, William Grant High School was eligible for the KHSAA district tournament. In that tournament, its first, the school's team won the 34th District championship and was runner-up to the Ninth Region winner, Dixie Heights High School. In the eight years from 1957 to 1965, William Grant High School won four regional championships and six district championships; it was runner-up in the district once and in the region twice. The basketball team has the best winning percentage within the region.

After Henry R. Merry retired in 1955, having served 30 years as principal, teacher Charles L. Lett became principal. Lett resigned in 1964 and was replaced by Matthew L. Mastin. It was during Mastin's tenure that Lincoln-Grant School was integrated, placed in the Covington school district system, and renamed Twelfth District School. Mastin left the school in 1973 and was replaced by James K. Burns. The school closed in 1976 and was later purchased by the Northern Kentucky Community Center. Facing fiscal problems, the community center was closed; the building is currently vacant.

Crosby, Leconia Franklin. "A Study of Pupil Marks, William Grant High School, Covington, Kentucky, 1918–1929." MA thesis, Univ. of Cincinnati, 1929, 4–7.

Hargraves, William F. "Comparative Study of the Educational Effectiveness of the White and Negro Schools of Covington, Kentucky." MA thesis, Miami Univ., 1935, 1–20.

Harris, Theodore H. H. "Creating Windows of Opportunity: Isaac E. Black and the African American Experience in Kentucky, 1848–1914." *RKHS* 98, no. 2 (Spring 2000): 155–77.

Jackson, Jewell Rebecca Smith. "A Proposed Course of Study in Speech in William Grant High School, Covington, Kentucky." MA thesis, Univ. of Cincinnati, 1945, 1–25.

Newspapers: "Colored Graduates," *KP,* June 22, 1894, 4; "Colored Night School Opens," *KP,* October 6, 1914, 1; "To Dedicate New School,"

KP, March 31, 1932, 3; "Famed Negro Composer Heads Music Institute," KP, November 30, 1938, 2; "Reader Traces Effort to Build First School for Blacks," KP, July 29, 1991, 4K.

Nordheim, Betty Lee. *Echoes of the Past—A History of the Covington Public School System.* Covington, KY: Covington Independent Schools, 2002.

—*Theodore H. H. Harris*

LINCOLN INDEPENDENT PARTY, political party that sought equal political rights for African Americans. In August 1921, the Lincoln Independent Party (LIP) was formed when leaders of the Louisville branch of the **National Association for the Advancement of Colored People** (NAACP) could no longer tolerate the feelings of political slavery that pervaded the local African American community at that time. One leader, **Arthur D. Porter,** noted that blacks were "in the very unenviable position of being owned by the Republican Party and hated by the Democrats." The LIP was formed to consolidate the black community's political voice within Louisville.

Until 1921, there were understood restrictions on where blacks could go in city parks. Officially, the city government was generally unwilling to segregate parks but in 1921 signs were erected in the parks designating areas for blacks. In 1924, the Louisville Board of Park Commissioners adopted a resolution specifying certain parks within the city as exclusively for whites and other parks as exclusively for blacks. The segregation signs were removed when **I. Willis Cole** and **William Warley,** prominent black journalists, protested vehemently. Then, at the state fair, blacks were confronted with signs designating hot dog stands and toilets "For Colored People." Although this treatment was not unusual, for black community leader and local businessman **Wilson Lovett** it was an impetus for action. Outraged by these segregation attempts, Lovett announced his candidacy for the state legislature. After receiving the endorsement of several black groups, Lovett was disqualified from the election by a legal suit filed by the Republican Party.

After this maneuver by the Republicans, Cole, Warley, Lovett, Porter, and other young community leaders met to form the LIP. Citing the link between the Republican political machine and political corruption and crime in the black communities, along with terrible race relations and insufficient black political power within the Republican Party, the founders announced that on the LIP ticket, Porter would run for mayor, Lovett for the state legislature, Cole for the state senate, and Warley for magistrate. Their platform called for absolute equality of opportunity, racial representation "at the forum where laws are made to tax our property," and a "proportional share of the emoluments of official preferment," and it insisted that they owed no allegiance to either party and could not be "bought or bluffed."

The formation of the party was denounced by conservative black leaders and, of course, the Republican Party. Conservative blacks hinted that the LIP had been created by the Democratic Party to dilute black political power and foster racial animosity. The party was also not strongly supported by local African American religious leaders, a fact that Cole attributed to the political machine.

Besides this verbal opposition, physical abuse was also visited on the party leaders. At one LIP meeting, a black opponent of the party fired a shot into the crowd. The police appeared immediately, as if on cue, and ordered the members to leave the area, claiming that they had incited the disturbance. As party members left, rocks and eggs were thrown at them by a group of black men and women involved in the Protective Aid Society, which had ties to Louisville underworld leader Harvey Burns. The candidates themselves were especially subject to violent attacks; each had his home or office ransacked by opposing blacks. The violence culminated in a physical assault on Lovett while he was waiting to vote. His assailant was allowed to go free, and police arrested Lovett for disturbing the peace.

The LIP was predictably defeated. Porter received only 274 votes for the mayor's office versus 63,332 Republican votes and 56,199 Democratic votes. The other candidates faced similar defeats. Although they suspected that there had been some tampering with ballot boxes, the LIP members were not discouraged. Indeed, they had never really expected victory. Their party experiment was still a success. Efforts to reconcile dissenting black community members after the split allowed each group to better understand, if not agree with, the stance taken by the other.

Warley and his cohorts insisted on changes within the Republican Party before they would return. The Republican Party began hiring blacks for clerical and lower-echelon city government jobs, and blacks were finally hired as policemen and firemen in the city. Although it would be years before the black community could unite more completely to oppose the standard political practices that continued to oppress them, the Lincoln Independent Party had proved that blacks were to be taken seriously in Louisville politics and that they would not continue to settle for less power than they knew they deserved.

Wright, George C. *Life Behind a Veil: Blacks in Louisville, Kentucky, 1865–1930.* Baton Rouge: Louisiana State Univ. Press, 1985, 246–52.

LINCOLN INSTITUTE, educational facility for African Americans in Shelby Co., KY. On October 1, 1912, the Lincoln Institute opened as a result of the passage of the **Day Law,** which the Kentucky legislature had enacted in 1904 to prohibit biracial education at **Berea College.** The college, which had been integrated since 1866, fought the law all the way to the Supreme Court of the United States, which ruled in *Berea College v. Kentucky* that even though Berea was a private college, it was subject to state law mandating racially segregated schools.

In order to educate Berea's black students, the college collected enough money to purchase 444.4 acres of farmland near Simpsonville in Shelby Co. and create what black newspaper editor Julia Young called the "new Berea" for blacks. Although Lincoln Institute offered some college-level courses until 1932, it essentially functioned as a prominent and private secondary boarding school for black students who could not get an education in their home school districts. Vocational education was offered, as well as a six-year normal training course that certified high school teachers.

Lincoln Institute faculty.

Girls basketball team, Lincoln Institute.

The institute's endowment suffered during the 1930s Great Depression, which led to state funding. First, the institute contracted with Shelby Co. to educate the county's black high school students. Then the Kentucky Board of Education contracted with the institute to provide a student teacher-training center for Kentucky State College (later known as **Kentucky State University**).

In 1946, the Kentucky legislature authorized the state to acquire Lincoln Institute. The following year, the institute's governing body deeded the property to the state at no cost. The state selected Kentucky State College to operate the institute.

After the *Brown* decisions (**Brown v. Board of Education,** 347 U.S. 483 [1954]; *Brown v. Board of Education,* 349 U.S. 294 [1955]), the state could no longer operate a legally segregated school. The last class graduated in 1966. The final president was **Whitney M. Young Sr.,** whose son, **Whitney M. Young Jr.,** and daughters, **Arnita Young Boswell** and **Eleanor Young Love,** were among the institute's more distinguished alumni.

Lincoln Institute was replaced by the Lincoln School, an integrated, "statewide school devoted to children who are intellectually gifted but whose exceptional talents are handicapped by their home life and poverty." Faced with external criticisms of management, the Lincoln School closed in 1970.

Berea College v. Kentucky, 211 U.S. 45 (1908).
Ecton, Gayle Webb. "A History of the Lincoln School, Simpsonville, Kentucky, 1966–1970." EdD dissertation, Univ. of Kentucky, 1979.

Faculty women's group at Lincoln Institute.

Hardin, John A. *Fifty Years of Segregation: Black Higher Education in Kentucky, 1904–1954*. Lexington: Univ. Press of Kentucky, 1997, 23, 130.
Kentucky Revised Statutes 166.191.
Wright, George C. "The Founding of the Lincoln Institute." *FCHQ* 49 (January 1975): 57–70.

—*Charles F. Faber*

LITTLE, JOHN (b. 1874, Tuscaloosa, AL; d. 1948, Louisville, KY), Presbyterian minister. After graduating from the University of Alabama, John Little came to Louisville, where he enrolled in Louisville Presbyterian Theological Seminary. While he was a student at the seminary, he founded the city's first settlement houses for African Americans. In February 1898, Little, along with five other members of the seminary's Student's Missionary Society, embarked on what was supposed to be a temporary project in home missions when they opened the Hope Mission Station in an old lottery office at 642 Preston St. as a Sunday school for the surrounding black community. The success of Hope prompted the decision to open a second mission in the spring of 1899, at Jackson and Lampton Sts., serving the **Smoketown** community as Grace Mission. After graduating from the seminary in 1899, Little, who had originally intended to serve in the mission fields of Africa, was persuaded by the Louisville Presbytery to stay on as the director of Grace and Hope Missions, a position he held until his death nearly 50 years later. Gradually, services at the missions expanded. Although Little's primary purpose was to teach Christianity, he also placed great importance on vocational and educational training, as well as basic health and hygiene. In fact, Hope Mission was responsible for Louisville's first public bathhouse for blacks. Thus what started as two experimental Sunday schools evolved into nationally recognized, top-rated African American settlement houses under Little's

guidance. In the mid-1950s, the name of the missions was changed to the John Little Presbyterian Centers in honor of their founder, who had died in 1948. In 1965, the name was changed again when the two centers were merged into one Presbyterian Community Center in the old Grace building at 760 S. Hancock.

Little, who was also one of the founders of **Grace Hope Presbyterian Church** (1910), remarried after the death of his first wife and was survived by his second wife, Bertha (Tarrent) Little, and a daughter and a son. He is buried in Cave Hill Cemetery.

LCJ, October 27, 1948.
Vouga, Anne F. "Presbyterian Mission and Louisville Blacks: The Early Years, 1898–1910." *FCHQ* 58 (July 1984): 310–35.

LITTLE AFRICA, African American community in Louisville, KY. Little is recorded about the community known as Little Africa, and its reputed boundaries have ranged as far north as Virginia Ave., east to Wilson Ave., south to Algonquin Pkwy., and west to Southwestern Pkwy. After the Civil War, the area became known as Needmore after thousands of poor freedman settled on the swampy lands during their northern migration. It was also known as black **Parkland,** and its flimsy shacks (although some sturdier houses existed) and muddy streets stood in stark contrast to the elegant homes and tree-lined boulevards in "white Parkland" farther east along Virginia Ave. and Dumesnil St. By the turn of the century, African Americans living in downtown Louisville began calling the community Little Africa, and the name Needmore was forgotten.

Local leaders such as educator **Joseph S. Cotter** and Dr. A. J. Duncan, the "mayor" of Little Africa, worked through the Parkland Improvement Club to better the community by adding sidewalks and mailboxes and by cleaning and leveling the streets. In 1916, Little Africa proudly celebrated its 25th anniversary after tracing its origin back to the erection of several houses on Virginia and Dumesnil and the opening of Virginia Avenue Baptist Church in 1891. During the festivities, Cotter boasted in a report of 700 homes, six churches, six groceries, and a public school serving the area.

However, by the mid-1940s, conditions in the community, known by then as Southwick, had improved very little. The destitute conditions caught the eye of Louisville officials, who earmarked the area for a public housing project. Despite the clearance of slums and the completion of the $7-million, 650-unit Cotter Homes in 1953, a *Louisville Courier-Journal* reporter visiting the area two years later related the continuing squalor. Claiming that he heard frogs croaking in the muddy streets, the reporter called Southwick "a generally shabby, rundown area with a high percentage of unmade streets, vacant, rubbish filled lots, open dumps, many poor people and many poor dwellings." The addition of the $8-million, 500-unit Lang Homes five years later alleviated further housing problems but did not bring about the neighborhood's turnaround. In 1956, the Lucie Duvalle Junior High School was moved into the area from Ninth and Chestnut Sts. After that time, the community began to be known informally as **Park Duvalle.**

As the area's crime, drug, infant-mortality, and poverty rates escalated throughout the 1960s, 1970s, and 1980s, city officials and federal agencies such as the Urban Renewal Agency continued to pump money into failing rehabilitation and renovation efforts. In the early 1990s, the city, along with local residents, discussed the best way to solve the area's numerous problems. It was decided that in order to revive the community, it was necessary to raze 118 public housing buildings and start over. In mid-1996, the city started a $165-million redevelopment plan. Funded by local and federal dollars, the project involved replacing the public housing with a mix of apartment buildings, duplexes, townhouses, and single-family homes.

Discussions about neighborhood improvement continued into 2013. Federal Community Development Block Grant money funded a $50,000 Parkland Corridor Improvement Study, which included Little Africa. Architects Kristin Booker and Charles Cash worked on the project.

Cotter, Joseph S., Sr. *Twenty-Fifth Anniversary of the Founding of Little Africa.* Louisville, KY: self-published, 1916.
Newspapers: *LCJ,* July 4, 1972; *LCJ,* February 1, 1989; *LCJ,* January 14, 1996; *LCJ,* June 26, 2013.

LITTLE GEORGETOWN, African American community in Fayette Co., KY. As with many Kentucky **African American hamlets,** the origins of Little Georgetown in western Fayette Co. remain debated. Geographer Peter Craig Smith claimed that the hamlet possibly resulted from manumitted slaves receiving land before the end of the Civil War, or landowner George Waltz giving 200 acres of land to former slaves after the Civil War. The community was presumably named for Waltz, and "Little" was later added to distinguish it from Georgetown, KY, in Scott Co. However, local residents believe that the settlement was named for George Washington, an African American who owned property in the area and sold lots to other African Americans. Smith located an 1877 map that showed a G. Washington as a property owner in the area identified as Little Georgetown. Also in the vicinity, three other families possessed small acreages of land, and there were two large estates, one owned by Waltz and the other by a Mrs. Parker. Most of Little Georgetown's citizens worked as farm laborers on these nearby estates. Another version of the origin of the hamlet is that Ned and Caroline Lewis, slaves of the Parker family, founded the community.

Group of students standing in front of Little Georgetown school house, 1865–1940.

Little Georgetown had a church, a cemetery, a school, and a general store. Bethany Baptist Church and its cemetery have been on Parkers Mill Rd. since 1896. The church building burned in 1992 but was rebuilt the following year. In the early twentieth century, the town's one-room schoolhouse held almost 30 students with one teacher, Nannie Faulconer, a white woman. The general store was demolished during the expansion of Lexington's Blue Grass Airport in 1981. Few residents remain in Little Georgetown since the airport built steel light towers literally in their backyards. Noisy planes, fear of crashes, and hopes of financial reward from selling their property encouraged most residents to move out of the community.

Newspapers: "Roots Run Deep in Little Georgetown," *LHL,* January 6, 1983, B1, B2; "Little Georgetown—Parkers Mill Road," *LHL,* April 21, 1999,17.
Smith, Peter Craig. "Negro Hamlets and Gentlemen Farms: A Dichotomous Rural Settlement Pattern in Kentucky's Bluegrass Region." PhD diss., Univ. of Kentucky, 1972.

—*Sallie L. Powell*

LITTLETON, ROBERT (b. 1850, Tennessee; d. 1909, Newport, KY), civic leader. Robert Littleton spent most of his life in Newport, where he was one of the leading African American figures for more than 35 years. He married Josephine Smith of Covington on September 15, 1884; they raised two daughters and a son. In November 1872, Robert Littleton was involved in the organization of the **Corinthian Baptist Church,** located in Newport on Roberts St. In February 1873, Littleton, Rev. Dennis Lightfoot, **Washington Rippleton,** and a delegation from Newport attended the Colored Education Convention held in Louisville, where attendees were informed of the proposed new state law that would allow for public schools for black children. After the convention, Littleton and the other Newport delegates took the next step by encouraging the Newport Board of Education to include African American children in its plans for new schools. The delegation's efforts resulted in the establishment of the **Southgate Street School** in Newport.

Littleton, along with his close friend Rippleton, became involved in Republican politics in Campbell Co. during the 1890s. In August 1891, Littleton, Rippleton, and a group of other black Republicans from Campbell Co. formed the first Republican League Club. Littleton was one of five people who served on its executive committee. In March 1892, when the league elected new officers for the ensuing year, Littleton was chosen as secretary. At this time, the league had 80 members. In May 1894, the African American Republican League was renamed the Crispus Attucks Club.

In 1882, Littleton was employed by the Cincinnati and Newport Iron and Pipe Company. His family continued to attend the Corinthian Baptist Church, and his children went to the Southgate Street School. From 1888 until his death in 1909, Littleton and his family lived at 837 Putnam St. Littleton died at age 59 and was buried in Evergreen Cemetery in Southgate.

Annual Report of Board of Education of Newport, Kentucky. Newport: Newport Printing, 1873.

Newspapers: "First in the State," *Kentucky Journal,* August 13, 1891, 5; "The Colored League," *Kentucky Journal,* March 4, 1892, 4; "Colored Club," *Kentucky Journal,* May 25, 1894, 6; "Newport Briefs," *Cincinnati Enquirer,* August 2, 1909.

—*Theodore H. H. Harris*

LIVERMORE LYNCHING, event that resulted in the arrest of multiple white men for the lynching of an African American. The victim of the lynching at Livermore in McLean Co., KY, on April 20, 1911, was Will Porter (or Potter), a black man who shot and wounded Frank Mitchell, a white man, after a barroom quarrel. Porter was then arrested by the sheriff, V. P. Stabler. The incident received national and international news coverage; except for the shooting and the arrest, the accounts vary. The *New York Times* said that Stabler, concerned for Porter's safety, hid him in the basement of the opera house and locked the doors; however, a mob of 50 men reached Porter, tied his hands and feet, brought him to center stage, and shot him standing there. A second version, reported in several Kentucky newspapers, maintained that the mob took Porter from the jail to the opera house, where they charged admission to his hanging. Those who purchased orchestra seats were allowed to empty their guns into the hanging figure, while those in the gallery had only one shot.

On May 2, the **National Association for the Advancement of Colored People** (NAACP) adopted a resolution condemning the lynching and sent letters to President William Howard Taft, Congress, and Kentucky governor A. E. Willson (1907–1911), requesting that they do the same. After Willson and other whites demanded the arrest of the lynchers, warrants were issued for 18 of the men involved. Frank Mitchell's brother, Lawrence, and two other men identified as the leaders of the lynch mob were separately indicted and tried on the charge of murder. All the defendants were quickly acquitted.

LOCKE-MATTOX, BERNADETTE (b. 1958, Rockwood, TN), athlete, first female assistant coach in a Division I men's basketball program, and the first black woman to serve as head coach of the University of Kentucky women's basketball team. Bernadette Locke-Mattox was born in 1958 to Alfred M. Locke and Nola Gillespie Locke and attended Roane State Community College in Harriman, Tennessee, from 1977 to 1979. After transferring to the University of Georgia, she became the university's first All-American with the Lady Bulldogs basketball team during her senior year and graduated with a degree in education in 1981.

After brief stints as an academic adviser at the University of Georgia (1982–1983) and as a customer service representative at Xerox Corporation (1984–1985), Locke-Mattox became an assistant coach of the University of Georgia women's basketball team in 1985. In 1990, at age 31, she was named an assistant coach of the University of Kentucky men's basketball team by head coach Rick Pitino. This appointment made Locke-Mattox the first woman to hold an assistant "bench" coach position in a Division I men's basketball program. During Locke-Mattox's tenure, the Wildcats had a 108–24 record and a Final Four appearance in 1993.

Locke-Mattox was promoted to assistant athletics director at the University of Kentucky in 1994 but returned to coaching one year later as the first female African American head coach of the women's basketball team. She has served as an assistant coach with the WNBA's Connecticut Sun.

Almond, Elliott. "Pitino Hires Woman at Kentucky." *Los Angeles Times,* June 14, 1990, C1.
"Locke-Mattox, Bernadette." In *Who's Who among African Americans,* 22nd ed., edited by Kristin B. Mallegg, 761. Detroit: Gale, 2008.
Nelson, Kathleen. "Pioneers of NCAA Women's Basketball." *St. Louis (MO) Post-Dispatch,* April 4, 2009, B7.
Plummer, William. "Woman among Wildcats." *People Weekly* 39, no. 11 (1993): 51.
Ross, Betsy M. *Playing Ball with the Boys: The Rise of Women in the World of Men's Sports.* Cincinnati: Clerisy Press, 2011.

—*Jennifer Bartlett*

LOCUST GROVE HISTORIC HOME, national historic landmark. Built in 1790 by William Croghan and his wife Lucy Clark Croghan, sister of George Rogers Clark, the 12-room brick Locust Grove Historic Home stands on 55 acres of the original 693.5-acre Locust Grove Plantation tract six miles east of downtown Louisville. The architecture is Georgian, reflecting a popular style in the colonies during the eighteenth century. William Croghan served as his own architect, and the five-bay house is simple and symmetrical. Most construction materials came from the property, but brass hardware and glass windowpanes were transported from Pennsylvania. Another imported element was the French arabesque wallpaper designed by the Reveillon Studio in Paris, France. It dates back to 1786 and is reflective of the neoclassical revival. Enslaved Africans and other laborers, possibly indentured servants, provided labor for the construction. Some detail work likely was completed by traveling craftsmen, as elements of very similar design are found in other Jefferson Co. houses at this time.

An Irish immigrant, William Croghan briefly served with the British army during the Revolutionary War before joining the 8th Virginia Regiment. He was captured and held in Charleston, SC, where he met Jonathon Clark, oldest son of John and Ann Clark. Croghan later became acquainted with Jonathon's brother, Revolutionary War hero George Rogers Clark. In 1784, William Croghan traveled to Kentucky with a commission to survey military lands. Clark's parents, Ann and John, and his siblings still residing at home moved from Virginia to Kentucky in 1785, and Croghan married Lucy Clark in 1789. They began construction of their home on the Locust Grove Plantation in the following year.

Locust Grove served as a social center at the end of the eighteenth and in the early nineteenth century. In 1805, former vice president Aaron Burr (1801–1805) visited Locust Grove during his travels through the region. In 1806, Meriwether Lewis and William Clark, younger brother of Lucy and George Rogers, stopped at Locust Grove after their famed discovery expedition to the Pacific Ocean. In 1809, George Rogers Clark, aging and in poor health, moved to Locust Grove and lived there until his death in 1818. Other famous visitors included President James Monroe (1817–1825) and Gen. Andrew Jackson, who visited in 1819 during

a tour of western military installations. Jackson later returned with his wife, Rachel. Neighbor and future president Zachary Taylor (1849–1850) grew up on his father's farm, Springfield, about one mile east of Locust Grove, and likely was a frequent visitor. Naturalist and artist John James Audubon was a family friend and did some of his Louisville-area work at Locust Grove. In 1841, noted abolitionist Cassius Marcellus Clay fought a duel there with Robert Wickliffe Jr. Neither participant was wounded.

William and Lucy Croghan reared eight children at Locust Grove. Their eldest, Dr. John Croghan, was an important early developer of Mammoth Cave during the 1840s. Their third son, William Croghan Jr., inherited Locust Grove from his father in 1822. He married Pittsburgh heiress Mary Carson O'Hara in 1823 and resided at Locust Grove until her death in 1828. At that time, William moved to Pittsburgh to manage the O'Hara estate, and Locust Grove was sold to his brother-in-law, George Hancock, who had married Eliza Croghan in 1819. Eliza died in 1833 in a cholera epidemic, and Hancock sold Locust Grove to Dr. John Croghan. John Croghan maintained the property until his death in 1849, when Locust Grove fell to the supervision of nephew St. George Croghan. St. George rented out the property until his death in 1861. Then Locust Grove was placed in trust for his infant son. In 1878, the property was purchased by riverboat captain James Paul. The Paul family held the property for only five years before it was sold to Richard Waters, whose family operated Locust Grove as a general farm.

In 1961, after almost 80 years of ownership by the Waters family, Locust Grove was to be sold at auction. There was much local interest in saving the property from demolition, and the Commonwealth of Kentucky and Jefferson Co. purchased the site to ensure its preservation. Research on the history of Locust Grove, restoration of the main house, and archaeological studies of the outbuildings began soon after. The house museum opened for public tours in 1964.

Locust Grove Historic Home is a national historic landmark, is listed on the National Register of Historic Places, and is only the second site, after Mount Vernon, listed on the National Register of the Surveyors Historical Society.

Bryant, Gwynne, ed. *The Croghans of Locust Grove.* Louisville, KY: Locust Grove Division of Historic Homes Foundation, 1988.
Lancaster, Clay. *Antebellum Architecture of Kentucky.* Lexington: Univ. Press of Kentucky, 1991.
Thomas, Samuel W., *The Restoration of Locust Grove.* Louisville, KY: S. W. Thomas, 1984.

—*Julia C. Parke*

LOGAN, GEORGE LESLIE (b. 1929, Stanford, KY), first African American official in the Kentucky Department of Education. George Leslie Logan was born in Stanford, KY, on February 27, 1929, and grew up in what he described as a typical black middle-class family. His father, James Logan, was a truck driver for a milling company, and his mother, Mary Woodford Logan, was a dietician at a local hospital. After graduating from nearby Lincoln High School in 1947, he attended Kentucky State College (later known as **Kentucky State University**), where he graduated in 1951.

That same year, he was accepted to graduate school at the University of Kentucky. The graduate school opened to African Americans after **Lyman T. Johnson**'s successful desegregation lawsuit in 1949. At the time of his arrival at the University of Kentucky in 1951, Logan was one of only three African Americans on the campus. Working on his master's degree in education, history, and government, Logan encountered racism and resentment from the nearly all-white institution. After buying a student ticket to a men's basketball game, Logan was turned down by the ticket collector at Memorial Coliseum. After Logan protested that he was a student and pulled out his student ID card, the ticket collector told him, "We don't care, you're not wanted." In a history class with Dr. Thomas Clark, classmates roped off a seat and placed a sign on it that read, "For Colored Only." Despite the racism he encountered, he successfully graduated with a master's degree in 1953.

That same year, he enlisted in the air force, where he served as an officer in the Philippines and Saigon. After he completed his four-year tour of duty, he lived briefly in Detroit before taking a teaching position in history and drivers' education at Lexington's (Paul Laurence) **Dunbar High School.** Throughout the rest of the 1960s, he continued to teach drivers' education at Dunbar and Henry Clay High Schools until he was appointed Kentucky's director of drivers' education supervisors in 1969. In assuming this position, he became the first African American professional hired by the Kentucky Department of Education. He remained in this position for the next 20 years. During this time, he also served as the director of social studies in the Division of Curriculum and Staff Development, where he fought to include more black history in Kentucky elementary and high school textbooks.

As a state employee, he was also one of Kentucky's most vocal advocates for a Martin Luther King Jr. holiday. During the 1980s, he persuaded Governor Martha Layne Collins to allow him and others to celebrate King's life during their lunch hour. He was also selected as a member of the national Martin Luther King Commission, which lobbied for a state holiday in all 50 states.

In 1991, as a member of the Lexington Unity Group Redistricting Committee, he played a major role in updating Fayette Co.'s legislative district lines and was largely responsible for drawing lines that ensured that African American communities were represented in Frankfort. In 1990 and 1992, he ran unsuccessfully in the Democratic primaries for state representative for Lexington's 77th District. In 2000 and 2003, he was nominated to the Kentucky Civil Rights Hall of Fame.

Logan, George. Interview by Betsy Brinson, March 14, 2001 (20 B 81). Kentucky Civil Rights Oral History Project, Kentucky Historical Society, Frankfort, KY.

Newspapers: "Black District in Fayette Wins House Approval," *LHL*, December 17, 1991, A1; "Ex-Educator to Seek 77th District House Seat," *LHL*, February 5, 1990, B2.

—*Joshua D. Farrington*

LOGAN, MOLLY (b. unknown; d. unknown), one of the first known female slaves in Kentucky. As with many of the first slaves in frontier Kentucky, little is known about Molly Logan.

Although slaves accompanied Daniel Boone's explorations in 1775, and there is a mention of "a coloured male child of a black woman" in Boonesborough, Molly Logan is the first known female slave to have lived in Kentucky.

During the winter of 1775, Benjamin Logan, who later became one of the state's most prominent early politicians, began the process of moving his family from Virginia through the remote Kentucky wilderness. He eventually established a residency inside a tiny fort named St. Asaph's, near present-day Stanford. On March 8, 1776, his female slave, Molly, arrived at the fort with her three sons, Matt, Dave, and Isaac.

Molly Logan confronted many of the same dangers as other early settlers. On May 20, 1777, she was tasked with assisting two white women in milking a cow outside the fort's gate. Although they were protected by four armed guards, the party was attacked by Indians. Molly successfully retreated back into the fort, but one guard was killed during the raid.

Besides her noteworthy arrival as one of the first African American women in Kentucky and her life-threatening encounter with Indians, little else is known about Molly Logan's life. However, her life and struggles prove that African American women were present at the earliest moments of Kentucky's exploration.

Harrison, Lowell H. *The Antislavery Movement in Kentucky.* Lexington: Univ. Press of Kentucky, 1978.

Talbert, Charles Gano. *Benjamin Logan: Kentucky Frontiersman.* Lexington: Univ. of Kentucky Press, 1962.

Wolfe, Margaret Ripley. *Daughters of Canaan: A Saga of Southern Women.* Lexington: Univ. Press of Kentucky, 1995.

—*Joshua D. Farrington*

LOUISVILLE CENTRAL LAW SCHOOL, one of the first law schools for African Americans. Louisville Central Law School was a major professional school for African Americans. Prof. John H. Lawson, who taught Greek and Latin at Kentucky Normal and Theological Institute (later known as State University and **Simmons College of Kentucky**), established Central Law School at the institute in 1890 and became its first dean. Lawson received his bachelor of arts degree from Howard University and his law degree from Harvard University. Central Law School became the fourth law school for blacks in the nation after Howard University, Walden University School of Law, and Shaw University Law School.

Central Law School was a proprietary school owned by a private corporation and operated by instructors in affiliation with State University and was the only black-supported law school in the country. On May 10, 1892, the first five Central Law School graduates held their commencement at the Masonic Temple Theater. The graduates were Isaac W. Thomas of Hemphill, TX; Charles W. Mason of Evansville, IN; Robert A. Goodall of Church Hill in Christian Co.; and John P. Jetton and **William H. Perry,** both of Louisville. The school was located on the campus at Seventh and Kentucky Sts.

Lawson died in 1896, and Albert S. White became the new dean, a position he held until 1911. In that year, W. C. Brown, a graduate of the school in 1903, became the next and last dean. In

1930, the University of Louisville purchased the property of Simmons University, which later became the site of **Louisville Municipal College.** Simmons University was renamed Simmons Bible College and moved to its present location at 18th and Dumesnil Sts. After 1930, the law classes continued to be conducted in the law offices of its dean. Between 1911 and 1941, there were approximately 100 graduates of the school, including Sallie J. White, the first black female law graduate to be admitted to the Kentucky bar. After 1941, the records of Simmons University Central Law School ended.

Kentucky's Black Heritage: The Role of the Black People in the History of Kentucky from Pioneer Days to the Present. Frankfort: Kentucky Commission on Human Rights, 1971.
Williams, Lawrence H. *Black Higher Education in Kentucky, 1879–1930: The History of Simmons University.* Lewiston, NY: Edwin Mellen Press, 1987.
Wilson, George D. *A Century of Negro Education in Louisville, Kentucky.* Louisville, KY: Louisville Municipal College, 1941. Reprint, Louisville, KY: Univ. of Louisville, 1986.
Wright, George C. *Life Behind a Veil: Blacks in Louisville, Kentucky, 1865–1930.* Baton Rouge: Louisiana State Univ. Press, 1985.

—*Bruce M. Tyler*

LOUISVILLE COLORED MUSICAL ASSOCIATION, African American group that held concerts and trained musicians. The establishment of the Louisville Colored Musical Association in 1867 was made possible by the development of a talented cadre of musicians and a tradition of participation by black churches in musical events. Since the 1830s, several of the most popular string and bass bands in Louisville had been led by African American musicians, such as **James C. Cunningham** and **William Cole.** Stringed instruments and organs were first introduced into black churches by music teacher **William H. Gibson.** Some of the churches held fund-raising fairs with musical entertainment as they struggled to establish themselves in antebellum Louisville.

On June 3, 1867, the Louisville Colored Musical Association held its first concert at the Center Street C.M.E. Church. The program featured the talented Lexington pianist **Julia A. Britton (Hooks).** The first president of the association was Peter Lewis. Other leaders of the group included **Nathaniel R. Harper,** who was musical director from 1871 to 1881; **William H. Lawson,** a painter and photographer who served as president in 1877; and William H. Gibson, who was president in the 1880s. By 1877, the association had grown to over 100 members, and its Excelsior Brass Band provided accompaniment for its choral group, which was drawn from many of the city's black churches. In 1881 and 1882, it hosted two large musical festivals that featured outstanding performers from all over the country. The Louisville Colored Musical Association played an important role in the training of musicians, in providing concerts and music festivals for public enjoyment, and in the raising of funds for benevolent purposes.

Gibson, W. H., Sr. *History of the United Brothers of Friendship and Sisters of the Mysterious Ten: In Two Parts, a Negro Order.* Louisville, KY: Bradley & Gilbert Co., 1897.

Weeden, H. C. *Weeden's History of the Colored People of Louisville.* Louisville, KY: H. C. Weeden, 1897.

—*Cornelius Bogert*

LOUISVILLE DEFENDER, African American newspaper. A leading weekly newspaper, the *Louisville Defender* is the oldest still published by African Americans in Kentucky. It produced its first edition on March 20, 1933—an eight-page issue that sold for a nickel. The founders were Alvin H. Bowman, a Louisville mortician, and John H. Sengstacke, owner of a black newspaper chain then expanding into the southern states whose flagship publication was the *Chicago Defender,* now a daily tabloid. Louisville then had two established black-owned papers: the ***Louisville Leader*** founded by **I. Willis Cole** in 1917, which dissolved after his death in 1950; and the *Louisville News,* founded in 1913 by **William Warley,** which continued to be published sporadically until the 1940s shortly before he died in 1947.

Initially the *Defender* operated with part-time office staff, freelance writers, and commission-only advertising salespeople. By 1936, it had six full-time employees producing 2,500 copies weekly from offices at 623 W. **Walnut St.** (now **Muhammad Ali** Blvd.). In April of that year, Sengstacke bought controlling interest from Bowman and hired as general manager **Frank Stanley Sr.,** who would become the paper's publisher and driving force for the next 37 years, until his death in 1974.

The *Defender* grew steadily in influence and circulation in the following years and became Kentucky's leading advocate for racial justice. For example, in 1942 it published an exposé of segregated army units at Ft. Knox, where black soldiers without barracks slept in tents. News stories and editorials pushed aggressively in the 1950s for integrated public accommodations and in the 1960s and 1970s for open housing, equal job opportunities, and desegregated public schools.

By 1943, the newspaper was circulating 15,000 copies weekly from offices at 418 S. Fifth St. It employed 35 news and business staff and operated bureaus in Lexington and Hopkinsville. Since 1968, it has occupied offices at 1720 Dixie Hwy.

Circulation peaked at 17,000 copies in 1948, dropped to about 15,000 when the paper became a tabloid in 1953, and fell to about 10,000 through the 1960s, when major daily papers such as the *Louisville Courier-Journal* and the *Lexington Herald-Leader* began hiring black newsmen to cover civil rights issues and compete successfully for African American readers. But the *Defender's* clout always exceeded its press run, thanks largely to its crusading publisher, Frank Stanley, who had become majority stockholder in 1950.

Stanley's sudden death prompted intrafamily legal strife, with his oldest son, **Frank Stanley Jr.,** unsuccessfully challenging the stock ownership of his brother and copublisher, Kenneth, and his stepmother, Vivian Stanley, then board chairman. Circulation plummeted to 2,600 weekly by 1985, when Vivian Stanley sold her controlling interest to Consumer Communications Industries Corporation, a holding company headed by Clarence Leslie, *Defender* general manager and executive vice president.

Hardin, John. "William Warley." In *The Encyclopedia of Louisville,* edited by John Kleber, 921–22. Lexington: Univ. Press of Kentucky, 2001.

Kentucky's Black Heritage: The Role of the Black People in the History of Kentucky from Pioneer Days to the Present. Frankfort: Kentucky Commission on Human Rights, 1971.

Newspapers: *LCJ,* March 22, 1983; *LD,* March 24, 1983.

—*Lawrence Muhammad*

LOUISVILLE LEADER, one of a number of black-owned and operated newspapers published in Louisville, KY. The *Louisville Leader* was established by **I. Willis Cole,** a migrant from Memphis, TN. In 1917, he borrowed $50 and founded the I. Willis Cole Publishing Company, which published the *Leader.* It soon became the leading black newspaper in Louisville. By the 1930s, the *Leader*'s circulation was 22,000. It employed more blacks than any other publisher in Kentucky and vigorously challenged racial inequality. Cole described the *Leader* as the "voice of the minority" and advertised the paper by saying, "It Champions your cause . . . it prints your news . . . [and] it employs your people."

Under Cole's guidance, the *Louisville Leader* became a central institution in black Louisville during its existence. It contained vital international, national, and local news specifically of interest to African Americans. At a time when few white newspapers reported on black communities or often portrayed blacks negatively when they did, the *Leader* provided an important venue for African Americans to represent themselves. The *Leader* advertised black businesses, announced births and deaths, and often promoted black unity. The *Leader* even had a "Hometown Correspondence" section catering to the large number of black migrants in the city by carrying news from around the state.

Although its reporting on the black community was central to its appeal, the *Leader*'s uncompromising denunciation of racial inequality made it the premier newspaper in black Louisville. The *Leader* opposed segregation, demanded that black votes not be taken for granted by either the Republican or Democratic Parties, and highlighted the problem of police brutality. For instance, it ran a series of editorials encouraging African Americans to boycott any businesses that "**Jim Crow**ed" them or failed to serve them on an equal basis. In the realm of politics, the *Leader* directed particular attention to the Republican Party, which billed itself as the "Party of Lincoln" while neglecting blacks' needs. The *Louisville Leader* captured the sentiments of many black Louisvillians when it said that blacks received "nothing but promises and hard times" from Republicans. Nor did the Democratic Party fare any better; ultimately, journalist Russell P. Lee reported that Democratic political leader W. W. Wilson stated that it was time for African Americans "to take advantage of the moment, to think independently, and in terms of Negroes, first, last and always." The *Leader* also drew attention to chronic police brutality. After Fletcher P. Martin reported that two white police officers had beaten two black women, he opined that the police should be regarded "not as public benefactors, but as public enemies." During its tenure, the *Louisville Leader* was unparalleled in its advocacy of equality. The paper went out of business soon after Cole died in 1950.

Adams, Luther. *Way Up North in Louisville: African American Migration in the Urban South, 1930–1970.* Chapel Hill: Univ. of North Carolina Press, 2010.

Collins, Ernest M. "The Political Behavior of Negroes in Cincinnati, Ohio, and Louisville, Kentucky." PhD diss., Univ. of Kentucky, 1950.

"Louisville Leader." In *The Encyclopedia of Louisville,* edited by John E. Kleber, 557. Lexington: Univ. Press of Kentucky, 2001.

Newspapers: Russell Lee, "Negroes Urged to Play Politics like White Man," *Louisville Leader,* April 20, 1935, 1; "Cops Brutally Beat Two Women" and "Editorials and Opinions: I Think What I Please," *Louisville Leader,* June 3, 1939, 1, 4.

"Souvenir Program." Broadway Temple, A.M.E. Zion Church, April 9, 1944. Box 13, folder 8, Wade Hall Collection, Kentucky Historical Society.

Wright, George C. *Life Behind a Veil: Blacks in Louisville, Kentucky, 1865–1930.* Baton Rouge: Louisiana State Univ. Press, 1985.

—*Luther Adams*

LOUISVILLE MUNICIPAL COLLEGE, African American college. Louisville Municipal College, a liberal arts college for African Americans, enrolled its first students on February 9, 1931. Raymond A. Kent, then president of the University of Louisville, selected **Rufus Early Clement** as dean of the new institution, which was a division of the university. The school was located at Seventh and Kentucky Sts. on property previously occupied by Simmons University, which continued to offer religious instruction only as Simmons Bible College at another location.

Louisville Municipal was the result of a demand by a coalition of leading black taxpayers and white supporters that the city make provision for higher education for blacks. After a bond issue was defeated in 1920, a second bond issue was passed in 1925 that set aside $100,000 for African American higher education. The school was one of three such liberal arts colleges for blacks established in the United States at that time, and it assumed the role that Simmons University had once played as the principal institution for blacks in the city. The University of Louisville desegregated on the graduate level in June 1950 and on the undergraduate level in 1951. In April 1950, the university's board of trustees voted to close Municipal and terminate its faculty and staff when desegregation occurred. After a bitter controversy, Municipal staff and nontenured faculty received severance pay. Three of the four tenured faculty—Dr. William Bright, Dr. George D. Wilson, and Dr. Henry Wilson—received assistance in securing jobs at other universities. The remaining Municipal faculty member, Dr. **Charles H. Parrish Jr.,** became the first African American faculty member on the main campus of the university when he joined the Department of Sociology in 1951.

Williams, Lawrence H. *Black Higher Education in Kentucky, 1879–1930: The History of Simmons University.* Lewiston, NY: Edwin Mellen Press, 1987.

Wilson, George D. *A Century of Negro Education in Louisville.* Louisville, KY: Louisville Municipal College, 1937, 1941, and University of Louisville Archives, 1986.

—*Nettie Oliver*

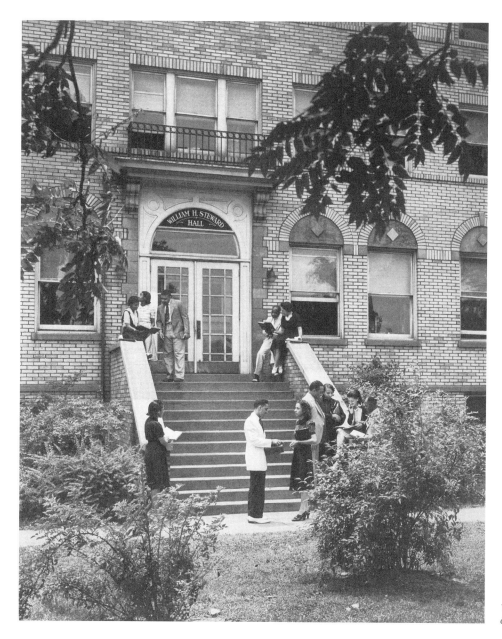

William H. Steward Hall on the campus of Louisville Municipal College.

LOUISVILLE NATIONAL MEDICAL COLLEGE (1886–1912), medical school that trained Kentucky African American physicians and nurses. In 1886, the founders of the Louisville National Medical College applied to the Kentucky General Assembly for authorization to create a regular medical college for blacks in Louisville. On April 24, 1888, the Louisville National Medical College was chartered with its founding members listed as the board of regents.

The founders also served as faculty at the college, and all of them had experience in providing instruction to students on the essentials of medicine and surgery. Those faculty members were Dr. **Henry Fitzbutler,** Dr. Rufus Conrad, Dr. W. A. Burney, and Dr. W. O. Vance. Fitzbutler hailed from Ontario, Canada, and was the first black graduate of the University of Michigan School of Medicine in 1872 Fitzbutler, along with the other three founders, received the charter to operate the Louisville National Medical

College in 1888. With an official charter from the Kentucky state legislature, the college had the power to confer degrees on its graduates. Located on the corner of Ninth and Magazine Sts. in Louisville, the college actually opened in 1886 and therefore held its first commencement in the spring of 1889. The location on Ninth and Magazine was the **United Brothers of Friendship** Hall, but the college later moved to a larger facility on Green (Liberty) St. between First and Second Sts.

Between 1888 and 1912, the Louisville National Medical College trained 150 African American doctors. In 1892, Henry Fitzbutler's wife, **Sarah Helen McCurdy Fitzbutler,** became the first African American woman to graduate from the Kentucky medical school. **Artishia Garcia Gilbert** graduated the following year and became the first African American female from Kentucky to pass the Kentucky State Medical Boards. By 1896, the college had received its accreditation as a four-year medical college and was able to operate a 12-room training hospital. Just one year later, the college enrolled 54 students, who came from 10 different states and Jamaica.

Unfortunately, the tuition received from these students was not sufficient to keep Louisville National Medical College operational. In 1907, the college merged with what was then called State University in Louisville. Five years later, on April 29, 1912, the university closed Louisville National Medical College, and the hospital became the nursing department for what was known as Simmons University, which later became **Simmons College of Kentucky.**

"Henry Fitzbutler: Medical School's First Black Graduate," *Michigan Alumnus* (Ann Arbor, MI), vol. 80 (December 1973): 4, 29.

Kleber, John E., ed. *The Encyclopedia of Louisville.* Lexington: Univ. Press of Kentucky, 2001, 562.

Kletzing, Henry F., and William Henry Crogman. *Progress of a Race; or, The Remarkable Advancement of the Afro-American.* Atlanta: J. L. Nichols & Company, 1903.

Lamb, Daniel Smith. *Howard University Medical Department, Washington, D.C.: A Historical, Biographical, and Statistical Souvenir.* Washington, DC: Medical Faculty of Howard University, 1900.

Lewis, Alvin Fayette. *History of Higher Education in Kentucky.* Washington, DC: Government Printing Office, 1899.

—*Sheila Pressley*

LOUISVILLE RIOT OF 1968, violent reaction to police misconduct in the West End. On May 8, 1968, police officers in Louisville's predominantly black West End pulled over a car that matched the description of a vehicle used in an earlier burglary. The owner of the car, a black schoolteacher named Charles Thomas, cooperated with police, but officers called in backup after the arrival of a large crowd. One of the officers called in for support, Michael A. Clifford, scuffled with Manfred Reid, a friend of Thomas's, and both Reid and Thomas were arrested. Although the crowd was angry with the situation, it dispersed peacefully.

In the next three weeks, the incident fed into increased resentment toward the state of racial relations in the city. Mayor Kenneth Schmied suspended Clifford for his mishandling of the situation, but the Civil Service Board overturned the suspension after a hearing, at which neither Reid nor Thomas appeared. The Black Unity League of Kentucky and the Southern Conference Educational Fund protested the decision and called for a rally to be held on May 27. At the rally, leaders in the Black Power movement issued calls for black unity and resistance to white oppression before James Cortez, a member of the Student Nonviolent Coordinating Committee who claimed to be a personal friend of Stokely Carmichael, falsely declared that white officials were keeping Carmichael from entering Louisville to deliver a speech.

The rally dissolved without incident despite angry reactions to Cortez's claim, but a few youths began throwing bottles and other items from the roofs of buildings. When police cars immediately arrived on the scene and an officer exited his car with his weapon drawn, a riot broke out; rioters broke windows and looted various businesses while the police made a series of arrests. Tensions escalated again after Governor Louie B. Nunn authorized the use of six units of the National Guard in keeping the peace. More effective was the employment of 40 black marshals in some

of the worst trouble spots, as well as appeals by local black leaders to end the violence. With the exception of a few flare-ups, most of the conflict had ended by the weekend, and the riot was effectively concluded with the pullout of National Guard in the first days of June.

The final toll of the riots included over $250,000 in property damage and the deaths of two bystanders, 14-year-old James Groves and 19-year-old Matthias Washington Browder. Over 400 people were arrested in connection with the riots; all those arrested in the West End were black. In the aftermath of the conflict, authorities attempted to eliminate continued black activism through the prosecution of the **Black Six**—Cortez, Reid, Walter "Pete" Crosby, Sam Hawkins, Robert Sims, and Ruth Bryant—for an alleged conspiracy to dynamite an oil refinery and other businesses as an act of black terrorism. The trial of the Black Six, however, resulted in an acquittal because of lack of evidence and succeeded only in providing additional fuel for leaders of the **civil rights movement** in Louisville.

Fosl, Catherine, and Tracy E. K'Meyer. *Freedom on the Border: An Oral History of the Civil Rights Movement in Kentucky.* Lexington: Univ. Press of Kentucky, 2009.

K'Meyer, Tracy E. *Civil Rights in the Gateway to the South: Louisville, Kentucky, 1945–1980.* Lexington: Univ. Press of Kentucky, 2009.

Newspapers: "Rioting Breaks Out in Louisville; State Police, Guard Called to Help," *LCJ*, May 28, 1968; "Witnesses Say Disorder Was Sparked by Rumor," *LCJ*, May 28, 1968; "Price Tag of Riot Placed at $200,000 First Day," *LCJ*, May 29, 1968; "Riots Flare Anew in Louisville's West End," *LCJ*, May 29, 1968, 1; "17 Treated at Hospital, 4 with Gunshot Wounds," *LCJ*, May 29, 1968.

Williams, Kenneth H. "'Oh Baby . . . It's Really Happening': The Louisville Race Riot of 1968." *Kentucky History Journal* 3 (1988): 48–64.

—*Stephen Pickering*

LOUISVILLE URBAN LEAGUE, association that helped African American businesses and workers. When African Americans began migrating from rural areas to urban communities after the Civil War, they encountered an industrial world for which they were unprepared. In Louisville, a group of progressive African American women became involved in the Big Brothers / Big Sisters program as a way of providing guidance and role models within the black community.

In 1920, the Louisville Urban League emerged and became a member agency of the Community Chest. Incorporated in August 1921, it was initially known as the Urban League of Louisville for Social Service among Negroes and later as the Louisville Branch of the **National Urban League** before it became the Louisville Urban League. It was started with $1,000 raised at a public dinner. Elwood Street, serving as temporary chairman, appointed a five-person committee to create the framework for the local Urban League. Ehner S. Carter became the first executive secretary (1921–1924).

J. M. Ragland was the second executive secretary (1924–1929), and J. A. Thomas was the third (1929–1943). During these early years, the league opened up new opportunities in local businesses for African Americans, helped create two junior high schools for blacks, and coordinated an award-winning effort though the Negro Health Week campaigns to improve the health of black families. **Louisville Municipal College** grew out of a bond issue led by the league during this period. By the end of the term of Robert E. Black, the fourth executive secretary (1943–1946), African Americans held positions on the Municipal Housing Commission, the Louisville Free Public Library Board of Trustees, the defense council and subcommittee, and the mayor's interracial committee.

When Charles T. Steele assumed leadership of the league (1946–1970), his title changed from executive secretary to executive director. During his tenure, former state representative **Mae Street Kidd** organized the Louisville Urban League Guild in 1948. It was the second guild formed in any of the affiliates nationwide. Guilds were organized as local information departments for the Urban League. Members identified particular areas of concern and aided the central organization in fund-raising and educational programs (always open to both sexes). In 1964, the league was the first agency in the Louisville area to develop and win a $210,000 Department of Labor grant for on-the-job training of disadvantaged workers. The grant, which preceded the National Urban League's involvement in on-the-job training, was a significant factor in integrating Louisville's nonunion workforce.

Under the leadership of **Arthur M. Walters** (1970–1987), the Louisville Urban League became the first affiliate to select a female chairperson of the board, Thelma Clemmons. It created a personnel policy manual and an organization chart, with a job description for each function, which became a model for the National Urban League.

In the late 1970s, the league established an affirmative-action-monitoring program directed to the downtown Galleria project, designed as part of the downtown revitalization effort. The project won one of five national awards based on the involvement of racial minorities and women in the workforce, the subcontractors, and the owned or operated businesses within the completed Galleria, as well as on the amount of money awarded to the project. Named an agent for affirmative action by the city of Louisville, the league held official status and negotiated with management and organized labor to include minorities in the Galleria project workforce. It instituted a preapprenticeship program permitting those involved to spend two nights a week learning educational basics. This allowed unskilled workers to move to the skilled labor force while earning income during their training.

In 1985, the league relocated its headquarters to the entire third floor of Lyles Mall. Approval also was given to plan and implement a capital campaign to raise $1.2 million to purchase that space. Benjamin K. Richmond assumed leadership in June 1987 under the new title of president and CEO. His first responsibility was to revive the capital campaign. Having its own permanent location would be a first for an Urban League affiliate. Corporate Louisville contributed about 90 percent of the money needed.

After construction of the new building (which was not at the Lyles Mall site) at 1535 W. Broadway (at the corner of 16th St.), the league purchased new state-of-the-art personal computer equipment and expanded its computer and office skills training program to include classes relating to telemarketing. From late 1989 to 1991, the league offered a Telemarketing Training Institute. Most graduates were hired to work in the telemarketing operation at Humana Inc. In 1992, the training curriculum was again expanded to include entry-level customer service skills for the retail and fast-food markets.

Attempting to avoid a local outbreak similar to the 1992 riots among young African Americans in Los Angeles, Louisville mayor Jerry Abramson assembled a group of African American civic leaders to discuss preventive measures. The group determined that employment assistance for young adults was needed. With support from the mayor and the city and in partnership with the local Private Industry Council, the league developed the Mayor's Urban Employment Program, which primarily targeted at-risk African American males between the ages of 16 and 25. To guide them toward productive citizenship, these young men were given life skills training as well as other support services and were then found suitable employment.

In 1993 REBOUND Inc. (Rebuilding Our Urban Neighborhood Dwellings) was created to increase community development and neighborhood revitalization. REBOUND is a nonprofit, cooperative effort among the Louisville Urban League, the city of Louisville, and Main Street Realty, the private real estate firm of David A. Jones. Its goal was to build and sell 90 quality homes in the historic Russell neighborhood. REBOUND became one of the first single-family housing projects to act as a cornerstone in a neighborhood revitalization project involving diverse housing.

Wright, George C. *Life Behind a Veil: Blacks in Louisville, Kentucky, 1865–1930.* Baton Rouge: Louisiana State Univ. Press, 1985.

—*Hope L. Hollenbeck*

LOVE, ELEANOR YOUNG (b. 1922, Lincoln Ridge, KY; d. 2006, Louisville, KY), first African American administrator at the University of Louisville. Eleanor Young Love was destined to be an educator as the daughter of **Whitney M. Young Sr.** and **Laura Ray Young.** She was born on the campus of **Lincoln Institute** in Lincoln Ridge, an area near Simpsonville, KY, where her father was the school's president. After completing her high school education at Lincoln Institute, Eleanor, like her older siblings, **Arnita Young Boswell** and **Whitney M. Young Jr.,** graduated from Kentucky State College, now **Kentucky State University,** with a degree in English in 1944. Two years later, she earned her library science degree at what is now Clark Atlanta University. She earned her master's and doctoral degrees in education at the University of Louisville (UL) and the University of Illinois, respectively.

From 1946 to 1951, she was a librarian at Florida Agricultural and Mechanical University before becoming the head librarian at Fairleigh Dickinson's Bergen Junior College campus. In 1953, at the request of her father, Eleanor returned home, where for the next 14 years she served Lincoln Institute first as librarian, then as a counselor, and finally as principal. During this time, she continued to pursue other degrees. In an interview, she revealed, "Every time that Daddy needed something at his institution, I went back to school and got another degree." Then she accepted the required position at Lincoln Institute.

Eleanor began her tenure at the University of Louisville as director of the Upward Bound Program in 1967. She also worked as the administrative assistant and director of student personnel before becoming UL's first black assistant dean in 1969. In 1993, after 25 years at UL and having earned the rank of full professor, Eleanor retired from the Educational Psychology Department.

Retirement freed Love to continue her counseling service for the Human Development Company and to pursue other interests. As president of the Lincoln Foundation Board of Trustees, she maintained her involvement with black youth, rewarding gifted, impoverished students with four-year college scholarships. In the community, she served as chairperson of the Human Relations Commission of Louisville and Jefferson County. She was an active member of the Louisville Public Library Task Force and the Westwood Presbyterian Church.

Socially, she belonged to many organizations, including **Alpha Kappa Alpha Sorority,** Project Women, M.O.L.E.S., and the Kentucky State University National Alumni Association. For her community involvement, she received the Governor's Appreciation Citation twice and was named a Kentucky Colonel by two different Kentucky governors. Additionally, she received the Urban League's Equality Award, the **National Association for the Advancement of Colored People** Worthington Award twice, the YMCA Black Achievers Award, the University of Louisville Minority Affairs Award twice, and the Kentucky State University Outstanding Alumni Award, among other awards, commendations, citations, and honors.

Dr. Eleanor Young Love died on July 14, 2006. **A. D. Porter** and Sons Funeral Home handled the funeral arrangements, and she was buried in Resthaven Memorial Park in Louisville.

"Love, Eleanor Young." In *Who's Who among African Americans*, 22nd ed., edited by Kristin B. Mallegg, 767. Detroit: Gale, 2008.

McDaniel, Karen Cotton. "Eleanor Young Love." In *Notable Black American Women*, vol. 2, edited by Jessie Carney Smith, 415–17. Detroit: Gale Research, 1996.

"Obituaries: Dr. Eleanor Young Love." *LCJ*, July 18, 2006.

Outstanding Alumni: Centennial Booklet. Frankfort: Kentucky State Univ., 1986.

—*Karen Cotton McDaniel*

LOVETT, WILSON STEPHEN (b. 1885, New York; d. 1951, Parma, MI), businessman and political leader. Wilson Stephen Lovett was raised by his widowed mother, Annie Lovett, in Pennsylvania, where he also received his commercial training at Dickinson College in Carlisle, PA. By 1910, he worked as a clerk and stenographer at the Tuskegee Institute in Alabama. Frustrated by the judgmental authority that the elder Tuskegee men held over the younger employees, Lovett left the institution without a job and only $2.50 in his pocket.

By 1911, Lovett worked as an agent for Atlanta Mutual Insurance in Louisville, KY. A few years later, in his early 30s, he was agency director of Louisville's Standard Life Insurance Company with his office at the **Knights of Pythias** Temple on Chestnut St. He became active in the **National Association for the Advancement of Colored People** and connected with other African American leaders in Louisville.

In 1920, Lovett, along with **A. E. Meyzeek, William Warley,** J. A. C. Lattimore, and Bishop **George C. Clement,** challenged a million-dollar bond proposal for the upgrade of the University of Louisville and requested assurances that funds would be used for black education. School officials ignored the request, and

the bond was defeated by 4,000 votes. During this time, Lovett also announced his candidacy for the Louisville Board of Education. He voiced the need for someone to protect the scholastic interests of Louisville's African Americans. Lovett's plan was to single-shoot him into office by having all black voters vote only for him and not divide their votes among the other three white candidates, and it caused an uproar among many whites. White political leaders blocked the plan by having one candidate drop out of the race; the Republicans then endorsed the Democratic candidate. Lovett later tried to run for the state legislature but was disqualified by a legal suit filed by the Republican Party.

Also, in 1920, Lovett headed the opening of the first black-owned bank in Kentucky, Louisville's **First Standard Bank.** The bank was capitalized at $100,000, with a surplus of $10,000. The entire stock was sold to African Americans in less than six months. The bank invested in property, a realty company, and two loan companies—the Standard Building and Loan Association and the Parkway Building and Loan Association.

In 1935, Lovett left Kentucky after he resigned as vice president and treasurer of the Supreme Liberty Life Insurance Company. He worked for various insurance companies in Detroit, MI, and Chicago, IL. He died in a car wreck in Parma, MI, in 1951.

Newspapers: "Negroes May Put Black on City Education Board," *Mt. Sterling Advocate,* October 12, 1920, 6; "Congratulations Fellow Kentuckians," *St. Paul (MN) Appeal,* December 18, 1920, 2.

U.S. Federal Census (1900, 1910, 1920, 1930).

World War I Draft Registration Cards, 1917–1918.

Wright, George C. *Life Behind a Veil: Blacks in Louisville, Kentucky, 1865–1930.* Baton Rouge: Louisiana State Univ. Press, 1985.

—*Sallie L. Powell*

LUNDERMAN, CHARLES J., JR. (b. 1922, Paducah, KY; d. 1973, Louisville, KY), civil rights activist and attorney in Louisville. Charles J. Lunderman was born in Paducah on December 26, 1922. After graduating from high school, he attended Kentucky State College (later known as **Kentucky State University**) in Frankfort for three years until he enlisted in the army in 1943. After he completed his tour of duty, Lunderman obtained his law degree from Lincoln University in St. Louis in 1949. He immediately returned to Kentucky, establishing a practice in Louisville and working on civil rights lawsuits. As a member of the **National Association for the Advancement of Colored People**'s Legal Redress Committee, he was heavily involved in the first lawsuit that ultimately led to the desegregation of the city's swimming pools.

His connections with the Louisville NAACP during the 1950s, however were brief because of his affiliation with the local Republican Party. Lunderman and fellow attorney Bishop **C. Ewbank Tucker** felt that the local NAACP was quickly becoming a "fifth wheel of the Democratic Party" after its support for Adlai Stevenson in the 1952 presidential election. That same year, he severed ties with the NAACP and deepened his ties with the Republican establishment. He soon became the cochair of the Louisville Young People for Eisenhower organization.

His association with local Republicans eventually led to his appointment as an assistant city attorney and membership on the Jefferson County Republican Party Executive Committee during the 1960s. During this time, he reestablished his ties with the NAACP and even served as the organization's president for a brief period.

Despite his ties to powerful local whites, Lunderman never quit fighting for civil rights in Louisville. In 1968, following a Louisville riot in which a black youth was shot by police, Republican mayor Kenneth A. Schmied responded by calling for the establishment of a committee to determine the causes of the riot. Lunderman, one of the few remaining African American figures in the city's Republican Party, immediately joined with the NAACP and called for a boycott of the mayor's committee. Lunderman said that if the mayor "really wants to know the cause of the riot . . . all he had to do was read the paper," and he noted that the black community wanted action and justice, not simply debate on a committee.

Similarly, in the late 1960s, Lunderman helped organize the Jefferson County Clean Air Committee, a group that opposed pollution that affected the residents of the predominantly black West End and Shively neighborhoods. Lunderman noted that nearby industrial plants were pumping over 11 tons of toxic gases into the neighborhoods on a daily basis.

Charles Lunderman's ties with the Republican Party ensured him power and a voice in Louisville politics, but they never moderated his views on civil rights. During his tenure as a powerful attorney and Republican committeeman, Lunderman pressed for integrated public accommodations, open housing, an end to police brutality, and clean air for the city's black residents. He died in Louisville on September 24, 1973.

K'Meyer, Tracy E. *Civil Rights in the Gateway to the South: Louisville, Kentucky, 1945–1980.* Lexington: Univ. Press of Kentucky, 2009.
Newspapers: "Call for Boycott of Mayor's Group," *Middlesboro Daily News,* June 4, 1968, 2; "Black History Month," *LCJ,* February 13, 2009, B3.

—*Joshua D. Farrington*

LYLES, LEONARD "LENNY" EVERETT (b. 1936, Nashville, TN; d. 2011, Louisville, KY), collegiate and professional football player and businessman. Born on January 26, 1936, in Nashville, TN, Leonard "Lenny" Everett Lyles grew up with his mother, Alice, and his sister, Doris, in Louisville, KY. He graduated from **Central High School.** In 1954, as a running back, the 6-feet-2, 202-pound Lyles was one of the first African Americans to cross the color barrier of the University of Louisville Cardinals football team and also ran track. Between 1954 and 1957, he scored 42 touchdowns, a school record, and became the first Cardinals player to rush for more than 1,000 yards in a season.

Known as the "fastest man in football," Lyles was selected 11th overall by the Baltimore Colts in the 1958 National Football League draft. He was initially a kickoff returner and later switched to right cornerback. He was traded to the San Francisco 49ers after his first year but returned to the Colts on waivers in 1961. Lyles played in the 1966 Pro Bowl and was in the starting lineup during the Colts' loss in Super Bowl III in 1969. During his final two seasons, he was also Baltimore's defensive captain. Altogether, Lyles returned 81 kicks for 2,161 yards and 3 touchdowns. Playing most of his career on defense, he also intercepted 16 passes and recovered 13 fumbles.

In 1969, Lyles retired and took a position as training coordinator for Brown and Williamson Tobacco Corporation. He owned several businesses, including a shopping center and a tavern in Louisville. He also developed the Lyles Mall on West Broadway and helped revitalize his home neighborhood of **Smoketown.** Living in Jefferson Co., KY, with his wife and three sons, he worked with several charities and served as a motivational speaker to youth.

On October 12, 2000, the University of Louisville dedicated a statue of Lenny Lyles in Cardinal Park. **Edward Hamilton Jr.** was the sculptor. Lyles died at age 75 on November 20, 2011. His body was cremated, and his memorial was held in January 2012.

"Ed Hamilton, Sculptor: Images from the Dedication Ceremony of the Lenny Lyles Statue." http://www.edhamiltonworks.com/lyles_dedication.htm (accessed July 26, 2013).
Newspapers: "Lenny Lyles Inks Pact with Colts, Set for Camp," *BAA,* May 26, 1964; "Lenny Lyles Is Trying to Instill Unity, Understanding in Others," *Lewiston (ID) Morning Tribune,* January 26, 1972; "Lenny Lyles Scores as Entrepreneur," *Black Enterprise,* April 1977; "Lenny Lyles (1936–2011): 'He Was Simply the Best,'" *LCJ,* November 22, 2011, C1; "Celebrating Lenny Lyles: Memorial Honors U of L Football Great," *LCJ,* January 26, 2012.

—*Kevin Hogg*

LYRIC THEATER, major business enterprise that provided entertainment opportunities. In December 1948, the Lyric Theater opened its doors as a movie house on the corner of **Deweese** and E. Third Sts. in segregated Lexington, KY. Built at a cost of $250,000 by white entrepreneurs, the Art Deco building provided air-conditioned entertainment. African American George Walston Jr., age 27, managed the enterprise along with his assistant manager, John Twyman, age 32. Although Lexington's other white-owned theaters allowed African Americans only in their balconies, the Lyric offered open seating to everyone. People from Lexington and the surrounding counties enjoyed not only movies but also live entertainment in the 924-seat theater.

Performers such as Count Basie, Duke Ellington, Cab Calloway, Jackie "Moms" Mabley, Ray Charles, Redd Foxx, Ike and Tina Turner, and countless others generally provided two shows in one night. Although the acts were paid $500, the admission was under $1, and the Lyric was frequently sold out. This "Mecca of Black entertainment" became a cultural icon with its children's Christmas parties, vaudeville acts, concerts, and pageants. In April 1950, **Alpha Kappa Alpha Sorority** hosted a fashion show including Marva Louis, the former wife of heavyweight champion boxer Joe Louis, modeling her own clothes. Proceeds from the event went to scholarships for African American women. Small black-owned businesses operated in and around the theater, including an ice cream parlor owned by **Dunbar High School**'s coach, **Sanford Roach.** In October 1960, the police raided the theater and charged two female impersonators, Verrano Willis and William Campbell Jr. (stage names Tuesday Taylor and Princess De Carlo), and the Lyric's manager, Donald Garrison, under a city lewdness ordinance.

Integration in the 1960s spurred the downfall of the Lyric Theater and the African American businesses around it. The theater officially closed in April 1963, and the entertainment arena was

Lyric Theater, ca. 1950.

condemned in 1974. Over a decade later, the dilapidated, steel-beamed concrete structure seemed doomed for the wrecking ball when the Lexington Outreach Ministry purchased it for $17,000. The ministry planned to open a mission for street people. In 2000, a nonprofit organization, God's Center Foundation, owned the Lyric, but the city again condemned the building. A lengthy court battle ensued.

By 2005, the city of Lexington owned the property. The next year, the Lyric Theater Task Force, consisting of 15 city leaders and community members, opened the theater's doors to the public. Over 700 people experienced a four-hour open house. The Task Force encouraged citizens to offer suggestions on how the Lyric should be used. On October 30, 2010, the music venue reopened under a new name, the Lyric Theatre and Cultural Center, with a sold-out concert. The renovation cost $6 million.

Lexington Lyric Theatre and Cultural Arts Center. http://www .lexingtonlyric.com/ (accessed June 4, 2012).
Newspapers: "Manage New Theater Here for Negroes," *LH,* December 16, 1948, 9; "Lyric Theater Destined to Be Mission for Street People," *LHL,* March 11, 1984, A1; "A Bright New Life—Silent for Decades, Theater Channels Its Past Glory," *LHL,* October 31, 2010, A1.

—*Sallie L. Powell*

LYTLE, HENRY HOPKINS (b. 1802, Maryland; d. 1890, Lexington, KY), Methodist minister. Born in Maryland under the institution of slavery and without any formal education, Henry Hopkins Lytle managed to learn to read and write. He began to preach at the age of 21. When he came to Kentucky, he laid the foundation for Methodism in Lexington when he and 12 others founded Asbury Methodist Episcopal Church in Lexington in 1847. Services were held in rented buildings until the congregation built its own church building in 1854. At the end of the Civil War, the church's membership had grown to about 500 people.

After the Baptist organization, Methodists formed the second-largest denomination among Kentucky African Americans but later divided into various branches. In 1866, the Methodist Episcopal Church–South organized under the authority of one white man and appointed African American ministers to churches throughout the state. The following year, the church divided into two districts centered on Lexington's Asbury Church and Louisville's Jackson Street Methodist Church under the leadership of African American minister Hanson Talbot. In 1868, the Methodist white officials appointed Lytle the second African American administrator. A year later, under pressure for a separate organization, the Methodist Church established an all-black Lexington Conference, and Edward Thomson, an African American, was appointed bishop. Lytle was considered one of the conference's leaders.

In this era, travel conditions were difficult in Kentucky, and Lytle frequently walked about 75 miles from Lexington to Louisville to preach. He and his wife, Rosetta, had two sons, Fletcher and Henry Hopkins Jr. He subsidized his minister's income by working as a farm hand along with his son Fletcher. Lytle died at age 88 in 1890.

Lucas, Marion B. *A History of Blacks in Kentucky: From Slavery to Segregation, 1760–1891.* 2nd ed. Frankfort: Kentucky Historical Society, 2003.
Riley, Walter H. *Forty Years in the Lap of Methodism: History of Lexington Conference of Methodist Episcopal Church.* Louisville, KY: Mayes Printing Company, 1915.
U.S. Federal Census (1880).

—*Sallie L. Powell*

M

MACK, EDGAR L. (b. 1930, Pleasureville, KY; d. 1991, Brentwood, TN), civil rights activist and pastor. Civil rights activist and religious leader Edgar Leroy Mack was the son of Edgar W. and Sarah L. Johnson Mack. He attended the **Lincoln Institute** and in 1953 graduated from Wilberforce College in Ohio. In 1955, he received an MA in divinity from Payne Theological Seminary in Wilberforce, OH. Later he received an MA in social work from Ohio State University in Columbus. For most of his adult life, Mack was a leader in the **National Association for the Advancement of Colored People** and the African Methodist Episcopal (A.M.E.) Church. In 1963, he served as president of the Frankfort NAACP and as the leadership-training director for the Kentucky NAACP youth councils and college chapters. In 1964, he was made pastor at **St. Paul A.M.E. Church** in Newport and was elected executive secretary of the Northern Kentucky NAACP.

Mack was blessed with excellent organizational skills, which he used frequently in civil rights activities throughout the state. He served as cochair of the northern Kentucky organizing committee for the March 5, 1964, Freedom **March on Frankfort,** which featured Martin Luther King Jr. Mack was instrumental in taking 300 people from northern Kentucky to that important civil rights event. In April 1968, soon after King was assassinated, Mack planned numerous memorial services around northern Kentucky and was active in quelling violent responses. In 1973, Mack was named chairman of the United Negro College Fund Advisory Committee in Cincinnati. He moved to Lexington, where he became pastor of **Quinn Chapel A.M.E. Church** and a professor of social work at the University of Kentucky. Mack was named general secretary of the A.M.E. Church in 1980 and moved to the Nashville, TN, area. In that position, he developed interdenominational relationships that created enduring church partnerships. In 1988, he authored the book *Our Beginning: The African American Methodist Episcopal Church.* Mack held his office in the A.M.E. Church until his death in 1991. He was buried in the Lexington Cemetery in Lexington.

African American Episcopal Church. http://www.ame-church.com (accessed January 17, 2007).
"Funeral Obituary." Read at Quinn Chapel A.M.E. Church, Lexington, KY, April 27, 1991.
NAACP Papers. Microform version, Univ. of Virginia Library. http://www.lib.virginia.edu (accessed January 14, 2007).
Newspapers: "Mack Head of College Fund Unit," *CP,* May 2, 1973, 29; Jim Reis, "King Marched in Frankfort in 1964," *KP,* January 20, 2003, 4K.

—*Jim Embry*

MACK, ESSIE (DORTCH) (b. 1883, Louisville, KY; d. 1940, Louisville, KY), educator. Essie (Dortch) Mack was the daughter of John and Emma (Talbert) Dortch. She graduated from **Central High School** in 1902 and attended **Louisville Municipal College.** A lifelong promoter of African American education,

Mack played a major role in the organization of the first kindergarten at the Phillis Wheatley Colored School (later known as Wheatley Elementary). Her belief that parents' involvement in their children's education was essential prompted her to serve as an officer of the Congress of Kindergarten Mothers, president of the Kentucky Colored Parent-Teacher Association for nine years, and president of the National Congress of Colored Parent-Teacher Associations for two terms.

Mack was married to Oliver P. Mack. She is buried in the Louisville Cemetery.

Second Report of the Board of Education of Louisville, KY, July 1, 1912, to June 30, 1913. Louisville, KY: Gross Parsons and Hambleton, n.d.
Third Report of the Board of Education of Louisville, KY, July 1, 1913, to June 30, 1914.

MADDOXTOWN, African American hamlet in Fayette Co. Maddoxtown, occasionally misspelled "Mattoxtown," is located on Huffman Mill Pike five miles north of Lexington, KY, and five miles east of the Kentucky Horse Park. In 1867, former slaves organized a Baptist church, but the village was officially established when white landowner Samuel Maddox and his wife, Sarah, sold one-half- to two-acre lots to freed African Americans in 1871. Six years later, seven African American families lived in Maddoxtown. Most of the citizens worked as laborers and domestics for nearby estates, such as Mount Brilliant Farm and Spendthrift Farm. They also earned an income raising tobacco, chicken, and pigs.

The community centered on the Maddoxtown Baptist Church, the cemetery, and the school. In 1908, Rev. R. Quarles held a camp meeting that included a drama on the Prodigal Son, which included a celebration of feeding lamb and bread to about 1,000 people. In 1912, plans were discussed to build a new two-story school. The next year, Fayette Co. school superintendent Nannie G. Faulconer wrote to the state school superintendent that the Maddoxtown School was "the best colored rural school house in the south" and possessed "an up-to-date kitchen." During the Great Depression in 1929, students were fed a hot meal. However, it was not until 1932 that Maddoxtown's Junior League assisted the school's Parent-Teacher Association in financing the installation of electric lights. In 1985, many homes did not have a city sewer or garbage pickup, and some did not have city water, but the U.S. Department of Housing and Urban Development planned $25,000 in housing rehabilitation for Maddoxtown.

One of Maddoxtown's most famous residents was **Will Harbut,** who worked for 15 years as the groomsman for the great racehorse Man o' War. The famed horse died shortly after Harbut in 1947.

Biennial Report of the Superintendent of Public Instruction of Kentucky for the Two Years, Ending June 10, 1913. Frankfort, KY: State Journal Co., 1913.
Newspapers: "Prodigal Son in Real Life," *LL,* August 6, 1908 1; Merelene Davis, "Settlement Tales Part of Fayette Heritage," *LHL,* October 10, 1999 J1.
Smith, Peter Craig. "Negro Hamlets and Gentlemen Farms: A Dichotomous Rural Settlement Pattern in Kentucky's Bluegrass Region." PhD diss., Univ. of Kentucky, 1972.

—*Sallie L. Powell*

344 MÁJOZO, ESTELLA MARIE CONWILL

MÁJOZO, ESTELLA MARIE CONWILL (b. 1949, Louisville, KY), poet, playwright, and university professor. "I am a Black woman artist," proclaimed Estella Marie Conwill Májozo in her memoir, *Come out the Wilderness.* Born in Louisville, KY, to Mary Luella Herndon and Giles Adolph Conwill, Májozo, the only daughter among five brothers, was profoundly influenced by her Catholic upbringing, racism, sexism, and her father's death when she was only nine years old. She lived in the Louisville African American community known as **Little Africa** and graduated from Holy Rosary Academy. As the only African American in the white Catholic school, she faced further discrimination by answering questions about Rev. Dr. Martin Luther King Jr.'s 1964 march in Frankfort. In 1966, in an effort to obtain a college scholarship, Májozo entered and won Louisville's Miss Exposition. She briefly attended Tennessee State and later received her BA and MA from the University of Louisville. In 1980, she earned her PhD in English from the University of Iowa.

Along with her memoir, Májozo authored various literary works, including the play *Purgatory* and the poetry collections *The Middle Passage, Jiva Telling Rites,* and *Blessings for a New World.* Along with her brother **Houston Conwill,** an artist, and architect Joseph DePace, she has created several commissioned public art monuments, including the terrazzo floor plan *Rivers,* located in New York's Schomburg Center for Research in Black Culture and completed in 1991. She has taught English at Frankfort's **Kentucky State University,** New York's Hunter College, and the University of Louisville. Some of her courses include creative writing and women in literature.

Májozo constructed her last name from the first names of three distinguished African American women: Mary McLeod Bethune, Josephine Baker, and Zora Neale Hurston.

"Estella Conwill Majozo, the Self as Writer: Speaking from a Position of a New World." University of Louisville. http://louisville.edu /womenscenter/kwbf/kwbf-2008/presenter-pages/estella-conwill -majozo.html (accessed January 17, 2012).
Májozo, Estella Conwill. *Come Out the Wilderness: Memoir of a Black Woman Artist.* New York: Feminist Press at the City University of New York, 1999.
Okoampa-Ahoofe, Kwaame, Jr. "Untangling the Jungle." *New York Amsterdam News* 90, no. 8 (February 1999): 32.

—Sallie L. Powell

MALONE, ROBERT EMMICK (b. 1889, Louisville, KY; d. 1949, Louisville, KY), educator and businessman. The son of post office porter Edward Cornelius Malone and Cora (Hansberry) Malone, Robert Emmick Malone graduated from Louisville's **Central High School** in 1906. Three years later, he graduated from Hampton Institute in Virginia. By 1912, he had earned a degree in agriculture from Cornell University, taught at Tuskegee Institute, and married Mattie F. Holmes. A few years later, he became director of agriculture at Topeka Institute in Kansas. From 1918 to 1920, he served as supervisor of the State Board of Vocational Education in North Carolina.

Malone later became the youngest African American man elected president of the Arkansas Agricultural, Mechanical, and Normal School (AM&N) in Pine Bluff, which was created as a racially segregated branch of the University of Arkansas. He pushed to improve the institution's poor academic performance, added more faculty members, and upgraded the curriculum. In 1925, AM&N was granted junior college status. Two year later, plans were made to separate AM&N from the University of Arkansas. For unknown reasons, Malone left the institution and joined the faculty of Oklahoma's Langston University in 1928. He later returned to Pine Bluff to become the president of Southwestern Life Insurance Company.

By 1949, Malone was divorced, living on Magazine St. in Louisville, and working as a biological assistant. His youngest daughter, Ethel, found him after he died suddenly of a heart attack. He was buried in Louisville's Greenwood Cemetery.

Boris, Joseph J., ed. *Who's Who in Colored America, 1927.* New York: Who's Who in Colored America Corp., 1927.
Dunnigan, Alice Allison, comp and ed. *The Fascinating Story of Black Kentuckians: Their Heritage and Traditions.* Washington, DC: Associated Publishers, 1982.
Kentucky Death Records, 1852–1953.
U.S. Federal Census (1900, 1910, 1920, 1930).
Williams, C. Fred. "Frustration amidst Hope: The Land Grant Mission of Arkansas AM&N College, 1873–1972." *Agricultural History* 65, no. 2 (Spring 1991).
Yenser, Thomas, ed. *Who's Who in Colored America, 1941–1944.* 6th ed. Brooklyn, NY: Thomas Yenser, 1942.

—Sallie L. Powell

MAMMOTH LIFE AND ACCIDENT INSURANCE COMPANY, insurance company originally created for African Americans. Opened on July 12, 1915, at Sixth and Green (Liberty) Sts., Mammoth Life and Accident Insurance Company was founded by B. O. Wilkerson, Rochelle I. Smith, **William H. Wright,** and **Henry E. Hall,** who served as president of the company from its inception until his death in 1944. Mammoth was established as an alternative company for African Americans who were often forced to pay inflated premiums by white-managed insurance companies and many times were denied coverage.

Originally, most of Mammoth's policies were of the home-service type, also called weekly debit, whereby an agent would make weekly door-to-door premium collections. This practice was intended to make it easier for low-wage earners to purchase insurance because they were better able to pay small weekly installments than larger monthly or annual premiums. The company discontinued the sale of weekly debit policies in the 1980s in the face of consumer advocates' claims that the policies were more expensive in the long term.

The company received instant support from the black community and quickly became Louisville's largest black-owned and operated company. Within two years of its founding, Mammoth had outgrown its facilities and moved into a three-story building at 422 S. Sixth St. It also established branch offices in cities throughout Kentucky, including Lexington, Hopkinsville, Bowling Green, and Paducah. Although it was initially started as a mutual company, Mammoth became a legal reserve stock institution in 1924 after a statewide sale of capital stock. The next year, Mammoth's success was shown in the construction of a six-story home office building at 604–612 W. **Walnut St.** (now **Muhammad Ali** Blvd.). The previous building was maintained as the Louisville district office.

Mammoth Life and Accident Insurance Company, Lexington, Kentucky, 1949.

In 1928, Mammoth extended into other states, eventually establishing offices in eight states: Michigan, Illinois, Indiana, Ohio, Missouri, Tennessee, and Wisconsin, as well as Kentucky. Although many companies foundered during the years of the Great Depression, Mammoth weathered the storm, in part because of the loyalty of its employees, many of whom voluntarily donated a portion of their wages back to the company to help it meet its client obligations. During the flood of 1937, hundreds of people found temporary housing in the company's two downtown offices.

In the 1960s, Mammoth, along with many other minority insurers, began to face increasing competition from white-owned firms that not only had discovered the profitability of doing business with the African American community but also had begun to entice accomplished black salesmen by offering higher salaries. Although this trend slowed Mammoth's growth, business remained strong, and in 1967 a $680,000 remodeling project of the company's headquarters was completed. In response to white competition, the company initiated a management training program in 1981 in an effort to "replenish the cells" of upper management.

In the mid-1980s, two other African American insurance companies, North Carolina Mutual and Atlanta Life Insurance, made unsuccessful attempts to take over Mammoth Life. However, in 1985 two years later, Atlanta Life Insurance Company succeeded in taking over Mammoth, and in 1992 Mammoth was merged into Atlanta Life. By 1994, Atlanta Life had closed the Mammoth office in Louisville.

Dunnigan, Alice Allison, comp. and ed. *The Fascinating Story of Black Kentuckians: Their Heritage and Traditions.* Washington, DC: Associated Publishers, 1982.

"Insurance," *Black Enterprise,* June 1989, 317.

Newspapers: *LCJ,* August 9, 1981; *LCJ,* June 3, 1985.

Wright, George C. *Life Behind a Veil: Blacks in Louisville, Kentucky, 1865–1930.* Baton Rouge: Louisiana State Univ. Press, 1985.

MARABLE, FATE (b. 1890, Paducah, KY; d. 1947, St. Louis, MO), bandleader for riverboats on the Ohio and Mississippi Rivers. Fate Marable learned how to read music and play the piano from his mother as a child in Paducah, KY. He parlayed his musical talents into a job on a riverboat in 1907, joining the crew of the *J.S.* as a bandleader at the age of 17. Despite his youth, Marable quickly established himself as a successful entertainer, leading a small band composed of white musicians until racial tension in nearby St. Louis necessitated the organization of an all-black band in 1917.

After switching to a format more pleasing to an audience accustomed to **Jim Crow** laws, Marable recruited several talented musicians to his Society Syncopators, including Louis Armstrong. The band, known for its strong and danceable rhythms, combined skilled improvisers with formally trained musicians, although Marable's preference for formal training led him to fire Armstrong after he skipped lessons to teach him to read music. Marable's bands remained powerful throughout the 1920s and early 1930s, but the onset of the Great Depression lowered the appeal of excursion boats. Reduced audiences and an injured finger forced Marable to withdraw from his career as a bandleader. He died of pneumonia in St. Louis on January 16, 1947. In 2002, he was inducted into the National Rivers Hall of Fame.

Bradley, Arthur. *On and Off the Bandstand.* Lincoln, NE: iUniverse, 2005.

"Fate Marable." *NYT,* January 19, 1947, 53.

Kenney, William Howard. *Jazz on the River.* Chicago: Univ. of Chicago Press, 2005.

—*Stephen Pickering*

MARCH ON FRANKFORT, civil rights demonstration at the Kentucky State Capitol. In January 1964, Governor Edward T. Breathitt met with a group of civil rights leaders, including **Frank L. Stanley Jr.,** to discuss a civil rights bill recently introduced in the General Assembly. Not comfortable with the progress or the strength of the bill, Stanley and other leaders decided to push the issue with the formation of the **Allied Organizations for Civil Rights** (AOCR). An interracial assembly of organizations

Dr. Martin Luther King Jr. speaking at the 1964 March on Frankfort.

Martin Luther King Jr. (right) and Jackie Robinson (left).

across Kentucky, the AOCR was designed to promote a civil rights bill in the state.

Stanley, who had been a participant in the March on Washington, called for a similar demonstration at the State Capitol to draw attention to the coalition's cause. With the support of cochairmen Olaf Anderson, John Loftus, and Eric Tachau, as well as help from **Georgia Davis Powers** and Lucretia Ward, the AOCR scheduled the March on Frankfort for March 5, 1964. In addition to speeches and performances by several local leaders and groups, Martin Luther King Jr., Jackie Robinson, and Peter, Paul, and Mary were all to appear as part of the demonstration. Although many politicians resisted the march as unnecessary interference in a legislative process, government agencies cooperated, and Frankfort police prepared to handle as many as 50,000 marchers.

Crowd gathering at the March on Frankfort.

On the day of the march, inclement weather and cold temperatures reduced initial projections for the crowd that assembled, but most sources agree that at least 10,000 activists joined in the march down Capitol Ave. Upon arriving at the Capitol, marchers listened to a truncated version of King's "I Have a Dream" speech and performances from Peter, Paul, and Mary and local bands. Among the people in the crowd was Mary Fran Breathitt, the 13-year-old daughter of the governor; Breathitt's wife also briefly appeared at the sidelines, but the governor did not attend. Instead, he met privately with eight leaders of the march in his office, where he professed support for their mission even as he claimed to lack the votes to get the civil rights bill passed in the current session.

Several demonstrators participated in a brief hunger strike at the Capitol in a last-ditch effort to sway the assembly, but the bill failed. The leaders of the **civil rights movement,** however, carried on the momentum from the March on Frankfort and continued to push for a stronger civil rights bill. Their efforts were finally rewarded two years later with the passage of the **Civil Rights Act of 1966.** In March 2014, a commemoration of the march drew several thousand people. The event was a rally for House Bill 70, which would allow some felons to regain their voting rights after they had served their sentences. Former state senator **Georgia M. Powers** was present at the march. She acknowledged the "50 years of progress" but declared "our efforts are not complete."

Blackford, Linda. "50 Years after Civil Rights March in Frankfort, Re-enactment Becomes a Rally for Voting Rights," *LHL,* March 5, 2014.

Horton, John Benjamin. *Not without Struggle.* New York: Vantage Press, 1979.

Kentucky's Black Heritage: The Role of the Black People in the History of Kentucky from Pioneer Days to the Present. Frankfort: Kentucky Commission on Human Rights, 1971.

Newspapers: "Gov. Breathitt Losing Support of Rights Advocates in Kentucky," *NYT,* February 25, 1964, 21; "10,000 March on Capitol for Accommodations Bill; Leaders Meet Breathitt," *LCJ,* March 6, 1964, 1; "King Holds Listeners despite March Rain," *Middlesboro Daily News,* March 6, 1964, 8; "Historic March Replayed—40 Years after Frankfort Civil Rights Demonstration First Black State Senator Speaks," *LHL,* March 4, 2004.

Williams, Jim. *The March on Frankfort: A Study in Protest Organization.* New York: Political Education Project, 1965.

—*Stephen Pickering*

MARRS, ELIJAH P. (b. 1840, Shelby Co., KY; d. 1910, Louisville, KY), minister, teacher, and Civil War veteran. Born into slavery in January 1840 in Shelby Co., KY, Elijah P. Marrs was the son of Andrew and Frances Marrs, natives of Culpeper Co., VA. His father, a carpenter, was a freeman, but his mother was a slave, one of about 30 owned by Jesse Robinson. Although education was generally forbidden to slaves in Kentucky, Marrs learned to read and write as a child, taught by white playmates and an old black man conducting a surreptitious night school.

Rev. Elijah P. Marrs.

In his childhood, his lifelong interest in education was fully established, as were his religious convictions.

Marrs's longing to escape from slavery was also formed in his early years. He gained his freedom when he joined the Union army, enlisting on September 28, 1864, along with a group of 27 fellow slaves, whom he led to Louisville to enlist with him. He was assigned to the 12th U.S. Colored Cavalry, but when it was discovered that he was literate, he was reassigned as the 3rd duty sergeant, Company L, 12th U.S. Heavy Artillery. After training at **Camp Nelson,** he fought in engagements at Glasgow and Big Springs. He was mustered out on April 20, 1866, and soon began a career as a schoolteacher, in Simpsonville, where he was the first African American teacher in La Grange, New Castle, and Louisville. He spent the fall term of 1874 at Roger Williams University in Nashville.

Along with his teaching, Marrs had begun preaching in Baptist churches in the early 1870s; in 1873, he was licensed to preach, and he was ordained on August 22, 1875. He founded the Beargrass Colored Baptist Church at Crescent Hill in Louisville and served as pastor there and at St. John Baptist Church from the early 1880s until his death. In 1879, he and his older brother, Henry C. Marrs, founded the Kentucky Normal and Theological Institute (later known as **Simmons College of Kentucky**) in Louisville; in 1879 and 1880, Elijah was the first president or superintendent, while his brother was the principal.

In addition to his other activities, Marrs was treasurer of the General Association of Colored Baptists and a delegate to the first Convention of Colored Men in 1882, and the National Convention of Colored Men in 1883. According to historian Marion Lucas, he was a "delegate to every major statewide political convention Kentucky blacks held in the postwar era." On August 30, 1910, Elijah P. Marrs died in Louisville and was buried in Greenwood Cemetery.

Kleber, John E., ed. *The Kentucky Encyclopedia.* Lexington: Univ. Press of Kentucky, 1992.

Lucas, Marion B. *A History of Blacks in Kentucky.* Vol. 1, *From Slavery to Segregation, 1760–1891.* Frankfort: Kentucky Historical Society, 1992.

Marrs, Elijah P. *Life and History of the Rev. Elijah P. Marrs.* Louisville, KY: Bradley & Gilbert Company, 1885.

Simmons, William. *Men of Mark: Eminent, Progressive and Rising.* Cleveland: George M. Rewell, 1887.

Smith, Jessie Carney, ed. *Notable Black American Men.* Detroit: Gale Research, 1998.

—*Richard D. Sears*

MARSHALL, HARRIET "HATTIE" GIBBS (b. 1868, Victoria, British Columbia; d. 1941, Washington, DC), founder of the music school at Eckstein-Norton Institute in Cane Springs, KY, and the Washington Conservatory of Music in Washington, DC. Harriet "Hattie" Gibbs was born to Mifflin and Maria Ann Gibbs in Victoria, British Columbia, in 1868. Her father, who later became one of the first African American judges in the United States, moved his family to Oberlin, OH, soon after Hattie's birth. A musical prodigy, she entered the Oberlin Conservatory of Music at age 11 and had graduated from high school, with an emphasis on Greek, Latin, and mathematics, before she turned 15.

In 1891, after refining her piano skills in Boston, Chicago, and Paris, France, Gibbs came to Kentucky to form a conservatory of music at **Charles H. Parrish**'s **Eckstein-Norton Institute** in Cane Springs. A contemporary wrote that "the people of Kentucky should be proud that one so able has placed her services within reach." After a fire burned the main building of Eckstein Norton in 1892, Marshall organized a musical company that included **Lulu Vere Childers,** later the first director of Howard University's School of Music, and raised money through a nationwide tour.

In 1900, Gibbs moved to Washington, DC, where she was named director of music for the city's black public schools. In 1903, she founded the Washington Conservatory of Music, which lasted for over 50 years as one of the city's premier musical institutions. During its long history, the school's board featured such luminaries as W. E. B. DuBois, W. C. Handy, and Eleanor Roosevelt. In 1906, she married Napoleon B. Marshall, a Harvard-educated lawyer.

Dedicated to training African American musicians her entire life, upon her death in 1941, Hattie Gibbs Marshall left the bulk of her property to the Washington Conservatory of Music. Her will further stipulated that the conservatory "shall preserve her aims through the development and preservation of Negro music and art and of a center of research and composition."

Abbott, Lynn, and Doug Seroff. *Out of Sight: The Rise of African American Popular Music, 1889–1895.* Jackson: Univ. Press of Mississippi, 2002.

Newspapers: "Career Women of the Capital," *BAA,* July 22, 1939, 17; "Director's Will Leaves Property to Conservatory," *BAA,* March 18, 1941, 9.

Richings, G. F. *Evidences of Progress among Colored People.* Philadelphia: George S. Ferguson Co., 1896.

—*Joshua D. Farrington*

MARTIN, CORNELIUS A. (1948, Greenville, KY; d. 2006, Bowling Green, KY), businessman. Born on August 4, 1948, Cornelius A. Martin, the son of Herbert and Beatrice Martin, graduated from Muhlenberg County Central High School, attended West Kentucky State Vocational School and Wright State University, and graduated from the highly selective General Motors Dealer Academy of the General Motors Institute. The ultimate entrepreneur, he created and owned automobile dealerships, insurance operations, general aviation terminal operations, motorcycle dealerships, and a real estate development company. After opening his first dealership in Bowling Green, KY, in 1985, Martin proceeded to operate 15 automobile dealerships in Arizona, California, Iowa, Kentucky, Ohio, and West Virginia. He formed the Martin Automotive Group in 1990. In February 1998, he formed Co-Mar Aviation, a full-service, fixed-based operation that provided mechanical services, aircraft positioning, aviation fuel, and pilot comfort facilities for aircraft arriving at and departing from Bowling Green–Warren County Municipal Airport. When he opened his Harley-Davidson Motorcycle business in Bowling Green in December 2003, he became only the third African American to own and operate a Harley-Davidson franchise.

Martin was chief executive officer of Martin Management Group, Martin Automotive Group, Co-Mar Aviation Group, and the Corporate Center at Hartland. The entire organization generated revenues in excess of $250 million. He and his wife created scholarships for deserving students attending Western Kentucky University and Wright State University. He provided funds and leadership to the United Way of Kentucky, the Girls and Boys Club of Bowling Green, the Girl Scouts of Kentuckiana, and Junior Achievement. Martin's numerous awards included Bowling Green–Warren County Small Business Person of the Year (1989), *Black Enterprise* magazine's Auto Dealer of the Year (1997), and the Junior Achievement's Business Hall of Fame Laureate (2003). He was awarded the Automotive News Automotive Dealership Service Excellence Award (1996) and Ward's Automotive Report's Mega 100 Award (2005).

Martin held prestigious board positions in a number of public organizations. He was appointed twice to the Board of Directors of the Federal Reserve Bank of St. Louis, served as chairman of the St. Louis Branch of the Federal Reserve Bank, served twice as chairman of the Board of Regents of Western Kentucky University, served on the Board of Directors of the Wright State University Foundation, founded and served as vice president of the South Central Kentucky Minority Economic Development Council, and served as chairman of the Bowling Green Municipal Utilities Board. Additionally, he served on the Bowling Green–Warren County Chamber of Commerce and the Advisory Board of the Western Kentucky University Institute for Economic Development.

On June 3, 2006, Martin was killed on U.S. 79 a few miles from Russellville, KY, in a motorcycle accident.

Co-Mar Aviation. http://www.martingp.com/comar/ (accessed July 30, 2009).
"Cornelius A. Martin, Car Dealer, Regent, Dies," *BGDN,* June 5, 2006.
Hayes, Cassandra. "Selling into the Stratosphere." *Black Enterprise* 27, no. 11 (June 1997): 176–81.
JC Kirby Obituary Directory. http://www.bmpv.net/view.php?id=222&page=1&cat=1 (accessed July 30, 2009).
Martin Automotive Group. http://www.martingp.com/TheMartinAutomotiveGroup/ (accessed July 30, 2009).
"Survivor Recalls Tragic Day." http://www.bgdailynews.com/news/survivors-recall-tragic-day/article_cb729305-67f1-5783-7c1b1d1fcb3a.html (accessed June 28, 2013).
Western Kentucky University. "WKU Remembers Former Regent Chair Cornelius Martin." WKU news release, July 20, 2006. http://www.wku.edu/news/releases06/july/martin.html (accessed July 30, 2009).

—*Harold T. Little Jr.*

MARTIN, FLETCHER P. (b. 1916, McMinnville, TN; d. 2005, Indianapolis, IN), first accredited black war correspondent. Born in McMinnville, TN, Fletcher P. Martin grew up in Louisville and graduated from **Central High School** and **Louisville Municipal College.** In 1939, just one year after finishing his college degree, he was named the city editor of the *Louisville Leader,* and three years later he became a feature writer for the *Louisville Defender.* In 1943, he became the first accredited black war correspondent, spending almost two years in the South Pacific and conducting personal interviews with Gen. Douglas MacArthur and Adm. William Halsey.

In 1946, Martin became the first African American to win Harvard University's coveted Nieman Fellowship, which provided a full scholarship to the university alongside a cash reward equal to his current salary. Despite Martin's impressive résumé, upon his return to Louisville he was denied a job at the *Louisville Courier-Journal* out of fear that white employees would quit. During the late 1940s and early 1950s, he resumed his work at the *Defender,* serving as city editor. In 1952, he became the first black reporter hired by the *Chicago Sun-Times.* While working for the *Sun-Times,* he covered the **civil rights movement** throughout the 1950s and 1960s. Years later, the newspaper praised his reporting, noting that "Fletcher Martin introduced Chicago to the Rev. Martin Luther King Jr." He published his first book in 1953, *Famous Americans,* which featured profiles of influential African Americans across the country.

In 1963, the U.S. Information Agency hired Martin; he served as a press attaché at various embassies in Africa. From the 1970s though the 1990s, he retired to Spain's Mallorca Island in the Mediterranean. In 1997, he returned to the United States and settled near his children in Indiana. He died of complications from diabetes in Indianapolis on November 27, 2005.

Newspapers: "Nieman Fellowship Won by Ex–War Correspondent," *BAA,* July 23, 1946, 1; "Groundbreaking Journalist Fletcher P. Martin Dies at 89," *LCJ,* December 1, 2005, B6.
Roberts, Gene, and Hank Klibanoff. *The Race Beat: The Press, the Civil Rights Struggle, and the Awakening of a Nation.* New York: Alfred A. Knopf, 2006.

—*Joshua D. Farrington*

MARTIN, JANICE REED (b. 1956, Union Co., KY), first black female judge in Kentucky. A native of Union Co., KY, Janice Reed Martin has dedicated most of her life to the practice of law within her home state. After receiving her undergraduate degree in political science at the University of Louisville, she stayed on at that institution to earn a law degree. When she graduated from the university's Brandeis School of Law in 1977, she was the only African American woman in her class. Martin moved into private practice after her graduation, but she left that position to work as a bar counsel for the Kentucky Bar Association. In 1988, she shifted into governmental work, serving as chief of the Jefferson County Attorney's Juvenile Division.

Her work in that office earned her the approval of the county's judicial nominating commission, which recommended her to Governor Brereton Jones for an open position in the district court. Upon being sworn in on March 6, 1992, Martin became the state's first black female judge. Her position, however, was secured only until she could win an election in her own right at the end of the year. Martin was chosen as one of two candidates for the position in a primary held two months later, and she easily won the November election over Martin McDonald with the support of the *Louisville Courier-Journal* and a nonpartisan group named Citizens for Better Judges.

After the election, Martin served for 17 more years as a circuit judge. She also dedicated herself to a number of causes within the local community, such as supporting parents facing homelessness and serving as a mentor for students interested in law in the Louisville area. Martin has been the recipient of several awards, including the Trailblazer Award from the Louisville Bar Association and the Distinguished Law and Alumni Award from the University of Louisville. In 2009, she retired from her position as district judge, leaving Jefferson Co. with no black judges, although she continued to try cases as a senior judge.

Newspapers: "Kentucky's First Black Female Judge Appointed," *Louisville Defender,* March 12, 1992, 1; "Martin Sweeps Past McDonald to Keep Post," *LCJ,* November 4, 1992, B1.
Who's Who in Black Louisville. 3rd ed. Columbus, OH: Who's Who Publishing Co., 2009.

—*Stephen Pickering*

MARTIN, JOE ELSBY (b. 1916, Louisville, KY; d. 1996, Louisville, KY), police officer and boxing coach. The son of Joe and Margaret (Shaw) Martin, Joe Elsby Martin was orphaned before the age of one. He was reared by an aunt in Phoenix, AZ, where he received his basic education. Martin returned to Louisville in 1937 and soon joined the city's police force, serving until his retirement in 1974. In 1938, he became a boxing coach at the Columbia Gym, which was located in the old Knights of Columbus building on Fourth St., south of York St. It later became a unit of Spalding University. The gym, which was operated by the Louisville Parks Department, provided a place of recreation for children off the streets. One of Martin's first acts was to integrate the gym racially.

It was at Columbia Gym in 1954 that Martin began his association with future heavyweight boxing champion **Muhammad Ali,** then known as Cassius Clay. The 12-year-old youngster went to police officer Martin to report the theft of his new bicycle and expressed his desire to "whip" the thief. Martin offered to teach him how to fight and became the guiding influence in the young boxer's career for the next six years. Beginning in the 1950s, Martin helped produce the weekly WAVE television show *Tomorrow's Champions,* which was broadcast for 12 years and featured matches of amateur boxers. This was Ali's first television exposure. In 1960, Martin was chosen as U.S. boxing coach for the Olympic Games in Rome, where Ali won a gold medal. Upon returning from Rome, Ali began his professional career but kept in touch with Martin through the years.

Martin was known as a tough disciplinarian who stressed the fundamentals of boxing. While continuing his work as a full-time police officer, he was the sustaining force in amateur boxing in Louisville during four decades. In 1977, he was inducted into the Amateur Boxing Hall of Fame. He was the owner of the Joe Martin Auction Co. and twice ran unsuccessfully for sheriff of Jefferson Co.

Martin married Christine Fentress on March 4, 1941. They had one son, Joe Jr. Martin is buried in Leitchfield Memorial Gardens in Leitchfield, KY.

LCJ, September 15, 1996.

—*Kenneth Dennis*

MARTIN, SARA (b. 1884, Louisville, KY; d. 1955, Louisville, KY), blues singer, actress, and church worker. The daughter of William Dunn and Kate Pope, Sara Martin began singing in her church choir and in 1908 made one of her earliest appearances as a popular singer at the White City Amusement Park. In 1922, her recording of "Sugar Blues" was a hit, and she became one of the reigning **blues** queens, touring the country. Occasionally, her travels brought her back to Louisville, where she performed at the Lincoln Theater, located at 814 W. **Walnut St.** (now **Muhammad Ali** Blvd.). She made over 100 records, recording on the Okeh label, and appeared in several movies. In 1930, she retired from popular music and returned to Louisville, where she devoted the rest of her life to serving her church. In 1939, she opened a nursing home at 1728 W. Walnut, which she managed until 1949. She was survived by three adopted children. She was buried in an unmarked grave for nearly sixty years. In September 2014, a dedication ceremony was held to lay a pictorial headstone at her grave site.

Harris, Sheldon. *Blues Who's Who.* New Rochelle, NY: Arlington House, 1979.
"New Headstone to Honor 1920s Blues Singer Sara Martin," *LCJ,* July 19, 2014.

—*Cornelius Bogert*

MARTIN, WILLIAM HENRY, JR. (b. 1895, Lexington, KY; d. 1952, Dayton, OH), businessman. Businessman William Henry Martin Jr. was the only child of William Henry and Alice M. Martin, who brought him to Covington at age six. William Jr. attended **Lincoln-Grant School** and graduated from William Grant High School in 1913 and from Miami University in Oxford, OH, in 1917. In 1918, he joined the U.S. Army and served during World War I. Upon his discharge, Martin went to Lexington, where he worked for a tailor named George Washington. Sometime later, Martin moved back to Covington and by 1927 had opened his first dry cleaning and tailor business at Athey Ave. and Craig St. That same year, he married Alice Arnold, a schoolteacher in Lexington. In 1928, he moved his business to 508 Scott St. In 1932 Martin opened a second dry cleaning business at 1015 Greenup St., near the corner of Clinton Ct. and Scott St. In the late 1930s, Martin closed the Greenup location to concentrate his business at 508 Scott St., which he moved in 1948 to 522 Scott St.

Martin was a member of the **First Baptist Church** and was actively involved in church affairs, the American Legion, the Utopian Club, and the **African American Businessmen's Association.** He was a charter member and the first commander of **Charles L. Henderson** American Legion Post No. 166.

Martin died at Veterans' Hospital in Dayton, OH, on February 10, 1952, and was buried in Mary E. Smith Cemetery, **Elsmere.** His wife kept the business open until 1957. Martin's son William III "Bill" was the longtime executive director of the Northern Kentucky Community Center.

Martin, Alice Arnold. Interview by Theodore Harris, Covington, KY, January 15, 1992.
Martin, William Henry, III. Interview by Theodore Harris, Covington, KY, January 14, 1992.
Newspapers: "Journey's End," *KE,* February 12, 1952, 23; Ted Harris, "Reader Recollection," *KP,* March 2, 1992, 4K.

—*Theodore H. H. Harris*

MARTIN LUTHER KING JR. UNITY BREAKFAST, annual event held in Lexington since 1995. In 1995, **Alpha Phi Alpha Fraternity** sponsored Lexington's first Martin Luther King Jr. Unity Breakfast. Although the breakfast started small, it became one of the marquee events in the city's celebration of the Martin Luther King Jr. holiday every January. Initially held at the Hyatt Regency, the breakfast was designed to start the day's activities, which typically culminated in a march downtown. In addition to serving countless cups of coffee, the 7:30 a.m. breakfasts included speeches by local ministers and leaders, musical performances, and awards to outstanding citizens.

After the second annual breakfast, Don Edwards of the *Lexington Herald-Leader* criticized whites for not participating in the breakfast, noting that only 40 people in the audience of over 300 were white. By 2009, however, the breakfast had moved to a larger facility at Heritage Hall and was described by one reporter as "Lexington at its best." That year's breakfast, still hosted by Alpha Phi Alpha Fraternity, was attended by over 1,300 people of all races, including representatives from many of central Kentucky's leading institutions and corporations. Previous speakers at the breakfast have included Lexington mayors, state representatives, and the presidents of the University of Kentucky and **Kentucky State University.**

Newspapers: "It's Simply a Matter of Black and White," *LHL,* January 16, 1996, B1; "Unity Breakfast, March Show Lexington at Its Best," *LHL,* January 20, 2009, C1.

—*Joshua D. Farrington*

MASHBURN, JAMAL (b. 1972, New York, NY), professional basketball player and entrepreneur. Jamal Mashburn, a six-feet-nine forward, played basketball for Cardinal High School in the Bronx, NY. He was a Parade Magazine All-American and Mr. Basketball in the state of New York in 1990. He played his college basketball at the University of Kentucky and became affectionately known to fans as the Monster Mash. He was selected to the All–Southeastern Conference freshman team.

During his sophomore season, he led the University of Kentucky squad known as the Unforgettables to a 29–7 record. This 1991–1992 team was one game from going to the Final Four before losing to the Duke Blue Devils in overtime in what has been considered one of the best college games ever played. The 1993 Wildcat team made the Final Four, and Mashburn was named a consensus first-team All-American and Southeastern Conference Player of the Year.

That same year, Mashburn was selected by the Dallas Mavericks as the fourth overall National Basketball Association (NBA) draft pick. He had a successful first year in the NBA, averaging nearly 20 points a game and being voted onto the All-Rookie team. In 1997, he was traded to the Miami Heat. Three years later, he was traded to the Charlotte Hornets, later known as the New Orleans Hornets. In 2003, Mashburn played for the East squad during that year's NBA All-Star Game. He was traded again in 2005 to the Philadelphia 76ers before retiring the following year. He finished his career averaging 19 points per game.

After retirement, Mashburn went to work as an NBA commentator for ESPN. He became a successful businessman, owning several Outback Steakhouses, Papa John's restaurants, and car dealerships. Mashburn's University of Kentucky jersey was retired in Lexington's Rupp Arena. In 2013, the University of Kentucky awarded him an honorary doctorate of humanities.

Basketball-Reference.Com. "Jamal Mashburn." http://www.basketball-reference.com/players/m/mashbja01.html (accessed August 7, 2013).
Clark, Ryan, and Joe Cox. *One Hundred Things Wildcat Fans Should Know and Do before They Die.* Chicago: Triumph Books, 2012.
"UK Classic Player Profile: Jamal Mashburn." UK Wildcats Blog. 2009. http://www.ukywildcatsblog.com/2009/10/uk-classic-player-profile-jam (accessed December 13, 2012).

—*Gerald L. Smith*

MASSIE, JOHN DANIEL FRANK (b. 1900, Hopkinsville, KY; d. 1977, Hopkinsville, KY), political and civic leader. The third child of Daniel B. and Ella M. Massie, John Daniel Frank Massie spent most of his life in Hopkinsville, KY. He graduated from Attucks High School. In 1928, he earned a degree from Worsham Embalming School (later known as Worsham College of Mortuary Science) in Wheeling, IL. In 1930, he worked in Hopkinsville's public transit system.

Sources disagree on whether Massie, a Democrat, was first elected a magistrate in Hopkinsville's First District in 1940 or 1945. In either case, when he died he had held public office longer than any other African American elected official. The First District was three-fourths African American, and black magistrates had served it since its formation in 1905. In most elections, Massie faced African American opponents, but he encountered white opposition in 1961.

In 1975, Massie was in the minority opposition on funding of the Hopkinsville / Christian County Public Library. His argument against the financial support was based on previous spending commitments for a new county jail and a water system. He declared, "This spending has got to stop somewhere." In 1977, just before his death, he served on the committee for Black Discovery that created African American history displays at the local library.

Active in the **National Association for the Advancement of Colored People,** Massie served as the local chapter's treasurer for 29 years. He also was treasurer of Pioneers, Inc., and trustee of Freeman Chapel Colored Methodist Episcopal (C.M.E.) Church. He died of a heart attack at Hopkinsville's Jennie Stuart Hospital and was buried in Cave Springs Cemetery. He was survived by his wife, Lottie R. Massie, a daughter, Vivian Hicks, and a son, Daniel F. Massie from Louisville. His son, who died in 2001, was also a civil rights leader. In his honor, the NAACP offers the Magistrate Daniel Massie Award for NAACP Involvement above and beyond the Call of Duty.

Kentucky Directory of Black Elected Officials. Frankfort: Kentucky Commission on Human Rights, 1972.
"Magistrate Dan Massie, 76, Dies." *KNE,* January 31, 1977, 1.

—*Sallie L. Powell*

MASTERSON, EDWARD I. (b. 1871, Boyle Co., KY; d. unknown), businessman. Little is known about Edward I. Masterson's personal life, but during the early 1900s, he was one of Louisville's most successful tailors. Census evidence suggests that he was most likely the son of a shoemaker from Boyle Co. After graduating from Louisville's **Central High School,** he learned his trade at the Tuskegee Institute's tailoring department, where he studied for 18 months.

E. I. Masterson, as he was frequently called, returned to Louisville in September 1896 and opened his own tailoring business. His advertisements in the ***American Baptist*** featured the slogan "It Is the Clothes That Make the Man" and claimed that "I cater to good dressers, and quote the very lowest price." By 1902, his shop at the corner of West and **Walnut** Sts. was one of the most successful clothing businesses in the city, bringing in at least $2,500 a year. His high-end gowns and suits were so popular with both white and black customers that he had to request that additional workers be sent from the Tuskegee Institute to help him keep up with demand. Many of the young workers sent to his shop went on to start their own repair shops and laundry businesses. A 1904 report presented before Booker T. Washington at the National Negro Business League's annual conference in Indianapolis estimated that businesses started by Masterson's apprentices were making over $15,000 a year. In 1906, Masterson designed a suit that was displayed at the Tuskegee Institute's 25th-anniversary exhibit.

The historical record is silent regarding Masterson's life after 1906. By 1907, his shop was no longer listed in the Louisville city directory, and there is no evidence that he opened a new business elsewhere.

"In the Metropolis of Kentucky." *IF,* April 5, 1902, 1.
Lewis, C. B. "Louisville and Its Afro-American Citizens." *Colored American Magazine,* April 1906, 263.
Masterson, C. L. "Merchant Tailoring." National Negro Business League, 5th Annual Convention, Indianapolis, IN, August 31–September 2, 1904. Records of the National Negro Business League, pt. 1, Annual Conference Proceedings and Organizational Records, 1900–1919, reel 1, frame 412.
Wright, George C. *Life Behind a Veil: Blacks in Louisville, Kentucky, 1865–1930.* Baton Rouge: Louisiana State Univ. Press, 1985.

—*Joshua D. Farrington*

MATHEWS, COURTNEY (b. 1868, Jessamine Co., KY; d. 1940, Lexington, KY), horseman. Courtney Mathews, the oldest child of Robert "Robin" and Louisa Mathews, grew up around horses because his father was a horse trainer and farmer. By age 10, he was working as a hostler. Six years later, he handled a breeding stallion named Deceiver at Sam Smith's farm on Harrodsburg Pike near Lexington, KY. Mathews later worked for Sanford C. Lyne of Larchmont Stud and also guided Lyne's son, Lucien, to become a top white American jockey.

In 1897, Mathews joined Major Thomas Clay McDowell, Henry Clay's great-grandson, at Ashland Stud and Breeding Farm in Lexington. He was responsible for breaking yearlings. When he started at the farm, both Thoroughbreds and Standardbreds were raised there. He worked with many outstanding racehorses, including Woodlake, a Latonia Derby winner, King's Daughter, Waterblossom, and Distinction. According to a 1938 interview, he broke and trained Alan-a-Dale, the 1902 **Kentucky Derby** winner, ridden by African American jockey **Jimmy Winkfield.** He also raised the 1912 American Horse of the Year, the Manager.

After jockey Lucien Lyne had great success in Belgium, he invited Mathews to join him. World War I prevented that trip.

In 1928, Mathews and his wife, Louisa "Lula," moved from 530 Ohio St. to a two-story, carved sandstone home at 547 Breckinridge St. in a predominantly white neighborhood. The home was a block from Lexington's Kentucky Association racetrack. Mathews remained at Ashland Stud until June 1935. For 38 years, he worked as a trainer and then foreman of the stud farm. He left only one time for one month and eight days because of a salary depute.

After a two-week illness, Mathews died at his home. Jones Funeral Service handled the funeral arrangements, and he was buried in Greenwood (now Cove Haven) Cemetery.

Kentucky Death Records, 1852–1953.
Leach, Brownie. "Major McDowell's Courtney." *Blood-Horse,* January 29, 1938.
Newspapers: "Colored Notes," *LL,* June 5, 1940; "Lexington House Offers Clues into Life of Little-Known Yet Acclaimed Black Trainer," *LHL,* July 24, 2011.
U.S. Federal Census (1870, 1880, 1910).

—*Sallie L. Powell*

MATHIS, HOWITT CONWAY (b. 1912, Greenville, KY; d. 1986, Paducah, KY), educator. H. C. Mathis was born in Greenville, KY, to John R. and Maggie Lee Mathis on January 2, 1912. After graduating from Greenville Training School, he attended Tennessee Agricultural and Industrial State University, from which he received a bachelor's degree in the early 1920s. He later returned to Tennessee A&I in the mid-1950s, writing his master's thesis on the history of the **Kentucky Negro Educational Association** and serving briefly as the head coach of the men's basketball team.

Mathis began his career as an educator in his hometown of Greenville in the 1930s and worked his way up from teacher to principal of a local elementary school. During the next two decades, he served in numerous positions, including principal and basketball coach at Muhlenberg County High School and principal of Drakesboro Community School. In 1957, he was appointed president of Paducah's West Kentucky State Vocational Training School (later known as **West Kentucky Community and Technical College**). During the early 1960s, he served as a consultant on school desegregation for the Human Relations Center at Western Kentucky University. In 1967, he became the first black president of the Kentucky Vocational Association. In 1971, he served on the Black History Committee of the **Kentucky Commission on Human Rights,** which was responsible for publishing the textbook *Kentucky's Black Heritage.*

Although Mathis retired from West Kentucky State Vocational Training School in 1972, he remained active throughout the rest of the decade. In 1976, he was named to the state board of education, and during the late 1970s, he served as executive director of West Kentucky Allied Services Inc., a pilot project that provided in-home services to the elderly. The program was so successful that it was eventually taken over by the Kentucky Department of Human Resources and expanded into a statewide service. Mathis died in Paducah on May 12, 1986.

In 1971, Paducah's mayor and city council changed the name of Thompson Avenue to H. C. Mathis Drive, and in 2011, the

Housing Authority of Paducah opened the H. C. Mathis Apartment Community, funded by a $2.6-million grant from the U.S. Department of Housing and Urban Development.

Horton, John Benjamin. *Profiles of Contemporary Black Achievers of Kentucky.* Louisville, KY: J. Benjamin Horton & Associates, 1983.
Kentucky's Black Heritage: The Role of the Black People in the History of Kentucky from Pioneer Days to the Present. Frankfort: Kentucky Commission on Human Rights, 1971.
"School Board." *KNE,* September 10, 1976, 3.

—*Joshua D. Farrington*

MAUPIN, MILBURN TAYLOR (b. 1926, Louisville, KY; d. 1990, Louisville, KY), educator. The son of Miller R. and Mary T. Maupin, Milburn Taylor Maupin was the oldest of seven children. He was educated in the public schools of Louisville and at the Oakwood Academy in Huntsville, AL. He received his bachelor of arts degree from the **Louisville Municipal College** in 1949. In 1951, he was awarded a master's in education from Indiana University.

Maupin began his career in education in 1949 as a junior high social studies teacher in the Louisville public school system. In 1958, he became the assistant principal of the Jackson Junior High (later known as Meyzeek Middle School)–Booker T. Washington Elementary complex. The next year, he was promoted to principal, a position he held until 1965, when he was appointed the director of the board of education's community school program.

As such, Maupin became the school system's first African American central office administrator. He also gained recognition as the first black president of the Louisville Education Association (1968–1970). Maupin held a number of administrative posts, including assistant superintendent for federally related programs (1968–1970), chairman of employee personnel services (1970–1973), deputy superintendent of operations (1973–1974), and interim superintendent (January–June 1975). He retired from the school system in July 1978 as the deputy superintendent of Jefferson County Public Schools.

Maupin also showed an interest in civic affairs, and in 1977 he was elected Louisville's First Ward alderman. He resigned in 1979 after he moved outside the city limits. Maupin was also a veteran of World War II, having served in the U.S. Army Medical Corps. He and his wife, Madeline Taylor Maupin, were the parents of two daughters, Madeline and Jacqueline. Maupin is buried in Evergreen Cemetery. In 1985, **Parkland** Elementary School was renamed Milburn T. Maupin Elementary in his honor.

MAY-MILLER, ZEPHRA (b. 1943, Indianapolis, IN; d. 2004, Louisville, KY), textile artist. Born to a 13-year-old mother, Zephra May moved to Louisville, KY, when she was only a few weeks old. She was raised by her great-aunt and great-uncle in the African American neighborhood known as **Smoketown,** the same area in which **Muhammad Ali** had been born the previous year. She worked as a mortician in the family business of R. G. May and Sons Funeral Home, the first African American funeral home in Louisville. She married multiple times and briefly lived in Spain when one husband served in the military. Her final marriage was to George H. Miller in 1986.

For over two decades, the four-feet-eight Miller created textile art using plastic garbage bags as her raw material. Cutting various colored bags into strips and then weaving the narrow pieces by using the crocheting technique of her great-aunt, Big Mamma, Miller fashioned wearable clothing. Many of her outfits included hats, purses, and shoes. She viewed people as "two-face-ted" and often made her garments reversible to indicate the dual nature of people. She believed that the commonality of everyday items like garbage bags helped break barriers between other people and herself that allowed them briefly to enter "her space." Her functional art included *Hit the Mark,* which demonstrated through black-and-white bull's-eyes the binary meaning of how people remain vulnerable while protecting themselves with clothing and the flirtatious concept of "hit on." She crafted other ensembles, such as *Snowflake, Fit to Be Tied,* and *Love Is Blind.* In 1992, she collaborated with sculptor **Ed Hamilton** on the work *Unity-Strength-Love: Smoketown Monument.* She exhibited in the Kentucky Museum of Art and Craft and Runako Gallery. As much as $700 was paid for her fashions, which she frequently modeled herself.

Miller commonly carried her Bible and proselytized. She offered the downtrodden transportation in her "Jesus car," a white limousine, and would give away the shoes off her feet. She varied between offering hugs and tongue-lashings and would sometimes burst into song. She enjoyed her title as the Bag Lady of Louisville. Like her art, the moniker had a double meaning based on her use of garbage bags and her eccentric behavior.

After suffering a stroke in July 2004, Miller died at Louisville's Norton Healthcare Pavilion in December 2004.

African-American Folk Art in Kentucky. Morehead, KY: Kentucky Folk Art Center, 1998.
Newspapers: "Searching for Zephra May," *CJ,* February 4, 2004, V8; "Artist Zephra May-Miller Dies at 61," *CJ,* December 21, 2004, B6.

—*Sallie L. Powell*

MAYSVILLE COLONIZATION SOCIETY, association that tried to encourage African Americans to move to the African colony of Liberia. The Maysville Colonization Society of Mason Co., which was active from at least 1822 to 1827, was associated with the state and national colonization societies. The group first met on December 26, 1822, in the Methodist Meeting House to "form a colonization Society in this place, auxiliary to the American Colonization Society of Washington City for the purpose of colonizing blacks of the United States on the Continent of Africa." Meetings were generally held in church meetinghouses, and Rev. John T. Edgar, one of the organizers, chaired the first meeting. Many prominent citizens were involved in the original group, including George Corwine, Peter Grant (the uncle of future U.S. president Ulysses S. Grant), William Grinstead, and Andrew Wood. Later members included Lewis Collins, a newspaper editor and an early Kentucky historian, and A. M. January. The Maysville Colonization Society met again two days after its first meeting and approved a constitution that stated the goal of raising money to pay for "the emigration and colonization of all people of colour who are willing to join the colony." Much of the local society's time was occupied with the administration of the group, although it also informed the public of its goals and raised money for its stated purpose. On February 23, 1824, the Maysville Colonization Society petitioned Henry Clay, a U.S. senator from Kentucky, to support the congressional incorporation of the American Colonization Society.

In 1825, the group selected members to meet with the Marquis de Lafayette, if he were to stop in Maysville, and ask him to meet with the society. There is no record that such a meeting took place, but Reverend Edgar and Johnston Armstrong, members of the Maysville Colonization Society, were selected to be part of the welcoming committee for the French general. There is no evidence that the local society's endeavors were very successful, despite its efforts to have the "managers of the Society see and converse with free blacks in our town and neighborhood and show them the advantages resulting to them by their moving to the colony of Liberia."

Maysville Colonization Society Record Book, 1822–1827. Kentucky Gateway Museum Center, Maysville, KY.

—*John Klee*

MCAFEE, ALONZO B. "A. B." (b. 1872, Harrodsburg, KY; d. 1919, Louisville, KY), **prominent undertaker, attorney, organizational leader, and newspaper editor.** Alonzo B. McAfee was born in Harrodsburg, KY. When he was a child, he and his mother, Mattie, moved from Mercer Co. to Louisville and lived with his maternal uncle. He graduated from Louisville's **Central High School** in 1894. He then taught at the Eighth and Kentucky Streets School. During his teaching years, he trained in stenography and bookkeeping. In 1896, as a member of the Grand United Order of Odd Fellows, he joined other young men to organize the political group Race Protective Association and became its first president. In that same year, he edited the *Informer,* a Louisville newspaper.

McAfee worked in various careers. According to the *Indianapolis Freeman,* after studying at Clarke's School of Embalming in Cincinnati, OH, McAfee became the first African American to obtain an embalmer's license in Kentucky. He worked with William Watson, owner of the oldest funeral business in Louisville. He also matriculated at Central Law School, worked with the school's dean and attorney Albert S. White, and was admitted to the bar in 1898. He married his wife, Minnie, in 1904. By 1906, he owned the Palace Rink and worked for the U.S. Revenue Service.

In 1907, the African American Undertakers' Association met in Frankfort, KY. Its officers included **Thomas Kenney Robb,** president, from Frankfort; **Lucas B. Willis,** vice president, originally from Louisville but operating a funeral home in Indianapolis; A. B. McAfee, secretary, W. M. J. Silkman, assistant secretary; **James Harris Hathaway,** treasurer, both from Louisville; and J. A. Agnew, sergeant-at-arms, from Owensboro. Robb, Willis, McAfee, and Hathaway were reelected to their positions at the Frankfort meeting. The group adopted a resolution asking the Falls City Undertakers' Association, a white organization, not to bury African Americans since African Americans were not allowed to bury white people.

In 1908, McAfee traveled with two other African American Republican leaders to the Republican National Convention. He had served as the secretary of the Louisville and Jefferson County Republican Convention. Along with working as the secretary of the Colored Jefferson County Fair Association, he wrote a pamphlet on the history of the Colored National Funeral Directors and edited a newspaper, the *New South* and later the *Ohio Falls Express.* He also established his own undertaking business on W. Chestnut in 1908.

Considered to have the most modern facilities, McAfee's equipment included an "ebonized" funeral carriage for adults and a child's funeral cart drawn by "milk white ponies." By 1912, he was president of the State Funeral Directors, and **Daisy Saffell** of Shelbyville was the secretary. McAfee died on February 3, 1919. He was buried in Louisville's Greenwood Cemetery.

Kentucky Death Records, 1852–1953.
Newspapers: "Undertakers Will Meet," *IF,* July 13, 1907, 1; "Want All Negro Funerals: Colored Undertakers Will Make the Request," *IF,* August 10, 1907, 1; "Race Progress," *IF,* December 26, 1908, 3; "A. B. McAfee," *IF,* December 24, 1910, 4.
U.S. Federal Census (1880).

—*Sallie L. Powell*

MCALPIN, HARRY S. (b. 1906, St. Louis, MO; d. 1985, Fairfax, VA), **journalist, attorney, and civil rights activist.** Harry S. McAlpin, the son of Harry S. and Louise (Scott) McAlpin, followed his father in his abhorrence of injustice and made fighting discrimination his life's work. His father died when McAlpin was 15, but he had taught his son that all men were created equal in God's sight. McAlpin did not use the suffix "Junior." In 1926, he earned a journalism degree from the University of Wisconsin and his law degree from Robert H. Terrell Law School in Washington, DC, in 1933.

Among his accomplishments, McAlpin served as the chief of information services in the Office of Negro Affairs from 1941 to 1942. His primary function was to find jobs for African Americans. His zeal provoked antagonism from his supervisors and cost him his job, but he fought for his reinstatement in what was called "the McAlpin case" and was back at his desk in three months. On February 8, 1944, he became the first African American reporter credentialed to the White House. He covered Presidents Franklin D. Roosevelt and Harry S. Truman for 51 black newspapers. He was also a naval war correspondent with the rank of lieutenant commander. During this time, he traveled to Korea on an inspection tour and fought for the rights of African American troops. In 1947, he became the director of information for the Sugar Rationing Administration.

In 1949, McAlpin joined the law firm of (Charles) Anderson and McAlpin in Louisville, Kentucky. In 1951, he attacked the advertising policy that stated the desired race for a job applicant. Three years later, civil service jobs were filled in Louisville without regard to race. He served as president of the Louisville branch of the **National Association for the Advancement of Colored People** and was the only African American commonwealth's attorney in the state when he resigned in 1953.

In Kentucky, McAlpin fought segregation in distinctive ways. He threatened a lawsuit if the Louisville public park system allowed African Americans to attend a play based on the life of Abraham Lincoln while simultaneously prohibiting African

Americans from using most of the park system's facilities. He said that police should arrest all blacks who attended or the city should void its archaic segregation resolution. In 1964, as a member of the Kentucky Board of Education, he pushed that racially segregated schools should lose their state financial aid. Three years later, he joined others in a proposal for an African American boycott of Louisville's downtown businesses for not supporting open-housing policies.

In 1972, McAlpin became the first African American administrative law judge when he was appointed chief judge at the U.S. Department of Agriculture. He and his wife, Alice B. Stokes of Washington, DC, had one child, Karlen S. McAlpin. In 1985, McAlpin died in Fairfax, VA, almost two years after his wife's death.

Fleming, G. James, and Christian E. Burckel, eds. *Who's Who in Colored America.* 7th ed. *Supplement.* Yonkers-on-Hudson, NY: Christian E. Burckel & Associates, 1950.

McAlpin, Harry S. "The Courage to Change the Things I Can." *This I Believe* (radio program). http://thisibelieve.org/essay/16794/ (accessed February 13, 2012).

Newspapers: "Negro Attorney Threatens Suit Unless Segregation Law Upheld," *LHL,* June 7, 1953; "Racial Ban to Affect Eight Local Schools," *KNE,* June 25, 1964, 1.

Stone, Gertrude B. "The McAlpin Case." *Crisis,* January 1941, 13, 20.

—*Sallie L. Powell*

MCANULTY, WILLIAM EUGENE, JR. (b. 1947, Indianapolis, IN; d. 2007, Louisville, KY), first African American to sit on the Kentucky Supreme Court. The youngest of three children in a working-class family in Indianapolis, IN, William Eugene McAnulty Jr. learned respect for others from his father, a postal worker. He encountered racial prejudice when he became one of the first African Americans to integrate a local all-white high school. After graduation, McAnulty briefly worked as a clerk in the governor's office, where he came in contact with several politicians and lawyers. After receiving a bachelor's degree at Indiana University and a master's degree in special education at the University of Louisville, he decided that a career in law offered him the best opportunity to "change things for the better." He then enrolled in the University of Louisville Law School.

McAnulty became the first African American to be elected president of the University of Louisville's Student Bar Association, beating out future Kentucky Supreme Court justice Joseph Lambert in the process. While he was still a law student, he worked for Judge Todd Hollenbach of Jefferson Co. as an assistant safety director. Hollenbach began McAnulty's career as a judge by appointing him to juvenile court in 1975. McAnulty was elected district court judge for Jefferson Co. in 1977 and moved further up the ranks after winning election as circuit judge in 1983. After a brief interlude in private practice following the completion of his term, he returned to the bench when he was appointed to the circuit court in 1993.

McAnulty's skill as a judge earned him the respect of lawyers throughout Louisville, who rated him highly on judicial evaluations conducted by the bar association. In 1997, the Kentucky Trial Attorneys Association named him Henry V. Pennington Outstanding Judge of the Year, and the Leadership Louisville

Foundation honored him with the Thomas C. Simons Distinguished Leadership Award in the same year. A year later, he was elected to the Kentucky Court of Appeals.

On August 15, 2006, William E. McAnulty Jr. became the first African American to serve on the Supreme Court of Kentucky when he was appointed by Governor Ernie Fletcher. Three months later, he won election to a full eight-year term over Ann O'Malley Shake with support from Citizens for Better Judges and the *Louisville Courier-Journal.* In July 2007, he announced that he would undergo treatment for lung cancer but planned to write opinions from his bed. He retired from the bench a month later after his condition worsened. On August 23, 2007, cancer claimed his life at his home in Louisville, KY. He was cremated and interred in Cave Hill Cemetery.

Newspapers: "Supreme Court Justice Resigns—McAnulty Cites Health Reasons," *LHL,* August 10, 2007, A1; "'We Have Lost a Good Friend': Irreverent, Trailblazing Jurist Dies after Bout with Cancer," *LCJ,* August 24, 2007, A1.

Who's Who in Black Louisville. 2nd ed. Columbus, OH: Who's Who Publishing Co., 2008.

"William E. McAnulty Jr. Sworn In as Justice of the Supreme Court of Kentucky." Supreme Court of Kentucky. August 15, 2006. http://courts.ky.gov/NR/rdonlyres/2C150E2F-E422-4918-BA1B-ED7F075978C0/0/JusticeMcAnultyInvestitureRelease081506.pdf (accessed July 22, 2011).

—*Stephen Pickering*

MCCANN, LES (b. 1935, Lexington, KY), famous jazz pianist. Growing up in Lexington, KY, Les McCann developed an affinity for gospel music from services at the nearby Shiloh Baptist Church. His parents, James and Anna McCann, later noted his natural talent for music from his attempts to bang out a tune on the piano at the age of three and his ability to play by ear in the **Dunbar High School** marching band. After a brief career in the navy between 1953 and 1956, McCann moved to Los Angeles and decided to make music his life, graduating from Westlake College of Music and playing piano in coffeehouses across the city.

After releasing a few albums in the early 1960s, McCann attracted some attention for *Stormy Monday,* an album he released with soul and **jazz** icon Lou Rawls in 1962. In 1969, McCann had his biggest hit with the single "Compared to What" from his album *Swiss Movement.* Established as a preeminent jazz pianist by these successes, McCann continued to make music for the next few decades. He was slowed by a stroke in 1994 but released several more albums afterward that he recorded in his own studio. In 2008, he was inducted into the Kentucky Music Hall of Fame.

Doerschuk, Robert L. *88: The Greats of Jazz Piano.* San Francisco: Backbeat Books, 2001.

"Jazz Legends of Los Angeles: Les McCann." *Los Angeles Sentinel,* May 27, 2004, B4.

"Les McCann Recognized Worldwide, and in his Home State." *LHL,* February 17, 2008, E1.

—*Stephen Pickering*

MCCLAIN, RICHARD POLLARD (b. 1890, Nicholasville, KY; d. 1965, Cincinnati, OH), medical doctor and Ohio state legislator. Born to Meredith and Ellen McClain in Nicholasville,

KY, on January 3, 1890, Richard Pollard McClain spent his formative teenage years in Cincinnati, OH. After graduating from high school in Ohio in 1908, McClain studied medicine at Howard University. He received his medical degree in 1913 and interned at Freedmen's Hospital in Washington, DC. In 1918, he married Alice E. Martin, a nurse at Freedmen's Hospital. During the 1920s, he returned to Cincinnati, where he opened his own practice. During his 30-year medical career, McClain became one of the city's most renowned African American doctors, serving as manager of the Model Drug Corporation, manager of Mercy Hospital, and president of the Buckeye Medical Association.

In 1934, McClain was elected to the Ohio House of Representatives after receiving the endorsement of the Hamilton County Republican Party. In 1935, he sponsored a bill that banned racial discrimination in employment by companies with public-works contracts. The McClain Law was ultimately signed by the governor and became effective on July 24, 1935. After its passage, McClain resigned from the legislature to run for the Cincinnati City Council. During his two terms on the council, he rose to the position of president pro tempore.

In 1939, McClain retired from politics to focus on his medical career. He remained active in the city's social life as a member of the Knights of Pythias and the Elks, a 32nd-degree Mason, and a trustee of the Antioch Baptist Church. He died at University Hospital of Cincinnati General on October 28, 1965.

Dabney, Wendell P. *Cincinnati's Colored Citizens: Historical, Sociological and Biographical.* Cincinnati: Dabney, 1926.

Fleming, G. James, and Christian E. Burckel, eds. *Who's Who in Colored America.* 7th ed. Yonkers-on-Hudson, NY: Christian E. Burckel & Associates, 1950.

Giffin, William Wayne. "The Negro in Ohio, 1914–1939." PhD diss., Ohio State Univ., 1968.

—*Joshua D. Farrington*

MCCLELLAN, GEORGE MARION (b. 1860, Belfast, TN; d. 1934, New York, NY), educator and poet. George Marion McClellan was born to George Fielding and Eliza McClellan in Belfast, TN, on September 29, 1860. He graduated from Fisk University in 1885 and then studied for two years at Hartford Theological Seminary in Connecticut. In 1887, he moved to Louisville, KY, to accept a position as a Congressionalist minister. In 1890, he returned to Fisk to obtain a master's degree and simultaneously commuted to Hartford to finish his divinity degree. After a brief period as a Fisk teacher and recruiter, he returned to Louisville. From 1899 to 1911, he taught geography and Latin at **Central Colored High School** and from 1911 to 1919 served as the principal of (Paul Laurence) **Dunbar High School.**

Although McClellan had a moderately successful career as an educator, his true passion was poetry. His first book of poetry, *Poems,* published in 1895, was later reviewed favorably by the *New York Times.* In 1896, he published *Songs of a Southerner.* James Weldon Johnson described McClellan as "a gentle poet of nature, of the seasons, of birds and flowers and woodland scenes." Many of his later works, however, addressed issues of racism and were known for their refusal to use a supposed "black dialect," a common practice among many black poets of the period.

Despite critical acclaim for his poetry from both white and black reviewers, McClellan struggled financially throughout his career. In 1906, he spent $500 to publish *Old Greenbottom Inn, and Other Stories.* The novella "Old Greenbottom Inn" was later described by a scholar as "one of the most complicated works from this period" by an African American writer. The tragic story of interracial love was a harsh critique of southern racism and one of the few works by a black author at the turn of the century to address the theme of gender and the unique struggles faced by black women.

In 1916, McClellan's 21-year-old son, Theodore, contracted tuberculosis. McClellan wrote letters asking for assistance from some of the nation's leading hospitals, all of which denied his request because they did not accept black patients. In order to raise money to visit an integrated hospital outside Kentucky, McClellan published *The Path of Dreams,* a compilation of his most successful works. In June, McClellan wrote a heartbreaking article featured in the **National Association for the Advancement of Colored People**'s *Crisis* that described the refusal of white hospitals to treat his son and offered readers a copy of his book if they sent $1.50 to his Louisville address. McClellan spent the donations on a visit to a Los Angeles, CA, hospital, but the trip proved to be too late. Theodore died in early 1917.

McClellan was devastated by the loss of his son, and his life unraveled during the 1920s. He died on May 17, 1934, in New York City and was buried in Louisville, KY. One Louisville African American school was renamed the George M. McClellan Colored School in his honor. It closed during the desegregation era in 1956.

Bruce, Dickson D., Jr. *Black American Writing from the Nadir: The Evolution of a Literary Tradition, 1877–1915.* Baton Rouge: Louisiana State Univ. Press, 1989.

Dunnigan, Alice Allison, comp. and ed. *The Fascinating Story of Black Kentuckians: Their Heritage and Traditions.* Washington, DC: Associated Publishers, 1982.

Jefferson County Public Schools. http://media.jefferson.k12.ky.us /groups/jcpshistory/wiki/dbc72/ (accessed October 28, 2013).

Schmidt, Peter. *Sitting in Darkness: New South Fiction, Education, and the Rise of Jim Crow Colonialism, 1865–1920.* Jackson: Univ. Press of Mississippi, 2008.

Sherman, Joan R. *Invisible Poets: Afro-Americans of the Nineteenth Century.* 2nd ed. Urbana: Univ. of Illinois Press, 1989.

—*Joshua D. Farrington*

MCCURINE, JAMES "BIG STICK" (b. 1921, Clinton, KY; d. 2002, Chicago, IL), power hitter for the Chicago American Giants from 1946 to 1949. Born into a religious family on May 8, 1921, James McCurine showed a talent for baseball in his teenage years in Clinton, KY. When he was 15 years old, he began playing with the semipro teams the Hartford Giants and the Brown Bombers before settling into a consistent role with the Lincoln Giants in Chicago. His father limited his playing time, requiring $25 from teams for him to play on Sundays, but he still managed to attract the attention of the Chicago American Giants in an exhibition game.

In 1945, the American Giants signed McCurine, and he quickly earned the nickname Big Stick for his ability to hit home runs. Although he was primarily an outfielder, he played other positions, which included pitching. He averaged around 20 home runs a season in the four years he played for the American Giants, which earned him a tryout with the Boston Braves. However, McCurine's right arm had deteriorated from extended use in his semipro days, and he rejected an offer to switch to first base for the team's minor-league affiliate. He retired the same year and briefly took a job with the Chicago Transit Authority before working for Golden State Mutual Insurance. On May 24, 2002, he died of heart and kidney failure and was buried in Burr Oak Cemetery in Chicago.

Heaphy, Leslie A., ed. *Black Baseball and Chicago: Essays on the Players, Teams, and Games of the Negro League's Most Important City.* Jefferson, NC: McFarland, 2006.

"James McCurine: Played for Giants in Negro League—Outfielder Who Was Lethal with Bat Was Known as 'Big Stick.'" *Chicago Sun-Times,* May 30, 2002, 64.

Kelley, Brent. *The Negro Leagues Revisited: Conversations with 66 More Baseball Heroes.* Jefferson, NC: McFarland, 2000.

—*Stephen Pickering*

MCDANIELS, JIM "BIG MAC" (b. 1948, Scottsville, KY), collegiate and professional basketball player. The son of James and Sendy Marie McDaniels, Jim McDaniels was born in Scottsville, Kentucky, on April 2, 1948. After graduating from Allen County High School, McDaniels began his varsity basketball career as a Hilltopper at Western Kentucky University (WKU) under Coach John Oldham in 1968. The 6-feet-11 center was named an All-American three times and was distinguished as a consensus All-American his senior year in 1971. He was also named Ohio Valley Conference Player of the Year in 1970 and 1971. During the 1970–1971 season, McDaniels led the Hilltoppers to the school's first Final Four appearance. After losing the NCAA Mideast Regional final in double overtime to Villanova, WKU beat Kansas in the consolation game. During his collegiate career, McDaniels became WKU's all-time leading scorer with 2,238 points. He held this record until 2008, when it was tied by senior guard Courtney Lee. McDaniels also remains one of Western's top-ten all-time leaders in rebounds with 1,118. After graduating from WKU in 1971 with a bachelor of science in physical education, McDaniels played professionally for seven years in both the American Basketball Association and the National Basketball Association, as well as in Italy. In 2000, Western Kentucky University honored McDaniels by retiring his number 44 jersey.

McDaniels, Jim. Interview by Hilltopper Haven, January 4, 2000. http://www.hilltopperhaven.com/interviews/mcdaniels.html (accessed January 16, 2009).

———. Telephone interview by Joanna Lile, October 10, 2009.

Western Kentucky University. Press release, June 27, 2008. http://www.wku.edu/news/releases08/june/mcdaniels.html (accessed December 28, 2008).

—*Joanna Lile*

MCDOWELL, CYRUS R. (b. 1854, Bowling Green, KY; d. 1950, Hannibal, MO), educator, minister, and founder of the *Bowling Green Watchman*. Cyrus R. McDowell was born to Cyrus and Lucinda McDowell in Bowling Green, KY, on February 4, 1854. Although little is known about the first 20 years of his life, during the 1870s and early 1880s, he taught at various schools in Rockfield, Woodburn, and Bowling Green, where he emerged as one of Warren Co.'s leading educators. In 1881, he was elected president of the Bowling Green Colored School (later known as **Bowling Green Academy**), an institution he helped establish.

In 1887, McDowell joined C. C. Strumm in founding the *Bowling Green Watchman* and served as its editor through 1889. In 1890, he began his transition from educator to minister and was ordained in the Baptist Church. During the rest of the decade, he served as pastor at churches in Hartford and Greenville, KY. As a minister, he played an instrumental role in the establishment of the Green River Valley Association. By 1915, the association represented 29 churches with 3,490 members.

In 1900, McDowell was called to pastor a church in Missouri, the state where he spent the rest of his life. During the next 50 years, McDowell earned his doctor of divinity degree from Missouri's Western College, served several years as moderator of the Northern Missouri Baptist Association, and pastored churches in Independence, St. Louis, and Hannibal. He also established his own insurance company and served as a trustee at Western College. His wife, Mary Thurmon of Louisville, was active in the National Association of Colored Women and was elected national treasurer in 1922. McDowell died of a stroke in Hannibal, MO, on November 16, 1950.

Mather, Frank Lincoln, ed. *Who's Who of the Colored Race: A General Biographical Dictionary of Men and Women of African Descent.* Vol. 1. Chicago: Memento Edition, 1915.

Parrish, C. H. *Golden Jubilee of the General Association of Colored Baptists in Kentucky: From 1865–1915.* Louisville, KY: Mayes Printing Co., 1915.

Penn, I. Garland. *The Afro-American Press, and Its Editors.* Springfield, MA: Willey & Co., 1891.

—*Joshua D. Farrington*

MCFARLAND, RICHARD LAWRENCE "R. L." (b. 1917, Owensboro, KY; d. 2002, Owensboro, KY), and MCFARLAND, RUBY TAYLOR (b. 1920, Sorgho, KY), funeral home owners. The youngest of eight children of James Dan McFarland, a custodian and church deacon, and Elizabeth "Lizzie" McFarland, Richard Lawrence "R. L." McFarland was taught to be involved in the church. As a youth, he was also politically active when he handed out election materials in 1929. In that same year, he first met his future wife, Ruby Taylor, when he was 12 and she was 9. As a teenager, McFarland worked as a custodian. In 1935, he graduated as valedictorian from Owensboro's all-black Western High School and soon went to work as a delivery driver while continuing his custodial job at night, beginning his lifelong practice of simultaneously working multiple jobs. He and Ruby married in 1939. During World War II, he drove almost an hour to Evansville, IN, to work as a janitor in the Chrysler defense plant.

On January 26, 1947, McFarland preached his first sermon. He ministered to several small churches in the Owensboro area. In 1950, while continuing his ministry, he went to work for the telephone company. Six years later, he began his 46-year pastorate of

Mount Calvary Baptist Church. Like R. L., Ruby also held multiple jobs in order to support their family of eight children. She worked full-time as a nurse on the maternity floor at Owensboro–Daviess County Hospital for 25 years and part-time at Haynes Funeral Home. She worked nights while R. L. worked days. In 1968, the McFarlands purchased Haynes Funeral Home with a hired mortician to run the business. **Dr. Reginald Claypool Neblett,** the only African American doctor in Owensboro, persuaded Ruby to get her funeral director's license. In 1974, she graduated from Louisville's Kentucky School of Mortuary Science.

In 1985, R. L. retired from BellSouth Telephone Company and was approached and encouraged by an interracial group of Owensboro citizens to run for the city commission. The next year, he became the first African American candidate elected to a paid public office in Owensboro or Daviess Co. He served six terms as an Owensboro city commissioner, and by receiving the most votes in 1992 and 1994, he acted as mayor pro tem. The Owensboro Human Relations Commission created the Rev. R. L. McFarland Leadership Award in 1992.

R. L. continued his ministry until his death in 2002. McFarland Funeral Home handled the arrangements. Ruby continued in the funeral business, aided by two of her sons. In 2006, they built a state-of-the-art mortuary on about one acre of land on W. Fifth St. The next year, Ruby was honored by 100 Black Women of Funeral Services, Incorporated.

Montell, William Lynwood. *Tales from Kentucky Funeral Homes.* Lexington: Univ. of Press of Kentucky, 2009.
Newspapers: "Old-Time Preacher McFarland Won't Retire from God's Work, but He's Slowing Down," *OMI,* August 11, 2001, 6; "McFarland, Former Mayor pro Tem, Dies at 85; Minister Opened Door for Black Politicians," *OMI,* September 14, 2002, 1; "Mourners Celebrate His Legacy at Funeral; 'A Giant Has Fallen,' Pastor Tells Hundreds," *OMI,* September 19, 2002, 1; "Funeral Director Recognized by National Organization," *OMI,* November 16, 2007, C1.
—*Sallie L. Powell*

MCFATRIDGE, JAMES MORGAN (b. 1914, Lexington, KY; d. 2000, Los Angeles, CA), Tuskegee Airman and Bronze Star recipient. James Morgan McFatridge was born in Lexington, KY, the first son of James Andrew and Jessie Hickman (Williams) McFatridge. The family moved to Cincinnati, OH, when McFatridge was still a child. His father worked as a dining car waiter for the Louisville and Nashville Railroad.

In 1934, McFatridge studied for two years at Ohio's Wilberforce University and then at West Virginia State College, 1936–1937. Three years later, he married Ruth Ernestine Kelsor of Huntington, WV. On September 20, 1942, McFatridge enlisted in the air corps in Ft. Thomas, KY. The next year, he graduated with distinction from an armorers course at Army Air Forces Buckley Army Air Field, Colorado, and was commissioned a 2nd lieutenant.

As a **Tuskegee Airman,** McFatridge served with the 301st Fighter Squadron in Italy. In 1944, he was awarded the Bronze Star for designing an armament device on the P-39 fighter plane. The next year, he received the Presidential Distinguished Unit Citation Medal. McFatridge later served in the Korean War before

retiring at the rank of lieutenant colonel. He was a member of **Alpha Phi Alpha Fraternity.**

Most of the McFatridge siblings resided in California in their elder years. McFatridge died in Los Angeles one year after one of his younger sisters. He was buried in Forest Lawn Memorial Park, Cypress, CA.

Fleming, G. James, and Christian E. Burckel, eds. *Who's Who in Colored America.* 7th ed. *Supplement.* Yonkers-on-Hudson, NY: Christian E. Burckel & Associates, 1950.
U.S. Federal Census (1920, 1930).
U.S. Veterans Gravesites, ca. 1775–2006.
U.S. World War II Army Enlistment Records, 1938–1946.
—*Sallie L. Powell*

MCGILL, CHARLOTTE SMITH (b. 1919, Louisville, KY; d. 1988, Louisville, KY), and MCGILL, HUGHES E. (b. 1920, Louisville, KY; d. 1970, Louisville, KY), state representatives in Kentucky's 42nd District. Hughes E. McGill played an active role in the **civil rights movement** in Louisville, KY, and broke down barriers to establish fair-housing laws in the state. Born in 1920 in Louisville, he graduated from West Virginia State College, the Mondell Business Institute, and the University of Louisville. He married Charlotte Smith in 1949. McGill served as a state representative in the Kentucky General Assembly from 1968 to 1970, representing the 42nd District. He was best known for securing the passage of Kentucky's Fair Housing Act.

His wife, Charlotte Smith, born in 1919, was accustomed to being involved in Louisville's black community. Her father, **James Edward Smith,** was a very active and influential member of the Louisville and Jefferson Co. black community in business and in politics. He cofounded the **Domestic Life and Accident Insurance Company** and other organizations. He was a state representative for Kentucky's 42nd District in the House of Representatives from 1964 to 1968. Charlotte's mother, **Verna Smith,** was also actively involved in the local community, serving as the first African American president of a local Democratic club. She was also the first African American female cocaptain of a precinct.

With both parents actively engaged in the Louisville community, government, and politics, Charlotte followed closely in their footsteps. She was a Howard University graduate and obtained her master's degree from Indiana State University. In 1949, after her marriage to Hughes McGill, the couple moved to New York City. She initially worked for the Wage Stabilization Board in Washington, DC, before she obtained a job with New York's YWCA executive offices. The couple returned to Louisville in 1957.

When her husband died in 1970 before his term expired, Charlotte served out the remainder of his term. In this position, she also became a member of the Governor's Special Committee on Reapportionment. She was elected to the Kentucky House of Representatives in 1971 and served three full terms of her own. She also served as a **National Association for the Advancement of Colored People** board member, was vice chairman of the Louisville–Jefferson County Democratic Executive Committee, and was an active member of the Democratic Women's Club. She died in December 1988 and was buried in the Louisville Cemetery.

"Black History Month: Charlotte Smith McGill, 1919–1988." *LCJ*, February 4, 2011, B3.

Fosl, Catherine, and Tracy E. K'Meyer. *Freedom on the Border: An Oral History of the Civil Rights Movement in Kentucky.* Lexington: Univ. Press of Kentucky, 2009.

K'Meyer, Tracy E. *Civil Rights in the Gateway to the South: Louisville, Kentucky, 1945–1980.* Lexington: Univ. Press of Kentucky, 2009.

Smith-McGill Family Papers, 1879–1987. University Archives and Special Collections, Ekstrom Library, Univ. of Louisville.

—*Karen Cotton McDaniel*

MCKINLEY, JOHN JORDAN CRITTENDEN (b. 1852, Russellville, KY; d. 1912, Louisville, KY), educator and journalist.

Born on March 1, 1852, to William J. and Mildred (Bibb) McKinley, John Jordan Crittenden McKinley, also known as J. J. C., moved with his family to Louisville, KY, when he was only six months old. He later studied under famous Kentucky African American educators Rev. **Henry Adams** and **William Gibson.** In 1870, he attended **Berea College** but was later forced to leave because of his mother's financial hardship after losing her money in the Freedmen's Bank.

In 1874, he became the principal at a school in Danville, KY. The next year, he accepted a teaching position in Louisville, joined the Odd Fellows, and also began a journalism career with Lexington's *American Citizen.* He used the nom de plume Video at this newspaper. In 1878, he worked as a correspondent and wrote under the pseudonym Mack for the *Western Review,* published in Cincinnati, OH. Two years later, he joined Louisville's *Bulletin* as one of its editors and frequently pushed for equal rights in his writings.

In 1881, McKinley began his role as the Odd Fellows' grand secretary of the state and served for 17 years. He authored the first historical sketch of the Grand United Order of Odd Fellows in America in 1893. He worked to have Kentucky secure funds to construct a building for troubled youths instead of sending them to prison.

In 1912, McKinley died and was buried in Louisville's Eastern Cemetery. After his death, McKinley's wife, Julia, continued in education as a member of the **Kentucky Negro Educational Association** (KNEA). His son, J. J. C. Jr., also entered teaching and became treasurer of the KNEA in 1926. In 1930, he followed in his father's journalism footsteps and worked as a newspaper reporter in Chicago, IL.

Hamilton, G. P. *Biographical Sketches of Prominent Negro Men and Women of Kentucky.* Memphis: E. H. Clarke & Brother, 1911.

Kentucky Death Records, 1852–1953.

U.S. Federal Census (1900, 1910, 1930).

—*Sallie L. Powell*

MCLEOD, JOHN C. (b. 1877, Covington, KY; d. 1962, New Rochelle, NY), veterinarian.

John C. McLeod, a black veterinarian, was the son of John S. and Anna McLeod. His father was the first principal of **Lincoln-Grant School** in Covington. The family eventually moved to Cincinnati, where McLeod attended public schools and graduated from Hughes High School. He was employed at the Phoenix Grain and Stock Exchange in Cincinnati as an assistant bookkeeper. On October 5, 1901, he married Elvira Cox of Cincinnati, and the couple had a son. John McLeod entered the Cincinnati Veterinary College, where he studied veterinary surgery and earned a DVM. After graduation, he was appointed the U.S. veterinary inspector in the Bureau of Animal Husbandry and served in the stockyards at Chicago. Before he left for Chicago, McLeod was the only African American veterinarian in Cincinnati.

McLeod was active in the Masonic Lodge; he was 32nd-degree Mason, a Shriner, and a past master of St, John's Lodge in Cincinnati. During the 1930s, he moved to New Rochelle, NY, where he continued working as a veterinarian with the U.S. Public Health Service. He died in that city in 1962 and was buried in Malden, MA.

Dabney, Wendell P. *Cincinnati's Colored Citizens: Historical, Sociological and Biographical.* Cincinnati: Dabney, 1926.

Newspapers: "Births," *KTS*, August 9, 1902, 11; "Death Notices," *CP*, March 26, 1962, 4; "Journey's End," *CE*, March 26, 1962, 37.

—*Theodore H. H. Harris*

MCRIDLEY, WENDELL H. (b. 1842, Tennessee; d. 1932, Cadiz, KY), minister, educator, and editor and publisher of the *Cadiz Informer.*

Little is known about the first 40 years of Wendell H. McRidley's life. There is even confusion surrounding his name. He was typically referred to simply as W. H. McRidley, and some sources claim that his first name was William, while others refer to him as Wendell H. McRidley. Born in Tennessee in 1842, he had become a moderately successful middle-class African American lawyer and preacher in Louisville by the late 1870s. In 1880, he served as treasurer of the city's Mt. Olive No. 34 Masonic Lodge. In 1881, he was called to the Second Baptist Church of Cadiz, KY, where he remained pastor for 51 years.

In 1894, McRidley founded Cadiz Normal and Theological School, which had 269 elementary through eighth-grade students during its first year and was operated by the local Baptist Association. McRidley served as principal and a teacher of the school for the next two decades. He was also the founder, editor, and publisher of the *Cadiz Informer,* a four-column, four-page weekly newspaper "devoted to the advancement of the negro," first printed in 1904. According to the *Paducah Evening Sun,* the newspaper had a large circulation, and some of its editorials were even reprinted in the nation's largest black newspapers, including the *New York Age.* The paper continued to thrive until its offices burned down after a lightning strike in 1931. His wife, Anna M. Crump McRidley, assisted him in the daily operations of the newspaper and also taught alongside him at Cadiz Normal and Theological School.

Although the *Cadiz Informer*'s primary focus was on reporting news from the Baptist Church, it also advanced McRidley's partisan Republican politics. He wrote to Republican officials in 1908 that "I have been fighting the battle for my party forty odd years in the State. . . . The Cadiz Informer has done more in breaking the backbone of [the Democratic Party] than any one thing in this section." During the early 1900s, he served as secretary of the Trigg County Republican Executive Committee and was a delegate to the Republican National Convention in 1900 and 1916.

W. H. McRidley remained the pastor of Cadiz's Second Baptist Church until his death on February 21, 1932.

Jones, Thomas Jesse. *Negro Education: A Study of the Private and Higher Schools for Colored People in the United States.* Vol. 2. Washington, DC: Government Printing Office, 1917.

Newspapers: "New Paper in Cadiz," *Paducah Sun,* April 15, 1904, 6; W. H. McRidley, letter to the editor, *Barbourville (KY) Mountain Advocate,* February 28, 1908, 1; "Cadiz Informer Plant Burns," *BAA,* July 18, 1931, 19.

Parrish, C. H. *Golden Jubilee of the General Association of Colored Baptists in Kentucky: From 1865–1915.* Louisville, KY: Mayes Printing Co., 1915.

—*Joshua D. Farrington*

MCWHORTER, "FREE FRANK" (b. 1777, Union Co., SC; d. 1854, New Philadelphia, IL), **founder of New Philadelphia, IL, a biracial town.** "Free Frank" McWhorter was born in South Carolina to a slave named Juda and Juda's owner, George McWhorter, in 1777. In 1795, McWhorter brought Frank to frontier Kentucky, where he started a farm in Pulaski Co. and they worked side by side. Frank was granted permission to rent his labor out to surrounding farms for his own profit. In 1799, he married a slave on a nearby farm named Lucy.

In 1810, George McWhorter moved to Tennessee and left Frank in charge of the Kentucky farm. Frank began to manufacture saltpeter, an essential ingredient of gunpowder. In 1815, George McWhorter died, and his heirs offered Frank his freedom for $500. Frank, however, first paid $800 for the freedom of his wife in 1817. Two years later, he purchased himself, and he registered as "Free Frank" in the 1820 census.

Throughout the 1820s, Frank and Lucy invested in land, expanded their farming operation, established a permanent saltpeter factory in Danville, KY, and used profits to purchase the freedom of their children. In 1819, Lucy's previous owner sued her, claiming that he had loaned her $212 when she was a slave. In court, Frank turned Kentucky's slave codes to his own benefit by arguing that the debt was void because of the legal inability of slaves to enter into contractual agreements. Although the Pulaski Co. court ruled against him, the Kentucky Court of Appeals ultimately ruled in his favor in 1829.

The following year, Free Frank moved to Illinois and sold his saltpeter factory for the freedom of his son, also named Frank. Before moving, Frank obtained the signatures of 19 prominent Pulaski Co. white citizens who vouched for his character—a requirement of freed blacks who sought to move into Illinois. Using $355 he obtained by selling the remainder of his farmland, Frank, Lucy, and their four free children settled in Pike Co., IL.

In 1836, Frank established the biracial town of New Philadelphia. Because it was an incorporated town, New Philadelphia was one of the few legally established black settlements in the country before the Civil War. The town had a post office, a Baptist church, and a private school and operated as a stagecoach stop. In 1836, after Frank obtained the support of prominent citizens in Kentucky and Illinois, the Illinois legislature passed an act that allowed Free Frank to change his name to Frank McWhorter. Additionally, the act gave him full rights to sue, purchase and sell property, and testify in court.

Over the course of the 1830s and 1840s, Frank McWhorter continued to purchase remaining enslaved family members in Kentucky. Rumored to have participated in the **Underground Railroad,** he strategically built his house to hide slaves and provide them assistance. Even after his death in 1854, his will provided for the purchase of his enslaved grandchildren. From the 1820s through the 1850s, Frank and Lucy spent around $15,000 to purchase 16 family members.

In 1988, McWhorter's grave in New Philadelphia was entered into the National Register of Historic Places, and in 2005, a portion of Interstate 72 was named in his honor.

Calarco, Tom. *Places of the Underground Railroad: A Geographical Guide.* Santa Barbara, CA: Greenwood, 2011.

Lucas, Marion B. *A History of Blacks in Kentucky: From Slavery to Segregation, 1760–1891.* 2nd ed. Frankfort: Kentucky Historical Society, 2003.

Morgan, Ted. *A Shovel of Stars: The Making of the American West, 1800 to the Present.* New York: Touchstone, 1995.

Shackel, Paul. *New Philadelphia: An Archaeology of Race in the Heartland.* Berkeley: Univ. of California Press, 2011.

Walker, Juliet E. K. *Free Frank: A Black Pioneer on the Antebellum Frontier.* Lexington: Univ. Press of Kentucky, 1983.

—*Joshua D. Farrington*

MEREDITH V. JEFFERSON COUNTY BOARD OF EDUCATION, **U.S. Supreme Court desegregation case.** In 2001, the Jefferson County schools system implemented a "managed choice" program that required the district's elementary schools to maintain black enrollment between 15 and 50 percent of a school's entire population. This measure passed after the conclusion of 25 years of federal oversight of desegregation intended to maintain racial integration in a school district where roughly 35 percent of enrolled students were black, and initial polls of the local population returned an 80 percent approval rating.

In 2002, Crystal Meredith, a white single mother in Louisville, requested a transfer for her son from a kindergarten on the other side of town to a local school. Her request was denied, however, because the removal of her son from the kindergarten would have pushed the school's black enrollment past the 50 percent mark required by the district. After seeking legal redress, Meredith had her name added to a federal lawsuit against the school district that claimed that the policy was discriminatory.

Arguing that it promoted education and tolerance and that it was sufficiently "narrowly tailored," Judge John Heyburn II upheld the program for public schools in a U.S. district court ruling in 2004. The following year, the court of appeals affirmed the district court's ruling without writing its own opinion. Ted Gordon, the lead attorney, appealed to the U.S. Supreme Court, which agreed to hear the case on June 5, 2006.

The Supreme Court heard arguments for *Meredith v. Jefferson County Board of Education,* along with a similar case, *Parents Involved in Community Schools v. Seattle School District,* in December 2006 and issued a ruling the following June. In a 5–4 decision, the Supreme Court struck down the desegregation policy on the basis of the equal protection clause of the Fourteenth Amendment. Chief Justice John Roberts declared, "The way to stop discrimination on the basis of race is to stop discriminating on the basis of race." Although civil rights groups protested the decision, Justice Anthony Kennedy penned a concurring opinion that allowed for the possibility of future programs that used race as a component, noting that the ruling "should not prevent school districts from continuing the important work of bringing together students of different racial, ethnic and economic backgrounds." After the decision, Jefferson Co. school officials implemented a new program that combined the previous plan's emphasis on racial integration with a new focus on socioeconomic conditions as a qualification for school assignment.

Tracy E. K'Meyer. *From Brown to Meredith: The Long Struggle for School Desegregation in Louisville, Kentucky, 1954–2007.* Chapel Hill: Univ. of North Carolina Press, 2013.

Newspapers: "Supreme Court to Hear Jefferson's School Suit," *LCJ,* June 6, 2006, A1; "Justices, 5–4, Limit Use of Race for School Integration Plans," *NYT,* June 29, 2007, A1; "Supreme Court Desegregation Decision," *LCJ,* June 29, 2007, K1; "The Next Kind of Integration," *NYT,* July 20, 2008, A38.

—*Stephen Pickering*

MERIWETHER, JESSE (b. 1812, near Louisville, KY; d. 1892, Louisville, KY), carpenter and educator. Jesse Meriwether was born a slave on the Samuel Churchill farm. He was emancipated in 1847 on condition that he agree to be sent to Liberia. He did so but returned to Louisville in 1849. He prospered as a carpenter and took an active role in the affairs of the African American community. In 1850, the first black Masonic lodge in Louisville was organized in secret at his house on **Walnut St.** (now **Muhammad Ali** Blvd). He traveled to the Free Soil Convention in Pittsburgh in 1852, where he heard Frederick Douglass and others give impassioned speeches against slavery. After the Civil War, Meriwether was appointed to the black Board of Visitors by the school board, and he also served on the boards of the Freedman's Savings and Trust Company and the Louisville Cemetery Association. He is buried in Eastern Cemetery.

Gibson, W. H., Sr. *History of the United Brothers of Friendship and Sisters of the Mysterious Ten: In Two Parts, a Negro Order.* Louisville, KY: Bradley & Gilbert Co., 1897.

—*Cornelius Bogert*

MERRITT, JOHN AYERS (b. 1926, Falmouth, KY; d. 1983, Nashville, TN), football coach. "Big John" Merritt, who became a football coach, was the son of Bradley and Grace Merritt. He received his early education in the segregated public school system of Falmouth. During summers, John often visited his aunt and uncle at the Gene and Bess Lacey Grocery Store in Covington, where they discussed various topics. **Eugene Lacey** was a member of Covington's **African American Businessmen's Association.** In later years, these exchanges to his aunt and uncle's store inspired Merritt to become involved in community activities in Nashville. When Merritt reached high school age, he moved to Louisville, where he attended **Central High School** and played guard on the football team; he graduated in 1943. He served in the U.S. Navy during World War II and was discharged in 1946. Thereafter, he enrolled at Kentucky State College (later known as **Kentucky State University**) in Frankfort, where he again played football and earned his BS in 1950. In 1952, he re-

ceived his MA degree from the University of Kentucky in Lexington and immediately was appointed head football coach at segregated Versailles High School in Woodford Co.

Merritt began his college coaching career in 1953 as the head football coach at Jackson State College in Mississippi. He spent 10 highly successful years at Jackson State before accepting the head football coaching position at Tennessee State College in Nashville in 1963. While coaching at Tennessee State, he had 21 consecutive winning seasons. Over the course of his high school and college football coaching career, Merritt achieved more than 30 straight winning seasons. In 1982, Merritt's coaching record totaled 215–64–9, third best behind Bear Bryant of the University of Alabama and Eddie Robinson at Grambling University. Merritt placed more than 200 players in the National Football League. In 1982, the city of Nashville honored him by renaming Centennial Blvd., running from 28th to 44th Aves., John Ayers Merritt Blvd. Merritt died in Nashville in 1983 at age 57 and was buried in Greenwood Cemetery there. In 1994, he was elected to the College Football Players Hall of Fame.

Climer, David. "One of a Kind Merritt Nears 200th Victory." *Tennessean,* August 1980.

"Coach John Merritt." Special Collections, Brown Daniel Library, Tennessee State Univ. Memorial Service, Coach "Big" John Ayers Merritt, Tennessee State Univ., December 18, 1983.

—*Theodore H. H. Harris*

MERRITT, MARY ELIZA (b. 1881, Berea, KY; d. 1953, Louisville, KY), first African American nurse licensed in Kentucky. Born in Berea, KY, on April 27, 1881, Mary Eliza Merritt was the only child of Thomas and Catherine "Kitty" Dorsey Merritt. She taught school to earn money for tuition at **Berea College,** where she graduated from the two-year nursing school in 1902. When the **Day Law** forced Berea College to close its doors to black students in 1904, Merritt entered the Freedmen's Hospital in Washington, DC, to continue her training as a nurse in 1904. She graduated as a registered nurse in 1906, becoming the first Kentucky native black or white graduate nurse, meaning someone who graduated from an accredited school of nursing. After returning to Kentucky, as the first black nurse to be licensed in Kentucky, she worked as a private-duty nurse at White Hall, the home of Cassius Clay. She then worked for two years as a housekeeper and matron for the Frost family. William G. Frost was the president of Berea College, and Merritt had worked previously for the Frost family when she attended Berea College. She later moved to Leavenworth, KS, where she supervised the Protective Home and Mitchell Hospital. While she was in charge, the first and only class of nurses graduated from Mitchell Hospital.

In 1911, Merritt became superintendent of Louisville's **Red Cross Hospital,** which had been established in 1899. She operated the hospital for 34 years and increased the number of beds from 12 to 100. The Red Cross Hospital, the first school of nursing for blacks in Kentucky, later became fully licensed by the Kentucky State Board of Health and accredited by the Joint Commission on the Accreditation of Hospitals. Merritt was an active member of the National Association of Colored Graduate Nurses. On August 25, 1949, she received the Mary Mahoney Award for Distinguished Service in the field of nursing. Mary

Mahoney, who had graduated from the New England Hospital for Women and Children in 1879, was the first black nurse to graduate from a white professional school of nursing.

After retiring, Merritt spent most of her time caring for her daughter and working with her church and various clubs. On January 8, 1953, Merritt died at age 71, leaving her adopted daughter as her only surviving family member. She was buried in Louisville's Eastern Cemetery.

Carnegie, Mary Elizabeth. *The Path We Tread: Blacks in Nursing, 1854–1984*. Philadelphia: Jones & Bartlett, 1995.

Dunnigan, Alice Allison, comp. and ed. *The Fascinating Story of Black Kentuckians: Their Heritage and Traditions*. Washington, DC: Associated Publishers, 1982.

Kentucky, Death Records, 1852–1953.

—*Sheila Pressley*

MERRIWEATHER, CLAYBORN W. (b. ca. 1869, Christian Co., KY; d. 1952, Hopkinsville, KY), newspaper publisher, poet, artist, and attorney. Sources differ on Clayborn W. Merriweather's birth date and parentage. According to his death certificate, he was born to John and Mary Gwynn Merriweather on January 10, 1874. However, his gravestone has his birth as May 7, 1869. The 1880 U.S. federal census listed him as 10 years old and his parents as Clabe and Anna Merriweather. The son of former slaves, Clayborn Merriweather grew up in rural western Kentucky, where local schools were poorly funded. Despite this absence of strong pedagogy, he used his education wisely. He worked on local farms and then traveled to Earlington in Hopkins Co., where he shined shoes in his brother's barbershop and later worked as a barber.

By 1889, Merriweather had enough resources to attend State Colored Baptist University in Louisville (later known as **Simmons College of Kentucky**). With his education in hand, he wrote and published five books of black dialect poetry, such as *Light and Shadows* in 1907. His work was similar to Paul Laurence Dunbar's poetry but differed in that he did not question racial discrimination practices and the challenges produced by its defenders. He also had several one-man exhibitions of his watercolor and oil paintings.

Merriweather taught school in his home county and established two newspapers, the *Paducah Bee* and the *Hopkinsville New Age*. Moreover, he studied law through Blackstone Institute's home study course and by 1908 had set up a successful local practice. Married to Hopkinsville schoolteacher Rosa Morgan Merriweather (1874–1935), Clayborn Merriweather was one of the oldest practicing attorneys in Kentucky when he died in Hopkinsville on February 16, 1952. The couple was buried in Cave Spring Cemetery in Christian Co., KY.

"C. W. Merriweather Dies Here Saturday." *KNE*, February 18, 1952, 1.

Glazier, Jack. *Been Coming through Some Hard Times: Race, History, and Memory in Western Kentucky*. Knoxville: Univ. of Tennessee Press, 2012.

Kentucky, Death Records, 1852–1953.

Kentucky's Black Heritage: The Role of the Black People in the History of Kentucky from Pioneer Days to the Present. Frankfort: Kentucky Commission on Human Rights, 1971.

U.S. Federal Census (1880).

—*John A. Hardin*

MEYZEEK, ALBERT ERNEST (b. 1862, Toledo, OH; d. 1963, Louisville, KY), educator and civil rights activist. Albert E. Meyzeek was the product of mixed parentage. His father, John E. Meyzeek, was a white Canadian, and his mother, Mary Lott, was an African American. Meyzeek's maternal grandfather, John Lott, was one of the organizers of the Ohio River **Underground Railroad** in Madison, IN. Shortly after his birth, Meyzeek and his mother returned to the family's home in Toronto, where he received his early years of schooling. In 1875, the family moved to Terre Haute, IN, and he enrolled in Terre Haute Classical High School. The only black student in his class, Meyzeek graduated as valedictorian.

Meyzeek initially enrolled at the Indiana State Normal School for teacher education. He continued his studies and later received a bachelor's degree in 1884 from Indiana University and a master's degree from Wilberforce University in 1917.

Beginning in 1884, Meyzeek taught school in Terre Haute. He moved to Louisville in 1890, where he began an extraordinary tenure of more than 50 years of service in public education in Kentucky. His first appointment in Louisville was at the Maiden Lane School in Butchertown, which later became Benjamin Banneker School. He was soon transferred to Western Colored School and then to Eastern Colored School, where he served as principal from 1891 through 1893. For the next three years, he was the principal at **Central High School,** where he expanded the curriculum from three to four years and established a reference library.

In 1896, Meyzeek married Pearl E. Hall, who had been an elementary teacher in the public school system. That same year, he was appointed principal of the Eastern School District, which included Jackson Junior High School and the Colored Normal School. While serving as principal of the Normal School for 14 years, he trained three-fourths of Louisville's black teaching staff. As a school principal, he reorganized the internal structure, offered new courses, sought college-educated teachers, established a school library, organized clubs for parents, and implemented discipline in his schools.

When enrollment at Jackson Junior High increased, Meyzeek decided to concentrate all his talents on that institution. He remained principal of Jackson Junior High School until he retired in 1943. In April 1967, the Louisville Board of Education renamed the school after Meyzeek as a tribute to his civic and educational accomplishments. Throughout his teaching career, he sought opportunities to improve the schools in which he served. One of his accomplishments was having Louisville's black schools named for notable persons of African descent.

A champion of civil rights causes, Meyzeek pressed to desegregate the General Hospital, open libraries to blacks, protest against ordinances mandating segregation in public facilities, worked to open the University of Louisville to blacks, and helped open a colored branch of the YMCA as early as 1892. He was also one of the founders of the **Louisville Urban League,** which he chaired for 29 years. Meyzeek served as president of the **Kentucky Negro Educational Association** in 1927 and was appointed to the Kentucky Board of Education from 1948 to 1956.

Among his many accomplishments, Meyzeek was one of the founders of the Louisville chapter of a national black fraternity,

Kappa Alpha Psi. He was the first man initiated into this organization. Meyzeek was also a successful businessman, serving as one of the founders of **Domestic Life and Accident Insurance Company** in Louisville, which became one of the leading black businesses in Kentucky. Meyzeek and others helped establish the Citizens Amusement Company and the Palace Theater Company of Louisville to provide entertainment opportunities for blacks. After Meyzeek retired from teaching, he also worked as an assistant in the Office of Price Administration for Kentucky during World War II. Meyzeek is buried in Eastern Cemetery.

Dunnigan, Alice Allison, comp. and ed. *The Fascinating Story of Black Kentuckians: Their Heritage and Traditions.* Washington, DC: Associated Publishers, 1982.

Horton, John Benjamin. *Old War Horse of Kentucky.* Louisville, KY: J. Benjamin Horton & Associates, 1986.

Smith, Jessie C., ed. *Notable Black American Men.* Detroit: Gale Research, 1999.

Yenser, Thomas, ed. *Who's Who in Colored America, 1941–1944.* 6th ed. Brooklyn, NY: Thomas Yenser, 1942.

—*Karen Cotton McDaniel*

MIDNIGHT STAR, entertaining pop, soul, and funk band that recorded major hits in the 1980s. Students Reginald Calloway, a trumpeter, his brother Vincent, a trombone player, and vocalist Belinda Lipscomb formed the nine-member band Midnight Star at **Kentucky State University** in 1976. "I went around the school and picked out the best players I could find," Reginald recalled. "We had played in marching band and **jazz** ensemble, so the players all knew what the others could do. We just found a room and started rehearsing." Dick Griffey, chief of Solar Records, signed the group in 1978. Among the group's early albums were *The Beginning, Standing Together,* and *Victory.* Their 1983 album *No Parking on the Dance Floor* reached number 27 on the Billboard 200 chart and number 2 on the rhythm and blues (R&B) charts. This album included hits such as "No Parking on the Dance Floor," "Freak-a-Zoid," which climbed to number 2 on the R&B Charts, and "Wet My Whistle," which reached number 8 on the R&B charts.

In 1984, the group released its fifth album, *Planetary Invasion,* which included the hit song "Operator." It reached number 1 on the R&B charts. The group had three more albums in that decade, but they did not achieve the level of success of those in the mid-1980s. When the Calloway brothers left the band to pursue other opportunities, the other members toured internationally and took a hiatus to work on other projects. Lipscomb appeared in comedies and gospel musicals. By 2000, the band had reunited and, with the exception of the Calloways, was once again giving live performances. "We just love doing this," said Melvin Gentry, one of the band's early members. "We never really get used to the effect this music has on people . . . what the songs mean to them, and that's what keeps us going. We love giving people a good time."

"Building the Perfect Storm: Second Annual Model Music Fest to Feature Music Midnight Star and Comedian Jimmie Walker." *Anniston Star,* June 30, 2012.

"Midnight Star Bio." http://www.midnightstarband.com/bio (accessed December 13, 2012).

"Midnight Star Hits Charts with Hot-Selling LLP, Single Band Midnight Star Is at the Dawn of a Skyrocketing Career." *LHL,* January 15, 1984.

—*Gerald L. Smith*

MILES, HENRY (b. 1905, Samuels, KY; d. 1984, Louisville, KY), fiddler and jug band leader. The son of Henry and Mattie Miles, Henry Miles came to Louisville at the age of 17 and learned to play the fiddle, guitar, and mandolin. From 1929 to 1932, he was a member of the immensely popular Ballard Chefs, whose music was heard on Monday nights over WHAS radio in a program sponsored by Ballard and Ballard Company flour mills. In 1965, the Henry Miles **Jug Band** performed at the World's Fair in New York. In January 1974, his band, without a jug player, appeared at the Smithsonian Folklife Festival in Washington, DC. He is buried in Brownsboro Cemetery.

—*Brenda K. Bogert*

MILES, JULIET (b. unknown, Bracken Co., KY; d. 1861, Frankfort, KY), freed slave. Juliet Miles began life enslaved on the John Fee Jr. farm near Germantown. She married Add Miles, a slave on a neighboring farm, but continued to care for the Fee children. Fee's son John Gregg Fee purchased Juliet from his father after the elder Fee threatened to send her "down south." Although Fee emancipated Juliet, she preferred to continue living at Fee's farm in order to be closer to her children. After much persuasion, coupled with Add's ability to purchase his own freedom, the couple and their freed son Henry moved to Felicity, OH. However, Juliet's other children and her grandchildren remained in bondage in Bracken and Mason Counties, KY, where their owner, the elder Fee, threatened to sell Juliet's family to a slave trader.

In 1858, Juliet made plans to return to Kentucky, collect her children, and flee with them back across the Ohio River. She first retrieved her children from the Elijah Currens plantation west of Germantown before entering Feeland to lead her remaining family to the appointed crossing at Rock Springs, west of Augusta in Bracken Co. Whoever was to provide them with skiffs for the crossing at Clalfont Creek did not show up, and Juliet was met by local patrollers who seized the fugitive band and escorted them to the Bracken Co. jail. After a few days, the children were released but then were sold to a trader and shipped to New Orleans.

Juliet remained in jail until her trial, where she was found guilty and sentenced to three years in the penitentiary at Frankfort. There she found favor with the penitentiary warden, who recognized Juliet's Christian values. She died at the penitentiary two years later. Her son Henry continued his life in Ohio and joined the Union army during the Civil War. The other children's fates remain unknown.

Bracken Co. Court Records, October 28, 1850, and October 4, 1858, Brooksville, KY.

Fee, John Gregg. *Autobiography of John G. Fee, Berea, Kentucky.* Chicago: National Christian Association, 1891.

Miller, Caroline R. "Juliet Miles and Matilda Fee: Willing Participants in John G. Fee's Anti-slavery Crusade." Northern Kentucky Univ. Borderlands Conference, Highland Heights, KY, 2004.

—*Caroline R. Miller*

MILES, WILLIAM HENRY (b. 1828, Lebanon, KY; d. 1892, Louisville, KY), first bishop of the Colored Methodist Episcopal (C.M.E.) Church. Born a slave in Lebanon, KY, on December 26, 1828, William Henry Miles was freed by his master's will in 1854. In August 1855, he joined Lebanon's Methodist Episcopal Church and was licensed to preach in 1857. Two years later, he married Frances Ellen Arnold in Lebanon, and the couple had eight children. By 1867, he was living and ministering in Louisville. The Colored Methodist Episcopal (C.M.E.) Church in America (later known as the Christian Methodist Episcopal Church) was organized in Jackson, TN, on December 21, 1870. Miles was ordained its first bishop.

Three years later, Bishop Miles was responsible for 14 annual conferences that included 600 traveling preachers, almost 600 local ministers, and about 70,000 church members. He announced that he opposed integrated schools and church membership but believed that the races should behave amicably toward each other. In August 1874, he became the first African American to preach a sermon from a Louisville white church pulpit. A large interracial crowd attended the service at **Walnut Street** Methodist Church.

Miles was the owner and publisher of the *Christian Index,* a monthly publication of the Colored Methodist Episcopal Church. The magazine was printed at 146 Fifth St. in Louisville, and subscriptions were $1 a year. By 1884, the CME Church had grown to 125,000 members. In March 1886, Miles helped encourage the organization of a cemetery for African Americans.

On November 14, 1892, Miles died of heart disease in Louisville. He had served as bishop for almost 22 years and had preached for more than 40 years. His funeral was held at Center Street C.M.E. Church, and blacks and whites attended his service. He was interred in the "colored grave yard" of which he was one of the founders. The Miles Memorial Tabernacle in Washington, DC, and Miles College in Fairfield, AL, were named in his honor.

Kentucky, Death Records, 1852–1953.

Newspapers: "A Black Bishop in a White Pulpit," *Washington (DC) Evening Star,* August 21, 1874, 1; advertisement for the *Christian Index, Washington (DC) People's Advocate,* April 19, 1879, 4; "Congregational Notes," *LCJ,* February 11, 1884, 6; "Grievances in Kentucky," *New York Freeman,* March 20, 1886, 4; "Bishop W. H. Miles," *IF,* November 26, 1892, 1; "Death of Bishop Miles," *Cleveland Gazette,* November 26, 1892, 3; "C.M.C. Church," *Maysville Daily Public Ledger,* January 16, 1895, 4.

Phillips, C. H. *The History of the Colored Methodist Episcopal Church in America: Comprising Its Organization, Subsequent Development and Present Status.* Jackson, TN: Publishing House C.M.E. Church, 1925.

Schaff, Philip, and S. Irenaeus Prim, eds. *History, Essays, Orations, and Other Documents of the Sixth General Conference of the Evangelical Alliance, Held in New York, October 2–12, 1873.* New York: Harper & Brothers, 1874. University of Michigan. http://quod.lib.umich.edu/m/moa/ajg4344.0001.001/633?page=root;print=1;rgn=full+text;size=100;view=image;q1=w+h+miles (accessed October 8, 2013).

—*Sallie L. Powell*

MILLER, DELLA BRIDGES (b. 1886, Harrodsburg, KY; d. 1946, Middlesboro, KY), educator, civil rights activist, and church and club leader. Born on July 4, 1886, in Harrodsburg, KY, to Robert and Fannie Johnson Bridges, Davie Della Bridges initially attended Harrodsburg's **Wayman Institute,** an African Methodist Episcopal (A.M.E.) Church school, and later Louisville's **Central High School.** Her college education included Kentucky State College (later known as **Kentucky State University**) in Frankfort, Louisville's Simmons University, and the Teachers College in Indianapolis, IN. After marrying Dr. Isaac Miller, she lived in Middlesboro and taught at the Lincoln School from 1921 to 1930 before becoming a local insurance agent.

Miller, active in the local A.M.E. church, served as a stewardess, a Sunday school superintendent, and a missionary president. She was a delegate to the A.M.E. General Conference in 1940 and 1944 and became president and a member of the Executive Board of the Kentucky Conference Branch of the A.M.E. Women's Missionary Society. From 1936 to 1937, she was president of the **Kentucky Association of Colored Women's Clubs.** She was an active member of the Order of the Eastern Star of Kentucky, served as its grand royal matron, and also was grand directress of the Household of Ruth in Kentucky.

In 1940, Miller became president of the Bell County **National Association for the Advancement of Colored People** (NAACP), which was a chapter of the Regional NAACP of Eastern Kentucky. In 1942, the NAACP publication, the *Crisis,* recognized her as one of the First Ladies of Colored America for her contributions. The Della Miller African Scholarship Fund was established to aid African students and to honor her. Della Bridges Miller died on June 19, 1946, in Middlesboro, KY.

"First Ladies of Colored America." *Crisis* 49, no. 9 (September 1942): 287; "First Ladies of Colored America—13." *Crisis* 50, no. 10 (October 1943): 305.

Wright, Richard Robert, Jr. *Encyclopaedia of the African Methodist Episcopal Church.* 2nd ed. Philadelphia: Book Concern of the A.M.E. Church, 1947.

—*Karen Cotton McDaniel*

MILLER, RAYMOND "JUNIOR" (b. 1927, Lebanon Junction, KY; d. 2004, Lowell, MI), baseball player. Raymond "Junior" Miller was born to Raymond and Leatta Miller in Lebanon Junction, KY, on October 11, 1927. His father, who formed a baseball club with family members and was a talented pitcher in his own right, taught Miller how to play the game. As a teenager, he first played for the Lebanon Junction Hustlers, where he drew attention from teams in Louisville. In the early 1940s, he played for the Louisville Black Colonels, and Charlie Henry's Alabama Zulu Cannibal Giants signed him when he was 16 years old in 1943.

Throughout the rest of the decade, Miller became one of the most successful .300 heavy hitters of the Negro leagues, described by a teammate as his generation's Hank Aaron. During the 1944 and 1945 seasons, he played for the Indianapolis Clowns, the Louisville Black Colonels, and the Birmingham Black Barons. From 1947 to 1954, he played alongside Satchel Paige for the Detroit Black Sox and the Kansas City Monarchs. During the off-season, he also played for a barnstorming team that toured California. In 1955, eight years after Jackie Robinson integrated the major leagues, Miller was signed by the Cincinnati Reds. By that time, however, Miller was past his prime and could not compete at the same level as he had in the early 1940s. As a member of the Reds' franchise, he practiced with the team in Cuba and Mexico and played on a Reds' minor-league farm team in Texas for one season.

By 1960, Miller settled in Lowell, MI, where he worked for 30 years at a Meijer's store. He was a member of the Negro League Legends Hall of Fame. He died in Lowell on November 18, 2004.

Kelley, Brent. *The Negro Leagues Revisited: Conversations with 66 More Baseball Heroes.* Jefferson, NC: McFarland, 2000.
"Miller Waited for His Shot at Big Leagues." *Grand Rapids Press,* November 23, 2004, D8.
"Raymond Miller." Negro League Baseball Players Association. 2000–2007. http://www.nlbpa.com/miller__raymond.html (accessed March 13, 2012).

MILLER, ROHENA (b. 1961, Louisville, KY), businesswoman. The daughter of Logan Miller, the first black chief arson investigator for the Louisville Fire Department, Rohena Miller was born in 1961. As an ambitious public-relations major at the University of Louisville in the 1980s, she started her own advertising agency, which produced posters for fraternities and sororities. After gaining experience in the advertising world following her graduation, she founded Niche Marketing in 1990 and began printing a popular business directory targeting African Americans, the *Louisville Black Pages.*

In 2001, Miller became disheartened by the lack of black celebrities invited to attend the **Kentucky Derby** and persuaded local black business leaders **Allan Wade Houston Sr.,** Alice Houston, **"Junior" Bridgeman,** and Charlie Johnson to sponsor a post-derby party hosted by Niche Marketing and attended by black celebrities. In 2002, her first Grand Gala sold $200 tickets to nearly 1,000 guests. Attendees at the first-ever black celebrity derby after-party included sports stars Ron Harper and Julius Erving, Kim Coles, Bernie Mac, Vivica A. Fox, and hundreds of other leading black stars. Over the next seven years, the gala continued to thrive as one of the marquee derby events, with proceeds given to the United Negro College Fund and other black charitable organizations. The *Louisville Courier-Journal* described Miller as "the hostess with the mostest this Derby season" because her parties consistently received some of the highest-profile guests of the entire derby, including Michael Jordan, Wesley Snipes, Kevin Garnett, **Muhammad Ali,** Jerome Bettis, Chris Tucker, Nelly, Cedric the Entertainer, and scores of other black celebrities. The parties received widespread coverage not only in Kentucky's major papers but also in national publications like *Ebony, Upscale,* and *Savoy.*

Miller's event was not immune from effects of the economic recession of 2008, and in 2010, she canceled her Grand Gala. In its place, she hosted a post-derby business seminar, the First Annual Business Summit, attended by leading black businesspeople, who discussed strategies for promoting minority-owned businesses. Niche Marketing, however, continued to thrive, and its numerous projects outside the Kentucky Derby included promotion of **Edward Hamilton Jr.'s** African American soldiers' monument in Washington, DC, and a major new Ohio River bridge project in Louisville. Miller also founded Planet Mogul, an online mentoring and networking website designed to educate and promote young black entrepreneurs.

Newspapers: "Big Race, Big Names, Big Parties, Big Fun," *LHL,* April 28, 2002, J1; "Grand Gala Lands Grand Celebs," *LCJ,* April 8, 2003, C1; "Saturday Night Live!," *LCJ,* March 31, 2004, X2; "Liftoff to Planet Mogul," *Minority Business News,* March 15, 2008; "Grand Gala Is 2nd Derby Event Lost to the Economy," *LCJ,* February 24, 2010.

—*Joshua D. Farrington*

MINNIFIELD, FRANK (b. 1960, Lexington, KY), professional football player for the Cleveland Browns. Born on January 1, 1960, Frank Minnifield graduated from Lexington's Henry Clay High School before attending the University of Louisville. He played cornerback for the Cardinals football team from 1979 to 1982, leading the country in kickoff returns during the 1981 season with an average of 30.4 yards. He joined the United States Football League's Chicago Blitz in 1982 and moved with the team when it became the Arizona Wranglers. After suing to obtain free-agent status, he signed with the Cleveland Browns of the National Football League in 1984. With Cleveland, he had 20 interceptions between 1984 and his retirement in 1992. He was also named to the Pro Bowl every year from 1986 to 1989. During this time, Minnifield and teammate Hanford Dixon created the "Dawg Pound" cheering section in Cleveland by barking like dogs after successful plays.

Having worked as a realtor during the football off-season, Minnifield returned to Lexington to create a home-building company, Minnifield All-Pro Homes, after retiring from the NFL. He later founded Minnifield Enterprises, a purchasing agent for Toyota. He serves on the board of the Community Trust Bank and was the first African American named to the Lexington Chamber of Commerce. He and his wife, Diane, have two children, a daughter, Chanel, and a son, Chase, who played cornerback for the University of Virginia Cavaliers and signed with the Washington Redskins. Frank Minnifield was inducted into the Kentucky Athletic Hall of Fame in 1998 and was elected chairman of the University of Louisville's Board of Trustees in 2011.

"Frank Minnifield Elected Chairman of U of L Trustees." *LHL,* September 14, 2011. http://www.kentucky.com/2011/09/14/1881190/frank-minnifield-elected-chairman.html (accessed April 27, 2012).
Newspapers: "Browns Waive Bobby Jones," *Pittsburgh Post-Gazette,* July 24, 1984; "Minnifield Signs with Browns," *Pleasant Point (WV) Register,* October 3, 1990.

—*Kevin Hogg*

MINSTRELSY, popular form of entertainment in the nineteenth and twentieth centuries. Minstrel shows became a popular form of entertainment in the nineteenth century throughout the United States because they united whites of all social classes by reinforcing the notion of white superiority. Early minstrelsy helped justify the institution of slavery because white performers in blackface, which accentuated the impression of big lips and eyes, used stereotypical caricatures to demonstrate that slaves were so well treated and happy that they were constantly singing and dancing. Stereotypes were also developed to show that slaves were childlike and unintelligent and thus to justify the need to keep them in a subordinate position. One famous caricature from that era was created by Thomas Dartmouth "Daddy" Rice, who became famous for his portrayal of "**Jim Crow**" in the Louisville City Theatre's production of *The Kentucky Rifle* in 1830. By the 1850s, minstrel shows were common throughout the Commonwealth of Kentucky because many communities had facilities to support those types of performances.

With the rise of abolition into the mainstream during the 1850s, minstrel shows increasingly moved away from directly supporting slavery to generally disparaging all Africans and African Americans. After the conclusion of the Civil War, minstrel shows provided some African American entrepreneurs an entry into show business. Like white performers, the African Americans wore blackface since that was what the form required. Although minstrelsy promoted negative stereotypes about African Americans, after 1865, it also provided artistic and economic opportunities for African Americans associated with the industry. By the twentieth century, minstrelsy was supplanted by other forms of entertainment, most notably vaudeville shows. Despite the demise of minstrelsy, the stereotypical caricatures of African Americans developed by minstrels have continued to reappear in other forms of popular entertainment.

Bogert, Cornelius. "Minstrelsy." In *The Encyclopedia of Louisville,* edited by John E. Kleber, 624–34. Lexington: Univ. Press of Kentucky, 2001.

Lott, Eric. *Love and Theft: Blackface Minstrelsy and the American Working Class.* New York: Oxford Univ. Press, 1995.

Mahar, William J. *Behind the Burnt Cork Mask: Early Blackface Minstrelsy and Antebellum American Popular Culture.* Urbana: Univ. of Illinois Press, 1999.

Robinson, Cedric J. *Forgeries of Memory and Meaning: Blacks and the Regimes of Race in American Theater and Film before World War II.* Chapel Hill: Univ. of North Carolina Press, 2007.

—*John R. Burch Jr.*

MITCHELL, ROBERT (b. 1864, Fulton Co., KY; d. 1926, Lexington, KY), minister, educator, and activist.

Robert Mitchell, the son of slaves from North Carolina brought to Kentucky just before the Civil War, was born in Fulton Co. on March 1, 1864. Converted to Christianity at a young age, Mitchell was known throughout the county as the "boy preacher," speaking at churches throughout the area. As a young teenager, he studied at Rust University in Holly Springs, MS, until he was called to preach at Seventh Street Baptist Church in Paducah in the early 1880s. Under his watch, the church grew from 25 members to 175 members in just four years. While he was in Paducah, he studied at Wesleyan University in Illinois and received a master's degree from State Colored Baptist University in Louisville (later known as **Simmons College of Kentucky**). He obtained a doctor of divinity degree from Guadalupe College in Texas.

In 1887, Mitchell was called to State Street Baptist Church in Bowling Green. During his nine years with the church, Mitchell also served for seven years as the president of Simmons Memorial College in Bowling Green and for two years as the president of the Colored Teachers' State Association (later known as the **KNEA**). He was an active participant in the **Anti–Separate Coach Movement,** joining 200 other African Americans in a Frankfort protest against the passage of a segregated coach bill in 1892. He was one of six elected spokesmen of the group who presented its case before the General Assembly. According to a summary of his speech published by the *Louisville Courier-Journal,* "He dwelt eloquently upon the chastity of the Negro home as it is today, and concluded with the statement that they were not . . . seeking social rights, but civil rights." The following year, he was a member of a committee appointed by the National Baptist Convention to meet with President Grover Cleveland.

In 1896, Mitchell moved to Lexington after being called to Main Street Baptist Church. Two years later, he became pastor of **First Baptist Church** in Frankfort, where he oversaw the purchase of new property and the construction of a new church building. The city's whites attempted to stop the construction through a court injunction, claiming that its new location made it a "nuisance," but Mitchell's church ultimately won the case after an appeal. In 1903, Mitchell was called to the First Baptist Church of Kansas City, KS. He returned to Kentucky in 1906 and eventually settled in Lexington, where he died of a heart attack in 1926. He was buried in Bowling Green.

During Mitchell's illustrious career, he baptized over 1,500 individuals and served as a trustee of Louisville's Colored Baptist University (later known as Simmons College of Kentucky), as commissioner of Kentucky to the Atlanta Exposition, and as vice president of the National Baptist Convention.

Hamilton, Green Polonius. *Biographical Sketches of Prominent Negro Men and Women of Kentucky.* Memphis: E. H. Clarke & Brother, 1911.

Smith, S. E. *History of the Anti–Separate Coach Movement of Kentucky.* Evansville, IN: National Afro-American Journal and Directory, 1895.

Underwood, Elsworth E. *A Brief History of the Colored Churches of Frankfort.* Frankfort, KY: Elsworth E. Underwood, 1906.

—*Joshua D. Farrington*

MODEL-EVANS PHARMACY, first African American–owned and operated pharmacy in northern Kentucky.

The Model-Evans Pharmacy was the first pharmacy owned and operated by African Americans in northern Kentucky, and thus far it is the only one. In 1923, **Charles W. Anderson** was the manager of the Model Drug Store at 1039 Greenup St. (on the northwest corner of Lynn and Greenup Sts.) in Covington. It was one of the branches owned by the Model Drug Stores Company of Cincinnati, a chain owned and operated by African Americans. In 1926, Mrs. Richie Kyles Smith, a pharmacist, was manager of the chain's Covington store. Smith had received her training at Meharry Medical School in Nashville, graduating in 1916. Before coming to Covington, she was employed at Bright's Pharmacy in Louisville for two years.

In 1928, the Covington drugstore was sold to Evans Noble, a pharmacist, and thus became known as Model-Evans Pharmacy. In October 1930, thieves ransacked the building and stole money, cigars, and sundry drug articles. As a result of this break-in, an investigation by the Covington license inspector cited Evans in police court and charged him with violation of the city's license law for failure to secure a separate license for the sale of bottled soft drinks. Evidence of his and his store's importance in the African American community is that Evans was selected in March 1932 to represent the African American businessmen at the dedication of the new **Lincoln-Grant School** in Covington. Evans operated his drugstore until late 1932, when it closed. He and his wife, Ethel, lived in Covington at 207 Lynn St. until 1939.

In 1936, the store at 1039 Greenup St. became a shoe repair shop operated by Napoleon Waddell. Later during the 1940s and 1950s, Raleigh Fender had a restaurant there. Throughout the late 1950s and early 1960s, the Walton family ran a candy and soda fountain shop at this address. From the late 1960s through 1971, Claude Grubbs had a barbershop in the building. Various other businesses were located there until finally, in the early years of the twenty-first century, the old Model-Evans Pharmacy building was torn down.

Dabney, Wendell P. *Cincinnati's Colored Citizens: Historical, Sociological and Biographical.* Cincinnati: Dabney, 1926.
Newspapers: "Docket Is Light," *KP,* October 20, 1930; "Drug Store Looted," *KP,* October 20, 1930; "To Dedicate New School," *KP,* March 31, 1932.

—*Theodore H. H. Harris*

MONROE, CHAPMAN COLEMAN (b. 1859, near Georgetown, KY; d. unknown), one of the first faculty members (1887) of Kentucky Normal and Industrial Institute, known today as Kentucky State University.

Chapman Coleman Monroe, the son of Tom and Mariah Monroe, was born near Georgetown, KY, on October 16, 1859. He attended "private subscription schools" in Scott Co. until he was 12 years old. At that point, he moved to Lexington and enrolled at the Chandler Normal School operated by the **American Missionary Association.** After completing its academic program and additional private tutoring, he taught in a local school in Fayette Co. and served as principal of Russell High School in Lexington from 1880 to 1887.

In 1887, Monroe was named one of the first faculty members of Kentucky Normal and Industrial Institute (now **Kentucky State University**). In 1886, he was elected president of the Colored Teachers State Association (later known as the **Kentucky Negro Educational Association**). During his tenure at Kentucky Normal (1887–1893), he served as professor of natural science and agriculture and received an honorary MA from State University (later known as **Simmons College of Kentucky**) in 1891. He completed additional course work at the University of Illinois in the summers of 1891 and 1892.

Professor Monroe was reported in the July 11, 1890, *Ohio Falls Express* as the faculty member who successfully sought dismissal of four Kentucky Normal female students found "under the bushes" with four white men. The entire faculty stated that they would resign if the girls were reinstated.

In December 1891, a **Jim Crow** bill that required separate seating for blacks and whites was introduced in the Kentucky General Assembly. As elected chairman of the **Anti–Separate Coach Movement,** Monroe was the first Kentuckian to speak out against what became the **Separate Coach Law.** He lost his job at Kentucky Normal School because of his opposition to that law.

After he left Kentucky Normal, he received appointments as principal at black schools in Owensboro and Mayfield, KY, and Evansville, IN. He also founded the Lexington Polytechnic Institute. He published the *Southern Teacher's Advocate* (1905–1908),

and his wife, Mary Bell Monroe, managed the office. In April 1910, Monroe was convicted in Todd Co. of selling teachers' examination questions. Mary filed for divorce six months later.

Two years later, Monroe opened a normal and commercial school in Lexington at 151 W. Short St. The school offered courses in bookkeeping, stenography, typewriting, and business. By 1916, he was living in Muskogee, OK, working as a stenographer. Four years later, he was principal of Ward School in Eufaula, OK. His date and place of death are unknown.

Jones, Paul W. L. *A History of the Kentucky Normal and Industrial Institute.* 1912, 67–68. Blazer Library Archives, Kentucky State Univ.
Kentucky's Black Heritage: The Role of the Black People in the History of Kentucky from Pioneer Days to the Present. Frankfort: Kentucky Commission on Human Rights, 1971.
Newspapers: "A Colored School," *LL,* June 15, 1894, 7; "A Credit to the Race," *LL,* June 22, 1905, 4; "Lexington Man Found Guilty," *LL,* April 1, 1910, 3; "Wife Asks for Divorce," *LL,* October 17, 1910, 9; "Colored School," *LL,* February 2, 1912, 2.
Russell, Harvey C. *The Kentucky Negro Education Association, 1877–1946.* Norfolk, VA: Guide Quality Press, 1946.
Simmons University: Past and Present. Louisville: Simmons University, 1964.
U.S. City Directories, 1821–1989 (1916).
U.S. Federal Census (1870, 1920).

—*John A. Hardin*

MONROE, JAMES (b. unknown; d. 1875, Lexington, KY), Baptist minister.

Although little is known about Rev. James Monroe's personal life, he was among many Kentucky African American ministers who enjoyed productive and long pastorates. In 1845, he began his ministry at Frankfort's black **First Baptist Church** and remained there for more than a decade. In 1858, John G. Fee, an abolitionist and founder of interracial and coeducational **Berea College,** attended one of Monroe's services. Fee, a minister, described Monroe as "a portly, fine-looking" man and was emotionally moved by Monroe's preaching and the sermon's effect on the congregation. Rev. **George W. Dupee,** one of the organizers of Covington's **First Baptist Church** (African American), called Monroe "the best preacher he [had] ever heard." In 1861, Monroe joined other Baptist preachers and organized the first ministers' and deacons' meeting among Kentucky African American Baptists.

After moving to serve the Lexington **First African Baptist Church,** Monroe was among the throng of Baptist ministers who organized the first State Convention of Colored Baptists in Kentucky in Louisville after the Civil War in August 1865. Four trustees were elected from two towns: Frankfort and Louisville. Monroe was the only trustee elected from Lexington. In the fall of that same year, under Monroe's leadership, Lexington's First Baptist Church opened a school with 27 students taught by **Eliza Isabel "Belle "(Mitchell) Jackson.** By March 1866, 95 pupils were enrolled. Monroe also began in that year his service as a trustee of State University (later known as **Simmons College of Kentucky**) and gave the keynote address at the second State Convention of Colored Baptists in Kentucky in Frankfort.

The next year, the convention was held at Monroe's church in Lexington, and he was part of a committee that changed the organization's name to the General Association of Colored Baptists in Kentucky. In 1870, Monroe served as the group's moderator pro tem in Paducah. Three years later, Monroe preached the introductory sermon when the association met in Georgetown. Monroe died on November 25, 1875. His wife, Evalene, died in 1902.

Lucas, Marion B. *A History of Blacks in Kentucky: From Slavery to Segregation, 1760–1891.* 2nd ed. Frankfort: Kentucky Historical Society, 2003.

Parrish, C. H. *Golden Jubilee of the General Association of Colored Baptists in Kentucky: From 1865–1915.* Louisville, KY: Mayes Printing Co., 1915.

Simmons, William. *Men of Mark: Eminent, Progressive and Rising.* Cleveland: George M. Rewell, 1887.

Spencer, John H., and Burrilla B. Spencer. *A History of Kentucky Baptists: From 1769 to 1885.* Cincinnati: J. R. Baumes, 1886.

—*Sallie L. Powell*

MOONGLOWS, musical group. Harvey Fuqua (1928–2010) and Bobby Lester (Robert L. Dallas, 1930–1980) were born in Louisville and began singing together there in 1948, but it was in Cleveland in 1952 that they joined Prentiss Barnes and Alexander "Pete" Graves and formed a singing group called the Crazy Sounds. They soon met Alan Freed, who became their manager, and, perhaps in connection with his nickname, Moondog, they changed the group's name to the Moonglows. In the mid-1950s, they were one of the premier rhythm and blues (R&B) and doo-wop groups in the nation. They recorded first on the Chance label, and their version of "Secret Love" was a success in 1954. Later that year, they moved to the Chess label and recorded "Sincerely," which topped the R&B charts and hit number 20 on the pop charts as well, although the McGuire Sisters' cover version of this song soon hit number 1 on the pop charts. They also performed in Alan Freed's movie *Rock, Rock, Rock* in 1956. In addition, the Moonglows were successful with "In My Diary" and "Most of All" in 1955, "See Saw" and "We Go Together" in 1956, "Please Send Me Someone to Love" in 1957, and "The Ten Commandments of Love" in 1958. The lead singers then split and formed other groups, some of which used the Moonglows' name, but their hits were in the past. The Moonglows were selected for the Vocal Group Hall of Fame in 1999 and the Rock & Roll Hall of Fame in 2000.

Groia, Philip. *They All Sang on the Corner.* West Hempstead, NY: Phillie Dee Enterprises, 1983, 22–26.

Nite, Norm N. *Rock On: The Illustrated History of Rock n' Roll.* New York: Crowell Co., 1974, 445–46.

Propes, Steve. "The Moonglows: The Ten Commandments of Doo-Wop." *Goldmine*, February 8, 1991, 11–13, 32.

Stambler, Irwin. "The Moonglows." In *Encyclopedia of Pop, Rock & Soul*, 471–72. New York: St. Martin's Press, 1989.

—*Richard Weigel*

MOORE, KIDD LEON "K. L.," JR. (b. 1923, Chicago, IL; d. 2006, Frankfort, KY), Baptist minister. Kidd Leon "K. L." Moore Jr. was born on November 7, 1923, in Chicago, IL, to Kidd Leon Moore Sr. and Emma Mane Moore. The elder Moore had worked as a minister before the marriage. In 1941, the younger Moore graduated from high school and was drafted two years

later. K. L., as he was often called, received three Bronze Stars for his bravery in France and Germany. Upon his return stateside, he graduated from Roosevelt University of Chicago. In 1950, he was licensed to preach and earned his master of divinity degree from Virginia Union University seven years later.

He married his wife, Sara, in 1958. After two years, the couple moved to Frankfort, KY, when Moore began his 46-year ministry at **First Baptist Church,** Frankfort's oldest and largest African American Baptist church, formed in 1833. Under his leadership, the congregation grew, and he initiated the Pastor's Aid Club and various musical groups. Moore, considered by some a principal organizer of the 1964 **March on Frankfort,** marched for civil rights with Dr. Martin Luther King Jr., Jackie Robinson, and Kentucky State senator **Georgia Powers.**

Moore was active in the community. In 1976, he offered his first invocation at the Kentucky General Assembly and periodically continued in that role for 30 years. The General Assembly posthumously honored him with a resolution in memory of his service. He served as chaplain of the Frankfort branch of the **National Association for the Advancement of Colored People,** president of the Franklin County Ministerial Association, chairman of the Mission Board of the **General Association of Baptists in Kentucky,** recording secretary of the Progressive National Baptist Convention, and board member of the Kentucky Student Loan Department and the Ethics Board of Franklin County.

Moore at times voiced opinions on local issues, including the Frankfort Country Club's exclusion from membership of a Japanese executive and **Kentucky State University** president **Raymond Burse.** He also questioned the wisdom of the financially strapped General Association of Baptists in Kentucky excluding churches that allowed women to preach. In 2004, he met with Kentucky governor Ernie Fletcher regarding the reorganization of the **Kentucky Commission on Human Rights.** Two years later, he again met with Governor Fletcher regarding casino gambling.

Moore died at his home in Frankfort less than a month before his 83rd birthday. He was buried in **Camp Nelson** National Cemetery in Nicholasville, KY.

First Baptist Church, Frankfort, KY. http://www.firstbaptistfrankfort.com/ History.html (accessed June 3, 2011).

Kentucky Historical Society. Oral History Project. http://205.204.134.47/civil_rights_mvt/search.aspx?terms=k+l+moore (accessed June 2, 2011).

Kentucky Legislature. http://www.lrc.ky.gov/record/07rs/SR3.htm (accessed June 2, 2011).

Newspapers: "Taking a Moment," *LHL,* February 2, 2002, C14; "Obituaries and Memorials," *LHL,* October 20, 2006, C4.

U.S. Department of Veterans Affairs. Nationwide Gravesite Locator. http://gravelocator.cem.va.gov/j2ee/servlet/NGL_v1 (accessed June 2, 2011).

U.S. Federal Census (1920, 1930).

United States Obituary Collection.

—*Sallie L. Powell*

MOORE, MARY ANN (b. 1915, Bath Co., KY; d. 1996, Carlisle, KY), inventor. Born on February 9, 1915, Mary Ann Jones grew up in Bath Co., Kentucky. Her parents were Carrie Boyd and Richard Jones. According to the 1930 U.S. federal census, at the age of 15, she lived with her mother, a washerwoman, and worked as a servant for a private family in Carlisle, KY. She later married Arthur Moore.

On December 4, 1979, at age 64, Mary Ann Moore obtained patent number 4,177,266 for her pain-relief creation. She combined the roots of burdock plants and the roots of the Phytolacca family in a heated mixture. Isopropyl alcohol was added after the product cooled. The blend was then applied to the skin to fight pain. Her son, James Richard Bean, was the patent assignee and thus had the property rights to her pain remedy.

On January 23, 1996, Mary Ann Moore, a homemaker and mother of three, died at St. Joseph Hospital in Lexington, KY. Mathers-Gaunce Funeral Home in Carlisle handled the arrangements. Moore was buried in Bethel Cemetery in Bath Co.

"Mary Ann Moore." *Nicholas Countian,* January 29, 1996, 3.
U.S. Federal Census (1930).
U.S. Patent and Trademark Office. http://patft.uspto.gov/netacgi/nph
    -Parser?Sect1=PTO2&Sect2=HITOFF&p=1&u=%2Fneta
    html%2FPTO%2Fsearch-bool.html&r=1&f=G&l=50&col=AND
    &d=PTXT&s1=4,177,266.PN.&OS=PN/4,177,266&RS=PN
    /4,177,266 (accessed April 2, 2013).

—*Sallie L. Powell*

MOORER, OLIVER D. (b. 1907, Dutch Bend, AL; d. 2004, Newark, OH), first African American member of the Lynch, KY, City Council. Born in Dutch Bend, AL, on September 29, 1907, Oliver D. Moorer moved north on several occasions in pursuit of work. Census records for 1930 identify him as a laborer at an aluminum plant in the factory town of Alcoa, TN. By 1940, he had moved to Lynch, KY, where he worked for U.S. Steel as a coal miner.

In Kentucky, Moorer owned his own businesses, including a restaurant and a grocery. In 1964, he successfully ran for the city council in Lynch and became the first African American member of the council. In 1966, he was reelected for another two-year term and was elected without opposition for the position in 1971.

After retiring as a coal miner, Moorer moved north again to Newark, OH, where he was a member of Shiloh Missionary Baptist Church and the local Masonic lodge. On April 12, 2004, he died at the Selma Markowitz Care Center and was buried in Newark Memorial Gardens. He was survived by his wife of 71 years, Gussie Lee Moorer.

Kentucky Commission on Human Rights. *Kentucky Directory of Black Elected Officials.* Frankfort: Commonwealth of Kentucky, 1972.
"Obituary." *Newark Advocate,* April 19, 2004.
U.S. Federal Census (1910, 1920, 1930, 1940).

—*Stephen Pickering*

MOORMAN, MARNEL C., SR. (b. 1943, Central City, KY; d. 1994, Wolfe Co., KY), first African American president of the Kentucky Education Association. A native of Central City, KY, Marnel C. Moorman Sr. experienced the setbacks of segregation when he attended an underfunded high school for black children in Muhlenburg Co. Reluctant to attend college, he finally agreed to visit Western Kentucky University at the urging of his school's valedictorian. He earned his bachelor's degree in education in 1965 and later earned a master's degree from Georgetown College.

Marnel Moorman.

Friends later recalled Moorman moving to Shelbyville, KY, "with a suitcase and an extra pair of shoes" to teach biology in Shelby Co. schools. He was part of the county's school system for over 30 years in various administrative and teaching roles, including coaching the basketball team. Moorman made history when he became the first African American elected vice president of the Kentucky Educational Association in 1986, a position he held for six years.

In 1992, he was elected president of the Kentucky Educational Association; the delegates at the group's annual convention voted for him by a two-to-one margin. As the first African American to hold that position, Moorman took over at a difficult time in the association's history, when education reform was under way across the state. He championed the implementation of the Kentucky Education Reform Act even as he cautioned against moving forward with reform too quickly. In editorials and presentations, he pointed out that teachers were having difficulty implementing changes in curriculum while enduring significantly increased hours and stress levels. Moorman also called for pay raises for teachers affected by these changes, noting that the expanded workload during educational reform coincided with salary freezes due to budget constraints.

On October 14, 1994, Moorman's car hit a coal truck as he was traveling to a board meeting of the Kentucky Educational Association. He died on the scene in Wolfe Co., KY. Over 1,200 people attended his funeral, which was held at Shelby County High School. He was buried in Calvary Cemetery. In 1995, Georgetown College established a scholarship in his name "to provide funds for qualified African-American students who wish to pursue teaching as a profession." Two years later, Western Kentucky

University inducted him into its Hall of Distinguished Alumni. On November 20 and 21, 1999, Clay Street Baptist Church, where he had served as chairman of the trustees, dedicated its new Marnel C. Moorman Sr. Family Life Center in his honor.

Newspapers: "Union Chief Seeks More Pay for Teachers," *LHL*, February 2, 1994, A9; "Death of KEA President Moorman in Crash Stuns Education Leaders," *LHL*, October 16, 1994, B2; "Marnel Moorman, Sr.," *OMI*, October 16, 1994, 2C.

—Stephen Pickering

MORGAN, GARRETT AUGUSTUS (b. 1877, Paris, KY; d. 1963, Cleveland, OH), inventor. Garrett Augustus was born March 4, 1877, in Paris, Bourbon Co. In his early years he did not allow a hostile social environment to stifle his determination to improve himself. By 1891, living in Cincinnati, Ohio, industriousness enabled him to engage a tutor. In 1895 his interests took him to Cleveland where as a result of his success as a sewing machine mechanic he married Madge Nelson in 1896.

In 1907 Morgan embarked on a series of successful business ventures with a sewing machine and shoe repair shop using devices of his own design. The following year he cofounded the Cleveland Association of Colored Men and wed Mary Anne Harsek. They had three sons. The business soon offered custom tailoring for men and women.

Later in 1909 his inventor's serendipity identified a lubricant that both prevented sewing machine needles from singeing fabric and straightened tough fibers. Finding that the formula straightened his own hair, he started the profitable G. A. Morgan Hair Refining Company and soon introduced hair dye products and a unique metal comb to maintain treated hair.

By 1912, motivated by the deaths in the Triangle Shirtwaist Factory fire, Morgan invented one of his most significant international contributions. His patented breathing device called a Safety Hood inspired the modern gas mask. He became the general manager of the National Safety Device Company. The Lake Erie Crib Disaster of 1916 took place during Cleveland Water Work's construction of an intake tunnel under the lake. Alerted to the explosion, Morgan and a brother employed Safety Hoods to rescue some workers. For his heroism, Morgan received awards from Cleveland and the International Association of Fire Engineers. However, many public safety departments around the country revoked orders for his equipment when they learned of his race. Chemical weapons use during World War I assured product sales. In 1920, he also began publishing a successful newspaper, *The Cleveland Call*.

As the first African-American automobile owner in the city, Morgan sought to reduce the increasing number of accidents by inventing in 1923 an improved traffic signal that made safe remote control possible at busy intersections. General Electric Company paid Morgan the considerable sum of $40,000 for this invention.

Progressive vision loss impaired his inventiveness but he remained active professionally and in the African American community. The Federal Highway Administration awarded Morgan a citation for his contributions to traffic safety only months before his death in Cleveland on August 27, 1963.

William M. King, "Guardian of the Public Safety," *Journal of Negro History*, 1985; *Inventive Genius* (Time-Life, 1991); Molefi Kete Asante, *100 Greatest African Americans: A Biographical Encyclopedia* (2002); *The Kentucky Encyclopedia* (1992); http://en.wikipedia.org/wiki/Garrett_Morgan.

—Eric Howard Christianson

MORRIS, HORACE (b. 1832, Louisville, KY; d. 1897, Louisville, KY), African American leader and businessman. Horace Morris was born a free person. His father, Shelton Morris, moved to Louisville in 1828 after being emancipated in Virginia and became a barber, bathhouse owner, and real estate speculator. After the death of Morris's mother, Evalina Spradling Morris, in 1841 and a controversy over whether his father violated the law by voting in the 1840 presidential election, the family moved to Ohio. There Morris completed his education and became an active worker in the **Underground Railroad.** He returned to Louisville in the late 1850s with his wife, Willeann, worked both as a riverboat steward and as a storeroom clerk, and became involved in civic affairs.

After the Civil War, Morris became prominent in local and state Republican Party politics. An eloquent speaker, he was politically moderate but was committed to the struggle for civil rights. He was considered a responsible leader by black and white Louisvillians. In December 1868, Morris was appointed cashier of the Louisville branch of the **Freedman's Savings and Trust Company.** He helped make his branch one of the most successful in the nation and was the only African American cashier called to Washington in 1881 to assist in resolving bank accounts after the nationwide collapse of the bank.

He also led campaigns for suffrage and efforts that resulted in the creation of public elementary schools for African Americans in 1870 and a high school in 1873. As a secretary of the Colored Board of Visitors, he monitored these schools, and he helped found the **Colored Orphans' Home** in 1878. Morris later became the first African American to serve as steward at Louisville's Marine Hospital. He was also a pioneer, although unsuccessful, black newspaper publisher, launching the short-lived *Kentuckian* in the early 1870s and the *Champion* in the early 1890s.

Morris, a longtime resident at 1930 Magazine St., had five children. He was active in **Quinn Chapel A.M.E. Church** and was a prominent Mason. He is buried in Eastern Cemetery.

Gibson, W. H., Sr. *Historical Sketch of the Progress of the Colored Race, in Louisville, Ky., as Noted by the Writer during a Period of Fifty Years.* Louisville, KY: Bradley & Gilbert, 1897.

Graham, Ruth Morris. *The Saga of the Morris Family.* Columbus, GA: Brentwood Christiana Communications, 1984.

Louisville City Directories, 1870–1900.

Lucas, Marion B. *A History of Blacks in Kentucky.* Vol. 1, *From Slavery to Segregation, 1760–1891.* Frankfort: Kentucky Historical Society, 1992.

Newspapers: *Louisville Courier,* January 2, 1866; *Louisville Commercial,* October 8, 1873; *Louisville Courier,* March 2, 1886; *LCJ,* December 2, 1873.

Weeden, H. C. *Weeden's History of the Colored People of Louisville.* Louisville, KY: H. C. Weeden, 1897.

Wilson, George D. *A Century of Negro Education in Louisville, Kentucky.* Louisville, KY: Louisville Municipal College, 1941.

Wright, George C. *Life Behind a Veil: Blacks in Louisville, Kentucky, 1865–1930*. Baton Rouge: Louisiana State Univ. Press, 1985.

—*J. Blaine Hudson*

MORRIS, LOIS WALKER (b. 1919, Okolona, MS; d. 1989, Louisville, KY), alderman and civil rights leader. Morris was one of eight children of Tom and Clara (Lomax) Walker. She attended Clark College in Atlanta and received a master's degree in international law and political science from Catholic University in Washington, DC. After graduation, she returned to Mississippi and taught history at Alcorn College (later Alcorn State University). She also taught history at high schools in Maryland, Mississippi, and Virginia. In 1955, she moved to Louisville.

In Louisville, Morris became actively involved in the struggle for the rights of African Americans, women, and the disadvantaged. In addition to being a member of the **Louisville Urban League,** Morris was the founder and president of the Louisville chapter of the National Council of Negro Women and the founder and executive director of the National Black Women for Political Action. She also served as a board member of the state chapter of the **National Association for the Advancement of Colored People** (NAACP). From 1979 to 1987, she served on the NAACP's task force on desegregating institutions of higher learning. She also served on various committees and commissions, including Louisville's first Human Relations Commission, the **Kentucky Commission on Human Rights,** and the Second Charter Commission on the merger of Louisville and Jefferson Co.

In 1969, Morris ran in the Democratic primary for 12th Ward alderman. She won the primary and the next three general elections. She was defeated by **E. Porter Hatcher** in 1975. In 1977, she ran unsuccessfully for mayor in the Democratic primary.

In addition to her political contributions, Morris wrote, without compensation, a column for the *Louisville Defender* called "Scribbling Socially." Morris, who was known for her fashionable dress and for wearing hats, was named to *Ebony* magazine's list of 21 best-dressed women in 1963. She also helped organize the Miss Exposition beauty and talent contest and the Miss Defender best-dressed list. Morris had several businesses at property she owned at 2000 W. Broadway, including a consignment shop called Lois' Old House of Bargains.

Morris was married to Dr. Ralph Morris, and they had one daughter, Roslyn. At **Kentucky Derby** time, the Morrises held a party at their West End home that attracted many celebrities and also received local and national newspaper coverage. Morris died in January 1989 of stomach cancer. She is entombed at the Evergreen Mausoleum. In 1996, the Board of Aldermen commissioned a bust of Morris to be placed in the Shawnee Branch of the Louisville Free Public Library.

LCJ, January 28, 1989.
Women's Manuscript Collection. University Archives, Univ. of Louisville.

MORRIS, WILLIAM RICHARD (b. 1859, Flemingsburg, KY; d. 1929, Minneapolis, MN), one of the first black lawyers in Minnesota. The son of Hezekiah and Elizabeth Morris, William Richard Morris was born in Flemingsburg, Ky, on February 22, 1859. His older brother, **Edward H. Morris,** eventually became a respected lawyer in Chicago. When Richard was a small child, his enslaved father died, and his free mother moved the family to Cincinnati, OH. When he was 17 years old, Morris moved to Tennessee to attend school at Fisk University and received a bachelor's degree in 1884. He stayed at the school for the next five years, where he worked toward a master's degree and taught classes in math, language, and science. At the time, he was the school's only African American teacher. During his time at Fisk, Morris also taught himself law, was admitted to the Tennessee and Illinois state bars, and was the representative of southern blacks at the national meeting of the **American Missionary Association** in 1885.

In 1889, Morris moved to Minneapolis, MN, to establish a law practice. That same year, he became the second African American admitted to the Minnesota bar, and by 1890, he was the first black lawyer to appear before a court in Hennepin Co. (Minneapolis). During the next 30 years, Morris became one of the most successful black criminal attorneys not just in Minnesota but in the United States. In 1912, he was admitted to practice before the U.S. Supreme Court. In 1911, Morris and two other African Americans became the first black lawyers admitted to the American Bar Association (ABA). By 1912, word of their membership had spread to southern lawyers, who protested their presence within the previously all-white national organization. Although the other two black lawyers persisted, Morris quietly resigned. Many believe that his decision to resign was not because he sought to accommodate whites, but because he wanted to embarrass a rival Minnesota lawyer who had eyes on the presidency of the ABA.

Morris was politically and socially active during his years in Minnesota. Around the turn of the century, he helped organize the Afro-American Law Enforcement League, designed "to secure moral and legal rights for Negroes." In 1913, he appeared before the Minnesota House Judiciary Committee to protest a proposed miscegenation law. A 33rd-degree Mason, he served for over 20 years as the master of finance and deputy supreme chancellor for the Knights of Pythias in Minnesota and was a charter member of numerous lodges throughout the state.

Morris died in Minneapolis on December 30, 1929.

Boris, Joseph J., ed. *Who's Who in Colored America, 1927.* New York: Who's Who in Colored America Corp., 1927.
Gibson, John W., and William H. Crogman. *The Colored American from Slavery to Honorable Citizenship.* Naperville, IL: J. L. Nichols & Co., 1903.
Smith, J. Clay, Jr. *Emancipation: The Making of the Black Lawyer, 1844–1944.* Philadelphia: Univ. of Pennsylvania Press, 1993.
Williams, Ephie Augustus, S. W. Green, and Joseph L. Jones. *History and Manual of the Colored Knights of Pythias.* Nashville, TN: National Baptist Publishing Board, 1917.

—*Joshua D. Farrington*

MORTON-FINNEY, JOHN (b. 1889, Uniontown, KY; d. 1998, Indianapolis, IN), attorney, civil rights activist, buffalo soldier, and educational leader. John Morton-Finney was born to the son of a former slave in Uniontown, KY, on June 25, 1889. His mother died when he was 14, and Morton-Finney's father, unable to care for his seven children, sent them to live with their grandfather on a farm in Missouri. From 1911 to 1914, Morton-Finney served in the U.S. Army as a member of the all-black cavalry regiment known as the **Buffalo Soldiers.** During this time, he served in the Philippines, and upon returning home, he enrolled at Lincoln College in Missouri, where he earned the first of 11 college degrees. He completed his master's degree in education and French from Indiana University in 1925, and two years later, he became one of the first teachers hired at the all-black Crispus Attucks High School in Indianapolis as head of the Foreign Languages Department.

Morton-Finney had a lifelong passion for learning. He completed his 11th and final degree from Butler University at the age of 75. In addition to his contributions to education, John Morton-Finney practiced law for more than 80 years, the longest-practicing lawyer in history. He was inducted into the National Bar Association Hall of Fame in 1991. He died on January 28, 1998, at the age of 108. He was given a full-honor military memorial service and was buried in Crown Hill Cemetery in Indianapolis, IN.

Buffalo Soldier Research Museum. "Trooper John Morton-Finney: 24th U.S. Infantry, World War I." Indianapolis, IN, 2005. http://www.buffalosoldiersresearchmuseum.org/research/books/morton-finney.htm (accessed September 10, 2009).

Indiana University. "Alumni Profile: John Morton-Finney." Bloomington, IN, 2009. http://alumni.indiana.edu/profiles/alumni/jmortonfinney.shtml (accessed September 8, 2009).

Weaver, Carmon, and George Hicks. *Our Journey with the Buffalo Soldiers.* Philadelphia: Xlibris, 2006.

—*Benjamin Rawlins*

MOUNTAIN ISLAND, African American community. Mountain Island, which is unique because it came to be entirely owned by African American families, is a 110-acre island in Eagle Creek in northern Owen Co. That stream flows northwest into the Kentucky River just south of Carrollton, splitting into two channels on the eastern side of Mountain Island. The island is composed of limestone bedrock that resisted the flow of Eagle Creek, which divided instead of carving through the hill. The two channels rejoin on the southwest corner of the island, where Caney Fork Creek merges into Eagle Creek. The island consists of three microtopographic zones: floodplains, steep hillslopes, and a narrow ridge top.

A road right-of-way reference to Mountain Island as early as 1792 has been found in Scott Co. records; at that time Owen Co. was part of Scott Co. The earliest record of settlers on the island coincides with the founding of the Mountain Island Baptist Church in 1801. By 1932, the church had moved several miles up Eagle Creek and had changed its name, first to Rocky Point Baptist Church and then to Pleasant View Baptist Church. The initial church membership rolls include no reference to the Herndons or the Rogers, the two families that were most influential in Mountain Island's earliest history, but James Herndon is mentioned in the later records of the Mountain Island Baptist Church. The Herndon and Rogers families (Herndon's sister) were apparently not active in the church. Several disputes occurred, after which members with abolitionist tendencies left

the rolls. Since both James Herndon and Susannah Herndon Rogers freed their slaves upon their deaths, perhaps they stayed away from the church because most of its membership supported slavery.

James Herndon first appears in Scott Co. records in 1797. In 1802, Herndon was the administrator of Lewis Herndon's will; he and his sister later took control of the property that had been owned by Lewis Herndon. James Herndon owned Mountain Island and some of the surrounding mainland until his death in 1853. He built a mill "on main Eagle Creek on the lower part of the Mountain Island above the mouth of Caney Fork [Creek]" in 1812. His sister Susannah Herndon Rogers owned land on the mainland east of Mountain Island. She died in 1847; provisions of her will freed her slaves and gave them land surrounding the island. James Herndon applied to the Owen Co. court in 1850 in an attempt to free his slaves but was told to pay a high bond on each one. He refused and freed 23 persons in his will. He divided his estate among them and gave allotments of property to the adults. The settlement contained 21 parcels, with lots 1 to 15 on the island and lots 16 to 21 on the mainland. All the lots included creek frontage. Herndon took care to ensure that each lot had access to the creek and to either bottomland or tillable ridgetop land. The list of the recipients of this land division survives. Twenty-one of the 23 persons listed received property; only Joshua Junior and Masiat did not. Perhaps they were minors at the time of emancipation. The family names Vinegar, Carroll, and Smith dominate these lists.

The 1883 atlas for Owen Co. depicts the division of Mountain Island but is silent about the African American owners of the island. The atlas shows no structures on the island or in the immediate surroundings. Apparently, either the surveyors did not approach the African American owners, or those owners did not subscribe to the atlas in order to obtain a listing therein (a common practice when such maps were made). Census records from the late nineteenth century identify several members of the Vinegar and Carroll families.

Mountain Island contains significant archaeological resources related to the black families. In 1998, the Behringer-Crawford Museum in Covington conducted an archaeological survey of the island to document the locations of the sites associated with the African American ownership and occupation. The survey found the following archaeological sites that are associated with the families who took ownership after the resolution of James Herndon's will in 1860: five house sites, a barn, a limestone wall, scattered historic artifacts, and a mill site on the mainland bank of Eagle Creek.

The Mountain Island community lasted until the early twentieth century. The Great Depression and local hardships forced inhabitants to look elsewhere for employment. Family members still own the island but do not live there. Perhaps the foremost descendant of the island's families was the successful horse trainer **Theodore Vinegar.**

Bryant, James C. *Mountain Island in Owen County, Kentucky: The Settlers and Their Church.* Owenton, KY: Owen Co. Historical Society, 1986.

—*Jeannine Kreinbrink*

MT. MORIAH CEMETERY (BOWLING GREEN), believed to be the oldest African American cemetery in Warren Co., KY. In 1860, African Americans, the majority of them enslaved, constituted 32 percent of Warren Co.'s population. They were frequently buried in unmarked graves outside the white family cemeteries. Others were interred in a segregated section of Pioneer Cemetery, including five markers that indicated the entombment of "free" African Americans.

During the Civil War, the Pioneer Cemetery filled to capacity. Therefore, the city of Bowling Green purchased land northeast of the city near the Barren River in 1862. Union soldiers from the U.S. Colored Calvary and the U.S. Colored Heavy Artillery were buried there. Six years later, the city bought property for St. Joseph Cemetery. Although substantiation is lacking, it is believed that African Americans were buried north of St. Joseph Cemetery as early as 1870. The deed was recorded in 1878. The cemetery's board of directors named the few acres Mt. (sometimes Mount) Moriah Cemetery in homage to Solomon's Temple in Jerusalem. On April 6, 1900, Mt. Moriah Cemetery Association was incorporated.

Operations under a board of directors continued into the mid-1980s, when complaints arose over the cemetery's maintenance and bookkeeping. In 1984, the Mt. Moriah Cemetery Association voted to allow the city of Bowling Green to maintain the cemetery and to collect burial fees. Although the cemetery no longer sold gravesites, people with proof of burial rights were still permitted interment.

Some of the more noteworthy people buried in Mt. Moriah Cemetery include **Reuben Ernest Crowdus** (a.k.a. Ernest Hogan), **Ora F. Porter, Otho Dandrith Porter, Zacharia K. Jones,** and Lucy Rodes. Crowdus, the first African American producer and star on Broadway, helped create **ragtime** music. Ora Porter was the first African American registered nurse in Bowling Green. Otho Dandrith Porter and Z. K. Jones practiced medicine in Bowling Green. Rodes, a cook and laundress, willed her estate to needy African Americans for hospital and medical care.

Civil War 150: Bowling Green's Mt. Moriah Cemetery; A Resting Place for African American Union Soldiers. http://buylocalbg.wordpress .com/2011/06/16/bowling-green-buy-local-civil-war-kentucky -african-american-soldiers/ (accessed October 17, 2012).
Jeffrey, Jonathan, and Mike Wilson, comps. *Mt. Moriah Cemetery: A History and Census of Bowling Green, Kentucky's African-American Cemetery.* Bowling Green, KY: Landmark Association, 2002.
—*Sallie L. Powell*

MOUNT VERNON A.M.E. CHURCH, one of the oldest African American churches in Kentucky. In 1802, freed slaves of William Howard formed the African American community of Freetown in Monroe Co. By the 1840s, Freetown had numerous homes built on 400 acres of land that had been given at a later date by Howard to his freed slaves.

Known to many locals as Freetown Church, Mount Vernon A.M.E. Church was built in 1848. One of the oldest black religious structures in the state and the first black church in Monroe Co., Mount Vernon was constructed by local residents George Pipkin, Albert Howard, and Peter West. West, one of the few residents who was not a former slave of Howard, was a freed

Methodist-trained minister from Tennessee. He served as the church's first pastor. The church was located on a plot donated by Albert Martin, less than a mile south of Freetown and just five miles from the Tennessee border. The simple one-room, one-story church was made with hand-hewn logs, wooden pegs, and clay.

For 70 years after its construction, the church also served as a school for Freetown's residents. Desks for the school were carved by church members, and "they used whatever the white students had rejected" for school supplies. The school continued to teach Freetown's children into the 1920s.

During the 1930s, the church was known throughout Monroe Co. for its decorated Maypole. Once a year, the pole was decorated with colorful streamers, and young girls danced around it. One former resident recalled, "Everyone went from miles around to see it," and a nearby white resident remarked that "it was such a pretty sight." The Maypole festivities were concluded by a large dinner on the church's lawn that was even attended by some whites.

Mount Vernon, already serving a small rural community, closed its doors in the following decade as the remaining residents of Freetown died or moved away. Given the historic nature of the church, however, many former members, like Joyce Thomas of Louisville, helped maintain and preserve the church building. In 1977, Mount Vernon was added to the National Register of Historic Places. In 1982, Thomas and other former members started what would become an annual reunion on the second Saturday in June. As in the 1930s, the church's lawn was once again used as the location for a large dinner and celebration.

Except for a tin roof, which was installed to replace the original wooden one, and double-pane windows, the remaining church structure maintains its original construction from 1848. Many of the school desks constructed in the mid-1800s also remain inside the church. Mount Vernon A.M.E. Church is located north of Gamaliel on Kentucky Route 100.

Curtis, Nancy. *Black Heritage Sites: The South.* Chicago: ALA Editions, 1996.
Rennick, Robert. *Kentucky Place Names.* Lexington: Univ. Press of Kentucky, 1988.
Savage, Beth. *African American Historic Places.* Hoboken, NJ: John Wiley & Sons, 1994.
—*Joshua D. Farrington*

MOXLEY, FRANK OTHA (b. 1908, Bowling Green, KY; d. 2004, Bowling Green, KY), educator. Frank Otha (F. O.) Moxley, the son of insurance agent James F. Moxley and Elizabeth Moxley, was born in Bowling Green, KY, on June 29, 1908. Like most African Americans in the South, he had sparse educational opportunities in early childhood. Traveling wherever he could for a quality education, he attended Wilberforce University and received his bachelor's degree in 1926.

Once he earned his degree from Wilberforce, Moxley came back to Bowling Green to grant the same opportunities that had been afforded to him. Education being his mainstay, he was considered an early pioneer in the Kentucky educational system. In 1958, he became the first African American to receive a master's degree in psychology and guidance from Western Kentucky University. He put his master's to good use, virtually alone creating the guidance counselor position for the Kentucky school system. In 1974, he received his doctorate in psychology from East Coast University/National University in Florida.

Moxley became a fixture not only in the greater Bowling Green community but also throughout western Kentucky. Some of his achievements included being commissioned by the governor's office to write "The Elementary Guidance Program," coaching a successful basketball program for 20 years at all–African American High Street School, serving as a member of the Board of Directors of the South Central Kentucky Minority Economic Development Council, and being inducted into the Western Kentucky University Hall of Distinguished Alumni. The Bowling Green Parks and Recreation gymnasium was named in his honor. Moxley died at the age of 96 in 2004.

"Dr. Frank Otha Moxley—Obituary 2004—Warren-Family History & Genealogy Message Board." August 16, 2004. http://boards.ancestry .com/localities.northam.usa.states.kentucky.counties.warren /4950/mb.ashx (accessed January 26, 2010).

"F. O. Moxley Opened Doors for Many Blacks." *BGDN*, August 10, 2004.

"Kentucky: Kentucky Commission on Human Rights—Great Black Kentuckians." February 23, 2009. http://kchr.ky.gov/gallergreat black.htm (accessed January 26, 2010).

—*Vincent Gonzalez*

MULLINS, PAMELA E. (b. 1953, Covington, KY.), civil rights activist. Pamela Mullins is one of six children of Robert and Shirley Jennings Mullins. During her early childhood, Mullins's father and mother worked long hours as a factory worker and a day laborer, respectively, in Covington. As she observed their circumstances, she came to believe in the link between a quality education and the expansion of one's socioeconomic opportunities. In her early years, Mullins did not desire a life as a social activist or a career in public service. However, her goals gradually changed. Mullins became a student activist at Covington's Holmes High School, partly because of her admiration of various national and local leaders of the **civil rights movement** during the 1960s and early 1970s. She and several of her classmates organized a student demonstration at Holmes in response to the school's inability to hire an adequate number of African American teachers, as well as the use of a history curriculum that disregarded the experience of black Americans.

After Mullins graduated from Holmes High School in 1971 and earned a BS degree in marketing from the University of Cincinnati in 1983, she became the first African American woman elected to the Covington Board of Education, where she served until 1996. During her tenure there, Mullins aimed at improving public education for African American students and other underrepresented pupils. When she was asked about some of her major accomplishments as a member of the school board, Mullins proclaimed, "Although it was a hard fight, I was successful in enhancing the educational experience of African American students in the Covington school system as well as the sponsoring of legislation that focused on such issues as site-based management, diversity, and multicultural [education]."

In 1996, Mullins was elected to the Covington City Commission, the first African American to hold such a position in north-

ern Kentucky. She left this position in 1998. Among her many achievements in the political arena, Mullins sponsored several neighborhood economic development projects, worked on a regional transportation commission, and helped create the Covington Human Rights Commission. In all her activities, she has worked to improve the lives of all the residents of Covington.

Covington Board of Education Meeting Minutes, Board of Education, Covington, KY, 1996.

Mullins, Pamela. Telephone interviews by Eric R. Jackson, September 15 and October 4, 2006.

Newspapers: "Covington Elects First Black to School Board," *Suspension Press,* November 1988, 1; "African-American Day Celebrates Roots," *KP,* April 27, 1990, 2K; Debra Ann Vance, "Chapman Returns as School Chair," *KP,* January 19, 1991, 3K; "Covington Board Member Pushes for Race-Gender Data," *KP,* September 14, 1991, 3K; "School Board Won't Seek Test-Score Breakdown—Gender, Race Analysis Rejected," *KP,* September 18, 1991; Bob Driehaus, "Mullins Brings Diversity to Covington Commission," *KP,* November 6, 1996, 1K; Pamela E. Mullins, "Editorial: A Graduation of Sorts," *KP,* September 27, 1998, 4K.

—*Eric R. Jackson*

MUNDY, JAMES AHYLN (b. 1886, Maysville, KY; d. 1978, Chicago, IL), choir leader. James Ahyln Mundy, the son of a former slave, became one of the premier choir leaders in the United States. He directed choirs, primarily in Chicago, from 1913 to 1978. While Mundy lived in Maysville, he served as organist of the Bethel Baptist Church there, and the church gave him some support while he attended Simmons Normal School (later known as **Simmons College of Kentucky**) in Louisville. Upon the death of his father, Mundy moved to Chicago with his mother. He later commented, "I had heard that up in Chicago a colored man could even work in the post office." Actually employed at a post office in Chicago, Mundy attracted the attention of local civil rights leader Ida Wells Barnett, who learned of his musical ability and asked him to form a choir to perform as part of an appearance of W. E. B. DuBois in Chicago. The day when James Mundy led the choir, January 12, 1913, was the first time an African American group performed in Chicago's Orchestra Hall. Mundy enjoyed creating combined choirs from Chicago's black churches in addition to arranging music and giving private voice and piano lessons. In 1916, he directed his group, named the Mundy Choristers, at the dedication of Chicago's Navy Pier. In 1931, Mundy was chosen to lead the choir at the rededication of Abraham Lincoln's tomb in Springfield, IL, where President Herbert Hoover (1929–1933) gave the address. When Chicago hosted the World's Fair in 1933 and 1934, the Mundy Jubilee Singers provided biweekly entertainment. Mundy took pride that only his group and a police band were invited to reappear at the closing, where 400,000 people witnessed the performances. Beginning in 1935, Mundy directed a Works Progress Administration–funded group of singers that delivered more than 5,000 performances in Chicago-area schools over the course of seven years. In 1946, Mundy directed a choir of 1,000 voices at Carnegie Hall in New York City. Mundy directed tens of thousands of singers, and his choirs performed for combined audiences numbering in the hundreds of thousands. He led his last choir, the Olivet Baptist

Church Choir, on Thanksgiving Day in 1978. Mundy was still teaching and directing when he died on Christmas Day of 1978.

Reife, Janice L., Keating, Ann Durkin, and Grossman, James R., eds., *The Encyclopedia of Chicago.* Chicago: Univ. of Chicago Press, 2004.
Newspapers: Vernon Jarrett, "James Mundy Still Stirs Yule Spirit," *Chicago Tribune,* December 29, 1974, A6; "Prof. Mundy, Who Raised Black Voices in Song, Dies," *Chicago Tribune,* December 27, 1978, A11.

—*George Vaughn and John Klee*

MURPHY, DONNA L. J. (b. 1958, Hutchinson, KS), basketball pioneer and coach. Born on January 18, 1958, in Hutchinson, KS, Donna Murphy spent her early life in Newport, KY. In 1974, she was the Class 2A state high jump champion. The Kentucky High School Athletic Association reinstated girls' basketball in 1974–1975. As a junior, Murphy, a five-feet-ten forward, led Newport High School in the return of the Girls' Sweet Sixteen Basketball Tournament, scoring 42 points and seizing 25 rebounds in the school's first game. Her "fluid moves, leaping ability, and patented left hand jump shot" attracted attention, and she was selected the Most Valuable Player of the state tournament. She also became the first recipient of the Joe Bill Mansfield Award, an honor that recognized athletic and academic achievement. In her senior year, she became the first Miss Basketball in Kentucky and was one of two high school female players invited to try out for the 1976 U.S. Olympic basketball team.

Murphy continued playing basketball at Morehead State University. In her college career, she scored 2,059 points, becoming the school's lead scorer. She was also named Ohio Valley Conference Player of the Year (1977–1978) and Ohio Valley Conference Woman Athlete of the Year (1979–1980). In 1999, Morehead retired her jersey; she was the first female basketball player to receive that honor from the school.

After college, Murphy briefly played professional basketball for the St. Louis Streak, part of the Women's Professional Basketball League, a forerunner of the Women's National Basketball Association. She then pursued her passion for basketball through coaching. She worked at several academic institutions, including the University of Kentucky, the University of Florida, the University of Memphis, the University of Cincinnati, and her alma mater, Morehead State University. She created the women's intercollegiate basketball program at Asbury College and coached there for over a decade.

In 2008, doctors gave Murphy only 72 hours to live because of autoimmune hepatitis, which attacks the liver cells. She survived a six-hour liver-transplant procedure. From 2011 to 2013, she coached at Bryan Station High School in Lexington. Along with coaching, she has worked as a counselor and instructor at Bluegrass Community and Technical College since 1985. Murphy has received various honors for her athletic accomplishments, including induction into the Dawahares–Kentucky High School Athletic Association Sports Hall of Fame (1989) and the Kentucky High School Basketball Hall of Fame (2013).

Kentucky High School Basketball Hall of Fame Inductees. http://www.khsbhf.com/inductees.asp (accessed May 24, 2013).
Newspapers: "Forward Helped Girls' Basketball Return with Bang," *LHL,* July 25, 1999, 13; "Murphy Receives Liver Transplant—Doctors Cautiously Optimistic," *LHL,* June 28, 2008, B2; "'Friends of 44' Aid Ex-MSU Hoops Star," *LHL,* January 8, 2009, A1; "Murphy Stressing Basics as Station's New Coach—Kentucky Icon Has Passion to Mentor," *LHL,* June 23, 2011, B3; *LHL,* http://kentucky.com/2013/06/2668358/lca-bryan-station-girls-coaches.html (accessed June 19, 2013).
1989 Dawahares–Kentucky High School Athletic Association Sports Hall of Fame Inductees. http://khsaa.org/hallfame/1989.pdf (accessed May 24, 2013).

—*Sallie L. Powell*

MURPHY, ISAAC BURNS (b. 1861, Clark Co., KY; d. 1896, Lexington, KY), legendary jockey. Isaac Burns was born in Clark Co., KY, on January 1, 1861. His mother, America Murphy, was a slave born on the Pleasant Green farm owned by David Tanner. She was the daughter of Anne and Green Murphy. Anne was a slave and Green likely shared the same status. Isaac's father is believed to have been Jerry Skillman, a slave on John Whitney Skillman's farm in Bourbon Co. Isaac learned to break horses from James T. Williams in 1873 and to ride from trainer Eli Jordan. He rode in his first race in May 1875 and won his first official race on September 15, 1876, on Glentina at Lexington or, as he claimed, the Crab Orchard track, Lincoln Co., KY. He changed his surname to Murphy shortly after that first victory. According

Isaac Murphy.

Lucy Murphy.

to trainer Jordan, the name change occurred because Isaac's mother requested that he ride "under the name of her father."

In 1879, Murphy gained a national reputation for his victories on J. W. Hunt Reynolds's horse Falsetto, later sold for an American record $18,000. Although Murphy began having trouble making weight starting in 1880, he continued to win consistently. Riding for Edward Corrigan in 1884, he won his first **Kentucky Derby** and added victories in the Clark Handicap, the Kentucky Oaks, and the first American Derby. Corrigan changed the name of horse Harry White to Isaac Murphy. As Murphy achieved notoriety on the track, a significant change occurred in his personal life. He married Lucy Carr on January 24, 1883, at St. John's African Methodist Church in Frankfort, KY. Ten years later the couple celebrated their tenth wedding anniversary. The *Kentucky Leader* reported that "Murphy's comfortable home on East Third Street was gaily lighted and decorated for the occasion." Guest were served an "elaborate" dinner. "Mrs. Murphy, the hostess, was dressed in white silk, trimmed with pearls and white lace, and wore ornaments of diamonds and gold."

In 1885, Murphy won the American Derby on Elias "Lucky" Baldwin's Volante, earning the then-immense fee of $1,000, and three of four races on Freeland against Miss Woodford, the first American $100,000 Thoroughbred winner. Baldwin paid Murphy an American jockey record of $12,000 in 1887. In 1888–1889,

Murphy enjoyed great success on the Dwyer brothers' Kingston, America's most winning Thoroughbred. He won consecutive Kentucky Derbies on Corrigan's Riley in 1890 and on Kingman in 1891. He raced less after 1891 and began buying and training horses in 1893. He rode his last race in 1895.

Edward Corrigan said of Murphy: "He has not a superior, if indeed, an equal, as a rider, and is the very embodiment of honesty and integrity. The later quality, combined with his great ability, makes him immensely popular." Murphy, famous for his keen judgment of pace, won many races by small margins. The *Spirit of the Times* noted, "No man with a touch of heart disease should ever back his mounts."

On February 12, 1896, Murphy died of heart failure in Lexington, KY, and was buried in **African Cemetery No. 2.** He was reinterred at Man o' War Park in 1967 and the Kentucky Horse Park in 1976. Inducted into the National Museum of Racing Hall of Fame in 1955, Murphy was also in the National Jockeys Hall of Fame. Named in his honor are the Arlington Race Track's Isaac Murphy Handicap and the Isaac Murphy Award, presented annually to the North American jockey with the highest winning percentage. Isaac Murphy was the first jockey to win three Kentucky Derbies, four American Derbies, and five Latonia Derbies; he won 628 of 1,412 races, a record 44 percent of all his starts.

Borries, Betty Earle. *Isaac Murphy: Kentucky's Record Jockey.* Berea, KY: Kentucke [sic] Imprints, 1988.
Borries, Frank. "His Record Is His Best Monument." *Thoroughbred Record* 173 (May 6, 1961): 14, 34.
Ginsburg, Debra. "Lucky Baldwin's Racing School." *Thoroughbred of California* 98 (June 1994): 38–39, 42–43, 46.
"Isaac B. Murphy, Colored Jockey." *New York Sportsman* 15 (January 20, 1883): 33–34.
"Isaac Murphy's Death." *Thoroughbred Record* 43 (1896): 79
McDaniels, Pellom, III. *The Prince of Jockeys: The Life of Isaac Burns Murphy.* Lexington: Univ. Press of Kentucky, 2013, 43–62, 259, 367–68.
"Miscellaneous Turf Gossip." *Live Stock Record* 36 (November 12, 1892): 327.
Murphy, Isaac B. Certificate of Death no. 1025, Fayette Co., KY.
Newspapers: "Freeland's Easy Victory over Miss Woodford," *NYT,* September 15, 1885, 2; "Isaac Murphy: Biographical Sketch of the Great Lexington Jockey," *LL,* March 20, 1890, 3; "Isaac Murphy's History," *Detroit (MI) Plaindealer,* August 14, 1891, 1.
Tarlton, L. P. "Isaac Murphy: A Memorial." *Thoroughbred Record* 43 (1896): 136.
Wall, Maryjean. "Isaac Murphy." In *Members in the National Museum of Racing Hall of Fame,* by the National Turf Writers Association. Saratoga Springs, NY: 1976.
"Was Isaac Murphy Poisoned [sic]?" *Live Stock Record* 32 (November 22, 1890): 329.

—*Steven P. Savage*

"MY OLD KENTUCKY HOME," Kentucky's official state song. Many Kentuckians believe that the song "My Old Kentucky Home," written by Stephen Collins Foster in 1850, was composed in the parlor of Federal Hill, the home of Foster's cousins, the **Rowan family,** in Bardstown. The mansion has been made a state shrine and the centerpiece of My Old Kentucky Home State Park. However, no historical evidence exists that Foster ever visited

Bardstown. The line about darkies rolling on the little cabin floor does not sound descriptive of a stately mansion, but it could have referred to a slave cabin in back of the house.

Another view is that Foster wrote the song to depict a slave longing to be reunited with his family after being sold to a sugar-cane plantation down South. The original title of the song, "Poor Uncle Tom, Good Night," buttresses this interpretation, as do such words as "The time has come when the darkies must part" and "The head must bow and the back will have to bend, Wherever the darky may go; A few more days, and the trouble all will end, In the field where the sugar-canes grow." It has also been suggested that Harriet Beecher Stowe's wildly popular antislavery novel **Uncle Tom's Cabin** and the plays based on it inspired the song. However, the first draft of Foster's song is believed to have been written in 1850, and Stowe's book was published in 1852. When the song was published in 1853, the title was changed to "My Old Kentucky Home," and poor Uncle Tom was not mentioned by name.

The song became popular when it was performed by the Christy Minstrels on the vaudeville stage. During the Civil War, both Union and Confederate troops sang it beside army campfires. Foster called it a plantation melody, and it became one of the most popular parlor songs of the latter half of the nineteenth century. Called maudlin by some, the song is sentimental and emotional, evoking feelings of homesickness and nostalgia in many listeners.

In 1924, the song replaced "The Star Spangled Banner" as the anthem of the **Kentucky Derby.** In 1928, it was designated the official state song by the Kentucky General Assembly. By resolutions of the legislature in 1986, the word "darkies" was replaced by "people" in the official version of the song. The song is played at all University of Kentucky and University of Louisville basketball and football games. Usually only the first two verses and the chorus are sung at these events.

Kelly, Mary Ann. *My Old Kentucky Home, Good-Night.* Hicksville, NY: Exposition Press, 1979.
Kentucky Department for Libraries and Archives. "Kentucky's State Song: My Old Kentucky Home." Frankfort, KY, 2008. http://www.kdla.gov/resources/KYsong.htm (accessed August 12, 2008).

—*Charles F. Faber*

N

NAPPY ROOTS, Grammy-nominated, platinum hip-hop group. Considered the most influential hip-hop group to come out of Kentucky, Nappy Roots was formed by Ronald Wilson ("Clutch") of Louisville, Brian Scott ("B. Stille") of Louisville, Vito Tisdale ("Big V") of Bowling Green, William Hughes ("Skinny DeVille") of Louisville, Melvin Adams ("Fish Scales") of Georgia, and Kenneth Anthony ("R. Prophet") of California. In 1995, DeVille and Clutch attended Western Kentucky University and often wrote lyrics in their house near campus. They were joined by Big V, who lived around the corner when he was not attending school at Eastern Kentucky University. The following year, Scales joined their rap sessions after receiving a basketball scholarship. The group was complete in 1997 once R. Prophet and B. Stille were admitted to Western Kentucky University.

Starting off with gigs at local skating rinks and parties, the hip-hop group quickly reached cult status within fraternities and sororities at Kentucky colleges. In 1998, it released its debut album, *County Fried Cess,* which drew the attention of Atlantic Records. In 2002, Atlantic released *Watermelon, Chicken & Gritz.* According to one reviewer, it was "the first rap album to put Kentucky on the map," and it was one of the most successful hip-hop releases of the year. The album quickly became certified platinum, selling over one million copies, and the song "Po' Folks" was nominated for a Grammy. The album was reviewed favorably by the *New York Times, Spin, Vibe,* and *Rolling Stone,* whose reviewer wrote that it was "the best thing to come out of Kentucky since the Colonel's chicken." The group's music video for the song "Awnaw" was frequently played on major cable television channels like MTV, MTV2, and BET. That same year, Governor Paul Patton named all six members of the group Kentucky Colonels and proclaimed September 16 Nappy Roots Day.

During the middle of the first decade of the twenty-first century, the group experienced setbacks after artistic disputes with Atlantic Records and after R. Prophet left to pursue a solo career. Publishing its music independently, however, proved successful for the group, which maintained its popularity into the 2010s. In 2003, it released *Wooden Leather,* which was certified gold and was ranked as high as 12th on the Billboard 200 chart (and 9th on the R&B / Hip-Hop chart). By the release of its next album, *The Humdinger,* in 2008, it had formed its own recording label, NREG (Nappy Roots Entertainment Group). In 2010, it released *The Pursuit of Nappyness,* and in 2011, it partnered with the production company Organized Noize in releasing its sixth album, *Nappy Dot Org.*

Despite its success, Nappy Roots also emphasized community involvement. It has made numerous appearances in Louisville, serving Thanksgiving turkey dinners to Louisville's homeless or accompanying groups of at-risk kids through tours of the **Muhammad Ali** Center. In 2007, it was featured on billboards across the city designed to attract children to positive role models. In 2005, it held a benefit concert for Hurricane Katrina vic-

tims on Louisville's waterfront, and in 2006, members of the group released *Hip Hop Multiplication,* a rap CD to help young children learn math. It has also toured with the United Service Organizations in Kuwait, Qatar, and Iraq.

"Nappy Roots." 2012. http://www.nappyroots.com (accessed March 12, 2012).
Newspapers: "Rap Group Stays True to KY Birthplace," *WP,* May 31, 2002, Weekender, 24; "Never Far from Their Roots," *LHL,* October 26, 2003, E1; "Deeper Roots," *LCJ,* May 27, 2009, V38.

—*Joshua D. Farrington*

NATIONAL ASSOCIATION FOR THE ADVANCEMENT OF COLORED PEOPLE, civil rights organization instrumental in the desegregation of education, housing, and public accommodations, as well as ending all forms of racial discrimination. Organized in 1909, the National Association for the Advancement of Colored People (NAACP) was at the forefront of the struggle for racial equality. Founded by black and white activists, the organization established local and state offices around the country to protest racial discrimination, publicize the existence of inequality, and lobby for the passage of federal and state laws that would assure equality in voting rights and in the justice system. Louisville, KY, was the site of the national office's first successful legal victory. On November 5, 1917, the U.S. Supreme Court declared that the city's residential segregation law was unconstitutional in the case **Buchanan v. Warley.** National president and attorney Morefield Story considered the ruling "the most important decision that has been made since the Dred Scott case, and happily this time it is the right way." After this case, local chapter membership increased in Louisville. A Frankfort chapter was established in 1919 and for several years held the second-highest membership total. The leader of the Frankfort chapter was civil rights activist Dr. **Edward E. Underwood.** On two occasions in the 1920s, this local branch played a role in saving African American men from execution in both Richmond and Lynch, KY.

On several occasions, local NAACP branches protested lynchings and fought to ensure that African Americans received fair trials. In 1935, Joe Hale, an African American, was indicted for murdering a white man in Paducah. His attorneys requested a change of venue because no African Americans had served on juries in McCracken Co. in nearly 30 years. The NAACP ultimately waged a successful campaign up to the Supreme Court (*Hale v. Kentucky*) to ensure that Hale would receive a new trial. Although Hale pleaded guilty to the crime, African Americans were no longer excluded from serving on juries as a result of the NAACP's efforts. Local NAACP chapters were eventually formed around the state. Middlesboro, Harlan, Lynch, Barbourville, and Benham made up the Regional NAACP of Eastern Kentucky in the 1940s. By the mid-twentieth century, NAACP chapters on both the state and the national level had embarked on a movement to desegregate schools. In 1949, the NAACP argued successfully for the desegregation of the University of Kentucky's graduate school. After the Supreme Court's ruling in *Brown v. Board of Education* (1954), Kentucky chapters filed lawsuits against local school boards to desegregate their institutions and campaigned for the retention of African American teachers. Across the state, local

NAACP members were active in civil rights demonstrations in the 1950s and 1960s.

Among the active NAACP leaders in the state were **Charles Anderson, I. Willis Cole, James A. Crumlin, Lyman T. Johnson, Frank Stanley Jr.,** and **C. Ewbank Tucker** (Louisville), **Helen Fisher Frye** (Danville), **Audrey Grevious** (Lexington), **Helen Holmes** (Frankfort), and **Osceola A. Dawson** (Paducah). **John J. Johnson** eventually served for 14 years as the state president and was also the youngest person to serve as president of a local chapter at the age of 17 in Franklin, KY, in the early 1960s.

Over the years, local NAACP branches have continued to hold fund-raising banquets and publicize and press for racial equality. The organization remains the oldest existing civil rights vanguard in the state. More than 50 branches list offices throughout Kentucky.

Smith, Gerald L. "Direct-Action Protests in the Upper South: Kentucky Chapters of the Congress of Racial Equality." *RKHS* 109, nos. 3–4 (Summer / Autumn 2011): 351–93.

Wright, George C. *A History of Blacks in Kentucky.* Vol. 2, *In Pursuit of Equality, 1890–1980.* Frankfort: Kentucky Historical Society, 1992.

———. *Racial Violence in Kentucky, 1865–1940: Lynchings, Mob Rule, and "Legal Lynchings."* Baton Rouge: Louisiana State Univ. Press, 1990.

—*Gerald L. Smith*

NATIONAL UNDERGROUND RAILROAD MUSEUM, MAYSVILLE, museum.

Because of its proximity to the Ohio River, and because it contained one of the largest holding pens for recaptured slaves along the North-South border, Maysville was a hotbed of pro- and antislavery forces during the first half of the nineteenth century. Many concerned individuals, churches, and organizations began a movement to assist slaves attempting to escape to the North. Maysville and nearby Ripley, OH, were among the first communities to support antislavery societies and set up **Underground Railroad** stations. The Underground Railroad consisted of a vast network of people who worked together to provide assistance to the fugitives. The operation was risky, and many whites and free persons of color were jailed or fined, or both, for aiding or encouraging the flight of slaves. Secret codes and special railway jargon often were used to protect the participants and to conceal their operations. "Conductors" took fugitives to safe houses, situated about 20 miles apart, where they could get food, clothing, and rest for a short time before moving on to the next station.

Two stations set up in Maysville were Phillip's Folly, at 227 Sutton St., and the Bierbower House, at 38 W. Fourth St. Carriage makers Frederick and Jonathon Bierbower owned the Bierbower House and were known to hide slaves in their home, which soon became an important stop on the Underground Railroad. The Bierbower House is now the home of the National Underground Railroad Museum of Maysville. The building has been restored to resemble closely the way it may have looked when slaves were hidden there. Many photos, slave artifacts, and memorabilia are on display at the museum.

Crawford, Byron. "Maysville's Own Underground Railroad Museum Tells Story of Slavery." *KE,* September 14, 1998, B1.

"National Underground Railroad Museum." http://www.cityofmaysville.com (accessed January 23, 2007).

PBS. "The Underground Railroad." http://www.pbs.org (accessed January 23, 2007).

NATIONAL URBAN LEAGUE, organization that studies the social and economic conditions of African Americans in urban centers and assists them in securing economic self-reliance, parity, power, and civil rights and in adjusting to urban life.

The National Urban League (NUL) came into existence in 1910 in New York as the Committee on Urban Conditions among Negroes. Its purpose was to assist African American migrants to assimilate into urban life. A year later, it merged with three other bodies: the Association for the Protection of Colored Women, the Committee for Improving the Industrial Conditions among Negroes, and the National League for the Protection of Colored Women. The merged organization was called the National League on Urban Conditions among Negroes. In 1920, the organization became known as the National Urban League.

The primary mission of the NUL was to study the social and economic conditions of blacks in urban centers of the North, find housing and jobs for the migrants, and assist them in adjusting to urban life. This mission was geared in particular to those migrants fleeing the institutionalized racism in the South in quest of freedom and greater economic empowerment in the North.

Among the leadership of the NUL have been two Kentuckians, **Eugene Kinckle Jones** and **Whitney M. Young Jr.** Jones, who served as executive secretary from 1917 to 1941, was influential in shaping the early organization. He emphasized the importance of vocational guidance to the new migrants and worked with industrialists and other northern employers to open employment opportunities for black migrants. Young served as the NUL's executive director from 1961 until his death in 1971 and made the NUL one of the major civil rights organizations during that era when he became one of the first black civil rights leaders to promote affirmative-action initiatives that were put in place in the late 1960s and early 1970s. Young played a significant role in the passage of the **Civil Rights Act of 1964** and the Voting Rights Act.

The National Urban League has continued its efforts by promoting affirmative action and economic and political empowerment and working to reduce violence and poverty in urban black America in the 21st century.

Fay, Robert. "National Urban League." In *Africana: The Encyclopedia of the African and African American Experience,* 2nd ed., edited by Kwame Anthony Appiah and Henry Louis Gates Jr. Oxford African American Studies Center. http://www.oxfordaasc.com/article/opr/t0002/e2853 (accessed April 18, 2012).

Frusciante, A. K., B. DeAguiar, D. Galarza, and J. Joseph. "National Urban League." In *Encyclopedia of Activism and Social Justice,* vol. 3, edited by Gary L. Anderson and Kathryn Herr, 1012–13. Thousand Oaks, CA: Sage Publications, 2007.

Jaynes, G. D., ed. "National Urban League." In *Encyclopedia of African American Society,* vol. 2, 845–46. Thousand Oaks, CA: Sage Publications, 2005.

Moore, Jesse T., Jr. "Urban League, National." In *The Oxford Companion to United States History,* edited by Paul S. Boyer. Oxford African American Studies Center. http://www.oxfordaasc.com/article/opr/t119/e1580 (accessed April 18, 2012).

National Urban League. http://www.blackpast.org/?q=aah/national-urban-league-1910 (accessed June 12, 2012).

Nelson, V. H. "National Urban League." In *Encyclopedia of the Harlem Renaissance*, vol. 2, edited by C. D. Wintz and P. Finkelman, 870–73. New York: Taylor and Francis, 2004.

Schuler, Anja. "National Urban League." In *Encyclopedia of African American History, 1896 to the Present: From the Age of Segregation to the Twenty-first Century*, edited by Paul Finkelman. Oxford African American Studies Center. http://www.oxfordaasc.com/article/opr/t0005/e0879 (accessed April 18, 2012).

—*Nkechi Amadife*

NEAL, GERALD A. (b. 1945, Louisville, KY), first African American male Kentucky state senator. The second son of community activists and union organizers **Sterling Neal** and Mildred "Millie" Neal, Gerald Neal grew up in Louisville, KY. According to his mother, when Jerry was 14 years old, he worked at a drugstore and filed a grievance over unfair wages with the Workmen's Compensation Board. He was fired from his job, but he received his back pay.

In 1967, Neal graduated from Kentucky State College (later known as **Kentucky State University**) and earned his law degree from the University of Louisville Brandeis School of Law in 1972. He was admitted to the bar and began his law firm, Gerald A. Neal and Associates, the next year. In 1979, he ran unsuccessfully for the senate against the first African American female Kentucky senator, **Georgia Davis Powers.** He married Kathy Cooksie in 1987. The next year, he won Powers's Senate seat and became the first African American male Kentucky senator.

Among his myriad positions and community contributions, Neal founded the Kentucky Education Reform African-American and All Children's Caucus to assist implementation of the 1990 Kentucky Education Reform Act. He served as assistant director of public health and safety for Louisville, a hearing officer for the State Workers' Compensation Board, a juvenile probation officer, and a United Nations observer / monitor for the historic April 1994 all-race elections in South Africa. In 2004, as a Democrat, he challenged Republican governor Ernie Fletcher to lead Kentucky's efforts to overcome racial barriers by appointing African American cabinet secretaries. In 2008, Neal was one of 60 Kentucky delegates to the Democratic National Convention. In 2012, he presented a resolution to establish a task force regarding the cost of the death penalty in Kentucky.

Gerald A. Neal. http://geraldneal.com/news_events/23.html (accessed June 5, 2012).

Newspapers: "Senator Says Governor Must Lead on Diversity—Issue Is Absence of Black Cabinet Secretaries," *LHL*, February 25, 2004, B3; "Nine from Ky. Are 'Super Delegates,'" *LHL*, August 25, 2008; "Readers' Views," *LHL*, March 21, 2012.

—*Sallie L. Powell*

NEAL, STERLING ORLANDO, SR. (b. 1918, Cleveland, OH; d. 1997, Louisville, KY), labor and civil rights organizer. Born in Cleveland, OH, to Kentuckians A. Robert and Anna Harper Neal, Sterling Orlando Neal moved with his family to Kentucky when he was young. He graduated from Louisville's **Catholic Colored High School** and later from Jefferson Community College. He married his wife, Mildred "Millie," in 1940. The couple had four children: Velma, Sterling Jr., Beverly, and Gerald.

Neal worked in the shipyards during World War II and supported his family by selling insurance. In 1946, International Harvester Company hired him when it established its factory in Louisville. As a shop steward, Neal joined the racially integrated United Farm Equipment and Metal Workers Union, which pushed for fair and equal pay. Two years later, Local 236 elected Neal a delegate to the Harvester Council, an executive board position. In 1949, International Harvester became the largest factory in Kentucky.

That same year, Local 236 established a women's auxiliary coordinated by civil rights activist Anne Braden. Neal's wife, Millie, chaired the organization in 1950. Since the company did not hire women employees, the auxiliary worked primarily as a support system for union men and their families, including feeding strikers through its "strike kitchen."

Neal rose in the union ranks to become the first African American district president and the first African American vice president of the United Electrical Workers Union in 1952. He traveled extensively for his union work and was home only on weekends. He served as one of the union's spokesmen with a demand to the Ohio Un-American Activities Commission to "disband and cease operation." In 1953, International Harvester fired Neal along with other union organizers for a work stoppage. Because he was on furlough, Neal's filed grievance took extra time to decide, but his reinstatement was still denied. He remained employed with the union, and he and his wife, Millie, continued their civil rights activism with close friends Anne and Carl Braden.

In 1957, Neal was forced to travel to Washington, DC, to answer questions by the Senate Internal Security Subcommittee about his connections with the Communist Party. He refused to answer and cited his constitutional rights under the Fifth Amendment. His union fired him, the first time in union history that a member had been fired for invoking the Fifth Amendment. Neal never recovered from this betrayal and, according to his wife, remained "very bitter."

While his wife worked in health care, Neal returned to the insurance business and also worked as a construction contractor. He became a city housing inspector in Louisville. In 2003, the **Kentucky Commission on Human Rights** posthumously inducted him into its Civil Rights Hall of Fame. His two sons demonstrated his influence. Sterling Jr. became a War on Poverty community activist and the director of Neighborhood Place Ujima, a social service center. **Gerald (Neal)** became an attorney and was elected the first African American male Kentucky senator.

Gilpin, Toni. "Left by Themselves: A History of the United Farm Equipment and Metal Workers Union, 1938–1955." PhD diss., Yale Univ., 1992.

Kentucky Legislature. http://www.lrc.ky.gov/recarch/97ss/SR42/bill.doc (accessed June 5, 2012).

Labor Relations Reporter 21 (1954): 243.

Neal, Millie. Interview, June 25, 1991. Anne Braden Oral History Project, Univ. of Kentucky.

3

Newspapers: "Ohio Un-American Inquiry Unit Rejects Plea to Quit," *Toledo Blade,* March 18, 1952, 2; "Machinist Union Fires Aide Who 'Took 5th,'" *Afro-American,* June 1, 1957, 47.

—*Sallie L. Powell*

NEBLETT, REGINALD C. (b. 1900, Clarksville, TN; d. 1978, Owensboro, KY), and Neblett, Hattie L. (b. 1903, Georgia; d. 1993, Owensboro, KY), founders of the H. L. Neblett Community Center in Owensboro. The grandson of a runaway slave who fought for the Union army, Reginald Neblett was born in Clarksville, TN. He spent much of his youth in the state, receiving a bachelor of science degree from Tennessee A&I State Normal College and a medical degree from Meharry Medical College in Nashville. In 1926, he married Hattie L. Neblett, a local home economics and music teacher, and four years later the two moved to Owensboro, KY.

Reginald Neblett was the first African American to join the Daviess County Medical Society and the second to join the Kentucky Medical Society. He ran a medical practice out of his home while his wife, Hattie, taught piano lessons and was active in community affairs. On his first day working as a physician, a local black youth died of a gunshot wound, an event that moved both the Nebletts to become more active in aiding the children of the city.

In 1936, Reginald and Hattie Neblett formed a permanent organization, the Community Recreation Council, that sought ways to improve the lives of local youths. At first, the council held meetings in churches and schools, but the Nebletts began raising funds for a more permanent location in 1940. They used these funds to purchase a decrepit former tobacco warehouse, which was renovated and then used as an educational center and, briefly, as sleeping quarters and a USO for visiting soldiers during World War II. The Nebletts frequently supported the Community Recreation Center with their own money and time; Reginald contributed through his salary as a physician, and Hattie served as president, fund-raiser, and, on occasion, janitor.

Shortly before Reginald's death of a stroke in 1978, the Nebletts received the Jane Addams Medal from the National Federation of Settlements and Neighborhood Centers. Although Hattie formally retired as president of the center in 1973, she continued to support the institution as president emeritus, and the facility was renovated and renamed the H. L. Neblett Center in her honor in June 1979. In 1993, Hattie Neblett died and was buried next to her husband in Evergreen Cemetery in Clarksville, TN.

In 2006, the original center was torn down to be replaced by a new building with a budget of $3,000,000, where it continues to provide programs in education and recreation. In 2010, the Nebletts were elected to the Kentucky Civil Rights Hall of Fame.

Newspapers: "H. L. Neblett Center's Namesake President Emeritus, Dies Thursday." *OMI,* August 28, 1993, 1B; "The Dream Lives On," *OMI,* August 29, 1999, 3E; "Kentucky Hall of Famers Nebletts, Acton Honored for Civil Rights Work," *OMI,* October 29, 2010, 1C.

—*Stephen Pickering*

NEGRO REPUBLICAN PARTY, one of the first black political organizations founded after the Civil War. After the Civil War, African Americans throughout Kentucky saw an opportunity to use the political turmoil of Reconstruction to their advantage. At a January 1, 1867, celebration of the **Emancipation Proclamation** in Louisville, a previously obscure African American named William F. Butler took the platform to demand equal rights. "We ask no man for pity," he declared. "We only ask you to take your hand off the black man's head and let him grow to manhood." Within two months, Butler joined other blacks in Louisville in forming the Law League, designed to provide attorney fees for African Americans denied their civil rights.

Although Kentucky was a Unionist state, its Republican Party did not support political equality for blacks. Because the Democratic Party was not a viable option for most black voters, African Americans like Butler sought to reform the state's Republican organization. In the summer of 1867, black Republicans from across the state agreed to hold a political convention in the fall. Although some African Americans, such as Malcolm Ayers and Benjamin Tibbs of Danville, feared that such a gathering would be met with hostility by local whites, the convention proceeded as planned.

On November 26, 1867, African American representatives gathered at Lexington's Second Methodist Church on Upper St. and agreed to form their own political organization called the Negro Republican Party. They elected William Butler president and Henry King, **Gabriel Burdett, Elisha Green,** E. Wren, and C. Clarke vice presidents. **Henry Scroggins** was elected corresponding secretary, and **Bartlett Taylor** treasurer. In his passionate opening address, William Butler exclaimed, "First we had the cartridge box, now we want the ballot box, and soon we'll get the jury box." He pledged that they would actively pursue liberty not with "our fists, but by standing up and demanding our rights." He even attempted to pacify the state's conservatives by claiming to stand for "universal suffrage," including former Confederate rebels. "I am not afraid of rebels voting," he continued, as long as "you give us the same weapon of defense." Butler saved some of his fiercest attacks for the conservatives who dominated the state party, claiming that he would rather vote for former Confederate president Jefferson Davis than "any half-hearted, rotten-at-the-core Republican conservative."

During a subsequent debate, the convention passed a series of resolutions demanding the right to vote, the right to testify in court, the right to equal accommodations on public transportation, and the continuation of services provided by the **Freedmen's Bureau.** Although the *Lexington Observer and Reporter* urged the members of the Negro Republican Party to abandon the organization, it commented that the "personal behavior" of the participants at the convention "was in the highest degree orderly, sober and decorous."

The state Republican Party, however, continued to resist providing full civil rights to African Americans. At the March 1868 Republican State Convention in Frankfort, white party officials barred blacks from the convention floor, and many members remained firmly against extending the right to vote to African Americans. It was not until the national ratification of the Fifteenth Amendment on February 3, 1870, that the right to vote was secured for blacks throughout the state.

The Negro Republican Party continued to critique the state's official Republican organization during the early 1870s and held meetings throughout the state in places that included Nicholas Co., Lebanon, Hardinsburg, Paris, and Owensboro. Although it failed in its immediate goal to reform the Republican Party of Kentucky—a party that would eventually count African Americans as one of its key constituencies by the early twentieth century—the Negro Republican Party was an important early attempt at political organization in the tumultuous era of postwar Kentucky.

"Colored Republican Convention of Kentucky." *Louisville Commercial*, February 25, 1870, 2.

Howard, Victor B. "Negro Politics and the Suffrage Question in Kentucky, 1866–1872." *RKHS* 72, no. 2 (April 1974): 111–33.

King, Cyrus Baldwin. "Ante-bellum Free Negroes as Race Leaders in Virginia and Kentucky during Reconstruction." MA thesis, Univ. of Kentucky, 1949.

Marshall, Anne E. *Creating a Confederate Kentucky: The Lost Cause and Civil War Memory in a Border State.* Chapel Hill: Univ. of North Carolina Press, 2010.

—*Joshua D. Farrington*

NELSON, WILLIAM STUART (b. 1895, Paris, KY; d. 1977, Washington, DC), educator and theologian. William Stuart Nelson, educator and theologian, was born on October 15, 1895, in Paris, KY, to William Henry and Emma (Kersands) Nelson. The family later moved to Paducah, where Nelson graduated from Lincoln High School. Stuart Nelson Park in Paducah was built and named for him in the 1940s, when the town's Bob Noble Park was restricted to whites.

Nelson joined the army in World War I and became a combat officer in the 2nd Army's 92nd Division, whose members were awarded 21 Distinguished Service Crosses. He earned a bachelor of arts degree from Howard University in Washington, DC, in 1920 and a bachelor of divinity degree from Yale in 1924. He also studied in France at the Sorbonne and the Protestant Theological Seminary, both in Paris.

Nelson began teaching philosophy at Howard University in 1924 and became an assistant to the president there. He left to become president of Shaw University in Raleigh, NC, and then served as president of Dillard University in New Orleans. Nelson returned to Howard in 1940 as dean of the School of Religion. He became dean of Howard in 1948 and vice president in 1961. Nelson was considered an authority on the practice of nonviolence. In 1958, he mailed Martin Luther King Jr. a copy of his article, "Satyagraha: Gandhian Principles of Non-Violent Non-Cooperation." King considered it "one of the best and most balanced analyses of the Gandhian principles of nonviolence, and noncooperation that I have read." Nelson wrote King often. He established the *Journal of Religious Thought* at Howard, where he also taught. Nelson retired in 1968. He died in Washington, DC, on March 26, 1977, and was buried there in Lincoln Memorial Cemetery. He was married to Blanche Louise (Wright) Nelson, who also taught at Howard.

"Nelson, William Stuart (1895–1977)." http://mlk-kpp01.stanford.edu /index.php/encyclopedia/encyclopedia/enc_nelson_william _stuart_1895_1977/ (accessed August 6, 2014).

"William Stuart Nelson." http://whospeaks.library.vanderbilt.edu /interviewee/william-stuart-nelson (accessed August 6, 2014).

—*Berry Craig*

NEW ZION, one of the oldest African American hamlets in Kentucky. Former slaves Calvin Hamilton and Primus Keene purchased 23 acres from a white landowner and then sold plots to other freedmen who formed the community originally named Briar Hill. Later it became known as New Zion, a biblical reference to a safe place for wandering people. On the border of Fayette and Scott Counties, on Newtown Pike, the area was inhabited and a Methodist church was established in 1868. However, the hamlet was not officially recognized until 1872.

In 1903, New Zion held its first annual Colored Farmers and Business Congress, later known as the Colored Farmers' Congress and Business Men's League. This organization's two-day event began with a parade led by the New Zion Brass Band. The conference included lectures and exhibits on animal care, plants, cooking, housekeeping, and mechanics as a business. At its peak from 1900 to 1920, New Zion's population was about 160 people. Businesses included a barber, a mechanic's garage, two dry goods stores, a candy store, and an ice cream parlor. The one-street village also had a school, a lodge, and a cemetery. Three of New Zion's five **buffalo soldiers,** slaves, and other war veterans were buried in the cemetery.

In 1956, six New Zion schoolchildren filed a discrimination lawsuit against the Scott Co. school system. The lawsuit was dropped two years later after the school system became integrated. In 1993, the Kentucky Historical Society placed a marker that highlights New Zion's historical value.

Well-known Thoroughbred horse trainer Oscar Dishman Jr. was born in New Zion and began training horses as a teenager in Scott Co. Outstanding Kentucky basketball player **Ukari Figgs** honed her shooting skills on a dirt court in New Zion.

Apple, Lindsey, Frederick A. Johnston, and Anne Bolton Bevins, eds. *Scott County, Kentucky: A History*. Georgetown, KY: Scott County Historical Society, 1993.

The Historical Marker Database. http://www.hmdb.org/marker.asp ?marker=35851 (accessed January 17, 2012).

Newspapers: "Colored Congress," *LL,* November 17, 1909, 9; "New Zion Residents Want to Preserve Area's Past," *LHL,* July 21, 1993, 8.

—*Sallie L. Powell*

NICHOLS, GEORGE, III (b. 1960, Bowling Green, KY), first African American commissioner of the Department of Insurance in Kentucky. The son of George and Vera Nichols, George Nichols III, at age 13, witnessed his father's job loss from Firestone, which closed its Bowling Green, KY, plant because of a labor strike. The event influenced Nichols's future career decisions. After graduating from Bowling Green High School, he earned his associate degree from Alice Lloyd College in Pippa Passes, KY, and graduated from Bowling Green's Western Kentucky University in sociology and economics. He then earned his master's degree in labor studies from the University of Louisville.

An internship at Louisville's Central State Hospital led Nichols to become the executive assistant to the commissioner of the Department for Mental Health / Mental Retardation Services in

1984. Five years later, he was appointed Central State Hospital's chief executive officer. He improved the hospital by increasing salaries, recruiting staff, and affiliating the hospital with the University of Louisville Medical School.

In 1992, Nichols served as executive director for product development of Blue Cross / Blue Shield of Kentucky and then as vice president of marketing for Athena of North America. In 1995, Kentucky governor Paul Patton appointed him executive director of the Kentucky Health Policy Board, quickly followed by his selection as Kentucky's commissioner of the Department of Insurance. He was the first African American to hold this position.

As insurance commissioner, Nichols regulated Kentucky's $10-billion insurance industry, eliminated the annuities tax, and increased inspection and investigation personnel. In 1999, the National Association of Insurance Commissioners elected Nichols its president; he was the first African American and first Kentuckian to hold the position.

In 2000, Nichols resigned as Kentucky's insurance commissioner and joined New York Life Insurance Company as senior vice president and assistant to the chairman. Six years later, he became senior vice president of the Office of Governmental Affairs. He became the first African American elected to New York Life's Executive Management Committee. In 2012, *Savoy* magazine named him one of the Top 100 Most Influential Blacks in Corporate America.

While residing in Potomac, MD, Nichols and his wife, Cynthia, a former Western Kentucky University basketball player, continued to support Kentucky education through their Cynthia and George Nichols III Scholarship for African American and Hispanic undergraduate students at the University of Louisville. Nichols has also served on the Board of Trustees of Alice Lloyd College.

"Insurance Commissioner Reflects Back on Tenure George Nichols Reformed State's Health Coverage for the Poor." *LHL,* December 31, 2000.
Kentucky Legislature. http://www.lrc.state.ky.us/recarch/98RS/SR69/bill.doc (accessed April 30, 2012).
New York Life. http://www.newyorklife.com/nyl/v/index.jsp?vgnextoid=c4d1387169616310VgnVCM100000ac841cacRCRD (accessed April 2, 2012).

—*Sallie L. Powell*

NICODEMUS, KS, all-black settlement founded by Kentucky migrants. The community of Nicodemus, located in the shortgrass prairie of northwestern Kansas, was founded in 1877 by a group of African Americans from central Kentucky seeking a better life. More than half a dozen black communities sprang up in Kansas after the Civil War, but Nicodemus is the only one that survives. The first families lived in dugouts, homes dug into the earth. The 308 refugees who arrived in 1877 were joined by some 150 others, mostly from Kentucky and Tennessee. By 1880, Nicodemus had a population of about 500 and a school, a livery stable, a post office, a bank, a newspaper, a drug store, three churches, and three general stores. It was surrounded by 12 square miles of cultivated land that its residents had homesteaded.

During the 1880s, the community continued to grow, but it needed a railroad to transport its farm products to eastern markets. The town approved a bond issue of $16,000 in an attempt to entice the Union Pacific Railroad to the community. However, the railroad bypassed Nicodemus, and the town fell into a decline, which was exacerbated by twin disasters in the 1930s. First came the Depression, which caused farm prices to fall. Then came severe droughts and the ensuing Dust Bowl. Entire families had to abandon an area that was no longer productive.

By 1935, the population had been reduced to about 75 persons. Most of the businesses closed. In 1938, the Works Progress Administration built a community center, but the population continued to decline. The post office closed in 1953. In recognition of its historic significance, Nicodemus was designated a national historic landmark in 1979. On November 12, 1996, the designation was changed to national historical site. The National Park Service assists the community in the preservation of historic structures and the interpretation of history for the benefit of residents and visitors. Five historic buildings have been preserved. The Nicodemus Historical Society is the only business currently operating. According to the official U.S. census of 2000, the population of Nicodemus Township was 52 persons.

Under the direction of Dr. Margaret Wood of Washburn University, students have conducted archaeological testing on one of the earliest farms in the Nicodemus area. The objective of the research is to identify and explore archaeological sites related to the settlement period and early occupation of the town.

Hamilton, Kenneth Marvin. *Black Towns and Profit: Promotion and Development in the Trans-Appalachian West, 1877–1915.* Urbana: Univ. of Illinois Press, 1991.
National Park Service. "Wake Nicodemus: African American Settlement on the Plains of Kansas." Washington, DC, 2008. http://nps.gov/archeology/sites/npSites/nicodemus.htm.
Schwendemann, Glen. "Nicodemus: Negro Haven on the Solomon." *Kansas Historical Quarterly* 34 (Spring 1968): 10–31.
U.S. Department of the Interior. *Promised Land on the Solomon: Black Settlement at Nicodemus, Kansas.* Washington, DC: Government Printing Office, 1986.

—*Charles F. Faber*

NICODEMUS TOWN COMPANY, business to encourage freed slaves to populate Nicodemus, KS. By the end of Reconstruction, the plight of many of the freed slaves in the South was desperate. The promise of "forty acres and a mule" proved illusory. Poverty, customs, and laws limited their economic opportunities. Many resumed working for their former masters as sharecroppers. In 1877, a white entrepreneur from Indiana, W. R. Hill, saw a way to help some of the former slaves and make some money for himself at the same time. Hill joined forces with William H. Smith, a black minister from Tennessee, who had settled in Kansas in 1874. With five other individuals, they formed the Nicodemus Town Company with Smith as president and Hill as treasurer. An African American minister from Kentucky, Simon P. Roundtree, became the secretary. The vice president was an African American, Benn Carr. Other members of the original company were Jerry Allsap, Jeff Lenze, and William Edmons, all from Kentucky.

Hill and Smith recruited poverty-stricken blacks in Kentucky and Tennessee, telling them about a sparsely settled land with lots of game, wild horses that could be tamed, and an opportunity to own land by homesteading. The company produced circulars exaggerating the wonders of the land. Roundtree and a black carpenter from Nashville, Benjamin Singleton, distributed circulars and recruited settlers. In 1877, **Nicodemus, KS,** was founded near the Solomon River in Kansas. In the summer of 1877, 308 men, women, and children boarded a train at Lexington, KY, headed for the railhead at Ellis, KS. From there, the families walked the remaining 55 miles to Nicodemus.

The settlers lived the first winter in homes dug into the earth along the Solomon River south of town. Hill collected a five-dollar fee from each emigrant—two dollars for government filing charges, two dollars for his commission, and one dollar for the company treasury. Conditions in northwestern Kansas were much harsher than the emigrants had been led to believe. Some returned to their former homes, but most stayed and were joined by 150 more from Kentucky and Tennessee in the spring of 1878. Smith and Hill had intended Nicodemus to be an all-black town, but the census of 1880 showed 58 whites and 258 blacks living in the township.

It is not clear when the company disbanded, but Hill and Smith soon moved on to develop the nearby town of Hill City. Sometime in the 1880s, the Nicodemus Town Company ceased promoting development of the town it had founded.

Hamilton, Kenneth Marvin. *Black Towns and Profit: Promotion and Development in the Trans-Appalachian West, 1877–1915.* Urbana: Univ. of Illinois Press, 1991.
Schwendemann, Glen. "Nicodemus: Negro Haven on the Solomon." *Kansas Historical Quarterly* 34 (Spring 1968): 10–31.

—*Charles F. Faber*

NINTH ST. METHODIST EPISCOPAL CHURCH, church in Covington, KY. The Ninth St. Methodist Episcopal (M.E.) Church of Covington, established in the mid-nineteenth century, originally met in a small building at Second and Scott Sts. Several church members began to sponsor weekly prayer meeting and worship sessions in hopes of inspiring the local African American community to continue to resist racial segregation and daily discrimination. These objectives were pursued more intensively during the 1870s and early 1880s, when the congregation, under the successive direction of Rev. G. S. Griffin, Rev. James Courtney, and Rev. G. W. Giegler, formed a coherent mission statement and developed an outstanding outreach program that sought to make the facility a shining "light in the community."

During the late 1880s, as the African American population of Covington increased, the church's membership also increased greatly. As a result, in 1889, the church moved to 18 E. Ninth St. This property was provided by the Board of Church Extension of the Methodist Church, and funds to construct a new building were obtained through an enormous membership drive campaign and a generous donation by Amos Shinkle, a prominent local businessman. The church was designed by noted regional architect James W. McLaughlin.

From the late 1880s to the 1920s, the membership of the Ninth St. M.E. Church continued to grow dramatically because of the vision and activities of several dynamic church leaders during this period, such as Rev. C. E. Ball, Rev. R. F. Broaddus, Rev. W. H. Evans, Rev. John W. Robinson, and Rev. J. H. Ross. These pastors encouraged the church to organize events such as annual revival meetings, weekly family-oriented entertainment programs, and weekend social activities for the youth. Various community leaders and civil rights organizations, galvanizing the local black community over the issues of political oppression and racial violence, also used the facility. For instance, in 1922, a vocal rally and endorsement meeting for the passage of a national antilynching bill was held at the church.

From the 1930s to the 1980s, the church's membership continued its community-based agenda by sponsoring numerous local and church events, such as the regional Women's Society of Christian Service conference in 1931, a daylong dedication service celebrating acquisition of the church's new pipe organ in 1954, a powerful prayer service led by Bishop Frank Robinson in 1978, and several community activities throughout the 1980s. In 2006, the church closed, the victim of a dwindling congregation.

"The Church Record of the 9th Street Methodist Episcopal Church, 1887–1901." Box 1, folder 13, Northern Kentucky African American Heritage Task Force Collection, W. Frank Steely Library, Northern Kentucky Univ.
Newspapers: "Religious," *Daily Commonwealth,* October 29, 1881, 1; "The City," *Daily Commonwealth,* October 3, 1881, 1; February 6, 1882, 2; February 14, 1882, 2; July 11, 1883, 4; "Local News," *Daily Commonwealth,* July 9, 1884, 4; "Anti-lynching Bill Endorsed," *Daily Commonwealth; KTS,* September 30, 1922, 14; "Knights of Pythias Born in 1864," *KP,* October 24, 1994, 4K; Jim Reis, "Four Churches That Made a Difference," *KP,* January 20, 1997, 4K; "When History Is Overlooked," *KP,* February 8, 1999, 4K.
"Ninth Street Methodist Episcopal." Vertical files, Kenton Co. Public Library, Covington, KY.

—*Eric R. Jackson*

NON-PARTISAN REGISTRATION COMMITTEE, organization to register black voters in Louisville. The Non-Partisan Registration Committee (NPRC) was formed during the 1960 and 1961 protests against segregated public accommodations in Louisville. The organization's founders, **Frank L. Stanley Jr., Woodford R. Porter Sr.,** and Neville Tucker, sought the removal of Mayor Bruce Hoblitzell and the Democratic-controlled board of aldermen, which twice rejected ordinances that would have integrated restaurants, theaters, and hotels.

Under the slogan "50,000 voting Negroes can totally desegregate Louisville," the NPRC had a large task ahead of it because only about 20,000 of the city's 51,000 eligible African Americans were registered. With over 800 volunteers, door-to-door registration efforts, and voter-education drives at Louisville's Armory Building, the group reached most of Louisville's potential black voters. The centerpiece of the NPRC efforts was a rally featuring Martin Luther King Jr. King proclaimed to the city's black voters that they could soon enter "the promised land of constructive integration by registering and voting" and called for the community to conduct a "vote-in" by electing an entirely new mayor and board of aldermen.

The NPRC succeeded in almost doubling the number of registered black voters in Louisville. Between its formation in the spring of 1960 and the deadline for registration in September, over 15,000 new African American voters had been registered; some estimates were as high as 22,000 county-wide. This was in addition to the 20,000 already registered. In one precinct alone in Louisville's Eighth Ward, registration jumped from 328 in January 1960 to over 1,000 by September. In less than a year, the city's percentage of registered black voters had jumped from around 40 percent of those eligible in January to almost 70 percent by September.

The NPRC's goal of removing the recalcitrant Democratic Party from power was more than fulfilled because the new influx of determined black voters was instrumental in shifting the political makeup of the city. After the votes were counted, William Cowger became the city's first Republican mayor in 28 years, and the entire Republican slate of candidates, from alderman to county judge to sheriff, swept to victory. Two African Americans, Russell P. Lee and **Louise Reynolds,** were elected to the Louisville Board of Aldermen, a historic first for the city. The sole Democrat left in office after the election was the city controller. Additionally, **Amelia Tucker** won a seat in the state legislature and became the first black woman to serve in a legislature of a southern state since Reconstruction.

Farrington, Joshua D. "Standing in the Wings: Black Voters in Louisville, Kentucky, and the Elections of 1960 and 1961." MA thesis, Univ. of Kentucky, 2008.
Horton, J. Benjamin. "We Are for Candidates Who Care." *Kentucky Negro Journal* 4, no. 3 (Summer 1961): 10.
"Non Partisan Committee Registers 22,000 Voters." *LD,* September 15, 1960, 1.

—*Joshua D. Farrington*

NORTHERN KENTUCKY AFRICAN AMERICAN HERITAGE TASK FORCE, association that strives to preserve Kentucky African American history. On June 23, 1992, the Kentucky Heritage Commission started a campaign that included more than 60 individuals from across the state to organize the Kentucky African American Heritage Task Force (KAAHTF). Two years later, in 1994, Governor Brereton Jones (1991–1995) disbanded the task force but replaced it with the **Kentucky African-American Heritage Commission,** under the direction of the Education, Arts, and Humanities Cabinet. On the basis of the pathbreaking work of the KAAHTF, the commission subsequently established several regional groups to uncover, document, and preserve the history of African American Kentuckians. Established in 1995 by numerous individuals, such as Bennie Butler, Susan Cabot, Rhonda Culver, Theodore "Ted" Harris, Leslie Henderson, Robert Ingguls, Hensley Jemmott, Basil Lewis, Mary Northington, Jim Reis, Larry Wright, and Martha Wright, the Northern Kentucky African American Heritage Task Force (NKAAHTF) is an outgrowth of this effort. The goals of the NKAAHTF mirror those of the Kentucky African American Heritage Commission in its quest to educate the public by documenting, preserving, and promoting African American history. The NKAAHTF emphasizes the role African American Kentuckians played in the inception and development of the 12 northernmost counties of the state: Boone, Bracken, Campbell, Carrol, Fleming, Gallatin, Kenton, Lewis, Mason, Owen, Pendleton, and Robertson.

At its inception, NKAAHTF had about 50 members. Over the years, membership has fluctuated between 100 and 300.

The NKAAHTF has been involved in annual African American church celebrations, has participated in numerous local history-day events, has established connections to northern Kentucky African American cemetery documentation projects, and has contributed to yearly historical conferences throughout Kentucky. At times, personnel changes, financial problems, irregular meeting schedules, and the lack of a comprehensive recruitment plan have plagued the organization, but despite these obstacles, the NKAAHTF continues to have a major impact on black American life in northern Kentucky. For example, in 2003, the organization became involved in a successful campaign to preserve the **Rosella Porterfield** Park in **Elsmere.** In 2005, the NKAAHTF participated in the documentation and preservation of the "colored" Julius **Rosenwald School** of Dry Ridge. Today, the NKAAHTF remains in the forefront of providing assistance to individuals, organizations, and communities in the region whose goal is to identify and promote the significant role black Kentuckians have played in the history and culture of northern Kentucky.

Northern Kentucky African American Heritage Task Force Newsletter. Kenton Co. Public Library, Covington, KY.
Whitehead, Shelly. "Black Graveyards at Risk." *KP,* February 13, 2001, 1K.

—*Eric R. Jackson*

NORTHINGTON, NATE "NAT" (b. 1947, Louisville, KY), football player. Nate "Nat" Northington was born to William E. and Flossie Northington in Louisville, KY, on October 17, 1947. He was an outstanding high school football player. In his junior year at Thomas Jefferson High School in Louisville, he led the team in touchdowns. In his senior year, he excelled in academics as well, becoming an officer and member of the Beta Club and the National Honor Society. He was recruited by the University of Kentucky as a wide receiver alongside **Greg Page,** also African American, with the intent of being a model for other southern schools to integrate their athletic teams. The recruitment process was led in part by former Kentucky governor Edward T. Breathitt, who at the time was the chairman of the University of Kentucky Board of Trustees.

In 1967, Page, Northington's roommate, suffered a neck injury during practice that left him paralyzed from the nose down, and he died 38 days later from his injuries. The next afternoon, September 30, 1967, Northington broke the Southeastern Conference color barrier as a wide receiver for the University of Kentucky in a home loss to the University of Mississippi. The conference had been openly reluctant to desegregate racially. Northington left the university in the weeks after the Mississippi game. He expressed the loneliness and distress that he felt as the only black varsity player: "I can tell you every brick in my room. All I do is talk to my walls." Shortly after he left the team in 1967, he transferred to Western Kentucky University, where he received a bachelor's degree in business administration.

After graduation, Northington headed the Bowling Green Housing Authority and later was a staffer at the Louisville Housing Authority. He eventually became the regional director of

Nat Northington.

property management with the Louisville Metro Housing Authority and served as a licensed minister at his church.

Breathitt, Edward. Interview, Civil Rights in Kentucky Oral History Project. Kentucky Historical Society, February 24, 2000.

Northington, Nate. *Still Running: The Autobiography of Nate Northington, the First African American Football Player in the Southeastern Conference.* Bloomington, IN: iUniverse, 2013.

Wharton, David. "The Great Barrier." *Los Angeles Times,* September 3, 2004, D1.

Wolff, Alexander. "Ground Breakers." *Sports Illustrated,* November 7, 2005, 58–67.

—*Vincent Gonzalez*

NOTABLE KENTUCKY AFRICAN AMERICANS DATA-BASE, first database to provide historical information on African Americans from a particular state. In September 2003, in response to patrons' requests for biographical information on African American Kentuckians, University of Kentucky librarians Reinette F. Jones and Robert A. Aken II created the website Notable Kentucky African Americans (NKAA). The site collected information from various sources on people who were Kentucky African American natives or residents who made significant contributions within the state and beyond its borders. The response to the site's 200 biographical entries was overwhelming. Patrons offered more names and information, thus directing librarians instead of librarians guiding patrons.

Employed at the University of Kentucky since 1988, Jones, the diversity and multicultural activities librarian and author of *Library Service to African Americans in Kentucky,* researched and verified contributors' submissions. Aken, a Web administration librarian, edited the entries and added them to the website. By 2007, the site had grown to over 1,000 vignettes of individuals, events, and communities, and its popularity also increased. The website became a database that year. Patrons could freely search entries by subjects, dates, or keywords.

In 2009, the Reference and User Services Association bestowed the Gale Cengage Learning Award for Excellence in Reference and Adult Library Services on Jones and Aken for the NKAA. This cash award of $3,000 acknowledged the NKAA for the "development of an imaginative and unique resource to meet patrons' reference needs." The NKAA had expanded from 200 entries to 2,000 and, at times, had 1,000 hits per day.

With entries covering the period from the 1700s to the present, the NKAA has served a broad audience with its user-friendly search interface. It has regularly updated information on Kentucky African American achievements and has offered knowledge through its free electronic collection of data.

Jones, Reinette. "Creating a Web Resource: African American Kentuckian Profiles." *Journal of Library Administration* 43, nos. 3 / 4 (2005): 149–59.

Newspapers: "Web of History: Listing of Notable Black Kentuckians to Become Online Searchable Database," *LHL,* January 31, 2007, E1, E3 E1, E3; "UK Database Traces Key Ky. African-Americans," *LHL,* April 14, 2009.

Notable Kentucky African Americans Database. http://www.uky.edu /Libraries/NKAA/aboutus.php (accessed September 10, 2012).

"University of Kentucky Libraries' Online African American History Tool Wins RUSA Award." American Library Association. http:// www.ala.org/news/news/pressreleases2009/april2009/rusagale cengagewinner (accessed September 19, 2012).

—*Sallie L. Powell*

NOTHING-NEW-FOR-EASTER BOYCOTT, boycott in Louisville in 1961. On February 20, 1961, several black students staged a stand-in at Stewart's Department Store in Louisville, KY. These students, frustrated by recent internal divisions within the local black freedom movement, were part of a new surge of activity on the part of Louisville's youth that sought to desegregate downtown businesses without going through official channels. When employees of the store "knocked down," "pushed around," and "violently hit" the students and had five of them arrested, several local civil rights organizations became directly involved.

Two days later, the **National Association for the Advancement of Colored People** (NAACP) announced the Nothing-New-for-Easter campaign against downtown stores from Main to W. Oak St. and First to Ninth Sts. Noting that 98 percent of the stores did not employ African Americans in clerical or sales positions, **William J. Hodge,** the president of the Louisville branch of the NAACP, called for a boycott of stores to last through the Easter season, when businesses relied heavily on purchases from the black community. **Frank L. Stanley Jr.,** cochairman of the **Non-Partisan Registration Committee,** led the movement and became the chief voice of the protesters.

At the urging of Governor Bert T. Combs, Mayor Bruce Hoblitzell formed an emergency committee on the subject of integration at the beginning of March. Although the committee pushed for stores to integrate by April 1, protesters were unconvinced. Over the next month, the Louisville police arrested numerous activists. The *Louisville Defender* reported a total of 278 arrests in three weeks, including 170 students and 10 adults in one day; Hodge, Stanley, and Frederick G. Sampson, another leader of the integration movement, were among the individuals arrested.

The boycott proved to be fairly effective. Most African Americans avoided downtown institutions that remained segregated, and white businesses suffered; some admitted a substantial decline in sales. In April, Stanley announced that the protests would continue throughout the month and become the Nothing-New-for-Derby boycott in light of the impending **Kentucky Derby.**

In May, the leaders of the boycott officially signaled its transition to a Selective Buying campaign that would be directed "only toward those businesses that refuse to hire qualified Negroes as clerks or in other capacities than menial." Although integration remained partial, Stanley identified 92 restaurants that had desegregated either voluntarily or through outside pressure. Unfortunately, it later became evident that most cooperation from local government and businesses was more superficial than a legitimate gesture, and the city's aldermen continued to resist any movement toward a desegregation ordinance.

Adams, Luther. *Way Up North in Louisville: African American Migration in the Urban South, 1930–1970.* Chapel Hill: Univ. of North Carolina Press, 2010.

Farrington, Joshua David. "Standing in the Wings: Black Voters in Louisville, Kentucky, and the Election of 1960 and 1961." MA thesis, Univ. of Kentucky, 2008.

Newspapers: "Stewart's Has CORE-NAACP Members Arrested—NAACP Starts Easter 'Non-Buying' Protests," *LD,* February 23, 1961; "Community Backs NAACP Non-buying," *LD,* March 9, 1961, 1; "Non-buying Campaign to Continue Downtown," *LD,* April 6, 1961, 1; "Non-buying Campaign Ended—Leaders to Seek Jobs," *LD,* May 11, 1961, 1.

Wright, George C. "Desegregation of Public Accommodations in Louisville." In *Southern Businessmen and Desegregation,* edited by Elizabeth Jacoway and David R. Colburn, 191–210. Baton Rouge: Louisiana State Univ. Press, 1982.

—*Stephen Pickering*

NUGENT, GEORGIA ANNE (b. 1873, Louisville, KY; d. 1940, Louisville, KY), and NUGENT, ALICE EMMA (b. ca. 1875, Louisville, KY; d. 1971, Louisville, KY), teachers and clubwomen. Daughters of George and Anna (Foster) Nugent, Georgia Anne, the eldest, and Alice Emma grew up in Louisville, KY, primarily on Sixth St. Both graduated from **Central High School,** State University (later known as **Simmons College of Kentucky**), and Kentucky State Industrial College (later known as **Kentucky State University**) in Frankfort. In 1889, Georgia began teaching school, and Alice initiated her teaching career in 1896.

In the same year in which Georgia started teaching, she joined her mother and some other citizens for a "storm party" to provide food and clothing to the Louisville **Colored Orphans' Home** after a severe storm. On September 25, 1896, Georgia and some other Louisville women attended a lecture by Ida B. Wells-Barnett, which influenced them to organize the Woman's Improvement Club with a membership of between 30 and 40. Georgia was elected secretary. The organization's civic work included sponsoring the first kindergarten training class for Louis-

ville's African Americans, launching Louisville's first day nursery, and introducing the city's first "Volunteer Probation work."

By the early 1900s, Alice had joined her sister in civic involvement, but she usually stayed in the background in a hostess role while Georgia held more leadership positions. In November 1903, Georgia joined **Nannie Helen Burroughs** and other Kentucky clubwomen in a meeting in Louisville to form the State Federation of Colored Women's Clubs (later known as the **Kentucky Association of Colored Women's Clubs**). In January 1904, the Federation of Women's Clubs was formed; Alice was appointed to the Committee on Credentials, and Georgia was elected president.

Georgia traveled considerably in her clubwoman's work. In September 1904, she was a representative to the National Negro Business League in Indianapolis. The next month, she traveled to Lexington, KY, as a member of the **Baptist Women's Educational Convention.** Years later, she worked with Chicago's Phyllis Wheatley Women's Club. In 1914, Georgia was elected corresponding secretary of the National Federation of Colored Women's Clubs when Margaret Washington, wife of Booker T. Washington, was reelected president. Four years later, she was elected chairman of the organization's executive board.

Georgia retired from teaching in 1938. She had taught Sunday school at Louisville's Lampton Street Baptist Church for 50 years. She died on November 25, 1940. The club she helped organize was renamed the Georgia A. Nugent Improvement Club.

Although Georgia's activities garnered more attention, Alice served on the **Kentucky Negro Educational Association**'s Scholarship Loan Fund Committee, penned Kentucky's clubwomen's song, "Kentucky Clubs," and, as a member of **Delta Sigma Theta Sorority,** donated money for scholarships for women seeking a college education. In 1971, she died, like Georgia, in November. During their lives, Georgia and Alice, who never married, lived with parents, sisters, a grandmother, an uncle, an aunt, and a brother-in-law in one house. The sisters were buried along with their parents, two sisters, and one brother-in-law in Louisville's Eastern Cemetery with only one marker to designate their burial.

Newspapers: "The Falls City," *St. Paul (MN) Appeal,* November 16, 1889, 1; "Points about People," *AB,* December 18, 1903, 2; "Federation of Women's Clubs," *AB,* January 8, 1904, 1; "Wilberforce Notes," *St. Paul (MN) Appeal,* August 15, 1914, 2; "Miss Georgia Nugent," *Louisville Times,* November 26, 1940, 4; "Obituaries," *CJ,* December 1, 1971, B3.

Smith, Lucy Harth, comp. and ed. *Pictorial Directory of the Kentucky Association of Colored Women.* Lexington: Kentucky Association of Colored Women, 1945, 32.

U.S. Federal Census (1870, 1900, 1910, 1920).

—*Sallie L. Powell*

NURSE, JOHN ROBERT (b. 1899, Louisville, KY; d. 1964, Louisville, KY), physician. A native of Louisville, Dr. John Robert Nurse was the son of Robert L. Nurse, a cook, and his wife, Pattie. He had three sisters: Freda, Ida, and Virginia. Nurse attended Howard University in Washington, DC, where he played football for the school. Even though he suffered a dislocated wrist, he managed to continue in sports and with his education. In 1921, he graduated with a bachelor of science degree. Four years later, he earned his MD and interned at Washington's Freedmen's Hospital. He returned to Louisville immediately after completing his medical education. He served as physician-in-charge in infant welfare at Central Louisville Health Center, which provided health services, including medical and surgical services, for the vast majority of Louisville's African Americans.

In 1938, Nurse became the medical director of **Mammoth Life and Accident Insurance Company.** Three years later, he married Jonniebelle Winlock, the daughter of mail carrier Benjamin Winlock and his wife, Elizabeth. In 1946, as an active leader in the National Medical Association, Nurse became the director of exhibits, a position he held for almost two decades. After the loss of his first wife, in 1953, he married another member of the National Medical Association, Elizabeth Howland, a newly retired registered nurse.

Nurse, a resident of W. Chestnut St. in Louisville, remained active throughout his life in various organizations, including the American Red Cross, the **National Association for the Advancement of Colored People,** the YMCA, and **Omega Psi Phi Fraternity.** He died on August 5, 1964.

Fleming, G. James, and Christian E. Burckel, eds. *Who's Who in Colored America.* 7th ed. *Supplement.* Yonkers-on-Hudson, NY: Christian E. Burckel & Associates, 1950.

Kentucky Death Index, 1911–2000.

Journal of the National Medical Association. http://www.ncbi.nlm.nih .gov/pmc/articles/PMC2617441/pdf/jnma00605-0003b.pdf (accessed April 9, 2012).

U.S. Federal Census (1900, 1910, 1920).

World War I Draft Registration Cards, 1917–1918.

—*Sallie L. Powell*

O

OLDHAM, SAMUEL (b. ca. 1796; d. unknown, Virginia), businessman. Little is known about Samuel Oldham's early life. Born a slave around 1796 in Virginia, Oldham was moved to Kentucky, where he bought his freedom from his owner, James Harper of Lexington, in 1826. He also bought the freedom of his wife, Daphney, as well as that of his children. In 1835, he purchased a 45-foot lot on South Mulberry St. for $200, thus becoming the first free African American to own property in Lexington. In the following two years, he constructed a two-story dwelling at 245 Main St. that would remain a landmark in the black community for nearly two centuries.

Oldham worked as a barber in addition to opening a store that sold fine items to the community. In an 1834 advertisement in the *Lexington Observer and Reporter,* he hoped to attract patrons with "moderate charges," as well as a selection of "fancy articles"; he concluded by noting the recent addition of a bathing house. In 1840, his estate was appraised at over $7,000, marking him as one of the city's richest free blacks, but other sources indicate that debts were beginning to accumulate. By 1841, he had to settle a $1,000 debt with another free African American by turning over a variety of household goods. In 1845, he finally went bankrupt, and his entire property was sold by John B. Johnson, a white saddle maker to whom Oldham had executed a deed of assignment. His sons continued his barber business, but Samuel Oldham then largely disappeared from public record.

In 2004, public interest in the Oldhams reemerged when the owner of the still-standing Oldham House requested a permit for its demolition from Lexington's Board of Architectural Review. Historical preservationists and the African American community united to demand that the house, which had been condemned in 2000, be refurbished and preserved. Businessman Stephen Dawahare bought the property "primarily to protect it from vandalism" in December 2004, but it was put back on the market a year later. The following March, Coleman D. Callaway III, president of Broadview Buildings, bought the home with the intention of refurbishing it as a location for meetings or retreats, although several squabbles ensued over planned additions to the property. Callaway completed the renovations to include a first floor office and a two bedroom/two bath apartment on the second floor. In 2013, the house was listed for sale at $725,000.

The increased visibility of the house also fostered interest in the lives of Samuel and Daphney Oldham in the form of a play by Ain Gordon. The one-person play, titled "In This Place," features a fictionalized account of the couple's lives through the eyes of a ghostly Daphney Oldham.

"BGT Detours: Oldham House." Bricks+Mortar: Thoughts on Historic Preservation, Community, and Design. http://bricksandmortar preservation.wordpress.com/tag/samuel-oldham/ (access August 6, 2014).

Kennedy, Rachel. "Preserving African American Material Culture: A Study of the Free Black Community in Lexington, Kentucky from 1800 to 1850." MA thesis, Univ. of Kentucky, 1999.

Newspapers: "S. Oldham, Barber & Hair Dresser," *Lexington Observer and Reporter,* April 17, 1834, 2; "Former Slave Was Owner," *LHL,* March 1, 2006, B1; "Historic Home's Owner Has Squabble in Present," *LHL,* January 25, 2007, A1; "Our New History: House of Freed Slave Inspiration for Lexarts Play," *LHL,* May 22, 2008, A1.
—*Stephen Pickering*

OMEGA PSI PHI FRATERNITY, INC., African American fraternity. Omega Psi Phi Fraternity, Incorporated, was founded on November 17, 1911, at Howard University in Washington, DC. It was the first predominantly African American fraternity to be founded on the campus of a historically black college. The founders were three undergraduates, Edgar Amos Love, Oscar James Cooper, and Frank Coleman, and their adviser, Dr. Ernest Everett Just. Omega Psi Phi was incorporated under the laws of the District of Columbia on October 28, 1914.

The fraternity is guided by the Supreme Council, which includes the grand basileus and his staff, the undergraduate representatives, and the district representatives. The national meeting is called a conclave. Omega Psi Phi has over 750 chapters throughout the world. The motto is "Friendship Is Essential to the Soul," and the fraternity colors are royal purple and old gold. Omega Psi Phi is a member of the National Pan-Hellenic Council.

The symbol of the fraternity is the lamp, and the national publication is the *Oracle.* The men of Omega Psi Phi are called Omegas, Sons of Blood and Thunder, Omega Men, Da Bruhz, and Q Dogs. The national headquarters is located at 3951 Snapfinger Pkwy., Decatur, GA, 30035.

At the Nashville Grand Conclave in 1920, **Carter G. Woodson** inspired the establishment of National Achievement Week to promote the study of Negro life and history. In 1924, the fraternity launched Negro History and Literature Week, which was renamed Negro Achievement Week in 1925 and later was given an expanded national presence in 1926 by Woodson's Association for the Study of Negro Life as Negro History Week. In 1976, this celebration was expanded to the full month of February and continues today as Black History Month under the guidance of the Association for the Study of African American Life and History.

In addition to Black History Month, Omegas support social action programs, such as voter registration, Assault on Illiteracy, Habitat for Humanity, and mentoring; participate in the Charles Drew Blood Drive; and partner with the American Diabetes Association.

Omega Psi Phi's oldest chapter in Kentucky is Theta Omega Graduate Chapter in Louisville, founded in 1922. Psi Phi Chapter at **Kentucky State University,** chartered on April 1, 1934, was the first undergraduate chapter of the fraternity in the state. There are Omega chapters in Kentucky at most state universities and in most major cities.

Omega Psi Phi Fraternity celebrated its centennial in July 2011 in Washington, DC.

Jenkins, Chris L. "Omega Psi Phi Brothers Celebrate Centennial at D.C. Birthplace." July 27, 2011. http://www.washingtonpost.com/local/omega-psi-chi-brothers-celebrate-centennial-at-dc-birthplace/2011/07/26/gIQAitkgd_story.html (accessed October 5, 2013).

Official Website of Omega Psi Phi Fraternity. http://omegapsiphifraternity.org (accessed October 5, 2013).

Ross, Lawrence C., Jr. *The Divine Nine: The History of African American Fraternities and Sororities.* New York: Kensington, 2000.

—*Fenobia I. Dallas*

OUR SAVIOR CATHOLIC CHURCH, first Roman Catholic church for African Americans in Covington. Our Savior Catholic Church, located on E. 10th St. in Covington, was the first Roman Catholic parish for African Americans in the Diocese of Covington. For a number of years, the parish also operated a grade and high school. The parishioners are primarily from northern Kentucky.

Before 1943, a few African Americans attended the Cathedral Basilica of the Assumption in Covington. That year it was decided, at the encouragement of Bishop Francis W. Howard, to form a separate African American church and school in northern Kentucky as a mission of the cathedral. The site selected was on E. 10th St. in Covington. The plan was to convert a two-family home into classrooms and a convent for the Sisters of Divine Providence, who were going to teach at the school. The school opened in September 1943, after the renovations for the school and convent were completed. Because of illness, Bishop Howard was unable personally to dedicate Our Savior Church, so Rev. Msgr. Walter Freiberg, pastor of the parish of the cathedral, officiated at the dedication.

In 1946, the pastor of Our Savior Church was Rev. Henry Haacke, and Rev. Anthony Deye directed the school's athletic program. Deye set up baseball, football, and basketball teams. The church was part of the Northern Kentucky Catholic High School League and the Northern Kentucky Holy Name Basketball League. In 1945, **William Lane,** an associate at the cathedral and the only African American priest in the diocese, was assigned to work at the parish. On September 19, 1948, a new school building was finished and blessed by Bishop William T. Mulloy. The building had four spacious, well-lighted classrooms and a cafeteria, and there was a large recreation room in the building next door.

The high school closed in 1956 because of the movement toward integration. One of the most famous students affected by its closing was **Thomas Thacker,** a basketball player who attended William Grant High School and later played on the University of Cincinnati's national championship teams. The grade school closed on May 31, 1963. In 1981, Our Savior Church became an independent parish with its own pastor, Daniel Saner. Today, the parish is overseen by Sr. Janet Butcher, CDP.

Newspapers: "Catholic Schools Merged and Split over the Years," *KP*, April 17, 1987, 2K; Jim Reis, "Our Savior Fills Unique Niche," *KP*, January 17, 1994, 4K.

—*Theodore H. H. Harris*

OVERTON, WILL ALFRED "MONK" (b. ca. 1867; d. 1935, Cincinnati, OH), jockey. Although some sources documented Overton's name as Will F. and others listed him as Alfred, all knew him as Monk. Described as "a square, powerful young man" who excelled in controlling robust horses, Overton rode in eight **Kentucky Derby**s between 1890 and 1900 but never won. He placed sixth in his first race in 1890 behind his comparable counterpart **Isaac Murphy.** He won the Chicago Derby that year on his Kentucky Derby mount, Prince Fonso. He also ended the year with the highest winning percentage of any jockey.

In the 1891 Kentucky Derby, Overton placed second behind Murphy in what was called the "funeral derby" because it was such a slow race. Two months later, he reportedly used "good judgment, good placing and masterly finishing" and broke the jockey record by winning six races in one day at Chicago's Washington Park. Frustrated bookmaking companies bet against him in every race and lost $120,000, but many of the crowd of 4,500 successfully wagered on him. Mrs. Henry Brown was one of those winning fans with one ticket having odds of 400 to 1. Overton won the Clipsetta Stakes at Latonia, KY, shortly after he married Lucy Britton, the sister of jockey **Tom Britton** and Dr. **Mary Britton,** in Lexington, KY.

The 1892 Kentucky Derby was supposed to be Overton's victory. Ed Corrigan owned Phil Dwyer, ridden by Overton, and Huron, ridden by Overton's brother-in-law, Tom Britton. Corrigan designed a plan for Britton to dash ahead of the pack in the hopes of tiring the other horses so Overton could pass everyone to win. However, Overton's horse did not have the capacity to follow the plan and finished in third place.

Overton continued to compete in the 1894, 1895, 1896, and 1899 Kentucky Derbys. In 1900, he raced in his last Kentucky Derby, and renowned jockey **Jimmy "Wink" Winkfield** entered his first one. Overton, wearing the pink and black of the Woodford Buckner stable and to the crowd's applause, rode Kentucky Farmer onto the track. As in his first Kentucky Derby, Overton finished sixth.

The news media covered Overton's racing accomplishments and his struggles. In 1893, the *New York Times* reported, "As was expected . . . Overton . . . made trouble." Contract issues between Ed Corrigan and Overton led to confusion at Chicago's American Derby. Overton refused to ride Corrigan's horse, but he did ride another horse and won. He also dealt with "the bogie of a jockey's life," weight gain. In order to lose nine pounds, he remained in a Turkish bath from 10:00 p.m. until 2:00 p.m. the next day, consuming only a cup of tea and some toast.

Five years after Overton's wife, Lucy, died, Overton "became violently insane," and it took six Chicago police officers to force him into a cell. He then "beat his head against the bars" until he became unconscious. A few months later, Overton was breaking yearlings for the Kentucky Association in Louisville. In 1913, he traveled so much as a trainer and horse buyer that his sister requested assistance in locating him from the readers of the *Daily Racing Form* when their mother was ill.

By 1927, Overton worked for the Kenton Farm Stable in Latonia. He trained various winning horses, including General Haldeman, winner of the Queen City Handicap, and Typhoon, champion of the Churchill Downs Bashford Manor Stakes. He died in Cincinnati, OH, of bladder disease in March 1937.

Hotaling, Ed. *Wink: The Incredible Life and Epic Journey of Jimmy Winkfield.* New York: McGraw-Hill, 2005.

Newspapers: "Colored Wedding," *LL*, September 21, 1891, 5; "Azra Won the Derby," *NYT*, May 12, 1892, 2; "A Great Stake for Boundless," *NYT*, June 25, 1893, 3; "The American Jockey Record," *DRF*, March 22, 1898, 1; "Women Turf Plungers," *NYT*, February 10, 1901, 17; "The Jockey's Peril," *NYT*, May 26, 1901, 25; "'Monk' Overton Violently Insane," *Atlanta Constitution*, April 24, 1910, sec. D, p. 8; "First Shipment of Season to Juarez," *DRF*, October 25, 1910, 1; "Notes of the Turf," *DRF*, February 11, 1913, 2; "Overton Dies: Famous Jockey of 1890 Era," *CE*, March 29, 1935, 25.

Saunders, James Robert, and Monica Renae Saunders. *Black Winning Jockeys in the Kentucky Derby*. Jefferson, NC: McFarland, 2003.

—*Sallie L. Powell*

OWENS, DARRYL T. (b. 1937, Louisville, KY), first African American to serve as assistant attorney general for the Commonwealth of Kentucky. Born and raised in Louisville, KY, Darryl T. Owens attended **Central High School,** graduating in 1955. He cited **Lyman T. Johnson** as the teacher who most influenced his future life. After receiving a bachelor's degree from Central State University in Ohio and a law degree from Howard University, Owens returned to Louisville and practiced civil and criminal law beginning in 1965. He took part in the **civil rights movement** in the city and joined four other African Americans who ran as a slate in the 1969 primary in an attempt to secure the Democratic Party's nominations for traditionally white elected positions. From 1970 to 1976, he served as president of the Louisville chapter of the **National Association for the Advancement of Colored People.**

After becoming prominent in local politics for fighting a possible city-county merger in the early 1980s, Owens was elected to the Fiscal Court in 1983, the first African American to hold that position. He remained on the Fiscal Court for 20 years, the longest tenure in the office's history. He became the first African American member of the Kentucky Workman's Compensation Board and the first black assistant attorney general for the Commonwealth. Owens continued to combat the possibility of a city-county merger, but he also became a spokesman on behalf of the underprivileged in Jefferson Co., creating the African American Strategic Planning Group that developed the Economic Opportunities Act to promote minority businesses; in 1999, the Kentucky legislature accepted the initiative.

Owens retired from his job as commissioner in 2002 but quickly reentered politics. In 2004, he defeated Mike Czerwonka for the office of state representative for the 43rd House District, a position he held for four consecutive terms. In his second term, he was appointed chairman of the House Committee on Elections, Constitutional Amendments, and Intergovernmental Affairs, the only sitting African American lawmaker to hold a position of that stature. Owens continued to support programs that targeted inferior conditions for minorities and the underprivileged, attacking budget cuts for the Kentucky Center for African American Heritage and the removal of gays from anti-discrimination legislation in 2006.

In recognition of his service to minorities, Owens was elected to the Kentucky Civil Rights Hall of Fame in 2005. He was also awarded Louisville's Dr. Martin Luther King Jr. Freedom Award in 2012, which celebrates recipients who embody "justice, peace, freedom, nonviolence, racial equality, and civic activism." In announcing the award, Mayor Greg Fischer described Owens as "a pioneering public servant and a tireless advocate for civil and human rights."

K'Meyer, Tracy E. *Civil Rights in the Gateway to the South: Louisville, Kentucky, 1945–1980.* Lexington: Univ. Press of Kentucky, 2009.

Newspapers: "Class of 1955 50th Reunion: Central's Special Class," *LCJ*, August 7, 2005, E1; "Owens to Receive 2012 Freedom Award," *LCJ*, January 9, 2012, B1.

Who's Who in Black Louisville. 3rd ed. Columbus, OH: Who's Who, 2009.

—*Stephen Pickering*

OWSLEY, DONALD EDWARD (b. 1930, Owensboro, KY; d. 1999, Owensboro, KY), community leader. Donald Edward Owsley spent his life in his native town, Owensboro, KY. He graduated from all-black Western High School. He and his wife, Anetta, raised five daughters and two sons while he worked for Green River Steel. After 33 years, the closing of the company forced Owsley into retirement at age 55 in 1986.

Always involved in his community, Masonic organizations, and his church, Owsley increased his activism after retirement. In 1989, as a member of the Urban County Charter Commission's Services and Taxation Committee, he voted to merge the governments of Owensboro, Whitesville, and Daviess Co. without a tax increase. In 1990, Owsley continued his vigorous involvement in Masonic organizations and was installed as deputy grand master of the Prince Hall Grand Lodge, the Free and Accepted Masons of Kentucky, part of the largest worldwide secret society. As a 50-year member of Owensboro's Center Street Baptist Church, he served in the positions of treasurer, trustee, and moderator.

In 1992, Owsley addressed a potential conflict between his denomination and the **Freemasons** regarding possible satanic influence on the Masons. For him, the big issue was not between the two organizations, but the work relationship between African American and white Masonic organizations. He stated that the Masons believed in God and that their purpose was to develop respectful men and enhance their community involvement.

Two years later, Owsley received a one-year appointment to Owensboro's Human Relations Commission. His goal to improve his community led him through various leadership positions, including president of the local chapter of the **National Association for the Advancement of Colored People,** president of the American Association of Retired Persons Yellow Banks Chapter, hearing officer for the Owensboro Housing Authority, executive committee member of the Green River Area Development District, and chairman of Audubon Area Community Services (AACS). The AACS began with President Lyndon Johnson's War on Poverty in 1964. Along with other community action agencies, the AACS struggled financially when President Ronald Reagan took office in 1981. In memory of Owsley, the organization renamed its building the Donald E. Owsley Human Services Center in 1999. In 2000, Owsley was posthumously inducted into the **Kentucky Commission on Human Rights** Civil Rights Hall of Fame.

Audubon Area Community Services, Inc. IntraNet. http://www.audubon-area.org/NewFiles/dowsley.htm (accessed July 25, 2008).

Newspapers: "Merger Panel's Plan Calls for No Tax Hike," *OMI,* January 24, 1989; "A Front for Satan? Southern Baptists Split over Whether to Scorn Freemasonry,"*OMI,* July 6, 1992.

—*Sallie L. Powell*

OXMOOR PLANTATION, Kentucky plantation. Oxmoor Plantation, located eight miles from Louisville on Beargrass Creek, was originally owned by William Christian, who gave 1,000 acres to his daughter, Priscilla, and her new husband, Alexander Scott Bullitt, for their marriage in February 1786. The name Oxmoor was taken from Laurence Sterne's *Tristram Shandy.* Bullitt purchased an additional 1,000 acres, and the family lived in a log cabin on the farm until 1791, when a four-room clapboard house was completed. William C. Bullitt acquired the property at his father's death in 1816, and he built a brick addition to the original home for his wife and eight children in 1829.

The Bullitt family owned up to 120 slaves in the nineteenth century, and many worked on the Oxmoor plantation cultivating hemp, corn, and wheat and tending to sheep, cattle, hogs, and horses. The 1850 Slave Schedule indicates that 54 slaves lived at Oxmoor—37 male and 17 female. Thomas W. Bullitt, the son of William, wrote about his childhood at Oxmoor and remembered that the slaves lived in brick quarters in the fields near the front of the house, and that they worked from sunrise to sunset throughout the year. The male slaves worked primarily in the hemp fields, cutting hemp in the summer months and breaking it throughout the winter. Slaves were required to break 100 pounds per day, but Bullitt paid one penny per pound over that amount. Female slaves worked in the house as cooks, seamstresses, and maids. Thomas W. also recounted the singing of the plantation's slaves, which varied in tempo and style depending on the work and carried a meaning that only the slaves understood. Bullitt wrote, "There was real pathos in them which, as a master instead of a slave, it was not possible for me to receive or realize."

In 1863, William C. Bullitt closed the house because he felt unsafe after the **Emancipation Proclamation** and federal troop occupation of the area. He rented the farm to tenants. Bullitt and his wife moved in with a daughter in Louisville, and the house remained closed until the early twentieth century, when William Marshall Bullitt, Alexander's great-grandson, purchased some of the farm and the house from relatives with plans to restore it. Thomas Walker Bullitt, the son of William Marshall, left the original house, outbuildings, and 70 acres to the Filson Club Historical Society in 1991.

Bullitt, Thomas W. *My Life at Oxmoor: Life on a Farm in Kentucky before the War.* Louisville, KY: John P. Morton & Company, 1911.

"Oxmoor." In *The Encyclopedia of Louisville,* edited by John E. Kleber, 682. Lexington: Univ. Press of Kentucky, 2001.

Thomas, Samuel W. "Oxmoor: The Bullitt House in Jefferson County, Kentucky." *Kentucky Review* 9 (Autumn 1989): 29–40.

—*Andrea S. Watkins*

P

PAGE, GREGORY DEWAYNE (b. 1948, Middlesboro, KY; d. 1967, Lexington, KY), football player. The second African American scholarship athlete to sign with the University of Kentucky (UK), Greg Page was the son of Robert, a former coal miner who later worked at a tannery, and Wilma Page, a registered nurse. Greg was an all-state defensive end at Middlesboro High School. In 1966, he received a scholarship to play for the UK football team. At 6-feet-1 and 190 pounds, Page made an immediate impression playing on the freshman team. Known for his quickness and mobility, Page was expected to serve an important role on the team as a backup player his sophomore year, but on August 22, 1967, during the team's third practice in preparation for the coming season, he was paralyzed during a noncontact drill. The defensive line was not moving at full speed, but Page's neck snapped after a collision with another player.

Page was taken to the University of Kentucky Medical Center. A tracheotomy was performed, and Page was able to speak with his parents. He received visitors and watched television before dying 38 days later at 11:25 p.m. on September 29, 1967. A

Greg Page.

memorial was held at Stoll Field on the UK campus to celebrate his life. The UK football team traveled to Middlesboro for his funeral, and he was buried in Green Hills Memorial Gardens. In 1979, the UK Board of Trustees voted to name a new apartment complex for students located across from the football stadium in Page's memory. Upon seeing the complex and sign, "Greg Page Stadium View Apartments," Page's father said, "That's nice. That's mighty nice."

Newspapers: "Page in Critical Condition with Severe Neck Injury," *LH*, August 23, 1967, 13; "Greg Page," *LH*, September 30, 1967, 1; "Greg Page," *LH*, October 2, 1967, 1; "UK Apartments Fitting Memorial to Son, Greg Page's Parents Say," *LHL*, November 4, 1979, A1.
—Gerald L. Smith

PAGE, THEODORE ROOSEVELT "TED" (b. 1903, Glasgow, KY; d. 1984, Pittsburgh, PA), pioneering African American baseball player. Born in Glasgow, KY, on April 22, 1903, Theodore Roosevelt Page, son of Joe and Marie Page, grew up in Youngstown, OH. He briefly attended Ohio State University on a football scholarship but dropped out to play baseball. Page, also known as Terrible Ted, played outfielder (1931) for the Homestead, PA, Grays, which was considered one of the greatest teams in the history of the Negro leagues, as well as the Pittsburgh Crawfords (1932–1934). Cline Thomas, "the Black DiMaggio," called Page "the best right-fielder I have seen. He made playing the outfield one of the fine arts." Page injured his knee and finally retired in 1937 with a .316 batting average in recorded Negro League games.

After he retired, Page worked briefly in public relations for Gulf Oil Company and then started a bowling alley catering to African Americans. He became a prominent person in bowling circles and even wrote a regular bowling column for a newspaper for many years. Page, like many of the early Negro League players, spent his life trying to gain recognition for his accomplishments and those of his fellow players. His best legacy was that he played for the love of the game. In 1977, he was inducted into the Negro Baseball Hall of Fame.

Remembered for his generous spirit, Page took in a young man from the Pittsburgh streets after his wife, Juanita, died. Page found the man robbing his home and confronted him. The man beat Page to death with a baseball bat on December 1, 1984.

Rogosin, Donn. *Invisible Men: Life in Baseball's Negro Leagues.* New York: Atheneum, 1983.

—Nancy Richey

PALMER, ZIRL A. (b. 1919, Bluefield, WV; d. 1982, Lexington, KY), business owner and civil rights activist. Zirl A. Palmer was born in Bluefield, WV, on December 11, 1919. After completing elementary and secondary education, he earned his bachelor of science degree from Bluefield State College and completed additional premedicine courses at Howard University. In 1951, he earned his pharmacy degree at Xavier University in New Orleans. In 1952, he opened his own drugstore in Lexington, KY. He claimed that he was the first African American person to hold a Rexall Drugstore franchise. On September 3, 1968, an unexplained explosion occurred in the West End Plaza Shopping

Zirl Palmer.

Center on Georgetown St., where Palmer's pharmacy was located. Three businesses were damaged, and eight people were injured. The explosion briefly trapped Palmer, his wife, Marian, and their four-year-old daughter, Andrea. The damage forced Palmer to close his business and retire.

Palmer was an active member of the Lexington community. He participated in the Lexington Urban League, the **Kentucky Commission on Human Rights,** the Lexington Human Rights Commission, the Salvation Army, the National Association of Retail Druggists, the American Pharmaceutical Association, the Fayette County Board of Health, the Fayette County Recreation Board, and other organizations. Appointed by Governor Wendell Ford, Palmer served from August 1972 to September 1979 as the first black trustee of the University of Kentucky. On May 1, 1982, he died at Lexington's Central Baptist Hospital. As a World War II veteran, Palmer was buried in **Camp Nelson** National Cemetery in Jessamine Co., KY.

Fifty Years of the University of Kentucky African American Legacy, 1949–1999. Lexington: Univ. of Kentucky, 1999.

Newspapers: "Explosion and Fire Rock Five Shops; 8 Persons Injured," *LL,* September 4, 1968, 1; "Palmer Looks Back on Work as First Black UK Trustee" and "Zirl Palmer Is No Stranger to Racial Discrimination," *LHL,* September 16, 1979, E1; "Zirl A. Palmer Dies at 62; First Black Trustee of UK," *LHL,* May 21, 1982, A1.

U.S. Veterans Gravesites, ca. 1775–2006.

—*John A. Hardin*

PARK DUVALLE, Louisville neighborhood. Park Duvalle is a neighborhood in western Louisville bounded by the Shawnee Expressway to the west, the Norfolk Southern railroad tracks to the north, Cypress St. to the east, and a combination of Bells Ln. and Algonquin Pkwy. to the south. The neighborhood's name appears to reflect the existence of several parks in the area, such as Algonquin Park, Harris Drive Park, and Russell Lee Park, and also the presence of DuValle Junior High School. The school was moved from downtown to the area in 1956 and was named after **Lucie DuValle,** an educator and the first female principal of a public high school in Louisville. Today the school is the site of the DuValle Education Center, which offers various learning opportunities to the surrounding community.

Although development of the area began in the late nineteenth century, a majority of the subdivisions were platted after the 1940s. Originally considered part of greater **Parkland,** the neighborhood included **Little Africa,** a community that was home to thousands of blacks beginning in the years after the Civil War. Because of urban renewal and integration, Little Africa with its shanty houses disappeared, to be replaced by the Cotter and Lang Homes housing projects.

In the mid-1990s, the neighborhood became the focus of a $180-million revitalization effort as the dilapidated Cotter and Lang Homes housing projects were cleared to make way for over 1,200 new homes and townhouses. The project—under a partnership that included the federal and Louisville city governments, the Housing Authority of Louisville, and the private sector—continued to change the neighborhood through 2012. Among improvements were new shopping and commercial investments.

"First Choice Market Opens in Park Duvalle." Economic Development Newsroom, LouisvilleKY.gov, June 12, 2012. http://www.louisvilleky.gov/economicdevelopment/News/2012/FirstChoiceMarketOpensinParkDuValle.htm (accessed August 7, 2014).

LCJ, December 16, 1997; *LCJ,* January 18, 1999.

PARKER, JOHN P. (b. 1827, Norfolk, VA; d. 1900, Ripley, OH), Underground Railroad conductor, businessman, and inventor. John P. Parker, born enslaved in Norfolk, VA, was a prolific **Underground Railroad** conductor. Parker made numerous unsuccessful attempts to escape from slavery until 1845. He was then allowed to purchase his freedom for $1,800 through work as an iron molder.

Parker married Miranda Boulden, with whom he had six children, and lived in Ripley, OH, overlooking the Ohio River. He was employed in the iron industry. In his oral autobiography, Parker explained that from his unsuccessful escape attempts, he learned valuable lessons for his later work. As a conductor, Parker helped between 315 and 1,000 enslaved African Americans escape from Kentucky, working closely with white Presbyterian minister John Rankin.

After the Civil War, Parker purchased a blacksmith shop and foundry in Ripley, where he invented farm and industrial instruments and registered several patents, including ones for a soil pulverizer and a tobacco press. In holding a patent before 1900, Parker was among a select group of only 55 African Americans.

Parker narrated his life story to white journalist Frank Moody Gregg in the 1880s. Robert Newman discovered the autobiographical manuscript at Duke University Library and collaborated with Charles Nuckolls and Stuart Seely Sprague to publish it as *His Promised Land* in 1996. Proceeds from the sale of the book go to the John P. Parker Historical Society, which maintains the Parker house in Ripley, OH.

Gonzalez, David. "Rise for Freedom: The John P. Parker Story." Unpublished opera libretto, 2006.
Hagedorn, Ann. *Beyond the River: The Untold Story of the Heroes of the Underground Railroad.* New York: Simon & Schuster, 2002.
Parker, John P. *His Promised Land: The Autobiography of John P. Parker, Former Slave and Conductor on the Underground Railroad.* Edited by Stuart Seely Sprague. New York: Norton, 1996.
Rappaport, Doreen, and Bryan Collier. *Freedom River.* New York: Hyperion, 2000.

—*Kristine Yohe*

PARKER, WILLIAM C. (b. 1925, Cairo, IL; d. 2008, Cumberland Falls, KY), vice chancellor for minority affairs at the University of Kentucky. The son of a railroad worker and a teacher, William C. Parker grew up in the black communities of Cairo, IL. The oldest of several children, Parker was encouraged to provide for his family while still pursuing an education. He managed to accomplish two tasks: finishing in the top 10 percent of his class in high school and receiving a tuition scholarship to Illinois State University. After completing a bachelor's degree, he pursued a master's degree before he exhausted his funds. He then held a series of teaching and social work jobs in the area around Cleveland, OH.

While working with a catering company, Parker met his future wife, Emily Miles. Although he had a steady job as a teacher, his wife encouraged him to accept an opportunity to teach at Oberlin College and, a few years later, a position as a program administrator at Princeton University. Seventeen years later, he accepted a job as vice chancellor for minority affairs at the University of Kentucky.

As vice chancellor from 1984 to 1990, Parker worked as an advocate for greater diversity, supporting efforts to hire more minorities as faculty and pursuing a higher retention rate among black students at the university. In 1984, he organized the **Kentucky Association of Blacks in Higher Education.** He also helped establish the Martin Luther King Cultural Center and organized activities that would "enhance human relations" during Martin Luther King Day. Parker received numerous awards for his advocacy, including Most Outstanding Alumni Award from Illinois State and the Brotherhood/Sisterhood Award from the National Conference of Christians and Jews.

After retiring as vice chancellor in 1990, Parker, who held a degree in psychology from Columbia Pacific University, continued to publish articles and books on diversity and psychology. He also established Parker and Parker Associates, a consulting firm, and served as an adjunct professor at Bluegrass Community and Technical College. In 2008, he suffered an apparent heart attack while giving a presentation at Cumberland Falls and died. The University of Kentucky named the William C. Parker Scholarship Program, which promotes diversity, in his honor.

Newspapers: "A Family Portrait—Couple Bring Their Children, Lives Together," *LHL,* January 17, 1988, J1; "Kentucky State University Graduates Set Out to Find Their Passion," *Frankfort State-Journal,* May 11, 2008; "Longtime Educator Dies—William Parker Was Head of Minority Affairs at UK," *LHL,* June 2, 2008, B1.
Parker, William C. Interview by Emily Parker, September 5, 1988. Blacks in Lexington Oral History Project, Louie B. Nunn Center for Oral History, Univ. of Kentucky.

—*Stephen Pickering*

PARKLAND, residential neighborhood in Louisville. Parkland is a primarily residential neighborhood west of downtown Louisville and bounded by 26th St. to the east, Broadway to the north, 34th St. to the west, and a combination of Woodland and Wilson Aves. and Catalpa St. to the south. In the mid-nineteenth century, the land, designated on some maps as Homestead, was inhabited by sparse settlements of German and African American farmers. Civil War soldiers roamed the area after Union forces constructed Ft. Karnasch, located near Wilson Ave. (then Cane Run Rd.) between 26th and 28th Sts.

Residential development began in the area in 1871 when the real estate firm of Morris Southwick and Co. subdivided a 346-acre rural tract into 1,072 lots and auctioned them to the public. Prompted by alluring ads, speculative fever raced through Louisville, impelling business owners to close on July 10, 1871, as approximately 2,000 people attended the auction. The developers had ensured transportation to the then-distant community by contracting with the Central Passenger Railway Company to extend its **Walnut St.** (now **Muhammad Ali** Blvd.) tracks to 28th St. and then southward to Greenwood Ave. In 1874, the town of Parkland was incorporated.

By 1890, Parkland had become a prestigious and fashionable address. Large Victorian, Queen Anne, and Romanesque homes were erected along tree-lined Dumesnil and Virginia Aves. Town ordinances prohibited bars, hunting, odor-spewing factories, and other nuisances. However, the prosperity temporarily came to a halt after the tornado of March 27, 1890, touched down just south of Parkland and cut a diagonal path toward the northeast, destroying a dozen homes and damaging many others. Parkland never recovered financially and was annexed by Louisville in 1894.

Many of the grand houses were rebuilt and others were added, but the area also witnessed a change as working-class people began moving into the community and constructing bungalows and shotgun cottages along Hale and Woodland Aves. Nearby, a small community of African Americans, known initially as black Parkland and later as **Little Africa,** developed on swampland southwest of Parkland. Much of the construction in the area was completed by 1915.

In the early decades of the twentieth century, an area centered around 28th St. and Dumesnil Ave. had become a thriving business district. Ultimately, it included establishments such as Schneider's Department Store, office buildings, the Parkland Theatre, the Royal Bank, an A&P grocery store, and a branch of the public library. By the 1950s, however, some white families had started to leave Parkland for the suburbs, a trend that continued well into the 1960s after the desegregation of public schools. Neighborhood businesses followed this lead after civil unrest erupted at the intersection of 28th St. and Greenwood Ave. in May 1968 on the heels of the assassination of Martin Luther King Jr. After days of looting and random outbursts of violence, many owners closed their shops, leaving the business district virtually deserted. Between 1970 and 1980, Parkland lost roughly 25 percent of its population.

In 1980, the business district was designated a local preservation district, and the neighborhood was placed on the National Register of Historic Places, spurring some revitalization efforts in the area. Further plans to rehabilitate the neighborhood stalled through the 1980s until a feasibility study in 1987 prompted the city to inject millions of dollars into the community. By restoring historic buildings, providing loans to new businesses, erecting new housing, and improving the area's roads, the city has continued its efforts to lure residents and businesses back to the area.

King, Ethel I. *From Parkland to the River's Edge.* Louisville, KY: Peter's Publications, 1990.
Parkland Historic Preservation District (Louisville, KY). http://www.louisvilleky.gov/NR/rdonlyres/6C73BA2B-3ABE-4139-BA0C-7E1B3432C37E/0/ParklandNG.pdf (accessed August 7, 2014).
Yater, H. George. *Two Hundred Years at the Falls of the Ohio.* Louisville, KY: Filson Club, Inc. 1987.

PARKS, SUZAN-LORI (b. 1963, Ft. Knox, KY), Pulitzer Prize-winning playwright. Born on May 10, 1963, at the Ft. Knox, KY, army base, Suzan-Lori Parks grew up in a military family and moved frequently. She attended schools in six different states and overseas in Germany. She then went to Mt. Holyoke College, receiving her BA in English and German literature in 1985. Parks took an advanced fiction-writing class there from famed playwright James Baldwin, who encouraged her to write plays for a vocation, stating that she was "an utterly astounding and beautiful creature who may become one of the most valuable artists of our time."

Parks's artistic endeavors have won her considerable acclaim. She received Obie Awards for her plays *Imperceptible Mutabilities in the Third Kingdom* (1989) and *Venus* (1996) and was the first African American woman to win a Pulitzer Prize for Drama for her play *Topdog/Underdog* (2001). She was also awarded a 2001 McArthur Genius Award and the 2008 Kentucky Governor's National Award in the Arts. Another play, *In the Blood*, was a 2000 Pulitzer Prize finalist, and *365 Plays/365 Days* (2007) was produced in over 700 theaters. She has also written numerous other plays and movie screenplays, a novel (*Getting Mother's Body*, 2003), and a musical on Ray Charles (*Unchain My Heart*).

Als, Hilton. "The Show-Woman." *New Yorker*, October 30, 2006.
"Governor's Awards in the Arts Recognizes Outstanding Achievements and Contributions." Press release, Kentucky Arts Council, August 29, 2008.
Parks, Suzan-Lori. "Info." The Official Site of Suzan-Lori Parks. http://www.suzanloriparks.com/info/ (accessed July 25, 2012).

—*David Lai*

PARRISH, CHARLES HENRY, JR. (b. 1899, Louisville KY; d. 1989, Newark, NJ), educator and first black faculty member at the University of Louisville. Charles Henry Parrish Jr., the son of **Charles Henry Parrish Sr.** and **Mary V. (Cook) Parrish,** was educated in the city's black public schools and graduated in 1916 from **Central High School.** After earning his bachelor's degree in mathematics from Howard University in 1920 and a master's degree in sociology from Columbia University in 1921, he served on the faculty of Simmons University (later known as **Simmons College of Kentucky**) from 1921 to 1930.

From 1931 to 1950, Parrish was a professor of sociology and education at **Louisville Municipal College,** an all-black division of the University of Louisville. He taught during the entire existence of the college and directed several scholarly studies at the state level, including the 1936 Works Progress Administration–funded "Study of Urban Negro Workers." In 1938, he married educator Frances Elizabeth Murrell, and in 1944, he received his PhD in sociology from the University of Chicago.

When Louisville Municipal College was closed in 1950 and its students matriculated at the University of Louisville's Belknap Campus, Parrish became the University of Louisville's first black faculty member. Initially he was assigned to advise black students and teach elective sociology courses. Parrish published nationally recognized scholarly articles on color caste and race relations, was a guest lecturer at colleges and professional organizations across the United States, and served as a resource person on race relations for the Kentucky and Louisville governments. From 1959 to 1964, he served as chairperson of the university's Department of Sociology, the first black to do so. Although he retired as a professor of sociology at the University of Louisville in 1969, he continued to teach at other universities in the United Sates and Africa and to serve in numerous Louisville civic and social welfare organizations.

Charles Henry Parrish Jr. Papers. Univ. of Louisville Archives and Records Center.
LCJ, July 21, 1989.

—*John A. Hardin*

PARRISH, CHARLES HENRY, SR. (b. 1859, Lexington, KY; d. 1931, Louisville, KY), educator and Baptist church leader. Parrish was born to Hiram and Harriet Parrish, who were slaves. After emancipation, he attended local segregated schools until 1874, when he temporarily dropped out to help his family. In 1880, at the urging of his pastor, Rev. **William J. Simmons,** Parrish enrolled at the Kentucky Normal and Theological Institute (later known as **Simmons College of Kentucky**) in Louisville. Although he worked his way through college, he excelled. By the time he received his bachelor's degree, the institute had become the State Colored Baptist University. His bachelor's degree was one of the first and he was named class valedictorian in 1886.

Parrish was appointed professor of Greek and secretary-treasurer at State Colored Baptist University in 1886, pastored Louisville's **Calvary Baptist Church** from 1886 to 1931, was selected as a delegate to the Kentucky Republican State Convention, was president of the Executive Board of the **General Association** of Negro Baptists in Kentucky, and from 1890 to 1912 served as president of **Eckstein Norton Institute** in Cane Springs, KY. He also established the Kentucky Home Society for Colored Children

The Rev. Charles H. Parrish Sr. (front center) and university secretaries, 1920s.

in Louisville (1908), was a member and secretary of the Board of Trustees of **Lincoln Institute** (1909–1919), and served as president of Simmons University in Louisville (1918–1931).

Parrish became renowned nationally for his religious activities after serving as a delegate to both Baptist and ecumenical meetings in London, Jamaica, Jerusalem, Sweden, and New York City. In 1905 he preached in 17 German towns. He was a founder of the National Baptist Convention and served as its chairman.

In 1898, he married **Mary V. Cook Parrish** of Bowling Green, KY. The following year, she gave birth to their son, **Charles H. Parrish Jr.** The elder Parrish is buried in Louisville Cemetery.

Hampton, George A. *Diamond Jubilee of the General Association of the Colored Baptists in Kentucky.* Louisville, KY: American Baptist, 1943.

Johnson, William D. *Biographical Sketches of Prominent Negro Men and Women of Kentucky.* Lexington, KY: Standard Print, 1897.

Richardson, Clement. *The National Cyclopedia of the Colored Race.* Montgomery, AL: National Publishing, 1919.

—*John A. Hardin*

PARRISH, MARY VIRGINIA COOK (b. 1863, Bowling Green, KY; d. 1945, Louisville, KY), educator, speaker, writer, and community leader. Born on April 8, 1863, the daughter of Ellen Buckner, Mary Virginia Cook spent her early years in Bowling Green, KY, and attended local African American schools, where she won prizes for spelling and reading. In 1881, she began teaching at the private **Bowling Green Academy.** Her scholarly aptitude, diligence, and dedication attracted attention, and she soon enrolled at Louisville's State Colored Baptist University (later known as **Simmons College of Kentucky**) as a protégée of the institution's president, Dr. **William Joseph Simmons,** and area

Baptist women and of the American Baptist Woman's Hope Society of Maine and Massachusetts.

Cook graduated as valedictorian in the normal school in 1883, completed college courses in 1887, and was awarded an honorary master's degree in 1889. In the mid-1880s, she joined the faculty of the normal school and became its principal and a Latin and mathematics instructor at State University. She combined these duties with those of a fund-raiser for the university and an advocate of Christian education. Her activities took her to New England and the Deep South and as far west as California. She delivered speeches at meetings of the American Baptist National Convention (1887), the National Press Convention (1887), and the American Baptist Home Mission Society (1888). In 1886, she published an article, "Nothing but Leaves," in the ***American Baptist,*** and soon she began writing educational articles for *Our Women and Children,* a Louisville-based African American religious magazine. She also contributed to the *South Carolina Tribune,* using the pen name Grace Ermine.

In 1892, Cook, along with three other young women, participated in an unsuccessful protest effort before the legislature in Frankfort against the **Separate Coach Law.** Also, in 1892, she joined the faculty of **Eckstein Norton Institute** at Cane Springs in Bullitt Co. The school's president was Rev. **Charles Henry Parrish,** the minister of Louisville's **Calvary Baptist Church** and the young teacher's future spouse. Marrying early in 1898, she returned to Louisville, where she was the financial secretary of her husband's church. The couple's only child, **Charles Henry Jr.,** was born in 1899.

The early 1900s saw Mary Cook Parrish's involvement in many church activities. She was an active member of the **Baptist Women's Educational Convention of Kentucky,** organized the

Mary Parrish.

PASSMORE, NORMAN L., SR. (b. 1915, Columbus, GA; d. 2003, East Chicago, IN), educator and athlete. A lifelong educator and leader in Lexington, KY, Norman L. Passmore Sr. was born in Columbus, GA, on April 1, 1915. Raised in East Chicago, IN, Passmore matriculated at Kentucky State Industrial College for Colored Persons (later known as **Kentucky State University**) on an athletic scholarship; he played quarterback and won two national championships with the football team in 1934 and 1937. He participated in track and was vice president of the senior class. After graduation, he earned a master's degree from the State University of Iowa before accepting a job in Lexington as a chemistry and physics teacher at **Dunbar High School.**

At Dunbar, Passmore served as assistant basketball coach under **Sanford T. Roach** for over 20 years in the 1930s and 1940s. The two men served together in the Merchant Marine during World War II, and Roach introduced Passmore to his future wife, Lillian Beatrice McGee. Football remained Passmore's primary sport, however, and he coached Kentucky State University for a single abbreviated season in 1944. He then took over the football team at Dunbar High in 1950, leading the team to over 90 wins and three titles during his tenure as coach. In a four-year term on the Board of Control of the Kentucky High School Athletic Association, he also helped push for the integration of black athletes.

Passmore was equally committed to his role as educator. In the 1960s, Dunbar was converted to a junior high school as part of the movement toward integration. Passmore later transferred to Henry Clay High School, where he became assistant principal. He implemented the National Honor Society, which he had established at Dunbar, and quickly earned a reputation as a fair administrator and confidant for the students. Even though he retired in 1984, he continued to support educational efforts in the area, running for the school board in 1986.

Passmore, who also served as a minister in the African Methodist Episcopal Church, received numerous awards and recognitions after his retirement. In 1989, he was named to the Kentucky High School Athletic Association Hall of Fame, and in 2001, the Dunbar Alumni Association established the Norman Passmore Classic, an annual football game in his honor. Although Passmore died two years later in East Chicago, IN, the game is still played annually, and a Passmore Classic Award is given at halftime to a person who "exemplifies the characteristics of Norman Passmore."

first parent-teacher organization in Louisville's African American schools, chaired a committee to establish a playground for African American children, served as the first president of the Colored Republican Women's Club, cofounded the **Phillis Wheatley YWCA** (West End), and sat on the board of the Kentucky Home Society for Colored Children. She was an alternate delegate to the 1932 Republican Convention in Chicago.

Active in church work until her death, Mary Virginia Cook Parrish died on October 14, 1945. She was buried in Zachary Taylor National Cemetery in Louisville.

Dunnigan, Alice Allison, comp. and ed. *The Fascinating Story of Black Kentuckians: Their Heritage and Traditions.* Washington, DC: Associated Press, 1982.

Higginbotham, Evelyn Brooks. *Righteous Discontent: The Women's Movement in the Black Baptist Church, 1880–1920.* Cambridge, MA: Harvard Univ. Press, 1994.

Kleber, John, ed. *The Encyclopedia of Louisville.* Lexington: Univ. Press of Kentucky, 2001.

Williams, Lawrence H. " 'Righteous Discontent': Mary Virginia Cook Parrish and Black Baptist Women." *Baptist History and Heritage* 42 (Summer/Fall 2007).

Wright, George C. *Life Behind a Veil: Blacks in Louisville, Kentucky, 1865–1930.* Baton Rouge: Louisiana State Univ. Press, 1985.

—*Carol Crowe Carraco*

Newspapers: "9 Are Seeking Appointment to School Board," *LHL,* July 26, 1986, B1; "Bowling, Garland among 15 Tapped for Hall of Fame," *LHL,* June 6, 1989, C1; "Dunbar Alumni Honor Passmore: Football Hero, Coach, Teacher," *LHL,* September 29, 1991, B1; "Longtime Educator Dies at 87," *LHL,* March 19, 2003, B1; "A Classic Game for a Classic Educator," *LHL,* August 29, 2004, C1.

Passmore, Norman. Interview by Edward Owens, August 17, 1978. Blacks in Lexington Oral History Project, Louie B. Nunn Center for Oral History, Univ. of Kentucky.

———. Interview by Emily Parker, September 8, 1986. Blacks in Lexington Oral History Project, Louie B. Nunn Center for Oral History, Univ. of Kentucky.

—*Stephen Pickering*

PAYNE, GARY (b. 1948, Paducah, KY), first black judge in Fayette Co., KY. A native of Paducah, KY, Gary Payne left his home state to attend Pepperdine College before returning to the University of Kentucky, where he earned his law degree in 1978. After deciding to stay in the Lexington area, Payne held a variety of legal jobs that included serving as an attorney for the Kentucky National Guard and as assistant to Fayette Co.'s county attorney, Norrie Wake, in 1986.

In 1988, Payne was one of three candidates whose names were submitted to Governor Wallace Wilkinson to fill a vacancy on the Fayette District Court. When Wilkinson selected Payne to fill the position, he became Fayette Co.'s first black judge. Payne regarded the position as an opportunity to act as a role model for young people and minorities. The following year, he won a tightly contested election against Byron Ockerman and became the first black judge elected to his position. Payne held this position until 1994, when he was appointed to the position of Fayette circuit judge by Governor Brereton Jones and won an election for the job in his own right later the same year. He has also served on a task force aimed at curbing domestic violence and as a member of the newly instituted Family Court system in 2003.

Newspapers: "New Judge Hopes to Be Role Model; Gary Payne Is First Black Judge in Fayette," *LHL,* December 4, 1988, B1; "Former Prosecutors Square Off in Race for Fayette District Judge," *LHL,* October 17, 1989, B1.
Smith, Jessie Carney. *Black Firsts: 4,000 Ground-Breaking and Pioneering Historical Events.* 2nd ed. Detroit: Visible Ink Press, 2003.

—*Stephen Pickering*

PAYNE, WILLIAM HERMAN (b. 1943, Covington, KY; d. 1970, Bel Air, MD), civil rights activist. William Payne, the son of Emmett Payne Jr. and Emma F. Robinson Payne, became the first African American from Covington killed during the modern **civil rights movement.** Payne was raised in Covington, attended **Lincoln-Grant School,** and graduated in 1963 from William Grant High School, where he was the manager of the basketball team. After graduation, he served with the U.S. Naval Reserves for two years of active duty during the Vietnam War. He attended Xavier University in Cincinnati, and while he was in college, he became active in the Student Non-violent Coordinating Committee (SNCC), the youth organization of the Southern Christian Leadership Conference, which was formed by Martin Luther King Jr. Payne has been described as highly intelligent and an organizer.

In 1967, he moved to Atlanta, GA, and traveled throughout Alabama, Georgia, and Mississippi on civil rights and voter-registration drives. He became a friend of the SNCC's national chairman, Herbert "H. Rap" Brown, and its former leader, Stokely Carmichael. It was while Payne was in Atlanta that he became known as Che, a name also used by the well-known revolutionary leader Ernesto "Che" Guevara from Cuba. In 1970, Brown went to Bel Air, MD, where the SNCC had established a presence because of civil rights issues; he was to face charges stemming from various protest marches and rallies. While traveling in Maryland to support Brown, Payne and a companion, Ralph Featherstone, were killed on March 9, 1970, when their car exploded. The incident was publicized nationally as part of the civil rights movement. Payne was buried in Mary E. Smith Cemetery in **Elsmere,** KY.

Newspapers: "Nobody Can Say He Was a Militant," *KP,* March 13, 1970, 1K–2K; "Black Struggle Leader Buried," *KP,* March 16, 1970, 4K; John Harris, "Black Leaders Eulogize Payne," *KP,* March 17, 1970, 1K–2K; "Services Held for Bomb Blast Victim," *KP,* March 17, 1970, 5K.

—*Theodore H. H. Harris*

PEEPLES, PORTER G. (b. 1945, Lynch, KY), director of the Urban League in Lexington. Porter G. Peeples grew up in Lynch, KY, a small coal-mining town in the Appalachian Mountains. Educated in a school subsidized by United States Steel, Peeples decided that he had no desire to work in a coal mine. In 1964, he

P. G. Peeples.

started attending classes at a community college in nearby Cumberland, KY, while spending his summers working as a messenger boy in Manhattan. This experience prepared him for his junior year of college, when he transferred to the University of Kentucky as one of a handful of African Americans on a predominantly white campus. In 1968, he graduated with a dual teaching certificate in elementary and special education and taught for one semester in Fayette Co.

While living at the YMCA in Lexington, Peeples met Walter Brown, who had come to Lexington to open a branch of the National Urban League. Brown offered him a job with the organization, which he accepted after working for a summer for the Community Action Agency. After Brown left the administration of the branch following a brief tenure, Peeples moved into the position of acting director, which he held for a year and a half. He then became full-time director, the youngest person to hold that position in the national organization.

As director, Peeples moved the headquarters to Main St. in order to "present a business image" to the community, which established the direction of the organization during his early years in charge. Identifying some of the greatest challenges facing blacks as chronic unemployment and lack of job skills, the Lexington branch implemented a program to teach clerical skills to women and brought in the Small Business Administration's financial counselor to advise minority business owners. Peeples also strongly recommended the policy of affirmative action and defended it against attacks from the federal government.

In 1994, Peeples was selected for the National Conference's Humanitarian Award in recognition of his commitment to improving race relations. In 1998 he supported moving the Lexington Urban League's headquarters to **Deweese St.,** once a hub for local black businesses, and began a process of urban renewal in the local community. Peeples also promoted initiatives to increase adoptions among African Americans and to create affordable housing. In addition to his work with the Urban League, Peeples was involved in several city organizations, including the Fayette County Schools Equity Council and the Lexington Chamber of Commerce, and he was elected chair of the Kentucky Community and Technical College System Board in 2011.

Newspapers: "Black Leaders Want Clout for Their Race," *L-L,* February 16, 1982, C1; "Urban League's Work Far from Done, Director Says," *LHL,* February 21, 1983, A1; "Peeples, Hensley to Receive Humanitarian Awards," *LHL,* January 26, 1994, 7.

Peeples, Porter G. Interview by Betsy Brinson, October 5, 2000. Kentucky Civil Rights Oral History Project, Kentucky Oral History Commission, Kentucky Historical Society.

———. Interview by Gerald Smith, November 5, 1982. Blacks in Lexington Oral History Project, Louie B. Nunn Center for Oral History, Univ. of Kentucky.

—Stephen Pickering

PENDLETON, CLARENCE M., JR. (b. 1930, Louisville, KY; d. 1988, San Diego, CA), first African American chairman of the U.S. Commission on Civil Rights. Born in Louisville, KY, and raised in Washington, DC, Clarence M. Pendleton Jr. lived in a primarily black neighborhood as a child and endured segregation in public schools and in swim meets. After graduating from high school, Pendleton enrolled at Howard University, where he earned a BS degree in 1954 and an MA in education in 1961. He took over as the swimming coach at the university and enjoyed substantial success with the team, but he decided to take a job as a recreation coordinator with the Model Cities program in Baltimore for more pay. Over the next few years, he held a series of jobs in government, becoming the director of the Urban Affairs Department of the National Recreation and Parks Association in Washington in 1970 and the head of the San Diego Urban League in 1975.

Pendleton's work with the Urban League, which focused on aiding minorities through the free-market sector, attracted the attention of President Ronald Reagan in 1981. Reagan appointed Pendleton chairman of the U.S. Commission on Civil Rights, the first African American to hold that office. His policies in office, including a disavowal of affirmative action and opposition to desegregation in neighborhood schools through **busing,** established his credentials as a conservative in line with the president's policies. He also clashed with Congress, claiming that budget cuts to the commission were an attempt to force him to resign. However, he remained in office until his term was cut short by his death after he collapsed at a health club in San Diego in 1988.

Moritz, Charles, ed. *Current Biography Yearbook, 1984.* New York: H. W. Wilson Company, 1985.

Newspapers: "Reagan Dismisses Civil Rights Chief, Busing Supporter," *NYT,* November 17, 1981, A1; "Clarence M. Pendleton, 57, Dies; Head of Civil Rights Commission," *NYT,* June 6, 1988, A1.

—Stephen Pickering

PERKINS, CHRISTOPHER WALLACE "C. W.," SR. (b. 1915, Florence, AL; d. 1998, Cincinnati, OH), jazz musician. Jazz musician C. W. Perkins was the son of **Constantine Perkins Jr.** and Willie Bertha McMillian Perkins. C. W. was named after his father's childhood friend William Christopher Handy, the "Father of the Blues," and his father's favorite teacher, Professor Y. A. Wallace. C. W. moved with his parents and older brother Carranza to Covington, KY, in 1921, when he was six years old. He briefly attended **Lincoln-Grant School** in Covington, but his father later enrolled him in a Catholic school in Cincinnati because it had a better arts program. C. W.'s father was his first music teacher; like his father, C. W. had a strong love for music and exhibited great talent at an early age. Even though he learned to play mainly religious and classical music at school, he was drawn to the sound of jazz music at school and turned to his father for help in improving his jazz-playing skills. When the Cincinnati Cotton Club opened in 1934 in the city's West End, Perkins became its first-chair trumpet player. From 1934 to the 1950s, Perkins was one of the best-known black musicians in Greater Cincinnati. He was nicknamed the Granddaddy of the Cotton Club by his protégé **Nelson Burton.** Perkins also performed as a backup musician for King Records in Cincinnati in 1947.

The only time Perkins was not playing for the Cotton Club during those years was when he was drafted and served in the U.S. Army. He became a member of the army band and achieved the rank of sergeant because of his advanced talents. During those years, he also traveled for less than a year with a well-known entertainer, Maurice Morocco.

When Josephine Baker, an internationally known entertainer, performed at the Albee Theatre in Cincinnati in 1951, she refused to go on stage until the theater provided her with an integrated band. Perkins was one of four men that the Albee hired from the Cotton Club to play for Baker. The Albee planned to have the "colored" musicians just be on standby and not perform, but Baker insisted that they play. In retaliation, the Albee selected an extremely difficult part for Perkins to perform, hoping that he would fail and that it could dismiss all four African American musicians. Instead, Perkins hit every note, high or fast, with perfection. After his performance, the Albee kept its band integrated. In the *Cincinnati Times Star,* a writer who did not realize that Perkins was a local musician reported that Baker had a "very hot trumpet player." Perkins was asked by many famous entertainers (for example, Josephine Baker, Count Basie, and Nat King Cole) to go on the road after he performed with them during the famous musical jam sessions at the Cotton Club, but Perkins would not leave because he did not want to be away from his young sons. Even after the Cotton Club closed, he continued to perform with local bands, such as the Frank Payne Quartet. He was a much-sought-after backup musician, performing with entertainers like Tony Bennett and Luther Vandross when they were in town.

In the 1980s, Perkins began serving as a musician at Holy Name Church in Mt. Auburn, OH. He performed every Sunday until he became ill in 1998. He died one month before his 83rd birthday and was buried in Gate of Heaven Cemetery, Montgomery, OH.

Burton, Nelson. *Nelson Burton: My Life in Jazz.* Cincinnati: Clifton Hills Press, 2000.
Cincinnati Times Star, June 15, 1951, 8.
Perkins, Christopher W., Sr. to Jessica Knox-Perkins, April 1997.
Ruppli, Michel. *The King Labels: A Discography.* Westport, CT: Greenwood Press, 1985.

—*Jessica Knox-Perkins*

PERKINS, CONSTANTINE "CONSTANT," JR. (b. 1870, Florence AL; d. 1942, Covington, KY), musician. Constantine Perkins, a musician and the father of **Christopher Wallace "C. W." Perkins,** was born to former slaves Constantine T. Perkins Sr. and Victoria Simpson Perkins. When he was only five, Constant was skilled as a pianist and quickly mastered several musical instruments, especially the cornet. He became known in Florence, AL, as a musical prodigy. His father became a wealthy businessman after slavery and owned a barbershop at which young Perkins would play the piano. Musicians from traveling minstrel shows who frequented the shop during their travels were astounded at the young musician's talent. By the time he was 20, Perkins was known throughout Alabama for having one of the finest black bands in the state.

W. C. Handy, the "Father of the Blues," was a childhood friend of Perkins. In Handy's autobiography, he recognized Perkins as a strong musical influence on his life: he was responsible for teaching Handy how to play **ragtime** and the **blues,** the type of music that brought fame and notoriety to Handy. Perkins and Handy joined the Mahara Minstrel Show and performed widely in the United States, Canada, and Cuba. Both were very popular musicians with the show, and their unique style of music made a major impact on other musicians.

Perkins left the show and returned home when his young daughter became very ill, a twist of fate that removed Perkins from the music world while Handy continued to advance. Back in Alabama, Perkins joined his father's barber business and became even more prosperous than his father. However, his success was interrupted when he refused to comply with Alabama's expanding laws requiring segregation. He had to leave Alabama and everything that he had accomplished and acquired. In Alabama, Perkins had worked with organizations like the **National Association for the Advancement of Colored People** to help put an end to segregation and the lynching of blacks, and when he moved to the Greater Cincinnati area, he continued his work for civil rights. He did not live to see the passing of the antilynching law (1947) or the **Civil Rights Act (1964),** though. Perkins died of a stroke in 1942 while residing at 1209 Russell St. in Covington. He was buried in St. Mary Cemetery, Ft. Mitchell.

Handy, W. C. *W. C. Handy: Father of the Blues.* New York: Macmillan, 1941.
Kentucky Death Certificate no. 24816 for the year 1942.
Newspapers: *Florence (AL) Times,* August 22, 1890, 3; "What's Happening," *Florence (AL) Herald,* August 5, 1891, 1.
Perkins, Willie Bertha, to Jessica Knox-Perkins, Cincinnati, June 1980.

—*Jessica Knox-Perkins*

PERKINS, JAMES (b. 1925, Woodford Co., KY; d. 1984, Lexington, KY), distinguished police officer. A native of Woodford Co., KY, James Perkins moved with his family to Fayette Co. when he was in the ninth grade. He attended **Dunbar High School,** where he played football, and received a degree from Western Kentucky Industrial College (now **West Kentucky Community and Technical College**) before joining the Lexington police force in 1952.

Later described as an "excellent officer" with a "real dislike for lawbreakers," Perkins joined a force that had been integrated only since the 1930s. He admitted that there was initial resistance from the white community, although most of that receded after he demonstrated that he would work impartially. He also avoided trouble by staying distant from the **civil rights movement,** although he disagreed with several of his fellow officers, as well as some of the laws on the books. He did his best to contribute when he had an opportunity, however, going through neighborhoods and warning residents of the possibility of arson when tensions grew high.

In 1959, Perkins was promoted to sergeant, the first African American in Lexington to hold that distinction, and he was considered a strong candidate for lieutenant in 1964. The Civil Service Board, however, ignored arguments that Lexington needed African Americans in positions of authority within the department and refused to place Perkins on its list of men eligible for promotion. Despite protests from representatives of activist groups like the **National Association for the Advancement of Colored People,** the **Congress of Racial Equality,** and the Lexington Commission on Human Rights, as well as the mayor and heads of the police department, the board stood firm in its decision. In response, the Lexington Board of City Commissioners created an additional lieutenancy and named Perkins to the new position. Protesters were conflicted by the result, noting that although the new role was deserved, he should have been promoted rather than selected by an outside board.

Perkins took on several roles during the 1960s, working as an undercover FBI agent for a while and traveling to Louisville to help break up a narcotics ring. He was especially respected as an investigator, earning a commendation from the Treasury Department after recovering $300,000 in veterans' bonus checks and another from the American Legion of Shively and the National Police Officers Association for solving the Westside Plaza bombing in 1968. In 1969, he was promoted to the rank of captain, a position he held until his retirement in March 1984. He died shortly afterward on July 12, 1984, in Lexington, KY.

Newspapers: "Police Post Is Created; Sgt. Perkins Gets Job," *LH,* December 24, 1964, 1; "J. E. Perkins, Four Others Promoted," *LH,* February 21, 1969, 1; "Former Policeman James Perkins Dies," *LHL,* July 12, 1984, B7.
Perkins, James. Interview by Edward Owens, August 16, 1978. Blacks in Lexington Oral History Project, Louie B. Nunn Center for Oral History, Univ. of Kentucky.

—Stephen Pickering

PERKINS, JAMES "SOUP" (b. 1880, Lexington, KY; d. 1911, Hamilton, Ontario, Canada), jockey. James Perkins's mother died shortly after his birth. His father, Jacob, worked with trotting horses and evidently influenced four of his five sons to pursue the equine business. Known for his favorite meal, Soup won his first race in Latonia, KY, at age 11. In 1893, he won five of six races in one day in Lexington, KY, at age 13. He signed a $4,000 annual contract with Fleischmann Stable that made him possibly one of the highest-paid teenagers in the country. The contract offered him a percentage for winning races and allowed him to compete independently when his stable was not racing.

In the same year, Perkins's career nearly ended when he fell from Merry Eyes in a race in Nashville, TN. He was unconscious for several hours, and some doubted that he would return to racing with his aggressive style. However, he continued to compete and won five of six races at Saratoga. The *New York Times* portrayed him as "the best lightweight jockey of the West." In 1895, he tied **Alonzo "Lonnie" Clayton** as the youngest **Kentucky Derby** winner at age 15. In the same year, Perkins became the leading jockey with 192 wins. A white rider was the second-place winner with 187 victories. The following year, Perkins won the St. Louis Derby and the Tennessee Oaks.

Although Perkins won horse races, he suffered from personal troubles. His 18-year-old sister died when he was racing in New Orleans in 1896. He was arrested a year later for shooting a horse with a Roman candle. The following year, he was charged with drunkenness and attempting to carve a woman with a razor. Although one brother described him as a very generous provider to his family and a gambler, Perkins and his brother Frank, a trainer, had a combative relationship. In 1900, Frank died from a gunshot wound inflicted by Thomas Christian. In the same year, Perkins was fined $200 for "a disorderly house."

At 88 pounds, Perkins was described as "diminutive" and "one of the most famous and successful jockeys of the turf." His earn-

James "Soup" Perkins.

ings afforded him considerable property in his lifetime. In 1903, he retired from racing because he became too heavy to ride, and he turned his skills to horse training. He purchased a colt and was training it at Louisville Downs when he traveled to Canada to watch some horse races. Only in his early 30s, he died there of heart failure. His body was returned to Lexington, where he was buried in **African Cemetery No. 2.** An obelisk marker, a duplicate of the famous jockey **Isaac Murphy**'s marker, was placed on the site. Perkins was survived by his wife, Frankie, a sister, and two brothers, including the famous trainer **William Perkins.**

Hotaling, Edward. *The Great Black Jockeys: The Lives and Times of the Men Who Dominated America's First National Sport.* Rocklin, CA: Forum, 1999.
Newspapers: untitled article, *Lexington Morning Transcript,* October 21, 1893, 1; "The Eleventh Suburban: A Good Field for the Great Sheepshead Bay Race To-day," *NYT,* June 21, 1894, 3; "Perkins Had a Good Day," *NYT,* August 14, 1894, 6; "Eliza Perkins," *LL,* January 18, 1896, 8; "State Siftings," *Hazel Green (KY) Herald,* December 30, 1897, 1; "Too Heavy to Ride," *Maysville (KY) Daily Public Ledger,* March 11, 1899, 2; "Frank Perkins Killed," *Mt. Sterling (KY) Advocate,* October 9, 1900, 6; "Colored Notes," *LL,* August 21, 1911, 7.
Ontario, Canada, Deaths, 1869–1936, and Deaths Overseas, 1939–1947.
Renau, Lynn S. *Racing around Kentucky.* Louisville, KY: L. S. Renau, 1995.
Saunders, James Robert, and Monica Renae Saunders. *Black Winning Jockeys in the Kentucky Derby.* Jefferson, NC: McFarland, 2003.
U.S. Federal Census (1880).

—Sallie L. Powell

PERKINS, JOSEPH P., JR. (b. 1933, Owensboro, KY; d. 1976, New York, NY), civil rights activist. Joseph P. "Joe" Perkins Jr., the first child of Joseph and Florence Perkins, grew up in Owensboro, KY. His father was a teacher at Western High School and was so beloved by his community that Kendall-Perkins Park was named in his memory for his devotion to the neighborhood and to children. After Joe Jr. graduated from Kentucky State College (later known as **Kentucky State University**), he enlisted in the army for two years in 1954. He then attended graduate school at the University of Michigan, where he joined demonstrations to support the southern sit-in movement. After earning his graduate degree, he later taught biology in New York.

In 1960, Perkins joined the **Congress of Racial Equality** (CORE). He became a regional field secretary and assisted in the organization of the Covington, KY, chapter, which quickly expanded into nearby counties and became the Northern Kentucky chapter in January 1961. During this time, Perkins also visited Richmond, KY, when three African American and three white Eastern Kentucky State College (later University) faculty members formed a committee to help the needy and examine racial discrimination in the community. Perkins's field report related the racial hostility he witnessed.

In May 1961, 27-year-old Joe Perkins joined CORE's first freedom riders for the purpose of desegregating southern public transportation. Perkins, "the group's official shoeshine segregation tester," was the first arrested when he refused to leave a "whites-only" bus station barbershop shoeshine chair. After two days in jail in Charlotte, NC, he rejoined the rest of the group and was the leader of the Greyhound bus riders.

On May 14, 1961, a mob attacked the bus with a small bomb six miles west of Anniston, AL, and initially would not allow the riders to leave the burning vehicle. Many of the riders were hospitalized, but the African American riders did not receive medical care. One black newspaper praised the uninjured Perkins as being "one of the smoothest operators on the tour."

It is unknown when Perkins returned to New York. However, in 1976, he died after a confrontation in his apartment building's elevator. The Perkins family was unable to get the New York police department to investigate his murder.

Arsenault, Raymond. *Freedom Riders: 1961 and the Struggle for Racial Justice.* New York: Oxford Univ. Press, 2011.
"Freedom Riders." *The American Experience.* http://www.pbs.org/wgbh/americanexperience/freedomriders/people/joseph-perkins (accessed April 23, 2012).
Newspapers: "Bi-racial Traveler Arrested in N.C.," *Tuscaloosa News,* May 6, 1961; "Determination, Courage Mark 'Freedom Riders,'" *BAA,* May 16, 1961; Merlene Davis, "Students Can Relive History in Freedom Rides," *LHL,* January 13, 2011.
Smith, Gerald L. "Direct-Action Protests in the Upper South: Kentucky Chapters of the Congress of Racial Equality." *Register of the Kentucky Historical Society* 109, nos. 3–4 (Summer/Autumn 2011): 351–93.

—*Sallie L. Powell*

PERKINS, WILLIAM "WILL" (b. 1875, Lexington, KY; d. 1927, Lexington, KY), horse trainer. William Perkins, son of Jacob Perkins, who worked with trotting horses, and older brother of celebrated jockey **James "Soup" Perkins,** initially attempted to be a jockey but found that his skills better suited him to be a horse trainer. In 1922, he trained the three-year-old chestnut colt Thibodaux that won the Latonia Derby. Considered one of the greatest Thoroughbred horse trainers, Perkins never had a horse win the **Kentucky Derby.** He saddled six horses for the event, but only John Finn (1922) and Son of John (1925), who placed third in the Kentucky Derby, were the best showings in the Kentucky Derby of horses he trained. He often worked for eminent white owners, including Kentucky senator Allie W. Young.

One year before his death, Perkins saddled 82 wins and won almost $128,000 in stakes and purses. His 13-year career garnered 622 wins and a little more than $619,000 in winnings. Perkins died of diabetes-induced blood poisoning. In the middle of the night, he had injured a toe, but he traveled several days later to the funeral of African American horse trainer Moses Moore in Dayton, OH. Perkins was hospitalized on his return to Lexington at St. Joseph's Hospital, where he died.

Perkins was preceded in death by his older brother Frank, also a horse trainer, and his younger brother James. He was survived by his older sister, Carrie, and another younger brother, Edward, who worked as a stable agent for him. Several well-known African American horsemen, including jockey and trainer William Walker and trainer Raleigh Colston, acted as his pallbearers. Colston received charge of Perkins's stable of 50 horses at the Kentucky Association track in Lexington.

Hotaling, Edward. *The Great Black Jockeys: The Lives and Times of the Men Who Dominated America's First National Sport.* Rocklin, CA: Forum, 1999.
Newspapers: "Thibodaux First in Latonia Derby," *NYT,* July 2, 1922, 14; "Will Perkins, Race Horse Man, Died," *LL,* April 18, 1927, 6; "Perkins Funeral," *LH,* April 19, 1927, 8; "Racing Fans of Country Mourn 'Bill' Perkins," *BAA,* April 23, 1927, 11.
Renau, Lynn S. *Racing around Kentucky.* Louisville, KY: L. S. Renau, 1995.
Wright, George C. *A History of Blacks in Kentucky.* Vol. 2, *In Pursuit of Equality, 1890–1980.* Frankfort: Kentucky Historical Society, 1992.

—*Sallie L. Powell*

PERRY, JULIA AMANDA (b. 1924, Lexington, KY; d. 1979, Akron, OH), composer and pianist. Julia Amanda Perry was born in Lexington on March 25, 1924, and studied composition, voice, and piano at Westminster Choir College in Princeton, NJ, from 1943 to 1948. She continued her studies at the Berkshire Music Center in Tanglewood in 1951 and the Juilliard School of Music. She worked with Nadia Boulanger in Paris and Luigi Dallapiccola in Italy. She received an award from the National Institute of Arts and Letters, as well as two Guggenheim Fellowships, and was awarded the Boulanger Grand Prix for the *Violin Sonata* in 1952.

In 1957, Perry organized a series of European concerts for the U.S. Information Service, and in the 1960s, she taught at Florida State University in Tallahassee and served as a consultant at the Atlanta Colleges Center. In 1973, she suffered a series of strokes that paralyzed her right side; nevertheless, she taught herself to write with her left hand and continued composing. Perry wrote in a number of musical genres, including orchestra, symphonic band, piano pieces, chamber music, and opera. Her best-known works are *Stabat mater* (1951) for contralto and string orchestra; *Homage to Vivaldi* (1973) for symphony orchestra; *Homunculus C.F.* (1960) for piano, harp, and percussion; and the opera *The Cask of Amontillado* (1954). She died in Akron, OH, on April 24, 1979.

Cohen, Aaron I. "Perry, Julia Amanda." In *International Encyclopedia of Women Composers,* 2nd ed., vol. 1, 541. New York: Books & Music, 1987.
"Perry, Julia (1924–1979)." In *Dictionary of Women Worldwide: 25,000 Women through the Ages,* vol. 2, edited by Anne Commire and Deborah Klezmer, 1501. Detroit: Yorkin Publications, 2007.
"Perry, Julia (Amanda)." In *Baker's Biographical Dictionary of Musicians,* vol. 4, edited by Nicolas Slonimsky, 2767. New York: Schirmer Books, 2001.
Southern, Eileen. *The Music of Black Americans: A History.* 3rd ed. New York: Norton, 1997, 551.

—*Jennifer Bartlett*

PERRY, WILLIAM HENRY, SR. (b. 1860, Terre Haute, IN; d. 1946, Louisville, KY), teacher, principal, and medical educator. The son of Charles and Anna Hill Perry, William Henry Perry Sr. was born in Terre Haute, IN, on March 5, 1860. After the death of his father, he and his mother moved to Louisville, where he graduated from **Central High School** in 1877. A gifted teenager, Perry received special permission from the Louisville Board of Education to teach in Louisville public schools before his graduation at the age of 16.

Perry continued serving the city's public school system for the next 50 years, including 10 years as principal of Eastern School before his tenure of over 35 years as principal of Western School (1891–1927). One of the city's most respected African American elementary school principals, he initiated a number of innovative programs at Western School, including kindergarten, manual training, organized play, and nutrition classes. He played an influential role in the early years of what became the **Kentucky Negro Educational Association** (KNEA), serving as one of the organization's first secretaries and as its fourth president between 1884 and 1887. In 1892, he was one of the first five graduates of Central Law School in Louisville.

An avid scholar, Perry furthered his own education while serving as principal at Western School, attending the University of Chicago and graduating from Illinois Medical College, and passed the examination of the Kentucky State Board of Medical Examiners. He had previously participated in cofounding Louisville's **Red Cross Hospital** in 1899. Focused more on educating medical professionals than on practicing medicine himself, Perry established the state's first nurse-training program that admitted African Americans. Almost all of Kentucky's first black nurses were educated in his program, receiving their training under the instruction of **Mary Eliza Merritt.**

Perry's wife, Ana Ridley of Nashville, was an acclaimed pianist and vocalist, and his son, William Henry Perry Jr., followed in his father's footsteps by later serving in leadership roles in the KNEA and on the **Kentucky Commission on Negro Affairs.** After Perry's death from chronic heart inflammation on Octo-

ber 13, 1946, the ***Louisville Defender*** reflected on his prodigious career, remarking that he was "truly one of the builders of Louisville." He was buried in the Louisville Cemetery.

In 1952, Western School was renamed Perry School in his honor. The school later merged with Roosevelt School to become Roosevelt-Perry Elementary School, which continued to educate Louisville's school children through the 2010s.

Kentucky, Death Records, 1852–1953.
"Prof. William H. Perry, Sr., Passes." *KNEAJ* 18, no. 1 (January–February 1947): 12–13.
Wright, George C. *A History of Blacks in Kentucky.* Vol. 2, *In Pursuit of Equality, 1890–1980.* Frankfort: Kentucky Historical Society, 1992.
———. *Life Behind a Veil: Blacks in Louisville, Kentucky, 1865–1930.* Baton Rouge: Louisiana State Univ. Press, 1985.

—*Joshua D. Farrington*

PETERS, AMO LUCILLE POWELL (b. 1912, Cynthiana, KY; d. 2010, Maysville, KY), nurse and civil rights activist. Amo Lucille Powell Peters, the leader of the **civil rights movement** in Maysville, as a child dreamed of serving as a missionary in Africa but later dedicated her life to the enrichment of the lives of African Americans in Mason Co. She married James Peters, and the couple had six children, three sons and three daughters. A longtime member of Maysville's Bethel Baptist Church, Amo Peters served as a Sunday school teacher, president of the Senior Choir, and president of the Women's Missionary Society; in 1985, at age 73, she received her church's Woman of the Year Service Award. She served as a trustee on the church's administrative board into her nineties.

Peters was the first African American hired at the former Hayswood Hospital in Maysville, where she worked for 30 years. At first a nurse's aide, Peters earned her licensed practical nurse degree and eventually was promoted to night nurse in charge. Later she worked as coordinator for the hospital's information and referral services.

In the 1960s, Peters organized local marches and peaceful demonstrations to end segregation and unfair conditions for African Americans. She became chairman of the Maysville–Mason Co. Human Rights Commission and helped plan the 1964 **March on Frankfort** in support of the public-accommodations bill. More than 10,000 people attended the march, which featured singer Mahalia Jackson, Rev. Martin Luther King Jr., and former baseball player Jackie Robinson. Although the bill never made it out of committee, local organizers such as Peters worked for the next two years to persuade their state representatives to pass the 1966 Kentucky Civil Rights Act. Her personal visits with the owners of local businesses and civic leaders led many to support her efforts to hasten integration. Under her leadership, Maysville saw the integration of its theater, its hospital, its restaurants, its local stores, and other facilities. Because of her persistent efforts at negotiation, the first black postal worker and the first black employee at the Social Security office in Maysville were hired. She also led the first local black troop of the Girl Scouts of America. The Black Caucus of Maysville arranged for Peters to receive a Kentucky Colonel commission in 1985.

Continuing in her local activism long after her retirement, Peters worked on behalf of disabled, elderly, and poor citizens. She served on the Board of Commissioners of the Five County Aging Council, the Buffalo Trace Aging Advisory Council, the Licking Valley Handicapped Board, the American Red Cross's local chapter, the Comprehend Foster Grandparents Board, the Low Income Advocacy Committee, the Interagency Council, and the Buffalo Trace Senior Olympics Steering Committee. In 1982, Governor John Y. Brown (1979–1983) appointed Peters a member of the Kentucky Institute for Aging. She was the first black to serve on the Planning and Aging Commission. Peters served as the physical fitness coordinator for the Buffalo Trace Adult Day Care Center and was coordinator of activities for senior centers. In 1988, Maysville mayor Harriet Cartmell appointed Peters to the local Housing Commission, where she served as commissioner, chairman, and vice chairman. Peters also served on the Committee for the Revitalization of Downtown Maysville. As a member of the Mason Co. Homemakers Association, she served on the board for the Martin Luther King Jr. Scholarship. In her 80s, Peters continued to volunteer in local organizations, such as the Hospice of Hope and the Licking Valley Community Action Program. She remained active in the Retired Senior Volunteer Program, where in the past she had organized physical education programs.

Peters received a number of prestigious awards, including the Outstanding Black Women's Award from the National Black Coalition in 1981 and the Community Service Award for Outstanding Leadership and Devotion from the Black Caucus at Morehead State University in 1985. In 1989, the National Black Caucus presented her with the National Community Service Award in Washington, DC. Local honors included Maysville's Community Service Award in 1988 and recognition of outstanding community service in 1996 from the Students United for Minority Awareness at Maysville Community and Technical College; she was named Maysville's Lady of the Year in 1988 by Alpha Nu Chapter of Beta Sigma Phi Sorority.

In 1998, the Maysville Housing Authority named its new building on Meadow Dr. the Amo Peters Community Center. In 2000, the Kentucky Gateway Museum's curator, Sue Ellen Grannis, nominated Peters for the Kentucky Civil Rights Hall of Fame, and she was nominated two more times in subsequent years. In 2003, Christian Women United of the Maysville–Mason Co. area (an organization she had formerly served as president) presented her with its first Valiant Woman Award. On January 15, 2004, the Kentucky State legislature passed resolutions honoring Peters and recognizing her as the recipient of the Martin Luther King Jr. Citizenship Award from the Martin Luther King Jr. State Commission. The Mason Co. Fiscal Court honored her the next month with the Frontiersman Award, and Maysville gave her a key to the city. Asked during an interview in 1996 to sum up her philosophy, Amo Peters said, "I am a firm believer that the good Lord does his part, and he expects you to do your part."

Amo Peters died on May 26, 2010, at the Maysville Nursing and Rehabilitation Facility and is buried in Green Acres Cemetery.

Kentucky House of Representatives Resolution No. 77 and Senate Resolution No. 28, January 15, 2004.
Newspapers: Amo Peters, "How Much Farther Do We Have to Go?," *Maysville Independent-Ledger,* 1994, clipping in the collection of Robert S. Peters; Barbara Phillips Long, "Donating their Time: R.S.V.P. Volunteers Provide a Wide Range of Services," *Maysville Independent-Ledger,* April 20, 1996, C1–C2; Matt Stahl, "Amo Peters Community Center to Be Dedicated in Friday Ceremony," *Maysville Independent-Ledger,* May 7, 1998, B1–B2; "Maysville Community College Offers Computer Classes at Amo Peters Center," *Maysville Independent-Ledger,* December 8, 2000, A3.

—*Randolph Hollingsworth*

PETERSON, ROY PHILLIP (b. 1934, Louisiana; d. 1998, Lexington, KY), Secretary of Kentucky Education and Humanities Cabinet. A native of Louisiana, Roy Phillip Peterson attended historically black Southern University in Louisiana and graduated with degrees in biology and liberal arts in 1957. After receiving an MS in biology from the University of Oregon, he moved to the University of Iowa, where he earned a PhD in endocrinology and met his wife, Juanita Betz Peterson. He taught at several schools before accepting a position as deputy executive director for academic and health programs on the Kentucky Council on Higher Education in 1980.

While serving on the Council of Higher Education staff throughout most of the 1980s, Peterson focused on minority recruitment. He also worked with the YMCA Black Achievers Program and served as interim president of Tennessee State University from 1985 to 1986; he was twice nominated as a candidate for the presidency of **Kentucky State University.** In 1995, Governor Paul Patton appointed Peterson as secretary or head of the Education and Humanities Cabinet. Peterson supported a movement toward a "virtual university" and literacy campaigns while he was in office before dying of lung cancer in 1998. He was buried in **Camp Nelson** cemetery in Nicholasville.

Peterson and his wife were named the winners of the Lauren K. Weinberg Humanitarian Award in 1999. In his memory, the Dr. Roy P. and Juanita Betz Peterson Scholarship Fund offers a scholarship to a student in the Black Achievers Program through a vocal competition as part of the annual Musical Heritage Celebration in Lexington.

Newspapers: "Patton Completes a Diverse Cabinet," *LHL,* December 9, 1995, A1;
"Education Secretary Roy Peterson, 64, Dies," *LHL,* November 29, 1998, B1; "Two Community Awards Honor Two Special People," *LHL,* April 18, 1999, C1.

—*Stephen Pickering*

PEYTON, ATHOLENE MARY (b. 1880, Louisville, KY; d. 1951, Louisville, KY), author of the earliest cookbook published in Kentucky by an African American. Born in Louisville, KY, to Dr. William and Mary Peyton, Atholene Mary Peyton was an 1898 graduate of Louisville's segregated **Central High School,** where she later became a domestic science teacher and adviser to the Girl's Cooking Club. In 1900, she was the Louisville city editor of her father's newspaper, the *Columbia,* which was published for eight years. She also taught domestic science at the Neighborhood Home and Training School for Colored Boys and Girls in Louisville and a 1910 summer session of the National Training School for Women and Girls in Washington, DC, under its president, **Nannie Helen Burroughs.**

Peyton had deep roots in Louisville, where her *Peytonia Cook Book* was published in 1906. Burroughs wrote the preface of the 256-page book. The cookbook was well received. An *Indianapolis Freeman* news item said that it "has achieved a wonderful degree of popularity among the best authorities on the culinary art." Her work was consistent with the domestic science movement, which influenced many aspects of the food-related occupations of the era before World War I. Most recipes in the *Peytonia Cook Book* were presented in the format that was introduced by the famous Boston Cooking School cookbooks. Typical of cookbooks oriented to domestic science, the recipes were described as thoroughly tested and were presented with standard, precise measures. And like other cookbooks with this orientation, the *Peytonia Cook Book* had didactic purposes. Peyton included a teacher's discussion of waitress service oriented toward employment in upper-class homes or elegant restaurants, the work of a culinary expert, not a housewife. Although her work was a general cookbook without a regional orientation, there were some references to southern and perhaps African American cuisine. For example, in her narrative associated with cooking greens, Peyton notes, "In fact, in the South jowl is used in preference to bacon with greens."

Peyton died in Louisville's **Red Cross Hospital** on April 26, 1951. Hathaway and Clark Funeral Home, originally started by **James Harris Hathaway,** handled the funeral arrangements. Peyton was buried in Greenwood Cemetery in the west end of Louisville.

Egerton, John. *Side Orders: Small Helpings of Southern Cookery and Culture.* Atlanta: Peachtree, 1990.

Hayes, Mrs. W. T. *Kentucky Cookbook: Easy and Simple for Any Cook.* St. Louis: J. H. Tomkins Printing Company, 1912.

Kentucky, Death Records, 1852–1953.

Newspapers: "Thompson's Weekly Review," *IF,* July 21, 1906, 8; "Facts from the Falls City," *IF,* February 23, 1907, 1; "The Primary at Louisville," *IF,* May 2, 1908, 5.

Peyton, Atholene. *Peytonia Cook Book.* Louisville, KY: Marshall Publishing, 1906.

—*John van Willigen*

PEYTONTOWN, almost entirely African American community near Richmond, KY. According to one source, Peytontown, located about four miles south of Richmond, KY, may have predated the Civil War. It was named for a prominent slave owner, Guffy (or Guffrey) Peyton. Cora Campbell, an African American, purchased 12 acres of land from Peyton for a church. Under the guidance of Rev. T. R. Reed from Berea, Peytontown Baptist Church was organized in 1886. The church and the school held their services in the same building. Two general stores serviced the community in its early years. The African American and the white stores were across the street from each other. Charlie Embry, Ed Mason, Henry Tevis, and Mac Miller operated the Black Diamond, the African American store.

Some citizens, like Hattie Harris and Mary V. White, matriculated at nearby **Berea College** in the late 1890s and early 1900s. The town's post office was established in 1899 and closed in 1910. In the early 1900s, along with surrounding communities, Peytontown struggled with smallpox, but it was the only hamlet that was not policed.

In 1903, the Independent Order of Good Samaritans and Daughters of Samaria held a picnic in Peytontown. The organization had formed as a white organization in New York City in 1847. After the Civil War, it became an exclusively black society. Three years after the Peytontown picnic, the 26th annual gathering of the Right Worthy State Grand Council of the fraternity met in the Peytontown Baptist Church. Rev. S. M. Watts presided as state grand chief. Nearly all of Kentucky's lodges were represented in the large assembly.

James Burnam, an illiterate Peytontown farmer, was awarded a patent for a hemp brake in 1905. His relative Charles Burnam Jr. ("Bicycle Charlie"), also from Peytontown, was a mechanical genius and operated a bicycle and motorcycle shop in Richmond, KY. Even though he also could neither read nor write, he constructed two small-scale steam engines, the first one in 1902. In 1913, he charged five cents for passengers to ride his trains at Ft. Boonesborough and Lexington's Joyland Park. By 1923, he had operated his trains at Daytona Park in Covington. Two white men later stole his trains.

Peytontown was primarily a farming community, but its citizens also found employment at the Old Teller Distillery, which purchased grain from local farmers. The interracial community had two churches, one predominantly African American and the other white. Both used the same name, Peytontown Baptist Church. In 1994, Rev. Clifford Campbell, pastor of the black church, joined Rev. Lee Morris from the white church to begin an annual event of sharing their Thanksgiving worship services. They alternated the location and which minister preached, and donations of food and clothing went to the needy.

Burnside, Jacqueline Grisby. *Berea and Madison County.* Black America. Charleston, SC: Arcadia, 2007.

Newspapers: "As to Small-pox in This County," *Richmond (KY) Climax,* January 31, 1900, 3; "State Grand Council," *L-L,* June 28, 1906, 2; "Churches Worship Together and Give Thanks for Diversity," *LHL,* November 24, 1997, A1.

Rennick, Robert M. *Kentucky Place Names.* Lexington: Univ. Press of Kentucky, 1984.

—*Sallie L. Powell*

PHI BETA SIGMA FRATERNITY, INC., historically black fraternity with early chapters in Kentucky black colleges. Established at Howard University in 1914 as a social fraternity emphasizing brotherhood, scholarship, and service, Phi Beta Sigma Fraternity, Incorporated, established additional chapters at other historically black institutions across the United States. It emphasized the use of culture for service and service to all humanity regardless of race, creed, or color.

In 1926, Tau Chapter of the fraternity was established at Simmons University (now **Simmons College of Kentucky**). By 1934, Xi Lambda Chapter was established at Kentucky State College (later known as **Kentucky State University**). Among its members were historian and Kentucky State professor **Henry Ellis Cheaney.** In 1984, the fraternity inducted Dr. Cheaney into its Distinguished Service Chapter.

In subsequent decades, collegiate chapters were created at Eastern Kentucky University, Western Kentucky University, the University of Kentucky, Morehead State University, Murray State University, and Northern Kentucky University. Alumni chapters of the fraternity have been created in Louisville (1928), Frankfort/Lexington (1980), and Bowling Green (2009).

Additional notable Kentucky members of Phi Beta Sigma Fraternity are **Frank X Walker,** University of Kentucky professor and one of the originators of the literary concept Affrilachian poetry; **John Benjamin Horton,** journalist and newspaper publisher; Dr. **Samuel Robinson,** former director of the **Lincoln Institute;** and **Samuel Plato,** Louisville architect and contractor. Among its nationally known members are civil rights activist and congressman John Lewis; labor activist A. Philip Randolph; President William Jefferson Clinton; the first black Rhodes scholar, Alain Leroy Locke; scientist George Washington Carver; composer James Weldon Johnson; and African leader Kwame Nkrumah. At present, the fraternity has had over 150,000 members come through its ranks worldwide.

Phi Beta Sigma Fraternity, Inc., International Corporate Headquarters, Washington, DC. http://www.phibetasigma1914.org/our-history/ (accessed December 1, 2013).

Samad, Anthony A. *March On, March On, Ye Mighty Host: The Comprehensive History of Phi Beta Sigma Fraternity, Inc., 1914–2013.* Washington, DC: Phi Beta Sigma Fraternity, 2013.

—*John A. Hardin*

PHILLIPS, JOSEPH "JOKER," JR. (b. 1963, Franklin, KY), first African American head football coach at the University of Kentucky.

The son of Joseph and Cressie Phillips, Joseph Phillips Jr. was born in Franklin, KY, on May 12, 1963. When he was two years old, his grandfather gave him the moniker Joker to distinguish him from his father, Joe Sr. At Franklin-Simpson High School, Joker participated in three different sports: football, basketball, and track. He was an all-state quarterback who also played cornerback in football.

Phillips played wide receiver for the University of Kentucky (UK) (1981–1984). One of his teammates was running back **Mark Higgs** from Owensboro, KY. Phillips finished fifth in the university's career receiving list with 75 catches for 935 yards and scored nine touchdowns. He competed in the 1983 and 1984 Hall of Fame Bowl Games. He was a professional wide receiver for the Washington Redskins (National Football League) and the Toronto Argonauts (Canadian Football League).

Phillips returned to UK and earned his bachelor's degree in advertising in 1986. He then climbed the ranks in UK's football coaching staff, beginning as a graduate assistant coach (1988–1989), assistant recruiting coordinator (1990), and wide receivers coach (1991–1996). After holding coaching positions at Cincinnati, Minnesota, Notre Dame, and South Carolina, Phillips returned to Kentucky as wide receivers coach (2003–2009), recruiting coordinator (2003–2004), and offensive coordinator (2005–2008). In 2009, he shifted to head coach of the offense. In 2010, the University of Kentucky hired Joker Phillips as its head football coach, the first African American to hold the position and the second black head football coach in the Southeastern Conference. In the same year, Kentucky became the first state in the country to have three African American Division I-A head college football coaches.

In his third season, UK fired Phillips because of his 13–24 record. Within a month, the University of Florida hired him as its wide receivers coach and recruiting coordinator. Phillips resigned from this position in 2014.

ESPN. "Joker Phillips Out at Kentucky." http://espn.go.com/blog/sec/post/_/id/54896/joker-phillips-out-at-kentucky (accessed October 10, 2013).

Jones, David. "Joker Phillips Resigns as Florida Wide Receivers Coach." *USA Today,* June 12, 2014.

Newspapers: "A Big Win for Diversity," *LHL,* January 10, 2010, A1; "Florida Hires Joker Phillips as Assistant," *Huntington (WV) Herald-Dispatch,* December 4, 2012, 8.

University of Florida Athletics. http://www.gatorzone.com/football/staff/phillips (accessed October 10, 2013).

University of Kentucky Athletics. http://www.ukathletics.com/sports/m-footbl/mtt/phillips_joker00.html (accessed October 10, 2013).

Vaught, Larry. "Being a Receiver Is No Joking Matter." *Cats' Pause,* November 24, 1984, 25.

—*Sallie L. Powell*

PHILLIS WHEATLEY YWCA, religion-focused community-service organizations for women.

The development of local Young Women's Christian Association of the U.S.A. (YWCA) branches in black communities began slowly. However, as part of the student movement, there were Young Men's Christian Association (YMCA) and YWCA student chapters at some black colleges, including State Colored Baptist University (later known as **Simmons College of Kentucky**) in Louisville. It was at State University that both **Mary Cook Parrish** and **Elizabeth "Lizzie" Fouse** became familiar with the work of the YWCA. Parrish served as president of the combined Young Men and Women's Christian Association in the 1880s. In 1915, the YWCA's first national Conference on Colored Work was held in Louisville, where the national body developed a policy to organize each city under one local administrative unit or central branch.

Parrish's and Fouse's early exposure to the work of the YWCA as students led them to establish "colored" branches of the YWCA in Louisville and Lexington, respectively. As was the practice of black YWCA branches across the country, they named their branches in honor of black female poet Phillis Wheatley. In 1917, Parrish and a committee of black women organized the Louisville Phillis Wheatley branch of the YWCA. Three years later, clubwomen Lizzie Fouse, **Eliza Isabel Mitchell Jackson,** and others established the Lexington Phillis Wheatley branch.

Both branches were committed to the YWCA goals to "promote growth in Christian character and service through physical, social, mental and spiritual training and to become a social force for the extension of the kingdom of God." The branches offered a multitude of programs and had increasingly large memberships in their infancy. Among the activities and services were employment services, girls' basketball teams, arts and crafts projects, sewing classes, and the Girl Reserve clubs. Of the 143 Kentucky Girl Reserve clubs in the 1920s, 31 were black girls' clubs.

Additionally, the YWCAs held worship services, conducted weekend conferences and institutes for their local areas, including neighboring cities, and published newsletters and pamphlets on a variety of topics of interest. The girls also participated in interracial summer camps that provided outdoor recreational activities. The two branches often boasted memberships of between 300 and 700, and attendance at various activities averaged over 100 participants. The Louisville branch also had resident housing for 18 girls and women and maintained a small library.

When the United States entered World War I, the YWCA established separate "colored" Industrial War Service Centers and Hostess Houses, expanding colored city branches under the national leadership of Eva Bowles. The centers provided rest and recreational opportunities for industry's women workers. The Hostess Houses supplied servicemen a place to relax and visit with female friends and family in a wholesome environment. Additionally, the YWCAs raised money and recruited war workers to assist war relief efforts in the United States and overseas.

For many years, both branches enjoyed the support of local black women's clubs, which frequently held their meetings at the YWCAs. The Louisville branch closed in the 1970s, while the Lexington Phillis Wheatley YWCA branch continued after moving to 647 Chestnut St. in 1966. It later became known as the YWCA Phillis Wheatley Center. In 2004, financially struggling, it ended its connection with the national organization and became a part of the **Brenda D. Cowan** Coalition for Kentucky, named for a firefighter killed on the job. In August 2009, the YWCA Phillis Wheatley Center building was auctioned for $114,000.

Fouse Family Papers. University Archives and Special Collections, Univ. of Kentucky.

Newspapers: "A Step toward Oversight," *LHL,* July 8, 2004, A1; "The 'Hub' of East End to Be Auctioned," *LHL,* August 18, 2009, C1; "Wheatley Center Is Sold," *LHL,* August 29, 2009, D1.

Penn, I. Garland. *The Afro-American Press, and Its Editors.* Springfield, MA: Willey & Co., 1891.

Sims, Mary S. *The YWCA—An Unfolding Purpose.* New York: Woman's Press, 1950.

Young Women's Christian Association of Louisville Records, 1911–1979. Univ. of Louisville Archives and Records Center, Louisville, KY.

Young Women's Christian Association of the U.S.A. National Board Records. Sophia Smith Collection, Social Work Archives, Smith College, Northampton, MA.

—*Karen Cotton McDaniel*

PLATO, SAMUEL M. (b. 1882, Montgomery Co., AL; d. 1957, Louisville, KY), architect and contractor. Samuel M. Plato, one of the first African American building contractors and architectural designers, was the son of James and Katie (Hendricks) Plato. His father, who passed his carpentry skills to his son, was a farmer who had apprenticed in carpentry under black artisan Samuel Carter, for whom the younger Plato was named. Samuel Plato as a youngster attended Mt. Meigs Training School near Waugh, AL. He spent a year of study in Winston-Salem, NC, and then enrolled at State Colored Baptist University (later known as **Simmons College of Kentucky**) in Louisville in 1898. Plato took a teachers' training course and liberal arts courses, with plans to study law.

While attending State University he took correspondence courses in architecture and carpentry from the International Correspondence School.

In 1902, Plato moved to Marion, IN, where he lived until sometime between 1919 and 1921. In Marion, he formed a partnership with black building contractor Jasper Burden that lasted about 10 years. Plato then moved to Louisville, where he practiced building design both independently and for a time with **William L. Evans Sr.** At a time when few blacks were practicing architecture, Plato's contract to build a U.S. post office in Decatur, AL, was the first such contract awarded to a black. He built more than 39 post offices at various locations throughout the United States. During World War II, he was one of the few blacks to be awarded contracts to build defense housing. He designed and built numerous residences, apartment houses, and office buildings and several banks, as well as schools and churches, in Louisville and Marion. He served as contractor for Westover, a subdivision developed between 1925 and 1947 in Louisville's West End. Among the buildings Plato is credited with designing are the Classical Revival–style Broadway Temple A.M.E. Church (1915) at 13th and Broadway, the Lampton Street Baptist Church, and his own Tudor-style home (ca. 1929) on W. **Walnut St.** (now **Muhammad Ali** Blvd).

Plato was married twice, first to a Marion native, Nettie Lusby. After her death, he married Elnora Davis Lucas. Plato is buried in the Louisville Cemetery.

Jourdan, Kathrine. "The Architecture of Samuel M. Plato." *Black History News and Notes* 37 (August 1989): 4–7.

—*Joanne Weeter*

PLESSY V. FERGUSON, 1896 U.S. Supreme Court case regarding racial segregation. Although *Plessy v. Ferguson* was concerned with the constitutionality of a Louisiana law requiring the separation of the races in intrastate railway coaches, its outcome had wide applicability to other facilities. The case arose when Plessy, a person of seven-eighths Caucasian and one-eighth African descent, took a seat in a coach reserved for whites. The conductor ordered Plessy to vacate said coach. When Plessy refused, a police officer forcibly ejected him and took him to the parish jail. He was charged with criminal violation of a state statute.

Plessy challenged the constitutionality of this act on the grounds that it conflicted with the Thirteenth and Fourteenth Amendments of the Constitution of the United States. The Supreme Court of Louisiana upheld the law, whereupon the plaintiff appealed to the Supreme Court of the United States. Justice Henry Brown, writing for the majority in a 7–1 decision, made short shrift of the Thirteenth Amendment issue, saying that it was too clear for argument that the Louisiana statute did not conflict with the amendment abolishing slavery. However, Justice Brown did go into considerable detail on the matter of the Fourteenth Amendment, especially the section prohibiting states from denying persons within their jurisdiction the equal protection of the laws. He extensively cited case law to establish that courts had generally held that separation of the races was permissible if the facilities accorded to both were equal. As a result of this case, "separate but equal" became the law of the land for several decades. In a strongly worded dissent, Justice **John Marshall Harlan** (a native of Kentucky) wrote, "In my opinion, the judgment this day rendered will, in time, prove to be quite as pernicious as the decision made by this tribunal in the Dred Scott Case."

The separate-but-equal doctrine was used in Kentucky and elsewhere to justify racial segregation in schools and other public facilities. Kentucky's infamous **Day Law** even prohibited the mingling of races in private schools, forcing **Berea College** to exclude African Americans from its main campus and leading to the founding of the **Lincoln Institute.** In many places, separate was enforced; equal was not.

Many courts agreed with the Supreme Court of North Carolina that "much must be left to the good faith, integrity and judgment of local boards in working out the difficult problem of providing equal facilities for each race" (*Lowery v. Board of Graded School Trustees,* 52 S.E. 267 [1905]). In 1954, the Supreme Court of the United States, in a unanimous ruling written by Chief Justice Earl Warren, held that in the field of education the doctrine of separate but equal has no place (***Brown v. Board of Education,*** 347 U.S. 483 [1954]). The **Civil Rights Act (1964)** outlawed segregation in public accommodations. As far as the public schools were concerned, *Plessy v. Ferguson* was no longer the law, but its effects lingered and can still be seen.

Berea College v. Kentucky, 211 U.S. 45 (1908).

Faber, Charles F., and Thomas Diamantes. *School Law for Kentucky Teachers and Administrators.* 8th ed. Crestview Hills, KY: Rhinegold, 1996.

Plessy v. Ferguson, 163 U.S. 537, 16 S. Ct. 1138, 41 L. Ed. 256 (1896).

—*Charles F. Faber*

PLYMOUTH CONGREGATIONAL UNITED CHURCH OF CHRIST, largely African American church. Formed as a Methodist church in the 1870s, the church became Congregational in the early 1880s when a small group of dissidents with a taste for dignified church services switched their affiliation. The church changed its name from Congregation Methodist Church to Congregation Church and by 1884 to Congregational Plymouth Church. It had moved to its present location in the **Russell neighborhood** at 1630 W. Chestnut St. by 1893, when Rev. **Everett G. Harris** arrived to be its pastor. The church developed a strong, influential base during those years and grew to be a small but leading African American congregation dominated by black professionals and college graduates.

The national Congregational Church subsidized Harris. A civic-minded man, Harris led Plymouth Church for more than four decades. In 1910, he began planning the Plymouth Settlement House (later the Plymouth Community Renewal Center) as an extension of his ministry. Between 1914 and 1917, he raised enough money from white supporters and the Welfare League to build a $20,000 structure.

During the nineteenth century, there were few Congregational churches in the South because that church was associated with the **antislavery** movement before the Civil War and the black educational movement afterward. For many years, Plymouth was the only Congregational church in the city and had no white members. **Lyman Johnson,** a prominent twentieth-century civil rights leader, began attending Plymouth Church shortly after he

moved to Louisville in 1930 and remained a member until his death in 1997.

Hall, Wade. *The Rest of the Dream: The Black Odyssey of Lyman Johnson.* Lexington: Univ. Press of Kentucky, 1988.

Wright, George C. *Life Behind a Veil: Blacks in Louisville, Kentucky, 1865–1930.* Baton Rouge: Louisiana State Univ. Press, 1985.

POLK INFIRMARY (a.k.a. Polk's Infirmary), African American hospital in Lexington, KY. John Knox Polk, the son of James Polk, a Baptist preacher, and Carrie Polk, was born in 1882 in Woodford Co., KY. At age 18, he worked as a grocery porter in Versailles. In 1905, he graduated from Rhode Island's Roger Williams University. He later earned a degree in pharmacy at Illinois University and then worked as a dining-room waiter for the Canada Steamship Lines while he studied at Howard University in Washington, DC.

After earning his medical degree, Dr. John Knox Polk practiced medicine at 166 **Deweese St.** in Lexington, KY, in 1914. In 1921, he moved to a two-story brick building at 148 Deweese St. and operated his own hospital, Polk's Infirmary. He performed minor surgeries at the infirmary and major operations at St. Joseph and Good Samaritan Hospitals, being one of only four African American doctors with operating-room privileges at these white hospitals. Louisville's Fraternal and **Red Cross Hospitals** also used his services. Polk and his wife, Anna, cared for overnight patients and orphans. In 1931, he served as the president of the Blue Grass Medical Society and later as the president of the Kentucky State Medical Society. Because of poor health, in May 1935, Polk and his wife moved to Lakeland, FL, where he died on March 12, 1936. His body was returned to Lexington for burial.

In 1940, Dr. J. Rufus Dalton became the next owner of the infirmary. A native of Cairo, IL, Dalton, the son of Rufus and Jenny Dalton Sr., earned his medical degree from Meharry Medical College in Nashville, TN, and served his internship at Tuskegee, AL. In 1930, he and his wife, Anna Dell, moved to Georgetown, KY, where he started his medical practice. When the family moved to Lexington, they lived upstairs at the infirmary, and Dalton cared for patients downstairs. Like Polk, Dalton was a member of the Blue Grass Medical Society and the National Medical Society. He died in Bardstown, KY, in 1953. Lexington's Cunningham Funeral Home handled the burial arrangements, and Rev. H. H. Greene officiated the services. Dalton was buried in Greenwood Cemetery (now Cove Haven Cemetery).

Other doctors worked at Polk's Infirmary, including Chaplain McCabe Stevenson, a Lexington native whose sister, **Willie Belle Stevenson,** was internationally known for her musical skills as a pianist and composer. McCabe Stevenson graduated from Lexington's Russell High School in 1903. Like Dalton, he earned his medical degree from Nashville's Meharry Medical College. Like Polk, his father was a Baptist minister, and he also served as a physician/surgeon at St. Joseph Hospital while working at Polk's Infirmary beginning in 1923. Stevenson was also a member of the Blue Grass Medical Society and the Kentucky State Medical Society. He died in 1955 and was buried in Greenwood Cemetery.

In January 1998, the Lexington–Fayette County Urban League, under the leadership of **P. G. Peeples Sr.,** president, purchased the landmark building of Polk's Infirmary for $25,000 to house the Urban League. In 2008, the University of Kentucky changed the name of its Clinic North to Polk-Dalton Clinic in honor of Dr. John Knox Polk and Dr. J. Rufus Dalton.

Jester, Art. "Clinic Renamed for 2 Black Doctors, Medical Pioneers, Polk, Dalton Honored." *LHL,* March 5, 2008, B2.

Kentucky Death Records, 1852–1953.

Newspapers: "Dr. John Polk Dies," *Woodford Sun* (Versailles, KY), March 19, 1936, 3; "Colored Notes," *LL,* September 11, 1953, 18.

Official Souvenir Program of Lexington Sesqui-centennial Jubilee Celebration, May 31–June 6, 1925. Lexington, KY: General Committee of the Lexington Sesquicentennial Jubilee Celebration, 1925.

U.S. Federal Census (1900, 1920, 1930).

World War I Draft Registration Cards, 1917–1918.

Yenser, Thomas, ed. *Who's Who in Colored America, 1941–1944.* 6th ed. Brooklyn, NY: Thomas Yenser, 1942.

—*Sallie L. Powell*

POMPEY (b. unknown; d. 1778), slave interpreter for Shawnee Indians. Pompey was captured as a slave child in Virginia by the Shawnee Indians. He lived with the Shawnees and by February 1778 was an interpreter for Chief Blackfish when Daniel Boone and other settlers were captured on a salt-making trip near Blue Licks. Pompey sat for hours quietly translating negotiations on the treatment of the captured men for Boone.

Later, in September 1778, when Blackfish with a group of Indians and French Canadians under British command arrived at Boonesborough, Pompey again acted as translator. During the siege, Pompey took part in "blackguarding," the hurling of insults and taunts at those inside the fort. He appeared at different points along the siege line to shout and take an account of the size and strength of the American forces.

One of the settlers, either Daniel Boone or William Collins, aimed and fired at Pompey's head when he emerged again. Pompey disappeared, and the Americans taunted the Indians with questions about his whereabouts. The Indians replied that he was hunting or asleep, but they finally shouted back, "Pompey nee-poo," meaning that he was dead. A body left behind by the Indians after the 10-day siege was believed to be that of Pompey.

Lofaro, Michael A. *Daniel Boone: An American Life.* Lexington: Univ. Press of Kentucky, 2003.

Lucas, Marion B. "African Americans on the Kentucky Frontier." *RKHS* 95 (Spring 1997): 121–34.

———. *A History of Blacks in Kentucky.* Vol. 1, *From Slavery to Segregation, 1760–1891.* Frankfort: The Kentucky Historical Society, 1992.

—*Andrea S. Watkins*

PORTER, ARTHUR D. SR. (b. 1877, Bowling Green, KY; d. 1942, Louisville, KY), funeral director. Arthur D. Porter came to Louisville as a young adult to attend **Central High School.** After graduation, he moved to Cincinnati to train as an embalmer. He returned to Louisville and worked for local funeral homes until 1908, when he opened his own business, which grew to be known as one of the best-managed black-owned establishments in the city. Business was not the only area in which he excelled, for Porter was known as an important leader in Louisville's African American community, gaining a reputation as a "race man" who was deeply concerned about the injustices that African Americans suffered and was committed to bringing about change.

Porter attempted to maintain friendly relations with the city's older black leaders, but he let it be known that they did not speak for him. Porter's status in the black community reached its peak when he became the mayoral candidate of the newly formed **Lincoln Independent Party** in 1921. Although he received only 274 votes, his campaign was seen as a success. The Lincoln Independent Party was a sign that change was long overdue, and the Republican Party later admitted spending a considerable sum of money to ensure an overwhelming defeat of the newly formed party. W. E. B. DuBois and the **National Association for the Advancement of Colored People** applauded the campaign and claimed that the 274 votes reported were a mere 10th of the total votes cast for Porter. The rest were allegedly dumped into the Ohio River or simply not counted at the polls. After the election, Porter went back to operating his funeral home. He was survived by his wife, Imogene, and four children: Arthur Jr., **Woodford R.,** Ferda Burden, and Clara. He is buried in Louisville Memorial Gardens. In 2014, A. D. Porter and Sons, Inc. is still owned and operated by the Porter family.

A.D. Porter and Sons. http://www.adporters.com/ (accessed August 7, 2014).

Wright, George C. *Life Behind a Veil: Blacks in Louisville, Kentucky, 1865–1930.* Baton Rouge: Louisiana State Univ. Press, 1985.

PORTER, JAMES RICE (b. ca. 1870, Nashville, TN; d. 1943, Lexington, KY), racetrack official and businessman. James Rice Porter, born in Nashville, TN, was the son of Sandy Porter, a fruit peddler, and Lizzie Porter. In the early 1880s, Nashville did not have a high school for African Americans. In 1886, Porter's mother, Lizzie, challenged the segregated school system of Nashville when she attempted to enroll her two sons, Tolbert Calvin and James Rice, in the city's only public high school. Even though they were refused admittance, Lizzie's boldness encouraged other black parents to attempt to enroll their children. The school board's admission rejections led to mass meetings and petitions that resulted in the board's capitulation. Meigs High School became the first black high school in Nashville when Tolbert, one of three boys in a class of seven, graduated in 1888. James Rice Porter graduated the next year.

Writer **Alice Dunnigan** wrote that Porter attended Purdue University in Lafayette, IN, and, at age 20, he worked in Chicago as a lunch-counter waiter. His job introduced him to racetrack patrons and helped him obtain a job as a horse clocker at the Chicago track. The 1900 U.S. federal census recorded that Porter, age 29, was working as a day laborer and living with his family in Nashville. By 1907, Porter lived in Louisville, KY, and, according to Dunnigan, "was soon named an official identifier of race horses, the first of his race to hold such a position in the state." He owned two horses that were quartered at Louisville's Churchill Downs. The *Louisville Courier-Journal* described his horse Nine as a "rheumatic horse" and quoted Porter about the horse's abilities and failures.

In 1919, Porter, considered one of the oldest timers in the country, became the racing secretary of the Colored Fair Association in Lexington, KY. The next year, he and his wife, Carrie, were rooming in New Orleans, LA, while he worked as a racetrack timer. By 1926, Porter was back in Lexington, and the Colored

Fair Association elected him president. Many horse people considered him a respected authority not only on horses but also on racetracks. One newspaper reported his evaluation of Kentucky's Latonia track as one of the best.

Porter was active not only in the horse industry but also in civic organizations and businesses. In the 1930s, he worked in real estate and served as executive chairman of the Colored Voters League, treasurer of the A&M Realty Company, vice president of the Domestic Realty Company, and chairman of the Board of Directors of the **Mammoth Life and Accident Insurance Company** of Louisville. He was a member of the Elks, the Masons, and the Knights of Pythias. In 1935, he and other prominent leaders pushed for African American police officers and firefighters in Lexington. The next year, two black men were appointed to the city police force. Porter's older brother, Tolbert Calvin, who had also moved to Lexington and worked as a bricklayer, died in 1941. James Rice Porter died two years later in 1943.

Cox, Deborah Oeser. "Friends of Metropolitan Archives of Nashville and Davidson County: Meigs School." Metro Nashville Archives, 2012, http://freepages.school-alumni.rootsweb.ancestry.com/~nashvillearchives/meigs.html (accessed April 17, 2012).
Dunnigan, Alice Allison, comp and ed. *The Fascinating Story of Black Kentuckians: Their Heritage and Traditions*. Washington, DC: Associated Publishers, 1982.
Kentucky Death Records, 1852–1953.
Lovett, Bobby L. *The African-American History of Nashville, Tennessee, 1780–1930: Elites and Dilemmas*. Fayetteville: Univ. of Arkansas Press, 1999.
Newspapers: "Turf Gossip from South," *CJ*, December 9, 1907, 6; "Colored Fair Association Organized," *DRF*, July 27, 1919, 2.
U.S. Federal Census (1870, 1880, 1900, 1920, 1930).

—*Sallie L. Powell*

PORTER, ORA FRANCES (b. 1879, Sugar Grove, KY; d. 1970, Bowling Green, KY), first registered nurse in Bowling Green, KY. Although many sources list Ora Frances Porter's birth year as 1880, the Social Security Death Index documented her birthdate as October 15, 1879. She and her mother, Sarah Porter, frequently lived with relatives. When Porter was 10, they moved from her birthplace of Sugar Grove in Butler Co. to nearby Bowling Green. She attended Tuskegee Institute School of Nursing and, during school vacations, worked as a nurse for white Tuskegee contributors in Florida. On the basis of a recommendation from Booker T. Washington, she worked for the family of John D. Rockefeller Jr., a Tuskegee donor.

After her 1904 graduation, Porter returned to Bowling Green to live with her mother and worked at St. Joseph Hospital, a privately owned institution. She also assisted in the State Laboratory. She later obtained additional training at Lincoln Hospital in New York. In 1916, she became the first registered nurse in Bowling Green. Some sources expanded her registered nurse role to the first in western Kentucky or the state.

In 1920, Porter purchased a two-story home at 715 College St. She entered private practice, nursing mostly for white families. Understanding the importance of sanitation, she supervised the cleaning of houses and when necessary for sanitary purposes,

cooked meals in her patients' homes. Her reputation as a quality nurse increased during the 1922 typhoid fever epidemic.

In 1946, Porter, along with some other African American women, organized the George Washington Carver Club, which became a youth center for the community. She served as one of its directors for many years. In 1949, she helped coordinate the Interracial Commission and served on its board of directors for the entire three years of the association's existence.

In 1960, Porter retired from nursing but continued to substitute for registered nurses at Bowling Green's City-County Hospital. She died at age 90 on February 4, 1970, and was interred in **Mt. Moriah Cemetery.**

Jeffrey, Jonathan, and Mike Wilson, comps. *Mt. Moriah Cemetery: A History and Census of Bowling Green, Kentucky's African-American Cemetery*. Bowling Green, KY: Landmark Association, 2002.
Newspapers: "Letters to the Editor: Miss Porter First Registered Nurse," *BGDN*, January 14, 1968, 9; "Black Heritage Grant Funding Sought for Center," *Park City Daily News* (Bowling Green, KY), September 25, 2007, 3A.
Potter, Eugenia K., ed. *Kentucky Women: Two Centuries of Indomitable Spirit and Vision*. Louisville, KY: Big Tree Press, 1997.
Social Security Death Index.
U.S. Federal Census (1880, 1900, 1910, 1930).

—*Sallie L. Powell*

PORTER, OTHA DANDRITH (b. 1865, Logan Co., KY; d. 1936, Bowling Green, KY), physician and civic leader. Born in December 1865 in Logan Co. and the son of Robert and Amanda Foster Porter, Otha Dandrith Porter attended African American public schools in Bowling Green and taught in local county schools. In 1878, realizing the need for educated health professionals, he enrolled at Nashville's Fisk University, where his first college roommate was the future **National Association for the Advancement of Colored People** leader W. E. B. DuBois; the two remained friends for life. Financial difficulties required Porter to continue teaching, but he graduated with a bachelor's degree in 1891. He earned a medical degree from Tennessee's Meharry Medical College in 1894 and returned to Bowling Green, where he established his practice as the town's first African American physician.

In April 1895, he married Carolyn "Carrie" Bridges, a Fisk acquaintance, in an impressive ceremony in Macon, Noxubee Co., MS. The wedding party numbered 10, the groom wore a double-breasted Prince Albert suit, and the bride wore a white silk dress with a train and white kid gloves and slippers. The Porters' wedding clothes are preserved in the Costume Collection of the Kentucky Library and Museum in Bowling Green.

As a medical college graduate, Porter held a unique position among Kentucky doctors, both black and white, many of whom had not attended undergraduate or medical schools. He became a lifelong member of the National American Negro Medical Association of Physicians, Dentists, and Pharmacists (later the National Negro Medical Association and now, since 1908, the National Medical Association). He was elected the organization's president in 1899. He helped found the State Medical Association and was a member of the state associations of both African American and white doctors.

Beginning in 1894, from various locations on Main and State Sts. in Bowling Green, Porter practiced medicine in south central Kentucky for the next 40 years; in 1906, he built the Porter Building, an office building on Main St. After 1901, the Porters lived in a two-story brick house on State St.

Although it is impossible to estimate the extent of Porter's practice because no business records have survived, local funeral home records from 1894 and vital statistics after 1911 indicate that he treated patients for a variety of diseases. The health of African Americans in south central Kentucky improved after Porter's arrival. No longer did death certificates indicate "too much whiskey" or simply "chills"; instead, a specific diagnosis with Latin terminology was provided.

The Porters had no children; they did act as guardians of a niece. They attended State Street Baptist Church, where Dr. Porter was a trustee and Mrs. Porter was active in the missionary society. Mrs. Porter has been described as aloof, but Dr. Porter became a mentor for local black youths, including **Z. K. Jones,** who opened a medical practice in Bowling Green in 1912.

Dr. O. D. Porter remained an active practitioner until his unexpected death from a stroke on January 21, 1936. Mrs. Porter died in 1968. Her will bequeathed the couple's portraits to Fisk University. They are both buried in Bowling Green's **Mt. Moriah Cemetery.**

Baird, Nancy. Interview, Western Kentucky University-Kentucky Library, October 1, 2009.

Jeffrey, Jonathan, and Mike Wilson. *Mt. Moriah Cemetery: A History and Census of Bowling Green, Kentucky's African-American Cemetery.* Bowling Green, KY: Landmark Association, 2002.

Richardson, Clement. *The National Cyclopedia of the Colored Race.* Vol. 1. Montgomery, AL: National Publishing Co., 1919.

Vertical Files, Kentucky Library and Museum, Western Kentucky Univ., Bowling Green.

—*Carol Crowe Carraco*

PORTER, WOODFORD ROY (b. 1918, Louisville, KY; d. 2006, Louisville, KY), first African American elected to the Louisville Board of Education and the University of Louisville Board of Trustees. The son of Imogene Stewart Porter and **Arthur D. Porter Sr.,** Woodford Roy Porter was born in Louisville, KY, in 1918. His father was the owner and operator of A. D. Porter and Sons Funeral Home, one of the first African American businesses in the city of Louisville. After graduating from **Central High School** in 1936, Woodford had aspirations to go to college, but the local institution of higher education, University of Louisville, did not accept African Americans at the time.

During World War II, Woodford was drafted and served in the navy throughout the whole campaign. After his service in the military, he became the director of his father's funeral business. Porter continued as a sound patron of and participant in the educational system. He was the first African American to serve on the Louisville Board of Education. As a board member, he played an integral part in the merger of the city and Jefferson Co. school systems. He simultaneously served on the Board of Trustees of the University of Louisville for 32 years, also the first African American to hold this position. He served four terms as the chairman of the University of Louisville board. He was a key person

on the board when it sought to make Louisville a full-fledged university.

As recognition of his contributions to the campus, the University of Louisville established the Woodford Porter Scholarship Fund in 1980, as well as the Society of Porter Scholars. It also awarded him the Presidential Medal in 2004. In 2005, Porter established the Harriett Bibb Porter Cancer Education and Prevention Endowment with a $250,000 donation for the James Brown Cancer Center. He died at the age of 87 on August 2, 2006.

"Whereas, Woodford R. Porter August 2, 2006." http://www.louisvilleky.gov/www.louisvilleky.gov/downloads/council/3228.doc (accessed January 27, 2010).

"Woodford Porter Made Louisville a Better Place." *Business First: Louisville,* 2006. http://louisville.bizjournals.com/louisville/stories/2006/08/07/editorial4.html (accessed January 27, 2010).

—*Vincent Gonzalez*

PORTERFIELD, ROSELLA FRENCH (b. 1918, near Owensboro, KY; d. 2004, Florence, KY), educator. Teacher, librarian, and civil rights pioneer Rosella French Porterfield was one of eight children born to a poor farming couple. The family lived about 12 miles south of Owensboro, KY, on a 40-acre farm that her father had inherited, in a community known as Crane Pond Frog's Ankle Station. Rosella's early education was in an all-black one-room schoolhouse about three miles from her home. After she finished there, she attended all-black Western High School in Owensboro, where she was valedictorian of her graduating class. She then entered Kentucky State College (later known as **Kentucky State University**) at Frankfort and earned a BA in English in 1940. Rosella married Vernon Porterfield in 1944, and they had one son, David. The family moved into a home on Chambers Rd. in Walton, where Rosella lived for the remainder of her life.

Porterfield's first teaching position was at the all-black **Dunbar School** in **Elsmere.** She had no automobile, so she traveled to school each morning on a Greyhound bus that operated between Lexington and Cincinnati. One morning, she started to sit near the front of the bus and was told by the driver that blacks had to sit in the back. She sternly informed him that she had three brothers in U.S. military service, fighting for their country, and that fact entitled her to sit anywhere she chose. The other passengers all applauded her action, and a white serviceman, home on furlough, stood up and offered her his seat. Porterfield said that she never considered herself an activist or even a role model, but she did not appreciate being treated like a second-class citizen. She taught the first three grades at Dunbar School for seven years and then became head teacher at the new, all-black Wilkins Heights School, part of the Erlanger-Elsmere Schools. When she arrived at her new position, she found no books or supplies, not even an encyclopedia. She immediately told the Erlanger-Elsmere school superintendent, Edgar Arnett, that she needed materials to teach properly, and he saw that they were provided. When the U.S. Supreme Court ruling in **Brown v. Board of Education** in 1954 made segregated schools illegal, the Erlanger-Elsmere School District, at the urging of Porterfield, became one of the first districts in Kentucky to desegregate peacefully. Porterfield retired from teaching in 1980, and the community honored her by naming an Elsmere playground and a school library for her.

For many years, she was a member of Zion Baptist Church in Walton, where she served as Sunday school superintendent, organist, teacher, and choir director. She died at age 85 in St. Luke Hospital West in Florence, KY. Funeral services were held at the First Baptist Church in Elsmere, and she was buried in Richwood Cemetery in Walton.

Newspapers: "Civil-Rights Pioneer Porterfield Honored," *KE*, July 25, 2002, C1; "Before Rosa, There Was Rosella," *CP*, December 18, 2003, 1C; "Rosella French Porterfield," *KP*, November 8. 2004, 8A; "Rosella French Porterfield, 85, Helped Integrate Schools," *CE*, November 10, 2004, C4.

POSTELL, PETER (b. 1841, unknown; d. 1901, Hopkinsville, KY), prominent businessman. Posy J. Glass, a Virginian, bought a boy named Peter, who was born into slavery in an unknown place in one of the Carolinas. In 1858, Glass brought Peter to Hopkinsville, KY. According to one newspaper source, three years later, Peter ran away and joined Company H, 16th U.S. Colored Infantry. However, his service records show that Peter Glass enlisted at Clarksville, TN, about 30 miles south of Hopkinsville, with the rank of 1st sergeant on January 29, 1864. On September 14, 1865, Glass lost rank through a court-martial sentence.

His court-martial or his desire to begin a new life as a freeman may have caused him to change his last name to Postell. He returned to Hopkinsville and opened a grocery store. In 1866, he married his wife, Pauline. The couple had 10 children and lived in a two-story brick home on the corner of Fifth and Clay Sts. The 1880 U.S. federal census listed his 61-year-old mother, C. Kirkpatrick, and stepfather, Ned Kirkpatrick, living with the family. After his grocery store burned in 1882, Postell built a two-story brick building on the corner of Sixth and Virginia Sts. As the business prospered, he purchased more property and owned nearly the full city block. He was known for financing public improvements, including purchasing $1,000 worth of shares in the Hotel Latham.

In 1896, Kentucky governor William O. Bradley nominated Postell's oldest son, John, age 27, steward of the Western Kentucky Asylum for the Insane. However, the Kentucky Senate refused to confirm an African American in that position. He was then assigned a position with the Internal Revenue Service.

Postell's second son, Peter Postell Jr., helped manage the grocery store and later became the assistant secretary at the Republican State Convention in Louisville, KY. He and his wife, Fannie, were active in education. He served on the school board, and she served as teacher, principal, and school superintendent.

All of Postell's daughters attended Fisk University. His youngest son, Zachariah, died at age 22, one year before Postell.

Described as a "light mulatto of almost gigantic frame," Postell died of heart disease on May 22, 1901, and was buried in East Hill Cemetery. Sources' estimates of the value of his estate ranged from $100,000 to $500,000. Some labeled him "the richest negro in the South." Others thought that he was the wealthiest black man in Kentucky.

Postell left everything to his wife on the condition that she never would remarry. Pauline left Kentucky with some of their daughters in 1904. Between 1912 and 1914, the family home was used as a hospital by eight Hopkinsville doctors. John later moved to Henderson, KY, where he died in 1918. Pauline died in 1922, and Peter Jr. died in 1944.

Civil War Pension Index: General Index to Pension Files, 1861–1934.
Newspapers: "Peter Postell," *HK*, May 24, 1901, 5; "Richest Negro in the South Dead," *Keowee Courier* (Walhalla, SC), May 29, 1901, 1; "Postell Example of Black Who Made Mark in Business," *KNE*, September 30, 1997, A1–A2.
U.S. Colored Troops Military Service Records, 1861–1865.
U.S. Federal Census (1870, 1880, 1900).
—Sallie L. Powell

POSTON, ERSA HINES (b. 1921, Mayfield, KY; d. 2009, Bethesda, MD), first African American woman to serve on the U.S. Civil Service Commission. Born on May 3, 1921, in Mayfield, KY, to Vivian Johnson Hines and Robert Hines, Ersa Poston (née Hines) moved to Paducah, KY, at age four when her mother died. She graduated from Kentucky State College for Negroes (later known as **Kentucky State University**) in 1942 and then completed a master's degree in social work at Atlanta University (later named Clark Atlanta University) in 1946.

Poston held positions in the New York state government before being named an assistant to Governor Nelson Rockefeller in 1966. She was named the director of the state's Office of Economic Opportunity in 1965. From 1967 to 1975, Poston served as president of the state's Civil Service Commission. She later served as a delegate to the United Nations and was appointed by President Gerald Ford to the National Commission on the Observance of International Women's Year.

Poston was nominated to the U.S. Civil Service Commission under President Jimmy Carter, a position she had declined under the Nixon administration. When the commission was divided, Poston was named vice chair of the Merit System Protection Board. She held that position until she retired in 1983, although she continued to serve as a consultant to the U.S. State Department. In 1983, she observed that "a lot has changed, but I'm a little upset. I'm not sure I agree with the figures that tell us black women are rising in government. I see a diminishing level of black women in strategic positions where they can serve as mentors for black and white younger women."

Poston was married twice, to John Clinton and Ted Poston, and divorced both men. She died of pneumonia on January 7, 2009, in Bethesda, MD.

The American Presidency Project. "Civil Service Commission Nomination of Ersa H. Poston to Be a Commissioner." http://www.presidency.ucsb.edu/ws/index.php?pid=7445 (accessed January 1, 2011).
"Ersa H. Poston, 87, Female Pioneer in US Civil Service, January 24, 2009." http://www.boston.com/bostonglobe/obituaries/articles/2009/01/24/ersa_h_poston_87_female_pion (accessed July 2, 2013).
Goddard, Alison. "Hers Is Not a 'Female' Job." *Rock Hill (SC) Herald-Leader*, March 26, 1973.
"Poston Exits Merit Board: Take This Job and Shove It." *Jet* 64, no. 19 (July 18, 1983): 36–37.
—Kevin Hogg

POSTON, ROBERT LINCOLN (b. 1890, Hopkinsville, KY; d. 1924, on a ship in the Atlantic Ocean) and POSTON, ULYSSES

SIMPSON (b. 1891, Hopkinsville, KY; d. 1955, Brooklyn, NY), newspapermen. At a time when many African Americans were illiterate, teachers Ephraim and Mollie Poston emphasized education to their eight children. They named most of their sons after historic individuals, beginning with Frederick Douglass, Robert Lincoln, and Ulysses Simpson and ending with their youngest child, **Theodore Roosevelt Augustus Poston.** The children also learned to confront discrimination. In 1908, Mollie Poston filed a lawsuit against the Illinois Central Railroad Company for $2,000 damages because the company had removed her from one of its trains. She was awarded $325.

Between 1912 and 1914, Ephraim commuted between Hopkinsville and Frankfort as a professor at Kentucky Normal and Industrial Institute (later known as **Kentucky State University**). In 1916, Robert taught school and attended the Kentucky Educational Association conference in Louisville, where blacks and whites attended the meetings. In 1918, Robert and Ulysses served in the military as sergeants but became outraged by the brutal treatment of black soldiers by their white superiors in Louisville. Their protests garnered them demotions.

After their discharge, the brothers launched their newspaper, the *Hopkinsville Contender;* Ted worked as the paper's copyboy. After upsetting local white residents with their editorials against segregation, Robert and Ulysses moved to Detroit and renamed their paper the *Detroit Contender.* The brothers then became very active with Marcus Garvey, founder of the Universal Negro Improvement Association, and followed his message of pan-Africanism. They then moved to New York. Robert quickly advanced and became the group's assistant secretary general, and Ulysses administered the organization's various business enterprises. In 1922, Garvey launched the association's newspaper, *Negro Times,* and chose Ulysses as its managing editor.

In 1924, a month after his 34th birthday, while returning from a mission trip in Africa (Liberia), Robert died of double pneumonia. Marcus Garvey delivered his eulogy. Robert's body was returned to Hopkinsville and was interred in Cave Spring Cemetery.

After Robert's death, Ulysses increased his political activity as president of the National Colored Political Association in the interest of forming a third political party for African Americans. He also became a real estate broker and continued his journalistic activism with the Calvins News Service. He died on May 14, 1955, and was buried in Long Island National Cemetery, Farmingdale, NY.

González, Juan, and Joseph Torres. *News for All the People: The Epic Story of Race and the American Media.* London and New York: Verso, 2011.

Hauke, Kathleen A. *The Dark Side of Hopkinsville: Stories by Ted Poston.* Athens: Univ. of Georgia Press, 1991.

Newspapers: "Many Caiming [*sic*] Indictments," *HK,* October 22, 1908, 4; "Christian Has Sixty White and Colored Teachers Attending These Meetings," *HK,* April 20, 1916, 1; "Colored Paper," *HK,* September 24, 1919, 4; "R. L. Poston of U.N.I.A. Dead," *Cleveland Gazette,* March 29, 1924, 1; "Third Party Hopes for Negro Support," *NYT,* September 7, 1924, E1; "Ulysses S. Poston, Real Estate Man," *NYT,* May 16, 1955, 23.

U.S. Federal Census (1910, 1930).

U.S. Passport Applications, 1795–1925.

U.S. Veterans Gravesites, ca. 1775–2006.

—*Sallie L. Powell*

POSTON, THEODORE ROOSEVELT AUGUSTUS MAJOR (b. 1906, Hopkinsville, KY; d. 1974, Brooklyn, NY), first full-time African American reporter for a daily newspaper. Born in Hopkinsville to Ephraim and Mollie Cox Poston, Ted Poston was the youngest of eight children in a politically active and well-connected family. After working for a series of family-owned regional papers and completing a bachelor's degree in journalism, Poston moved to New York, where he ran his brother **Ulysses Poston**'s *New York Contender* and wrote regular columns for the *Pittsburgh Courier;* the *Amsterdam News* hired him full-time in 1931.

Poston was one of the founding members of the Newspaper Guild, and his attempts to organize the *News* resulted in his acrimonious departure from that paper in 1935, the same year in which he began working on an inch-rate basis for the *New York Post.* Later that year, Ted Poston became the first African American reporter hired full-time by a major white daily. Poston worked closely with Roosevelt administration officials as a member of the Black Cabinet and in the Office of War Information. With exception of this five-year break, his career at the *Post* spanned 35 years. During his tenure, Poston covered the boycotts, court decisions, and untimely deaths of the **civil rights movement,** pricking the conscience of the *Post*'s large readership with a witty style imbued with that movement's hope.

Hauke, Kathleen A. *Ted Poston: Pioneer American Journalist.* Athens: Univ. of Georgia Press, 1998.

—*Kristy Howell*

POTTER, MARY ETTA PORTER (b. 1882, Bowling Green, KY; d. 1929, Louisville, KY), medical doctor. The daughter of Woodford and Annie Porter, Mary Etta Porter was born in Bowling Green, KY, in 1882. She was educated at Bowling Green's black State Street High School and graduated from State Colored Baptist University (later known as **Simmons College of Kentucky**) in Louisville. She also matriculated at Hampton Industrial Institute and Dixie Hospital in Virginia. She returned to Louisville and taught at the Kentucky Institute for the Colored Blind for three years. In 1907, she earned her medical degree from **Louisville National Medical College.**

By 1911, Porter had married Joseph Virgil Potter, a chauffeur and mechanic, and had established her medical practice at her residence at 532 S. Eighth St., which she later called Mary Etta Apartments. As a physician who specialized in women's and children's diseases, Potter was elected to the faculty of Louisville National Medical College where she served as a faculty member for three years. She established the Fraternal Hospital Training School for Nurses in 1922. This organization met the standard requirements of Kentucky's Board of Nurse Examiners.

Potter was a member of various medical associations, including the Falls City Medical Society and the State Association of Negro Physicians, Pharmacists and Dentists of Kentucky. She served as a medical examiner for five female organizations.

Active in diverse fraternal groups, Potter also founded and organized the Women's Business, Civic and Political Club in 1925 and was chief of the editorial staff of the club's journal.

Potter died of complications from hay fever on September 12, 1929. Her half brother, **Arthur D. Porter,** a Louisville undertaker, handled the burial arrangements. She was interred in the Louisville Cemetery.

Boris, Joseph J., ed. *Who's Who in Colored America, 1928–1929.* New York: Who's Who in Colored America Corp., 1929.

Directory of Deceased American Physicians, 1804–1929. Vol. 2. Chicago: American Medical Association, 1993.

Kentucky, Death Records, 1852–1953.

U.S. City Directories, 1821–1989: Louisville, Kentucky, City Directory (1905, 1911, 1922).

U.S. Federal Census (1920).

—*Sheila Pressley*

POWELL, RUTH MARIE (DAVIDSON) (b. 1912, Madisonville, KY; d. 2000, Flint, MI), religious author. Ruth Marie Davidson was the first child of John S. and Louise Davidson, who were in their mid-30s when she was born near Madisonville, KY, in Hopkins Co., on February 4, 1912. John, originally from North Carolina, was a coal miner. The family soon moved to nearby Providence, KY, in Webster Co., where John began his funeral home business and Louise became a teacher.

Ruth attended Paducah's West Kentucky Industrial College (previously known as West Kentucky Industrial College and now as **West Kentucky Community and Technical College**). She married Rev. John Lewis Powell on June 6, 1935. Five years later, she earned her AB degree from Johnson C. Smith University in Charlotte, NC. Her father, in his 60s, had also moved the family to his native state of North Carolina, where he continued in the undertaking business and Ruth's younger sister taught school.

In 1947, Ruth M. Powell and her husband, John, moved to Nashville when he became the dean of students and professor of missions at American Baptist Theological Seminary. In 1953, Powell earned her MS degree from Tennessee State University. Two years later, she became an assistant professor in education at her alma mater. In 1964, she published *Lights and Shadows: The Story of American Baptist Theological Seminary,* which provided historical information on the seminary's training of ministers. In 1981, she authored *Ventures in Education with Black Baptists in Tennessee, 1883–1968.*

Powell died two weeks after her 88th birthday. A few years later, Powell's church, Faith United Missionary Baptist Church, memorialized her with the Ruth Marie Powell Women's Conference.

Dunnigan, Alice Allison, comp. and ed. *The Fascinating Story of Black Kentuckians: Their Heritage and Traditions.* Washington, DC: Associated Publishers, 1982.

Social Security Death Index.

U.S. Federal Census (1910, 1920, 1930, 1940).

Who's Who in Religion. 2nd ed. Chicago: Marquis Who's Who, 1977.

—*Sallie L. Powell*

POWERS, GEORGIA MONTGOMERY DAVIS (b. 1923, Springfield, KY), first woman and first African American elected to the Kentucky Senate. Born on October 29, 1923, in Springfield, KY, as Georgia Montgomery, the second of nine children and the only girl of Frances (Walker) and Ben Montgomery, Georgia was always determined to rise above the discrimination her gender and interracial heritage imposed on her. In 1925, the Montgomery family moved to Louisville, where Georgia received the majority of her education. She attended Virginia Avenue Elementary School (1929–1934), Madison Junior High School (1934–1937), **Central High School** (1937–1940), and **Louisville Municipal College** (1940–1942). Additionally, she received certificates from the Central Business School and the United States Government IBM Supervisory School. A year after her graduation from Louisville Municipal College, she married Norman F. Davis. The couple had one son, William F. Davis. In 1968, the couple divorced, and Georgia married James F. Powers in 1973.

Powers began her political career training volunteers for Wilson Wyatt's U.S. Senate campaign in 1962. She led campaigns for candidates for governor of Kentucky, mayor of Louisville, the U.S. House and Senate, and U.S. president within the next five years. Additionally, she participated in many civil rights activities throughout the 1960s. As one of the organizers of the **Allied Organizations for Civil Rights,** a group that worked toward the enactment of fair-employment and public-accommodations laws, she helped organize the 1964 **March on Frankfort.** Dr. Martin Luther King Jr. was the keynote speaker. The next year, Powers helped organize the **Kentucky Christian Leadership Conference** and attended the historic march in Selma, AL, supporting the national Voting Rights Act. Among many other important civil rights activities, she marched with Dr. King in the Memphis sanitation struggle.

In 1967, Powers ran for the Kentucky State Senate with endorsements from the AFL-CIO, the Kentucky Medical Association, the Kentucky and Louisville Education Associations, and the Louisville Chamber of Commerce. She won that seat easily,

Georgia Powers.

and her first bill for statewide housing passed in no time. She collaborated with Representatives **Mae Street Kidd** and **Hughes E. McGill** in introducing the first open-housing law in the South, which was passed in 1968. Other legislation that she either sponsored or cosponsored included bills for low-cost housing, the Equal Rights Amendment Resolution, and a bill to omit "race" from Kentucky driver's licenses. She was also the secretary of the Kentucky Democratic Caucus during her entire senatorial career. While serving in the Kentucky Senate for 21 years, she chaired the Health and Welfare Committee (1970–1976) and served as a member of the Rules Committee (1976–1978) and the Labor and Industry Committee for 10 years (1978–1988).

Since her retirement in 1988, Powers has received numerous accolades. In 1995, she published her memoirs, *I Shared the Dream: The Pride, Passion, and Politics of the First Black Woman Senator from Kentucky.* She also published *The Adventures of the Book of Revelation* in 1998 and *Celia's Land, a Historical Novel* in 2004.

"Georgia M. Powers, Mrs." *Who's Who among African Americans.* 17th ed. Detroit: Gale Group, 2004.

Georgia M. Powers Papers. Special Collections, Paul G. Blazer Library, Kentucky State Univ., Frankfort.

"Georgia Powers." *Notable Black American Women,* vol. 1, edited by Jessie Carney Smith. Detroit: Gale Research, 1992.

Powers, Georgia Davis. *I Shared the Dream: The Pride, Passion, and Politics of the First Black Woman Senator from Kentucky.* Far Hills, NJ: New Horizon Press, 1995.

—*Karen Cotton McDaniel*

PRALLTOWN, the oldest African American neighborhood in Lexington, KY. A few years after the Civil War, Colonel John A. Prall, a white attorney and legislator, bought land prone to flooding on S. Limestone St. for $1.25 an acre. He divided the property into lots, which later became the predominantly African American neighborhood of Pralltown. Prall named two of the streets after family members. Lottie St. was named in honor of his oldest daughter, and Winnie St. (which still exists) was named for his wife's sister. The community was created in stages between 1868 and 1877. Most of the inhabitants were farm laborers and freed slaves. Unlike many Kentucky **African American hamlets,** Pralltown did not have a school or church.

In 1952, the citizens of Pralltown began their first of many battles against the University of Kentucky's attempts to engulf the community and their fight against what scholar Jennifer Kopf called "purification." In September, the Lexington Slum Clearance and Redevelopment Agency, which was part of the national organization of the Division of Slum Clearance of the Housing and Home Finance Agency, surveyed the area with plans for clearance, redevelopment, and relocation of citizens. The University of Kentucky was one organization that expressed interest in the area once it was redeveloped.

In the 1960s, the University of Kentucky did purchase some property in Pralltown. In 1975, urban renewal brought discussions of single-family units versus multifamily units for the university. Although urban renewal destroyed some homes in the 1970s, after a change in political administration, funds were no longer available to provide low-income housing. Louis Watkins,

a Pralltown resident since 1914, questioned whether the urban-renewal efforts truly sought to help the community. He believed that the organization was "a tool of the university [the University of Kentucky] that bought our land and sold it to the university for its purposes or to private developers who wanted to build expensive housing on the land so that blacks wouldn't have been able to move back into the community after they were displaced."

In some sense, Pralltown was an enclave shut off from society by its boundaries of S. Limestone St., Virginia Ave., and the Southern Railroad. However, beginning in the 1960s, its citizens celebrated Pralltown Day on the Saturday of Labor Day weekend at Lou Johnson Park, which was named for **Louis Brown "Sweet Lou" Johnson,** the first African American major-league baseball player from Lexington. Johnson frequently returned for the event, which was filled with food, a parade, and games. By the end of the twentieth century, most of the remaining buildings of Pralltown have been surrounded by student housing of the University of Kentucky and facilities of Lexingon Theological Seminary.

Kopf, Jennifer. "Neighborhood Hygiene and 'Removal' in the U.S. South: The Purification of Pralltown during the Civil War Reconstruction and 1960s Urban Renewal Eras." *Historical Geography* 25 (1997), 148–64.

Newspapers: "Col. John A. Prall," *Bourbon News,* October 8, 1907, 1; "Pralltown May Be Redeveloped for U.K., College of Bible," *L-L,* September 28, 1952, 1; "Housing Project, Rent Subsidies Give Home to Pralltown Residents," *L-L,* July 24, 1977, A-1; "Protecting Pralltown," *LHL,* Bluegrass Communities, September 2, 1998, 3; "Old Neighboorhood Still Having Fun," *LHL,* September 5, 1999, B1.

—*Sallie L. Powell*

PREWITT, CLIFTON BLACKBURN (b. 1826, Scott Co., KY; d. unknown), real estate dealer. Born into slavery in Scott Co. on July 4, 1826, Clifton Blackburn Prewitt struggled to acquire an education. By the end of the Civil War, he had gained a basic understanding of reading and mathematics. He spent several years sharecropping, saving his money, and investing wisely. He was able to purchase his own farm after five years, where he grew hemp and wheat.

After deciding that "to make money one must spend money," Prewitt took 18 years' worth of earnings from his farm and invested in real estate. Frequently in competition with local white businessmen, he advertised extensively and purchased several homes in Georgetown, KY. At one point, he owned more than 20 lots in the city, and he eventually owned several homes that he rented out to white residents. One of his properties was a rock quarry with an accompanying "stately three-bay house" on the corner of Elley Alley and W. Jackson St., which he purchased from Mettie and Paul O'Neill in 1892.

Prewitt was also actively engaged in the Georgetown area. He, along with his wife, Harriet Fauntroy, was a longtime member of the First Baptist Church, and he held stock in the Georgetown Electric Street Railway and the City Ice Factory. A contemporary noted that he was held in high esteem by the local community for his honesty and integrity.

Prewitt was the father-in-law of **W. D. Johnson,** founder and editor of the *Lexington Standard.*

Bevins, Ann Bolton. *Involvement of Blacks in Scott County Commerce during the Postbellum Period (1865–1918)*. Georgetown, KY: Georgetown–Scott County Joint Planning Commission, 1989.

Hamilton, G. P. *Biographical Sketches of Prominent Men and Women of Kentucky*. Memphis: E. H. Clarke & Brother, 1911.

U.S. Federal Census (1880, 1900).

—*Stephen Pickering*

PRICE, JACOB (b. 1839, Woodford Co., KY; d. 1923, Covington, KY), pastor and businessman. Born in central Kentucky, clergyman Jacob Price spent most of his life in Covington, where for more than 60 years he was one of the city's leading African Americans. Price, a freeman before the end of slavery, was listed in the 1860 census as a laborer and a minister of the Gospel. He lived on Bremen St., which was renamed Pershing Ave. during World War I, and it was rumored that he was a conductor on the **Underground Railroad** from that location. Price formed the **First Baptist Church, Covington** (African American), and at the church, the first private school for African American children in the city. He was a businessman and was involved in civil, political, and education rights.

Price was the first pastor of the First Baptist Church, and after a dispute split the church's membership, he became the pastor of Ninth St. Baptist Church. While he was at the First Baptist Church, Price was instrumental in the founding of **Ninth St. Methodist Episcopal Church.**

In 1869 Price, **Isaac Black,** and **William Blackburn** served as members of a delegation representing Covington at the Freedmen's Bureau for Education convention in Louisville. After they returned, Price and the other Covington delegates organized a board of trustees for the city's proposed first two public schools for blacks, one housed in a Baptist church and the other in a Methodist church.

On February 25, 1870, during the statewide African American political convention in Frankfort, some of the newly enfranchised African Americans wanted to vote the straight Republican ticket. However, Price, Black, and Blackburn preferred to vote for anyone who favored policies in the best interests of the African American community. This political position later benefited Covington's African American community when William L. Grant, a white politician, asked Price and other African American community leaders for their support. Grant was an influential businessman and Covington City Council member seeking the Democratic nomination for the office of Kenton Co. representative in the Kentucky legislature. Grant proposed that if the African American voters supported him for office, he would have the city charter of Covington amended to provide for a public school for black children. Grant received the nomination, and a new Covington city charter soon provided for an African American school. Price's political acumen had been demonstrated.

In 1882, Price owned and operated a lumberyard and sheds in the area of Fourth St. and Madison Ave. The sheds occupied an area of 60 by 90 feet and had a storage capacity of half a million board feet of lumber. He continued in the lumber business until 1894. In 1899, Price was named president of the Colored Laborers' Union.

Price died in 1923 at age 84 in Covington and was buried in Evergreen Cemetery in Southgate. On Janaury 26, 1939, the Covington Municipal Housing Commission named the new housing complex for blacks in honor of Price, stating that "no Negro citizen is better known than the late Jacob Price."

Newspapers: "School Opened Oct. 14 in Basement of Methodist Church on Madison St. between 2 & 2," *CJ*, October 19, 1872, 3; "Headquarters for Lumber," *Daily Commonwealth* (Frankfort, KY), November 28, 1882, 2; "Colored Labor Union," *KE*, March 5, 1899, 3; "Negro Pastor Dies," *KP*, March 2, 1923, 1; "Organized First Negro Church," *KTS*, March 2, 1923, 37; "Housing Project to Be Named Latonia Terrace: Negro Settlement to Be Known as 'Jacob Price Homes' in Honor of Leader, Board Reports," *KP*, January 26, 1939, 1.

—*Theodore H. H. Harris*

PRIEST, JAMES M. (b. 1816, Paris, KY; d. 1883, Greenville, Liberia), missionary and Liberian statesman. James M. Priest was born into slavery in Paris, KY. His owner, Jane Anderson Meaux, educated him while they lived in Jessamine Co., KY. Meaux was a devout Presbyterian and believer in the American Colonization Society movement to send freed African Americans to Africa. In 1835, she sent Priest, age 19, as a missionary to Liberia. He returned stateside and arrived in Philadelphia on June 29, 1839.

The next year, Priest entered the Presbyterian-established New Albany Theological Seminary of Chicago, IL (later known as McCormick Theological Seminary). On April 9, 1842, as a member of the Church of Nicholasville, he was licensed, becoming "the first of his race who was called to this work within its bounds." In 1843, after he graduated from seminary, was ordained, and married, the Presbyterian Foreign Board sent him to Liberia.

Priest established a church in Greenville, Sinoe County, Liberia. His wife, Ann, a member of Philadelphia's Central Presbyterian Church, was also a missionary and advocated a school for girls. Additionally, Priest served as Liberia's vice president under President Daniel Bashiel Warner from 1864 to 1867. He and his wife continued to promote their mission work. In 1870, in a fundraising effort, Priest addressed a public meeting of the Pennsylvania Colonization Society in Philadelphia. By 1879, he was considered "the oldest Presbyterian missionary in Africa." Ann died the next year. In 1883, Priest died while serving as one of the justices of the Liberian Supreme Court.

African Repository and Colonial Journal. Washington, DC: American Colonization Society, 1879, 1880.

Halsey, Leroy J. *History of the McCormick Theological Seminary of the Presbyterian Church.* Chicago: McCormick Theological Seminary of the Presbyterian Church, 1893.

Hendrick, William Jackson. *James P. Hendrick, D.D.: Memoirs with an Appendix Containing History of Ebenezer Presbytery and Other Papers.* Cambridge, MA: Riverside Press, 1907.

Newspapers: *Philadelphia Daily Evening Telegraph,* June 14, 1870, 3; "Death of Judge Priest, of Liberia," *Washington (DC) National Republican,* July 23, 1883, 4.

Philadelphia, Passenger and Immigration Lists, 1800–1850.

—*Sallie L. Powell*

PROGRESSIVE BUILDING AND LOAN ASSOCIATION, African American business group. The Progressive Building and Loan Association, a creation of the African American community in Covington, KY, was formed to provide otherwise scarce home financing and business loans for that community. The association submitted its articles of incorporation to the Kenton Co. clerk's office in June 1906. The new corporation's officers were F. L. Williams, principal of Covington's **Lincoln-Grant School,** president, and **Wallace A. Gaines,** a funeral director, secretary. The board of directors included **Charles E. Jones,** a funeral director, and Lawson Thompson, the owner of Steam Carpet Cleaners. The other incorporators were James C. Campbell, a laborer; Charles Carson, a janitor; Nathan A. Fleming, a teacher at Lincoln-Grant School; Ollie B. Havelow, pastor at Lane Chapel C.M.E. Church; and Robert P. Johnson, the principal of the Latonia Colored School. The corporation's capital stock of $50,000 was divided into four classes of shares: $400 shares required payments of 80 cents per week; $200 shares required payments of 40 cents per week; $100 shares required payments of 20 cents per week; and $50 shares required payments of 10 cents per week. Indebtedness of the firm was capped at $20,000. The office was located at the corner of Seventh and Scott Sts., adjacent to the W. A. Gaines Funeral Home.

The Progressive Building and Loan Association was a milestone for the African American community of Covington. The association drew its leaders from all walks of life, and many of them remained in business locally for three or four decades. The distinguished educators and religious leaders who served with the association were consistently chosen for both their abilities and their dedication to service within Covington's African American community. Available records do not indicate what happened to the association after 1910.

Newspapers: "Building Association Will Be Organized," *KP,* May 31, 1906, 2; "Negroes File Papers," *KP,* June 12, 1906, 2; "Estill Is President," *KP,* May 6, 1910, 3.

—*Theodore H. H. Harris*

PRUITT, EARLE ELIAS (b. 1903, Louisville, KY; d. 1959, Louisville, KY), public housing official. The son of Richard Pruitt, a railroad porter, and Minnie Pruitt, Earle Elias Pruitt, a native of Louisville, worked after high school in a machine shop. In 1922, he married Della Evans from Stanford, KY, and worked for several years as a railroad porter. He graduated from Louisville's Simmons University (later known as **Simmons College of Kentucky**) with a bachelor of laws degree in 1931. He became active in the Democratic Party and was "credited with assuring the Democratic Party a majority" beginning in 1932. He served as party chairman in 1936.

From 1937 to 1940, under the U.S. Housing Authority, Pruitt managed the College Court Apartments, the first public housing unit for Louisville's African Americans, and it became "a model for public housing throughout the United States." He then managed Kentucky's largest housing project, Beecher Terrace, for four years. He subsequently secured the position of welfare and finance officer for the United Nations Relief Rehabilitation Administration. In this role, he traveled to Europe to promote public housing. In March 1945, he presented a lecture, "Public Housing in Louisville," over the British Broadcasting Corporation. On November 25, 1945, he returned stateside on the ship *Europa* and continued his managerial work at Beecher Terrace.

Pruitt actively worked for various housing policy groups, like the Management Division of the National Association of Housing Officials, and charitable organizations, like the Red Cross and the War Fund. For over a decade, he advised Louisville mayors. In 1950, he was appointed racial relations assistant with the Louisville Municipal Housing Commission. Six years later, he was awarded an honorary bachelor of laws degree from Monrovia College and Industrial Institute in Liberia, West Africa.

Pruitt died at Louisville's **Red Cross Hospital** on March 15, 1959. Beckett Funeral Home handled the arrangements, and he was interred in Calvary Cemetery. His wife, Della, died in 1966.

Fleming, G. James, and Christian E. Burckel, eds. *Who's Who in Colored America.* 7th ed. *Supplement.* Yonkers-on-Hudson, NY: Christian E. Burckel & Associates, 1950.
"Funeral Service Held for Earle E. Pruitt, Housing Official with an Amazing Record." *LD,* March 19, 1959, 1.
"Inventory of the Papers of Earle E. Pruitt, ca. 1925–1956." Kentuckiana Virtual Library: Digital Library. http://kdl.kyvl.org/ (accessed July 11, 2012).

—*Sallie L. Powell*

PRYOR, MARGARET (b. ca. 1835, Kentucky; d. 1910, Lexington, KY), heiress. Little is known about the early life of Margaret Pryor. Census records indicate that she was born in February 1835, although reports of her age in later life fluctuated. Several relatives recalled that she was born into slavery in Macon, GA, before moving to Danville, KY, while still enslaved. In 1850, she traveled with her master's family to Lexington, KY, where she was eventually purchased by horse breeder Maj. Barak G. Thomas. She remained with him as a "housekeeper and servant" after gaining her freedom at the conclusion of the Civil War.

Newspapers remarked that Pryor, or Aunt Margaret, "as she was known to practically every horseman of note in this country and Europe," was a fixture at Thomas's farm. One account claimed that she had saved Thomas, a former Confederate major, from a beating by opponents during the Civil War, and she possibly had an intimate relationship with her former master, although the evidence is inconclusive. When he passed away on May 16, 1906, it was revealed that Thomas had listed Pryor as the primary beneficiary in his will, bequeathing to her his farm, his remaining Thoroughbreds, and his house in Lexington.

The estate, valued at around $50,000, made Pryor the richest black woman in Kentucky, as well as the target of several lawsuits. Several of Thomas's relatives in South Carolina, who had received relatively small amounts in the will, sued to recover the property, but they were unsuccessful. Her opponents did succeed, however, in challenging a less publicized feature of the will that required that she be buried in Lexington Cemetery, which was segregated at the time. She agreed that she would be buried in a different cemetery and succeeded in retaining the inheritance.

After a long illness that began in December of the preceding year, Margaret Pryor passed away on May 12, 1910. As specified in the earlier conflict over the will, she was not buried next to Barak G. Thomas; instead, she was interred in Cove Haven Cemetery, an African American cemetery adjacent to Lexington Cemetery. Her will left most of her estate to a local white family, the des Cognets, who had been close friends of Thomas. Although she specified that she had no kin, several individuals claiming to be relatives challenged the will, noting that it was "unnatural for a colored woman to leave all her property to white people." Their attempts were unsuccessful, and the will stood.

Newspapers: "Will of Maj. Thomas," *LL,* May 22, 1906, 3; "Margaret Thomas—Ex-Housekeeper for Major Thomas," *LL,* May 12, 1910, 1; "Death of Rich Ex-Slave," *WP,* May 13, 1910, 11; "To Break Will," *LL,* September 15, 1910, 5; "A Mysterious Relationship—In 1906, Servant Inherited Farm, Main St. Home," *LHL,* February 27, 2011, A1.

—*Stephen Pickering*

PURCE, CHARLES L. (b. 1856, Charleston, SC; d. 1905, Louisville, KY), president of Selma University. The son of a slave and a freeman, Charles L. Purce was moved from his birthplace of Charleston, SC, to Georgia at the age of five to avoid being "taken by the Yankees" in 1861. At the conclusion of the Civil War, Purce's family returned to Charleston, where he attended both public and private schools. In 1875, Purce had a religious awakening at Morris Street Baptist Church, and four years later he enrolled in Richmond Theological Seminary in Virginia, graduating with honors in 1883.

After finishing school, Purce returned to South Carolina, where he briefly served as a minister before being elected president of Alabama's Selma University in November 1886. During his tenure as president, he earned a doctorate of divinity from State Colored Baptist University in Louisville (later known as **Simmons College of Kentucky**) and helped rid the Alabama institution of several thousand dollars of debt. By the time he left Selma University, enrollment had increased to over 500 students.

In 1894, Purce accepted the presidency of State University (later known as Simmons College of Kentucky). He was well loved in the community, which celebrated his 10th anniversary at the institution with a rally and an attempt to raise $1,000 to support education in 1904. Purce died in August of the following year.

Newspapers: "University Notes," *AB,* September 16, 1904, 3; "University Notes," *AB,* October 21, 1904, 2.

Pegues, A. W. *Our Baptist Ministers and Schools.* Springfield, MA: Willey & Co., 1892.

Simmons, William. *Men of Mark: Eminent, Progressive and Rising.* Cleveland: George M. Rewell, 1887.

—*Stephen Pickering*

Q

QUILLINGS, CHARLES HARDIN (b. August 30, 1920, Muskogee, OK; d. March 22, 2011, Atlanta, GA), band director and educator. Born in Muskogee, OK, Charles Hardin Quillings graduated from Manual Training High School in Louisville, KY, in 1938. He had been a member of the high school marching band, and he received a music scholarship to Kentucky State College (later known as **Kentucky State University**), where he played in the Kentucky State Collegiate **Jazz** Band. After graduating in 1942, Quillings served in the U.S. Army for four years as an assistant warrant officer while also directing the Jazz Orchestra. In 1947, Quillings was hired as band director at **Dunbar High School,** as well as four elementary schools in Fayette Co., KY: Constitution, **Green P. Russell,** Booker T. Washington., and George Washington Carver. He developed the Dunbar program from just 9 students in 1947 to a 128-member band when the historically black Dunbar High School closed in 1967.

In 1949, Quillings was one of the first five African Americans to enroll in the newly integrated graduate school at the University of Kentucky. He earned a master's degree in music education. After Dunbar High School closed in 1967, Quillings continued to work in the Fayette County Public School District in an administrative capacity. He served as the first African American president of the Kentucky Band Directors from 1968 to 1969. He was also honored as Kentucky's first African American all-state band director. Quillings retired in 1982 and later moved to Atlanta, GA, with his wife, Marie Cruse.

Quillings died in Atlanta on March 22, 2011, and was buried in Cove Haven Cemetery in Lexington, KY.

Newspapers: "Dozens Honor Former Dunbar Band Director—Quillings Calls 20-Year Tenure His 'Dream Job,'" *LHL,* May 27, 2002, D1; "Recognition of Musical Mentor Is Long Overdue," *LHL,* October 23, 2005, A6; "Respected Music Director Taught at First Dunbar—He Kept Playing Long Past Retirement," *LHL,* March 25, 2011, A6.

Quillings, Charles H. Interview by Edward Owens, July 14, 1978. Blacks in Lexington Oral History Project, Louie B. Nunn Center for Oral History, Univ. of Kentucky, Lexington.

—*Elizabeth Schaller*

QUINN CHAPEL AFRICAN METHODIST EPISCOPAL CHURCH, African American church in Louisville, KY. One of Louisville's oldest African American congregations, Quinn Chapel African Methodist Episcopal (A.M.E.) Church was established in 1838 as Bethel, House of God, in a room over a public stable at Second and Main Sts. The church is named after the Right Reverend William Paul Quinn, a senior bishop in the A.M.E. Church from 1848 to 1873 and the first African American bishop to visit the city. About 10 years after its founding, the church relocated to Fourth and Green (Liberty) Sts., where it became known also as the Old Fourth Street Church. With the financial aid of Quaker Friends, Dr. W. R. Revels, pastor, opened the doors of the first school for blacks within the city of Louisville. After another move and a short stay at Ninth and Green Sts., a new brick building for the church was completed and dedicated in 1854 at Ninth St. and **Walnut St.** (now **Muhammad Ali** Blvd.). There the chapel remained until 1910, when it moved to its fifth location at 912 W. Chestnut St.; later the church moved to its final location at 1901 W. Muhammad Ali Blvd. The building was purchased from Weaver Memorial Baptist Church, a white congregation. This building is noted as a prime example of the Gothic Revival architectural style and is listed on the National Register of Historic Places. Carrying on the A.M.E. tradition of resistance to discrimination, Quinn Chapel early became known as the Abolitionist Church, and many slaveholders forbade their slaves to attend services there. Over the years, Quinn Chapel has continued to protest actively against discrimination in streetcar access (1870), for open housing (1914), and for access to public accommodations (1961). On May 3, 1967, Quinn Chapel was the starting point for an open-housing march to city hall and through the downtown area led by Rev. Dr. Martin Luther King Jr. It was his second visit to the city in support of local open-housing efforts.

Gibson, W. H., Sr. *History of the United Brothers of Friendship and Sisters of the Mysterious Ten: In Two Parts, a Negro Order.* Louisville, KY: Bradley & Gilbert Co., 1897.

Jenkins, Horace G., and J. Bryant Cooper. *One Hundred Years of Celebration of Quinn Chapel AME Church, 1838 to 1938.* Louisville, KY: n.p., 1938.

Kentucky's Black Heritage: The Role of the Black People in the History of Kentucky from Pioneer Days to the Present. Frankfort: Kentucky Commission on Human Rights, 1971.

Tate, Monica Newton. "Faith in Action: Quinn Chapel to Revisit Its Four Former Homes." *LCJ,* February 22, 1997.

Weeden, H. C. *Weeden's History of the Colored People of Louisville.* Louisville, KY: H. C. Weeden, 1897.

—*Walter W. Hutchins*

R

RABB, MAURICE F., JR. (b. 1932, Shelbyville, KY; d. 2005, Chicago, IL), prominent ophthalmologist. The son of an anesthesiologist and a math teacher, Maurice F. Rabb Jr. spent much of his childhood experimenting with photography in Shelbyville, KY. After completing his secondary education at **Central High School** and attending the University of Indiana before switching to the recently desegregated University of Louisville, Rabb parlayed his interest in visual media into a career in ophthalmology. Having earned a degree from the University of Louisville's Medical School in 1958 and studying the subject at New York University, he became the first black ophthalmology resident at the University of Illinois Hospital and eventually the first black chief resident in 1963.

Although Rabb always preferred to be known simply as an ophthalmologist rather than as an African American ophthalmologist, during his extensive and distinguished career he achieved several firsts, including first African American director of an eye bank and first African American to help write a book on ophthalmology. In 1972, he cofounded the Comprehensive Sickle Cell Center at the University of Illinois, where his research led to techniques to prevent blindness and retinal detachment in sickle-cell patients. In 2000, the National Medical Association created the Rabb Venable Ophthalmology Award for Outstanding Research in honor of Rabb and Dr. H. Philip Venable. A month after Rabb's death in 2005, he was elected to the Kentucky Civil Rights Hall of Fame.

"Dr. Maurice Rabb, 72, Leading Ophthalmologist." *Chicago Sun-Times,* June 9, 2005, 69.

"Eyeing the Future of Optical Care." *Black Enterprise,* October 1988, 78.

Routledge, Chris. "Rabb, Maurice F., Jr." In *Contemporary Black Biography,* vol. 58, edited by Sara Pendergast, Tom Pendergast, and Pamela M. Kalte, 148–49. Detroit: Gale, 2007.

—*Stephen Pickering*

RAGTIME, musical genre associated with several Kentucky African American performers. Ragtime is defined by music historian John Edward Hasse as a "dance-based American vernacular music, featuring a syncopated melody against an even accompaniment." It is often associated with solo piano performances but may be played by a full band or even a single banjo. The works of Scott Joplin (1868–1917), including "Maple Leaf Rag" and "The Entertainer," are among the most famous examples of ragtime.

Early antecedents of ragtime were performed by roustabouts along inland rivers, such as the levees in Kentucky's Ohio River cities. Cincinnati newspaper journalist Lafcadio Hearn (1850–1904) reported on various forms of the roots of ragtime along the Ohio River near Covington during the 1870s, nearly 20 years before the musical genre was nationally known. Other inspirations included homegrown banjo and fiddle music played by African Americans and Appalachians. Early ragtime pianists were often heard playing in saloons.

Although sources vary on the roots of ragtime's birth, all sources agree about its contemporaneous midwestern and southeastern origins. Ultimately, the ragtime revolution opened the door for African American professional musicians. It prompted Bowling Green native Ernest Hogan (born **Ernest Reuben Crowdus;** 1865–1909) to become one of the earliest great black entertainers in the United States. Hogan is credited with one of the first published ragtime-influenced songs (1895), "La Pas Ma La." He was called the "Father of Ragtime Music" in a 1909 *Chicago Record-Herald* news story.

Ragtime was initially associated with rebellious youth and hence took some time to achieve acceptance by mainstream popular culture. Although ragtime was soon displaced by **jazz** in the 1920s, Fats Waller (1904–1943) incorporated some of its spirit into his performances for WLW radio in Cincinnati in the early 1930s. During this time, Waller was known to play stride piano (a form of ragtime) for live venues, late-evening audiences in Covington and Newport.

Abbott, Lynn, and Doug Seroff. *Out of Sight: The Rise of African American Popular Music, 1889–1895.* Jackson: Univ. Press of Mississippi, 2002.

Hasse, John Edward, ed. *Ragtime: Its History, Composers, and Music.* New York: Schirmer Books, 1985.

Library of Congress. "History of Ragtime." *Performing Arts Encyclopedia.* http://lcweb2.loc.gov/diglib/ihas/loc.natlib.ihas.200035811/default.html (accessed September 3, 2011).

Newspapers: "'Father of Ragtime Music' Who Had Passed Away," *Chicago Record-Herald,* May 22, 1909, 9; "Origin of Ragtime: Fred Stone Credits Ernest Hogan, a Negro, with Starting the Jazz Era in Music," *NYT,* March 23, 1924, 2.

Waldo, Terry. "Ragtime." In *Encyclopedia of African American History, 1896 to the Present,* vol. 4, *O–T,* edited by Paul Finkelman. Oxford: Oxford Univ. Press, 2009.

—*John Schlipp*

RAMSEY, ARTHUR, SR. (b. 1921, Kentucky; d. 1985, Detroit, MI), member of the Negro League Hall of Fame. A native of Kentucky, Arthur Ramsey Sr., began a career in baseball in 1945 when he joined the Knoxville Giants. A teammate described him as "a heckuva hitter" and "a good defensive second baseman and a good base runner." During his career, Ramsey played for the Homestead Grays and the Pittsburgh Crawfords, and he appeared alongside baseball legends like Satchel Paige and "Cool Papa" Bell. In 1954, he moved to Detroit, MI, after finishing his career with teams in Minneapolis and Saskatoon.

After his retirement, Ramsey was elected to the Negro League Hall of Fame in Ashland, KY. He was also a member of the Afro-American Sports Hall of Fame Gallery and a charter member of the Old-Timers' All-Stars, a team of retired players assembled in Detroit in 1982. In 1985, after a long struggle with illness, Ramsey passed away in his home in Detroit. His funeral was held in Ashland, KY, and he was buried in Woodlawn Cemetery.

Newspapers: "Short Stops," *Argus-Press* (Owosso, MI), August 6, 1985, 12; "Tuesday's Notebook," *Orlando (FL) Sentinel,* August 7, 1985, C5.

—*Stephen Pickering*

RAMSEY, DERRICK KENT (b. 1956, Hastings, FL), football player and member of the Kentucky Athletic Hall of Fame. Born on December 23, 1956, in Hastings, FL, Derrick Kent Ramsey grew up with his parents, a chef and a mechanic. During his junior year, he moved in with his uncle in New Jersey and attended Camden High School. He later chose the University of Kentucky because he wanted to help the Wildcats basketball and football teams. Ramsey was the school's first African American quarterback, and he helped lead the team to a sixth-place national ranking in his senior year.

Ramsey was selected in the fifth round of the 1978 National Football League draft by the Oakland Raiders, who moved him to tight end. He recorded 952 yards and 7 touchdowns in 75 games and helped win the Super Bowl in 1981. In 1983, he was traded to the New England Patriots, with whom he recorded 1,412 yards and 14 touchdowns in 46 games. Ramsey and the Patriots lost the 1986 Super Bowl to the Chicago Bears. He later joined the Indianapolis Colts but was quickly traded to the Detroit Lions. Ramsey played one game for the Lions before retiring from football.

Ramsey later served as the University of Kentucky's community relations officer before taking a position as director of athletics at **Kentucky State University** in 1999. Ramsey was inducted into the Kentucky Athletic Hall of Fame in 1999. He became athletic director at Maryland's Coppin State University in 2008.

Newspapers: "Derrick Ramsey—Man of Destiny," *Hendersonville (NC) Times-News,* February 24, 1982, 11; "Ex-UK Quarterback Takes Job at KSU," *LHL,* June 3, 1999, D2; "New Vision for Coppin," *Baltimore Sun,* August 19, 2008, 16Z.

—*Kevin Hogg*

RANDOLPH, JAMES E. (b. 1888, Hannibal, MO; d. 1981, Newport, KY), physician. James E. Randolph was an African American medical doctor who practiced in Covington for 59 years. He was the first African American permitted to practice in any northern Kentucky hospital. Randolph graduated from Meharry Medical College in Nashville, TN, in 1917. The grandson of a slave, he worked his way through medical school as a railroad Pullman porter. Randolph began his practice in Shelbyville, TN. He served in the U.S. Army Medical Reserve Corps in World War I. In 1922, Randolph moved to Covington. He lived first at 1039 Greenup St. and in 1950 moved across the street to 1002 Greenup.

Randolph was the staff physician at **Lincoln-Grant School** in Covington for more than 40 years. In 1973, after the school's name was changed to Twelfth District School, he began treating children from the school at his nearby office.

A grove of trees on the campus of Northern Kentucky University in Highland Heights memorializes Randolph's achievements. In 1974, the city of Covington named an Eastside neighborhood park in his honor. In 1976, he received a gold medal for service to the community from the parochial La Salette Academy in Covington. He was an active member of **St. James A.M.E. Church** in Covington. He died after cataract surgery in 1981, at age 93, at the Baptist Convalescent Center in Newport and was buried in the Mary E. Smith Cemetery in **Elsmere.**

On May 9, 1997, Randolph was inducted into the region's Leadership Hall of Fame during ceremonies held by the North- ern Kentucky Chamber of Commerce. He was acknowledged as the first African American physician on staff at St. Elizabeth Hospital in Covington and as the first African American member of the Campbell-Kenton Medical Society. A Kentucky Historical Society highway marker along Greenup St. was dedicated to Randolph on September 10, 2004.

Newspapers: "He's 85 . . . Still One of the Busiest Doctors," *KP,* February 15, 1973, 11; "Dr. Randolph Was 'There to Help Us,'" *KP,* May 25, 1981, 1K; "Portrait of an Epic Journey," *KP,* June 1, 1995, 1K; "Students' Book Celebrates Covington's Black History," *KP,* February 26, 1997, 2K; "Leaders Who Made Mark Inducted in Hall of Fame," *KP,* April 29, 1997, 3K; "N. KY Hall Adds Three," *KE,* May 9, 1997, C1–C2; "Pioneering Covington Physician Recognized," *KP,* September 11, 2004, B1.

—*Theodore H. H. Harris*

RANDOLPH, LORETTA CORRYNE BACON LUNDERMAN SPENCER (b. 1903, Paducah, KY; d. 1975, Cincinnati, OH), educator and church leader. Born Loretta Corryne Bacon to Rev. Benjamin and Mary Bacon in Paducah in 1903, Loretta grew up appreciating both education and religion and therefore was driven both to enhance Kentucky's education system and to serve its churches. After graduating from Paducah's Lincoln High School with top honors, Bacon attended both Lane College in Tennessee and Southern Illinois Teachers College before graduating with her AB from Kentucky State College (later known as **Kentucky State University**). She completed her graduate work at Fisk University and Indiana University.

While taking and teaching classes, Bacon found time to dedicate to the church and community, serving as district president of the Sunday School Convention, a position she held from the age of 17. She married Charles J. Lunderman Sr. in 1921. In addition, she was the anti-basileus for Beta Upsilon Omega Chapter of **Alpha Kappa Alpha Sorority** and became vice president of the Conference Branch Missionary Society in 1929.

Loretta worked as a high school teacher in her hometown for five years before becoming principal of Robertstown High School. She then accepted several consecutive principal jobs before taking a principal position at Ballard Co.'s La Center High School in 1932. She became chairman of the High School Group of the First District Teachers' Association that same year. When the high school was destroyed in a fire, she worked tirelessly to raise the funds needed to construct a modern high school with the latest equipment.

Loretta married Benjamin Franklin Spencer in 1934. Although her husband owned a shoe shop and could provide for the family, Loretta was unwilling to end her career or her community service. The couple moved to Frankfort, where she joined St. John African Methodist Episcopal Church and became president of the Busy Bee Club and a member of the Artistic Ten, a women's organization that promoted the domestic arts. In addition, she became the dean of girls and assistant principal at **Lincoln Institute** near Simpsonville.

Although she was a dedicated principal, Spencer eventually returned to teaching and continued to work in Kentucky high schools long after her husband died in 1950. Ten years later, at the age of 57, Spencer moved to Lexington and began a new job teaching at (**Frederick**) **Douglass High School.** She later married Dr. **James E. Randolph** of Covington. While residing there, she died in Bethesda Oak Hospital in Cincinnati, OH, on June 24, 1975.

Polk's Lexington City Directory, 1960. Cincinnati: R. L. Polk & Co., 1960.

Smith, Lucy Harth, comp. and ed. *Pictorial Directory of the Kentucky Association of Colored Women.* Lexington: Kentucky Association of Colored Women, 1945.

U.S. Federal Census (1920, 1930, 1940).

Wright, Richard Robert, Jr. *The Centennial Encyclopedia of the African Methodist Episcopal Church.* Philadelphia: s.n., 1916.

Yenser, Thomas. *Who's Who in Colored America.* 4th ed., *1933–1937.* Brooklyn, NY: Thomas Yenser, 1937.

—*Dana Caldemeyer*

RANKIN V. LYDIA, Kentucky court case on laws governing slavery and freedom. *Rankin v. Lydia,* decided in Kentucky's Court of Appeals in 1820, centered on the rights of Lydia, a slave who was suing for her freedom from her current master, John W. Rankin. Born into slavery in Kentucky in 1805, Lydia was moved to Indiana and registered as an indentured servant because of the Northwest Ordinance's prohibition of slavery within the territory. Before her term of service expired, however, she was sold to Rankin, who brought her back to Kentucky as a slave. After six years, she sued for her freedom and won.

The decision was appealed to the Kentucky Court of Appeals, which was headed by Judge Benjamin Mills. In a careful and lengthy decision, he upheld the lower court's decision, ruling that Lydia's master's legal right to her involuntary servitude ceased during her residence in Indiana. Moreover, he held that slavery was not protected as a natural right and thus could be protected only by positive law, thus entailing that the laws that granted freedom in Indiana continued in operation upon Lydia's return to Kentucky.

The precedent established in *Rankin v. Lydia* influenced decisions on questions of freedom between free and slave states for the next 40 years.

Cover, Robert M. *Justice Accused: Antislavery and the Judicial Process.* New Haven, CT: Yale Univ. Press, 1975.

Finkelman, Paul. *An Imperfect Union: Slavery, Federalism, and Comity.* Chapel Hill: Univ. of North Carolina Press, 1981.

Marshall, Alexander K. *Decisions of the Court of Appeals of Kentucky, Commencing with the Fall Term, 1817, and Ending with the Fall Term, 1821.* Vol. 2. Cincinnati: Henry W. Derby, 1848.

—*Stephen Pickering*

RAWLINGS, SIMON PETER (b. 1914, Stamping Ground, KY; d. 1991, Lexington, KY), bishop and leader in a religious denomination. Simon Peter Rawlings was born on August 2, 1914, in Stamping Ground, KY, approximately eight miles northeast of Georgetown, KY. At age 17, he joined the House of God, a small Pentecostal church in Georgetown, in 1931. The next year, he became a minister, and his first ministerial appointment was to copastor alongside Marvin Pentz Gay Sr. in Mirsmill, SC, in 1934. A second appointment in 1936 brought him back to Kentucky as pastor of the House of God in Lexington.

Bishop S. P. Rawlings achieved the position of chief apostle and general overseer of the House of God, the Holy Church of the Living God, the Pillar and Ground of the Truth, the House of Prayer for All People, Inc. He reestablished its headquarters in Lexington, KY, in 1950.

During his 40-year tenure as chief bishop of the House of God, the denomination grew from approximately 10 churches with $200 in its national coffers to a multimillion-dollar corporation with over 150 churches throughout the United States, Jamaica, the West Indies, Canada, Africa, and Australia. He also established the Kentucky College of Contemporary Religion in Lexington.

Rawlings received his bachelor of sacred theology from Coopers Institute in Jacksonville, FL, and a doctor of divinity degree from the Kentucky College of Contemporary Religion in October 1967. From 1987 to 1988, he served a term as president of the Lexington Coalition of Black Churches, an organization established to provide economic assistance to disadvantaged citizens of Lexington.

President Jimmy Carter recognized Rawlings as an outstanding black leader in March 1984. At the time of his death on January 2, 1991, he had pastored his church for 55 years, longer than any other African American pastor in Lexington. In August 1991, Lexington mayor Scotty Beasler posthumously gave Rawlings the Distinguished Citizen's Award, and Governor Wallace Wilkerson posthumously declared him a Kentucky Colonel.

"Bishop Remembered as Being Dedicated to Serving God." *LHL,* January 7, 1991, B1.

Johnson, Larry L. *Chosen.* Lexington, KY: author, 2012.

Rawlings, Simon Peter. Interview by Larry Johnson, no date.

—*Larry L. Johnson*

RAY, JOSEPH REYNOLDS "JOIE," JR. (b. 1923, Louisville, KY; d. 2007, Louisville, KY), race-car driver. Joseph Reynolds "Joie" Ray Jr. was born in Louisville in 1923 into a prominent family. His father was a bank president and community activist who spent the last six years of his life in Washington, DC, as a public housing administrator in President Dwight D. Eisenhower's administration. Joseph Jr. declined to follow in his father's business and civic footsteps. Instead, he forged a career as a race-car driver in the minor-league racing circuits that existed in the Upper South and Midwest after World War II.

Ray's racing career lasted from 1947 to 1963. He drove both open-wheel vehicles and stock cars at county fairgrounds and small racetracks throughout Middle America. Usually relegated to driving inferior machines on a limited budget, he experienced the thrill of victory only three times. But as the lone African American driver in most of the races in which he participated, Ray broke the color barrier in several racing associations. He was not an official NASCAR stock car driver and never realized his dream of participating in the Indianapolis 500.

"Joseph Reynolds "Joie" Ray, Jr." Legends of NASCAR.com (not an official NASCAR site). http://www.legendsofnascar.com/Joie_RayJr.htm (accessed July 31, 2014).

Newspapers: Tom Archdeacon, "Pioneer Black Race Driver Teaching 'Dare to Be First,'" *CP,* April 16, 2003; Michael Grant, "Pioneer Auto Racer Ray Dies at 83," *LCJ,* April 17, 2007.

Sullivan, Patrick. *Brick by Brick: The Story of Auto Racing Pioneer Joie Ray*. Fishers, IN: American Scene Press, 2008.

—*Roger D. Hardaway*

RED CROSS HOSPITAL, hospital in Louisville, KY, founded by African Americans. Despite its name, Red Cross Hospital in Louisville, KY, was never associated with the American Red Cross but rather was established in 1899 by a group of African American physicians led by W. T. Merchant and Ellis D. Whedbee. Because of their color, they were prevented from practicing in local hospitals. Red Cross Hospital was started to provide medical services for the black community and was opened in a rented two-story house on Sixth St. between **Walnut St.** (now **Muhammad Ali** Blvd.) and Green (Liberty) St. In 1905, the hospital moved to a new, larger facility at 1436 S. Shelby St.

Recognizing that the cost of medical treatment was a serious issue for many poor black families, the hospital offered its services at a fraction of the amount charged by other hospitals; it also offered a free preventive care clinic. Another prominent feature was its nurse-training program. Red Cross was the only Kentucky hospital to admit African American women to a nurse-training program. The program was discontinued in 1937 because of insufficient funds and loss of certification but was reinstated in 1948. That same year, Red Cross Hospital was the country's first private black hospital authorized by the American Cancer Society to operate a small cancer clinic.

Throughout its history, Red Cross Hospital was plagued by financial worries. It depended heavily on support from the white community, specifically from prominent families like the Speeds and the Belknaps, who were instrumental in founding the Red Cross Club and the Red Cross Advisory Board, which, among other things, paid for numerous renovation projects. At different times, the hospital also received funds from the state, the Community Chest, and various foundations. Although the hospital struggled through its first three decades, hampered by inadequate facilities and substandard equipment, the 1940s and 1950s brought major modernization efforts that briefly improved the hospital's economic status.

By the early 1960s, however, the move toward racial integration of Louisville's hospitals and increasing operational costs resulted in the facility's ultimate decline. Many of Red Cross's past patients chose to go to bigger, more technically advanced hospitals. Red Cross, which changed its name to Community Hospital in 1972, continued attempting to upgrade its facilities until 1975, by which time it was in debt, and the lack of patients forced a closure. The last patient was admitted in September 1975. Bankruptcy was declared the following January. In 1978, Volunteers of America purchased the hospital's building, which now houses the organization's Men's Transitional Living Center.

LCJ, February 21, 1988.

Wright, George C. *Life Behind a Veil: Blacks in Louisville, Kentucky, 1865–1930*. Baton Rouge: Louisiana State Univ. Press, 1985.

REED, STEVEN S. (b. 1962, Munfordville, KY), first black U.S. attorney in Kentucky. One of seven children born to working-class parents, Steven S. Reed learned to value education at an early age in Munfordville, KY. Known as a serious and bright pupil at Munfordville Elementary, Reed went on to be a star high school student before graduating from Western Kentucky University. Afterward, he attended the University of Kentucky Law School, received his degree in 1986, and began work as a corporate and banking lawyer for Brown, Todd, and Heyburn in Louisville. He left the firm two years later for a lower-paying job as a clerk for a federal judge and eventually moved up the ranks to become deputy general counsel to Governor Brereton Jones and assistant U.S. attorney.

In 1999, President Bill Clinton appointed Reed to replace Mike Troop as acting U.S. attorney for western Kentucky, the first African American to hold that position in the state. On July 3 of the following year, he was sworn in after receiving confirmation from the Senate, a task aided by U.S. senator and Republican leader Mitch McConnell. Reed and McConnell, despite their activity on behalf of the Democratic and Republican Parties respectively, worked together on several occasions, and McConnell offered a tribute on Reed's behalf in the Senate on June 16, 2003. As U.S. attorney for western Kentucky, Reed earned several plaudits for aggressively cracking down on methamphetamine production in the region.

In 1994, Reed was appointed to the University of Kentucky Board of Trustees, where he pursued a course that would make the university more accessible to students and privilege its academic pursuits over athletics. Five years later, he supported Billy Joe Miles in his campaign to be chairman of the board and accepted a role as vice chairman. The two played a strong role in the selection of Lee Todd as the next president of the University of Kentucky. In 2002, Reed became chairman of the board in his own right—the first African American to obtain that role—where he remained a loyal ally of President Todd.

Although friends and family assumed that Reed would eventually move into politics, he turned down an opportunity to run for lieutenant governor in 2007. Since 2003, he has served on the Board of directors of ResCare, a human services company that supports individuals with intellectual and developmental disabilities and others with special needs, while continuing to practice law at Reed Wicker in Louisville, KY, where he is the managing member.

Newspapers: "Black U.S. Attorney Is a First for Kentucky, Swearing-In a Milestone for One Man and His Family," *LHL*, July 4, 2000, B1; "UK Board Set to Get First Black Leader—Steve Reed Has Been Panel's Vice Chairman for 3 Years," *LHL*, September 17, 2002, A1; "A Bright Future—From Poverty to Politics, Chairman of UK Trustees Adapts," *LHL*, May 11, 2003, A1.

—*Stephen Pickering*

REED, WILLIAM B. "CHIEF" (b. 1912, Bourbon Co., KY; d. 1996, Redford, MI), first black member of the Paris City Council. One of nine children born to Frank and Susie Reed in Bourbon Co., KY, William B. Reed entered a lifelong career in education when he attended Paris Western High School as a youth. He then enrolled at Kentucky State College (later known as **Kentucky State University**), where he played for the basketball and football teams. In basketball, he made the All-American and All-Midwestern Teams, while the football team won the national championship after he was named captain his senior year.

He was later named to the Kentucky State University Hall of Fame.

Reed returned to all-black Western High School as a teacher. He received accolades for his performances coaching the football and basketball teams, leading the latter to the national high school championship and receiving a commendation from the *Pittsburgh Courier* in 1953. He became principal of the school after the former principal died, but when Western High was converted to a junior high after desegregation in 1963, he joined Paris High School as an assistant principal. He remained an educator for 36 years.

In addition to his work in education, Reed served his local community in a variety of positions during his life in Bourbon Co. Locals praised Reed for his desire to improve "community relationships, working with blacks and whites, in trying to make integration a smooth transition." In 1977, he was elected to the Paris City Council, the first African American to hold that position, and he was an active member of the Seventh Street Christian Church and the Paris–Bourbon County YMCA. On July 4, 1981, local and state governments recognized his service by renaming a public park William "Chief" Reed Park and declaring the day Bill Reed Day.

On December 7, 1996, William B. Reed died of Alzheimer's disease in a nursing home in Redford, MI. His wife, Willanna Patterson Reed, passed away two hours later. Services were held at Paris High School, and he was buried in Evergreen Memory Gardens.

Newspapers: "July 4 Observed as 'Bill Reed Day,'" *Paris (KY) Citizen-Advertiser,* July 6, 1981, 1; "William Reed, Retired Educator, Coach, Dies," *LHL,* December 11, 1996, B2; "Obituaries," *Paris (KY) Citizen-Advertiser,* December 16, 1996, 8.

—*Stephen Pickering*

REID, BARNEY FORD, JR. (b. 1890, Garrard Co., KY; d. 1951, Cincinnati, OH), president of Cincinnati Theological Seminary. Born on August 19, 1890, Barney Ford Reid Jr. grew up in Garrard Co., Kentucky, and worked numerous odd jobs for most of his young adult life. In 1917, he identified himself as a tailor when he was drafted for World War I out of Richmond, KY. He was transferred to Camp Zachary Taylor, where he quickly rose through the ranks. By the end of his service, he had achieved the rank of sergeant and was the principal of the Consolidated Army School.

At the conclusion of the war, Reid returned to civilian life as a clergyman. Possessor of a doctorate of divinity from Simmons University (later known as **Simmons College of Kentucky**), where he also served on the faculty, he joined the faculty at Cincinnati Theological Seminary, which had recently consolidated with Zion Baptist Church School. In 1931, he was named president of the institution and simultaneously served as the pastor of Zion Baptist Church, a position he had held since 1927.

Among Reid's accomplishments during his tenure at the church were the addition of an annex, significant expansion of the institution's services and furnishings, and the hosting of the National Sunday School and Baptist Training Union in 1943. On November 10, 1951, his death concluded 24 years of service to the church and the community.

Fleming, G. James, and Christian E. Burckel, eds. *Who's Who in Colored America.* 7th ed. *Supplement.* Yonkers-on-Hudson, NY: Christian E. Burckel & Associates, 1950.
General Association of Colored Baptists. *Diamond Jubilee of the General Association of Colored Baptists in Kentucky.* Louisville, KY: American Baptist, 1943.
Zion Baptist Church. "Who We Are." http://zioncincinnati.org/page17.php (accessed July 17, 2012).

—*Stephen Pickering*

REYNOLDS, LOUISE ELLIOT "MATTIE" (b. 1916, Cornersville, TN; d. 1995, Louisville, KY), politician. Louise Elliot Reynolds was brought to Louisville as a child and graduated from Louisville **Central High School.** She attended **Louisville Municipal College** and the University of Louisville after it was integrated in 1951. That same year, Reynolds went into real estate and was elected president of the Real Estate Brokers Association six years later. Her political career began in 1952 when she became secretary to U.S. representative John M. Robison; she was the first African American woman to be secretary to a Kentucky congressman.

Reynolds became the first black female alderman in Louisville when she was elected 11th Ward alderman in 1961 as a Republican. In 1967, when the party's six-year control of city government ended with the election of 11 Democratic aldermen, Reynolds was the only Republican survivor. When Mayor William O. Cowger and aldermanic president Kenneth A. Schmied visited out of town for three days in 1965, Reynolds became the first black female to serve as mayor of a southern city. For her accomplishments, she received national recognition and dined at the White House with President Lyndon B. Johnson. Reynolds was later appointed to a national Republican task force on human rights and responsibilities. After leaving elected office, she handled minority affairs for the Small Business Administration's office.

Reynolds married James Elwood, and they had one child, Linda. Reynolds died at Brownsboro Hills Nursing Home and is buried in Cave Hill Cemetery.

LCJ, March 5, 1995.

RHEA, LA JULIA (b. ca. 1904, Louisville, KY; d. 1992, Evanston, IL), first black opera singer to perform on the stage of a major American opera company. A performer even as a toddler, La Julia Rhea learned to sing before she learned to walk in her home in Louisville, KY. After moving with her mother to Chicago, Rhea decided to put her vocal abilities to use and enrolled at the Chicago Musical College in the early 1920s. She drew the attention of famous voice coach Romano Romani, who got her an audition for the Metropolitan Opera Company. Although both teacher and student understood that the racial climate of the time would preclude any real chance of her being hired, she tried out on the stage of the Met on March 17, 1933.

After the Metropolitan Opera Company rejected her, Rhea moved on to break other color barriers when she became the first African American to perform for the Chicago Civic Opera Company on December 26, 1937. Her performance in *Aida* earned high marks from reviewers; the *Chicago Daily Tribune* praised her "large [voice] of excellent quality" and "emotional force." Rhea performed in opera and in Broadway musicals for several more years, but she retired to take care of her family in 1949. On July 2, 1992, she passed away in St. Francis Hospital in Evanston, IL.

Newspapers: "Two Colored Singers Take Roles in 'Aida,'" *Chicago Daily Tribune,* December 27, 1937, 12; "A Month of Dreams and Courage: La Julia Rhea Typifies Black Achievements," *Chicago Daily Tribune,* January 31, 1986, CS5; "La Julia Rhea, 94, Early Black Opera Star," *Chicago Daily Tribune,* July 7, 1992, sec. 2, p. 5.
Southern, Eileen. *The Music of Black Americans: A History.* 3rd ed. New York: Norton, 1997.

—*Stephen Pickering*

RIPPLETON, WASHINGTON (b. 1842, Danville, KY; d. 1911, Newport, KY), coachman. Although Washington Rippleton was born in Danville, KY, he spent most of his life in Newport and for more than 50 years was one of Newport's leading African American figures. Rippleton married a local woman named Lucy, and they resided in Newport on Rickey St., raising four children. From 1867 through 1876, Rippleton's occupation was listed in the local city directory as either hostler or coachman. He was involved in other aspects of the community as well.

In 1866, Washington Rippleton, Beverly Lumpkin, and others formed a board of trustees for the newly established African American school, which opened under the direction of the Missionary Aid Association and the **Freedmen's Bureau.** In April 1870, Rippleton led a delegation of Newport's residents during a parade celebrating the passage of the Fifteenth Amendment to the U.S. Constitution. That parade wound its way from Newport to Covington. In November 1872, Rippleton helped organize the **Corinthian Baptist Church,** located on Roberts St. in Newport. In February 1873, continuing his activities in social and educational issues, Rippleton, along with Rev. Dennis Lightfoot, **Robert Littleton,** and a delegation from Newport, attended the Colored Education Convention in Louisville. The convention informed the attendees of the proposed new state law that would allow for public schools for African American children. In August, when the **Southgate Street School** was authorized, Rippleton was active in the planning for it.

In February 1883, the African-American Literature Circle was organized in Newport, with Washington Rippleton as president. He remained involved in Campbell Co. Republican politics throughout the 1890s, as did his close friend Robert Littleton. In July 1891, the Campbell Co. Republican executive committee named Rippleton a delegate to its county convention. In August, Rippleton, Littleton, and other African American Republicans formed the first Republican League Club. Rippleton was one of five men to serve on the executive committee. In March 1892, the league elected Rippleton president for the ensuing year. At the July meeting, held at the African Methodist Episcopal Church on Southgate St. in Newport, the club announced that the membership was 80 strong and increasing daily. In May 1894, the African-American Republican League was renamed the Crispus Attucks Club; Rippleton remained as president.

From 1878 through 1892, Rippleton worked at the Newport Barracks and lived nearby at 249 Liberty St. Throughout the 1890s, he served as a storekeeper in government service under a Republican administration. Afterward, Rippleton operated a

shoeshine parlor at 405 York St. in Newport until his death in 1911. He was buried in Evergreen Cemetery in Southgate.

Annual Report of Board of Education of Newport, Kentucky. Newport, KY: Newport Printing, 1873.
Newspapers: "Colored Schools," *Cincinnati Daily Enquirer,* August 1, 1866, 2; *Cincinnati Daily Gazette,* April 15, 1870; *Cincinnati Daily Gazette,* November 29, 1872; *Cincinnati Daily Gazette,* February 11, 1873; *Covington Ticket,* August 14, 1875; "The City," *Kentucky State Journal,* February 10, 1883, 1; "Delegates Selected," *Kentucky Journal,* July 7, 1891, 3; "First in the State," *Kentucky Journal,* August 13, 1891, 5; "The Colored League," *Kentucky Journal,* March 4, 1892, 4; "The Outs Knock Out the Bloody In," *Kentucky Journal,* March 8, 1892, 4; "A Card to the Colored Citizens," *Kentucky Journal,* May 13, 1892, 4; "Colored Club," *Kentucky Journal,* May 25, 1894, 6; "Deaths in Newport," *KP,* May 13, 1911, 5.

—*Theodore H. H. Harris*

ROACH, SANFORD T. (b. 1916, Frankfort, KY; d. 2010, Lexington, KY), educator, basketball coach, and civic leader. Sanford T. Roach was born in Frankfort, KY, in February 1916, the son of Jessie and T. W. Roach. When Sanford was five, the family moved to Danville, where his mother was a schoolteacher and his father a dentist. He lettered in football and basketball at Bate High School, as well as being salutatorian of his graduating class in 1933. At Kentucky State College (later known as **Kentucky State University**), from which he graduated in 1937, he captained the basketball team, starred in track and field, edited the student newspaper, and served on the student council. In 1955, he earned a master of arts in education degree from the University of Kentucky. In 2002, he received an honorary doctor of humanities degree from the university.

After his graduation from Kentucky State, Roach taught for one year at Kentucky Village, later known as Blackburn Institute. For the next three years, he taught science and coached basket-

Sanford T. Roach.

Dunbar High School 1960 43rd district champions. Head coach S. T. Roach (standing left) and assistant coach Norman Passmore (standing right).

ball at Bate High School, where his success led to his recruitment to teach and coach at **Dunbar High School** in Lexington. After two years as assistant coach, he became the head coach and compiled a record of 512 wins and 142 losses over the next 22 years. His teams won two state championships in the Kentucky High School Athletic League and finished second twice in the Kentucky High School Athletic Association state tournaments after desegregation. In a 2007 KET interview, Roach said, "I always would insist that our young men have good character and abide by the rules."

After his first wife, Mary, died in 1965, Roach retired from coaching but remained active as an educator and civic leader. He served as both the first black principal of an integrated Fayette Co. elementary school (George W. Carver) and secondary school (Lexington Junior High). In 1974, he was appointed to the University of Kentucky Athletic Association Board of Directors. Among the civic organizations in which he worked were the Good Samaritan Foundation, the **Kentucky Commission on Human Rights,** the Big Brothers / Big Sisters program, the **National Association for the Advancement of Colored People,** and the Kiwanis Club. He was a leader in the struggle against racial injustice and a role model not only for his students but for all citizens of the commonwealth. In 2004, he received the John Sherman Cooper Award for Outstanding Public Service. He is a member of the National High School Sports Hall of Fame, the Kentucky Athletic Hall of Fame, and the Kentucky State University Athletic Hall of Fame.

In 1967, Roach married Lettie, his second wife. He had two children, Sandra Cole and Thomas Roach. S. T. Roach died on September 2, 2010.

"Legendary Lexington Basketball Coach S. Roach Dies at Age 94." http://www.kentucky.com/2010/09/03/1418055/legendary-basketball-coach-st.html (accessed July 3, 2013).

"Legendary Prep Coach S. T. Roach Dies." Kentucky School News and Commentary. http://theprincipal.blogspot.com/2010/09/legendary-prep-coach-s-t-roach-dies.html (accessed July 3, 2013).

Roach, Sanford T. Interview by Betsy Brinson, Lexington, KY, October 23, 1999.

Stout, Louis. *Shadows of the Past: A History of the Kentucky High School Athletic League.* Lexington, KY: Host Communications, 2006.

"S. T. Roach, 2003–2004 John Sherman Cooper Award Winner." http://www.kchp.eku.edu. (accessed September 7, 2010).

—*Charles F. Faber*

ROBB, JACKSON KENNEY (b. 1910, Frankfort, KY; d. 1977, Frankfort, KY), musician and undertaker. Jackson Kenney Robb was born in Frankfort, KY, the youngest child of funeral home owner **Thomas Kenney Robb** and music teacher **Mary Etta Jackson Robb.** He was profoundly influenced by his mother and music. In 1918, he performed as a drummer boy for a World War I musical group and later sang as a soloist with the Kentucky State College Singers. His mother taught him to play the piano, and afterward, he taught himself to play the organ.

Even though he had no interest in the funeral business, Robb, in his early 20s, was forced to manage Robb Funeral Home on Clinton St. after the death of his father in 1932. He became a successful funeral director, and his wealth grew. He married Kathryn (Katie) Taylor, a nurse intern at Louisville's **Red Cross Hospital,** in 1934. The couple lived with their children and Robb's mother, Mary, in the funeral home building.

Robb continued his fascination with entertainment. He and his wife wrote, produced, and acted in plays at Mayo-Underwood High School and Kentucky State College (later known as **Kentucky State University**). In 1933, he organized the Grad Club from alumni of Mayo-Underwood and Clinton Street Schools. The group held fund-raising dances at the Stagg Distillery specifically

Jackson Robb playing the organ.

for the schools' athletic programs until the 1950s. In 1943, Robb participated in a "womanless wedding" for a Mayo-Underwood School benefit. All of the performers were male, and many, including Robb, were dressed in female attire.

Robb also operated a dancing school in the upstairs of his home and charged students only a quarter. At one of his musical engagements for which he planned a piano/organ duet, his organist did not show up. Robb pushed the two instruments together and played both simultaneously. He performed across the United States and in Europe and became locally known as "the beloved pale-skinned, singing-and-dancing undertaker."

In 1965, along with managing the funeral home, Robb became a relocation adviser for Urban Renewal and Community Development. As a wealthy member of the Frankfort community, he opened his home rent free to **Mae Street Kidd,** an African American businesswoman and politician, when she was first elected to the Kentucky legislature in 1968. She was impressed with his skills as a pianist and organist and told how his neighbors enjoyed his music into the early morning hours.

Robb died in Frankfort on January 13, 1977. He was interred in the Frankfort Cemetery.

Boyd, Douglas A. *Crawfish Bottom: Recovering a Lost Kentucky Community.* Lexington: Univ. Press of Kentucky, 2011.

Dunnigan, Alice Allison, comp. and ed. *The Fascinating Story of Black Kentuckians: Their Heritage and Traditions.* Washington, DC: Associated Publishers, 1982.

Fletcher, Winona L., sr. ed. *Community Memories: A Glimpse of African American Life in Frankfort, Kentucky.* Frankfort: Kentucky Historical Society, 2003.

Franklin County, Kentucky, Frankfort 200 Celebration, 1786–1986. Paducah, KY: Turner, 1987.

Hall, Wade. *Passing for Black: The Life and Careers of Mae Street Kidd.* Lexington: Univ. Press of Kentucky, 1997.

—*Sallie L. Powell*

ROBB, THOMAS KENNEY (b. 1862, Frankfort, KY; d. 1932, Frankfort, KY), and ROBB, MARY ETTA JACKSON (b. 1870, Washington Court House, OH; d. 1972, Frankfort, KY), prominent business persons and community activists. Born in Frankfort, KY, to James and Kate Kenney Robb, Thomas Kenney

Robb left school at age 14 to work as a water boy for R. N. Archer and Company, a sawmill. When he was not carrying water, he educated himself in the lumber business. In 1880, he lived in Frankfort with his mother and stepfather, Anderson Williams, and was later promoted to yard master in Point Burnside, KY. Three years later, he moved to Williamstown, KY, to work for the Kentucky Lumber Company and was quickly advanced to lumber inspector. In 1888, he moved to Louisville to work as yard master and head inspector for the Frank Ingram Lumber Company. His duties included purchasing and shipping lumber across the country. The panic of 1891 caused the company to close, and because Robb was a company stockholder, he suffered great financial loss. One source claimed that Robb traveled to the South to recover from his economic damage and returned to Kentucky in 1895. The next year, the State Board of Sinking Fund Commissioners elected him lumber inspector for the Frankfort Penitentiary over 11 white competitors. His salary was $100 a month.

By 1910, Robb and his wife, Mary Etta Jackson Robb, had two daughters, ages seven and four. The couple established the Robb Funeral Home in 1898. Before her marriage, Mary Etta Jackson, an Ohio native, had moved to Frankfort to teach English and music at Kentucky Normal and Industrial Institute for Colored Persons (later known as **Kentucky State University**), becoming one of the first faculty at the school. After her marriage, she helped develop Frankfort's only African American hospital, the **Winnie A. Scott Memorial Hospital.** She also served on its board and was involved in club work and active in her church.

Behind their funeral home, the Robbs also owned a livery stable that they purchased in 1904. They provided ambulance service to Frankfort's African American citizens and nearby communities. In 1915, Thomas Robb served as master of ceremonies for a Booker T. Washington memorial service at Frankfort's **First Baptist Church.** After Robb died of throat cancer in 1932, his son, **Jackson Kenney Robb,** managed the funeral home. Thomas K. Robb was buried in the Frankfort Cemetery. His wife, Mary, lived to be 102 years old. She was also buried in the Frankfort Cemetery.

Franklin County, Kentucky, Frankfort 200 Celebration, 1786–1986. Paducah, KY: Turner, 1987.

Johnson, W. D. *Biographical Sketches of Prominent Negro Men and Women of Kentucky.* Lexington, KY: Standard Print, 1897.

Kentucky, Death Records, 1852–1953.

U.S. Federal Census (1880, 1900, 1910, 1920).

—*Sallie L. Powell*

ROBINSON, JAMES HATHAWAY (b. 1888, Sharpsburg, KY; d. unknown), social work leader in Cincinnati and first African American to receive a fellowship from Yale University. The son of a former slave, James Hathaway Robinson was born in Sharpsburg, KY, to Nathaniel Robinson, a dairyman, and Martha Robinson on October 6, 1888. After attending public schools in Winchester and Lexington's Russell High School, he pursued a degree at Fisk University, which he received in 1912. He then attended Yale, where he became the first African American to receive a fellowship from that university. For one year, he studied sociology and social service in the Graduate School of Columbia University before moving to Cincinnati, where he taught at the **(Frederick) Douglass School.**

From 1917 to 1925, Robinson served as executive secretary of the Negro Civic Welfare Association, Department Community Chest and Council of Social Agencies in Cincinnati. The organization selected Robinson to draft a plan of action for social work in the city based on a survey of the recent influx of African Americans to the city and of housing conditions. After discerning that many of the problems faced by African Americans in the city were institutional, Robinson recommended that the black community develop its own set of services, including "colored departments" of white agencies and a YWCA and YMCA. Simultaneously, he argued for a federation of churches in the city, as well as an education campaign among white citizens. These suggestions guided the direction of social work in Cincinnati until the 1940s, when a more integrationist approach prevailed.

In 1934, Robinson earned his PhD in sociology from Yale University for his dissertation, "A Social History of the Negro in Memphis and in Shelby County." He then became director of the Department of Social Administration at Wilberforce University and later dean of the College of Liberal Arts.

Boris, Joseph J., ed. *Who's Who in Colored America, 1927.* New York: Who's Who in Colored America Corp., 1927.

Dabney, Wendell P. *Cincinnati's Colored Citizens: Historical, Sociological and Biographical.* Cincinnati: Dabney, 1926.

Greene, Henry Washington. *Holders of Doctorates among American Negroes.* Boston: Meador, 1946.

Kornbluh, Andrea Tuttle. "James Hathaway Robinson and the Origins of Professional Social Work in the Black Community." In *Race and the City: Work, Community, and Protest in Cincinnati, 1820–1970,* edited by Henry Louis Taylor Jr., 209–31. Urbana: Univ. of Illinois Press, 1993.

Proctor, Mortimer Robinson, comp. *History of the Class of 1912, Yale College.* Vol. 1. New Haven, CT: Yale Univ., 1912.

Social Work Year Book. Vol. 4. New York: Russell Sage Foundation, 1937.

—*Stephen Pickering*

ROBINSON, SAMUEL (b. 1935, Memphis, TN), educator. One of nine children, Samuel Robinson was born in Memphis, TN, in 1935. After graduating from Tennessee State University in 1956 with a bachelor's degree in biology, he served for two years in the army before moving to Kentucky to work at **Lincoln Institute** in Shelby Co. in 1960. After teaching biology and math at the Lincoln Institute, he ultimately became dean of education and administrative assistant to the president.

As of 1966, Lincoln Institute had closed and would become the Lincoln School. The Commonwealth of Kentucky changed the mission from educating black students to educating gifted but disadvantaged students, regardless of race. Robinson became principal. Unexpectedly, and for unannounced reasons, the General Assembly eliminated funding for the Lincoln School. This action forced the school to close in 1970. There was only one class of graduates; however, according to Robinson, all 42 graduates had four-year scholarships to colleges, including Harvard and Yale. Thus Robinson was the last principal of the Lincoln Institute and the first and only principal of the Lincoln School.

Robinson was principal at Louisville's Shawnee High School for a few years and then enrolled at Indiana University to earn a doctorate in education. When he returned to Louisville in 1974,

he became executive director of the **Lincoln Foundation;** he became its president in 1991.

In 1994, the James Graham Brown Foundation offered the Lincoln Foundation a challenge grant of $500,000 for its **Whitney M. Young** Scholars Program. The grant allowed the Lincoln Foundation to raise $500,000 in matching money in a little over a year. Because of Robinson's leadership, the goal was reached in less than six months. In Robinson's opinion, the Whitney Young Scholars Program, which chose students in the seventh grade and guided them through high school with the promise of a college scholarship if they maintained their grades, was his signature achievement.

Robinson retired as president of the Lincoln Foundation and became president emeritus in 2000. He has received over 100 honors throughout his career, including induction into the National African-American Hall of Fame, honorary doctorates from Northern Kentucky and Bellarmine Universities, and Louisville's second Dream Award, given to a person who reflects the principles of Dr. Martin Luther King Jr.

Lincoln Foundation Files, 705 W. Broadway, Louisville, KY.

Robinson, Samuel. *The Gentle Agitator: Lessons from the Life of Dr. Samuel Robinson as Told to Gail Ritchie Henson,* edited by Gail Ritchie Henson. Louisville, KY: Bellarmine Univ. Press, 2008.

———. Interview by Andrew Baskin, Louisville, KY, June 11, 2008.

Robinson, Samuel, and Hugh Ella Robinson. Interview by Andrew Baskin, Louisville, KY, June 6, 2006.

—*Andrew Baskin*

ROOTS AND HERITAGE FESTIVAL, annual cultural celebration in Lexington, KY. The Roots and Heritage Festival was cofounded by Chester and Ann Grundy and Catherine Warner in Lexington, KY, in 1989. Warner, who initially brought the idea to the Grundys, was inspired by similar celebrations of African American cultural heritage in large metropolitan areas throughout the United States. Chester and Ann Grundy had previously been involved in developing an African Heritage Festival in Louisville, KY, which faded out after the couple moved to Lexington. According to Ann Grundy, Warner convinced them that the timing for a Lexington festival was ideal because **Deweese Street,** the old black business district, was being renovated. They connected with the neighborhood youth organization, led by Ed Holmes, who supported the idea, and proceeded to seek financial backing from Lexington mayor Scotty Baesler.

Mayor Baesler agreed to support the festival. Warner, Holmes, and the Grundys had originally intended to refer to the event as the African American Heritage Festival. However, Mayor Baesler requested that they change the name to the Roots and Heritage Festival in order to receive funding. The grant also required community collaboration. The Ann/Goodloe Street neighborhood and the Bluegrass Aspendale Association joined the effort.

Together, they assembled a festival featuring artists, performers, vendors, and speakers, all intended "to bring historical and cultural awareness to the Black community." The first festival was a daylong celebration that took place along the newly renovated Deweese St. on Saturday, September 23, 1989. The opening ceremony began with an African dance, and the day's entertainment included storytelling, a talent show, a fashion show with traditional African dress, and various musical performances. Booths set up along the street offered visitors to the free event the opportunity to purchase African art and cultural objects. The event culminated with a keynote address by Pulitzer Prize–winning author Alex Haley.

Since 1989, the festival has grown significantly and has attracted crowds of over 40,000 people. The celebration has expanded from a one-day event to a monthlong exploration of the heritage of the African American community in Lexington. Event themes have included "Blacks in Sports: Myth or Reality" and "My Brother's Keeper: Lending a Helping Hand to the Community." In 2002, the first annual Lexington Heritage Football Classic was played at Paul Laurence Dunbar Stadium and featured Clark Atlanta and Lincoln Universities. In 2007, the game was moved to the University of Kentucky's Commonwealth Stadium, and since 2005 the Football Classic has featured **Kentucky State University** and Central State University from Wilberforce, OH. This popular football game, as well as the numerous social, cultural, and educational experiences that are part of the monthlong celebration, have made the Roots and Heritage Festival a vibrant tradition in central Kentucky.

Grundy, Ann. Interview by Betsy Brinson, June 23, 1999. Kentucky Civil Rights Oral History Project, Kentucky Oral History Commission, Kentucky Historical Society, Lexington.
Muhammad, Patrice. "Twenty Years Later, the Roots and Heritage Festival Is Still Going." *Key Newsjournal.* http://keyconversationsradio.com/?p=478 (accessed July 16, 2012).
Newspapers: "Lexington to Celebrate Roots in Day-long Festival," *LHL,* September 7, 1989, B1; "Downtown Festival to Celebrate Black Culture, History," *LHL,* September 22, 1989, B1; "Festival Gets to Roots of Black Culture Sociologist: Sports Priorities Misplaced," *LHL,* September 8, 1991, C1; "Game Added to Lexington Festival—Heritage Classic Clash Is Sept. 7," *LHL,* June 8, 2002, D6; "UK Will Help Host Heritage Classic—Commonwealth Game Might Give School P.R. Boost," *LHL,* February 28, 2006, C3.
Roots and Heritage Board, Inc. "Lexington's Annual Roots & Heritage Festival." Lexington, KY, 2012. http://www.rootsfestky.com/ (accessed July 17, 2012).

—*Elizabeth Schaller*

ROSENWALD SCHOOLS, nearly 5,000 schools built in the early 1900s to educate African American students in the South. In 1911, Julius Rosenwald, president of Sears, Roebuck and Company and noted philanthropist, met Booker T. Washington in Chicago. The two men quickly became friends, and Rosenwald became a trustee of Washington's Tuskegee Institute in 1912. Both men expressed an interest in education, especially among southern African Americans. After Washington's death three years later, Rosenwald moved forward with a plan to fund the creation of schools throughout the South for the purpose of educating blacks in rural areas. He agreed to pay for one-third of the construction costs of these schools as long as local communities furnished land and contributed labor, materials, and funds.

By the time of Rosenwald's death in 1932, he had supported the construction of over 5,000 schools, shops, and teachers' homes in over a dozen states. The schools were noted for their architectural improvements on traditional schoolhouses, which later led white builders to mimic the schools' style. Architects insisted that

Clay City School (Rosenwald School) in Powell Co., KY, ca. 1927.

New Zion School (Rosenwald School) in Scott Co., KY, ca. 1920.

the schools be placed on one acre of land so that there would be room for playgrounds, and each building featured windows facing east to allow for sunlight in the mornings. Rosenwald contributed $4.3 million to his project, with an additional $4.7 million in contributions raised by the black community.

In Kentucky, the Julius Rosenwald Fund aided in the construction of 158 schools and buildings. Much of this support was a result of the **Kentucky Negro Educational Association's** (KNEA) decision to use its relationship with the Rosenwald building program to further the interests of black education in the state. **Francis M. Wood,** Rosenwald building agent and president of the KNEA from 1909 to 1916, made continuous efforts to bridge gaps between white and black educators, which contributed to the program's success.

Many of the schools were abandoned at the beginning of integration in the 1950s, and several were converted into residential and commercial buildings. By the end of the twentieth century, however, several movements had emerged to identify and preserve these sites. In 1997, Alicestyne Turley-Adams compiled a list of Rosenwald School sites in Kentucky, and many communities petitioned to have local schoolhouses restored and preserved during the following decade. In 2001, the National Trust Southern Office established the Rosenwald School Initiative to aid individuals and groups in organizing to protect historic sites, and in 2002, the National Trust for Historic Preservation included Rosenwald Schools on its list of America's Most Endangered Historic Places, leading to renewed interest in the schools as an important site in African American history.

Hoffschwelle, Mary S. *The Rosenwald Schools of the American South.* Gainesville: Univ. Press of Florida, 2006.

Newspapers: "History Lesson—Researcher Hopes to Find and Save Rosenwald Schools in Kentucky," *LHL,* August 11, 2004, A1; "Finding Rosenwald Schools," *LCJ,* August 16, 2004, A1.

Turley-Adams, Alicestyne. *Rosenwald Schools in Kentucky, 1917–1932.* Frankfort: Kentucky Heritage Council, 1997.

—*Stephen Pickering*

ROSS, GERALD D. (b. 1908, Washington, KY; d. 1991, Washington, DC), aide to Supreme Court justice Stanley F. Reed. As a child, Gerald D. Ross served as a golf caddy for Stanley F. Reed, an up-and-coming lawyer in Maysville, KY. Ross, who was born in the nearby town of Washington, hoped to save up money to attend college after high school, but when the Great Depression arrived, he moved to Washington, DC, in search of work. Ross had difficulty finding a job until he asked Reed, who was then solicitor general, for help. Reed helped him find a job as a butler at a local woman's home, but he quit after facing the prospect of a pay cut.

Reed became a justice on the Supreme Court in 1938 and then offered Ross a job as his personal messenger and aide. As an aide, Ross's responsibilities included keeping Reed's library up to date, serving as a personal chauffeur, and working as a butler and chef. In his free time, he moonlighted as a server at dinner parties and read books that he sneaked out of the Library of Congress for his personal use. For the next 19 years, he served as Reed's aide until Reed left the Supreme Court in 1957.

After suffering a stroke, Ross retired from his work in the city. In December 1991, he passed away in Washington, DC.

Dunnigan, Alice Allison, comp and ed. *The Fascinating Story of Black Kentuckians: Their Heritage and Traditions.* Washington, DC: Associated Publishers, 1982.

Fassett, John D. *New Deal Justice: The Life of Stanley Reed of Kentucky.* New York: Vantage Press, 1994.

Ross, Gerald D. Interview by Edward Gilson, March 18, 1981. Stanley F. Reed Oral History Project, Louie B. Nunn Center for Oral History, Univ. of Kentucky Libraries, Lexington.

—*Stephen Pickering*

ROSS, J. ALLEN (b. ca. 1847, Lexington, KY; d. unknown), Democratic politician. A native of Lexington, KY, J. Allen Ross first gained prominence as a charismatic speaker and controversial figure in Washington Co., MS. He engaged heavily in local politics, speaking on behalf of both the Republican and the Democratic Parties. He also earned the enmity of local partisans by attending their speeches and interrupting them with numerous irrelevant questions. On several occasions, he was wounded by gunmen for antagonizing local businesses or politicians. He was elected at different times as chancery clerk and sheriff, although he forfeited the latter position after failing to provide the necessary bond.

After numerous incidents that had made him somewhat infamous in Mississippi, Ross reemerged in Kentucky as a firm supporter of the Democrats. He attended the Mass State Convention of black voters held in Columbus, OH, where he was appointed a delegate to the Democratic National Convention in Louisville in 1883. In 1888, his reputation as a party organizer in the state earned him a role as a delegate to the Democratic Colored National Conference, where he served as secretary. Widely regarded as one of the finest black orators of his time, he was hired to deliver stump speeches on behalf of his party both within Kentucky and in other states, which at one point resulted in his being wounded by a thrown rock. He continued to speak on behalf of unpopular causes by delivering an impassioned speech for the **Anti–Separate Coach Movement,** arguing that blacks should "not be put in a separate cage like a criminal when they traveled."

In 1895, Ross moved to Louisville to practice law and remained active in politics by continuing to serve on the Negro State Democratic Committee.

Garner, James Wilford. *Reconstruction in Mississippi.* New York: Macmillan, 1901.

Newspapers: "Mississippi," *Nashville Union and American,* August 18, 1875, 1; "A Prostrate Party," *NYT,* May 6, 1876, 1; "Colored Democrat Assaulted," *Western Appeal* (St. Paul, MN), November 17, 1888, 1; *LH,* December 28, 1897, 1.

Smith, S. E., ed. *History of the Anti–Separate Coach Movement of Kentucky.* Evansville, IN: National Afro-American Journal and Directory, 1895.

—*Stephen Pickering*

ROSS, WILLIAM HENRY (b. 1869, Madisonville, KY; d. unknown), businessman and political activist in Hopkins Co., KY. William Henry Ross, son of John and Amanda Ross, was born in Madisonville, KY, in 1869. He was the oldest of 10 children. His father worked for a time as a blacksmith, and Ross learned the trade while also attending the Normal School in Hopkins Co., KY. After graduating from the Normal School, he taught at a public school in Muhlenburg Co., KY, in 1885. In 1887, he returned to Madisonville and went into business with his father, opening the John Ross and Son grocery store. Between 1887 and 1892, the grocery store changed locations several times. By 1897, Ross owned a large permanent store in downtown Madisonville.

In addition to his entrepreneurial interests, Ross became involved in local politics. In 1892, he began his political activity by participating in a protest demonstration at the state capitol in Frankfort, KY, regarding passage of the **Separate Coach Law.** A later account in W. D. Johnson's *Biographical Sketches of Prominent Negro Men and Women of Kentucky* described Ross defending African American Republican voters during an election in Madisonville. His actions frustrated the Democrats, who proceeded to attack Ross.

This incident made Ross an even more influential figure in local politics. He served as a delegate to the 1896 Republican State Convention and again to the 1900 convention. In 1900, several newspapers mistakenly identified him as a delegate to the Republican National Convention because reporters confused him with Dr. William P. Ross, also of Madisonville. He became secretary of the Republican Committee of Hopkins County in 1898 and continued to serve in that capacity until 1900. Ross was devoted to public service and furthering the cause of the Republican Party in Kentucky.

Johnson, W. D. *Biographical Sketches of Prominent Negro Men and Women of Kentucky.* Lexington, KY: The Standard Print, 1897.

Newspapers: "Colored People's Column," *Earlington (KY) Bee,* July 7, 1892, 3; "Colored People's Column," *Earlington (KY) Bee,* July 20, 1893, 3; "Hopkins County and the Second District at the State Convention," *Earlington (KY) Bee,* April 23, 1896, 2; "Republican Conventions,"*Earlington (KY) Bee,* August 18, 1898, 2; "Hopkins County Republicans," *Earlington (KY) Bee,* May 3, 1900, 1; "Republican District Convention," *Earlington (KY) Bee,* May 10, 1900, 1; "Announcements," *HK,* May 15, 1900, 4; "Senatorial Convention," *Earlington (KY) Bee,* March 7, 1901, 1.

—*Elizabeth Schaller*

ROWAN FAMILY, owners of Federal Hill Plantation, popularly believed to have been the site of the composition of "My Old Kentucky Home." In the late eighteenth century, John Rowan, a lawyer and future U.S. senator in Bardstown, KY, began construction of a large house. The actual work of crafting materials for the building and the assembly of its various parts fell to a large number of slaves owned by Rowan; they lived in cabins at the rear of the house. Ownership of the plantation, Federal Hill, passed through the hands of several members of the family before Madge Frost, John Rowan's granddaughter, sold it to become the site of My Old Kentucky Home State Park. A widely held legend asserted that the residence was Stephen Foster's inspiration for **"My Old Kentucky Home."**

Aside from a small plaque "dedicated to the faithful retainers of Judge John Rowan," slavery largely disappeared from the public history of Federal Hill until Ida Roberts, an administrator for IBM, began to research her ancestry. Drawing from a family story that claimed that her great-grandfather was the son of John Rowan Jr., the second owner of Federal Hill, she tracked down available slave records from various institutions around Nelson Co. before publishing her findings in a book, *Rising above It All: A Tribute to the Rowan Slaves of Federal Hill.*

According to Roberts, evidence suggested that Rowan Jr. fathered children with two slaves, one of whom was Mary Lyons Rowan in 1855. After the publication of the book, Roberts began an annual tradition of holding reunions at My Old Kentucky Home State Park for descendants of the household slaves. At the first reunion, about 300 relatives were expected to participate, and many wore shirts with the statement "Yes, I'm a Rowan."

Several changes to the park to emphasize the place of slavery have been proposed since the revelation of the extent of the Rowan family. Park director Alice Heaton successfully moved a golf course fairway that separated a slave cemetery from the house, although an adjacent fairway remained in place. Additionally, the commissioner for state parks ordered a review of how African American history would be interpreted at historical sites within the state.

Bradby, Marie. "Whose Old Kentucky Home?" *Louisville* 47 (September 1996): 32–39.

Capps, Randall. *The Rowan Story: From Federal Hill to My Old Kentucky Home.* Bowling Green, KY: Homestead Press, 1976.

Newspapers: "Descendants of Slaves Gather to Unveil Book," *LHL,* June 19, 1994, B1; "Where the Sun Shone Less Bright," *LHL,* August 2, 2009, A1.

Roberts, Ida M. K. (Rowan). *Rising above It All: A Tribute to the Rowan Slaves of Federal Hill.* Louisville, KY: Harmony House, 1994.

—*Stephen Pickering*

RUDD, DANIEL (b. 1854, Bardstown, KY; d. 1933, Bardstown, KY), Roman Catholic publisher, activist, and founder of the National Black Catholic Congress. Daniel Rudd was born on August 7, 1854, in Bardstown, KY. Both of his parents were slaves on local plantations. His father, Robert Rudd, lived on the Rudd plantation, and his mother, Elizabeth, was enslaved on the Hayden plantation. One of 12 children, Daniel Rudd followed his parents' Catholic faith during his lifetime.

After the Civil War, Rudd moved to Springfield, OH, and obtained a secondary school education there. In 1886, he established the *American Catholic Tribune* newspaper. This national publication became the first newspaper owned and directed by black Catholics and addressed issues affecting blacks in general and the Catholic faith community nationally. Rudd believed that the Catholic Church was a positive force to oppose racial segregation in the nineteenth century.

Under Rudd's leadership, black Catholics were urged to create a Congress of Colored Catholics to encourage the church to promote civil rights. The first such congress met in 1889 and elected Rudd president. Successive congresses had denominational support, promoted the establishment of schools, and pushed the church's bishops and clergy to reject racist practices inherent in American society.

In 1899, the *Tribune* ceased publication, and Rudd moved first to Mississippi and then to Madison, AR, serving as an accountant for a well-to-do black farmer. In 1932, he returned to Bardstown after suffering a stroke. On December 3, 1933, he died at age 79 and was buried in Bardstown's Saint Joseph's Cemetery. His legacy to African Americans was the National Black Catholic Congress, which continues to exist as a coalition of black Catholic organizations.

Davis, Cyprian. *The History of Black Catholics in the United States.* New York: Crossroad, 1990.

Kentucky, Death Records, 1852–1953.

—*John A. Hardin*

RUSSELL, ALFRED FRANCIS (b. 1817, Lexington, KY; d. 1884, Liberia), missionary, plantation owner, and government official in Liberia. Alfred Francis Russell was born a slave on August 25, 1817, in Lexington, KY. He was the son of Milly Russell, an octoroon slave, and was rumored to have been fathered by John Russell, the son of Mary Owen Todd Russell, the daughter of early Kentucky settler John Todd, who was killed at the Battle of Blue Licks in 1782. Mary Russell never publicly acknowledged Alfred as her only grandson, but his paternity was the subject of a protracted court case involving Todd family heirs and Mary's second husband, Robert Wickliffe, the largest slaveholder in Kentucky and well known for his proslavery views.

Russell and his mother were emancipated by Mary Owen Todd Russell in March 1833 and traveled on the ship *Ajax* to Liberia. Settling in the **Clay-Ashland** district, Russell worked for the Methodist Church as a missionary and later joined the Protestant Episcopal Church as a priest. He owned a large farm in Montserrado Co. where coffee and sugarcane were grown. He served as a senator and commissioner of education in Liberia and in 1881 became vice president for the winning True Whig Party ticket with Anthony William Gardner. Russell assumed the presidency in 1883 when Gardner resigned after losing territory along the western Liberia border. He was not nominated for re-election and died on April 4, 1884, shortly after leaving office.

Ramage, Andrea S. "Love and Honor: The Robert Wickliffe Family of Antebellum Kentucky." *RKHS* 94 (Spring 1996): 115–33.
Smith, David, Jr. *The First 10 African American Presidents, 1848–1904: The Nation Builders.* Atlanta: Black History Collection, 2010.
Watkins, Andrea S. "Patriarchal Politics: Robert Wickliffe and His Family in Antebellum Kentucky." PhD diss., Univ. of Kentucky, 1999.

—Andrea S. Watkins

RUSSELL, GREEN PINCKNEY (b. 1864, Russellville, KY; d. 1936, Waukegan, IL), president of Kentucky Normal and Industrial Institute.

Born on Christmas Day of 1864 in Russellville, KY, Green Pinckney Russell received an extensive education as a child with the help of a private tutor hired by his mother. He attended the public schools of Russellville before entering **Berea College** to pursue a degree, which he earned after six years. He taught briefly at a segregated school in Chilesburg before accepting a position as principal of a school in Lexington in 1890. In 1894, Russell was promoted to the newly created position of supervisor of Negro schools. In that position, Russell attracted some attention by advocating manual training as part of his curriculum.

In 1912, Russell was selected to fill the vacant position of president of Kentucky Normal and Industrial Institute for Colored Persons (later known as **Kentucky State University**) with the support of his friends and fellow Democrats Judge Rogers Clay and Auditor Henry Bosworth. During his tenure, he expanded the school's operating budget and added a new dormitory and housing for the president. He also gained a reputation as an authoritarian figure who tolerated little disagreement. Dissension at Kentucky Normal grew in 1914 after Russell's heavy-handed mishandling of a supposed "riot" on campus, and by the end of the decade, a strong movement had gained traction among students and teachers alike to have Russell dismissed from the presidency.

In 1923, the campaign to remove Russell succeeded when George Colvin, chairman of the board of trustees and Republican hopeful for governor, chose **Francis M. Wood** to replace him. However, Colvin's political aspirations proved to be short lived,

and when he lost the election for governor in November of the same year, Russell made a move to regain his position. Again with the support of state Democrats, Russell took back the presidency when Wood resigned in 1924.

His second term as president, however, proved to be as controversial as the first. After charges of financial misconduct surfaced, the board of trustees investigated Russell's administration in the late 1920s. The trustees discovered that he had hired his wife and daughter to work in the school's tiny library and that his mismanagement of the school had resulted in disappointing educational and professional standards. Russell resigned in 1929, although he resisted to the end and attempted for several years to regain his position from his successor, **Rufus B. Atwood.** He passed away on October 18, 1936, in Waukegan, IL, and was buried in Greenwood (Cove Haven) Cemetery in Lexington.

Hardin, John A. *Fifty Years of Segregation: Black Higher Education in Kentucky, 1904–1954.* Lexington: Univ. Press of Kentucky, 1997.
———. "Green Pinckney Russell of Kentucky Normal and Industrial Institute for Colored Persons." *Journal of Black Studies* 25 (1995): 610–21.
Smith, Gerald L. *A Black Educator in the Segregated South: Kentucky's Rufus B. Atwood.* Lexington: Univ. Press of Kentucky, 1994.

—Stephen Pickering

RUSSELL, HARVEY CLARENCE, JR. (b. 1918, Louisville, KY; d. 1998, Yonkers, NY), corporate executive and Coast Guard Officer.

From a family of educators, Harvey Clarence Russell Jr. was one of five children. His father, **Harvey Clarence Russell Sr.,** had served as dean of Frankfort's Kentucky State College (later known as **Kentucky State University**) and president of West Kentucky Industrial College (later known as **West Kentucky Community and Technical College**). His mother, Harriet Tucker Russell, a Fisk graduate, taught Latin, and his maternal grandmother, Annie C. Vance Tucker, a **Berea College** graduate, was known as the Lady Principal at Livingstone College in Salisbury, NC.

Russell, an Eagle Scout and graduate of Kentucky State College, became the second African American admitted to the Coast Guard Academy's Reserve Officer Training Course in September 1943. Five months later, he was promoted to lieutenant junior grade and served as navigation officer on the nation's first integrated naval vessel, the USS *Sea Cloud*. In October 1945, he became the "second recognized African American" to helm an American sea service vessel when he was commissioned his own vessel, the *TY-45*, which included an all-white crew, in the Philippines.

After leaving the service, Russell joined W. B. Graham Associates, an African American advertising agency in New York. He worked for six months free as a trainee and earned a salary after he signed a contract as a sales manager for Joe Louis Punch, a soft drink promoted primarily in the South. In 1950, PepsiCo hired Russell to manage "Negro sales." In 1962, he became the first African American vice president of a leading national company when PepsiCo promoted him to be in charge of "special markets" that included African American and Latin American consumers. A year later, he encouraged the company to finance an audio series on black history that included study guides for public schools.

Russell retired as PepsiCo's vice president of community affairs in 1983. While dealing with prostate cancer, he died of a heart attack in Yonkers, NY, in 1998. In his lifetime, he served as a board member of the **National Association for the Advancement of Colored People** Legal Defense and Educational Fund, helped develop the Congressional Black Caucus Foundation, and became chairman of the Interracial Council for Business Opportunities. In 2003, PepsiCo established the Global Harvey Russell Inclusion Award in his honor.

"Big Business Names a VEEP." *Ebony,* June 1962.

Dunnigan, Alice Allison, comp. and ed. *The Fascinating Story of Black Kentuckians: Their Heritage and Traditions.* Washington, DC: Associated Publishers, 1982.

"Harvey C. Russell Jr., 79; Broke Ground for Blacks in Corporations," *NYT,* March 1, 1998, 34.

Thiesen, William H. "Pioneers of Ethnic Diversity in the American Sea Services." United States Coast Guard. http://www.uscg.mil/history /articles/Bulletin_HistoryLesson_Oct_11.pdf (accessed June 29, 2012).

"Who Was Harvey C. Russell?" and "Harvey C. Russell-Pioneer In Diversity and Involvement." Pepsico. https://www.pepsicochairmans award.com/ca/hraward1.shtml (accessed June 28, 2012).

—*Sallie L. Powell*

RUSSELL, HARVEY CLARENCE, SR. (b. 1883, Bloomfield, KY; d. 1949, Louisville, KY), educator.

Harvey Clarence Russell Sr. attended Kentucky State Normal School (later known as **Kentucky State University**) and later earned an AB degree from Simmons University (later known as **Simmons College of Kentucky**) in Louisville and an MA degree from the University of Cincinnati. In his long and distinguished career, Russell taught in the Bloomfield public schools and at Frankfort Normal School, **Booker T. Washington** Elementary School in Louisville, and Louisville Normal School.

Russell served as dean of Kentucky State College, then as president of West Kentucky Industrial College (1937–1938) and its successor, West Kentucky Vocational College (1943–1947) in Paducah, and from 1939 to 1942 as director of the National Youth Administration. Between 1917 and 1922, Russell was president of the **Kentucky Negro Educational Association** (KNEA); he was instrumental in establishing African American parent-teacher associations as part of the KNEA and organizing the State High School Athletic Association. Russell was also one of the founders of the **Domestic Life and Accident Insurance Company,** a national grand master of the **United Brothers of Friendship,** an educational columnist for the *Louisville Leader,* and a business manager for Simmons University in his later years.

In 1926, Russell and his wife, Julia, moved from 1029 W. Madison St. to 2345 W. Chestnut, where he lived until his death. Russell had six children: **Harvey Jr.,** George, Anna, Howard, Bessie, and Rhonda. Several of them became successful elsewhere, most notably Harvey Jr., who was a vice president of PepsiCo in the 1960s. Because of Harvey Sr.'s many achievements, the **Russell neighborhood** in West Louisville came to bear his name, as did the former Madison Street Junior High School, which was rededicated as Harvey C. Russell Junior High School on February 9, 1960.

Dunnigan, Alice Allison, comp. and ed. *The Fascinating Story of Black Kentuckians: Their Heritage and Traditions.* Washington, DC: Associated Publishers, 1982.

Newspapers: *LCJ,* September 23, 1949; *Louisville Times,* September 23, 1949; *Louisville Leader,* September 24, 1949; *LD,* February 9, 1960.

—*J. Blaine Hudson*

RUSSELL NEIGHBORHOOD, Louisville community.

The Russell neighborhood, named for nationally recognized black educator **Harvey C. Russell Sr.,** is a primarily residential area west of downtown Louisville, bounded by Market St. to the north, 32nd St. to the west, Broadway to the south, and Roy Wilkins Ave. to the east. The eastern section of the area was inhabited by numerous free African American families in the years before the Civil War. The Russell area attracted substantially more people in the 1870s. At first, into the 1880s, the "suburban" community became a fashionable address for wealthy white families spurred by crowded downtown conditions, mule-drawn streetcar lines, and the romantic connotations associated with rural living. They were further enticed by developers such as Basil Doerhoefer, who was also president of the American Tobacco Works. Russell was home to architect Max Drach, Falls City Stone Works owner Michael Blatz, and Phillip Stitzel of the U. P. Stitzel Brothers Distillery. Scattered among the grand Victorian and Italianate homes on Chestnut, **Walnut** (now **Muhammad Ali** Blvd.), and Jefferson Sts., African Americans and working-class whites, some of whom were employed as servants, constructed smaller frame and shotgun-style houses on the minor streets and along back alleys.

With the development of the eastern and southern portions of the city in the 1890s, white residents began leaving the Russell neighborhood. Concentrated primarily in the eastern portion of the community before this time, middle-class African Americans slowly replaced the white families in a westward pattern; professionals purchased the larger homes, and the working class moved into the more modest dwellings. The continued settlement of African Americans was affected by the city's Residential Segregation Ordinance in 1914, which was intended to slow housing integration by prohibiting African Americans from moving onto a predominantly white street and vice versa. After the U.S. Supreme Court declared the measure unconstitutional in *Buchanan v. Warley* (1917), African Americans continued to migrate into the community and pushed west of 21st St. A substantial concentration of African Americans existed by the 1920s, evidenced by the establishment of the **Western Colored Branch Library** in 1908 at 10th and Chestnut Sts. and the Plymouth Settlement House in 1917 at 16th and Chestnut Sts.

By the 1940s, Russell was the city's premier African American neighborhood. Businesses lined the bustling Walnut St. corridor, and popular night spots such as the Top Hat Club, Charlie Moore's, and Joe's Palm Room dotted the area. However, in the years after World War II, many of the wealthier African American residents abandoned the area, an action that increased dramatically during the 1960s as housing became more integrated throughout the city. Many of the abandoned homes were bulldozed during the 1960s after heirs frequently refused to claim their relatives' property. Urban renewal was an important factor of change that leveled old, abandoned buildings. Crime, drugs, and poverty became so rampant that the city had difficulty finding people to purchase lots even when they were offered for one dollar in the 1970s and early 1980s.

The 1980s witnessed the beginning of Russell's rebirth. After years of neglect, the placement of a large section of the neighborhood on the National Register of Historic Places in 1980 prompted organizations such as Habitat for Humanity, the Louisville Central Development Corp., and REBOUND (Rebuilding Our Urban Neighborhood Dwellings) to begin rehabilitating old houses and building new houses in the area. The Old Walnut Street Capital Campaign, a $3-million fund-raising drive organized by the Louisville Central Community Center, also planned several new facilities, including a neighborhood services center, an entrepreneurial development center, a youth and adult training center, and a child development center. By 1996, 100 new homes and 170 apartments (such as Hampton Place) had been built in the area, and a $33.7-million renovation project was announced for the large Village West (now called City View Park–Walnut) housing development that had been constructed in 1973. In 2014, the Russell Neighborhood's population was close to 11,000, representing 1 percent of Jefferson Co.'s total population. African Americans comprised more than 85 percent of the residents.

Louisville Survey West: Final Report. Louisville, KY: Preservation Alliance of Louisville, 1977.

A Place in Time: The Story of Louisville's Neighborhoods. Louisville, KY: Courier-Journal, 1989.

"Russell Neighborhood Profile, January 2014." Prepared by the Network Center for Community Change. http://makechangetogether .org/wp-content/uploads/2014/04/Russell-Data-Profile-Final.pdf (accessed August 15, 2014).

S

SAFFELL, DAISY MORGAN (b. 1875, Louisville, KY; d. 1918, Shelbyville, KY), and SAFFELL, GEORGE WILLIAM (b. 1873, Frankfort, KY; d. 1953, Shelbyville, KY), educators, undertakers, and club organizers. Daisy Morgan Grubbs was born in Louisville, KY, and matriculated at Fisk University and Roger Williams University in Nashville, TN. Known for her musical ability, she was also regarded as a skillful writer and an eloquent speaker. She taught school in Frankfort and Lawrenceburg, where she served as principal for three years. In 1897, she married "Professor" George William Saffell, also an educator. In 1901, the couple worked at Harrodsburg's **Wayman Institute,** where George served as principal and Daisy taught music.

Not only educators, Daisy and George were very active in club work. In 1904, Daisy organized the Women's Improvement Club in Lawrenceburg. Five years later, George, as district grand master, presided over "the largest convention in the history of the Colored Odd Fellows" in Kentucky, held in Nicholasville. This convention unanimously elected George grand master for the upcoming year. Daisy was elected secretary of the Household of Ruth. In a speech at the convention, she advocated for enforcement of a compulsory insurance law.

According to the 1910 U.S. census, Daisy had left teaching and was working as an undertaker, while George served as a school principal in Shelbyville, KY. After training at Clark's School for Embalming (later known as Cincinnati College of Mortuary Science) in Cincinnati, OH, Daisy had become the first African American female licensed embalmer in Kentucky. She operated Saffell and Saffell Funeral Home, located on Clay St. in Shelbyville. She later became the secretary of the Colored Funeral Director's Association of Kentucky, treasurer of the National Association of Colored Funeral Directors, and editor of the *Kentucky Club Woman.* In August 1912, she addressed the National Negro Business League in Chicago. That same year, as secretary of the District Household of Ruth of Kentucky, she spoke in Atlanta, encouraging African American girls to get into business by declaring: "I believe that there is a place for every girl of my race. . . . The only thing is for her to make up her mind to find it."

Before her death on October 2, 1918, Daisy worked toward the building of the Amanda Smith Hospital for African Americans in Shelbyville. The hospital was posthumously renamed the Daisy M. Saffell Hospital in her honor. Prominent undertaker **Thomas K. Robb** handled the funeral arrangements, and Daisy was buried in the Frankfort Cemetery.

George continued to work in education while simultaneously managing the funeral home and purchased land to establish Calvary Cemetery in Shelbyville. In 1924, he was elected the first president of the newly formed Independent National Funeral Directors Association. In 1933, as an active member of the **Kentucky Negro Educational Association,** he appealed for the organization to support assistance for the young males arrested in

Scottsboro, AL, known as the Scottsboro Boys. In his mid-60s, George married Mildred Stone, age 27, in 1939. Mildred also trained in the undertaking business and primarily managed Saffell Funeral Home. George died of a heart attack on March 22, 1953. He and Mildred, who died in 2003, were buried together in Saffell Calvary Cemetery in Shelbyville.

Kentucky, Death Records, 1852–1953.

Newspapers: "Peace and Good Will the Text," *CJ,* July 14, 1909, 3; "Negro Odd Fellows Elect Grand Master," *CJ,* July 15, 1909, 3; "Race Progress in Kentucky," *Broad Ax* (Chicago), March 29, 1913, 4; "Colored Woman Dies," *Shelby Sentinel,* October 11, 1918, 5; "Heart Attack Fatal to Prof. Saffell," *Shelby Sentinel,* March 27, 1953, 1.

Parrish, C. H. *Golden Jubilee of the General Association of Colored Baptists in Kentucky: From 1865–1915.* Louisville, KY: Mayes Printing Co., 1915.

U.S. Federal Census (1900, 1910, 1920, 1930, 1940).

—*Sallie L. Powell*

ST. AUGUSTINE CATHOLIC CHURCH, one of the oldest African American Catholic churches in the United States. St. Augustine Roman Catholic Church, located at 1310 W. Broadway in Louisville, was founded on February 20, 1870. It is the sixth-oldest African American Catholic church in the United States. Louisville's first African American Catholics migrated from Maryland in 1785, but not until 1868 did Bishop William McCloskey appoint Father John L. Spalding to organize an African American parish. St. Augustine was selected as the patron of the congregation. The first parishioners worshipped in the basement of the Cathedral of the Assumption until the first church was built on Broadway between 14th and 15th Sts. On February 20, 1870, 75 members marched from the cathedral's basement to the new site. Facilities included a school on the ground level, a church on the second floor, and a rectory next door. The school opened in 1871 and was operated by the Sisters of Charity of Nazareth.

The growth of the congregation necessitated a new building. The second church building was blessed on May 18, 1902, and the first church was remodeled and used as a parish hall. The third and present site of the church was blessed on September 10, 1912.

A high school was established in 1921. In 1929, the high school was moved to Eighth and Cedar Sts. and was operated by the Archdiocese of Louisville until 1958 under the name **Catholic Colored High School.** The cornerstone for the new elementary school was laid in 1961 and was blessed in March 1962 by the Most Reverend Charles G. Maloney. In 1967, the schools of three parishes—St. Louis Bertrand, St. Philip Neri, and St. Augustine—consolidated into one school named Pope Paul VI Consolidated School. In 1969, the school merged with Pope John XXIII Consolidated School to become Popes Paul and John Consolidated Schools. It was closed in 1973. Renovation of the church began on January 6, 1974, and was completed in early April. Murals and icons were designed by Kinshasha and **Houston Conwill.** Sculptor **Ed Hamilton** created a bronze crucifix.

St. Augustine was the first parish in the Archdiocese of Louisville to have the ordination of a deacon, Robert J. Mueller, in 1973. It had the first black permanent deacon, Robert Grundy, in

1977. Father Edward Branch, the first archdiocesan black priest, offered his first mass at St. Augustine in 1974.

—*Angela Partee*

ST. JAMES A.M.E. CHURCH, African American church in Covington, KY. St. James African Methodist Episcopal (A.M.E.) Church of Covington began in 1869, only a few years after the Civil War ended. The church was started by Martha Ann Taylor, a devoted local Christian woman who for years conducted numerous church services, taught weekly Sunday school classes, and organized nightly prayer meetings from her home in Covington. With the growth of church membership, Taylor moved the congregation to a newly built schoolhouse located in the Austinburg area of Covington. Several years later, the congregation moved to a building in Covington on Maryland Ave. near Oliver St. and later to a structure on Ninth St. between Greenup and Prospect Sts. Two subsequent moves took the congregation to downtown Covington, at the corner of Seventh St. and Madison Ave., and to the Domestic Science Department at **Lincoln-Grant School.** Finally, in 1922, under the leadership of Rev. J. A. G. Grant, the congregation developed a plan to construct a permanent structure on several acres of land located in Covington at 120 Lynn St. that the church had purchased in 1918. Under Grant's direction, donations and pledges were collected from hundreds of local African Americans for the construction of the new church. Grant also gained the support of Bishop A. J. Carey, who appealed to A.M.E. church members throughout Kentucky and Tennessee to invest in this venture. The first phase of the building program, which included a large sanctuary and several meeting rooms, was completed in late 1922.

After Grant's departure, each subsequent pastor contributed substantially to guiding the continuous construction at St. James A.M.E. Church. For instance, Rev. S. R. Reid, who served as the church's pastor for only one year (1925–1926), created a church building fund that later was used to acquire furniture and a new furnace for the church. By the late 1950s, most of the building was completed through the use of these funds. Today, St. James A.M.E. Church continues to serve the spiritual and community needs of hundreds of African American northern Kentuckians.

"Diamond Jubilee Celebration and Mortgage Burning of St. James A.M.E. Church—September 10th to 16th, 1945." Northern Kentucky African American Heritage Task Force Collection, W. Frank Steely Library, Northern Kentucky Univ.

Reis, James. "Black Churches Offered Stability in Troubled Times," *KP*, January 20, 1997, 4K.

"St. James A.M.E. Church—118th Anniversary 1987—Covington, KY." Northern Kentucky African American Heritage Task Force Collection, W. Frank Steely Library, Northern Kentucky Univ.

—*Eric R. Jackson*

ST. JULIEN, MARION (b. 1972, Lafayette, LA), jockey. Marion St. Julien was born in Lafayette, LA. His mother, Cynthia Sargent, an elementary school teacher, introduced him to horse racing. However, his ambition was to play football. After the 5-feet-2, 110-pound high school honor student experienced some hard hits on the football field, he decided in the summer before his senior year to apply for his jockey's license. At age 17, he competed in his first race and had his first victory in the same year.

St. Julien, nicknamed the Saint, rode in Lone Star Park, part of the Texas-Louisiana-Arkansas circuit. As Lone Star's leading rider for two years, he accumulated nearly 1,000 career victories and $8 million in purse winnings by 1998. Well aware of the history of **African American jockeys,** he struggled when he was overlooked as a possible rider by many owners and trainers.

In May 2000, St. Julien became the first African American jockey in 79 years to compete in the **Kentucky Derby.** He rode Curule, a 50-to-1 long shot, and finished 7th in a 19-horse field. Based in Louisville, KY, he was rated in the top five in jockey standings. Later that year, he became the first African American to ride in the Breeders' Cup since that championship was established in 1984.

At age 40, St. Julien had over 2,250 wins and rode primarily in Indiana and Kentucky. In January 2013, the Turfway Park stewards suspended him indefinitely pending the completion of a drug-treatment program. He admitted to the use of "an unprescribed controlled substance." A few months later, African American jockey Kevin Krigger rode in the Kentucky Derby.

"Blacks Make History at Kentucky Derby with Black Chairman and Black Jockey." *Jet,* May 22, 2000, 51–53.

"'A Feeling of a Lifetime': St. Julien Will Be First Black Jockey in 79 Years at Derby." CNN/Sports Illustrated, May 4, 2000. http://sportsillustrated.cnn.com/more/horseracing/2000/triplecrown/kentucky/news/2000/05/04/stjulien_derby_ap/ (accessed September 11, 2013).

"It's a Long, Uphill Ride to Racing's Big Leagues." *NYT,* July 21, 1998, C1.

McGee, Marty. "Turfway Park Notes: Jockeys St. Julien, Gonzalez Given Lengthy Suspensions." *Daily Racing Form,* January 4, 2013. http://www.drf.com/print/news/turfway-park-notes-jockeys-st-julien-gonzalez-given-lengthy-suspensions (accessed September 11, 2013).

—*Wardell Johnson*

ST. MARK'S EPISCOPAL CHURCH (COLORED), church that opened the first black high school in Louisville, KY. St. Mark's was the first Episcopal church founded for Louisville blacks and, after the Civil War, was a site for local black education until its decline in 1868. The church started when white Episcopal missionary William Ira Waller organized St. Mark's Episcopal Mission as a distinct organization for local blacks in 1861. The mission soon bought an old church building at Green and Ninth Sts. for its programs. In February 1865, Kentucky bishop B. B. Smith recruited D. D. Dennehy, a white teacher, to run a school there. According to one estimate, night school attendance at the school ranged from 60 to 80 students.

In February 1867, the church opened the first local public high school for African Americans. According to one supporter, the school would help "prepare those who aspire for any of the positions in the walks of life," in contrast to previous black educational efforts, which "aim only at dispensing that degree of culture which will make the colored men more intelligent hewers of wood and drawers of water." The school hired Cordelia A.

Jennings, a black woman who had graduated from the Colored Institute of Philadelphia and was principal of a distinguished school in Philadelphia, to run the school.

Bishop Smith specifically recruited West Indians for black educational work, once writing a friend to ask that "any educated colored men in Barbados who are sufficiently interested in the American freedmen come over and assist him." One Barbados native involved in St. Mark's was Rev. Joseph Sandiford Atwell, the first black deacon ordained in the state diocese. Shortly before the school's opening, the **American Missionary Association** sent Atwell to St. Mark's as rector. According to Bishop Smith, Atwell served with "singular wisdom and discretion . . . greatly for the benefit of his race," and during his time there, he also married Jennings.

In August 1868, Atwell resigned from St. Mark's to pursue a pastorate in Virginia, and his wife followed him. After their departure, Barbados native D. A. Straker immigrated to Kentucky to work at St. Mark's. However, local white violence toward black schools convinced Straker that he needed a law degree to fight effectively for black education, and he left to study law at Howard University. The church faded out of existence soon afterward. Two years later the Episcopal Diocese of Kentucky founded the **Church of Our Merciful Savior** to continue its ministry to local blacks.

Gibson, W. H., Sr. *Historical Sketch of the Progress of the Colored Race, in Louisville, Ky., as Noted by the Writer during a Period of Fifty Years.* Louisville, KY: Bradley & Gilbert, 1897.

Lucas, Marion B. *A History of Blacks in Kentucky.* Vol. 1, *From Slavery to Segregation, 1760–1891.* Frankfort: Kentucky Historical Society, 1992.

Newspapers: "Schools in Louisville, Ky.," *Freedmen's Record,* May 1865, 72–73; "St. Mark's Colored High School," *Louisville Daily Courier,* February 12, 1867, 1.

Phillips, Glenn O. "The Response of a West Indian Activist: D. A. Straker, 1842–1908." *JNH* 66 (Summer 1981): 128–39.

—David Lai

ST. PAUL AFRICAN METHODIST EPISCOPAL CHURCH (LEXINGTON), African American church organized during slavery.

Saint Paul African Methodist Episcopal (A.M.E.) Church has been identified as a house of worship that can trace its existence to 1820. The congregation evolved from the Hill Street Methodist Church associated with the local Conference of the Methodist Episcopal Church South. During 1820, several black members of the Hill Street Church decided to form their own congregation and rented a stable on N. Upper St. from Charles Wilkins, a white banker, who promised to protect those blacks who worshipped there from any harassment.

William Smith, a local black preacher, presided over the first meetings of the new church. Under his leadership, new members were attracted. Subsequently, the church purchased the rented stable and the surrounding lot for $280 in 1827. Parts of the stable were removed, and a small brick building had already been built before the purchase. Although the building experienced significant remodeling in 1850, 1877, 1906, and 1986, part of the original stable is thought to remain in the basement of the current building.

In 1865, the church, then known locally as Upper Street Methodist Church, withdrew from the Conference of the Methodist

Church South and briefly operated as an independent church. In 1866, the church joined the Ohio Conference of the African Methodist Episcopal Church. Reverend Grafton Graham was appointed its first A.M.E. pastor.

The congregation engaged in civic activities as well. Before the Civil War, the church functioned in the **Underground Railroad** as a resting place for runaway slaves. It became a venue for black community events, such as statewide meetings of black teachers and fraternal organizations. During World War I, the church participated in community Fourth of July celebrations by showing films of African American soldiers serving in combat and other roles. During World War II, the American War Mothers group met at the church. **Jordan C. Jackson,** a prominent local African American businessman and politician, was a member of the church.

Newspapers: "Colored Notes," *LHL,* July 23, 1903; "Colored Notes," *LHL,* April 13, 1911; "Colored Notes," *LHL,* August 2–4, 1925.

Perrin, William Henry. *History of Fayette County.* Chicago: O. L. Baskin, 1882, 472.

—John A. Hardin

ST. PAUL AFRICAN METHODIST EPISCOPAL CHURCH (NEWPORT), African Methodist Episcopal church in Newport, KY.

St. Paul African Methodist Episcopal (A.M.E.) Church of Newport was formed in 1901 and changed its name in 1914. An A.M.E. church had existed in Newport since 1880, and on several occasions it was confused with the Colored Methodist Episcopal (C.M.E.) denomination, of which there was at least one congregation in Newport; however, there is a difference between the two denominations. In February 1880, the A.M.E. congregation, under the leadership of Rev. Henry Harris, dedicated the recently leased and repaired church previously pastored by Peter H. Jeffries, a Lutheran minister. The building was at the corner of Mayo St. and Central Ave. in Newport. In April 1884, at the Kentucky Methodist conference held in Covington, Rev. H. G. Jenkins was appointed pastor of the A.M.E. Church in Newport.

In June 1901, a new A.M.E. church was dedicated in Newport at 714 Saratoga St. The group performed at the camp meeting held at Nelson Pl. in East Newport. In July, Tanner's Chapel was the name first given to the A.M.E. church. In August, Rev. J. W. Frazier, presiding elder of the Lexington District A.M.E. Church, preached and served Communion at the Saratoga St. church. In September, the church's annual festival was held at Memorial Hall next to the church. The following year, Rev. J. H. Clark, formerly of Payne Theological Seminary, Wilberforce, OH, and pastor at the A.M.E. church, engaged the famous singing group African Missionary Singers.

In December 1905, the A.M.E. church began negotiations to purchase the property of the former Corpus Christi Catholic Church on Chestnut St. in Newport. The church had been abandoned for several years after the Catholics opened a new church in town at Ninth and Isabella Sts. Rev. J. R. Rooks, who had served as pastor of Tanner's Chapel for less than a year, was instrumental in completing the purchase for $2,000 in January 1906; afterward, the church building on Saratoga St. was abandoned. In April, a large celebration of the formal opening of the newly acquired church building was held; Rev. J. W. Frazier was in town again to deliver the sermons.

From 1908 to 1917, church services continued to be held at the building on Chestnut St. In 1914, the congregation's name had changed from Tanner's Chapel to St. Paul A.M.E. Church. By 1923, St. Paul A.M.E. Church had moved to 210 W. Seventh St. in Newport, and Rev. Elmer Reid was pastor. On October 4, 1925, at the Kentucky Annual Conference of A.M.E. churches held in Danville, KY, Rev. D. C. Carter was made pastor of St. Paul A.M.E. Church. Carter died in 1926, and Rev. Edward J. McCoo was appointed his successor. In 1942, W. M. Mitchell served as pastor, and from 1944 through 1946, Rev. J. L. Madison served. In the eight years between 1946 and 1954, various ministers attended to the spiritual needs of the congregation.

On Sunday evening, March 28, 1954, Eugene Russell, who was then St. Paul A.M.E. Church's pastor, brought the Wright Gold musical ensemble from Cincinnati to perform at the church. On October 15, 1959, the Kentucky Annual Conference of A.M.E. Churches held in Lexington appointed Rev. F. L. Durden pastor of St. Paul A.M.E. Church. The following year, on October 16, at the same conference, held again in Lexington, Rev. M. H. Johnson was appointed pastor of St. Paul and served until he was replaced by Rev. **Edgar L. Mack.**

Mack was one of the most active pastors within the local African American community. He helped organize and led the northern Kentucky delegation from Boone, Campbell, and Kenton Counties in the 1964 civil rights **March on Frankfort.** Rev. Martin Luther King Jr. and legendary baseball player Jackie Robinson led an estimated 10,000 persons in the march. In 1971, Mack led a delegation of northern Kentucky clergy to attend the funeral of **Whitney M. Young Jr.,** a Kentucky native who had been executive director of the **National Urban League.** In 1983, Rev. R. Mitchell arrived at St. Paul A.M.E. Church as its last pastor. In the late 1980s, the church was dissolved because of a lack of members. The lot where the church once stood is now vacant.

Williams' Covington and Newport directory, 1894.
Newspapers: "Church Notes," *State Journal,* February 28, 1880, 1; "Newport News," *KTS,* August 25, 1902, 3; "Sale Is under Way; Old Corpus Christi Church Is to Become African M.E. Church," *KP,* December 6, 1905, 5; "Freedom! Freedom! Freedom!," *KE,* March 6, 1964, 2; "Kentucky Rites Set for Young," *KE,* March 16, 1971, 16; "King Marched in Frankfort in 1964," *KP,* January 20, 2003, 4K.

—*Theodore H. H. Harris*

ST. PAUL UNITED METHODIST CHURCH (PARIS), oldest African American church in Bourbon Co. On March 14, 1853, the deed for Cottontown Methodist Church was recorded. In 1865, a tornado destroyed the building. Two years later, Rev. George Downey led the rebuilding of the church at 1117 High St., Paris, KY, where it was named St. Paul Methodist Church. The two-story brick building was in transitional Greek Revival/Italianate style and became the cornerstone of the black community when it was finished in 1876.

While the building was being constructed, the church became a member of the Lexington Conference, part of the Methodist Episcopal Church. Rev. George W. Hatton, a Maryland native, served as pastor in the 1870s. Hatton, a former soldier who was

later buried in Arlington National Cemetery, was an energetic political speaker and community activist. In March 1899, Bishop John H. Vincent, noted white leader of the American Methodist Episcopal Church, opened the Colored Methodist Conference in Paris. Visiting ministers stayed in the homes of local church members. Nearly 2,000 people attended the next conference in Paris in 1901. In that same year, Rev. L. M. Hagood, who was also a physician and surgeon, became the pastor of the church. In 1905, the Colored Charity Organization held its meeting at St. Paul Methodist Church in the hopes of educating the public about consumption. Two years later, the church sponsored Rev. Father C. F. Checizzle, an Ethiopian priest, as a guest speaker, an event that garnered a story in the local paper.

In 1911, Rev. J. B. Redmond, the newly appointed minister of St. Paul Church, organized the black community to raise funds for the "colored annex" of the white W. W. Massie Memorial Hospital in Paris. The submitted proposition stated that if the African American citizens raised $1,500, then the white inhabitants of Paris would provide $6,000 toward the annex building. After the African American community raised the money, it celebrated at St. Paul Methodist Church on **Emancipation Day,** January 1, 1913. Over three years later, Redmond, as president of the Massie Memorial Hospital Annex Association, wrote a full column in the local newspaper asking how much longer they were expected to wait patiently for completion of the annex.

In 1968, the Methodist Church and the Evangelical United Brethren Church joined to form the United Methodist Church. The Paris church became known as St. Paul United Methodist Church. About 50 ministers have served the church. In 1983, Rev. Mallonee Hubbard, a white woman, was the church's first female pastor. In 2005, Rev. Connie L. Mitchell, an African American woman, became the church's third female minister.

Coates, Ta-Nehisi, and Andy Hall. "George W. Hatton's Long Road." *Atlantic,* January 20, 2011. http://www.theatlantic.com/national/archive/2011/01/george-w-hattons-long-road/69924/ (accessed July 26, 2012).
Newspapers: "Bishop Vincent Coming," *Bourbon News,* March 3, 1899, 5; "An Intelligent Etheopian," *Bourbon News,* February 8, 1907, 1; "Proposed Hospital Annex to Massie Memorial Hospital," *Bourbon News,* November 6, 1916, 1.

—*Sallie L. Powell*

SALES, MARY ELIZABETH ANN (b. 1892, Lexington, KY; d. unknown), registered nurse. Mary Elizabeth Ann Sales, daughter of Jack and Elizabeth "Lizzie" Sales, was born in Lexington, KY, on July 3, 1892. Her mother died in 1906. After graduating from John A. Andrew Memorial Hospital's Nursing and Training School in 1913, Sales attended the neighboring school, Tuskegee Institute in Tuskegee, AL, in 1915. Between 1918 and 1920, she was the head nurse at Sisters of Charity Hospital in Indianapolis, where she was considered to be a "friendly visitor with patients who had tuberculosis." In 1924, she became a school nurse after gaining experience as a private nurse practitioner with the American Red Cross. On September 7, 1934, in Nashville, TN, she was elected second vice president of the National Association of Colored Graduate Nurses.

In 1940, Sales earned her BS at Butler University in Indianapolis, IN. She was a member of several clubs and organizations throughout her lifetime, including nationally recognized organizations: the Women's Federated Clubs in Indiana, the Indiana Health Advisory Center, the National Organization of Public Health, the National Association of Colored Graduate Nurses, the American Nurses Association, the Indiana Central District Association, and the Indiana Public Health Organization. She was the president of the local Colored Graduate Nurses Club and the Hubbard Center Civic Club. She also served as chairman and health commissioner of the **Phillis Wheatley YWCA** in Indianapolis and vice president of the Central Region of the Indiana State Federation of Colored Women's Clubs. In 1949, Sales attended the International Congress of Nurses in Stockholm, Sweden. How she spent the rest of her life is unknown.

Butler University Alumni Services, Indianapolis, IN.

"Estelle Massey Heads Nurses." *Wichita (KS) Negro Star,* September 7, 1934, 1.

Fleming, George James, and Christian E. Burckel, eds. *Who's Who in Colored America.* 7th ed. Yonkers-on-Hudson, NY: Christian E. Burckel & Associates, 1950, 450.

Nursing and Allied Health—History. "Tuskegee University School of Nursing and Allied Health: 1892–2003." June 24, 2008. http://www.tuskegee.edu/Global/story.asp?S=1236562 (accessed June 5, 2008).

U.S. Federal Census (1900, 1930).

—Debra Bulluck

SAMPLE, PRINCE ALBERT (P. A.) (b. 1878, Mt. Sterling, KY; d. unknown), businessman and club leader.

Prince Albert (P. A.) Sample, the son of Prince Albert Sample Sr., a Colored Methodist Episcopal minister, and Kitty (Freeman) Sample, was born in Mt. Sterling, Kentucky, on September 28, 1878. When he was two years old, the family lived in Elkton, KY, in Todd Co. The family later moved to Paducah, KY, where Sample worked as a hotel porter and earned his high school diploma from Lincoln High School in 1902.

In the early 1900s, Sample moved to Milwaukee, WI, and worked as a waiter. He was also the city editor and business manager of the *Wisconsin Advocate* (1903–1908) and a special correspondent for the *Evening Wisconsin* (1906–1907). Described as "an orator and a sound reasoner," he later earned his bachelor of laws degree from the University of Michigan in Ann Arbor. By 1908, he worked in Jersey City, NJ, as an attorney. He married Bertha Tarpley on September 18, 1912.

By 1920, Sample was employed as a railroad porter, and his wife worked as a dressmaker. By 1930, the couple owned their home, which was valued at $5,000. Sample served as president of Jersey City's branch of the **National Association for the Advancement of Colored People,** was a legislative candidate in the state in 1925, and worked as an investigator and welfare worker for the Pullman Company in New York City (1922–1932). Known as one of the founders of the Pullman Porters Benefit Association of America, he began his career as a comptroller at that association in 1931 and continued in that role into the mid-1940s.

Newspapers: "Annual Sermon," *IF,* June 27, 1891, 1; "Cream City Notes," *Wisconsin Weekly Advocate* (Milwaukee), April 28, 1904, 1; "Cream City Notes," *Wisconsin Weekly Advocate* (Milwaukee), June 28, 1906, 1.

U.S Federal Census (1880, 1900, 1920, 1930, 1940).

Yenser, Thomas, ed. *Who's Who in Colored America, 1941–1944.* 6th ed. Brooklyn, NY: Thomas Yenser, 1942.

—Kim Nguyen

SANDERS, HENRY LIGHTER (b. 1854, Lexington, KY; d. 1939, Indianapolis, IN), businessman.

According to the 1900 U.S. census, Henry Lighter Sanders was born near Lexington in 1854 and spent his early years as a farm laborer. In 1874, he migrated to Indianapolis and worked as a pan washer and later as a cook in the Grand Hotel. After their marriage, his wife, Sadie, made his white jacket uniform. His coworkers then asked him to have her sew white work jackets and aprons for them.

By 1898, Sanders had invested in six electric sewing machines and had his teenaged son, Edward, traveling in Indiana, Ohio, Michigan, and Illinois to sell to more customers. Active in the Business Men's League, Sanders was praised by peers as a man from humble beginnings who rose to become a leading manufacturer of white khaki uniforms for both men and women and an employer of 40 people.

By the time Sanders died on April 11, 1939, he had been director and still held office as treasurer of the Senate Avenue YMCA in Indianapolis, which had served as registration headquarters during World War I for both white and black men's military enlistments. Sanders and his family were pioneer residents of the Indianapolis historic Ransom Place District in Marion Co., IN.

Notable Kentucky African Americans. http://www.uky.edu/Libraries/NKAA/record.php?note_id=270 (accessed July 9, 2008).

Thornbrough, Emma Lou. *Indiana Blacks in the Twentieth Century.* Bloomington: Indiana Univ. Press, 2000.

Washington, Booker T. *The Negro in Business.* Boston: Hertel, Jenkins & Co., 1907, 240–42.

Yenser, Thomas. *Who's Who in Colored America. 1933–1937,* 4th ed. Brooklyn, NY: Thomas Yenser, 1937.

—Jackie Burnside

SANDUSKY, ANNIE L. (b. 1900, Louisville, KY; d. 1976, Washington, DC), author and child welfare advocate.

Annie Lee Sandusky was born in Louisville, KY, on January 10, 1900. She graduated from Louisville Normal School and later became an elementary teacher there for 10 years. Desiring to continue her education, Sandusky attended the University of Chicago with hopes of earning a degree in higher education. However, because of a clerical mistake, she was enrolled in the School of Social Administration, where she earned her bachelor's degree in social work in 1938. She proved to excel in the field as a respected author and probation officer, as well as a consultant.

From the early 1940s to the 1970s, Sandusky was a key advocate for child welfare in Washington, DC, with the Children's Bureau, later named the American Humane Association. The author of four books, Sandusky was a pioneer in social work, specializing in child welfare with an emphasis on African American children and families. From 1954 until 1974, when she retired, Sandusky was a consultant in the Children's Bureau of the Department of Health, Education, and Welfare.

As a faithful member of Michigan Park Christian Church in Washington, DC, she led the Christian Women's Fellowship, organized the child day care center, and served as a church board member. She was also featured on the National Association of Social Workers Pioneer list. On August 10, 1976, Annie Lee Sandusky died at the Washington Hospital Center. In 2002, the University of Chicago's School of Social Administration posthumously recognized Sandusky as a pioneer in the field of social work with an exhibition that included a brief biography and a list of her contributions to social work.

"Annie Sandusky, 76, Dies, Retired Social Worker." *WP*, August 13, 1976, C8.

Bowden, Jane A., ed. *Contemporary Authors: A Bio-Bibliographical Guide to Current Writers in Fiction, General Nonfiction, Poetry, Journalism, Drama, Motion Pictures, Television, and Other Fields.* Detroit: Gale Research, 1978, 511.

Church, Gertrude M. "Understanding Each Other to Achieve a Common Goal." *American Journal of Nursing* 56, no. 2 (February 1956): 201–4. http://www.jstor.org/stable/3469214?seq=1 (accessed June 18, 2008).

Counts-Spriggs, Margaret S. E. E-mail to Debra Bulluck, June 24, 2008.

"NASW Foundation National Program: NASW Social Work Pioneers." http://www.naswfoundation.org/pioneers/defaulty.asp (accessed June 15, 2008).

Roots Web. Social Security Death Index. June 25, 2008. http://ssdi .rootsweb.ancestry.com/cgi-bin/ssdi.cgi?lastname=Sandusky &firstname=Annie&nt=exact (accessed June 25, 2008).

SSA/Chicago. "SSA Report 2002: School of Social Service Administration, the University of Chicago." http://www.ssa.uchicago.edu /publications/annual-report-2002.pdf (accessed June 17, 2008).
—*Debra Bulluck*

SANSBURY, LOUIS (b. 1806, Springfield, KY; d. 1861, Springfield, KY), enslaved health care provider. Considered the "scourge of the nineteenth century," Asiatic cholera struck fear in the 618 citizens of Springfield, KY, when a female slave died from it on June 2, 1833. According to one account, in only two weeks, 180 residents died from the disease. People panicked, closed businesses, and left town. George Sansbury, a white hotel owner, left his business keys with his 27-year-old slave Louis Sansbury. Other white business owners also trusted him and left their shop and house keys with him. Sansbury managed the hotel, cared for the sick, and buried the dead along the road to the Springfield Cemetery. A female cook, Matilda Sims, assisted him in feeding and treating the black and white cholera victims.

Springfield's townspeople returned after the epidemic ended in about three weeks. In 1845, George Sansbury died, and his children inherited his slaves, except for Louis Sansbury. In honor of his heroic service to the community, Springfield's citizens collected funds, purchased his freedom, built a livery stable, and stocked it with horses for Sansbury to start a business. In 1854, Sansbury witnessed another cholera outbreak in the town, with fewer fatalities than the first epidemic. He again stayed to care for the diseased.

Sansbury continued his successful livery business on the corner of Walnut and Main Sts. until his death on April 12, 1861. He was buried in an unmarked grave in Springfield's Saint Rose Cemetery. On August 6, 2004, Springfield held its first African-American Heritage Week celebration and included a public tribute to Louis Sansbury.

Baird, Nancy D. "Asiatic Cholera's First Visit to Kentucky: A Study in Panic and Fear." *FCHQ* 48, no. 4 (1974): 228–40.

Newspapers: "Cholera Days," *Springfield (KY) News-Leader,* March 13, 1902, 1; Byron Crawford, "Slave Stayed to Nurse Town in Epidemics," *LCJ,* July 30, 2004, B1.

O'Malley, Mimi. *It Happened in Kentucky.* Guilford, CT: Morris, 2006.
—*Sallie L. Powell*

SCOTT, ISAIAH BENJAMIN (b. 1854, Midway, KY; d. 1931, Nashville, TN), educator and religious leader. Born in Midway, KY, on September 30, 1854, Isaiah Benjamin Scott sought an education even while he and his parents were enslaved. After his family's emancipation, he became one of the first students to attend Clark Seminary (later known as Clark Atlanta University) in Atlanta, GA. He then studied theology at Central Tennessee College, earning a bachelor's degree in 1880 and a master's degree in 1883. For the next decade, he preached in churches in both Tennessee and Texas before he was selected to be the first black president of Wiley College in Marshall, TX.

In 1896, Scott left Wiley College to accept a position as editor of the *Southwestern Christian Advocate.* Because of his performance as an administrator and writer, the General Conference of the Methodist Episcopal Church elected him missionary bishop of Africa. He spent 12 years on the continent, primarily in Liberia, and spoke on behalf of further missionary work. In 1909, he shared the stage with President William Howard Taft at the African Methodist Diamond Jubilee as a featured speaker.

After retiring in 1919, Scott returned to his home in Nashville, TN, where he stayed active in religious administration. He died on July 4, 1931, and was buried in Greenwood Cemetery, Nashville, TN.

Arters, John M., ed. "Bishop Isaiah Benjamin Scott." In *Journal of the Thirty-First Delegated General Conference of the Methodist Episcopal Church,* 895–96. New York: Methodist Book Concern, 1932.

Hartshorn, W. N. *An Era of Progress and Promise, 1863–1910.* Boston: Priscilla, 1910.

Sherer, Robert G. "Scott, Isaiah Benjamin." *Handbook of Texas Online.* http://www.tshaonline.org/handbook/online/articles/fsc61 (accessed November 1, 2010).

"Taft to Speak at Jubilee." *Palestine (TX) Daily Herald,* December 13, 1909, 6.
—*Stephen Pickering*

SCROGGINS, HENRY (b. 1841, KY; d. unknown), one of the organizers of the Kentucky Negro Republican Party. A freeman, Henry Scroggins, age 18, married Diademia Akers, age 15, in Boyle Co., KY, in 1859. The next year, Scroggins worked as a barber. He and his wife lived in Lexington, KY, with S. A. Oldham, an African American barber, and his wife.

On March 22, 1866, Scroggins and several other Lexington African American leaders of the Kentucky State Benevolent Association (also known as the **Colored People's Union Benevolent Society,** which helped care for needy African Americans) met in the Ladies Hall to encourage members to become politically knowledgeable and active. The group elected Scroggins recording secretary and appointed him to the Revisory and Publishing Committee in order to document the convention's proceedings in a pamphlet. The next year, before African Americans could vote, Scroggins joined other African American leaders to organize Kentucky's **Negro Republican Party** and hold its convention in Lexington. Scroggins was elected corresponding secretary. In 1869, the first local Agricultural and Mechanical Association was established. Scroggins served as the organization's secretary for several years.

By 1870, Scroggins, his wife, two sons, and his mother, Leanna, lived in Lexington's Ward 4. His business as a barber provided him with an estate worth $1,000. The following year, Scroggins, along with two other appointed black leaders, met with some white Fayette Co. farmers in an effort to preserve law and order in the area. The goal of the black leaders was to obtain the right for African Americans to testify in Kentucky's courts. When they were unsuccessful, Scroggins joined others to establish the Fayette County Justice Association to aid African Americans in carrying their cases to the federal courts in hopes of a fair trial.

In July 1873, Llew P. Tarlton, Fayette Co.'s white sheriff, appointed Scroggins a deputy sheriff. One newspaper claimed that the purpose of Tarlton's appointment was to irritate the Democrats, but Scroggins was viewed as "a more capable, decent and whiter man than the sheriff." However, according to the *Lexington Leader*, Scroggins "was used . . . solely to serve court processes issued for colored persons and for no other service."

The next year, at the Republican State Convention, **Jordan C. Jackson,** a prominent African American Republican, nominated Scroggins for jailer. White Republicans argued that it was too soon for an African American to have such a prominent political position. Scroggins won three voice ballots but lost the written vote. Since many African American delegates were illiterate, they had asked white delegates to write Scroggins's name on their ballots. Several well-known Lexington blacks asked Scroggins to run for jailer as an independent, but, as a devout Republican Party man, he refused. His devotion to the party reaped him a federal job as storekeeper.

In 1875, as managing editor of Lexington's *American Citizen,* Scroggins joined other Kentucky African Americans in promoting quality education for black students by encouraging the newspaper's readers to sign a petition that would be sent to Kentucky's Senate and House of Representatives. In 1884, he served as an alternate delegate at the Republican National Convention in Chicago, IL.

Kentucky, Marriage Records, 1852–1914.

King, Cyrus Baldwin. "Ante-bellum Free Negroes as Race Leaders in Virginia and Kentucky during Reconstruction." MA thesis, Univ. of Kentucky, 1949.

Newspapers: "Negro Deputy Sheriff," *Lexington Dollar Weekly Press,* July 9, 1873, 1; untitled article, *Lexington Dollar Weekly Press,*

July 23, 1873, 1, 4; "Educational Convention," *Lexington American Citizen,* November 13, 1875, 1; "Lexington Democrats Once Nominated a Negro," *LL,* October 22, 1911, 9.

Proceedings of the First Convention of Colored Men of Kentucky: The Constitution of the Kentucky State Benevolent Association. Louisville, KY: Civill & Calvert Printers, 1866.

U.S. Federal Census (1860, 1870, 1880).

—*Sallie L. Powell*

SEAL, CATHERINE (b. ca. 1874, Hustonville, KY; d. 1930, Lexington, KY), religious leader in New Orleans. Little is known about the early life of Catherine Seal. Her will states her original name as Nanny Cowans and lists her birthplace as Hustonville, KY. After moving to New Orleans at a young age, Seal was kicked in the stomach by her third husband and as a result suffered from partial paralysis. After being rejected by a local faith healer who was "not treating colored folks that day," she began to pray intensely for her own healing. When she recovered, she decided to work as a healer and religious leader in her own right.

In 1922, Seal and several followers built the Holy Manger, an enclosure with a high wooden fence that served as a gathering place for her congregation. Her services featured a multiracial following, as well as a feminist theology that favored women because of their role in childbearing. In 1929, she moved her congregation to a new building, the Temple of the Innocent Blood, and continued her work. After suffering from heart problems, she returned to Lexington, KY, to visit her sister and rest. She died shortly thereafter on August 11, 1930. Her followers had her body returned to New Orleans, where she was interred in a vault at St. Vincent de Paul Cemetery.

Jacobs, Claude F., and Andrew J. Kaslow. *The Spiritual Churches of New Orleans: Origins, Beliefs, and Rituals of an African-American Religion.* Knoxville: Univ. of Tennessee Press, 2001.

"Physicking Priestess." *Time,* April 20, 1931, 63.

Smith, Jessie Carney, ed. *Notable Black American Women.* Book II. Detroit: Gale Research, 1996.

—*Stephen Pickering*

SEAL, DENNIS (b. ca. 1784, Kentucky; d. unknown), early Lexington businessman. Little is known about Dennis Seal's early life. According to census records, he was born in Kentucky around 1784. By the 1830s, he had established himself as a successful businessman in Lexington. Between 1831 and 1850, Seal successfully pursued several endeavors, buying his own grocery store and operating a livery stable on E. Water St. He also bought and sold real estate and owned several rental properties.

Seal's wealth eventually became so substantial that he was able to endorse the bank notes of white citizens and serve as security for them. On several occasions, Seal even received slaves from whites who were indebted to him, including a "Negro boy, a slave about fourteen years of age and named George."

In 1863, Seal created a last will and testament that revealed the extent of his personal fortune. Describing himself as "sound in mind but much afflicted in body," he left several properties to his children and to several creditors. To his son, David, he left his stable and grocery, although he requested that the tenants of these buildings pay their rent to Sawney Lewis, a creditor and free person of color, until his debts were extinguished. He also owned multiple homes in Lexington, including a log house on Mill St. and a brick house on Mulberry St., which he deeded to another son, Daniel. Additional houses and lots were to be given to other children, as well as a lump sum of $1,200 to a daughter upon the sale of his personal estate. Although little information is available about the rest of his life, Seal's personal wealth and financial success at a time when most persons of color in Lexington were enslaved marked him as an early leader of the black business community in Fayette Co.

Lucas, Marion B. *A History of Blacks in Kentucky*. Vol. 1, *From Slavery to Segregation, 1760–1891*. Frankfort: Kentucky Historical Society, 1992.

MacCabe, Julius P. Bolivar. *Directory of the City of Lexington and County of Fayette for 1838 & 1839*. Lexington, KY: J. C. Noble, 1838.

Strother, William Bruce. "Some Aspects of Negro Culture in Lexington, Kentucky." PhD diss., Univ. of Kentucky, 1939.

Will Book Y. Fayette County Records, reel 127, Special Collections, Univ. of Kentucky Libraries.

—*Stephen Pickering*

SEBREE, CHARLES (b. 1914, White City, KY; d. 1985, Washington, DC), artist.

Charles Sebree was born in White City, KY, two and one-half miles from Madisonville, on November 16, 1914. He spent his early years in White City and attended elementary school in Madisonville. He began to take an interest in art at the age of four, working with his uncle, John Robinson. What piqued Sebree's interest in art were the figures he and his uncle created out of mud and twigs.

In 1924, at age 10, Sebree moved with his mother to Chicago and attended school. On the weekends, he attended the University of Chicago Art Institute through one of its scholarships. He later joined the Chicago Renaissance Society, in addition to earning a formal art degree at the Art Institute. In 1932, his career skyrocketed when he began to produce several works of art, choreographed dances, wrote plays, and made numerous other contributions to the field of visual arts. His style was a "combination of Picasso and Paul Klee, yet he produces an abstract that is still his own."

Sebree participated in the Works Progress Administration, part of the New Deal, from 1936 to 1938. The organization helped give people jobs and improve the community during the Great Depression. Drafted into the navy in 1942, he served until 1944, in the heat of World War II, and was stationed at the Great Lakes Naval Base in an all-black division.

Sebree continued to pursue his craft after his military service. By creating his own type of artwork in several media, such as beeswax and crayons, among other things, he made significant contributions to art. His work in the theater and painting has helped improve the cultural makeup of the United States and Kentucky. Sebree's influence in art and theater inspired other artists with his form and methods and helped others recognize the talent Kentucky is capable of producing. Some examples of his outstanding work include *Woman with Lemons, Figure of a Woman,* and *War Worker*. He additionally contributed to a few plays: *Dry August* and *Juno and the Paycock*. Sebree died in Washington, DC, on September 27, 1985.

"Charles Sebree." *Artcyclopedia: The Guide to Great Art on the Internet*. http://www.artcyclopedia.com/artists/sebree_charles.html.

"Charles Sebree." In *The Negro Artist Comes of Age: A National Survey of Contemporary Artists*, 59. Albany: Albany Institute of History and Art, 1945.

"Charles Sebree, 70, a Washington Artist Who Also Had Been a Dancer, Playwright and Set Designer, Died of Cancer Sept. 27 at George Washington University Hospital." *WP*, October 7, 1985.

Shine, Ted. "Charles Sebree, Modernist." *Black American Literature Forum* 19 (Spring 1985): 6–8.

—*Aaron Clark*

SECOND BAPTIST CHURCH (MAYS LICK), African American church in Mays Lick, KY.

Mays Lick in Mason Co. is home to an African American church congregation that dates back to 1789. Records indicate that in that year slaves were holding worship services and that the white Baptist church ministered to the black population. **Elisha Green,** a Mays Lick slave who became a founder of African American churches and a Republican leader, was a member of the church. According to oral tradition, black worshippers at the town's Baptist church sat along the walls and in the back of the church during services. This segregated but united system of worship continued until June 17, 1855, when the white congregation granted the 175 black members permission to form their own church, the Second Baptist Church of Mays Lick. For more than a decade, this congregation met in homes, barns, and whatever other places could be found. After William and Mitchell donated land to the Maysville and Lexington Turnpike Company for a school and a church for the African American Baptists of Mays Lick, Andrew M. January, as the authority of the turnpike company, deeded the property on August 27, 1868, to the trustees of what was termed the "Colored" Baptist Church and their successors. Those first trustees were Stephen Breckinridge, Henry Jackson, and John Middleton. A church and a school were built on the property. A Reverend Natis, the first pastor in 1855, was there for the building of the first church. The original deed stated that other black congregations should be allowed to use the church for services when it was not being used by the local black Baptists.

The first church burned, and the structure built to replace it in 1913 continues to serve the congregation. The first black school in the town was replaced by a larger structure next door, and the original school building is used by the church. In 1889, the Second Christian Church opened in Mays Lick, giving the community two predominantly African American churches. The Second Christian Church closed in the 1990s, and the Second Baptist congregation has declined to around 30 members. Approximately 30 pastors have served the Mays Lick Baptist Church since its beginning.

American Association of University Women (Maysville Branch). *From Cabin to College: A History of the Schools of Mason County.* Maysville, KY: G. F. McClanahan, 1976.

Kentucky Gateway Museum Center. Vertical files. Maysville, KY.

Ramsey, William, elder of the Second Baptist Church. Interview by John Klee, Mays Lick, KY, October 2, 2006.

—John Klee

SECOND BAPTIST CHURCH (NEWPORT), African American church in northern Kentucky. On December 28, 1945, the Second Baptist Church of Newport was formed as a mission of the Ninth St. Baptist Church in Covington. Albert Lowe served as pastor of this mission, and the congregation purchased a lot at 315 Isabella St. for $250. In 1947, the mission became the Second Baptist Church, with Rev. Edward Smith serving as moderator. After Pastor Lowe died on April 16, 1950, Robert J. Brown became pastor; at the time, the church had only six members and $6 in the treasury. In 1951, the Housing Authority of Newport purchased the church's property on Isabella, and the congregation decided to relocate to 112 Central Ave. in Newport, where Brown constructed a church building himself. In 1957, the Housing Authority of Newport took the church's property on Central Ave., and the church was forced to look for yet another home. Land was purchased at the church's current location, 713 Brighton St. in Newport, and another building was built, again without needing to obtain a loan. Reverend Brown again, along with friends, did the work. The name of the church was changed to Mount Zion Baptist Church with this move. Brown remained pastor until 1976. From 1976 to 1979, several ministers served at the church: James Streeter, James Crawford, Elmore Morris, and Herman L. Harris. In 1979, the church's name was changed back to Second Baptist Church. In March 1980, Rev. Paul D. McMillan was called to lead the Second Baptist Church. Under his leadership, the church became involved in many community and civic activities, such as the Martin Luther King Jr. celebration held at the Northern Kentucky Convention Center on January 16, 2001.

Historical notes on file at Second Baptist Church, Newport, KY.
Installation Service for Rev. H. L. Harris, Sunday, May 20, thru Sunday, May 27, 1979, Mount Zion Baptist Church, Newport, Kentucky. Newport, KY: Mount Zion Baptist Church, 1979. Pamphlet.
"Simpson Recalls Rights Struggle." *KP,* January 16, 2001, 3K.

—Theodore H. H. Harris

SEPARATE COACH LAW, law that allowed segregated coaches on trains. Racial segregation of railroad passenger traffic was legalized in Kentucky when the General Assembly on March 15, 1892, enacted the Separate Coach Law, which stipulated that all passenger trains operating in the state must provide clearly labeled individual coaches for "colored" and "white" passengers. The law was similar to those of other states throughout the South. The act was challenged by a black minister and his wife, **W. H. and Sarah Anderson,** who boarded a train in Evansville, IN, and remained in a coach marked for whites as the train entered Kentucky. The Andersons were ejected from the train in Henderson, KY. They immediately purchased two more first class tickets for Madisonville and were again ejected when they refused to move to the segregated car. They filed suit against the Louisville and Nashville Railroad Company. In the ensuing lawsuit, federal district judge John W. Barr ruled on June 4, 1894, that the Kentucky statute was unconstitutional because it interfered with interstate

commerce, an area of law reserved to the U.S. Congress (*Anderson v. Louisville & Nashville Railroad Co.*). Two years later, in a case originating in Louisiana, the U.S. Supreme Court ruled that separate intrastate railroad coaches for the races were legal (***Plessy v. Ferguson,*** 1896), and in 1900 the court upheld Kentucky's Separate Coach Law as it applied to intrastate commerce (*Chesapeake & Ohio Railway v. Kentucky*). In 1920, the court upheld the law as it applied to interstate commerce (*South Covington & Cincinnati Street Railway v. Kentucky*), thus in effect overruling *Anderson v. Louisville & Nashville.*

Reflecting increased sympathy for civil rights, the U.S. Supreme Court in 1946 placed Kentucky's Separate Coach Law in jeopardy when it invalidated a Virginia statute requiring segregated interstate bus travel (*Morgan v. Virginia*). In 1955, the Interstate Commerce Commission banned racial discrimination in interstate railroad passenger traffic, thus rendering Kentucky's law invalid as it applied to train traffic to and from other states. The Kentucky statute's validity in regard to intrastate traffic came into question in light of ***Brown v. Board of Education*** (1954), which held that state-mandated public school segregation violated the *Constitution.* In 1966, the Kentucky General Assembly repealed the Separate Coach Law.

Barnes, Catherine A. *Journey from Jim Crow: The Desegregation of Southern Transit.* New York: Columbia Univ. Press, 1983.

SEYMOUR, WILLIAM (b. 1843, Nicholasville, KY; d. 1920, Colorado Springs, CO), juror. The son of a slave woman of both African and Native American descent, William Seymour grew up on the Martin Plantation in Nicholasville, KY. While he was a slave, he met his future wife, Elizabeth Wright, with whom he lived along with his five children. After the conclusion of the Civil War, he decided to join a larger migration of freed slaves to the West, settling on a ranch in Kansas and fathering seven more children.

In the 1890s, Seymour packed up his family and moved farther west, where he founded a dairy in the Black Forest region of Colorado. He was well respected by his peers and became a valuable member of the local community after he retired and moved within the city limits of Colorado Springs. When the city opened a new courthouse in 1903, Seymour served on the jury for the first trial, the first African American to serve as a juror in El Paso Co. In 1920, he died and was buried in Evergreen Cemetery.

In 2002, the Pioneers Museum in Colorado Springs unveiled a bronze statue of Seymour in recognition of his contribution to the African American community. The statue was placed on the northwest corner of the museum's property on S. Tejon St., near the original location of the courthouse where he served as a juror.

Newspapers: "Lawyerly Lore of County Bar Goes by the Book," *Colorado Springs Gazette,* April 25, 1995, 1; "Springs Statue Honors Ex-Slave, Black Pioneer," *Colorado Springs Gazette,* February 10, 2002, 1.
Turpin, Ruth Elizabeth Seymour. *"Chips off the Old Block": A Compilation of the Memories of the Morgan-Seymour Family.* Detroit: Harlo Press, 1990.

—Stephen Pickering

SHAKE RAG, African American community in Bowling Green, KY. Shake Rag is an African American community located on the northern part of Bowling Green, KY. In 1802, Robert Moore, the founder of Bowling Green, donated a plot of land known as Lee Square to the black community for use as a public square. After the Civil War, the community grew, becoming more prosperous and thriving as State St. became part of the Dixie Hwy. in the early twentieth century.

The community consisted of churches, schools, grocery stores, a hotel, beauty shops, barbershops, restaurants, nightclubs, a community center, and other black-owned businesses. The lives of the residents of Shake Rag revolved around church, school, and family activities.

State Street Missionary Baptist Church, located at 340 State St., the oldest African American church in Bowling Green, was established in 1830. In the 1940s and 1950s, the church also operated a preschool for black students. The church still exists today.

In the early 1880s, the Bowling Green Colored School (later known as **Bowling Green Academy**), a boarding school for black students, was in existence. Students from as far away as Nashville, TN, attended this school. In 1885, racially segregated State Street High/Elementary School, located at the corner of Second and State Sts., was established. The school existed until 1955, when a new school, High Street High/Elementary School, located at 200 High St., was built. This was the only high school within a 30-mile radius that black students could attend. After completing elementary school in their local community, they came to the Shake Rag community to continue their education.

The Southern Queen Hotel, one of the more prosperous and popular businesses in the community, was built in 1906 by James Covington. It served black travelers who were unable to stay in Bowling Green's white hotels. The hotel was popular with black musicians, such as Ray Charles, Chuck Berry, and Ike and Tina Turner, who worked the Chitlin' Circuit between Louisville and Nashville. Shake Rag had also several restaurants and nightclubs that provided entertainment not only for Shake Rag but also for other small black communities within a 30-mile radius. Jimmy's (JC's) Barber Shop has operated in the neighborhood since 1948.

Civic activities were served by the George Washington Carver Center, which was established in 1946 by a group of teachers who saw a need for a place for students to go after school. The students could finish their homework and play games. A Girl Scouts troop was also located at the center, and it was used for birthday parties, showers, weddings, and other community activities. It is still in existence today.

From the late 1800s through the 1960s, several doctors and a nurse lived in the neighborhood. Dr. **Z. K. Jones** worked out of his home at 506 State St. Dr. **Otha D. Porter** worked from his home at 439 State St. Dr. Isaac B. Bruton also worked from his home at 139 State St. Dr. W. F. Becket worked from his office on State St. **Ora Porter** was the first registered nurse (black or white) in Warren Co. Although she was not allowed to work in the hospital, she did private nursing for patients in their homes.

We may never know the true origin of the name Shake Rag. Monday was wash day in the community, and the ladies would put their clothes on the line, where the breeze would be blowing them. Others say that on the weekend people were out in the clubs dancing and shaking those "rags" or fancy clothes.

In September 2000, the Shake Rag District was placed on the National Register of Historic Places. It is Bowling Green's first National Register district recognized for its significance to African American history. On October 21, 2004, a Kentucky Historical

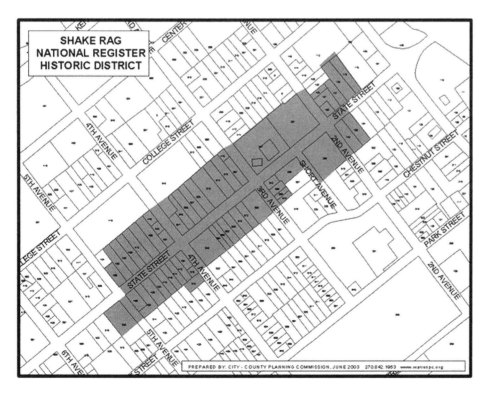

Map of Shake Rag district.

Society highway marker was placed on the grounds of the George Washington Carver Center at 201 State St. to commemorate the community and its residents.

Edmonds, John B. Interviews by Maxine Ray, Bowling Green, KY, June 2002 and May 2003.

Offutt, Don C., Sr. Interviews by Maxine Ray, Bowling Green, KY, September 1999, May 2002, and June 2004.

Oldham, Herbert A. Interview by Maxine Ray, Bowling Green, KY, February 1999.

—*Maxine Ray*

SHANKS, IRVINE LEE (b. 1930, Kenton Co., KY; d. 2004, Lexington, KY), first African American basketball player at Berea College since the passage of the 1904 Day Law. In 1904, the Kentucky legislature enacted the **Day Law,** which prohibited integrated education in Kentucky schools, including private schools. It was aimed specifically at **Berea College**'s interracial educational system. Kentucky amended the law in 1950 to allow black and white persons to attend the same school.

Born in Kenton Co., Kentucky, Irvine Lee Shanks grew up in Richmond and matriculated in all-black schools. He attended Nashville's Tennessee A&I (later named Tennessee State University) on a basketball scholarship. Dissatisfied there, he returned home and joined the army. He served on the front lines in the Korean War.

By the time he entered Berea College in 1953, Shanks, age 23, was married with two children. He lived off campus but roomed with white teammates on road trips. Six-feet-five, he played center for Berea College. His first game was against Ohio's Wilmington College on February 4, 1954. Many believed that the pivot man was the first African American to integrate an all-white Kentucky college team. However, Theodore "Ted" Wade played for Louisville's Bellarmine College in 1950, and Freeman Franklin played there in 1952–1953.

Nevertheless, Shanks was the first African American to integrate basketball at Berea College since the passage of Kentucky's Day Law. **Jim Crow** laws resonated throughout Kentucky and the South. Some hotels and restaurants would not serve the team. In movie theaters, Shanks was forced to sit in the balcony separate from his teammates. Despite this environment, his teammates and the college accepted him. No riots, boycotts, or violence interrupted his sports career. No team refused to play Berea College because of Shanks's participation.

Shanks helped the Berea Mountaineers win the 1955 Kentucky Intercollegiate Athletic Conference Tournament. He majored in mathematics in college but struggled in trigonometry. After the 1955–1956 season, he left school before finishing his final year. He worked for a Lexington construction company for over 30 years.

Toward the end of his life, Shanks suffered from diabetes and had daily kidney dialysis. He died at the Veterans Affairs Medical Center in Lexington on March 5, 2004. Kentucky senator Jim Bunning, believing that Shanks had broken college basketball's color barrier in Kentucky, posthumously paid tribute to Shanks at the Capitol on March 9, 2004.

Chase, Tom. *B for Berea: The Amazing Story of Berea College Basketball in the Words of the Men Who Played It.* Vol. 1, *Triumph and Toil, 1895–1969.* Johnson City, TN: Overmountain Press, 2000.

Newspapers: "The Jackie Robinson of Kentucky Basketball," *LHL,* November 17, 2001, A1; "Irvine Shanks, Sports Pioneer," *LHL,* March 9, 2004, B4; "What's Up with Ted Wade," *LCJ,* April 12, 2004, E1.

"Tribute to Irvine Lee Shanks." Capital Words. http://capitolwords.org /date/2004/03/09/S2434-2_tribute-to-irvine-lee-shanks/ (accessed October 21, 2013).

—*Sallie L. Powell*

SHANNON, JOHN W. (b. 1933, Louisville, KY), decorated Army officer. John W. Shannon was born on September 13, 1933,

Basketball team with Irvine Shanks (far left).

in Louisville, KY. He earned his BS degree from Central State University in Wilberforce, OH, in 1955. During that same year, Shannon was commissioned an infantry 2nd lieutenant in the U.S. Army. From 1972 to 1974, Shannon served as a congressional liaison officer in the Office of the Secretary of the Army. He then furthered his education at Shippensburg State College, Shippensburg, PA, and received his master of science degree in 1975. He supplied support to the assistant secretary of defense for legislative affairs as the special assistant for manpower, reserve affairs, and logistics from 1979 to 1981.

During the Vietnam War, Shannon served two tours of active duty as an adviser and an infantry battalion commander. A decorated Vietnam War veteran, Shannon retired from active duty with the rank of colonel after 23 years in service. He earned high military awards, such as the Bronze Star, the Combat Infantryman Badge, the Defense Superior Service Medal, the Legion of Merit, Parachutist Wings, the Ranger Tab, and the Republic of Vietnam Gallantry Cross with Palm, and Vietnam Battle Campaign. He also received numerous honors, including the Anderson Medal, the Defense Meritorious Civilian Service Award, the Rock of the Year Award for 1987, the Korean Gugseon Award, the Roy Wilkins Meritorious Service Award, and the Secretary of Defense Awards for Distinguished and Outstanding Public Service.

After Shannon retired, he continued to serve in the number two civilian position, under secretary of the army, from 1989 until his pending appointment to the number one civilian position as acting secretary of the army in 1993. Unfortunately, Shannon's appointment as acting secretary of the army was short lived; he was forced to take administrative leave after being accused of shoplifting.

Shortly after this accusation, the army dropped the misdemeanor charges in return for Shannon's agreement to perform 50 hours of community service and participate in a support group. Despite these legal issues, he was hired by James Klugh, a deputy under secretary, as a month-to-month consultant for the Pentagon in November 1993 until early 1994.

Shannon is married to Jean, and they have one son, John Jr., who serves in the Army Reserves.

"Former Under Secretary, US Army: John W. Shannon." Archived Biography from the Department of the Army at the Wayback Machine. https://web.archive.org/web/20040118144217/www.army.mil/leaders/FormerUSAs/bios/Shannon.htm (accessed August 12, 2014).
Hawkins, Walter L. *African American Biographies: Profiles of 558 Current Men and Women.* Jefferson, NC: McFarland, 1992, 378–79.
Newspapers: "Acting Army Secretary, Accused of Shoplifting, Is Placed on Leave," *NYT,* August 28, 1993, http://www.nytimes.com/1993/08/28/us/acting-army-secretary-accused-of-shoplifing-is-placed-on-leave.html; "Arrested Official Hired by Pentagon," *NYT,* December 9, 1993, http://articles.dailypress.com/1993-12-09/news/9312090049_1_army-secretary-john-w-shannon-pentagon; "Official in Shoplifting Case to End Duties for Pentagon," *NYT,* January 22, 1994, http://www.nytimes.com/1994/01/22/us/official-in-shoplifting-case-to-end-duties-for-pentagon.html.
"Rock of the Year." The Rocks Inc. http://www.rocksinc.org/content.aspx?page_id=22&club_id=459944&module_id=56537 (accessed August 12, 2014).

—*Debra Bulluck*

SHAW, THOMAS (b. 1846, Covington, KY; d. 1895, Rosslyn, VA), sergeant. Thomas Shaw was born into slavery to an African American mother and a white father. He spent his youth in the Mississippi River town of Louisiana, MO. In January 1864, he joined the Union army and served with the 67th Infantry Regiment of the U.S. Colored Troops. Despite the hardship of being garrisoned and bivouacked in the swamps of Port Hudson, LA, Shaw remained with the regiment until the newly formed 9th U.S. Cavalry Regiment was organized in Louisiana in 1866. His 31-year army career stretched over both the Civil War and the Indian Wars. Shaw saw firsthand the expansion and settlement of the West, where he served as a guardian of settlers and travelers at some very remote outposts. His regiment moved to Texas, and within 10 years Shaw rose to the rank of 1st sergeant. There he trained a fellow Kentuckian, African American trooper and future Medal of Honor winner **Brent Woods.** While Shaw was in the New Mexico Territory, he participated in the pursuit of renegade warriors from the Southern Ute and Apache tribes. He helped enforce the law and patrol the area during the Colfax and Lincoln Co. wars. As a result of his troop's pursuit of the Apache subchief Nana in 1881, after the death of Chief Victorio, Shaw earned a Medal of Honor. However, he did not receive his medal until December 7, 1890, while he was serving with K Troop, 9th Cavalry, at Ft. Robinson, NE. While serving in Nebraska, Shaw fought in the last major Indian war against the Sioux Indians of South Dakota. Shaw and the K Troop were then reassigned in April 1892 to Ft. Myer, VA, where they performed ceremonial garrison duty. Shaw retired from the army in January 1895. Later that year, he died at his home in Rosslyn, VA, and was buried with full military honors in Arlington National Cemetery, Arlington, VA.

"Battle of Carrigo Canyon." In *The Black Military Experience in the American West,* edited by John M. Carroll. Ft. Collins, CO: Old Army Press, 1970.
Newspapers: Jim Reis, "Acts of Heroism Won Local Men Nation's Highest Military Award," *KP,* November 29, 1982, 4K; "Monument to Honor War Heroes," *KP,* August 10, 2001, 16A.
Register of Enlistments, United States Army, 26 September 1871. Washington, DC: National Archives and Record Service (NARS), Government Printing Office, 1871.
Reis, Jim. "A Slave Who Earned Honors as a War Hero." In *Pieces of the Past,* vol. 2. Covington: Kentucky Post, 1991.

—*Theodore H. H. Harris*

SHAWNEE, predominantly African American neighborhood in Louisville. Carved out of property owned by tobacco manufacturer Basil Doerhoefer in the 1890s, the neighborhood of Shawnee originated as a fairly well-to-do part of the West End in Louisville, KY. Owners of corporations purchased much of the land in the community, and Doerhoefer constructed a notable three-story mansion in the area. Residents also had the luxury of visiting nearby **Fontaine Ferry Park** after its opening in 1905.

For blacks, however, Shawnee presented little in the way of opportunity. Fontaine Ferry Park was strictly segregated, and white residents of the neighborhood fiercely protected their community from any supposed threat of racial integration. In 1950, 100 families formed the Shawnee Foundation with the express purpose of keeping a black family from buying a house in the area. They successfully raised over $15,000 to purchase the house, claiming that race relations in the area had been amicable and "that's the way we want to keep it." In the same year, other concerned locals formed the Shawnee Home Owners Association, which featured bylaws aimed at "restoring the use of property-deed restrictions against sale to persons of African descent."

By the 1960s, the black community had begun to make a stronger push for integration in housing and accommodations. A 1961 clash at Fontaine Ferry Park resulted in the arrest of 28 African Americans and began a long struggle to integrate the park, which finally succeeded in 1964. Tensions in the community ran especially high after the **Louisville Riot of 1968.** The riot, which consumed much of Louisville's West End and lasted for days, resulted from lingering resentment over the arrest of two innocent black men in May 1968. Rioters inflicted over $250,000 in property damage, and two black youths were shot and killed. The following year, conflict returned to Fontaine Ferry Park, where violence erupted on opening day. Several black youths, some of whom were participants in other recent uprisings, vandalized buildings and smashed cash registers, which forced the park to close.

The threat of violence accelerated a process that the risk of integration had begun a decade earlier, as whites families fled from Louisville's West End. In less than a decade, over 40,000 people had been involved in real estate transactions in the area. By 1970, Shawnee had transformed almost entirely. Once exclusively populated by the white middle class, it was now predominantly the home of black middle-class residents of Louisville.

Bierman, Don E., ed. *An Introduction to the Louisville Region: Selected Essays.* Washington, DC: Association of American Geographers, 1980.

K'Meyer, Tracy E. *Civil Rights in the Gateway to the South: Louisville, Kentucky, 1945–1980.* Lexington: Univ. Press of Kentucky, 2009.

Newspapers: "Neighbors Buy House to Keep It from Negroes," *LCJ,* May 14, 1950; "Troubled Waters Calm Now at Fairdale and Shawnee," *Louisville Times,* May 14, 1980, A1.

A Place in Time: The Story of Louisville's Neighborhoods. Louisville, KY: Courier-Journal and the Louisville Times Co., 1989.

Wolcott, Victoria W. *Race, Riots, and Roller Coasters: The Struggle over Segregated Recreation in America.* Philadelphia: Univ. of Pennsylvania Press, 2012.

—*Stephen Pickering*

SHELBY, JOHN T. (b. 1958, Lexington, KY), professional baseball player who played on two different World Series championship teams. After graduating from Lexington's Henry Clay High School in 1976, John "T-Bone" Shelby enrolled in Columbia State Community College in Columbia, TN. He was a first-round pick of the Baltimore Orioles in 1977 and was called up to the majors in September 1981. He became the Orioles' center fielder in 1983, played in 126 games, batted .258, and stole 15 bases. That year, the Orioles won the World Series, and Shelby produced a game-winning RBI in game four. The Orioles closed out the series by beating the Phillies in five games. While playing for the Orioles, he was given the nickname T-Bone by some-

one who made light of his middle initial, T., which he was formerly called by friends and teammates.

In 1987, Shelby was traded to the Los Angeles Dodgers and was a member of the championship team that defeated the Oakland Athletics in 1988. He finished his playing career with the Detroit Tigers in 1991, with a lifetime batting average of .239 and 70 home runs. In 1993, he entered the coaching profession, managing the Pioneer League's independent team, the Butte Copper Kings. In five years of managing four different minor-league teams, he compiled a 265–286 won/loss record. In June 1998, he was selected as the Dodgers' first base and outfield coach. He joined the Pittsburgh Pirates as first base coach in 2006 before returning to the Orioles in the same coaching position in October 2007. In 2011, Shelby joined the Milwaukee Brewers' coaching staff.

In recognition of his professional baseball career, his childhood neighborhood in Lexington honored him with the first Smithtown Neighborhood Achievement Award in 1999. Nearly 10 years later, he was inducted into the Henry Clay High School of Fame. Shelby and his wife, Trina, are the parents of six children and live in Lexington during the off-season.

"Managers and Coaches, John Shelby #31." Milwaukee Brewers Baseball: Witness Every Moment. http://milwaukee.brewers.mlb.com /team/coach_staff_bio.jsp?c_id=mil&coachorstaffid=122112 (accessed January 15, 2013).

PressBox. "The Return of John Shelby." http://www.pressboxline.com /story.cfm?id=3810 (accessed December 12, 2012).

"Smithtown's Slugger—Neighborhood Celebrates L.A. Dodgers' John Shelby." *LHL,* August 8, 1999.

—*Gerald L. Smith*

SHEPPARD, WILLIAM HENRY (b. 1865, Waynesboro, VA; d. 1927, Louisville, KY), minister. William Henry Sheppard was born in Waynesboro, VA, in 1865. He was a freedman because Fannie, his mother, was a freedwoman. William, his father, was the sexton at the First Presbyterian Church. Sheppard attended Hampton Institute (later known as Hampton University) in Hampton, VA. Afterward, he matriculated at the Theological Institute (now Stillman College) in Tuscaloosa, AL, and was ordained as a Presbyterian minister. He was appointed to churches in Montgomery in 1887 and Atlanta in 1888; however, his desire was to be a missionary in Africa, a goal he achieved in 1890.

As a missionary in the Congo (1890–1910), Sheppard tried to Christianize the Kuba tribe, which had a history of beheading intruders. Sheppard was also an excellent ethnographer who studied and provided details about Kuba culture. In 1911, the Hampton Institute purchased the bulk of his collection of African artifacts.

Sheppard revealed information in missionary magazines about the brutality of Belgian king Leopold's private ownership and exploitation of the people of the Congo, which was devastating Kuba culture. Sheppard was sued and charged with libel because of his writings. He won the court case, which propelled him to international celebrity status. Unfortunately, in 1910, adulterous affairs with Congolese women led to his suspension by the Presbyterian Church and permanent return to the United States.

Sheppard spent the remaining years of his life in Louisville, KY. He began an urban ministry at Hope Mission and Grace Mission (which later merged to become **Grace Hope Presbyterian Church**) in the **Smoketown** neighborhood in Louisville. In 1924, William H. Sheppard Park at 17th and Magazine Sts. was named in his honor.

In 1926, Sheppard suffered a stroke and died the following year. More than 1,000 people attended his funeral, where he was eulogized by African American and white ministers. In 1942, the Sheppard Square Housing Project opened as a tribute to Sheppard.

Hochschild, Adam. *King Leopold's Ghost: A Story of Greed, Terror and Heroism in Colonial Africa.* New York: Houghton Mifflin, 1999.

Morrin, Peter. "Cutting a Swath." *Kentucky Humanities,* October 2007, 8–14.

Phipps, William E. *William Sheppard: Congo's African American Livingstone.* Louisville, KY: Geneva Press, 2002.

Turner, John G. "A 'Black-White' Missionary on the Imperial State: William H. Sheppard and Middle-Class Black Manhood." *Journal of Southern Religion* 9 (2006). http://jsr.fsu.edu/Volume9/Turner.htm.

—*Andrew Baskin*

SHIMFESSEL, ALICE THORNTON (b. 1901, Xenia, OH; d. 1983, Cincinnati, OH), civil rights activist.

Alice Thornton was the daughter of Rev. Isaac and Laura Thornton and married Elmer T. Shimfessel. In 1941, she became the first secretary of the newly opened **Jacob Price** Homes housing project in Covington. During the early 1950s, she was at the forefront of the **civil rights movement** and accepted a challenge from the city of Covington and neighborhood residents to find a place for African American youth to play. She stated in a local newspaper: "Now that the sun is about to shine on both sides of the street the kids in this end of town are looking for a place to go. They do not have a YMCA, Boys' Club, canteen, Community Center, picture show or any place where they might find recreation. Not even a ball field where they can play a game of ball. Friends, this really is serious to me. We talk about juvenile delinquency but are we doing anything about it? I still say any old building or even a prefab building would solve the problem. I am anxious to get started on a drive for just such a place. I wonder if anyone is willing to help?" She appeared before the Covington Board of City Commissioners to request aid. Shimfessel also encouraged the African American community to support the Covington–Kenton Co. Tuberculosis Sanatorium.

Several attempts were made to establish a YMCA in Peaselburg (central Covington) on a site owned by the L. B. Fouse Civic League. This civic activity evolved into the effort to start the community center on E. Bush St. that became the L. B. Fouse Civic League building. Shimfessel served as its president for many years. Many civil rights activities, including **Congress of Racial Equality** freedom riders' protest demonstrations, and **National Association for the Advancement of Colored People** meetings were launched out of the L. B. Fouse Civic League.

During the late 1950s and early 1960s, Shimfessel was involved in protest activities against segregated restaurants, movie theaters, and department stores in Covington. She led the protesters who were carrying signs in front of the Madison and Liberty movie theaters. In 1958, she found herself in federal district court supporting the enrollment of an African American student, Jesse Moore, at Holmes High School. Shimfessel's efforts were successful; Jesse Moore was permitted to enter the high school, thereby breaking the color barrier that existed there. In later years, Shimfessel was instrumental in getting the Civic League to participate in serving senior citizens locally through the Meals on Wheels program. She also taught preschool at the Civic League.

Shimfessel was a member of the **First Baptist Church** of Covington for more than 50 years and served as church clerk and financial secretary for most of that time. She received a plaque from the local chapter of the NAACP for outstanding community service and also was named an outstanding senior citizen by the Junior Chamber of Commerce. She was a charter member of the Charles Henderson American Legion Post Ladies Auxiliary. Shimfessel died in 1983 at age 82 and was buried in Mary E. Smith Cemetery in **Elsmere.**

Newspapers: "A Check for $525," *KTS,* April 22, 1952, 5; "Early Start Planned for Negro Center," *KTS,* February 9, 1955, 2A; "Negro Building in Dispute," *KTS,* September 21, 1956, 1A; "Fouse League Is Getting Results," *KP,* August 1, 1957, 1; "White Only Sign in Store Is Hit," *KP,* July 19, 1960, 1K; "Alice T. Shimfessel: A Clear Voice Who Espoused Concern, Involvement," *CP,* December 6, 1983, 10A; John C. K. Fisher, "Blacks Join Together on a Positive Note; Program Teaches Children about Heritage," *KP,* February 29, 1988, 1K–2K.

—*Theodore H. H. Harris*

SHOBE, BENJAMIN F. (b. 1920, Bowling Green, KY), first African American in Kentucky to serve as a circuit judge since Reconstruction.

Born on October 2, 1920, Benjamin F. Shobe spent his childhood in Bowling Green, KY. The son of educators, Shobe received a bachelor's degree from Kentucky State College (later known as **Kentucky State University**) in 1941, but he was unable to attend law schools at the University of Kentucky or the University of Louisville because of segregation. He earned his law degree at the University of Michigan with funds acquired from the **Anderson-Mayer State Aid Act** in 1946 and began his career as a trial attorney the same year in Kentucky.

Shobe was part of several prominent civil rights cases during his tenure as a lawyer. In 1949, he was one of the attorneys who represented **Lyman T. Johnson** in *Johnson v. Board of Trustees,* which successfully forced the University of Kentucky to integrate its graduate school. The following year, he represented P. O. Sweeney for the **National Association for the Advancement of Colored People** in a case aimed at the integration of parks in Louisville, eventually achieving desegregation of golf courses in 1952; the city's parks became fully open in 1955.

On January 6, 1953, Shobe made history when he became the first African American appointed to Jefferson County Circuit Court in the twentieth century. His selection was technically illegal—he was 32 years old at the time, but the state constitution required a minimum age of 35 for circuit court judges—but he was intended to serve for only one day as a replacement for an absent justice. In 1960, Shobe became the assistant commonwealth's attorney, and in 1973, he was elected police court judge.

In 1975, Shobe was again appointed Jefferson Circuit Court judge, and he remained in that position after winning an election for the office two years later. His associates elected him chief judge in 1979, a position he held for two years. He continued to serve as a judge until his retirement in 1992, ending a career of over 45 years in law.

In the years since his retirement, Shobe has received several honors and awards. The Louisville Bar Association presented Shobe with its Trailblazer Award to recognize his contributions in promoting racial and ethnic diversity, and it created the Judge Shobe Civility and Professionalism Award for bar association members who "embody professionalism, civility, honesty, and courtesy" in the following year. Soon after, the Louisville Black Lawyers Association established a scholarship in his name. Even in retirement, he remained committed to using his acquired skills to serve the community, serving as alternative dispute resolution specialist for Retired Judges and Associates in Louisville.

K'Meyer, Tracy E. *Civil Rights in the Gateway to the South: Louisville, Kentucky, 1945–1980.* Lexington: Univ. Press of Kentucky, 2009.
Newspapers: "Eckert, Shobe Re-elected; Most Primary Victors Win District Seats." *LCJ*, November 9, 1977, A16; "BG Native, Retired Judge Humbled by Honors," *BGDN*, April 8, 2012.

—*Stephen Pickering*

SHOCKLEY, ANN ALLEN (b. 1927), author, critic, and university librarian. Ann Allen Shockley, born on June 21, 1927, to Henry and **Bessie (Lucas) Allen,** has a well-established career as a librarian, novelist, and critic. She received her college education from Fisk University, where she earned a bachelor of arts in history in 1948. The following year she married William Shockley, with whom she had two children and whom she later divorced. Shockley returned to college at Case Western Reserve University, where she received a master of arts in library science in 1959.

Her career in the library field has included working as a curator, librarian, and archivist at Delaware State College, Fisk University, and the University of Maryland. Shockley has received a great deal of attention and sometimes criticism for her literary works, which often explore black feminist thought and lesbian themes. She has received several awards for her contributions to the world of literature, including the Martin Luther King Award for Literary Output, the American Library Association Black Caucus Award, the National Short Story Award, and the Hatshepsut Award for Literature.

Shockley's literary work carries a great deal of significance because she initiated the idea of including lesbian subject matter and feminist thought in her works long before well-known authors Toni Morrison, Maya Angelou, and Alice Walker. Her published works include *Loving Her* (1970), *Living Black American Authors* (1973), *A Handbook for Black Librarianship* (1977), *The Black and White of It* (1980), *Say Jesus and Come to Me* (1982), and *Afro-American Women Writers, 1746–1933: An Anthology and Critical Guide* (1988).

Shockley has a distinguished career as a reviewer, journalist, and librarian. Her literary works and the themes included in them have helped pave the way for a new expression of African American literature and thought.

Matthews, Tracye A. "Ann Allen Shockley." In *Black Women in America: An Historical Encyclopedia*, 1029–30. Brooklyn, NY: Carlson, 1993.

—*Kimberly Renee McDaniel*

SIGMA GAMMA RHO SORORITY, INC. historically African American sorority. Sigma Gamma Rho Sorority Inc. is an international service and social organization with a membership exceeding 85,000 sisters in over 500 chapters in the United States, the Virgin Islands, Bermuda, Korea, and Germany. The founders of Sigma Gamma Rho were a group of young African American teachers: Nannie Mae Gahn Johnson, Mary Lou Allison Little, Vivian White Marbury, Bessie M. Downey Martin, Cubena McClure, Hattie Mae Dulin Redford, and Dorothy Hanley Whiteside. These founders organized the sorority on November 12, 1922, at Butler University in Indianapolis, IN, a significant accomplishment at a time and in an area rife with racism. The first national convention was held in Indianapolis on December 27–29, 1925. On December 30, 1929, Alpha Chapter at Butler University was chartered, and Sigma Gamma Rho was incorporated as a national collegiate sorority.

In 1938, Louisville, KY's, graduate chapter Pi Sigma was the first chapter of the sorority organized in the state. Sigma Gamma Rho's first undergraduate chapter in Kentucky, Lambda, was organized at Kentucky State College for Negroes (now **Kentucky State University**) on April 15, 1947. In Kentucky, an undergraduate chapter exists at each of the eight state universities. There are also three graduate chapters, one each in Ft. Knox, Lexington, and Louisville. In May 1993, Pi Sigma hosted the Central Region's conference in Louisville at the Galt House.

Sigma Gamma Rho Sorority's mission is "to enhance the quality of life within the community. Public service, leadership development and education of youth are the hallmarks of the organization's programs and activities. Sigma Gamma Rho addresses concerns that impact society educationally, civically, and economically."

The sorority has sponsored countless service initiatives during its rich history as it has focused on scholarship, sisterhood, and service around the globe. Project Reassurance provides health education and services for teen parents and expectant mothers. Operation Bookbag assists at-risk school-age children and is associated with the sorority's yearly Youth Symposiums. Wee Savers educates youth between 6 and 18 years of age on financial matters. The Hattie McDaniel Cancer Awareness and Health Program provides education and support of early detection and prevention research for cancer. The National Marrow Donor Program educates and recruits race-appropriate bone marrow donors. Project Africare provides financial and educational assistance in economics and HIV/AIDS awareness in Africa. Project Mwanamugimu is an essay contest for American youth who research and write about Africa and African culture. Additionally, Sigma Gamma Rho sponsors three foundations, both national and international in scope, with the goal of improving the welfare of all people: the National Education Fund, the Sigma Public Education and Research Foundation, and the Seven Pearls Foundation.

Sigma Gamma Rho Sorority is a nonprofit, collegiate sorority dedicated to the encouragement and promotion of high scholastic attainment, community service, and improvement of the quality of lives and of society. The sorority flower is the yellow tea rose; its mascot is the poodle; and its colors are royal blue and gold. The Sigma Gamma Rho slogan is "Greater Service, Greater Progress."

Sigma Gamma Rho Sorority, Inc. "About Sigma—Mission Statement." Cary, NC, 2009. http://www.sgrho1922.org/page.php?page_id=115396&parent_id=0 (accessed April 28, 2010).
———. "Central Region Chapter Profiles." Cary, NC, 2009. http://sgrhocentral.com/chapter-profiles (accessed July 8, 2010).
———. "HER-story." Cary, NC, n.d. http://www.sigmagammarho.org/her.html (accessed April 28, 2010).
———. "History." Cary, NC, 2009. http://www.sgrho1922.org/page.php?page_id=115397&parent_id=115396 (accessed April 28, 2010).
———. "Programs." Cary, NC, 2009. http://www.sgrho1922.org/page.php?page_id=115399&parent_id=115396 (accessed April 28, 2010).
White, Pearl Schwartz, and Lillie Wilkes. *Behind These Doors—A Legacy: The History of Sigma Gamma Rho Sorority.* Chicago: Sigma Gamma Rho Sorority, 1974.

—Karen L. Gilbert and Jojuana Leavell Greene

SIMMONS, WILLIAM JOSEPH (b. 1849, Charleston, SC; d. 1890, Cane Springs, KY), minister, educator, editor, and writer. William Joseph Simmons was born in slavery on June 24, 1849, to Edward and Esther Simmons. His mother escaped along with young William and his two siblings from slavery and settled in

Dr. William J. Simmons.

Bordertown, NJ (the history of his father is unknown). In Bordertown, Simmons worked as a dentist's apprentice before he joined the Union army in 1864, and he resumed this type of work after the war. Among the schools he attended for his undergraduate studies were Madison University, Rochester University, and Howard University, where he earned his bachelor of arts degree in 1873. In Washington, DC, Simmons also taught at Hillsdale Public School while studying at Howard University and later became principal of the school. From 1874 to 1879, he resided in Florida with his wife, Josephine A. Silence. It was in Florida that he first entered politics. He held positions of deputy county clerk and county commissioner. He also served as chairman of the county campaign committee, and member of the district congressional committee.

From 1879 to 1880, Simmons was the sixth pastor at the **First African Baptist Church** in Lexington, KY. A year later, he accepted the offer to be the president of Kentucky Normal and Theological Institute (1880–1890), which later was named Simmons University in his honor (then later known as **Simmons College of Kentucky**). In September 1883, he organized the **Baptist Women's Educational Convention** for fund-raising purposes. In his writing career, he was elected editor of the *American Baptist* and president of the Colored Press Convention. His best-known work is *Men of Mark: Eminent, Progressive and Rising,* a biographical work he published in 1887. The book features 177 notable African American men of his time.

In 1890, Simmons resigned from the theological school, which had been renamed State Colored Baptist University. He and **Charles Henry Parrish** founded **Eckstein Norton Institute** at Cane Springs, KY, that same year. A few months later, on October 30, 1890, Simmons died of heart failure in Cane Springs, according to Kentucky's death records and the *Indianapolis Freeman.* However, some sources identify Louisville as his place of death. His body lay in state at the university for two days, and he was buried in Louisville's Eastern Cemetery.

Boone, Theodore S. *Negro Baptist Chief Executives in National Places.* Detroit: A. P. Pub. Co., 1948.
"The Falls City." *IF,* November 15, 1890, 2.
Kentucky, Death Records, 1852–1953.
Logan, Rayford Whittingham, and Michael R. Winston, eds. *Dictionary of American Negro Biography.* New York: Norton, 1982.
Melton, J. Gordon. *Religious Leaders of America: A Biographical Guide to Founders and Leaders of Religious Bodies, Churches, and Spiritual Groups in North America.* Detroit: Gale Research, 1999.
Simmons, William J. *Men of Mark: Eminent, Progressive and Rising.* Cleveland: George M. Rewell, 1887.

—Kim Nguyen

SIMMONS COLLEGE OF KENTUCKY, African American college. In August 1865, the General Association of Colored Baptists of Kentucky, under the leadership of Rev. **Henry Adams** of Louisville's **Fifth Street Baptist Church,** voted to establish a college for Kentucky African Americans. However, translating their intent into a viable school would require sustained commitment over more than a decade amid the turbulence of Reconstruction in the commonwealth.

In 1869, the General Association applied to the Kentucky General Assembly for a charter and began raising funds with which they purchased the Old Fort Hill property in Frankfort as a future site for a college. This property proved unsatisfactory and was soon sold, after which a more suitable site was purchased at Seventh and Kentucky Sts. in Louisville. After more years of planning and fund-raising, Kentucky Normal and Theological Institute opened on November 25, 1879, headed initially by Rev. **Elijah P. Marrs.** It was the first African American–controlled higher educational institution in Kentucky.

In September 1880, the General Association was fortunate in attracting Rev. **William J. Simmons,** a former slave and well-educated young minister beginning to gain a national reputation, to the presidency of the fledgling college. Simmons held BA and MA degrees from Howard University. Under his leadership, the college developed preparatory (elementary), academic (secondary), normal (teacher training), and religious education programs. After a college department was added in 1883, the institute was renamed State Colored Baptist University. Simmons acquired financial support from both Northern and Southern Baptists. Simmons resigned in 1890, but the university continued to evolve. By 1893, 159 students had completed the normal school program, and 30 had graduated from the college department. By 1900, State University was offering nurse-training programs and professional education in medicine and law through its affiliation with **Louisville National Medical College** and **Louisville Central Law School,** respectively.

Nevertheless, State University was a religious institution committed to liberal arts education and, as a result, received neither public funds nor private support from the white philanthropic organizations that sustained "industrial education" schools such as Tuskegee and Hampton Institute. Consequently, despite its achievements, the university was constantly beset by financial troubles that, after 1900, made it difficult to maintain physical facilities and to attract and retain the most qualified faculty.

In 1918, Rev. **Charles H. Parrish Sr.,** a State University graduate, was appointed president. Parrish renamed the school in honor of former president Simmons, his early mentor, and launched a determined campaign to revitalize the school's curriculum and improve its facilities. By 1922, there were 467 students in the college department, 33 theological students, and property valued at

Simmons University nursing students.

President Charles H. Parrish Sr. (seated, in center) with faculty, 1920s.

George Hampton (front center), a 1905 graduate, pictured with the 1924 Simmons graduating class.

$750,000. With an endowment of only $54,000, fund-raising efforts in 1922 and 1925 were moderately successful, and Parrish's tireless labors were repaid when, in March 1930, Simmons University was awarded a B rating as a senior college by the Committee on Accredited Relations of the University of Kentucky. However, this reversal of fortunes proved short lived when, with the onset of the Great Depression, Simmons became insolvent.

On August 31, 1930, the University of Louisville purchased the Simmons University property as the future location of **Louisville Municipal College** for Negroes—the black branch of the University of Louisville that opened on February 9, 1931, only two months before Parrish's death on April 8, 1931. Simmons retained the temporary use of one building and agreed to limit its offerings to religious instruction. In 1934, the University of Louisville exercised its option on the remaining Simmons property, and the school, then known as Simmons Bible College, moved to its present location at 18th and Dumesnil Sts. in Louisville. By 2013 Simmons had expanded its theological offerings and included a new liberal arts focus as Simmons College of Kentucky.

Dunnigan, Alice Allison, comp. and ed. *The Fascinating Story of Black Kentuckians: Their Heritage and Traditions.* Washington, DC: Associated Publishers, 1982.

Hardin, John A. *Fifty Years of Segregation: Black Higher Education in Kentucky, 1904–1954.* Lexington: Univ. Press of Kentucky, 1997.

Hudson, J. Blaine. "The Establishment of Louisville Municipal College: A Case Study in Racial Conflict and Compromise." *Journal of Negro Education* 64 (1995): 111–23.

———. "The History of Louisville Municipal College: Events Leading to the Desegregation of the University of Louisville," PhD diss., Univ. of Kentucky, 1981.

Newspapers: *Louisville Leader,* August 24, 1929; March 15, 1930; August 9, 1930; August 23, 1930; September 6, 1930; September 20, 1930; February 7, 1931; April 11, 1931.

Williams, Lawrence H. *Black Higher Education in Kentucky, 1879–1930: The History of Simmons University.* Lewiston, NY: Edwin Mellen Press, 1987.

Wilson, George D. *A Century of Negro Education in Louisville, Kentucky.* Louisville, KY: Louisville Municipal College, 1941.

—J. Blaine Hudson

SIMMS, JAMES NELSON (b. ca. 1870, Port Royal, KY; d. unknown), attorney, publisher, and inventor. The son of Henry Simms, a farmer, and Frances Simms, James Nelson Simms was born in Port Royal, KY, in Henry Co. Sources vary on the exact year of his birth, but the 1870 U.S. federal census listed him as a year old. However, his World War I draft registration card noted his birthdate as November 24, 1872.

In 1886, Simms graduated from Louisville's State Colored Baptist University (later known as **Simmons College of Kentucky**). He also matriculated at Ohio Wesleyan University in Delaware, OH. In 1897, he earned a law degree from the University of Indianapolis. By 1900, he was practicing law in Chicago, IL, at 3532 S. State St.

A spirited defense attorney, Simms was also politically active and frequently addressed political issues in multicolumn opinion articles in Chicago's *Broad Ax* newspaper. He was also an inventor. On January 3, 1916, he filed for a patent on an ornamental clock case. On April 25, 1923, he applied for a patent on "new and useful improvements in dinner pails" to increase the ease of cleaning the product.

That same year, Simms published *Simms' Blue Book and National Negro Business and Professional Directory* in order to promote African American businesses. He continued his Chicago law practice through the late 1930s and possibly into the early 1940s. Research has yet to locate his death information.

Newspapers: "The Colored Allies of the Democratic Party," *Broad Ax* (Chicago), January 24, 1903, 1; "Lawyer James N. Simms Deserts the Ranks of the Insurgents," *Broad Ax* (Chicago), August 13, 1910, 1; "Municipal Judge Wade Stored Attorney J. N. Simms Away in Unpleasant Quarters," *Broad Ax* (Chicago), October 25, 1913, 2.

Official Gazette of the United States Patent Office. Vol. 234. Washington, DC: Government Printing Office, 1917.

Simms, James N., comp. *Simms' Blue Book and National Negro Business and Professional Directory.* Chicago: James N. Simms, 1923.

U.S. Federal Census (1870, 1880).

U.S. Patent and Trademark Office. http://pdfpiw.uspto.gov/.piw?Docid =01482271&homeurl=http%3A%2F%2Fpatft.uspto.gov%2Fne tacgi%2Fnph-Parser%3FSect1%3DPTO2%2526Sect2%3DHITOFF %2526p%3D1%2526u%3D%25252Fnetahtml%25252FPTO%2525 2Fsearch-bool.html%2526r%3D1%2526f%3DG%2526l%3D50%25 26co1%3DAND%2526d%3DPALL%2526s1%3D%252522si mms,%252Bjames%252Bn%252522.INNM.%2526OS%3DIN %2F%2526RS%3D&PageNum=&Rtype=&SectionNum=&idkey =NONE&Input=View+first+page (accessed September 5, 2013).

U.S. World War I Draft Registration Cards, 1917–1918.

Yenser, Thomas, ed. *Who's Who in Colored America, 1938–1940.* Brooklyn, NY: Thomas Yenser, 1940.

—Amanda Hoover

SIMMS, WILLIAM "WILLIE" (b. 1880, Augusta, GA; d. 1927, Asbury Park, NJ), jockey and horse trainer, Preakness and Belmont winner, and two-time Kentucky Derby champion.

William "Willie" Simms entered the horse business as a young stable boy for George Cunningham, a wealthy white liveryman, in Augusta, GA. In 1892, he began his winning turf career riding for Philip J. Dwyer at Gravesend's First and Second Specials and Sheepshead Bay's Flatbush Stakes and Tidal Stakes. He then won the Belmont Stakes two consecutive years. In 1894, Simms was the top American winning jockey with 228 victories and a year later earned a reported $20,000 in salary and winnings. With his income, he bought his mother a palatial home in Augusta, but a tornado destroyed it.

In 1895, Dwyer's brother, Michael F. Dwyer, contracted Simms and sent him to ride in England for four months; he was possibly the first African American to ride there. Simms introduced to the English "the American seat," an aerodynamic, low-crouched riding style that eventually ended the British spurring style that frequently cut open the sides of the horses. The English ridiculed the technique as "monkeyship" instead of jockeyship. It was not until Tod Sloan, a white jockey, used the method a few years later that they accepted it.

In 1896, Simms won his first **Kentucky Derby** on Ben Brush, a horse he rode into the winner's circle in several other races, including the Latonia Derby. He won the Kentucky Derby again in 1898, on Plaudit, a horse owned by John E. Madden of Lexington, KY. That same year, he won the Preakness on Sly Fox. Simms remains the only African American jockey to win all three Triple Crown races: the Kentucky Derby, the Preakness, and the Belmont.

In 1901, the *New York Times* reported that jockeys who had "outgrown their usefulness" were in great demand in Europe. These riders who were unable to locate work in the United States were able to find "all the riding they could do" overseas. Simms raced in France. Weight gain and the ousting of African Ameri-

William "Willie" Simms.

can jockeys from the Thoroughbred industry forced Simms to retire from racing in the early 1900s, and he became a trainer. He never married and lived with his widowed mother, Ida Pleasant, in Asbury Park, NJ, where he died at age 47.

Henderson, Edwin Bancroft. *The Negro in Sports.* Washington, DC: Associated Publishers, 1949.

Hotaling, Edward. *Wink: The Incredible Life and Epic Journey of Jimmy Winkfield.* New York: McGraw-Hill, 2005.

Newspapers: "Windstorm," *Maysville (KY) Daily Public Ledger,* March 21, 1895, 3; "Pleased with English Racing," *NYT,* May 2, 1895, 6; "Kentucky Conquers," *LCJ,* May 6, 1898, 6; "Yankee Jockeys Abroad," *NYT,* February 25, 1901, 8; "Horse World," *LL,* April 6, 1903, 7; "Simms, Noted Rider, Dies," *NYT,* March 1, 1927, 24; "Will Simms Won Laurels in Famous Kentucky Derby," *BAA,* March 26, 1927, 18.

Renau, Lynn S. *Racing around Kentucky.* Louisville, KY: L. S. Renau, 1995.

Saunders, James Robert, and Monica Renae Saunders. *Black Winning Jockeys in the Kentucky Derby.* Jefferson, NC: McFarland, 2003.

—Sallie L. Powell

SIMPSON, ABRAM LYNN (b. 1894, Louisville, KY; d. 1955, Washington, DC), World War I captain. A soldier and a teacher, Abram Lynn Simpson was born and raised in Louisville, KY. He attended Wilberforce University in Ohio, where he joined **Alpha Phi Alpha, Inc.** and wrote the text for the fraternity's national hymn before beginning a career as a teacher at Morris Brown College in Atlanta. During World War I, he entered the U.S. Army in June 1917. Later that year, he achieved the rank of captain as a member of the 349th Machine Gun Battalion at the age of 23, becoming perhaps the youngest black captain in the military. His role in the war provided the inspiration for one of the characters in *On the Fields of France,* a play by his childhood friend Joseph S. Cotter Jr.

After returning from Europe, Simpson resumed his career in education, serving as president of Allen University in South Carolina from 1932 to 1937. He then became acting president of Bethune-Cookman College in Florida. However, he wanted to place more emphasis on industrial education at the school, which put him at odds with the school's founder, Mary McLeod Bethune, who decided against renewing his contract in 1939.

Simpson then moved to Washington, DC, where he served on the draft board before his death in 1955. He was buried in Arlington National Cemetery.

Hanson, Joyce A. *Mary McLeod Bethune and Black Political Women's Activism.* Columbia: Univ. of Missouri Press, 2003.
Hatch, James V., and Leo Hamalian, eds. *Lost Plays of the Harlem Renaissance, 1920–1940.* Detroit: Wayne State Univ. Press, 1996.
Ihle, Elizabeth L., ed. *Black Women in Higher Education: An Anthology of Essays, Studies, and Documents.* New York: Garland, 1992.
Jamieson, J. A., Jack Allen, John Graham, H. White, and G. L. Williams. *Complete History of the Colored Soldiers in the World War.* New York: Bennett & Churchill, 1919.

—*Stephen Pickering*

SIMPSON, ARNOLD R. (b. 1952, Somerset, KY), politician. Arnold Ray Simpson is the first African American to serve as Covington's city manager and the first of his race to be elected a state representative in Kentucky's 65th District. The son of funeral directors **James Simpson** and Zona Pennington Simpson, he was educated in the public schools of Covington and attended **Kentucky State University** in Frankfort and the University of Kentucky College of Law in Lexington. On October 10, 1981, he married Jo Ann Hill of Cincinnati.

In October 1986, Simpson was appointed city manager of Covington after serving as the assistant city manager since 1980. He was picked for the top job after City Manager Donald Eppley's resignation. In November 1989, Simpson resigned from the city manager position. In November 1993, Mary Sheehan, having been elected a Kenton Co. district court judge, resigned as the state representative of Kentucky's 65th District, and the Kenton Co. Democratic Party selected Simpson as its candidate to compete in a special election. Simpson defeated Republican Jerry Hatfield in that January 1994 election. Later that year, Simpson won both the Democratic primary in May against James Redwine and the November election, in which his opponent was Republican Eileen Wendt; he continues to serve in the Kentucky legislature. Simpson lives in Covington with his family.

Newspapers: "Covington Picks Simpson to Be Manager," *KP,* October 15, 1986, 1K–2K; "City Manager Leaving," *KP,* October 30, 1989, 1K–2K; "Simpson Likely Candidate to Fill Vacated Seat in General Assembly," *KP,* November 25, 1993, 1K; "Simpson to Run for State House," *KP,* December 13, 1993, 1K–2K; "Simpson Elected in 65th," *KP,* January 12, 1994, 1K–2K; "Redwine Challenges Simpson Again for Party's Nod," *KP,* May 20, 1994, 5K; "Simpson Wins Right to Try and Keep Seat," *KP,* May 25, 1994, 5K; "Stage Set for Fall," *KP,* May 25, 1994, 1K; "Simpson Victory Decisive," *KP,* November 9, 1994, 7K.

—*Theodore H. H Harris*

SIMPSON, JAMES "JIM," JR. (b. 1928, Somerset, KY; d. 1999, Covington, KY), funeral home operator and local government official. Jim Simpson, the first African American to be elected and serve on the Covington City Commission, was the son of James and Zetta West Simpson. He was educated in public schools in Covington and then joined the U.S. Army in 1947. After his tour of duty in the army, he entered the Cincinnati College of Mortuary Science, graduating in 1951. In 1952, Simpson began working for Anna Jones, the owner of **C. E. Jones** Funeral Home in Covington. In 1961, after the retirement of Jones, Simpson took over the operation of the funeral home and became part owner of the business; the firm's name changed to Jones and Simpson Funeral Home. In 1972, the city of Covington acquired the funeral home's property at 633–635 Scott St., and the business moved to its current location at 1129 Garrard St.

In 1971, Simpson ran successfully for the Covington City Commission. He served the full two-year term and later completed an unexpired term of Nyoka Johnston on the commission in 1991. Simpson served on the Kenton Co. Airport Board for eight years and in 1978 was elected its chairman; he also served on the boards of People's Liberty Bank; Booth Memorial Hospital, Covington; St. Elizabeth Hospital, Covington; and the Kenton Co. Tuberculosis Sanatorium. Simpson was the father of **Arnold R. Simpson,** a Covington city manager and a Kentucky state representative. James Simpson Jr. died on February 18, 1999, and was buried in Highland Cemetery, Ft. Mitchell. In June 2001, Simpson was nominated for the Kentucky Civil Rights Hall of Fame.

Newspapers: "Simpson Wins at Wire: Covington Vote Close," *KE,* November 3, 1971, 1A; "Funeral Directors Assumed Civic Roles," *KP,* February 2, 1987, 4K; "Kentucky Deaths," *KP,* February 20, 1999, 13A; "Dignified Leader Laid to Rest: James Simpson, Jr. Called a 'True Friend,'" *KP,* February 23, 1999, 2K; "Simpson Is Nominated for Rights Hall of Fame," *KP,* June 28, 2001, 3K.

—*Theodore H. H. Harris*

SIMPSON, PETER (b. 1848, Clark Co., KY; d. unknown), pioneer Kentucky African American educator. A son of slaves, Peter Simpson was born near Winchester in Clark Co., KY, in August 1848. He was about 19 years old when the Civil War ended but without money or education, he had few options at that time

Simpson later divided his time between work and school. In 1874, he had obtained enough schooling to teach while simultaneously continuing his education. In 1878, he entered **Berea College** but was forced to quit school in 1882 for financial reasons.

He then taught at various African American schools, many of which he helped build, until 1893. He frequently earned only $12 for months of work.

Simpson then became a grocer in Winchester, KY. Prominent in the community, he was successful in this business and a member of the local Baptist church. According to the 1900 U.S. federal census, he was single and owned his home. In 1911, he was "highly esteemed by both whites and blacks" in Winchester.

Hamilton, G. P. *Biographical Sketches of Prominent Negro Men and Women of Kentucky.* Memphis: E. H. Clarke & Brother, 1911.
U.S. Federal Census (1880, 1900).

—*Sallie L. Powell*

SIMPSONVILLE SLAUGHTER (1865), massacre of African American soldiers marching from Camp Nelson to Louisville. In January 1865, members of the 5th U.S. Colored Cavalry, a volunteer unit composed primarily of former slaves, departed **Camp Nelson** in Kentucky and began a journey north to Louisville. Their task was to escort a herd of nearly 1,000 cattle to a slaughterhouse in the city, which would then use the meat as rations for poorly provisioned Union soldiers in that city and across the South. Although initial progress was good, intensely cold temperatures and the arrival of snow hindered the column midway through its journey as it approached Simpsonville.

On January 25, the train had largely divided into two large groups as it passed through the town of Simpsonville, with most of the officers toward the front of the herd and the remaining soldiers struggling to keep pace in the rear. Taking advantage of the cattle guard's disorganization, a band of over a dozen Confederate guerrillas, led by Isaiah Coulter and including infamous raider Henry C. Magruder, attacked the rear of the column, catching the soldiers by surprise. According to most accounts, the cavalry offered little or no resistance, and this led some to suggest that the men had surrendered to their attackers; however, the guerrillas showed no mercy, killing between 19 and 35 black soldiers and gravely injuring several more. Newspapers reported the massacre as the "Simpsonville Slaughter."

Early accounts differed on the causes and extent of the massacre. The first report, published in the *Louisville Daily Journal* the following day, claimed that the "officers in command of the negro troops should be held responsible for the slaughter," arguing that they had abandoned their command to "warm at various houses along the road." An account in the *Shelby Record* in 1913, on the other hand, presented a significantly different portrait. According to a resident of Simpsonville, a guerrilla spy had thrown the column into disarray by stealing the commanding officer's boots and then tearing down a fence that separated the herd of cattle from a nearby cornfield; these tricks had contributed to the cavalry's disorganization the following day. The two narratives of the events of January 25 also diverged on the end results of the slaughter, with the *Journal* reporting 35 killed and the *Record* listing 19 dead and over 20 more injured.

The massacre was largely forgotten in historical accounts until 2008, when the **Kentucky African American Heritage Commission** awarded a Lincoln Preservation Grant to the Shelby County Historical Society to investigate the Simpsonville Slaughter. Locals

assumed that the victims of the attack had been buried in a mass grave in a nearby African American cemetery that had been abandoned for 40 years. Most of the grant funds were intended for the use of "ground-penetrating radar to identify, rehabilitate, and preserve" the burial site. Although the mass grave was not identified, the Historical Society did succeed in funding a roadside marker that was dedicated on January 25, 2009. Proponents of the marker have also begun the process of nominating the site for the National Register of Historic Places.

Newspapers: "Horrible Butchery," *Louisville Daily Journal,* January 26, 1865, 3; "Nineteen Negro Soldiers Shot Down," *Shelby Record,* February 21, 1913, 7; "Marker Revives Memory of 'Simpsonville Slaughter,'" *LHL,* January 21, 2009, B1.

—*Stephen Pickering*

SISNEY, RICARDO (b. 1939, Henderson, KY), educator and civil rights activist. Born in Henderson, KY, on February 18, 1939, Ricardo Sisney was an only child. His father's family was from Henderson, and his mother's family lived in Poole, KY, in Webster Co. Both of Sisney's parents, as well as Sisney himself, attended school in a segregated district in Henderson Co. Sisney's experiences first at Alvis Street Elementary School and then at Henderson (**Frederick**) **Douglas High School** helped shape his interest in education. In 1957, Sisney graduated from Henderson Douglas and went on to attend Kentucky State College (later known as **Kentucky State University**) on a band scholarship. He graduated in 1962 with a major in biology and a minor in French.

After graduating from Kentucky State, Sisney was employed in the Bowling Green city school system. He taught seventh- and eighth-grade general science at High Street School. Sisney remained at High Street School after it became an elementary school when the school district desegregated in 1965. He taught at the newly desegregated school for several years before becoming a team leader with the National Teacher Corps. His experience training intern teachers translated into a brief stint as the assistant director of the Teacher Corps Program at Western Kentucky University.

In 1971, Sisney was recruited from Western Kentucky University by the Bowling Green city school system to help alleviate some of the racial problems at the new campus of Bowling Green High School. Sisney became the assistant principal at the school, a position in which he served for 27 years. Sisney also began coaching a Little League baseball team. His opposition to the segregated league became a major concern for him. He became involved in the **Kentucky Commission on Human Rights,** a forum that allowed him to pursue various community and civil rights interests.

While Sisney was active in the commission, he often intervened in disputes, but at that time no formal local commission was established to receive complaints. In 1971, Sisney was appointed by the governor to the statewide commission. During the 1970s and 1980s, he was appointed three separate times to serve as a hearing commissioner. He dealt with several housing disputes, as well as other racial and gender discrimination. Throughout his tenure on the commission, Sisney continued to serve as the assistant principal at Bowling Green High School until his retirement in 1998. Unable to forgo his involvement in education, Sisney shortly thereafter returned to work at Western

Kentucky University, where he served as academic adviser for athletics.

Fosl, Catherine, and Tracy E. K'Meyer. *Freedom on the Border: An Oral History of the Civil Rights Movement in Kentucky.* Lexington: Univ. Press of Kentucky, 2009.

Newspapers: "Teacher Corps Offers Aid to Disadvantaged Children," *BGDN,* December 17, 1968, 2; "Dismissals Rejected in Lady Cop Hearing," *KNE,* November 21, 1974, 1; "Human Rights Commission Announces Three Settlements," *BGDN,* November 20, 1981, 5-A; "Tradition Ends as Administrator Takes His Leave," *BGDN,* June 7, 1998, 15-B.

Sisney, Ricardo. Interview by Betsy Brinson, Bowling Green, KY, June 5, 2000. Kentucky Civil Rights Oral History Project, Kentucky Oral History Commission, Kentucky Historical Society, Frankfort.

—*Elizabeth Schaller*

SISTERS OF LORETTO, the first black Roman Catholic sisterhood organized in the United States. Organized religious life for African Americans was created in central Kentucky's "Catholic Holy Land" in 1824 with the formation of an all-black ancillary community of the Sisters of Loretto, the first Catholic sisterhood established in the United States without a European foundation. In May 1824, three black female youths who had been adopted and educated by the Loretto Sisters were accepted into the congregation as postulants (petitioners for full membership) and received the Loretto veil. Acceptance of the black Loretto postulants was championed by Loretto founder Father Charles Nerinckx, and likely necessitated by an increasing African American desire for the consecrated state. The black Loretto postulants were accepted specifically to serve the catechetical and educational needs of Kentucky's expanding and largely neglected African American Catholic population, especially girls.

Because the Sisters of Loretto, like most religious orders of men and women in the Americas, was a slaveholding community and upheld white supremacy, the inaugural black Loretto sisters were also seemingly organized to be a separate congregation. According to Nerinckx, the black sisters were slated to wear a different habit than their white counterparts and hold different "offices and employment." Moreover, although the black Loretto sisters were bound to keep the main rules of the congregation and take vows, they could not make perpetual vows before 12 years of profession. Despite these restrictions and challenges, it is believed that sometime later in 1824, two additional free black women joined the community as postulants.

However, the institution of black Loretto Sisters proved to be short lived. White antipathies toward African American religion, the stranglehold of white supremacy on the church and wider American society, and Father Nerinckx's forced departure from Kentucky (and subsequent death in Missouri) in 1824 spelled a quick demise for the fledgling black congregation. Father Guy Chabrat, Nerinckx's successor and later the coadjutor bishop of Bardstown, dismissed the black Loretto sisters from their vows and sent them back into the world seemingly because he disapproved of the black congregation's existence.

Although very little else is known about the pioneering black Loretto congregation (partly because of two fires at the Loretto motherhouse before the turn of the twentieth century), its postulants were likely members or descendants of the generations of enslaved black Catholic Marylanders transported to Kentucky in the late eighteenth and early nineteenth centuries. It is also known that the members of the black Loretto congregation were not the first black Loretto sisters. Recent archival work at the Loretto motherhouse has revealed that Sister Clare (Nellie) Morgan, the sixth member of the congregation, who entered in 1812 and was the first Loretto to take a religious name, was the daughter of Winifred Abell, a former slave widow of color, and John Morgan, a white man who received Revolutionary War land grants in Kentucky in the late eighteenth century. It is also important to note that Loretto Sisters had at least 14 free and enslaved black oblates (persons who voluntarily promised themselves to the religious observances and obedience to the rule of the congregation) attached to their convents in Kentucky (8), Pine Bluff, AR (1), and Cape Girardeau, MO (5). Although they were not official members of the white Loretto community, these black women of God took religious names, were seemingly called sisters, and arguably should be recognized as such.

Maes, Camillus P. *The Life of Rev. Charles Nerinckx.* Cincinnati: Robert Clarke, 1880.

Miller, Randall, and Jon Wakelyn, eds. *Catholics in the Old South: Essays on Church and Culture.* Macon, GA: Mercer Univ. Press, 1999.

Minogue, Anna Catherine. *Loretto: Annals of the Century.* New York: American Press, 1912.

"Nuns Apologize for Slave Legacy." *BGDN,* December 4, 2000, 3-A.

Reilly, L. W. "Negro Sisters of Loretto" *Colored Harvest,* October 1898, 54.

Sisters of Loretto Motherhouse. Archival records, Nerinx, KY.

—*Shannen Dee Williams*

SISTERS OF THE MYSTERIOUS TEN, female and youth division of the United Brothers of Friendship fraternal organization. The Sisters of the Mysterious Ten (SMT) became an organized arm of the Order of the **United Brothers of Friendship** (UBF) in 1876, 15 years after its all-male counterpart was constituted. Initially, the organization was made up of the wives, daughters, and sisters of the men who were members of the UBF. Their assemblage as a formal organization was a testament to the efforts expended by the women of the order to proclaim their worth also as a benefit society for women by women. It was during the Louisville Convention of 1875 that the Sisters of the Mysterious Ten received initial approval to organize under the United Brothers of Friendship.

During the 1875 convention, two successful charters were conferred, leading to the creation of the first temples concurrently in Louisville and Covington, KY. As progressive expansion and change led to membership increasing by the thousands and the chartering of new temples throughout Kentucky, incorporation became essential to perpetuate this advancing national black society. After the addition of a unit for youth in July 1882 and a name change on October 9, 1905, the Grand Lodge of the United Brothers of Friendship–Sisters of the Mysterious Ten and Juveniles and its Subordinate Branches of the State of Kentucky was duly incorporated on September 11, 1911, in Lexington, KY.

Each of the branches of the SMT was called a temple. Each temple was composed of women who ranged in age from 16 to

50, as well as precisely three men who offered protection. There were also juvenile temples made up of young girls ranging in age from 5 to 16. By April 1914, there were 128 recorded temples in Kentucky. The organizational charge of the SMT was to help build a strong and financially viable benevolent institution whose purpose was to aid and care for its members when necessary because of illness and disability, as well as offering relief, via monetary payments, housing, or infirmary services, to the families of members who had died.

The African American women of this fraternal order were pioneers of their time. They worked skillfully and strategically in tandem with the men of the UBF to promote this organization through contributions of their own finances and labor and the use of their ties to the church and the community. Their leadership and guidance were also fundamentally required for the success of the juvenile arm of the State Grand Lodge of Kentucky.

Gibson, W. H., Sr. *History of the United Brothers of Friendship and Sisters of the Mysterious Ten: In Two Parts, a Negro Order.* Louisville, KY: Bradley & Gilbert Company, 1897.
Palmer, Edward N. "Negro Secret Societies." *Social Forces* 23, no. 2 (December 1944): 207–12.
Skocpol, Theda, Ariane Liazos, and Marshall Ganz. *What a Mighty Power We Can Be: African American Fraternal Groups and the Struggle for Racial Equality.* Princeton, NJ: Princeton Univ. Press, 2006, 49–50.
United Brothers of Friendship Collection. Special Collections and Archives, Paul G. Blazer Library, Kentucky State Univ., Frankfort.

—*Dantrea Hampton*

SLAUGHTER, ELIZABETH B. (b. ca. 1874, Louisville, KY; d. unknown), milliner. The oldest child of railroad porter Carter Slaughter and Henrietta Slaughter, Elizabeth B. Slaughter received her basic education in Louisville. In the late 1890s, she graduated from the Millinery Department of Armour Institute in Chicago, IL. An 1899 Washington, DC, African American newspaper column declared that Slaughter was "Womanhoods True Type" and praised her "extraordinary business ability." Her millinery shop was located in the home she shared with her parents on 1200 W. Chestnut St. She maintained a substantial stock of hats and hired local African American female employees.

While she was building her business, Slaughter became involved with John V. "Mushmouth" Johnson, a notorious Chicago gambler and businessman, and the couple planned to marry. In 1903, Slaughter moved to Chicago, IL, lived with an aunt at 3544 Dearborn St., and opened her shop, the Green-Lilly Millinery Company, at 128 E. 30th Street. A local newspaper described her as "an expert in making all kinds of art or fancy needle work."

In 1907, "Mushmouth" Johnson died without a will and with an estimated worth of $800,000. A year later, Slaughter sued his sister, Eudora Johnson, for $10,000 for libel and slander. Slaughter's friend, Kentucky native and Chicago attorney **Edward Hezekiah Morris**, won the case. However, an appellate court overturned the case in 1913.

In 1916, Slaughter married businessman and Bahamian native Terrevous La Fayette Douglas. The couple later moved to Evanston, IL, where they established the South American Art Novelty Store. A handmade ebony pipe they gave to Vice President Charles Gates Dawes became his favorite smoking instrument. On March 4, 1931, Terrevous Douglas died. Research has yet to locate any further information on Elizabeth B. Slaughter Douglas.

Cook County, Illinois, Marriages Index, 1871–1920.
"Elizabeth B. Slaughter, Appellee, v. Eurdora Johnson, Appellant." Gen. No. 17,448. *Reports of Cases Determined in the Appellate Courts of Illinois*, vol. 181. Chicago: Callaghan & Company, 1913.
Newspapers: "Womanhoods True Type," *Colored American* (Washington, DC), June 3, 1899, 5; "Chips," *Broad Ax* (Chicago), November 26, 1904, 4; "The Green-Lilly Millinery Company," *Broad Ax* (Chicago), April 1, 1911, 2; "The Slaughter-Douglas Nuptial," *Broad Ax* (Chicago), December 30, 1916, 1; "Mr. and Mrs. Terrevous L. Douglas Successfully Conduct a Unique Art Store at Evanston, Illinois," *Broad Ax* (Chicago), May 22, 1926, 2.
Richings, G. F. *Evidences of Progress among Colored People.* 10th ed. Philadelphia: Geo. S. Ferguson Co., 1903.
U.S. Federal Census (1880, 1900, 1920).

—*Sallie L. Powell*

SLAUGHTER, HENRY PROCTOR (b. 1871, Louisville, KY; d. 1958, Washington, DC), journalist. The son of Charles Henry and Sarah Jane (Smith) Slaughter, Henry Proctor Slaughter began his involvement in the newspaper business at an early age. When Slaughter was six, his father died, and he began selling newspapers to help support the family. After graduating as salutatorian of his class at Louisville **Central** (Colored) **High School,** he accepted a journalistic apprenticeship as a printer with the *Louisville Champion.* Slaughter became associate editor of the *Lexington Standard* in 1894. He studied at Livingstone College in Salisbury, NC, and at the same time served as the manager of that city's A.M.E. Zion Publishing House.

In 1896, he was appointed a compositor at the U.S. Government Printing Office in Washington, DC, and occupied that position until 1937. Committed to education, Slaughter did not allow his responsibilities at the printing office to interfere with his learning. Although he was not a practicing attorney, he received a bachelor of laws degree (1899) and a master of laws (1900) from Howard University in Washington. Slaughter, who was active in such fraternal organizations as the Masons and the Odd Fellows, also edited the *Odd Fellows Journal* from 1910 to 1937. Although he lived outside Kentucky for most of his life, Slaughter remained in contact with his home state as a correspondent for the *Bardstown (KY) Standard.* He also served as secretary of the Kentucky Republican Club in Washington, DC.

In addition to his professional pursuits, Slaughter spent a lifetime collecting materials associated with African American history and culture. His private library had a particular emphasis on the Civil War and slavery and was estimated to contain more than 10,000 volumes. The collection is now at Clark Atlanta University, Atlanta, GA.

Slaughter married Ella M. Russell on April 27, 1904; she died on November 2, 1914. On November 24, 1925, he married Alma Level, whom he later divorced. Slaughter, who died in Washington, DC, was cremated.

LD, February 20, 1958.

SLAVE LAWS, laws that defined the status of slaves. In 1798, the Kentucky state legislature enacted a slave code intended to govern slave behavior and the relationship between masters and slaves. The 43-article code, which replaced temporarily adopted statutes that had been inherited from Virginia, explicitly labeled slaves as property, dictating that "all negro, mulatto, or Indian slaves . . . shall be held, taken, and adjudged to be real estate." Other articles reduced slaves' mobility, restricted meetings among slaves, and required that any slave who would "lift his or her hand in opposition to any person not being a negro, mulatto or Indian" receive 30 lashes.

Several additions to the code in subsequent years targeted possible criminal behavior on the part of slaves. In 1811, the legislature listed 4 crimes as punishable by death for slaves: conspiracy and rebellion, the administration of poison, voluntary manslaughter, and rape of white women. The list expanded to 11 by the end of the slavery era, with arson, robbery, and shooting or wounding a white person among the new capital offenses. Accused slaves had little recourse in their defense. The 1798 slave code allowed masters to testify on their slaves' behalf, but slaves' testimony in their own defense was strictly limited.

Another class of laws dealt with the importation of slaves. The Kentucky Constitution of 1792 included a provision that the legislature would have "full power to prevent slaves being brought into this commonwealth as merchandise," and in 1815 the legislature increased existing penalties for importing foreign slaves. On February 2, 1833, the General Assembly passed the **Slave Nonimportation Law,** which again increased penalties for participating in illegal exchanges and, more notably, forbade citizens from importing slaves from outside the state for personal use. Although the law was controversial and poorly enforced, it initially had the support of the state's slave owners, many of whom opposed the **slave trade** and feared that the introduction of new slaves would foster insurrections.

The nonimportation laws and increased debate over slavery led to reactionary legislation in the 1840s and 1850s. In 1849, antislavery reformers hoped to use an impending constitutional convention to pursue gradual emancipation, but proslavery forces dominated the proceedings. They successfully adopted an article stating that "the right of the owner of a slave to such slave and its increase is the same and as inviolable as the right of any property whatsoever" and defeated an effort to include the nonimportation laws in the constitution. Proslavery Kentuckians also led drives for a stronger Fugitive Slave Law, which was enacted as part of the Compromise of 1850 and, pushed for more consistent enforcement.

In 1865, the ratification of the Thirteenth Amendment to the U.S. Constitution ended slavery in Kentucky.

Harrison, Lowell H., and James C. Klotter. *A New History of Kentucky.* Lexington: Univ. Press of Kentucky, 1997.
Lucas, Marion B. *A History of Blacks in Kentucky.* Vol. 1, *From Slavery to Segregation, 1760–1891.* Frankfort: Kentucky Historical Society, 1992.
McDougle, Ivan E. *Slavery in Kentucky, 1792–1865.* Lancaster, PA: New Era Printing Company, 1918.
Morehead, C. S., and Mason Brown. *A Digest of the Statute Laws of Kentucky, of a Public and Permanent Nature, from the Commencement of the Government to the Session of the Legislature, Ending on the 24th February, 1834.* Frankfort: Albert Hodges, 1834.
Tallant, Harold. *Evil Necessity: Slavery and Political Culture in Antebellum Kentucky.* Lexington: Univ. Press of Kentucky, 2003.

—*Stephen Pickering*

SLAVE NONIMPORTATION LAW, law stating that only immigrants who intended to become residents could bring slaves into Kentucky. In 1833, a coalition of diverse elements of Kentucky's population—humanitarians, abolitionists, slave owners, and others—was successful in pressuring the General Assembly

Slave ordinance, 1832.

to prohibit the importation of slaves into the commonwealth. Under the nonimportation legislation of 1833, only immigrants to Kentucky who swore within 60 days of their arrival their intention to become residents could bring slaves into Kentucky. All others who purchased, sold, or hired illegally imported slaves were subject to heavy fines.

The 1833 law proved to be virtually unenforceable, and its effect is difficult to assess. The percentage of blacks in the population declined thereafter, but maturing economic forces and the exportation of slaves to the Southwest may have been more important factors. Furthermore, interpretations that the 1833 law was evidence of an increasing determination of Kentuckians to end slavery were overly optimistic. The anticipated constitutional convention that was to provide for gradual emancipation never materialized, and opponents of the 1833 law soon weakened its force by allowing newcomers to Kentucky to avoid fines by pleading ignorance of the law. Meanwhile, the threatened clash between the North and the South over slavery so strengthened opponents of the 1833 law that they achieved its repeal, including exculpation of all who had violated the measure, in 1849. In the 1850s, Kentucky increasingly became a clearinghouse for the sale of slaves southward.

Coleman, J. Winston, Jr. *Slavery Times in Kentucky.* Chapel Hill: Univ. of North Carolina Press, 1940.

Harrison, Lowell H. *The Antislavery Movement in Kentucky.* Lexington: Univ. Press of Kentucky, 1978.

—*Marion B. Lucas*

SLAVE PATROL, organized group of white men who had authority to monitor slave activities throughout the South. The patter-rollers or "Padaroes," as they were sometimes called by slaves, were the white slave patrols that were established to protect whites from slave insurrections. These patrols were formed by South Carolina and Virginia in 1704 and 1724, respectively. In 1798, Kentucky passed the state's first slave code, which required slaves to have passes if they were away from their master's residence for more than four hours. In 1799, the Kentucky General Assembly passed an act giving county courts the right to organize into five districts, and each district was given the authority to pay a company of patrollers. There were a captain and a maximum of four patrollers in each company at that time. Because Kentucky was a border state, located on the Ohio River, whites felt compelled to guard their property from the activity of abolitionist and free blacks. They were vigilant in their search for runaway slaves and those who violated local ordinances. Slaves in Henderson, KY, had a 10:00 p.m. curfew. In Paris, KY, blacks had to have a pass to come into the city. Louisville prohibited more than three blacks from gathering at the market.

The slave patrols searched for slaves "strolling about" without proper passes from their masters. They observed large gatherings of blacks where insurrections could be organized. Those slaves apprehended for violating local laws were punished. A slave could "receive any number of lashes on his or her bare back, at the discretion of the captain of the patrol not exceeding ten." If the slave was brought before the magistrate, the level of punishment was given at the discretion of the magistrate but could not exceed 39 lashes. Captains were paid "four shillings" and the other patrollers "three shillings for twelve hours of service." The number of hours they worked was determined by courts, but the time served could not be less than 12 hours each month.

Whether on horseback or foot, the slave patrols questioned the activities of slaves who were away from their masters in both rural and urban communities. They freely confiscated items considered dangerous from slaves, and they broke up questionable meetings, which included church services. Slave patrols were established in Lexington and in Fayette and Mason Counties. In May 1861, 42 men patrolled the Knottsville District in Daviess Co. The slave patrols played an important role in maintaining the institution of slavery. In the words of Daniel Daly, a former slave, "The patter-rollers were everywhere."

Smith, Gerald L. "Slavery and Abolition in Kentucky: 'Patter-rollers' Were Everywhere." In *Bluegrass Renaissance: The History and Culture of Central Kentucky, 1792–1852,* edited by James C. Klotter and Daniel Rowland, 75–92. Lexington: Univ. Press of Kentucky, 2012.

—*Gerald L. Smith*

SLAVE TRADE, business that shaped the nature of Kentucky slavery. Although slavery in Kentucky was characterized as benign, the state possessed a thriving slave trade that made it a major exporter of slaves to the Lower South. The slave trade arrived with the first settlers in Kentucky in the late 1780s and lasted until 1865, when the Thirteenth Amendment outlawed slavery in the United States. The commerce was an important mechanism that facilitated the circulation of slave labor in local communities but also maintained the overall value of slave property in a state that relied on a diverse agricultural economy rather than staple-crop production.

The earliest slave trading in Kentucky took the form of local sales among the pioneers, who after initial settlement sold their excess slaves to newly arrived settlers. However, by the beginning of the 1800s, slave trading was a daily occurrence, and masters sold slaves for various reasons, from settling debts to ridding themselves of rebellious bondsmen. A number of variables affected slave prices, including sex, age, health, and job skills. Most Kentucky slaves were sold on the local market until the mid-1840s, when cotton cultivation in the Southeast provided an interstate dimension to the state's slave trade and raised prices for bondsmen. Although the financial panic of the late 1830s caused slave prices to dip temporarily, prices continually increased so that by 1860 young healthy slaves of either sex brought from $1,500 to $2,000. Kentucky slave traders created profitable connections with firms in New Orleans and Natchez. Historians estimate that roughly 77,000 Kentucky slaves were "sold down the river" between 1830 and 1860.

Despite some sentiment against slave trading, there were few efforts to limit the practice. In 1833, the Kentucky legislature passed the **Slave Nonimportation Law,** making it illegal to import slaves into the state for resale. But by the 1840s, professional traders openly advertised to purchase slaves, and in 1849, the Slave Nonimportation Law was repealed. Meanwhile, large slave-trading firms established themselves in Lexington and Louisville, which became centers of the slave commerce. From these cities, traders or their agents traveled throughout central Kentucky, which contained a large slave population, paying cash for "number one" slaves until they had gathered enough to ship to the southern markets in the early fall.

The slave trade was a flexible enterprise that also included the hiring of slaves. Whites who could not afford to buy a bondsman could hire a slave for a year or any length of time. Slave leasing provided a means for masters who did not want to sell their surplus slaves to make a profit from their labor.

Clark, T. D. "The Slave Trade between Kentucky and the Cotton Kingdom." *Mississippi Valley Historical Review* 21, no. 3 (December 1934): 331–42.

Deyle, Steven. *Carry Me Back: The Domestic Slave Trade in American Life.* Oxford: Oxford Univ. Press, 2005.

Gudmestad, Robert H. *A Troublesome Commerce: The Transformation of the Interstate Slave Trade.* Baton Rouge: Louisiana State Univ. Press, 2003.

Lucas, Marion B. *A History of Blacks in Kentucky.* Vol. 1, *From Slavery to Segregation, 1760–1891.* Frankfort: Kentucky Historical Society, 1992.

—*Benjamin Fitzpatrick*

SLEET, ANNE (b. 1931, Crab Orchard, KY), first African American mayor of Perryville, KY. Born in Crab Orchard, KY, on August 14, 1931, to Morris and Annie B. Ross, Anne Ross graduated from Lincoln High School in Stanford, KY. After earning her nursing degree at Danville School of Practical Nursing, she worked as a psychiatric nurse at the Kentucky State Hospital in Lexington. On May 13, 1951, she married Raymond Sleet, one of the descendants of the Sleet family from the historic African American community of **Sleettown,** near Perryville, KY.

Anne and Raymond had three children, Marshall, Steven, and Regina. Raymond was elected to the Perryville City Council four times. After his death in 1998, Anne succeeded him. She later won election on her own and was reelected to three more two-year terms, including two as mayor pro tem.

In 2006, Anne Sleet ran unopposed for mayor of Perryville. At age 75, she became the first African American mayor of Perryville and one of the few African American female mayors in Kentucky. As Perryville's first female mayor, Sleet planned to attract new businesses to the town. She wanted Perryville to become "the biggest little city in Kentucky." In 2007, the Kentucky Department of Parks purchased Sleettown to become part of the Perryville Battlefield State Historic Site. Mayor Sleet stressed the importance of people learning the history of the hamlet.

Active in her community, Anne Sleet has served in various capacities, including member of the Planning and Zoning Committee for four years and president of the Missionary Society. She is a member of the First Baptist Church, the Heritage Hospice Family Services, and the Human Rights Commission.

"Anne Sleet, Perryville Mayor (#210)." *Connections with Renee Shaw,* Kentucky Educational Television, February 10, 2007.

Cartwright, Regina Sleet, daughter of Anne and Raymond Sleet. E-mail to Sallie L. Powell, January 28, 2013.

"Perryville's Next Mayor: Anne Sleet Adds New Chapter to Family's Proud History in Boyle County" *LHL,* November 27, 2006, A1.

—*Sallie L. Powell*

SLEET, MONETA J., JR. (b. 1926, Owensboro, KY; d. 1996, Long Island, NY), photojournalist who was considered "one of the greatest photographers of the Freedom Movement." Moneta J. Sleet Jr. was born to Moneta J. and Ozetta L. Sleet in Owensboro, KY, on February 14, 1926. His parents sparked his interest in photography when they gave him an old box camera in his childhood. Photography was a hobby for Sleet during his high school and college years and a two-year stint in the U.S. Army. In 1947, after he graduated from Kentucky State College (later known as **Kentucky State University**) with a BA degree in business, photography became his career. In 1948, he established a photography department at Maryland State College. He then left to pursue graduate work, eventually receiving a MA degree in journalism from New York University in 1950. Afterward, he began a career of 46 years working exclusively with the black press, the last 41 with Johnson Publishing Company, the publisher of *Jet* and *Ebony.*

During his career, Sleet took pictures of famous and not-so-famous African Americans and people of color throughout the world. His most important contributions are his photographs of the American **civil rights movement** and the freedom movements in Africa, such as the Independence Day celebrations in Kenya. His personal and professional interests in civil rights led him to develop a relationship with Dr. Martin Luther King Jr. and his family. The result was the largest collection of candid photos of the King family, much of which Sleet donated to the University of Texas.

In 1968, Sleet took a picture of Coretta Scott King comforting her daughter, Bernice, at Dr. King's funeral. For this picture, Sleet became the first African American to win the Pulitzer Prize in Photography; his prize was the first given to a journalist working for a black publication. Sleet received awards from the Overseas

Mayor Anne Sleet.

Moneta Sleet, 1959.

Press Club of America, the **National Urban League,** and the National Association of Black Journalists. In 1989, he was inducted into the Kentucky Journalism Hall of Fame at the University of Kentucky. On September 30, 1996, he died of cancer and was buried in Calverton National Cemetery in Long Island, NY.

Crawford, Joe, ed. *The Black Photographers Annual.* Brooklyn, NY: Black Photographers Annual, 1972, 1973.
"Moneta J. Sleet, Jr., Pulitzer Prize–Winning Photographer, Eulogized in New York." *Jet,* October 21, 1996, 12–18.
Willis-Thomas, Deborah, ed. *Black Photographers, 1940–1988: An Illustrated Bio-Bibliography.* New York: Garland, 1989.

—*Andrew Baskin*

SLEETTOWN, African American community founded during the antebellum era. The story of Sleettown began in neighboring Mercer Co. In his will, dated August 4, 1836, slave owner Reubin Sleet gave his daughter Lucy Ann Peter a slave named Warner, the patriarch of the African American Sleets. The will did not mention whether Warner had a wife, but the 1870 census records his wife as an African American named Octavia. (The Sleet family claims that she was mainly Native American.) Warner and Octavia had three sons—Henry (ca. 1842), Preston (ca. 1844), and George (ca. 1850); all were born in Boyle Co.

Both Henry and Preston joined the Union army in 1864, using their middle name, Brown, as their last name. Henry enlisted as Henry Brown in the 5th U.S. Colored Heavy Artilley at Vicksburg, MS, on August 13, 1864. Preston enlisted as Preston Brown in Company G, 123rd U.S. Colored Troops, on September 29, 1864, at **Camp Nelson** in Jessamine Co. After the war ended, Henry and Preston returned to Boyle Co. and helped develop Sleettown, located in Boyle Co. approximately two miles northwest of Perryville.

Sleet family members, ca. 1880.

Records indicate that the Sleet family lived on the property as sharecroppers as early as 1865. In response to a lawsuit filed in Boyle Circuit Court on January 3, 1880, the master commissioner gave Henry and Preston nearly 150 acres for $141.00. The duo continued to buy property. As a result, Sleettown increased in size in the following years.

Sleettown was a refuge during the **Jim Crow** era. The residents had their own stores, restaurant, churches, and cemeteries. The men labored as sharecroppers, and the women worked at home. Although there were a few whites in the neighborhood, there was no open racial hostility. According to Hattie Sleet in a 1998 interview, the races lived in harmony.

The vibrant community of Sleettown had declined by 1931. Many of the residents had moved to Perryville. However, the legacy of the Sleets continued through the work of the descendants of Henry and Preston. Raymond Sleet coached Little League baseball for 27 years and received the Holman Cotton Leadership Award in 1983 for his work with the youth of Boyle Co. In 1998, the city of Perryville named a street in his honor to recognize his contributions. He was elected four times to the Perryville City Council.

After Raymond's death, his wife, **Anne Sleet,** was appointed to the Perryville City Council. She was reelected to three consecutive terms. In 2006, she ran unopposed for mayor of Perryville. With her election, she became the first African American woman mayor in Kentucky. Amelia Burton, Raymond and Anne's first cousin, began her teaching career in a one-room schoolhouse in Perryville and then taught for 14 years at Bate, the all-black school in Danville. In 1967, she became the first African American to teach at predominantly white Jennie Rogers Elementary School in Danville. In 1983, she became the first recipient of the Distinguished Teacher Award given by the Kentucky Department of Education and the Kentucky Board of Education for her commitment to education.

The best-known member of the Sleet family, **Moneta Sleet Jr.,** worked for more than 40 years as a photographer for Johnson Publishing Company, the publisher of *Jet* and *Ebony*. Moneta's son, Gregory, was appointed a federal judge by President Bill Clinton.

In 2007, the Kentucky Department of Parks purchased 96 acres where Sleettown was located. The department will use walking trails, interpretive signs, and research to tell the story of the Battle of Perryville, the largest Civil War battle in Kentucky, and the history of Sleettown.

Newspapers: "Sleettown Tells a Part of the Tale," *LHL*, September 30, 2001, J3; "Perryville's Next Mayor—Anne Sleet Adds New Chapter to Family's Proud History in Boyle County," *LHL*, November 27, 2006, A1; "Sleettown to Become Part of Historic Sites," *LHL*, June 5, 2007, CB3.
Perryville Battlefield Preservation Association. *Sleettown: Gateway to Freedom.* Perryville, KY.

—*Andrew Baskin*

SMITH, ANDREW JACKSON (b. 1843, Lyon Co., KY; d. 1932, Grand Rivers, KY), Medal of Honor recipient. In January 1862, Andrew Jackson Smith heard his master tell his sons that he planned to take his slaves to the Confederate army. Smith, who had been a slave since his birth in Lyon Co., KY, in 1843, took this opportunity to strike out for his freedom by joining the Union army at nearby Smithland. After walking 25 miles, he and a companion reached the camp of the 41st Illinois Volunteers, where they were given food and protection.

Unable to join the army, Smith became a servant to Maj. John Warner, with an order to bring Warner's belongings to his family in Illinois if he fell in battle. The two eventually participated in the Battle of Shiloh, where Smith twice replaced Warner's horse after the first two were shot out from under him. Smith, too, was struck in the head by a minié ball and almost killed. Afterward, Warner returned to Clinton, IL, along with his servant. However, after learning of the possibility of joining the war effort, Smith left to enroll in the 54th Massachusetts Colored Volunteers.

So many volunteers enlisted in the 54th Massachusetts that a second unit was created immediately, and Smith joined Company B of the 55th Massachusetts in 1863. He engaged in several campaigns across South Carolina before receiving honors for his role in the Battle of Honey Hill. After seeing the color sergeant downed by an artillery shell, he seized the falling Union flag, which he carried for the remainder of the battle. He also rescued the regimental colors, thus finishing the battle with two flags.

Promoted to the noncommissioned rank of color sergeant, Smith returned to Kentucky after the conclusion of the Civil War, where he purchased land in Lyon Co. In 1916, he was nominated for the Medal of Honor, but a lack of records, along with reluctance to award high honors to a black man, stalled the initiative. On March 4, 1932, he died and was buried in Mount Pleasant Cemetery in Logan Co.

Smith's daughter, Caruth Smith Washington, remained determined that he receive the award he deserved, and after her grandson, Andrew Bowman, researched his story for over 10 years, they succeeded in their attempt to restore the memory of a Civil War hero. On January 16, 2001, President Bill Clinton awarded the Medal of Honor to Andrew Jackson Smith posthumously. A historical marker near his grave in Lyon Co. records his service to the Union army.

Craig, Berry. *Hidden History of Kentucky in the Civil War.* Charleston, SC: History Press, 2010.
Hubbard, Mark, ed. *Illinois's War: The Civil War in Documents.* Athens: Ohio Univ. Press, 2013.
Newspapers: "Black Soldier's Kin Battle to Make Sure He's Honored," *Houston Chronicle*, February 16, 2000, 12; "U.S. 'Makes Things Right' for Roosevelt, Black Civil War Hero," *LHL*, January 17, 2001, B3; "A Civil War Hero Finally Gets His Due," *LHL*, January 21, 2001, J1.

—*Stephen Pickering*

SMITH, EFFIE WALLER (b. 1879, Pikeville, KY; d. 1960, Neenah, WI), poet. Effie Waller, a native of Pikeville, KY, was born on January 6, 1879. Her parents, Frank Waller and Sibbie (Ratliff) Waller, were former slaves. Raised along with three other siblings, Effie was provided with a strong educational and religious background. She began writing poetry at the age of 16 and then attended Kentucky Normal School for Colored Persons (later known as **Kentucky State University**) from 1900 to 1901.

Effie Waller Smith.

In her lifetime, Effie wrote three volumes of poetry, three short stories, and poems for literary magazines. Her first collection of poems, titled *Songs of the Month,* was published in 1904. In 1909, *Rhymes of the Cumberland* and *Rosemary and Pansies* were published. Smith also wrote short stories and published her poems in literary magazines. Her last published piece, "Autumn Winds," appeared in the September 1917 issue of *Harper's Magazine.* This piece was presented to the public when Smith was only 38 years old, but she lived until the age of 80. The reasons she stopped publishing her work despite enjoying 13 years of literary success remain a mystery.

Effie married twice. Her first marriage, in 1904, was to Lyss Cockrell and ended a year later; at the height of her writing career, she married Charles Smith, a deputy sheriff, in 1908. During the same year, the couple separated, and Charles Smith was killed while serving a warrant in Pikeville. In addition, Effie Smith adopted a daughter, Ruth (1918–2005), when Ruth's mother who was a friend of Smith, died at an early age. According to Ruth, Effie Smith was an avid gardener who constructed a large garden that was open to visitors. She recorded the names of thousands of visitors to the garden. She died on January 2, 1960, in Neenah, WI.

Pipkin, James Jefferson. *The Story of a Rising Race.* Black Heritage Library Collection. Freeport, NY: Books for Libraries Press, 1971.
Smith, Effie Waller. *The Collected Works of Effie Waller Smith.* Schomburg Library of Nineteenth-Century Black Women Writers. New York: Oxford Univ. Press, 1991.

—*Kim Nguyen*

SMITH, JAMES EDWARD (b. 1883, unknown; d. 1969, Louisville, KY), businessman. James Edward "J. E." Smith attended Jacksonian College in Jackson, MI, before settling in Louisville. He started in the insurance business with **Mammoth Life and Accident Insurance Company.** He and two other coworkers, **Green Percy "G. P." Hughes** and W. F. Turner, founded the **Domestic Life and Accident Company** in 1920. Smith also served as president of the National Negro Insurance Association. His business activities included work with the Falls City Chamber of Commerce, and he founded the Fidelity Industrial Plan, a loan company, in 1962.

In addition to being a businessman, Smith was a political activist. He was a member of the **National Association for the Advancement of Colored People** and of the Jefferson County Kentucky Democratic Executive Committee. This political activity reached its height when Smith was chosen to serve as a Kentucky delegate to the 1964 Democratic National Convention. He served in the Kentucky House of Representatives in Frankfort from 1964 to 1968, representing the 42nd District in Louisville, and introduced a public-accommodations bill.

Political participation ran in the family. Smith's wife, **Verna Smith,** served as an alternate delegate to the 1944 Democratic National Convention and also as president of a local Democratic club and cocaptain of her precinct. Similarly, James and Verna's daughter, **Charlotte Smith McGill,** was vice chair of the Democratic Executive Committee of Louisville–Jefferson County and a member of the Kentucky General Assembly.

J. E. Smith died on April 24, 1969. He was buried in the Louisville Cemetery alongside his wife, who had died in 1966.

Kentucky Death Index, 1911–2000.
Univ. of Kentucky Libraries. "Smith, James E. 'J. E.'" Notable Kentucky African Americans Database. http://www.uky.edu/Libraries/NKAA/record.php?note_id=1160 (accessed March 23, 2009).
Univ. of Louisville Libraries. Special Collections and Archives. "Smith-McGill Family Papers." http://special.library.louisville.edu/display-collection.asp?ID=561 (accessed March 23, 2009).

—*Joseph Gershtenson*

SMITH, JOSHUA I. (b. 1941, Garrard Co., KY), founder of the Maxima Corporation. A native of Garrard Co., KY, Joshua I. Smith taught biology in high school and at the University of Akron before becoming interested in information technology in the late 1960s. After moving to Washington, DC, Smith began to take classes in business while he worked at the American Society for Information Science from 1970 to 1976. He then joined Herner and Company, a consulting firm, for two years before forming his own business, the Maxima Corporation, in 1978.

Smith's company, an information technology firm, turned a profit almost immediately, earning revenues of $321,000 in 1979 and surging to $28 million by 1985. Smith's business acumen landed him in prominent positions in both private and public sectors. He served on the board of directors of three Fortune 100 companies—Fedex, Allstate Insurance, and Caterpillar—and was appointed chairman of the U.S. Commission on Minority Business Development in 1989. In 2003, he chaired the special Task Force on Minority Business Reform in Maryland, continuing a lifelong commitment to minority and women-owned business enterprises. In 2007, he was named a Business Legend in Maryland and was inducted into the African American Hall of Fame the following year. He has hosted a radio show, *Biz Talk with Josh Smith*, which gives advice to business owners.

Hawkins, Walter L. *African American Biographies: Profiles of 558 Current Men and Women*. Jefferson, NC: McFarland, 1992.
"Host Bio." *Biz Talk with Josh Smith*. http://www.biztalkwithjosh.com/bio.html (accessed June 11, 2012).
"Maxima Corp. Struggles to Regain the Success That Made It One of the Nation's Biggest Black-Owned Firms." *Baltimore Sun*, February 27, 1994, 1D.

—*Stephen Pickering*

SMITH, LUCY CORNELIA HARTH (b. 1888, Roanoke, VA; d. 1955, Lexington, KY), educator. Born in Roanoke, VA, in 1888, Lucy Cornelia Harth was the daughter of schoolteachers Daniel W. and Rachel (Brockington) Harth. She initially studied at Hampton Institute and later earned her undergraduate degree magna cum laude at Kentucky State Industrial College for Colored Persons (later known as **Kentucky State University**) in 1932. She obtained her master's in education at the University of Cincinnati. From 1908 to 1910, Smith taught in Roanoke, VA. She married Paul Vernon Smith, a teacher, in 1910. The couple taught school in Lexington, KY. Lucy worked as an assistant principal for 17 years at the Booker T. Washington Academy. Between 1935 and 1955, she served as principal of the school.

Aside from her career as an educator, Smith's greatest contributions include her service in many organizations, including the

Lucy Harth Smith.

Lexington YWCA Interracial Council, the State Interracial Council, the Governor's Committee on Youth and Children, the Association for the Study of Negro Life and History (ASNLH), the Executive Council of ASNLH, **Kentucky Association of Colored Women's Clubs,** and the National Association of Colored Women. In addition, she was one of the founders of the National Association of Colored Girls, which worked to raise the self-esteem for young African American females. She was also the founder of the Colored Health Camp, whose purpose was to improve the health of malnourished black children. In 1939, Mildred Chandler, the wife of Kentucky governor Albert Benjamin "Happy" Chandler, selected her to represent Kentucky at the World's Fair in New York City. As the second woman to become president of the **Kentucky Negro Educational Association,** she carried out her mission to increase knowledge of African American history by bringing textbooks about African Americans into classrooms. Through her leadership in the American Association for the Study of Negro Life and History, she was able to carry out this mission nationwide.

Smith died of complications from diabetes in Lexington, KY, on September 21, 1955.

"Lucy Harth Smith." *Journal of Negro History* 41, no. 2 (April 1956): 177–79. http://www.jstor.org/stable/2715588 (accessed June 12, 2008).
McDaniel, Karen C. "Lucy Harth Smith." In *Notable Black American Women*, vol. 2. edited by Jessie Carney Smith. Detroit: Gale Research, 1996, 603–4. Reproduced in *Biography Resource Center*. Farmington Hills, MI: Gale, 2008. http://galenet.galegroup.com/servlet/BioRC (accessed June 12, 2008).
Smith, Camie. 1975. "Mrs. Lucy Cornelia Harth Smith." Unpublished manuscript.
Smith, Lucy Harth, comp. and ed. *Pictorial Directory of the Kentucky Association of Colored Women*. Lexington: Kentucky Association of Colored Women, 1945.

—*Kim Nguyen*

SMITH, LUCY WILMOT (b. 1861, Lexington, KY; d. 1890, Louisville, KY), journalist. Lucy Wilmot Smith lived her life "by voice and pen." She was born, most likely into slavery, on November 16, 1861, to a single mother, Margaret Smith, who resided in Lexington, KY. Reverend **James Monroe** of the **First African Baptist Church** baptized her in December 1872. She began her career as a teacher at the young age of 16 and managed to put herself through school and support her mother.

In 1877, she graduated from the normal school at Kentucky Normal and Theological Institute (later known as **Simmons College of Kentucky**) in Louisville, KY. She continued teaching and served as personal secretary to Dr. **William J. Simmons.** In 1883, Simmons called together a Baptist women's conference. Smith was instrumental in the organization and served on the board of managers. She was also the secretary of the Children's Band, which was an auxiliary of the Baptist women's group. In 1885, Smith returned to State Colored Baptist University as a financial clerk and city missionary to the Young Men's and Women's Christian Association, where she also served as president. In 1887, she held the position of historian at the American National Baptist Convention and became a professor at State University.

During her short but eventful career, Smith was editor of the "Women's Department" in *Our Women and Children* and was chair of the Women's Baptist Educational and Missionary Convention in Kentucky. She died in December 1890, leaving the message of women's equality and suffrage to live on in the work she had accomplished.

Brown, Hallie Quinn. *Homespun Heroines and Other Women of Distinction.* Xenia, OH: Aldine, 1926.

Higginbotham, Evelyn Brooks. *Righteous Discontent: The Women's Movement in the Black Baptist Church, 1880–1920.* Cambridge, MA: Harvard Univ. Press, 1994.

Penn, I. Garland. *The Afro-American Press, and Its Editors.* Springfield, MA: Willey & Co., 1891.

—*Amanda Hoover*

SMITH, MARVIN PENTZ (b. 1910, Nicholasville, KY; d. 2003, New York, NY), and Smith, Morgan Sparks (b. 1910, Nicholasville, KY; d. 1993, New York, NY), artists. Twin brothers Marvin and Morgan Smith were born in Nicholasville, KY, on February 16, 1910. Their parents, Allena and Charles, worked as tenant farmers until they moved the family to Lexington, KY, in 1922. The young boys attended (Paul Laurence) **Dunbar High School** and were both employed by prominent white families: Marvin worked for the Headley family, while Morgan served as chauffeur for Dr. John C. Hanley, president of Sayre School. These contacts gave both brothers the opportunity to develop as artists despite the lack of art studios and materials at Dunbar High School.

After graduating in 1933, the Smiths traveled first to Cincinnati, OH, but ultimately ended up in New York City in order to pursue careers in the fine arts. After settling in Harlem, the Smiths took jobs performing manual labor through the Works Progress Administration. In 1936, they married Anna and Florence McLean, also identical twins, whom they divorced three years later. Around this same time, the brothers began experimenting with photography. They sold images to African American newspapers and eventually opened M. Smith Photo Studio in 1937. That same year, Morgan won honorable mention in a national photo contest for his image *Robert Day Playing Hi-Li,* and he was hired as the first staff photographer at the *Amsterdam News.*

Located at 243 W. 125th Street, the studio was next door to the Apollo Theater in the cultural center of Harlem. The brothers photographed well-known figures like Jackie Robinson and Josephine Baker, as well as young African American women looking to establish modeling careers. Marvin volunteered for the navy during World War II and was the first African American to attend the Naval Air Station School of Photography and Motion Pictures. Morgan continued to sell photographs to newspapers and began working for the *People's Voice* in 1942. In the 1950s, Marvin traveled to Paris to study abstract art, while Morgan began working in the motion picture industry as a sound technician. The brothers became union members and continued to work in television and film until they retired in 1975. Morgan Smith died on February 17, 1993, in New York City. Marvin died ten years later, on November 9, 2003. He was buried in Lexington's Cove Haven Cemetery.

Finney, Nikky. *M & M Smith: For Posterity's Sake.* Directed by Heather Lyons. Lexington, KY: Little City Productions, 1995. Videocassette, 57 min.

Miller, James A. *Harlem: The Vision of Morgan and Marvin Smith.* Lexington: Univ. Press of Kentucky, 1998.

Newspapers: "Stars in Harlem but Little Known in Lexington Smith Brothers Photographed Prominent Blacks," *LHL,* April 11, 1993, J1; "Portrait of Black Life, Minus the Bad News," *NYT,* December 12, 1997, E39; "The Heartbeat of a Photogenic Life," *NYT,* December 25, 1997, F1; "Marvin Smith, 93, Whose Photographs Defined Harlem Life," *NYT,* November 12, 2003, C13; "Artist Marvin Smith, 93, Dies in Manhattan—Photographer and His Twin Known for Shots of Celebrities, Harlem," *LHL,* November 13, 2003, B4.

Rachleff, Melissa. *Images of Harlem, 1935–1952: A Brief Biography of Marvin and Morgan Smith.* Lexington: Univ. of Kentucky Art Museum, 1993.

—*Elizabeth Schaller*

SMITH, MARY ELIZABETH HYATT (b. ca. 1872, Estill Co., KY; d. 1946, Indianapolis, IN), physician and author. Born in Estill Co., KY, Mary Elizabeth Hyatt was the third child of Richard Hyatt, a blacksmith, and Nancy Jane (McCarley) Hyatt. By the time she was eight years old, the family had moved to Indiana. She attended public school in Crawfordsville, IN, and later attended the Marion Normal Conservatory of Music in Marion, IN. She worked as a dressmaker, milliner, and music teacher. She married her first husband, William Tennyson Thomas, on April 27, 1896. They had one son, Fred Hyatt Thomas, born on June 1, 1897.

Mary returned to Kentucky and earned her medical degree at **Louisville National Medical College** (1895–1909). After her medical training, she married her second husband, Woodford Robert Milton Smith, on May 18, 1909. That same year, she became a lecturer on eugenics. She worked at the National Relief Hospital as a nurse and matron in North Marion, IN. As a physician, she specialized in women and children and diseases that affected them.

Smith wrote many articles pertaining to medical care and health for various newspapers and magazines. She compiled a book on poetry and health topics, and wrote "My Little Hoosier Song" and "Consecration." She also belonged to many community and professional organizations. On December 3, 1946, she died and was buried in Crown Hill Cemetery in Indianapolis, IN.

Beckford, Geraldine Rhoades, comp. *Biographical Dictionary of American Physicians of African Ancestry, 1800–1920.* Cherry Hill, NJ: Africana Homestead Legacy, 2011.

Boris, Joseph J., ed. *Who's Who in Colored America, 1928–1929.* New York: Who's Who in Colored America Corp., 1929, 341.

U.S. Federal Census (1880, 1930).

—*Amanda Hoover*

SMITH-STOWE, MARY LEVI (b. 1936, Hazelhurst, MS), first African American woman president of a state university in Kentucky. Born on January 30, 1936, Mary Levi, a native of Hazelhurst, MS, was one of seven children born to Rev. William and Byneter (Markham) Levi. She graduated from Jackson State College (later known as Jackson State University), where she married Lexington native Leroy Smith in March 1957, three months before her college graduation. Her early career included teaching

Dr. Mary Smith.

in public elementary schools in Mississippi, Alabama, and Tennessee. She also taught at Tuskegee University. She spent her summers in graduate school at the University of Kentucky, where she earned both her master of arts (1964) and doctor of education (1980).

In 1970, Smith began her career at Kentucky State College (later known as **Kentucky State University**) (KSU) as assistant coordinator of a reading program for Kentucky's classroom teachers. In 1981, she became chairperson of the Division of Education, Human Services, and Technology and was appointed dean of the College of Applied Sciences in 1983. The KSU faculty conferred the outstanding faculty award on Smith in 1985. In 1988, she was appointed vice president of academic affairs, and in 1989, she became interim president for 14 months until the new president took office. Controversy at the university led to the dismissal of the new president one year later. Subsequently, in October 1991, Mary Levi Smith was appointed the 11th president of Kentucky State University, the first female president in the university's 105-year history and the first African American woman to become a university president in Kentucky. During her presidency, she improved the university's financial stability and established the campus's technology infrastructure.

Among Smith's numerous honors are outstanding alumnus of Jackson State University in 1988, the Torchbearers and Trailblazers Education Award given by **Alpha Kappa Alpha**'s Phi Lambda Omega Chapter of Louisville in 1989, the Citizen Award presented by the Frankfort Alumnae Chapter of **Delta Sigma Theta Sorority** in 1990, the Lexington YWCA Women of Achievement Award in 1990, the **National Association for the Advancement of Colored People**'s Woman of the Year Award in 1990, the Woman of Achievement Award from the Frankfort Business and Professional Women in 1994, and the 1994 Professional Achievement Award from the *Louisville Defender.* She was inducted into the University Of Kentucky Hall of Distinguished Alumni in 1995.

Smith retired from the university after 28 years of dedicated service in 1998. Her husband died on October 25, 2002. In 2005, she published her memoirs, *In Spite of the Odds: Using Roadblocks, Potholes, and Hurdles as Stepping Stones to Success.* In 2007, she married Rev. James Howard Stowe. She remains actively involved in the work of several local community groups, including the Frankfort Alumnae Chapter of Delta Sigma Theta Sorority, Inc. and her church.

McDaniel, Karen C. "Mary Levi Smith." In *Notable Black American Women,* vol. 2, edited by Jessie Carney Smith, 605–6. Detroit: Gale Research, 1996.
Smith, Mary Levi. *In Spite of the Odds: Using Roadblocks, Potholes, and Hurdles as Stepping Stones to Success.* Louisville, KY: Goose Creek, 2005.

—*Karen Cotton McDaniel*

SMITH, MARY SIMON (VINCENT), SVD, OCSO (b. 1894, Lebanon, KY; d. 1952, Piffard, NY), first Kentucky-born African American Catholic priest, one of the first four African American priests of the Society of the Divine Word, and first African American Trappist monk in Kentucky. Vincent Smith was born on August 2, 1894, in Lebanon, KY, to Pious and Mary Eliza (née Spalding) Smith. He was raised in a devout Catholic family that attended Lebanon's segregated St. Augustine Catholic Church, where he was baptized, made all his holy sacraments, and served as an altar boy.

Called to religious life as a child, Smith first professed his desire to join the monastic life while assisting his father (a plasterer) in construction work at the Abbey of Gethsemani, the Trappist monastery near Bardstown, the epicenter of Kentucky's "Catholic Holy Land." However, his desire was delayed for several decades because he was forced to enter the workforce as a teenager to assist his family and because of persistent racial discrimination practices in the U.S. Catholic Church.

Smith served for 18 months in the U.S. Army during World War I but renewed his pursuit to enter religious life in 1919. With the support of Bishop Ferdinand Brossart of Covington, KY, for whom he had previously worked as a chauffeur and valet, he entered the all-black and Catholic St. Emma's Military Institute in Rock Castle, VA. While he was there, he applied to enter Baltimore's St. Joseph's Seminary, one of only three U.S. seminaries known to have admitted black men and helped them secure ordination in the United States. However, the refusal of most U.S. bishops to ordain and appoint black priests in their jurisdictions prompted the Josephite Fathers to reject Smith's application on the basis of race.

In 1921, Smith transferred to Sacred Heart College (later named St. Augustine's), a minor seminary operated by the Society

Father Vincent Simon, SVD, conducting mass at St. Elizabeth's Catholic Church in Chicago, March 1942.

of the Divine Word (SVD), which specifically trained African Americans for the priesthood. In 1926, he was a member of the seminary's first graduating class. The following year, he entered the SVD novitiate in East Troy, WI, with the institute's first group of African American seminarians, took his first vows in 1928, and advanced through his major seminary training back at St. Augustine's for the next six years.

On May 23, 1934, Smith, along with three other African American men, made history when they were ordained to the priesthood by Bishop Richard Gerow of the Diocese of Natchez-Jackson in Mississippi. They were the first African American priests ordained in the South and the first to secure positions in a southern diocese. Father Vincent conducted his first mass at his home church in Lebanon on June 10, 1934.

In 1940, Father Vincent was appointed assistant pastor at Chicago's all-black St. Elizabeth's Catholic Church. He was only the second African American priest to serve in the archdiocese of Chicago. By 1943, his desire to become a Trappist monk returned, and he took a leave of absence in Lebanon to seek admission into the Order of the Cistercians of the Strict Observance (OCSO) at the Abbey of Gethsemani. However, he was initially rejected. He then served two churches in New Jersey.

In 1949, Father Vincent left to reapply to the Trappists in Lebanon. Finally accepted into the community, he received the Trappist robes on May 15, 1949. He took his final vows on May 20, 1951, using the name Father Mary Simon. Soon thereafter, he was

transferred to the Abbey of Genesee in Piffard, NY, where he served as the novice master until he suffered a major heart attack on May 22, 1952. He died three days later and was buried at the Trappist monastery in Piffard.

Brandewie, Ernest. *In the Light of the Word: Divine Word Missionaries of North America.* Maryknoll, NY: Orbis Books, 2000.
Davis, Cyprian. *The History of Black Catholics in the United States.* New York: Crossroad, 1990.
Foley, Albert S. *God's Men of Color: The Colored Catholic Priests of the United States, 1854–1954.* New York: Farrar, Straus, 1955.
Ochs, Stephen J. *Desegregating the Altar: The Josephites and the Struggle for Black Priests, 1871–1960.* Baton Rouge: Louisiana State Univ. Press, 1990.

—*Shannen Dee Williams*

SMITH, MARY VICTORIA CUNNINGHAM (b. 1842, Louisville, KY; d. 1919, Covington, KY), teacher and pianist who challenged the institution of segregation with a lawsuit in the late nineteenth century. Daughter of **James C. Cunningham** and Lucy Cunningham, Mary Victoria Cunningham was raised in a musical environment. Her father, born in Bermuda, was a violinist, bandleader, and dancing teacher in Louisville. Her younger brother, **James R. Cunningham,** was the leader of a brass band. Mary, a teacher, became a well-known organist and pianist. In 1869, she married Early Smith, a barber and saloon owner. The couple lived with the Cunninghams. After Louisville's **St. Augustine Catholic Church** was opened to black worshippers that same year, Smith served as one of its choir directors.

On May 8, 1870, a chilly, damp, gloomy day, Mary Victoria Cunningham Smith and her six-year-old stepson, Gustavus Smith, paid five cents to ride a streetcar owned by the Louisville City Railway Company, which had been organized in 1864. For unknown reasons, the streetcar operator ejected Smith and her stepson from the car about eight blocks from their home. On June 2, Smith and her husband, Early, filed a lawsuit, *Early Smith and Wife v. Louisville City Railway Company.* The lawsuit questioned whether the company had the right to expel passengers because of race. Three white attorneys, including James Speed, represented the couple. The case was heard in U.S. circuit court on October 28. There were many delays in the case, including the birth of Mary's first child, Richard T. Smith, in April 1871. On October 17, 1872, the Smiths won their case. They had filed for $10,000 in damages but were awarded only one cent and the costs incurred from the lawsuit.

Smith continued with her music. In May 1880 and 1881, at a musical festival sponsored by the Colored Musical Association, she accompanied performers on the organ. Her husband, Early, died in 1896. She then lived with her son, Richard, and worked as a domestic. After Richard became a banker in Cincinnati, they moved to Covington. Smith died after suffering a cerebral hemorrhage on December 13, 1919. A Covington undertaker, E. E. Jones, handled the burial arrangements. Smith was buried in Louisville's Eastern Cemetery near her parents.

Bogert, Pen. "A Woman of Courage: Mary Victoria Cunningham Smith." *Griot* 1 (Summer 2000). http://www.kcaah.org/site/essay/c/marycvictoriacunningham.htm (accessed November 28, 2012).

Kentucky, Death Records, 1852–1953.
Lucas, Marion B. *A History of Blacks in Kentucky: From Slavery to Segregation, 1760–1891.* 2nd ed. Frankfort: Kentucky Historical Society, 2003.
U.S. Federal Census (1870, 1880).

—*Sallie L. Powell*

SMITH, ORLANDO "TUBBY" (b. 1951, Scotland, MD), basketball coach. Orlando "Tubby" Smith was born on June 30, 1951, in Scotland, MD, the son of Parthenia and Guthrie Smith. After playing basketball at and graduating from High Point College, Smith coached high school basketball for 6 years and assisted at colleges for 12 years. He then became head coach at the University of Tulsa, rebuilt the team, and led it to two Missouri Valley Conference championships. At the University of Georgia, he guided the Bulldogs to their first back-to-back 20-win seasons. In 1997, he became coach at the University of Kentucky and led the Wildcats to the national championship in his first year. He was conference Coach of the Year five times (twice in the Missouri Valley and three times in the Southeastern Conference) and won three National Coach of the Year awards. In 2007, he moved to the University of Minnesota and turned a losing program into a winner, winning 20 games his first season at a school that had lost 22 games the previous season. On April 1, 2013, Texas Tech announced its hiring of Smith. He replaced another former University of Kentucky coach, Billy Gillispie.

Smith and his wife, Donna, have three sons—G. G., Saul, and Brian—all of whom played basketball in the Southeastern Conference. Smith has been very active in community work. The Tubby Smith Foundation has raised over $1 million to help underprivileged children. Several community centers have been named Tubby's Clubhouse to honor his efforts.

Kosmider, Nick. "It's Official: Texas Tech Hires Tubby Smith as Basketball Coach." *Lubbock Avalanche-Journal,* April 1, 2013.
Krawczynski, Jon. "Tubby's Rapid Turnaround Stuns Gophers." *LHL,* January 12, 2009.
University of Minnesota Athletics. Official Web Site. "Tubby Smith." http://www.gophersports.com (accessed December 31, 2008).

—*Charles F. Faber*

SMITH, ROBERT W., JR. (b. 1923, Indianapolis, IN; d. 1998, Prospect, KY), business executive. Robert W. Smith Jr., son of Esther and Robert W. Smith Sr., was born in Indianapolis, IN, on October 10, 1923. He graduated from Crispus Attucks High School in Indianapolis in 1943. He attended Central State College in Wilberforce, OH, and graduated in 1947. He married his wife, Irene, one year later, and the couple moved back to Indianapolis. Smith, like his father, began working at Bob Kuhn Chevrolet. He eventually became the first African American general sales manager in the Midwest while he was employed at Don Young Chevrolet in Indianapolis.

Smith and his wife moved to Louisville, KY, in 1971. He purchased the facilities of the Universal Chevrolet Company of Louisville, located at 2500 W. Broadway, reopened the business, and renamed the dealership Bob Smith Chevrolet. He thus became the first minority to open an automobile dealership in Kentucky and the third African American in the country to own a Chevrolet dealership. By 1986, he had developed the business enough to need more space. He moved the dealership to Westport Rd. in eastern Jefferson Co.

Smith was active in the Louisville community and gained recognition as a successful businessman. He was included five times on *Black Enterprise* magazine's list of the top 100 black-owned businesses. In 1986, he was named Minority Entrepreneur of the Year by the Louisville Minority Business Development Center, and he earned the same title from the Kentuckiana Minority Supplier Development Council in 1991. In 1988, Philip Morris USA inducted him into the Louisville Gallery of Greats. He was a sponsor of the Black Junior Achievement of Kentuckiana Inc., and served on the Board of Directors of the Russell Area Revitalization Project. He also served as vice president of the Greater Louisville Automobile Dealers Association. Smith died in Louisville on February 6, 1998. He was buried in Crown Hill Cemetery in Indianapolis.

Horton, John Benjamin. *Profiles of Contemporary Black Achievers of Kentucky.* Louisville, KY: J. Benjamin Horton & Associates, 1982.
Newspapers: "Chevrolet Dealership Owner Bob Smith Dies," *LCJ,* February 7, 1998, B4; "Obituaries—Robert W. Smith, Jr.," *LD,* February 12, 1998, A8; "Two Auto Dealerships Get Changes in Name," *LCJ,* January 16, 2007, D1; "Obituaries—Irene E. Smith," *LCJ,*

Tubby Smith.

November 14, 2008, B6; "Black History Month: Robert W. Smith," *LCJ,* February 9, 2011. http://www.courier-journal.com/article/2011 0210/NEWS01/302100003/Black-History-Month (accessed July 10, 2012).

—*Elizabeth Schaller*

SMITH, S. E. (b. 1860, Glasgow, KY; d. 1907, Lexington, KY), preacher at First African Baptist Church and Republican delegate. Born in Glasgow, KY, on June 7, 1860, S. E. Smith faced a difficult childhood after the death of his father. Forced to earn a living for his mother and himself, he worked to provide for the family while beginning his education. In 1881, his efforts resulted in his entry into the Kentucky Normal and Theological Institute (later known as **Simmons College of Kentucky**) in Louisville, where he graduated with honors. He later became a trustee of the university for several years.

Smith was prominently involved in state politics, particularly on behalf of the Republican Party. He was a delegate to the National Republican Convention on many occasions and seconded the nomination of H. Clay Evans for vice president at the St. Louis convention in 1896. He was nominated for the position of register of the Treasury several times but failed to win. In Kentucky, his political activism often took the form of resistance to the **Separate Coach Law,** including the publication of a history of the **Anti–Separate Coach Movement** in 1895.

Perhaps Smith's most visible and controversial role in the community was as a Baptist minister. He served as the preacher at Fourth Street Colored Baptist Church in Owensboro, where he erected a $30,000 brick house of worship. However, parishioners confronted him with charges of mismanagement. Eventually, members of his congregation obtained an injunction against Smith after charging that he was attempting to install as his replacement a "political servant" who would allow him to "continue as the chief dictator of the Negroes' political consciences" in the church.

In 1904, Smith was installed as the eighth pastor of **First African Baptist Church** in Lexington, KY. During his three years as the church's leader, he renovated the building and improved its exterior; he also orchestrated the final installation of a pipe organ. Again, his leadership was a source of controversy. In 1907, a faction in the church seized an opportunity to convert a prayer meeting into a business meeting and called for Smith to respond to grievances. The dispute, well publicized in the *Lexington Leader,* eventually concluded after he agreed to resign as pastor.

Smith announced his intention to accept the pastorate of a large congregation in Columbus, OH, but he became ill and was unable to leave the city. On August 7, 1907, he died in Lexington of acute gastritis. Contemporaries suggested that the illness was a product of stress from the battles of the preceding months.

Hamilton, G. P. *Biographical Sketches of Prominent Negro Men and Women of Kentucky.* Memphis: E. H. Clarke & Brother, 1911.

McIntyre, L. H. *One Grain of the Salt: The First African Baptist Church West of the Allegheny Mountains.* Lexington: L. H. McIntyre, 1986.

Newspapers: "Dissensions among Colored Baptists," *LL,* May 2, 1907, 7; "Colored Church Troubles Settled," *LL,* July 2, 1907, 1; "Rev. S. E. Smith," *LL,* August 7, 1907, 7; "Rev. Smith's Body," *LL,* August 8, 1907, 7.

—*Stephen Pickering*

SMITH, SAM (b. 1944, Hazard, KY), basketball player. A native of Hazard, KY, Sam Smith began his sports fame at Hazard High School. In 1962, the six-feet-two center played on the Kentucky High School All-Star basketball team against the Indiana All-Star team. In the same year, without any fanfare, the University of Louisville's basketball coach, Bernard "Peck" Hickman, recruited Smith, along with **Wade Houston Sr.** and Eddie Whitehead. These three players broke color barriers, becoming the first African American basketball players at the University of Louisville, the first African American basketball players at a traditionally white Kentucky university, and most likely the first African American basketball players in the Southeast. Smith joined Houston and Whitehead on the freshman team and later on the varsity squad. In his first varsity year, Smith was lead scorer but later was ruled academically ineligible to play. He then transferred to Owensboro's Kentucky Wesleyan College (KWC).

KWC had a losing record, 9–12, in the 1964–1965 season, but that changed when Smith joined the team, which included Dallas Thornton and **George Tinsley.** In the championship basketball game of the NCAA Division II in March 1966, Smith scored with 15 seconds left in the game to defeat Southern Illinois 54–51, and he became the tournament's Most Valuable Player after scoring over 20 points in that game. This basketball tournament victory was the first of five championships for KWC.

After Smith scored a career 1,102 points and 714 rebounds, he left college to play guard/forward for the professional ranks. The Cincinnati Royals of the American Basketball Association (ABA) recruited him in 1967. He later played for the Kentucky Colonels and finished his ABA career with the Utah Stars in 1971. In 1977, the Atlanta Hawks of the National Basketball Association recruited him. He played one season for the Milwaukee Bucks and one season for the Chicago Bulls, finishing his career in 1980.

Smith later returned to Owensboro and continued to play basketball in the recreational Dust Bowl. KWC fans voted him to the KWC All-Century team. The school also inducted him, along with teammates George Tinsley and Dallas Thornton, into its inaugural Athletics Hall of Fame in 2013.

Basketball-Reference.com. http://www.basketball-reference.com/players/s/smithsa01.html (accessed September 9, 2013).

Cox, Dwayne D., and William J. Morison. *The University of Louisville.* Lexington: Univ. Press of Kentucky, 2000.

"Leaping over Barriers." *University of Louisville Magazine.* Spring 2004. https://louisville.edu/ur/ucomm/mags/spring2004/barriers.html (accessed September 9, 2013).

Newspapers: "Hazard's Sam Smith Named to Kentucky All-Star Squad," *Park City Daily News* (Bowling Green, KY), June 19, 1962, 8; "Wesleyan Wins NCAA College Crown 54–51," *KNE,* March 12, 1966, 6; "Colonels Win, 106–101," *NYT,* November 29, 1969, 42; "KWC's Gathering of Champions First Title Came from Players Who 'Wanted to Win So Badly,'" *OMI,* February 25, 1993, 1B; "KWC Honors Inaugural Hall of Fame Class," *OMI,* February 23, 2013, C3.

—*Wardell Johnson*

SMITH, VERNA MCDONALD (b. 1889, Lyons, IN; d. 1966, Louisville, KY), political leader. Born in March 1889 in Lyons, IN, Verna McDonald married **James Edward Smith** in Clark Co., IN, on January 24, 1913. By 1920, the couple lived in Louisville,

KY; James had founded the **Domestic Life and Accident Company;** and they had a newborn daughter, Charlotte. **Charlotte Smith McGill** later became a member of the Kentucky House of Representatives.

Smith and her husband were vigorously involved in the Louisville community. While James ascended in the insurance business and political activism, Verna worked as a salesperson in a corset store, was a member of the **Kentucky Negro Educational Association** through its Parent-Teacher Association, and became publicity chair of the National Congress of Colored Parents and Teachers. She was also the president of the National Housewives League of America.

Smith served as the first black president of a Louisville Democratic club and became the first African American woman to be cocaptain of a precinct. In 1944, she acted as an alternate delegate to the Democratic National Convention held at the Chicago Stadium in Chicago, IL.

Smith died in Louisville, KY, on June 23, 1966. She was buried beside her husband in the Louisville Cemetery.

Kentucky Death Index, 1911–2000.

Newspapers: "National Parent-Teachers Congress to Meet in Georgia," *Wichita (KS) Negro Star,* July 24, 1936, 2; "Many Negroes Attend Dem Convention; Writer Finds Rumors A-Plenty, Friends and Enemies at Meet," *Plaindealer* (Kansas City, KS), July 28, 1944, 2.

Proceedings of the Kentucky Negro Education Association: Parent Teacher Association Enrollment (April 23–26, 1924), 70.

Smith/McGill Family Papers, ca. 1879–1978. University Archives and Records Center, Univ. of Louisville, Louisville.

U.S. Federal Census (1920, 1930, 1940).

—*Kim Nguyen*

SMOKETOWN, African American community in Louisville, KY. Louisville's Smoketown neighborhood is a compact and cohesive residential, commercial, and industrial enclave. Located just east of Louisville's central business district, it is bounded to the north by Broadway, to the south by Kentucky St., to the east by Beargrass Creek and the CSX Railroad, and to the west by Floyd St. It is Louisville's only surviving neighborhood that reflects the continuous presence of African Americans since before the Civil War.

The name apparently came from the large number of brick kilns in the area, which produced great volumes of smoke. Brick making started early. An advertisement for the sale of the farm and residence of "the late Mark Lampton" (*Louisville Public Advertiser,* April 16, 1823) noted that included were a brickyard and utensils, as well as up to 150,000 bricks. The advertisement also stated that the buyer could hire "Negro men well skilled in the brickmaking business." Lampton St., south of and parallel to Broadway, probably takes its name from Mark Lampton.

In 1841, the Louisville City Council adopted a resolution introduced by John J. Jacob that digging in Prather St. (Broadway) west of Preston St. be stopped. The mayor was directed to require those responsible "to restore the street to its original grade" (council minutes, March 29, 1841). *Caron's Louisville City Directory* for 1871 listed 9 brickyards concentrated in the Smoketown area out of 20 in the city. The others were scattered in various locations. By 1880, none were left in Smoketown as now defined, although two

were nearby in the Ft. Hill and Germantown neighborhoods. Apparently the clay that lay under Smoketown had been mined out. By that year, a portion of Smoketown had acquired the name Frogtown. It was located around Lampton and Jackson Sts., and the name may reflect abandoned, water-filled clay pits that attracted frogs (*Louisville Courier-Journal,* January, 1880, 4).

Whites of German ancestry began some residential development in Smoketown in the 1850s. By the end of the Civil War, freed slaves settled there, and an African American community was firmly established by 1870.

Smoketown developed as a thriving business and industrial center in part because of the opening of a streetcar line on Preston St. to Kentucky St. in 1865. Beargrass Creek, an important water source, also attracted industry. Tobacco-processing plants were major employers. While whites performed skilled labor and held managerial positions, Smoketown's African American residents were employed in low-paying, labor-intensive jobs. An exception to this pattern was a tiny enclave of African American–owned businesses on Preston St. near College St., where two blacksmiths and a wagon maker's shop were located.

Because Smoketown's white residents were more affluent than their black neighbors, they had the means to build and own more substantial brick and frame houses. African Americans, by contrast, lived in modest rental housing owned by whites and situated in densely settled blocks and minor streets and alleys. For both races, the shotgun house was the most prevalent building type.

Because of the economic and social climate in Smoketown during its early years, examples of African American property ownership were rare. There were, however, a few exceptions to the rule. Washington Spradling Jr., one of Louisville's most prominent African American citizens, owned a large amount of real estate in the area. In another instance, a group of enterprising African Americans built simple shotgun houses on land leased from whites. They later lost ownership when the panic of 1873 wiped out their savings and they were unable to pay their rent.

Smoketown has historically been home to many churches and institutions that have provided important social services in the community for generations. Most notable were the **Booker T. Washington School** (built in 1874 as the Eastern Colored School and one of Louisville's earliest schools for blacks), the Presbyterian Colored Mission (begun with the founding of Hope Mission in 1898 and Grace Mission in 1899), the **Eastern Colored Branch Library** (a Carnegie-endowed library for African Americans that opened in 1914), and Sheppard Square Housing Project (built in 1942 as segregated war-worker housing and named for **William Sheppard,** the first African American missionary to the Congo).

In time, the industrial base left the area. Housing developments replaced the old single-family units. Smoketown has experienced a renaissance in recent years as neighborhood groups have emerged, businesses have relocated to the area, houses have been built, and older homes have been restored. In 1996, select residential portions of the Smoketown neighborhood most closely associated with African American settlement were listed on the National Register of Historic Places for their historic significance.

Kemp, Janet E. *Report of the Tenement House Commission of Louisville.* Louisville, KY: Tenement House Commission, 1909.

Louisville Survey East Report. Louisville, KY: City of Louisville Development Cabinet, 1979.

Weeden, H. C. *Weeden's History of the Colored People of Louisville.* Louisville, KY: H. C. Weeden, 1897.

Wright, George C. *Life Behind a Veil: Blacks in Louisville, Kentucky, 1865–1930.* Baton Rouge: Louisiana State Univ. Press, 1985.

—*Joanne Weeter*

SNEED, LAVINIA B. (b. 1867, New Orleans, LA; d. 1932, Louisville, KY), journalist, lecturer, educator, and performing artist. Little is known about Lavinia Sneed's early life after she was born on May 15, 1867, in New Orleans, LA, to Letta A. (Jones) and Joseph Elliot. In 1880, she was living with her mother, brother, and grandmother, Rachael Jones, in Louisville, KY. She graduated as valedictorian of the 1887 class at State Colored Baptist University (later known as **Simmons College of Kentucky**). After graduation, she taught at State and was a member of its board of managers. The following year, she married Charles F. Sneed, a professor at State University. When **Eckstein Norton Institute** was established, she served on its Ladies Board of Care, which consisted of 18 women, including **Nannie Helen Burroughs** and **Mary V. Cook Parrish.** As a professor, she taught English and Latin and was proclaimed "a singer of merit as well as an elocutionist of superior ability."

Lavinia Sneed, 1887.

Sneed, along with Parrish, **Lucy Wilmot Smith,** and **Ione E. Wood,** wrote for the nationally acclaimed Baptist publication *Our Women and Children.* Although she was a well-known public speaker, writer, and friend of such people as Madame C. J. Walker, her articles were written to appeal to everyday people. Lavinia B. (Elliot) Sneed died on June 23, 1932, in Louisville and was buried in the Louisville Cemetery.

Kentucky Death Records, 1852–1953.

Lowry, Beverly. *Her Dream of Dreams: The Rise and Triumph of Madame C. J. Walker.* New York: Alfred A Knopf, 2004.

Penn, I. Garland. *The Afro-American Press, and Its Editors.* Springfield, MA: Willey & Co., 1891.

Scruggs, L. A. *Women of Distinction: Remarkable in Works and Invincible in Character.* Raleigh, NC: Scruggs, 1893.

U.S. Federal Census (1880).

Urban, Wayne J., ed. *Essays in Twentieth-Century Southern Education: Exceptionalism and Its Limits.* New York: Garland, 1999.

—*Karen Cotton McDaniel*

SNOW, WILLIE (b. 1931, unknown; d. 2011, Cincinnati, OH), rescuer of fire victims. Although little has been recorded about his early life, Willie Snow was born in 1931. In 1957, he began working for Richard Schilling, owner and operator of the Newport Steel Mill. Snow continued his employment under Schilling at several of his restaurants before beginning work at the Beverly Hills Supper Club in Southgate, KY, when Schilling reopened the club in 1971. It was here that Snow experienced one of the most deadly nightclub fires in U.S. history, which claimed 164 lives.

Snow was working as the head dishwasher at the supper club on May 28, 1977. Early in the evening, Snow overheard fellow employees relaying several complaints from patrons about the heat. Shortly after the complaints were reported, smoke was sighted in the club's Zebra Room. Snow went to investigate. Upon witnessing the flames, he immediately sprang into action, pulling bodies out of the smoke-filled building. He continued to enter the building and extracted bodies until doctors at the scene ordered him not to reenter the burning building.

In 1988, Willie Snow had a second run-in with a fatal fire. After the supper-club fire, Snow continued his employment with Schilling, eventually taking a job at Islands, the first riverboat restaurant in Newport, KY. The boat was moved to Louisville, KY, in 1986. Snow continued to work at the restaurant and therefore began to commute between Louisville and his home in northern Kentucky. On May 14, 1988, during his evening commute along Interstate 71, Snow once again found himself in the role of rescuer.

A school bus returning from a church trip to Kings Island amusement park was involved in a serious accident after a drunk driver going the wrong way on the interstate collided with the vehicle. Snow was on the other side of the interstate but saw the bus immediately after the accident. He rushed over to the burning school bus, entered through the back door, and began pulling people out of the vehicle. Despite his heroic efforts, the bus crash was the worst drunken-driving crash in U.S. history, killing 24 children and 3 adults.

Willie Snow, a man whom chance and circumstance led to save many lives over the course of his 80-year existence, died in

Cincinnati, OH, on Tuesday, August 9, 2011. Snow's remaining family members were unable to pay the funeral and burial expenses, but after several friends of Willie Snow publicized their predicament, a funeral home agreed to handle the services. Snow was buried in Vine Street Hill Cemetery in Cincinnati, OH, on Tuesday, November 1, 2011.

Elliott, Ron. *Inside the Beverly Hills Supper Club Fire.* Paducah, KY: Turner, 1996.
Newspapers: "Beverly Hills 'Family' Recalls Night of Horror," *CP,* May 18, 1992, 4A; "Proper Burial Sought for Rescuer in Beverly Hills Fire," *CE,* October 27, 2011.

—Elizabeth Schaller

SNOWDEN, LEANNA C. HOLLAND (b. ca. 1879, Lexington, KY; d. 1930, Lexington, KY), and SNOWDEN, JOHN B. (b. 1875, Lexington, KY; d. 1944, Lexington, KY), educators and club organizers. A native of Lexington, KY, Leanna C. Holland, daughter of John and Susan Holland, served the community through her church leadership at **St. Paul A.M.E. Church.** Her religious dedication included her roles as recording secretary of the church's missionary society and later as conference branch president of the Women's Missionary Society of Kentucky. She also taught at Russell School. In 1898, she married former teacher and postal carrier John B. Snowden, son of John Snowden Sr. and Ellen Snowden. The couple resided at 563 N. Upper St., and their only child, a daughter, Leland Weldon, was born in 1901.

Devoted club leaders, both Leanna and John helped their fraternal organizations through difficult financial troubles. In 1906, John, assistant secretary of the Colored Agricultural and Mechanical Fair Association of Lexington, was elected grand chancellor of the Knights of Pythias in Kentucky and proceeded to help increase the fraternity's coffers. In 1918, Leanna was elected grand worthy counselor of the Calanthe of Kentucky and guided the organization through the rigid economy of World War I. Moreover, Leanna was a member of the Eastern Star, the Daughter of Elks, and the Mosaic Templars.

Along with her church involvement, club work, and teaching, Leanna operated a successful millinery trade that served both African Americans and whites. She also taught classes in that business. In 1927, the **Kentucky Negro Educational Association** unanimously elected her director.

Preceded in death by their daughter, a teacher, Leanna died on March 4, 1930, and John died on January 21, 1944. They were buried in Greenwood Cemetery in Lexington, KY. Some of Lexington's prominent African American leaders served as Leanna's pallbearers, including Dr. J. M. McInham, Professor **William Henry Fouse,** horseman **James Rice Porter,** and Dr. **Thomas T. Wendell.**

Wright, Richard Robert, Jr. *Centennial Encyclopaedia of the African Methodist Episcopal Church.* Philadelphia: Book Concern of the A.M.E. Church, 1916, 211.
Newspapers: "Progress of the Knights of Pythias in Kentucky," *IF,* August 18, 1906, 8; "In the Woman's World," *IF,* August 25, 1906, 1; "Lenna Snowden," *Plaindealer* (Topeka, KS), August 12, 1921, 6; "Colored Notes," *LL,* March 5, 1930, 2.

—Sallie L. Powell

SOUTHGATE STREET SCHOOL (NEWPORT), African American school in northern Kentucky. Newport's Southgate Street School, organized in 1873 for the African American citizens of Campbell Co., was located on the north side of Southgate St. between Saratoga and Washington Sts. The school would not have been finished without the help of Dennis Lightfoot, **Robert Littleton,** and **Washington Rippleton,** who were involved from the very beginning, along with educators, such as Dennis Anderson, Lavina Ellis, **Charles D. Horner,** and Elizabeth Hudson. But the commitment of two important local governmental bodies, the Newport City Council and the Newport Board of Education, was also essential. Each of these bodies used state legislation and the **Freedmen's Bureau** to establish the school.

Early teachers at the Southgate Street School were Elizabeth Hudson, who taught from 1873 to 1878; Mr. F. Mackoy, 1878 to 1879; and Dennis R. Anderson, 1879 to 1890. The 1880s witnessed an increase of more than 50 percent in the African American population in both Newport and Campbell Co. The Southgate Street School served the entire county and even some children from nearby Bracken Co. On June 26, 1893, the school held its first graduation exercise at the Park Avenue School hall; the first two graduates were Louisa Smith and Lavina Ellis. In attendance were the president of the board of education, E. G. Lohmeyer, and a representative from the local school, C. W. H. Johnson. Johnson was one of the committee members who had originally petitioned the Newport City Council for free public education for African American children in the city. Lohmeyer addressed the audience, urging parents to persevere in keeping their children in school; he said that education, not legislation, would prove the best solution to the race question. The second graduating class consisted of only one person, Beatrice Genevieve Johnson. The commencement exercise took place on June 19, 1896, again at the Park Avenue School hall.

In 1901, the city school board determined the curriculum for the high school, based on a three-year school program. Southgate School's principal, Charles D. Horner, asked to have the course requirements extended to cover four years so the students would have the same educational advantages as students at the white Newport High School; however, a four-year program was never implemented. With the addition of a second floor, two more classrooms were added to the building and another teacher was hired. Each teacher had to teach three grades, and the principal taught the three high school grades. On June 5, 1921, Superintendent E. F. Sporing recommended to the Newport Board of Education that the Southgate High School be discontinued for the coming school year because of unsatisfactory conditions, and that the high school students be sent to William Grant High School in Covington (later known as **Lincoln-Grant School**). He believed that there they would receive an "all grade high school education, and upon graduation, the students would be eligible for admission to the leading Universities and Colleges which are open to African-American students." Given the small number of graduates from the Southgate high school and the cost of only $50 in tuition per student to send them to the Covington high school, it was an easy decision for the board to send students to Covington. African American students did not again attend high school in Newport until the fall of 1955.

From 1916 through 1940, the Southgate Street School principals were chosen from within the school. In August 1921, W. S. Blanton, who had been principal at the Southgate Street School since 1909, resigned and was replaced by Nora H. Ward, who had been a teacher of domestic science in the sixth and seventh grades at the school. The teacher's dedication to the school and the community was a source of pride for all African Americans in Newport. Lavina Ellis, who had been in the first graduating class of 1893, returned to teach at the school about 1900 and stayed until she retired in 1936. She saw a need and opened a day nursery for African American children nearby. Ellis lived on Covert Road Pk. in Bellevue. She had the longest tenure of any teacher, serving under three principals: Charles D. Horner, W. E. Blanton, and Nora H. Ward. Elise Gooch, who began teaching at the school in 1910, was the sister of Elizabeth Gooch, a teacher at Covington's Lincoln-Grant School from 1912 until 1953. Elise had direct contact with all the new students from Newport. Most faculty members at the Southgate Street School were lifelong residents of Covington with connections throughout northern Kentucky. Ruth Bond taught at Southgate from 1936 to 1957. She was from Louisville, where her family had strong educational ties. When the Southgate Street School was closed because of integration, she was transferred to another Newport school and retired in 1957.

In 1926, Anderson D. Owens was appointed superintendent of the Newport schools. Under his direction, the Southgate Street School received considerable attention. For example, Owens wanted to replace the old Southgate Street School building with a larger, modern school. In 1938, he proposed to the city's school board that a new school for African Americans be built. The board proposed building the new school under the federal Public Works Administration (PWA). The application to the PWA for funding was supplemented with a local bond issue and sent to the Newport City Council, which approved both applications and placed the issue on the ballot for voters. The law required that all bond issues be approved by voters with a two-thirds majority. Owens, the board, and the council had done their part, but in the general election on November 8, 1938, the voters defeated the new school bond issue; a majority, but not the required two-thirds majority, voted in favor of the bond issue.

In 1940, Charles Harris, who had been a teacher at the Southgate Street School since November 1932, replaced Nora Ward as principal. Harris's staff of teachers included Ruth Bond, Melissa Bruce, and Leila Patton. This staff remained at the school until after the 1954 U.S. Supreme Court rendered its decision mandating school desegregation.

On July 27, 1955, Superintendent Owens submitted to the city board of education a program for the desegregation of Newport public schools. He asked the board to adopt a policy requiring that all African American children through the 11th grade attend Newport schools during the 1955–1956 school year; under this policy, the segregated Southgate Street School would be closed. All African American students in the 12th grade who were attending William Grant High School in Covington were given the choice of either finishing their senior year there or attending Newport High School. The superintendent also placed African American teachers in desegregated schools. The Newport school system thereby became the first public school system in northern Kentucky to integrate. The closing of the Southgate Street School was much like its beginning, accomplished without the hostility, lawsuits, and study groups that many communities experienced during the period of school desegregation. But Superintendent Owens's concern for the equitable placement of the now-defunct school's former teachers was equally important. Charles Harris retired in 1956; Ruth Bond, Melissa Bruce, and Leila Patton continued teaching at their new schools, and all three of them retired after the 1957–1958 school year.

The old Southgate Street School building has remained very much a part of Newport's African American heritage. In 1959, Newport Masonic Lodge No. 120 purchased the building. The Southgate Street School Alumni Association is leading the restoration project for the school building as part of the neighborhood's historic district. A Kentucky State Historical Society highway marker was dedicated in front of the former Southgate Street School on October 6, 2011.

Annual Report of the Board of Education, Newport, Kentucky. Newport, KY: Newport Printing, 1873.

Harris, Theodore H. H. "Southgate School Newport, Kentucky (1866–1955)." *Northern Kentucky Heritage* 4, no. 2 (Spring–Summer 1997): 34–42.

Newport City Council Records, 1874, Newport, KY.

Newspapers: "Negro Educational Convention," *Cincinnati Commercial,* February 19, 1873, 3; "Newport," *Cincinnati Daily Gazette,* August 28, 1873, 2; August 30, 1873, 3; September 8, 1873, 3; "Newport School Appointments," *Newport Local,* June 11, 1878, 3; "Newport School Committee on Salaries," *Newport Local,* June 3, 1879, 1; "Colored School Graduation Exercises," *State Journal* (Frankfort) June 6, 1893, 4; "Newport Voters Defeat Bond Issues," *KP,* November 9, 1938, 1; "Integration Will Begin in Newport," *KP,* August 15, 1955, 1; "Integration Delay May Bring Suit," *KP,* September 1, 1955, 1; "Local Schools Openings to See Changes," *KP,* September 5, 1955, 1; "First Day School Figures Go Up," *KP,* September 7, 1955, 1; Jim Reis, "Superintendents Notable for Longevity, Leadership," *KP,* March 6, 1995, 7.

—*Theodore H. H. Harris*

SPAULDING, JANE MORROW (b. 1897, Keysburg, KY; d. 1965, Chicago, IL), assistant to the secretary of health, education, and welfare. Born in rural Logan Co., KY, to Ben W. and Ollie Morrow, Jane Morrow moved with her family to Nashville, TN, at the age of seven. After attending school at Napier Elementary and Pearl High, she decided to continue her education in Nashville by enrolling at Fisk University. There, she met Albert Spaulding, whom she married in 1918. The couple moved to Charleston, WV, where he worked as a physician and assistant health commissioner while she engaged in various forms of social work.

Spaulding's sterling record with the Charleston Woman's Improvement League and the Central Association of Colored Women's Clubs earned her accolades from several leading women's groups, as well as the attention of the Eisenhower administration. In 1953, she was named assistant to the secretary of the newly formed Department of Health, Education, and Welfare, becoming one of the highest-ranking black governmental appointees. After a feud over racial policy with Secretary Oveta

Culp Hobby, she was shifted to the Foreign Claims Settlement Commission, where she was dropped from her position. The resultant public outcry forced the government to find her another role, and she was named consultant to the Foreign Operations Administration in 1954.

Spaulding continued to serve as an advocate for African American women until she suffered two strokes in the space of eight years. She died in Chicago, IL, on September 10, 1965.

Christmas, Walter. *Negroes in Public Affairs and Government.* Vol. 1. Chicago: Educational Heritage, 1966.

Newspapers: "Welfare Worker Named Hobby Aide," *NYT,* April 15, 1953, 20; "Mrs. Spaulding Gets Position with F.O.A.," *NYT,* December 30, 1954, 3; "Mrs. Jane Spalding Viewed for FOA Job," *Plain Dealer* (Kansas City), January 7, 1955, 4.

Smith, Jessie Carney, ed. *Notable Black American Women.* Vol. 2. New York: Gale Research, 1996.

—Stephen Pickering

SPENCER, BENJAMIN FRANKLIN, SR. (b. 1853, Scott Co., KY; d. 1934, Franklin, KY), first former slave to receive a teacher's certificate in Kentucky. According to his grandson, John C. Spencer, Benjamin Spencer was born into slavery in Scott Co., KY, on December 30, 1853. He was raised on a small plantation with several slave families. The plantation's owner, Edward Spencer, had a son about the same age as Benjamin. His relationship with the owner's son, Edward, allowed Benjamin the opportunity to learn to read and write. Edward's parents were concerned that he was not serious about his studies. They had Benjamin sit in classes with Edward, and "the teacher would call on him to identify some of the words and the sums of numbers in order to shame Edward."

Benjamin Spencer began to study discarded books, magazines, and newspapers, and eventually he became a source of current events for the other slaves on the plantation. For instance, he was able to read well enough by age 10 to explain the significance of the Civil War to his parents. His father then passed on the information to the other slaves in the field, several of whom decided to leave the plantation in order to fight with the Union troops.

At the end of the war, Spencer moved with his parents to Georgetown, KY. He worked delivering telegrams until he was 22, at which time he chose to take the teacher's examination at the county courthouse. On March 16, 1878, he passed the examination and was certified to teach the first four grades in the Colored Common Schools in Scott Co., becoming the first former slave in Kentucky to receive a teacher's certificate. He proceeded to organize the first school for African Americans in the county and taught there for two years before moving to Frankfort, KY, in 1880.

In Frankfort, Spencer became interested in making boots. He worked as an apprentice for one year and eventually opened his own shop in 1883. On April 6, 1881, he married Sue Thomason. They had six children, including three sons whom Spencer trained as boot makers. Their eldest daughter, Julia, became a teacher at a public school in Frankfort. Benjamin Spencer died on April 30, 1934. He was buried in Frankfort's Greenhill Cemetery. After his death, Benjamin Spencer Jr. took over the boot shop, B. F. Spencer and Son, and continued to operate the business until 1950. The shop was subsequently run by the next generation of the Spencer family until it eventually closed in 1973.

Four men working in a shoe shop.

Benjamin F. Spencer and his wife.

Spencer, Benjamin Franklin. Teacher's certificate, Scott Co., KY, issued March 16, 1880. Spencer Family Papers, Univ. of Kentucky Special Collections—Manuscripts Collection, Lexington.

Spencer, John C. "Spencer Family History." Spencer Family Papers, Univ. of Kentucky Special Collections—Manuscripts Collection, Lexington.

Wright, George C. *A History of Blacks in Kentucky.* Vol. 2, *In Pursuit of Equality, 1890–1980.* Frankfort: Kentucky Historical Society, 1992.

—Elizabeth Schaller

SPENCER, MIKE (b. 1954, Spencer Co., KY), horse trainer.

Born in Spencer Co., KY, Mike Spencer grew up surrounded by horses. His grandfather, who helped raise him, worked for the Bennetts, a family known for training and breeding Saddlebred horses. Spencer, too, came to love horses after moving to Simsonville with his family. While attending Simpsonville High School, Spencer began to work as a groom for Charles and Helen Crabtree—renowned figures in the equestrian world—despite having only just entered his teenage years. He eventually managed to save enough money to buy his own horse, which he trained and sold at a profit, before Charles Crabtree offered to sell him a prize stud for a marginal price. After he accepted, Spencer went on to become one of the more prominent trainers in the state.

In 2004, Spencer entered the World's Championship at Freedom Hall in Louisville with Spider Red, a five-year-old mare owned by Minna Hankin Mintz of Pennsylvania. He had been the horse's trainer since she was purchased as a yearling and had ignored advice that he should train her for the "three-gaited division," choosing instead to push for the more complex "five-gaited division." Initial returns were mixed, with Spider Red finishing third at the Mercer County Fair as a three-year-old and again third at the Penn National Horse Show the following year. At the World's Championship, however, she stunned the crowd by defeating several previous champions to win the title of Five-Gaited Mare World's Champion.

After this success, Spencer returned to Gold Leaf Farm in Simpsonville, where he continued to train horses. Asked about the possibility of retirement, he replied, "You don't retire from this. It don't come out of your blood." In 2007, he was among several black horsemen featured in *Out of the Shadows: Bringing to Light Black Horsemen in Saddlebred History,* an exhibition at the Kentucky Horse Park in Lexington, KY, that also featured a documentary sponsored by Minna Mintz in honor of Mike Spencer and the recently deceased Spider Red, who had collapsed of a heart attack during an earlier performance; the documentary won a Silver Telly Award. A year later, Spencer's contributions to the equestrian world were recognized by the American Saddlebred Horse Association, which presented him with the C. J. "June" Cronan Sportsmanship Award.

Carter, Eryn. "A World Champion Feature . . . Spider Red." Saddle Horse Report Online. http://www.saddlehorsereport.com/news .aspx?cid=1914 (accessed August 29, 2012).

Newspapers: "World's Championship Horse Show: Spider Red Captures 5-Gaited Mare Stake," *LCJ,* August 25, 2004, C10; "Show Heralds Achievements of Black Trainers," *LCJ,* February 5, 2007, 1E.

"Out of the Shadows: Bringing to Light Black Horsemen in Saddlebred History." BlackHorsemen.com. http://www.blackhorsemen.com /graphics/ExhibitOpening/exhibit.html (accessed August 29, 2012).

Reichert, Walt. "From the 'Back Barn' to the Show Ring." *Shelby County Life Magazine,* April 2010.

—Stephen Pickering

SPRADLING, MARY ELIZABETH MACE (b. 1911, Winchester, KY; d. 2009, Kalamazoo, MI), educator.

Mary Elizabeth Mace Spradling, a community activist and educator, taught young African Americans and others about African American ancestry and heritage. Throughout her career, she touched the lives of others, especially African American youth. Spradling was born to Ella Nora Trivers (a teacher) and Minor Jeremia Mace (a minister) in Winchester, KY, on December 31, 1911.

In 1933, she earned an AB in English from Kentucky State Industrial College for Colored Persons (later known as **Kentucky State University**) and a bachelor of library science degree from Atlanta University in 1949. She taught French at the Lynch Colored School in Lynch, KY, from 1933 to 1937. With the exception of a one-year teaching position in South Carolina, she spent her career as a schoolteacher in Kentucky. In 1936, she married Louis Lee Spradling, a teacher and elementary school principal. From 1948 until 1957, Spradling served as a branch librarian at the Louisville Public Library in Louisville, KY.

Spradling left Kentucky in 1957 to become the first professional African American librarian at the Kalamazoo (MI) Public Library. There she served as head of the Young Adult Department until her retirement in 1976. During her tenure at the library, Spradling established the Alma Powell branch on the north side of the city.

At an early age, Spradling started her personal collection of books by and about African Americans, often going without lunch to save money to buy more books. Spradling was active in many organizations throughout her life. Her 1971 reference book *In Black and White: Afro-Americans in Print* became a valuable resource for students and others. It referenced nearly 2,000 notable African Americans. Spradling created the source because she could find no reference pertaining to African Americans to give to library patrons. A second (1976) and a third (1980) edition of *In Black and White* and a supplement (1985) were also published. Spradling also authored "Black Librarians in Kentucky" in *The Black Librarian in the Southeast,* edited by A. L. Phinazee (1980). In 1998, Spradling donated the Mary Mace Spradling African-American Book Collection to the Kalamazoo Valley Community College Arcadia Commons Campus Library.

Spradling passed away on January 19, 2009. A close friend of Spradling's found it ironic that she died on the day of the national holiday honoring Martin Luther King Jr. since she played an influential role in Kalamazoo's official recognition of his accomplishments.

Kentucky Birth Index, 1911–1999.

Kentucky State Industrial College (Kentucky State University), Records Card College Department, Registrar's Office, transcript.

"Mary Elizabeth Mace Spradling." Contemporary Authors Online. Detroit: Gale, 2002. Literature Resource Center. Blazer Library, Kentucky State Univ. http://go.galegroup.com/ps/start.do?p=LitRC&u =ksu_blazer (accessed January 28, 2010).

Newspapers: Kristine Pioch, "Obituary: Longtime Kalamazoo Librarian, Also Wrote African-American Reference Book," *Kalamazoo*

Gazette, January 24, 2009, http://blog.mlive.com/kzgazette_impact/print.html?entry=/2009/01/obituary_longtime_kalamazoo_li.html (accessed January 28, 2010); "Mrs. Mary Mace Spradling of Kalamazoo, Age 97," *Kalamazoo Gazette (MI), Section: Obits_Mem,* April 19, 2009.

—*Sharon R. McGee*

SPRADLING, WASHINGTON, SR. (b. 1805, Jefferson Co., KY; d. 1868, Louisville, KY), barber, real estate speculator, and legal adviser. Washington Spradling was the son of William Spradling, an overseer, and Maria Dennis, a slave on the Isaac Miller farm. William provided for the emancipation of Maria and their children in his will in 1814. After his emancipation in 1825, Spradling moved to Louisville and established a barbershop, serving mostly wealthy clients. He was a shrewd businessman and soon saved enough money to buy, sell, and lease real estate in Louisville. As Louisville grew, the value of his land appreciated. By building dwellings and subdividing his holdings, Spradling was responsible for establishing an African American presence in the **Russell neighborhood** by the 1840s. His son Washington Spradling Jr. was responsible for founding the **Smoketown** neighborhood after the Civil War on East End property inherited from his father.

By 1860, Spradling's real estate was valued at more than $25,000, making him one of the wealthiest men in the city. Spradling also gave many African Americans helpful legal advice, and his wealth enabled him to purchase 33 slaves in order to give them their freedom. Spradling also was instrumental in founding at least two antebellum African American churches in the area (Centre St. Church, which is now Brown Memorial C.M.E. Church and Jackson St. C.M.E.). He married Lucy Ann Jackson in 1828, and later Henrietta Richardson. His children included **William,** Will, Washington, Julia, and Martha. Spradling is buried in Eastern Cemetery.

Blassingame, John W., ed. *Slave Testimony: Two Centuries of Letters, Speeches, Interviews, and Autobiographies.* Baton Rouge: Louisiana State Univ. Press, 1977.
Gibson, W. H., Sr. *Historical Sketch of the Progress of the Colored Race, in Louisville, Ky., as Noted by the Writer during a Period of Fifty Years.* Louisville, KY: Bradley & Gilbert, 1897.

—*Pen Bogert*

SPRADLING, WILLIAM WALLACE (b. 1866, Louisville, KY; d. 1940, Louisville, KY), prominent businessman. William Wallace Spradling was the son of **Washington Spradling Sr.** and his wife, Henrietta Richardson Spradling. His father was a shrewd businessman who operated a barbershop and became a real estate mogul. Spradling, educated in Louisville's public schools, followed his father into the real estate business in 1887. In 1905, he married Mary E. Wilson.

In 1910, Spradling became the first treasurer of the Kentucky Home Society for Neglected, Abandoned, and Helpless Colored Children in Louisville. He worked alongside people like Rev. **Charles Henry Parrish Sr.,** who was the president of the board of directors.

Spradling also worked as the financial secretary of Louisville's Colored Republican League. He was the director of the Falls City Realty Company and vice president of the Louisville Cemetery Association. He eventually owned more real estate in Louisville than any other African American at that time.

In 1920, Spradling was prominent in the organization of the **Domestic Life and Accident Insurance Company.** After the death of **Green Percy Hughes** in 1930, he was elected president of the company and worked with **Mary Virginia Cook Parrish,** who was the company's second vice president and the wife of Rev. Charles H. Parrish. Ten years later, Spradling died of heart disease on June 24, 1940. In November 1960, the sale of Domestic Life and Accident Insurance Company to a white insurance company was approved by the board of directors, much to the chagrin of Spradling's widow, who asserted, "I don't like it. I'm just grieved. The company has always been held by Negroes."

Kentucky, Death Records, 1852–1953.
Mather, Frank Lincoln. *Who's Who of the Colored Race: A General Biographical Dictionary of Men and Women of African Descent.* Vol. 1. Chicago: Memento Edition, 1915.
"Past Week at Louisville," *Indianapolis Freeman Supplement,* October 15, 1910, 1.
"Say Negro Insurance Co. May Sell to White Ky. Firm," *Jet,* November 10, 1960, 24.
Stuart, M. S. *An Economic Detour: A History of Insurance in the Lives of American Negroes.* New York: Wendell, Malliet & Co., 1940.
U.S. Federal Census (1920, 1930, 1940).

—*Sallie L. Powell*

STANLEY, FRANK L., JR. (b. 1937, Louisville, KY; d. 2007, Smyrna, TN), civil rights leader in Louisville. The son of **Frank L. Stanley Sr.,** editor of the *Louisville Defender,* Frank L. Stanley Jr. followed in his father's footsteps shortly after graduating magna cum laude with a degree in journalism from the University of Illinois in 1958. Although he initially intended to accept a graduate fellowship at Boston University with the recommendation of Martin Luther King Jr., he instead decided to return to Louisville and participate in the local movement to desegregate public accommodations.

Stanley quickly made a name for himself in the community by joining the Integration Steering Committee as its youngest member. He called for greater unity and support among civil rights groups, and his **Non-Partisan Registration Committee** (NPRC) was one of the few organizations to receive attention from both the **Congress of Racial Equality** and the **National Association for the Advancement of Colored People** after its organization in 1960. The NPRC proved to be a particularly successful institution, leading a voter-registration drive that had increased the black electorate in Louisville by 15,000 by the end of 1960.

In February 1961, Stanley helped lead a movement to desegregate downtown businesses called the **Nothing-New-for-Easter Boycott.** Designed to affect Louisville department stores' profits during the holiday season, the campaign succeeded in integrating numerous restaurants and businesses by its conclusion in May. Unfortunately, the city's entrenched Democratic government remained opposed to formal desegregation.

In response, Stanley and the NPRC increased their efforts to enlarge the black vote. In November 1961, his efforts were rewarded when Louisville Republicans won a surprising and sweeping victory, in part due to pronounced resistance to the election

Frank L. Stanley Sr.

of segregationist mayoral candidate William Milburn. After briefly leaving to obtain his master's degree at Boston University, Stanley returned to Louisville to push the state government to enact a civil rights bill. The spokesman for the Kentucky delegation to the March on Washington, Stanley began a movement for a similar march in his home state. On March 5, 1964, over 10,000 activists took part in the **March on Frankfort,** where they listened to speeches by Martin Luther King Jr. and Jackie Robinson and petitioned Governor Edward Breathitt for action on their behalf.

In 1967, Stanley took a job with the **National Urban League,** moving to Los Angeles the next year as the executive director of the Greater Los Angeles Urban League. He resigned from his new position after clashing with the board of directors and took over the editorship of the *Defender* after his father's death. He left the newspaper in 1976 and ran unsuccessfully for mayor of Louisville in 1984. On February 23, 2007, he died in a nursing home in Smyrna, TN, at age 70.

Adams, Luther. *Way Up North in Louisville: African American Migration in the Urban South, 1930–1970.* Chapel Hill: Univ. of North Carolina Press, 2010.
Newspapers: "Rights Leaders 'Angry Men,'" *LD,* March 30, 1961, 1; "10,000 March on Capitol for Accommodations Bill: Leaders Meet Breathitt," *LCJ,* March 6, 1964, 1; "Frank Stanley, Jr., Champion of Civil Rights in Louisville, Dies at Age 70," *LCJ,* March 2, 2007, B4.

Stanley, Frank L., Jr. Blacks in Louisville Oral History Project. Louie B. Nunn Center for Oral History, Univ. of Kentucky, Lexington, George C. Wright, interviewer, January 6, 1976, and March 7, 1978.
—*Stephen Pickering*

STANLEY, FRANK LESLIE, SR. (b. 1906, Chicago, IL; d. 1974, Louisville, KY), newspaper publisher, political activist, and civil rights advocate. Frank Leslie Stanley's father, Frank Leslie Stanley, was a railroad steward from Moline, IL, and his mother, Helen (Cole) Stanley, was a **domestic worker** from Nashville, TN. In 1912, he moved with his mother to Louisville, where he graduated from **Central High School** in 1925. He attended Atlanta University, graduated in 1929 with a degree in English and journalism, and afterward taught English at Jackson State College in Jackson, MS. From 1931 to 1933, he taught English and coached football at Central High School in Louisville. In 1933, he joined the staff of the *Louisville Defender* as a reporter.

In 1936, Stanley married Ione Garrett, a Louisville businesswoman. They had two sons: **Frank Stanley Jr.,** who became a noted civil rights activist, and Kenneth, a musician who graduated from the Berklee School (later College) of Music and the Boston Conservatory of Music. Also in 1936, he became the editor and general manager of the *Louisville Defender,* founded three years earlier as part of the *Defender* newspaper chain headquartered in Chicago. He sold ads, wrote and edited the news, pasted galleys, and in rapid succession became a board member in 1938, secretary in 1940, secretary/treasurer in 1943, and finally chairman and largest stockholder in 1950, buying out its previous owners.

Under Stanley, the *Defender* became Kentucky's top black newspaper, outselling the *Louisville Leader,* which stopped publishing in 1950. He was a crusading editor whose advocacy for racial justice in jobs, schools, housing, and public accommodations and for integrated military units during World War II predated the postwar **civil rights movement.** He was a founder in 1940 of the National Newspaper Publishers Association, the trade group of America's 200 black-owned newspapers. In 1946 and 1948, he led delegations appointed by the U.S. State Department to study racial segregation of American troops in occupied Europe and wrote a report that paved the way for integration of the armed forces.

In Kentucky, with the support of Governor Earle Clements, Stanley in 1950 wrote Senate Resolution No. 53, which integrated state colleges. In 1960, with the support of Governor Bert Combs, he drafted the organizational structure of the **Kentucky Commission on Human Rights** and later served as its vice president. In 1955, as national president of **Alpha Phi Alpha,** his college fraternity, Stanley won financial support for the Montgomery, AL, bus boycott led by fraternity brother Martin Luther King Jr., and he hand-delivered the check.

Stanley divorced his wife in 1960 and in 1961 married Vivian Clarke, a Memphis social scientist educated at Smith College. He continued to build the circulation and influence of the *Defender,* enhancing his stature as a trusted adviser to civic and government leaders on the local, state, and national level.

Stanley suffered a heart attack and died at the *Defender*-sponsored **Black Expo** held at Louisville Gardens. During his life, he received numerous honors and awards, including an honorary doctorate of laws from the University of Kentucky. He was posthumously named to the Kentucky Journalism Hall of Fame in 1983, one of the first African Americans so honored.

Kentucky's Black Heritage: The Role of the Black People in the History of Kentucky from Pioneer Days to the Present. Frankfort: Kentucky Commission on Human Rights, 1971, 119
Newspapers: *LCJ Magazine,* February 6, 1966; *LD,* March 24, 1983; *LCJ,* February 23, 1992.

—*Lawrence Muhammad*

STEED, MAGGIE (b. 1877, Tennessee; d. 1924, Paducah, KY), businesswoman. Born in Tennessee in 1877, Maggie Steed moved to Paducah, KY, in 1893. Drawn to the city in part by camps established for former colored regiments, she recognized the need for housing for dislocated blacks and took lodgers in her home until 1908. According to some sources, her late husband, Henry Steed, in his will, deeded their home at 724 Jackson St. to her. However, the *Paducah Evening Sun* reported that the couple had married in 1902 and separated two years later. Two months after a fire destroyed the Steed home in March 1908, Maggie sued her husband for divorce, alleging abandonment.

Whether via her husband's death or divorce, Maggie Steed, a laundress, decided to use the space to construct a new hotel for the city's black population. After having the house razed, she paid a lumber company over $1,000 in 62 installments to build her hotel. In 1909, the Hotel Metropolitan—opened its doors to the public for the first time.

During her time as owner and proprietor of the Hotel Metropolitan, Steed witnessed the growth of her property from a small business venture to an important community center in Paducah's Upper Town. Her upscale hotel—with lights and running water—attracted a wide variety of clients, who paid two dollars per day. In only five years, Steed earned enough from her business to pay off her debts and gain full title to the property. During her lifetime, she had little competition from other businesses, and the Hotel Metropolitan worked in cooperation with the Jefferson Hotel to serve their black clientele after the latter opened in 1923.

After her death in 1924, Steed's hotel passed into the hands of Steed's son Edward who managed the hotel for two to three years before selling it. The hotel changed hands several times and among its owners were Mamie Burbridge and Lucille Wright. Over the next few decades, the hotel retained its position at the heart of Paducah's black community, with guests including Thurgood Marshall, Louie Armstrong, and Jesse Owens. In the early 1950s, future Hall of Fame basketball coach **Clarence Edward "Big House" Gaines** and his parents Lester and Olivia Gaines purchased the hotel. It ceased operation as a hotel in 1996, but the Upper Town Heritage Foundation pursued and received several grants to renovate the property as a site for a museum of African American life in Paducah. In 2002, the Hotel Metropolitan was added to the National Register of Historic Places. As a "Save America's Treasures" project, the hotel has been restored. In April 2014, the hotel hosted an African American quilt exhibit that included lectures on the history of **Underground Railroad** quilts.

"Black History in the Jackson Purchase." *Jackson Purchase Historical Society.* http://www.jacksonpurchasehistory.org/2010/01/31/black -history-in-the-jackson-purchase-part-1-hotel-metropolitan/ (accessed November 29, 2012).

National Register of Historic Places. Hotel Metropolitan. Paducah, McCracken Co., KY. National Register 01001251.

Newspapers: "House Burned," *PES,* March 17, 1908, 7; "News of Courts," *PES,* May 29, 1908, 4; "Divorce Suits," *PES,* May 30, 1908, 5; "Paducah Works to Restore Segregation-Era Hotel," *KNE,* March 12, 2001, A10; "Landmark State," *LHL,* February 5, 2003, E1; "Hotel Where Famous Blacks Stayed Will Get a Makeover," *LHL,* January 20, 2004, B3.

Parrish, C. H. *Golden Jubilee of the General Association of Colored Baptists in Kentucky: From 1865–1915.* Louisville, KY: Mayes Printing Co., 1915.

"Much to Do at Paducah's Metropolitan Hotel." http://www.examiner .com/article/much-to-do-at-paducah-s-metropolitan-hotel (accessed August 17, 2014).

U.S. City Directories, 1821–1989 (1908, 1910, 1916).

—*Stephen Pickering*

STEVENSON, WILLIE BELLE (b. 1904, Lexington, KY; d. unknown), composer, poet, pianist, and organist. Willie Belle Stevenson was born on November 8, 1904, in Lexington, KY, to William H. and Lucy Allen Stevenson. Willie Belle was known in her community as a talented poet, composer, and musician. In 1925, she received her teaching certificate from the Chicago Musical College and was the only African American student in her class. Her talent and dedication to music allowed her to excel in her studies, and while attending the Chicago Musical College, she won a piano contest that awarded her a Percy Grainger Scholarship, a distinguished musical honor.

Stevenson initially opened a studio in the Chicago area where she taught piano, voice, and theory. She later became the Kentucky state manager of the International Music Foundation and the supervisor of instrumental and vocal music at Western High School in Paris, KY. Stevenson's artistic and musical contributions were widely recognized, and she received several awards, such as the Walsh Literary Prize, a special commendation from the Dramatists Alliance of California, and first prize for a poem she presented in San Francisco at the Golden State Anthropology Exposition. She was an active participant in community and professional organizations, including the **Phillis Wheatley YWCA** branch, the Order of the Eastern Star, and the Mosaic Templars. Her professional memberships included the Lexington Harmonic Promoters Music Club, the **Roland Hayes** Choral Society, the Bozart Society, the Music Community Service League, the Church of Music, the International League of Nations of Literature, and the National Song Writers Guild. The place and date of her death are unknown.

Dunnigan, Alice Allison, comp. and ed. *The Fascinating Story of Black Kentuckians: Their Heritage and Traditions.* Washington, DC: Associated Publishers, 1982.

Fleming, G. James, and Christian E. Burckel, eds. *Who's Who in Colored America.* 7th ed. *Supplement.* Yonkers-on-Hudson, NY: Christian E. Burckel & Associates, 1950.

Yenser, Thomas, ed. *Who's Who in Colored America: A Biographical Dictionary of Notable Living Persons of African Descent in America.* Brooklyn, NY: Thomas Yenser, 1933.

—*Kimberly Renee McDaniel*

STEWARD, MAMIE E. LEE (b. 1858, Lexington, KY; d. 1931, Louisville, KY), educator, musician, author, and church and club leader. Mamie E. Lee's parents, Isaac and Caroline Lee, were prominent free persons of color in Lexington's black community and sent her to private schools, where she excelled in music. On April 25, 1878, she married **William Henry Steward,** and they had four children.

Mamie E. Lee Steward.

Mamie Steward taught and headed the music department at Louisville's State Colored Baptist University (later known as **Simmons College of Kentucky**) for 40 years. She also wrote for Baptist publications regarding women's moral responsibility for racial uplift, child upbringing, and community improvements. Steward served as organist of Louisville's **Fifth Street Baptist Church** for 47 years. She was one of the founders of the **Baptist Women's Educational Convention** in 1883 and was selected as its first president, a position she held for 30 years.

Steward worked with the women's club movement on the local, state, and national levels. In 1896, she was one of the founders of Louisville's Woman's Improvement Club, which she served as club secretary for 34 years. She was a charter member of the **Kentucky Association of Colored Women's Clubs** (KACWC) in 1903. In 1908, she became the second KACW president. She was president of the Ladies Sewing Circle and secretary on the **Colored Orphans' Home** Board of Directors. Beginning in 1904, Steward served as an officer with the National Association of Colored Women's Clubs when she assumed the position of second recording secretary. She continued to serve in a variety of national offices for the next 12 years. After women were granted suffrage, Steward became secretary of Louisville's West-End Republican League of Colored Women.

Steward's feminist perspective was often expressed through Baptist publications. In an 1898 article, Steward articulated her feminist frustrations about the dedicated work among the church's women and pronounced her concerns to the Baptist community in a bold statement that "no good work is inaugurated or prosecuted in which she [woman] is not an interested and ardent worker." Steward documented the prominence of women in the church and reminded her readers that most of the "money raised for denominational enterprises comes from her [woman's] scantily filled pocket book." She concluded her remarks by advising Baptist men to use the church's women to further the work of the National Baptist Convention because the women were the denomination's strength.

On May 22, 1930, 12 Louisville women established a club, the Mamie E. Steward Friendly Group, in her honor. Its goals were "improvement, civic, and racial uplift." Mamie Steward died on March 21, 1931, in Louisville.

"Colored Women Elect Officers." *IF,* July 23, 1904, 8.

Davis, Elizabeth Lindsay. *Lifting as They Climb.* Washington, DC: National Association of Colored Women, 1933.

Smith, Lucy Harth, comp. and ed. *Pictorial Directory of the Kentucky Association of Colored Women.* Lexington: Kentucky Association of Colored Women, 1945.

Steward, Mamie E. "Woman in the Church." *National Baptist Magazine* 6 (August–October 1898): 147–48.

—*Karen Cotton McDaniel*

STEWARD, WILLIAM HENRY (b. 1847, Brandenburg, KY; d. 1935, Louisville, KY), religious leader and publisher. Born in Brandenburg, Meade Co., KY, on July 26, 1847, William Henry Steward at the age of nine moved with his family to Louisville, where he studied in private schools and displayed extraordinary abilities, according to his teachers. After graduation, he worked as a teacher in Frankfort and Louisville in the 1870s. The turning point in Steward's life came in 1876 when he became a letter carrier for the Louisville post office; he was the first black man to hold that position in Kentucky. The job introduced him to many influential whites in the city who claimed to admire and respect

William Henry Steward.

him. He used this experience to advance his career, as well as to assist people of color.

After embracing Christianity in 1867, Steward was baptized and joined the **Fifth Street Baptist Church** in Louisville. He served as a Sunday school teacher, secretary of the choir, and later as the superintendent of the Sunday school. Although he had a position as a postman, he pursued a successful career in publishing. As the publisher and editor of the ***American Baptist,*** the oldest weekly colored newspaper in the United States, founded in 1879, Steward used his popular, scholarly columns not only to disseminate the principles of racial equality but also to help educate African Americans. For more than 50 years, he used the *American Baptist* to reach a wide audience and earned the title "Dean of Colored Editors."

Steward was also deeply involved in politics and civil rights issues. He used his position as the judge of registration and election for the 15th Precinct of the 9th Ward in Louisville (the first black person to hold that position in Kentucky) to spread political consciousness among blacks. Likewise, he championed the campaign against the prevailing practices of residential segregation, as well as the unjust segregation policies of city parks in Louisville.

Steward was also elected to chair the Board of Trustees of Colored Baptists (later known as **Simmons College of Kentucky**), a position he held until his death. He was the vice president of the National Afro-American Council and the president of the National Afro-American Press Association in the 1890s. He was also the secretary of the **General Association of Colored Baptists of Kentucky** and the first secretary of the National Baptist Convention. For two terms, Steward was elected grand master of the Masons of Kentucky, and, recognizing his years of national service, Shaw University honored him with a master of arts degree. As G. F. Richings stated in *Evidences of Progress among Colored People,* Steward was "one of those clear-headed and bright-minded men peculiar to Kentucky." He died on January 3, 1935, and was buried alongside his wife, **Mamie E. Lee Steward,** in Louisville's Eastern Cemetery.

Richings, G. F. *Evidences of Progress among Colored People.* 4th ed. Philadelphia: George S. Ferguson Co., 1897.

Smith, Jessie Carney, ed. *Notable Black American Men.* Detroit: Gale, 1999.

—*Ogechi Anyanwu*

STEWART, CHARLES (b. 1869, Frankfort, KY; d. 1925, Guthrie, OK), journalist and orator. Born May 28, 1869, in Frankfort, KY, Charles Stewart was the son of Henry and Harriet Stewart. One of six children, Stewart excelled in school and sought a college education despite his impoverished circumstances. In 1883, he left his home in Frankfort for Louisville, KY, where he was able to attend State University (later known as **Simmons College of Kentucky**). While he was in Louisville, he worked for the *Louisville Courier-Journal,* and he continued to pursue a career in newspaper work after moving to Chicago, IL, in 1886. He received his MA from Alabama A&M College in Normal, AL, and his DD from Campbell College in Jackson, MS.

Stewart worked for numerous newspapers during his career as a journalist. He was a member of the National Negro Press

Association, and he became a press agent for the National Baptist Convention in 1896. He served as president and manager of Stewart's General Press Bureau in Chicago. In 1900, he worked as a correspondent for the *Baltimore Afro-American Ledger*. He was also employed as a staff writer for the *Chicago Inter-ocean*. In 1911, he reported on the Kentucky Conference of the African Methodist Episcopal Church for the *Lexington Leader*. By 1914, Stewart worked as a correspondent of the Associated Press, and he was often referred to as "the press agent of the Negro race."

While traveling in Oklahoma, Stewart, also known as Charles E. Stump for his speaking skills, suffered an illness that required him to stay in Guthrie's Park Sanitarium for two weeks. When he was released, he searched the hospital corridors for a phone and collapsed from a heart attack. His body was transferred to Chicago, where he was interred in Lincoln Cemetery.

Bacote, Samuel William. *Who's Who among the Colored Baptists.* Kansas City, MO: Franklin Hudson, 1913.

Newspapers: "A Little Humor," *Atlanta Independent,* March 18, 1905, 4; "Roosevelt Guest of Negro League," *NYT,* August 17, 1910, 2; "Sambo Waxed Fat and Kicked," *LL,* May 21, 1911, 25; "A.M.E. Conference Given Glad Hand," *LL,* October 19, 1911, 5; "Colored Notes," *LL,* March 28, 1912, 11; "Negro Writer," *LL,* May 15, 1912, 3; "At the Nation's Capital," *Atlanta Independent,* October 3, 1914, 7; "Charles Stewart Noted Journalist and Orator, Dies in Oklahoma," *Topeka Plaindealer,* July 17, 1925, 1.

Washington, Booker T. *The Booker T. Washington Papers.* Vol. 5, *1899–1900.* Edited by Louis R. Harlan. Urbana: Univ. of Illinois Press, 1977.

—*Elizabeth Schaller*

STEWART, FANNIE BELLE CALDWELL (b. 1877, Louisville, KY: d. 1957, Indianapolis, IN), owner and publisher of the *Indianapolis Recorder* newspaper in 1924. Fannie Belle Caldwell was born in Louisville, KY, in 1877. In September 1898, she married George Pheldon Stewart from Vincennes, IN. The couple had four children: Joyce Caldwell, Marcus C., twins Theodore Douglass and Fredonia Helen. They also raised two other children, Henry Sweetland and Clarence Porter.

A few years before his marriage to Fannie, George and his partner, William H. Porter, founded an African American newspaper called the *Indianapolis Recorder*. In 1899, Porter sold his share of the paper to the Stewarts, making them sole owners with George serving as editor of the *Recorder*. George died in 1924, at which time Fannie became the sole owner and publisher of the newspaper. Her sons Marcus and Clarence became editor and collector, respectively, of the *Recorder*. The newspaper remained in the Stewart family until it was sold to Eunice Trotter in 1988.

Fannie died after a stroke at her daughter Fredonia's house in Indianapolis in November 1957. She was buried in Crown Hill Cemetery beside her husband and her son Clarence.

George P. Stewart Papers. http://www.indianahistory.org/our-collections/collection-guides/george-p-stewart-papers-1894-1924.pdf (accessed September 17, 2013).

Mather, Frank Lincoln. *Who's Who of the Colored Race: A General Biographical Dictionary of Men and Women of African Descent.* Vol. 1. Chicago: Memento Edition, 1915.

"This Week's Census." *Jet,* November 28, 1957, 45.

U.S. Federal Census (1910, 1920, 1930).

—*Christine Kindler*

STILL, ART (b. 1955, Camden, NJ), defensive end for the University of Kentucky, the Kansas City Chiefs, and the Buffalo Bills. A native of Camden, NJ, Art Still turned heads with his outstanding performances on the football field at Camden High School. Rejected by Bethune-Cookman College for being "too tall" for its football team, Still joined the University of Kentucky team in 1974. For the next four years, he anchored a dominating defensive line, leading the team to an 11–1 record and receiving recognition as an All-American in 1977. He was selected second overall in the 1978 National Football League (NFL) draft by the Kansas City Chiefs and was awarded a seven-year contract.

During his career in the NFL, Still was selected to four Pro Bowls and was named to the All-Pro Team in 1980 and 1984. Still was twice voted the Chiefs' Most Valuable Player, and his sacks total ranks in the top five in the team's history. He was traded to the Buffalo Bills in 1988, where he played for two more years before retiring. After his retirement, Still became involved in several charitable organizations, including the Special Olympics, Big Brothers and Sisters, and the DARE program. In 2005, he was inducted into the Kentucky Athletic Hall of Fame, where he joined his sister, **Valerie Still,** the all-time leader in points and rebounds for the University of Kentucky's women's basketball team.

"Arthur B. Still." *UK Alumni Association.* Univ. of Kentucky. http://www.ukalumni.net/s/1052/index-no-right.aspx?sid=1052&gid=1&pgid=1017 (accessed May 30, 2012).

"Defense Led by Still Drove Team to Triumphs in '77." *LHL,* October 12, 1990, Special 7.

"Kentucky Player Nearly Went to Bethune-Cookman." *Daytona Beach Morning Journal,* November 12, 1977, 1B.

—*Stephen Pickering*

STILL, VALERIE RENEE (b. 1961, Camden, NJ), the University of Kentucky's all-time leading basketball scorer and rebounder (male or female). Camden, NJ, native Valerie Renee Still was the 9th of 10 children of James and Gwendolyn Still. She was the younger sister of **Art Still,** all-pro defensive end of the Kansas City Chiefs, and followed him to his alma mater, the University of Kentucky (UK). The six-feet-one center played basketball there from 1979 to 1983, leading the team to the Southeastern Conference championship in 1982. In her senior year, *Sports Illustrated* reported that she surpassed UK's Dan Issel to become the school's all-time leading scorer with 2,763 points. She also became the university's all-time leading rebounder with 1,525. UK's assistant sports information director Rena Koier assessed, "If Val were a man, the local media would have immortalized her and the fans would have built a statue downtown."

Since female basketball players had no professional playing opportunities in the United States in the 1980s, Still joined the Italian Professional League after she graduated from UK with a bachelor of science degree in animal science. After about 15 years, she returned stateside. She became a charter member of the American Basketball League, playing for the league's champions, the Columbus Quest, in 1996. Still became a two-time Most Valuable Player. After the league folded, she joined the Washington Mystics of the Women's National Basketball Association in 1999, the same year in which she formed the Valerie Still Foundation, a nonprofit organization that assists young girls to grow into

Valerie Still.

healthy, confident, mature women through various programs. After retiring as a player, she became an assistant coach for the team.

In 2003, the University of Kentucky retired Still's jersey, and two years later, she was inducted into the Kentucky Athletic Hall of Fame, at UK. After her divorce from former UK basketball player Rob Lock, she had sole responsibility of their son, Aaron. She continued her education and earned a master's degree in African and African American studies at Ohio State University in 2007. She pursued her doctorate in sports humanities with plans to write her dissertation on race and gender discrimination in high school athletics.

Still developed a children's book series, *Still Alive on the Underground Railroad: Recollections of an American Family,* based on her family's history. Through her research, she learned that her great-great-granduncles had been enslaved on the grounds of her alma mater, the University of Kentucky. In 2013, she headed the Dr. James Still Preservation Trust, named for her great-great-grandfather. One of his properties became New Jersey's first and only African American historic site.

Newspapers: "Valerie Still Recounts Slave Heritage in Book," *LHL,* January 22, 2012, B1; "Palmyra Grads Winners of New Scholarships," *Philadelphia Inquirer,* June 15, 2013, B1.

Ramsey, Guy. "Where Are They Now: Still a Fighter, School's Leading Scorer Perseveres after Playing Career." *Cat Scratches,* July 1, 2011, UK Athletics. http://www.ukathletics.com/blog/2011/07/where-are -they-now-still-a-fighter-all-time-leading-scorer-perseveres-in -life-after-playing-career.html (accessed September 18, 2013).

Reed, Billy. "This Still's a Potent Producer." *Sports Illustrated,* January 17, 1983. http://sportsillustrated.cnn.com/vault/article/magazine /MAG1120432/1/index.htm (accessed September 17, 2013).

Still Publications. http://stillpublications.com/?page_id=40 (accessed September 18, 2013).

—*Wardell Johnson*

STITCH, RUDELL (b. 1933, Louisville, KY; d. 1960, Louisville, KY), professional boxer. Rudell Stitch was the son of Lena Mae Henderson Stitch and Charles Rudell Stitch. He became one of only four people in the twentieth century to be awarded two Carnegie Hero Medals for risking his life to save another.

In his teens, Rudell Stitch started boxing as an amateur in Louisville. As a lightweight and welterweight, he won 45 of 57 amateur bouts. He won Kentucky state titles in 1951, 1952, 1953, 1955, and 1956 and reached the semifinals of the Chicago Golden Gloves and the finals of the National AAU Tournament in 1956. He rose to become second-ranked welterweight in world rankings in early 1960.

Stitch was on his way to a brilliant career, but critics claimed that he was too nice to be a successful boxer. On September 15, 1958, Stitch rescued a stranger, Army Corps of Engineers worker Joseph Shifcar, who fell into the Ohio River. He was awarded his first Carnegie Hero Medal for that rescue. In another incident, during a fight with world-class contender Gaspar Ortega in 1959, there was an accidental clashing of heads. Stitch was not hurt, but Ortega was staggering and bleeding profusely from a cut near his eye. Instead of resuming the fight, as instructed by the referee, Stitch walked to Ortega, touched gloves, apologized, and stepped back and waited until Ortega's head had cleared. When asked about it later, Stitch said that he did not believe in taking advantage of an opponent in that kind of situation.

Stitch died on June 5, 1960, while trying to save the life of a boxer friend, Charles Oliver, who was fishing with him. Oliver slipped from a ledge and fell into the Ohio River. Stitch started swimming to shore but turned when he heard Oliver yelling for help and went back to get him. Stitch and Oliver, weighed down by heavy waders and coats, disappeared in the turbulent water. Stitch was awarded a second Carnegie Hero Medal posthumously for sacrificing his life in an effort to save his friend.

Crawford, Byron. "Boxer Made the Greatest Sacrifice of All." *LCJ,* November 25, 2005, B1.

Notable Kentucky African Americans. Univ. of Kentucky. http://nkaa .uky.edu/.

—*Myrte Nudd*

STOCKS, JAMES "JIM" RICHARD, JR. (b. 1948, Akron, OH), athlete and news anchor. Son of James Richard Stocks Sr. and Inez (Greene) Stocks, James Stocks Jr. came to Kentucky on a basketball scholarship at Murray State University (MSU) (1965–1970). In the 1968 Ohio Valley Conference Tournament, Murray State finished second after it lost to Tennessee Tech. The six-feet-seven Stocks led the reserves in tournament scoring with a 6.1 average.

On January 11, 1969, Stocks and fourteen other African American male students chartered Murray State's chapter of **Alpha Phi Alpha Fraternity Inc.,** the first African American Greek-letter organization at the school. That same month, Western Kentucky

University beat Murray State with a last-second tap-in basket, 84–82. Stocks scored seven points and had only one rebound.

As "the first African-American scholarship basketball player to graduate from MSU," Stocks earned his bachelor of science in speech and physical education. He then played briefly for the Kentucky Colonels of the American Basketball Association. While still living in Kentucky, Stocks became the first African American radio announcer for Murray's WNBS and WAAW and Paducah's WDXR. He also became the first African American news anchor at Paducah's WDXR-TV.

Stocks returned to his home state of Ohio to teach and coach basketball. In 1975, he married Debbie Rene Spencer, who later worked as marketing director for the Columbus Quest of the American Basketball League, a women's professional basketball program. Two of their daughters followed their parents into careers in basketball. Amber, a University of Cincinnati basketball player, became an assistant basketball coach at Xavier University. Tamara, a University of Florida basketball player, played in the Women's National Basketball Association for the Washington Mystics.

Alpha Phi Alpha Fraternity, Inc., Murray State University. http://campus.murraystate.edu/org/alpha_phi_alpha/zohistory.htm (accessed (October 4, 2012).

Newspapers: "Bright's Tap-In Wins for Western over Murray by 84–82," *BGDN*, January 30, 1969, 7–8; "Douglass Reunion Set," *Murray Ledger Times*, July 25, 2012.

Shield (Murray State University yearbook) (1968, 1969).

Summit County, Ohio, Marriage Records, 1840–1980.

—*Sallie L. Powell*

STONE, GEORGE E. (b. 1946, Covington, KY; d. 1993, Columbus, OH), basketball player. A native of Covington, KY, George Stone enjoyed a successful basketball career beginning at William Grant High School (see **Lincoln-Grant School**), from which he graduated in 1964. After being heavily recruited by Coach Ellis T. Johnson, he joined the team at Marshall University, where he was part of a lineup nicknamed the Iron Five, known for its fast-break offense and trapping defenses. Referred to by a teammate as "the best pure shooter I ever saw," he set a scoring record at Madison Square Garden with 46 points in the 1967 National Invitational Tournament.

After Stone graduated from Marshall in 1968, the Carolina Cougars of the American Basketball Association (ABA) drafted him and then traded him to the Los Angeles Stars. He averaged over 15 points per game for two seasons before the franchise relocated to Utah in 1970. In his first season with the Utah Stars, he helped the team win its first and only ABA championship. He played for another year before retiring and moving to Columbus, OH, where he worked in various entertainment and recreation services. On December 30, 1993, he suffered a heart attack while driving and died at age 47. In 1999, he was posthumously inducted into the Marshall University Athletic Hall of Fame.

Newspapers: "George Stone: What Is He Really Like?," *Parthenon* (Marshall University, Huntington, WV), March 21, 1968, 2; "Former MU Great, George Stone, Dies," *Huntington (WV) Herald-Dispatch*, January 1, 1994, B1; "Six Inducted into 18th Athletic Hall of Fame," *Parthenon*, November 2, 1999.

Reger, George M. "Integration and Athletics: Integrating the Marshall University Basketball Program, 1954–1969." MA thesis, Marshall Univ., 1996.

—*Stephen Pickering*

STONE, JAMES COLEMAN "COLIE" (b. Bloomfield, KY; d. 1893, Auburn, NY), jockey who was the subject of a highly publicized murder trial. Raised as a slave in Bloomfield, KY, James Coleman Stone gained a reputation as an obedient servant, praised for his cheerful disposition by both his fellow slaves and his masters. After gaining his freedom, however, he earned a different reputation after being accused of murder in Brooklyn, NY, on June 21, 1888. According to reports, Stone—by this time working as a jockey—accused a bartender of trying to keep his change after buying a drink. Although the bartender apologized for his mistake, Stone returned later that night, entered into an argument with the bartender, and then shot him in the head.

A well-publicized series of trials followed. The first two trials resulted in hung juries, with six in favor of conviction and six opposed. On April 25, 1889, a third jury convicted him of murder. Initially sentenced to death, Stone almost became the last person to die by hanging in the state of New York; however, the sibling of his former master wrote to the presiding judge on his behalf, and his sentence was commuted to life in prison at Sing Sing. He died in Auburn, NY, on January 11, 1893.

Newspapers: "Jockey Stone Found Guilty," *NYT*, April 26, 1889, 5; "A Kentucky Negro," *Newark (NJ) Daily Advocate*, May 15, 1889; "Jockey Stone's Sentence Commuted," *NYT*, February 1, 1890, 2.

—*Stephen Pickering*

STOUT, LOUIS (b. 1939, Cynthiana, KY; d. 2012, Lexington, KY), first African American state high school athletic association commissioner in Kentucky. Louis Stout, the son of Elizabeth Wilson Ford and John Stout, was born in Cynthiana, KY, on May 17, 1939. He attended Banneker School, where he made the varsity basketball team as a sixth-grader. As a result of desegregation, he then attended Cynthiana High School for three years, leading his team in scoring and to the state tournament each year. In his senior season, he led the state in scoring with 30.9 points per game and averaged 24 rebounds per game. He was selected to the 1959 all-state team. He attended Regis College and led the team in scoring and made the all-conference team all four years. In 1962–1963, he made the Catholic Digest All-American team. After college, he went into high school coaching at Lexington's (Paul Laurence) **Dunbar High School** and Tates Creek High School, the first African American coach at a predominantly white Kentucky high school. While coaching, he embarked on a long career as a high school and college baseball and softball umpire.

In 1971, Stout became the first African American assistant commissioner of the Kentucky High School Athletic Association (KHSAA), and in 1994, he became the first African American to serve as commissioner of a state athletic association anywhere in the United States. At the national level, he chaired the Amateur Athletic Union (AAU) Coaches Education Program, the AAU Sullivan Committee, and the National Federation of High Schools (NFHS) Hall of Fame Screening Committee and served on the

Louis Stout (left) shakes hands with S. T. Roach.

NFHS Board of Directors. He was inducted into the Kentucky Basketball Coaches Hall of Fame in 1997, the Kentucky High School Athletic Association Hall of Fame in 1999, the Regis University Athletics Hall of Fame in 2006, and the National High School Hall of Fame in 2008. He was also a member of the AAU Hall of Fame and the AAU Softball Umpire Hall of Fame.

In 2006, his *Shadows of the Past,* a history of the Kentucky High School Athletic League, was published by Host Communications. He died in Lexington, KY, on September 9, 2012.

Newspapers: "Former KHSAA Commissioner Louis Stout Dies," *LHL,* September 9, 2012; "Obituary," *LHL,* September 13, 2012.
Stout, Louis. Interview by Edward Owens, August 15, 1978. Louie B. Nunn Center for Oral History, Univ. of Kentucky, Lexington.
———. *Shadows of the Past: A History of the Kentucky High School Athletic League.* Lexington, KY: Host Communications, 2006.

—*Charles F. Faber*

STOVAL, JOHN "KID" (b. 1864, Louisville, KY; d. 1900, New York, NY), jockey. John "Kid" Stoval began and ended his racing career exercising horses. At age 13, he began riding for Colonel Milton Young, helping build his fortune near Lexington, KY. In one year, Stoval won 41 out of 119 races. He competed in six **Kentucky Derby**s, but the closest he came to winning was third place in 1885 and 1887, when **African American jockeys Erskine "Babe" Henderson** and **Isaac Lewis,** respectively, won.

Even though Stoval never won a Kentucky Derby, he had numerous victories, including three wins at Kentucky Oaks and five triumphs at the Churchill Downs Tobacco Stakes. In 1881, he rode a Kentucky horse, Getaway, to the finish line at Saratoga by "applying whip and steel mercilessly" to the horse. He won at Latonia in 1887 and 1888, the St. Louis Derby in 1883, and several others.

Stoval's biggest challenge on the track was suspensions. In 1879, he was terminated "for two days for disobeying orders." Two years later, along with three other jockeys, he received a one-day moratorium for "uncalled-for breakaways." In 1889, he was suspended pending an investigation of the way he rode a horse that lost the race. The next year, Philadelphia's Linden Park judges, suspicious of his riding, ruled him off the track. Three days later, he was reinstated. In 1894, the American Turf Congress License Committee refused to license him, but two years later he won the Ideal Park race in Wisconsin. In 1897, the American Turf Congress rejected his jockey license application for the last time.

Stoval also encountered trouble off the track. In 1891, while traveling by ferry between Gloucester and Philadelphia and accompanied by two white women, he shot a sheriff's clerk who had made an offensive remark. The clerk was taken to a local hospital in serious condition, and Stoval was taken to prison.

On September 13, 1900, while exercising a horse at Gravesend in New York, John Stoval leaned forward and fell from his saddle. He died of a heart attack.

Leach, George B. *The Kentucky Derby Diamond Jubilee.* Louisville, KY: Gibbs-Inman Co., 1949.
Newspapers: "Fine Racing in Saratoga," *NYT,* July 26, 1879, 2; "Stovall's Good Riding," *NYT,* August 10, 1881, 2; "Results at Saratoga," *NYT,* August 6, 1889, 3; "Shot by a Colored Jockey," *NYT,* September 21, 1891, 5; "Chat from Track and Stable," *NYT,* April 3, 1894, 7; "Ex-Jockey Stoval Dead," *NYT,* September 14, 1900, 9.
Renau, Lynn S. *Racing around Kentucky.* Louisville, KY: L. S. Renau, 1995.
Saunders, James Robert, and Monica Renae Saunders. *Black Winning Jockeys in the Kentucky Derby.* Jefferson, NC: McFarland, 2003.

—*Sallie L. Powell*

STOWERS, WALTER HASLIP (b. 1859, Owensboro, KY; d. 1932, Detroit, MI), lawyer, government worker, and author. Walter Haslip Stowers, the son of Jesse and Hester Stowers, was born in Owensboro, KY, on February 7, 1859, during the time of American slavery. His family eventually relocated to Detroit, MI, where Walter attended Detroit High School. In 1881, he graduated from Mayhew Business University in Detroit. Desiring to become an attorney, he enrolled at the Detroit College of Law and graduated in 1895. He was admitted to the Michigan bar that same year.

Stowers had a very distinguished professional career. An active Republican in Wayne Co., MI, he served as deputy sheriff for 4 years, clerk of the Assessor's Office for 4 years, and deputy county clerk for 12 years. He began a law practice with Robert C. Barnes, called Barnes and Stowers, and according to one source, the men "made a name for themselves" and were "known throughout the state as competent attorneys." He served as an attorney for the White Sewing Machine Company, the Acme Repair and Tire Company, and the Almo Amusement Company, to name only a few. In addition to his legal work, he held stock in several commercial corporations.

Stowers served as grand master of the Masons in Michigan for two years. He also served on the local draft board during the entire period of World War I and was a trustee at the Phyllis Wheatley Home for Aged Colored Women. Although he had a busy life, he found time to author a novel, *Appointed,* which was published by the Detroit Law Printing Company in 1894. After a long and distinguished career as an attorney, Walter Stowers died in 1932.

Boykin, Ulysses W. *A Hand Book on the Detroit Negro: A Preliminary Edition.* Detroit: Minority Study Associates, 1943.

Mather, Frank Lincoln. *Who's Who of the Colored Race: A General Biographical Dictionary of Men and Women of African Descent.* Vol. 1. Chicago: Memento Edition, 1915.

Warren, Francis H. *Michigan Manual of Freedmen's Progress.* Detroit: Michigan Freedmen's Progress Commission, 1915.

Yenser, Thomas. *Who's Who in Colored America.* 4th ed., *1933–1937.* Brooklyn, NY: Thomas Yenser, 1937.

—*David H. Jackson Jr.*

STRADER V. GRAHAM, U.S. Supreme Court case that included the question whether slaves traveling in a free state became free. In December 1850, the U.S. Supreme Court heard *Strader v. Graham,* which originated in a suit filed by slave owner Christopher Graham against the owners (Jacob Strader and James Gorman) and captain (John Armstrong) of the steamboat *Pike* for the loss of three slaves. Graham often permitted three of his slaves, George, Henry, and Reuben, to travel with a musician named Williams to Louisville and from there to other locations as determined by Williams to engage in public performances. Williams took several trips with his band, bringing Reuben and Henry with him, to Cincinnati, OH, and New Albany and Madison, IN. In 1841, Reuben and Henry, along with George, escaped Kentucky by leaving their owner's home in Harrodsburg, boarding the steamboat *Pike* in Louisville, disembarking in Cincinnati, and then fleeing to Canada. Graham filed suit in the Louisville Chancery Court, arguing that Kentucky law held the steamboat

owners and captain liable for the loss of the slaves. Among other defenses, the defendants (plaintiffs in the Supreme Court case) argued that the African Americans were no longer slaves at the time of their 1841 travel to Ohio and escape to Canada by virtue of their previous travel to the free state of Ohio.

The Chancery Court ruled in favor of Graham and ordered Strader, Gorman, and Armstrong to pay $3,000 in damages. The Kentucky Court of Appeals affirmed this ruling, and the case went to the Supreme Court on a writ of error on the judgment by the Kentucky court. The Supreme Court did not rule directly on whether travel to a free state released slaves from their servitude. Rather, the court, in a unanimous decision issued by Chief Justice Roger Taney on January 6, 1851, dismissed the case on the grounds that it lacked jurisdiction. This decision was grounded in the logic that a state is responsible for determining the standing of persons in that state provided that the Constitution of the United States does not contain provisions precluding such authority. The lack of any constitutional control on Kentucky law therefore meant that Kentucky statutes were the only relevant law and were to be interpreted by Kentucky courts.

The fate of the African Americans was consequently determined by a Kentucky statute of 1824 and its amendments in 1828. These statutes placed responsibility on the master (and owners, mate, clerk, and other officers) of any vessel taking slaves out of Kentucky without the slave owner's permission and permitted the owner to seek restitution. *Strader v. Graham* figured prominently in the high-profile *Dred Scott v. Sanford* case of 1857 regarding the potential freedom of African American slaves. Interestingly, in *Dred Scott,* the Supreme Court did not rely on *Strader v. Graham* as a precedent to dismiss the case based on the ultimate authority of Missouri law and state courts; instead, it considered different legal questions and more broadly tackled the issue of the status of African Americans.

Finkelman, Paul. "Prelude to the Fourteenth Amendment: Black Legal Rights in the Antebellum North." *Rutgers Law Journal* 17 (1986): 415–82.

Hyman, Harold M., and William M. Wiecek. *Equal Justice under Law: Constitutional Development, 1835–1875.* New York: Harper & Row, 1982.

Strader v. Graham. 51 U.S. 82, 10 How. 82, 1850 WL 6936, 13 L. Ed. 337 (1850).

Wiecek, William M. "Slavery and Abolition before the United States Supreme Court, 1820–1860." *Journal of American History* 65, no. 1 (June 1978): 34–59.

—*Joseph Gershtenson*

STRADFORD, JOHN THE BAPTIST "J. B." (b. 1861, Versailles, KY; d. 1935, Chicago, IL), prominent business leader accused of initiating the Tulsa, OK, race riot of 1921. Born into slavery in Versailles, KY, John the Baptist Stradford decided to go by his initials, J. B., after his father bought his freedom. Stradford moved to various cities in pursuit of a career and education, receiving a degree from Oberlin College and completing work at Indiana Law School at the age of 38. Soon thereafter, he moved to Tulsa, OK, where he earned a reputation both as a prominent lawyer and businessman and as an agitator for black rights in Tulsa's black community of Greenwood.

Stradford's numerous lawsuits against **Jim Crow** practices and his personal wealth made him the target of white backlash. In 1921, a riot broke out in the city after whites alleged that a young black man had committed rape, and angry locals attacked prominent African Americans, storming Greenwood and torching a three-story hotel belonging to Stradford.

Although he had tried to keep tensions from escalating into violence earlier in the day, Stradford was accused of initiating the riot and was forced to flee to Chicago after jumping bail. He rebuilt his life as a lawyer there, but he remained furious over his financial and personal losses until his death in 1935. His descendants succeeded in having Stradford cleared of any wrongdoing after a commission was created to investigate the riots in 1997.

Brophy, Alfred L. *Reconstructing the Dreamland: The Tulsa Riot of 1921.* New York: Oxford Univ. Press, 2002.

Hirsch, James S. *Riot and Remembrance: The Tulsa Race War and Its Legacy.* Boston: Houghton Mifflin, 2002.

Newspapers: "Oklahoma Clears Black in Deadly 1921 Race Riot." *NYT,* October 26, 1996, 8; "Unearthing," *NYT,* December 19, 1999, SM64.

Oklahoma Commission to Study the Tulsa Race Riot of 1921. "Tulsa Race Riot." February 28, 2001. http://www.okhistory.org/trrc /freport.pdf (accessed August 18, 2010).

—*Stephen Pickering*

STRAWS, DAVID (b. 1799, Kentucky; d. 1872, Louisville, KY), barber and Methodist church leader. David Straws was born into slavery but purchased his freedom and came to Louisville around 1830. He opened a barbershop and in 1848 bought a lot on Sixth St. at the rear of the Louisville Hotel. His business prospered, and by 1860 his real estate holdings were valued at $10,000. In 1845, Straws provided much of the funding to purchase a church at Fourth and Green (Liberty) Sts. for the use of a black Methodist congregation. The church was organized as Fourth Street Colored Methodist Church, and he was one of the first trustees. In 1848, Straws figured prominently in the successful attempt by the church (now Asbury Chapel) to secede from the white Methodist Episcopal Church South and join with the African Methodist Episcopal Church. He is buried in Eastern Cemetery.

Gibson, W. H., Sr. *History of the United Brothers of Friendship and Sisters of the Mysterious Ten: In Two Parts, a Negro Order.* Louisville, KY: Bradley & Gilbert Company, 1897.

Weeden, H. C. *Weeden's History of the Colored People of Louisville.* Louisville, KY: H. C. Weeden, 1897.

—*Cornelius Bogert*

STRIDER, MAURICE WILLIAM (b. 1913, Lexington, KY; d. 1989, Savannah, GA), artist and art educator. Born in Lexington, KY, in 1913, Maurice Strider was greatly influenced by his paternal grandfather and his parents. His paternal grandfather was a former slave and founder of Gunn Tabernacle (now Wesley) Church. His mother was a strong, educated woman who loved music and flowers; his father worked as a jeweler. After graduating from (Paul Laurence) **Dunbar High School** in 1929, Strider earned a bachelor of arts degree in history and education from Fisk University and studied art in New York.

After five years in New York City, Strider returned to Lexington and began teaching art at Dunbar High School. From 1934

Maurice Strider.

to 1966, he developed Dunbar's first art and black history classes and taught driver education. After the University of Kentucky relented and accepted African Americans as students, Strider enrolled and earned his master of education in art degree and a minor in art in 1960.

In 1966, he became the first African American appointed an assistant professor of art at Morehead State University (MSU) and was promoted to associate professor in 1972. When he retired from MSU in 1979, Strider was named professor emeritus of art. In the capacity of consultant to MSU on Afro-American studies, he continued to teach one class a semester until 1983.

In addition to being an educator, Strider was a photographer for the *Pittsburgh Courier* and the ***Louisville Defender*** and an active painter. In 1960, his painting *The Carnival* won Atlanta University's John Hope Art Award. He received the Chicago Defender Award in 1958 and a distinguished service award from the Kentucky Art Education Association in 1981. His work was exhibited at many locations, including Chicago's DuSable Museum, the Carnegie Institute, and **Kentucky State University.** The Bluegrass Chapter of the National Conference of Christians and Jews presented Strider with its Brotherhood Award in 1986 because of his work with inner-city youth. The Strider Gallery on the second floor of the Claypool-Young Art Building at MSU and the Maurice Strider Library/Media Center at Lexington's Paul Laurence Dunbar High School are named in his honor.

Strider, who died in February 1989, was survived by his wife, Mildred Goff-Steele Strider, and a daughter, Maureen Cook.

"Educator, Artist, Historian Maurice Strider Dies at 75." *LHL*, February 23, 1989, B1.

"Interview with Maurice Strider, September 16th, 1986." Guide to Blacks in Lexington Oral History Project, 1900–1989. Kentuckiana Digital Library. http://www.uky.edu/Libraries/libpage (accessed August 18, 2010).

"Maurice William Strider." In *Who's Who among African Americans*, 13th ed., 1277. Farmington Hills, MI: Gale, 2000.

—*Andrew Baskin*

STUBBLEFIELD, WILKER HARRISON THELBERT "MICKEY" (b. 1926, Mayfield, KY; d. 2013, Smyrna, GA), **first African American baseball player in the Kitty League.** A native of Mayfield, KY, and son of Harrison and Mary Wilker Stubblefield, Wilker Harrison Thelbert Stubblefield earned the nickname Mickey by playing baseball in a pair of oversized cleats as a youth, reminding his friends of the popular cartoon character Mickey Mouse. The nickname and a love for baseball persisted throughout his life. After spending two years in the navy, Stubblefield played baseball during the summer while attending trade school. He joined the Kansas City Monarchs in 1948 as a starting pitcher, a position he held for two years.

After a brief stint with the McCook Cats in Nebraska, Stubblefield signed with the Mayfield Clothiers in the Kentucky-Illinois-Tennessee (Kitty) League, the first black player to do so. The other clubs in the league reacted negatively to his presence, and fears of violence or diminished attendance at hostile stadiums forced him to pitch primarily in home games. After a year with the Clothiers, he bounced around a few semipro clubs before retiring from baseball to begin a career working for the automotive industry. Stubblefield was honored for his bravery in breaking the racial barrier at the fifth annual Negro Leagues Tribute Game in 2008, and he was named grand marshal of the Heritage Days community celebration in McCook, NE, in 2011.

Stubblefield died in Smyrna, GA, on February 19, 2013. He was buried in Mayfield Memory Gardens Cemetery.

Adelson, Bruce. *Brushing Back Jim Crow: The Integration of Minor-League Baseball in the American South.* Charlottesville: Univ. Press of Virginia, 1999.

Kelley, Brent. *The Negro Leagues Revisited: Conversations with 66 More Baseball Heroes.* Jefferson, NC: McFarland, 2000.

Newspapers: "Honor Goes to McCook's 'Little Satchel,'" *Omaha World-Herald*, May 15, 2011; "Wilker H. T. 'Mickey' Stubblefield," *McCook (NE) Daily Gazette*, February 21, 2013, http://www.mccookgazette.com/story/1943446.html/ (accessed July 10, 2013).

—*Stephen Pickering*

STUMM, CHASTEEN C. (b. 1848, Airdrie, KY; d. 1895, Washington, DC), **educator, pastor, and publisher.** Chasteen C. Stumm was born in Airdrie, KY, near the Green River in rural Muhlenburg Co. on April 11, 1848. He attended school in Greenville and then very briefly received additional education in a white school. He taught in his first school in Christian Co. in 1869. Beginning in 1871, he attended several institutions to prepare himself to be a teacher, including **Berea College** and the Baptist Theological Institute in Nashville.

In 1875, Stumm married Elizabeth Penman from Louisville. He taught at several Kentucky black schools, including Chaplaintown and Elizabethtown, where his wife aided him in establishing a successful school. He briefly served as president of Bowling Green Colored School (later known as **Bowling Green Academy**). He also taught at Hartsville and Lebanon schools in Tennessee.

In addition, Stumm, as a Baptist minister, pastored small churches until his call to Union Baptist Church in Philadelphia on October 4, 1885. He used his pastorships and contributions to Baptist journals to become an active writer and sometime editor with the *Baptist Herald* (Paducah), the *Pilot* (Nashville) and the *American Baptist* (Louisville). In 1890, Stumm and his wife published the *Christian Banner,* a religious home journal, and he served as editor of the Philadelphia office of the Brooklyn-based *National Monitor.* At the same time, State University of Louisville (later known as **Simmons College of Kentucky**) conferred an honorary doctor of divinity degree on him.

In 1891, Stumm moved to Staunton, VA, to serve Mt. Zion Baptist Church. Four years later, he died in Washington, DC. His funeral service was held at Mt. Zion Baptist Church, and he was interred in Fairview Cemetery in Staunton, VA.

Newspapers: "Accepted a Position," *IF*, August 8, 1891, 1; "Death of Rev. C. C. Stumm," *Staunton (VA) Spectator*, November 20, 1895, 3.

Pegues, A. W. *Our Baptist Ministers and Schools.* Springfield, MA: Willey & Co., 1892.

Penn, I. Garland. *The Afro-American Press, and Its Editors.* Springfield, MA: Willey & Co., 1891.

—*John A. Hardin*

SUBLETT, JOHN WILLIAM "BUBBLES" (b. 1902, Tennessee; d. 1986, Palos Verdes Peninsula, CA), **entertainer and pioneer in tap dance.** Described as the "father of rhythm tap," John William "Bubbles" Sublett developed an innovative style of dance that became known as "rhythm tap" or "jazz tap," a complex technique that involved peppering each bar of music with more taps than the usual two, combined with syncopated heel drops. These techniques were eventually incorporated into modern tap and helped redefine the genre.

According to his death records, Sublett was born in Tennessee on February 19, 1902, the second child of John and Katie Sublett. The family lived in Nashville, TN, in 1910. In a 1967 interview, Sublett stated that the family moved to Indianapolis, IN, when he was nine years old, but later moved to Louisville, where he met Louisville native **Ford Lee "Buck" Washington.** The two spent several years crafting a song and dance and comedy act, Buck and Bubbles, that later featured Sublett's tap dancing with Washington accompanying on piano. Both teenagers were living with their families in Louisville and were listed as actors in the 1920 U.S. federal census. Sublett's father died the next year, and the pair later moved, along with Sublett's mother, to New York City, where they achieved swift success and broke numerous color barriers, becoming the first African Americans to entertain at Radio City Music Hall. They performed on stage in *Porgy and Bess* and *Carmen Jones* and in such films as *Varsity Show* and *A Song Is Born.*

The partnership continued until 1952, when the pair and Sublett's wife were arrested in Canada for marijuana possession.

Washington was fined $200 and sentenced to six months in jail, but Sublett and his wife were released. The act never reunited, and Washington died three years later.

As a solo act, Sublett participated in Bob Hope's USO tours in Vietnam and appeared on a number of television variety shows. He was the first African American entertainer on Johnny Carson's *Tonight Show.* A stroke left him partially paralyzed in 1967. John Bubbles, as he was frequently called, died on May 18, 1986, in Palos Verdes Peninsula, CA. He was posthumously inducted into the Tap Dance Hall of Fame in 2002.

African American Registry. http://www.aaregistry.com/detail.php?id=707 (accessed on October 12, 2008).

Appiah, Anthony, and Henry Louis Gates, eds. *Africana: The Encyclopedia of the African and African-American Experience.* New York: Civitas Books, 1999.

Gates, Henry Louis, and Evelyn Brooks Higginbotham, eds. *African American Lives.* Oxford: Oxford Univ. Press, 2004.

Kentucky, Death Records, 1852–1953.

Newspapers: "New Yorker Jailed in Canada," *NYT,* October 29, 1952, 9; "Entertainer Wins Acquittal," *NYT,* November 6, 1952, 36; "Theatrical Whirl," *Washington (DC) Afro American,* February 8, 1955, 5.

Stevenson, James. "Bubbles." *New Yorker,* August 26, 1967. http://archives.newyorker.com/?i=1967-08-26#folio=021 (accessed November 5, 2013).

U.S. Federal Census (1900, 1910, 1920, 1930, 1940).

—*Rebecca J. Williams*

SUDDUTH, HORACE (b. 1888, Covington, KY; d. 1957, Washington, DC), businessman.

Businessman Horace Sudduth was the son of Charles Sudduth and Mattie Lee Howard Sudduth. In 1906, Horace graduated from Covington's African American high school, William Grant High School (see **Lincoln-Grant School**), while also working as a messenger for the U.S. Post Office. One of Sudduth's teachers stated, "Horace was a dedicated pupil and his high school education was all the formal training he received. But he obtained the skill and confidence needed to pursue a career in business." It was during his high school graduation commencement that Sudduth first acknowledged in public his personal admiration for business. His oration was "The Growth of Industrial Pursuits."

By marrying Melvina Jones, the sister of **Charles E. Jones,** a funeral director in Covington, Sudduth established the family bonds necessary to proceed with the new business development he had planned for Covington. But it was across the Ohio River in Cincinnati that Sudduth became a business and civic leader. He soon proved to be astute both in developing modern business practices and in establishing organizations to promote his endeavors. He founded the Horace Sudduth and Associates Real Estate Agency and was owner of the Manse Hotel, where influential African American visitors such as Sammy Davis Jr. stayed while they were in the area.

Sudduth served as president of two national organizations, the National Negro Business League, whose sole purpose was to promote black-owned businesses, and the Industrial Federal Saving and Loan Association. He was also president of the Crawford Old Men's Home and the New Orphan Asylum for Colored Children of Cincinnati. Sudduth's greatest impact, however, was in help-

ing promote progressive business thinking among fellow African Americans both in Cincinnati and his hometown, Covington. Along with Charles Jones, his father-in-law, Sudduth helped establish and lead Covington's **African American Businessmen's Association.** For many years, he and his wife were members of the **Ninth St. Methodist Episcopal Church.** Sudduth died at age 68 in 1957 in Washington, DC, where he had traveled on business. He was buried in the United American Cemetery in the Madisonville, OH, suburb of Cincinnati.

Middleton, Stephen. "We Must Not Fail!!!" Horace Sudduth: Queen City Entrepreneur." *Queen City Heritage* 49, no. 2 (Summer 1991): 3–20.

Newspapers: "Wm. Grant High School Commencement," *KTS,* June 8, 1908, 1; "Open House at New Manse Hotel," *CE,* April 1, 1950, 12; "A Tribute to a Negro Hotel Operator," *CE,* April 16, 1950, sec. 2, p. 3; "Long Illness Fatal to Horace Sudduth," *CP,* March 20, 1957, 6.

—*Theodore H. H. Harris*

SUL-TE-WAN, MADAME (b. 1873, Louisville, KY; d. 1959, Los Angeles, CA), first African American actor to sign a Hollywood film contract.

Madame Sul-Te-Wan, born Nellie Crawford on September 12, 1873, was raised in Louisville, KY, by her parents, Mary Kennedy Crawford, an African American washerwoman, and Silas Crawford, a Hawaiian minister. To help her mother, Nellie delivered laundry to theaters in Louisville, and she was sometimes allowed to stay and watch shows. This exposure to dance and theater inspired her to pursue a career in entertainment, first in Louisville and later in Cincinnati, OH. While she was touring the East Coast with a minstrel group, she married Robert Reed Conley, and they had three sons: Otto, Onest, and James. She moved with her husband and children to Arcadia, CA, in 1912.

Two years later, her husband abandoned her and their children, and in order to support her family, Nellie Crawford Conley created the stage name Madame Sul-Te-Wan and pursued a film career in Los Angeles, CA. In 1915, she met fellow Kentuckian D. W. Griffith, who hired her first as a maid on the set; he later gave her a minor role in *The Birth of a Nation,* for which she signed the first film contract for an African American actor. Sul-Te-Wan appeared in over 40 films between 1915 and 1959. She was often cast as a servant. These roles included Hattie in the 1938 film *In Old Chicago* and Lily in *Kentucky,* also produced in 1938. Sul-Te-Wan was also cast in roles that emphasized her unique ancestry, including Voodoo Sue in the 1931 film *Heaven on Earth.* Her final film appearance was in *Porgy and Bess,* released in 1959. Sul-Te-Wan died that same year on February 1. She was buried in Valhalla Memorial Park Cemetery in North Hollywood, CA.

Beasley, Delilah. *The Negro Trail Blazers of California.* New York: Negro Universities Press, 1969.

Hine, Darlene Clark, Elsa Barkley Brown, and Rosalyn Terborg-Penn, eds. *Black Women in America: An Historical Encyclopedia.* Brooklyn, NY: Carlson, 1993.

Regester, Charlene. *African American Actresses: The Struggle for Visibility, 1900–1960.* Bloomington: Indiana Univ. Press, 2010.

—*Rebecca J. Williams*

SUMMERS, JANE ROBERTA WHATLEY (b. 1895, Selma, AL; d. 1992, Covington, KY), community advocate. Community activist Jane Roberta Whatley Summers was the daughter of Calvin and Minerva Kendall Whatley. In 1934, at age 39, she moved with her family to Covington. She soon developed a community-service mind-set. She joined **St. James A.M.E. Church** and became one of the denomination's most active members, both locally and nationally. In addition to being both a wife and a mother, it seemed that daily Summers was helping someone in need. For example, if she encountered a person who required medical attention, she would contact a local physician and stay at the person's side until medical help arrived. Throughout the years, because of such generosity, most local African American Kentuckians described Summers as an angel of mercy.

At age 50, Summers became the first African American manager of Covington's **Jacob Price** Homes housing community, which was built in 1939. As manager, she helped numerous residents by conducting yearly fund-raising events, offering individual counseling sessions on health care topics, and sponsoring workshops on how to gain access to local governmental agencies. During these years, many local residents referred to Summers as "Mama Janie."

Even after leaving her Jacob Price Homes position at age 75, Summers continued to serve her community. She was a member of the Northern Kentucky Community Action Commission, the Northern Kentucky Interfaith Commission, the local Meals on Wheels program, and the **Kentucky Commission on Human Rights.** She also was active in the local **National Association for the Advancement of Colored People** chapter and helped organize a regional Poor People's Campaign.

In 1992, as a testament to her various humanitarian activities and extraordinary community service, Summers was inducted into the Northern Kentucky Leadership Hall of Fame. After her death that year, Summers continued posthumously to receive notable awards, celebrity plaques, and recognition decrees, such as a key to the city of Covington, a proclamation from the Kenton Co. Fiscal Court, an honorary and recognition letter from U.S. senator and former Kentucky governor Wendell Ford (1971–1974), a Community Service Award from the Covington–Kenton Co. Jaycees, and election to the Gallery of Great Black Kentuckians by the **Kentucky Commission on Human Rights.** Throughout her 97 years, Summers was an essential and preeminent community activist who waged a lifetime battle against racism, homelessness, illiteracy, and hunger.

African American National Biography, s.v. "Jane Roberta Summers," by Lois Schultz. Oxford Univ. Press, forthcoming.

"Happy Birthday—Our Role Model—This Is Your Life—Jane Summers: 96 Years Young—May 5, 1991." Northern Kentucky African American Heritage Task Force Collection, W. Frank Steely Library, Northern Kentucky Univ.

Northington, Mary. Interview by Eric R. Jackson, Covington, KY, September 2004.

Newspapers: "Jane Summers, 97, Mentor to Many in Covington," *KP,* July 1, 1992, 10A; "Jane Summers," *KP,* July 2, 1992, 10A; "African American History Has a Devoted Caretaker," *KP,* October 18, 1997, 1K; "Local Activist Added to Gallery," *KP,* November 14, 2001, 21A.

—*Eric R. Jackson*

SUMMERS, WILLIAM E., III (b. 1917, Louisville, KY; d. 1996, Louisville, KY), minister and radio executive. William E. Summers III was the son of Mima (Sweat) and William E. Summers II. Summers started his career in journalism as a writer for the *Louisville Defender* in 1941. In the late 1940s, he coordinated a talent show for WGRC (which became WAKY) radio. In 1951, he became a part-time sportscaster for WLOU radio and later moved into a full-time position. From that position, he moved into management on Rounsaville Radio, a company that owned seven radio stations with a black format, including Louisville-based WLOU. In 1967, he became vice president and general manager of WLOU.

Summers incorporated Summers Broadcasting and purchased WLOU in 1971 and WNUU-FM in 1973 (sold in 1976). WLOU was the first Kentucky broadcast property to be owned and operated by a minority group. It was sold in 1982 to Johnson Publishing Company (Chicago), but Summers remained with WLOU as a consultant until 1988. The Kentucky Broadcasters Association awarded Summers the Golden Mike award for his services to broadcasting. He was also inducted into the University of Kentucky Journalism Hall of Fame in 1996, a month before his death.

Summers also served numerous congregations as an African Methodist Episcopal minister, pasturing churches in Taylorsville, Georgetown, Shelbyville, and Louisville. His longest pastorate was at St. Paul A.M.E. Church in Louisville, where he served from 1968 until his retirement in 1988. Active in civic affairs, he was a board member of the **Louisville Urban League,** the Boys Club of America, the Transit Authority of River City; board member and ultimately president of the Kentucky Derby Festival; president of the Food for the Elderly consortium; and a local and national board member of the YMCA. He marched in Selma, AL, in 1965 with Rev. Martin Luther King Jr. For his work, Summers was awarded such honors as the Distinguished Service Award of the Louisville Urban League, the **National Association for the Advancement of Colored People** Educational Award, Black Achiever of the Year, the City of Louisville's Freedom Award, and the National Association of Christians and Jews Brotherhood Award.

His family included his wife, Feryn (Stigall) Summers; three children: a son, William E. Summers IV, and two daughters, Seretha Summers-Tinsley and Sherryl S. Summers; and seven grandchildren. He is buried in Cave Hill Cemetery.

—*Gail Henson*

SWEENEY, PRUITT OWSLEY (b. 1891, Kentucky; d. 1960, Louisville, KY), dentist who filed suit to desegregate Louisville golf courses. Pruitt Owsley Sweeney was born to Florence and Edgar Sweeney on June 6, 1891. He spent his childhood in Lincoln Co., KY, and by age 18 was living with his parents and five younger siblings in Junction City, KY. By 1917, Sweeney was working as a teacher in Louisville, KY, where he lived with his wife, Minerva. Two years later, they had their first and only child, Florence. That same year, Sweeney received his bachelor's degree from Simmons University (later known as **Simmons College of Kentucky**). In 1920, he worked as a principal in a public school in Clinton, KY.

Sweeney earned a degree in dentistry from Meharry Medical College in Nashville, TN, in 1925. Shortly after, he established a dental practice in an office in the **Domestic Life and Accident Insurance** Building in Louisville. Sweeney was a member of the National Medical Association, although he was repeatedly denied admission to the city and county dental societies because of his race. Minerva (Jones) Sweeney died in 1930. Sweeney did not remarry.

In 1947, Sweeney brought a lawsuit against Louisville City Parks and Recreation. He was an avid golfer and sought the right to play golf on the municipal course, as well as to have access to other segregated city park facilities, including Iroquois Amphitheater. The suit, backed by the local chapter of the **National Association for the Advancement of Colored People,** was initially dismissed by Kentucky Court of Appeals judge Lawrence Speckman, who stated that "social equality between persons of the white race and colored races or, in fact, between persons of the same race cannot be enforced by legislation or the courts." In 1950, the NAACP followed up with a new federal suit involving three plaintiffs, including Sweeney. The lawsuit was heard by Judge Roy Shelbourne in 1951. He issued a temporary ruling opening city golf courses to the African American community. However, rather than integrate the courses, Louisville chose to build a golf course in the segregated park. In response, Shelbourne ordered the immediate integration of the golf courses in 1952.

In the late 1950s, Sweeney purchased a farm outside Louisville. Having served as the vice president of the Board of Directors of **Mammoth Life and Accident Insurance,** Sweeney had earned a place on *Ebony*'s list of 100 Richest Negroes. A political, social, and economic leader in Louisville, Pruitt Sweeney died in 1960.

Hall, Wade. *The Rest of the Dream: The Black Odyssey of Lyman Johnson.* Lexington: Univ. Press of Kentucky, 1988.
K'Meyer, Tracy E. *Civil Rights in the Gateway to the South: Louisville, Kentucky, 1945–1980.* Lexington: Univ. Press of Kentucky, 2009.
"Ky. Dentist Quits South Because of Jim Crow." *Jet,* September 3, 1953, 27.
"Louisville Risk Firm Elects New Vice-President." *Jet,* December 1, 1960, 21.
"The 100 Richest Negroes." *Ebony,* May 1962, 135.
"Stereotypes and Prejudices." *Ebony,* June 1969, 116.
"This Week's Census," *Jet,* October 27, 1960, 27.

—*Elizabeth Schaller*

SWOPE, WILLIAM "BILL," JR. (b. 1959, Lexington, KY), first African American state fire marshal in Kentucky. Lexington native William "Bill" Swope Jr. was born to Mildred Swope and William Swope Sr. on December 3, 1959. After graduating from Lexington's Bryan Station High School, Swope Jr. earned a degree in communications and organizational management at the University of Kentucky. He is a member of **Kappa Alpha Psi Fraternity.**

Swope began working for Lexington's Division of Fire and Emergency Services in 1985. Beginning in 1995, as part of the Fire Prevention Bureau, he managed field inspectors and presented public education programs for five years. In 2002, he became the division's chief of administration and directed the day-to-day administrative operations. He also served as assistant fire chief.

In 2008, Kentucky governor Steve Beshear appointed Swope state fire marshal, the first African American to hold that position in Kentucky. Continuing in the position, he led the first brainstorming session among Kentucky's fire officials in April 2013. Kentucky suffered a high risk of fatal fires because of poverty, an excessive smoking rate among its citizens, and the widespread use of supplemental heating sources. Looking for some type of intervention to reduce the exorbitant number of fire fatalities in the state, Swope challenged the group that it could no longer "sit by and hope that this changes on its own."

"Department of Public Protection." Kentucky Government. http://migration.kentucky.gov/Newsroom/eppc_dpp/firemarshalswope.htm (accessed July 12, 2012).
"NASFM News, May 2009." National Association of State Fire Marshals. www.firemarshals.org/pdf/MayNewsfromNASFM.pdf (accessed July 12, 2012).
Newspapers: "Swope Appointed State Fire Marshal," *LHL,* April 17, 2008, B3; "Officials Share Ideas to Fight Rise in Fire Deaths," Associated Press State Wire: Kentucky, April 16, 2013.

—*Sallie L. Powell*

SYKES, HARRY N. (b. 1927, Starkville, MS; d. 2012, Lexington, KY), city commissioner, civil rights activist, educator, and Harlem Globetrotter player. One of 13 children of minister and sharecropper Pinkie Kirk Sykes and Parkay Marie Hall Sykes, Harry N. Sykes, born on April 1, 1927, stood six-feet-six at age 15.

Harry Sykes.

He was still in the sixth grade at that time because he and his siblings had to work on the farm instead of spending time in school. In the 1940s, the family moved to Illinois, and Sykes was able to improve his education. In 1948, he accepted an athletic scholarship to Kentucky State College (later known as **Kentucky State University**) in Frankfort. He played basketball, ran track, and met his future wife, Geraldine Higgins, a cheerleader. The couple married on July 1, 1951, at Geraldine's home in Lexington, KY.

After graduating with a physical education degree in 1952, Sykes played two seasons for the Harlem Globetrotters. After returning to Lexington, he taught math and was assistant basketball coach at (Paul Laurence) **Dunbar High School.** He earned his master's degree in mathematics from the University of Minnesota. In 1963, he was elected Lexington's first African American city commissioner. Eighty percent of the registered voters in the precinct were white. Reelected three times, he became Lexington's first African American mayor pro tem (the council member with the most votes) in 1967. A year later, he cofounded the Lexington–Fayette County Urban League and served as its first president. He was instrumental in the integration of the city's fire department and in assisting **James Perkins,** Lexington's first African American sergeant, to climb the police department's ranks.

In 1971, Sykes announced his run for mayor by proclaiming, "A sick society is one that will put prejudices before principles." After losing the race, he was appointed acting city manager and oversaw the merger of the Lexington and Fayette Co. governments. Later, he served as personnel director for the Kentucky Cabinet for Natural Resources and compliance officer for the Kentucky Finance Cabinet. He retired in 1992.

In 2005, Sykes was elected to the Kentucky Civil Rights Hall of Fame. Lexington mayor Jim Gray declared Harry Sykes Day on October 25, 2012. Sykes died at age 85 on November 28, 2012. His funeral was held at the **Historic Pleasant Green Missionary Baptist Church,** of which he was a faithful member. He was interred in Lexington Cemetery.

Newspapers: "Harry Sykes Knew the Score for Leadership," *LHL,* February 25, 2000, B1; "Color Our Mayoral Race White and Green," *LHL,* July 7, 2001, C1; "How They Met 'We Just Started Going Around Together,'" *LHL,* July 29, 2001, J6.

—*Sallie L. Powell*

T

TANDY, HENRY A. (b. ca. 1855, Estill, KY; d. 1918, Lexington, KY), prominent Lexington brick mason. Little is known about Henry A. Tandy's early life. Born in Estill Co., KY, to unknown parents, Tandy moved to Lexington in the 1860s. After a brief stint as a photographer, he began a career as a bricklayer for G. D. Wilgus in 1867. He had considerable success in this occupation, rising to the position of foreman before his employer's death in 1892. Tandy then joined another African American laborer to form a partnership that operated under the name Tandy and Byrd.

Tandy rapidly became one of the more sought-after brick masons in Lexington. He helped build Morton Middle School, several buildings for the University of Kentucky, and the original buildings of Eastern Kentucky University. He also gained a reputation as an excellent business manager, employing numerous black workers and becoming perhaps the richest African American in the state of Kentucky. As of September 1897, he employed between 40 and 50 black and white workers. In 1898, he achieved his greatest fame when he was contracted for the brickwork on the Lexington Courthouse. In 1918, Tandy died of a septic infection in Lexington and was buried in Greenwood Cemetery (later named Cove Haven Cemetery). His son, **Vertner Woodson Tandy Sr.,** became a famed architect in his own right, designing several notable buildings in New York during the Harlem Renaissance.

"Black Businesses Prospered after Civil War; End of Segregation Brought Failure for Many Black Enterprises." *LHL,* March 1, 1992, Special 15.
Hamilton, G. P. *Biographical Sketches of Prominent Negro Men and Women of Kentucky.* Memphis: E. H. Clarke & Brother, 1911.
Richings, G. F. *Evidences of Progress among Colored People.* 8th ed. Philadelphia: Geo. S. Ferguson Co., 1902.

—*Stephen Pickering*

TANDY, OPAL L. (b. 1917, Hopkinsville, KY; d. 1983, Indianapolis, IN), journalist and publisher. Opal L. Tandy was born on March 25, 1917, in Hopkinsville, KY, to Roxie Moss and Elzie Tandy. In 1921, at the age of four, Opal and his mother moved to Indianapolis, IN, where he attended Crispus Attucks High School. He studied journalism and political science at Indiana University's extension campus in Indianapolis (now Indiana University, Purdue University–Indianapolis). During World War II, Tandy was on the communications staff of Gen. George S. Patton. After his honorable discharge, Tandy became a deputy coroner in Marion Co., IN, for 22 years. At least twice, he ran unsuccessfully for political office.

In the 1930s, Tandy began his career in journalism at African American newspapers by writing editorials and crime stories for the *Indianapolis Recorder.* During the 1950s, he worked for the *Hoosier Herald.* In 1956, the newspaper was the *Indiana Herald-Times,* and Tandy was the city editor. In 1958, Tandy bought control of the newspaper and became the owner and publisher. He changed the name to the *Indiana Herald* in 1960. Mary Bryant was the business manager. Eventually, they married, and she became the publisher after his death.

Tandy was a member of Mount Zion Baptist Church, the **National Association for the Advancement of Colored People,** and the Indianapolis Urban League. Professionally, he was affiliated with the National Publishers Association, the National Negro Publishers Association, and the Indiana Democratic Editorial Association. He died on June 13, 1983. His survivors included Mary, his wife; a son; and four stepdaughters and stepsons.

Indiana Herald. http://www.indianaherald.com.
Matheson, Bernice. E-mails to author, July 2008.
"Opal L. Tandy Collection, 1951–1983." Indiana Historical Society—Manuscripts and Archives. http://www.indianahistory.org/library/manuscripts/collection_guides/sc2485.html.

—*Andrew Baskin*

TANDY, VERTNER WOODSON, SR. (b. 1885, Lexington, KY; d. 1949, New York, NY), New York architect and one of the founders of Alpha Phi Alpha Fraternity Inc. The son of **Henry A. Tandy,** a successful brick contractor in Lexington, KY, Vertner Woodson Tandy Sr., followed in his father's footsteps by pursuing a career in architecture, studying at the local Chandler Normal School before moving on to Tuskegee Institute. After three years at Tuskegee, Tandy enrolled at Cornell University to further his studies. At the university, he, along with six other African American students, founded **Alpha Phi Alpha Fraternity, Inc.**

After graduating in 1908, Tandy began a flourishing career as an architect in New York City. The movement of various churches and businesses to Harlem as part of the Harlem Renaissance bolstered his business, and his commissions included some of the most familiar buildings in the city. Madame C. J. Walker's Villa Lewaro was considered a pinnacle of black architecture for years after its completion in 1916. Tandy's business declined with the arrival of the Great Depression, but he earned praise for other contributions, becoming the first African American to pass the military commissioning exam, as well as the first to be accepted into the American Institute of Architects. In 1949, he died after suffering from pneumonia for three months in New York City. In Lexington, members of Alpha Phi Alpha unveiled a highway marker in his honor in 2009.

"Fraternity Puts Its Founder on Map—Road Marker to Note Architect's Place in History." *LHL,* September 15, 2009, C1.
Smith, Jessie Carney, ed. *Encyclopedia of African American Business.* Vol. 2. Westport, CT: Greenwood Press, 2006.
Wilson, Dreck Spurlock, ed. *African American Architects: A Biographical Dictionary, 1865–1945.* New York: Routledge, 2004.

—*Stephen Pickering*

TAYLOR, ASA (b. before 1800, Virginia; d. after 1839, Kentucky), preacher. Asa Taylor, an enslaved African American who lived in Kentucky, has been called the first African American preacher in Boone Co. He and his siblings, all enslaved, came from Virginia to Kentucky with Rev. John Taylor, a Baptist evangelist who had many slaves. Asa Taylor was one of 31 African

Americans who were accepted into the fellowship of the Bullittsburg Baptist Church in August 1800. That summer, John Taylor baptized by immersion a few young people, including Asa, whom Taylor had raised and taught to read. Another man, a slaveholder named Christopher Wilson, was baptized at the same time. Wilson was later called as the first moderator or pastor of the Baptist Church at Middle Creek (present-day Belleview Baptist Church). Asa Taylor and Wilson often traveled throughout Boone Co. together, teaching and preaching. John Taylor said of Asa, "May he be useful among his fellow Blacks as there is the greatest sphere of his action."

Asa Taylor's sister, Letty, also raised by John Taylor, did not share her brother's religious fervor. Letty had so great an aversion to religion that it took stern measures by John Taylor to force her to join the Taylor family prayers and worship. Taylor described Letty as having "masculine strength" and an unflagging determination. After Asa Taylor's conversion, Letty was apparently stricken by her own "consciousness of guilt," and she called on Asa for his counsel. Asa responded that Letty was "of the Devil" and was not ready for baptism or acceptance into any Baptist church. Despite Asa's assessment of her, Letty made a confession of faith three weeks after Asa's conversion and was baptized and accepted as a member of the Bullittsburg Baptist Church.

Unlike Wilson, who was ordained on May 2, 1807, Asa Taylor was never officially ordained as a Baptist preacher. For the first 18 years of his ministry, the Baptist elders held Asa in tight rein. The church finally relaxed its hold and allowed him to share freely his "gift of exhortation."

Boone Co. slave schedules indicate that Asa was a slave of several Boone Co. men. When John Taylor left Boone Co. for Gallatin Co. in 1802, Asa Taylor was listed with John Graves. From 1819 to 1835, two other slaveholders claimed ownership of Asa. In 1839, the Bullittsburg Baptist Church minutes recorded the request of a "Brother Ezra Ferris, who asked that Asa [Taylor] and his wife, Rachel, be granted dismissal from the Bullitsburg congregation." It is possible that Ferris, who lived in Dearborn Co., IN, had manumitted Asa and Rachel. It is believed that Asa Taylor lived at least until 1839; there is no record of his death or burial.

Jackson, Eric R. *Northern Kentucky.* Black America. Charleston, SC: Arcadia, 2005.
Taylor, John. *Baptists on the American Frontier: A History of Ten Baptist Churches of Which the Author Has Been Alternately a Member.* Edited by Chester Raymond Young. 3rd ed. Macon, GA: Mercer Univ. Press, 1995.

—*Jannes W. Garbett*

TAYLOR, BARTLETT (b. 1815, Henderson, KY; d. 1901, Louisville, KY), pastor and businessman. Bartlett Taylor was born enslaved in Henderson, KY, on February 14, 1815. His father, Jonathan Taylor, owned him and his mother. When Bartlett was seven, his mother and five of her other children were taken by the local court to settle Jonathan Taylor's debts. Two years later, the remaining children were sold to other family members when the Taylors—both owners and remaining slaves—relocated to La Grange in Oldham Co.

During his adolescent years, young Bartlett Taylor learned the meat-butchering trade from a member of his owner's family. Using these skills and an innate but shrewd business sense, he was able to buy his freedom by bidding for himself at a slave auction in 1840. Once he was free, he married his first wife, Jane McCune, and had three daughters by her. She died in 1846. Taylor became a successful retailer and wholesaler in the meat-butchering industry and used those proceeds to purchase multiple houses and lots in Louisville. In 1848, he married Mariam McGill and they had one son, who became a principal in one of the black schools in Louisville.

Taylor's self-taught business skills enabled him to become successful in a parallel career as a builder of churches and schools for the African Methodist Episcopal (A.M.E.) Church after his ordination as an itinerant elder (pastor) in the denomination. His service to the A.M.E. Church included serving both as treasurer and trustee of Wilberforce University in Ohio and financing the construction of A.M.E. churches in Bowling Green, Cynthiana, and Louisville. While pastoring a church in Shelbyville in 1881, he persuaded the blacks and whites of the town to create, build, and open an elementary school for blacks where there had been none.

Toward the end of his life, Taylor became widely recognized in the A.M.E. Church as an active and forceful preacher. By 1887, he had bought a lot and built a home in the southeastern area of Louisville. On July 3, 1901, Bartlett Taylor died and was buried in the black Eastern Cemetery in Louisville on July 6, 1901.

Family Search The Church of Jesus Christ of Latter-day Saints. http://familysearch.org/pal:/MM9.1.1/FWPT-W3N (accessed July 17, 2012).
Gibson, W. H., Sr. *Historical Sketch of the Progress of the Colored Race, in Louisville, Ky., as Noted by the Writer during a Period of Fifty Years.* Louisville, KY: Bradley & Gilbert, 1897, 27.
Simmons, William. *Men of Mark: Eminent, Progressive and Rising.* Cleveland: George M. Rewell, 1887, 627–30.

—*John A. Hardin*

TAYLOR, JAMES H. "J. H." (b. 1838, James City Co., VA, 1838; d. 1901, Louisville, KY), undertaker. Little is known about James H. Taylor's early life. Born in James City Co., VA, in 1838, Taylor moved to Louisville in 1865, where he worked as a house carpenter for two years. In 1867, he formed a partnership with Yarmouth Carr and opened an undertaking business, becoming the first African American mortician in Louisville. In a city where white undertakers charged double for black clients, he quickly established a strong customer base, first in separate partnerships with Carr and R. C. Fox and then as a business owner on his own. In 1897, he was considered one of the wealthier black residents of the city, with an estate worth several thousand dollars.

A respected citizen of Louisville, Taylor was a member of several lodges; one biography suggested that he was "possibly connected with more secret societies than any one man in Louisville." On May 10, 1901, J. H. Taylor died at his home at 610 Ninth St. of apoplexy. At his death, he left his business to his son, Robert J. Taylor, but turmoil followed. The *Louisville Courier-Journal* reported that Robert J. Taylor shot at rival undertaker Andrew Taylor (possibly a relative). Both operated their businesses on the same street. A bystander was injured, and the men were arrested and charged with "malicious shooting."

After J. H. Taylor's sons died, his wife, Mary H. Taylor, carried on the family business, which continued to flourish as "one of the best equipped offices in the city."

Buck, D. D. *The Progression of the Race in the United States and Canada.* Chicago: Atwell Printing and Binding, 1907.

Kentucky, Death Records, 1852–1953.

Newspapers: "Doings of the Race," *Cleveland Gazette,* January 2, 1886, 1; "Negro Riot," *LCJ,* October 29, 1901, 8; "Progress of Undertakers," *IF,* July 7, 1906, 1.

U.S. Federal Census (1880, 1900)

Weeden, H. C. *Weeden's History of the Colored People of Louisville.* Louisville, KY: H. C. Weeden, 1897.

—*Stephen Pickering*

TAYLOR, MARSHALL WILLIAM (b. 1846, Lexington, KY; d. 1887, Louisville, KY), hymn writer.

The son of free parents in Lexington, KY, Marshall William Taylor was born the youngest of three brothers on July 1, 1846. His mother encouraged him to get an education, so he attended schools in Louisville, as well as in Indiana and Ohio. After pursuing his education farther north, he returned to Louisville to work as a messenger in the law firm of J. B. Kincaid and John W. Barr before beginning a teaching career in Breckinridge Co. Even though local whites resisted his efforts to provide black students with an education, Taylor was elected president of a convention for educators in Owensboro in 1868.

The following year, the quarterly conference of the Hardinsburg Circuit in Kentucky licensed Taylor to preach. A member of the Methodist Episcopal Church, he traveled to Arkansas to spend one year in missionary work before returning to enter the Lexington Conference in 1872. He began his own work in Indianapolis, becoming a pastor in 1875 and an elder in 1876 and receiving an honorary doctorate of divinity from Central Tennessee College in 1879. The next year, he was nominated to be a bishop at the General Conference in Cincinnati, but whites successfully resisted his appointment.

Taylor also tried his hand in the realm of publishing, penning several biographical sketches, contributing to the Methodist press, and editing a collection of revival songs and plantation spirituals. He served as editor of the *Southwestern Christian Advocate,* based in New Orleans, LA, although he primarily stayed in Kentucky, Indiana, and Ohio while he worked for the newspaper. After discovering a growth on his throat, Taylor returned to his home in Indianapolis and contributed to his paper when health allowed. Eventually, doctors informed him that the growth was a "fibrous tumor" that would soon kill him, but he continued to write for the paper until his death in Louisville, KY, on September 11, 1887.

Perhaps Taylor's most important contribution was his collection of spirituals that he edited into a hymnal titled *A Collection of Revival Hymns and Plantation Melodies.* The hymnal, originally published in 1882, went into multiple editions and featured songs that were intended to keep the memories of the slave experience alive. Historians continue to use the collection to provide insight into the lives and experiences of African Americans in the nineteenth century.

Abbott, Lynn, and Doug Seroff. *Out of Sight: The Rise of African American Popular Music, 1889–1895.* Jackson: Univ. Press of Mississippi, 2002.

Hough, Robin. "Choirs of Angels Armed for War: Reverend Marshall W. Taylor's *A Collection of Revival Hymns and Plantation Melodies.*" In *Feel the Spirit: Studies in Nineteenth-Century Afro-American Music,* edited by George R. Keck and Sherrill V. Martin, 17–33. Westport, CT: Greenwood Press, 1988.

"Marshall W. Taylor, D.D." *Southwestern Christian Advocate,* September 22, 1887, 4.

Simmons, William. *Men of Mark: Eminent, Progressive and Rising.* Cleveland: George M. Rewell, 1887.

—*Stephen Pickering*

TEVIS, ELIZABETH CURTIS HUNDLEY (b. 1802, Virginia; d. 1880s, Jefferson Co., KY), landowner and businesswoman.

Eliza Curtis Hundley Tevis, one of the most fascinating and imposing women and African Americans in Louisville's history, was born enslaved in Virginia and brought to Kentucky. She was freed in 1833 in recognition of her service to John and, later, Thomas Hundley, owners of the land on which Bashford Manor Mall now stands and from whom she also inherited money and property in Louisville.

On June 17, 1843, she married Henry Tevis (ca. 1804–1869), a freeman of color, after first formalizing a prenuptial agreement that protected her premarital property from her husband's control. According to oral tradition, Tevis was given enslaved children separated from their families by sale on the Louisville slave market. These she employed or hired out as farm laborers and, consequently, became one of the few African American slave owners listed in the records of Jefferson Co. On February 22, 1851, Tevis and her husband purchased 40 acres of land near the Hundley property, constructed a large log house near present-day Newburg Rd. and Indian Trail, and began farming. The Tevis land was subdivided and sold or rented to other African Americans after the Civil War. Along with an adjacent 40 acres purchased by Peter Laws from Col. George Hikes in the 1870s, the entire area evolved into the African American community of Petersburg.

Tevis had a reputation as a healer, was deeply religious, and was instrumental in founding Forest Baptist Church in 1867. She and her husband had no children, although he had five children from a previous union. She was buried, along with family members and other early settlers, in Forest Home Cemetery near her house.

LCJ, September 16, 1979.

U.S. Federal Census (1850, 1860, 1870, 1880).

—*J. Blaine Hudson*

THACKER, THOMAS (b. 1939, Covington, KY), basketball player.

Thomas Porter Thacker, the son of William T. and Velma M. Arvin Thacker, played basketball on national championship teams of three associations: the NCAA (at the University of Cincinnati, 1960–1961 and 1961–1962), the NBA (for the Boston Celtics, 1967–1968), and the ABA (for the Indiana Pacers, 1970–1971).

Thacker's success in basketball began in grade school at the Roman Catholic African American school in Covington, Our Savior. His team played in the Northern Kentucky Holy Name Basketball League, winning the league's championship in 1955. In 1956, when integration closed **Our Savior Catholic Church** High School, Thacker enrolled at William Grant High School. In 1956, African American schools were admitted to the Kentucky High School Athletic Association. That year, his basketball team won the district tournament but lost in the regional tournament. William Grant had a season record of 23–4. In 1957–1958, Thacker's second year, William Grant High School won the district and regional basketball tournaments but lost in the first round of the state tournament. The school's basketball season ended with a record of 26–5. In 1958–1959, Thacker's final year, his high school won the district and regional tournaments but lost in the quarterfinals of the state tournament. The school's season ended with a record of 31–7.

Thacker, still needing a few high school credits to graduate, attended Holmes High School during the summer of 1959. In the fall, he entered the University of Cincinnati, where he earned a BA and an MA. As a six-feet-two forward, he had a distinguished college playing career that included twice being named a basketball All-American. After college, Thacker played basketball professionally for a time with the Cincinnati Royals alongside Oscar Robertson. After his NBA and ABA career, Thacker played and coached some minor-league professional basketball teams. He also coached the University of Cincinnati's Lady Bearcats basketball team for a short period.

Thacker was named to the Northern Kentucky Sports Hall of Fame in 1986 and the Northern Kentucky Black Hall of Fame in 1989. He retired in Cincinnati, occasionally substitute teaching for the Cincinnati Public School System.

Newspapers: "Our Savior Wins," *KTS*, January 5, 1955, 7A; "Brain Busters: Quick Quiz of Forgettable Facts," *KP*, August 13, 1982, 5K; "Thacker, Hils, Grant Top All-Time Hoop Picks," *KP*, December 25, 1984, 10K; "Black Hall of Fame Inductees Transcend Sports," *KP*, February 25, 1989, 1K; "Our Savior Fills Unique Niche," *KP*, January 17, 1994, 4K; "Many Tried, Few Defeated William Grant in '50s, '60s," *KP*, February 23, 1998, 4K.

—*Theodore H. H. Harris*

THOMAS, CLINTON (b. 1896, Greenup, KY; d. 1990, Charleston, WV), baseball player. Baseball player Clinton Thomas was born on November 25, 1896, in Greenup, KY, the son of James and Lutie Thomas. Instead of attending high school, he moved to Columbus, OH, in 1910 to play amateur baseball, and he worked in a restaurant and grocery store. Thomas served in the army during World War I. He began his professional career in 1920 as a second baseman with the Brooklyn Royal Giants and then played for the Columbus Buckeyes in 1921 and the Detroit Stars in 1922. Joining the Philadelphia Hilldale Giants, a black major-league team, in 1923, he became an outfielder who combined speed, power, and defense. He appeared in two Negro World Series and earned the nickname Hawk for his defensive

prowess. He played with the Atlantic City Bacharach Giants in 1928–1930. He closed out his career with the New York Black Yankees, with a lifetime .333 batting average. He then moved to Charleston, WV, where he worked for the West Virginia Department of Mines. He retired as staff supervisor of the state senate at 80 years of age. Thomas married Ellen Odell (Smith) Bland in 1963.

Baxter, Terry. "Thomas, Clinton." In *Biographical Dictionary of American Sports, Baseball,* edited by David L. Porter, 1534–35. Westport, CN: Greenwood Press, 2000.
Peterson, Robert. *Only the Ball Was White: A History of Legendary Black Players and All-Black Professional Teams.* New York: Oxford University Press, 1970, 250.
"Baseball's Clint Thomas Dies at Age 94 in W. Va." *Jet* 79 no. 11 (December 24, 1990): 48.

THOMAS, REGENA L. (b. 1957, Clinton, KY), politician. Regena L. Thomas, a native of Clinton, KY, earned a BA in university studies from Morehead State University, where she also played basketball. From 1980 to 1985, she was a legislative analyst for the Kentucky legislature's Legislative Research Commission. She worked with Jesse L. Jackson and his National Rainbow Coalition during Jackson's bid for the presidency of the United States in 1984 and 1988 and was on the staffs of Washington mayors Sharon Pratt Kelly and Marion Barry.

Thomas also served on the campaigns of Robert G. Torricelli for U.S. Senate in 1996, James E. McGreevy for governor of New Jersey in 1997, and Jon Corzine for U.S. Senate in 2000. New Jersey governor James McGreevey appointed her the 31st secretary of state of New Jersey; she served from 2002 to 2006. As secretary of state, she oversaw government organizations including the New Jersey Historical Commission, the New Jersey Historic Trust, and the New Jersey State Museum.

Hedges, Chris. "Public Lives: Fighting for the Arts and Yearning for a Spiritual Life." *NYT,* May 8, 2003, B2.
Kentucky Legislature. House of Representatives. *A Resolution Recognizing and Commending the Appointment of Regena L. Thomas as the 31st Secretary of State in New Jersey.* H.R. 118. Regular Session, 2002. http://www.lrc.state.ky.us/recarch/02rs/HR118.htm (accessed January 15, 2012).
Pulley, Brett. "On Politics: A Democratic Vote-Finder Who Does Take Prisoners." *NYT,* March 16, 1997, NJ2.
"Thomas, Regena L." *Who's Who in America 2010,* 64th ed. New Providence, NJ: Marquis Who's Who, 2009.

—*Jennifer Bartlett*

THOMAS, REGINALD "REGGIE" (b. 1953, Chicago, IL), attorney and elected legislator. After Reginald "Reggie" Thomas's father died, his mother moved the family to her hometown of Lexington, KY. Thomas was 14. He participated in the local Micro–City Government youth program and graduated from Lexington's Bryan Station High School in 1971. He graduated magna cum laude from Dartmouth College in 1975 and subsequently earned a law degree from Harvard University.

Thomas returned to Lexington and opened a law practice. He served the community in various capacities, including Bryan Station High School PTA president, Bluegrass Community and

Technical College board member, and chair of the Kentucky Conference for Community and Justice. He served as a University of Kentucky law professor until 1984. He then became associate professor in the Division of Social Work/Criminal Justice at **Kentucky State University.**

In 2012, Thomas ran in his first political race for the 88th Kentucky House District seat in southern Fayette Co. In a special election in 2013, he won the Senate District 13 seat that centered in downtown Lexington and encompassed the University of Kentucky. He was the first African American state senator elected outside Louisville. **Georgia Powers** and **Gerald A. Neal,** both from Louisville, had preceded him into the Senate.

Thomas ran on issues of education and jobs. In order to save the state money in pension benefits, he announced that he would not take the official oath of office until the beginning of 2014.

Kentucky Democratic Party. "Reggie Thomas for SD13." http://kyde mocrat.com/news/reggie-thomas-sd13 (accessed December 17, 2013).

Kentucky State University. Academics: School of Public Administration, Social Work and Criminal Justice. http://www.kysu.edu /academics/collegesAndSchools/collegeofprofessionalstudies /PASWCJ/schoolOfPublicAdministration/r_Thomas.htm (accessed December 17, 2013).

Muhammad, Patrice K. "Historic Special Election Set for December 10th." *Key Conversations Radio Show: Conversation Is the Key,* December 1, 2013. http://keyconversationsradio.com/historic-special -election-set-for-december-10th/ (accessed December 17, 2013).

Newspapers: "Holy Four-Year Scholarship!," *LHL,* May 14, 1988, B1; "Thomas for 88th," *LHL,* October 20, 2012, A15; "Candidates Offer Voters Stark Choice in Philosophy Size, Scope of Government at Issue," *LHL,* October 21, 2012, A1; "Democrat Reggie Thomas Victorious in 3-Man Race," *LHL,* December 11, 2013, A1.

—*Sallie L. Powell*

THOMPSON, DINNIE D. (b. 1857, Louisville, KY; d. 1939, Louisville, KY), freed slave and member of the Sisters of the Mysterious Ten. Dinnie D. Thompson was born to Diana (1818–1895) and Spencer Thompson (d. 1858), enslaved by the family of John and Lucy Fry Speed of **Farmington,** a Louisville hemp plantation. John Speed died in 1840, and his 57 slaves were parceled out to his wife and 11 children. Diana, Ned Russell, and their children, Lot, Lydia, and Robert Russell, were given to Mary Speed. In 1854, Mary moved her slaves from Farmington to her home on Fifth St. in downtown Louisville. When Ned Russell died, Diana married Spencer Thompson, who was enslaved by Peachy Speed Peay at Farmington. Spencer died in 1858, a year after Dinnie's birth.

Diana secreted Dinnie away from Mary Speed's home on several failed attempts to secure passage across the Ohio River to Indiana, but they were always caught and returned. When Diana and Dinnie were freed in 1864, they traveled to Indianapolis to view President Abraham Lincoln lying in state. Diana had been Mary Speed's personal slave when Lincoln had visited his friend Joshua, John's son, at Fry Speed's Farmington estate in 1841.

In 1870, Dinnie attended a Louisville public school for colored students. In 1913, she became the third-floor maid at the Neighborhood House at 428 S. First St., a settlement house, where she was employed until her death. There she befriended a young so-

cial worker named Elizabeth A. Wilson, who in 1974, 1978, and 1997 recounted to the *Louisville Courier-Journal* stories that Dinnie had told about her life. For many years, Dinnie Thompson was a member of the **Sisters of the Mysterious Ten,** a benevolent African American group organized in 1876 by the **United Brothers of Friendship.** She was an officer in the St. Mary chapter. Although her life appears to have been an ordinary one, in a larger sense she represented thousands of Kentucky African American women who after slavery persevered and triumphed in spite of horrendous obstacles.

Thompson never married. She lived for 54 years in a small cottage at 433 Roselane St. purchased in 1885 by her mother. Thompson is buried in Louisville's Eastern Cemetery.

Newspapers: *LCJ,* February 21, 1997; *LCJ,* May 13, 1997; *LCJ,* July 23, 1997.

Ottesen, Ann I. "A Reconstruction of the Activities and Outbuildings at Farmington, an Early Nineteenth Century Hemp Farm." *FCHQ* 59 (October 1985): 395–425.

—*Juanita White*

THOMPSON, LUCIA ELLEN MILLER (b. 1897, Paducah, KY; d. unknown, Chicago, IL), optometrist. Lucia Ellen Miller, the daughter of William and Grace (Story) Miller, was born in Paducah, KY, on October 23, 1897. Some sources list her first name as Lucy or Lucie. She received her bachelor's degree from West Kentucky Industrial College (later known as **West Kentucky Community and Technical College**) in Paducah in 1923. In 1929, she married Raymond Lee Thompson, a pharmacist.

In 1947, Thompson obtained her doctor of optometry degree from Monroe College of Optometry in Chicago, IL. For 10 years, she taught at West Kentucky Industrial College, and for 5 years, she taught adults at a private school. Thompson later became a very successful businesswoman and was a member of the Chicago Club of the National Association of Negro Business and Professional Women's Club, and the National Negro Business League. One of her business ventures included ownership of a club in Chicago called the Tuesday Two. She was also a member of the Baptist faith and a member of **Zeta Phi Beta Sorority Inc.**

Thompson and her husband operated Thompson Pharmacist Supplies Company in Chicago. In 1953, she was elected president of the National Association of Negro Business and Professional Women's Clubs and presided over its 20th-anniversary convention in Chicago in 1955.

Fleming, G. James, and Christian E. Burckel, eds. *Who's Who in Colored America.* 7th ed. *Supplement.* Yonkers-on-Hudson, NY: Christian E. Burckel & Associates, 1950.

Newspapers: "Ardent Club Worker," *Arkansas State Press* (Little Rock), May 1, 1953, 6; "Negro Business Women Organize $1,000,000 Finance Project," *Wichita Post Observer,* November 13, 1953, 12; "Dr. L. E. Thompson to Preside Over Conference," *Plaindealer* (Kansas City, KS), July 22, 1955, 1–2.

Wright, George C. *A History of Blacks in Kentucky.* Vol. 2, *In Pursuit of Equality, 1890–1980.* Frankfort: Kentucky Historical Society, 1992.

—*Sheila Pressley*

THOMPSON, ROBERT L. "BOB" (b. 1937, Louisville, KY; d. 1966, Rome, Italy), artist. Internationally recognized artist Robert L. "Bob" Thompson was born in Louisville, KY, on June 26, 1937. He was raised in Elizabethtown, KY, until age 13, when his father was killed in a car accident. The resulting trauma prompted him to move in with his older sister in Louisville. He attended Madison Junior High School and **Central High School** and, after graduating, enrolled in the premed program at Boston University in 1955. He decided to withdraw after his freshman year and returned to Louisville to study art on an Allen R. Hite Scholarship at the University of Louisville in 1957.

Thompson left Louisville for New York City after his first solo exhibition, *Arts in Louisville,* in 1958. His expressionist style, with an emphasis on the figurative as well as frequent allusions to classical art, resonated with his contemporary audience. In 1961, Thompson received a Walter Gutman Foundation Grant, which, combined with a John Hay Whitney Fellowship, allowed him to travel throughout Europe with his wife, Carol, for two years. In 1963, he returned to New York and participated in numerous solo and group exhibitions. Most notably, a 1965 solo exhibit at the Martha Jackson Gallery broke the influential gallery's attendance records. In November 1965, Thompson and his wife moved to Rome, Italy. Thompson, a heroin addict, had to undergo gall bladder surgery in March 1966. Refusing to follow the doctor's request to relax after the surgery, he died of a lung hemorrhage on May 30, 1966.

Bob Thompson: Important Works in New York Collections, 1960–1966. Edited by Martha Jackson Gallery. New York: Graphica, 1968.
"Bob Thompson, 29, Dies; Artist Succumbs in Rome." *NYT,* June 8, 1966, 42.
Golden, Thelma. *Bob Thompson.* Berkeley: Whitney Museum of American Art in association with University of California Press, 1998.
King, Richard H. "The Enigma of Bob Thompson." In *The Hearing Eye: Jazz and Blues Influences in African American Visual Art,* edited by Graham Lock and David Murray, 134–45. Oxford: Oxford Univ. Press, 2009.
Perry, Regenia A. *Free within Ourselves: African-American Artists in the Collection of the National Museum of American Art.* Washington, DC: National Museum of American Art in association with Pomegranate Art Books, 1992. http://americanart.si.edu/collections/search/artist/?id=4784 (accessed July 27, 2012).

—*Elizabeth Schaller*

TIMBERLAKE, CLARENCE L. (b. 1885, Elizaville, KY; d. 1979, Madisonville, KY), educator. Clarence L. Timberlake, who worked to expand educational opportunities for black Kentuckians, was born in Fleming Co., KY, in 1885. Timberlake was a graduate of the agriculture program of Kentucky Normal and Industrial Institute (later known as **Kentucky State University**) in 1904. After graduation, he accepted a position as a messenger in Kentucky's Department of Education. In 1914, he wrote a pamphlet, "Politics and the Schools," to protest politicians' interference in the development of schools. He was one of the supporters of the law passed by the General Assembly requiring that regents who governed state schools be selected from the state at large rather than from the community in which they served.

Timberlake organized a four-year high school in Madisonville and teacher-training schools in Pembroke and Greenville, KY. In 1948, he became the fourth president of West Kentucky Vocational School for Negroes (later known as **West Kentucky Community and Technical College**) in Paducah, a position he held until his retirement in July 1957. He died in 1979.

Dawson, Osceola A. *The Timberlake Story.* Carbondale, IL: Dunway-Sinclair, Inc., 1959.

—*Gerald L. Smith*

TINSLEY, GEORGE WILLIAM, SR. (b. 1946, Louisville, KY), and TINSLEY, SERETHA SUMMERS (b. 1949, Louisville, KY), athletes, businesspeople, and community activists. George William Penebaker was born in **Smoketown,** a Louisville inner-city neighborhood. His mother abandoned him when he was seven months old to an elderly babysitter, Willie Tinsley. Tinsley was widowed, had one leg, used a crutch, and survived on a $65 monthly Social Security check. She adopted George but died when he was 13. He then moved in with her son.

Sports, particularly basketball, provided George Tinsley an outlet from poverty. He led Louisville's Male High School to the state basketball championship and later spearheaded three NCAA Division II championships (1966, 1968, and 1969) for Kentucky Wesleyan College in Owensboro, KY. Nicknamed the Hat, he was also selected All-American twice and was the leading rebounder at 1,115 while scoring 2,014 points. He was later inducted into several sports halls of fame, including the Kentucky Athletic Hall of Fame, and was voted Kentucky Wesleyan College's top player for its all-century team.

One of seven African Americans at Kentucky Wesleyan College, Tinsley met and later married the first African American female to attend and graduate from the college. Seretha Summers, also a Louisville native and a graduate of Male High School, was the daughter of William and Eleanor Summers. Very active in college, Summers was a cheerleader, class officer, Judicial Council member, and a member of the Pacesetters, a group that entertained at the college's sports events. Both Tinsley and Summers became the first African Americans selected to the Order of Oak and Ivy, the school's prestigious honor society.

After graduation in 1969, Tinsley played professional basketball for several teams, including the Kentucky Colonels, in the American Basketball Association (ABA) and retired in 1972. Summers had traveled to Africa in hopes of fulfilling a childhood dream of becoming a missionary. Instead, she married George that year. They taught at Male High School for a short time before George went to work for Kentucky Fried Chicken (KFC) and Seretha joined her father at his radio station, WLOU. In 1979, Seretha moved to Atlanta to become WAOK's station manager. A few months later, George transferred there with KFC. Seretha later joined WPDQ in Jacksonville, FL, as vice president and general manager, the first African American female general manager in radio.

In 1983, George and Seretha went into business for themselves after purchasing a KFC franchise in Auburndale, FL. Their company, PenGeo, was named for their children, Penni and George Jr.

They amassed numerous restaurants and concessions, including the first African American–owned T.G.I. Fridays.

Residing in Winter Haven, FL, George and Seretha received numerous awards for their contributions to the community. George coached and sponsored local sports teams while serving on various local boards. Seretha cofounded Chain of Lake Achievers to tutor and inspire youth leadership. She presided over the local chamber of commerce, served as coadviser of the Winter Haven **National Association for the Advancement of Colored People** Youth Council, and worked with the Girl Scouts and Girls Inc. In 2010, their alma mater, Kentucky Wesleyan College, presented them honorary doctorates.

George W. Tinsley, Sr. http://www.georgetinsleysr.com/ (accessed June 20, 2012).

Kirkpatrick, Curry. "Gabriel and Owensboro Blow Their Horns." *Sports Illustrated,* January 13, 1969. http://sportsillustrated.cnn .com/vault/article/magazine/MAG1081983/2/index.htm (accessed June 21, 2012).

"Local Finds Success Comes from Within." *Lakeland Ledger,* January 31, 1994, 1A, 9A.

Rutherman, Kathy. "George Tinsley '69: Success despite the Odds." *KW Today,* Fall 2009.

Tinsley and Family. http://www.tfcfamily.com/web2/ (accessed June 20, 2012).

—*Sallie L. Powell*

TONY SULLIVAN INCIDENT, event that sparked a racial uprising in the Lexington area in 1994. On the morning of October 25, 1994, police officers stormed an apartment at 726 Breckinridge St. in Lexington, KY. The officers were in pursuit of an 18-year-old African American named Antonio Orlando Sullivan, a suspect in a recent drive-by shooting investigation. One of the residents of the apartment directed police to a closet where Tony Sullivan was hiding. Five officers then surrounded the closet and demanded that he exit with his hands up. When he left the closet, he initially did so with his hands at his sides, but he raised them to shoulder level upon repeated demands from police. Now aware that Sullivan was unarmed, Police Sergeant Phil Vogel, a white man, attempted to lower the hammer on his Beretta 9-mm pistol manually, but it discharged and shot Sullivan in the forehead. Sullivan was transported to the University of Kentucky Hospital, where he died shortly thereafter.

Upon hearing the news of the shooting death of a black youth by a white police officer, over 100 black residents of the Bluegrass-Aspendale housing project, where the incident took place, gathered in the streets. In the afternoon, the gathering turned violent; several youths damaged police cars and threw rocks and bottles at officers, several reporters were assaulted in the streets, and gunshots were heard in the area. Members of the community also criticized local police for abuse and violent responses.

Later in the day, a group of 30 protesters detached from the main crowd and marched on city hall, but they left quickly after Police Chief Larry Walsh gave the locals details on the incident. An hour later, a much larger group gathered on the second floor of city hall and met with black community leaders. The crowd largely dispersed after the meeting, but for the next week, isolated incidents of violence related to the incident were reported in the city, and at least 15 people were treated for injuries.

In the days after the shooting, four different law-enforcement agencies began independent investigations, chief among them the FBI. Mayor Pam Miller called for a grand-jury investigation of the case. On January 30, 1995, the grand jury met to hear details of the case from 42 witnesses, including Vogel and Sullivan's girlfriend. Four days later, the jury chose not to indict Sergeant Vogel for his actions, declaring that they were "unable to conclude that an indictable offense was committed." Vogel immediately retired from the police force, precluding any attempts by city officials to take administrative action. On May 9 of the same year, the FBI also concluded that the shooting was accidental and therefore not prosecutable under the **Civil Rights Act.** In response, Mary Clark, the mother of Tony Sullivan, filed a lawsuit alleging negligence on the part of both Vogel and the city of Lexington, noting that Vogel's attempt to uncock his gun manually was against police procedure. In November 1996, the city settled the lawsuit by agreeing to pay Clark $500,000.

Newspapers: "City Searches for Answers," *LHL,* October 27, 1994, A1; "Killing of Teen Sets Off Rampage," *LHL,* October 26, 1994, A1; "Vogel Won't Face Charges in Shooting," *LHL,* May 9, 1995, A1.

—*Stephen Pickering*

TOOLS, ROBERT (b. 1942, Mobile, AL; d. 2001, Louisville, KY), recipient of the first self-contained artificial-heart transplant. Born on July 31, 1942, in Mobile, AL, Robert Tools graduated from high school in Tampa, FL. He worked as a technical librarian at US West Communications in Denver, CO, before moving to Franklin, KY, in 1996. Tools, who suffered from congestive heart failure, diabetes, and kidney disease, moved to Franklin in order to receive a heart transplant in Nashville, TN. However, his deteriorated physical condition prevented him from being eligible for the transplant. Instead, Dr. Joseph Fredi encouraged him to explore the possibility of participating in the Abio-Cor clinical trial of a new artificial heart at Jewish Hospital in Louisville, KY.

The self-contained artificial heart was successfully transplanted on July 2, 2001. Tools experienced several health problems after the transplant, including difficulty breathing and internal bleeding. Despite these complications, he was able to make several trips to local parks and restaurants, including a dinner with Louisville mayor Dave Armstrong. The surgeons who implanted the device, Dr. Laman Gray and Dr. Robert Dowling, were hopeful that Tools would be healthy enough to return to his home in Franklin, KY, in December. On November 11, he suffered a stroke. Tools steadily declined thereafter, and he died of internal bleeding and multisystem organ failure on December 1, 2001. He had lived with the AbioCor artificial heart for 151 days.

McKellar, Shelley. "Artificial Hearts: A Technological Fix More Monstrous Than Miraculous?" In *The Technological Fix: How People Use Technology to Create and Solve Problems,* edited by Lisa Rosner. New York: Routledge, 2004, 11–26.

Newspapers: "Southern KY Man Identified as Heart Patient Friend Lauds Recipient's Strong Will," *LHL,* August 21, 2001, A1; "Whir of Artificial Heart Gives Patient New Reason to Smile," *NYT,*

August 22, 2001, A1; "Heart Story Led Patient to Surgery," *KP*, August 24, 2001, 1K; "After Stroke, Artificial Heart Recipient on Ventilator—Doctors Confident Tools Will Recover," *LHL*, November 15, 2001, B1; "Recipient of AbioCor Heart Dies—Surgeons Cite Abdominal Bleeding and Longstanding Health Problems," *LHL*, December 1, 2001, A1.

—*Elizabeth Schaller*

TRAVIS, ONETH MORVIEW (b. 1894, Albany, KY; d. 1991, Pittsburgh, PA), businessman and educator.

Born on October 27, 1894, in Albany, Clinton Co., KY, Oneth Morview Travis was the son of Jacob and Nancy (Overstreet) Travis. The family moved to Monticello in 1914. After he graduated from **Lincoln Institute** two years later, he operated Jacob Travis and Son, a family dry goods business founded by his father, in Monticello. He obtained further education in business administration at La Salle University, Philadelphia, PA, in 1920.

In 1931, Travis purchased land in Monticello to consolidate all schools for African Americans into one grade and high school. The school was named Travis School in his honor. After purchasing a bus from the Wayne Taxi Company, he established the first school transportation system in Wayne Co. He was one of the leaders in the integration of public schools in Monticello and Wayne Co. On November 14, 1945, Kentucky governor Simeon S. Willis appointed him the first African American on the Kentucky Board of Education. He also served on the Board of Trustees of Wilberforce University.

Travis was a loyal and dedicated member of the Republican Party on the local, state and national levels. He was one of two African Americans named to the Republican Party State Central Committee in 1952, a delegate to Republican national conventions, chairman of the Executive Committee of Black Republicans of the Second Congressional District, and a member of the Electoral College for the 1972 presidential election. In 1986, Travis moved to Pittsburgh, PA, where he died of a heart attack at age 96 in 1991.

Newspapers: "Oneth M. Travis," *Pittsburgh Post-Gazette*, August 20, 1991, B4; "Oneth M. Travis," *Wayne County Outlook*, August 28, 1991.

Wayne County, Kentucky, Museum. http://www.waynecountyky museum.com.

Wright, Richard Robert, Jr. *Encyclopaedia of the African Methodist Episcopal Church.* 2nd ed. Philadelphia: Book Concern of the A.M.E. Church, 1947.

—*Andrew Baskin*

TRIBBLE, ANDREW (b. 1879, Richmond, KY; d. 1935), famous female impersonator and actor.

Born in Richmond, KY, in 1879, Andrew Tribble, son of Alice Tribble, began a career in theater at an early age, joining a pickaninny band with the Old Kentucky Company and traveling throughout the state in 1894. Tribble's career took off in 1906 after Robert Allen Cole and Billy Johnson, two African American composers and playwrights, saw one of his performances in Chicago in which he wore a dress. The two men signed him for a female role in their next production, *Shoo Fly Regiment.*

Tribble's slender physique and short stature, along with his skill as an actor and dancer, made him a natural for impersonat-

ing women on stage, and his performance as Ophelia Snow over three seasons received rave reviews. Cole and Johnson, noting his popularity in the role, cast him in *Red Moon* as Lily White, a washerwoman. Reactions to this performance were even more enthusiastic; the *Toledo News-Bee* declared him "one of the funniest persons who ever grouped himself behind a bunch of footlights." Tribble, frequently joined on stage by his wife, Bessie, continued to perform for several decades until his career was cut short by his death in 1935.

"Editorials." *Messenger: World's Greatest Negro Monthly* 7 (1925): 20–23.
Sampson, Henry T. *Blacks in Blackface: A Source Book on Early Black Musical Shows.* Metuchen, NJ: Scarecrow Press, 1980.
Seniors, Paula Marie. *Beyond "Lift Every Voice and Sing": The Culture of Uplift, Identity, and Politics in Black Musical Theater.* Columbus: Ohio State Univ. Press, 2009.
"This Very Frenchy Play May Shock New Yorkers." *Toledo (OH) News-Bee,* May 8, 1909, 6.

—*Stephen Pickering*

TUCKER, AMELIA (MOORE) (b. 1908, Alabama; d. 1987, Los Angeles, CA), legislator.

The wife of civil rights activist Bishop **C. Ewbank Tucker,** Rev. Amelia M. Tucker was the first African American woman to be elected to the Kentucky state legislature. She was educated at Alabama State Teachers College, Indiana State University, and the University of Louisville. As a Republican representative from the 42nd District, Tucker served from 1961 to 1963. She worked tirelessly for the integration of public facilities and supported the public-accommodations bill. Although the bill did not pass, the Enabling Act did, and, as a result, second- and third-class cities were granted the ability to pass public-accommodation acts of their own. Tucker was also a member of the Jefferson County Republican Executive Committee in the 1960s and 1970s, and in the early 1970s she sat on President Richard Nixon's advisory council on ethnic groups.

Tucker was a retired minister of Brown Temple A.M.E. Zion Church and was involved in the Interdenominational Ministerial Alliance. She was also a charter member of the Interdenominational Ministerial Wives Association and was active in the United Council of Church Women. She and her husband married in 1922 and had two children, Neville and Olivia.

Newspapers: *LD,* February 11, 1971; *Louisville Times,* February 13, 1987.

TUCKER, CHARLES EWBANK (b. 1896, Baltimore, MD; d. 1975, Louisville, KY), minister, lawyer, and civil rights activist.

On January 12, 1896, C. Ewbank Tucker, as he was known, was born to William and Elivia Tucker in Baltimore, MD. He completed his education at Beckford-Smith College in Spanishtown, Jamaica, before moving on to Philadelphia's Lincoln and Temple Universities, where he received degrees in 1917 and 1919. In 1922, he married **Amelia Moore Tucker,** who later served as an African Methodist Episcopal (A.M.E.) Zion minister and was the first African American woman elected to the Kentucky state legislature.

As a pastor in the A.M.E. Zion church, C. Ewbank Tucker led congregations in Pennsylvania, Alabama, Mississippi, Georgia,

Florida, and Indiana before coming to Louisville, KY, in 1929. After becoming presiding elder, he became a bishop and chairman of the national A.M.E. Zion Church's Board of Bishops. In 1964, he led the Sixth District, encompassing Kentucky, Georgia, West Tennessee, and Mississippi. He retired as a bishop in 1972.

Despite Tucker's considerable achievements within the A.M.E. Zion Church, his nearly four decades of civil rights activism earned him notoriety. After arriving in Louisville, he gained a reputation as a militant race lawyer, becoming one of the black community's most outspoken and controversial leaders. In 1931, while he was defending two African Americans, a white mob physically attacked him, and he narrowly escaped being lynched outside the courthouse in Elizabethtown, KY.

In 1935, Tucker and **Charles W. Anderson** ran as the Democratic and Republican candidates for state representative. Anderson defeated Tucker to become the first African American elected to the state legislature. Five years later, Tucker formed and served as president of the **Kentucky Bureau for Negro Affairs.** In 1953, he initiated a successful one-man sit-in to desegregate the Greyhound Bus Lines depot.

A onetime member of the **National Association for the Advancement of Colored People,** Tucker became one of the most consistent critics of what he saw as the NAACP's elitism and willingness to compromise. In 1954, he served as the lawyer for Carl and Anne Braden during their sedition trial and was the leading attorney for the Andrew Wade Defense Committee, formed to defend an African American accused of bombing his own home, purchased in a white neighborhood. In 1960, Tucker, along with the Bradens, was central in the establishment of a branch of the **Congress of Racial Equality** (CORE) in Louisville. Through its direct-action campaigns of pickets, sit-ins, and demonstrations, CORE proved essential in the effort to desegregate public accommodations in Louisville.

Until his death on December 25, 1975, Tucker served as a member of the Louisville–Jefferson County Human Relations Commission.

Adams, Luther. *Way Up North in Louisville: African American Migration in the Urban South, 1930–1970.* Chapel Hill: Univ. of North Carolina Press, 2010.

"C. Ewbank Tucker." In *The Encyclopedia of Louisville,* edited by John E. Kleber, 893–94. Lexington: Univ. Press of Kentucky, 2001.

Wright, George C. *A History of Blacks in Kentucky.* Vol. 2, *In Pursuit of Equality, 1890–1980.* Frankfort: Kentucky Historical Society, 1992.

—*Luther Adams*

TUSKEGEE AIRMEN, all-black air force unit in World War II. On January 16, 1941, the U.S. War Department announced the creation of a new fighter squadron in the air force that would consist entirely of African Americans and be based in Tuskegee, AL. This decision marked a reversal of previous discriminatory practices that barred African Americans from flying for the military. A little over a year after the initial decision was made, five black men received qualifications as military pilots from the "Tuskegee Experiment," beginning a process in which over 1,000 African Americans received certification as pilots. Known collectively as the Tuskegee Airmen, these pilots engaged in numerous successful combat missions in World War II and never lost a bomber to enemies in escort missions.

Several Kentuckians played a prominent role in the initial creation and development of the Tuskegee Airmen. Although reports of the exact number vary, over 10 of the original cadets listed Kentucky as their home state. The commander of training at Tuskegee Field, Noel Parrish, was a native of Versailles, KY, and although he was a white commanding officer, he earned the respect of black cadets for judging candidates on merit and mitigating previous administrations' policies on segregation. Many of the cadets had been students at the Coffee School of Aeronautics and had been taught by **Willa Brown Chappell**—the first African American woman to earn a commercial pilot's license—who was born in Glasgow, KY. Recruit James T. McCullin, who had been a student at Kentucky State College (later known as **Kentucky State University**) before joining the unit, was one of the first two black pilots to be killed in the war.

According to Tuskegee University, the following Tuskegee pilot graduates listed Kentucky as their home: Julius Calloway (Louisville), Milton Hall (Owensboro), Jose Elfalan (Prospect), John Harris (Richmond), John Sloan (Louisville), Thomas Smith (Lebanon), and Frank D. Walker (Richmond).

Godman Army Airfield, part of Ft. Knox in Hardin Co., KY, served as a training base for the 477th Bombardment Group, a unit developed later in the Tuskegee program. However, the field was ill suited for training bomber pilots because its runways were unable to accommodate the B-25Js flown by the 477th, and most members of the unit recognized that they were transferred there in order to avoid racial tensions in their initial deployment area of Detroit. Circumstances were only marginally better in Kentucky, where black officers were excluded from Ft. Knox's facilities. In 1945, the unit was again transferred, this time to Freeman Field in Indiana, but an organized demonstration against segregation at the base resulted in the arrest of 101 black officers, including Kentuckian **Roy M. Chappell.** The men were detained and held by an armed guard at Godman Field until the army chief of staff, Gen. George C. Marshall, ordered their release. The 477th never saw combat.

Although frequently marginalized and discriminated against while they were in service, the Tuskegee Airmen received several honors in the decades after their military careers. In May 2007, Congress bestowed on the entire Tuskegee Airmen program the Congressional Gold Medal; five surviving airmen from Kentucky attended the ceremony. Three months later, a 23-mile stretch of Interstate 75 in Fayette Co. was renamed the Tuskegee Airmen Memorial Trail, and in 2010, the trail was extended to cover the entire span of I-75 within Kentucky in honor of the men who served their country in the face of war abroad and intolerance at home.

Moye, J. Todd. *Freedom Flyers: The Tuskegee Airmen of World War II.* New York: Oxford Univ. Press, 2010.

Newspapers: "Kentuckians to Be Honored as Tuskegee Airmen," *LHL,* March 29, 2007, B1; "The Road to Glory—I-75 Stretch Honors Tuskegee Airmen," *LHL,* August 11, 2007, B3; "I-75 in Ky. Becomes Tuskegee Airmen Trail," *LHL,* July 17, 2010, A3.

Osur, Alan M. *Blacks in the Army Air Forces during World War II: The Problem of Race Relations.* Washington, DC: Office of Air Force History, 1977.

Sandler, Stanley. *Segregated Skies: All-Black Combat Squadrons of WWII*. Washington, DC: Smithsonian Institution Press, 1992.
Tuskegee University: Legacy of Fame: The Tuskegee Airmen. http://www.tuskegee.edu/about_us/legacy_of_fame/tuskegee_airmen.aspx (accessed July 29, 2014).

—*Stephen Pickering*

TWYMAN, LUSKA JOSEPH (b. 1913, Hiseville, KY; d. 1988, Glasgow, KY), educator and mayor. On May 19, 1913, Luska Joseph Twyman was born at Hiseville, Barren Co., KY, to Edward and Eliza Twyman. He was educated in the rural schools of Barren Co. and in the public schools of Indiana. He received degrees from Kentucky State College (later known as **Kentucky State University**) (AB), Indiana University (MS) and Simmons University (LLD) (later known as **Simmons College of Kentucky**). He began his teaching career at Oak Grove, one of two black common schools in Barren Co., and he also taught in the Glasgow school system for two years before serving in the Philippines in World War II.

After his return, Twyman became principal of the Glasgow Training School. In 1950, when it was renamed Ralph J. Bunche School, a building to house all 12 grades was constructed, and the school became the first state-accredited, 12-year program for African Americans. Twyman served as principal, teacher, and coach for over 25 years. His reputation and efforts toward integration resulted in the 10th, 11th, and 12th grades of Bunche School merging with Glasgow High School in 1963. In that same year, he became the first Barren Co. African American elected to office as a member of the Glasgow Common Council, later known as the Glasgow City Council. In 1968, he became mayor of Glasgow when the city council selected him to fill a vacancy created by the resignation of the incumbent. In 1969, he ran and was elected to a full term beginning in January 1970, carrying all districts. He served as Glasgow's mayor until 1986, becoming the first African American elected to a full term as mayor of a Kentucky city and the third African American to become a mayor in the United States. An overwhelming majority elected Twyman each time.

Twyman continued to be the first of his race to be a member or officer of many associations, including the Kentucky Education Association and U.S. Commission of Human Rights and the U.S. Commission of Agriculture. He was also a member of the **Kentucky Negro Educational Association,** chairman of the **Kentucky State University** (KSU) Board of Regents in 1980, and a trustee of both KSU and Simmons Bible College.

Twyman continued receiving recognition throughout his life for his civic, educational, and church leadership. Other honors include Outstanding Citizens Award, *Louisville Defender;* Outstanding Alumni Award, Kentucky State College; and Southern Educational Foundation fellow. He was also appointed a member of the Governor's Conference on Education, the State Police Commission, and the Governor's Task Force on Transportation, and was one of two minorities to serve on the State Comprehensive Council. He was involved in many areas of improvement in Glasgow, with particular focus on the youth of the area and on the expansion of housing, employment, and recreational opportunities for all.

Twyman died in Glasgow at age 74 on January 28, 1988. He was buried in Bear Wallow Baptist Church Cemetery in Hart Co. A Kentucky historical marker and the Luska J. Twyman Memorial Park posthumously honored him.

Dilley, Amber. "Twyman Was a Pioneer." *Glasgow (KY) Daily Times,* February 16, 2009. http://www.glasgowdailytimes.com/local/x211922496/Twyman-was-a-pioneer.
Ebony Success Library. Vol. 1, *1000 Successful Blacks.* Nashville: Southwestern Co., 1973.
Spradling, Mary Mace. *In Black and White.* Detroit: Gale Research, 1980.

—*Nancy Richey*

UNCLE TOM'S CABIN, antislavery novel. Harriet (Beecher) Stowe's fiery antislavery novel *Uncle Tom's Cabin*, published in 1852, is believed to have been influenced by what she had seen and heard of slavery in Kentucky. The Connecticut-born author had visited Kentucky while living in Cincinnati, where her father was president of Lane Theological Seminary; she married Calvin Stowe, then a professor at Lane, during her residence there.

Harriet Stowe explained in *A Key to Uncle Tom's Cabin* (1853) that many of her characters—slaves and others—were composites of people she had heard about or met. She noted that the slave **Josiah Henson,** who once lived on the Amos Riley plantation near Blackford Creek in northeastern Daviess Co., KY, and who later became a clergyman in Canada, was one of the inspirations for the character she called Uncle Tom. She is believed to have obtained most of her information about Henson from his 1849 autobiography. In 1833, Stowe visited the family of Col. Marshall Key in the town of Washington, in Mason Co., where she is believed to have seen slaves being sold in front of the Maysville courthouse and to have observed slave life at a nearby plantation.

Another Kentucky site from which Stowe may have drawn impressions for her novel is the Garrard Co. community of Paint Lick, where Revolutionary War veteran Gen. Thomas Kennedy and his son owned a large plantation and many slaves. **Lewis Clarke,** an escaped slave from Kentucky who was acquainted with Stowe and who was born near Paint Lick, implied in an 1846 narrative of his life that he had once belonged to the Kennedys. His description of people and events during his years as a Kentucky slave closely parallel those of Stowe's fictional character George Harris.

Johnston, Johanna. *Runaway to Heaven: The Story of Harriet Beecher Stowe.* Garden City, NY: Doubleday, 1963.

—*Byron Crawford*

UNDERGROUND RAILROAD, system to assist persons to escape from slavery. In 1998, the National Park Service defined the Underground Railroad as "the effort—sometimes spontaneous, sometimes highly organized—to assist persons held in bondage in North America to escape from slavery." Wilbur Siebert in his 1898 work described a trajectory of freedom seeking that employed a secretive network he defined as an "underground railroad." Both Siebert and National Park Service officials identified the early evidence pointing to the importance of Kentucky in telling this national freedom story, primarily because of the state's geographic location.

The Underground Railroad network began operating in the United States as early as 1786 in Delaware, Pennsylvania, and Maryland, commanded by a network of secret agents, conductors, and safe houses that by 1804 extended southwest. Kentucky's association with Underground Railroad history formed with its founding connection to Virginia and the creation of the North-west Territory. Although evidence is unclear on exactly when American media began referring to assisted slave escapes as an "Underground Railroad," Kentuckians are given credit for popularizing the term. Reportedly, this occurred when escaping slave **Tice Davids** fled slavery and Kentucky in 1831. During his escape, Davids vanished from sight, leaving his owner to speculate that he had taken an "underground road." Writers of the period stated that Davids received assistance crossing the Ohio River from abolitionists in eastern Indiana.

Ironically, in Kentucky, open acceptance of violence and political action against antislavery advocates, as well as resistance to personal liberty laws that permitted slave owners to free slaves at their own discretion, served to create pockets of resistance in the Ohio and Mississippi River valley borderlands. These decisions were destined to make Kentucky a well-traveled Underground Railroad escape route. The fact that successful slave escapes were occurring throughout Kentucky was evidenced in countless newspaper articles, diaries, and court cases emanating from every part of the state complaining of the continuous loss of slave property. To stem this alarming loss, slave owners found it necessary to form alliances to improve the security of their enslaved populations, particularly in areas bordering the "River Jordan"—the Ohio River. Riverboat captain Rick Rhodes wrote, "Some of the most fierce struggles and gunfights between slave catchers and those helping runaways were fought in Madison, Indiana," a city directly across the river from Trimble Co., a well-known Kentucky escape route.

Kentuckians were aware of and actively engaged in national social reform movements that advocated black liberation and an abolitionist agenda. Kentucky played an important role in all three national escape corridors. The presence of Kentucky as a successful escape destination is evidenced particularly within the nation's so-called "Western," "Central," and "Eastern" Underground Railroad escape corridors. **J. Blaine Hudson** documented 12 major exit points on the Kentucky Underground Railroad, extending from the mountains of eastern Kentucky to the Ohio/Mississippi River valley.

The Ohio River and the Appalachian Mountains served as the two most important geographic features that forced Kentuckians into a national saga of African American resistance and freedom seeking. The Ohio River divided American slavery from American freedom, stretching the length of Kentucky's western and northern borders from Paducah to Ashland. This expanse of river bordered the free states of Illinois, Indiana, and Ohio. Eastern Kentucky's Appalachian Mountain chain provided an important avenue of escape for freedom seekers from the Deep South. Stretching from the heart of American slavery to freedom above the Mason-Dixon line into Canada, the Appalachian Mountains were a part of the nation's Eastern escape corridor encompassing the southeastern United States. Quaker and former North Carolina resident Levi Coffin, a relocated Cincinnati resident and Underground Railroad conductor, identified the Eastern escape route as a corridor he employed to aid slave escapes into Indiana and Cincinnati. The slave narrative of **Josiah Henson** (one of the inspirations for the character Uncle Tom in Harriet Beecher Stowe's *Uncle Tom's Cabin*) of Daviess Co. offers another example of an escaping Kentucky slave who benefited from Coffin's network of aided escape. Most African Americans who employed these escape routes made Canada their final destination; however, some remained in the region, well hidden in the mountains, where, after a change of clothes, names, and hairstyles, they created a new identity for themselves in one of the region's many isolated communities.

The Central escape corridor originated in the heart of the Deep South and extended through the entirety of Kentucky, other states, and Canada. The Western escape corridor proceeded up the Mississippi River valley through the Arkansas and Missouri Territories and into Iowa and Illinois, a route designed to aid southern slave escapes into Michigan and Canada skirting western Kentucky through Paducah as far north as Trimble Co. Kentucky formed the core of two of the nation's most heavily traveled escape routes, the Western and Central Underground Railroad corridors. Kentucky slave escapes were accomplished through a variety of creative and racially diverse networks that extended across cultural and religious boundaries of cooperation before the Civil War. Such an interwoven system was vitally necessary to create and sustain the large, geographically and culturally expansive network of assistance necessary to ensure success and black freedom.

Many noted leaders in Kentucky's Underground Railroad operations had formerly been enslaved African Americans who had taken or been granted their freedom. As free men and women, they worked to assist others. Kentucky Underground Railroad escapees who offered assistance to escaping slaves include **Lewis Hayden** and **William Wells Brown** of Fayette Co., and countless lesser-known freedom seekers. Kentucky served not only as an important pass-through state for escapees but also as home to many Kentucky communities actively engaged in organized resistance and systems of assisted escape. Those who participated in this illegal activity, such as Rev. John Gregg Fee in Madison, Lewis, and Bracken Counties, often did so as a demonstration of religious beliefs and a belief in universal freedom for all people.

After passage of the Fugitive Slave Law in 1850, southern slave escapes increased dramatically, and more slaves extended their search for freedom into Canada. In addition, Kentucky escape systems became more organized and more widely assisted over time through greater black participation and self-emancipation, as well as incidents of open rebellion. Kentucky counties with large numbers of enslaved African Americans in close proximity to free states made America's Western, Central, and Eastern Underground Railroad escape corridors the most highly traveled escape routes in the nation.

Buckmaster, Henrietta. *Let My People Go.* Columbia: Univ. of South Carolina Press, 1992.

Coffin, Levi, *Reminiscences of Levi Coffin, the Reputed President of the Underground Railroad.* Cincinnati: Robert Clarke Company, 1898.

Hudson, J. Blaine. *Fugitive Slaves and the Underground Railroad in the Kentucky Borderland.* Jefferson, NC: McFarland, 2002.

Rhodes, Rick. *The Ohio River in American History.* St. Petersburg, FL: Heron Island Guides, 2008.

Siebert, Wilbur. *The Underground Railroad from Slavery to Freedom.* New York: Macmillan, 1898.

Switala, William J. *Underground Railroad in Delaware, Maryland, and West Virginia.* Mechanicsburg, PA: Stackpole Books, 2004.

Tyler-McGraw, Marie, and Kira R. Badamo. *Underground Railroad Resources in the U.S. Theme Study,* September 2000. National Register of Historic Places Registration Form 10-900.

—*Alicestyne Turley*

UNDERWOOD, EDWARD ELLSWORTH (b. 1864, Mt. Pleasant, OH; d. 1942, Frankfort, KY), physician and minister.

On June 7, 1864, Edward Ellsworth Underwood was born in Mt. Pleasant, OH, to Rev. Johnson P. and Harriet (Clanton) Underwood. After he completed his studies in the segregated school, Underwood's family enrolled him in the white high school in Mt. Pleasant. His performance was outstanding, and he graduated in three years, third in his class in 1881.

After completing his high school education, Underwood taught in the Emerson Colored School in Ohio from 1881 to 1888. At age 19, he was licensed to preach in the African Methodist Episcopal (A.M.E.) Church. He followed in his father's footsteps and soon become a distinguished minister in the A.M.E. Church, which he served in many capacities over the years in Ohio and later in Kentucky, where he was a lay member of the Annual Conference and a lay delegate to the General Conference of the A.M.E. Church in 1920 and 1924.

Underwood began his medical career in Frankfort, KY, after completing his medical degree at Western Reserve University in Cleveland, OH. In Frankfort, he operated a very profitable private medical practice, which he was able to sustain from 1891 until his death in 1942.

Edward Elsworth Underwood, ca. 1930s.

In 1919, Underwood was one of the founders of the Frankfort **National Association for the Advancement of Colored People** branch and was elected its first president. He became an activist with the NAACP and the **Anti–Separate Coach Movement** (ASCM). Members of the ASCM worked to abolish the segregated railroad policy in Kentucky during the 1890s. In 1891, the black residents in Louisville, KY, became more politically active and launched the ASCM to challenge segregation laws by protesting a state law that mandated separate accommodations for blacks and whites on trains.

Underwood also served as Frankfort's assistant city physician from 1897 until 1900, the only African American appointed to the position. He was president of the State Medical Society of Kentucky and held memberships in the National Medical Association and the Kentucky Medical Association. He also worked as an editor for several newspapers, including the *Blue Grass Bugle* in Frankfort, and as the educational editor of the *Lexington News*. In addition, he was a member of many fraternal organizations, such as the **Freemasons** and the **United Brothers of Friendship.** Underwood was also politically active in the Republican Party and became the organizer and president of the Kentucky State League of Colored Republican Clubs.

Underwood died in Frankfort on May 31, 1942. He was interred in the Frankfort Cemetery. **Thomas K. Robb** Funeral Home handled the burial arrangements.

Kentucky, Death Records, 1852–1953.

Mjagkij, Nina. *Organizing Black America: An Encyclopedia of African American Associations.* Oxford, UK: Taylor & Francis, 2001.

Smith, Jessie Carney, ed. *Notable Black American Men.* Detroit: Gale Research, 1999.

Yenser, Thomas, ed. *Who's Who in Colored America, 1930–1932.* 3rd ed. Brooklyn, NY: Thomas Yenser, 1933.

—*Sheila Pressley*

UNION CYCLE CLUB (a.k.a. Afro-American Bicycle Club), African American bicycling organization in Louisville, KY. In September 1891, the Afro-American Bicycle Club of Louisville planned to provide an exhibition of three races at Daisy Line Park. Frederick "Fred" J. Scott, Robert Anderson, Dallas Pottinger, and C. B. Clay, the only African American tailor in Louisville, competed for the winning prize. The next year, "prominent" African American cyclists from Louisville formed the Union Cycle Club and elected Fred Scott president; James Fitzbutler, secretary; and Dallas Pottinger, treasurer. They presented "a fine show" to the public in a parade and challenged "any and all white cyclists" to race them in Louisville. According to the *Indianapolis Freeman,* Scott could match any cyclist in his weight category.

In February 1893, William Wagner Watts, a white Louisville attorney and chief counsel of the Kentucky division of the League of American Wheelmen (LAW), proposed an amendment to the LAW's constitution that would add the word "white." He bellowed to the assemblage, "Wipe out the nigger and we will give you many white members in his place." After two hours of heated debate and with only six African American riders in the LAW membership, the amendment was narrowly defeated.

The LAW appeared to accept African American wheelmen. In September 1893, its magazine, *Bicycling World,* covered, in nearly half a page with a drawing, John Pash, an African American native of Bardstown, KY, who had built his own bicycle from raw materials. However, it also included a letter from New York's Premier Cycle Company that warned retail bicycle distributors not to sell to African Americans, particularly African American women.

After losing a Louisville mayoral race, Watts again pushed the amendment when the LAW National Assembly met in Louisville in February 1894. He insisted that 5,000 southern men would join the organization if blacks were barred. He additionally read a supportive letter from Frederick J. Scott, the president of the Union Cycle Club. In the letter, Scott, as representative of the 25 members, expressed the belief that it was more important for the LAW to increase its membership in order to improve roads for all bicyclists. Some sources claimed that the Union Cycle Club was the largest African American club in the South and possibly in the country. A bicycle weekly reported Scott as saying, "We do not want to belong to an organization where we are not wanted." The LAW drew the color line with Watts's "white" amendment by a vote of 127 to 54. The Massachusetts delegates voted en bloc against it.

The African American community was outraged. The *Cleveland Gazette* called the bicycle organization "The League of *Prejudiced* Wheelmen" and the amendment un-American. The Riverside Cycle Club from Boston, MA, questioned the authenticity of Scott's letter. One Riverside member expressed the belief that Watts had bribed someone to write the letter. Another thought that Watts had written the letter himself.

However, according to one reporter who claimed to have interviewed Fred Scott, Scott wrote the letter after Watts visited him and explained the value of the amendment for increasing the organization's membership. Scott said that other African Americans had condemned him and that he had received a letter from Boston's Riverside Cycle Club, which he had not answered. He had no desire for notoriety and had spoken only as the representative of the Union Cycle Club, not of all African American cyclists.

Kentucky African American cyclists could then either compete in Kentucky **colored fairs** or travel outside the state. After this brief moment in the spotlight, the Union Cycle Club seemed to vanish. In 1900, Frederick J. Scott, age 40, worked as a porter in Louisville. Dallas Pottinger, a chef, died in Louisville in 1947.

Bearings: The Cycling Authority of America. "Leading Measures," February 24, 1893; "The National Assembly, February 23, 1894; "Negroes Are Indignant," March 9, 1894, n.p.

Bicycling World and L.A.W. Bulletin. "A Bicycle Built Out of Old Iron Scraps" and "A Protest from a Premier Company," September 22, 1893, 40, 75.

Newspapers: "Annual Conference," *IF,* September 12, 1891, 5; *IF,* July 30, 1892, 1; "Bicycle Race Riders," *NYT,* January 8, 1893, 3; *Cleveland Gazette,* February 24, 1894, 2.

—*Sallie L. Powell*

UNITED BROTHERS OF FRIENDSHIP, benevolent society formed in Louisville, KY. The United Brothers of Friendship

(UBF) originated as a benevolent order offering goodwill, support, and vigilance for free as well as enslaved men. The society's intent was to build and improve their conditions of living while pursuing a higher quality of life through acts of human kindness, generosity, Christianity, and friendship. Adopted as a network for aspiring blacks, the United Brothers of Friendship (UBF) was formed in Louisville, KY, at a private residence on August 1, 1861. Those duly recognized as the contributing founders include **Marshall W. Taylor,** Charles B. Morgan, William N. Hazelton, Wallace Jones, William H. Lawson, Charles Coats, William Anderson, and Benjamin Carter.

Two years after its inception, membership had grown tremendously. However, the Civil War's call for soldiers drastically reduced the society's active membership, but those who remained continued to minister to the sick and exchanged letters with soldiers. After the war, expansion and renewal gave way to many changes, including a new name: the Grand Lodge of the United Brothers of Friendship. On February 7, 1868, the Kentucky legislature granted the organization its first charter, constituting its rights and privileges as a corporate and legal entity. In 1871, the order began successful operations under its charter when many benevolent societies throughout the nation united as one. On April 10, 1871, the Grand Lodge of the UBF held its first formal state convention at Louisville's **Quinn Chapel African Methodist Episcopal Church.** In 1876, the all-male organization established the Ladies Temple, which became the **Sisters of the Mysterious Ten,** consisting of the wives, sisters, and daughters of UBF members and other upstanding women who were willing to support the existing mission.

As a means to finance operation costs and offer aid to members' dependent families, the order organized and incorporated the State Mutual Aid Insurance Department. From 1880 to 1888, this arm of the UBF prospered. Often, the gains collected from the insurance policies outperformed the collection of membership dues. In July 1888, the installation of new officers for the management of the order's insurance program was confirmed in St. Louis, MO, in a special session. The mission of the program and its managers was to insure all UBF members.

Kentucky lodges varied in their community involvement. Twenty-five African American men organized a lodge in Columbia, Adair Co., KY, in 1910. In contrast, in the same year, Hopkinsville's lodge closed after its Gala Day, which included a parade, athletic games, and music. A year later, the Illinois Central Railroad promoted a discount fare for the UBF's golden jubilee in Louisville. In 1912, in Hopkins Co., Earlington's lodge members placed an advertisement in the local newspaper inviting everyone to their 19th anniversary to hear speeches from such dignitaries as **Professor J. W. Bell** and to enjoy fun at the skating rink. Some lodges, like the one in Maysville, Mason Co., participated in **Emancipation Day** celebrations.

Staying true to its humble beginnings of benevolence and improvement of African Americans lives through supplication, education, and training remained the UBF's cornerstone throughout its existence. Scholar Anne S. Butler noted of the organization's collapse that its cemeteries were "the only tangible remnants of the ideals and existence of this fraternal order."

Brown, Tamara L., Gregory S. Parks, and Clarenda M. Phillips. *African American Fraternities and Sororities: The Legacy and the Vision.* Lexington: Univ. Press of Kentucky, 2005.

Gibson, W. H., Sr. *History of the United Brothers of Friendship and Sisters of the Mysterious Ten: In Two Parts, a Negro Order.* Louisville, KY: Bradley & Gilbert Co., 1897.

Newspapers: *Adair County News* (Columbia, KY), July 20, 1910, 1; "Grand Lodge Has Closed," *HK,* August 13, 1910, 5; "Golden Jubilee: United Brothers of Friendship and Sisters of Mysterious Ten," *HK,* July 29, 1911, 6; "Notice!," *Earlington (KY) Bee,* August 13, 1912, 4; "Our Colored Citizens," *Daily Public Ledger* (Maysville, KY), September 10, 1915, 4.

United Brothers of Friendship Collection. Special Collections and Archives, Paul G. Blazer Library, Kentucky State Univ., Frankfort.

—Dantrea Hampton

UNSELD, WESTLEY "WES" (b. 1946, Louisville, KY), collegiate and professional basketball player. Westley "Wes" Sissel Unseld was born in Louisville, KY, to Charles and Cornelia Unseld on March 14, 1946. He was one of nine children. Unseld's parents instilled a sense of a work ethic and the value of education in his mind at a young age. He was also a standout basketball player at the center position. During his secondary education, he led Seneca High School to two back-to-back state championships in 1963–1964. After high school, Unseld opted to go to the University of Louisville to further his academic and basketball interests.

From 1966 to 1968 (freshman were not allowed to play varsity sports during his tenure), Unseld averaged 20.6 points and 18.9 rebounds per game and was honored with selection as an All-American in his senior year, 1967–1968. After college, he was selected second overall in the National Basketball Association (NBA) college draft by the Baltimore Bullets. Listed at 6-feet-6 (considered undersized for the forward/center position), Unseld excelled through his superb basketball intellect and the proper use of his powerful 245-pound frame.

During his rookie year in the NBA, Unseld averaged 13.8 points and 18.2 rebounds a game and earned both the Rookie of the Year and the Most Valuable Player awards. The only other player to accomplish that feat was Wilt Chamberlain. When Unseld retired from the NBA in 1980, he left professional basketball as a five-time all-star and the captain of the 1977–1978 Baltimore Bullets team that won the NBA championship. In 1988, he was elected to the Naismith Memorial Basketball Hall of Fame and was named a member of the NBA 50th Anniversary All-Time Team.

After his playing career ended, Unseld accepted a position as executive vice president of basketball operations with the Washington Bullets and as a broadcaster for the team. In 1988, he was appointed head coach of the team and held that position until 1994. He served on the Board of Trustees of Baltimore's St. Mary's College and as head of Capital Center Charities in Washington. He and his wife, Constance, operate Unseld School, a private school in Baltimore, MD, whose enrollment includes students from infancy through eighth grade. It is the only accredited school in the nation with this diverse student population.

"Boys Past Winners." March 27, 2009. http://www.khsaa.org/records/basketball/boyspastwinners.pdf (accessed January 25, 2010).

"Eye on the Entrepreneur—Silver Anniversary for Unseld's School." *Baltimore Daily Record,* February 27, 2004, 1–3. http://findarticles.com/p/articles/mi_qn4183 (accessed January 22, 2010).
Kleber, John E., ed. *The Kentucky Encyclopedia.* Lexington: Univ. Press of Kentucky, 1992, 914.
"Wes Unseld Summary." 2010. http://www.nba.com/history/players/unseld_summary.html (accessed January 25, 2010).

—*Vincent Gonzalez*

UTTINGERTOWN, African American hamlet in Fayette Co., KY. In 1869, Samuel L. Uttinger, a 22-year-old white landowner in eastern Fayette Co., KY, divided his property and sold two-acre lots for about $100 per acre to freed slaves. The community was named for him. He later reportedly disappeared and was declared dead. However, the U.S. federal census in 1880 listed Sam Uttinger, age 31, as working on a farm in nearby Briar Hill for James Darnaby and in 1900 as working as a farm laborer in Sni-A-Bar, MO.

Located about six miles from Lexington on Royster Rd., off U.S. Highway 60, Uttingertown was near another **African American hamlet,** Chilesburg, whose most famous citizen was jockey **James "Jimmy" Winkfield,** a **Kentucky Derby** winner. From 1917 to 1920, Uttingertown's children attended a two-teacher, two-room **Rosenwald School.** The school cost $3,406 and continued to stand into the twenty-first century. In addition to the school, one of the primary centers of the rural community was the Baptist Church. Uttingertown also has a cemetery.

In a 1972 survey of **African American hamlets** near Lexington, Uttingertown was among those communities whose heads of households did not work on nearby estates, indicating that individual farms were the primary source of income. These small neighborhoods, with their proximity to Lexington, provided property ownership, including housing, for African Americans. For over a decade, the Uttingertown Baptist Church connected with other vicinity churches for an annual interdenominational Christmas service.

In 2005, with the help of University of Kentucky students and faculty, the Union Benevolent Society Lodge No. 28 was completed as a historic preservation project. Founded by Bettie Howard, the Sisters Benevolent Club No. 1 had met regularly on the first Thursday of each month for a century. The members made quilts to sell and funded various ventures, including care for the sick and needy and pulpit furniture for the Uttingertown Baptist Church, and maintained a public restroom as a dignified facility for African Americans on S. Broadway in Lexington.

"Historical Communities near Lexington." http://www.uky.edu/~dolph/scraps/towns.html (accessed July 18, 2013).
Newspapers: "5 Churches to Celebrate Christ's Birth," *LHL,* December 13, 1980, B-1; "Women's Club Carries On as It Has since 1905," *LHL,* April 6, 2004, E1.
Rennick, Robert M. *Kentucky Place Names.* Lexington: Univ. Press of Kentucky, 1984.
Smith, Peter Craig. "Negro Hamlets and Gentlemen Farms: A Dichotomous Rural Settlement Patter in Kentucky's Bluegrass Region." PhD diss., Univ. of Kentucky, 1972.
Turley-Adams, Alicestyne. *Rosenwald Schools in Kentucky, 1917–1932.* Frankfort: Kentucky Heritage Council, 1997.
U.S. Federal Census (1860, 1880, 1900).

—*Sallie L. Powell*

V

VAN LOWE, THEDA HOSKINS (b. 1890, Kentucky; d. 1968, Lexington, KY), high school principal, club member, and community leader. Born on December 7, 1890, according to the 1900 U.S. federal census, Theodosia E. Hoskins, who went by the name of Theda, was the daughter of Charles Hoskins, a blacksmith, and Martha Hoskins, a teacher, and the family lived in Campbellsville, KY. In 1910, Theda and her mother taught school in Harrodsburg, KY. She first attended college at Simmons University (later known as **Simmons College of Kentucky**) and then graduated from Kentucky State Industrial College (now **Kentucky State University**) with a bachelor of arts degree in 1934. She continued her education by completing a master of arts degree from the University of Denver. Research has not located her marriage information.

Theda Van Lowe taught in various Kentucky schools for about 10 years. However, the majority of her career was at Lexington's **(Frederick) Douglass High School,** where she was principal for 32 years before she retired in 1961. She was an active participant in educational, social, and civic affairs within the Lexington community. She was a faithful member of three Lexington women's clubs: the Woman's Improvement Club, the Committee for Health Camp for Colored Children (secretary), and the Flower and Garden Club. Her community activism was demonstrated through her service on the Steering Committee for Integration in the Fayette Co. schools. She was always concerned for the youth of the community and provided her wisdom and support as a member of the board of the Child Guidance Clinic and as a member of the Lexington YWCA's Board of Directors. Van Lowe received a citation by the Lexington Chapter of the National Conference of Christians and Jews for her role in the community.

Van Lowe, a member of the First Church of Christ, Scientist, died at age 77 in 1968. Lexington's Lafayette High School honored her with a scholarship in her name.

Newspapers: "Ex-Douglass Principal, Mrs. Van Lowe, 77 Dies," *LHL,* April 8, 1968, 8; "Noted Educator Buried," *LD,* April 18, 1968, 1.
Smith, Lucy Harth, comp. and ed. *Pictorial Directory of the Kentucky Association of Colored Women.* Louisville: Kentucky Association of Colored Women, 1945.
Twenty-Ninth Annual Catalogue of the Kentucky Normal and Industrial Institute for Colored Persons, Frankfort. Frankfort: Kentucky Institute Press, 1916.
U.S. Federal Census (1900, 1910).
U.S. Social Security Death Index, 1935–Current

—*Kimberly Renee McDaniel*

VAN ZANDT, JOHN (b. 1791, Mason Co., KY; d. 1847, Hamilton Co., OH), abolitionist and minister. John Van Zandt, an abolitionist, a minister, and a plantation owner, was the son of a wealthy plantation owner. In the early 1800s, Van Zandt operated a large plantation in Boone Co. on which there were several slaves. As a result of his religious convictions, it became increasingly obvious to him that "slavery was a sin." He sold his plantation and moved to the "free state" of Ohio, freeing his slaves. Van Zandt became a Methodist minister in the Glendale, OH, area.

Van Zandt played a pivotal part in the **Underground Railroad,** harboring many runaway slaves. It has been suggested that the character John Van Trompe in Harriet Beecher Stowe's book ***Uncle Tom's Cabin*** is based on John Van Zandt. Stowe once took a female runaway slave to Van Zandt, who then delivered the slave to safety. On April 23, 1842, while driving his wagon just north of the Ohio River, Van Zandt spotted nine runaway slaves and gave them a ride. Slave-catchers eventually caught them with Van Zandt, and all but one, named Andrew, escaped. Salmon P. Chase, who later became chief justice of the U.S. Supreme Court, argued for Van Zandt that slavery was prohibited by the 1787 Northwest Ordinance on the Northwest Territory, part of which later became the state of Ohio. The case reached the U.S. Supreme Court (***Jones v. Van Zandt***), and Chase lost. In 1841, Van Zandt was expelled from the Methodist Church for lying about his slave-related activities.

Once a prominent figure, Van Zandt sacrificed all for what he believed were injustices to humanity. Shunned by society, he was also ruined financially by his efforts on behalf of runaway slaves. After the trial, his 11 children were sent to live with relatives throughout the United States. He died at age 56 and was buried in Wesleyan Cemetery in the Northside area of Cincinnati. His property was sold to pay the staggering debts incurred in the courts.

Newspapers: "Fugitive Slave Case Outlived Protagonists," *CE,* June 16, 2005, A12; "Hero of the Underground Railroad Honored," *CE,* June 16, 2005, A1.

Lexington, KY, Douglass High School principal Theda Van Lowe congratulates senior student Rupert Seals, who won the Lexington Chamber of Commerce public speaking contest for Lexington, Fayette Co., high school students in 1949.

VAUGHN, C. C. (b. 1846, Dinwiddie Co., VA; d. 1923, Russellville, KY), preacher and educator. C. C. Vaughn—his first name is given as either Charles or Cornelius—was born into slavery in Dinwiddie Co., VA, on December 27, 1846. His parents gained their freedom when their master, Theodoric H. Grigg, sold his plantation and moved his former slaves to Ohio. However, by the time Vaughn was 13 years old, both of his parents had died, leaving him an orphan. He worked on a farm during the summer and did his best to attend a distant segregated school in the winter, learning to write while he earned a living.

In 1864, Vaughn enlisted in the U.S. Army and joined the Colored Heavy Artillery. A year later, he was transferred to a different company with the rank of orderly sergeant, a position he held until he was mustered out of service in November 1865. He attended Liber College in Indiana for a short time before moving to Kentucky, where he taught school in Cynthiana and Richmond from 1869 to 1870. He also briefly attended **Berea College** before being expelled and excommunicated after being implicated in a fornication scandal.

Vaughn continued to teach before establishing a long-term career in Russellville, KY, where he was the principal of Russellville Male School for over 20 years. Having joined the Baptist Church in 1875, he was licensed to preach in Allensville, KY. He was ordained in Hopkinsville in 1877.

Vaughn also enjoyed some success in politics. While he was at Liber College, he delivered a well-received oration titled "The Colored Man's Right to the Ballot" and was elected chairman of the State Convention of Colored Men that was held in Louisville in 1884. On October 21, 1923, he died at age 76 and was buried in Maple Grove Cemetery in Russellville, KY.

Haley, James T. *Afro-American Encyclopaedia; or, The Thoughts, Doings, and Sayings of the Race.* Nashville: Haley and Florida, 1895.

Pegues, A. W. *Our Baptist Ministers and Schools.* Springfield, MA: Willey & Co., 1892.

Sears, Richard D. *A Utopian Experiment in Kentucky: Integration and Social Equality at Berea, 1866–1904.* Westport, CT: Greenwood Press, 1996.

—*Stephen Pickering*

VINEGAR, THEODORE ROOSEVELT "TEDDY" (b. 1909, Owen Co., KY; d. 2001, Cincinnati, OH), farmer and horse trainer and breeder. Teddy Vinegar, an African American farmer who raised and trained horses in Owen Co., KY, was the youngest son of a former slave whose family owned **Mountain Island** Farm in Kentucky. His parents were Cord and Charlotte Vinegar.

Vinegar was born on the 110-acre family property at Mountain Island, where he learned his farming skills from his father. Horses and farming were part of the family culture, and Vinegar worked with horses most of his life. In the 1930s, he started to race horses at Mountain Island. He also used the roots of plants to make medicines to cure various horse ailments. The family moved away from Mountain Island in the 1940s but continued to own and maintain the farm. Vinegar bought a 40-acre farm on Kentucky Route 330 in Owen Co., where he farmed and also raised horses. During World War II, Vinegar served in the U.S. Army with the 318th Engineering Combat Battalion.

In the 1950s, Vinegar bred a black-and-white gaited pinto stallion named Hillrise from a mostly Thoroughbred mare with just a splotch of white on her and a gaited stallion named Rooster. For 50 years, Vinegar bred for gait with the pinto stallion and his offspring, and these horses were prized all around Owen, Grant, and neighboring counties. They undoubtedly represented a major contribution to the Spotted Saddle horse breed, first made official in the 1980s; hence a pool of compactly built, pinto gaited horses was first bred in the northern Kentucky region. Today, many Spotted Saddle horses are part- or full-blooded Tennessee walking breeds. Vinegar preferred a smoother and less "hip-jiggling" gait than that of many modern Tennessee walkers, a gait more like that of the Plantation Walker.

Vinegar introduced an innovative farming technique, planting crops on hillsides in a way that would not cause erosion; he used only a horse and a plow in his farming. This technique was taught to agricultural students from the surrounding counties and at the University of Kentucky in Lexington.

Teddy Vinegar died in 2001 at the Veterans Administration Medical Center in Cincinnati and was buried in the Newby-Vinegar Family Cemetery at New Columbus in Owen Co., KY.

Newspapers: "Land Given to Freed Slave Ties Grandson to His Past," *LHL,* March 1, 1992, 10–13; "Volunteers Unearth Remnants of Civil War Community," *KP,* November 18, 1998, 1KK; "Kentucky Obituaries," *CE,* August 9, 2001, B2.

—*Theodore H. H. Harris*

Wade, Helen Caise. Interview by Gerald Smith, July 13, 2009. History of Education in Kentucky Oral History Collection. Louie B. Nunn Center for Oral History, Univ. of Kentucky Libraries, Lexington.
—*Stephen Pickering*

WADE, HELEN CARY CAISE (b. 1939, Lexington, KY), first student to integrate schools in Lexington. Born on March 18, 1939, Helen Cary Caise Wade described her childhood as a pleasant one despite the constant presence of segregation in Lexington, KY. She attended all-black schools, including Chandler Normal School, (Paul Laurence) **Dunbar High School,** and **(Frederick) Douglass School,** and recalled not being allowed to enter several stores in the shopping district. Her stepfather, John Jacob Caise, made ends meet by working various construction jobs while her mother, Lucy Edna Cary, took care of the children.

In the summer of 1955, Wade decided that she would like to attend summer school. However, the unavailability of summer classes at any black school led her to inquire about attending all-white Lafayette High School. Wade—who admitted that she was unfamiliar with the recent **Brown v. Board of Education** decision at the time—received support from teachers at Douglass High School, as well as from her father. After receiving her request, Fayette Co. superintendent N. C. Turpen decided that "we have no grounds for excluding the girl, especially in view of the fact that there are no summer school facilities for colored students."

Despite receiving numerous threats against her and her family, Wade attended courses for the duration of the summer. She was taken to classes in a convoy of three cars, usually filled with around 10 armed relatives, and friends and family guarded her house from the numerous whites who drove by to harass the Caises. In school, Wade's classmates largely shunned her, although her teacher and a young Jewish classmate both treated her as they would any other student. Perhaps the most damage done was to her father's career when local businesses refused to offer him contracts; he was forced to move to Florence and travel to Lexington to see his family on weekends. Wade attempted to quit, but her father told her to continue so that she could help future generations.

Although Lexington schools formally desegregated in the following years, Wade returned to Douglass High School, where she graduated as valedictorian. After a miserable experience at the University of Kentucky in 1957 and 1958—she described it as "the worst experience of my life"—she attended Kentucky State College (later known as **Kentucky State University**) and eventually moved to Cleveland, OH, to work as a social studies teacher at John Adams High School. She retired after working for almost 30 years in the school system to work for a publishing company. In 2010, Wade was invited to tell her story to students at Rosa Parks Elementary School in Lexington, where she asserted that she did not regret her decision because it helped a new generation get an education "regardless of race, creed, or color."

Newspapers: "Douglass Student to Study at Lafayette," *LH,* June 7, 1955, 1; "Negro Girl Admitted," *NYT,* June 7, 1955, 13; "A Summer Class in '55 Cost More than Tuition," *LHL,* March 1, 1992, J1; "She Broke a Race Barrier," *LHL,* February 27, 2010, A3.

WADE-BRADEN AFFAIR, confrontation over housing discrimination in Louisville, KY. Just after midnight on June 27, 1954, a time of high racial tensions, an explosion ripped through the Louisville home of black electrician Andrew Wade IV. Since the 1940s, Louisville had integrated its libraries, city golf courses, amphitheaters, medical and car associations, civil service, police department, and university. However, rigid segregation still characterized the city's housing patterns.

Wade, a World War II veteran, wanted to move his family out of the **Jim Crow** urban area to a suburb but was unable to get anyone to sell him a house. He sought the help of two white acquaintances, Carl and Anne Braden. Carl Braden, a copy editor for the *Louisville Courier-Journal,* was an avowed socialist and trade unionist. Anne Braden was a writer, journalist, and civil rights activist who had returned to her native Louisville from Birmingham, AL, to work as a reporter for the *Louisville Times* in 1947. Being both native southerners and committed integrationists, the Bradens purchased a house on Rone Court (later Clyde Drive) in a previously all-white neighborhood just west of Shively and transferred the title to Wade.

When the Wades moved into the house in May, they immediately became, as they had expected, the victims of fierce harassment that included gunfire, burning crosses, and broken windows. On May 18, the day after the U.S. Supreme Court declared school segregation unconstitutional in **Brown v. Board of Education,** the *Courier-Journal* ran one editorial endorsing the court's decision and another castigating the Bradens and their attempts to "force the issue" of residential desegregation.

After the bombing of the Wades' house, the commonwealth's attorney, A. Scott Hamilton, developed a theory that the incident was part of a Communist plot hatched by the Bradens to arouse racial strife within the city. Nationally, the recent army-McCarthy hearings had undercut the credibility of unbridled anti-Communist emotions, but challenges to segregation gave anti-communism new life in the South. The Louisville case electrified the city. The Bradens, along with five others—Vernon Brown, I. O. Ford, Louise Gilbert, Lew Lubka, and Larue Spiker—were indicted for "criminal syndicalism and sedition" against the government of the United States and the Commonwealth of Kentucky.

Carl Braden was the only "conspirator" brought to trial as a test case for the state, which claimed that his Communist activities dated to early in 1947. No evidence was presented that linked Braden to the bombing, but surprise testimony by a supposed undercover FBI plant, a former family friend who could produce no proof of her employment by the government, told of Carl Braden's alleged Communist connections. The state also claimed that Braden had been involved in at least 27 Communist groups. The jury convicted Braden under a never-before-used 1920 sedition law and sentenced him to serve 15 years in prison and pay a $5,000 fine.

After serving seven months in the La Grange State Reformatory, Braden was released on bond. The Kentucky Court of Appeals overturned his conviction on June 22, 1956. The court followed the U.S. Supreme Court precedent in *Pennsylvania v. Nelson,* noting that the state did not have the right to prosecute a sedition case against the United States but could retry him for sedition against the commonwealth. In August, a judge dismissed the case against Braden. Three months later, all charges were dropped against everyone involved in the case.

The Bradens were charged with sedition a second time in 1967 when the Southern Conference Education Fund, an interracial South-wide organization seeking to bring white people into active participation in the **civil rights movement,** was helping people in Appalachia organize against strip mining. The Bradens won that case and were later successful in getting the Kentucky sedition law declared unconstitutional.

Andrew and Charlotte Wade and their children, however, were never able to return to their house because of financial losses and lingering neighborhood hostility. The actual bombers were never brought to justice.

Braden, Anne. *The Wall Between.* New York: Monthly Review 1958.
LCJ, December 11, 1954.
Thomas, Samuel W. *Louisville since the Twenties.* Louisville, KY: Courier Journal, 1978.

WALKER, FRANK X (b. 1961, Danville, KY), founder of the Affrilachian Poets. The second of 10 children, Frank Wesley Walker Jr. was born in Danville, KY, in 1961. A precocious child, he learned to read from magazines his mother brought home as he recuperated from an accident. During his attendance at Toliver Elementary, he also developed a love for the arts, supported by teachers who provided private lessons and art supplies. However, in high school, he was encouraged to focus on math and science, and he entered the University of Kentucky on an engineering scholarship in 1979.

After missing several classes because of hospital stays, Walker lost his scholarship at the end of his first year at the university. He decided to continue his education, working jobs on the side to pay for the few classes he could afford. As a form of therapy, he also began writing poems and plays, although he never shared them. Only after taking a course with Gurney Norman did Walker consider the arts as a possible career. He briefly contemplated working in journalism in Knoxville, TN, before returning

Frank X Walker, 1991.

to Lexington and accepting a position as the program director of the Martin Luther King Jr. Cultural Center in 1985.

By the end of the 1980s, Walker had assembled a small writing group that met at the center after it closed. Now writing under the name Frank X Walker—the X signified "the unknown"—he realized, after attending a lecture where **Nikky Finney** was flown in from California as the one black representative in a celebration of Kentucky writers, that black writers were not recognized in his home state. Further troubled after reading a definition of "Appalachian" that referred to "white residents from the mountains," Walker devised a new term, "Affrilachian," to give a name to the movement of black writers from the mountain region.

In 2000, Walker published *Affrilachia,* the first of several collections of poems. In addition to numerous published poems in various poems and journals, he also produced *Coal Black Voices,* a documentary on the Affrilachian poets, in 2001. His work has received numerous awards, including the $75,000 Lannan Literature Fellowship in Poetry, which he used to help establish *Pluck! The Journal of Affrilachian Arts and Culture* in 2007. Walker has published a variety of well-received books of poetry. Among them are two books of poetry on enslaved African explorer **York** in the Lewis and Clark expedition: *Buffalo Dance: The Journey of York* and *When Winter Come: The Ascension of York.* Another book of poems, *Isaac Murphy: I Dedicate This Ride,* focuses on the black jockey who won the **Kentucky Derby** in 1884, 1890, and 1891.

In addition to these extensive contributions in writing, Walker has also engaged in a lengthy teaching career. After receiving a master of fine arts in writing from Spalding University in 2003, he taught at the University of Louisville, Eastern Kentucky University, and Northern Kentucky University before finally returning to the University of Kentucky as an associate professor in English. He has served as director of the African American and Africana studies Program. Walker has honorary doctorates from the University of Kentucky and Transylvania University. He was the first African American named Kentucky poet laureate (2013–2014). In 2014 he received the NAACP Image Award for the category of Outstanding Literary Work in Poetry for his book *Turn Me Loose: The Unghosting of Medgar Evers.*

"The Frank X Walker Issue." *Iron Mountain Review* 25 (Spring 2009).
Newspapers: "EKU Hires Two Renowned Native Sons," *LHL,* April 20, 2004, A1; "Affrilachian Poets Mark 15th Year," *LHL,* June 30, 2006, B1; "The Journal Begins," *LHL,* March 11, 2007, E2.
Meehan, Mary. "Lexington Writer Frank X. Walker Named Kentucky Poet Laureate." http://www.kentucky.com/2013/02/14/2516910/lexington-writer-frank-x-walker.html (accessed August 18, 2014).
Walker, Frank X. Interview by Betsy Brinson, September 26 and October 3, 2001. Kentucky Writers Oral History Project, Louie B. Nunn Center for Oral History, Univ. of Kentucky Libraries, Lexington.
"What's in a Name?" The Affrilachian Poets. http://www.affrilachianpoets.org/history.html (accessed November 27, 2012).
—*Stephen Pickering*

WALKER, KENNETH "KENNY" (b. 1964, Roberta, GA), professional basketball player who won the 1989 NBA slam dunk competition. Born on August 18, 1964, in Roberta, GA, Kenneth

"Kenny" "Sky" Walker grew up outside the city with his father, Jerome, his mother, Ola Mae, and three brothers. He played basketball at Crawford County High School, where he was named Georgia's Player of the Year in his senior year and competed in two national all-star games.

Walker later played for the University of Kentucky and was chosen the Southeastern Conference Freshman of the Year. He was named a Second Team Associated Press All-American for the 1984–1985 season and made the First Team the following year. Altogether, Walker recorded 2,080 points in 132 games for the Kentucky Wildcats.

Walker was selected fifth in the 1986 National Basketball Association (NBA) draft by the New York Knicks. A six-feet-eight forward, he scored a career-high 826 points in his second season. He gained his greatest fame by winning the 1989 slam dunk championship but later suffered from knee problems and left the NBA to play in Spain and Italy. In 1993, he signed as a free agent with the Washington Bullets and played two seasons with the team before playing his final professional season in Japan. Walker scored 3,128 points in his 448 NBA games. After his basketball career ended, he hosted a radio show discussing the Kentucky Wildcats.

Howard-Cooper, Scott. "For Knicks' Walker, Slam Dunk Victory Occurs after a Loss." *Los Angeles Times,* February 12, 1989. http://articles.latimes.com/1989-02-12/sports/sp-3003_1_slam-dunk (accessed August 2, 2014).
Wheeler, Lonnie. "Kenny Walker's Career as a Sky King Advances by Leaps." *Miami News,* December 24, 1985.

—*Kevin Hogg*

WALKER, MELVIN WADDELL (b. 1909, Covington, KY; d. 1995, Cleveland, OH), Silver Star and Purple Heart recipient for service in World War II. War hero and educator Melvin W. Walker was born on April 13, 1909, the only child of John and Helen Walker. He was a graduate of William Grant High School (1929) and a classmate of Covington attorney **John W. Delaney Jr.** Walker graduated from Wilberforce College in Ohio with a BA in 1933. At Wilberforce, he took ROTC training. He later received a BS and an MA from Ohio State University in Columbus. Walker entered the U.S. Army as a lieutenant in March 1941, trained at Camp Benning, GA, and arrived in Italy as a member of the 366th Infantry Regiment, 92nd Infantry Division, in July 1944. In January 1945, Maj. Gen. Edward M. Almond, commanding officer of the 92nd Infantry Division, presented Walker the Silver Star for meritorious service. The award reads, "Lieutenant Walker took a raiding party across a canal, penetrating enemy lines, smashing installations, returning with German prisoners." Walker was wounded in action in Italy and received numerous other medals, including the Purple Heart. After World War II, he moved to Cleveland, OH, where he worked for the U.S. Veterans Administration and later taught in the Cleveland public school system. His teaching career as a mathematics teacher spanned 43 years, and he also did postgraduate work at Case Western Reserve University in Cleveland. Remaining in the Army Reserve, he obtained the rank of major. He often returned to Covington to visit his mother at the family residence on W. 15th St. At the age of 86, Walker died on January 19, 1995, in Cleveland and was buried there.

Newspapers: "Decorate 17 in 92nd Division," *Pittsburgh Courier,* January 13, 1945, 5; "Citations, Awards for Servicemen," *KTS,* January 19, 1945, 2; "Military Notes, Maj. Melvin W. Walker," *KTS,* July 23, 1956, 4A; "Melvin Walker, Cleveland Teacher," *Cleveland Plain Dealer,* December 29, 1995, 6; "Stories of African-Americans in WWII Went Untold," *KP,* February 28, 2002, 4K.

—*Theodore H. H. Harris*

WALKER, RENELDA ANN MEEKS HIGGINS (b. ca. 1950, Louisville, KY), activist, artist, and author. The only daughter of Eloise and Florian Meeks Jr., Renelda Ann Meeks spent her early life in Louisville, KY. In 1968, she graduated from Atherton High School and many years later was inducted into the school's hall of fame. As a student at the University of Louisville, Meeks participated in a sit-in at the school's Administration Building. She was arrested, lost her scholarship, and was forced to leave school.

In 1971, Meeks married photographer **Chester A. Higgins Jr.** in Tuskegee, AL. Both wrote articles for the *Crisis.* Chester became the editorial director, and Renelda, as the magazine's art director, illustrated some of the essays. The couple had two children. In 1983, she was appointed director of the Public Information Office at North General Hospital in Harlem. In 1994, she also worked for New York mayor Rudolph W. Giuliani as a deputy director of the Mayor's Community Assistance Unit in Manhattan.

Renelda married Benjamin J. Walker in the early 1990s. By 2009, she was senior associate director of public affairs for three hospitals in New York City. On July 6, 2012, the *New York Observer* reported the possible effect of the Affordable Care Act on one of Renelda's hospitals, the Lincoln Hospital. Its program, the Lincoln Art Exchange, allowed artists financial credit toward their health care when they volunteered at the hospital. Thirty-nine artists had enrolled in the program and had provided their creative skills to the hospital. Many of them planned to continue their work.

Harris, Robin R. "Sisters in Struggle: Women in the Civil Rights Movement, 1945–1975." *Owl,* March 2005. http://owl.library.louisville.edu/2005/owl0305.pdf (accessed July 9, 2008).
Newspapers: "Nataki Higgins, R. T. Montgomery," *NYT,* August 14, 1994, 52; "Adding to Success," *CJ,* April 15, 2009, A5; "After Affordable Care Act Upheld, Artists Pledge Loyalty to Community Healthcare Programs," *New York Observer,* July 6, 2012.
"Table of Contents." *Crisis* 88, no. 8 (October 1981): n.p.
"Transition." *Crisis* 90, no. 8 (October 1983): 36.

—*Sallie L. Powell*

WALKER, WILLIAM "BILLY" (b. 1860, Woodford Co., KY; d. 1933, Louisville, KY), jockey and horse trainer. Born into slavery on either John Harper's Nantura Farm or General Abe Buford's Bosque Bonita Farm near Versailles, KY, William "Billy" Walker began his jockey career at age 11 at New York's Jerome Park in 1871. He won his first race later that year in Lexington, KY. Walker was dubbed "the bravest jockey of them all" at age 15 and received a financial reward from Louisville Jockey Club

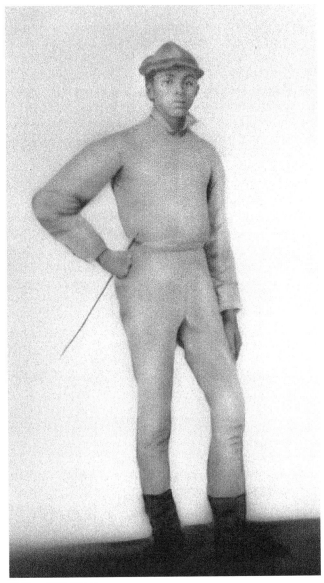

William "Billy" Walker.

president M. Lewis Clark after he barely escaped a disastrous fall when he and his horse were pushed against the railing in a Louisville race. Although his leg was badly bruised, he recovered to finish second in the competition.

Walker rode in the first and second **Kentucky Derby**s in 1875 and 1876, and in 1877, at age 17, he won on Baden Baden, trained by African American horse trainer **Edward Dudley Brown,** better known as "Brown Dick." The U.S. Congress adjourned that same year in order to watch him ride Ten Broeck in a race. Walker was named Churchill Downs' leading rider five times from 1875 to 1878.

Louisville Jockey Club president Clark later charged Walker with plans to throw a race and warned that he would be lynched if he did so. Walker tried to remove himself from the race, but Clark would not allow it. Onlookers disputed any plans of Walker to lose the race, and his large bet on his horse discredited Clark's claims.

Walker stated that he had taught the famous jockey **Isaac Murphy** some of the "rudiments of riding." Walker married his wife, Hannah, at Murphy's home in Lexington, KY, in 1891. He retired as a jockey in 1896 and became a respected Thoroughbred pedigree expert, advising horse breeders like John E. Madden, who had five Kentucky Derby winners. After Madden's death, Walker worked as a turf correspondent for several sporting papers. He also invested in real estate and attended 59 straight Kentucky Derbys. He was described as "one of the wealthiest African Americans in the state." In 1996, Walker's unmarked grave at Louisville Cemetery was awarded a headstone.

Hotaling, Edward. *The Great Black Jockeys: The Lives and Times of the Men Who Dominated America's First National Sport.* Rocklin, CA: Forum, 1999.

"Kentucky Derby: African Americans in the Kentucky Derby." Kentucky Derby. http://www.kentuckyderby.info/africanamerican-jockeys.php (accessed June 23, 2010).

Newspapers: "Colored Social Events," *LL,* June 10, 1891, 2; "Colored Jockey: Their Treatment in the States," *New Zealand Truth,* April 20, 1907, 2; "Veteran Derby Jockey Active in Turf Sport," *Sarasota Herald,* April 25, 1928, 3; "William Walker, Jockey Star of 70's, Dies at 73," *LCJ,* September 21, 1933, 15; "Passing of Negro Rider," *Daily Racing Forum* (Chicago), April 8, 1923, 1.

Renau, Lynn S. *Racing around Kentucky.* Louisville, KY: L. S. Renau, 1995.

—*Sallie L. Powell*

WALLS, MURRAY B. ATKINS (b. 1899, Indianapolis, IN; d. 1993, Louisville, KY), educator, organizational leader, and activist. Murray B. Atkins was born to Dr. Calvin R. Atkins, a native Kentuckian, and Dora Atkins in Indianapolis, IN, She studied at Butler University in Indiana, where she joined **Alpha Kappa Alpha Sorority, Inc.** After graduating in 1920, she began teaching high school and received a master's degree from Columbia University. In 1935, she married Dr. John H. Walls and moved to Louisville, where she volunteered at **Red Cross Hospital** and supervised tenant selection for the Louisville Housing Commission.

In 1940, Walls joined the Girl Scouts and played a critical role in establishing Kentucky's first **African American Girl Scout** troop. She was the first African American woman to serve on the Girl Scouts' Board of Directors and was an integral force in the Scouts' decision to desegregate its troops in 1954. While working with the Girl Scouts, she was also active in the **National Association for the Advancement of Colored People** and led the effort to desegregate Louisville's public libraries, beginning in 1941. Such a feat, she claimed, was nothing that happened overnight. Rather than taking on the entire library system, "we had to fight each one of them separately," so that desegregating Louisville's libraries took 11 years. The process was slow, she acknowledged, but "that was the way we had to work!"

In addition to this activism, Walls was appointed to Louisville mayor Bruce Hoblitzell's Civic-Religious Advisory Committee and joined the Louisville and Jefferson County Human Relations Commission. In each of her endeavors, her husband, also an activist, was by her side. Martin E. Pelrey, executive director of the Human Relations Commission, recognized both for their efforts, calling them "a couple who have together, dedicated and devoted their lives, talents, and activities to achieve harmony."

In September 1993, Walls died in Louisville, KY, and was buried in Crown Hill Cemetery in Indianapolis, IN.

U.S. Federal Census (1900).
Walls, John, and Murray A. Walls. Interview by Dwayne Cox, July 27, 1977. Univ. of Louisville Archives, tapes 398 and 399.

—*Dana Caldemeyer*

WALNUT STREET AFRICAN AMERICAN BUSINESSES, Louisville, KY, that housed a majority of the city's African American residents and businesses. "Old Walnut Street" has been described by locals as "a celebrated, colorful street," "a teeming avenue of commerce," "the heart and soul of the black community," and "a bustling microcosm of city life for blacks in a segregated society." This Walnut St. of legend extended westward from 6th St. to approximately 13th St. and included spillover developments along intersecting side streets. Its heyday was from the 1930s to the 1950s.

The roots of "old Walnut Street" are found in three slavery-time practices that gained prominence between 1830 and 1860 in most developing southern cities. The first practice was hiring out—permitting slaves to perform work for a fee whenever they were needed. As it became more common, slave owners soon found the practice of living out—whereby slaves did not have to return to their compound or enclosure each night—economically profitable. The burden of finding shelter was placed on the slave. Finally came board money, whereby slave owners actually made "payment to slaves of small sums in lieu of food and shelter" (Wade, *Slavery in the Cities*, 71). These situations amounted to quasi-freedom for many and, along with other factors, led to a nearly disintegrated system of slavery in southern cities by 1860.

Market forces soon began meeting the needs this created. First came rooms for rent and rooming houses, then boardinghouses, and eventually "eat" shops, sandwich shops, restaurants, cafés, and saloons. As slaves and free blacks intermingled and gradually became participants in the money economy, entrepreneurs, both white and black, took advantage of these business opportunities. Since strict segregation was the law, merchants and vendors catering nearly exclusively to "colored trade" began to appear. Although this activity was concentrated in urban perimeters, physical segregation was not the issue. Local authorities realized the importance of maintaining a residential racial mixture so as to prevent the buildup of a "cohesive" Negro society.

The first Louisville city directory, published in 1832, was organized alphabetically by last name and showed no racial designations for residents or businesses. In the 1841 city directory, the abbreviation "of col" was used to indicate businesses catering to African Americans. There were 41 businesses so listed out of a total of approximately 4,800 businesses. These businesses were distributed throughout the growing city, with no concentration in any one area.

Perhaps the first black business in the Walnut St. area was a boardinghouse in the 900 block operated by Martha A. Cozzens, who was described as "fwc" (free woman of color) in the 1860 city directory. In 1861, there was a "colored" barber at 10th and Walnut Sts., plus four other "colored" barbers in locations other than Walnut St.

In 1884, the first street listing was published. This allows a more precise analysis of Walnut St. from 6th St. to 13th St. It showed 51 "colored" residents interspersed among a total of approximately 254 residents and business owners. Under the "colored" designation for businesses, there were a church, a restaurant, two barbers, and a confectioner.

By 1900, Walnut St. black residents were showing near dominance in the blocks under review. There were 24 colored businesses in the area, including three each of barbers, restaurants, teamsters, and furnished rooming houses, plus another dozen assorted endeavors.

In the next 30 years, the number of colored businesses increased sixfold to reach 154 listings in the 1932 city directory. Notable during that period was the appearance of four insurance companies, three theaters, and two newspapers, along with a proliferation of doctors, dentists, and lawyers, all concentrated in the Walnut St. area.

The 1932 city directory was the last directory that contained a code to identify "colored" residents or businesses. The Walnut St. area survived the Great Depression and continued its growth during the early post–World War II years, which have been described as the "glory" years of old Walnut St. The variety of businesses increased. Important in the life of the street were the nightclubs, such as the Top Hat Tavern, which attracted nationally known musical entertainers, especially **jazz** performers. Young whites enjoyed hearing a type of music not presented in other parts of the city. Revelers came from across the nation, especially during **Kentucky Derby** time, to experience the Top Hat's exciting atmosphere and clientele.

In the 1950s, three significant events marked the beginning of the end of old Walnut St. First, the desegregation of stores, restaurants, theaters, and accommodations provided opportunities for colored citizens to spend their money in places where they previously could not. Second, white flight to new suburban housing developments and shopping malls began to decimate the former downtown area. Third, urban-renewal actions in the late 1960s demolished almost all buildings on Walnut St. between 6th St. and 13th St. and effectively eliminated the old Walnut St. area. In addition, the street has been renamed **Muhammad Ali** Blvd. Today, only two structures remain from the old Walnut St. era: the **Mammoth Life and Accident Insurance Company** building at 6th St. and the **Church of Our Merciful Savior** at 11th.

There have been efforts to preserve the memory of old Walnut St. In 1984, the Louisville Free Public Library presented a multimedia show that took a nostalgic look back at that vanished part of Louisville. Since 1985, the Kentucky Center for the Arts has produced an annual *Midnite Ramble* series—a re-creation of the revues that had added to the fame of old Walnut St. In 1997, a local civic organization launched a town-square renovation project to "rekindle that spirit of pride and entrepreneurship and . . . attract and redirect capital and business activity and disposable income back into the historic old Walnut St. area and western Louisville" (Louisville Central Communication Centers, *Vital Link*, Summer 1991, 2).

Coleman, Winston, Jr. *Slavery Times in Kentucky*. Chapel Hill: Univ. of North Carolina Press, 1940.

Mellon, James, ed. *Bullwhip Days: The Slaves Remember.* New York: Grove Press, 1988.

Tyler, Bruce M. *African-American Life in Louisville.* Charleston, SC: Arcadia Pub., 1998.

Wade, Richard C. *Slavery in the Cities: The South, 1820–1860.* New York: Oxford Univ. Press, 1964.

Weeden, H. C. *Weeden's History of the Colored People of Louisville.* Louisville, KY: H. C. Weeden 1897.

—Walter W. Hutchins

WALTERS, ALEXANDER (b. 1858, Bardstown, KY; d. 1917, New York City, NY), bishop of the A.M.E. Zion Church.

According to **Rufus Clement,** Alexander Walters was born in a room behind the kitchen of the Donohue Hotel in Bardstown, KY, on August 1, 1858. Clement also claimed that Walters was distantly related to Abraham Lincoln through his father, who was the son of his white master. At age eight, Walters began studying at the local church school, and he joined the A.M.E. Zion Church in 1870. In 1876, he moved to Indianapolis, IN, where he was licensed to preach by the Quarterly Conference of Blackford Street A.M.E. Zion Church in 1877.

Walters returned to Kentucky and worked in Corydon for two years before his ordination as deacon in St. Louis, MO, on July 8, 1879. In 1880, he was appointed to Cloverport, KY, and he was ordained an elder and stationed at Fifteenth Street Church in Louisville, KY, in 1882. Walters also spent time in San Francisco, CA, at the Stockton Street Church. In 1891, he received a DD from Livingstone College. In 1892, he became the youngest bishop of the AMEZ church elected in the United States. In 1889, he served as a delegate to the World's Sunday School Convention in London, England, and during his travel abroad, he also spent time preaching in continental Europe, Jerusalem, and Egypt. In 1898, he was appointed president of the Afro-American Council, and he spent 25 years as bishop of the New York and New England dioceses. Walters died at his home in New York City on February 1, 1917.

Anderson, James Harvey. *Biographical-Souvenir Volume of the 23rd Quadrennial Session of the General Conference of the African Methodist Episcopal Zion Church.* Philadelphia: African Methodist Episcopal Zion Church, 1908.

Clement, Rufus E. "Phylon Profile, VII: Alexander Walters." *Phylon* 7, no. 1 (1946): 15–19.

Hood, James Walker. *One Hundred Years of the African Methodist Episcopal Zion Church; or, The Centennial of African Methodism.* New York: A.M.E. Zion Book Concern, 1895.

Newspapers: "Bishop Alexander Walters," *Sun* (New York), February 3, 1917, 5; "Bishop Alexander Walters," *Sun* (New York), February 7, 1917, 7.

Quick, William Harvey. *Negro Stars in All Ages of the World.* Henderson, NC: D. E. Aycock, Printers, 1890.

—Elizabeth Schaller

WALTERS, ARTHUR M. (b. 1918, Magnolia, KY; d. 2010, Lexington, KY), Louisville Urban League executive director.

Born on November 6, 1918, Arthur M. Walters grew up on a 160-acre tobacco farm in Magnolia, KY. He split his time between working in the fields and earning an education, graduating as valedictorian from **Bond-Washington High School.** He then attended Kentucky State College (later known as **Kentucky State University**) before entering the army. He had a long and distinguished military career, serving for 20 years during both World War II and the Korean War in an engineering unit. He earned numerous decorations, including the Commendation Medal for Meritorious Service, the Bronze Star for Heroism, and the Soldier's Medal for Bravery, before retiring as a lieutenant colonel.

In 1963, Walters joined the **Louisville Urban League** as a staff member under Charles T. Steele, then executive director. He initially worked as a director of education and youth incentives. His more notable role, however, was as director of economic development and employment, where he tried to "open doors to some untraditional employment and find some persons who were qualified to enter those positions." He also began an on-the-job training program that was intended to provide job skills to underskilled individuals and encourage local companies to hire black workers. In 1970, he was named recipient of the Louisville Central Labor Council's Community Service Award for his "unheralded" behind-the-scenes work in creating job opportunities for the city's minorities.

In the same year, Walters became executive director of the Louisville Urban League. As director, he expanded services in the realms of education, adoption, and economic success. His accomplishments in the areas of training and job development were especially noteworthy. Programs he implemented accounted for nearly 5,000 persons trained annually for roughly 2,500 employers; his initiatives, according to one report, added $315,600 in local revenue. He also worked tirelessly to improve the Urban League's base of operations in Louisville, moving the headquarters to Lyles Mall in 1985.

The following year, Art Walters retired as executive director of the Louisville Urban League. On May 14, 1986, his service was recognized with a community celebration during Arthur Walters Day, where he was feted with a parade and recognized by federal, state, city, and county officials, including Senators Wendell Ford and Mitch McConnell and Governor Martha Layne Collins. On October 16, 2010, at age 91, Walters died in Lexington, KY, after struggling with a long illness. In his honor, the Louisville Urban League created the Arthur M. Walters Champion of Diversity Award, presented annually, and he was inducted into the Kentucky Civil Rights Hall of Fame in 2012.

Horton, John Benjamin. *Profiles of Contemporary Black Achievers of Kentucky.* Louisville: J. Benjamin Horton & Associates, 1982.

Newspapers: "Arthur Walters Receives Community Service Award," *LD,* January 29, 1970, A3; "City and Friends Honor LUL Director with Historic 'Art Walters Day,' " *LD,* May 21, 1987, 1; "Urban League President Reflects on 'Old Struggles, New Realities,' " *LD,* May 28, 1987, 1; "Former Louisville Urban League Director Arthur M. Walters Dies at 91," *LCJ,* October 18, 2010.

—Stephen Pickering

WARD, WILLIAM H. (b. unknown, Virginia; d. 1918, Louisville, KY), civil servant.

William H. Ward settled in Louisville in 1855. Known primarily for his more than 30 years of service as the chief custodian of city hall, Ward was also active in the Republican Party. His work meant that he was known to many political leaders. This might have generated his interest in politics.

He was the first African American member of the Louisville and Jefferson County Republican Committee. At the local Republican Party convention of 1870, he was among those nominated to run for the position of jailer but was defeated by John Mehringer. Ward made another unsuccessful bid for public office in 1878 when he ran for marshal of the city court. In 1890, he accompanied former mayor Charles D. Jacob on a trip around the world.

Weeden, H. C. *Weeden's History of the Colored People of Louisville.* Louisville, KY: H. C. Weeden, 1897.

WARDERS, JESSE PUCKETT (b. 1917, Russellville, KY; d. 1981, Louisville, KY), civil rights legislator. Born in Russellville, KY, Jesse Puckett Warders was raised by his mother, Perlina, and his stepfather, Frank Jackson. He attended Louisville's **Central High School** before joining the army during World War II. He served overseas as a 1st sergeant with the 600th Field Artillery Battalion and earned numerous awards and citations. Upon returning from his overseas tour of duty, he departed for Indiana University, where he received a BA in 1952 and an MS in 1966. He began his own business, Warders Real Estate and Insurance Agency, which he owned and operated for over 30 years. He also served as a director of the Plymouth Settlement House in Louisville.

On November 2, 1965, Warders was elected to the Kentucky House of Representatives from the 41st District. As a Republican and the only black member of the House, he encouraged bipartisan support for civil rights. He cosponsored a bill with Representative John Y. Brown Sr. that would promote open accommodations and end job discrimination in Kentucky in 1965. On January 17, 1966, Warders rose to give a speech in favor of the **Civil Rights Act of 1966,** noting, "It is wrong in modern America . . . that men should still have to rise to see that all men are treated equally." He later referred to this speech, which drew applause from his audience, as his finest hour. The bill passed the House of Representatives by a 76–12 vote and was approved by the Senate shortly thereafter. Warders then guided the passage of House Bill 475, which erased dead-letter discriminatory laws that Warders described as "an affront to Negro citizens."

Later in that same year, Warders resigned his seat to accept an appointment as the first black director of sanitation in the city of Louisville. He then became the district manager of the city's branch of the U.S. Census Bureau before joining the U.S. Small Business Administration office in 1971. He quickly earned an appointment as the area's deputy director of housing and urban development, which was at that time the highest federal office to be held by a black Kentuckian. By 1981, he referred to himself as "semi-retired," working with Mitch McConnell to increase local support for the Republican Party. In July of that year, he died of a heart attack at his mother's home in Louisville and was buried in Greenwood Cemetery. In 2001, he was elected to the Kentucky Civil Rights Hall of Fame.

Horton, John Benjamin. *Not without Struggle.* New York: Vantage Press, 1979.
———. *Profiles of Contemporary Black Achievers of Kentucky.* Louisville: J. Benjamin Horton & Associates, 1982.

Newspapers: "GOP Gets All Jefferson Senate Seats," *LCJ,* November 3, 1965, A3; "House Passes Rights Bill in Historic 76–12 Vote; Senate Approval Likely," *Louisville Times,* January 18, 1966, 1A; "Remove These Relics," *Washington (DC) Afro-American,* April 5, 1966, 4; "Black Political Leader Warders, Dead at 63," *LD,* July 9, 1981, 1.
—*Stephen Pickering*

WARING, MARY FITZBUTLER (b. 1869, Amherstburg, Ontario, Canada; d. 1958, Chicago, IL), leader in the National Association of Colored Women's Clubs. Daughter of Louisville, KY, physician **Henry Fitzbutler** and **Sarah Fitzbutler,** Mary Fitzbutler was born in Amherstburg, Ontario, on November 30, 1869. She moved to Louisville with her parents and attended public schools in the city. During high school, she assisted her father at the hospital he helped found. She began teaching in Louisville after graduating from the normal school and married Chicago native Frank Waring in Louisville in 1901. The couple moved to Chicago shortly thereafter.

Waring became involved in various women's clubs in Chicago. In 1913, she was elected secretary of the Illinois Federation of Colored Women's Clubs. That same year she was appointed chair of the National Association of Colored Women's Clubs (NACW) Department of Health and Hygiene. In this capacity, Waring wrote articles on public health issues and called for the inclusion of African American Red Cross nurses in World War I. In 1923, she graduated with a degree in medicine from National Medical College of Chicago. Waring was elected vice president-at-large of the NACW in 1930. This new leadership role required her to take up issues outside her interest in public health. For instance, she wrote a letter to President Franklin D. Roosevelt calling for the desegregation of railroad cars in 1933. She was elected president of the NACW that same year and served until 1937. Waring died in Chicago on December 3, 1958.

Lewis, Catherine, and J. Richard Lewis, eds. *Jim Crow America: A Documentary History.* Fayetteville: Univ. of Arkansas Press, 2009.
Smith, Jessie Carney, and Shirelle Phelps, eds. *Notable Black American Women.* Vol. 2. Detroit: Gale Research, 1996.
Wesley, Charles Harris. *The History of the National Association of Colored Women's Clubs: A Legacy of Service.* Washington, DC: National Association of Colored Women's Clubs, 1984.
—*Elizabeth Schaller*

WARLEY, WILLIAM (b. 1884, Louisville, KY; d. 1946, Louisville, KY), editor and civil rights activist. After graduating from Louisville's **Central High School** in 1902 and attending State Colored Baptist University University (later known as **Simmons College of Kentucky**) Law School, William Warley established a weekly newspaper, the *Louisville News,* in 1912. As advocates of racial justice, Warley, who was African American, and white Louisvillian Charles Buchanan, a real estate agent, set the stage for the overturn of the city's residential racial segregation law. The ordinance, passed in 1914, was designed to stop "the gradual influx of the negro into blocks or squares where none but whites reside." It forbade African Americans from occupying housing in any predominantly white block. Warley purchased from Buchanan a lot in the Portland neighborhood with the stated purpose of erecting a house in a predominantly white block. Buchanan then filed suit in Jefferson Circuit Court, charging that Warley had violated the law. The legislation was upheld by both the Jefferson Circuit Court (December 24, 1914) and the Kentucky Court of Appeals (June 18, 1915). The **National Association for the Advancement of Colored People** took the case to the U.S. Supreme Court. In a unanimous decision in ***Buchanan v. Warley***, the Supreme Court declared the ordinance unconstitutional because it interfered with property rights. However, racially restrictive covenants were placed in deeds, thus keeping residential segregation.

In 1926, Warley was fined $250 for editorial criticism of a Madisonville judge during the trial of two blacks for rape. For his activism, Warley lost his post office job and encountered other harassment.

Three weeks after surgery for an undisclosed illness, Warley died at Louisville General Hospital in 1946. He is buried in the Louisville Cemetery.

Newspapers: *Louisville Leader,* April 6, 1946; *LCJ,* September 25, 1961.
Wright, George C. *Life Behind a Veil: Blacks in Louisville, Kentucky, 1865–1930.* Baton Rouge: Louisiana State Univ. Press, 1985.

—*John A. Hardin*

WARNER, ANDREW JACKSON (b. 1850, Washington, KY; d. 1920, Charlotte, NC), A.M.E. Zion Church bishop.

Born on March 4, 1850, in Washington, KY, the son of a black freeman and a slave, Andrew Jackson Warner also grew up enslaved. He ran away to Ohio when he was 13 and enlisted in the army, becoming a sergeant by the end of the Civil War. Afterward, he attended Wilberforce College and worked in a law firm in Maysville, KY, before joining the ministry.

In 1877, Warner's preaching career began at Greenville, KY, where he stayed until 1880 and added more than 100 people to the church's membership. Over the next 30 years, he started or grew African Methodist Episcopal (A.M.E.) Zion churches at Little Rock, AR; Russellville, KY; St. Louis, MO; Knoxville, TN; Mobile and Birmingham, AL; and Charlotte, NC. His success in the South earned him the nickname Swamp Angel and helped him rise in the denomination. He became the first secretary of the denomination's church extension program in 1896.

Warner's ecclesiastical popularity even led to political endeavors; he ran for Congress in 1890 and for governor of Alabama in 1898. According to an estimate, more than 10,000 members joined A.M.E. Zion churches through his leadership. In 1908, Warner was consecrated bishop, and he was one of four A.M.E. Zion delegates at the Federal Council of Churches' founding meeting. He died of apoplexy in Charlotte, NC, on May 31, 1920.

Caldwell, A. B., ed. *History of the American Negro.* Vol. 4, *North Carolina Edition.* Atlanta: A. B. Caldwell, 1921.
Hood, James Walker. *One Hundred Years of the African Methodist Episcopal Zion Church; or, The Centennial of African Methodism.* New York: A.M.E. Zion Book Concern, 1895.
Mather, Frank Lincoln, ed. *Who's Who of the Colored Race: A General Biographical Dictionary of Men and Women of African Descent.* Vol. 1. Chicago: Memento Edition, 1915.

Walls, William J. *The African Methodist Episcopal Zion Church: Reality of the Black Church.* Charlotte, NC: A.M.E. Zion Publishing House, 1974.

—*David Lai*

WARREN, MARK EDWARD III (b. 1938, Harrodsburg, KY; d. 1999, Los Angeles, CA), producer and director.

Mark Edward Warren III was born in Harrodsburg, KY, on September 24, 1938. He spent six years in Toronto, Canada, as a producer and director with the Canadian Broadcasting Corporation. He left Canada for Hollywood in 1968.

In 1972, Warren became the first African American to win an Emmy Award for Outstanding Directorial Achievement for his direction of the series *Rowan & Martin's Laugh-In.* He also won the **National Association for the Advancement of Colored People**'s Image Award for Excellence in Directing for *The New Bill Cosby Show.* Other directorial accomplishments included *The Diahann Carroll Show, Burns and Schreiber Comedy Hour,* and episodes of *Barney Miller* and *The Dukes of Hazzard.* He directed several films, including *Come Back Charleston Blue* with Godfrey Cambridge. He and director/photographer Gordon Parks were the first African American directors to become members of the Directors Guild of America.

During his career, Warren worked with Flip Wilson, Robert Guillaume, **Muhammad Ali,** Dick Clark, Nancy Wilson, and many others. He was an instructor for the Directors Guild of America's Special Projects Workshops and Crossroads Academy. He was also an adjunct professor teaching a graduate course, Multi-camera Television Production, at the University of Southern California and continued to direct *The Apollo Theater Comedy Hour* until his death from cancer on January 15, 1999. He was survived by wife, Beryl, his mother, Mary, in Frankfort, KY, three children from a previous marriage, and step-great-grandchildren.

"Mark Edward Warren III." September 1, 2007. http://www.markedwardwarrenofficialwebsite.com/ (accessed September 5, 2008).
"Mark Warren, 60, TV and Film Director." *NYT,* January 25, 1999.

—*Amanda Hoover*

WASHINGTON, EDITH STUBBLEFIELD (b. 1948, Almo, KY), first African American woman elected president of the Construction Specifications Institute.

Although Edith Stubblefield was born in Almo, KY, she grew up in Toledo, OH, graduating from Scott High School in 1966. She went to Philander Smith College in Little Rock, AR, where she studied English from 1966 to 1970. Edith married Clarence Washington, who played for the Pittsburgh Steelers (1969–1971).

Washington attributes her interest in construction to childhood experiences with her grandfather, who was a carpenter. In the 1970s, while working in Alabama, she became interested in construction specifications writing. Through five years of on-the-job training and mentoring, she passed the Construction Specifications Institute (CSI) national certification examination. Washington has held numerous key positions in the construction industry for over 30 years. As a specifications writer, she develops construction specifications to accompany drawings for commercial, institutional, and industrial facilities.

She has worked on countless construction projects, including some in Japan, Mexico, and the Philippines. Her projects include hotels, schools, manufacturing facilities, hospitals, major retail establishments, athletic facilities, and airports. She is a member of the Owens Community College Engineering and Construction Advisory Committee and has taught specifications and contracts at Ohio community colleges and the University of Toledo's College of Engineering. She has owned and operated her own consulting firm, the Stubblefield Group, in Toledo since 1994.

In recognition of her contributions to continuing education in the design and construction industry, she was elevated to fellow of the CSI in 1997. She served for eight years on the CSI Board of Directors before becoming CSI's national president in 2003–2004. Edith Washington is the first African American woman president in the 60-year history of the Construction Specifications Institute, a nationwide organization with more than 17,000 members.

Deen, Lango. "Edith Washington: From Carpenter's Helper to Head of the CSI." January 5, 2004. http://www.blackengineer.com (accessed, July 10, 2013).
"Groundbreaking Women in Construction." January 1, 2006. http://www.pecklaw.com (accessed, July 12, 2013).
Mallegg, Kristin B., ed. Who's Who among African Americans. 22nd ed. Detroit: Gale Research, 2008, 1256.

—*Karen Cotton McDaniel*

WASHINGTON, FORD LEE "BUCK" (b. 1903, Louisville, KY; d. 1955, New York, NY), vaudeville and film entertainer. Born on October 16, 1903, in Louisville, KY, to Abe Washington, a musician, and Jennie Washington, Ford Lee "Buck" Washington began his musical career at an early age when he teamed up with fellow Louisville native **John William "Bubbles" Sublett.** The two formed a song and dance and comedy duo known as Buck and Bubbles, with Sublett displaying his innovative tap dancing while Washington accompanied him on the piano. In 1920, Washington lived with his mother, stepfather, older sister, and younger brother in Louisville.

The duo won numerous local talent contests before taking their act to the vaudeville circuit throughout the North and Northeast. In 1922, the pair played New York City's Palace Theatre, one of the nation's most famous vaudeville venues, and later in the decade broke color barriers by becoming the first African American entertainers to perform at Radio City Music Hall. They appeared in a number of Broadway shows, including *Porgy and Bess* and *Carmen Jones,* and later expanded into film with roles in movies such as *Varsity Show* (1937) and *A Song Is Born* (1943).

The artists also performed in England and Canada. While they were in Canada in 1952, Washington was arrested for illegal possession of marijuana. He was fined $200 and sentenced to six months in jail. Sublett and his wife were acquitted. The partnership then dissolved.

After a brief illness, Washington died on January 31, 1955, in New York City. He was interred in Cypress Hills Cemetery.

African American Registry. http://www.aaregistry.com/detail.php?id =707 (accessed October 12, 2008).
Newspapers: "New Yorker Jailed in Canada," *NYT,* October 29, 1952, 9; "Entertainer Wins Acquittal," *NYT,* November 6, 1952, 36; "Theatrical Whirl," *Washington (DC) Afro-American,* February 8, 1955, 5.
U.S. Federal Census (1910, 1920).

—*Rebecca J. Williams*

WASHINGTON STREET MISSIONARY BAPTIST CHURCH, Paducah, largest African American Baptist church in west Kentucky in the late nineteenth century. The founding members of Washington Street originally worshipped with the white congregation of First Baptist Church in Paducah. According to Deacon Robert Coleman, "The white slave owners brought their slaves to church and the numbers began to grow." As the number of black congregates attending the white church increased, they were allowed to organize their own separate body of worshippers. On the first Sunday of February 1855, the Rev. George Brent, pastor of First Baptist, led the organization of the new church in a small log cabin at its current location. Three years later, Rev. **George W. Dupee** became the pastor. Known as "Pappy Dupee," he had a reputation for the three foot long, two-inch

Washington Street Missionary Baptist Church.

hickory stick he had with him in the pulpit to convey his authority. Dupee pastored Washington Street for nearly forty years and baptized more than 3,000 people.

In 1893, the church constructed a Gothic style structure. A church fire led to the construction of the current sanctuary in 1969. The church has had 17 pastors during the course of its history. It is a multiracial and multicultural congregation that provides various ministries, which include a food pantry. As one senior member commented, "Washington Street is not what she once was, and not what she could be. But with your help and God's grace, she is constantly moving forward."

Bigham, Darrel E. *On Jordan's Banks: Emancipation and Its Aftermath in the Ohio River Valley.* Lexington: Univ. Press of Kentucky, 2006.
Kinsey, Angie. "Washington Street Missionary Baptist Church." *PS,* February 9, 2007. http://www.washingtonstreetbaptist.org/church-history/ (accessed August 18, 2014).

—*Gerald L. Smith*

WATKINS, LUEVENIA (b. 1934, Hopkinsville, KY; 1998, Madisonville, KY), first African American woman on the Hopkinsville City Council. A native of Hopkinsville, KY, Luevenia Watkins studied at **Booker T. Washington Elementary School** and Attucks High School before moving to Clarksville, TN, to attend Hughes Beauty College. Afterward, she returned home to Hopkinsville, where she worked as a **domestic worker** and raised nine children. Upset with negative images of the predominantly black neighborhood on Durrett Ave., she decided to become involved in local politics to promote economic development and combat a growing drug problem.

On July 7, 1987, Watkins became the first black woman on the Hopkinsville City Council when Mayor Tommy Gates appointed her to the position. She was elected to five consecutive full terms and held her job for over 10 years. While she was on the council, Watkins worked with the local neighborhood association to tackle persistent economic problems in her area by sponsoring job seminars and funding the Walnut Street Center, which provided activities for youths. She also helped launch the Hopkinsville Innercity Transition Squad, an organization designed to improve housing and fight crime.

Watkins received numerous awards for her work in the community, including the Pennyrile Allied Community Service Award, the Durrett Avenue Community Service Award, and the **National Association for the Advancement of Colored People**'s Magistrate Daniel Massie Award for NAACP Involvement above and beyond the Call of Duty. In addition to her duties as a member of the city council, she served as Democratic chairperson of her ward. She was named a member of the Honorable Order of the Kentucky Colonels.

In December 1997, Watkins became ill after attending the state football championship and was hospitalized with pneumonia a month later. On January 26, 1998, she died at the Regional Medical Center in Madisonville, KY. In honor of her service, Mayor Wally Bryan had flags on city property flown at half-mast in Hopkinsville.

Hawkins, Walter L. *African American Biographies: Profiles of 558 Current Men and Women.* Jefferson, NC: McFarland, 1992.

Newspapers: "City Council Gains 2 New Members," *KNE,* July 8, 1987, 1A; "Another Incumbent Files for Re-election," *KNE,* May 13, 1989, 15A; "Council Member Watkins Is Dead," *KNE,* January 27, 1998, 1A.

—*Stephen Pickering*

WATKINS, SIMON J. (b. 1868, Courtland, AL; d. 1948, Covington, KY), physician. Simon J. Watkins, the son of Anderson and Mary Watkins, was the first African American physician in Covington. He was a physician, a surgeon, and a dentist. Watkins attended Tennessee A&I State College and Meharry Medical College, both in Nashville, TN, receiving his degree in dentistry in 1888 and a degree in medicine in 1889. He served on the Meharry Medical College faculty until 1891. Later that year, he moved to Covington to begin his medical practice. He married a woman from Covington, Rosa A. Moore, on January 12, 1893. In 1894, Watkins's office was located at 429 Scott St. in Covington. Four years later he moved his office to 113 E. Ninth St. in Covington, where he maintained his practice until he retired in 1946. Watkins was appointed to the state Interracial Committee and was named a sanitary officer in Covington by the state medical board. In May 1912, he hosted the Kentucky Medical Association of Colored Physicians, Surgeons, Dentists, and Pharmacists at a meeting in Covington.

Watkins was a member of Lane Chapel Colored Methodist Episcopal (C.M.E.) Church. In March 1895, he gave the welcome talk to the Mt. Sterling District Conference of Colored Methodists meeting in Covington. He also served as a delegate to the Christian (Colored) Methodist Episcopal conference for three consecutive years. He was actively involved in the local Republican Party. Watkins died at his home in 1948 and was buried in Linden Grove Cemetery in Covington. His daughter, Anna Mae Jones, operated the C. E. Jones funeral home after the death of her husband, **Charles E. Jones.**

Dabney, Wendell P. *Cincinnati's Colored Citizens: Historical, Sociological and Biographical.* Cincinnati: Dabney, 1926.
Newspapers: "Colored Conference," *KP,* March 4, 1895, 5; "Colored Medical Men Meeting in Covington," *KP,* May 10, 1912, 11; "Historic Lane Chapel," *KP,* March 4, 1996, 4K.

—*Theodore H. H. Harris*

WATTS, BEVERLY L. (b. 1948, Nashville, TN), executive director of the Kentucky Commission on Human Rights. Beverly L. Watts, daughter of William and Evelyn Lindsley, was born in Nashville, TN, on February 4, 1948. She grew up in Tennessee and graduated with a degree in sociology from Tennessee State University in 1969. She earned a master's degree in sociology from Southern Illinois University in 1973. From 1972 to 1974, Watts worked for the Chicago Model Cities Program. She then worked for the U.S. Department of Health, Education, and Welfare for four years before securing a position as the regional director of the Civil Rights Division of the U.S. Department of Agriculture in 1978.

In 1992, Watts was chosen to be the executive director of the **Kentucky Commission on Human Rights.** She served in this capacity for 12 years. In 2000, Watts founded the Kentucky Civil Rights Hall of Fame. As executive director, she led a hate crimes commission within the state and established several awards and programs associated with Martin Luther King Jr. Day. She concurrently served as president of the International Association of Official Human Rights Agencies from 1999 to 2003. In that capacity, she had the opportunity to attend the 2001 United Nations World Conference against Racism, Racial Discrimination, Xenophobia, and Related Intolerance in South Africa. In 2003, she became the fifth recipient of the Martha Layne Collins Leadership Award.

Watts left the Kentucky Commission on Human Rights for a position as the first director of the National Fair Housing Training Academy in Washington, DC, in 2004. She was inducted into the Kentucky Civil Rights Hall of Fame in 2005. That same year, she also received the Louisville Metro Martin Luther King Jr. Freedom Award. She served as special adviser to the chair of the U.S. Equal Employment Opportunity Commission before being appointed executive director of the Tennessee Human Rights Commission in 2007. Watts was selected to join the National Neighbors Advisory Council in 2012.

Mallegg, Kristin B., ed. "Watts, Beverly L." In *Who's Who among African Americans*, 22nd ed., 1267. Detroit: Gale Research, 2008.

Newspapers: "How Rights Panel Chose Director Criticized," *LHL*, August 21, 1992, C1; "Human Rights Activists Honored," *KP*, July 30, 2005, K5; "People in Business," *Commercial Appeal* (Memphis, TN), April 11, 2012, C2.

Tennessee Human Rights Commission. "New Executive Director Appointed to the Tennessee Human Rights Commission." Press release, Nashville, July 2007.

—*Elizabeth Schaller*

WATTS, CATO (b. unknown; d. unknown), possibly Louisville's first African American resident. Cato Watts, traditionally Louisville's first African American resident, may have been among the group of first settlers who arrived with George Rogers Clark on May 27, 1778. Said to have been the slave of John Donne Sr., he would be unknown if he had not been accused of murdering his master. Other slaves may have accompanied their owners, but there is no way to tell. African Americans, as property, are all but invisible in early public records and private letters and journals. They appeared only in wills, in appraisals of estates, occasionally in letters, and in rare court appearances when they were accused of serious crimes.

The Jefferson County Court on July 26, 1786, examined Watts, who "pleaded that he had knocked Donne down, but not with the intention of killing him." Two witnesses, Benjamin Reeder and Thomas A. Winn, also appeared, but their testimony was not recorded, as was usual. Perhaps unsure of Watts's degree of guilt or its jurisdiction, the local court decided that he should be held without bail for trial before the higher Court of Oyer and Terminer in Danville in September. The prisoner was taken to Danville by guard George Dament. For this service, he was paid 300 pounds of tobacco, a frequent medium of exchange in early Kentucky.

There the paper trail ends. The records of the Danville court, which was discontinued when Kentucky was separated from Virginia in 1792, have vanished. Watts's fate is unknown. A mythical tale, often repeated, holds that he was hanged in Louisville on the south side of Jefferson St. between Sixth and Seventh.

This would have been the first hanging in Louisville and should have persisted in local lore, but it appears in no recollections of early settlers or in print until 1880. The same tale makes Watts the hero of the first Christmas in 1778 when he played his fiddle for the reels and jigs of the celebration. As with the hanging, there is no basis for this fanciful story. An unanswered question is why Watts had a last name, unusual among slaves. Did he take the name of a previous owner, or was he possibly a freeman?

Jefferson County Court Order Book 2, p. 20.
Jefferson County Court Order Book 3, p. 85.
LCJ, May 1, 1880.

—*George H. Yater*

WAYMAN INSTITUTE, private school in Harrodsburg, KY. In 1890, the Kentucky Conference of the African Methodist Episcopal (A.M.E.) Church founded Wayman Institute in honor of A.M.E. bishop Alexander Washington Wayman. As a denominational academy, it depended almost entirely on donations from the Kentucky Conference A.M.E churches, as well as minimal tuition from students. It had a limited staff of a male principal and two female teachers. According to one A.M.E. source, its instructional courses were "English, normal, academic, theological and industrial."

Wayman Institute was expected to fill a need for private education lacking in the area. During its existence from 1890 to 1919, 29 persons graduated from its courses of study. Its physical facilities consisted of 18.5 acres of land and four frame buildings. However, it competed for students with a local segregated public school with a seven-month term, a good teaching force, and a much larger attendance. When the school's trustees decided to close the school in 1919, the buildings and land were sold. Although the property was valued at $5,000, the proceeds from the sale were only $2,000; they given to Turner College of Tennessee.

Jones, Thomas Jesse. *Negro Education: A Study of the Private and Higher Schools for Colored People in the United States*. Vol. 2. Washington, DC: Government Printing Office, 1917, 278.

Wright, Richard Robert, Jr. *Encyclopaedia of the African Methodist Episcopal Church*. 2nd ed. Philadelphia: Book Concern of the A.M.E. Church, 1947, 525.

—*John A. Hardin*

WEAVER, SYLVESTER (b. 1896, Louisville, KY; d. 1960, Louisville, KY), blues guitarist and gospel singer. Sylvester Weaver was born in the **Smoketown** neighborhood of Louisville to Walter Weaver and Maria Cottrell. His recording career began in 1923 when he became the first **blues** guitarist to record. From 1923 to 1927, he made blues and gospel records and served as a talent scout, bringing singer **Helen Humes** and guitarist Walter Beasley to the attention of Okeh Records. His best-known recording is "Guitar Rag," which was made famous by Bob Wills and His Texas Playboys as "Steel Guitar Rag." Around 1928, he became the chauffeur for the family of Gertrude Lemon. He is buried in the Louisville Cemetery.

Garon, Paul, and Jim O'Neal. "Kentucky Blues: Part Two." *Living Blues* 52 (Spring 1982): 15–20.

Harris, Sheldon. *Blues Who's Who*. New York: Arlington House, 1979.

—*Brenda K. Bogert*

WEBB, WILLIAM (b. 1836, Georgia; d. unknown), abolitionist. Little is known about William Webb's early life. Webb was born a slave in Georgia and was taken by his master to Mississippi as a child. Upon his first master's death, he was separated from his family. He lived with several different masters, one of whom took him to Warren Co., KY. He returned to Mississippi shortly after, and it was there that he became involved in the abolitionist movement. In 1856, John C. Frémont's presidential campaign inspired him to look to "another Nation wishing for the slaves to be free."

Webb returned to Kentucky and worked to establish a line of communication between Mississippi and Kentucky. Through this communication network, he was able to transmit news to slaves throughout the South. He became a spy for the Union army at the outset of the Civil War. He was captured by slaveholders but escaped and traveled to Paducah, KY, in order to join the Union forces stationed there. He passed himself off as a Confederate prisoner and was able to escape to the North. He lived and worked throughout the Midwest before finally settling down with his wife, Maria, in Detroit, MI. Webb's life was primarily documented in his autobiographical narrative, *The History of William Webb, Composed by Himself,* which was transcribed by his wife and published in 1873.

Jeffrey, Julie Roy. *Abolitionists Remember: Antislavery Autobiographies and the Unfinished Work of Emancipation.* Chapel Hill: Univ. of North Carolina Press, 2008.

McCurry, Stephanie. *Confederate Reckoning: Power and Politics in the Civil War South.* Cambridge, MA: Harvard Univ. Press, 2010.

Ward, Andrew. *The Slaves' War: The Civil War in the Words of Former Slaves.* Boston: Houghton Mifflin, 2008.

Webb, William. *The Story of William Webb, Composed by Himself.* Detroit: Egbert Hoekstra, 1873. Documenting the American South, Univ. of North Carolina at Chapel Hill. http://docsouth.unc.edu/neh/webb/webb.html (accessed July 26, 2012).

—*Elizabeth Schaller*

WEBSTER, DELIA ANN (b. 1817, Vergennes, VT; d. 1876, Jeffersonville, IN), abolitionist. Delia Ann Webster, abolitionist, was born on December 17, 1817, in Vergennes, VT, the daughter of Benejah Webster. Educated at Vergennes Classical School, she became a teacher in the spring of 1835. In early 1843, Webster traveled with friends to Lexington, KY, where they remained to teach art. Prompted by several prominent Kentuckians, the three established the Lexington Female Academy.

On September 28, 1844, Webster accompanied abolitionist Calvin Fairbank to northern Kentucky. When they returned to Lexington two days later, they were arrested and charged with assisting three slaves to escape to Ohio. At her trial, Webster pleaded not guilty. The jury, many of whom were slaveholders, found Webster guilty, and she was sentenced to two years in the state penitentiary. Later, in the autobiographical *History of the Trial of Delia Webster* (1845), Webster wrote that Fairbank had left her in Millersburg, KY, while he continued to Ohio. She did not mention slaves or say what business Fairbank had in Ohio. Pardoned on February 24, 1845, despite the protests of many citizens, Webster returned to the Northeast and taught for several years in New York.

In 1854, with the financial help of northern abolitionists, Webster purchased a 600-acre farm in Trimble Co., KY, on the Ohio River. Her farm used the labor of freed blacks and operated as an **Underground Railroad** station for slaves seeking freedom in the North. After the disappearance of some slaves in the area in the spring of 1854, she fled to Madison, IN, to escape a warrant for her arrest. In her absence, her property was looted. In the fall of 1857, slaveholders successfully blocked Webster's attempts to secure a credit extension on her farm loan. The following year, Bostonians created the Webster Kentucky Farm Association, which helped save her property.

In August 1866, Webster, who remained unpopular after the war, was ordered to leave Kentucky, and in early November she lost $8,000 worth of property, including building materials for a school, in fires set by her opponents. Over time, arsonists destroyed 17 dwellings, 4 barns, and finally Webster's residence. Unable to pay her debts, and with the Webster Association defunct, she lost her farm in October 1869. Webster later taught school in Madison, IN. She died in 1876 in Jeffersonville, IN.

Runyon, Randolph. *Delia Webster and the Underground Railroad.* Lexington: Univ. Press of Kentucky, 1996.

WEEDEN, HENRY CLAY (b. 1862, La Grange, KY; d. 1937, Louisville, KY), author, educator, preacher, publisher, and editor. Henry Clay Weeden was born into slavery and was later educated in La Grange public schools and in Louisville, as well as in New Castle, KY, under Rev. **Elijah P. Marrs.** He worked and studied in Louisville under Dr. Stuart Robinson and Col. Bennett Young. Weeden became subeditor of the *Christian Index* and in 1881 became editor of *Zion's Banner,* a black religious newspaper. His editorials from the *Banner* were reprinted in the *New York Independent.* During the 1895 Grand Army of the Republic Encampment in Louisville, Weeden served as a special correspondent for the city's dailies. He was permitted access to all encampments and activities, both black and white.

A staunch Republican, Weeden was a member of the National Republican League of the United States. During the administration of President Benjamin Harrison (1889–1893), he held a high position in the postal service, the highest office of any black man in his district. He served as a delegate to the Republican National Convention for 10 years and was a member of the city and county committee for 8 years. In 1892, he was elected secretary of the Fifth-District Republican Convention, the first African American to hold the position.

In 1897, *Weeden's History of the Colored People of Louisville* appeared, giving recognition to many black ministers, educators, and political activists who had gone unrecognized for their work in improving the lives of the city's people of color, and to the institutions that were important in their lives. He noted in his introduction that he hoped that the pages would "inspire us that we may have a greater ambition to become more useful citizens." Weeden received praise for arousing the interest and pride of the colored people from such Louisville notables as Mayor George D. Todd. Although the material was sometimes sketchy and the facts often ambiguous, Weeden's book is a milestone in preserving local history of African Americans.

Weeden was socially active. He served as a secretary of the Louisville Cemetery Association, which organized the Louisville Cemetery, a cemetery on Poplar Level Rd. for African Americans. He earned a law degree later in life and was a trustee of Atkinson College in Madisonville, KY, and a 32nd-degree Mason. He was cofounder and served as president of the Mendelssohn Singing Association, which was formed in 1892 and filled many singing engagements. As a church worker, he was musical director and superintendent of the Sabbath schools of the Zion Church for 12 years.

In 1901, he married Anna Marshall Smith, a black Canadian whose grandparents had been active in the **Underground Railroad** in Ontario. After her death, she was recognized as a prominent black poet. They had three children and lived at 816 S. Hancock St. Weeden is buried in the Louisville Cemetery.

Dunnigan, Alice Allison, comp. and ed. *The Fascinating Story of Black Kentuckians: Their Heritage and Traditions.* Washington, DC: Associated Publishers, 1982.

Weeden, H. C. *Weeden's History of the Colored People of Louisville.* Louisville, KY: H. C. Weeden, 1897.

Wright, George C. "Blacks in Louisville, 1890–1930." PhD diss., Duke Univ., 1977.

WELLS, WILLIAM "DICKY" (b. 1907, Centerville, TN; d. 1985, New York, NY), jazz trombonist.

William "Dicky" Wells, son of George Washington and Florence Wells, was born in Centerville, TN. When he was 10 years old, his stepfather, Felix Murray, moved the family to Louisville, KY. Wells later joined **Bessie Lucas Allen**'s Sunday school band of the Booker T. Washington Community Center, where he began his musical career playing the baritone horn. After a fall caused him to break the horn, he played the trombone. He and some friends organized a seven-piece **jazz** band. The Sunday school band played in the daytime for county fairs, funerals, and parades. The jazz band played at night for dances. Wells credited Louisville as the place where he learned to play music as he felt it. By the time he was about 20, he had already traveled and played with various bands. In 1927, he moved to New York's Harlem "because they like to swing there."

After playing with numerous jazz artists, Wells joined Count Basie and his orchestra in 1938. He performed trombone solos in "Taxi War Dance" and "Dickie's Dream." In the mid-1940s, Basie fired Wells for excessive drinking but rehired him after he promised to control his use of alcohol. Wells also performed in Europe and led his own band with the release of the "Dicky Wells Blues." He never received much notoriety outside jazz circles for his exuberant, chancy style, which included "moans, wheezes and exclamations." Saxophonist Preston Love believed that "Mr. Bones," as he called him, would have destroyed famous white trombonist Tommy Dorsey if they had ever performed together.

In the 1960s, when musical engagements were harder to obtain, Wells went to work in the mail room of A. E. Ames and Company in New York City but still played music wherever he could. In 1976, he survived a brutal beating during a robbery. He recorded for the last time in 1981. Wells died of cancer in 1985, one year after his famous bandleader, Count Basie.

Love, Preston. *A Thousand Honey Creeks Later: My Life in Music from Basie to Motown.* Middletown, CT: Wesleyan Univ. Press, 1997.

Newspapers: "The Old Black Jazzmen: Where They Are Now," *NYT,* July 21, 1969, 38; "Dicky Wells at the West End," *NYT,* July 10, 1981, C22; "Dicky Wells, 78, Dies: Trombonist with Basie," *NYT,* November 14, 1985, B18.

Social Security Death Index.

Wells, Dicky, as told to Stanley Dance. *The Night People: Reminiscences of a Jazzman.* Boston: Crescendo, 1971.

—*Sallie L. Powell*

WENDELL, THOMAS TYLER (b. ca. 1877, Nashville, TN; d. 1953, Lexington, KY), pharmacist, physician, and psychiatrist.

Thomas Tyler Wendell, son of Alfred and Clara Wendell, was raised in a large family in Nashville, TN. Sources vary regarding his birth date. One early 1900s book noted that he was born on July 24, 1871. His World War I draft registration card listed his birth date as July 24, 1874; however, his death record chronicled his birth date as January 26, 1877. In 1886, Wendell's father died, but Wendell still managed to earn degrees in pharmacy and medicine from Nashville's Meharry Medical College. He was the school's pharmaceutical valedictorian in 1894.

Wendell then moved to Henderson, KY, to work as manager of the Citizens' Drug Company until Dr. **William Henry Ballard** offered him a position at his pharmacy in Lexington in 1898. A few years later, he practiced medicine at 314 W. Short St. and lived with his wife, Mary Alice, and their four children, John, Laura, Jennie, and Clara, at 335 E. Third St.

A leader in the community, Wendell participated in various organizations. In 1903, he was selected as grand marshal of the Knights of Pythias. Ten years later, he was elected president of the Medical Society of Negro Physicians, Pharmacists, and Dentists of Kentucky. He was involved in the effort to build Lexington's (Paul Laurence) **Dunbar High School** for African Americans in 1922. Three years later, he was elected grand master of Kentucky Colored Masons.

Wendell was a pioneer in the care of Kentucky's mentally ill. For 20 years, he worked to upgrade care for his African American patients at Lexington's Eastern State Hospital, the nation's second-oldest institution devoted to the treatment of mental disorders. To accomplish his objective, he was an advocate of new techniques, such as occupational therapy. Unfortunately, he died two years before Eastern State Hospital offered occupational therapy. He was also the resident psychiatrist. The Wendell Building at the hospital was named in his honor just a few months before his death.

Wendell died of apoplexy on October 6, 1953. He was interred in Lexington's all-black Greenwood Cemetery (later known as Cove Haven Cemetery). Decades later, he was featured in the **Kentucky Commission on Human Rights** Gallery of Great Black Kentuckians.

"Eastern State Hospital Project, Naming the Forgotten." http://kykinfolk.com/esh/index/htm (accessed July 16, 2013).

Gibson, J. W., and W. H. Crogman. *The Colored American from Slavery to Honorable Citizenship.* Naperville, IL: J. L. Nicholas & Co., 1902.

Kentucky Commission on Human Rights. "Great Black Kentuckians." http://www.kchr.ky.gov/about/gallerygreatblack.htm (accessed July 16, 2013).

Dr. T. T. Wendell in his office with his son, John.

Kentucky, Death Records, 1852–1953.

Newspapers: "Several Anniversaries," *IF,* February 10, 1894, 6; "Officers Chosen," *PS,* July 30, 1903, 5; "Kentucky Metropolis," *IF,* May 23, 1913, 1; "Dr. Wendell Heads Colored Masons," *LL,* August 6, 1925, 7; "Negro Building at Eastern to Be Named for Dr. Wendell," *LL,* March 2, 1953, 24.

U.S. City Directories, 1821–1989.

U.S. Federal Census (1910, 1920, 1930, 1940).

U.S. World War I Draft Registration Cards, 1917–1918.

—*Andrew Baskin*

WESLEY, CHARLES HARRIS (b. 1891, Louisville, KY; d. 1987, Washington, DC), distinguished educator, author, and minister. Born in Louisville, KY, Charles Harris Wesley, the son of Charles S. and Matilda Wesley, was a graduate of Fisk University. He received his master's degree from Yale University, and in 1925, he became the third African American to receive a doctorate from Harvard. A trained historian, Wesley published several books and articles. He taught history at Howard University in Washington, DC, and eventually became dean of the College of Liberal Arts and dean of the Graduate School. He worked closely with **Carter G. Woodson,** who founded the Association for the Study of Negro Life and History. Wesley became president of the association in 1950 and served in that position for 15 years before taking over as executive director, a position he held until 1972.

An ordained African Methodist Episcopal Church elder, Wesley served as pastor of the Ebenezer African Methodist Episcopal Church in Washington, DC, in 1918. He served as the president of two higher learning institutions in Ohio: Wilberforce University from 1942 to 1947 and Central State College of Education and Industrial Arts from 1947 to 1965. He was a member of Sigma Pi Phi and **Alpha Phi Alpha, Inc.** Fraternities, as well as the Prince Hall Masons. He wrote several widely acclaimed books, including *The History of Alpha Phi Alpha* and *Prince Hall: Life and Legacy.* Wesley received numerous awards throughout his lifetime. He died of pneumonia and cardiac arrest in Washington, DC, at the age of 95.

Barrett, Warrick L. "Park View, D.C.: A Great Place to Hang Your Hat." Historical Profile: Wesley (1891–1897). http://parkviewdc .com/2013/02/22/historical-profile (accessed August 5, 2013).

Dunnigan, Alice Allison, comp. and ed. *The Fascinating Story of Black Kentuckians: Their Heritage and Traditions.* Washington, DC: Associated Publishers, 1982.

Fleming, G. James, and Christian E. Burckel, eds. *Who's Who in Colored America.* 7th ed. *Supplement.* Yonkers-on-Hudson, NY: Christian E. Burckel & Associates, 1950.

"Wesley, Charles H. (1891–1897)." BlackPast.org. http://wwwblack pastorg/?q=aah/esley-charles-h-1891-1897 (accessed August 5, 2013).

—*Gerald L. Smith*

WEST, MILLARD (b. 1943, Lexington, KY), first African American Kentucky state trooper. Born in Lexington, KY, Millard West graduated from (Paul Laurence) **Dunbar High School.** In 1961, he won an all-state award as top male vocalist of popular tunes. He also attended Frankfort's Kentucky State College (later known as **Kentucky State University**), majoring in business administration. In 1962, West entered the U.S. Air Force for a four-year tour of duty.

The same year West entered the air force, Kentucky's Democratic governor, Bert T. Combs, appointed **Frank L. Stanley Sr.,** publisher of the *Louisville Defender,* to serve as consultant to the Kentucky Personnel Commission in an effort to promote the employment of more African Americans in state government positions. Nevertheless, according to James E. "Ted" Bassett III, the director of the Kentucky State Police (1963–1967), it was Governor

Edward T. "Ned" Breathitt Jr. who spurred the move to hire African Americans into the state police ranks in early 1967.

After West left the air force and was deciding on a career choice, he read an employment ad in the *Louisville Defender* for state troopers. He asked the agency whether it hired African Americans and was told that it did. On September 18, 1967, West entered the State Police Academy. He was the sole black trooper cadet. He was surprised that there were no other African Americans on the force and later stated that if he had known that he would be the only black officer, he "probably never would have applied."

On January 26, 1968, Governor Louie B. Nunn inducted 39 state troopers, including Millard West, age 25. Nunn specifically warned West that he had an added responsibility as the first African American state police officer and should conduct himself accordingly. Nunn also claimed that there soon would be other black state troopers.

West reported for duty the following Monday morning at Post Four in Elizabethtown, KY. He worked for four weeks with an experienced officer before traveling alone. He covered eight counties: Hardin, Jefferson, Grayson, Breckinridge, Meade, Bullitt, Nelson, and Larue. On June 26, 1972, West left the force "because of personal reasons."

Bassett, James E. "Ted," III, and Bill Mooney. *Keeneland's Ted Bassett: My Life.* Lexington: Univ. Press of Kentucky, 2009.
Newspapers: "First Negro among 39 New State Troopers Inducted," *LHL,* January 27, 1968, 13; "First Kentucky Tan Trooper Takes Oath," *Washington (DC) Afro-American,* January 30, 1968, 16; "Kentucky Gets Its First Negro State Trooper," *LD,* February 15, 1968, D1.
"Talking About." *Jet,* March 1968, 43.

—*Sallie L. Powell*

WESTERN COLORED BRANCH LIBRARY (LOUISVILLE), the first library solely for African Americans in the United States. One notable characteristic of early twentieth-century black middle-class and professional groups in the United States was a conscious effort to build community infrastructures primarily to facilitate the educational advancement of African Americans. These educated blacks understood that knowledge was the passport to life. **Albert Meyzeek,** a black educator, was one of those leaders in Louisville, KY. Meyzeek served for many years as principal at various schools and, during his tenure as principal at the segregated **Central High School,** led the campaign for the establishment of a black library in Louisville. His efforts and those of other middle-class blacks yielded fruit when the Western Colored Branch Library (WCBL) in Louisville was founded in 1905. This achievement inspired the subsequent establishment of the **Eastern Colored Branch Library** in Louisville in 1914. To many, the WCBL marked a fulfillment of the dreams of blacks in Kentucky to foster rapid social and intellectual empowerment.

At a time in the United States when libraries were closed to people of color, the WCBL established its place in history as the first in the country to provide free library services to African Americans. Just as black schools from Reconstruction through the 1940s were often housed in black churches and fraternal lodges, most black libraries before the 1960s were located in rented or converted facilities. Formally called the Carnegie Library at Tenth and Chestnut, the WCBL was initially sited in a home belonging to William M. Andrews, a waiter at the well-known Galt House Hotel. In 1908, the WCBL became the first public library for blacks in the South to be housed in a Carnegie-funded facility. Andrew Carnegie, who had set up a national

Western Colored Branch Library children's room, 1927.

foundation to build libraries in the United States, supported the growth of the library through generous charitable contributions.

For more than a century, the WCBL was a source of self-enlightenment for blacks. By opening the library free of charge to all regardless of race, securing reading rights for blacks, and acquiring thousands of volumes, the WCBL pioneered the diffusion of cultural awareness for blacks as it sought to remedy the inequalities of the past. Under the leadership of **Thomas F. Blue,** who became the librarian in 1908, the WCBL witnessed tremendous growth, serving the educational needs of blacks, as well as establishing itself as a community center dedicated to promoting exchange of ideas. Over time, the WCBL played an important role in the social advancement of African Americans in Louisville. The WCBL not only marked an unprecedented achievement by a new group of middle-class blacks but also helped train a new generation of African Americans who later played a prominent role in the politics of both Kentucky and the nation.

Fultz, Michael. "Black Public Libraries in the South in the Era of De Jure Segregation." *Libraries and the Cultural Records* 41, no. 3 (Summer 2006): 337–59.
Meier, August. "Negro Class Structure and Ideology in the Age of Booker T. Washington." *Phylon* 23, no. 3 (Fall 1962): 258–66.

—*Ogechi Anyanwu*

WEST KENTUCKY COMMUNITY AND TECHNICAL COLLEGE, school in Paducah, KY. In the early years of the twentieth century, a Methodist minister and a graduate of Lane College in Tennessee, **Dennis Henry Anderson,** came to western Kentucky with his wife, the former Artelia Harris, to provide educational opportunities for the African American youth of the area. Among the schools he established was West Kentucky Industrial College. In 1909, he began excavating a lot in Paducah donated by Armour Gardner. By 1911, he had excavated the entire basement, and the cornerstone for the building was laid. Anderson solicited trees from farmers, gravel from the railroad, and funds from anyone who would donate. He picked up loose bricks and lumps of coal that had fallen from trucks on city streets and deposited them on school property. Artelia Anderson put her entire salary of $55 per month from teaching at nearby White Oak into construction of the building, much of which was built with Dennis Anderson's own hands.

In 1912, Anderson asked the Kentucky General Assembly for state support. The legislature passed an appropriation, but the governor vetoed it. In 1914 and again in 1916, the Senate approved funding, but not the House of Representatives. Finally, in 1918, both houses passed a bill "to provide a training school for colored teachers, boys and girls." The bill pointed out that there was no normal school in the western part of the state, and the institute at Frankfort was too far away to serve the area. The governor signed the act, and West Kentucky Industrial College (WKIC) became a state school, with an appropriation of $8,000. Over the next 20 years, funding increased, and by 1938, WKIC was the third-largest Negro junior college in the United States. In that year, the legislature established a four-year liberal arts college for African Americans under the name Kentucky State College for Negroes (now **Kentucky State University**) and closed West Kentucky Industrial College.

At the same time, a new institution, known as West Kentucky Vocational School for Negroes, was established on the former WKIC campus. In 1979, the school moved to land donated by Paducah Junior College and instituted more advanced technical programs. Further name changes and curricula improvements occurred in the 1980s and 1990s. Now known as Western Kentucky Community & Technical College, the former WKIC is presently a part of the Kentucky Community and Technical College System.

Blythe, Janett Marie. *My West Kentucky: A History of West Kentucky Technical College, 1909–1999.* Paducah, KY: Turner, 2000.
Dunnigan, Alice Allison, comp. and ed. *The Fascinating Story of Black Kentuckians: Their Heritage and Traditions.* Washington, DC: Associated Publishers, 1982.
Hardin, John A. *Fifty Years of Segregation: Black Higher Education in Kentucky, 1904–1954.* Lexington: Univ. Press of Kentucky, 1997.

—*Charles F. Faber*

WHEAT, DEJUAN SHONTEZ (b. 1973, Louisville, KY), college and professional basketball player. DeJuan Wheat was a six-feet-two guard on the Louisville Ballard High School basketball team. In 1992, his senior year, he averaged 22.5 points a game and was first-team all-state and a candidate for the title of Kentucky's Mr. Basketball. From 1993 to 1997, he played for the University of Louisville (UL), where he became a standout player. He was recognized as the Freshman Player of the Year in the Metro Conference and the national Newcomer of the Year by *Basketball Times* in 1994. During his years as a Louisville Cardinal, the team compiled a 95–41 win-loss record and appeared in four NCAA tournaments, reaching the Sweet 16 and the Elite 8.

Wheat was recognized for several individual accomplishments. He became the first player in NCAA Division I history to have 200 steals, 300 three-point field goals, 450 assists, and 2,000 points. By the end of his career at UL, he was the school's second all-time scorer with 2,183 points and second in three-pointers. He had also started in 136 consecutive games. He was a 1997 runner-up for Conference USA Player of the Year, a finalist for the Naismith Player of the Year Award, and third-team All-American as selected by *Basketball Times*.

Wheat was drafted in the second round by the Los Angeles Lakers but was waived before signing with the Minnesota Timberwolves as a free agent on October 23, 1997. Less than two years later, he signed as a free agent with the Vancouver Grizzlies. Wheat played a total of 12 years of professional basketball, which included several years in Mexico with Soles de Mexicali.

After retiring from basketball in 2010, Wheat returned to Louisville to organize local projects, which included basketball camps for less fortunate children and raising funds for cancer research. In May 2012, Wheat's jersey was included among the UL jerseys hanging in the KFC Yum Center. That same year, he received his degree from the University of Louisville through the Houston-Bridgeman Fellows Cardinal Degree Completion Program.

Basketball Reference.Com. "DeJuan Wheat." http://www.basketball-reference.com/players/w/wheatde01.html (accessed July 9, 2013).
The Louisville Paper. "Catching Up with DeJuan Wheat." http://theLouisvillepaper.com/2011/12/02/catching-up-with-deju . . . (accessed December 13, 2012).

Rutherford, Mike. "DeJuan Wheat Will Be Honored at Halftime." CardChronicle. http://www.cardchronicle.com/2012/2/26/285999 /djuan-wheat-will-be-honored-at-halftime (accessed July 9, 2013). "Louisville Cardinals: Men's Basketball: DeJuan Wheat." http://www .gocards.com/sports/m-baskbl/mtt/wheat_dejuan00.html.

—*Gerald L. Smith*

WHITE, CLARENCE CAMERON (b. 1880, Clarksville, TN; d. 1960, New York, NY), opera composer and director. Clarence White, the son of James W. and Jennie Scott White, was a world-renowned African American opera composer and director. White studied at Howard University in Washington, DC, and at the Oberlin Conservatory of Music (Oberlin, OH) and later spent the years 1908–1911 in London, England, studying with the black British composer and conductor Samuel Coleridge-Taylor. White also traveled to Paris, France. He began his teaching career in the public schools of Washington, DC, and then served as director of music at West Virginia State College at Institute, WV. In 1937 he was named a music specialist for the National Recreation Association, established by President Franklin Roosevelt (1933–1945) under the Works Progress Administration. The association offered aid in organizing community arts programs.

In November 1938, White visited Covington to head a music institute for African Americans in northern Kentucky. During the mornings, he conducted several institutes on music at Covington's **Lincoln-Grant School.** The purpose of the institute was to advance the musical interests of the community and to develop participation in choral and instrumental groups. Mrs. Sadye L. Dunham, director of the Negro Youth Recreation Association of Northern Kentucky, was instrumental in bringing White to the community. To keep the community involved, training sessions were held nightly at the **First Baptist Church** and the Ninth St. Baptist Church. The training period resulted in a public concert in which African American spirituals were featured. In 1960, after a long and successful career in opera composition, White died at Sydenham Hospital in New York City. His most acclaimed composition was his 1932 opera *Ouanga,* which was first performed that year by the American Opera Society of Chicago.

Newspapers: "Famed Negro Composer Heads Music Institute," *KP,* November 30, 1938; "Clarence White, Composer, Was 79," *NYT,* July 2, 1960, 17. Smith, Jessie Carney, ed. *Notable Black American Men.* Detroit: Gale Research, 1999, 1206–1208.

—*Theodore H. H. Harris*

WHITE, SAMUEL L. (b. ca. 1804, New Jersey; d. 1870, Cincinnati, OH), musician and composer. According to census records, Samuel L. White was born in New Jersey; however, he was raised in the Philadelphia area. He was a celebrated musician who played guitar with Francis Johnson, a noted African American bandleader and composer. In the 1840s, White was one of many free black musicians who went westward to play music for steamboat trips along the Ohio River, and he eventually relocated to Louisville.

White became a prominent member of Louisville's antebellum free black community. Listed as a music teacher in the 1850 and 1870 federal censuses, White taught prominent citizens "of both sexes, white and colored." In December 1852, he also helped organize the Mozart Society, an African American musical organization that performed concerts in black churches. A noted composer in his own right, White arranged "Didst Thou Ever Think of Me" for the guitar and "The Heart That Loves Fondest of Any."

White's prominent status eventually upset some local whites, who targeted him in a successful harassment campaign that included throwing stones through his residence's windows. When he applied for police protection, he was instead advised to leave the state. He moved to Cincinnati soon after with his wife Lucy, where they lived until his death in 1870.

Gibson, W. H., Sr. *Historical Sketch of the Progress of the Colored Race, in Louisville, Ky., as Noted by the Writer during a Period of Fifty Years.* Louisville, KY: Bradley & Gilbert, 1897. "New Music," *New York Evening Post,* August 9, 1832. U.S. Federal Census (1850, 1870).

—*David Lai*

WHITE HALL, home of slave owner, emancipationist, and diplomat Cassius M. Clay. White Hall has the distinction of being the home of not only one of the largest slaveholders in Kentucky but also one of the most prominent emancipationists in the state. The original house was built by Gen. Green Clay in 1798–1799. The brick Georgian-style home was named Clermont and was the residence of Green, his wife, Sally Lewis, and their seven children. At the time of his death in 1828, Green Clay was considered the largest landowner and the largest slaveholder in the state of Kentucky. One hundred and five enslaved individuals were identified by name in his will. The family home and a number of slaves were passed to the youngest son, Cassius Marcellus Clay.

Cassius M. Clay grew up in this prominent family and had been indoctrinated with the general view that slavery was a necessary evil. Inspiration from his emancipationist brother, Sidney Clay, childhood experiences involving the injustices of the slavery system, and influences of his time in the North while he was at Yale all helped persuade the young Cassius to speak out against slavery. While traveling to political rallies and speaking on emancipation, Clay met Abraham Lincoln. The two men shared similar beliefs regarding the slavery issue, and when Lincoln ran for president, Clay campaigned for him. This earned Clay a position as minister to Russia once Lincoln became president. Although Clay's family traveled with him to Russia, his wife and children soon returned home to Kentucky. It was at this time, while Clay served overseas, that his wife oversaw the construction of an addition to the original house, Clermont. The home was transformed into a 10,000-square-foot Italianate mansion with such modern amenities as central heating and indoor plumbing. The new home was called White Hall.

Today the home is in a 13.6-acre park and historic site owned by the state of Kentucky. In addition to the mansion, also on the property are the original loom house and cooking kitchen used by the enslaved on the property. There are also foundations still visible of buildings that the enslaved once used and inhabited.

Clay, Cassius M. *The Life Memoirs, Writings, and Speeches of Cassius M. Clay.* Cincinnati: J. Fletcher Brennan & Co., 1886.

Clay, Green. Will. Madison County Courthouse, Book D, pp. 461–69, 1828.

Richardson, H. Edward. *Cassius Marcellus Clay: Firebrand of Freedom.* Lexington: Univ. Press of Kentucky, 1976.

—*Lashé D. Mullins*

WHITESIDE, BIRDIE L. (b. 1911, Hopkinsville, KY; d. Marion, IN, 2004), founder of Guiding Light Christian Service.

Birdie Mary Lee Whiteside was born to Argurtee Radford and Ockter Whiteside in Hopkinsville, KY. She completed a bachelor of missions degree from Simmons University (later known as **Simmons College of Kentucky**) in Louisville in 1949 and moved to Indianapolis. In 1953, she founded Guiding Light Christian Service, a tape ministry designed to provide recorded religious sermons to the infirm and convalescent. The organization's volunteers also prepared and delivered Easter baskets and Christmas stockings to shut-ins.

Eventually the group expanded to include institutions and shut-ins in adjacent counties. Whiteside received numerous honors and awards because of the organization's work, including a 1984 Birdie Whiteside Day proclamation from Indianapolis mayor William Hudnut III. She also received the 1983 and 1984 Ivy Award, sponsored by the Volunteer Action Center of the United Way, for her distinguished volunteer service.

Whiteside was an active member of Messiah Missionary Baptist Church who participated in the choir, missionary societies, the Baptist Training Union, and Sunday school. She also belonged to other groups, including Church Women United, the Council of Negro Women, Three Sisters Nursing Home, and the Juvenile Center Auxiliary. Whiteside died in 2004 and was buried in New Crown Cemetery in Indianapolis.

The Birdie L. Whiteside Collection is housed at the Indiana Historical Society as part of the Black Women in the Middle West Project.

Kentucky Birth, Marriage, and Death Databases: Births 1911–1999.
Guide to African American History Materials in Manuscript Collections. Indianapolis: Indiana Historical Society.
Hine, Darlene Clark, and Patrick Kay Bidelman, eds. *The Black Women in the Middle West Project: A Comprehensive Resource Guide Illinois and Indiana.* Indianapolis: Indiana Historical Bureau, 1986.
U.S., Social Security Death Index, 1935–Current.

—*Karen Cotton McDaniel*

WHITMAN, ALBERY ALLSON (b. 1851, Hart Co., KY; d. 1901, Atlanta, GA), teacher, poet, and minister.

Albery Allson Whitman was born on the Green River Plantation in Hart Co., KY, on May 30, 1851. Although he was born in bondage, in Whitman's view, he "never was a slave." His parents died when he was young: his mother in 1862 and his father in 1863. Whitman moved to Louisville and then to Cincinnati and Troy, OH. In Troy, he worked in a plow shop and later in railroad construction.

Whitman enrolled in a school for seven months. He taught in Carysville, OH. Around 1870, he attended Wilberforce University for six months. During this time, he met Daniel Alexander Payne, the president of Wilberforce and the bishop of the African Methodist Episcopal Church. The two became good friends, and through this friendship, Whitman gained a close affiliation

to the university. In 1877, Whitman was the general financial agent at Wilberforce. He was also the elder in the local A.M.E. church and later became pastor in many A.M.E. churches, some of which he founded in Ohio, Kansas, Texas, and Georgia. According to the 1880 federal census, he served a church in Danville, KY.

Whitman was considered one of the most influential black poets among his contemporaries. His verses, containing vivid imagery, have been compared to those of Edgar Allen Poe. One of his most famous works is *Not a Man and Yet a Man* (1877), an epic poem that features a slave hero, Rodney, and his struggles against racist antagonists. His other works include *Rape of Florida* (1884), *Twasinta's Seminoles* (1885), *The World's Fair Poem* (1893), and *An Idyl of the South* (1901).

On June 29, 1901, Whitman died of pneumonia. He was buried in Atlanta, GA.

"Albery A. Whitman—Poet." *IF*, August 8, 1891, 5.
Brawley, Benjamin Griffith. *The Negro Genius: A New Appraisal of the Achievement of the American Negro in Literature and the Fine Arts.* New York: Biblo & Tannen, 1972.
Harris, Trudier, and Thadious M. Davis. "Afro-American Writers before the Harlem Renaissance." *Dictionary of Literary Biography,* vol. 50. Detroit: Gale, 1986.
U.S. Federal Census (1880).

—*Kim Nguyen*

WHITNEY, DAVEY L. (b. 1930, Midway, KY), athlete and coach.

A native of Midway, KY, Davey L. Whitney was born on January 8, 1930. When he was 13, famed University of Kentucky basketball coach Adolph Rupp allowed him to observe his team practice. Whitney graduated with a bachelor's degree from Kentucky State College (later known as **Kentucky State University**) (KSU) in 1953. He earned more athletic letters than any other athlete in KSU history, including letters in basketball, baseball, football, and track. He was a two-time All–Midwest Conference selection in basketball. He played professional baseball as a shortstop for the Kansas City Monarchs of the Negro Baseball League from 1952 to 1954 with the nickname Wiz.

Whitney started his basketball coaching career at Burt High School in Clarksville, TN, where he won two state championships and compiled a record of 217–72. After his first collegiate coaching job at Houston's Texas Southern University, he moved to Alcorn State University in Mississippi, where he spent 26 years. While he was there, he earned a master's degree in 1990. At the time of his retirement, he was the oldest living African American current head basketball coach in the NCAA at the age of 73.

Even though his players towered over the 5-feet-6, 141-pound coach, Whitney had more winning seasons than any of his predecessors at Alcorn State and was the first Southwestern Athletic Conference coach to lead his team to play in an NCAA Division I basketball championship. His successes made him the first coach to lead a historically black college team to win in both NIT (1979) and NCAA (1980) tournament games.

Whitney's many awards and recognitions included National High School Coach of the Year (1961), the KSU Athletics Hall of Fame (1979), the Mississippi Sports Hall of Fame (1991), the Alcorn State University Hall of Fame (1996), and the National

Collegiate Basketball Hall of Fame (2010). In 1999, Mississippi senator Trent Lott paid tribute to Whitney's many athletic accomplishments on the U.S. Senate floor. In 2012, the Magnolia Bar Association honored him with the Harriet Tubman Award.

Congressional Record. Vol. 145, pt. 12, 106th Cong., Senate, July 19, 1999.

McDaniel, John, III. "Black Midway Native Makes Basketball History." *Midway Exchange* 3, no. 26 (February 2005). 1.

Negro Leagues Baseball Museum. "Davey Whitney." http://coe.k-state .edu/annex/nlbemuseum/history/players/whitney.html (accessed November 6, 2013).

Newspapers: "Small Wonder: Alcorn State Coach in Big Finale at Tiny SWAC School," *Pittsburgh Post-Gazette,* March 2, 2003, D6; "Alcorn's Whitney to Be Honored," Associated Press State Wire, Mississippi, January 12, 2012.

—*Amanda Hoover*

WHITNEY, FRANCIS EUGENE (b. 1916, Hopkinsville, KY; d. 2006, Hopkinsville, KY), businessman and politician. Born on August 3, 1916, the youngest child of Mary J. and James T. Whitney Jr., Francis Eugene Whitney grew up in segregated Hopkinsville, KY. He attended all-black **Booker T. Washington Elementary School** and Crispus Attucks High School, graduating from the latter in 1933. He then went to Kentucky State College (later known as **Kentucky State University**), where he majored in natural science and mathematics, before briefly serving as a substitute teacher in Paris, KY. After returning home to Hopkinsville, he worked for **Domestic Life and Accident Insurance Company,** and during this period he met his future wife, Georgia Evans, whom he married in 1941.

At the outbreak of World War II, Whitney moved to Wright Patterson Field outside Dayton to begin work as a mechanic, servicing the engines and fuselages of bombers and other planes as they arrived. In an attempt to avoid combat duty, he applied for a role with the Signal Corps, training with communication technologies at Transylvania University. However, white resistance reduced the number of assignments given to black servicemen, and by the end of the war, he and his fellow workers had few options for jobs within the military.

In 1945, Whitney returned to work in insurance with **Mammoth Life and Accident Insurance Company** before deciding to start his own real estate enterprise. His company, the F. E. Whitney Real Estate Agency, began operations in 1948 and remained open for over 50 years. In 1958, he was the first black to be accepted into the Kentucky Association of Realtors, and in 1986, he was chosen Realtor of the Year.

Whitney matched his successes in business with an equally extensive and productive career in local politics. In 1952, he was a charter member of Pioneers, a black male service group "for the purpose of Promoting, Advancing, and Stimulating Social, Cultural, and Civic Interest in Hopkinsville." In 1953, he was one of 12 citizens appointed to the city council after the local government's transition from a commission to a councilman form of representation. During his 23 years on the council, the city passed a fair-housing ordinance, and he helped establish the local Human Rights Commission. In 1970, he was elected mayor pro tem after the death of W. B. Moore. He also worked on the Board of Regents of Kentucky State University and was elected to the Christian County Fiscal Court in 1977.

On December 21, 2006, Francis Eugene Whitney died of natural causes at the Jennie Stuart Medical Center in Hopkinsville. He was interred in Cave Spring Cemetery.

Horton, John Benjamin. *Profiles of Contemporary Black Achievers of Kentucky.* Louisville, KY: J. Benjamin Horton & Associates, 1982.

Newspapers: "12 Democrats Are Appointed by Governor to Serve on Initial City Council for Hopkinsville," *KNE,* March 12, 1953, 1; "Whitney, Carver Gain City Council Positions," *KNE,* March 18, 1970, 2; "Local Black Pioneer Dies at 90," *KNE,* December 22, 2006, A1.

Whitney, Francis E. Interview by Betsy Brinson, June 7, 2000. Kentucky Civil Rights Oral History Project, Kentucky Oral History Commission, Kentucky Historical Society. Frankfort, KY.

—*Stephen Pickering*

WILKINSON, CRYSTAL (b. 1962, Casey Co., KY), Affrilachian poet. Raised in a rural community in Appalachia, Crystal Wilkinson spent her childhood roaming her grandparents' 64-acre farm, where she learned an appreciation for the land, as well as a desire to write. Painfully shy, she attended Middleburg Elementary School, where she, as one of three black students, endured racist comments from an abusive classmate. At Casey County High School, a counselor recognized her skill at writing and recommended that she join the journalism program at Eastern Kentucky University, which she did after her graduation in 1979.

At college, an unexpected pregnancy as well as her painful shyness slowed Wilkinson's progress, but she graduated with a degree in journalism in 1985. She then pursued a variety of jobs for the next decade, working at the *Lexington Herald-Leader* and for the local city government before discovering a passion for teaching creative writing to students while serving on the faculty of the Kentucky Governor's School for the Arts. Meanwhile, her own writing career was beginning to take off, and pieces appeared in several Appalachian and Kentucky magazines. In 2000, she published a collection of short stories, *Blackberries, Blackberries,* which won the Chaffin Award for Appalachian Literature in 2002.

Along with her close friend **Frank X Walker,** Wilkinson established herself as one of the leading writers in the Affrilachian movement. Her work, which she described as an attempt to "paint a landscape of rural black experience and small-town black experience," drew heavily on her own childhood in Casey Co., KY. A second book, *Water Street,* was well received after its publication in 2005, and her shorter works were published in numerous magazines and anthologies over the next decade. Along with her partner artist, Ron Davis, she founded and edited *Mythium: A Journal of Contemporary Literature Celebrating Writers of Color and the Cultural Voice.*

Even as she received increased attention for her writing, Wilkinson continued with her other passion: teaching. After earning an MFA from Spalding University in Louisville, she returned to Eastern Kentucky University, where she taught creative writing before a stint at the University of Kentucky. After a few years at Indiana University in Bloomington, she accepted a job as head of the Creative Writing Program at Morehead State University, where she was also named writer-in-residence.

In 2008, she won the Denny Plattner Award in Poetry from *Appalachian Heritage,* and the following year, she received the Sallie Bingham Award, which honors an artist for "outstanding contributions to feminist art and social justice in Kentucky." Berea College named Wilkinson as the Appalachian Writer-in-Residence, a three-year grant-funded position in both the English and Appalachian Studies departments, which began in the fall 2014 semester.

Brosi, George. "A Black Appalachian Treasure." *Appalachian Heritage* 34, 2 (Spring 2006): 8–12.

Buckner, Jay. "Esteemed Author Crystal Wilkinson Joins Berea College," June 13, 2014. BC News on the Web: Powered by Students. http://bcnow.berea.edu/esteemed-author-crystal-wilkinson-joins -berea-college/ (accessed August, 8, 2014).

Grubbs, Morris. "An Interview." *Appalachian Heritage* 34 (2006): 13–23.

Newspapers: "Crystal Sees Clearly Now," *LHL,* March 18, 2001, J1; "She Had a Dream—and She Followed It," *LHL,* July 7, 2002, J1; "Wilkinson to Be Honored," *LCJ,* September 12, 2009, A9.

Wilkinson, Crystal. *Blackberries, Blackberries.* London: Toby Press, 2000.

———. *Write with Your Spine.* http://crystal-wilkinson.blogspot.com/ (accessed October 30, 2012).

—*Stephen Pickering*

WILKINSON, DORIS Y. (b. 1936, Lexington, KY), sociologist and first full-time African American faculty member at the University of Kentucky. A (Paul Laurence) **Dunbar High School** homecoming queen who became a nationally recognized sociologist, Doris Y. Wilkinson was born to Howard T. and Regina L. Cowherd Wilkinson in Lexington, KY, in 1936. She was valedictorian of her class at Dunbar High School before becoming one of the early African American graduates of the University of Kentucky in 1958. She received her master's and doctorate from Case Western Reserve University. In 1967, she became the first full-time African American faculty member at the University of Kentucky. At the university, she created the first black social club for women, a faculty newsletter, the **Carter G. Woodson** Lecture Series, the Forum for Black Faculty, and the Black Women's Conference. She was also selected as the first director of the African American Studies and Research Program.

Wilkinson spent her time outside the university organizing and establishing education activities that brought knowledge and awareness of African American history to the Lexington community. She instituted an education tour in downtown Lexington called the African American Trail and also created exhibitions such as *Warriors in Shadows: Women of the Underground Railroad.* She was a professor of sociology, and her extensive work and interest in that field focused on topics such as the sociology of illness and health, as well as critical race theory. She was coeditor of *Race, Class, and Gender: Common Bonds, Different Voices* and was featured in *Imagine a World: Pioneering Black Women Sociologists.*

Wilkinson served in various professional organizations. She was president of the Society for the Study of Social Problems, vice president of the American Sociological Association, president of the District of Columbia Sociological Society, and president of the Eastern Sociological Society. Being an executive associate at the American Sociological Association afforded her the opportunity to receive a grant from the National Institute of Education to create a Research Skills Institute for minorities and women.

Wilkinson has received numerous professional honors and awards. In 2010, the American Sociological Association awarded her the Public Understanding of Sociology Award. She also garnered the Distinguished Arts and Sciences Professorship, a Ford Foundation Fellowship at Harvard University, and the American Sociological Association's National DuBois-Johnson-Frazier Award. In addition, she received the Great Teacher Award and the Lifetime Achievement Award from Women Leading Kentucky. The University of Kentucky has established the Doris Wilkinson Distinguished Professorship in Sociology and the Humanities, and the Sociology Department named a conference room in Breckinridge Hall in her honor.

Bailiff, Melody. "Professor Honored for New Work." *Kentucky Kernel* (University of Kentucky), April 14, 2010, 1.

Bonner, Florence, and Jean H. Shin. "Doris Wilkinson Receives Honors." *ASA Footnotes* 36, no. 5 (May–June 2008): 1.

"Doris Wilkinson Award Statement." American Sociological Association. http://www.asanet.org.

Fifty Years of the University of Kentucky African-American Legacy, 1949–1999. Lexington: Univ. of Kentucky, 1999.

"Hall of Distinguished Alumni: Doris Wilkinson." University of Kentucky. http://www.ukalumni.net/s/1052/semi-blank-noimg.aspx ?sid=1052&gid=1&pgid=1051 (accessed March 15, 2013).

Kentucky Department for Libraries and Archives.

—*Kimberly Renee McDaniel*

WILLIAMS, AUBREY (b. Harlan, KY, 1945), state legislator. One of nine surviving children of a coal-mining family in the Appalachian Mountains of Kentucky, Aubrey Williams was born in Harlan, Kentucky on February 27, 1945. He attended Harlan **Rosenwald School,** where he graduated as a member of the last segregated class in 1963. A member of the basketball team and editor in chief of the school newspaper, Williams enjoyed a mostly peaceful childhood, with life in the local community relatively integrated compared with other regions in the state. After graduation, he split his time between working in Detroit and attending Sue Bennett College in London, KY, on a basketball scholarship.

After stints at East Carolina University and Pikeville College, he graduated cum laude from Pikeville in 1970. Then Williams decided to pursue a career in law and enrolled in the University of Louisville Law School in the fall semester in 1970. After graduating law school, he accepted a job as an investigator for the **Kentucky Commission on Human Rights.** He then turned to local politics in Louisville, becoming president of the local chapters of the **National Association for the Advancement of Colored People** and the National Bar Association; he also worked as a legal adviser for the President Jimmy Carter Election Campaign in Kentucky. In 1977, Williams, then the appointed magistrate of Jefferson Co., ran successfully for state representative against incumbent **Charlotte S. McGill.**

From 1978 to 1985, Williams served as the state representative of the 42nd District for four consecutive terms. He was named the chairman of the Judiciary Criminal Committee, the first black chairman of a standing committee in the Kentucky

House of Representatives. During his term as a member of the committee, he figured prominently in debates over the "slammer bill," which increased penalties for drunk driving. After losing his reelection bid in 1984, he was appointed director of the Special Fund in the Kentucky Labor Cabinet. However, the end of his political career was marked by some controversy because he was suspended from the bar for failing to appear in a trial. In 1987, he was fired from his post with the Special Fund because of charges of "alleged harassment and intimidation of employees and the possible misuse of state equipment and personnel." He responded that his dismissal was a product of racial discrimination.

After his career in government, Williams returned to his career as a prominent attorney in Louisville.

Matney, William C., ed. *Who's Who among Black Americans.* 3rd edition. Detroit: Gale Research, 1981.
Newspapers: "Black Leader Says Brown Is Insensitive," *KNE,* August 14, 1979, 3; "Williams to Speak Sunday at College," *Harlan Daily Enterprise,* February 27, 1982, 6; "High Court Suspends Williams," *KNE,* December 19, 1984, 12B; "Aubrey Williams Fired from State Post," *Harlan Daily Enterprise,* September 3, 1987, 2.
Williams, Aubrey. Interviews by Eric Moyen, March 25 and April 20, 2004. Louie B. Nunn Center for Oral History, Univ. of Kentucky Libraries, Lexington.

—*Stephen Pickering*

WILLIAMS, EARLE HENRY (b. November 6, 1885, Cynthiana, KY; d. unknown), physician and surgeon. The son of Henry and Mary Williams, Earle Williams was born on November 6, 1885, in Cynthiana, KY. His preparatory educational training prepared him well enough to attend Butler College in Irvington, IN, and Baptist University in Indianapolis, IN. After completing his undergraduate training, he enrolled at Meharry Medical College in Nashville, TN, to study medicine. However, for some unknown reason he did not finish at Meharry and transferred to the Chicago Medical College, from which he graduated in 1907. That same year, he began practicing medicine. He married Lola Ailen in 1923, and they had one child, Mildred.

Earle Williams had a very successful career as a physician and surgeon. He worked on the surgical staff at Peoples Hospital in St. Louis, MO, and as a visiting surgeon at St. Mary's Hospital in East St. Louis, IL. Williams also worked as a surgeon for the Terminal Railway Association in St. Louis, the Illinois Railway (McKinley System), and the Illinois Transportation Company, located in Granite City, IL, among others.

In addition to his professional work, Earle Williams participated in several professional and fraternal organizations, including the National Medical Association, the Mound City Medical Forum, the Pan Missouri Medical Association, the Elks, and the Knights of Pythias. Moreover, he served as the president of the Board of Education of Brooklyn (popularly known as Lovejoy), IL. Under his leadership, two new modern schools were constructed, and the number of teachers in the district increased from 4 to 17.

Fleming, G. James, and Christian E. Burckel, eds. *Who's Who in Colored America.* 7th ed. Yonkers-on-Hudson, NY: Christian E. Burckel & Associates, 1950.

U.S. Federal Census (1930).
U.S. World War II Draft Registration Cards, 1942.
Yenser, Thomas, ed. *Who's Who in Colored America, 1930–1932.* 3rd ed. Brooklyn, NY: Thomas Yenser, 1933.

—*David H. Jackson, Jr.*

WILLIAMS, FRANCES HARRIET (b. 1898, Danville, KY; d. 1992, Newton, MA), federal administrator and civil rights activist. Frances Harriet Williams was born in Danville, KY, in 1898. Her parents, Frank L. and Fannie (Miller) Williams, moved the family to St. Louis, where Williams was raised. After graduating from Mt. Holyoke College in 1919 with an AB in economics and sociology, she studied at the New York School of Social Work and then at the University of Chicago, where she worked as a research assistant in the Political Science Department and graduated with her MA in political science in 1931.

From 1935 to 1940, Williams served as the interracial education secretary for the national YWCA. In 1944, she began working as the race relations adviser for the Office of Price Administration, a government agency that was originally established to control inflation during World War II. She later became the assistant to the executive secretary of President Harry S. Truman's Committee on Civil Rights in 1947. Two years later, Williams served as a consultant for the Office of the Assistant Secretary for United Nation Affairs in the State Department. In 1950, she was given a position as the only female legislative assistant to Senator Herbert H. Lehman.

Williams was a member of the Board of Directors of the **National Association for the Advancement of Colored People,** the YWCA, the Editorial Board of the American Society for Public Administration, and the Citizens Committee for the National Association of Colored Graduate Nurses. Her writings include *Negro Community Works in Behalf of Its Families* (1942) and "Minority Groups and OPA," which appeared in the *Public Administration Review* (1947). After spending many years advocating for civil rights, Williams died on March 15, 1992, in Newton, MA.

Dunnigan, Alice Allison, comp. and ed. *The Fascinating Story of Black Kentuckians: Their Heritage and Traditions.* Washington, DC: Associated Publishers, 1982.
Fleming, G. James, and Christian E. Burckel, eds. *Who's Who in Colored America.* 7th ed. Yonkers-on-Hudson, NY: Christian E. Burckel & Associates, 1950.
Houck, Davis W., and David E. Dixon. *Women and the Civil Rights Movement, 1954–1965.* Jackson: Univ. Press of Mississippi, 2009.
Massachusetts Death Index, 1970–2003.

—*Christine Kindler*

WILLIAMS, GEORGIA CLEOPATRA (b. ca. 1909, Tennessee; d. 1946, Louisville, KY), funeral home director. Georgia Cleopatra Williams was the daughter of Tennessee natives E. M. and Inez Thomas Williams. Her early life remains a mystery. Williams was among the few licensed female embalmers in Kentucky when she was in her early 20s and operated her funeral home at 1123 W. Chestnut St. in Louisville, KY, beginning in 1929.

Williams, a licensed mortician, lived with her cousin, Daniel H. Oberton, a railroad employee, and his wife, Amelia, a dressmaker, in 1930. She was first listed in the business section for undertakers in the Louisville city directory in 1936. Another source maintained that she was known as "the only Negro woman embalmer" in Louisville when she established G. C. Williams Funeral Director and Embalmer in 1937. Four years later, according to the U.S. census, she lived at the same location as her two-story funeral home, and the property was valued at $2,000. Her sister, Kathleen, listed as an embalmer, and her aunt, Blanche Bowen, lived with her.

One year before Williams's death, her sisters, Kathleen and Grace, became licensed funeral directors and embalmers and joined her in the undertaking business. The funeral home was renamed G. C. Williams and Sisters Funeral Directors and Embalmers. On September 25, 1946, Williams died of pneumonia in her home at age 37. She was survived by her two sisters, three aunts, and one cousin. She was buried in the Louisville Cemetery.

The sisters continued to manage the funeral home until their deaths. Grace, at age 55, died in 1961. Fifty-year-old Kathleen died the next year. Calvin R. Winstead then purchased the funeral home at auction. Two years later, he relocated the renamed G. C. Williams Funeral Home to 1935 W. Broadway. The business continued to prosper for many years.

G. C. Williams Funeral Home. "Our History." http://www.gcwilliams .com/Our_History.html (accessed July 13, 2012).
Kentucky Death Index, 1911–2000.
Kentucky Death Records, 1852–1953.
Newspapers: "First Negro Woman Embalmer in State Dies," *LCJ*, September 26, 1945, sec. 2, p. 9; "Mortician Calvin Winstead Dies," *LCJ*, October 5, 2003, B6.
U.S. Federal Census (1930, 1940).

—*Sallie L. Powell*

WILLIAMS, HENRY H. (b. 1790s, near Lexington, KY; d. 1850, Louisville, KY), musician and dancing teacher. Henry H. Williams was a free African American and a pioneer in many respects in Louisville's musical history. It is unknown how or when he arrived in Louisville, but in 1834 he opened a dancing school at Edward Lynch's Assembly Room on Main St. Williams was the first African American dancing teacher in Louisville and one of the most popular teachers; he often advertised his services in local newspapers. In 1835, he announced the formation of a cotillion band, the earliest African American–led band in the region, which would be "the very best in the country" (*Louisville Public Advertiser,* October 14, 1835). It included other free African Americans, slaves, and German immigrants. He chose exceptional musicians; several African American members, including **James C. Cunningham** and Samuel Hicks, later formed their own successful string and brass bands. By the late 1830s, Williams's band was the most popular in the region, playing not only in Louisville but from Cincinnati to New Orleans. In 1839, Williams played at the Oakland Race Course during the famous race between Grey Eagle and Wagner. His band was in constant demand on steamboats and at Kentucky's spas and resorts during the summers, particularly at Paroquet Springs and Drennon Springs.

Williams was a talented violinist and was capable of performing whatever type of music the situation required, from marches, waltzes, and polkas at cotillions and fancy balls to Virginia reels and breakdowns at country dances and barbecues. Louisville newspapers often commented favorably on his musical and teaching talents, and a benefit was given for him at William C. Peter's Apollo Rooms on Main St. in 1848. Despite his popularity, however, he was never included in the formal concerts given by white musical associations, such as the St. Cecilia Society, the Louisville Music Association, or the Louisville Mozart Society.

Newspapers: *Louisville Morning Courier,* September 18, 1846; *Louisville Morning Courier,* March 3, 1848.

—*Cornelius Bogert*

WILLIAMS, KERMIT (b. 1941, Frankfort, KY), first black player on the football, basketball, and track teams at Frankfort High School. Born in Frankfort, KY, Kermit Williams attended all-black Mayo-Underwood High School in 1955, the year after the landmark ***Brown v. Board of Education*** decision. Unhappy with that school's lack of an organized football team, Williams decided to transfer to the newly integrated Frankfort High School, where he became the first African American on the football, basketball, and track teams.

His first game with the football team occurred on September 8, 1956, at the end of a week that had featured Governor Albert B. "Happy" Chandler calling in the National Guard to enforce integration of Sturgis Consolidated School. Tensions were similarly high in Frankfort, where the game would be played on a field deeded to the school on the condition that it be used only by whites. Williams scored two touchdowns in a victory, but accounts of the game and a photo in *Life* magazine noted that a cross was burned on a hill adjacent to the football field.

Williams spent over two years in the army and briefly played football for Kentucky State College (now **Kentucky State University**) after high school, but he noted that the experience was not comparable to his earlier career. In his adult life, he moved to Dayton, KY, where he married Anita Blair and worked at a nursing home. On August 25, 2006, he was inducted into the Frankfort High School Football Hall of Fame for his role in integrating the team.

"The Enlightened One." *Frankfort State-Journal,* August 23, 2006. State-Journal.com (accessed June 6, 2012).
"The Halting and Fitful Battle for Integration." *Life,* September 17, 1956, 40.
"Panthers Topple Trojans 13–0; Elks Fall to Admirals 26–0." *Frankfort State-Journal,* September 9, 1956, 6.

—*Stephen Pickering*

WILLIAMS, MARGARET THOMAS YEAGER (b. 1917, Stanford, KY; d. 2006, Louisville, KY), activist, first black in the Louisville PTA, and first black president of the local United Methodist Women. Margaret Thomas was the daughter of John and Bertie Thomas of Stanford, KY. Her mother died in childbirth when Margaret was young, and she was raised by her father and grandmother. She eventually relocated to Louisville and married William Edward Yeager in 1936 and Samuel Taylor Williams in 1991. She and Yeager had four sons and three daughters, and she became a stay-at-home mother. As a parent, she was among the leadership of five black parent-teacher associations where her children attended school. When she could not get much-needed repairs at the Mary B. Talbert Elementary School, she contacted the *Louisville Courier-Journal* and the local television stations and encouraged them to visit the black school during a rainstorm. Her activism exposed the disparity of facilities in the black school and resulted in necessary maintenance at the school.

In 1965, Yeager was an outspoken advocate for the Head Start program for African American children. During that same year, she was accepted for the Federal Career Opportunities Program, which gave her the opportunity to attend college. At the age of 52, after graduating from the University of Louisville, Yeager became an elementary special-education teacher in Louisville. She became the first African American in the Louisville Parent-Teacher Association, providing oversight to the integration plan in the Jefferson Co. public school system.

Yeager was a lifelong member of the United Methodist Women and served as a delegate to its annual Jurisdictional and General Meetings. Because of her experience with integrated PTAs, she was selected as the first African American president of the United Methodist Women at the R. E. Jones Temple Methodist Church. She also was the first African American dean of the School of Missions for the Louisville Conference.

Yeager's children honored her in a celebration in 1978 in Los Angeles, where she received letters of commendation from the president of the United States and the mayors of Louisville and Los Angeles. When the *Louisville Courier-Journal* selected people to honor for the millennium celebration, she was the first of 52 persons honored.

In 2003, Margaret Thomas Yeager Williams was named a Woman of Distinction by the Center for Women and Children in Louisville. She died on December 29, 2006, and was buried in Evergreen Cemetery and Garden Mausoleum in Louisville.

Kentucky Birth, Marriage, and Death Databases: Births, 1911–1999.
Newspapers: "My Millennium: Postscripts," *LCJ*, December 26, 1999, A22; "6 'Women of Distinction' Are Honored," *LCJ*, March 24, 2003, C1; "Obituaries," *LCJ*, January 1, 2007, B7.
U.S. Federal Census (1920).
Women of Distinction Records. Center for Women and Children, Louisville, KY.

—*Kimberly Renee McDaniel*

WILLIAMS, STANLEY R. "FESS" (b. 1894, Danville, KY; d. 1975, Jamaica, Queens, NY), composer, orchestra leader, and entertainer. Born on April 10, 1894, Stanley R. Williams was raised by his grandmother, Maria Jane Durham, in Danville, KY. He studied under noted musician Major N. Clark-Smith at Tuskegee Institute, graduating in 1914. He then taught school in Winchester, KY, where he acquired the moniker Fess, short for "professor." Although Williams was able to play a variety of instruments, he primarily performed on the clarinet and the alto saxophone. The 1920 U.S. Federal Census listed him with the occupation "writer of music" and living in Winchester, KY, with his wife, Louise, and their three children, Estelle, Stanley, and Phillip.

Although sources do not agree on exactly how many orchestras he organized or where and when he performed in his early

career, Williams worked in Cincinnati and Chicago. In 1924, he moved to New York, where he later formed the Royal Flush Orchestra, which opened at the Savoy Ballroom, the band's home base, on March 12, 1926. In 1927, he left the Royal Flush to front for Dave Peyton's band and opened Chicago's Regal Theatre in early 1928. The ensemble became known as Fess Williams' Joy Boys and performed to sold-out crowds. He returned to his Royal Flush Orchestra and the Savoy in 1929.

Williams was known for his "magnetic personality," which made "**jazz** high class as well as low down." He inserted comedy within his music and filled the stage with "a sky-rocket of motion" in his top hat and diamond-studded tuxedo. He would holler to the crowd, "Hello, Folks," and they would respond, "Hello, Fess." His musical style of gas-pipe clarinet and saxophone fabricated animal sounds of squeaks and honks. He produced a slap-tongue style that manufactured popping sounds with the notes. He also used a circular breathing method whereby a note could be held in a continuous tone. He and his various orchestras created over 50 recordings, including his biggest seller, "Hot Town," and the lesser-known "Kentucky Blues."

In 1933, Williams and his 16-piece orchestra signed a radio contract with the Columbia Broadcasting System. The 1940 U.S. federal census recorded Williams as a musician who owned his business, and his oldest son Rudolph (a.k.a. Stanley) worked with him. All three of his adult children lived with him, his wife, and his mother, Maria Phillips. He occasionally performed in the 1940s but worked predominantly in real estate. In the early 1960s, he worked as a mail-room supervisor at New York's Musicians' Union Headquarters. Williams died on December 17, 1975, at the age of 81.

Newspapers: "Reviews: Regal (Chicago)," *Indianapolis Recorder*, August 4, 1928, 3; "Theatres and Performers Big, Little," *Indianapolis Recorder*, August 10, 1929, 3; "Williams at Hershey," *Reading (PA) Eagle*, July 26, 1931, 10; "Fess Williams for Radio," *Baltimore Afro-American*, July 29, 1933, 10; "Walter Winchell of New York," *Lakeland (FL) Ledger*, October 2, 1960, 4-A; "Fess Williams, 81, Jazz Band Leader," *NYT*, December 20, 1975, 30.
U.S. Federal Census (1900, 1920, 1930, 1940).
Yanow, Scott. *Classic Jazz*. San Francisco: Backbeat Books, 2001.

—*Sallie L. Powell*

WILLIAMS, WORTHY (b. 1922, Redfox, KY; d. 1989, Redfox, KY), elected constable. The fifth child of Harlan and Sopha Williams, Worthy Williams came from many generations of farmers. He lived the majority of his life in Knott Co.'s Redfox, KY. He worked as a school bus driver, county comptroller, and coal miner.

In 1969, Williams, a Democrat, was the first African American elected to public office in predominantly white Knott Co. He served as constable in the Second District. In 1973, he beat six white candidates to win reelection. In 1977, after beating four white opponents in the spring primary, Williams won unopposed in November. Nickname variations for him exist, including Butt Cutt, But Cut, and Cut Butt. Origins of the nickname have not been located.

Williams fathered six children. His first wife, Wilma Dean Gipson, died in 1981. On August 28, 1989, Williams, age 67, died of cancer due to black lung at Hazard Appalachian Medical Center. Hindman Funeral Services handled the arrangements, and the service was held at Little Home Regular Baptist Church in Redfox.

Newspapers: "Candidates Who Have Already Qualified," *Knott County Observer,* January 18, 1977, 6; "In Kentucky" (obituary), *LHL,* August 29, 1989.
1978 Kentucky Directory of Black Elected Officials: Fifth Report. Frankfort: Commission on Human Rights, Commonwealth of Kentucky, 1978.
Notable Kentucky African Americans Database. http://nkaa.uky.edu/.
Social Security Death Index.
U.S. Federal Census (1990).

—*Andrew Baskin*

WILLIAMSON, ANSEL (b. ca. 1806, Virginia; d. 1881, Lexington, KY), trainer of the first horse to win the Kentucky Derby. Born a slave in Virginia around 1806, Ansel Williamson achieved a small measure of fame as a trainer of horses after winning a race with his horse Brown Dick in Alabama in 1855. Purchased by a Kentucky horse owner named Keene Richards, Williamson gained his freedom after being purchased yet again by Robert A. Alexander, who gave him a job training his finest horses. Two of the horses he trained under Anderson, Norfolk and Asteroid, were undefeated. Williamson eventually moved to Versailles, KY, after Alexander's death to work with H. Price McGrath. Tom Bowling, a horse owned by McGrath, won 14 of 17 races under Williamson's training.

In 1875, Williamson selected **Oliver Lewis** to ride one of his trained horses, Aristides, in the first **Kentucky Derby.** His choice paid dividends because Lewis and Aristides won the inaugural derby by a length over a horse named Volcano. Williamson continued to train successfully for several years and established a strong reputation as one of the state's finest trainers, but he was forced to retire because of old age. He died on June 18, 1881, in Lexington, KY. In 1998, the National Museum of Racing elected Williamson—who had until recently been misidentified as Ansel Anderson—to its Hall of Fame.

"Hall of Fame Joins Past and Present." *NYT,* August 11, 1998, C5.
National Museum of Racing. "Ansel Williamson." *National Museum of Racing and Hall of Fame.* http://www.racingmuseum.org/hall-of-fame/horse-trainers-view.asp?varID=68 (accessed June 8, 2012).
Renau, Lynn S. *Racing around Kentucky.* Louisville: L. S. Renau, 1995.
Saunders, James Robert, and Monica Renae Saunders. *Black Winning Jockeys in the Kentucky Derby.* Jefferson, NC: McFarland, 2003.

—*Stephen Pickering*

WILLIS, EDWARD D. (b. 1870, Kentucky; d. 1930, Lexington, KY), horse jockey, trainer, and newspaper editor. Edward D. Willis was the trainer and superintendent of Patchen Wilkes Farm in Lexington, KY. In 1911, he established the world record for most wins by yearling trotters, which he broke in 1913. When he announced his resignation from the horse industry in 1914, the *Lexington Leader* stated, "No colored man and few of the Caucasian race have achieved as decided a success in their profession."

In 1912, Willis became the editor in chief of the *Lexington Weekly News,* "the leading colored newspaper of Central and Eastern Kentucky." To Willis, the "importance of a newspaper in which the Negroes may present the aims and aspirations of their race and freely discuss questions in which they are especially interested" was crucial. He used the editorial page to state his opinions. For example, in the October 25, 1912 issue, Willis opposed the 1912 presidential campaign of Theodore Roosevelt because of Roosevelt's derogatory statements about African Americans. Willis also participated in a local protest against the motion picture *The Birth of a Nation.*

Willis died on December 5, 1930. His obituary noted that he would be remembered as "one of the most noted Negro trainers of trotting horses in the history of the sport."

Newspapers: "Good Advice from Colored Editor" (editorial), *LL,* October 25, 1912, 4; "Lexington News," *LL,* December 22, 1912, sec. 1, p. 5; "Wilson Was Famous Horse Trainer," *LL,* December 6, 1930, 1.
University of Kentucky. "Willis, Edward D." Notable Kentucky African Americans Database. http://nkaa.uky.edu/.

—*Andrew Baskin*

WILLIS, LUCAS B. (b. 1874, Frankfort, KY; d. 1930, Indianapolis, IN), prominent undertaker and organizational leader. The middle child of Sam Willis, a barkeeper, and Appaline Willis, Lucas B. Willis was educated in Frankfort, KY. He then attended Massachusetts College of Embalming in Boston and graduated in 1898. He trained further at Renouard Training School for Embalming in New York City.

Willis returned to Frankfort, KY, and worked with noted mortician **Thomas K. Robb** until 1900. He then moved to Indianapolis and married Cora L. Christy, a schoolteacher, in 1903. The next year, he joined undertaker C. M. C. Willis and later partnered with James N. Shelton. They advertised their business as having a "lady attendant."

Willis donated time and money to various civic organizations. He organized and served as vice president of the Kentucky State Funeral Directors Association and executive secretary of the Independent National Funeral Directors Association. By 1910, he owned Lucas B. Willis Funeral Home at 413 W. Michigan St. in Indianapolis.

In 1929, Willis was one of the officers of the local branch of the National Negro Business League and helped organize its annual convention. He also expanded his business to include a quick-service garage. In April 1930, Willis died of acute cardiac dilatation. His wife, Cora, continued to own the business. She retired from teaching in June 1934.

Mather, Frank Lincoln. *Who's Who of the Colored Race: A General Biographical Dictionary of Men and Women of African Descent.* Vol. 1. Chicago: Memento Edition, 1915.
Newspapers: Advertisement, *IF,* December 10, 1904, 7; "Millions of Dollars Are Represented," *Indianapolis Recorder,* August 10, 1929, 1; "Deaths," *Indianapolis Recorder,* April 5, 1930, 7.
Yenser, Thomas, ed. *Who's Who in Colored America, 1930–1932.* 3rd ed. Brooklyn, NY: Thomas Yenser, 1933.

—*Sallie L. Powell*

WILL LOCKETT RIOT (LEXINGTON, 1920), incident in which Kentucky police officers prevented the lynching of African American Will Lockett, who had been convicted of murder

and sentenced to death. The Will Lockett riot of 1920 was an incident that affected Kentucky state law regarding mob violence and lynching. In the late nineteenth and early twentieth centuries, incidents of lynching of African Americans in the South occurred frequently. Kentucky experienced numerous incidents of racial violence as well. An event in Fayette Co., KY, in early 1920 forever changed the response of authorities to this brand of vigilante justice and served as a model for the rest of the country.

On February 4, 1920, in a Fayette Co. cornfield, a farmer discovered the body of Geneva Hardman, a 10-year-old white girl. The girl had been beaten and her skull crushed. Suspicion turned toward Will Lockett, an African American World War I veteran and ex-convict who had been seen in the vicinity shortly before the crime had occurred. Although an armed mob began a search for Lockett, the suspect was apprehended by a police officer and handed over to the Lexington Police Department.

In custody, Lockett confessed to the Hardman murder, as well as several others, doing so without benefit of counsel. When it was suspected that Lockett's life might be in danger while he was housed at the Fayette Co. jail, he was transferred to Frankfort. Told that a mob was indeed in pursuit, Governor Edwin P. Morrow ordered local police to prevent the crowd from entering the town.

Lockett was indicted by a Fayette Co. grand jury, and the trial was set for February 9, a date that coincided with Court Day, an event that typically attracted large numbers of people. As the trial began, a crowd of several thousand began to gather outside the courthouse, although it is impossible to ascertain how many were there specifically to lynch Lockett. The trial was brief. Lockett pleaded guilty and was sentenced to die by electrocution on March 11.

Nearly 100 state troopers, along with Lexington police, were dispatched to control the crowd. It was believed that the riot began when a newsman encouraged the crowd to behave more belligerently for the camera. The mob broke through police barricades and stormed the courthouse. The police were ordered to fire, and in the ensuing melee, 5 of the crowd lay dead. Another died several days later, and an estimated 50 were injured. From there, the crisis escalated, and federal troops were brought in to restore law and order.

The incident garnered national attention as the first case of a southern state making a stand against racially motivated lynching. Subsequently, in March 1920, the Kentucky General Assembly passed a law that established harsh penalties for anyone involved in lynching; Kentucky was the first state to enact such a law.

Wright, John D., Jr. "Lexington's Suppression of the 1920 Will Lockett Lynch Mob." *RKHS* 84, no. 3 (Summer 1986): 279–83.

—*Rebecca J. Williams*

WILSON, ATWOOD S. (b. 1895, Louisville, KY; d. 1967, Louisville, KY), educator and community leader. Atwood S. Wilson was born to Allen and Mary Wilson in Louisville, KY. He graduated from **Central High School** in Louisville in 1910. In 1915, he graduated from Fisk University in Nashville, TN, with a major in science and mathematics. He earned a second BS in chemistry in 1920 and an MS in education in 1934 from the University of Chicago. His career as an educator began at the **Shake Rag** District of Bowling Green, KY, in 1915. Two years later, he left that position to serve as a chemistry researcher at the American University Experiment Station during World War I. After returning to Louisville, he became the first principal of Madison Junior High. In 1934 he became principal of Louisville's **Central High School.** While serving as principal, Wilson was instrumental in choosing the site and planning the building for the school's new facility, which opened in 1952. After 29 years as Central High School's principal, Wilson retired in 1963. He returned to Central the following year to aid his successor J. Wayman Hatchett and to serve as a guidance counselor.

During his career, Wilson served as executive director, secretary-treasurer, and managing editor of the journal of the **Kentucky Negro Educational Association** (KNEA), chairperson of the KNEA's Merger Committee that led to the merger of the KNEA and the Kentucky Educational Association (KEA), and trustee of the Board of the Louisville Free Public Library, which presented a resolution to abolish segregation at the main library building in 1948. His list of honors included being the first African American in the South to be presented with a citation for his service on a library board, the Lincoln Institute Key Award for his contributions to the education of blacks in Kentucky, the Silver Beaver Award from the Boy Scouts of America, an honorary doctor of humanities from Simmons University (later known as **Simmons College of Kentucky**) in 1954, and being one of the first inductees into the Central High School Distinguished Alumni Hall of Fame. Since 1974, the Kentucky Education Association has annually given the **Lucy Harth Smith**–Atwood S. Wilson Award for Civil and Human Rights in Education. Wilson was credited with encouraging **Muhammad Ali** (Cassius Clay) to finish high school despite a poor academic record.

Wilson died on March 25, 1967. He was survived by his wife, Eunice, and five daughters. **Denise Clayton,** one of Wilson's grandchildren, was later appointed a judge on the Kentucky Court of Appeals.

"Atwood S. Wilson, Educator, Dies." *LCJ,* March 26, 1967, B15.
Edmonds, Anthony O. *Muhammad Ali: A Biography.* Westport, CT: Greenwood Press, 2005.
Guess, Susie. "Wilson, Atwood S." University of Kentucky Notable Kentucky African Americans. http://www.uky.edu/Libraries/NKAA.

—*Andrew Baskin*

WILSON, CLARENCE H. "CAVE," SR. (b. 1926, Horse Cave, KY; d. 1996, Louisville, KY), basketball player and juvenile probation officer. Son of Howard and Lillian Wilson, Clarence H. Wilson was born in Hart Co.'s Horse Cave, KY, on August 20, 1926. Even though Horse Cave Colored High School, a four-room building, did not have a gymnasium, Wilson begged Principal Newton S. Thomas to start a basketball team. In 1944 and 1945, Wilson led his team to the Kentucky High School Athletic League state basketball championship. Even more impressive, the team won 65 consecutive games. Wilson earned all-state and all-tournament honors in 1943, 1944, and 1945. All five starters of the Horse Cave School team enrolled at Nashville's Tennessee State University.

In 1949, the Harlem Globetrotters signed the six-foot Wilson. By 1951, he was not just the team's point guard, known for his two-handed set shot, but was also the captain and coach. He was given the nickname Cave because of his hometown of Horse Cave. He and his teammates performed in the 1952 movie *Harlem Globetrotters*.

Wilson played and traveled the world with the team until 1964. He then worked as a juvenile probation officer with the Cabinet for Human Resources in Louisville for the next 27 years. Well respected by his colleagues and clients, Wilson was known for going the extra mile.

For his basketball and baseball skills, Wilson was also voted into the Tennessee State University Hall of Fame in 1983. In 1995, he was inducted into the Dawahares Kentucky High School Athletic Association Hall of Fame. The next year, he died of complications from a stroke in Louisville on September 18. **A. D. Porter** and Sons Funeral Home handled the funeral arrangements. He was buried in Calvary Cemetery.

Kentucky High School Athletic Association Hall of Fame. http://www.khsaa.org/hallfame/1995.pdf (accessed November 6, 2013).

Newspapers: "Ex–Harlem Globetrotter Clarence Wilson Dies," *LCJ,* September 20, 1996, B5; "Former Harlem Globetrotter Clarence 'Cave' Wilson Dies," *LHL,* September 20, 1996, B2.

Stout, Louis. *Shadows of the Past: A History of the Kentucky High School Athletic League.* Lexington, KY: Host Communications, 2006.

U.S. Federal Census (1930, 1940).

—*Andrew Baskin*

WILSON, EDITH GOODALL (b. 1896, Louisville, KY; d. 1981, Chicago, IL), blues and jazz singer. Born on September 6, 1896, in Louisville, KY, to Hundley Goodall, a schoolteacher, and Susan Jones, a housekeeper, Edith Goodall was related to vice president John C. Breckinridge (Wilson's great-grandmother had two children by Breckinridge). She left her hometown as a teenager to pursue a career in music and acting, touring with Johnny Dunn and His Original **Jazz** Hounds and marrying the group's piano player, Danny Wilson, around 1919. She was signed by Columbia Records in 1921 as its first **blues** singer and was only the third African American woman to make phonograph records, approximately 40 recordings during the 1920s.

During the 1930s, she appeared with orchestras led by Cab Calloway, Jimmie Lunceford, and others and worked with Louis Armstrong in the Broadway musical *Memphis Bound* in 1945. Wilson's most notable film appearance was in *To Have and Have Not* (1944), starring Humphrey Bogart and Lauren Bacall. She was best known for appearing on the *Amos and Andy* radio and television programs, but her role as Aunt Jemima in Quaker Oats pancake mix commercials for radio and television and in live tours from 1948 to 1966 garnered criticism from some civil rights leaders as an exploitation of black stereotypes. Wilson sang at clubs and on television well into her 80s and appeared in the Newport Jazz Festival and the show *Blacks on Broadway* in 1980. She died in Chicago on March 30 of the following year.

Davis, Merlene. "Singer Did More than Belt Out Blues." *LHL,* September 18, 2003, E2.

"Edith (Née Edíth Goodall) Wilson." *Black Perspective in Music* 9, no. 2 (Autumn 1981): 242.

Harrison, Daphne Duval. "Wilson, Edith Goodall." In *American National Biography,* vol. 23, edited by John Garraty and Mark C. Carnes, 563–64. New York: Oxford Univ. Press, 2005.

—*Jennifer Bartlett*

WILSON, ELLIS (b. 1899, Mayfield, KY; d. 1977, New York, NY), artist. One of six children, Ellis Wilson, the son of a barber, was born in Mayfield, KY, to Frank and Minnie Wilson in 1899. Formal education for Wilson began at Mayfield Colored Grade School. He attended Kentucky Normal and Industrial Institute for Colored Persons (later known as **Kentucky State University**) for two years before leaving to pursue his dreams of becoming an artist at the Chicago Art Institute. He graduated in 1923. For the next five years, he worked as a commercial artist in Chicago. In 1928, he moved to New York City, his home for the remainder of his life. Wilson's works, according to the University of Kentucky Museum, concentrated on "scenes of daily activities of the African American community."

Wilson was an active participant in the New Negro Art movement of the 1920s and 1930s. From 1935 to 1940, while he was employed by the Works Progress Administration Federal Arts Project, he associated with other African American artists. In 1944, he received a Guggenheim Fellowship to finance his two-year project to travel and paint ordinary southern African Americans in their daily activities. The $3,000 he won at the Terry Art Exhibition in Miami in 1952 made it possible for him to travel to Haiti and to paint the activities of Haitian peasants.

By the late 1940s, Wilson began receiving recognition in Kentucky. His first exhibition in his hometown was in 1947. In 1950, Murray State University purchased his painting *End of the Day.* In 1951, he became the first African American to exhibit work at the J. B. Speed Art Museum's annual Kentucky and Southern Indiana Exhibition of Art.

Collections of Wilson's works are in many museums. He received more exposure during the 1980s because his painting *Funeral Procession* was used on *The Cosby Show.* Nonetheless, like other African American artists of his time, Wilson was unable to make a living as a painter. In 1977, he died in New York City and was buried in an unmarked pauper's grave. The location is unknown.

"Ellis Wilson (1899–1977)." University of Kentucky Art Museum. http://www.tfaoi.com/aa/1aa/1aa488.htm.

Ellis Wilson—So Much to Paint. Directed by Guy Mendes. Lexington: Kentucky Educational Television 2000. DVD.

King, Eva F. "Celebrating Ellis Wilson." Kentucky Educational Television. http://www.ket.org/elliswilson/bio1kentucky.htm.

—*Andrew Baskin*

WILSON, GEORGE W., SR. (b. 1943, Paris, KY; d. 2005, Lexington, KY), first African American to serve in the Kentucky Cabinet. Born on September 19, 1943, in Paris, KY, George W. Wilson Sr. graduated from Paris Western High School and later obtained a bachelor's degree in history and political science at what became **Kentucky State University.** Continuing his graduate studies, he earned a master's degree in social work and business administration from the University of Louisville.

In a predominantly white state, Wilson became the first black to hold a cabinet-level position in Kentucky when, in 1980, he became the commissioner of the Kentucky Department of Corrections. Governor John Y. Brown Jr. (1979–1983) later elevated the position to cabinet level, secretary of corrections. Governor Martha Layne Collins (1983–1987) recognized Wilson's worth by retaining him. During the eight years he served as secretary of corrections, Wilson established himself as a well-known figure in state politics, providing the needed leadership in recruitment, retention, and pay for women and minorities. By helping close 20 jails considered inadequate in the state and opening one in Marion Co.—the first private prison in the commonwealth—Wilson ushered in a new era in Kentucky's prisons system.

Wilson's contributions to the prison system did not go unnoticed by his colleagues and superiors alike. John D. Rees, commissioner of the Kentucky Department of Corrections, who had been a warden of the Kentucky State Reformatory at La Grange under Wilson's supervision, acknowledged Wilson's accomplishments. According to Rees, "The leadership he demonstrated with the federal consent decree, and bringing about a solution to those difficult times, was the foundation from which we operate today." Wilson chaired the Board of Regents of his alma mater, Kentucky State University, and served as the director of Morehead Girls Center and on the Commission on Accreditation for Corrections from 1982 to 1988.

Wilson's service went beyond the borders of Kentucky when, in 1988, Dick Celeste, the governor of Ohio (1983–1991), made him the director of the Ohio Department of Rehabilitation and Correction. After many decades of distinguished public service, Wilson returned to Kentucky in 1992, where he spent the rest of his life working as a warden of the minimum-security Blackburn Correctional Complex in Lexington, a Franklin Co. jailer, and a teacher of criminal justice at Kentucky State University. He retired in 1994.

Wilson died on March 1, 2005, at the University of Kentucky Medical Center in Lexington. He received state honors when Kentucky governor Ernie Fletcher ordered state flags to be lowered to half-staff. Reflecting on Wilson's legacy, the governor praised him as "a pioneer in Kentucky state government, who built an admirable record of public service and personal accomplishment during his long career."

"In Memory of George W. Wilson." *Correction Today* 67, no. 2 (April 1, 2005). http://www.thefreelibrary.com/In memory of George W. Wilson, 1943–2005.-a0131858610 (accessed August 09, 2014).
Newspapers: "Ex-Chief of Kentucky Prisons Gets Ohio Corrections Post," *LHL,* August 12, 1988, C4; "George W. Wilson, 1943–2005: First Black to Serve in State Cabinet Dies at 61," *LHL,* March 2, 2005, B1; *Frankfort State Journal,* March 2, 2005, Obituaries, 2.

—*Ogechi Anyanwu*

WINKFIELD, JAMES "JIMMY" (b. 1880, Chilesburg, KY; d. 1974, Paris, France), jockey. Born in 1880 in Chilesburg (near **Uttingertown**) in Fayette Co., KY, James "Jimmy" Winkfield was the youngest of 17 children in a family of sharecroppers. After dropping out of school in the seventh or eighth grade, Winkfield began to work at racetracks, starting as a stable hand. At the age of 16, he became a jockey with the nickname Wink. After plac-

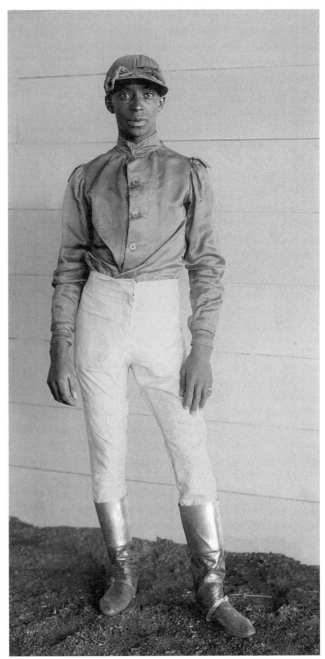

James "Jimmy" Winkfield.

ing third in 1900, he became the second African American jockey to win the **Kentucky Derby** in consecutive years on Eminence in 1901 and Alan-a-Dale in 1902. His 1902 victory was the last Kentucky Derby for an African American jockey.

Like other **African American jockeys,** Winkfield was forced out of racing in the United States; he then went to Russia, where he became the dominant jockey and won the Russian national riding championship three times. The Russian Revolution forced Winkfield to flee on a 1,000-mile odyssey to Poland, occasionally eating horseflesh to survive. His next stop was France, where he was successful once again.

In 1930, Winkfield retired with his stable of horses and more than 2,600 wins as a jockey. He was forced to leave France because of the Nazi occupation. From 1940 to 1953, he lived in the United States and worked at horse farms and racetracks in Maryland and South Carolina. In 1953, he returned to France to live. In 1961, racism intervened again at a Kentucky Derby banquet. Although Winkfield was an invited guest, initially he and his daughter were not allowed to enter through the front door of the Brown Hotel in Louisville.

Winkfield was married twice. His first wife was Alexandra, a Russian aristocrat, who died in 1921. They had one son, George, who died in 1934. His second wife was Frenchwoman Lydia de Minkiwitz, whom he married in 1922; she died in 1958. They had two children, Liliane and Robert. Winkfield died outside Paris, France, in 1974. He was one of horse racing's greatest jockeys, as evidenced by his long-overdue induction into the National Museum of Racing and Hall of Fame in 2004.

Hotaling, Edward. *Wink: The Incredible Life and Epic Journey of Jimmy Winkfield.* New York: McGraw-Hill, 2005.

"Jimmy Winkfield, a Horse Racing Legend!" *The African American Registry.* October 7, 2003. http://www.aaregistry.com.

Saunders, James Robert, and Monica Renae Saunders. *Black Winning Jockeys in the Kentucky Derby.* Jefferson, NC: McFarland, 2003.

—*Andrew Baskin*

WINNIE A. SCOTT MEMORIAL HOSPITAL (FRANK-FORT), the only African American hospital in Frankfort, KY. Born in 1865 in Franklin Co., KY, Winnie Annette Scott was the oldest child of Ephraim and Jane Scott. Her father, a farmer and carpenter, had served in the 5th U.S. Colored Calvary at **Camp Nelson,** KY. When Winnie's mother died, Ephraim placed his 10-year-old daughter in the home of Peter Smith, an African American barber, and Julia Smith as a family servant in exchange for her room, board, and education. Scott graduated from Frankfort's Anderson Female High School on Clinton St. and then earned her degree with the first graduating class of State Normal School (later known as **Kentucky State University**) in 1890. She taught school in Lawrenceburg, Bagdad, and Frankfort and later became the assistant principal at Clinton Street High School.

In 1903, Scott's two-story, white frame home at 228 E. Second St. was converted into a hospital sponsored by the Women's Improvement Club, also called the Women's Hospital Club. In 1910, Scott was elected president of the club. She was credited as the founder of the hospital, which was named the Winnie A. Scott Memorial Hospital in her honor and opened with nearly 10 rooms and one operating room on December 26, 1915. African American doctors, such as **Edward Ellsworth "E. E." Underwood** and **Thackery Louis Berry,** a renowned surgeon, worked at the hospital.

By 1920, Scott lodged with a Baptist minister, William H. Bellew, and his family. She died on May 19, 1920. Her physician was E. E. Underwood, and **Thomas K. Robb** served as her undertaker. After her death, the community continued its support of the hospital. In 1945, Kentucky State College's chapter of **Delta Sigma Theta, Inc.** completely furnished one of the hospital rooms. The Winnie A. Scott Memorial Hospital was the only hospital to serve African Americans until desegregation in 1959. The building was then used for apartments. In 1999, a historical marker was placed at the former hospital's site.

Davis, Elizabeth Lindsay. *Lifting as They Climb.* Washington, DC: National Association of Colored Women, 1933.

Fletcher, Winona, ed. *Community Memories: A Glimpse of African American Life in Frankfort, Kentucky.* Frankfort: Kentucky Historical Society, 2003.

Kentucky, Death Records, 1852–1953.

U.S. Colored Troops Military Service Records, 1861–1865.

U.S. Federal Census (1870, 1880, 1910).

—*Sallie L. Powell*

Winnie A. Scott Memorial Hospital.

WOMEN. When women of African descent arrived in Kentucky while it was a county in the state of Virginia, they came under the institution of chattel slavery. An enslaved woman, a cook, was one of the first women who lived and worked in Boonesboro, an early Kentucky settlement. The first black child was born to an unnamed wife of slave **Monk Estill** in 1782. Another black woman, **Molly Logan,** who came to present-day Kentucky in bondage with her three sons in 1776, later managed to survive an Indian attack. But Molly and thousands of enslaved black women who were brought to Kentucky remained under attack by the ironhanded constraints of slavery.

The slave statutes that defined Molly Logan and other black women as chattel property, governed their daily existence, sanctioned the violation of their bodies, and destroyed their families began before Kentucky statehood. They suffered the restrictions and indignities of slavery but were determined to make a new life for themselves and their families when freedom came. However, some, like Harriett McClain and her daughter Adah, cunningly escaped slavery across the river to northern freedom, where they were welcomed by the free black community.

During the last year of the Civil War, many more women and children freed themselves by leaving farms and towns to follow their fathers, husbands, and sons to Union camps, primarily **Camp Nelson.** At Camp Nelson, three local black women's groups, the Daughters of Zion, the Colored Soldiers' Aid Society, and the Daughters of Mourning, were formed to support and nurse black soldiers. In 1864, in Louisville, women organized the Ladies' Colored Soldiers Aid Society, which provided similar relief during the Civil War.

After emancipation, black women initially focused on education by establishing such institutions as Ladies Hall, which housed a school in Lexington. Additionally, they petitioned local governments for schools while they worked to open rudimentary schools in black churches. As they had done in slavery days, black women of all classes established networks of women who came together to address race, class, gender, self-definition, and economic, political, and sexuality issues. Interdependence among black women strengthened the African American community by providing shared consciousness through common effort. They created an informal system of social welfare and self-help programs within their communities, organizing schools, orphanages, old-folks homes, and basic health facilities, and supported the poor and underprivileged within their churches and in the secular community.

Women like Fannie Miller Williams, **Mayme L. Brooks Copeland,** and **Theda Hoskins Van Lowe** availed themselves of educational opportunities at what are now **Berea College, Simmons College of Kentucky,** and **Kentucky State University** to become teachers in the black schools. In 1877, black male and black female educators formed the State Association of Colored Teachers, which later became the **Kentucky Negro Educational Association** (KNEA).

Kentucky's black women more often focused on racial equality issues than on gender concerns, but some of them participated in suffrage and temperance organizations. At an 1887 State Association of Colored Teachers (later known as the **Kentucky Negro Educational Association**) meeting, **Mary E. Britton** verbalized women's displeasure with second-class citizenship and demanded full voting rights. **Elizabeth "Lizzie" Fouse** served as president of Kentucky's eight Women's Christian Temperance Union Sojourner Truth Unions (black chapters) for several years. However, beginning with the 1892 **Anti–Separate Coach Movement,**

The Chumney Club, Paducah, KY.

City Federation of Women's Clubs, Frankfort, KY.

Kentucky's black women participated in, voiced their concerns about, and supported every social justice action with their male counterparts over the course of the state's history. Among those who spoke before the General Assembly on this proposed coach legislation were Britton and **Mary V. Cook Parrish.**

Within the church, African American women, including **Nannie Helen Burroughs, Lucy Wilmot Smith,** and Parrish, expressed their need for autonomy, and their efforts led to the creation of the Woman's Convention of the Baptist Church in 1900. Similarly, women of other denominations, such as the Methodists, negotiated specific leadership positions for women. The continuous efforts of **Martha Jayne Keys** led to the eventual ordination of women, including **Laura J. Vance Lange,** not only as ministers but also as bishops in the African Methodist Episcopal Church.

In 1903, black women's groups (the Chumney Club of Paducah, and the City Federation of Women's Clulbs of Frankfort, and the Jolly Matrons Improvement Club) coalesced to form the **Kentucky Association of Colored Women's Clubs** (KACWC), through which they coordinated their community-uplift activities. Their gendered concerns were expressed through the KACW, the **Phillis Wheatley YWCA** branches, the Sojourner Truth chapters of the Women's Christian Temperance Union, and women's suffrage group activities. They chartered undergraduate and graduate chapters of the four black Greek-letter sororities, **Delta Sigma Theta, Inc.** (1922), **Alpha Kappa Alpha, Inc.** (1922), **Zeta Phi Beta, Inc.** (1928), and **Sigma Gamma Rho, Inc.** (1938). Additionally, they organized chapters of the Order of the Eastern Star, the **Sisters of the Mysterious Ten,** the Links, the Chums, and others.

During World War II, **Anna Mac Clarke, Willa Brown Chappell, Margaret Ellen Barnes Jones,** and many other black women enlisted in the military. On the local level, women planted victory gardens and organized patriotic clubs such as Lexington's Dorie Miller Chapter of American War Mothers to promote patriotic work and to aid wounded or incapacitated military men and women.

Employment opportunities for African American women after emancipation were limited to positions as **domestic workers,** which included positions as cooks, maids, laundresses, waitresses, day workers, general servants, and children's nurses. However, some, like **Elizabeth B. Slaughter,** used the same skills to establish businesses as dressmakers, caterers, florists, and milliners. A few black women pursued alternative careers, including hotel operator **Maggie Steed** and undertakers **E. Belle Jackson, Elizabeth B. Delaney,** and **Daisy Saffell.** By 1930, over 1,000 black women were teachers in segregated schools. These female educators paved the way for Kentucky State University president **Mary Levi Smith,** college administrator **Eleanor Young Love,** and college faculty such as **Doris Wilkinson.**

Some women went into the science professions, including nursing and medicine. In the late nineteenth and early twentieth centuries, practicing medical doctors included **Sarah Fitzbutler, Artishia Garcia Gilbert,** and Mary E. Britton. **Mary Fitzbutler Waring** followed her mother in the profession, and other women likewise became doctors, including **Mary Hyatt Smith, Mary Etta Potter,** and **Grace Marilynn James.** In the field of nursing, **Mary E. Merritt** became the first graduate nurse, black or white, in the state and was followed by other black nurses. Among them are **Mary Elizabeth Ann Sales, Anne Sleet, Amo Lucille Powell Peters,** and **Ora Frances Porter.** Additionally, Kentucky has produced chemist **Elmer Lucille Allen,** dentist Tracey Butler Ross, science educator and researcher **Mary Smith Lee,** inventor **Mary Ann Moore,** and optometrist **Lucia Ellen Miller Thompson.**

Black women's presence has been widely acknowledged in all areas of the literary, performing, cultural, and fine arts. Although the creative talents of textile artist Zephra May Miller and ceramic and textile artist **Elmer Lucille Allen** have enhanced the lives of many, few other black women have gained recognition in art around Kentucky. However, women's literary prowess has

The Jolly Matrons Improvement Club.

been demonstrated for many decades through the writings of such early authors as **Effie Waller Smith,** Lucy Wilmot Smith, and **Atholene Mary Peyton.** Some early newspaper editors include **Blanche Taylor Dickinson** and **Julia Sohmers Young.** White House correspondent and journalist **Alice Allison Dunnigan** also published her autobiography and a reference volume on Kentucky African Americans.

Affrilachian poet cofounder and National Book Award winner **Nikky Finney** and Chaffin Award winner **Crystal Wilkinson** top the list of acclaimed poets connected with Kentucky. Other published poets include **Margaret Danner, Emma Carson Green,** and **Harriet Price Jacobson.** Among Kentucky's female playwrights have been Pulitzer Prize winner **Suzan-Lori Parks, Mary Frances Gunner,** and **Estella Májozo.** The content of novels by critically acclaimed novelists **Ann Allen Shockley** and **Gayl A. Jones** has garnered much attention. Similarly, **bell hooks,** renowned feminist author and social critic, raised the consciousness level of women and men alike with influential books like *Ain't I a Woman?*

Beginning with circus performer **Winifred "Big Winnie" Johnson,** Kentucky has produced several talented performers in movies and on television. Often overlooked, **Madame Sul-Te-Wan** paved the way for black performers in Hollywood around 1915. Emmy Award–winning Atlanta news anchorwoman **Monica Kaufman** and comedy star **Telma Hopkins** are among the female television personalities. Hopkins has also enjoyed a career as a singer. Among the **jazz** singers were **Helen Humes** and **Edith Goodall Wilson.** **Blues** singers in the state included **Sara Martin, Jennie Katherine Henderson,** and **Mary Ann Fisher.** Opera lovers have enjoyed the remarkable voice of **La Julia Rhea** performing opera and singing in Broadway musicals. Several of the state's daughters had multiple musical gifts, such as **Mamie E. Steward, Julia Britton Hooks, Caroline Bourgard, Julia A.**

Perry, Willie Belle Stevenson, and **Lulu Vere Childers,** which they used for teaching youth as well as performing.

Athletic achievements among the state's women of color have been primarily in basketball, which has produced such athletes as **Valerie Still, Donna L. J. Murphy, Kym Michelle Hampton, Lisa Darlene Harrison,** and **Ukari Okien Figgs.** The sport has also witnessed first-time achievements for **Bernadette Locke-Mattox** and **Brenda Lee Garner Hughes.**

African American women's racial, social justice and political anxieties were communicated through **National Association for the Advancement of Colored People** and National Urban League memberships. In these groups, black women and men worked together, closely monitoring and strategizing ways to attack the segregated structures that restricted black citizenship. **Della Bridges Miller, Helen Fairfax Holmes, Audrey Grevious,** and **Helen Fisher Frye** were among the NAACP branch presidents during the height of the modern **civil rights movement** in Kentucky. These female leaders successfully coordinated voter-registration drives, sit-ins, boycotts, picketing, and other direct-action undertakings. Their leadership successfully integrated many establishments, such as libraries, restaurants, and housing, and increased employment opportunities.

By 1971, two women, **Mae Street Kidd** and **Charlotte Smith McGill,** were elected state representatives, and **Georgia Powers** was the state's only female and only black state senator. They successfully introduced and pushed civil rights legislation through Kentucky's legislature. Although today there are no black women in either the Kentucky House or the Senate, over the years, some women have been appointed to state offices, such as **Kim M. Burse,** secretary of the Revenue Cabinet, and **Eleanor Jordan,** executive director of the Kentucky Commission on Women. Others are judges, like Court of Appeals judge **Denise Clayton** and Lexington's **Pamela Goodwine.**

Over the years, Kentucky's black women have represented the state on the national level. When **Emma Clarissa Clement** was recognized as American Mother of the Year in 1946, Kentucky's African American women were elevated as the nation publicly reaffirmed what black women already knew: that they were good mothers and worthy of respect. Additionally, Kentucky has been represented at national beauty contests by black women **Lyda Lewis,** Miss Kentucky 1973, **Veronica Duka,** Miss Kentucky 1996, and Djuan Keila Trent, Miss Kentucky 2010.

Even though African American women have achieved major triumphs in spite of various obstacles, they still struggle for advancement. Overall, the state's black women lag behind white women in many areas of achievement because of recurring racist and restrictive policies and practices, for example, in attainment of college and graduate degrees, appointment as college faculty, and employment rate. By 2009, only 13.5 percent of Kentucky African American women over the age of 18 had bachelor's degrees. At the same time, women represented over 43 percent of the full-time faculty at the eight state-supported universities, but less than 3 percent of the full-time faculty were black women.

At 12 percent, the unemployment rate for Kentucky's black females is more than double that of white women in the state. The lack of accessible and affordable child care remains a factor. Although there has been an increase in the number of African American female physicians since the nineteenth century, health care for black women remained beyond reach for almost 20 percent of them who, before 2014, had limited or no access to health insurance, which could have negatively affected their life-expectancy rate. Until restrictive practices and policies in areas such as employment, educational opportunities, child care, and health care are changed significantly, the wider struggle for equal opportunity will likely continue.

Although black women have been in the state since the arrival of Daniel Boone in 1775, the historical canon has neglected to include fully their story of struggles and triumphs. Historical narratives about Kentucky blacks also have excluded or minimalized black women. Only a handful of published works, particularly biographies, document the lives of Kentucky black women. By 2010, Kentucky textbooks and monographs recognized a few of the better-known political and activist women but generally ignored the overall impact of black women in the state. Black women have made significant and varied contributions to all aspects of Kentucky's development, particularly as activists in the continuing struggle for full citizenship rights for black people. More historians need to uncover, interrogate, and give meaningful voice to the multifaceted lives of Kentucky's black women.

Bharmal, Nazleen, Chi-Hong Tseng, Robert Kaplan, and Mitchell D. Wong. "State-Level Variations in Racial Disparities in Life Expectancy." *Health Services Research* 47, no. 1, pt. 2 (February 2012): 544–55.

Harrison, Lowell H., and James C. Klotter. *A New History of Kentucky.* Lexington: Univ. Press of Kentucky, 1997.

Kentucky Association of Colored Women's Clubs. Records. Kentucky Historical Society, Kentucky State Univ., Univ. of Kentucky, and Univ. of Louisville.

Kleber, John E., ed. *The Kentucky Encyclopedia.* Lexington: Univ. Press of Kentucky, 1992.

Lucas, Marion B. *A History of Blacks in Kentucky.* Vol. 1, *From Slavery to Segregation, 1760–1891.* Frankfort: Kentucky Historical Society, 1992.

McDaniel, Karen Cotton. "Local Women: The Public Lives of Black Middle Class Women in Kentucky before the 'Modern Civil Rights Movement.'" PhD Diss., Univ. of Kentucky 2013.

The State of African Americans in Kentucky. Frankfort: Kentucky Commission on Human Rights, 2009.

Works Progress Administration. *Slave Narratives: A Folk History of Slavery in the United States from Interviews with Former Slaves; Indiana Narratives.* St. Clair Shores, MI: Scholarly Press, 1976.

Wright, George C. *A History of Blacks in Kentucky.* Vol. 2, *In Pursuit of Equality, 1890–1980.* Frankfort: Kentucky Historical Society, 1992.

———. *Life Behind a Veil: Blacks in Louisville, Kentucky, 1865–1930.* Baton Rouge: Louisiana State Univ. Press, 1985.

—*Karen Cotton McDaniel*

WOMEN'S SUFFRAGE, the fight for the right of women to vote and hold political office. Kentucky granted school suffrage to women in 1838, but in 1902, the Democratic majority in the Kentucky legislature voted to abolish school suffrage for women in second-class cities, which included Lexington, Covington, and Newport. The change was racially motivated by the large turnout of black female voters during the past election in Lexington. Although white women voters outnumbered black women voters by a large margin, the Democrats were concerned. However, throughout the rest of the state, women retained the right to vote in school elections.

Kentucky's black women more often focused on national racial issues than on gender concerns; nevertheless, some of them participated in suffrage and temperance organizations. In 1887, Lexington's **Mary E. Britton** delivered a speech on suffrage to the State Association of Colored Teachers (later known as the **Kentucky Negro Education Association**). In her oration, Britton argued that women's suffrage was based on the view that everyone had a right to determine her or his own fate on the basis of societal laws and that laws should be applied equally to both women and men. She asserted that if men and women were the same, then they should enjoy the same rights, but if they were different, then women still needed the vote to make laws that applied to them.

Kentucky suffragists found some support among black women temperance members and **Kentucky Association of Colored Women's Clubs** (KACW) members who believed that women's suffrage would assist virtuous women in electing moral leadership. KACW women attended the 1912 and 1913 conventions of the National Association of Colored Women's Clubs (NACW) and participated in various discussions on women's suffrage. They acknowledged the participation of Mary Church Terrell, Ida B. Wells, and the young women of **Delta Sigma Theta Sorority,** Inc. in the 1913 Suffrage Parade in Washington, DC.

In 1920, after the ratification of the Nineteenth Amendment to the U.S. Constitution granting women voting rights, voting rights again were emphasized at the NACW convention. Kentuckian

Georgia A. Nugent commented on the NACW proposal to establish citizenship schools, saying, "The ballot without intelligence back of it is a menace instead of a blessing and I like to believe that women are accepting their recently granted citizenship with a sense of reverent responsibility."

In Kentucky, after receiving suffrage rights, black women quickly engaged in all areas of politics, particularly the Republican Party. Across the state, various women established groups such as Louisville's West-End Republican League of Colored Women. **Mary V. Cook Parrish** served as president of this group, and **Mamie E. Steward** served as secretary. Many hesitant women voters were persuaded to exercise their suffrage rights by these two women's diplomatic approach and pleasant temperaments.

A few months after the ratification, **Annie Simms Banks,** a black schoolteacher from Winchester, was appointed a delegate to the state Republican Party Convention. She was the first black woman to become a delegate to a political convention in the South. Banks participated throughout the convention, serving on the Rules Committee. She stated, "We are just beginning to open our eyes in politics, but before long, we are going to make ourselves felt."

Britton, Mary E. "Woman's Suffrage: A Potent Agency in Public Reforms." *American Catholic Tribune,* July 22, 1887, 1.

Knott, Claudia. "Women's Suffrage." In *The Kentucky Encyclopedia,* edited by John E. Kleber, 949–50. Lexington: Univ. Press of Kentucky, 1992.

National Association of Colored Women's Clubs. *The Records of the National Association of Colored Women's Clubs, Inc., Part I.* Bethesda, MD: University Publications of America, 1994, reel 1, frame 613.

"School Suffrage in Kentucky: Boston Transcript." *Friend's Intelligencer* 59, no. 14 (April 15, 1902): 221.

Terborg-Penn, Rosalyn. *The African American Women in the Struggle for the Vote, 1850–1920.* Bloomington: Indiana Univ. Press, 1998.

—*Karen Cotton McDaniel*

WOOD, FRANCIS MARION (b. 1878, Glasgow, KY; d. 1943, Baltimore, MD), educator. Francis M. Wood was born in Glasgow, KY. His life was committed to improving educational opportunities for African Americans. He graduated from Kentucky Normal and Industrial Institute for Colored Persons (now **Kentucky State University**) in the academic and agricultural departments. In 1906, he received an MA degree from **Eckstein Norton Institute** (which later merged with **Lincoln Institute**).

Wood began his career by teaching in a one-room log schoolhouse. Wood's career as an administrator included serving as the principal of Western High School in Paris, KY, state superintendent of the Kentucky Negro Schools, president of the Kentucky Normal and Industrial Institute for Colored Persons. In 1925 he became supervisor of Colored Schools, which then changed to Director, Colored Schools of Maryland, a position he held until his death.

In addition, Wood was involved in educational organizations. He was the president of the **Kentucky Negro Educational Associational** for 10 years. Later, as the president of the National Association of Teachers in Colored Schools, he led the efforts that resulted in the creation of a permanent office for the association in Washington, DC.

In 1931, Wood was awarded an honorary degree of doctor of pedagogy by Morgan State College (now Morgan State University) for his accomplishments. Francis M. Wood Alternative High School in Baltimore was named in his honor. Wood died on May 8, 1943, at Johns Hopkins Hospital in Baltimore after a short illness. He left a widow, three sons, and a daughter to mourn his passing.

Archives of Maryland. *The First Colored Professional, Clerical and Business Directory of Baltimore City, 22nd Annual Edition, 1934–1935.* Vol. 512, p. 1. http://www.mdarchives.state.md.us (accessed August 19, 2010).

Newspapers: "Dr. Francis M. Wood, Educator, 65, Dead," *NYT,* May 9, 1943, 40; *LL,* May 22, 1943.

University of Kentucky. "Wood, Francis M." Notable Kentucky African Americans Database. http://www.uky.edu/Libraries/NKAA (accessed August 19, 2010).

Yenser, Thomas, ed. *Who's Who in Colored America, 1941–1944.* 6th ed. Brooklyn, NY: Thomas Yenser, 1942, 581–582.

—*Andrew Baskin*

WOOD, IONE ELVEDA (b. 1868, Burlington, NJ; d. 1923, Minneapolis, MN), educator, club leader, lecturer, and writer. Ione Elveda Wood, daughter of George and Emma (Simmons) Wood, was born in Burlington, NJ, in 1868. Her educational background included a high school diploma from Atlantic City (a mixed-race school), her college degree from Kentucky Normal and Theological Institute, and her AB degree from Louisville's State Colored Baptist University (later known as **Simmons College of Kentucky**) in 1888. In the same year, she was employed by *Our Women and Children* as the editor of the temperance department. In Louisville, she also worked in education and lectured in woman's work and temperance.

As a writer, Wood was well respected and gained popular attention to her work at the age of 20. After she enrolled at State University with aid from her uncle, Dr. **William J. Simmons,** she filled the position of teacher's assistant at the school. She taught Greek and German. As a leader, she served as president of Afro-American Women's Clubs of Minnesota, vice president of the National Association of Colored Women's Clubs, honorary president of the State Federation American Association of Woman's Clubs, and fraternal delegate to Minnesota's State Federation of Women's Clubs, a white organization.

In 1890, Wood married businessman Jasper Gibbs. After their marriage, they moved to Minneapolis, MN, and together they produced five sons. After her husband's death, she, along with her sons, operated a laundry company. On June 9, 1923, barely passed her 55th birthday, she died in her home and was buried in Lakewood Cemetery in Minneapolis.

Majors, Monroe A. *Noted Negro Women: Their Triumphs and Activities.* Jackson, TN: M. V. Lynk Publishing House, 1893.

Mather, Frank Lincoln. *Who's Who of the Colored Race: A General Biographical Dictionary of Men and Women of African Descent.* Vol. 1. Chicago: Memento Edition, 1915.

"Mrs. Ione E. Gibbs, Prominent Club Woman, Dies in Minneapolis." *Appeal* (St. Paul and Minneapolis), June 16, 1923, 1.

Penn, I. Garland. *The Afro-American Press, and Its Editors.* Springfield, MA: Willey and Co., 1891.

—*Kim Nguyen*

WOODS, BRENT (b. 1855, Pulaski Co., KY; d. 1906, Somerset, KY)Medal of Honor recipient. Brent Woods, awarded the Congressional Medal of Honor as a sergeant in the Indian campaigns, was a mulatto born into slavery in Pulaski Co., KY, in 1855. Freed at the age of eight, he joined the cavalry 10 years later, in 1873. Woods was assigned to Company B of the 9th Cavalry and was stationed in the West to fight in the Indian campaigns (1866–1891). During a battle with the Apache Indians led by Chief Nana on August 19, 1881, in Gavilan Canyon, NM, the men of Company B found themselves without a commanding officer when the first in command was killed and the second in command could not be found. Woods rallied the men of his company after taking a group of cowboy civilians, who had joined them the day before, to safety. Woods then led a charge against the Indians, making his way to the top of a ridge where he fought despite a wounded arm until the Indians retreated. A cowboy saved by Woods in the battle said, "If it had not been for him, none of us would have come out of that canyon." Thirteen years later, on July 21, 1894, Woods received the Congressional Medal of Honor. The delay is attributed to his race. Woods died on March 31, 1906, and was buried without notice in an unmarked grave in the black section of the First Baptist Church Cemetery in Somerset, KY. He was survived by his wife, Pearl Baker.

Woods went virtually unrecognized until 1982, when Loraine Smith of Somerset began a campaign to mark his grave. On June 20, 1984, Woods's body was moved to Mill Springs Cemetery near Nancy, KY, and on October 28, 1984, with the help of U.S. representative Harold Rogers and the Veterans Administration, an official military burial ceremony took place, attended by the secretary of the army, John O. Marsh Jr. Woods is Pulaski Co.'s only Medal of Honor winner.

Kentucky's Black Heritage: The Role of the Black People in the History of Kentucky from Pioneer Days to the Present. Frankfort: Kentucky Commission on Human Rights, 1971.
Lee, Irvin H. *Negro Medal of Honor Men.* New York: Dodd Mead, 1969.

—*Peggy M. Brock*

WOODS, GRANVILLE T. (b. 1846, Columbus, OH; d. 1910, New York, NY), inventor and businessman. Granville Woods, known as the black Thomas Edison, was a pioneer African American inventor and businessman. After mastering the trades of a machinist and a blacksmith, and after working as a railroad fireman and engineer, Woods completed a series of college courses in electrical and mechanical engineering between 1876 and 1878. In 1880, he came to Cincinnati and founded the Woods Electric Company. In 1888, he moved to Covington, KY, and resided on Lynn St. In late 1888, while operating the Woods Electric Company in Cincinnati, he started a similar enterprise in Newport, KY. He incorporated his manufacturing enterprise on January 21, 1889, as the G. T. Woods Manufacturing Company. The company manufactured electrical and mechanical devices, such as switches, telegraph systems, and appliances. Woods is credited with inventing the "induction telegraph," in 1887. This invention made voice communication between train stations over telegraph wires possible. A short time later, Woods moved to New York City, where he sold a number of his patents to Thomas A. Edison and his General Electric Company, the American Bell Telephone Company, and the Westinghouse Air Brake Company. Woods obtained some 60 patents during his life. He never married. Woods died in 1910 at Harlem Hospital after suffering a stroke and was buried in St. Michael's Cemetery, Astoria, in Queens Co., NY.

Christopher, Michael C. "Granville T. Woods: The Plight of a Black Inventor," *Journal of Black Studies* 11, no. 3 (1981).
"Granville T. Woods Biography." http://www.biography.com/people/granville-t-woods-9536481#synopsis (accessed August 18, 2014).
"Granville T. Woods 1856–1910." http://inventors.about.com/od/wstartinventors/a/GranvilleTWoods.htm (accessed August 18, 2014).
Low, W. Augustus, ed. *Encyclopedia of Black America.* New York: McGraw-Hill, 1981.
State Journal (Frankfort), January 3, 1889, 4.

—*Theodore H. H. Harris*

WOODSON, CARTER GODWIN (b. 1875, New Canton, VA; d. 1950, Washington, DC), educator and author known as the father of Black History Month. Carter Godwin Woodson was born on December 19, 1875, in New Canton, Buckingham Co., VA, to former slaves James and Eliza Riddle Woodson. His father, who had assisted Union soldiers during the Civil War, had a large family, which he moved to Huntington, WV, when he heard that a high school for blacks was being built there. In 1895, at the age of 20, Woodson entered (**Frederick**) **Douglass High School.** Graduating two years later, he taught in Fayette Co. and in 1900 became principal of Douglass High School. The following year he enrolled in **Berea College** and graduated with a bachelor of literature degree in 1903. (Subsequently, he asserted that the college should have awarded him a bachelor of arts degree.)

Woodson was a school supervisor in the Philippines from 1903 to 1907. In 1907, he received a BA degree from the University of Chicago, and an MA in 1908. In 1912, he was awarded a PhD in history from Harvard University; he was only the second black American to earn that degree (the first was W. E. B. Du-Bois). In 1915, with Jesse E. Moorland, Woodson founded the Association for the Study of Negro Life and History; a year later he established the *Journal of Negro History.* He was dean of liberal arts and head of the graduate faculty at Howard University (1919–1920) and dean of West Virginia State College (1920–1922). To encourage publication of books on African Americans, he founded Associated Publishers in 1920 and six years later helped establish Negro History Week (now Black History Month). He wrote many pathbreaking scholarly books, such as *The Negro in Our History* (1922) and *The Mis-education of the Negro* (1933), which continue to be read today. He died on April 3, 1950, and was buried in Lincoln Memorial Cemetery, Suitland–Silver Hill, MD. His home in Washington, DC, is preserved as a national historic site.

Durden, Robert F. *Carter G. Woodson: Father of African-American History.* Springfield, NJ: Enslow, 1998.
Goggin, Jacqueline Anne. *Carter G. Woodson: A Life in Black History.* Baton Rouge: Louisiana State Univ. Press, 1993.
Greene, Lorenzo Johnston. *Selling Black History for Carter G. Woodson: A Diary, 1930–1933.* Columbia: Univ. of Missouri Press, 1996.

—*Paul David Nelson*

WRIGHT, GEORGE C. (b. 1950, Lexington), teacher, scholar, and college president. April 4, 1968 impacted the life of George C. Wright for two reasons: it was the day Dr. Martin Luther King Jr. was assassinated in Memphis, TN, and institutions like the University of Kentucky began seriously recruiting African American students in the aftermath of King's death. That summer, Wright attended a summer program at the University of Kentucky that offered admission and financial support for students who completed the program. He had recently graduated from Lafayette High School in Lexington and it was during that summer program he met his future wife Valerie Ellison Wright. Both graduated from the university in 1972. Wright earned an MA degree in history in 1974 and a PhD in history from Duke University in 1977. Wright and his wife became parents of two children: Rebeca, who passed away in 2004, and Benjamin a college graduate.

Wright had an extensive teaching and administrative career that included positions at the University of Kentucky, University of Texas at Austin, Duke University, and the University of Texas at Arlington where he served as vice president and provost. He published three influential books on the Kentucky African American experience and won several teaching awards including the Jean Holloway Award for Teaching Excellence at the University of Texas at Austin. In 2003, he was appointed as the seventh president of Prairie View A&M University Texas. The following year he was awarded an honorary doctorate from the University of Kentucky and was included in the Hall of Distinguished Alumni in 2005.

In 2011, when the Prairie View faced a budget cut, Wright saved the university $50,000 when he made the decision to serve as president and teach an entry-level course on American history with 300 students. "I've been masquerading all these years as an administrator," said Wright, "but I'm really a teacher." When he is no longer president at Prairie Wright he said he did not "want to sit on an advisory board or a foundation, I plan to teach."

Hamilton, Reeve, "George C. Wright: The TT Interview," *The Texas Tribune,* August 22, 2011.

Minutes of the Special Telephonic Meeting of the Board of Regents of The Texas A&M University System held in College, Texas, July 8, 2003, 2.

Prairie View A&M University, "About the President, Dr. George C. Wright." http://www.pvamu.edu/president/about-the-president/ (accessed August 18, 2014).

Roenker, Robin, "George C. Wright: Presidential Success, Lexington Native Rose from Smart-aleck Kid to Be University President," *Kentucky Magazine,* Winter 2012, 16–19.

—*Gerald L. Smith*

WRIGHT, JAMES L. (b. 1919, Russellville, KY; d. 1999, Chicago, IL), union organizer and civil rights activist. Born on March 15, 1919, the son of sharecropper parents, James L. Wright grew up in Russellville in the midst of the Depression. After marrying his wife, Gladys, in 1936, Wright worked at a Civilian Conservation Corps camp and washed cars before moving to Louisville in 1941. He carried crossties, became a construction foreman, and assembled airplanes before he was inducted into

military service in 1944, during which he was wounded and captured.

Upon returning to Louisville from military service in 1946, Wright worked at an International Harvester factory and joined Local 236 of the interracial leftist-led Farm Equipment Workers (FE) Union. He emerged as a union leader during the contentious labor battles between International Harvester and FE, helping organize several strikes in protest of company policy. He was also exposed to national politics, spending considerable time campaigning for Henry Wallace in 1948.

Wright also was active in civil rights efforts, attempting to integrate both the factory and the city. In 1948, he was temporarily fired after sitting down in the whites-only area of the factory cafeterias but was soon reinstated after other factory workers walked out in protest. He also participated in union efforts to integrate the all-white **Cherokee State Park** area and several city hotels, joined the local branch of the **National Association for the Advancement of Colored People,** and served on the Andrew Wade Committee. Reflecting on his civil rights activity, Wright said that "we was struggling and fighting and getting put in jail, the same stuff that [Martin Luther King Jr.] did . . . back in '51, '50, '49, '48." His efforts even earned him FBI scrutiny as a suspected subversive.

In 1952, Wright was fired from his job after he was falsely accused of throwing a brick through the windshield of a strikebreaker's car. He became a full time staff member with the FE and followed it into the United Auto Workers (UAW) after the FE-UAW merger in 1955. Wright moved to Chicago soon after and rose in prominence in the UAW. Helping unionize more than 40 plants as an organizer, he additionally served as the head of the Fair Practice and Civil Rights Department of the UAW's Region 4, covering the north central United States. Wright was also active in civil rights as a member of the Chicago Urban League, a participant in the Chicago Freedom Movement, and president of the Chicago Area Community Action Program Council. He was selected as assistant director of Region 4 in 1975 and director in 1980 before resigning in 1984 because of illness. He died on July 25, 1999.

Devinatz, Victor G. "'We Had a Utopia in the Union': James Wright, the Farm Equipment Workers Union, and the Struggle for Civil Rights Unionism in Postwar Louisville, 1946–1952." *Nature, Society, and Thought* 20, nos. 3–4 (July/October 2007), 261–78.

Gilpin, Toni. "Left by Themselves: A History of the United Farm Equipment and Metal Workers Union, 1938–1955." 2 vols. PhD diss., Yale Univ., 1992.

Newspapers: "Leaders Draw Up Demands for Racial 'Summit' Meeting," *Chicago Defender,* August 17, 1966, 1; "Regional UAW Elects Wright to International," *Chicago Defender,* May 20, 1970, 8; Lorraine Forte, "James Wright, Former UAW leader," *Chicago Sun-Times,* July 28, 1999, 74.

—*David Lai*

WRIGHT, WILLIAM H. (b. 1876, Livingston, AL; d. 1926, Louisville, KY), cofounder of Mammoth Life and Accident Insurance Company and American Mutual Savings Bank. Born to slave parents on an Alabama farm, William H. Wright worked in the fields in the mornings and evenings while attending local schools in between, at one point walking 10 miles each day to get an education. In 1892, he attended Selma University, leaving to enter State Colored Baptist University (later known as **Simmons College of Kentucky**) in Louisville in 1896. Three years later, he enrolled in the Law Department of Howard University and earned his degree in 1902. He briefly worked for the Department of Printing before returning to Louisville to practice law in 1904.

Wright joined the faculty at State University and maintained a law practice in the city. In Louisville, he was one of several influential black citizens to attend **Fifth Street Baptist Church.** He also briefly dabbled in politics, announcing his decision to run for the state legislature in 1909. However, he received no support from the local Republican organization, whose leaders told him that "it was too early for a Negro to run for office," and their resistance doomed his independent campaign to failure.

After local white insurance companies promoted a bill that hindered the efficacy of out-of-state black insurance companies in Kentucky, Wright, along with **Henry Hall** and several black investors, organized **Mammoth Life and Accident Insurance Company** on July 12, 1915. The insurance company, which received its charter a year later, rapidly became Louisville's largest black-owned and black-operated business, with over $200,000 in assets by 1924. Wright's position on the board of trustees, as well as his law practice, efforts in real estate, and presidency of the **American Mutual Savings Bank,** combined to make him one of the richest black men in the city despite having been born in poverty.

On June 30, 1926, Wright died at his home on **Walnut St.** in Louisville.

Newspapers: *IF,* June 26, 1909, 1; "Negro Who Made Fortune Is Dead," *Louisville Times,* June 30, 1926, 15.

Stuart, M. S. *An Economic Detour: A History of Insurance in the Lives of American Negroes.* New York: Wendell Malliet & Company, 1940.

Wright, George C. *Life Behind a Veil: Blacks in Louisville, Kentucky, 1865–1930.* Baton Rouge: Louisiana State Univ. Press, 1985.

—*Stephen Pickering*

Y

YARBROUGH, MARILYN V. (b. 1945, Bowling Green, KY; d. Burnsville, NC, 2004), law school professor and dean. Marilyn V. Yarbrough Ainsworth was born in 1945 as Marilyn Yarbrough in Bowling Green, KY, to Merca Toole and William Yarbrough. Her family moved to North Carolina when Yarbrough was a child. She left the state to attend Virginia State University, a historically black school in Petersburg, VA, where she received her bachelor's degree in 1966. She subsequently moved to California to attend law school at the University of California, Los Angeles.

Yarbrough's winnings from the *Hollywood Squares Show* financed her law school education, and she enjoyed subsequent success in other television game shows. Beginning with her first law professor position at Boston College, Yarbrough specialized primarily in race and gender discrimination. From Boston College, Yarbrough went on to spend over a decade at the University of Kansas.

In 1987, Yarbrough became the first African American woman dean at a major southern law school when she received the position at the University of Tennessee. After her stint as dean, Yarbrough held the William J. Maier Jr. Chair of Law at West Virginia University for a year before moving to the University of North Carolina. In addition to teaching in the law school at North Carolina, Yarbrough served two years as associate provost.

Outside her teaching, Yarbrough contributed to the academic and collegiate community by serving on the Pulitzer Prize Board and on the NCAA Committee on Infractions. One example of recognition of her contributions is the Marilyn Yarbrough Dissertation/Teaching Fellowship at Kenyon College in Ohio. When she died in 2004 of natural causes, Dean Gene Nichol of the University of North Carolina School of Law commented that "the University of North Carolina has lost one of its greatest leaders and most prized friends. Yarbrough gave much of her professional life to us and we have all benefited greatly from her efforts, her humor, her insight and her care. Our entire community has been devastated by her loss."

American Bar Association Commission on Women in the Profession. "Dean Marilyn V. Yarbrough." http://www.abanet.org/women/bios/marilyn_yarbrough.pdf (accessed March 30, 2009).
Associated Press. "Obituaries in the News, Marilyn Yarbrough." *WP,* March 11, 2004.
Kenyon College. "Marilyn Yarbrough Dissertation/Teaching Fellowship." http://www.kenyon.edu/x27112.xml (accessed April 1, 2009).
"Marilyn Yarbrough, Law Prof, Ex-Tennessee Dean, Dies at 58." http://www.lawschool.com/yarbrough.htm (accessed August 18, 2014).
Stewart, Lizzie. "Yarbrough, 58, Law Professor." *Daily Tar Heel,* March 15, 2004.

—Joseph Gershtenson

YOKLEY, RAYTHA (b. 1910, East Bernstadt, KY; d. 2001, Buffalo, NY), one of the first African American professors at Western Kentucky University. Raytha Yokley was born to Emma and Edward Yokley in Laurel Co., KY, on September 12, 1910. He was the youngest of five children. He attended public schools in Laurel Co. before moving to Frankfort, KY, to finish high school at the Kentucky Normal and Industrial Institute (later known as **Kentucky State University**) in 1927. Yokley earned a bachelor's degree from Kentucky State College in 1937. He taught in public schools in both Manchester and London, KY, before pursuing his master's degree at Indiana University, Bloomington. His thesis, titled "The Negro Community in Bloomington," was completed in 1941. Shortly after receiving his degree, Yokley enlisted in the U.S. Army. He spent three years (1942–1945) as a classification specialist in the South Pacific.

Upon returning from the war, Yokley enrolled at Indiana University in order to pursue a PhD in sociology. In 1952, he received his degree, having completed his dissertation, "The Development of Racial Concepts in Negro Children." He taught first at what is now Kentucky State University, where he served as head of the Sociology Department for three years, beginning in 1956. He then held the position of associate professor of sociology at Fisk University for several years. In this capacity, he conducted research on the relationship of adolescents and college students to the law and the judicial system. In 1966, he directed the Pre-college Center at the university. This organization worked to improve education for high school students from low-income families in Nashville, TN.

In 1967, Yokley was appointed assistant professor of sociology at Western Kentucky University, one of its first African American professors. He was elected the first African American member of the Russellville Board of Education in 1968. During his 14-year term on the board, he served as vice chairman and for four years as chairman. In 1971, Yokley coauthored *The Black Church in America.*

Yokley continued to teach at Western Kentucky University until 1978. That year, Governor Julian Carroll appointed him to the Kentucky State Advisory Committee on Educational Improvement. In 1984, he received the Smith-Wilson Award for Civil and Human Rights in Education from the Kentucky Education Association.

Raytha Yokley died in Buffalo, NY, on July 3, 2001. His funeral was held in Russellville, KY.

Dunnigan, Alice Allison, comp. and ed. *The Fascinating Story of Black Kentuckians: Their Heritage and Traditions.* Washington, DC: Associated Publishers, 1982.
Newspapers: "20 Negroes Hold Elective Offices across Kentucky," *BGDN,* March 2, 1969, 29; "Award Winner Talks about His Experiences in Education," *BGDN,* April 20, 1984, 2; "Raytha L. Yokley," *BGDN,* July 7, 2001, 5A.

—Elizabeth Schaller

YORK (b. ca. 1770, Caroline Co., VA, d. ca. 1825), enslaved explorer with the Lewis and Clark expedition. York, the only black member of the Lewis and Clark Corps of Discovery (1804–1806), was the enslaved body servant of William Clark. He was born in 1770 or shortly thereafter at the Clark family plantation in Caroline Co., VA. His parents were York and Rose, slaves of Clark's father, John Clark. In 1784, he migrated with the Clark family to Mulberry Hill plantation near Louisville, KY. He grew to be a big, strong, athletic man. Chosen by Clark as a member of the expedition to the Pacific Ocean, he made invaluable contributions. He was a popular part of the team, plying the oars on the expedition's boats and doing all that everyone else did. On one occasion, he risked his life to save Clark from drowning, and he was a good hunter. In addition, he impressed the Indians, particularly their women.

Some time before 1811, York had a falling out with Clark and was hired out to a cruel taskmaster in Louisville. He married an unknown woman but lost her when her master moved to Natchez. Freed by Clark after 1811 and given a wagon and six horses, he was cheated by whites in business, forced to sell his property, and bonded to a man in Tennessee. He died of cholera sometime between 1814 and 1832, perhaps while attempting to return to Clark or (as some speculate) to reach the Indians who had befriended him in the West.

Ambrose, Stephen E. *Undaunted Courage: Meriwether Lewis, Thomas Jefferson, and the Opening of the American West.* New York: Simon & Schuster, 1996.
Betts, Robert B. *In Search of York: The Slave Who Went to the Pacific with Lewis and Clark.* Boulder: Univ. Press of Colorado and the Lewis and Clark Trail Heritage Foundation, 2000.

—*Paul David Nelson*

YOUNG, CHARLES DENTON (b. 1864, Mays Lick, KY; d. 1922, Lagos, Nigeria), educator and military officer. Charles Young, who became a colonel in the U.S. Army, was the son of former slaves. During the Civil War, his father served as a private in the Colored Artillery Volunteers when the U.S. Army was segregated.

Young's family moved to Ripley, OH, when he was a young child. He attended the white Ripley High School, from which he graduated with honors at age 16. Afterward, he taught at the black Ripley High School. Young was musically inclined and played the piano, the violin, and the guitar.

While he was a teacher, he took a competitive exam for appointment to the U.S. Military Academy at West Point, NY, and placed second among the applicants. He graduated from West Point in the class of 1889, becoming only the third black ever to graduate, and was commissioned as a 2nd lieutenant.

In 1903, he married Aida Barr, and they had two children. Also in 1903, he was named acting superintendent of the Sequoia and General Grant National Parks, the first black to hold that title. His duties as a military officer were to enforce park rules, supervise the activities of the rangers, and protect the park and its wildlife from harm. His greatest accomplishment during his tenure was the construction of more roads, and he encouraged the federal government to purchase additional park land. For his performance, he was promoted to the rank of captain. He served in the U.S. Army for 37 years, with assignments in the United States, Mexico, the Philippines, Haiti, and Liberia.

At the start of World War I, he was diagnosed with Bright's disease (a kidney disorder) and was medically discharged. For the next two years, he served as a professor of military science at Wilberforce University in Ohio. In 1916, he was awarded the Spingarn Medal, given annually by the **National Association for the Advancement of Colored People** for outstanding achievement by a black American. In the fall of 1918, Young rode a horse from Xenia, OH, to Washington DC, proving to government officials that he was physically fit, and he was subsequently allowed to rejoin the army.

On November 6, 1918, he was promoted to the rank of colonel, becoming the first African American to reach that rank in the U.S. Army. In 1919, he was appointed military attaché to the Republic of Liberia. At the age of 58, while on a reconnaissance mission there, Young died of a kidney infection. He was buried in Lagos, Nigeria. In June 1923, at his wife's insistence, his remains were reburied with full military honors in Arlington National Cemetery in Arlington, VA. In 2014, work began on restoring Young's log cabin birthplace in Mays Lick with plans to establish a museum.

Arlington National Cemetery Website: Where Valor Proudly Sleeps. "Charles Denton Young: Colonel United States Army." http://www.arlingtoncemetery.net (accessed July 27, 2014).
Buffalo Soldiers and Indian Wars. "Colonel Charles Young." http://www.buffalosoldier.net.
NPS.gov. "Capt. Charles Young." http://www.nps.gov.
Toncray Marla, "Restoration Begins on Young Cabin." *The Ledger Independent,* May 22, 2014.

—*Jack Wessling*

YOUNG, JULIA SOHMERS (b. ca. 1874, Maysville, KY; d. 1922, Frankfort, KY), journalist and teacher. Born in Maysville, KY, around 1874, Julia Sohmers Young spent much of her life in the city, as well as in neighboring towns in Mason Co. Her parents, William and Mary Young, were both born and raised in Kentucky as well. Young had a twin sister, Anna, and both girls attended the black school in Mason Co. By 1891, Julia Young was teaching in the Mason Co. public school district. In 1894, she graduated from **Eckstein Norton Institute** in Cane Springs, KY. Young returned to Mason Co. and received her first-class teaching certificate on July 25, 1894.

Julia Young taught in Maysville for several years and then returned to Eckstein Norton Institute and worked there as a stenographer. Between 1900 and 1902, Young was employed first as a stenographer and typist in Charlotte, NC, and later served briefly on the editorial staff of the *Colored American,* a Washington, DC, newspaper. In September 1902, she returned home to teach first in Maysville and later in Germantown, KY.

By 1907, Julia Young was an active member of the Negro Press Association, organized in Louisville, KY. The association held an initial meeting on August 26, 1907, in Mt. Sterling, KY, at which Young gave a presentation titled "Our Safeguard." During the next several years, Young served as the owner and editor of the *Kentucky Standard,* a newspaper published in Lexington, KY. She continued to be a leading member of the Negro Press Association and served as secretary of the organization in 1908.

Young continued to be closely involved in the State Association of Colored Teachers (later known as the **Kentucky Negro Educational Association**) and always maintained a passion for education. She was a major proponent of educational progress for African Americans in Kentucky. She opposed programs that focused on instruction in manual labor skills, such as that at

Lincoln Institute, in favor of a curriculum that was intellectually comparable to that available to white students.

Her interest in education continued long after circulation of the *Kentucky Standard* ended in 1911. Young took a job as the secretary to the president and director of the Commercial Department at the Kentucky Normal and Industrial Institute (later known as **Kentucky State University**) in Frankfort, KY. She worked at the school for over eight years and then returned to teaching, this time in Frankfort. She taught for several years before her death on November 27, 1922. Julia Young was buried in Maysville, KY.

Newspapers: "Successful Teachers," *Evening Bulletin* (Maysville, KY), July 25, 1894, 2; "Meeting of New Society Called for Aug. 26 at Mt. Sterling," *Mt. Sterling Advocate,* August 21, 1907, 6.

Students of the Kentucky Normal and Industrial Institute. *Students' Bulletin: Annual Edition Dedicated to Class of 1919.* Frankfort, KY: Middle Class, 1919.

—*Elizabeth Schaller*

YOUNG, LAURA RAY (b. ca. 1896, Lebanon, KY; d. 1962, Simpsonville, KY), postmistress and educator at Lincoln Institute, Lincoln Ridge, KY. Laura Ray Young was born around 1896 to Richard and Ella Ray of Lebanon, KY. The Rays were married in 1881 and had ten children. They owned a sulfur well and sold special water to an interracial clientele. By 1890, the Rays owned their home mortgage free.

Like many Kentucky African Americans of the early twentieth century, Laura left home to attend high school at **Lincoln Institute** in Lincoln Ridge, Shelby Co., KY. Besides obtaining a high school education at Lincoln, she met **Whitney Young Sr.,** whom she married in 1914. They were married for 45 years and had three children: **Arnita Young Boswell, Eleanor Young Love,** and **Whitney Young Jr.**

Laura attended Kentucky Normal and Industrial Institute (later known as **Kentucky State University**) after graduating from Lincoln Institute. Whitney Sr. served in the U.S. Army during World War I; after his discharge, the Youngs lived briefly in Detroit, MI, but returned to teach at Lincoln Institute in 1920. In 1940, Laura was appointed postmaster at Lincoln Ridge. She became the first African American postmaster in Kentucky and the second one in the United States. She was a member of the Red Cross Guild and the Urban League Guild of Louisville.

Known as Mother Dear to her children and grandchildren, Young was a firm but gracious disciplinarian. She would provide home-cooked meals and buy clothes for needy students. Sometimes, she would intervene with the police if she believed that students were being falsely accused. In addition, she openly defied **Jim Crow** practices. For example, contrary to a practice during segregation, before purchasing clothes, she would try them on. She was a full partner in helping her husband ensure the survival of Lincoln Institute until the 1960s.

Dickerson, Dennis. *Militant Mediator: Whitney M. Young, Jr.* Lexington: Univ. Press of Kentucky, 1998.

"1st Negro Postmaster, Mrs. W. M. Young, Dies." *LCJ,* October 4, 1962, 26.

Weiss, Nancy. *Whitney M. Young, Jr., and the Struggle for Civil Rights.* Princeton, NJ: Princeton Univ. Press, 1989.

—*Andrew Baskin*

YOUNG, MARGARET BUCKNER (b. 1922, Campbellsville, KY; d. 2009, Denver, CO), educator and author of children's books. Margaret Buckner was born in 1922 in Campbellsville, KY, to Frank Buckner and Eva Carter Buckner, both teachers in Kentucky's segregated school system. She graduated in 1942 from

Dr. Whitney M. Young Sr. and his wife, Laura Young (seated, far left), with Lincoln Institute students.

Kentucky State College (later known as **Kentucky State University**) and received a master's degree in educational psychology and testing from the University of Minnesota in 1945. She married **Whitney M. Young Jr.**, a Kentucky State College classmate, on January 2, 1944.

Beginning her career in education as an instructor at Kentucky State College from 1942 to 1944, Young later served as a professor of educational psychology at Spelman College (1957–1960). She also wrote several books for children focusing on the African American experience and civil rights, including *The First Book of American Negroes* (1966), *The Picture Life of Martin Luther King, Jr.* (1968), and *Black American Leaders* (1969).

Young's husband, Whitney M. Young, Jr. was appointed executive director of the **National Urban League** in 1961. After her husband's death in 1971, Young served as the chairwoman and executive director of the Whitney M. Young Jr. Memorial Foundation. She was also on the boards of directors of the Metropolitan Museum of Art in New York, Lincoln Center, and the Dance Theatre of Harlem, as well as those of the Philip Morris Company and the New York Life Insurance Company. In 1973, she was a U.S. delegate to the 28th General Assembly of the United Nations.

Young died at the age of 88 and was buried with her husband in Ferncliff Cemetery in Westchester Co., NY.

Culver, Virginia. "Margaret Buckner Young Dies at 88; Author, Widow of Civil-Rights Leader." *Denver Post*, December 9, 2009. http://www.denverpost.com/ci_13955713 (accessed July 28, 2014).

Dunnigan, Alice Allison. "Margaret Buckner Young." In *The Fascinating Story of Black Kentuckians: Their Heritage and Traditions*, compiled and edited by Alice Allison Dunnigan, 276. Washington, DC: Associated Publishers, 1982.

Fox, Margalit. "Margaret B. Young, Writer of Children's Books on Blacks, Dies at 88." *NYT*, December 18, 2009. http://www.nytimes.com/2009/12/18/us/18myoung.html?_r=0# (accessed July 28, 2014).

Horan and McConaty Funeral Home. "Margaret Young." Denver, CO, 2009. http://www.horancares.com/obituary/Margaret-Young/Denver-CO/733130 (accessed January 12, 2013).

"Young, Margaret Buckner." In *Who's Who among African Americans*, 22nd ed., edited by Kristin B. Mallegg, 1361. Detroit: Gale, 2008.

—*Jennifer Bartlett*

YOUNG, WHITNEY MOORE, JR. (b. 1921, Lincoln Ridge, KY; d. 1971, Lagos, Nigeria) National Urban League executive director. Whitney Moore Young Jr., civil rights advocate, was born at Lincoln Ridge, KY, on July 31, 1921. He was the son of **Whitney Moore Young Sr.** and **Laura Ray Young.** His father was an instructor and later education director (head) of **Lincoln Institute** in Shelby Co. Young graduated from Lincoln Institute as valedictorian in 1936 and from Kentucky State College (later known as **Kentucky State University**) in 1940 at the head of his class. He was a mathematics teacher at **Rosenwald High School** in Madisonville. Entering the army in 1941, he spent two years at the Massachusetts Institute of Technology studying electrical engineering and one as a sergeant in an all-black antiaircraft battery. He earned three Bronze Stars. On January 2, 1944, he mar-

Whitney Moore Young Jr., 1967.

ried **Margaret Buckner** (**Young**); they had two children. Denied admission to the University of Kentucky because of his race, he attended the University of Minnesota from 1944 to 1947, where he organized a chapter of the **Congress of Racial Equality** and received a master's degree in social work

In 1947, Young began working for the **National Urban League** in St. Paul, MN. Three years later, he became head of the Omaha (NE) Urban League office He was appointed dean of the Atlanta University of Social Work in 1954 and in 1961 became executive director of the National Urban League. Over the next 10 years he was a leader in the social work profession and the **civil rights movement.** He was president of the National Conference on Social Welfare and the National Association of Social Workers. He served on seven presidential commissions, wrote important books, and penned a weekly syndicated newspaper column. In 1969, he received the Medal of Freedom from President Lyndon B. Johnson. He died in a swimming accident in Lagos, Nigeria, on March 11, 1971, and was buried in Greenwood Cemetery (later named Cove Haven) in Lexington. His body was later reinterred in New Rochelle, NY.

Dickerson, Dennis C. *Militant Mediator: Whitney M. Young, Jr.* Lexington: Univ. Press of Kentucky, 1998.

Weiss, Nancy J. *Whitney M. Young, Jr., and the Struggle for Civil Rights.* Princeton, NJ: Princeton Univ. Press, 1989.

—*Paul David Nelson*

YOUNG, WHITNEY MOORE, SR. (b. 1897, Paynes Depot, KY; d. 1975, Louisville, KY), educator. Educator Whitney Moore Young Sr. was born in Paynes Depot, KY, on September 26, 1897, the son of Taylor and Annie Young. When **Lincoln Institute** opened in 1912, he enrolled and graduated four years later. He was employed by the Ford Motor Company in Detroit, MI. In 1914, he married **Laura Ray (Young)** of Lebanon, KY; they had three children. During World War I, Young served in the U.S. Army as a volunteer in France. He rejoined Ford after the war as an electrical engineer. In 1920, he accepted an appointment at reduced pay as head of the engineering department of Lincoln Institute. After later service as dean, he was appointed the first black educational director in 1935.

When Young took over as director of Lincoln Institute, the school was $10,000 in debt, losing enrollment, and in danger of closing. Over time, he successfully reversed its decline, initiating programs to raise money and bring in more students. Significant monetary gifts from William Henry Hughes, a wealthy black Lexingtonian, were instrumental in this process. Before long, the school was thriving and had become the premier black college preparatory institution in Kentucky. In 1947, the state took over Lincoln Institute and made it a public high school. Meanwhile, Young had graduated from **Louisville Municipal College** in 1938 and earned an MA degree from Fisk University in 1944. Eleven years later, he was awarded an honorary degree of doctor of education by Monrovia College in Liberia. In the 1950s, he twice served as president of the **Kentucky Negro Educational Association.**

After the U.S. Supreme Court declared school segregation unconstitutional in 1954, Young faced a significant decrease in enrollment at Lincoln Institute. In 1964, as the school began to close (the last class graduated in 1966), he retired and moved to Louisville. President Lyndon Johnson immediately appointed him to serve on a committee to implement the newly enacted **Civil Rights Act of 1964.** He also served on the Chief Justice's Housing Commission, the State Vocational Advisory Board, the **Kentucky Commission on Human Rights** and its Black History Committee, which published the 1971 textbook *Kentucky's Black Heritage.* Whitney M. Young Sr. died on August 18, 1975, and was interred in Greenwood Cemetery (later known as Cove Haven) in Lexington.

Dunnigan, Alice Allison, comp. and ed. *The Fascinating Story of Black Kentuckians: Their Heritage and Traditions.* Washington, DC: Associated Publishers, 1982.

Lee, Mary Elizabeth, "The Leadership of Whitney M. Young, Sr., in an Educationally Segregated School System." EdS thesis, Univ. of Louisville, 1983.

Weiss, Nancy J. *Whitney M. Young, Jr., and the Struggle for Civil Rights.* Princeton, NJ: Princeton Univ. Press, 1989.

—*Paul David Nelson*

YOUNG, WILLIAM "BILLY" (b. ca. 1860, Lexington, KY; d. 1914, Lexington, KY), entertainer. Little is known about William "Billy" Young's early life. In the early 1900s, the *Lexington Leader* frequently boasted of the town's native son, and in his autobiography, **blues** legend W. C. Handy noted Young's Kentucky origin. Young's death certificate listed Lexington as his birthplace, but his parents' names were unknown.

In an era when most minstrel companies were owned and operated by white men, Young formed McCabe and Young's Minstrels in partnership with D. W. McCabe from Boston in the late 1870s. They traveled and became known nationwide. They also performed annually in Cuba. In February 1889, the two refused to bow to pressure from white patrons in St. Augustine, FL, to provide special seating for white spectators. Their business continued to flourish until the dissolution of the partnership in 1891.

In 1895, Young signed with W. A. Mahara of Mahara's Colored Minstrels. Later, W. C. Handy joined the troupe. He claimed that "Clever Billy" Young earned his billing through his talent as a singer, dancer, imitator, actor, and improviser. Handy regarded Young as "the daddy of them all in his line of work." Young was known not only for his ability to hold a high note almost endlessly but also for his excessive drinking, womanizing, and money troubles.

In October 1913, the *Indianapolis Freeman* reported Young's poor health and need for financial assistance. Young died of tuberculosis in Lexington, KY, on January 27, 1914. Undertakers Williams and Reed handled the burial arrangements and requested assistance with the burial expenses in the Indianapolis newspaper since Young died without any funds. He was buried in Lexington's **African Cemetery No. 2.** His daughter, LaBlanche Young, followed in her father's performing footsteps and took the billing name Billy Young.

Abbott, Lynn, and Doug Seroff. *Out of Sight: The Rise of African American Popular Music, 1889–1895.* Jackson: Univ. Press of Mississippi, 2002.

Handy, W. C. *Father of the Blues: An Autobiography.* Edited by Arna Bontemps. New York: Macmillan, 1941.

Kentucky, Death Records, 1852–1953.

Newspapers: "The Stage," *IF,* February 16, 1889, 4; "Signed with Mahara," *IF,* July 13, 1895, 8; "Billy Young's Latest Song," *LL,* October 14, 1902, 7; "Billy Young," *LL,* May 12, 1903, 5; "Gossip of the Stage," *IF,* October 4, 1913, 5; "Stage Notes and Stroll News," *IF,* February 14, 1914, 5; "Parker & Young—Miss Billy Young, Daughter of the Famous Billy Young," *IF,* August 28, 1915, 5.

—*Andrew Baskin*

Z

ZETA PHI BETA SORORITY, INC., first Greek-letter organization to establish a chapter in Africa. Zeta Phi Beta Sorority, Incorporated, was founded on January 16, 1920, on the campus of Howard University in Washington, DC. The five founders, Arizona Cleaver (Stemons), Pearl Anna Neal, Myrtle Tyler (Faithful), Viola Tyler (Goings), and Fannie Pettie (Watts), sought to "establish an organization that focused on the societal mores, ills, prejudices, and poverty affecting humanity in general and the black community in particular." Through their work with **Phi Beta Sigma Fraternity** members Charles Robert Samuel Taylor and A. Langston Taylor, Zeta Phi Beta Sorority and Phi Beta Sigma Fraternity became the first constitutionally bound Greek-letter sister and brother organizations. In 1948, Zeta Phi Beta became the first Greek-letter organization to charter a chapter in Africa, in Monrovia, Liberia.

In 1928, the first Kentucky chapter, Eta Zeta, a graduate chapter, was chartered in Louisville, KY. The active Eta Zeta Chapter celebrated its 85th anniversary in May 2013. Eta Alpha Chapter was the first undergraduate chapter in Kentucky, chartered in 1935 at what is now **Kentucky State University.** Five graduate chapters and six undergraduate chapters remain active in Kentucky. Additionally, there is one Zeta Amicae Auxiliary Group in Kentucky, sponsored by Eta Zeta Chapter in Louisville. In 2013, there were approximately 135 active Zetas and four Amicae in Kentucky. The largest chapters in Kentucky were graduate chapters, Eta Zeta Chapter in Louisville, followed by Kappa Lambda Zeta Chapter in Lexington.

Several Kentucky women have held national elected offices in the sorority. Fannie R. Givens, a Louisville police officer, served as chairman of the National Executive Committee and was elected the seventh president (1930–1933). In 1934, Zeta Phi Beta began naming national honorary members, including Kentuckians **Abbie Clement Jackson** and Dorcas Ruthenburg. Other Kentuckians have served the sorority as national third vice president and as the regional director for the Great Lakes Region. Many other Kentucky Zetas, such as **Elizabeth B. Cook Fouse, Alberta Odell Jones,** and **Lucy Harth Smith,** have significantly improved the lives of black people in the state through their activism.

Kentucky Zetas build on their founding principle of service through community-service initiatives. These services have included the March of Dimes March for Babies, providing and preparing dinner for families staying at the Ronald McDonald House, serving meals with the Salvation Army, assisting with and providing gifts for children on the Angel Tree, establishing and implementing voter-registration campaigns, assisting with the Fayette County Back to School Rallies, providing scholarships for undergraduate Zetas to attend National Zeta Organizational Leadership Conferences, and collecting hats and mittens for distribution through local homeless shelters. Zeta Phi Beta Sorority, Incorporated, has continually endeavored to meet the needs of the people in diverse communities and has more than 850 chapters throughout the world. Its members have remained committed to their pledge as "a Community Conscious, Action Oriented Organization."

Harrison, Lullelia W. *Torchbearers of a Legacy: A History of Zeta Phi Beta Sorority, Inc., 1920–1997.* Washington, DC: Zeta Phi Beta Sorority, 1998.

Hine, Darlene Clark, Elsa Barkley Brown, and Rosalyn Terborg-Penn, eds. *Black Women in America: An Historical Encyclopedia.* Brooklyn, NY: Carlson, 1993.

Zeta Phi Beta Sorority, Incorporated, National Website. "Zeta Phi Beta Sorority, Inc." http://www.zphib1920.org (accessed August 13, 2013).

—Toni Thomas

ZION HILL, African American community in Scott Co., KY. Before the end of slavery, a slave owner named Harris deeded some land in the southwestern corner of Scott Co., bordered by Fayette and Woodford Counties, to some African American residents. The community was originally known as Lenerson and also as South Elkhorn Bend. With over 200 acres, the village grew to a population of around 250 inhabitants, 45 homes, two stores, and one church. One of the stores housed the post office. In 1901, the post office was moved to Midway.

The prominent **African American hamlet** was later named Zion Hill, occasionally called Zion's Hill. It then had two churches, Zion Hill Baptist and an African Methodist Episcopal Church, and Zion Hill Cemetery. Born in nearby Paynes Depot, **Whitney Moore Young Sr.,** president of **Lincoln Institute,** began his education at Zion Hill's elementary school. In 1905, the school had 154 students enrolled and only one teacher, John W. Dey. That same year, some community leaders organized the Booker T. Washington Club, composed of 190 businessmen, farmers, and laborers from Scott, Fayette, and Woodford Counties. The organization met regularly to discuss race issues and annually held a banquet. Some of the town's other civic groups included the Zion's Hill Union Benevolent Society and the Zion Hill Lodge.

Zion Hill continued to grow in the 1920s with the building program of the Zion Hill Baptist Church. Additionally, in 1929, a **Rosenwald school** was built and funded. With only one teacher, the school cost $3,200, and $2,000 worth of fire insurance was purchased. The school later closed, and elementary students were bused to White Sulfur and high school students to Ed Davis High School in Georgetown.

Zion Hill later received telephone service from Fayette Co., mail delivery from Woodford Co., and civic services like water, police, and fire from Scott Co. The Faith Way Church at Zion Hilll is located on Leestown Road.

Apple, Lindsey, Frederick A. Johnston, and Anne Bolton Bevins, eds. *Scott County, Kentucky: A History.* Georgetown, KY: Scott County Historical Society, 1993.

The Historical Marker Database. http://migration.kentucky.gov/kyhs/hmdb/MarkerSearch.aspx?mode=All (accessed January 7, 2013).

"Faith Way Church at Zion Hill." https://www.facebook.com/pages/Faith-Way-Church-at-Zion-Hill/570930456319016?sk=timeline&ref=page_internal (accessed August 18, 2014).

Newspapers: "Colored," *LL,* January 24, 1905, 5; "Colored Methodist Appointments Made," *CJ,* October 12, 1909, 4.

Notable Kentucky African Americans Database. http://nkaa.uky.edu/.

—Sallie L. Powell

Selected Bibliography

BOOKS, BOOK CHAPTERS, DISSERTATIONS, AND THESES

Aaseng, Nathan. *African-American Religious Leaders.* New York: Infobase Publishing, 2003.

Abbott, Lynn, and Doug Seroff. *Out of Sight: The Rise of African American Popular Music, 1889–1895.* Jackson: Univ. Press of Mississippi, 2002.

Abraham, H. *Freedom and the Court.* New York: Oxford Univ. Press, 1967.

Adams, Luther. *Way Up North in Louisville: African American Migration in the Urban South, 1930–1970.* Chapel Hill: Univ. of North Carolina Press, 2010.

Adams, Revels A. *Cyclopedia of African Methodism in Mississippi.* Natchez, MS, 1902.

Adelson, Bruce. *Brushing Back Jim Crow: The Integration of Minor-League Baseball in the American South.* Charlottesville: Univ. Press of Virginia, 1999.

Adoff, Arnold, ed. *The Poetry of Black America: Anthology of the Twentieth Century.* New York: Harper Row, 1973.

African-American Folk Art in Kentucky. Morehead: Kentucky Folk Art Center, 1998.

African American Heritage Guide. Lexington, KY: Isaac Scott Hathaway Museum, 2009.

Akins, C. B., Sr. *From Burden to Blessing: Herein Lies the History of a Small Rural Church with Portable Biblical Principles That Propelled It from 65 to over 700 Members.* Naperville, IL: Storybook, 2001.

Alexander, Sadie. *Who's Who among Negro Lawyers.* Washington, DC: National Bar Association, 1945.

Ali, Muhammad. *The Greatest: My Own Story.* New York: Random House, 1975.

Allen, James Lane. *Flute and Violin, and Other Kentucky Tales and Romances.* New York: Harper & Brothers, 1891.

Allen, L. P. *The Genealogy and History of the Shreve Family from 1641.* Greenfield, IL: Self-published, 1901.

Alvey, R. Gerald. *Kentucky Bluegrass Country.* Jackson: Univ. Press of Mississippi, 1992.

Ambrose, Stephen E. *Undaunted Courage: Meriwether Lewis, Thomas Jefferson, and the Opening of the American West.* New York: Simon & Schuster, 1996.

American Association of University Women (Maysville Branch). *From Cabin to College: A History of the Schools of Mason County.* Maysville, KY: G. F. McClanahan, 1976.

Anderson, James Harvey. *Biographical-Souvenir Volume of the 23rd Quadrennial Session of the General Conference of the African Methodist Episcopal Zion Church.* Philadelphia: African Methodist Episcopal Zion Church, 1908.

Anderson, Robert. *From Slavery to Affluence: Memoirs of Robert Anderson, Ex-Slave.* Steamboat Springs, CO: Steamboat Pilot, 1967.

Andrews, William L. *To Tell a Free Story: The First Century of Afro-American Autobiography, 1760–1865.* Urbana: Univ. of Illinois Press, 1988.

Andrews, William L., and Henry Louis Gates, eds. *Slave Narratives.* New York: Library of America, 2000.

Annual Catalogue of the Hopkinsville M. & F. College. Hopkinsville, KY: New Era Print, 1902.

Appiah, Anthony, and Henry Louis Gates, eds. *Africana: The Encyclopedia of the African and African-American Experience.* New York: Civitas Books, 1999.

Apple, Lindsey, Frederick A. Johnston, and Anne Bolton Bevins, eds. *Scott County, Kentucky: A History.* Georgetown, KY: Scott County Historical Society, 1993.

Applegate, Katherine. *The Story of Two American Generals: Benjamin O. Davis, Jr. and Colin L. Powell.* Milwaukee, WI: Gareth Stevens, 1995.

Appleton, Thomas H., Jr., Melba Porter Hay, James C. Klotter, and Thomas E. Stephens, eds. *Kentucky: Land of Tomorrow.* Frankfort: Kentucky Historical Society Foundation, 1998.

Aptheker, Herbert. *Anti-racism in U.S. History.* New York: Greenwood Press, 1992.

Ardery, Philip. *Heroes and Horses: Tales of the Bluegrass.* Lexington: Univ. Press of Kentucky, 1996.

Arnett, Maralea. *The Annals and Scandals of Henderson County, Kentucky, 1775–1975.* Corydon, KY: Fremar Publishing, 1976.

Arsenault, Raymond. *Freedom Riders: 1961 and the Struggle for Racial Justice.* New York: Oxford Univ. Press, 2011.

Ash, Lee, ed. *Who's Who in Library Service: A Biographical Directory of Professional Librarians in the United States and Canada.* Hamden, CT: Shoe String Press, 1966.

Ashe, Arthur R., Jr. *A Hard Road to Glory: A History of the African American Athlete since 1946.* New York: Warner Books, 1988.

Asher, Brad. *Kentucky.* Northampton, MA: Interlink Books, 2006.

Bacote, Samuel William. *Who's Who among the Colored Baptists of the United States.* Kansas City, MO: Franklin Hudson, 1913.

Badger, Reid. *A Life in Ragtime: A Biography of James Reese Europe.* New York: Oxford Univ. Press, 1995.

Baird, Nancy Disher. *Healing Kentucky: Medicine in the Bluegrass State.* Lexington: Univ. Press of Kentucky, 2007.

Baker, Henry E. *The Colored Inventor.* 1913. Reprint, New York: Arno Press, 1969.

Ballard, Chris. *Hoops Nation: A Guide to America's Best Pickup Basketball.* Lincoln: Univ. of Nebraska Press, 2004.

Bancroft, Edwin Henderson. *The Negro in Sports.* Rev. ed. Washington, DC: Associated Publishers, 1939.

Bankstone, C. L. *Racial and Ethnic Relations in America.* Pasadena, CA: Salem Press, 2000.

Barnes, Catherine A. *Journey from Jim Crow: The Desegregation of Southern Transit.* New York: Columbia Univ. Press, 1983.

Barnette, Henlee Hulix. *A Pilgrimage of Faith: My Story.* Macon, GA: Mercer Univ. Press, 2004.

Barnhart, Scotty. *The World of Jazz Trumpet: A Comprehensive History and Practical Philosophy.* Milwaukee, WI: Hal Leonard, 2005.

Barr, Frances Keller, and Rebecca Smith Lee. *The Great Elm Tree: The Heritage of the Episcopal Diocese of Lexington.* Lexington, KY: Faith House Press, 1969.

Bassett, James E. "Ted," III, and Bill Mooney. *Keeneland's Ted Bassett: My Life.* Lexington: Univ. Press of Kentucky, 2009.

Bastin, Bruce. *Red River Blues: The Blues Tradition in the Southeast.* Urbana: Univ. of Illinois Press, 1986.

Batterson, Jack A. *Blind Boone: Missouri's Ragtime Pioneer.* Columbia: Univ. of Missouri Press, 1998.

Beasley, Delilah. *The Negro Trail Blazers of California.* New York: Negro Universities Press, 1969.

Beckford, Geraldine Rhoades, comp. *Biographical Dictionary of American Physicians of African Ancestry, 1800–1920.* Cherry Hill, NJ: Africana Homestead Legacy, 2011.

Beito, David, and Linda Royster Beito. *Black Maverick: T. R. M. Howard's Fight for Civil Rights and Economic Power.* Urbana: Univ. of Illinois Press, 2009.

Bentley, George R. *A History of the Freedmen's Bureau.* Philadelphia: Univ. of Pennsylvania, 1955.

Berlin, Edward A. *Ragtime: A Musical and Cultural History.* Berkeley: Univ. of California Press, 1980.

Beth, Loren P. *John Marshall Harlan: The Last Whig Justice.* Lexington: Univ. Press of Kentucky, 1992.

Betts, Robert B. *In Search of York: The Slave Who Went to the Pacific with Lewis and Clark.* Boulder: Univ. Press of Colorado and the Lewis and Clark Trail Heritage Foundation, 2000.

Betz, Paul R., and Mark Christopher Carnes, ed. *American National Biography: Supplement 1.* Oxford: Oxford Univ. Press, 2002.

Bevins, Ann Bolton. *Involvement of Blacks in Scott County Commerce during the Postbellum Period (1865–1918).* Georgetown, KY: Georgetown–Scott County Joint Planning Commission, 1989.

Bibb, Henry. *Narrative of the Life and Adventures of Henry Bibb, an American Slave.* New York: Privately printed, 1849.

Bigham, Darrel E. *On Jordan's Banks: Emancipation and Its Aftermath in the Ohio River Valley.* Lexington: Univ. Press of Kentucky, 2005.

Billingsley, Andrew. *Mighty Like a River: The Black Church and Social Reform.* New York: Oxford Univ. Press, 1999.

Binstock, Jonathan. *Sam Gilliam: A Retrospective.* Berkeley: Univ. of California Press, 2005.

Birney, William. *James Birney and His Times.* New York: Appleton, 1890.

Bishop, Robert H., collector and arranger. *An Outline of the History of the Church in the State of Kentucky, during a Period of Forty Years. . . .* Lexington, KY: Thomas T. Skillman, 1824. Reprinted in *Essence of a Saga: A Complete History of the Oldest Black Baptist Congregation West of the Allegheny Mountains, Historic Pleasant Green Missionary Baptist Church (Formerly African Baptist Church),* edited by T. H. Peoples Jr. Lexington, KY, 1990.

Bland, Sterling Lecater, Jr., ed. *African American Slave Narratives: An Anthology.* Vol. 1. Westport, CT: Greenwood Press, 2001.

Blassingame, John W., ed. *Slave Testimony: Two Centuries of Letters, Speeches, Interviews, and Autobiographies.* Baton Rouge: Louisiana State Univ. Press, 1977.

Blesh, Rudi, and Harriet Janis. *They All Played Ragtime: The True Story of an American Music.* New York: Oak Publications, 1971.

Blythe, Janett Marie. *My West Kentucky: A History of West Kentucky Technical College, 1909–1999.* Paducah, KY: Turner, 2000.

Bodenhamer, David J., and Robert Graham Barrows, eds. *The Encyclopedia of Indianapolis.* Bloomington: Indiana Univ. Press, 1994.

Bogle, Donald. *Bright Boulevards, Bold Dreams: The Story of Black Hollywood.* New York: One World Books/Random House, 2005.

Bolin, James Duane. *Bossism and Reform in a Southern City: Lexington, Kentucky, 1880–1940.* Lexington: Univ. Press of Kentucky, 2000.

Bond, Horace M., and Julia W. Bond. *The Star Creek Papers.* Edited by Adam Fairclough. Athens: Univ. of Georgia Press, 1992.

Bontemps, Arna Wendell, and Jack Conroy. *Anyplace but Here.* Columbia: Univ. of Missouri Press, 1997.

Boone, Theodore S. *Negro Baptist Chief Executives in National Places.* Detroit: A. P. Publishing Co., 1948.

Booth, Charles E. *Bridging the Breach: Evangelical Thought and Liberation in the African American Preaching Tradition.* Chicago: Urban Ministries, 2000.

Bordewich, Fergus M. *Bound for Canaan: The Underground Railroad and the War for the Soul of America.* New York: Amistad-HarperCollins, 2005.

Boris, Joseph J., ed. *Who's Who in Colored America, 1927.* New York: Who's Who in Colored America Corp., 1927.

———. *Who's Who in Colored America, 1928–1929.* New York: Who's Who in Colored America Corp., 1929.

Borries, Betty Earle. *Isaac Murphy: Kentucky's Record Jockey.* Berea: Kentucky Imprints, 1988.

Bowden, Jane A., ed. *Contemporary Authors: A Bio-Bibliographical Guide to Current Writers in Fiction, General Nonfiction, Poetry, Journalism, Drama, Motion Pictures, Television, and Other Fields.* Detroit: Gale Research, 1978.

Bowen, Edward L. *Man o' War.* Lexington, KY: Eclipse Press, 2000.

Boyd, Carl B., Jr., and Hazel Mason Boyd. *A History of Mt. Sterling, Kentucky, 1792–1918.* Mt. Sterling, KY: C. B. Boyd Jr., 1984.

Boyd, Douglas A. *Crawfish Bottom: Recovering a Lost Kentucky Community.* Lexington: Univ. Press of Kentucky, 2011.

Boykin, Ulysses W. *A Hand Book on the Detroit Negro: A Preliminary Edition.* Detroit: Minority Study Associates, 1943.

Braden, Anne. *The Wall Between.* New York: Monthly Review Press, 1958.

Bradley, Arthur. *On and Off the Bandstand.* Lincoln, NE: iUniverse, 2005.

Brandewie, Ernest. *In the Light of the Word: Divine Word Missionaries of North America.* Maryknoll, NY: Orbis Books, 2000.

Brashear, Carl M., with Paul Stillwell. *The Reminiscences of Master Chief Boatswain's Mate Carl M. Brashear, U.S. Navy (Retired).* Annapolis, MD: U.S. Naval Institute, 1998.

Brawley, Benjamin Griffith. *The Negro Genius: A New Appraisal of the Achievement of the American Negro in Literature and the Fine Arts.* New York: Biblo & Tannen, 1972.

Brophy, Alfred L. *Reconstructing the Dreamland: The Tulsa Riot of 1921.* New York: Oxford Univ. Press, 2002.

Brown, Hallie Quinn. *Homespun Heroines and Other Women of Distinction.* Xenia, OH: Aldine, 1926.

Brown, Russ. *Cardinals Handbook: Stories, Stats and Stuff about Louisville Basketball.* Wichita, KS: Wichita Eagle and Beacon Publishing, 1996.

Brown, Tamara L., Gregory S. Parks, and Clarenda M. Phillips, eds. *African American Fraternities and Sororities: The Legacy and the Vision.* Lexington: Univ. Press of Kentucky, 2005.

Bruce, Dickson D., Jr. *Black American Writing from the Nadir: The Evolution of a Literary Tradition, 1877–1915.* Baton Rouge: Louisiana State Univ. Press, 1989.

Bruner, Peter. *A Slave's Adventures toward Freedom: Not Fiction, but the True Story of a Struggle.* Oxford, OH: A. W. McGraw, 1919.

Bryant, Gwynne, ed. *The Croghans of Locust Grove.* Louisville, KY: Locust Grove Division of Historic Homes Foundation, 1988.

Bryant, James C. *Mountain Island in Owen County, Kentucky: The Settlers and Their Church.* Owenton, KY: Owen County Historical Society, 1986.

Buck, D. D. *The Progression of the Race in the United States and Canada: Treating of the Great Advancement of the Colored Race.* Chicago: Atwell Printing and Binding Co., 1907.

Bullitt, Thomas W. *My Life at Oxmoor: Life on a Farm in Kentucky before the War.* Louisville, KY: John P. Morton & Company, 1911.

Burdette, Dick. *Jump, Johnny, Jump!* Bloomington, IN: AuthorHouse, 2007.

Burke, Jackie C. *Equal to the Challenge: Pioneering Women of Horse Sports.* New York: Howell Book House, 1997.

Burnside, Jacqueline Grisby. *Berea and Madison County.* Charleston, SC: Arcadia, 2007.

Burrowes, Carl Patrick. *Power and Press Freedom in Liberia, 1830–1970.* Trenton, NJ: Africa World Press, 2004.

Burton, Nelson, Lisa Ledin, and Simon Anderson. *Nelson Burton: My Life in Jazz.* Cincinnati: Clifton Hills Press, 2000.

Burton, Thomas William. *What Experience Has Taught Me: An Autobiography of Thomas William Burton.* Cincinnati: Press of Jennings and Graham, 1910.

Byars, Lauretta Flynn. *Lexington's Colored Orphan Industrial Home: Building for the Future.* Lexington, KY: I. B. Bold Publications, 1995.

Calarco, Tom. *Places of the Underground Railroad: A Geographical Guide.* Santa Barbara, CA: Greenwood Press, 2011.

Caldwell, Arthur Bunyan, ed. *History of the American Negro and His Institutions.* Atlanta: A. B. Caldwell, 1917.

Calvert, Jean, and John Klee. *Maysville, Kentucky: From Past to Present in Pictures.* Maysville, KY: Mason County Museum, 1983.

Campbell, Israel. *An Autobiography: Bond and Free; or, Yearnings for Freedom, from My Green Brier House; Being the Story of My Life in Bondage, and My Life in Freedom.* Philadelphia: C. E. P. Brinckloe & Co., 1861.

Campbell, Madison. *Autobiography of Elder Madison Campbell: Pastor of the United Colored Baptist Church.* Richmond, KY: Pantagraph Job Rooms, 1895.

Capps, Randall. *The Rowan Story: From Federal Hill to My Old Kentucky Home.* Bowling Green, KY: Homestead Press, 1976.

Carey, Mike, and Michael McClellan. *Boston Celtics: Where Have You Gone?* Champaign, IL: Sports Publishing, 2005.

Carnegie, Mary Elizabeth. *The Path We Tread: Blacks in Nursing, 1854–1984.* Philadelphia: Jones & Bartlett, 1995.

Carnes, Mark Christopher, ed. *American National Biography: Supplement 2.* Oxford: Oxford Univ. Press, 2005.

Carpenter, Bill. *Uncloudy Days: The Gospel Music Encyclopedia.* San Francisco: Backbeat Books, 2005.

Carraco, Carol Crowe. *Women Who Made a Difference.* Lexington: Univ. Press of Kentucky, 1989.

Carter, Leon J., III. *Black Windsongs.* London: Mitre Press, 1973.

Carter, Lillie Mae. *Black Thoughts.* London: Mitre Press, 1971.

———, comp. *Doing It . . . Our Way.* London: Mitre Press, 1975.

Cathcart, William. *The Baptist Encyclopedia.* Philadelphia: Louis H. Everts, 1881.

Chalmers, David Mark. *Hooded Americanism: The History of the Ku Klux Klan.* 3rd ed. Durham, NC: Duke Univ. Press, 1987.

Charles, Ray, and David Ritz. *Brother Ray: Ray Charles' Own Story.* Cambridge, MA: Da Capo Press, 2003.

Chase, S. P. *Reclamation of Fugitives from Service.* Cincinnati: B. P. Donogh & Co., 1847.

Childress, Morton O. *Louisville Division of Police: History and Personnel, 1806–2002.* Louisville, KY: Turner, 2005.

Christmas, Walter. *Negroes in Public Affairs and Government.* Vol. 1. Chicago: Educational Heritage, 1966.

Clarke, Lewis, and Milton Clarke. *Narrative of the Sufferings of Lewis and Milton Clarke, Sons of a Soldier of the Revolution, during a Captivity of More than Twenty Years among the Slaveholders of Kentucky, One of the So-Called Christian States of North America.* Boston: Bela Marsh, 1846.

Clarke, Lewis Garrard, and Milton Clarke. *Narrative of the Sufferings of Lewis and Milton Clarke.* 1846. Reprint, New York: Arno Press, 1969.

Clark-Lewis, Elizabeth. *Living In, Living Out: African American Domestics and the Great Migration.* New York: Kodansha America, 1994.

Clay, Cassius M. *The Life Memoirs, Writings, and Speeches of Cassius M. Clay.* Cincinnati: J. Fletcher Brennan & Co., 1886.

Clayton, Xernona, with Hal Gulliver. *I've Been Marching All the Time: An Autobiography.* Atlanta: Longstreet Press, 1991.

Cohen, William. *At Freedom's Edge: Black Mobility and the Southern White Quest for Racial Control.* Baton Rouge: Louisiana State Univ. Press, 1991.

Cohn, Lawrence. *Nothing but the Blues: The Music and the Musicians.* New York: Abbeville Press, 1993.

Cole, Olen. *The African-American Experience in the Civilian Conservation Corps.* Gainesville: Univ. Press of Florida, 1999.

Coleman, Bill. *Trumpet Story.* Boston: Northeastern Univ. Press, 1991.

Coleman, J. Winston. *Slavery Times in Kentucky.* Chapel Hill: Univ. of North Carolina Press, 1940.

Collier-Thomas, Betty. *Jesus, Jobs, and Justice: African American Women and Religion.* New York: Random House, 2010.

Contemporary Black Biography (multiple vols.). Detroit: Gale Research Group, 1992– .

Cotter, Joseph S., Sr. *Twenty-Fifth Anniversary of the Founding of Little Africa.* Louisville, KY: Self-published, 1916.

Cotterill, Robert S. *History of Pioneer Kentucky.* Cincinnati: Johnson and Hardin, 1917.

Cottrell, Robert Charles. *The Best Pitcher in Baseball: The Life of Rube Foster, Negro League Giant.* New York: New York Univ. Press, 2004.

Coulter, Charles. *"Take Up the Black Man's Burden": Kansas City's African American Communities, 1865–1939.* Columbia: Univ. of Missouri Press, 2006.

Cover, Robert M. *Justice Accused: Antislavery and the Judicial Process.* New Haven, CT: Yale Univ. Press, 1975.

Cowan, Alexander. *Liberia, as I Found It in 1858.* Frankfort, KY: A. G. Hodges, 1858.

Cox, Fred, John Randolph, and John Harris. *Jug Bands of Louisville.* Compiled by Laurie Wright. Chigwell, UK: Storyville Publications, 1993.

Craig, Berry. *Hidden History of Kentucky in the Civil War.* Charleston, SC: History Press, 2010.

———. *Hidden History of Kentucky Soldiers.* Charleston, SC: History Press, 2011.

Crawford, Joe, ed. *The Black Photographers Annual.* Brooklyn, NY: Black Photographers Annual, 1972, 1973.

Crosby, Leconia Franklin. "A Study of Pupil Marks, William Grant High School, Covington, Kentucky, 1818–1929." MA thesis, Univ. of Cincinnati, 1929.

Crump, William L. *The Story of Kappa Alpha Psi: A History of the Beginning and Development of a College Greek Letter Organization, 1911–1971.* Philadelphia: Kappa Alpha Psi Fraternity, 1972.

Cullen, Countee, ed. *Caroling Dusk: An Anthology of Verse by Negro Poets.* New York: Harper & Brothers, 1927.

Curtis, Nancy. *Black Heritage Sites: An African American Odyssey and Finders Guide.* Chicago: American Library Association, 1996.

Cusic, Don, ed. *Encyclopedia of Contemporary Christian Music: Pop, Rock, and Worship.* Santa Barbara, CA: ABC-CLIO, 2010.

Dabney, Wendell P. *Cincinnati's Colored Citizens: Historical, Sociological and Biographical.* Cincinnati: Dabney, 1926.

Dahl, Linda. *Stormy Weather: The Music and Lives of a Century of Jazzwomen.* New York: Limelight Editions, 1989.

D'Amico, Francine, and Laurie Weinstein, eds. *Gender Camouflage: Women and the U.S. Military.* New York: New York Univ. Press, 1999.

Dannheiser, Frieda J., ed. *History of Henderson County, Kentucky.* Henderson, KY: Henderson County Genealogical and Historical Society, 1980.

Davis, Benjamin O., Jr. *Benjamin O. Davis, Jr., American: An Autobiography.* Washington, DC: Smithsonian Institution Press, 1991.

Davis, Cyprian. *The History of Black Catholics in the United States.* New York: Crossroad, 1990.

Davis, Donald G., ed. *Dictionary of American Library Biography.* Westport, CT: Libraries Unlimited, 2003.

Davis, Elizabeth Lindsay. *Lifting as They Climb.* Washington, DC: National Association of Colored Women, 1933.

Davis, Jeffery. "A Kentucky Response: The Founding of the Kentucky Civil Liberties Union, 1955–1960." MA thesis, Univ. of Washington, 1981.

Dawson, Osceola A. *The Timberlake Story.* Carbondale, IL: Dunway-Sinclair, 1959.

Debono, Paul. *The Indianapolis ABCs: History of a Premier Team in the Negro Leagues.* Jefferson, NC: McFarland, 2007.

Delany, Martin Robison, and Robert Steven Levine. *Martin R. Delany: A Documentary Reader.* Chapel Hill: Univ. of North Carolina Press, 2003.

Dew, Lee A., and Aloma W. Dew. *Owensboro, the City on the Yellow Banks: A History of Owensboro, Kentucky.* Bowling Green, KY: Rivendell Publications, 1988.

Deyle, Steven. *Carry Me Back: The Domestic Slave Trade in American Life.* Oxford: Oxford Univ. Press, 2005.

Dickerson, Dennis C. *Militant Mediator: Whitney M. Young, Jr.* Lexington: Univ. Press of Kentucky, 1998.

———. *Out of the Crucible: Black Steelworkers in Western Pennsylvania, 1875–1980.* Albany: State Univ. of New York Press, 1986.

A Directory of Negro Graduates of Accredited Library Schools, 1900–1936. Washington, DC: Columbia Civic Library Association, 1937.

Doerschuk, Robert L. *88: The Greats of Jazz Piano.* San Francisco: Backbeat Books, 2001.

Doran, James. *Herman Chittison: A Bio-Discography.* Bel Air, MD: International Association of Jazz Record Collectors, 1993.

DuBois, W. E. B. *Economic Co-operation among Negro Americans.* Atlanta: Atlanta Univ. Publications, 1907.

Dunbar, Paul Laurence. *Works of Paul Laurence Dunbar.* N.p.: The Perfect Library, 2013.

Dunnigan, Alice Allison. *A Black Woman's Experience: From Schoolhouse to White House.* Philadelphia: Dorrance, 1974.

———, comp. and ed. *The Fascinating Story of Black Kentuckians: Their Heritage and Traditions.* Washington, DC: Associated Publishers, 1982.

Durden, Robert F. *Carter G. Woodson: Father of African-American History.* Springfield, NJ: Enslow, 1998.

Edmonds, Anthony O. *Muhammad Ali: A Biography.* Westport, CT: Greenwood Press, 2005.

Eger, Bob. *Maroon & Gold: A History of Sun Devil Athletics.* Champaign, IL: Sports Publishing, 2001.

Egerton, John. *Side Orders: Small Helpings of Southern Cookery and Culture.* Atlanta: Peachtree, 1990.

———. *Southern Food: At Home, on the Road, in History.* New York: Alfred A. Knopf, 1987.

Eisenberg, Theodore. *Civil Rights Legislation: Cases and Materials.* Charlottesville, VA: Michie Co., 1981.

Elliott, Ron. *Inside the Beverly Hills Supper Club Fire.* Paducah, KY: Turner, 1996.

Ellis, William E. *A History of Education in Kentucky.* Lexington: Univ. Press of Kentucky, 2011.

Elmore, Ronn. *How to Love a Black Woman.* New York: Warner Books, 1999.

Embry, Mike. *Basketball in the Bluegrass State: The Championship Teams.* New York: Leisure Press, 1983.

Engle, Fred A., and Robert N. Grise. *Madison's Heritage.* Richmond, KY: AA Printing Co., 1985.

Evans, Mari. *Black Women Writers (1950–1980): A Critical Evaluation.* Garden City, NY: Anchor Books, 1984.

Everman, H. E. *Bourbon County since 1865.* Richmond, KY: H. E. Everman, 1999.

Faber, Charles F., and Thomas Diamantes. *School Law for Kentucky Teachers and Administrators.* 8th ed. Crestview Hills, KY: Rhinegold, 1996.

Fairbank, Calvin. *Rev. Calvin Fairbank during Slavery Times.* Chicago: R. R. McCabe & Company, 1890.

Farrison, William Edward. *William Wells Brown: Author and Reformer.* Chicago: Univ. of Chicago Press, 1969.

Fassett, John D. *New Deal Justice: The Life of Stanley Reed of Kentucky.* New York: Vantage Press, 1994.

Fee, John Gregg. *Autobiography of John G. Fee, Berea, Kentucky.* Chicago: National Christian Association, 1891.

Fikes, Robert, Jr. *The Struggle for Equality in "America's Finest City": A History of the San Diego NAACP.* San Diego: San Diego Branch of the National Association for the Advancement of Colored People, 2012.

Finkelman, Paul. *An Imperfect Union: Slavery, Federalism, and Comity.* Chapel Hill: Univ. of North Carolina Press, 1981.

———. *Slavery in the Courtroom: An Annotated Bibliography of American Cases.* Washington, DC: Library of Congress, 1985.

Finkelman, Paul, and Bruce A. Lesh. *Milestone Documents in American History: Exploring the Primary Sources That Shaped America.* Dallas, TX: Schlager Group, 2008.

Finney, Nikky. *Heartwood.* Lexington: Univ. Press of Kentucky, 1997.

Fleming, G. James, and Christian E. Burckel, eds. *Who's Who in Colored America.* 7th ed. *Supplement.* Yonkers-on-Hudson, NY: Christian E. Burckel & Associates, 1950.

Fletcher, Winona L., sr. ed. *Community Memories: A Glimpse of African American Life in Frankfort, Kentucky.* Frankfort: Kentucky Historical Society, 2003.

Floyd-Thomas, Juan M. *The Origins of Black Humanism in America: Reverend Ethelred Brown and the Unitarian Church.* New York: Palgrave Macmillan, 2008.

Foley, Albert S. *God's Men of Color: The Colored Catholic Priests of the United States, 1854–1954.* New York: Farrar, Straus, 1955.

Foner, Eric. *Reconstruction, 1863–1877: America's Unfinished Revolution.* New York: Harper & Row, 1988.

Fosl, Catherine. *Subversive Southerner: Anne Braden and the Struggle for Racial Justice in the Cold War South.* Lexington: Univ. Press of Kentucky, 2006.

Fosl, Catherine, and Tracy E. K'Meyer. *Freedom on the Border: An Oral History of the Civil Rights Movement in Kentucky.* Lexington: Univ. Press of Kentucky, 2009.

Foster, Laurence, ed. *The Alumni Directory of Lincoln University.* Oxford, PA: Lincoln Univ., 1946.

Fouché, Rayvon. *Black Inventors in the Age of Segregation: Granville T. Woods, Lewis H. Latimer, and Shelby J. Davidson.* Baltimore: Johns Hopkins Univ. Press, 2003.

Franklin County, Kentucky, Frankfort 200 Celebration, 1786–1986. Paducah, KY: Turner, 1987.

Frazier, E. Franklin. *Negro Youth at the Crossways: Their Personality Development in the Middle States.* Washington, DC: American Council on Education, 1940.

Frederick, Francis. *Autobiography of Rev. Francis Frederick, of Virginia.* Baltimore: J. W. Woods, Printer, 1869.

Freund, Paul A., and Stanley N. Katz, eds. *History of the Supreme Court of the United States.* New York: Macmillan, 1984.

Friedman, Leon, and Fred L. Israel. *The Justices of the United States Supreme Court, 1789–1969: Their Lives and Major Opinions,* 4 vols. New York: Chelsea House, 1969.

Frost, Karolyn Smardz. *I've Got a Home in Glory Land: A Lost Tale of the Underground Railroad.* New York: Farrar, Straus & Giroux, 2007.

Fuller, George N., ed. *Michigan: A Centennial History of the State and Its People.* Chicago: Lewis, 1939.

Gaines, Clarence E., with Clint Johnson. *They Call Me Big House.* Winston-Salem, NC: John F. Blair, 2004.

Gannon, Barbara. *The Won Cause: Black and White Comradeship in the Grand Army of the Republic.* Chapel Hill: Univ. of North Carolina Press, 2011.

Gara, Larry. *The Liberty Line.* Lexington: Univ. of Kentucky Press, 1961.

Gardner, Washington. *History of Calhoun County, Michigan.* Chicago: Lewis, 1913.

Garner, James Wilford. *Reconstruction in Mississippi.* New York: Macmillan, 1901.

Garraty, John, and Mark Christopher Carnes, eds. *American National Biography.* Oxford: Oxford Univ. Press, 1999.

Gazda, Elaine, ed. *The Ancient Art of Emulation: Studies in Artistic Originality and Tradition from the Present to Classical Antiquity.* Ann Arbor: Univ. of Michigan Press, 2002.

Geenen, Paul. *Milwaukee's Bronzeville, 1900–1950.* Charleston, SC: Arcadia, 2006.

General Association of Colored Baptists. *Diamond Jubilee of the General Association of Colored Baptists in Kentucky.* Louisville, KY: American Baptist, 1943.

Gentry, Tony. *Paul Laurence Dunbar: Poet.* New York: Chelsea House, 1989.

Gibson, John W., and William H. Crogman. *The Colored American from Slavery to Honorable Citizenship.* Naperville, IL: J. L. Nichols and Co., 1902.

Gibson, W. H., Sr. *Historical Sketch of the Progress of the Colored Race, in Louisville, Ky., as Noted by the Writer during a Period of Fifty Years.* Louisville, KY: Bradley & Gilbert, 1897.

———. *History of the United Brothers of Friendship and Sisters of the Mysterious Ten: In Two Parts, a Negro Order.* Louisville, KY: Bradley & Gilbert Co., 1897.

Giddings, Paula. *In Search of Sisterhood: Delta Sigma Theta and the Challenge of the Black Sorority Movement.* New York: Morrow, 1988.

Glazier, Jack. *Been Coming through Some Hard Times: Race, History, and Memory in Western Kentucky.* Knoxville: Univ. of Tennessee Press, 2012.

Goggin, Jacqueline Anne. *Carter G. Woodson: A Life in Black History.* Baton Rouge: Louisiana State Univ. Press, 1993.

Golden, Thelma. *Bob Thompson.* Berkeley: Whitney Museum of American Art in Association with University of California Press, 1998.

Goldsby, Jacqueline. *A Spectacular Secret: Lynching in American Life and Literature.* Chicago: Univ. of Chicago Press, 2006.

Gore, Matthew Henry. *A History of the Cumberland Presbyterian Church in Kentucky to 1988.* Memphis, TN: Joint Heritage Committee of Covenant and Cumberland Presbyteries, 2000.

Gorn, Elliot J., ed. *Muhammad Ali: The People's Champ.* Urbana: Univ. of Illinois Press, 1995.

Graham, Ruth Morris. *The Saga of the Morris Family.* Columbus, GA: Brentwood Christiana Communications, 1984.

Grant, Nancy L. *TVA and Black Americans: Planning for the Status Quo.* Philadelphia: Temple Univ. Press, 1990.

Green, Ben. *Spinning the Globe: The Rise, Fall, and Return to Greatness of the Harlem Globetrotters.* New York: HarperCollins, 2005.

Green, Elisha W. *Life of the Rev. Elisha W. Green.* Maysville, KY: Republican Printing Office, 1888.

Green, Jacob D. *Narrative of the Life of J. D. Green, a Runaway Slave, from Kentucky, Containing an Account of His Three Escapes, in 1838, 1846, and 1848.* Huddersfield, UK: Henry Fielding, Pack Horse Yard, 1864.

Greene, Lorenzo Johnston. *Selling Black History for Carter G. Woodson: A Diary, 1930–1933.* Columbia: Univ. of Missouri Press, 1996.

Griffin, William Wayne. *African Americans and the Color Line in Ohio, 1915–1930.* Columbus: Ohio State Univ. Press, 2005.

Griffiths, Sian, ed. *Beyond the Glass Ceiling: Forty Women Whose Ideas Shaped the Modern World.* Manchester: Manchester Univ. Press, 1996.

Griffler, Keith P. *Front Line of Freedom: African Americans and the Forging of the Underground Railroad in the Ohio Valley.* Lexington: Univ. Press of Kentucky, 2004.

Gross, Viola. *Two Hundred Years of Freedom: A Genealogy and History of the Doram, Rowe, Barbee and Allied Families.* N.p.: Kinnersley Press, 2003.

Grossman, James R., Ann Durkin Keating, and Janice L. Reife. *The Encyclopedia of Chicago.* Chicago: Univ. of Chicago Press, 2004.

Gudmestad, Robert H. *A Troublesome Commerce: The Transformation of the Interstate Slave Trade.* Baton Rouge: Louisiana State Univ. Press, 2003.

Guelzo, Allen. *Lincoln's Emancipation Proclamation: The End of Slavery in America.* New York: Simon & Schuster, 2004.

Guzman, Jessie Parkhurst, ed. *Negro Year Book; a Review of Events Affecting Negro Life, 1941–1946.* Tuskegee, AL: Department of Records and Research, Tuskegee Institute, 1947.

Hagedorn, Ann. *Beyond the River: The Untold Story of the Heroes of the Underground Railroad.* New York: Simon & Schuster, 2002.

Halbrook, Stephen P. *Freedmen, the Fourteenth Amendment, and the Right to Bear Arms, 1866–1876.* Westport, CT: Praeger, 1998.

Haley, James T. *Afro-American Encyclopaedia; or, The Thoughts, Doings, and Sayings of the Race.* Nashville: Haley and Florida, 1895.

Hall, Wade. *Passing for Black: The Life and Careers of Mae Street Kidd.* Lexington: Univ. Press of Kentucky, 1997.

———, ed. *The Rest of the Dream: The Black Odyssey of Lyman Johnson.* Lexington: Univ. Press of Kentucky, 1988.

Hallenberg, Leone W. *Anchorage: A Casual Gathering of Facts and Stories from the Past and Present of a Unique Kentucky Town.* Anchorage, KY: Anchorage Press, 1959.

Halsey, Leroy J. *History of the McCormick Theological Seminary of the Presbyterian Church.* Chicago: McCormick Theological Seminary, 1893.

Hamilton, Ed. *The Birth of an Artist: A Journey of Discovery.* Louisville, KY: Chicago Spectrum Press, 2006.

Hamilton, G. P. *Biographical Sketches of Prominent Negro Men and Women of Kentucky.* Memphis: E. H. Clarke & Brother, 1911.

Hamilton, Kenneth Marvin. *Black Towns and Profit: Promotion and Development in the Trans-Appalachian West, 1877–1915.* Urbana: Univ. of Illinois Press, 1991.

Hammond, Theresa. *A White-Collar Profession: African American Certified Public Accountants since 1921.* Chapel Hill: Univ. of North Carolina Press, 2007.

Hampton, George A. *Diamond Jubilee of the General Association of the Colored Baptists in Kentucky: The Story of Seventy-Five Years of the Association and Four Years of Convention Activities.* Louisville, KY: American Baptist, 1943.

Hampton, Lionel, with James Haskins. *Hamp: An Autobiography.* New York: Amistad, 1993.

Handy, W. C. *Unsung Americans Sung.* New York: Handy Brothers Music Co., 1944.

———. *W. C. Handy: Father of the Blues.* New York: Macmillan, 1941.

Hanson, Joyce A. *Mary McLeod Bethune and Black Political Women's Activism.* Columbia: Univ. of Missouri Press, 2003.

Hardin, John A. *Fifty Years of Segregation: Black Higher Education in Kentucky, 1904–1954.* Lexington: Univ. Press of Kentucky, 1997.

———. *Onward and Upward: A Centennial History of Kentucky State University, 1886–1986.* Frankfort: Kentucky State University, 1987.

Harrell, Kenneth E., ed. *The Public Papers of Governor Edward T. Breathitt, 1963–1967.* Lexington: Univ. Press of Kentucky, 1984.

Harris, Lawrence. *The Negro Population of Lexington in the Professions, Business, Education, and Religion.* Lexington, KY, 1907.

Harris, Sheldon. *Blues Who's Who: A Biographical Dictionary of Blues Singers.* New York: Arlington House, 1979.

Harris, Trudier, and Thadious M. Davis. "Afro-American Writers before the Harlem Renaissance." *Dictionary of Literary Biography,* vol. 50. Detroit: Gale, 1986.

Harrison, Lowell H. *The Antislavery Movement in Kentucky.* Lexington: Univ. Press of Kentucky, 1978.

———. *Western Kentucky University.* Lexington: Univ. Press of Kentucky, 1994.

Harrison, Lowell H., and James Klotter. *A New History of Kentucky.* Lexington: Univ. Press of Kentucky, 1997.

Hartshorn, William Newton, and George W. Penniham. *An Era of Progress and Promise, 1863–1910: The Religious, Moral, and Educational Development of the American Negro since His Emancipation.* Boston: Priscilla Publishing Co., 1910.

Hartzman, Mark. *American Sideshow: An Encyclopedia of History's Most Wondrous and Curiously Strange Performers.* New York: Jeremy P. Tarcher/Penguin, 2005.

Hasse, John Edward, ed. *Ragtime: Its History, Composers, and Music.* New York: Schirmer Books, 1985.

Hatch, James V., and Leo Hamalian, eds. *Lost Plays of the Harlem Renaissance, 1920–1940.* Detroit: Wayne State Univ. Press, 1996.

Hauke, Kathleen A., ed. *The Dark Side of Hopkinsville: Stories by Ted Poston.* Athens: Univ. of Georgia Press, 1991.

———. *Ted Poston: Pioneer American Journalist.* Athens: Univ. of Georgia Press, 1998.

Hauser, Thomas. *Muhammad Ali: His Life and Times.* New York: Simon & Schuster, 1991.

Haviland, Laura S. *A Woman's Life-Work: Labors and Experiences.* 4th ed. Chicago: Publishing Association of Friends, 1889.

Hawkins, Walter L. *African American Biographies: Profiles of 558 Current Men and Women.* Jefferson, NC: McFarland, 1994.

Hayden, William. *Narrative of William Hayden: Containing a Faithful Account of His Travels for a Number of Years, Whilst a Slave, in the South.* Cincinnati, 1846.

Hayes, Mrs. W. T. *Kentucky Cookbook: Easy and Simple for Any Cook.* St. Louis: J. H. Tomkins Printing Co., 1912.

Hayne, Coe Smith. *Race Grit: Adventures on the Border-Land of Liberty.* Philadelphia: Judson Press, 1922.

Hazzard-Gordon, Katrina. *Jookin': The Rise of Social Dance Formations in African-American Culture.* Philadelphia: Temple Univ. Press, 1990.

Heady, Peyton. *History of Camp Breckinridge.* Morganfield, KY: Hites' International Printing, 1987.

Heaphy, Leslie, ed. *Black Baseball and Chicago: Essays on Players, Teams, and Games.* Jefferson, NC: McFarland, 2006.

Heermance, J. Noel. *William Wells Brown and Clotelle: A Portrait of the Artist in the First Negro Novel.* Hamden, CT: Archon Books, 1969.

Heglar, Charles J. *Rethinking the Slave Narrative.* Westport, CT: Greenwood Press, 2001.

Helm, MacKinley. *Angel Mo' and Her Son, Roland Hayes.* Boston: Little Brown, 1942.

Henderson, Edwin Bancroft. *The Negro in Sports.* Washington, DC, Associated Publishers, 1949.

Hendrick, William Jackson. *James P. Hendrick, D.D.: Memoirs with an Appendix Containing History of Ebenezer Presbytery and Other Papers.* Cambridge, MA: Riverside Press, 1907.

Henritze, Barbara K. *Bibliographic Checklist of African American Newspapers.* Baltimore, MD: Genealogical Print Company, 1995.

Higginbotham, Evelyn Brooks. *Righteous Discontent: The Women's Movement in the Black Baptist Church, 1880–1920.* Cambridge, MA: Harvard Univ. Press, 1994.

Hill, Ruth Edmunds, ed. *The Black Women Oral History Project.* Vol. 6. Westport, CT: Meckler, 1991.

Hine, Darlene Clark, Elsa Barkley Brown, and Rosalyn Terborg-Penn, eds. *Black Women in America: An Historical Encyclopedia.* Brooklyn, NY: Carlson, 1993.

Hine, Darlene Clark, and Patrick Kay Bidelman, eds. *The Black Women in the Middle West Project: A Comprehensive Resource Guide, Illinois and Indiana: Historical Essays, Oral Histories, Biographical Profiles, and Document Collections.* Indianapolis: Indiana Historical Bureau, 1986.

Hingeley, Joseph B. *Journal of the Twenty-Fourth Delegated General Conference of the Methodist Episcopal Church.* New York: Eaton & Mains, 1904.

Hirsch, James S. *Riot and Remembrance: The Tulsa Race War and Its Legacy.* Boston: Houghton Mifflin, 2002.

Hirsch, Joe, and Jim Bolus. *Kentucky Derby: The Chance of a Lifetime.* New York: McGraw-Hill, 1988.

Hischak, Thomas S. *American Theatre: A Chronicle of Comedy and Drama, 1969–2000.* Oxford: Oxford Univ. Press, 2001.

History of the Ohio Falls Cities and Their Counties: With Illustrations and Biographical Sketches. 2 vols. Cleveland: L.A. Williams, Co., 1882.

Hitchcock, H. Wiley, and Stanley Sadie, eds. *The New Grove Dictionary of American Music.* New York: Macmillan, 1986.

Hochschild, Adam. *King Leopold's Ghost: A Story of Greed, Terror and Heroism in Colonial Africa.* New York: Houghton Mifflin Harcourt, 1999.

Hoffschwelle, Mary S. *The Rosenwald Schools of the American South.* Gainesville: Univ. Press of Florida, 2006.

Hogan, Lawrence D. *Shades of Glory: The Negro Leagues and the Story of African-American Baseball.* Washington, DC: National Geographic, 2006.

Hogan, Roseann Reinemuth. *Kentucky Ancestry: A Guide to Genealogical and Historical Research.* Salt Lake City, UT: Ancestry Inc., 1992.

Holland, Antonio Frederick. *Nathan B. Young and the Struggle over Black Higher Education.* Columbia: Univ. of Missouri Press, 2006.

Holland, Jeffrey Scott. *Weird Kentucky: Your Travel Guide to Kentucky's Local Legends and Best Kept Secrets.* New York: Sterling, 2008.

Hollingsworth, Randolph. *Lexington: Queen of the Bluegrass.* Charleston, SC: Arcadia, 2004.

Honey, Maureen, ed. *Shadowed Dreams: Women's Poetry of the Harlem Renaissance.* New Brunswick, NJ: Rutgers Univ. Press, 2006.

Hood, James Walker. *One Hundred Years of the African Methodist Episcopal Zion Church; or, the Centennial of African Methodism.* New York: A.M.E. Zion Book Concern, 1895.

hooks, bell. *Ain't I a Woman? Black Women and Feminism.* Boston: South End Press, 1981.

———. *Belonging: A Culture of Place.* New York: Routledge, 2009.

———. *Remembered Rapture: The Writer at Work.* New York: Henry Holt, 1999.

Horton, J. Benjamin. *Flights from Doom: The Autobiography of the Life, Observations, Experiences and Involvements in America of an African-American Journalist, Author and Publicist.* Louisville, KY: J. Benjamin Horton & Associates, 1990.

———. *Not without Struggle: An Account of the Most Significant Political and Social-Action Changes That Have Occurred in the Lives of Black Kentuckians in the Twentieth Century.* New York: Vantage Press, 1979.

———. *Old War Horse of Kentucky: A Gripping Biographical Narrative about the Life and Achievements of Albert Ernest Meyzeek.* Louisville, KY: J. B. Horton & Associates, 1986.

———. *Profiles of Contemporary Black Achievers of Kentucky: A Brief Account of Individual Black Achievers of Kentucky Whose Qualities and Attainments against the Odds of Circumstance Distinguish Them from the Unexceptional.* Louisville, KY: J. Benjamin Horton & Associates, 1982.

Hotaling, Edward. *The Great Black Jockeys: The Lives and Times of the Men Who Dominated America's First National Sport.* Rocklin, CA: Forum, 1999.

———. *Wink: The Incredible Life and Epic Journey of Jimmy Winkfield.* New York: McGraw-Hill, 2005.

Houck, Davis W., and David E. Dixon. *Rhetoric, Religion and the Civil Rights Movement.* Waco, TX: Baylor Univ. Press, 2006.

———. *Women and the Civil Rights Movement, 1954–1965.* Jackson: Univ. Press of Mississippi, 2009.

Howard, Victor B. *Black Liberation in Kentucky.* Lexington: Univ. Press of Kentucky, 1983.

———. *The Evangelical War Against Slavery and Caste: The Life and Times of John G. Fee.* London: Associated Univ. Press, 1996.

Hubbard, Mark, ed. *Illinois's War: The Civil War in Documents.* Athens: Ohio Univ. Press, 2013.

Hudson, J. Blaine. *Encyclopedia of the Underground Railroad.* Jefferson, NC: McFarland, 2006.

———. *Fugitive Slaves and the Underground Railroad in the Kentucky Borderland.* Jefferson, NC: McFarland, 2002.

Hull, Debra Beery. *Christian Church Women: Shapers of a Movement.* St. Louis: Chalice Press, 1994.

Hyman, Harold M., and William M. Wiecek. *Equal Justice under Law: Constitutional Development, 1835–1875.* New York: Harper & Row, 1982.

Ihle, Elizabeth L., ed. *Black Women in Higher Education: An Anthology of Essays, Studies, and Documents.* New York: Garland, 1992.

Inge, M. Thomas, ed. *The New Encyclopedia of Southern Culture.* Chapel Hill: Univ. of North Carolina Press, 2008.

Innes, C. L., ed. *Slave Life in Virginia and Kentucky: A Narrative by Francis Fedric, Escaped Slave.* Baton Rouge: Louisiana State Univ. Press, 2010.

Jackson, Andrew. *Narrative and Writings of Andrew Jackson of Kentucky.* Syracuse, NY: Daily and Weekly Star Office, 1847. Reprint, Miami: Mnemosyne, 1969.

Jackson, Eric R. *Northern Kentucky.* Charleston, SC: Arcadia, 2005.

Jacobs, Claude F., and Andrew J. Kaslow. *The Spiritual Churches of New Orleans: Origins, Beliefs, and Rituals of an African-American Religion.* Knoxville: Univ. of Tennessee Press, 2001.

James, Amos N. *Historical Abstract of the Henry Wise Jones Family, 2007.* Washington, DC: Xanthas Express Press, 2007.

James, Portia P. *The Real McCoy: African-American Invention and Innovation, 1619–1930.* Washington, DC: Smithsonian Institution Press, 1989.

Jamieson, J. A., Jack Allen, John Graham, H. White, and G.L Williams. *Complete History of the Colored Soldiers in the World War.* New York: Bennett & Churchill, 1919.

Jarrett, Andrew Gene, and Thomas Lewis Morgan. *The Complete Stories of Paul Laurence Dunbar.* Athens: Ohio Univ. Press, 2005.

Jasen, David A., and Gene Jones. *Spreadin Rhythm Around: Black Popular Songwriters, 1880–1930.* London: Schirmer Books, 1998.

Jaspin, Elliot. *Buried in the Bitter Waters: The Hidden History of Racial Cleansing in America.* New York: Basic Books, 2007.

Jeffrey, Jonathan, and Mike Wilson, comps. *Mt. Moriah Cemetery: A History and Census of Bowling Green, Kentucky's African-American Cemetery.* Bowling Green, KY: Landmark Association, 2002.

Jeffrey, Julie Roy. *Abolitionists Remember: Antislavery Autobiographies and the Unfinished Work of Emancipation.* Chapel Hill: Univ. of North Carolina Press, 2008.

Jenkins, Horace G., and J. Bryant Cooper. *One Hundred Years of Celebration of Quinn Chapel AME Church, 1838 to 1938.* Louisville, KY: AME Church, 1938.

Jennings, Dorothy, and Kerby Jennings. *The Story of Calloway County, 1822–1976.* Murray, KY: Murray Democrat Publishing Co., 1980.

Jessamine County Historical Society. *History of Jessamine County, Kentucky.* Dallas: Taylor, 1993.

Johnson, Dorothy Sharpe, and Lula Goolsby Williams. *Pioneering Women of the African Methodist Episcopal Zion Church.* Charlotte, NC: A.M.E. Zion Publishing House, 1996.

Johnson, Isaac. *Slavery Days in Old Kentucky.* Introduction by Cornel J. Reinhart. Canton, NY: Friends of the Owen D. Young Library and the St. Lawrence County Historical Association, 1994.

Johnson, Larry L. *Chosen.* Lexington, KY: Self-published, 2012.

Johnson, W. D. *Biographical Sketches of Prominent Negro Men and Women of Kentucky.* Lexington, KY, 1897.

Johnston, Harry. *Liberia.* London: Hutchinson, 1906.

Johnston, Johanna. *Runaway to Heaven: The Story of Harriet Beecher Stowe.* Garden City, NY: Doubleday, 1963.

Johnston, J. Stoddard, ed. *Memorial History of Louisville from Its First Settlement to the Year 1896.* Chicago: American Biographical Publishing Co., 1896.

Johnston, Tyler. *Jeffersontown, Kentucky—The First 200 Years.* Jeffersontown, KY: City of Jeffersontown, 1997.

Jones, J. E. *A Profile of Z. K. Jones.* Bowling Green, KY: Master Printers, 1974.

Jones, Michael L. *Second-Hand Stories.* Louisville, KY: Weeping Buddha Press, 2006.

Jones, Reinette F. *Library Service to African Americans in Kentucky, from the Reconstruction Era to the 1960s.* Jefferson, NC: McFarland, 2001.

Jones, Thomas Jesse. *Negro Education: A Study of the Private and Higher Schools for Colored People in the United States.* Vol. 2. Washington, DC: Government Printing Office, 1917.

Kavanaugh, Frank. *Kentucky Directory: For the Use of Courts, State and County Officials, and General Assembly of the State of Kentucky.* Frankfort, KY: Perry, 1952.

Kelley, Brent. *"I Will Never Forget": Interviews with 39 Former Negro League Players.* Jefferson, NC: McFarland, 2003.

———. *The Negro Leagues Revisited: Conversations with 66 More Baseball Heroes.* Jefferson, NC: McFarland, 2000.

Kelly, Mary Ann. *My Old Kentucky Home, Good-Night.* Hicksville, NY: Exposition Press, 1979.

Kemp, Janet E. *Report of the Tenement House Commission of Louisville.* Louisville, KY: Tenement House Commission, 1909.

Kempf, Gary. *A History of Fort Knox: Battles, Extinct Communities, Churches, Schools, and Historic Vignettes.* Vine Grove, KY: Ancestral Trails Historical Society, 1998.

Kenner, Charles L. *Buffalo Soldiers and Officers of the Ninth Cavalry, 1867–1898: Black and White Together.* Norman: Univ. of Oklahoma Press, 1999.

Kenney, William Howard. *Jazz on the River.* Chicago: Univ. of Chicago Press, 2005.

Kenton Co. Public Library. *Covington.* Images of America. Charlestown, SC: Arcadia, 2003.

Kentucky's Black Heritage: The Role of the Black People in the History of Kentucky From Pioneer Days to the Present. Frankfort: Kentucky Commission on Human Rights, 1971.

Kernfeld, Barry, ed. *The New Grove Dictionary of Jazz.* 2nd ed. New York: Grove's Dictionaries, 2002.

Kern-Foxworth, Marilyn. *Aunt Jemima, Uncle Ben, and Rastus: Blacks in Advertising Yesterday, Today, and Tomorrow.* Westport, CT: Praeger, 1994.

King, Ethel I. *From Parkland to the River's Edge.* Louisville, KY: Peter's Publications, 1990.

King, Richard H. "The Enigma of Bob Thompson." In *The Hearing Eye: Jazz and Blues Influences in African American Visual Art,* edited by Graham Lock and David Murray, 134–49. Oxford: Oxford Univ. Press, 2009.

Kinnard, William, and Stephen Messner. *Effective Business Relocation: A Guide to Workable Approaches for Relocating Displaced Businesses.* Lexington, MA: D. C. Heath, 1970.

Kleber, John E., ed. *The Encyclopedia of Louisville.* Lexington: Univ. Press of Kentucky, 2001.

———, ed. *The Kentucky Encyclopedia.* Lexington: Univ. Press of Kentucky, 1992.

K'Meyer, Tracy E. *Civil Rights in the Gateway to the South: Louisville, Kentucky, 1945–1980.* Lexington: Univ. Press of Kentucky, 2009.

Laine, Henry Allen. *Foot Prints.* Richmond, KY: Daily Register Press, 1924.

Lamb, Daniel Smith. *Howard University Medical Department, Washington, D.C.: A Historical, Biographical, and Statistical Souvenir.* Washington, DC: Medical Faculty of Howard University, 1900.

Lancaster, Clay. *Antebellum Architecture of Kentucky.* Lexington: Univ. Press of Kentucky, 1991.

Lanctot, Neil. *Negro League Baseball: The Rise and Ruin of a Black Institution.* Philadelphia: Univ. of Pennsylvania Press, 2004.

Larkin, Colin, ed. *The Encyclopedia of Popular Music.* 3rd ed. New York: Muze, 1998.

Lawson, R. A. *Jim Crow's Counterculture: The Blues and Black Southerners, 1890–1945.* Baton Rouge: Louisiana State Univ. Press, 2010.

Leach, George B. *The Kentucky Derby Diamond Jubilee.* Louisville, KY: Gibbs-Inman Co., 1949.

Leckie, William H., with Shirley A. Leckie. *The Buffalo Soldiers: A Narrative of the Black Cavalry in the West.* Rev. ed. Norman: Univ. of Oklahoma Press, 2003.

Lee, Irvin H. *Negro Medal of Honor Men.* New York: Dodd, Mead, 1969.

Lesick, Lawrence Thomas. *The Lane Rebels: Evangelicalism and Antislavery in Antebellum America.* Metuchen, NJ: Scarecrow Press, 1980.

Lewis, Alvin Fayette. *History of Higher Education in Kentucky.* Washington, DC: Government Printing Office, 1899.

Lewis, Catherine, and J. Richard Lewis. *Jim Crow America: A Documentary History.* Fayetteville: Univ. of Arkansas Press, 2009.

Lewis, Selma. "Julia Britton Hooks, 1852–1942." In *The Tennessee Encyclopedia of History and Culture,* edited by Caroll Van West. Nashville: Tennessee Historical Society, 1968. http://tennessee encyclopedia.net/entry.php?rec=648.

Litwack, Leon, and August Meier. *Black Leaders of the Nineteenth Century.* Urbana: Univ. of Illinois Press, 1988.

Loevy, Robert D., ed. *The Civil Rights Act of 1964: The Passage of the Law That Ended Racial Segregation.* Albany: State Univ. of New York Press, 1997.

Lofaro, Michael A. *Daniel Boone: An American Life.* Lexington: Univ. Press of Kentucky, 2003.

Logan, Rayford. *Howard University: The First Hundred Years, 1867–1967.* New York: New York Univ. Press, 1969.

Logan, Rayford, and Michael Winston, eds. *Dictionary of American Negro Biography.* New York: Norton, 1982.

Long, Jerry. *Greenwood Cemetery: 1821 Leitchfield Road, Owensboro, Kentucky.* Utica, KY: McDowell Publications, 2006.

Lott, Eric. *Love and Theft: Blackface Minstrelsy and the American Working Class.* New York: Oxford Univ. Press, 1995.

Lotz, Rainer E. *Black People: Entertainers of African Descent in Europe and Germany.* Bonn: Birgit Lotz, 1997.

Love, Preston. *A Thousand Honey Creeks Later: My Life in Music from Basie to Motown.* Middletown, CT: Wesleyan Univ. Press, 1997.

Lovett, Bobby L. *The African-American History of Nashville, Tennessee, 1780–1930: Elites and Dilemmas.* Fayetteville: Univ. of Arkansas Press, 1999.

———. *How It Came to Be: The Boyd Family's Contribution to African American Religious Publishing from the 19th to the 21st Century.* Lavergne, TN: Lightning Source Press, 2007.

Lucas, Marion B. *A History of Blacks in Kentucky: From Slavery to Segregation, 1760–1891.* 2nd ed. Frankfort: Kentucky Historical Society, 2003.

Lydon, Michael. *Ray Charles: Man and Music.* New York: Routledge, 2004.

MacCabe, Julius P. Bolivar. *Directory of the City of Lexington and County of Fayette for 1838 & 1839.* Lexington, KY: J. C. Noble, 1838.

Mack, Dwayne. "Kentucky." In *Black America: A State-by-State Historical Encyclopedia,* edited by Alton Hornsby, 305–25. Santa Barbara, CA: ABC-CLIO, 2011.

MacLean, Nancy. *Behind the Mask of Chivalry: The Making of the Second Ku Klux Klan.* New York: Oxford Univ. Press, 1994.

Maes, Camillus P. *The Life of Rev. Charles Nerinckx.* Cincinnati: Robert Clarke, 1880.

Magill, Frank N. *Masterpieces of African-American Literature.* New York: HarperCollins, 1992.

Mahar, William J. *Behind the Burnt Cork Mask: Early Blackface Minstrelsy and Antebellum American Popular Culture.* Urbana: Univ. of Illinois Press, 1999.

Maher, Neil M. *Nature's New Deal: The Civilian Conservation Corps and the Roots of the American Environmental Movement.* New York: Oxford Univ. Press, 2008.

Majors, Monroe A. *Noted Negro Women: Their Triumphs and Activities.* Jackson, TN: M. V. Lynk Publishing House, 1893. Reprint, Freeport, NY: Books for Libraries Press, 1971.

Májozo, Estella Conwill. *Come Out the Wilderness: The Memoir of a Black Woman Artist.* New York: Feminist Press at the City Univ. of New York, 1999.

Mallegg, Kristin, ed. *Who's Who among African Americans.* 22nd ed. Detroit: Gale, 2008.

Malone, Jacqui. *Steppin' on the Blues: The Visible Rhythms of African American Dance.* Urbana: Univ. of Illinois Press, 1996.

Maltz, Earl M. *Slavery and the Supreme Court, 1825–1861.* Lawrence: Univ. Press of Kansas, 2009.

Manring, M. M. *Slave in a Box: The Strange Career of Aunt Jemima.* Charlottesville: Univ. Press of Virginia, 1998.

Marrs, Elijah P. *Life and History of the Rev. Elijah P. Marrs.* Louisville, KY: Bradley and Gilbert Co., 1885. Reprint, Freeport, NY: Books for Libraries, 1977.

Marshall, Alexander K. *Decisions of the Court of Appeals of Kentucky, Commencing with the Fall Term, 1817, and Ending with the Fall Term, 1821.* Vol. 2. Cincinnati: Henry W. Derby, 1848.

Marshall, Anne E. *Creating a Confederate Kentucky: The Lost Cause and Civil War Memory in a Border State.* Chapel Hill: Univ. of North Carolina Press, 2010.

Martin, Asa E. *The Anti-slavery Movement in Kentucky prior to 1850.* Louisville, KY: Standard Printing Company of Louisville, 1918.

Mason, Herman, Jr. *The Talented Tenth: The Founders and Presidents of Alpha.* Winter Park, FL: Four-G Publishers, 1999.

Masters, Frank M. *A History of Baptists in Kentucky.* Louisville: Kentucky Baptist Historical Society, 1953.

Materson, Lisa G. *For the Freedom of Her Race: Black Women and Electoral Politics in Illinois, 1877–1932.* Chapel Hill: Univ. of North Carolina Press, 2009.

Mather, Frank Lincoln, ed. *Who's Who of the Colored Race: A General Biographical Dictionary of Men and Women of African Descent.* Vol. 1. Chicago: Memento Edition, 1915.

Matney, William C., ed. *Who's Who among Black Americans.* Vol. 3. Detroit: Gale Research, 1981.

McCann, Bob, ed. *Encyclopedia of African American Actresses in Film and Television.* Jefferson, NC: McFarland, 2010.

McCulloch, James, ed. *Democracy in Earnest: Southern Sociological Congress, 1916–1918.* Washington, DC: Southern Sociological Congress, 1918.

McCurry, Stephanie. *Confederate Reckoning: Power and Politics in the Civil War South.* Cambridge, MA: Harvard Univ. Press, 2010.

McDaniel, Karen Cotton. "Local Women: The Public Lives of Black Middle Class Women in Kentucky before the 'Modern Civil Rights Movement.'" Ph.D. diss., Univ. of Kentucky, 2013.

McDougle, Ivan E. *Slavery in Kentucky, 1792–1865.* Lancaster, PA: New Era Printing Company, 1918.

McGuire, Phillip, ed. *Taps for a Jim Crow Army: Letters from Black Soldiers in World War II.* Lexington: Univ. Press of Kentucky, 1993.

McIntyre, L. H. *One Grain of the Salt: The First African Baptist Church West of the Allegheny Mountains.* Lexington, KY: L. H. McIntyre, 1986.

McKean, Else. *Up Hill.* New York: Shady Hill Press, 1947.

McKinney, Victor, Jr., and H. W. Jones Jr. "A Short History of the American Baptist." In *The American Baptist Newspaper Centennial Volume,* 2–7. Louisville, KY: American Baptist Newspaper, 1978.

McNeil, William. *Cool Papas and Double Duties: The All-Time Greats of the Negro Leagues.* Jefferson, NC: McFarland, 2001.

McPheeters, Annie L. *Library Service in Black and White: Some Personal Recollections, 1921–1980.* Metuchen, NJ: Scarecrow, 1988.

McQueen, Keven. *Offbeat Kentuckians.* Kuttawa, KY: McClanahan, 2001.

Mellon, James, ed. *Bullwhip Days: The Slaves Remember.* New York: Grove Press, 1988.

Melton, J. Gordon. *Religious Leaders of America: A Biographical Guide to Founders and Leaders of Religious Bodies, Churches, and Spiritual Groups in North America.* Detroit: Gale Research, 1999.

Merrill, Boynton, Jr. *Jefferson's Nephews: A Frontier Tragedy.* Lexington: Univ. Press of Kentucky, 1987.

Meyer, Leland Winfield. *The Life and Times of Colonel Richard M. Johnson of Kentucky.* New York, 1932.

Michaud, Denise, and the Madison Historical Society. *Madison.* Images of America. Charleston, SC: Arcadia, 2010.

Mikula, Mark, and L. Mpho Mabunda, eds. *Great American Court Cases.* Vol. 2, *Criminal Justice.* Detroit: Gale Group, 1999.

Miller, Adrian. "Presidential Cooks: Cooking Truth to Power." In *American I Am Pass It Down Cookbook: Over 130 Soul-Filled Recipes,* edited by Jeff Henderson and Ramin Ganeshram, 73–76. New York: SmileyBooks, 2011.

Miller, James A. *Harlem: The Vision of Morgan and Marvin Smith.* Lexington: Univ. Press of Kentucky, 1998.

Miller, Patrick B., and David K. Wiggins, eds. *Sport and the Color Line: Black Athletes and Race Relations in Twentieth-Century America.* New York: Routledge, 2004.

Miller, Penny. *Kentucky Politics and Government: Do We Stand United?* Lincoln: Univ. of Nebraska Press, 1994.

Miller, Randall, and Jon Wakelyn, eds. *Catholics in the Old South: Essays on Church and Culture.* Macon, GA: Mercer Univ. Press, 1999.

Milward, Burton. *William "King" Solomon, 1775–1854.* Lexington, KY: Larkspur Press, 1990.

Minogue, Anna Catherine. *Loretto: Annals of the Century.* New York: American Press, 1912.

Mize, J. T. H., ed. *The International Who Is Who in Music.* 5th ed. Chicago: Who Is Who in Music, 1951.

Mjagkij, Nina. *Organizing Black America: An Encyclopedia of African American Associations.* Oxford, UK: Taylor & Francis, 2001.

Montell, William Lynwood. *The Saga of Coe Ridge: A Study in Oral History.* Knoxville: Univ. of Tennessee Press, 1970.

———. *Tales from Kentucky Funeral Homes.* Lexington: Univ. Press of Kentucky, 2009.

Moore, Brenda L. *To Serve My Country, to Serve My Race: The Story of the Only African American WACs Stationed Overseas during World War II.* New York: New York Univ. Press, 1996.

Moore, Jacqueline M. *Leading the Race: The Transformation of the Black Elite in the Nation's Capital, 1880–1920.* Charlottesville: Univ. Press of Virginia, 1999.

Morehead, C. S., and Mason Brown. *A Digest of the Statute Laws of Kentucky, of a Public and Permanent Nature, from the Commencement of the Government to the Session of the Legislature, Ending on the 24th February, 1834.* Frankfort, KY: Albert Hodges, 1834.

Morgan, Ted. *A Shovel of Stars: The Making of the American West, 1800 to the Present.* New York: Touchstone, 1995.

Moritz, Charles, ed. *Current Biography Yearbook, 1984.* New York: H. W. Wilson Co., 1985.

Morrison-Reed, Mark. *Black Pioneers in a White Denomination.* 3rd ed. Boston: Unitarian Universalist Association, 1994.

Moye, J. Todd. *Freedom Flyers: The Tuskegee Airmen of World War II.* New York: Oxford Univ. Press, 2010.

Muraskin, William A. *Middle-Class Blacks in a White Society: Prince Hall Freemasonry in America.* Berkeley: Univ. of California Press, 1975.

Murray, Florence. *The Negro Handbook, 1944.* New York: Current Reference Publications, 1944.

The National Cyclopedia of American Biography. New York: J. T. White, 1950.

Needleman, Ruth. *Black Freedom Fighters in Steel: The Struggle for Democratic Unionism.* Ithaca, NY: Cornell Univ. Press, 2003.

Nell, William Cooper. *The Colored Patriots of the American Revolution, with Sketches of Several Distinguished Colored Persons: To Which Is Added a Brief Survey of the Condition and Prospects of Colored Americans.* Boston: Robert F. Wallcut, 1855.

Nercessian, Nora N. *Against All Odds: The Legacy of Students of African Descent at Harvard Medical School before Affirmative Action, 1850–1968.* Cambridge, MA: Harvard Medical School, 2004.

Nicholson, Stuart. *Ella Fitzgerald: A Biography.* New York: Da Capo Press, 1995.

Nieman, Donald G. *The Freedmen's Bureau and Black Freedom.* New York: Garland, 1994.

Nordheim, Betty Lee. *Echoes of the Past—A History of the Covington Public School System.* Covington, KY: Covington Independent Schools, 2002.

Ochs, Stephen J. *Desegregating the Altar: The Josephites and the Struggle for Black Priests, 1871–1960.* Baton Rouge: Louisiana State Univ. Press, 1990.

Oder, Barron Krieg. "Education, 'Race-Adjustment,' and the Military: The Life and Work of Chaplain Allen Allensworth, 24th Infantry, U.S. Army." PhD diss., Univ. of New Mexico, 1994.

O'Leary, Cecilia Elizabeth. *To Die For: The Paradox of American Patriotism.* Princeton, NJ: Princeton Univ. Press, 1999.

Oliver, Paul. *Songsters and Saints: Vocal Traditions on Race Records.* Cambridge: Cambridge Univ. Press, 1984.

———. *The Story of the Blues.* London: Cresset Press, 1969.

O'Malley, Mimi. *It Happened in Kentucky.* Guilford, CT: Morris, 2006.

Osur, Alan M. *Blacks in the Army Air Forces during World War II: The Problem of Race Relations.* Washington, DC: Office of Air Force History, 1977.

Ott, Virginia, and Gloria Swanson. *Man with a Million Ideas: Fred Jones, Genius/Inventor.* Minneapolis: Lerner, 1977.

Page, Yolanda, ed. *Encyclopedia of African American Women Writers.* Vol. 2. Westport, CT: Greenwood Publishing, 2007.

Painter, Nell Irvin. *Exodusters: Black Migration to Kansas after Reconstruction.* New York: Norton, 1992.

Parker, John P. *His Promised Land: The Autobiography of John P. Parker, Former Slave and Conductor on the Underground Railroad.* Edited by Stuart Seely Sprague. New York: Norton, 1996.

Parrish, C. H. *Golden Jubilee of the General Association of Colored Baptists in Kentucky: From 1865–1915.* Louisville, KY: Mayes Printing Co., 1915.

Passing the Torch: Lessons Learned—Wisdom Shared; Conversations with Louisville Leaders about Life, Leadership and Service. Louisville, KY: Butler Books, 2005.

Pegues, A. W. *Our Baptist Ministers and Schools.* Springfield, MA: Willey & Co. 1892.

Penn, I. Garland, *The Afro-American Press, and Its Editors.* Springfield, MA: Willey and Co., 1891.

Peoples, T. H., Jr. *Essence of a Saga: A Complete History of the Oldest Black Baptist Congregation West of the Allegheny Mountains, Historic Pleasant Green Missionary Baptist Church.* Lexington, KY, 1990.

Perrin, William Henry, and Robert Peter. *History of Fayette County with an Outline Sketch of the Blue Grass Region.* Chicago: O. L. Baskin, 1882.

Perry, Regenia A. *Free within Ourselves: African-American Artists in the Collection of the National Museum of American Art.* Washington, DC: National Museum of American Art in Association with Pomegranate Art Books, 1992.

Peterson, Robert. *Only the Ball Was White: A History of Legendary Black Players and All-Black Professional Teams.* New York: Oxford Univ. Press, 1970.

Peyton, Atholene. *Peytonia Cook Book.* Louisville, KY: Marshall Publishing, 1906.

Phillips, C. H. *The History of the Colored Methodist Episcopal Church in America.* Jackson, TN: Publishing House C.M.E. Church, 1925.

Phipps, William E. *William Sheppard: Congo's African American Livingstone.* Louisville, KY: Geneva Press, 2002.

Pipkin, James Jefferson. *The Story of a Rising Race.* Black Heritage Library Collection. Freeport, NY: Books for Libraries Press, 1971.

A Place in Time: The Story of Louisville's Neighborhoods. Louisville, KY: Courier-Journal and the Louisville Times Co., 1989.

Pluto, Terry. *Loose Balls: The Short, Wild Life of the American Basketball Association.* New York: Simon & Schuster, 1990.

Podoll, Brian A. *The Minor League Milwaukee Brewers, 1859–1952.* Jefferson, NC: McFarland, 2003.

Polk's Lexington City Directory, 1960. Cincinnati: R. L. Polk & Co., 1960.

Porter, David L. *Biographical Dictionary of American Sports, Baseball, Revised and Expanded Edition A–F.* Westport, CT: Greenwood Press, 2000.

Potter, Eugenia K., ed. *Kentucky Women: Two Centuries of Indomitable Spirit and Vision.* Louisville, KY: Big Tree Press, 1997.

Potter, Hugh O. *History of Owensboro, and Daviess County, Kentucky.* Owensboro, KY: Daviess County Historical Society, 1974.

Powers, Georgia Davis. *I Shared the Dream: The Pride, Passion, and Politics of the First Black Woman Senator from Kentucky.* Far Hills, NJ: New Horizon Press, 1995.

Pride, Armistead, and Clint Wilson II. *A History of the Black Press.* Washington, DC: Howard Univ. Press, 1997.

Proceedings of the First Convention of Colored Men of Kentucky: The Constitution of the Kentucky State Benevolent Association. Louisville, KY: Civill & Calvert Printers, 1866.

Putney, Martha S. *When the Nation Was in Need: Blacks in the Women's Army Corps during World War II.* Metuchen, NJ: Scarecrow Press, 1992.

Quick, William Harvey. *Negro Stars in All Ages of the World.* Henderson, NC: D. E. Aycock, Printers, 1890.

Rachleff, Melissa. *Images of Harlem, 1935–1952: A Brief Biography of Marvin and Morgan Smith.* Lexington: Univ. of Kentucky Art Museum, 1993.

Rappaport, Doreen, and Bryan Collier. *Freedom River.* New York: Hyperion, 2000.

Reed, Christopher Robert. *Black Chicago's First Century.* Vol. 1, *1833–1900.* Columbia: Univ. of Missouri Press, 2005.

Reemtsma, Jan Philipp. *More than a Champion: The Style of Muhammad Ali.* New York: A.A. Knopf, 1998.

Regester, Charlene. *African American Actresses: The Struggle for Visibility, 1900–1960.* Bloomington: Indiana Univ. Press, 2010.

Renau, Lynn S. *Jockeys, Belles, and Bluegrass Kings.* Louisville, KY: Herr House Press, 1996.

———. *Racing around Kentucky.* Louisville, KY: L. S. Renau, 1995.

Rennick, Robert M. *Kentucky Place Names.* Lexington: Univ. Press of Kentucky, 1987.

Richardson, Charles E. *Grace Hope Presbyterian Church.* Louisville, KY: 1998.

Richardson, Clement. *The National Cyclopedia of the Colored Race.* Montgomery, AL: National Publishing Co., 1919.

Richardson, H. Edward. *Cassius Marcellus Clay: Firebrand of Freedom.* Lexington: Univ. Press of Kentucky, 1976.

Richardson, Nathaniel. *Liberia's Past and Present.* London: Diplomatic Press and Publishing Co., 1959.

Richardson, Willis, ed. *Plays and Pageants from the Life of the Negro.* Jackson: Univ. Press of Mississippi, 1993.

Richings, G. F. *Evidences of Progress among Colored People.* 12th ed. Philadelphia: George S. Ferguson Co., 1905.

Riggs, Thomas, ed. *St. James Guide to Black Artists.* Detroit: St. James Press, 1997.

Riley, James A., ed. *The Biographical Encyclopedia of the Negro Baseball Leagues.* New York: Carroll & Graf, 1994.

Riley, Walter H. *Forty Years in the Lap of Methodism: History of Lexington Conference of Methodist Episcopal Church.* Louisville, KY: Mayes Printing Co., 1915.

Roberts, Gene, and Hank Klibanoff. *The Race Beat: The Press, the Civil Rights Struggle, and the Awakening of a Nation.* New York: Alfred A. Knopf, 2006.

Roberts, Ida M. K. (Rowan). *Rising above It All: A Tribute to the Rowan Slaves of Federal Hill.* Louisville, KY: Harmony House, 1994.

Robinson, Ann R. Taylor. *Childress Touched Many One Man.* Lexington, KY: Heart to Heart & Associates, 1998.

Robinson, Cedric J. *Forgeries of Memory and Meaning: Blacks and the Regimes of Race in American Theater and Film before World War II.* Chapel Hill: Univ. of North Carolina Press, 2007.

Robinson, George W., ed. *The Public Papers of Governor Bert T. Combs: 1959–1963.* Lexington: Univ: Press of Kentucky, 1979.

Robinson, Lottie Offett. *The Bond-Washington Story: The Education of Black People, Elizabethtown, Kentucky.* N.p.: Self-published, 1983.

Robinson, Samuel. *The Gentle Agitator: Lessons from the Life of Dr. Samuel Robinson as Told to Gail Ritchie Henson.* Edited by Gail Ritchie Henson. Louisville, KY: Bellarmine Univ. Press, 2008.

Rodriguez, Junius P., ed. *The Historical Encyclopedia of World Slavery.* Santa Barbara, CA: ABC-CLIO, 1997.

Rogers, Howard S. *History of Cass County, from 1825–1875.* Cassopolis, MI: Vigilant Book and Job Print, 1875.

Rogers, Naomi. *An Alternative Path: The Making and Remaking of Hahnemann Medical College and Hospital of Philadelphia.* New Brunswick, NJ: Rutgers Univ. Press, 1998.

Rogosin, Donn. *Invisible Men: Life in Baseball's Negro Leagues.* New York: Atheneum, 1983.

Ross, Betsy M. *Playing Ball with the Boys: The Rise of Women in the World of Men's Sports.* Cincinnati: Clerisy Press, 2011.

Ross, Charles. *Outside the Lines: African Americans and the Integration of the National Football League.* New York: New York Univ. Press, 2001.

Ross, Lawrence C. *The Divine Nine: The History of African American Fraternities and Sororities.* New York: Kensington, 2000.

Runyon, Randolph Paul. *Delia Webster and the Underground Railroad.* Lexington: Univ. Press of Kentucky, 1996.

Ruppli, Michel. *The King Labels: A Discography.* Westport, CT: Greenwood Press, 1985.

Rush, Theressa Gunnels, Carol Fairbanks Myers, and Esther Spring Arata. *Black American Writers Past and Present: A Biographical and Bibliographical Dictionary.* Metuchen, NJ: Scarecrow Press, 1975.

Russell, J. H. *Heads and Tails . . . and Odds and Ends.* Los Angeles: Thomas Litho and Printing Co., 1963.

Russell, Tony. *The Blues—From Robert Johnson to Robert Cray.* New York: Schirmer Books, 1997.

Ryan, Perry T. *The Last Public Execution in America.* KY: P. T. Ryan, 1992.

———. *Legal Lynching: The Plight of Sam Jennings.* Lexington, KY: Alexandria Printing, 1989.

Salem, Dorothy C., ed. *African-American Women: A Biographical Dictionary.* New York: Garland, 1993.

Samad, Anthony A. *March On, March On Ye Mighty Host: The Comprehensive History of Phi Beta Sigma Fraternity, Inc., 1914–2013.* Washington, DC: Phi Beta Sigma Fraternity, 2013.

Sampson, Henry T. *Blacks in Blackface: A Source Book on Early Black Musical Shows.* Metuchen, NJ: Scarecrow Press, 1980.

———. *The Ghost Walks: A Chronological History of Blacks in Show Business, 1865–1910.* Metuchen, NJ: Scarecrow Press, 1988.

Sandler, Stanley. *Segregated Skies: All-Black Combat Squadrons of WWII.* Washington, DC: Smithsonian Institution Press, 1992.

Sanford, Joseph, and John Hatfield. Interviews in *The Refugee; or, The Narratives of Fugitive Slaves in Canada*, by Benjamin Drew. Boston: J. P. Jewett, 1856. Reprint, Toronto: Prospero, 2000.

Saunders, James Robert, and Monica Renae Saunders. *Black Winning Jockeys in the Kentucky Derby.* Jefferson, NC: McFarland, 2003.

Savage, Beth. *African American Historic Places.* Hoboken, NJ: John Wiley & Sons, 1994.

Scheurer, Timothy, ed. *American Popular Music: The Nineteenth Century and Tin Pan Alley.* Madison, WI: Popular Press, 1989.

Schick, Elizabeth A., ed. *Current Biography Yearbook, 1998.* New York: H. W. Wilson Company, 640.

Schmidt, Peter. *Sitting in Darkness: New South Fiction, Education, and the Rise of Jim Crow Colonialism, 1865–1920.* Jackson: Univ. Press of Mississippi, 2008.

Schuller, Gunther. *The Swing Era: The Development of Jazz, 1930–1945.* New York: Oxford Univ. Press, 1989.

Scruggs, L. A. *Women of Distinction: Remarkable in Works and Invincible in Character.* Raleigh, NC: L. A. Scruggs, 1893.

Sears, Richard D. *Camp Nelson, Kentucky: A Civil War History.* Lexington: Univ. Press of Kentucky, 2002.

———. *The Day of Small Things: Abolitionism in the Midst of Slavery, Berea, Kentucky, 1854–1864.* Lanham, MD: Univ. Press of America, 1986.

———. *A Practical Recognition of the Brotherhood of Man: John G. Fee and the Camp Nelson Experience.* Berea, KY: Berea College Press, 1986.

———. *A Utopian Experiment in Kentucky: Integration and Social Equality at Berea, 1866–1904.* Westport, CT: Greenwood Press, 1996.

Seniors, Paula Marie. *Beyond "Lift Every Voice and Sing": The Culture of Uplift, Identity, and Politics in Black Musical Theater.* Columbus: Ohio State Univ. Press, 2009.

Shabazz, Julian L. D. *Black Stars of Professional Wrestling.* Clinton, SC: Awesome Records, 1999.

Shackel, Paul. *New Philadelphia: An Archaeology of Race in the Heartland.* Berkeley: Univ. of California Press, 2011.

Shelby County Historical Society. *The New History of Shelby County, Kentucky.* Prospect, KY: Harmony House, 2003.

Sherman, Joan R. *Invisible Poets: Afro-Americans of the Nineteenth Century.* 2nd ed. Urbana: Univ. of Illinois Press, 1989.

Shick, Tom W. *Behold the Promised Land: A History of Afro-American Settler Society in Nineteenth-Century Liberia.* Baltimore: Johns Hopkins Univ. Press, 1980.

Siebert, Wilbur. *The Underground Railroad from Slavery to Freedom.* New York: Macmillan, 1898.

Simmons, William. *Men of Mark: Eminent, Progressive and Rising.* Cleveland: George M. Rewell, 1887.

Simms, James N. *Simms' Blue Book and National Negro Business and Professional Directory.* Chicago: James N. Simms, 1923.

Simon, F. Kevin, ed. *The WPA Guide to Kentucky.* Lexington: Univ. Press of Kentucky, 1996.

Simon, George T. *The Big Bands.* 3rd ed. New York: Macmillan, 1973.

Sims, Mary S. *The YWCA—An Unfolding Purpose.* New York: Woman's Press, 1950.

Sinclair, Bruce, ed. *Technology and the African-American Experience: Needs and Opportunities for Studies.* Cambridge: MA: MIT Press, 2004.

Skelton, David E. *History of the Lexington Conference.* Lexington, KY: Self-published, 1950.

Skocpol, Theda, Ariane Liazos, and Marshall Ganz. *What a Mighty Power We Can Be: African American Fraternal Groups and the Struggle for Racial Equality.* Princeton, NJ: Princeton Univ. Press, 2006.

Sluby, Patricia Carter. *The Inventive Spirit of African Americans: Patented Ingenuity.* Westport, CT: Praeger, 2004.

Smith, David, Jr. *The First 10 African American Presidents, 1848–1904: The Nation Builders.* Atlanta: Black History Collection, 2010.

Smith, Effie Waller. *The Collected Works of Effie Waller Smith.* Schomburg Library of Nineteenth-Century Black Women Writers. New York: Oxford Univ. Press, 1991.

Smith, Gerald L. *A Black Educator in the Segregated South: Kentucky's Rufus B. Atwood.* Lexington: Univ. Press of Kentucky, 1994.

———. *Lexington, Kentucky.* Charleston, SC: Arcadia, 2002.

Smith, Harvey H. *Lincoln and the Lincolns.* New York: Pioneer Publications, 1931.

Smith, J. Clay, Jr. *Emancipation: The Making of the Black Lawyer, 1844–1944.* Philadelphia: Univ. of Pennsylvania Press, 1993.

Smith, Jessie Carney. *Black Firsts: 4,000 Ground-Breaking and Pioneering Historical Events.* 2nd ed. Detroit: Visible Ink Press, 2003.

———, ed. *Encyclopedia of African American Business.* Vol. 2. Westport, CT: Greenwood Press, 2006.

———. *Notable Black American Men.* Detroit: Gale Research, 1998.

———. *Notable Black American Women.* Detroit: Gale Research, 1992.

———. *Notable Black American Women.* Book II. Detroit: Gale Research, 1996.

Smith, Jessie Carney, and Shirelle Phelps, eds. *Notable Black American Women.* Book III. Detroit: Gale Research, 2003.

Smith, Lucy Harth, comp. and ed. *Pictorial Directory of the Kentucky Association of Colored Women.* Lexington: Kentucky Association of Colored Women, 1945.

Smith, Mary Levi. *In Spite of the Odds: Using Roadblocks, Potholes, and Hurdles as Stepping Stones to Success.* Louisville, KY: Goose Creek, 2005.

Smith, Peter Craig. "Negro Hamlets and Gentlemen Farms: A Dichotomous Rural Settlement Pattern in Kentucky's Bluegrass Region." PhD diss., Univ. of Kentucky, 1972.

Smith, R. J. *The Great Black Way: L.A. in the 1940s and the Lost African-American Renaissance.* New York: Public Affairs, 2006.

Smith, S. E., ed. *History of the Anti–Separate Coach Movement of Kentucky.* Evansville, IN: National Afro American Press, 1895.

Smith, Suzanne E. *To Serve the Living: Funeral Directors and the African American Way of Death.* Cambridge, MA: Belknap Press of Harvard Univ. Press, 2010.

Southern, Eileen. *Biographical Dictionary of Afro-American and African Musicians.* Westport, CT: Greenwood Press, 1982.

———. *The Music of Black Americans: A History.* 3rd ed. New York: Norton, 1997.

Spencer, John H., and Burrilla B. Spencer. *A History of Kentucky Baptists: From 1769 to 1885.* Cincinnati: J. R. Baumes, 1886.

Spradling, Mary Mace. *In Black and White.* 3rd ed. Detroit: Gale Research, 1980.

Standley, Fred L., and Louis Pratt. *Conversations with James Baldwin.* Jackson: Univ. Press of Mississippi, 1989.

Stokes, Carl B. *Promises of Power: A Political Autobiography.* New York: Simon & Schuster, 1973.

Stout, Louis. *Shadows of the Past: A History of the Kentucky High School Athletic League.* Lexington, KY: Host Communications, 2006.

Stowe, Harriet Beecher. *The Key to Uncle Tom's Cabin.* London: Clarke, Beeton, & Co., 1853.

Strangis, Joel. *Lewis Hayden and the War Against Slavery.* North Haven, CT: Linnet Books, 1999.

Stuart, M. S. *An Economic Detour: A History of Insurance in the Lives of American Negroes.* New York: Wendell, Malliet & Co., 1940.

Students of the Kentucky Normal and Industrial Institute. *Students' Bulletin: Annual Edition Dedicated to Class of 1919.* Frankfort, KY: Middle Class, 1919.

Styles, Fitzhugh Lee. *Negroes and the Law in the Race's Battle for Liberty, Equality, and Justice.* Boston: Christopher Publishing House, 1937.

Sue, Jacqueline Annette. *Black Seeds in the Blue Grass.* Corte Madera, CA: Khedcanron Press, 1983.

Sullivan, Patrick. *Brick by Brick: The Story of Auto Racing Pioneer Joie Ray.* Fishers, IN: American Scene Press, 2008.

Sutter, L. M. *Ball, Bat, and Bitumen: A History of Coalfield Baseball in the Appalachian South.* Jefferson, NC: McFarland, 2009.

Swisher, Carl B. *History of the Supreme Court of the United States.* Vol. 5, *The Taney Period, 1836–64.* New York: Macmillan, 1974.

Talbert, Charles Gano. *Benjamin Logan: Kentucky Frontiersman.* Lexington: Univ. of Kentucky Press, 1962.

Talbert, Horace. *The Sons of Allen: Together with a Sketch of the Rise and Progress of Wilberforce University, Wilberforce, Ohio.* Xenia, OH: Aldine Press, 1906.

Tallant, Harold. *Evil Necessity: Slavery and Political Culture in Antebellum Kentucky.* Lexington: Univ. Press of Kentucky, 2003.

Tapp, Hambleton, and James C. Klotter. *Kentucky: Decades of Discord, 1865–1900.* Frankfort: Kentucky Historical Society, 1977.

Taylor, John. *Baptists on the American Frontier: A History of Ten Baptist Churches of Which the Author Has Been Alternately a Member.* Edited by Chester Raymond Young. 3rd ed. Macon, GA: Mercer Univ. Press, 1995.

Tenkotte, Paul A., and James C. Claypool, eds. *The Encyclopedia of Northern Kentucky.* Lexington: Univ. Press of Kentucky, 2009.

Terhune, Jim. *Tales from the 1980 Louisville Cardinals.* Champaign, IL: Sports Publishing, 2004.

Thomas, Samuel W. *Louisville since the Twenties.* Louisville, KY: Courier Journal, 1978.

———. *The Restoration of Locust Grove.* Louisville, KY: S. W. Thomas 1984.

Thompson, Bob. *Bob Thompson: Important Works in New York Collections, 1960–1966.* Edited by Martha Jackson Gallery. New York: Graphica, 1968.

Thornbrough, Emma Lou. *Indiana Blacks in the Twentieth Century.* Bloomington: Indiana Univ. Press, 2000.

Thorpe, Earl E. *Black Historians: A Critique.* New York: William Morrow, 1971.

Titon, Jeff Todd. *Early Downhome Blues: A Musical and Cultural Analysis.* Chapel Hill: Univ. of North Carolina Press, 1977.

Todd County Historical Society. *Todd County, Kentucky, Family History.* Todd Co., KY: Turner, 1995.

Torok, George D. *A Guide to Historic Coal Towns of the Big Sandy River Valley.* Knoxville: Univ. of Tennessee Press, 2004.

Townsend, Dorothy Edwards, comp. and ed. *Kentucky in American Letters.* Vol. 3, *1913–1975.* Georgetown, KY: Georgetown College Press, 1976.

Tracy, Steven C. *Going to Cincinnati: A History of the Blues in the Queen City.* Urbana: Univ. of Illinois Press, 1993.

Trelease, Allen W. *White Terror: The Ku Klux Klan Conspiracy and Southern Reconstruction.* Baton Rouge: Louisiana State Univ. Press, 1995.

Tsesis, Alexander. *The Thirteenth Amendment and American Freedom.* New York: New York Univ. Press, 2004.

Turley-Adams, Alicestyne. *Rosenwald Schools in Kentucky, 1917–1932.* Frankfort: Kentucky Heritage Council, 1997.

Turner, William T., and Donna K. Stone. *Hopkinsville.* Charleston, SC: Arcadia, 2006.

Turpin, Ruth Elizabeth Seymour. *"Chips off the Old Block": A Compilation of the Memories of the Morgan-Seymour Family.* Detroit: Harlo Press, 1990.

Twenty-Ninth Annual Catalogue of the Kentucky Normal and Industrial Institute for Colored Persons, Frankfort. Frankfort: Kentucky Institute Press, 1916.

Twenty-Two Years Work of the Hampton Normal and Agricultural Institute at Hampton, Virginia. Hampton, VA: Normal School Press, 1891.

Tygiel, Jules. *Baseball's Great Experiment: Jackie Robinson and His Legacy.* New York: Vintage Books, 1984.

Tyler, Bruce M. *African-American Life in Louisville.* Charleston, SC: Arcadia, 1998.

———. *Louisville in World War II.* Charleston, SC: Arcadia Publishing, 2005.

Underwood, Elsworth E. *A Brief History of the Colored Churches of Frankfort, Kentucky.* Frankfort, KY: Elsworth E. Underwood, 1906.

Union Benevolent Society No. 1 of Lexington, Kentucky. *Constitution and By-Laws of the Colored People's Union Benevolent Society No. 1 of Lexington, Kentucky.* Lexington, KY: W. M. Purnell, 1877.

U.S. Department of the Interior. *Promised Land on the Solomon: Black Settlement at Nicodemus, Kansas.* Washington, DC: Government Printing Office, 1986.

U.S. Works Projects Administration. *Libraries and Lotteries: A History of the Louisville Free Public Library.* Cynthiana, KY: Hobson Book Press, 1944.

Urban, Wayne J. *Black Scholar: Horace Mann Bond, 1904–1972.* Athens: Univ. of Georgia Press, 1992.

Vann, Andre. *Vance County, North Carolina.* Charleston, SC: Arcadia, 2000.

Vlach, John Michael. *By the Work of Their Hands: Studies in Afro-American Folklife.* Charlottesville: Univ. Press of Virginia, 1991.

Wade, Richard C. *Slavery in the Cities: The South, 1820–1860.* New York: Oxford University Press, 1964.

Wagner, Thomas E., and Phillip J. Obermiller. *African American Miners and Migrants: The Eastern Kentucky Social Club.* Urbana: Univ. of Illinois Press, 2004.

Wagner, Tricia Martineau. *It Happened on the Underground Railroad.* Guilford, CT: Pequot Press, 2007.

Walker, Juliet E. K. *Free Frank: A Black Pioneer on the Antebellum Frontier.* Lexington: Univ. Press of Kentucky, 1983.

Wall, Maryjean. "Isaac Murphy." In *Members in the National Museum of Racing Hall of Fame* by the National Turf Writers Association. Saratoga Springs, NY: National Museum of Racing, 1976.

Wallace-Sanders, Kimberly. *Mammy: A Century of Race, Gender, and Southern Memory.* Ann Arbor: Univ. of Michigan Press, 2008.

Waller, Gregory A. *Main Street Amusements: Movies and Commercial Entertainment in a Southern City, 1896–1930.* Washington, DC: Smithsonian Institution Press, 1995.

Walls, William Jacob. *The African Methodist Episcopal Zion Church: Reality of the Black Church.* Charlotte, NC: A.M.E. Zion Publishing House, 1974.

Ward, Andrew. *The Slaves' War: The Civil War in the Words of Former Slaves.* Boston: Houghton Mifflin, 2008.

Warner, Jennifer S. *Boone County: From Mastodons to the Millennium.* Burlington, KY: Boone County Bicentennial Book Committee, 1998.

Warren, Francis H. *Michigan Manual of Freedmen's Progress.* Detroit: Michigan Freedmen's Progress Commission, 1915.

Washington, Booker T. *The Booker T. Washington Papers.* Vol. 5, *1899–1900.* Edited by Louis R. Harlan. Urbana: Univ. of Illinois Press, 1977.

———. *The Negro in Business.* Tuskegee, AL: Hertel, Jenkins & Co., 1907.

Weaver, Carmon, and George Hicks. *Our Journey with the Buffalo Soldiers.* Philadelphia: Xlibris, 2006.

Webb, William. *The Story of William Webb, Composed by Himself.* Detroit: Egbert Hoekstra, 1873. Documenting the American South, Univ. of North Carolina at Chapel Hill. http://docsouth.unc.edu/neh/webb/webb.html (accessed July 26, 2012).

Wedgeworth, Robert. *World Encyclopedia of Library and Information Services.* ALA Editions. Chicago: American Library Association, 1980– .

Weeden, H. C. *Weeden's History of the Colored People of Louisville.* Louisville, KY: H. C. Weeden, 1897.

Weisenburger, Steven. *Modern Medea: A Family Story of Slavery and Child-Murder from the Old South.* New York: Hill & Wang, 1998.

Weiss, Nancy J. *Whitney M. Young, Jr., and the Struggle for Civil Rights.* Princeton, NJ: Princeton Univ. Press, 1989.

Wells, Dicky, as told to Stanley Dance. *The Night People: Reminiscences of a Jazzman.* Boston: Crescendo, 1971.

Wesley, Charles H. *The History of Alpha Phi Alpha: A Development in College Life.* Chicago: Foundation Publishers, 1981.

———. *History of the Improved Benevolent and Protective Order of Elks of the World, 1898–1954.* Washington, DC: Association for the Study of Negro Life and History, 1955.

———. *The History of the National Association of Colored Women's Clubs: A Legacy of Service.* Washington, DC: The Association, 1984.

White, Charles Frederick. *Who's Who in Philadelphia.* Philadelphia: A.M.E. Book Concern, 1912.

White, Pearl Schwartz, and Lillie Wilkes. *Behind These Doors—A Legacy: The History of Sigma Gamma Rho Sorority.* Chicago: Sigma Gamma Rho Sorority, 1974.

White, Sol, and Jerry Malloy. *Sol White's History of Colored Base Ball with Other Documents on the Early Black Game, 1886–1936.* Lincoln: Univ. of Nebraska Press, 1996.

Who's Who in Black Louisville. 3rd ed. Columbus, OH: Who's Who Publishing Co., 2009.

Who's Who in Religion. 2nd ed. Chicago: Marquis Who's Who, 1977.

Wiggins, Lida Keck. *The Life and Works of Paul Laurence Dunbar.* New York: Dodd, Mead, 1907.

Wiggins, William H., Jr. *O Freedom! Afro-American Emancipation Celebrations.* Knoxville: Univ. of Tennessee Press, 1987.

Wilkinson, Crystal. *Blackberries, Blackberries.* New Milford, CT: Toby Press, 2000.

———. *Water Street.* New Milford, CT: Toby Press, 2002.

———. *Write with Your Spine.* http://crystal-wilkinson.blogspot.com/ (accessed October 30, 2012).

Williams, Albert. *Black Warriors: Unique Units and Individuals in African American Military History.* Haverford, PA: Infinity, 2003.

Williams, Ephie Augustus, S. W. Green, and Joseph L. Jones. *History and Manual of the Colored Knights of Pythias.* Nashville, TN: National Baptist Publishing Board, 1917.

Williams, Erma Brooks. *Political Empowerment of Illinois' African-American State Lawmakers from 1877 to 2005.* Washington, DC: Univ. Press of America, 2008.

Williams, Ethel. *Biographical Directory of Negro Ministers.* New York: Scarecrow Press, 1965.

Williams, Jim. *The March on Frankfort: A Study in Protest Organization.* New York: Political Education Project, 1965.

Williams, Lawrence. *Black Higher Education in Kentucky, 1879–1930: The History of Simmons University.* Lewiston, NY: Edwin Mellen Press, 1987.

Williams, Lillian Serece. *Strangers in the Land of Paradise: The Creation of an African American Community, Buffalo, New York, 1900–1940.* Bloomington: Indiana Univ. Press, 1999.

Williams, Robert L. *History of the Association of Black Psychologists: Profiles of Outstanding Black Psychologists.* Bloomington, IN: AuthorHouse, 2008.

Williams, Roger M. *The Bonds: An American Family.* New York: Atheneum, 1971.

Willis, Deborah, ed. *J. P. Ball: Daguerrean and Studio Photographer.* New York: Garland, 1993.

Willis-Thomas, Deborah, ed. *Black Photographers, 1940–1988: An Illustrated Bio-Bibliography.* New York: Garland, 1989.

Wills, Ridley, II. *The History of Belle Meade: Mansion, Plantation, and Stud.* Nashville: Vanderbilt Univ. Press, 1991.

Wilson, Dreck Spurlock, ed. *African American Architects: A Biographical Dictionary, 1865–1945.* New York: Routledge, 2004.

Wilson, George D. *A Century of Negro Education in Louisville, Kentucky.* Louisville, KY: Louisville Municipal College, 1941. Reprint, Louisville, KY: Univ. of Louisville, 1986.

Wilson, Shannon H. *Berea College: An Illustrated History.* Lexington: Univ. Press of Kentucky, 2006.

Witmark, Isidore, and Isaac Goldberg. *The Story of the House of Witmark: From Ragtime to Swingtime.* New York: Lee Furman, 1939.

Wolfe, Charles K. *Kentucky Country: Folk and Country Music of Kentucky.* Lexington: Univ. Press of Kentucky, 1996.

Wolfe, Margaret Ripley. *Daughters of Canaan: A Saga of Southern Women.* Lexington: Univ. Press of Kentucky, 1995.

Wolfe, Mrs. H. M. *Mission Schools and Their Value.* Bowling Green, KY: 1918.

Work, Monroe N., ed. *Negro Year Book, 1931–1932.* Tuskegee, AL: Negro Book Publishing Co., 1931.

Wright, George C. *A History of Blacks in Kentucky.* Vol. 2, *In Pursuit of Equality, 1890–1980.* Frankfort: Kentucky Historical Society, 1992.

———. *Life Behind a Veil: Blacks in Louisville, Kentucky, 1865–1930.* Baton Rouge: Louisiana State Univ. Press, 1985.

———. *Racial Violence in Kentucky, 1865–1940: Lynchings, Mob Rule, and "Legal Lynchings."* Baton Rouge: Louisiana State Univ. Press, 1990.

Wright, John D., Jr. *Lexington: Heart of the Bluegrass.* Lexington, KY: Lexington–Fayette County Historic Commission, 1982.

Wright, Richard Robert, Jr. *Centennial Encyclopaedia of the African Methodist Episcopal Church.* Philadelphia: Book Concern of the A.M.E. Church, 1916.

———. *Encyclopaedia of the African Methodist Episcopal Church.* 2nd ed. Philadelphia: Book Concern of the A.M.E. Church, 1947.

———. *Who's Who in the General Conference.* Philadelphia: A.M.E. Book Concern, 1924.

Wynn, Neil A., ed. *Cross the Water Blues: African American Music in Europe.* Jackson: Univ. Press of Mississippi, 2007.

Yanow, Scott. *Classic Jazz.* San Francisco: Backbeat Books, 2001.

Yarbrough, Tinsley E. *Judicial Enigma: The First Justice Harlan.* New York: Oxford Univ. Press, Inc., 1955.

Yater, George H. *Flappers, Prohibition and All That Jazz.* Louisville, KY: Museum of History and Science, 1984.

———. *Two Hundred Years at the Falls of the Ohio.* Louisville, KY: Filson Club, 1987.

Yenser, Thomas, ed. *Who's Who in Colored America, 1941–1944.* 6th ed. Brooklyn, NY: Thomas Yenser, 1942.

Young, Herman A., and Barbara H. Young. *Scientists in the Black Perspective.* Louisville, KY: Lincoln Foundation, 1974.

Zang, David W. *Fleet Walker's Divided Heart: The Life of Baseball's First Black Major Leaguer.* Lincoln: Univ. of Nebraska Press, 1995.

ARTICLES

Atwood, R. B. "Kentucky Faces the Problem of Training Colored Teachers." *KNEAJ* 1, no. 3 (February 1931): 21–26.

Baird, Nancy D. "Asiatic Cholera's First Visit to Kentucky: A Study in Panic and Fear." *FCHQ* 48, no. 4 (1974): 228–40.

Bradby, Marie. "Whose Old Kentucky Home?" *Louisville* 47 (September 1996): 32–39.

Brosi, George. "A Black Appalachian Treasure." *Appalachian Heritage* 34, no. 2 (2006): 8–12.

Burnside, Jacqueline G. "Black Symbols: Extraordinary Achievements by Ordinary Women." *Appalachian Heritage* 15 (Summer 1987): 11–16.

———. "Suspicion versus Faith: Negro Criticisms of Berea College in the Nineteenth Century." *RKHS* 83 (1985): 237–66.

Christopher, Michael C. "Granville T. Woods: The Plight of a Black Inventor." *Journal of Black Studies* 11, no. 3 (March 1981): 269–76.

Clark, T. D. "The Slave Trade between Kentucky and the Cotton Kingdom." *Mississippi Valley Historical Review* 21, no. 3 (December 1934): 331–42.

Coleman, J. Winston, Jr. "The Kentucky Colonization Society." *RKHS* 39 (January 1941): 1–9.

Finkelman, Paul. "Prelude to the Fourteenth Amendment: Black Legal Rights in the Antebellum North." *Rutgers Law Journal* 17 (1986): 415–82.

Gilbert, Abby L. "The Comptroller of the Currency and the Freedman's Savings Bank." *JNH* 57, no. 2 (April 1972): 125–43.

Griggs, Kristy Owens. "The Removal of Blacks from Corbin in 1919: Memory, Perspective, and Legacy of Racism." *RKHS* 100, no. 3 (Summer 2002): 293–310.

Hardin, John A. "Green Pinckney Russell of Kentucky Normal and Industrial Institute for Colored Persons." *Journal of Black Studies* 25 (1995): 610–21.

Harris, Theodore H. H. "Creating Windows of Opportunity: Isaac E. Black and the African American Experience in Kentucky, 1848–1914." *RKHS* 98, no. 2 (Spring 2000): 155–77.

———. "The History of Afro-American Elkdom and Benjamin Franklin (B. F.) Howard in Covington, Kentucky, 1889–1918." *Northern Kentucky Heritage* 1, no. 2 (Spring–Summer 1994): 43–44.

Hobgood, Patrick. "Constructing Community: An Exhibition of the Voices of Goodloetown." *Kaleidoscope: University of Kentucky Journal of Undergraduate Scholarship* 4 (2006): 39–44.

Howard, Victor B. "The Black Testimony Controversy in Kentucky, 1866–1872." *JNH* 58, no. 2 (April 1973): 140–65.

———. "The Struggle for Equal Education in Kentucky, 1866–1884." *Journal of Negro Education* 46, no. 3 (Summer 1977): 305–38.

Hudson, J. Blaine. "The Establishment of Louisville Municipal College: A Case Study in Racial Conflict and Compromise." *Journal of Negro Education* 64 (1995): 111–23.

Jones, Jeff. "A Sweet Evening Breeze in Lexington." *Chevy Chaser Magazine* (Lexington, KY), September 2002.

Jones, Reinette. "Creating a Web Resource: African American Kentuckian Profiles." *Journal of Library Administration* 43, nos. 3/4 (2005): 149–59.

Jourdan, Kathrine. "The Architecture of Samuel M. Plato." *Black History News and Notes* 37 (August 1989): 4–7.

Kellogg, John. "The Formation of Black Residential Areas in Lexington, Kentucky, 1865–1887." *Journal of Southern History* 48, no. 1 (February 1982): 21–52.

Kousser, J. Morgan. "Making Separate Equal: Integration of Black and White School Funds in Kentucky." *Journal of Interdisciplinary History* 10, no. 3 (Winter 1980): 399–428.

Leask, J. MacKenzie. "Jesse Happy, a Fugitive Slave from Kentucky." *Ontario History* 54 (June 1962): 87–98.

Lucas, Marion B. "African Americans on the Kentucky Frontier." *RKHS* 95 (Spring 1997): 121–34.

———. "Camp Nelson, Kentucky, during the Civil War: Cradle of Liberty or Refugee Death Camp?" *FCHQ* 63, no. 4 (October 1989): 439–52.

"Lucy Harth Smith." *JNH* 41, no. 2 (April 1956): 177–79.

Malone, Cheryl Knott. "Louisville Free Public Library's Racially Segregated Branches, 1905–35." *RKHS* 93 (Spring 1995): 159–79.

Middleton, Stephen. "We Must Not Fail!!! Horace Sudduth: Queen City Entrepreneur." *Queen City Heritage* 49, no. 2 (Summer 1991): 3–20.

Nelson, Paul David. "Experiment in Interracial Education at Berea College, 1858–1906." *JNH* 59 (1974): 13–27.

Norris, Marjorie M. "An Early Instance of Nonviolence: The Louisville Demonstrations of 1870–1871." *Journal of Southern History* 32 (1996): 487–504.

Ottesen, Ann I. "A Reconstruction of the Activities and Outbuildings at Farmington, an Early Nineteenth Century Hemp Farm." *FCHQ* 59 (October 1985): 395–425.

Pearce, John Ed. "Louisville Negro Breaks Vote Pattern." *Christian Science Monitor,* May 19, 1961.

Powell, Sallie L. "'It Is Hard to Be What You Have Not Seen': Brenda Hughes and the Black and White of the Zebra Shirt—Race and Gender in Kentucky High School Basketball." Special edition, *RKHS* 109, nos. 3–4 (Summer/Autumn 2011): 433–65.

Ramage, Andrea S. "Love and Honor: The Robert Wickliffe Family of Antebellum Kentucky." *RKHS* 94 (Spring 1996): 115–33.

Schmitzer, Jeanne Cannella. "CCC Camp 510: Black Participation in the Creation of Mammoth Cave National Park." *RKHS* 93, no. 4 (Autumn 1995): 446–64.

———. "The Sable Guides of Mammoth Cave." *FCHQ* 67 (April 1993): 240–58.

Silverman, Jason H. "Kentucky, Canada, and Extradition: The Jesse Happy Case." *FCHQ* 54, no. 1 (1980): 50–60.

Smith, Gerald L. "Direct-Action Protests in the Upper South: Kentucky Chapters of the Congress of Racial Equality." *RKHS* 109, nos. 3–4 (Summer/Autumn 2011): 351–93.

Smith, Peter C., and Karl B. Raitz. "Negro Hamlets and Agricultural Estates in Kentucky's Inner Bluegrass." *Geographical Review* 64, no. 2 (April 1974): 217–34.

Steely, Will Frank. "William Shreve Bailey: Kentucky Abolitionist." *FCHQ* 31 (1957): 274–81.

Thomas, Samuel W. "Oxmoor: The Bullitt House in Jefferson County, Kentucky." *Kentucky Review* 9 (Autumn 1989): 29–40.

Thomas, Samuel W., Eugene H. Connor, and Harold Meloy. "A History of Mammoth Cave, Emphasizing Tourist Development and Medical Experimentation under Dr. John Croghan." *RKHS* 68, no. 4 (October 1970): 319–41.

Trowbridge, John. "Union African American Soldiers Honored in Green Hill Cemetery, Franklin County." *Kentucky Ancestors* 36, no. 3 (Spring 2001): 125–29.

Turner, John G. "A 'Black-White' Missionary on the Imperial State: William H. Sheppard and Middle-Class Black Manhood." *Journal of Southern Religion* 9 (2006). http://jsr.fsu.edu/Volume9/Turner.htm.

Urbahns, Paul. "More Moremans, Pleasant Moreman: The Free Negro of Meade County." *Ancestral News* 19, no. 3 (Fall 1994): 101–4.

Vouga, Anne F. "Presbyterian Mission and Louisville Blacks: The Early Years, 1898–1910." *FCHQ* 58 (July 1984): 310–35.

Wax, Darold D. "Robert Ball Anderson, a Kentucky Slave, 1843–1864." *RKHS* 81 (Summer 1983): 255–73.

Westin, Alan F. "John Marshall Harlan and the Constitutional Rights of Negroes: The Transformation of a Southerner." *Yale Law Journal* 66 (1957): 637–710.

Williams, Kenneth H. "'Oh Baby . . . It's Really Happening': The Louisville Race Riot of 1968." *Kentucky History Journal* 3 (1988): 48–64.

Williams, Lawrence H. "'Righteous Discontent': Mary Virginia Cook Parrish and Black Baptist Women." *Baptist History & Heritage* 42, no. 3 (Summer/Fall 2007): 34–41.

Wright, George C. "The Founding of the Lincoln Institute." *FCHQ* 49 (January 1975): 57–70.

———. "The NAACP and Residential Segregation in Louisville, Kentucky, 1914–1917." *RKHS* 78 (Winter 1980): 39–54.

Wright, John D., Jr. "Lexington's Suppression of the 1920 Will Lockett Lynch Mob." *RKHS* 84, no. 3 (Summer 1986): 263–79.

Yanuck, Julius. "The Garner Fugitive Slave Case." *Mississippi Valley Historical Review* 40 (1953): 47–66.

NEWSPAPERS AND MAGAZINES

Akron Beacon Journal
American Baptist
Appalachian Heritage
Argus Press (Owosso, MI)
Arkansas State Press
Atlanta Constitution
Atlanta Independent
Atlanta Journal-Constitution
Atlanta Magazine
Atlantic
Baltimore Afro-American
Baltimore Daily Record
Baltimore Herald
Baltimore Sun
Barbourville Mountain Advocate
Battle Creek Enquirer
Battle Creek Tribune
Berea Citizen
Black Belt
Black Enterprise
Black Perspective in Music
Bloomington Herald-Times
Bluegrass Blade
Bourbon News (Paris, KY)
Bowling Green Daily News
Breathitt County News (Jackson, KY)
Broad Ax (Chicago)
Calgary Sun

Call and Post (Cleveland, OH)
Carrollton News Democrat
Central Record (Lancaster, KY)
Chapel Hill Herald
Chapel Hill News
Charleston Gazette
Chevy Chaser Magazine
Chicago Daily Tribune
Chicago Defender
Chicago Examiner
Chicago Record-Herald
Chicago Sun-Times
Chicago Tribune
Cincinnati Daily Enquirer
Cincinnati Daily Gazette
Cincinnati Enquirer
Cincinnati Magazine
Cincinnati Post
Cincinnati Times Star
Clay City Times
Cleveland Advocate
Cleveland Gazette
Cleveland Plain Dealer
College Heights Herald (Bowling Green, KY)
Colorado Springs Gazette
Colored American (Washington, DC)
Colored American Magazine

Corbin Times
Covington Journal
Covington Ticket
Crisis
Daily Commonwealth (Frankfort, KY)
Daily Public Ledger (Maysville, KY)
Daily Racing Form (Chicago)
Daily Tar Heel
Danville Advocate-Messenger
Dayton Daily News
Denver Post
Detroit News
Detroit Plaindealer
Dubuque Herald
Earlington (KY) Bee
Ebony
Evansville (IN) Courier
Evansville (IN) Courier-Press
Evansville (IN) Gleaner
Evansville (IN) Press
Florence (AL) Herald
Florence (AL) Times
Florida Evening Independent
Floyd County Times
Ft. Wayne Journal Gazette
Frankfort Roundabout
Frankfort State Journal
Frankfort Weekly Commonwealth

Freedmen's Record
Free South (Newport, KY)
Glasgow (KY) Daily Times
Grand Rapids Press
Grant County News
Greensboro News and Record
Harlan Daily Enterprise
Hartford Herald
Hartford Republican
Hazel Green Herald
Henderson Daily Gleaner
    (Henderson, KY)
Henderson Gleaner (Henderson, KY)
Henderson Gleaner and Journal
    (Henderson, KY)
Hendersonville (NC) Times-News
Hickman County Gazette
Hickman Courier
Historical Geography
Hopkinsville Kentuckian
Houston Chronicle
Huntington (WV) Herald-Dispatch
Indiana Alumni Magazine
Indianapolis Freeman
Indianapolis Recorder
Indianapolis Star
Iron Mountain Review
Irvington Herald
Jet
Kalamazoo Gazette
Kansas City Advocate
Kentucky Enquirer
Kentucky Irish American
Kentucky Journal
Kentucky Leader
Kentucky New Era
Kentucky Post
Kentucky Reporter
Kentucky Review
Kentucky State Bar Journal
Kentucky State-Journal
Kentucky Statesman
Kentucky Thorobred
Kentucky Times-Star
Knott County Observer
Knoxville News-Sentinel
KW Today
La Grange Daily News
Lakeland (FL) Ledger
Lawrence (KS) Weekly World
Lewiston (ID) Morning Tribune
Lexington American Citizen
Lexington Dollar Weekly Press
Lexington Herald
Lexington Herald-Leader
Lexington Leader
Lexington Morning Herald
Lexington Morning Transcript
Lexington Observer and Reporter
Licking Valley Register
Life
Los Angeles Daily News

Los Angeles Sentinel
Louisville Commercial
Louisville Courier
Louisville Courier-Journal
Louisville Courier-Journal and Times
Louisville Daily Courier
Louisville Daily Journal
Louisville Defender
Louisville Herald
Louisville Leader
Louisville Magazine
Louisville Morning Courier
Louisville Music News
Louisville Post
Louisville Times
Lubbock Avalanche-Journal
Maysville Daily Evening Bulletin
Maysville Daily Independent
Maysville Evening Bulletin
Maysville Independent-Ledger
Maysville Public Ledger
McCook (NE) Daily Gazette
Memphis Commercial Appeal
Messenger: World's Greatest Negro
    Monthly
Miami News
Michigan Chronicle
Middlesboro Daily News
Minority Business News
Montreal Gazette
Mt. Sterling (KY) Advocate
Mt. Sterling (KY) Reporter
Mount Vernon Signal
Murray Ledger and Times
Nashville Union and American
National Republican (Washington, DC)
Negro Star (KS)
Newark Advocate
Newark Daily Advocate
New Hampshire Union Leader
Newport Local
New York Amsterdam News
New York Beacon
New York Daily Tribune
New Yorker
New York Evening Post
New York Observer
New York Times
New York Tribune
New Zealand Truth
Oklahoman
Omaha World-Herald
Orlando Sentinel (Orlando, FL)
Owensboro Inquirer
Owensboro Messenger-Inquirer
Oxford (OH) Press
Paducah Daily Sun
Paducah Evening Sun
Paducah Sun
Palestine (TX) Daily Herald
Park City Daily News (Bowling Green,
    KY)

Parthenon (Huntington, WV)
People Weekly
Philadelphia Daily Evening Telegraph
Philadelphia Daily News
Pittsburgh Courier
Pittsburgh Dispatch
Pittsburgh Post-Gazette
Pittsburgh Press
Plaindealer (Kansas City, KS)
Plaindealer (Wichita, KS)
Pleasant Point (WV) Register
Post-Tribune (IN)
Queen City Heritage (Cincinnati)
Reading (PA) Eagle
Richmond Afro-American (VA)
Richmond Climax (KY)
Richmond (IN) Palladium-Item
Richmond Times-Dispatch (VA)
Rochester (NY) North Star
Rutland (VT) Herald
Sacramento Observer
Sacramento Record Union
St. Joseph (MO) News-Press
St. Louis (MO) Post-Dispatch
St. Paul (MN) Appeal
San Antonio Express-News
San Diego Union
San Diego Union-Tribune
San Francisco Call
Sarasota (FL) Herald
Seattle Times
Sentinel-News (Shelbyville, KY)
Shelby County Life Magazine
Shelby Record
Shelby Sentinel
Sports Illustrated
Springfield (KY) Sun
Tennessean
Tennessee Tribune
Time
Toledo (OH) Blade
Toledo (OH) News-Bee
Topeka Plaindealer
Topeka Tribune
Toronto Star
Tri-State Defender
Tuscaloosa News
University Missourian
USA Today
Ventura County Star
Washington (DC) AfroAmerican
Washington (DC) Bee
Washington Post
Wayne County Outlook
Western Appeal (St. Paul, MN)
Wichita Post Observer
Williamson (WV) Daily News
Winchester News
Winchester Sun
Winston-Salem Journal
Woodford Sun (Versailles, KY)
Youngstown (OH) Daily Vindicator

INTERNET SITES

African American Biographical Database, http://aabd.chadwyck
.com/

Ancestry, http://www.ancestry.com

Documenting the American South, http://www.docsouth.unc.edu

Find a Grave, http://www.findagrave.com/

HeritageQuest Online Database (Lexington Public Library),
www.lexpublib.org/database/heritagequest-online

Kentucky Commission on Human Rights, kchr.ky.go

Kentucky Historical Society, http://history.ky.gov/

Kentucky Virtual Library, http://www.kyvl.org/

Library of Congress, http://www.loc.gov/

Local History Index Database (Lexington Public Library),
http://www.lexpublib.org/database/local-history-index

Newsbank, http://www.newsbank.com/

Notable Kentucky African Americans Database, http://nkaa.uky
.edu/

Illustration Credits

Adams, Henry: General Research and Reference Division, Schomburg Center for Research in Black Culture, The New York Public Library, Astor, Lenox, and Tildon Foundations. **African American Jockeys**: Keeneland Library-Hemment. **Alpha Kappa Alpha Sorority, Incorporated**: Kentucky Historical Society. **Anderson, Nancy "Old Boss"**: Kentucky Digital Library. **Atwood, Rufus Ballard**: *Lexington Herald-Leader.* **Baptist Women's Educational Convention of Kentucky**: Image number 7.4.2, Simmons Bible College Records, Univ. Archives and Records Center, Univ. of Louisville, KY. **Bate, John W.**: Berea College Photographic Archives, Special Collections & Archives, Hutchins Library, Berea College. **Bishop, Stephen**: National Park Service. **Blue, Thomas Fountain, Sr.**: Univ. Archives and Records Center, Univ. of Louisville, KY. **Bond, James M.**: Berea College Photographic Archives, Special Collections & Archives, Hutchins Library, Berea College. **Bracktown**: UK Explore. **Bransford Family**: National Park Service. **Burleigh, Angus Augustus**: Berea College. Courtesy of Photographic Archives, Special Collections and Archives, Hutchins Library, Berea College. **Burse, Raymond Malcolm**: Archives of the Center of Excellence for the Study of Kentucky African Americans, Kentucky State Univ. **Business**: Bill Richardson. **Camp Nelson**: Berea College Photographic Archives, Special Collections & Archives, Hutchins Library, Berea College. **Chappell, Willa Brown**: Ron Spriggs. **Cheaney, Henry Ellis**: Kentucky Historical Society. **Chiles, James Alexander**: UK Explore. **Civil Rights Movement**: Calvert McCann. **Clayton, Alonzo "Lonnie"**: Keeneland Library. **Coletown**: UK Explore. **Crawfish Bottom**: Kentucky Historical Society. **Dawson, Dermontti Farra**: *Lexington Herald-Leader.* **Duka, Veronica Marie**: Stan Mckinney. **Dupee, George Washington**: General Research and Reference Division, Schomburg Center for Research in Black Culture, The New York Public Library, Astor, Lenox, and Tildon Foundations. **Eastern Kentucky Coalfields**: William H. Turner Collection. **Figgs, Ukari Okien**: *Lexington Herald-Leader.* **Finney, Nikky**: *Lexington Herald-Leader.* **First African Baptist Church (Lexington)**: Kentucky Heritage Council. **First Standard Bank (Louisville)**: Image CS035044, Caufield & Shook Collection, Photographic Archives, Univ. of Louisville, Louisville, KY. **Fontaine Ferry Park**: UK Explore. **Fouse, William Henry**: Kentucky Historical Society. **Freemasons**: Kentucky Historical Society. **Givens, Jack "Goose"**: *Lexington Herald-Leader.* **Haley, Sister Patricia, SCN**: Sisters of Charity of Nazareth Archival Center. **Hall, Henry Elliott**: General Research and Reference Division, Schomburg Center for Research in Black Culture, The New York Public Library, Astor, Lenox, and Tildon Foundations. **Hamilton, Anthony "Tony"**: Keeneland Library. **Harbut, William Luther**: UK Explore. **Hayes, Edythe Larsenia Jones**: UK Explore. **Hooks, Julia Britton**: Berea College Photographic Archives, Special Collec-

tions & Archives, Hutchins Library, Berea College. **Hooper, Ernest Jackson**: Kentucky Digital Library. **Houston, Allan Wade, Sr.**: *Lexington Herald-Leader.* **Hughes, Brenda Lee Garner**: *Lexington Herald-Leader.* **Jim Crow**: Image number P011441, R. G. Potter Collection, Photographic Archives, Univ. of Louisville, Louisville, KY. **Johnson, John J.**: Kentucky Commission on Human Rights. **Johnson, Lyman Tefft**: Kentucky Digital Library. **Jones, Paul William Lawrence**: Kentucky State Univ. Special Collections and Archives. **Jones, Robert Elliott "Jonah"**: Kentucky Commission on Human Rights. **Jug Bands**: Image CS 107364, Caufield & Shook Collection, Photographic Archives, Univ. of Louisville, Louisville, KY. **Kentucky Negro Educational Association**: Kentucky State Univ. Special Collections and Archives. **Kentucky State University**: Kentucky Historical Society; Kentucky State Univ. Special Collections and Archives. **Lee, James "Jimmy"**: Keeneland Library-Hemment. **Lewis, Oliver**: Keeneland Library. **Lincoln Institute**: Whitney M. Young Sr. Collection Archives of the Center of Excellence for Study of Kentucky African Americans, Kentucky State Univ. **Little Georgetown**: Kentucky Digital Library. **Louisville Municipal College**: Image number 197959 25, Small Groups, Photographic Archives, University of Louisville, Louisville, KY. **Lyric Theater**: *Lexington Herald-Leader.* **Mammoth Life and Accident Insurance Company**: Kentucky Digital Library. **March on Frankfort**: Jim Curtis photograph collection on Civil Rights in Kentucky, Univ. of Kentucky Special Collections. **Marrs, Elijah P.**: General Research and Reference Division, Schomburg Center for Research in Black Culture, The New York Public Library, Astor, Lenox, and Tildon Foundations. **Moorman, Marnel C., Sr.**: Kentucky Commission on Human Rights. **Murphy, Isaac Burns**: Keeneland Library-Hemment; Kentucky Historical Society. **Northington, Nate "Nat"**: UK Explore. **Page, Gregory Dewayne**: Univ. of Kentucky Athletic Department. **Palmer, Zirl A.**: UK Explore. **Parrish, Charles Henry, Sr.**: Image 6.9.2, Simmons Bible College Records, Univ. Archives and Records Center, Univ. of Louisville, Louisville, KY. **Parrish, Mary Virginia Cook**: General Research & Reference Division, Schomburg Center for Research in Black Culture, New York Public Library, Astor, Lenox, and Tilden Foundations. **Peeples, Porter G.**: *Lexington Herald-Leader.* **Perkins, James "Soup"**: Keeneland Library. **Powers, Georgia Montgomery Davis**: *Lexington Herald-Leader.* **Roach, Sanford T.**: Lettie Roach. **Rosenwald Schools**: Fisk University Archives. **Shake Rag**: Warren County Commission. **Shanks, Irvine Lee**: Berea College Office of Integrated Marketing & Communications. **Simmons, William Joseph**: General Research and Reference Division, Schomburg Center for Research in Black Culture, The New York Public Library, Astor, Lenox, and Tildon Foundations. **Simmons College of Kentucky**: Image numbers 6.15.2, 7.8.3, and 7.3.3, Simmons Bible College Records, Univ. Archives and

Records Center, Univ. of Louisville, KY. **Simms, William "Willie"**: Keeneland Library-Hemment. **Slave Laws**: Univ. of Kentucky Special Collections. **Sleet, Anne**: Charles Betram, *Lexington Herald-Leader.* **Sleet, Moneta J., Jr.**: UK Explore. **Sleettown**: Perryville Battlefield State Historic Site. **Smith, Effie Waller**: Kentucky Commission on Human Rights. **Smith, Lucy Cornelia Harth**: Kentucky Commission on Human Rights. **Smith-Stowe, Mary Levi**: Archives of the Center of Excellence for the Study of Kentucky African Americans. **Smith, Orlando "Tubby"**: *Lexington Herald-Leader.* **Sneed, Lavinia B.**: Image no. 7.1.6, Simmons Bible College Records, Univ. Archives and Records Center, Univ. of Louisville, Louisville, KY. **Stanley, Frank Leslie, Sr.**: UK Explore. **Steward, Mamie E. Lee**: General Research and Reference Division, Schomburg Center for Research in Black Culture, The New York Public Library, Astor, Lenox, and Tildon Foundations. **Steward, William Henry**: General Research and Reference Division, Schomburg Center for Research in Black Culture, The New York Public Library,

Astor, Lenox, and Tildon Foundations. **Still, Valerie Renee**: *Lexington Herald-Leader.* **Strider, Maurice William**: *Lexington Herald-Leader.* **Sykes, Harry N.**: *Lexington Herald-Leader.* **Underwood, Edward Ellsworth**: Kentucky Historical Society. **Walker, Frank X**: UK Explore. **Walker, William "Billy"**: Keeneland Library-Leach. **Washington Street Missionary Baptist Church**: William Carter. **Western Colored Branch Library (Louisville)**: Image number CS091520, Caufield & Shook Collection, Photographic Archives, Univ. of Louisville, Louisville, KY. **Winkfield, James "Jimmy"**: Keeneland Library-Cook. **Winnie A. Scott Memorial Hospital (Franfort)**: Kentucky Historical Society. **Young, Laura Ray**: Whitney M. Young Sr. Collection, Archives of the Center of Excellence for the Study of Kentucky African Americans, Kentucky State Univ. **Young, Whitney Moore, Jr.**: UK Explore.

All illustrations not attributed to some other source are from the collections of the editors in chief or public domain.

Index